Introduction to Drama

Introduction to Drama

ROBERT C. ROBY, *Department of English, Marquette University,*

BARRY ULANOV, *Department of English, Barnard College*

MC GRAW-HILL *Book Company, Inc., New York, San Francisco, Toronto, London, 1962*

CRITICAL EXCERPTS

Chapman, Percy Addison, *The Spirit of Molière: An Interpretation,* edited by Jean-Albert Bede. Reprinted by permission of and copyright by Princeton University Press.

Chute, Marchette, *Ben Jonson of Westminster.* Reprinted by permission of E. P. Dutton & Co., Inc.

Craig, Hardin, *English Religious Drama of the Middle Ages.* Reprinted by permission of Oxford University Press, Oxford, 1955.

Cunningham, Maurice P., "Medea Ex Machina," *Classical Philology.* Reprinted by permission of and copyright 1954 by the University of Chicago.

Downer, Alan S., *The British Drama.* Reprinted by permission of and copyright 1950 by Appleton-Century-Crofts, Inc.

Dryden, John, *Dramatic Essays.* Reprinted by permission of E. P. Dutton & Co., Inc., and Everyman's Library, J. M. Dent & Sons, Ltd.

Ehrenberg, Victor, *Sophocles and Pericles.* Reprinted by permission of Basil Blackwell and Mott, Ltd., Oxford, 1954.

Eliot, T. S., *Selected Essays,* copyright 1932 by Harcourt, Brace & World, Inc.; © 1960 by T. S. Eliot. Reprinted by permission of the publishers, and Faber and Faber, Ltd.

Ellis-Fermor, Una M., *The Frontiers of Drama.* Reprinted by permission of Methuen and Company, Ltd., London.

Ellis-Fermor, Una M., *The Jacobean Drama,* 3d ed., rev. Reprinted by permission of Methuen and Company, Ltd., London, 1953.

Enck, John J., *Jonson and the Comic Truth.* Reprinted by permission of the copyright owners, the Regents of the University of Wisconsin, University of Wisconsin Press.

Enright, D. J., "Crime and Punishment in Ben Jonson," *Scrutiny,* 9 (1940). Reprinted by permission of D. J. Enright.

Fergusson, Francis, *An Idea of a Theater.* Reprinted by permission of and copyright by Princeton University Press.

Fernandez, Ramon, *Molière: The Man Seen through the Plays,* translated by Wilson Follett, copyright © 1958 by Hill and Wang, Inc. Reprinted by permission of Hill and Wang, Inc.

Fowlie, Wallace, *Dionysus in Paris,* copyright © 1960 by Wallace Fowlie. Reprinted by permission of Meridian Books, The World Publishing Company, Cleveland and New York.

Frye, Northrop, *The Anatomy of Criticism.* Reprinted by permission of and copyright by Princeton University Press.

Herford, C. H. and Percy Simpson, *Ben Jonson,* vol. 2. Reprinted by permission of Oxford University Press, Oxford, 1925.

Holland, Norman N., *The First Modern Comedies.* Reprinted by permission of Harvard University Press, Cambridge, Mass., 1959.

Hudson, Lynton, *Life and the Theatre.* Reprinted by permission of George G. Harrap & Company, Ltd.

Huneker, James, *Iconoclasts.* Reprinted with the permission of Charles Scribner's Sons, pp. 256–257, 262–264.

Inskip, Donald, *Jean Giraudoux: The Making of a Dramatist.* Reprinted by permission of Oxford University Press.

Jaeger, Werner, *Paideia,* translated by Gilbert Highet. Reprinted by permission of Oxford University Press and Basil Blackwell, New York and Oxford, 1939.

Kenworthy, B. J., *Georg Kaiser.* Reprinted by permission of Basil Blackwell.

Kitto, H. D. F., *Greek Tragedy.* Reprinted by permission of Methuen & Co., Ltd., and Doubleday and Company, Incorporated.

Knights, L. C., *Drama and Society in the Age of Jonson.* Reprinted by permission of Chatto and Windus, Ltd., London, 1951.

Knoll, Robert E., "How to Read The Alchemist," *College English,* 21 (1960). Reprinted by permission of University of Nebraska.

Knox, Bernard, "Sophocles' Oedipus," *Tragic Themes in Western Literature,* edited by Cleanth Brooks. Reprinted by permission of Yale University Press, New Haven, 1955.

Kronenberger, Louis, *The Thread of Laughter*. Reprinted by permission of Alfred A. Knopf, Incorporated.

Lancaster, H. Carrington, *A History of French Dramatic Literature in the Seventeenth Century*, Part III, volume 2. Reprinted by permission of The Johns Hopkins Press.

Lattimore, Richmond, *The Poetry of Greek Tragedy*. Reprinted by permission of The Johns Hopkins Press.

Leech, Clifford, "An Addendum on Webster's Duchess," *Philological Quarterly*, 37 (1958). Reprinted by permission of the editors and Clifford Leech.

Leech, Clifford, *John Webster: A Critical Study*. Reprinted by permission of The Hogarth Press, Ltd., London, 1951.

Leefmans, Bert M-P., "Giraudoux's Other Muse," *Kenyon Review*. Reprinted by permission of the author.

LeSage, Laurent, *Jean Giraudoux: His Life and Works*. Reprinted by permission of The Pennsylvania State University Press.

Letters, F. J. H., *The Life and Work of Sophocles*. Reprinted by permission of Sheed and Ward, Ltd., London, 1953.

Lockert, Lacy, *Studies in French-Classical Tragedy*. Reprinted by permission of Vanderbilt University Press.

Lucas, D. W., *The Greek Tragic Poets*, 2d ed. Reprinted by permission of Cohen and West, Ltd., London, 1959.

Lucas, F. L., "General Introduction," *The Complete Works of John Webster*, vol. 1. Reprinted by permission from F. L. Lucas and Oxford University Press, Oxford, and Chatto and Windus, Ltd., London, 1927.

Lumley, Frederick, *Trends in 20th Century Drama*. Reprinted by permission of Oxford University Press and Barrie and Rockliff.

Magarshack, David, *Chekhov the Dramatist*. Reprinted by permission of Hill and Wang, Inc.

McFarlane, J. W., *Ibsen and the Tempo of Norwegian Literature*. Reprinted by permission of Oxford University Press.

Mortensen, B. M. E. and B. W. Downs, *Strindberg*. Reprinted by permission of Cambridge University Press.

Mueschke, Paul and Miriam, *A New View of Congreve's Way of the World* (1958). Reprinted by permission of and copyright by The University of Michigan.

Murray, Gilbert, *Euripides and His Age*. Reprinted by permission of Oxford University Press.

Nicoll, Allardyce, *World Drama*. Reprinted by permission of Harcourt, Brace & World, Inc.

Norwood, Gilbert, *Greek Tragedy*. Reprinted by permission of and copyright by Methuen & Co., Ltd., published by John W. Luce & Co., Boston, 1932.

Norwood, Gilbert, *Essays on Euripidean Drama*. Reprinted by permission of University of California Press, Berkeley, and University of Toronto Press, Toronto, 1954.

Palmer, John, *Ben Jonson*. Reprinted by permission of Routledge & Kegan Paul, Ltd.

Palmer, John, *The Comedy of Manners*. Reprinted by permission of G. Bell and Sons, Ltd., London, 1913.

Partridge, Edward B., *The Broken Compass*. Reprinted by permission of Columbia University Press, New York, 1958.

Paulson, Arvid, *Letters of Strindberg to Harriet Bosse*. Reprinted by permission of the author.

Peacock, Ronald, *The Poet in the Theatre*, copyright 1946, copyright © 1960 by Ronald Peacock. Reprinted by permission of Hill and Wang, Inc.

Post, L. A., *From Homer to Menander*. Reprinted by permission of University of California Press, Berkeley, 1951.

Poulet, Georges, *Studies in Human Time*. Reprinted by permission of The Johns Hopkins Press.

CONTENTS

Contents

INTRODUCTION

Drama is a much abused term. We hear it applied to tense moments in human life, in phrases such as "the drama of the courtroom." Newspaper feature writers often find "the drama of everyday life" in common situations which are charged with emotion: the faithfulness of a dog to a dead master, the bewilderment of a lost child. Advertisements trumpet as "dramatic" a lady's gown, a coiffure, a perfume. "Let me," says the television announcer, his garb and manner obscurely suggesting some connection with medical science, "let me dramatize this for you"; and imaginary acid eats a hole through a pocket handkerchief, a schematized valve drips liquid into a schematized stomach, diagrammatic pains torture a diagrammatic head. Such varied and inexact uses of the term *drama* do have at least one thing in common: they associate the dramatic with some effect—vivid, moving, or sensational—which events or objects may produce. By a strange transference, *drama* comes to refer not to the thing but to certain of its results; not to an action but to an interaction, real or supposed, between event and spectators.

The psychological reaction of the audience, as an ultimate end toward which drama is designed, is a necessary consideration. To the dramatist it is a compelling consideration, for drama is a form intended for presentation in action before a group. Nevertheless, defining drama in psychological terms is a pitfall, although an inviting one, from which even great critics have not always escaped with complete success. Aristotle found in relief through pity and fear the proper psychological effect of tragedy, thereby leaving succeeding ages to puzzle over just what he meant by that. The limitations of psychological analysis are obvious. Individual reactions vary; tastes and beliefs change; the terms employed often lack precision, and meanings change also. Objective analysis must begin with attention to drama as a form; otherwise, discussion easily degenerates into vague, subjective declarations of individual and often accidental emotions and experiences.

Our word *drama* originated in the Greek verb *dran*: to do; to act; to accomplish. From its beginnings, the drama of the western world has had action as its essential element. Action is vital to drama in two ways: as its matter or content and as its manner or form of presentation.

THE STRUCTURE OF DRAMA

In subject matter, a play is about an action, a happening in human life. Like other kinds of art, it seeks not to furnish a mere stenographic transcription from life, but to order its materials in a form from which emerge meaning and significance. The complete career of any man encompasses a great number of episodes, many of them seemingly insignificant. There is too little meaning—or too much—apparent here. So the dramatist is faced, as is any other artist, with the problem of selection. He must choose from the confused wealth of material available to him a chain of events which center on a particular action, with logically determined limits. He must discover or impose a unity.

One meaning of the Greek word *dran* is *to accomplish,* and in this meaning lies a further key to the structure of drama. A play concerns a human agent attempting to accomplish some purpose. In tragedy his attempt is, in personal terms at least, unsuccessful; in comedy it is successful; in the problem play final accomplishment is often either ambiguous or doubtful.

This action, from the beginning to the end of a movement toward a purposed goal, must also have a middle; it must proceed through a number of steps, the succession of incidents which make up the plot. Because the dramatist is concerned with the meaning and logic of events rather than with their casual relationship in time, he will probably select his material and order it on a basis of the operation, in human affairs, of laws of cause and effect. It is in this causal relationship of incidents that the element of conflict, present in virtually all plays, appears. The central figure of the play—the protagonist—encounters difficulties; his purpose or purposes conflict with events or circumstances, with purposes of other characters in the play, or with cross-purposes which exist within his own thoughts and desires. These difficulties threaten the protagonist's accomplishment; in other words, they present complications, and his success or failure in dealing with these complications determines the outcome. Normally, complications build through the play in order of increasing difficulty; one complication may be added to another, or one may grow out of the solution of a preceding one. At some point in this chain of complication and solution, achieved or attempted, the protagonist performs an act or makes a decision which irrevocably commits him to a further course, points toward certain general consequences. This point is usually called the crisis; the complications and solutions which follow work out the logical steps from crisis to final resolution, or denouement.

This, then, is typical dramatic structure: a human agent is presented in a situation which necessitates the removal of certain difficulties for the achievement of his purpose; the manner in which he meets these difficulties, in combination with the nature of the difficulties themselves, determines his success or failure. Within this general pattern, however, a dramatist has wide latitude for arrangement, and in a sense each play has its own particular structure.

CHARACTER IN DRAMA

The concept of character in drama is a more familiar one than that of action, and to many people it is a more interesting one. Character is rather easily discernible, and it engages a natural interest in personalities. Our reactions to "people" we recognize immediately, verbalize easily. The things that characters do and say are more obvious than are the logic and meaning of the pattern in which they say and do them.

For these very reasons it is easy to overemphasize those aspects of characterization which, although important, are not necessarily of greatest importance. In most cases it is readily apparent whether figures in a play are simple or complex, typed or unique, naturalistic or romanticized, realistic or artificial, sympathetic or antipathetic. Often, however, many such conditions of characterization are decided for the dramatist at the outset, by the dramatic genre in which he is working or by expectations in his audience which must be satisfied. Characters must not only be analyzed for the qualities which they possess and the attitudes which they embody. They must be judged within necessary limitations imposed upon them by the demands of art, in terms of their appropriateness and effectiveness in the particular plot which provides them with a dramatic life. It is the only life they have, and any illusion of a character's vitality extending beyond the bounds of the play in which he appears is merely illusion built on illusion.

The generalizations on structure have already suggested the importance of character in the pattern of complication and solution. The initial situation assumed for any particular play limits in some ways the nature of the characters and the modes of action open to them; their solutions come in answer to problems which help to form their dramatic environment. But a particular character is expected to arrive at particular solutions rather than at other available ones because of the kind of character that he is, because he has been given one set of qualities rather than another. In turn, in the solutions which a character provides he may create further difficulties for himself. Dramatic logic is the plausible working out, in terms of cause and effect, of this mutual relationship between plot and character. When a playwright violates probabilities inherent in this relationship in order to achieve a happy ending or a surprising theatrical effect, he has violated his own assumptions, tricked his audience, and betrayed his art.

SEEING AND READING PLAYS

The form of presentation characteristic of drama must be of acute concern to its readers. Other fictional forms address a reader as reader; they tell about an event or a train of events. But a play is not only about characters engaged in an action; it directly represents that action as taking place before the audience. This characteristic poses a number of problems for the playwright. He must restrict his play in length so that it will be neither wearisome to watch nor impossible to understand at a single sitting. He cannot comment or explain overtly, but must confine comments to those of the characters themselves. He must achieve an immediate emotional and intellectual impact upon a number of people simultaneously. These problems and more force themselves upon the writer of a play, and an awareness of them is indispensable for a thorough study of it. There are other matters, however, which are of more immediate concern to the reader of drama.

What is often ignored is the vast difference which can and often does exist between performances of a single play. A performance occurs at a particular time and place, by actors with certain abilities and training, before an audience with certain expectations and attitudes. The playwright's original conception is postulated on some definite sort of theater, with all

that this implies in terms of acting style, relationship between the play and its audience, and the visual and aural appurtenances at his disposal. A performance is always a reconstruction involving a number of variables which lead to uncertain results. A modern audience would not react in the same way to a presentation of *Oedipus Rex* as did that of Sophocles. Today's theatergoers might grant, in an antiquarian spirit, the idea of oracles; they might accept, as novelties, the masks and cothurni of the actors. But the amphitheater open to surrounding Athens and its temples, the holiday air compounded of religious festival and civic pageant—the setting and atmosphere so important to Sophocles—these are irretrievable. And, as eighteenth century productions of Shakespeare so painfully illustrate, Gresham's Law sometimes operates in the theater, too: bad money drives out good.

The reader of a play must be aware of the limitations which reading imposes. He can then compensate for them in some measure by exercising his visual and auditory imagination, supplying as best he can the sights and sounds of the theater. By familiarizing himself with the evolution of the theater he can, perhaps, go far in the attempt to know a play as it was known by its earliest audience.

Of necessity the student of drama is thrown back upon the written word, but this is neither a peculiar nor an unmitigated handicap. A play exists in the form of words before the fact of its performance, and it survives in words after the performance is over. Not only does the playwright provide the play in this form; the actors who are to perform in it, the director who guides them, the designers of sets and of costumes, all must begin with the written word. While these professionals of the theater enjoy certain advantages of training, experience, and cooperative endeavor, fundamentally they, too, are faced with the problem of fleshing in the skeleton, filling in the outline, which the written words constitute. Critics as formidable as Aristotle and Dr. Johnson have agreed that there is no *essential* difference between a play acted and a play read.

For a reader, the truth of this statement depends largely upon his attention to the complex functions which the words serve. One function is the obvious one of presenting plot. We know what is happening largely through the dialogue, through what is said.

Another function of the dialogue is the presentation of ideas. Any play contains some thought, and a serious play, be it comedy or tragedy or problem play, usually contains a great deal. Here the reader of a play enjoys certain advantages over an observer of its performance. For the latter, a speech is heard when delivered, then is accessible only in the memory. A reader can puzzle over entire speeches or individual lines; he can page back and forth at will. Consequently, he can know the ideas in a play more surely and completely than he could by simply watching a performance. Indeed, the danger is that he will allow the ideas to dominate his view of the play. If a play convinces intellectually it does so through the combination of all its elements; if a reader stresses concepts to the exclusion of the emotions which accompany them and the arrangement in which they appear, he distorts the real meaning of the play. Ideas are held by characters and influence their actions; they conflict just as desires do. The conceptual meaning or theme which a play embodies is usually presented in the dialogue, but it must be consistent with plot and characterization to be valid. It must be a part of the play's totality, not a separate entity.

Language in a play also has other uses: uses which would not require from a spectator the conscious attention necessary for a reader. It helps to establish and to explain character through a figure's choice of words, and the images and sound patterns which he characteristically employs. Further, variations in and departures from a character's typical mode of speech may be used to reflect not only changes in character but turns in the plot as a character's ideas and emotions alter. Finally, the tempo of the dialogue may help to establish changing tempo in the play. For these reasons, it is important that a reader catch the sounds and implications, as well as the sense, of the dialogue.

The complexities of language in drama burden a reader; they make outrageous demands upon a translator. While no translation can reproduce exactly the original style of a work, the translations which appear in this book have been chosen with careful attention to the measure in which they suggest for contemporary readers the flavor of the originals.

THE CRITICISM OF DRAMA

A full appreciation of drama is a critical appreciation. The reading of drama is most productive when we analyze and evaluate. Drama is, of course, entertainment, but it is often a very serious, sometimes even a grim, sort of entertainment, as a ballet may be, or a symphony, or a bullfight. As does any other good work of art, a good play stimulates the imagination, engages the intellect, and sustains lasting interest. Its meaning and value increase with close and continued examination. Understanding good plays of the past also sharpens our ability to perceive the quality and meaning of plays which we encounter for the first time.

Dramatic style extends over the full range of human performance. There are few commitments to a creed or a goal that have not found their voice in a drama, that have not been cheerfully accepted or noisily rejected. With mockery or with sympathy, by quiet agreement or jaunty disagreement, playwrights have opened every sort of idea and person to our inspection. The resultant revelation of character and conviction is among the particular delights of the theater. It is surely worth the special effort required to savor that delight to the fullest.

A special effort is required. There are a few ancient and odd vocabularies to be conned, some strange corridors of history to be entered. The obscurities of language and event are the least of the difficulties, however, and the most easily overcome. Of greater concern to the close reader of plays will be the idiosyncrasies of playwrights, the special idiom of each one. It is here that analysis must be most intense, most precise, and yet open to more than one conclusion. Wisdom in the drama, perhaps more than in any other art, comes through conflicting testimony, for it must follow the infinite oscillations of human character, whether it examines that character as a species, a type, or an individual.

The critical excerpts which accompany the plays in this book are quite capable of speaking for themselves. They all deal with crucial questions in the plays. All are written by critics of some stature. They represent a variety of critical approaches and assumptions; sometimes they represent divergent viewpoints. They are not furnished as counters in a game, the object of which is to guess which is the right answer. In drama, as in all art, there is seldom one right answer; there are a number of partial answers, and the final one has not yet been given. A work of art is not a mathematical problem; it adds up in many ways, and at the same time it equals only itself. In some cases, of course, differing opinions cannot both or all be right; one may preclude another. In such cases a student of drama will be able to make the correct choice for himself.

The point is that it will be his choice, not a directed one. It may even be a choice that the student will later on reject in favor of another. If he recognizes that in the process he has come a little closer to the inner workings of a particular art and to a certain number of persons, himself perhaps among them, then he will have realized the purpose of this book and will have come very close indeed to appreciating the nature of art in general.

SOPHOCLES

c. 497–406 B.C.

The long career of Sophocles overlapped those of Aeschylus and Euripides. His first plays were produced in 468 B.C., in competition with Aeschylus; he is first known to have competed against Euripides in 438 B.C. Unfortunately, only seven plays survive entire of the more than one hundred that he wrote. Apparently he won the prize for tragedy in the City Dionysia some eighteen times, never finishing as low as third. Ironically, Oedipus Rex *(429 B.C.), almost certainly Sophocles's finest play, was not among his victories. The Oedipus myth was familiar to Sophocles's audience. While he could select from among variations in the myth and include or reject minor details, he was committed to the main outlines of the story. The art of fashioning a play from it lay in the handling of known events rather than in the invention of new ones. Briefly, the myth went this way. It was prophesied to Laius, king of Thebes, that he would be murdered by his own son, who would then marry Laius's widow, Jocasta. Hoping to avert this catastrophe, Laius and Jocasta had their infant son's feet pierced and abandoned him on a mountain to die. The child, however, was saved by a shepherd, given to another shepherd, and taken to Corinth, where he was raised by the king and queen as their own. Some years later this prince, unaware that he was an adopted child, heard that it would be his fate to kill his father and marry his mother. Leaving Corinth in precaution, Oedipus (the name means Swell-foot or Clubfoot) killed an elderly man and his followers in a dispute at a crossroads. Going on, he arrived at Thebes when it*

1

was being devastated by the Sphinx. Solving her riddle, he saved the city and became king, marrying the recently widowed Jocasta. Years later, when Thebes again became a sterile waste, the oracle proclaimed the discovery of Laius's slayer to be a condition for the city's deliverance. Oedipus, seeking to solve this mystery, discovered his own guilt.

Oedipus Rex

A VERSION FOR THE MODERN STAGE BY WILLIAM BUTLER YEATS

Characters

OEDIPUS *King of Thebes*

JOCASTA *wife of Oedipus*

ANTIGONE *daughter of Oedipus*

ISMENE *daughter of Oedipus*

CREON *brother-in-law of Oedipus*

TIRESIAS *a seer*

A PRIEST

MESSENGERS

A HERDSMAN

CHORUS

The Palace of King Oedipus at Thebes.

OEDIPUS Children, descendants of old Cadmus, why do you come before me, why do you carry the branches of suppliants, while the city smokes with incense and murmurs with prayer and lamentation? I would not learn from any mouth but yours, old man, therefore I question you myself. Do you know of anything that I can do and have not done? How can I, being the man I am, being King Oedipus, do other than all I know? I were indeed hard of heart did I not pity such suppliants.

PRIEST Oedipus, King of my country, we who stand before your door are of all ages, some too young to have walked so many miles, some —priests of Zeus such as I—too old. Among us stand the pick of the young men, and behind in the market-places the people throng, carrying suppliant branches. We all stand here because the city stumbles towards death, hardly able to raise up its head. A blight has fallen upon the fruitful blossoms of the land, a blight upon flock and field and upon the bed of marriage—plague ravages the city. Oedipus, King, not God but foremost of living men, seeing that when you first came to this town of Thebes you freed us from that harsh singer, the riddling Sphinx, we beseech you, all we suppliants, to find some help; whether you find it by your power as a man, or because, being near the Gods, a God has whispered you. Uplift our State; think upon your fame; your coming brought us luck, be lucky to us still; remember that it is better to rule over men than over a waste place, since neither walled town nor ship is anything if it be empty and no man within it.

OEDIPUS My unhappy children! I know well

3

what need has brought you, what suffering you endure; yet, sufferers though you be, there is not a single one whose suffering is as mine—each mourns himself, but my soul mourns the city, myself, and you. It is not therefore as if you came to arouse a sleeping man. No! Be certain that I have wept many tears and searched hither and thither for some remedy. I have already done the only thing that came into my head for all my search. I have sent the son of Menoeceus, Creon, my own wife's brother, to the Pythian House of Phoebus, to hear if deed or word of mine may yet deliver this town. I am troubled, for he is a long time away —a longer time than should be—but when he comes I shall not be an honest man unless I do whatever the God commands.

PRIEST You have spoken at the right time. They have just signalled to us that Creon has arrived.

OEDIPUS O King Apollo, may he bring brighter fortune, for his face is shining!

PRIEST He brings good news, for he is crowned with bay.

OEDIPUS We shall know soon. Brother-in-law, Menoeceus' son, what news from the God?

CREON Good news; for pain turns to pleasure when we have set the crooked straight.

OEDIPUS But what is the oracle?—so far the news is neither good nor bad.

CREON If you would hear it with all these about you, I am ready to speak. Or do we go within?

OEDIPUS Speak before all. The sorrow I endure is less for my own life than these.

CREON Then, with your leave, I speak. Our lord Phoebus bids us drive out a defiling thing that has been cherished in this land.

OEDIPUS By what purification?

CREON King Laius was our King before you came to pilot us.

OEDIPUS I know—but not of my own knowledge, for I never saw him.

CREON He was killed; and the God now bids us revenge it on his murderers, whoever they be.

OEDIPUS Where shall we come upon their track after all these years? Did he meet his death in house or field, at home or in some foreign land?

CREON In a foreign land: he was journeying to Delphi.

OEDIPUS Did no fellow-traveller see the deed? Was there none there who could be questioned?

CREON All perished but one man who fled in terror and could tell for certain but one thing of all he had seen.

OEDIPUS One thing might be a clue to many things.

CREON He said that they were fallen upon by a great troop of robbers.

OEDIPUS What robbers would be so daring unless bribed from here?

CREON Such things were indeed guessed at, but Laius once dead no avenger arose. We were amid our troubles.

OEDIPUS But when royalty had fallen what troubles could have hindered search?

CREON The riddling Sphinx put those dark things out of our thoughts—we thought of what had come to our own doors.

OEDIPUS But I will start afresh and make the dark things plain. In doing right by Laius I protect myself, for whoever slew Laius might turn a hand against me. Come, my children, rise up from the altar steps; lift up these suppliant boughs and let all the children of Cadmus be called hither that I may search out everything and find for all happiness or misery as God wills.

PRIEST May Phoebus, sender of the oracle, come with it and be our saviour and deliverer!

[*The Chorus enters.*]

CHORUS What message comes to famous Thebes from the Golden House?
What message of disaster from that sweet-throated Zeus?
What monstrous thing our fathers saw do the seasons bring?
Or what that no man ever saw, what new monstrous thing?
Trembling in every limb I raise my loud importunate cry,
And in a sacred terror wait the Delian God's reply.

Apollo chase the God of Death that leads no shouting men,
Bears no rattling shield and yet consumes this form with pain.

Famine takes what the plague spares, and all
the crops are lost;
No new life fills the empty place—ghost flits
after ghost
To that God-trodden western shore, as flit be-
nighted birds.
Sorrow speaks to sorrow, but no comfort finds
in words.

Hurry him from the land of Thebes with a fair
wind behind
Out on to that formless deep where not a man
can find
Hold for an anchor-fluke, for all is world-
enfolding sea;
Master of the thunder-cloud, set the lightning
free,
And add the thunder-stone to that and fling
them on his head,
For death is all the fashion now, till even Death
be dead.

We call against the pallid face of this God-hated
God
The springing heel of Artemis in the hunting
sandal shod,
The tousle-headed Maenads, blown torch and
drunken sound,
The stately Lysian king himself with golden
fillet crowned,
And in his hands the golden bow and the
stretched golden string,
And Bacchus' wine-ensanguined face that all
the Maenads sing.

OEDIPUS You are praying, and it may be that
your prayer will be answered; that if you hear
my words and do my bidding you may find
help out of all your trouble. This is my proclamation, children of Cadmus. Whoever among
you knows by what man Laius, son of Labdacus, was killed, must tell all he knows. If he
fear for himself and being guilty denounce himself, he shall be in the less danger, suffering no
worse thing than banishment. If on the other
hand there be one that knows that a foreigner
did the deed, let him speak, and I shall give
him a reward and my thanks: but if any man
keep silent from fear or to screen a friend, hear
all what I will do to that man. No one in this
land shall speak to him, nor offer sacrifice beside him; but he shall be driven from their
homes as if he himself had done the deed. And
in this I am the ally of the Pythian God and of
the murdered man, and I pray that the murderer's life may, should he be so hidden and
screened, drop from him and perish away, whoever he may be, whether he did the deed with
others or by himself alone: and on you I lay
it to make—so far as man may—these words
good, for my sake, and for the God's sake, and
for the sake of this land. And even if the God
had not spurred us to it, it were a wrong to
leave the guilt unpurged, when one so noble,
and he your King, had perished; and all have
sinned that could have searched it out and did
not: and now since it is I who hold the power
which he held once, and have his wife for wife
—she who would have borne him heirs had he
but lived—I take up this cause even as I would
were it that of my own father. And if there be
any who do not obey me in it, I pray that the
Gods send them neither harvest of the earth nor
fruit of the womb; but let them be wasted by
this plague, or by one more dreadful still. But
may all be blessed for ever who hear my words
and do my will!

CHORUS We do not know the murderer, and it
were indeed more fitting that Phoebus, who laid
the task upon us, should name the man.

OEDIPUS No man can make the Gods speak
against their will.

CHORUS Then I will say what seems the next
best thing.

OEDIPUS If there is a third course, show it.

CHORUS I know that our lord Tiresias is the seer
most like to our lord Phoebus, and through him
we may unravel all.

OEDIPUS So I was advised by Creon, and twice
already have I sent to bring him.

CHORUS If we lack his help we have nothing
but vague and ancient rumours.

OEDIPUS What rumours are they? I would examine every story.

CHORUS Certain wayfarers were said to have
killed the King.

OEDIPUS I know, I know. But who was there
that saw it?

CHORUS If there is such a man, and terror can move him, he will not keep silence when they have told him of your curses.

OEDIPUS He that such a deed did not terrify will not be terrified because of a word.

CHORUS But there is one who shall convict him. For the blind prophet comes at last—in whom alone of all men the truth lives.
[Enter Tiresias, led by a boy.]

OEDIPUS Tiresias, master of all knowledge, whatever may be spoken, whatever is unspeakable, whatever omens of earth and sky reveal, the plague is among us, and from that plague, Great Prophet, protect us and save us. Phoebus in answer to our question says that it will not leave us till we have found the murderers of Laius, and driven them into exile or put them to death. Do you therefore neglect neither the voice of birds, nor any other sort of wisdom, but rescue yourself, rescue the State, rescue me, rescue all that are defiled by the deed. For we are in your hands, and what greater task falls to a man than to help other men with all he knows and has?

TIRESIAS Aye, and what worse task than to be wise and suffer for it? I know this well; it slipped out of mind, or I would never have come.

OEDIPUS What now?

TIRESIAS Let me go home. You will bear your burden to the end more easily, and I bear mine —if you but give me leave for that.

OEDIPUS Your words are strange and unkind to the State that bred you.

TIRESIAS I see that you, on your part, keep your lips tight shut, and therefore I have shut mine that I may come to no misfortune.

OEDIPUS For God's love do not turn away—if you have knowledge. We suppliants implore you on our knees.

TIRESIAS You are fools—I will bring misfortune neither upon you nor upon myself.

OEDIPUS What is this? You know all and will say nothing? You are minded to betray me and Thebes?

TIRESIAS Why do you ask these things? You will not learn them from me.

OEDIPUS What! Basest of the base! You would enrage the very stones. Will you never speak out? Cannot anything touch you?

TIRESIAS The future will come of itself though I keep silent.

OEDIPUS Then seeing that come it must, you had best speak out.

TIRESIAS I will speak no further. Rage if you have a mind to; bring out all the fierceness that is in your heart.

OEDIPUS That will I. I will not spare to speak my thoughts. Listen to what I have to say. It seems to me that you have helped to plot the deed; and, short of doing it with your own hands, have done the deed yourself. Had you eyesight I would declare that you alone had done it.

TIRESIAS So that is what you say? I charge you to obey the decree that you yourself have made, and from this day out to speak neither to these nor to me. You are the defiler of this land.

OEDIPUS So brazen in your impudence? How do you hope to escape punishment?

TIRESIAS I have escaped; my strength is in my truth.

OEDIPUS Who taught you this? You never got it by your art.

TIRESIAS You, because you have spurred me to speech against my will.

OEDIPUS What speech? Speak it again that I may learn it better.

TIRESIAS You are but tempting me—you understood me well enough.

OEDIPUS No; not so that I can say I know it; speak it again.

TIRESIAS I say that you are yourself the murderer that you seek.

OEDIPUS You shall rue it for having spoken twice such outrageous words.

TIRESIAS Would you that I say more that you may be still angrier?

OEDIPUS Say what you will. I will not let it move me.

TIRESIAS I say that you are living with your next of kin in unimagined shame.

OEDIPUS Do you think you can say such things and never smart for it?

TIRESIAS Yes, if there be strength in truth.

OEDIPUS There is; yes—for everyone but you. But not for you that are maimed in ear and in eye and in wit.

TIRESIAS You are but a poor wretch flinging

taunts that in a little while everyone shall fling at you.

OEDIPUS Night, endless night has covered you up so that you can neither hurt me nor any man that looks upon the sun.

TIRESIAS Your doom is not to fall by me. Apollo is enough: it is his business to work out your doom.

OEDIPUS Was it Creon that planned this or you yourself?

TIRESIAS Creon is not your enemy; you are your own enemy.

OEDIPUS Power, ability, position, you bear all burdens, and yet what envy you create! Great must that envy be if envy of my power in this town—a power put into my hands unsought—has made trusty Creon, my old friend Creon, secretly long to take that power from me; if he has suborned this scheming juggler, this quack and trickster, this man with eyes for his gains and blindness in his art. Come, come, where did you prove yourself a seer? Why did you say nothing to set the townsmen free when the riddling Sphinx was here? Yet that riddle was not for the first-comer to read; it needed the skill of a seer. And none such had you! Neither found by help of birds, nor straight from any God. No, I came; I silenced her, I the ignorant Oedipus, it was I that found the answer in my mother-wit, untaught by any birds. And it is I that you would pluck out of my place, thinking to stand close to Creon's throne. But you and the plotter of all this shall mourn despite your zeal to purge the land. Were you not an old man, you had already learnt how bold you are and learnt it to your cost.

CHORUS Both this man's words and yours, Oedipus, have been said in anger. Such words cannot help us here, nor any but those that teach us to obey the oracle.

TIRESIAS King though you are, the right to answer when attacked belongs to both alike. I am not subject to you, but to Loxias; and therefore I shall never be Creon's subject. And I tell you, since you have taunted me with blindness, that though you have your sight, you cannot see in what misery you stand, nor where you are living, nor with whom, unknowing what you do—for you do not know the stock you come of—you have been your own kin's enemy be they living or be they dead. And one day a mother's curse and father's curse alike shall drive you from this land in dreadful haste with darkness upon those eyes. Therefore, heap your scorn on Creon and on my message if you have a mind to; for no one of living men shall be crushed as you shall be crushed.

OEDIPUS Begone this instant! Away, away! Get you from these doors!

TIRESIAS I had never come but that you sent for me.

OEDIPUS I did not know you were mad.

TIRESIAS I may seem mad to you, but your parents thought me sane.

OEDIPUS My parents! Stop! Who was my father?

TIRESIAS This day shall you know your birth; and it will ruin you.

OEDIPUS What dark words you always speak!

TIRESIAS But are you not most skillful in the unravelling of dark words?

OEDIPUS You mock me for that which made me great?

TIRESIAS It was that fortune that undid you.

OEDIPUS What do I care? For I delivered all this town.

TIRESIAS Then I will go: boy, lead me out of this.

OEDIPUS Yes, let him lead you. You take vexation with you.

TIRESIAS I will go: but first I will do my errand. For frown though you may you cannot destroy me. The man for whom you look, the man you have been threatening in all the proclamations about the death of Laius, that man is here. He seems, so far as looks go, an alien; yet he shall be found a native Theban and shall nowise be glad of that fortune. A blind man, though now he has his sight; a beggar, though now he is most rich; he shall go forth feeling the ground before him with his stick; so you go in and think on that, and if you find I am in fault say that I have no skill in prophecy.

[*Tiresias is led out by the boy. Oedipus enters the palace.*]

CHORUS The Delphian rock has spoken out, now must a wicked mind,
Planner of things I dare not speak and of this bloody wrack,

Oedipus Rex

Pray for feet that are as fast as the four hoofs
    of the wind:
Cloudy Parnassus and the Fates thunder at his
    back.

That sacred crossing-place of lines upon Par-
    nassus' head,
Lines that have run through North and South,
    and run through West and East,
That navel of the world bids all men search the
    mountain wood,
The solitary cavern, till they have found that
    infamous beast.

[*Creon enters from the house.*]

CREON Fellow-citizens, having heard that King
Oedipus accuses me of dreadful things, I come
in my indigation. Does he think that he has
suffered wrong from me in these present troubles, or anything that could lead to wrong,
whether in word or deed? How can I live under
blame like that? What life would be worth
having if by you here, and by my nearest
friends, called a traitor through the town?

CHORUS He said it in anger, and not from his
heart out.

CREON He said it was I put up the seer to speak
those falsehoods.

CHORUS Such things were said.

CREON And had he his right mind saying it?

CHORUS I do not know—I do not know what
my masters do.

[*Oedipus enters.*]

OEDIPUS What brought you here? Have you a
face so brazen that you come to my house—
you, the proved assassin of its master—the certain robber of my crown? Come, tell me in
the face of the Gods what cowardice, or folly,
did you discover in me that you plotted this?
Did you think that I would not see what you
were at till you had crept upon me, or seeing
it would not ward it off? What madness to
seek a throne, having neither friends nor followers!

CREON Now, listen, hear my answer, and then
you may with knowledge judge between us.

OEDIPUS You are plausible, but waste words
now that I know you.

CREON Hear what I have to say. I can explain
it all.

OEDIPUS One thing you will not explain away—
that you are my enemy.

CREON You are a fool to imagine that senseless
stubbornness sits well upon you.

OEDIPUS And you to imagine that you can
wrong a kinsman and escape the penalty.

CREON That is justly said, I grant you; but what
is this wrong that you complain of?

OEDIPUS Did you advise, or not, that I should
send for that notorious prophet?

CREON And I am of the same mind still.

OEDIPUS How long is it, then, since Laius—

CREON What, what about him?

OEDIPUS Since Laius was killed by an unknown
hand?

CREON That was many years ago.

OEDIPUS Was this prophet at his trade in those
days?

CREON Yes; skilled as now and in equal honour.

OEDIPUS Did he ever speak of me?

CREON Never certainly when I was within earshot.

OEDIPUS And did you enquire into the murder?

CREON We did enquire but learnt nothing.

OEDIPUS And why did he not tell out his story
then?

CREON I do not know. When I know nothing I
say nothing.

OEDIPUS This much at least you know and can
say out.

CREON What is that? If I know it I will say it.

OEDIPUS That if he had not consulted you he
would never have said that it was I who killed
Laius.

CREON You know best what he said; but now,
question for question.

OEDIPUS Question your fill—I cannot be proved
guilty of that blood.

CREON Answer me then. Are you not married
to my sister?

OEDIPUS That cannot be denied.

CREON And do you not rule as she does? And
with a like power?

OEDIPUS I give her all she asks for.

CREON And am not I the equal of you both?

OEDIPUS Yes: and that is why you are so false
a friend.

CREON Not so; reason this out as I reason it,
and first weigh this: who would prefer to lie

awake amid terrors rather than to sleep in peace, granting that his power is equal in both cases? Neither I nor any sober-minded man. You give me what I ask and let me do what I want, but were I King I would have to do things I did not want to do. Is not influence and no trouble with it better than any throne, am I such a fool as to hunger after unprofitable honours? Now all are glad to see me, every one wishes me well, all that want a favour from you ask speech of me—finding in that their hope. Why should I give up these things and take those? No wise mind is treacherous. I am no contriver of plots, and if another took to them he would not come to me for help. And in proof of this go to the Pythian Oracle, and ask if I have truly told what the Gods said: and after that, if you have found that I have plotted with the Sooth-sayer, take me and kill me; not by the sentence of one mouth only—but of two mouths, yours and my own. But do not condemn me in a corner, upon some fancy and without proof. What right have you to declare a good man bad or a bad good? It is as bad a thing to cast off a true friend as it is for a man to cast away his own life—but you will learn these things with certainty when the time comes; for time alone shows a just man; though a day can show a knave.

CHORUS   King! He has spoken well, he gives himself time to think; a headlong talker does not know what he is saying.

OEDIPUS   The plotter is at his work, and I must counterplot headlong, or he will get his ends and I miss mine.

CREON   What will you do then? Drive me from the land?

OEDIPUS   Not so; I do not desire your banishment—but your death.

CREON   You are not sane.

OEDIPUS   I am sane at least in my own interest.

CREON   You should be in mine also.

OEDIPUS   No, for you are false.

CREON   But if you understand nothing?

OEDIPUS   Yet I must rule.

CREON   Not if you rule badly.

OEDIPUS   Hear him, O Thebes!

CREON   Thebes is for me also, not for you alone.

CHORUS   Cease, princes: I see Jocasta coming out of the house; she comes just in time to quench the quarrel.

[*Jocasta enters.*]

JOCASTA   Unhappy men! Why have you made this crazy uproar? Are you not ashamed to quarrel about your own affairs when the whole country is in trouble? Go back into the palace, Oedipus, and you, Creon, to your own house. Stop making all this noise about some petty thing.

CREON   Your husband is about to kill me—or to drive me from the land of my fathers.

OEDIPUS   Yes: for I have convicted him of treachery against me.

CREON   Now may I perish accursed if I have done such a thing!

JOCASTA   For God's love believe it, Oedipus. First, for the sake of his oath, and then for my sake, and for the sake of these people here.

CHORUS   King, do what she asks.

OEDIPUS   What would you have me do?

CHORUS   Not to make a dishonourable charge, with no more evidence than rumour, against a friend who has bound himself with an oath.

OEDIPUS   Do you desire my exile or my death?

CHORUS   No, by Helios, by the first of all the Gods, may I die abandoned by Heaven and earth if I have that thought! What breaks my heart is that our public griefs should be increased by your quarrels.

OEDIPUS   Then let him go, though I am doomed thereby to death or to be thrust dishonoured from the land; it is your lips, not his, that move me to compassion; wherever he goes my hatred follows him.

CREON   You are as sullen in yielding as you were vehement in anger, but such natures are their own heaviest burden.

OEDIPUS   Why will you not leave me in peace and begone?

CREON   I will go away; what is your hatred to me? In the eyes of all here I am a just man. [*He goes.*]

CHORUS   Lady, why do you not take your man in to the house?

JOCASTA   I will do so when I have learned what has happened.

CHORUS   The half of it was blind suspicion bred of talk; the rest the wounds left by injustice.

JOCASTA It was on both sides?

CHORUS Yes.

JOCASTA What was it?

CHORUS Our land is vexed enough. Let the thing alone now that it is over.

[Exit Leader of Chorus.]

JOCASTA In the name of the Gods, King, what put you in this anger?

OEDIPUS I will tell you; for I honour you more than these men do. The cause is Creon and his plots against me.

JOCASTA Speak on, if you can tell clearly how this quarrel arose.

OEDIPUS He says that I am guilty of the blood of Laius.

JOCASTA On his own knowledge, or on hearsay?

OEDIPUS He has made a rascal of a seer his mouthpiece.

JOCASTA Do not fear that there is truth in what he says. Listen to me, and learn to your comfort that nothing born of woman can know what is to come. I will give you proof of that. An oracle came to Laius once, I will not say from Phoebus, but from his ministers, that he was doomed to die by the hand of his own child sprung from him and me. When his child was but three days old, Laius bound its feet together and had it thrown by sure hands upon a trackless mountain; and when Laius was murdered at the place where three highways meet, it was, or so at least the rumour says, by foreign robbers. So Apollo did not bring it about that the child should kill its father, nor did Laius die in the dreadful way he feared by his child's hand. Yet that was how the message of the seers mapped out the future. Pay no attention to such things. What the God would show he will need no help to show it, but bring it to light himself.

OEDIPUS What restlessness of soul, lady, has come upon me since I heard you speak, what a tumult of the mind!

JOCASTA What is this new anxiety? What has startled you?

OEDIPUS You said that Laius was killed where three highways meet.

JOCASTA Yes: that was the story.

OEDIPUS And where is the place?

JOCASTA In Phocis where the road divides branching off to Delphi and to Daulia.

OEDIPUS And when did it happen? How many years ago?

JOCASTA News was published in this town just before you came into power.

OEDIPUS O Zeus! What have you planned to do unto me?

JOCASTA He was tall; the silver had just come into his hair; and in shape not greatly unlike to you.

OEDIPUS Unhappy that I am! It seems that I have laid a dreadful curse upon myself, and did not know it.

JOCASTA What do you say? I tremble when I look on you, my King.

OEDIPUS And I have a misgiving that the seer can see indeed. But I will know it all more clearly, if you tell me one thing more.

JOCASTA Indeed, though I tremble I will answer whatever you ask.

OEDIPUS Had he but a small troop with him; or did he travel like a great man with many followers?

JOCASTA There were but five in all—one of them a herald; and there was one carriage with Laius in it.

OEDIPUS Alas! It is now clear indeed. Who was it brought the news, lady?

JOCASTA A servant—the one survivor.

OEDIPUS Is he by chance in the house now?

JOCASTA No; for when he found you reigning instead of Laius he besought me, his hand clasped in mine, to send him to the fields among the cattle that he might be far from the sight of this town; and I sent him. He was a worthy man for a slave and might have asked a bigger thing.

OEDIPUS I would have him return to us without delay.

JOCASTA Oedipus, it is easy. But why do you ask this?

OEDIPUS I fear that I have said too much, and therefore I would question him.

JOCASTA He shall come, but I too have a right to know what lies so heavy upon your heart, my King.

OEDIPUS Yes: and it shall not be kept from you now that my fear has grown so heavy. Nobody is more to me than you, nobody has the same right to learn my good or evil luck. My father was Polybus of Corinth, my mother the Dorian Merope, and I was held the foremost man in all that town until a thing happened—a thing to startle a man, though not to make him angry as it made me. We were sitting at the table, and a man who had drunk too much cried out that I was not my father's son—and I, though angry, restrained my anger for that day; but the next day went to my father and my mother and questioned them. They were indignant at the taunt and that comforted me—and yet the man's words rankled, for they had spread a rumour through the town. Without consulting my father or my mother I went to Delphi, but Phoebus told me nothing of the thing for which I came, but much of other things—things of sorrow and of terror: that I should live in incest with my mother, and beget a brood that men would shudder to look upon; that I should be my father's murderer. Hearing those words I fled out of Corinth, and from that day have but known where it lies when I have found its direction by the stars. I sought where I might escape those infamous things—the doom that was laid upon me. I came in my flight to that very spot where you tell me this king perished. Now, lady, I will tell you the truth. When I had come close up to those three roads, I came upon a herald, and a man like him you have described seated in a carriage. The man who held the reins and the old man himself would not give me room, but thought to force me from the path, and I struck the driver in my anger. The old man, seeing what I had done, waited till I was passing him and then struck me upon the head. I paid him back in full, for I knocked him out of the carriage with a blow of my stick. He rolled on his back, and after that I killed them all. If this stranger were indeed Laius, is there a more miserable man in the world than the man before you? Is there a man more hated of Heaven? No stranger, no citizen, may receive him into his house, not a soul may speak to him, and no mouth but my own mouth has laid this curse upon me. Am I not wretched? May I be swept from this world before I have endured this doom!

CHORUS These things, O King, fill us with terror; yet hope till you speak with him that saw the deed, and have learnt all.

OEDIPUS Till I have learnt all, I may hope. I await the man that is coming from the pastures.

JOCASTA What is it that you hope to learn?

OEDIPUS I will tell you. If his tale agrees with yours, then I am clear.

JOCASTA What tale of mine?

OEDIPUS He told you that Laius met his death from robbers; if he keeps to that tale now and speaks of several slayers, I am not the slayer. But if he says one lonely wayfarer, then beyond a doubt the scale dips to me.

JOCASTA Be certain of this much at least, his first tale was of robbers. He cannot revoke that tale—the city heard it and not I alone. Yet, if he should somewhat change his story, King, at least he cannot make the murder of Laius square with prophecy; for Loxias plainly said of Laius that he would die by the hand of my child. That poor innocent did not kill him, for it died before him. Therefore from this out I would not, for all divination can do, so much as look to my right hand or to my left hand, or fear at all.

OEDIPUS You have judged well; and yet for all that, send and bring this peasant to me.

JOCASTA I will send without delay. I will do all that you would have of me—but let us come in to the house.

[They go in to the house.]

CHORUS For this one thing above all I would
    be praised as a man,
That in my words and my deeds I have kept
    those laws in mind
Olympian Zeus, and that high clear Empyrean,
Fashioned, and not some man or people of
    mankind,
Even those sacred laws nor age nor sleep can
    blind.

A man becomes a tyrant out of insolence,
He climbs and climbs, until all people call him
    great,
He seems upon the summit, and God flings him
    thence;
Yet an ambitious man may lift up a whole
    State,

Oedipus Rex

11

And in his death be blessed, in his life fortunate.

And all men honour such; but should a man forget
The holy images, the Delphian Sibyl's trance,
And the world's navel-stone, and not be punished for it
And seem most fortunate, or even blessed perchance,
Why should we honour the Gods, or join the sacred dance?

[*Jocasta enters from the palace.*]

JOCASTA It has come into my head, citizens of Thebes, to visit every altar of the Gods, a wreath in my hand and a dish of incense. For all manner of alarms trouble the soul of Oedipus, who instead of weighing new oracles by old, like a man of sense, is at the mercy of every mouth that speaks terror. Seeing that my words are nothing to him, I cry to you, Lysian Apollo, whose altar is the first I meet: I come, a suppliant, bearing symbols of prayer; O, make us clean, for now we are all afraid, seeing him afraid, even as they who see the helmsman afraid.

[*Enter Messenger.*]

MESSENGER May I learn from you, strangers, where is the home of King Oedipus? Or better still, tell me where he himself is, if you know.

CHORUS This is his house, and he himself, stranger, is within it, and this lady is the mother of his children.

MESSENGER Then I call a blessing upon her, seeing what man she has married.

JOCASTA May God reward those words with a like blessing, stranger! But what have you come to seek or to tell?

MESSENGER Good news for your house, lady, and for your husband.

JOCASTA What news? From whence have you come?

MESSENGER From Corinth, and you will rejoice at the message I am about to give you; yet, maybe, it will grieve you.

JOCASTA What is it? How can it have this double power?

MESSENGER The people of Corinth, they say, will take him for king.

JOCASTA How then? Is old Polybus no longer on the throne?

MESSENGER No. He is in his tomb.

JOCASTA What do you say? Is Polybus dead, old man?

MESSENGER May I drop dead if it is not the truth.

JOCASTA Away! Hurry to your master with this news. O oracle of the Gods, where are you now? This is the man whom Oedipus feared and shunned lest he should murder him, and now this man has died a natural death, and not by the hand of Oedipus.

[*Enter Oedipus.*]

OEDIPUS Jocasta, dearest wife, why have you called me from the house?

JOCASTA Listen to this man, and judge to what the oracles of the Gods have come.

OEDIPUS And he—who may he be? And what news has he?

JOCASTA He has come from Corinth to tell you that your father, Polybus, is dead.

OEDIPUS How, stranger? Let me have it from your own mouth.

MESSENGER If I am to tell the story, the first thing is that he is dead and gone.

OEDIPUS By some sickness or by treachery?

MESSENGER A little thing can bring the aged to their rest.

OEDIPUS Ah! He died, it seems, from sickness?

MESSENGER Yes; and of old age.

OEDIPUS Alas! Alas! Why, indeed, my wife, should one look to that Pythian seer, or to the birds that scream above our heads? For they would have it that I was doomed to kill my father. And now he is dead—hid already beneath the earth. And here am I—who had no part in it, unless indeed he died from longing for me. If that were so, I may have caused his death; but Polybus has carried the oracles with him into Hades—the oracles as men have understood them—and they are worth nothing.

JOCASTA Did I not tell you so, long since?

OEDIPUS You did, but fear misled me.

JOCASTA Put this trouble from you.

OEDIPUS Those bold words would sound better, were not my mother living. But as it is—I have some grounds for fear; yet you have said well.

SOPHOCLES

JOCASTA Yet your father's death is a sign that all is well.

OEDIPUS I know that: but I fear because of her who lives.

MESSENGER Who is this woman who makes you afraid?

OEDIPUS Merope, old man, the wife of Polybus.

MESSENGER What is there in her to make you afraid?

OEDIPUS A dreadful oracle sent from Heaven, stranger.

MESSENGER Is it a secret, or can you speak it out?

OEDIPUS Loxias said that I was doomed to marry my own mother, and to shed my father's blood. For that reason I fled from my house in Corinth; and I did right, though there is great comfort in familiar faces.

MESSENGER Was it indeed for that reason that you went into exile?

OEDIPUS I did not wish, old man, to shed my father's blood.

MESSENGER King, have I not freed you from that fear?

OEDIPUS You shall be fittingly rewarded.

MESSENGER Indeed, to tell the truth, it was for that I came; to bring you home and be the better for it—

OEDIPUS No! I will never go to my parents' home.

MESSENGER Oh, my son, it is plain enough, you do not know what you do.

OEDIPUS How, old man? For God's love, tell me.

MESSENGER If for these reasons you shrink from going home.

OEDIPUS I am afraid lest Phoebus has spoken true.

MESSENGER You are afraid of being made guilty through Merope?

OEDIPUS That is my constant fear.

MESSENGER A vain fear.

OEDIPUS How so, if I was born of that father and mother?

MESSENGER Because they were nothing to you in blood.

OEDIPUS What do you say? Was Polybus not my father?

MESSENGER No more nor less than myself.

OEDIPUS How can my father be no more to me than you who are nothing to me?

MESSENGER He did not beget you any more than I.

OEDIPUS No? Then why did he call me his son?

MESSENGER He took you as a gift from these hands of mine.

OEDIPUS How could he love so dearly what came from another's hands?

MESSENGER He had been childless.

OEDIPUS If I am not your son, where did you get me?

MESSENGER In a wooded valley of Cithaeron.

OEDIPUS What brought you wandering there?

MESSENGER I was in charge of mountain sheep.

OEDIPUS A shepherd—a wandering, hired man.

MESSENGER A hired man who came just in time.

OEDIPUS Just in time—had it come to that?

MESSENGER Have not the cords left their marks upon your ankles?

OEDIPUS Yes, that is an old trouble.

MESSENGER I took your feet out of the spancel.

OEDIPUS I have had those marks from the cradle.

MESSENGER They have given you the name you bear.

OEDIPUS Tell me, for God's sake, was that deed my mother's or my father's?

MESSENGER I do not know—he who gave you to me knows more of that than I.

OEDIPUS What? You had me from another? You did not chance on me yourself?

MESSENGER No. Another shepherd gave you to me.

OEDIPUS Who was he? Can you tell me who he was?

MESSENGER I think that he was said to be of Laius' household.

OEDIPUS The king who ruled this country long ago?

MESSENGER The same—the man was herdsman in his service.

OEDIPUS Is he alive, that I might speak with him?

MESSENGER You people of this country should know that.

OEDIPUS Is there any one here present who knows the herd he speaks of? Any one who has seen him in the town pastures? The hour has come when all must be made clear.

CHORUS   I think he is the very herd you sent for but now; Jocasta can tell you better than I.

JOCASTA   Why ask about that man? Why think about him? Why waste a thought on what this man has said? What he has said is of no account.

OEDIPUS   What, with a clue like that in my hands and fail to find out my birth?

JOCASTA   For God's sake, if you set any value upon your life, give up this search—my misery is enough.

OEDIPUS   Though I be proved the son of a slave, yes, even of three generations of slaves, you cannot be made base-born.

JOCASTA   Yet, hear me, I implore you. Give up this search.

OEDIPUS   I will not hear of anything but searching the whole thing out.

JOCASTA   I am only thinking of your good—I have advised you for the best.

OEDIPUS   Your advice makes me impatient.

JOCASTA   May you never come to know who you are, unhappy man!

OEDIPUS   Go, some one, bring the herdsman here —and let that woman glory in her noble blood.

JOCASTA   Alas, alas, miserable man! Miserable! That is all that I can call you now or for ever. [She goes out.]

CHORUS   Why has the lady gone, Oedipus, in such a transport of despair? Out of this silence will burst a storm of sorrows.

OEDIPUS   Let come what will. However lowly my origin I will discover it. That woman, with all a woman's pride, grows red with shame at my base birth. I think myself the child of Good Luck, and that the years are my foster-brothers. Sometimes they have set me up, and sometimes thrown me down, but he that has Good Luck for mother can suffer no dishonour. That is my origin, nothing can change it, so why should I renounce this search into my birth?

CHORUS   Oedipus' nurse, mountain of many a hidden glen,

Be honoured among men;

A famous man, deep-thoughted, and his body strong;

Be honoured in dance and song.

Who met in the hidden glen? Who let his fancy run

Upon nymph of Helicon?

Lord Pan or Lord Apollo or the mountain Lord

By the Bacchantes adored?

OEDIPUS   If I, who have never met the man, may venture to say so, I think that the herdsman we await approaches; his venerable age matches with this stranger's, and I recognize as servants of mine those who bring him. But you, if you have seen the man before, will know the man better than I.

CHORUS   Yes, I know the man who is coming; he was indeed in Laius' service, and is still the most trusted of the herdsmen.

OEDIPUS   I ask you first, Corinthian stranger, is this the man you mean?

MESSENGER   He is the very man.

OEDIPUS   Look at me, old man! Answer my questions. Were you once in Laius' service?

HERDSMAN   I was: not a bought slave, but reared up in the house.

OEDIPUS   What was your work—your manner of life?

HERDSMAN   For the best part of my life I have tended flocks.

OEDIPUS   Where, mainly?

HERDSMAN   Cithaeron or its neighbourhood.

OEDIPUS   Do you remember meeting with this man there?

HERDSMAN   What man do you mean?

OEDIPUS   This man. Did you ever meet him?

HERDSMAN   I cannot recall him to mind.

MESSENGER   No wonder in that, master; but I will bring back his memory. He and I lived side by side upon Cithaeron. I had but one flock and he had two. Three full half-years we lived there, from spring to autumn, and every winter I drove my flock to my own fold, while he drove his to the fold of Laius. Is that right? Was it not so?

HERDSMAN   True enough; though it was long ago.

MESSENGER   Come, tell me now—do you remember giving me a boy to rear as my own foster-son?

HERDSMAN   What are you saying? Why do you ask me that?

MESSENGER   Look at that man, my friend, he is

the child you gave me.

HERDSMAN A plague upon you! Cannot you hold your tongue?

OEDIPUS Do not blame him, old man; your own words are more blameable.

HERDSMAN And how have I offended, master?

OEDIPUS In not telling of that boy he asks of.

HERDSMAN He speaks from ignorance, and does not know what he is saying.

OEDIPUS If you will not speak with a good grace you shall be made to speak.

HERDSMAN Do not hurt me for the love of God, I am an old man.

OEDIPUS Some one there, tie his hands behind his back.

HERDSMAN Alas! Wherefore! What more would you learn?

OEDIPUS Did you give this man the child he speaks of?

HERDSMAN I did: would I had died that day!

OEDIPUS Well, you may come to that unless you speak the truth.

HERDSMAN Much more am I lost if I speak it.

OEDIPUS What! Would the fellow make more delay?

HERDSMAN No, no. I said before that I gave it to him.

OEDIPUS Where did you come by it? Your own child, or another?

HERDSMAN It was not my own child—I had it from another.

OEDIPUS From any of those here? From what house?

HERDSMAN Do not ask any more, master; for the love of God do not ask.

OEDIPUS You are lost if I have to question you again.

HERDSMAN It was a child from the house of Laius.

OEDIPUS A slave? Or one of his own race?

HERDSMAN Alas! I am on the edge of dreadful words.

OEDIPUS And I of hearing: yet hear I must.

HERDSMAN It was said to have been his own child. But your lady within can tell you of these things best.

OEDIPUS How? It was she who gave it to you?

HERDSMAN Yes, King.

OEDIPUS To what end?

HERDSMAN That I should make away with it.

OEDIPUS Her own child?

HERDSMAN Yes: from fear of evil prophecies.

OEDIPUS What prophecies?

HERDSMAN That he should kill his father.

OEDIPUS Why, then, did you give him up to this old man?

HERDSMAN Through pity, master, believing that he would carry him to whatever land he had himself come from—but he saved him for dreadful misery; for if you are what this man says, you are the most miserable of all men.

OEDIPUS O! O! All brought to pass! All truth! Now, O light, may I look my last upon you, having been found accursed in bloodshed, accursed in marriage, and in my coming into the world accursed! [*He rushes into the palace.*]

CHORUS What can the shadow-like generations of man attain
But build up a dazzling mockery of delight that under their touch dissolves again?
Oedipus seemed blessed, but there is no man blessed amongst men.

Oedipus overcame the woman-breasted Fate;
He seemed like a strong tower against Death and first among the fortunate;
He sat upon the ancient throne of Thebes, and all men called him great.

But, looking for a marriage-bed, he found the bed of his birth,
Tilled the field his father had tilled, cast seed into the same abounding earth;
Entered through the door that had sent him wailing forth.

Begetter and begot as one! How could that be hid?
What darkness cover up that marriage-bed? Time watches, he is eagle-eyed,
And all the works of man are known and every soul is tried.

Would you had never come to Thebes, nor to this house,
Nor riddled with the woman-breasted Fate, beaten off Death and succoured us,

That I had never raised this song, heartbroken Oedipus!

SECOND MESSENGER [*coming from the house*] Friends and kinsmen of this house! What deeds must you look upon, what burden of sorrow bear, if true to race you still love the House of Labdacus. For not Ister nor Phasis could wash this house clean, so many misfortunes have been brought upon it, so many has it brought upon itself, and those misfortunes are always the worst that a man brings upon himself.

CHORUS Great already are the misfortunes of this house, and you bring us a new tale.

SECOND MESSENGER A short tale in the telling: Jocasta, our Queen, is dead.

CHORUS Alas, miserable woman, how did she die?

SECOND MESSENGER By her own hand. It cannot be as terrible to you as to one that saw it with his eyes, yet so far as words can serve, you shall see it. When she had come into the vestibule, she ran half crazed towards her marriage-bed, clutching at her hair with the fingers of both hands, and once within the chamber dashed the doors together behind her. Then called upon the name of Laius, long since dead, remembering that son who killed the father and upon the mother begot an accursed race. And wailed because of that marriage wherein she had borne a two-fold race—husband by husband, children by her child. Then Oedipus with a shriek burst in and running here and there asked for a sword, asked where he would find the wife that was no wife but a mother who had borne his children and himself. Nobody answered him, we all stood dumb; but supernatural power helped him, for, with a dreadful shriek, as though beckoned, he sprang at the double doors, drove them in, burst the bolts out of their sockets, and ran into the room. There we saw the woman hanging in a swinging halter, and with a terrible cry he loosened the halter from her neck. When that unhappiest woman lay stretched upon the ground, we saw another dreadful sight. He dragged the golden brooches from her dress and lifting them struck them upon his eyeballs, crying out, "You have looked enough upon those you ought never to have looked upon, failed long enough to know those that you should have known; henceforth you shall be dark." He struck his eyes, not once, but many times, lifting his hands and speaking such or like words. The blood poured down and not with a few slow drops, but all at once over his beard in a dark shower as it were hail. [*The Chorus wails; stepping further on to the stage*] Such evils have come forth from the deeds of those two and fallen not on one alone but upon husband and wife. They inherited much happiness, much good fortune; but to-day, ruin, shame, death, and loud crying, all evils that can be counted up, all, all are theirs.

CHORUS Is he any quieter?

SECOND MESSENGER He cries for someone to unbar the gates and to show to all the men of Thebes his father's murderer, his mother's—the unholy word must not be spoken. It is his purpose to cast himself out of the land that he may not bring all this house under his curse. But he has not the strength to do it. He must be supported and led away. The curtain is parting; you are going to look upon a sight which even those who shudder must pity.

[*Enter Oedipus.*]

OEDIPUS Woe, woe is me! Miserable, miserable that I am! Where am I? Where am I going? Where am I cast away? Who hears my words?

CHORUS Cast away indeed, dreadful to the sight of the eye, dreadful to the ear.

OEDIPUS Ah, friend, the only friend left to me, friend still faithful to the blind man! I know that you are there; blind though I am, I recognise your voice.

CHORUS Where did you get the courage to put out your eyes? What unearthly power drove you to that?

OEDIPUS Apollo, friends, Apollo, but it was my own hand alone, wretched that I am, that quenched these eyes.

CHORUS You were better dead than blind.

OEDIPUS No, it is better to be blind. What sight is there that could give me joy? How could I have looked into the face of my father when I came among the dead, aye, or on my miserable mother, since against them both I sinned such things that no halter can punish? And what to me this spectacle, town, statue, wall, and what to me this people, since I, thrice wretched, I, noblest of Theban men, have doomed myself to banishment, doomed myself when I commanded all to thrust out the unclean thing?

CHORUS It had indeed been better if that herdsman had never taken your feet out of the spancel or brought you back to life.

OEDIPUS O three roads, O secret glen; O coppice and narrow way where three roads met; you that drank up the blood I spilt, the blood that was my own, my father's blood: remember what deeds I wrought for you to look upon, and then, when I had come hither, the new deeds that I wrought. O marriage-bed that gave me birth and after that gave children to your child, creating an incestuous kindred of fathers, brothers, sons, wives, and mothers. Yes, all the shame and the uncleanness that I have wrought among men.

CHORUS For all my pity I shudder and turn away.

OEDIPUS Come near, condescend to lay your hands upon a wretched man; listen, do not fear. My plague can touch no man but me. Hide me somewhere out of this land for God's sake, or kill me, or throw me into the sea where you shall never look upon me more.

[Enter Creon and attendants.]

CHORUS Here Creon comes at a fit moment; you can ask of him what you will, help or counsel, for he is now in your place. He is King.

OEDIPUS What can I say to him? What can I claim, having been altogether unjust to him.

CREON I have not come in mockery, Oedipus, nor to reproach you. Lead him in to the house as quickly as you can. Do not let him display his misery before strangers.

OEDIPUS I must obey, but first, since you have come in so noble a spirit, you will hear me.

CREON Say what you will.

OEDIPUS I know that you will give her that lies within such a tomb as befits your own blood, but there is something more, Creon. My sons are men and can take care of themselves, but my daughters, my two unhappy daughters, that have ever eaten at my own table and shared my food, watch over my daughters, Creon. If it is lawful, let me touch them with my hands. Grant it, Prince, grant it, noble heart. I would believe, could I touch them, that I still saw them. [Ismene and Antigone are led in by attendants.] But do I hear them sobbing? Has Creon pitied me and sent my children, my darlings? Has he done this?

CREON Yes, I ordered it, for I know how greatly you have always loved them.

OEDIPUS Then may you be blessed, and may Heaven be kinder to you than it has been to me! My children, where are you? Come hither —hither—come to the hands of him whose mother was your mother; the hands that put out your father's eyes, eyes once as bright as your own; his who, understanding nothing, seeing nothing, became your father by her that bore him. I weep when I think of the bitter life that men will make you live, and the days that are to come. Into what company dare you go, to what festival, but that you shall return home from it not sharing in the joys, but bathed in tears? When you are old enough to be married, what man dare face the reproach that must cling to you and to your children? What misery is there lacking? Your father killed his father, he begat you at the spring of his own being, offspring of her that bore him. That is the taunt that would be cast upon you and on the man that you should marry. That man is not alive; my children, you must wither away in barrenness. Ah, son of Menoeceus, listen. Seeing that you are the only father now left to them, for we their parents are lost, both of us lost, do not let them wander in beggary—are they not your own kindred?—do not let them sink down into my misery. No, pity them, seeing them utterly wretched in helpless childhood if you do not protect them. Show me that you promise, generous man, by touching me with your hand. [Creon touches him.] My children, there is much advice that I would give you were you but old enough to understand, but all I can do now is bid you pray that you may live wherever you are let live, and that your life be happier than your father's.

CREON Enough of tears. Pass into the house.

OEDIPUS I will obey, though upon conditions.

CREON Conditions?

OEDIPUS Banish me from this country. I know that nothing can destroy me, for I wait some incredible fate; yet cast me upon Cithaeron, chosen by my father and my mother for my tomb.

CREON Only the Gods can say yes or no to that.

OEDIPUS No, for I am hateful to the Gods.

CREON If that be so you will get your wish the quicker. They will banish that which they hate.

OEDIPUS Are you certain of that?

CREON I would not say it if I did not mean it.

OEDIPUS Then it is time to lead me within.

CREON Come, but let your children go.

OEDIPUS No, do not take them from me.

CREON Do not seek to be master; you won the mastery but could not keep it to the end.

[*He leads Oedipus into the palace, followed by Ismene, Antigone, and attendants.*]

CHORUS Make way for Oedipus. All people said,
  "That is a fortunate man";
And now what storms are beating on his head!
  "That is a fortunate man";
Call no man fortunate that is not dead.
  The dead are free from pain.

SINCE ARISTOTLE'S TIME the plot of Oedipus Rex has commanded high and virtually universal praise. Considerably less agreement appears in the attempts to define the particular nature of its excellence. Are its incidents fitted together realistically, or does Sophocles shape them with an artifice which conceals an essential lack of realism? And what qualities in the general action of the play does Sophocles's handling of these incidents reveal?

By . . . subtle strokes [of characterization] Sophocles makes the curious features of the archaic story fit his Oedipus. Whatever improbable or grotesque elements the legend had are transmuted with consummate skill into this convincing and coherent plot. [C. M. Bowra, *Sophoclean Tragedy*, Oxford University Press, New York, 1947, p. 192.]

All words seem drab for the plot of the *Oedipus*. . . . But its extraordinary cleanness of line was not won without finesse. We must not make unfair exactions, or sight the work from improper angles. There is that recapitulation early in the play [page 4]. . . . To explain such a sequence as this is, quite strictly, to tamper with the drama, for the last thing that Sophocles desired was that we should pause and test the passage. . . . What he is really proposing is a tacit agreement: if we will concede him this slight improbability then he undertakes to economize in his workmanship. . . . Finally, if one

examines the play one comes across many little adjustments that make for smoothness of line, though by canons of meticulous realism most of them would be hard to defend. . . . When dramatists blur some detail it is because they desire it blurred; when they take pains not to raise a question then that question is *not in the play*. [A. J. A. Waldock, *Sophocles the Dramatist*, Cambridge University Press, New York, 1951, pp. 160–166.]

[The] firm control of rhythm, both in the gross and in detail, is [quite] noticeable in the *Tyrannus*. Here we find a spaciousness and a leisureliness in the early scenes which goes well with their position in the play, with the assured and lofty position of Oedipus, and with the apparent remoteness of the catastrophe. We are given plenty of time in which to look at our Oedipus. As the drama progresses and suspicion grows, so the pace quickens and the scenes shorten. It is no accident that the first stages of the investigation, between Oedipus and Creon in the prologue, proceeds in leisurely couplets, the later ones in tense line-by-line dialogue. The pace grows so fast that the final scene in the discovery is packed into seventy-five amazing verses. [H. D. F. Kitto, *Greek Tragedy*, Anchor edition, Doubleday & Company, Inc., New York, 1955, p. 186.]

The action which Sophocles shows is a quest, the quest for Laius' slayer; and . . . as Oedipus' past is unrolled before us his whole life is seen as a kind of quest for his true nature and destiny. But since the object of this quest is not clear until the end, the seeking action takes many forms, as its object appears in different lights. The object, indeed, the final perception, the "truth," looks so different at the end from what it did at the beginning that Oedipus' action itself may seem not a quest, but its opposite, a flight. Thus it would be hard to say, simply, that Oedipus either succeeds or fails. He succeeds, but his success is his undoing. He fails to find what, in one way, he sought; yet from another point of view his search is brilliantly successful. The same ambiguities surround his effort to discover who and what he is. [Francis Fergusson, *The Idea of a Theater*, Princeton University Press, Princeton, N. J., 1949. Citations are from the Anchor edition, Doubleday & Company, Inc., New York, 1954, p. 30.]

The tightly organized and relentless process by which Oedipus finds his way to the truth is the operation of the human intellect in many aspects; it is the investigation of the officer of the law who identifies the criminal, the series of diagnoses of the physician who identifies the disease —it has even been compared by Freud to the process of psychoanalysis—and it is also the working out of a mathematical problem which will end with the establishment of a true equation. [Bernard Knox, "Sophocles' Oedipus," in Cleanth Brooks (ed.), *Tragic Themes in Western Literature*, Yale University Press, New Haven, Conn., 1955, pp. 14 15.]

The meaning, or spiritual content of the play, is not to be sought by trying to resolve such ambiguities as [appear in its ironies and reversals]. The spiritual content of the play is the tragic action which Sophocles directly presents; and this action is in its essence [ambiguous]: triumph and destruction, darkness and enlightenment, mourning and rejoicing, at any moment we care to consider it. But this action has also a shape: a beginning, middle, and end, in time. It starts with the reasoned purpose of finding Laius' slayer. But this aim meets unforeseen difficulties, evidences which do not fit, and therefore shake the purpose as it was first understood; and so the characters suffer the piteous and terrible sense of the mystery of the human situation. From this suffering or passion, with its shifting visions, a new perception of the situation emerges; and on that basis the purpose of this action is redefined, and a new movement starts. This movement, or *tragic rhythm of action,* constitutes the shape of the play as a whole; it is also the shape of each episode, each discussion between principals with the chorus following. Mr. Kenneth Burke . . . gives the three moments traditional designations which are very suggestive: *Poiema, Pathema, Mathema.* They may be called, for convenience, Purpose, Passion (or Suffering) and Perception. It is this tragic rhythm of action which is the substance or spiritual content of the play, and the clue to its extraordinarily comprehensive form. [Fergusson, *op. cit.,* pp. 30–31.]

Oedipus is a fascinating figure, but critics disagree, as in the two selections immediately below, over the relative emphasis which his character receives in the play. The nine subsequent excerpts deal with possible flaws in that character, an issue raised by Aristotle's remarks on hamartia.

The man who is to be taught his own utter insignificance must be endowed with special gifts of character and intellect; for only in such conditions is the lesson worth learning. Such Oedipus undeniably is. But in presenting him Sophocles has boldly faced certain difficulties inherent in the legend and turned them to good account. His Oedipus must be a man who has killed his father, solved the riddle of the Sphinx, married his mother, and become king of Thebes, and at the same time he must be convincing enough to win sympathy in his fate and fall. Sophocles shirks none of these difficulties. The past events of Oedipus' life are worked into the play in the most natural way possible. Through the greater part of it Oedipus shows himself as the sort of man to defend himself when attacked, to answer riddles and assume great responsibilities. But the same characteristics which brought him to success make his downfall more tragic and are almost instruments to it. It is because he is such a superior being, angry when attacked, capable of brief and brilliant action, self-confident and rapid in decision, that his discovery of the truth takes so tragic a turn. His fated life is his own life. It is his character, his typical actions, that make his mistakes so intelligible and fit so naturally into the gods' plan to humble him. [Bowra, *op. cit.,* pp. 185–186.]

The character of Oedipus is not itself in dispute; the question is of the emphasis that this character has received in the play. I do not think for my own part that the portrayal of Oedipus is a masterpiece. . . . We recognize that he has this or that quality, but do we ever quite reach the core? And his qualities have to some extent to adapt themselves to the exigencies of the plot. There is not a perfect coherence between that sagacious Oedipus of the past and this present unpredictable Oedipus whose brain seems so often befogged and who is swayed so easily by his passions. Oedipus is an assembly of qualities; they are a little loosely collected, and there is no clear *soul* in the man that makes qualities largely irrelevant; unless we are content just to speak of nobility. He becomes clearer to us after his downfall; we begin then really to see him, and perceive that his structure is truly heroic. But his character is not the point of the play. [Waldock, *op. cit.,* pp. 166–167.]

The predominant quality of Sophocles' Oedipus is his high temper. . . . This was an ambiguous quality. On the one side it worked for good and made men active and enduring. . . . But it . . . could have a destructive side when it was applied to unreasoning violence. So in Oedipus, his high spirits and temper, admirable when the end is good, are liable to get out of control, and do damage. That he is a man of this kind is seen by Jocasta [page 12]. There is in Oedipus a tendency to uncontrolled anger, to unreasonable passion. This is part of his high spirit and essential to his character. [Bowra, *op. cit.,* pp. 192–193.]

We do not feel that he was inexcusably rash— do not feel that he was very injudicious. . . . He has heard certain bodeful things; it is obvious that he must take care. Well, he has made his dispositions—dispositions that, in all the circumstances, are logical and reasonably safe. We have no right, as we read this drama, to blame him for taking *some* risks. (Indeed, as we read the drama, there is not the slightest temptation to blame him; the blame comes later—in criticism —when we have a little withdrawn from the play.) He feels, and is justified in feeling, that he has taken fair measures of security; to have made the security absolute would have meant resigning himself to a half-life; more accurately, perhaps, it would have meant a retirement from life *in toto*. He prefers to accept that margin of danger, and, with moderate luck, all would have been well. [Waldock, *op. cit.*, p. 148.]

Oedipus acts in self defense, and even though he kills his own father and thereby incurs an appalling pollution, he is none the less innocent of any criminal intent or of acting consciously against what he knows to be right. It seems unlikely that Sophocles intended to portray Oedipus as punished for wanton pride; for the proud are punished by the gods for acts of quite a different character.

The view that Oedipus is punished for insolent pride can, however, be stated and defended in a different way. It can be claimed that he is punished not for the single act of killing Laius but for being in general proud and aggressive, as he certainly shows himself in the scenes with Teiresias and Creon. . . . For in these scenes Oedipus transgresses the Mean and is almost swept away in a blind frenzy of pride. . . . Moreover, the Chorus are distressed by Oedipus and afraid that he may prove to be a tyrant [page 11]. . . . Yet despite this, we may doubt whether Sophocles intended his Oedipus to be punished for aggressive insolence. Even Teiresias does not speak of his coming woes as if they were a punishment; the Chorus do not return to their suspicion but form a different view of Oedipus' fall when it comes; Oedipus himself, in the horror of his humiliation, does not think that it is a punishment for pride. . . . Proud he may be, but pride is not the direct cause of his fall. [Bowra, *op. cit.*, pp. 165–166.]

The man who sets out on his new task by sending first for the venerable seer is not lacking in pious reverence; but all we see of him in the play shows unrestrained pride in his own intellectual achievements. No seer found the solution, this is Oedipus' boast; no bird, no god revealed it to him; he, "the utterly ignorant," had to come, and to hit the mark by his own wit [page 7]. Pride and self-confidence induce Oedipus to despise prophecy, and to feel almost superior to the gods. [Victor Ehrenberg, *Sophocles and Pericles*, Basil Blackwell, Ltd., Oxford, 1954, p. 68.]

He does not shrink from the possibility that his birth may be humble [page 14]. What matters for him is the sense of freedom, of irresponsibility, which is for the moment his. He feels that Luck looks after him and that therefore all is well. This confidence is unfounded and irrational, a mere feeling, a manifestation of Oedipus' confident spirit in its least reasonable form. . . . There is no need to accuse him of irreverence, of denying the rule of the gods. Implicitly perhaps or logically he does, but he cannot be judged by such standards. He is wildly excited, carried away by a last desperate hope. [Bowra, *op. cit.*, p. 198.]

"I will know my origin, burst forth what will." He knows that it will be good. Chance governs the universe and Oedipus is her son. Not the son of Polybus, nor of any mortal man but the son of fortunate chance. In his exaltation he rises in imagination above human stature. "The months, my brothers, have defined my greatness and smallness"; he has waned and waxed like the moon, he is one of the forces of the universe, his family is time and space. It is a religious, a mystical conception; here is Oedipus' real religion, he is equal to the gods, the son of chance, the only real goddess. [Knox, *op. cit.*, p. 21.]

Oedipus is connected by the terms he uses, and which are used to and about him, with the whole range of human achievement which has raised man to his present level. All the items of this triumphant catalogue recur in the *Oedipus Tyrannos*: the images of the play define him as helmsman, conqueror of the sea, and ploughman, conqueror of the land, as hunter, master of speech and thought, inventor, legislator, physician. Oedipus is faced in the play with an intellectual problem, and as he marshals his intellectual resources to solve it, the language of the play suggests a comparison between Oedipus' methods in the play and the whole range of sciences and techniques which have brought him to mastery, made him tyrannos of the world. [*Ibid.*, pp. 9–10.]

Sophocles makes him a man of powerful intelligence and shows that it is of the kind to solve problems. . . . His energy in looking for the murderer belongs to his vigorous mental equipment. But by a hideous irony, this time the answers are all wrong. They are based on some kind of evidence; they sound plausible. But they do not touch the truth. The man who could answer riddles is still keen-witted and live-minded, but he is no longer right. He is in fact really the "ignorant Oedipus" such as in mock modesty he thinks that he once was [page 7]. . . . Just as his fall is all the greater because he is a great king, so it is all the more poignant because despite his acute intelligence he is unable to see the truth until it is forced upon him. [Bowra, *op. cit.*, pp. 190–191.]

One of Oedipus' favorite words is "measure" and this is of course a significant metaphor: measure, mensuration, number, calculation—these are among the most important inventions which have brought man to power. . . . The play is full of equations, some of them incomplete, some false; the final equation shows man equated not to the gods but to himself, as Oedipus is finally equated to himself. For there are in the play not one Oedipus but two.

One is the magnificent figure set before us in the opening scenes, tyrannos, the man of wealth and power, first of men, the intellect and energy which drives on the search. The other is the object of the search, a shadowy figure who has violated the most fundamental human taboos, an incestuous parricide, "most accursed of men." And even before the one Oedipus finds the other, they are connected and equated in the name which they both bear, Oedipus. *Oedipus*— "Swollen-foot"; it emphasizes the physical blemish which scars the body of the splendid tyrannos, a defect which he tries to forget but which reminds us of the outcast child this tyrannos once was and the outcast man he is soon to be. The second half of the name *pous*, "foot," recurs throughout the play, as a mocking phrase which recalls this other Oedipus. . . .

These mocking repetitions of one-half the name invoke the unknown Oedipus who will be revealed: the equally emphatic repetition of the first half emphasizes the dominant attitude of the man before us. *Oidi*—"swell," but it is also *Oida*, "I know," and this word is often, too often, in Oedipus' mouth. . . . *Oida*, "I know" —it runs through the play with the same mocking persistence as *pous*, "foot," and sometimes reaches an extreme of macabre punning emphasis. [Knox, *op. cit.*, pp. 11–13.]

Because the oracle had foretold the outcome of Oedipus's career, one conclusion often advanced in explanation of the play is that fate, rather than Oedipus himself, is responsible for his tragic end. The three following selections present different approaches to the part which fate plays in the action.

Had [Oedipus] chosen to spurn the oracle when first he learnt it by staying on where he was, he must have been saved. Yet this mistake was insufficient to complete his doom. It was enough to lead him straight to parricide, but in order that he might wed his mother and ultimately discover his double pollution, the Sphinx's intervention was imperative. Now since these two decisive moments of his life, and the course of action to which they commit him, occur long before we see him on the stage, we have proof not only that Oedipus is the victim of Fate, but that his doings, moods and character in the drama cannot make matters either better or worse. They can only affect the length of time to elapse before self-discovery. All this, while making no difference to the logic of his situation, adds an immense psychological emphasis: it denies the audience the emotional illusion that it was the distracted hero's loss of self-control in their presence that brought him to this pass. [F. J. H. Letters, *The Life and Work of Sopho-*

cles, Sheed and Ward, Ltd., London, 1953, pp. 225–226.]

The overthrow of the tyrannos is . . . a terrible reversal, and it raises the question, "Is it deserved? How far is he responsible for what he has done? Were the actions for which he is now paying not predestined?" No, they were committed in ignorance, but they were not predestined, merely predicted. An essential distinction, as essential for Milton's Adam as for Sophocles' Oedipus. His will was free, his actions his own, but the pattern of his action is the same as that of the Delphic prophecy. The relation between the prophecy and Oedipus' actions is not that of cause and effect. It is the relation suggested by the metaphor [of measurement], the relation of two independent entities which are equated. [Knox, *op. cit.,* p. 22.]

Kitto goes further. Oedipus has been told what lies in wait for him: "No one can accuse Destiny of not playing fair: its victims are given every chance"—its victims being Jocasta as well as Oedipus. Are they? Doubtless God's mere foreknowledge that Brown will murder Jones does not rescind Brown's free will, but a divine proclamation of that foreknowledge surely does not give Brown every chance. . . . Even if Kitto were right, to go so far without arguing the matter out is unsatisfactory. He has merely left it open to an objector to maintain that the most pious thing Jocasta and Oedipus could have done was deliberately and conscientiously to fulfill the oracles; the most inexcusable, to try to circumvent them, since the attempt must not only fail, but convict them of a gross lack of respect and proper submission to the divine will. It is to be admitted that in a sense Oedipus' tragedy is his character. . . . Even so we must protest against the insinuation that his case suggests no real question. The question is there. But does Sophocles answer it? [Letters, *op. cit.,* p. 219.]

A number of the preceding critical statements have concerned characterization, and some have either assumed or implied an interpretation of the play's meaning. The four selections which follow deal directly with the relationship between the two. Is the conflict in the play between man and the gods, and if so, is the emphasis on man's deficiencies or on his greatness in defeat? Is the play's meaning to be looked for, rather, in man's character alone? Or is character completely inoperative in the events of the play?

The play depicts a conflict between two worlds, the world of gods and the world of a man. The first drives home its truth to the second. Oedipus learns it at last. But before he learns it he resists, not indeed consciously but with all the force of his unconscious nature. The tragic conclusion lies in the fearful character of the truth. The gods insist that their victim shall know who and what he is. And this conflict is all the more stubborn and painful because Oedipus is the high creature that he is. . . . His love of action, his desire to know everything, his occasional ruthlessness in forcing the truth from an unwilling witness, lead to nothing but his own humiliation. The core of the drama is Oedipus' discovery of the truth about himself. Sophocles has dramatized the illusions and the ignorance of Oedipus and their collapse. In their ruin is his climax, in their discord with reality his conflict, in their failure to resist the truth his tragic fall. [Bowra, *op. cit.,* pp. 199–200.]

The supernatural factor in the motivation operates through character. There is no divine interference in the play: "Apollo knows the future, but does not create it." . . . what really functions is the mind of man, and its success reveals its failure. The failure has been emphasized, in terms of human nothingness, the folly of human wisdom, the gap between man and the gods, the emptiness of human good fortune. But these facts were all well known before Sophocles. Rather the essential interest lies in the strength of Oedipus, the keenness of human wisdom which can find out its own secret, the function of a divine necessity within man which makes a standard of its own and holds the standard to be worth more than empty good fortune. The darkness and discouragement of the play, on the other hand, come from the bitterness of the truth itself, and the fact that the arete of Oedipus brings him no praise for the victory over his own mystery and no reward for his courage and intellectual integrity. [Cedric H. Whitman, *Sophocles,* Harvard University Press, Cambridge, Mass., 1951, pp. 140–141.]

The story is not moralized. Sophocles could have put Oedipus in the wrong at the crossroad; he could have suggested that blind ambition made him accept the crown and Queen of Thebes. He does neither of these things; Oedipus is not being given his deserts by an offended Heaven. What happens is the natural result of the weaknesses and virtues of his character, in combination with other people's. It is a tragic chapter from life, complete in itself, except for the original oracle and its repetition. [Kitto, *op. cit.,* pp. 143–144.]

It is not quite proper to put the question in this form: whether a man of another character would have acted differently. The question is rather this: whether the character of Oedipus can reasonably be charged with his downfall— whether, in a sufficiently emphatic and pointed way, it can be seen as the source of his troubles. . . . It is easy to think of any number of effective rejoinders to the formulated threats of the oracle—the simplest would have been plain suicide. But all this is rather beside the point and does not prove that Oedipus, in a human way of speaking, was ill-advised in the line he took. Critics who stand or fall by character adopt curious manoeuvres here. Some have as good as said that if Oedipus had been a more lackadaisical person he would have found himself in no trouble at all. . . . This is a very neat illustration of the absurdities that sometimes follow from believing that, in every play worth its salt, we simply must show that "character is destiny." In strict aesthetics this, no doubt, ought to be so, but in fact we do not always see it. The implication of the view just mentioned is that Oedipus pays a price for being normal. [Waldock, *op. cit.,* pp. 143–144.]

As the statements on character and meaning indicate, any explanation of meaning in Oedipus Rex *must take into account the role played by the gods. They may be directing events for their own obscure purposes, or to provide man with an object lesson; if the latter, it is necessary to explain why Oedipus should be singled out to serve as an example, and what he is an example of. Perhaps the gods are merely symbols for something else—for irrational evil or for an order in the universe. A final recourse is to reject meaning in the play entirely.*

King Oedipus shows the humbling of a great and prosperous man by the gods. This humbling is not deserved. . . . The gods display their power because they will. But since they display it, man may draw a salutary lesson. This is kept till the end of the play when the Chorus, or perhaps Oedipus himself, point to the extent of his fall, and comment [page 24]. . . . After the hideous and harrowing events this finale of *King Oedipus* may seem a little tame. Yet it provides a quiet end, such as the Greeks liked, and it is Sophocles' conclusion on what has taken place. [Bowra, *op. cit.,* p. 175.]

The Gods act "because they will," but at least they accomplish something; they give man "a salutary lesson," and with this we reach bedrock at last. There is nothing deeper in the play than this, we are at the end of explanation, this is the ultimate moral of the drama. It seems, to speak bluntly, a fiasco. The meaning that had to be probed for, all the care to keep on the track, the patient following of clues, the rejection of inadequate hypotheses—to find this at the end of the search! I do not think that there is the slightest immoderation in suggesting that, in that case, Sophocles has been wasting our time. It would have been far better, for all concerned, if we had never once thought of a significance. [Waldock, *op. cit.,* p. 156.]

No amount of preconception can drive [the play] into a shape consistent with a religious attitude of faithful trust in the justice of the gods. . . . Insofar as the gods appear or are mentioned at all, they contrive evil. But the gods as personages are not in the plays; they do nothing that life could not do. Whatever divinity meant to Sophocles, it was not summed up in the public religion of Athens. . . . The fear [behind the play is] that human excellence, which has its own divinity, may not be sufficient to assert itself in the face of the irrational evil which descends without plan or justice, and whence no one knows. [Whitman, *op. cit.,* pp. 142–143.]

This is Apollo; this is life. An awful sin is committed in all innocence; children are born to a life of shame; virtuous intentions go awry. What are we to think of it? Of course, moral and prudential lessons can be drawn from it—though Sophocles draws very few—but what are we to think of it? . . . What, in other words, is the catharsis? That Oedipus accepts his fate? But when you are knocked flat, you must accept it; and if you cannot get up again, you must be resigned. There is little illumination in this.

The catharsis that we are looking for is the ultimate illumination which shall turn a painful story into a profound and moving experience. It has been suggested by Professor Ellis-Fermor [in *Frontiers of Drama*] that the catharsis of plays like the *Tyrannus* and *Macbeth* lies in the perfection of their form, which, by implication, represents the forces of righteousness and beneficence. . . .

While Greek life was still healthy and stable, the Greek believed, as if by instinct, that the universe was not chaotic and "irrational," but was based on a *logos,* obeyed law. . . . To the mind of Sophocles this *logos* shows itself . . . as a balance, rhythm, or pattern in human affairs. "Call no man happy until he is dead," for the chances of life are incalculable. But this does not mean that they are chaotic; if so they seem to us, it is because we are unable to see the whole pattern. But sometimes, when life for a moment becomes dramatic, we can see enough pattern to give us faith that there is a meaning in the whole. [Kitto, *op. cit.,* pp. 147–148.]

Let us suppose that the hero is not just *Oedipus,* a mere man who for inscrutable reasons has been picked out for special attention by the gods. Let us suppose that he stands for something—"human suffering" will conveniently do. Let us also depersonalize the gods—treat them a little abstractly by referring rather to the "universe of circumstance as it is." Immediately the play seems lifted; once more a new dignity accrues. It is unnecessary to argue for a thesis, we need not maintain that the play makes a point; but to have embodied human suffering—there already is an achievement. To have given dramatic expression to the universe of circumstance as it is—no work accomplishing that could be thought of as destitute of content.

This is a neat manoeuvre, but quite as illegitimate, in my opinion, as the others. It is just one more way of smuggling significance into the *Oedipus Tyrannus.* . . . But the action of this play is exceptional; no argument can alter that. Oedipus is a world-wonder in his suffering, in his peculiar destiny he is a freak . . . that is why his story is so fascinating. . . . We can imagine it all so vividly, we can live in every one of his emotions; yet we should as reasonably fear to be hit by a thunderbolt as to be embroiled in his particular set of misfortunes. And if Oedipus, by the extreme rarity of his destiny, is outside the common lot of mankind, so is the special malignance that strikes him a thing quite apart from the universe of circumstance as it is. Circumstance has its practical jokes and its sinister-seeming moods, but a concatenation of malevolences on this scale is an absolutely unparalleled thing. . . . That is why it is so misleading to reduce this play to the normal. . . . Here the terror of sheer coincidence is vital; to suppress that terror here is to rob the play of its essence. . . . We have no feeling here of the nature of things; what we feel is an *interference* with nature. The play quintessentializes misfortune; it is an epigram in ill-luck. [Waldock, *op. cit.*, pp. 159–160.]

Oedipus . . . is a paradigm, an example to all men; and the fact that he is tyrannos, self-made ruler, the proverbial Greek example of worldly success won by individual intelligence and exertion, makes him an appropriate symbol of civilized man, who was beginning to believe, in the fifth century B.C., that he could seize control of his environment and make his own destiny, become, in fact, equated to the gods. . . .

Oedipus became tyrannos by answering the riddle of the Sphinx. It was no easy riddle, and he answered it, as he proudly asserts, without help . . . alone, with his intelligence. The answer won him a city and the hand of a queen. And the answer to the Sphinx's riddle was—Man. In Sophocles' own century the same answer had been proposed to a greater riddle. "Man," said Protagoras the sophist, "is the measure of all things." . . .

With the fulfillment of the prophecy Oedipus knows himself for what he is. He is not the measurer but the thing measured, not the equator but the thing equated. . . . In this self-recognition of Oedipus, man recognizes himself. Man measures himself and the result is not that man is the measure of all things. The chorus, which rejected number and all that it stood for, has learned to count; and states the result of the great calculation. "Generations of man that must die, I add up the total of your life and find it equal to zero." [Knox, *op. cit.*, pp. 8–9; 221–22.]

Oedipus is indisputably a victim; that fact is at the very heart of the drama. "O Zeus, what hast thou willed to do unto me?"—this is the central cry of the play. A thorough thinking through of the facts could have led only to an indictment of the gods. Sophocles draws back from such an indictment. But this is merely an abstinence, and does not bestow "meaning" on the drama. There is no meaning in the *Oedipus Tyrannus*. There is merely the terror of coincidence, and then, at the end of it all, our impression of man's power to suffer, and of his greatness because of this power. [Waldock, *op. cit.*, pp. 167–168.]

EURIPIDES

c. 484–407 B.C.

*Only thirteen years younger than Sophocles, Euripides came to
maturity during a period of doubt and disillusion which apparently
had little effect upon his older contemporary. He did not compete
for the prize until he was twenty-nine, and it was to be some
thirteen or fourteen years before success came. Despite the number
of plays which he produced (ninety-two by most estimates),
Euripides won the tragic prize only five times, once posthumously.
His great popularity and influence came after he was dead. Lack of
stature in the eyes of his contemporary judges was the price he
paid for nonconformity. His drama encompassed both more realism
and more artificiality than were common. He was interested in the
sensational and the highly emotional. He seemed to lack piety.
And he tended, particularly in his late plays, toward tragicomedy.
In* Medea *(431 B.C.), little of the romance of the Golden Fleece
legend remains, but the background of the play's two principals is
important. Jason's uncle, King Pelias, sent him from Thessaly to
Colchis in quest of the golden fleece of a ram. Jason eventually
arrived in Colchis, where the king, Aeetes, promised him the fleece
if he would yoke two fire-breathing bulls and sow a field with
dragons' teeth. With the help of Aeetes' sorceress daughter, Medea,
Jason subdued the bulls and the armed giants who sprang up from
the sown teeth. Aeetes still withheld the fleece, and Jason again
enlisted Medea's aid. She gave a sleeping potion to the dragon
guarding the prize, which the hero then stole. Aeetes pursued the
fleeing Argonauts, now accompanied by Medea and her younger*

brother, but the sorceress chopped her brother's body into pieces, scattering them in the Argo's wake. Her father abandoned the chase to retrieve his son's remnants. After various perils, the Argonauts arrived in Thessaly, to find that Pelias had done away with Jason's parents. In revenge, Medea persuaded Pelias' daughters to try rejuvenating their aging father with a formula which she possessed. But she withheld from the boiling cauldron in which Aeetes was immersed the magic herbs which had proved successful in her demonstration with a ram, and the king died horribly. Jason and Medea found it expedient to leave for Corinth, where, some years later, the action of Euripides's play begins.

Medea

TRANSLATED BY GILBERT MURRAY

Characters

MEDEA *daughter of Aeetes, King of Colchis*

JASON *chief of the Argonauts, nephew of Pelias, King of Iôlcos*

CREON *ruler of Corinth*

AEGEUS *King of Athens*

NURSE *servant of Medea*

TWO CHILDREN *sons of Jason and Medea*

ATTENDANT *servant for the children*

A MESSENGER

CHORUS OF CORINTHIAN WOMEN WITH THEIR LEADER

SOLDIERS AND ATTENDANTS

In front of Jason's house at Corinth.

NURSE Would God no Argo e'er had winged the seas
To Colchis through the blue Symplêgades:[1]
No shaft of riven pine in Pelion's glen[2]
Shaped that first oar-blade in the hands of men
Valiant, who won, to save King Pelias' vow,
The fleece All-golden! Never then, I trow,
Mine own princess, her spirit wounded sore
With love of Jason, to the encastled shore
Had sailed of old Iôlcos: never wrought
The daughters of King Pelias, knowing not,
To spill their father's life: nor fled in fear,
Hunted for that fierce sin, to Corinth here
With Jason and her babes. This folk at need
Stood friend to her, and she in word and deed
Served alway Jason. Surely this doth bind,
Through all ill days, the hurts of humankind,
When man and woman in one music move.
But now, the world is angry, and true love
Sick as with poison. Jason doth forsake
My mistress and his own two sons, to make
His couch in a king's chamber. He must wed:[3]
Wed with this Creon's child, who now is head

[1] The Symplêgades ("Clashing") or Kuaneai ("Dark blue") were two rocks in the sea which used to clash together and crush anything that was between them.

[2] Pelion was a great mountain in Thessaly. Iôlcos lay between Pelion and the sea.

[3] Medea was not legally married to Jason, and could not be, although he is loosely referred to at times as her husband. Intermarriage between the subjects of two separate states was possible only through a special treaty, with which Colchis was not favored.

29

And chief of Corinth. Wherefore sore betrayed
Medea calleth up the oath they made,
They two, and wakes the claspèd hands again,
The troth surpassing speech, and cries amain
On God in heaven to mark the end, and how
Jason hath paid his debt.

     All fasting now
And cold, her body yielded up to pain,
Her days a waste of weeping, she hath lain,
Since first she knew that he was false. Her eyes
Are lifted not; and all her visage lies
In the dust. If friends will speak, she hears no
 more
Than some dead rock or wave that beats the
 shore:
Only the white throat in a sudden shame
May writhe, and all alone she moans the name
Of father, and land, and home, forsook that day
For this man's sake, who casteth her away.
Not to be quite shut out from home . . . alas,
She knoweth now how rare a thing that was!
Methinks she hath a dread, not joy, to see
Her children near. 'Tis this that maketh me
Most tremble, lest she do I know not what.
Her heart is no light thing, and useth not
To brook much wrong. I know that woman, aye,
And dread her! Will she creep alone to die
Bleeding in that old room, where still is laid
Lord Jason's bed? She hath for that a blade
Made keen. Or slay the bridegroom and the king.
And win herself God knows what direr thing?
'Tis a fell spirit. Few, I ween, shall stir
Her hate unscathed, or lightly humble her.
Ha! 'Tis the children from their games again,
Rested and gay; and all their mother's pain
Forgotten! Young lives ever turn from gloom!
[*Enter The Children and their Attendant.*]

ATTENDANT Thou ancient treasure of my lady's
 room,
What mad'st thou here before the gates alone,
And always turning on thy lips some moan
Of old mischances? Will our mistress be
Content, this long time to be left by thee?

NURSE Grey guard of Jason's children, a good
 thrall
Hath his own grief, if any hurt befall
His master's. Aye, it holds one's heart! . . .
 Meseems
I have strayed out so deep in evil dreams,

I longed to rest me here alone, and cry
Medea's wrongs to this still Earth and Sky.

ATTENDANT How? Are the tears yet running in
 her eyes?

NURSE 'Twere good to be like thee! . . . Her
 sorrow lies
Scarce wakened yet, not half its perils wrought.

ATTENDANT Mad spirit! . . . If a man may speak
 his thought
Of masters mad.—And nothing in her ears
Hath sounded yet of her last cause for tears!
[*He moves towards the house, but the Nurse
checks him.*]

NURSE What cause, old man? . . . Nay, grudge
 me not one word.

ATTENDANT 'Tis nothing. Best forget what thou
 hast heard.

NURSE Nay, housemate, by thy beard! Hold it
 not hid
From me. . . . I will keep silence if thou bid.

ATTENDANT I heard an old man talking, where
 he sate
At draughts in the sun, beside the fountain gate,
And never thought of me, there standing still
Beside him. And he said 'twas Creon's will,
Being lord of all this land, that she be sent,
And with her her two sons, to banishment.
Maybe 'tis all false. For myself, I know
No further, and I would it were not so.

NURSE Jason will never bear it—his own sons
Banished—however hot his anger runs
Against their mother!

ATTENDANT   Old love burneth low
When new love wakes, men say. He is not now
Husband nor father here, nor any kin.

NURSE But this is ruin! New waves breaking in
To wreck us, ere we are righted from the old!

ATTENDANT Well, hold thy peace. Our mistress
 will be told
All in good time. Speak thou no word hereof.

NURSE My babes! What think ye of your father's
 love?
God curse him not, he is my master still:
But, oh, to them that loved him, 'tis an ill
Friend . . .

ATTENDANT And what man on earth is different?
 How?
Hast thou lived all these years, and learned but
 now

That every man more loveth his own head
Than other men's? He dreameth of the bed
Of this new bride, and thinks not of his sons.

NURSE Go: run into the house, my little ones:
All will end happily! . . . Keep them apart:
Let not their mother meet them while her heart
Is darkened. Yester night I saw a flame
Stand in her eye, as though she hated them,
And would I know not what. For sure her wrath
Will never turn nor slumber, till she hath . . .
Go: and if some must suffer, may it be
Not we who love her, but some enemy!

MEDEA [*within*] Oh shame and pain: O woe is
    me!
Would I could die in my misery!
[*Exeunt Children and Attendant.*]

NURSE Ah, children, hark! She moves again
Her frozen heart, her sleeping wrath.
In, quick! And never cross her path,
Nor rouse that dark eye in its pain;

That fell sea-spirit, and the dire
Spring of a will untaught, unbowed.
Quick, now!—Methinks this weeping cloud
Hath in its heart some thunder-fire,

Slow gathering, that must flash ere long.
I know not how, for ill or well,
It turns, this uncontrollable
Tempestuous spirit, blind with wrong.

MEDEA [*within*] Have I not suffered? Doth it call
No tears? . . . Ha, ye beside the wall
Unfathered children, God hate you
As I am hated, and him, too,
That gat you, and this house and all!

NURSE For pity! What have they to do,
Babes, with their father's sin?
Thy curse on these? . . . Ah, children, all
These days my bosom bleeds for you.

Rude are the wills of princes: yea,
Prevailing alway, seldom crossed,
On fitful winds their moods are tossed:
'Tis best men tread the equal way.

Aye, not with glory but with peace
May the long summers find me crowned:
For gentleness—her very sound
Is magic, and her usages

All wholesome: but the fiercely great
Hath little music on his road,

And falleth, when the hand of God
Shall move, most deep and desolate.
[*During the last words the Leader of the Chorus
has entered. Other Women follow her.*]

LEADER I heard a voice and a moan,
A voice of the eastern seas:
Hath she found not yet her ease?
Speak, O aged one.
For I stood afar at the gate,
And there came from within a cry,
And wailing desolate.
Ah, no more joy have I,
For the griefs this house doth see,
And the love it hath wrought in me.

NURSE There is no house! 'Tis gone. The lord
Seeketh a prouder bed: and she
Wastes in her chamber, nor one word
Will hear of care or charity.

MEDEA [*within*] O Zeus, O Earth, O Light,
Will the fire not stab my brain?
What profiteth living? Oh,
Shall I not lift the slow
Yoke, and let Life go,
As a beast out in the night,
To lie, and be rid of pain?
[*Some Women from the Chorus speak.*]

ONE WOMAN "O Zeus, O Earth, O Light":
The cry of a bride forlorn
Heard ye, and wailing born
Of lost delight?

SECOND WOMAN Why weariest thou this day,
Wild heart, for the bed abhorrèd,
The cold bed in the clay?
Death cometh though no man pray,
Ungarlanded, un-adorèd.
Call him not thou.

THIRD WOMAN If another's arms be now
Where thine have been,
On his head be the sin:
Rend not thy brow!

FOURTH WOMAN All that thou sufferest,
God seeth: Oh, not so sore
Waste nor weep for the breast
That was thine of yore.

MEDEA [*within*] Virgin of Righteousness,
Virgin of hallowed Troth,
Ye marked me when with an oath
I bound him; mark no less
That oath's end. Give me to see

Him and his bride, who sought
My grief when I wronged her not,
Broken in misery,
And all her house. . . . O God,
My mother's home, and the dim
Shore that I left for him,
And the voice of my brother's blood . . .

NURSE Oh, wild words! Did ye hear her cry
To them that guard man's faith forsworn,
Themis and Zeus? . . . This wrath new-born
Shall make mad workings ere it die.

[*Other Women from the Chorus speak.*]

FIFTH WOMAN Would she but come to seek
Our faces, that love her well,
And take to her heart the spell
Of words that speak?

SIXTH WOMAN Alas for the heavy hate
And anger that burneth ever!
Would it but now abate,
Ah God, I love her yet.
And surely my love's endeavour
Shall fail not here.

SEVENTH WOMAN Go: From that chamber drear
Forth to the day
Lead her, and say, Oh, say
That we love her dear.

EIGHTH WOMAN Go, lest her hand be hard
On the innocent: Ah, let be!
For her grief moves hitherward,
Like an angry sea.

NURSE That will I: though what words of mine
Or love shall move her? Let them lie
With the old lost labours! . . . Yet her eye—
Know ye the eyes of the wild kine,

The lion flash that guards their brood?
So looks she now if any thrall
Speak comfort, or draw near at all
My mistress in her evil mood.

[*Exit Nurse into the house.*]

A WOMAN Alas, the bold blithe bards of old
That all for joy their music made,
For feasts and dancing manifold,
That Life might listen and be glad.

But all the darkness and the wrong,
Quick deaths and dim heart-aching things,
Would no man ease them with a song
Or music of a thousand strings?

Then song had served us in our need.
What profit, o'er the banquet's swell
That lingering cry that none may heed?
The feast hath filled them: all is well!

OTHER WOMEN I heard a song, but it comes no
more.
Where the tears ran over:
A keen cry but tired, tired:
A woman's cry for her heart's desired,
For a traitor's kiss and a lost lover.
But a prayer, methinks, yet riseth sore
To God, to Faith, God's ancient daughter—
The Faith that over sundering seas
Drew her to Hellas, and the breeze
Of midnight shivered, and the door
Closed of the salt unsounded water.

[*During the last words Medea has entered from
the house.*]

MEDEA Women of Corinth, I am come to show
My face, lest ye despise me. For I know
Some heads stand high and fail not, even at night
Alone—far less like this, in all men's sight:
And we, who study not our wayfarings
But feel and cry—Oh we are drifting things,
And evil! For what truth is in men's eyes,
Which search no heart, but in a flash despise
A strange face, shuddering back from one that
ne'er
Hath wronged them? . . . Sure, far-comers any-
where,
I know, must bow them and be gentle. Nay,
A Greek himself men praise not, who alway
Should seek his own will recking not. . . . But
I—
This thing undreamed of, sudden from on high,
Hath sapped my soul: I dazzle where I stand,
The cup of all life shattered in my hand,
Longing to die—O friends! He, even he,
Whom to know well was all the world to me,
The man I loved, hath proved most evil.—Oh,
Of all things upon earth that bleed and grow,
A herb most bruised is woman. We must pay
Our store of gold, hoarded for that one day,
To buy us some man's love; and lo, they bring
A master of our flesh! There comes the sting
Of the whole shame. And then the jeopardy,
For good or ill, what shall that master be;
Reject she cannot: and if he but stays

His suit, 'tis shame on all that woman's days.
So thrown amid new laws, new places, why,
'Tis magic she must have, or prophecy—
Home never taught her that—how best to guide
Toward peace this thing that sleepeth at her
    side.
And she who, labouring long, shall find some
    way
Whereby her lord may bear with her, nor fray
His yoke too fiercely, blessèd is the breath
That woman draws! Else, let her pray for death.
Her lord, if he be wearied of the face
Withindoors, gets him forth; some merrier place
Will ease his heart: but she waits on, her whole
Vision enchainèd on a single soul.
And then, forsooth, 'tis they that face the call
Of war, while we sit sheltered, hid from all
Peril!—False mocking! Sooner would I stand
Three times to face their battles, shield in hand,
Than bear one child.
                        But peace! There cannot be
Ever the same tale told of thee and me.
Thou hast this city, and thy father's home,
And joy of friends, and hope in days to come:
But I, being cityless, am cast aside
By him that wedded me, a savage bride
Won in far seas and left—no mother near,
No brother, not one Kinsman anywhere
For harbour in this storm. Therefore of thee
I ask one thing. If chance yet ope to me
Some path, if even now my hand can win
Strength to requite this Jason for his sin,
Betray me not! Oh, in all things but this,
I know how full of fears a woman is,
And faint at need, and shrinking from the light
Of battle: but once spoil her of her right
In man's love, and there moves, I warn thee
    well,
No bloodier spirit between heaven and hell.

LEADER   I will betray thee not. It is but just,
Thou smite him.—And that weeping in the dust
And stormy tears, how should I blame them?
    . . . Stay:
'Tis Creon, lord of Corinth, makes his way
Hither, and bears, methinks, some word of
    weight.

[*Enter from the right Creon, with armed Attendants.*]

CREON   Thou woman sullen-eyed and hot with
    hate
Against thy lord, Medea, I here command
That thou and thy two children from this land
Go forth to banishment. Make no delay:
Seeing ourselves, the King, are come this day
To see our charge fulfilled; nor shall again
Look homeward ere we have led thy children
    twain
And thee beyond our realm's last boundary.

MEDEA   Lost! Lost!
Mine haters at the helm with sail flung free
Pursuing; and for us no beach nor shore
In the endless waters! . . . Yet, though stricken
    sore,
I still will ask thee, for what crime, what thing
Unlawful, wilt thou cast me out, O King?

CREON   What crime? I fear thee, woman—little
    need
To cloak my reasons—lest thou work some deed
Of darkness on my child. And in that fear
Reasons enough have part. Thou comest here
A wise-woman confessed, and full of lore
In unknown ways of evil. Thou art sore
In heart, being parted from thy lover's arms.
And more, thou hast made menace . . . so the
    alarms
But now have reached mine ear . . . on bride
    and groom,
And him who gave the bride, to work thy doom
Of vengeance. Which, ere yet it be too late,
I sweep aside. I choose to earn thine hate
Of set will now, not palter with the mood
Of mercy, and hereafter weep in blood.

MEDEA   'Tis not the first nor second time, O King,
That fame hath hurt me, and come nigh to
    bring
My ruin. . . . How can any man, whose eyes
Are wholesome, seek to rear his children wise[4]
Beyond men's wont? Much helplessness in arts
Of common life, and in their townsmen's hearts
Envy deep-set . . . so much their learning brings!

[4] Medea was a "wise woman," which in her time
meant much the same as a witch or enchantress. She
did really know more than other women; but most
of this extra knowledge consisted—or was supposed
to consist—either in lore of poisons and charms or
in useless learning and speculation.

Come unto fools with knowledge of new things,
They deem it vanity, not knowledge. Aye,
And men that erst for wisdom were held high,
Feel thee a thorn to fret them, privily
Held higher than they. So hath it been with me.
A wise-woman I am; and for that sin
To divers ill names men would pen me in;
A seed of strife; an eastern dreamer; one
Of brand not theirs; one hard to play upon. . . .
Ah, I am not so wondrous wise!—And now,
To thee, I am terrible! What fearest thou?
What dire deed? Do I tread so proud a path—
Fear me not thou!—that I should brave the wrath
Of princes? Thou: what hast thou ever done
To wrong me? Granted thine own child to one
Whom thy soul chose.—Ah, *him* out of my heart
I hate; but thou, meseems, hast done thy part
Not ill. And for thine houses' happiness
I hold no grudge. Go: marry, and God bless
Your issues. Only suffer me to rest
Somewhere within this land. Though sore oppressed,
I will be still, knowing mine own defeat.

CREON Thy words be gentle: but I fear me yet
Lest even now there creep some wickedness
Deep hid within thee. And for that the less
I trust thee now than ere these words began.
A woman quick of wrath, aye, or a man,
Is easier watching than the cold and still.
Up, straight, and find thy road! Mock not my will
With words. This doom is passed beyond recall;
Nor all thy crafts shall help thee, being withal
My manifest foe, to linger at my side.

MEDEA [*suddenly throwing herself down and clinging to Creon*] Oh, by thy knees! By that new-wedded bride . . .

CREON 'Tis waste of words. Thou shalt not weaken me.

MEDEA Wilt hunt me? Spurn me when I kneel to thee?

CREON 'Tis mine own house that kneels to me, not thou.

MEDEA Home, my lost home, how I desire thee now!

CREON And I mine, and my child, beyond all things.

MEDEA O Loves of man, what curse is on your wings!

CREON Blessing or curse, 'tis as their chances flow.

MEDEA Remember, Zeus, the cause of all this woe!

CREON Oh, rid me of my pains! Up, get thee gone!

MEDEA What would I with thy pains? I have mine own.

CREON Up: or, 'fore God, my soldiers here shall fling . . .

MEDEA Not that! Not that! . . . I do but pray, O King . . .

CREON Thou wilt not? I must face the harsher task?

MEDEA I accept mine exile. 'Tis not that I ask.

CREON Why then so wild? Why clinging to mine hand?

MEDEA [*rising*] For one day only leave me in thy land
At peace, to find some counsel, ere the strain
Of exile fall, some comfort for these twain,
Mine innocents; since others take no thought,
It seems, to save the babes that they begot.
Ah! Thou wilt pity them! Thou also art
A father: thou hast somewhere still a heart
That feels. . . . I reck not of myself: 'tis they
That break me, fallen upon so dire a day.

CREON Mine is no tyrant's mood. Aye, many a time
Ere this my tenderness hath marred the chime
Of wisest counsels. And I know that now
I do mere folly. But so be it! Thou
Shalt have this grace. . . . But this I warn thee clear,
If once the morrow's sunlight find thee here
Within my borders, thee or child of thine,
Thou diest! . . . Of this judgement not a line
Shall waver or abate. So linger on,
If thou needs must, till the next risen sun;
No further. . . . In one day there scarce can be
Those perils wrought whose dread yet haunteth me.

[*Exit Creon with Attendants.*]

CHORUS O woman, woman of sorrow,
Where wilt thou turn and flee?
What town shall be thine to-morrow,
What land of all lands that be,

What door of a strange man's home?
Yea, God hath hunted thee,
Medea, forth to the foam
Of a trackless sea.

MEDEA Defeat on every side; what else?—But Oh,
Not here the end is: think it not! I know
For bride and groom one battle yet untried,
And goodly pains for him that gave the bride.
Dost dream I would have grovelled to this man,
Save that I won mine end, and shaped my plan
For merry deeds? My lips had never deigned
Speak word with him: my flesh been never stained
With touching. . . . Fool, Oh, triple fool! It lay
So plain for him to kill my whole essay
By exile swift: and, lo, he sets me free
This one long day: wherein mine haters three
Shall lie here dead, the father and the bride
And husband—mine, not hers! Oh, I have tried
So many thoughts of murder to my turn,
I know not which best likes me. Shall I burn
Their house with fire? Or stealing past unseen
To Jason's bed—I have a blade made keen
For that—stab, breast to breast, that wedded pair?
Good, but for one thing. When I am taken there,
And killed, they will laugh loud who hate me. . . .
            Nay,
I love the old way best, the simple way
Of poison, where we too are as strong as men.
Ah me!
And they being dead—what place shall hold me then?
What friend shall rise, with land inviolate
And trusty doors, to shelter from their hate
This flesh? . . . None anywhere! . . . A little more
I needs must wait: and, if there ope some door
Of refuge, some strong tower to shield me, good:
In craft and darkness I will hunt this blood.
Else, if mine hour be come and no hope nigh,
Then sword in hand, full-willed and sure to die,
I yet will live to slay them. I will wend
Man-like, their road of daring to the end.
So help me She who of all Gods hath been

The best to me, of all my chosen queen
And helpmate, Hecatê, who dwells apart,
The flame of flame, in my fire's inmost heart:
For all their strength, they shall not stab my soul
And laugh thereafter! Dark and full of dole
Their bridal feast shall be, most dark the day
They joined their hands, and hunted me away.
Awake thee now, Medea! Whatso plot
Thou hast, or cunning, strive and falter not.
On to the peril-point! Now comes the strain
Of daring. Shall they trample thee again?
How? And with Hellas laughing o'er thy fall
While this thief's daughter weds, and weds withal
Jason? . . . A true king was thy father, yea,
And born of the ancient Sun! . . . Thou know'st the way;
And God hath made thee woman, things most vain
For help, but wondrous in the paths of pain.

[*Exit Medea into the house.*]

CHORUS Back streams the wave on the ever-running river:
Life, life is changed and the laws of it o'ertrod.
Man shall be the slave, the affrighted, the low-liver!
Man hath forgotten God.

And woman, yea, woman, shall be terrible in story:
The tales too, meseemeth, shall be other than of yore.
For a fear there is that cometh out of Woman, and a glory,
And the hard hating voices shall encompass her no more!

The old bards shall cease, and their memory that lingers
Of frail brides and faithless, shall be shrivelled as with fire.
For they loved us not, nor knew us: and our lips were dumb, our fingers
Could wake not the secret of the lyre.

Else, else, O God the Singer, I had sung amid their rages
A long tale of Man and his deeds for good and ill.

But the old World knoweth—'tis the speech of
    all his ages—
Man's wrong and ours: he knoweth and is still.

SOME WOMEN   Forth from thy father's home
Thou camest, O heart of fire,
To the Dark Blue Rocks, to the clashing foam,
To the seas of thy desire:

Till the Dark Blue Bar was crossed;
And, lo, by an alien river
Standing, thy lover lost,
Void-armed for ever,

Forth yet again, O lowest
Of landless women, a ranger
Of desolate ways, thou goest,
From the walls of the stranger.

OTHER WOMEN   And the great Oath waxeth weak;
And Ruth, as a thing outstriven,
Is fled, fled, from the shores of the Greek,
Away on the winds of heaven.

Dark is the house afar,
Where an old king called thee daughter;
All that was once thy star
In stormy water,

Dark: and, lo, in the nearer
House that was sworn to love thee,
Another, queenlier, dearer,
Is thronèd above thee.

[*Enter from the right Jason.*]

JASON   Oft have I seen, in other days than these,
How a dark temper maketh maladies
No friend can heal. 'Twas easy to have kept
Both land and home. It needed but to accept
Unstrivingly the pleasure of our lords.
But thou, for mere delight in stormy words,
Wilt lose all! . . . Now thy speech provokes not
    me.

Rail on. Of all mankind let Jason be
Most evil; none shall check thee. But for these
Dark threats cast out against the majesties
Of Corinth, count as veriest gain thy path
Of exile. I myself, when princely wrath
Was hot against thee, strove with all good will
To appease the wrath, and wished to keep thee
    still
Beside me. But thy mouth would never stay
From vanity, blaspheming night and day
Our masters. Therefore thou shalt fly the land.

Yet, even so, I will not hold my hand
From succouring mine own people. Here am I
To help thee, woman, pondering heedfully
Thy new state. For I would not have thee flung
Provisionless away—aye, and the young
Children as well; nor lacking aught that will
Of mine can bring thee. Many a lesser ill
Hangs on the heels of exile. . . . Aye, and
    though
Thou hate me, dream not that my heart can
    know
Or fashion aught of angry will to thee.

MEDEA   Evil, most evil! . . . Since thou grantest
    me
That comfort, the worst weapon left me now
To smite a coward . . . Thou comest to me,
    thou,
Mine enemy!

[*Turning to the Chorus*]
          Oh, say, how call ye this,
To face, and smile, the comrade whom his kiss
Betrayed? Scorn? Insult? Courage? None of
    these:
'Tis but of all man's inward sicknesses
The vilest, that he knoweth not of shame
Nor pity! Yet I praise him that he came . . .
To me it shall bring comfort, once to clear
My heart on thee, and thou shalt wince to hear.
I will begin with that, 'twixt me and thee,
That first befell. I saved thee. I saved thee—
Let thine own Greeks be witness, every one
That sailed on Argo—saved thee, sent alone
To yoke with yokes the bulls of fiery breath,[5]
And sow that Acre of the Lords of Death;
And mine own ancient Serpent, who did keep
The Golden Fleece, the eyes that knew not
    sleep,
And shining coils, him also did I smite
Dead for thy sake, and lifted up the light
That bade thee live. Myself, uncounsellèd,
Stole forth from father and from home, and fled
Where dark Iôlcos under Pelion lies,

[5] Among the tasks set him by Aeetes, Jason had
to yoke two fire-breathing bulls, plough with them a
certain Field of Ares, sow the field with dragons'
teeth, and reap a harvest of earth-born or giant warriors that sprang from the seed. When all this was
done, there remained the ancient serpent coiled
round the tree where the Golden Fleece was hanging.

With thee—Oh, single-nearted more than wise!
I murdered Pelias, yea, in agony,
By his own daughters' hands, for sake of thee;
I swept their house like War.—And hast thou then
Accepted all—O evil yet again!—
And cast me off and taken thee for bride
Another? And with children at thy side!
One could forgive a childless man. But no:
I have borne thee children. . . .
                 Is sworn faith so
  low
And weak a thing? I understand it not.
Are the old gods dead? Are the old laws forgot,
And new laws made? Since not my passioning,
But thine own heart, doth cry thee for a thing
Forsworn.
[*She catches sight of her own hand which she
has thrown out to denounce him.*]
          Poor, poor right hand of mine, whom
  he
Did cling to, and these knees, so cravingly,
We are unclean, thou and I; we have caught the
  stain
Of bad men's flesh . . . and dreamed our dreams
  in vain.
Thou comest to befriend me? Give me, then,
Thy counsel. 'Tis not that I dream again
For good from thee: but, questioned, thou wilt
  show
The viler. Say: now whither shall I go?
Back to my father? Him I did betray,
And all his land, when we two fled away.
To those poor Peliad maids? For them 'twere
  good
To take me in, who spilled their father's
  blood. . . .
Aye, so my whole life stands! There were at
  home
Who loved me well: to them I am become
A curse. And the first friends who sheltered
  me,[6]
Whom most I should have spared, to pleasure
  thee
I have turned to foes. Oh, therefore hast thou
  laid
My crown upon me, blest of many a maid

[6] The kindred of Pelias.

In Hellas, now I have won what all did crave
Thee, the world-wondered lover and the brave
Who this day looks and sees me banished,
  thrown
Away with these two babes, all, all, alone. . . .
Oh, merry mocking when the lamps are red:
"Where go the bridegroom's babes to beg their
  bread
In exile, and the woman who gave all
To save him?"
              O great God, shall gold withal
Bear thy clear mark, to sift the base and fine,
And o'er man's living visage runs no sign
To show the lie within, ere all too late?

LEADER Dire and beyond all healing is the hate
When hearts that loved are turned to enmity.

JASON In speech at least, meseemeth, I must be
Not evil; but, as some old pilot goes
Furled to his sail's last edge, when danger blows
Too fiery, run before the wind and swell,
Woman, of thy loud storms.—And thus I tell
My tale. Since thou wilt build so wondrous high
Thy deeds of service in my jeopardy,
To all my crew and quest I know but one
Saviour, of Gods or mortals one alone,
The Cyprian. Oh, thou hast both brain and wit,
Yet underneath . . . nay, all the tale of it
Were graceless telling; how sheer love, a fire
Of poison-shafts, compelled thee with desire
To save me. But enough. I will not score
That count too close. 'Twas good help: and
  therefor
I give thee thanks, howe'er the help was
  wrought.
Howbeit, in my deliverance, thou hast got
Far more than given. A good Greek land hath
  been
Thy lasting home, not barbary. Thou hast seen
Our ordered life, and justice, and the long
Still grasp of law not changing with the strong
Man's pleasure. Then, all Hellas far and near
Hath learned thy wisdom, and in every ear
Thy fame is. Had thy days run by unseen
On that last edge of the world, where then had
  been
The story of great Medea? Thou and I . . .
What worth to us were treasures heapèd high
In rich kings' rooms; what worth a voice of gold
More sweet than ever rang from Orpheus old,

Unless our deeds have glory?
                              Speak I so,
Touching the Quest I wrought, thyself did throw
The challenge down. Next for thy cavilling
Of wrath at mine alliance with a king,
Here thou shalt see I both was wise, and free
From touch of passion, and a friend to thee
Most potent, and my children. . . . Nay, be still!
When first I stood in Corinth, clogged with ill
From many a desperate mischance, what bliss
Could I that day have dreamed of, like to this,
To wed a King's daughter, I exiled
And beggared? Not—what makes thy passion
    wild—
From loathing of thy bed; not over-fraught
With love for this new bride; not that I sought
To upbuild mine house with offspring: 'tis
    enough,
What thou hast borne: I make no word thereof:
But, first and greatest, that we all might dwell
In a fair house and want not, knowing well
That poor men have no friends, but far and near
Shunning and silence. Next, I sought to rear
Our sons in nurture worthy of my race,
And, raising brethren to them, in one place
Join both my houses, and be all from now
Prince-like and happy. What more need hast
    thou
Of children? And for me, it serves my star
To link in strength the children that now are
With those that shall be.
                          Have I counselled ill?
Not thine own self would say it, couldst thou
    still
One hour thy jealous flesh.—'Tis ever so!
Who looks for more in women? When the flow
Of love runs plain, why, all the world is fair:
But, once there fall some ill chance anywhere
To baulk that thirst, down in swift hate are trod
Men's dearest aims and noblest. Would to God
We mortals by some other seed could raise
Our fruits, and no blind women block our ways!
Then had there been no curse to wreck man-
    kind.

LEADER   Lord Jason, very subtly hast thou twined
Thy speech: but yet, though all athwart thy will
I speak, this is not well thou dost, but ill,
Betraying her who loved thee and was true.

MEDEA   Surely I have my thoughts, and not a few
Have held me strange. To me it seemeth, when
A crafty tongue is given to evil men
'Tis like to wreck, not help them. Their own
    brain
Tempts them with lies to dare and dare again,
Till . . . no man hath enough of subtlety.
As thou—be not so seeming-fair to me
Nor deft of speech. One word will make thee
    fall.
Wert thou not false, 'twas thine to tell me all,
And charge me help thy marriage path, as I
Did love thee; not befool me with a lie.

JASON   An easy task had that been! Aye, and
    thou
A loving aid, who canst not, even now,
Still that loud heart that surges like the tide!

MEDEA   That moved thee not. Thine old bar-
    barian bride,
The queen out of the east who loved thee sore,
She grew grey-haired, she served thy pride no
    more.

JASON   Now understand for once! The girl to
    me
Is nothing, in this web of sovranty
I hold. I do but seek to save, even yet,
Thee: and for brethren to our sons beget
Young kings, to prosper all our lives again.

MEDEA   God shelter me from prosperous days
    of pain,
And wealth that maketh wounds about my heart.

JASON   Wilt change that prayer, and choose a
    wiser part?
Pray not to hold true sense for pain, nor rate
Thyself unhappy, being too fortunate.

MEDEA   Aye, mock me; thou hast where to lay
    thine head,
But I go naked to mine exile.

JASON   Tread
Thine own path! Thou hast made it all to be.

MEDEA   How? By seducing and forsaking thee?

JASON   By those vile curses on the royal halls
Let loose . . .

MEDEA   On thy house also, as chance
    falls,
I am a living curse.

JASON   Oh, peace! Enough
Of these vain wars: I will no more thereof.

If thou wilt take from all that I possess
Aid for these babes and thine own helplessness
Of exile, speak thy bidding. Here I stand
Full-willed to succour thee with stintless hand,
And send my signet to old friends that dwell
On foreign shores, who will entreat thee well.
Refuse, and thou shalt do a deed most vain.
But cast thy rage away, and thou shalt gain
Much, and lose little for thine anger's sake.

MEDEA I will not seek thy friends. I will not take
Thy givings. Give them not. Fruits of a stem
Unholy bring no blessing after them.

JASON Now God in heaven be witness, all my heart
Is willing, in all ways, to do its part
For thee and for thy babes. But nothing good
Can please thee. In sheer savageness of mood
Thou drivest from thee every friend. Wherefore
I warrant thee, thy pains shall be the more.
[*He goes slowly away.*]

MEDEA Go: thou art weary for the new delight
Thou wooest, so long tarrying out of sight
Of her sweet chamber. Go, fulfill thy pride,
O bridegroom! For it may be, such a bride
Shall wait thee—yea, God heareth me in this—
As thine own heart shall sicken ere it kiss.

SOME WOMEN Alas, the Love that falleth like a flood,
Strong-winged and transitory:
Why praise ye him? What beareth he of good
To man, or glory?
Yet Love there is that moves in gentleness,
Heart-filling, sweetest of all powers that bless.
Loose not on me, O Holder of man's heart,
Thy golden quiver,
Nor steep in poison of desire the dart
That heals not ever.

The pent hate of the word that cavilleth,
The strife that hath no fill,
Where once was fondness; and the mad heart's breath
For strange love panting still:
O Cyprian, cast me not on these; but sift,
Keen-eyed, of love the good and evil gift.
Make Innocence my friend, God's fairest star,
Yea, and abate not
The rare sweet beat of bosoms without war,

That love, and hate not.

OTHER WOMEN Home of my heart, land of my own,
Cast me not, nay, for pity,
Out on my ways, helpless, alone,
Where the feet fail in the mire and stone,
A woman without a city.
Ah, not that! Better the end:
The green grave cover me rather,
If a break must come in the days I know,
And the skies be changed and the earth below;
For the weariest road that man may wend
Is forth from the home of his father.

Lo, we have seen: 'tis not a song
Sung, nor learned of another.
For whom hast thou in thy direst wrong
For comfort? Never a city strong
To hide thee, never a brother.
Ah, but the man—cursèd be he,
Cursèd beyond recover,
Who openeth, shattering, seal by seal,
A friend's clean heart, then turns his heel,
Deaf unto love: never in me
Friend shall he know nor lover.

[*While Medea is waiting downcast, seated upon her door-step, there passes from the left a traveller with followers. As he catches sight of Medea, he stops.*]

AEGEUS Have joy, Medea! 'Tis the homeliest
Word that old friends can greet with, and the best.

MEDEA [*looking up, surprised*] Oh, joy on thee too, Aegeus, gentle king
Of Athens!—But whence com'st thou journeying?

AEGEUS From Delphi now and the old encaverned stair . . .

MEDEA Where Earth's heart speaks in song? What mad'st thou there?

AEGEUS Prayed heaven for children—the same search alway.

MEDEA Children? Ah God! Art childless to this day?

AEGEUS So God hath willed. Childless and desolate.

MEDEA What word did Phoebus speak, to change thy fate?

AEGEUS Riddles, too hard for mortal man to read.

MEDEA Which I may hear?

AEGEUS Assuredly: they need
A rarer wit.

MEDEA How said he?

AEGEUS Not to spill
Life's wine, nor seek for more . . .

MEDEA Until?

AEGEUS Until
I tread the hearth-stone of my sires of yore.

MEDEA And what should bring thee here, by Creon's shore?

AEGEUS One Pittheus know'st thou, high lord of Trozên?

MEDEA Aye, Pelops' son, a man most pure of sin.

AEGEUS Him I would ask, touching Apollo's will.

MEDEA Much use in God's ways hath he, and much skill.

AEGEUS And, long years back he was my battle-friend,
The truest e'er man had.

MEDEA Well, may God send
Good hap to thee, and grant all thy desire.

AEGEUS But thou . . . ? Thy frame is wasted, and the fire
Dead in thine eyes.

MEDEA Aegeus, my husband is
The falsest man in the world.

AEGEUS What word is this?
Say clearly what thus makes thy visage dim?

MEDEA He is false to me, who never injured him.

AEGEUS What hath he done? Show all, that I may see.

MEDEA Ta'en him a wife; a wife, set over me
To rule his house.

AEGEUS He hath not dared to do,
Jason, a thing so shameful?

MEDEA Aye, 'tis true:
And those he loved of yore have no place now.

AEGEUS Some passion sweepeth him? Or is it thou
He turns from?

MEDEA Passion, passion to betray
His dearest!

AEGEUS Shame be his, so fallen away
From honour!

MEDEA Passion to be near a throne,
A king's heir!

AEGEUS How, who gives the bride? Say on.

MEDEA Creon, who o'er all Corinth standeth chief.

AEGEUS Woman, thou hast indeed much cause for grief.

MEDEA 'Tis ruin.—And they have cast me out as well.

AEGEUS Who? 'Tis a new wrong this, and terrible.

MEDEA Creon the king, from every land and shore . . .

AEGEUS And Jason suffers him? Oh, 'tis too sore!

MEDEA He loveth to bear bravely ills like these!
But, Aegeus, by thy beard, oh, by thy knees,
I pray thee, and I give me for thine own
Thy suppliant, pity me! Oh, pity one
So miserable. Thou never wilt stand there
And see me cast out friendless to despair.
Give me a home in Athens . . . by the fire
Of thine own hearth! Oh, so may thy desire
Of children be fulfilled of God, and thou
Die happy! . . . Thou canst know not; even now
Thy prize is won! I, I will make of thee
A childless man no more. The seed shall be,
I swear it, sown. Such magic herbs I know.

AEGEUS Woman, indeed my heart goes forth to show
This help to thee, first for religion's sake,
Then for thy promised hope, to heal my ache
Of childlessness. 'Tis this hath made mine whole
Life as a shadow, and starved out my soul.
But thus it stands with me. Once make thy way
To Attic earth, I, as in law I may,
Will keep thee and befriend. But in this land,
Where Creon rules, I may not raise my hand
To shelter thee. Move of thine own essay
To seek my house, there thou shalt alway stay,
Inviolate, never to be seized again.
But come thyself from Corinth. I would fain
Even in foreign eyes be alway just.

MEDEA 'Tis well. Give me an oath wherein to trust
And all that man could ask thou hast granted me.

AEGEUS Dost trust me not? Or what thing troubleth thee?

MEDEA I trust thee. But so many, far and near,
Do hate me—all King Pelias' house, and here
Creon. Once bound by oaths and sanctities
Thou canst not yield me up for such as these
To drag from Athens. But a spoken word,
No more, to bind thee, which no God hath
   heard . . .
The embassies, methinks, would come and go:
They all are friends to thee. . . . Ah me, I
   know
Thou wilt not list to me! So weak am I,
And they full-filled with gold and majesty.

AEGEUS Methinks 'tis a far foresight, this thine
   oath.
Still, if thou so wilt have it, nothing loath
Am I to serve thee. Mine own hand is so
The stronger, if I have this plea to show
Thy persecutors: and for thee withal
The bond more sure.—On what God shall I
   call?

MEDEA Swear by the Earth thou treadest, by the
   Sun,
Sire of my sires, and all the gods as one . . .

AEGEUS To do what thing or not do? Make all
   plain.

MEDEA Never thyself to cast me out again.
Nor let another, whatsoe'er his plea,
Take me, while thou yet livest and are free.

AEGEUS Never: so hear me, Earth, and the great
   star
Of daylight, and all other gods that are!

MEDEA 'Tis well: and if thou falter from thy
   vow . . . ?

AEGEUS God's judgement on the godless break
   my brow!

MEDEA Go! Go thy ways rejoicing.—All is
   bright
And clear before me. Go: and ere the night
Myself will follow, when the deed is done
I purpose, and the end I thirst for won.
[*Aegeus and his train depart.*]

CHORUS Farewell: and Maia's guiding Son
Back lead thee to thy hearth and fire,
Aegeus; and all the long desire
That wasteth thee, at last be won:
Our eyes have seen thee as thou art,
A gentle and a righteous heart.

MEDEA God, and God's Justice, and ye blinding
   Skies!

At last the victory dawneth! Yea, mine eyes
See, and my foot is on the mountain's brow.
Mine enemies! Mine enemies, oh, now
Atonement cometh! Here at my worst hour
A friend is found, a very port of power
To save my shipwreck. Here will I make fast
Mine anchor, and escape them at the last
In Athens' wallèd hill.—But ere the end
'Tis meet I show thee all my counsel, friend:
Take it, no tale to make men laugh withal!
Straightway to Jason I will send some thrall
To entreat him to my presence. Comes he here,
Then with soft reasons will I feed his ear,
How his will now is my will, how all things
Are well, touching this marriage-bed of kings
For which I am betrayed—all wise and rare
And profitable! Yet will I make one prayer,
That my two children be no more exiled
But stay . . . Oh, not that I would leave a
   child
Here upon angry shores till those have laughed
Who hate me: 'tis that I will slay by craft
The king's daughter. With gifts they shall be
   sent,
Gifts to the bride to spare their banishment,
Fine robings and a carcanet of gold.
Which raiment let her once but take, and fold
About her, a foul death that girl shall die
And all who touch her in her agony.
Such poison shall they drink, my robe and
   wreath!
Howbeit, of that no more. I gnash my teeth
Thinking on what a path my feet must tread
Thereafter. I shall lay those children dead—
Mine, whom no hand shall steal from me away!
Then, leaving Jason childless, and the day
As night above him, I will go my road
To exile, flying, flying from the blood
Of these my best-beloved, and having wrought
All horror, so but one thing reach me not,
The laugh of them that hate us.

                              Let it come!
What profits life to me? I have no home,
No country now, nor shield from any wrong.
That was my evil hour, when down the long
Halls of my father out I stole, my will
Chained by a Greek man's voice, who still, oh,
   still,
If God yet live, shall all requited be.

For never child of mine shall Jason see
Hereafter living, never child beget
From his new bride, who this day, desolate
Even as she made me desolate, shall die
Shrieking amid my poisons. . . . Names have I
Among your folk? One light? One weak of
    hand?
An eastern dreamer?—Nay, but with the brand
Of strange suns burnt, my hate, by God above,
A perilous thing, and passing sweet my love!
For these it is that make life glorious.

LEADER Since thou hast bared thy fell intent
    to us
I, loving thee, and helping in their need
Man's laws, adjure thee, dream not of this deed!

MEDEA There is no other way.—I pardon thee
Thy littleness, who art not wronged like me.

LEADER Thou canst not kill the fruit thy body
    bore!

MEDEA Yes: if the man I hate be pained the
    more.

LEADER And thou made miserable, most miser-
    able?

MEDEA Oh, let it come! All words of good or ill
Are wasted now.

[*She claps her hands: the Nurse comes out from
the house.*]
                Ho, woman; get thee gone
And lead lord Jason hither. . . . There is none
Like thee, to work me these high services.
But speak no word of what my purpose is,
As thou art faithful, thou, and bold to try
All succours, and a woman even as I!
[*The Nurse departs.*]

CHORUS The sons of Erechtheus, the olden,
Whom high gods planted of yore
In an old land of heaven upholden,
A proud land untrodden of war:
They are hungered, and, lo, their desire
With wisdom is fed as with meat:
In their skies is a shining of fire,
A joy in the fall of their feet:
And thither, with manifold dowers,
From the North, from the hills, from the morn,
The Muses did gather their powers,
That a child of the Nine should be born;
And Harmony, sown as the flowers,
Grew gold in the acres of corn.

And Cephîsus, the fair-flowing river—
The Cyprian dipping her hand
Hath drawn of his dew, and the shiver
Of her touch is as joy in the land.
For her breathing in fragrance is written,
And in music her path as she goes,
And the cloud of her hair, it is litten
With stars of the wind-woven rose.
So fareth she ever and ever,
And forth of her bosom is blown,
As dews on the winds of the river,
An hunger of passions unknown,
Strong Loves of all godlike endeavour,
Whom Wisdom shall throne on her throne.

SOME WOMEN But Cephîsus the fair-flowing,
Will he bear thee on his shore?
Shall the land that succours all, succour thee,
Who art foul among thy kind,
With the tears of children blind?
Dost thou see the red gash growing,
Thine own burden dost thou see?
Every side, Every way,
Lo, we kneel to thee and pray:
By thy knees, by thy soul, O woman wild!
One at least thou canst not slay,
Not thy child!

OTHER WOMEN Hast thou ice that thou shalt bind
    it
To thy breast, and make thee dead
To thy children, to thine own spirit's pain?
When the hand knows what it dares,
When thine eyes look into theirs,
Shalt thou keep by tears unblinded
Thy dividing of the slain?
These be deeds not for thee:
These be things that cannot be!
Thy babes—though thine hardihood be fell,
When they cling about thy knee,
'Twill be well!
[*Enter Jason.*]

JASON I answer to thy call. Though full of hate
Thou be, I yet will not so far abate
My kindness for thee, nor refuse mine ear.
Say in what new desire thou hast called me here.

MEDEA Jason, I pray thee, for my words but
    now
Spoken, forgive me. My bad moods . . . Oh,
    thou

At least wilt strive to bear with them! There be
Many old deeds of love 'twixt me and thee.
Lo, I have reasoned with myself apart
And chidden: "Why must I be mad, O heart
Of mine: and raging against one whose word
Is wisdom: making me a thing abhorred
To them that rule the land, and to mine own
Husband, who doth but that which, being done,
Will help us all—to wed a queen, and get
Young kings for brethren to my sons? And yet
I rage alone, and cannot quit my rage—
What aileth me?—when God sends harbourage
So simple? Have I not my children? Know
I not we are but exiles, and must go
Beggared and friendless else?" Thought upon
    thought
So pressed me, till I knew myself full-fraught
With bitterness of heart and blinded eyes.
So now—I give thee thanks: and hold thee wise
To have caught this anchor for our aid. The
    fool
Was I; who should have been thy friend, thy
    tool;
Gone wooing with thee, stood at thy bed-side
Serving, and welcomed duteously thy bride.
But, as we are, we are—I will not say
Mere evil—women! Why must thou to-day
Turn strange, and make thee like some evil
    thing,
Childish, to meet my childish passioning?
See, I surrender: and confess that then
I had bad thoughts, but now have turned again
And found my wiser mind.
[*She claps her hands.*]

                        Ho, children! Run
Quickly! Come hither, out into the sun,
[*The Children enter from the house, followed
by their Attendant.*]
And greet your father. Welcome him with us,
And throw quite, quite away, as mother does,
Your anger against one so dear. Our peace
Is made, and all the old bad war shall cease
For ever.—Go, and take his hand. . . .
[*As the Children go to Jason, she suddenly
bursts into tears. The Children quickly return
to her: she recovers herself, smiling amid her
tears.*]
                                Ah, me,

I am full of hidden horrors! . . . Shall it be
A long time more, my children, that ye live
To reach to me those dear, dear arms? . . .
    Forgive!
I am so ready with my tears to-day,
And full of dread. . . . I sought to smooth
    away
The long strife with your father, and, lo, now
I have all drowned with tears this little brow!
[*She wipes the Child's face.*]

LEADER O'er mine eyes too there stealeth a pale
    tear:
Let the evil rest, O God, let it rest here!

JASON Woman, indeed I praise thee now, nor
    say
Ill of thine other hour. 'Tis nature's way,
A woman needs must stir herself to wrath,
When work of marriage by so strange a path
Crosseth her lord. But thou, thine heart doth
    wend
The happier road. Thou hast seen, ere quite the
    end,
What choice must needs be stronger: which to
    do
Shows a wise-minded woman. . . . And for
    you,
Children, your father never has forgot
Your needs. If God but help him, he hath
    wrought
A strong deliverance for your weakness. Yea,
I think you, with your brethren, yet one day
Shall be the mightiest voices in this land.
Do you grow tall and strong. Your father's
    hand
Guideth all else, and whatso power divine
Hath alway helped him. . . . Ah, may it be
    mine
To see you yet in manhood, stern of brow,
Strong-armed, set high o'er those that hate
    me. . . . How?
Woman, thy face is turned. Thy cheek is swept
With pallor of strange tears. Dost not accept
Gladly and of good will my benisons?

MEDEA 'Tis nothing. Thinking of these little
    ones . . .

JASON Take heart, then. I will guard them from
    all ill.

MEDEA I do take heart. Thy word I never will

Mistrust. Alas, a woman's bosom bears
But woman's courage, a thing born for tears.

JASON What ails thee?—All too sore thou weepest there.

MEDEA I was their mother! When I heard thy prayer
Of long life for them, there swept over me
A horror, wondering how these things shall be.
But for the matter of my need that thou
Should speak with me, part I have said, and now
Will finish.—Seeing it is the king's behest
To cast me out from Corinth . . . aye, and best,
Far best, for me—I know it—not to stay
Longer to trouble thee and those who sway
The realm, being held to all their house a foe . . .
Behold, I spread my sails, and meekly go
To exile. But our children. . . . Could this land
Be still their home awhile: could thine own hand
But guide their boyhood. . . . Seek the king, and pray
His pity, that he bid thy children stay!

JASON He is hard to move. Yet surely 'twere well done.

MEDEA Bid her—for thy sake, for a daughter's boon . . .

JASON Well thought! Her I can fashion to my mind.

MEDEA Surely. She is a woman like her kind . . .
Yet I will aid thee in thy labour; I
Will send her gifts, the fairest gifts that lie
In the hands of men, things of the days of old,
Fine robings and a carcanet of gold,
By the boys' hands.—Go, quick, some handmaiden,
And fetch the raiment.

[A handmaid goes into the house.]

                    Ah, her cup shall then
Be filled indeed! What more should woman crave,
Being wed with thee, the bravest of the brave,
And girt with raiment which of old the sire
Of all my house, the Sun, gave, steeped in fire,
To his own fiery race?

[The handmaid has returned bearing the gifts.]

                    Come, children, lift

With heed these caskets. Bear them as your gift
To her, being bride and princess and of right
Blessèd!—I think she will not hold them light.

JASON Fond woman, why wilt empty thus thine hand
Of treasure? Doth King Creon's castle stand
In stint of raiment, or in stint of gold?
Keep these, and make no gift. For if she hold
Jason of any worth at all, I swear
Chattels like these will not weigh more with her.

MEDEA Ah, chide me not! 'Tis written, gifts persuade
The gods in heaven; and gold is stronger made
Than words innumerable to bend men's ways.
Fortune is hers. God maketh great her days:
Young and a crownèd queen! And banishment
For those two babes. . . . I would not gold were spent,
But life's blood, ere that come.

                    My children, go
Forth into those rich halls, and, bowing low,
Beseech your father's bride, whom I obey,
Ye be not, of her mercy, cast away
Exiled: and give the caskets—above all
Mark this!—to none but her, to hold withal
And keep. . . . Go quick! And let your mother know
Soon the good tidings that she longs for. . . . Go!

[She goes quickly into the house. Jason and the Children with their Attendant depart.]

CHORUS Now I have no hope more of the children's living;
No hope more. They are gone forth unto death.
The bride, she taketh the poison of their giving:
She taketh the bounden gold and openeth;
And the crown, the crown, she lifteth about her brow,
Where the light brown curls are clustering. No hope now!
O sweet and cloudy gleam of the garments golden!
The robe, it hath clasped her breast and the crown her head.
Then, then, she decketh the bride, as a bride of olden
Story, that goeth pale to the kiss of the dead.
For the ring hath closed, and the portion of

death is there;
And she flieth not, but perisheth unaware.

SOME WOMEN O bridegroom, bridegroom of the
  kiss so cold,
Art thou wed with princes, are thou girt with
  gold,
Who know'st not, suing
For thy child's undoing,
And, on her thou lovest, for a doom untold?
How art thou fallen from thy place of old!

OTHER WOMEN O Mother, Mother, what hast
  thou to reap,
When the harvest cometh, between wake and
  sleep?
For a heart unslaken,
For a troth forsaken,
Lo, babes that call thee from a bloody deep:
And thy love returns not. Get thee forth and
  weep!

[*Enter the Attendant with the Two Children:
Medea comes out from the house.*]

ATTENDANT Mistress, these children from their
  banishment
Are spared. The royal bride hath mildly bent
Her hand to accept thy gifts, and all is now
Peace for the children.—Ha, why standest thou
Confounded, when good fortune draweth near?

MEDEA Ah God!

ATTENDANT This chimes not with the news I
  bear.

MEDEA O God, have mercy!

ATTENDANT Is some word of wrath
Here hidden that I knew not of? And hath
My hope to give the joy so cheated me?

MEDEA Thou givest what thou givest: I blame
  not thee.

ATTENDANT Thy brows are all o'ercast: thine
  eyes are filled. . . .

MEDEA For bitter need, Old Man! The gods have
  willed,
And my own evil mind, that this should come.

ATTENDANT Take heart! Thy sons one day will
  bring thee home.

MEDEA Home? . . . I have others to send home.
  Woe's me!

ATTENDANT Be patient. Many a mother before
  thee
Hath parted from her children. We poor things
Of men must needs endure what fortune brings.

MEDEA I will endure.—Go thou within, and lay
All ready that my sons may need to-day.
[*The Attendant goes into the house.*]
O children, children mine: and you have found
A land and home, where, leaving me dis-
  crowned
And desolate, forever you will stay,
Motherless children! And I go my way
To other lands, an exile, ere you bring
Your fruits home, ere I see you prospering
Or know your brides, or deck the bridal bed,
All flowers, and lift your torches overhead.
Oh, cursèd be mine own hard heart! 'Twas all
In vain, then, that I reared you up, so tall
And fair; in vain I bore you, and was torn
With those long pitiless pains, when you were
  born.
Ah, wondrous hopes my poor heart had in you,
How you would tend me in mine age, and do
The shroud about me with your own dear
  hands,
When I lay cold, blessèd in all the lands
That knew us. And that gentle thought is dead!
You go, and I live on, to eat the bread
Of long years, to myself most full of pain.
And never your dear eyes, never again,
Shall see your mother, far away being thrown
To other shapes of life. . . . My babes, my
  own,
Why gaze ye so?—What is it that ye see?—
And laugh with that last laughter? . . . Woe
  is me,
What shall I do?

                    Women, my strength is gone,
Gone like a dream, since once I looked upon
Those shining faces. . . . I can do it not.
Good-bye to all the thoughts that burned so hot
Aforetime! I will take and hide them far,
Far, from men's eyes. Why should I seek a war
So blind: by these babes' wounds to sting again
Their father's heart, and win myself a pain
Twice deeper? Never, never! I forget
Henceforward all I laboured for.

                              And yet,
What is it with me? Would I be a thing
Mocked at, and leave mine enemies to sting
Unsmitten? It must be. O coward heart,
Ever to harbour such soft words!—Depart
Out of my sight, ye twain.

Medea

[*The Children go in.*]
                                    And they whose eyes
Shall hold it sin to share my sacrifice,
On their heads be it! My hand shall swerve not
    now.
Ah, Ah, thou Wrath within me! Do not thou,
Do not. . . . Down, down, thou tortured thing,
    and spare
My children! They will dwell with us, aye, there
Far off, and give thee peace.
                                    Too late, too late!
By all Hell's living agonies of hate,
They shall not take my little ones alive
To make their mock with! Howsoe'er I strive
The thing is doomed; it shall not escape now
From being. Aye, the crown is on the brow,
And the robe girt, and in the robe that high
Queen dying.
                        I know all. Yet . . . seeing that
    I
Must go so long a journey, and these twain
A longer yet and darker, I would fain
Speak with them, ere I go.
[*A handmaid brings the Children out again.*]
                                    Come, children;
    stand
A little from me. There. Reach out your hand.
Your right hand—so—to mother: and good-
    bye!
[*She has kept them hitherto at arm's length: but
at the touch of their hands, her resolution
breaks down, and she gathers them passionately
into her arms.*]
Oh, darling hand! Oh, darling mouth, and eye,
And royal mien, and bright brave faces clear,
May you be blessèd, but not here! What here
Was yours, your father stole. . . . Ah God,
    the glow
Of cheek on cheek, the tender touch; and Oh,
Sweet scent of childhood. . . . Go! Go! . . .
    Am I blind? . . .
Mine eyes can see not, when I look to find
Their places. I am broken by the wings
Of evil. . . . Yea, I know to what bad things
I go, but louder than all thought doth cry
Anger, which maketh man's worst misery.
[*She follows the Children into the house.*]
CHORUS My thoughts have roamed a cloudy
    land,

And heard a fierier music fall
Than woman's heart should stir withal:
And yet some Muse majestical,
Unknown, hath hold of woman's hand
Seeking for Wisdom—not in all:
A feeble seed, a scattered band,
Thou yet shalt find in lonely places,
Not dead amongst us, nor our faces
Turned alway from the Muses' call.
And thus my thought would speak: that she
Who ne'er hath borne a child nor known
Is nearer to felicity:
Unlit she goeth and alone,
With little understanding what
A child's touch means of joy or woe,
And many toils she bareth not.
But they within whose garden fair
That gentle plant hath blown, they go
Deep-written all their days with care—
To rear the children, to make fast
Their hold, to win them wealth; and then
Much darkness, if the seed at last
Bear fruit in good or evil men!
And one thing at the end of all
Abideth, that which all men dread:
The wealth is won, the limbs are bred
To manhood, and the heart withal
Honest: and, lo, where Fortune smiled,
Some change, and what hath fallen? Hark!
'Tis death slow winging to the dark,
And in his arms what was thy child.
What therefore doth it bring of gain
To man, whose cup stood full before,
That God should send this one thing more
Of hunger and of dread, a door
Set wide to every wind of pain?
[*Medea comes out alone from the house.*]
MEDEA Friends, this long hour I wait on For-
    tune's eyes,
And strain my senses in a hot surmise
What passeth on that hill.—Ha! even now
There comes . . . 'tis one of Jason's men, I
    trow.
His wild-perturbèd breath doth warrant me
The tidings of some strange calamity.
[*Enter Messenger.*]
MESSENGER O dire and ghastly deed! Get thee
    away,
Medea! Fly! Nor let behind thee stay

One chariot's wing, one keel that sweeps the
  seas. . . .
MEDEA And what hath chanced, to cause such
  flights as these?
MESSENGER The maiden princess lieth—and her
  sire,
The king—both murdered by thy poison-fire.
MEDEA Most happy tiding! Which thy name
  prefers
Henceforth among my friends and well-wishers.
MESSENGER What say'st thou? Woman, is thy
  mind within
Clear, and not raving? Thou art found in sin
Most bloody wrought against the king's high
  head,
And laughest at the tale, and hast no dread?
MEDEA I have words also that could answer
  well
Thy word. But take thine ease, good friend, and
  tell,
How died they? Hath it been a very foul
Death, prithee? That were comfort to my soul.
MESSENGER When thy two children, hand in
  hand entwined,
Came with their father, and passed on to find
The new-made bridal rooms, Oh, we were glad,
We thralls, who ever loved thee well, and had
Grief in thy grief. And straight there passed a
  word
From ear to ear, that thou and thy false lord
Had poured peace offering upon wrath fore-
  gone.
A right glad welcome gave we them, and one
Kissed the small hand, and one the shining hair:
Myself, for very joy, I followed where
The women's rooms are. There our mistress
  . . . she
Whom now we name so . . . thinking not to
  see
Thy little pair, with glad and eager brow
Sate waiting Jason. Then she saw, and slow
Shrouded her eyes, and backward turned again,
Sick that thy children should come near her.
  Then
Thy husband quick went forward, to entreat
The young maid's fitful wrath. "Thou wilt not
  meet
Love's coming with unkindness? Nay, refrain
Thy suddenness, and turn thy face again,

Holding as friends all that to me are dear,
Thine husband. And accept these robes they
  bear
As gifts: and beg thy father to unmake
His doom of exile on them—for my sake."
When once she saw the raiment, she could still
Her joy no more, but gave him all his will.
And almost ere the father and the two
Children were gone from out the room, she
  drew
The flowerèd garments forth, and sate her down
To her arraying: bound the golden crown
Through her long curls, and in a mirror fair
Arranged their separate clusters, smiling there
At the dead self[7] that faced her. Then aside
She pushed her seat, and paced those chambers
  wide
Alone, her white foot poising delicately—
So passing joyful in those gifts was she!—
And many a time would pause, straight-limbed,
  and wheel
Her head to watch the long fold to her heel
Sweeping. And then came something strange.
  Her cheek
Seemed pale, and back with crooked steps and
  weak
Groping of arms she walked, and scarcely
  found
Her old seat, that she fell not to the ground.
Among the handmaids was a woman old
And grey, who deemed, I think, that Pan had
  hold
Upon her, or some spirit, and raised a keen
Awakening shout; till through her lips was seen
A white foam crawling, and her eyeballs back
Twisted, and all her face dead pale for lack
Of life: and while that old dame called, the cry
Turned strangely to its opposite,[8] to die
Sobbing. Oh, swiftly then one woman flew
To seek her father's rooms, one for the new
Bridegroom, to tell the tale. And all the place
Was loud with hurrying feet.

[7] The reflection in the glass, often regarded as
ominous or uncanny in some way.
[8] The notion was that an evil spirit could be scared
away by loud cheerful shouts—*ololugae*. But while
this old woman is making an ololugê, she sees that
the trouble is graver than she thought, and the
cheerful cry turns into a wail.

Medea

So long a space
As a swift walker on a measured way
Would pace a furlong's course in, there she lay
Speechless, with veilèd lids. Then wide her eyes
She oped, and wildly, as she strove to rise,
Shrieked: for two diverse waves upon her
    rolled
Of stabbing death. The carcanet of gold
That gripped her brow was molten in a dire
And wondrous river of devouring fire.
And those fine robes, the gift thy children
    gave—
God's mercy!—everywhere did lap and lave
The delicate flesh; till up she sprang, and fled,
A fiery pillar, shaking locks and head
This way and that, seeking to cast the crown
Somewhere away. But like a thing nailed down
The burning gold held fast the anadem,
And through her locks, the more she scattered
    them,
Came fire the fiercer, till to earth she fell
A thing—save to her sire—scarce nameable,
And strove no more. That cheek of royal mien,
Where was it—or the place where eyes had
    been?
Only from crown and temples came faint blood
Shot through with fire. The very flesh, it stood
Out from the bones, as from a wounded pine
The gum starts, where those gnawing poisons
    fine
Bit in the dark—a ghastly sight! And touch
The dead we durst not. We had seen too much.
But that poor father, knowing not, had sped,
Swift to his daughter's room, and there the dead
Lay at his feet. He knelt, and groaning low,
Folded her in his arms, and kissed her: "Oh,
Unhappy child, what thing unnatural hath
So hideously undone thee? Or what wrath
Of gods, to make this old grey sepulchre
Childless of thee? Would God but lay me there
To die with thee, my daughter!" So he cried.
But after, when he stayed from tears, and tried
To uplift his old bent frame, lo, in the folds
Of those fine robes it held, as ivy holds
Strangling among young laurel boughs. Oh,
    then
A ghastly struggle came! Again, again,
Up on his knee he writhed; but that dead
    breast

Clung still to his: till, wild, like one possessed,
He dragged himself half free; and, lo, the live
Flesh parted; and he laid him down to strive
No more with death, but perish; for the deep
Had risen above his soul. And there they sleep,
At last, the old proud father and the bride,
Even as his tears had craved it, side by side.
For thee—Oh, no word more! Thyself will
    know
How best to baffle vengeance. . . . Long ago
I looked upon man's days, and found a grey
Shadow. And this thing more I surely say,
That those of all men who are counted wise,
Strong wits, devisers of great policies,
Do pay the bitterest toll. Since life began,
Hath there in God's eye stood one happy man?
Fair days roll on, and bear more gifts or less
Of fortune, but to no man happiness.
[*Exit Messenger.*]

SOME WOMEN   Wrath upon wrath, meseems, this
    day shall fall
From God on Jason! He hath earned it all.

OTHER WOMEN   O miserable maiden, all my heart
Is torn for thee, so sudden to depart
From thy king's chambers and the light above
To darkness, all for sake of Jason's love!

MEDEA   Women, my mind is clear. I go to slay
My children with all speed, and then, away
From hence; not wait yet longer till they stand
Beneath another and an angrier hand
To die. Yea, howsoe'er I shield them, die
They must. And, seeing that they must, 'tis I
Shall slay them, I their mother, touched of
    none
Beside. Oh, up and get thine armour on,
My heart! Why longer tarry we to win
Our crown of dire inevitable sin?
Take up thy sword, O poor right hand of mine,
Thy sword: then onward to the thin-drawn
    line
Where life turns agony. Let there be naught
Of softness now: and keep thee from that
    thought,
"Born of thy flesh," "thine own belovèd." Now,
For one brief day, forget thy children: thou
Shalt weep hereafter. Though thou slay them,
    yet
Sweet were they. . . . I am sore unfortunate.
[*She goes into the house.*]

SOME WOMEN   O Earth, our mother; and thou
All-seër, arrowy crown
Of Sunlight, manward now
Look down, Oh, look down!
Look upon one accurst,
Ere yet in blood she twine
Red hands—blood that is thine!
O Sun, save her first!
She is thy daughter still,
Of thine own golden line;
Save her! Or shall man spill
The life divine?
Give peace, O Fire that diest not! Send thy
    spell
To stay her yet, to lift her afar, afar—
A torture-changèd spirit, a voice of Hell
Wrought of old wrings and war!

OTHER WOMEN   Alas for the mother's pain
Wasted! Alas the dear
Life that was born in vain!
Woman, what mak'st thou here,
Thou from beyond the Gate
Where dim Symplêgades
Clash in the dark blue seas,
The shores where death doth wait?
Why hast thou taken on thee,
To make us desolate,
This anger of misery
And guilt of hate?
For fierce are the smitings back of blood once
    shed
Where love hath been: God's wrath upon them
    that kill,
And an anguished earth, and the wonder of
    the dead
Haunting as music still. . . .

[A cry is heard within.]

WOMAN   Hark! Did ye hear? Heard ye the chil-
    dren's cry?

ANOTHER WOMAN   O miserable woman! O abhor-
    red!

CHILD [within]   What shall I do? What is it?
    Keep me fast
From mother!

OTHER CHILD   I know nothing. Brother! Oh,
I think she means to kill us.

WOMAN   Let me go!
I will—Help! Help!—and save them at the
    last.

CHILD   Yes, in God's name! Help quickly ere
    we die!

OTHER CHILD   She has almost caught me now.
    She has a sword.

[Many of the Women are now beating at the
barred door to get in. Other Women are standing apart.]

WOMEN [at the door]   Thou stone, thou thing of
    iron! Wilt verily
Spill with thine hand that life, the vintage
    stored
Of thine own agony?

OTHER WOMEN   A Mother slew her babes in days
    of yore,[9]
One, only one, from dawn to eventide,
Ino, god-maddened, whom the Queen of Heaven
Set frenzied, flying to the dark: and she
Cast her for sorrow to the wide salt sea,
Forth from those rooms of murder unforgiven,
Wild-footed from a white crag of the shore,
And clasping still her children twain, she died.
O Love of Woman, charged with sorrow sore,
What hast thou wrought upon us? What beside
Resteth to tremble for?

[Enter hurriedly Jason and Attendants.]

JASON   Ye women by this doorway clustering
Speak, is the doer of the ghastly thing
Yet here, or fled? What hopeth she of flight?
Shall the deep yawn to shield her? Shall the
    height
Send wings, and hide her in the vaulted sky
To work red murder on her lords, and fly
Unrecompensed? But let her go! My care
Is but to save my children, not for her.
Let them she wronged requite her as they may.
I care not. 'Tis my sons I must some way
Save, ere the kinsmen of the dead can win
From them the payment of their mother's sin.

LEADER   Unhappy man, indeed thou knowest not
What dark place thou art come to! Else, God
    wot,
Jason, no word like these could fall from thee.

JASON   What is it?—Ha! The woman would kill
    me?

LEADER   Thy sons are dead, slain by their
    mother's hand.

9 Ino, wife of Athamas, King of Thebes, nursed
the infant Dionysus. For this Hera punished her
with madness.

Medea

JASON How? Not the children. . . . I scarce understand. . . .

O God, thou hast broken me!

LEADER   Think of those twain

As things once fair, that ne'er shall bloom again.

JASON Where did she murder them? In that old room?

LEADER Open, and thou shalt see thy children's doom.

JASON Ho, thralls! Unloose me yonder bars! Make more

Of speed! Wrench out the jointing of the door.

And show my two-edged curse, the children dead,

The woman. . . . Oh, this sword upon her head . . .

[*While the Attendants are still battering at the door Medea appears on the roof, standing on a chariot of winged dragons, in which are the children's bodies.*]

MEDEA What make ye at my gates? Why batter ye

With brazen bars, seeking the dead and me

Who slew them? Peace! . . . And thou, if aught of mine

Thou needest, speak, though never touch of thine

Shall scathe me more. Out of his firmament

My father's father, the high Sun, hath sent

This, that shall save me from mine enemies' rage.

JASON Thou living hate! Thou wife in every age

Abhorrèd, blood-red mother, who didst kill

My sons, and make me as the dead: and still

Canst take the sunshine to thine eyes, and smell

The green earth, reeking from thy deed of hell;

I curse thee! Now, Oh, now mine eyes can see,

That then were blinded, when from savagery

Of eastern chambers, from a cruel land,

To Greece and home I gathered in mine hand

Thee, thou incarnate curse: one that betrayed

Her home, her father, her . . . Oh, God hath laid

Thy sins on me!—I knew, I knew, there lay

A brother murdered on thy hearth that day

When thy first footstep fell on Argo's hull . . .

Argo, my own, my swift and beautiful!

That was her first beginning. Then a wife

I made her in my house. She bore to life

Children: and now for love, for chambering

And men's arms, she hath murdered them! A thing

Not one of all the maids of Greece, not one

Had dreamed of; whom I spurned, and for mine own

Chose thee, a bride of hate to me and death,

Tigress, not woman, beast of wilder breath

Than Skylla shrieking o'er the Tuscan sea.

Enough! No scorn of mine can reach to thee,

Such iron is o'er thine eyes. Out from my road,

Thou crime-begetter, blind with children's blood!

And let me weep alone the bitter tide

That sweepeth Jason's days, no gentle bride

To speak with more, no child to look upon

Whom once I reared . . . all, all for ever gone!

MEDEA An easy answer had I to this swell

Of speech, but Zeus our father knoweth well,

All I for thee have wrought, and thou for me.

So let it rest. This thing was not to be,

That thou shouldst live a merry life, my bed

Forgotten and my heart uncomforted,

Thou nor thy princess: nor the king that planned

Thy marriage drive Medea from his land,

And suffer not. Call me what thing thou please,

Tigress or Skylla from the Tuscan seas:

My claws have gripped thine hearth, and all things shine.

JASON Thou too hast grief. Thy pain is fierce as mine.

MEDEA I love the pain, so thou shalt laugh no more.

JASON Oh, what a womb of sin my children bore!

MEDEA Sons, did ye perish for your father's shame?

JASON How? It was not my hand that murdered them.

MEDEA 'Twas thy false wooings, 'twas thy trampling pride.

JASON Thou hast said it! For thy lust of love they died.

MEDEA And love to women a slight thing should be?

JASON To women pure!—All thy vile life to thee!

MEDEA Think of thy torment. They are dead, they are dead!

JASON No: quick, great God; quick curses round thy head!

MEDEA The Gods know who began this work of woe.

JASON Thy heart and all its loathliness they know.

MEDEA Loathe on. . . . But, Oh, thy voice. It hurts me sore.

JASON Aye, and thine me. Wouldst hear me then no more?

MEDEA How? Show me but the way. 'Tis this I crave.

JASON Give me the dead to weep, and make their grave.

MEDEA Never! Myself will lay them in a still
Green sepulchre, where Hera by the Hill
Hath precinct holy, that no angry men
May break their graves and cast them forth again
To evil. So I lay on all this shore
Of Corinth a high feast for evermore
And rite, to purge them yearly of the stain
Of this poor blood. And I, to Pallas' plain
I go, to dwell beside Pandion's son,
Aegeus.—For thee, behold, death draweth on,
Evil and lonely, like thine heart: the hands
Of thine old Argo,[10] rotting where she stands,
Shall smite thine head in twain, and bitter be
To the last end thy memories of me.

[*She rises on the chariot and is slowly borne away.*]

JASON May They that hear the weeping child

[10] Jason, left friendless and avoided by his kind, went back to live in his old ship, now rotting on the shore. While he was sleeping under it, a beam of wood fell upon him and broke his head.

Blast thee, and They that walk in blood!

MEDEA Thy broken vows, thy friends beguiled
Have shut for thee the ears of God.

JASON Go, thou art wet with children's tears!

MEDEA Go thou, and lay thy bride to sleep.

JASON Childless, I go, to weep and weep.

MEDEA Not yet! Age cometh and long years.

JASON My sons, mine own!

MEDEA   Not thine, but mine . . .

JASON Who slew them!

MEDEA   Yes: to torture thee.

JASON Once let me kiss their lips, once twine
Mine arms and touch. . . . Ah, woe is me!

MEDEA Wouldst love them and entreat? But now
They were as nothing.

JASON   At the last,
O God, to touch that tender brow!

MEDEA Thy words upon the wind are cast.

JASON Thou, Zeus, wilt hear me. All is said
For naught. I am but spurned away
And trampled by this tigress, red
With children's blood. Yet, come what may,
So far as thou has granted, yea,
So far as yet my strength may stand,
I weep upon these dead, and say
Their last farewell, and raise my hand
To all the daemons of the air
In witness of these things; how she
Who slew them, will not suffer me
To gather up my babes, nor bear
To earth their bodies; whom, O stone
Of women, would I ne'er had known
Nor gotten, to be slain by thee!

[*He casts himself upon the earth.*]

CHORUS Great treasure halls hath Zeus in heaven,
From whence to man strange dooms be given,
Past hope or fear.
And the end men looked for cometh not,
And a path is there where no man thought:
So hath it fallen here.

EURIPIDES'S TIME saw the rise of the Sophists and their rhetoric. Euripides was affected, perhaps in rather complex ways, by this development.

The language used by tragic poets now approximated to the language of ordinary life, in the same way as the myths had been transformed into symbols of everyday problems. At the same time, the new devices of polished logical argument were imported from the elaborate art of forensic oratory into the dialogues and speeches of tragedy. . . . Throughout [Euripides's] plays we can trace a novel competition between tragedy and the rhetorical contests of opposing litigants which so delighted the Athenians, for now verbal duels between contrasting characters on the stage became one of the principal excitements of tragic drama. [Werner Jaeger, *Paideia,* vol. one, Oxford University Press, New York, 1939, pp. 343–344. Translated by Gilbert Highet from the second German edition.]

Here the Greek and the Norwegian [Ibsen] agree heartily; for the "sophistry" with which many at Athens were disgusted is only Euripides' way of putting his conviction that there is no fixed rule of conduct, still less any fixed rule for our self-satisfied attempts to praise or blame the abnormal. . . . This consciousness that effort brings about results different from its aims, that chance, whatever chance may be, is too potent to allow any faith in orthodox deities, only in moods of despair wrings from the poet such out-

cry as Hecuba's that Fate is "a capering idiot." But it has planted surely in his mind the conviction that there is no golden rule of conduct. And hence that "love of forensic rhetoric" of which we hear so much—each case must be considered on its own merits. [Gilbert Norwood, *Greek Tragedy,* John W. Luce and Co., Boston, n.d., pp. 317–318.]

Rhetoric, as taught by the sophists, aimed at putting forward the subjective view of an accused person with every possible persuasive device. . . . For Euripides . . . the passionate subjective self-vindications of his heroes are always expressed as bitter accusations of the deadly injustice of man's fate. We know that in the age of Pericles the problem of legal responsibility in Athenian penal law and in the speeches of defendants was coming to be viewed more and more from the subjective point of view, so that the distinction between guilt and innocence sometimes entirely disappeared: for example, many held that acts done under the influence of passion were not voluntary acts at all. This attitude went very deep in tragic poetry. . . . [Its appearance] can be described as the invasion of tragedy by rhetoric, but it was very much more than a stylistic device. [Jaeger, *op. cit.,* pp. 344–345.]

Aristotle's early objection to Euripides's use of the chorus has been followed by a number of attacks and defenses.

The chorus too must be regarded as one of the actors. It must be part of the whole and share in the action, not as in Euripides but as in Sophocles. [Aristotle, *Poetics,* William Heinemann, Ltd., London, 1927, p. 71. Translated by W. Hamilton Fyfe, Loeb Classical Library.]

The Chorus in the *Medea* finds itself in a famous difficulty at the murder of the children;

it ought to participate in the action and may not. Fifteen women of Corinth stand by doing nothing while Medea murders her children indoors—or rather they stand by deliberating whether to do anything or not. In meeting this improbability nothing is gained by saying that the Chorus was a body of Ideal Spectators and that a Greek audience would not expect them to interfere. They have in fact always taken part in the action when circumstances suggested it. . . . Moreover, Euripides himself feels that they should naturally interfere now, for if no thought of the possible intervention of Ideal Spectators could have arisen in the mind of the audience, why does he go out of his way to suggest that thought? [H. D. F. Kitto, *Greek Tragedy,* Doubleday & Company, Inc., New York, p. 200.]

The answer to that is given in the play itself. They do not rush in; there is no question of their rushing in: because the door is barred. When Jason in the next scene tries to enter the house he has to use soldiers with crowbars. The only action they can possibly perform is the sort that specially belongs to the Chorus, the action of baffled desire. [Gilbert Murray, *Euripides and His Age,* rev. ed., Williams & Norgate, Ltd., London, 1914, pp. 240–241.]

This chorus is a little surprising too in the ode that it sings . . . when Medea has finally resolved that her children must die, and just before we hear the horrible story of Glauce's death. If we have in mind the tremendous effects that Sophocles produced with his chorus at moments like these, it is a little chilling to find Euripides going off into his study, as it were, and writing, in anapests too, on the advantages of being childless. . . .

The subject is germane to the context, but the treatment is not; such generalized reflection breaks the emotional rhythm of the play. When such desperate deeds are afoot, why does Euripides insert this pleasant little essay? . . . [Whatever] the true explanation of the passage, we can draw one deduction from it, and that is that Euripides' attitude to his tragic heroine is quite different from Sophocles'. . . . For all the sympathy and the tragic power with which Euripides draws his characters . . . it seems clear that fundamentally he is detached from them. He can, as Sophocles cannot, retire for a moment and invite us to think of something else. [Kitto, *op. cit.,* p. 201.]

The important thing to observe is . . . that a Greek tragedy normally proceeds in two planes or two worlds. When the actors are on the stage we are following the deeds and fates of so many particular individuals, lovers, plotters, enemies, or whatever they are, at a particular point of time and space. When the stage is empty and the Choral Odes begin, we have no longer the particular acts and places and persons but something universal and eternal. The body, as it were, is gone and the essence remains. We have the greatness of love, the vanity of revenge, the law of eternal retribution, or perhaps the eternal doubt whether in any sense the world is governed by righteousness.

Thus the talk about improbability . . . falls into its proper insignificance. The Chorus in Euripides is frequently blamed by modern scholars on the ground that "it does not further the action," that its presence is "improbable," or its odes "irrelevant." The answer is that none of these things constitute the business of the Chorus; its business is something considerably higher and more important. [Murray, *op. cit.,* pp. 232–233.]

The conflict in the Medea *has been described as social, as personal, and as a combination of the two.*

Medea's first speech must be read with attention. Its sententious opening is deliberately designed to disappoint those who had expected the flame and fire of an inhuman or superhuman heroine on her first appearance. She appears to have won control over her wild grief. There is strength in that. There is strength too in the quiet, cold bitterness of her polite exordium, and in the contempt with which she describes a society where men are supreme and women their chattels. . . . The words, designed for heavy irony, are the echo of many a reproach of Jason, and introduce the famous passage of protest against male morality which makes the play important as a social document. [E. M. Blaiklock, *The Male Characters of Euripides,* New Zealand University Press, Wellington, N.Z., 1952, p. 25.]

Euripides invented domestic drama. *Medea,* with its conflict between the boundless egoism of the husband and the boundless passion of the wife, was a completely up-to-date play. Accordingly, the disputes, the abuse, and the logic used by all its characters are essentially bourgeois. Jason is stiff with cleverness and magnanimity; while Medea philosophizes on the social position of women. . . . It is impossible for us to admire the play wholeheartedly; yet it was a revolution in its time, and it shows the true fertility of the new art. [Jaeger, *op. cit.,* p. 342.]

In Sophocles we have observed how that collision of wills and emotions, which is always the soul of drama, arises from the confrontation of two persons. In the present drama that collision takes place in the bosom of a single person. Sophocles would probably have given us a Jason whose claim upon our sympathy was hardly less than that of Medea. Complication, with him, is to be found in his plots, not in his characters. But here we have a subject which has since proved so rich a mine of tragic and romantic interest—the study of a soul divided against it-

self. Medea's wrongs, her passionate resentment, and her plans of revenge do not merely dominate the play, they *are* the play from the first line to the close. [Norwood, *op. cit.,* p. 196.]

Euripides does not make society responsible for the isolation of Medea. In fact, he shows her aided against her husband by the women of Corinth. Nor is tragedy allowed to treat of love except its effects, and before the play begins it has turned to hate. Thus the play is one of personal conflict assuming various aspects as the intrigue and revelation of character proceed. There is of course the contrast between man's world and its concerns and woman's preoccupation with her own intimate feelings; there is the conflict of the apparently helpless deserted creature against the king and his cohorts; and above all we are reminded in the end of the difference between Greek and barbarian. There is no singleness of mind, however . . . to give consistency to any one issue. The Athenians could hardly award the *Medea* more than the third prize which they did award, if they had any regard for consistent support of principles. Its perspective is too ingenious. [L. A. Post, *From Homer to Menander,* University of California Press, Berkeley, Calif., 1951, pp. 130–131.]

In the Medea, *characterization, and its relation to structure, is certainly* not *Sophoclean. It is somewhat difficult to decide what it is: a manifestation of naturalism, sentimentality, sensationalism, or an individual perspective.*

How . . . does Medea fit Aristotle's definition of a tragic hero? Not at all. Aristotle's tragic hero is "like" us, for we should not feel pity and fear for one unlike us. He must not be a saint, or his downfall would be revolting, nor a villain, whose downfall might be edifying but would not be tragic. He must be intermediate, better rather than worse, and find his ruin through some hamartia. . . . Medea is no character compounded of good and bad, in whom what is bad tragically brings down in ruin what is good, and

we certainly cannot fear for her as for one of ourselves. In fact, treated as a genuinely tragic heroine she will not work. . . .

Medea is certainly not all villainy; she loves her children, loved Jason (if that is a merit), and was popular in Corinth; but it is the essential part of this tragedy that she was never really different from what we see her to be. Euripides could easily have represented her as a good but passionate woman who plunges into horrors only when stung by deadly insult and injury. There was no need for him to rake up her past as he does—except that this is his whole point. She never was different; she has no contact with Aristotle. [Kitto, *op. cit.,* pp. 197–198.]

Here, it has been said, we see inside the soul of a woman as no Greek writer ever made us see before. And this is entirely true; but the analysis exacts its price. The high horror of the action comes when Medea kills her children. Why does she kill them? We are given, not one compelling motive but a whole assortment of motives. . . . In the end she does not know why she kills them and neither do we. But . . . we ought perhaps not to think too much about rational or psychological motivation, but only the inevitable sequences of action. We can think of several reasons why Oedipus should blind himself, but these too many reasons do not stunt the force of his act. That is because the act is self-expressive and motives come as after-thoughts. Medea acts, or is supposed to act, on sheer drive of feeling, irrational or barbaric or simply female. But we do not feel the drive, because the motives are constantly being forced on our attention. Instead of striding forward with irresistible momentum, Medea keeps getting stuck and having to lash herself along. And here is the insincerity. From the outset, in the text and not in our imagination, we are given a woman who enrages herself. "There," says the nurse, "children, do you hear? Your mother stirs up her heart, stirs up her gall." Or, again, "she will kindle the stormcloud of her sorrow with growing anger" [page 31]. By the time she reaches the great monologue in which she harangues herself forward toward her acts, self-flagellation has involved self-dramatization too. I cannot help feeling that, by this time, Medea, who is practiced in deceit of others, is putting on an act for her own benefit, that the mother-love is phony and that Jason, cold and smug though he may be, loves the children better than Medea does. All this is horribly natural.

This is what people are like . . . but the pace and force of action in dramatic illusion have been sacrificed. The gain is naturalistic detail. [Richmond Lattimore, *The Poetry of Greek Tragedy,* Johns Hopkins Press, Baltimore, 1958, pp. 106–107.]

For none of [the prominent] characters do the spectators feel either pity or fear. If one of these emotions is aroused the cause must be looked for somewhere else, and . . . it is to be found in the part of the children. It is fear for them and pity for their fate that the poet stirs up. . . . They are silent characters except for a word or two uttered behind the scenes, but they have an important part in the drama. In fact the plot largely centres about their fate; and their death becomes the culmination of the tragedy. [William Nickerson Bates, *Euripides,* University of Pennsylvania Press, Philadelphia, 1930, p. 166.]

The tragedy of the Sophoclean hero is that such strength is nullified by such weakness; of Medea, that such a character should exist at all. She is bound to be a torment to herself and to others; that is why Euripides shows her blazing her way through life leaving wreckage behind her; that is why the suffering of others, of Glauce and of Creon, are not to be glozed over. That she suffers herself is a great and no doubt a necessary part of the drama, but it is not the point of the tragedy, which is that passion can be stronger than reason, and so can be a most destructive agent. Destructive to whom? Here, to the children, Glauce, Creon, Jason, and to Medea's peace—but not to her life; in short, destructive to society at large.

It follows that Euripides had either to describe Glauce's death horribly or to enfeeble his theme; the sufferings of Medea's victims are as much part of the tragedy as those of Medea herself, possibly a greater part. Hence the contrast with Sophocles. [Kitto, *op. cit.,* p. 203.]

The Aegeus episode is troublesome because of the chance appearance of a character who does not serve the function for which he is apparently introduced.

It is right . . . to censure . . . improbability where . . . no use is made of the improbability. An example is Euripides' introduction of Aegeus. . . . [Aristotle, *op. cit.*, p. 111.]

There is something lifelike in the solution of Medea's problem by a chance arrival. Since she was prepared to act according to circumstances, there is nothing forced in arranging a circumstance to produce this result rather than that. No doubt the Athenians liked to see their kings on the stage and to hear choruses in praise of Athens. Aegeus is not necessary to Medea's vengeance, but Euripides could not easily leave him out, once he had got into the story. Euripides is satisfied to make the intervention of Aegeus as inoffensive as possible. With Aristotle, Aegeus is a byword for the character who arrives unexpectedly and opportunely, but if there were no chance arrivals in life the resourceful heroine would have fewer opportunities to exercise her charm. [Post, *op. cit.*, p. 129.]

In the Sophoclean tragedy of character [the validity of the Aristotelian law of necessary or probable sequence] is absolute. . . . Evidently the whole point of such drama depends on this, that the character shall be a convincing one and that the circumstances, though they may be exceptional, shall develop normally, and always in significant relation with the character of the hero. It would be stultification if the dramatist had to produce a railway-accident without which the hero's doom would not be achieved. But Aegeus comes out of the blue, like a railway-accident. If the *Medea* were really a tragedy of character . . . and if an Aegeus had to be introduced after all in order to bring [her inevitable ruin] to pass, then the play would be meaningless. . . . But Euripides is not doing this at all. He is presenting to us his tragic conception that the passions and unreason to which humanity is subject are its greatest scourge. This implies no tragic interlock between character and situation; the situation is nothing but the setting for the outburst of unreason, the channel along which it rushes. What matters now is not that the situation must be convincing and illuminating, not even that the heroine must be convincing as a person; but that her passion must be, in however extreme a form, a fundamental and familiar one. If Medea is in this sense true, we shall not stay to object that she is not likely.

The situation then being only a setting, Euripides is philosophically justified in manipulating it in order to present his tragic thesis in its strongest colours. . . . Medea was in any case certain to work some ruin; Aegeus only allows her, and Euripides, to go to the logical extreme. [Kitto, *op. cit.*, pp. 205–206.]

A number of critics have considered the deus ex machina *in the play a theatrical device, disagreeing only on Euripides's motives for introducing it.*

The "dénouement" of each play should . . . be the result of the plot itself and not produced mechanically as in the *Medea.* [Aristotle, *op. cit.*, p. 57.]

In regard to his introduction, at the end, of the *deus ex machina* . . . it must be remembered that Euripides was a practical playwright; that he knew the spectacular effect which could be produced by it; and that he undoubtedly used it in the *Medea,* as in other plays, for this purpose. There can be no question that the audience approved of it, as, in fact, a modern audience would do. [Bates, *op. cit.*, pp. 164–165.]

Many plays of Euripides have endings like this. Perhaps he had antiquarian tastes and collected out-of-the-way tales for their own sake; it would not be the only way in which he anticipated the Hellenistic writers of a century and a half later. There is nothing to be done but to recognize the trait and admit that it is very odd. [D. W. Lucas, *The Greek Tragic Poets*, 2d ed., Cohen and West, London, 1959, p. 200.]

Of course, Medea's sudden godlike powers at the end make Aegeus unnecessary for her purpose, but it might be supposed that she had not herself expected such divine assistance as a chariot drawn by dragons. At any rate, it is a convention in Greek tragedy that the play is over when the gods intervene. [Post, *op. cit.*, p. 129.]

Aristotle's objection to this opportune though ostentatious equipage is amusingly mild: that it does not arise out of the action. So momentous a resource clashes ruinously with the repeated assertion of Medea's helpless isolation. Euripides

has sorely injured a fine tragedy in his effort to give it the average length. [Gilbert Norwood, *Essays on Euripidean Drama*, University of California Press, Berkeley, Calif., 1954, p. 34.]

Dr. Verrall's theory [stated in *Four Plays of Euripides*] meets all these difficulties. He supposes that several of Euripides' plays were originally written for private performance. The *Medea*, so acted, had no obtrusive chorus, and no miraculous escape of the murderess. To the episode of Aegeus corresponded a *finale* in which Medea, by allowing her husband to bury the bodies of his children, and by instituting the religious rites referred to in our present text [page 49] induced both Jason and the Corinthians to allow her safe passage to Athens. This view, or a view essentially resembling it, must be accepted, not so much because of the absurdity involved (as it appears to us) by the presence of the chorus, as the utter futility of the Aegeus-scene in the present state of the text. [Norwood, *Greek Tragedy*, pp. 196–197.]

The deus ex machina *has also been defended as functioning organically in the play.*

If we look carefully into the last scene we shall see more than dramatic convenience in the chariot. Medea has done things which appal even the chorus. . . . Their prayer now is "O Earth, O thou blazing light of the Sun, look upon this accursed woman before she slays her own children. . . . O god-given light, stay her hand . . ." [page 50]. In the same vein Jason says, when he has learnt the worst, "After doing this, of all things most unholy, dost thou show thy face to the Sun and the Earth?" [page 52]. Sun and Earth, the most elemental things in the universe, have been outraged by these terrible crimes; what will they do? How will they avenge their sullied purity? What Earth will do we shall not be told, but we are told what the Sun does: he sends a chariot to rescue the murderess.

Is this illogical? Could anything be finer, more imaginative? . . . Jason and the chorus think that "Gods should be wiser than men." Perhaps

so, but these gods are not. They exist; as well deny the weather as deny Aphrodite; but they are not reasonable and can make short work of us. Zeus, "whoever he is," is another matter. There may be a *Nous,* a Mind, in the universe; but there are other powers too, and these we may worship in vain. The magic chariot is a frightening glimpse of . . . the existence in the universe of forces that we can neither understand nor control—only participate in. [Kitto, *op. cit.*, pp. 208–209.]

By having her appear on the machine, Euripides forces the audience to seek for ways in which the character of Medea resembles that of a *deus ex machina*. We perceive in her an arbitrary fixity of will; she seems to hold herself aloof and remote from the ordinary concerns of men; and she speaks with authority. By the tone of her speech and by the use of the machine

Euripides seems to suggest that the price Medea has paid for her own course of action has been to suffer the loss of her own humanity. On this interpretation the final scene of the play presents visually and strikingly the dehumanizing effect upon Medea of what she has done. Certainly its effect is not and cannot be to present us with a happy Medea about to become a bride, nor with a Medea so fortunate that she has become a goddess. When the spectator sees Medea appear no longer where mortals appear and speak, but aloft in the place reserved for *theoi*, he ought to feel that she has received not reward but some awful and terrible retribution. When Medea first explains her plans to the Chorus, they say she will become a most unhappy woman [page 42]. When she goes in to commit the murder, she calls herself an unfortunate woman [page 48]. To Jason, she has become a [tigress] rather than a woman [pages 50–51]. But, to the audience, under the spell of the dramatic illusion of Medea's final appearance and disappearance through the air, she has indeed lost her humanity, though not in exchange for bestiality but for something of the awful, implacable, inhuman character of a *theos*. [Maurice P. Cunningham, "Medea ex Machina," *Classical Philology,* Vol. 49, 1954, pp. 158–159.]

TITUS MACCIUS PLAUTUS

c. 255–184 B.C.

*Plautus, foremost of the Roman comic dramatists, furnishes a link,
even if a somewhat tenuous one, between ancient Greece and the
Renaissance. His plots, characters, and dramatic devices were for
the most part taken from Greek New Comedy, particularly that of
Menander, who had been influenced by Euripides. However,
Plautus did not merely adapt Greek comedies; he habitually mixed
plots from different plays to create something new, a practice
referred to as "contamination." Nor did Plautus deal in subtleties.
Writing primarily for the crowd, he ignored tidiness of construction
in favor of the absurdity of situation characteristic of farce.*

*His swiftly moving though loosely constructed plots, his exuberant
if often coarse dialogue, and his broad portrayal of character types
account for Plautus' popularity among his contemporaries and
his influence upon the dramatists of the Renaissance, both on the
Continent and in England. The* miles gloriosus, *title character of
the play which follows (written c. 205 B.C.), was a favorite type in
Roman comedy, and Pyrgopolynices, "Taker of Towered Towns,"
is its outstanding representative. Shakespeare's Falstaff is only the
best known and most complex of his numerous progeny.*

ARGUMENT I (ACROSTIC)

A soldier carries off a courtesan from Athens to Ephesus. The young man in love with the girl is on an embassy abroad; his slave tries to get word of the abduction to his master, but is himself captured at sea and handed over as a gift to this same soldier. The slave summons his master from Athens and secretly digs a passage through the party wall of the two houses so that the two lovers may meet. The girl's watchman sees them embracing each other from the roof, and, by an amusing deception, he is made to believe that she is another girl. Moreover, Palaestrio persuades the soldier to give up his concubine, saying that the wife of the old man next door wants to marry him. The soldier of his own accord begs the girl to go away, and gives her many presents. He himself is caught in the home of the old man and is punished as an adulterer.

ARGUMENT II

A young man of Athens and a freeborn courtesan were madly in love with each other; he left home and went to Naupactus on an embassy. A soldier comes upon the girl and carries her off to Ephesus against her will. The slave of the Athenian sets sail to tell his master of the abduction; he is captured and is handed over as a captive to that same soldier. The slave writes to his master and tells him to come to Ephesus. The young man hurries there and puts up at the house next door with a friend of his father. The slave digs a hole in the wall between the two houses so that the lovers may meet secretly. He pretends that the girl's twin sister is next door. Then the master of the house furnishes Palaestrio with a protégée of his own to arouse the soldier's passion. The soldier is deceived, hopes for marriage, sends away his mistress, and is flogged as an adulterer.

Miles Gloriosus

THE BRAGGART WARRIOR

Characters

PYRGOPOLYNICES *the braggart warrior*

ARTOTROGUS *his parasite*

PALAESTRIO *slave of Pleusicles, now in the power of Pyrgopolynices*

PERIPLECTOMENUS *an old gentleman of Ephesus*

SCELEDRUS *slave of Pyrgopolynices*

PHILOCOMASIUM *a girl abducted by Pyrgopolynices*

PLEUSICLES *a young Athenian, in love with Philocomasium*

LURCIO *a slave boy, belonging to Pyrgopolynices*

ACROTELEUTIUM *a courtesan*

MILPHIDIPPA *her maid*

A SLAVE BOY *belonging to Periplectomenus*

CARIO *the cook of Periplectomenus*

The play takes place on a street in Ephesus in front of the adjoining houses of Pyrogopolynices and Periplectomenus.

Act One

Enter Pyrgopolynices from his house, followed by Artotrogus and orderlies; the latter carry an enormous shield.

PYRGOPOLYNICES [*to the orderlies, as he struts about*] Take pains to make my shield shine far more brilliantly than do the rays of the sun when the sky is cloudless; when the need arises and the conflict commences, I want it to dazzle the enemy's sight on the battle-site. [*Examining his sword*] Now I wish to comfort this poor blade of mine, so that it won't be miserable or downcast at heart because it's been hanging here at my side so long on a holiday; it's awfully eager to make mincemeat of the enemy. But where is Artotrogus?

ARTOTROGUS [*stepping forward*] He stands beside a man who's brave and blessed and as beautiful as a prince; and as to your fame as a fighter—Mars himself wouldn't dare mention it, or compare his achievements with yours.

PYRG. Was that the fellow I saved in the battle

61

of Weevil Plains, where the commander in chief was Bumbomachides Clutomestoridysarchides, the grandson of Neptune?

ART. Ah, I remember. You mean the one with the golden armour, whose legions you puffed away with a breath, just as the wind blows away leaves or a thatched roof.

PYRG. Heavens! That was a mere nothing.

ART. A mere nothing, to be sure, compared to the other deeds I could mention—[aside] which you never did. [To the audience, in a disgusted tone] If anyone has seen a greater liar or a bigger bundle of conceit than this fellow, he can have me as his own and I'll guarantee the title. [Pauses.] There's one thing to consider, though; his olive salad is excellent eating.

PYRG. [looking around] Where are you?

ART. [coming to attention] Right here, sir. Gad! That elephant in India, for instance! How you smashed its forearm with your fist!

PYRG. What? Forearm?

ART. Foreleg, I meant to say.

PYRG. I didn't hit very hard.

ART. Of course not. If you had really put your strength into it, your arm would have transpierced the elephant all the way through, hide, flesh, bone, and all.

PYRG. I'd rather not talk about this now.

ART. Heavens! It really isn't worth while for you to tell me about it; I know all your achievements. [Aside] It's my belly that's responsible for all my sufferings. I have to 'ear him with my ears, so that my dental work can make dents in food; and I have to agree to any lie he tells.

PYRG. What was it that I was saying?

ART. Ah! I know already what you want to say. Heavens! You did it. I remember that you did it.

PYRG. Did what?

ART. Whatever it is you did.

PYRG. Do you have—

ART. [interrupting] You want a tablet. I have it, and a pen, too.

PYRG. Clever of you to be so attentive with your attention.

ART It's right for me to know your character through and through and to take pains that I get the first whiff of your wishes.

PYRG. Well, what do you recall?

ART. [calculating] Let me see. I recall there were one hundred and fifty in Cilicia, a hundred in Scythobrigandia, thirty Sardians, sixty Macedonians—those are the men you slaughtered in one day.

PYRG. And what's the sum total of the men?

ART. Seven thousand.

PYRG. Yes, that's what it ought to be. Your calculation is quite correct.

ART. I don't write any of it down, either; I just rely on my memory.

PYRG. Well, you've a damned excellent one.

ART. [aside] The thought of food helps it.

PYRG. If you behave as you have in the past, you'll have plenty to eat; I shall always share my table with you.

ART. [eager for more praise] What about the time in Cappadocia, when you would have killed five hundred men all with one stroke, if your sword hadn't been dull?

PYRG. But they were worthless infantrymen; I let them live.

ART. Why should I tell you what all mortals know, that you are the one and only Pyrgopolinices on earth, unsurpassed in valour, in beauty, and in brave deeds? All the women are in love with you, and not without reason, since you're so handsome. Take, for instance, those girls yesterday who caught me by my cloak.

PYRG. [concealing his eagerness] What did they say to you?

ART. They kept asking about you. "Is this fellow Achilles?" one of them says to me. "No," says I, "but it is his brother." Then the other one says to me, "Dear me, but he's handsome, and such a gentleman, too. Just look how lovely his hair is. The women that sleep with him are certainly lucky."

PYRG. Did they really say that?

ART. Why, didn't both of them beg me to lead you past there today, as if you were on parade?

PYRG. [pretending indifference] It's such a nuisance for a man to be so handsome.

ART. Absolutely right, sir. They're a bother to me; they beg, urge, beseech to be allowed to see you; they keep sending for me, so that I can't devote myself to your business.

PYRG. Well, I guess that it's time for us to go to the forum, so that I can pay the recruits I enlisted here yesterday. King Seleucus earnestly requested me to collect and enlist recruits for him. I've decided to devote this day to the king.

ART. Well, then, let's do it.

PYRG. [*to the orderlies*]   After me, you attendants!

[*All march off towards the forum.*]

Act Two

SCENE ONE[1]

Enter Palaestrio from the house of Pyrgopolynices.

PALAESTRIO [*to the audience*]   I wish to oblige you by outlining the plot of our play, if you will all be kind enough to listen. Moreover, if anyone should not desire to listen, he may arise and leave, so that there will be a seat for the person who does so desire. Now as to your reason for assembling in this festive spot, I shall tell you both the plot and the name of the comedy which we are about to present. The name of this comedy in Greek is *Alazon,* and we translate it into Latin as *Gloriosus.*[2] This is the city of Ephesus. That soldier who just went off to the forum is my master, a bragging, impudent stinker, filled with lies and lechery; he says all the women chase after him. Actually, wherever he goes, he's the laughingstock of them all. And consequently most of the harlots you see here have wry mouths from twisting their lips at him.

Now, I've not been a servant in his service very long. I want you all to know how I came into his service and ceased to serve my former master. Give me your attention, for now I shall begin the plot.

My master in Athens was an excellent young man. He was in love with a courtesan who lived in Athens in Attica, and she returned his love —which is the nicest kind of love to cherish. He was sent as state envoy to Naupactus on a matter concerning the welfare of the state. Meanwhile this soldier happens to come to Athens and works his way to an acquaintance with my master's sweetheart. He began to entice her mother with wine and jewelry and dainty delicacies, and he gets on most intimate terms with the old procuress there. Then, as soon as he had the chance, he bamboozled the procuress, the mother of the girl my master loved; for he put the daughter on board ship without the knowledge of her mother and carried the girl here to Ephesus against her will.

When I learned that my master's mistress had been carried off from Athens, I got myself a ship as quickly as I possibly could and set sail to tell the news to my master at Naupactus. When we were out on the deep, the will of the gods was done; pirates captured the ship on which I was sailing; I was lost before I could get my message to my master. The man who captured me gave me as a gift to this same soldier. When he takes me home to his dwelling, I see there the girl who had been my master's mistress at Athens. When she saw me there before her, she gave me a signal with her eyes not to let on that I knew her; later, when there was an opportunity, she complained to me of her bitter fate; she said that she was anxious to get away from the house and escape to Athens, for she loved that master of mine who lived in Athens and detested no one more thoroughly than that soldier.

When I realised how the girl really felt, I seized a tablet, sealed it, and slipped it to a certain merchant to deliver to my master, the Athenian one who loved her; I urged him to come here. He didn't disregard the message; he's arrived and is staying here next door with a friend of his father's, a lovely old gentleman, who is assisting his guest in his love affair and

---

[1] This scene is really a prologue, but is deferred to permit the introduction of Pyrgopolynices in the opening scene, since his character is extremely important to the later action of the play. For a similarly postponed prologue, cf. *The Casket,* Act One, Scene III.

[2] *Alazon* and *Gloriosus* both mean "braggart."

aiding and abetting us with his help and advice. Consequently, I've prepared a delightful device inside here, to enable the lovers to be together. The soldier gave his concubine a certain room where no one but herself was to set foot; I dug a hole through the wall of that room so that the girl could have a secret passage from the soldier's house to this one [*pointing to the house of Periplectomenus*]; I did this with the knowledge of the old gentleman; in fact, he suggested it.

Now, this fellow slave of mine that the soldier selected to keep watch over his concubine is an utterly worthless fellow. With clever contrivances and deceitful devices we'll throw dust in his eyes and make him admit that he hasn't seen what he has seen. And to keep you from being confused, this one girl today will play the part of two girls, one from each house; she'll be the same one, but will pretend to be a different one. In that way the guard of the girl will be completely fooled. But I hear the door of the old man's house next door. The man's coming out. This is the charming old gentleman I just mentioned.

SCENE TWO

Enter Periplectomenus from his house.

PERIPLECTOMENUS [*to slaves within*] Damn it! I'll cut your sides into strips if you don't break the legs of any stranger you see on the roof after this. Already, I suppose, my neighbours know what's going on in my house; imagine, their looking in through the skylight! Here are my orders now to all of you: any person from the soldier's house that you see on our roof, with the one exception of Palaestrio, is to be hurled headlong down to the street! It doesn't make any difference whether he says he's chasing a chicken, or a dove, or a monkey; you're done for if you don't batter his body to death! And to keep them from breaking the Dicing Law, be sure that they haven't any bones left when they give a party at home.

PAL. [*aside*] Something's amiss, to judge from his words, and somebody from our house is to blame; that's why the old man wants the bones of my fellow slaves to be crushed. But he made an exception of me, and I don't give a damn what happens to the rest of them. I'll approach him. [*He advances.*]

PER. Isn't this Palaestrio coming towards me?

PAL. How do you do, Periplectomenus?

PER. There aren't many men, if I had my choice, that I'd rather see and meet right now than you.

PAL. What's up? What trouble are you having with our household?

PER. We're ruined!

PAL. What's the matter?

PER. It's known.

PAL. What's known?

PER. Somebody from your house, on the roof just now, looked in through the skylight and saw Philocomasium and my guest kissing each other here in my house.

PAL. Who's the person that saw it?

PER. A fellow slave of yours.

PAL. Who was he?

PER. I don't know. He dashed off too quickly.

PAL. I suspect that I'm done for!

PER. As he hurried off, I shouted after him. "Hey, you!" says I, "What are you doing on the roof?" "Chasing a monkey," says he, and off he goes.

PAL. Damnation! To be ruined on account of a worthless beast like that! But is Philocomasium still here in your house?

PER. She was when I came out.

PAL. Go, please, and tell her to come over to our house as quickly as possible, so that the slaves can see her at home—that is, unless she wants all of us slaves to be admitted to the Companionship of the Cross just on account of her love affair.

PER. I did tell her that. Anything else you wish?

PAL. Yes. Tell her this too: she's not to depart a single inch from women's wiles, and she's to cherish all the cleverness and skill they have.

PER. In what way?

PAL. So that she can convince the fellow who saw her here that he didn't see her. Even if she were seen here a hundred times, she's still to deny it. She's got plenty of cheek and a smooth tongue, and she's treacherous, cunning, and confident; she's full of conceitedness, resoluteness, deceitfulness. If anyone accuses her, she's to prove the opposite on her solemn oath; she's got a goodly supply of crooked talk, crooked tricks, crooked oaths; she's stocked with cunning, with captivating caresses, with crafty contraptions. As a matter of fact, sir, a woman who's wicked enough never applies to a gardener; she has her own garden stuff with plenty of seasoning for serving up every kind of corruption.

PER. [*a little weary*]   I'll tell her all this, if she's still inside. [*Palaestrio becomes thoughtful.*] What is it, Palaestrio, that you're turning over in your mind?

PAL.   Be silent a moment, please, while I call together a council in my heart and consider what to do, what device to draw up against my devilish fellow slave who saw her kissing here, so that what was seen will be unseen.

PER.   Think carefully. In the meantime I'll step over here a bit. [*He moves away and comments to himself as he watches Palaestrio's gesticulations.*] Just look at that, now, how he stands there, with frowning brow, considering and cogitating. With his fingers he's knocking at the door of his breast; he's going to invite his intelligence to come out, I imagine. There, he turns away. He rests his left hand on his left thigh, and with the fingers of his right does some calculating. Now he slaps his right thigh! A right lusty blow! He's having a difficult time deciding what to do. Now he's snapped his fingers; what a struggle! He constantly changes his position. But look at that! He's shaking his head; he doesn't like that notion. No matter what it is, he won't put forth a half-baked idea; he'll provide one well done. And now look! [*Palaestrio rests his head on his arm.*] He's doing some building; supporting his chin on a column. The devil with it! I don't like that style of building. I've heard it said that a foreign poet had a columned countenance and two guards always on watch day and night.[3] [*Palaestrio changes his position.*] Bravo! How becoming! By Jove,

he stands there just like slaves in comedies. He'll never rest today until he succeeds in what he is seeking. There! He's got it, I think. [*Aloud, as Palaestrio seems to hesitate*] If you're going to do anything, do it! Wake up; don't sink into slumber, that is, unless you want to keep watch here battered with blows until you're black and blue. Yes, I'm talking to you. You didn't get drunk yesterday, did you?[4] Hey, Palaestrio! It's you I'm speaking to. Wake up, I say! Arouse yourself, I say! It's dawn, I say!

PAL. [*without enthusiasm*]   I hear you.

PER.   Don't you see that the enemy is upon you and attacking your rear? Take counsel; seize aid and assistance for this emergency. Now's the time for sweeping on, not sleeping. Steal a march in some way, lead around your army by some route; blockade the enemy, but aid our troops; shut off supplies from the foe, procure a passage so that provisions and supplies can reach you and your legions in safety. Attention! The need is urgent! Devise something, hit upon something, make haste to hatch a plot that's hot; the things that have been seen here must be unseen, or the things that have been done will be undone. The man is reaching for something big; high-reaching are the ramparts he's raising. If you say that you'll undertake it yourself, I'm confident that we can crush the foe.

PAL.   I say it and I undertake it.

PER.   And I say that you'll gain your wish.

PAL.   May Jupiter bless you!

PER.   Won't you inform me of your scheme?

PAL.   Hush, while I conduct you to the land of my machinations, that you may know my plots as well as I.

PER.   You shall take back the same in safety.

PAL.   My master is covered with the hide of an elephant, instead of his own skin; he's as stupid as a stone.

PER.   I know that.

PAL.   Now, sir, this is the plan I'll begin; this is the cunning scheme I'll set up. I'll say that Philocomasium's own true twin sister has arrived from Athens with a certain lover of hers, and that the two sisters are as much alike as two drops of milk; I'll say that they're being

---

[3] This refers to the Roman ("foreign," i.e., non-Greek) poet Naevius, who was imprisoned for his attacks on the aristocratic family of the Metelli, probably about 206 B.C. The "two guards" are the chains on his hands and feet.

[4] The text is corrupt here.

lodged and entertained at your house.

PER. Excellent! Excellent! Perfect! I praise your scheme.

PAL. [continuing] So if that fellow slave of mine should complain to the soldier that he saw Philocomasium here kissing a strange man, I'll assert in reply that he saw the sister here in your house embracing and kissing her own lover.

PER. Splendid! I'll tell the same story, if the soldier asks me about it.

PAL. Be sure to say that they're exactly alike. And Philocomasium must be instructed so that she'll know about this and won't make a slip, if the soldier should ask her.

PER. A most clever contrivance! But if the soldier wants to see both of them at one time, what are we to do?

PAL. That's easy. A thousand pretexts can be provided. "She's not at home, she's gone for a walk, she's asleep, she's dressing, she's bathing, she's dining, she's drinking; she's occupied; she's not at leisure, it's impossible." There are lots of ways of putting him off, provided we convince him at the beginning to accept our lies as the truth.

PER. I like what you say.

PAL. Go in, then, and if the girl's there, tell her to return home quickly, and inform her, instruct her, advise her, so that she'll understand the scheme about the twin sister that we've started.

PER. I'll make her as skilled as skilled can be. Anything else?

PAL. Just be off indoors.

PER. I'm off. [He goes into his house.]

PAL. [to himself] And now I'll go home and aid him secretfully by digging out the identity of that fellow slave of mine who was chasing a monkey today. He couldn't keep from informing someone in the house about his master's mistress, how he saw her kissing some strange young man here next door. I know the habit: "I just can't keep a secret all to myself." If I find the man who saw her, I'll bring up my sheds and my siege-works. Everything's prepared; I'm determined to take the fellow by force and violence. If I don't find him, I'll go sniffing about like a hunting dog until I track

down the fox and overtake him. [He pauses.] But the door of our house creaked; I'll lower my voice. Here is my fellow slave, the guard of Philocomasium, coming out.

SCENE THREE

Enter Sceledrus, much troubled.

SCELEDRUS [to himself] Unless I was walking around on the roof in my sleep today, I know for certain that I saw Philocomasium, my master's mistress, here in the house next door bringing trouble on herself.

PAL. [aside] He's the one that saw her kissing, as far as I can tell from his words.

SCEL. [hearing his voice] Who's here?

PAL. [stepping forward] Your fellow slave. How are you, Sceledrus?

SCEL. Awfully glad I've met you, Palaestrio.

PAL. What is it? What's the trouble? Tell me.

SCEL. I'm afraid—

PAL. Afraid of what?

SCEL. Damn it! That all of us slaves in the household today are going to be plunged into painful punishment.

PAL. You plunge in alone, then; I don't care for that sort of plunging and lunging.

SCEL. Maybe you don't know about the horrible new crime that has occurred at our house.

PAL. What sort of crime?

SCEL. Oh, a shameless one!

PAL. You keep it to yourself then; don't tell me. I don't want to know it.

SCEL. Well, I won't stop until you do know it. I chased our monkey today on their roof.

PAL. By Jove, Sceledrus! A worthless beast chased by a worthless man!

SCEL. Damn you!

PAL. You, I'd prefer— [changing his tone] to speak on, since you've begun.

SCEL. It just so happened that I chanced to look down through the skylight into the house next door; and there I saw Philocomasium kissing some strange young man, I don't know who.

PAL. What's this villainy that I hear from you, Sceledrus?

SCEL. I certainly saw her.

PAL. You yourself?

SCEL. I certainly did, with these two eyes of mine.

PAL. Get out! What you say isn't likely. You didn't see her!

SCEL. You don't think I have sore eyes, do you?

PAL. You'd better ask a doctor about that. But, for the love of the gods, don't be rash in fathering that fable; you're creating here a fatal disaster for your head and heels. If you don't put a stop to this stultiloquy of yours, you're destined to die a double death.

SCEL. How do you mean, double?

PAL. I'll tell you. In the first place, if you accuse Philocomasium falsely, you're done for; in the second place, if it's true, you're done for because you're her guard.

SCEL. [*worried, but stubborn*] What will happen to me I don't know; but I do know for certain that I saw this.

PAL. Keeping right on, you poor wretch?

SCEL. What do you want me to say, except what I really saw? Why, even now she's here in the house next door.

PAL. What! Isn't she at home?

SCEL. Go and see. Go inside yourself. I don't expect anyone to believe me.

PAL. [*rushing towards the door*] I'm determined to do it.

SCEL. I'll wait for you here! At the same time I'll be on watch to see how soon the heifer comes back from pasture to her stall here. [*To himself, as Palaestrio goes into the house of Pyrgopolynices*] What am I to do now? The soldier made me her guard; now if I reveal it, I'm ruined; I'm ruined just the same if I keep silent, if the truth leaks out. What is there more worthless or more audacious than a woman? She slipped away from her house while I was on the roof. Gad! She did a daring deed, all right. If the soldier finds out about it, damned if he won't hurl the whole house, me included, to the devil! Whatever the outcome, I'll keep still rather than come to a bad end. I just can't guard a woman that's always putting herself up for sale. [*Reenter Palaestrio.*]

PAL. Sceledrus, Sceledrus, where on earth is there a more impudent person than you? Who was ever born when the gods were more angry and enraged?

SCEL. What's the matter?

PAL. Why don't you order someone to gouge out your eyes, since they see things that nowhere exist?

SCEL. What? Nowhere exist?

PAL. I wouldn't pay a rotten nut for your life.

SCEL. What's the trouble?

PAL You ask what's the trouble?

SCEL. Why shouldn't I ask?

PAL. Have that talkative tongue of yours torn out, won't you?

SCEL. What for?

PAL. Well, there Philocomasium is at home, whom you said you saw kissing and hugging some man next door.

SCEL. It seems strange that you live on darnel,[5] when wheat is so cheap.

PAL. What do you mean?

SCEL. Because you're blear-eyed.

PAL. You hangman's delight! You're not blear-eyed, you're blind-eyed! She's right there at home.

SCEL. What, at home?

PAL. Damn it! She certainly is.

SCEL. Get out! You're playing with me, Palaestrio.

PAL. Then my hands are filthy.

SCEL. How so?

PAL. Because I'm playing with filth.

SCEL. You go to the devil!

PAL. That'll be your fate, Sceledrus, I promise you, if you don't get yourself different eyes and ideas. [*Listening*] But our door's creaked. [*The door opens and Philocomasium is visible in the doorway.*]

SCEL. [*with his back to the door of Pyrgopolynices' house and his eyes intent on Periplectomenus' door*] And I'm keeping my eyes fixed on this door, for there's no way that she can get from this house to the other except right through this door.

PAL. But look! There she is at home! Some

---

[5] Darnel was said to be bad for the eyes.

deviltry or other possesses you, Sceledrus.

SCEL. [*refusing to turn his head*] I see for myself, I think for myself, I have faith most of all in myself. No man shall keep me from believing that she is right here in this house. [*Blocking Periplectomenus' door*] I'll take my stand right here, so that she can't slip by without my knowledge.

PAL. [*aside, as Philocomasium disappears and Pyrgopolynices' door is closed*] I've got the fellow now. I'll hurl him down from his stronghold. [*To Sceledrus*] Want me to make you admit that you're fool-sighted?

SCEL. Go on, do it.

PAL. And that you have neither sense in your brains nor sight in your eyes?

SCEL. [*still defiant*] Yes, I want you to.

PAL. Do you still say that master's concubine is in there?

SCEL. [*watching Periplectomenus' door*] Yes. And I maintain that I saw her and a strange man kissing each other inside here.

PAL. You know, don't you, that there's no passage between our house and this one?

SCEL. I know that.

PAL. And that there's no sun deck, no garden, no means of communication except through the skylight?

SCEL. I know that.

PAL. Well then! If she's at home, if I have you see her come out of the house here, do you deserve a good thrashing?

SCEL. Of course.

PAL. You watch that door, then, so that she doesn't secretly slip away from there and cross over to our house.

SCEL. Just what I'm going to do.

PAL. I'll stand her right here in the street in front of you. [*He goes into the house of Pyrgopolynices.*]

SCEL. [*a little less confident*] Just go and do it, then. [*To himself*] I'd like to know whether I saw what I saw, or whether he can do what he says he'll do—prove that she's home. I certainly have eyes of my own in my head, and I don't have to go borrowing a pair from other people. [*Reflecting*] This fellow, though, is always flattering her, he's her right-hand man; he's the first to be called to dinner, he's the first to get

his fodder. And yet he's been with us only about three years, and there isn't a single servant in the entire household better treated than he. But I must tend to my business here and watch this door. [*Spreading his arms before Periplectomenus' door*] I'll stand like this. They'll never pull the wool over my eyes, I know that, by gad!

SCENE FOUR

Enter Palaestrio and Philocomasium from the house of Pyrgopolynices.

PAL. [*aside to Philocomasium*] Be sure you remember my instructions.

PHILOCOMASIUM [*aside to Palaestrio*] I'm surprised that you warn me so often.

PAL. [*to Philocomasium*] I'm afraid that you won't be quite cunning enough.

PHIL. [*to Palaestrio*] Why, give me ten women without a trace of deceit; I'll teach them to be full of deceit and still have an abundant supply left over for myself. Come now, push on with your trickery. I'll step aside a bit.

PAL. [*to Sceledrus*] Look here, Sceledrus.

SCEL. [*not turning his head*] I'm tending to my job here. I have ears; say whatever you want.

PAL. [*seeing his position*] You'll soon perish outside the gate in that pose, I guess, with your arms outstretched, when you're on the cross.

SCEL. What for?

PAL. Just look here to the left. What woman is this?

SCEL. [*turning his head at last*] Immortal gods! [*Horrified*] Why, it's master's concubine!

PAL. [*dryly*] Damned if I don't think the same. But come now, when you wish—

SCEL. To do what?

PAL. Make haste to die.

PHIL. [*advancing angrily*] Where is that excellent slave who falsely accused me, an innocent woman, of such shameful behaviour?

PAL. [*to Philocomasium*] There he is. He's the one that told me what I told you.

PHIL. You say that you saw me here in the house next door kissing, you rascal?

PAL. You and some strange young man, so he told me.

SCEL. Yes, I did say it, by heaven!

PHIL. It was me you saw?

SCEL. Yes, confound it! With my own eyes.

PHIL. You'll soon lose them, I daresay, since they see more than they see.

SCEL. Never, by heaven, will I be frightened out of having seen what I did see.

PHIL. I'm a stupid and foolish person to waste my breath on this idiot; by the powers, I'll punish him to perfection!

SCEL. Don't threaten me. I know the cross will be my tomb. That's where my ancestors lie, my father, my grandfather, my great-grandfather, my great-great-grandfather.[6] You can't dig out these eyes of mine with your threats. Palaestrio, I want a few words with you. [*He draws him aside.*] In the name of heaven, where did she come from?

PAL. Where but from home?

SCEL. From home?

PAL. You see me, don't you?

SCEL. Yes, I see you. [*Pondering*] It's awfully strange how she got from that house to ours. For there certainly isn't any sun deck in our house nor any garden nor any window that isn't grated. [*To Philocomasium*] And yet I certainly saw you here next door.

PAL. Keeping right on with your accusation, you rogue?

PHIL. Good gracious! The dream that I had last night has turned out to be true, then.

PAL. What was your dream?

PHIL. I'll tell you. Both of you pay attention, please. Last night in my dream my own twin sister seemed to have come from Athens to Ephesus with a certain lover of hers; they both seemed to be visiting here next door.

PAL. [*aside*] She's relating the dream of Palaestrio. [*Aloud*] Go right on.

PHIL. I seemed happy that my sister had come, but on her account I seemed to incur a most outrageous suspicion. For in my dream my own servant seemed to accuse me, just as you are now doing, of having been kissing some strange young man, when actually that twin sister of mine had been kissing her own sweetheart. And thus I dreamed that I was wrongly, falsely accused.

6 Sceledrus' enumeration of his ancestors is particularly amusing, since a slave in Roman law had no father.

PAL. And doesn't the same thing happen to you when you're awake that you say you saw in your sleep? Jupiter! How well the dream fits! Inside now, and make a prayer. I recommend that the soldier be told.

PHIL. I intend to do so. I shan't permit such a false accusation of dreadful behaviour to go unpunished. [*She goes into the house of Pyrgopolynices.*]

SCEL. [*in alarm*] I'm afraid that I've done it now; my back itches all over.

PAL. You realise you're done for, don't you?

SCEL. Anyway, she's certainly home now. [*Placing himself in front of Pyrgopolynices' door*] Now I've made up my mind to watch our door, wherever she is.

PAL. But just think, Sceledrus, how like was the dream she dreamed to reality, to your suspicion that you saw her kissing!

SCEL. [*wavering*] Now, I don't know what to believe; I'm beginning to think that I didn't see what I believe I did see.

PAL. You'll come to your senses when it's too late, by Jove! If this story gets to master first, you'll die a fine death.

SCEL. I realise now at last that there was a mist before my eyes.

PAL. Gad! That's been obvious for some time, since she's been inside here all along.

SCEL. I don't know what to say for sure. I didn't see her, but I did see her.

PAL. Damned if your folly didn't almost destroy us all. You just about ruined yourself, trying to be faithful to your master. But our neighbour's door creaked. I'll hush.

SCENE FIVE

Enter Philocomasium as the twin sister from the house of Periplectomenus.

PHIL. [*to a slave within*] Light the fire on the altar, that I may gratefully give praises and thanks to Diana of Ephesus and offer her the pleasing odour of Arabian incense; she saved me in the realms and boisterous abodes of Neptune, where I was so tossed about by angry waves.

SCEL. Palaestrio! Oh, Palaestrio!

PAL. Oh, Sceledrus! Sceledrus! What do you want?

SCEL. This woman that just came out here—is she master's concubine, Philocomasium, or isn't she?

PAL. [pretending amazement] By Jove, I think so! She seems to be. But it's an awfully strange thing how she could get from our house over here to our neighbour's, if it is she.

SCEL. Do you have any doubt that it's Philocomasium?

PAL. She seems to be.

SCEL. Let's approach and speak to her. [To Philocomasium] Hey, Philocomasium! What's going on here? What are you doing in that house? What's your business there? Why are you silent? I'm talking to you.

PAL. [amused] Hell, no! You're talking to yourself. She doesn't answer a single word.

SCEL. [angrily] I'm talking to you, you vehicle of vice and corruption, you who go roaming around among our neighbours.

PHIL. [coolly] To whom are you speaking?

SCEL. To whom, indeed, except to you?

PHIL. Who are you? What business have you with me?

SCEL. What? You ask me who I am?

PHIL. Why not, since I don't know?

PAL. Who am I, then, if you don't know him?

PHIL. A great nuisance to me, whoever you are; you and he both.

SCEL. [incredulous] You don't know us?

PHIL. No, neither of you.

SCEL. I'm fearfully afraid—

PAL. Afraid of what?

SCEL. That we've lost our identity somewhere or other; she says that she doesn't know either you or me.

PAL. I want to find out here, Sceledrus, whether we're really ourselves or somebody else; maybe one of our neighbours changed us when we weren't looking.

SCEL. [examining himself] Well, I'm certainly myself.

PAL. Gad, and so am I! [To Philocomasium] Woman, you're looking for trouble. [She pays no attention.] I'm talking to you, Philocomasium. Hey, there!

PHIL. What sort of insanity possesses you, that you keep addressing me wrongly by an unintelligible name?

PAL. Oho! What is your name, then?

PHIL. My name is Dicea.

SCEL. You're wrong, Philocomasium; you're trying to take a false name. You're not Dicea, you're Deceit-ea, and you're playing the hypocrite with my master.

PHIL. I?

SCEL. Yes, you.

PHIL. Why, I arrived in Ephesus last evening from Athens, with my sweetheart, an Athenian youth.

PAL. Tell me; what is your business here in Ephesus?

PHIL. I heard that my own twin sister was here. I came to look for her.

SCEL. You're a bad one!

PHIL. Mercy me! I'm certainly a very foolish one to be chattering with the two of you. [Turning away] I'm going.

SCEL. [seizing her arm] I won't let you go.

PHIL. Let me loose.

SCEL. You're caught in the act! I won't let you loose.

PHIL. My hands will smack and your cheeks will crack, if you don't let me loose.

SCEL. [to Palaestrio] What the devil are you standing still for? Grab her on the other side, won't you?

PAL. I don't care to have my back battered with blows. How do I know that she is Philocomasium? Maybe she's another person just like her.

PHIL. Will you let me loose or not?

SCEL. I will not. Unless you go along willingly, I'm going to drag you home by force, willy-nilly.

PHIL. [pointing to the house of Periplectomenus] This is my lodging while I'm abroad. My home is in Athens and so is my master.[7] I have no interest in that home of yours and I don't know who you are.

SCEL. Go to law about it, then. I won't let you go anywhere, unless you give me your solemn promise that you'll enter our house here, if I let you loose.

PHIL. You're using force, whoever you are. I'll

[7] The text is uncertain here. Periplectomenus later speaks of the twin sister as being free.

TITUS MACCIUS PLAUTUS

promise that I'll go inside where you say, if you let me loose.

SCEL. [*releasing her*] There, you're loose!

PHIL. And now that I am, I'm going in. [*She darts into the house of Periplectomenus.*]

SCEL. There's a woman's word for you!

PAL. Sceledrus, you let the booty slip through your fingers. It's as sure as can be that she's master's mistress. Do you want to act like a man of spirit?

SCEL. What am I to do?

PAL. Bring me out a sword from inside.

SCEL. What'll you do with it?

PAL. I'll burst right into the house. And any person I see inside kissing Philocomasium I'll slaughter right on the spot!

SCEL. You think it was she, then?

PAL. Damned right it was!

SCEL. But how she did pretend!

PAL. Go on! Bring me the sword!

SCEL. I'll have it here in a minute. [*He goes into the house of Pyrgopolynices.*]

PAL. [*to himself*] There isn't a single soldier, on horse or on foot, that can do anything as bravely and as boldly as a woman can. How cleverly she changed her speech for each part! And how my fellow slave, the wary guard, is being gulled! A very happy thought—that passage piercing the wall!

[*Reenter Sceledrus, much confused.*]

SCEL. Hey, Palaestrio! You don't need the sword.

PAL. What now? What's the matter?

SCEL. Master's mistress—she's inside the house.

PAL. What? Inside?

SCEL. She's lying on the couch.

PAL. Well! Damned if you haven't brought disaster on yourself! I can see that from your words.

SCEL. How so?

PAL. Why, because you dared to lay your hands on the lady here next door.

SCEL. Gad! I'm getting scared!

PAL. Now, no one shall ever make her be anything but the twin sister of the girl in our house. She's the one, obviously, that you saw kissing.

SCEL. It's clear now that she's the one, just as you say. How close I would have been to destruction, if I had mentioned it to master!

PAL. You'll keep quiet, then, if you're wise. A slave ought to know more than he tells. I'm going to leave you, so that I won't get mixed up in this muddle of yours. I'll be here in the neighbour's house. Your troubles don't interest me. If master comes and wants me, I'll be here, and you can send for me. [*He goes into the house of Periplectomenus.*]

SCENE SIX

SCEL. [*to himself*] Has he really gone? Doesn't he care any more for master's affairs than if he weren't a slave in slavery? Well, the girl is surely in our house now, I know that, for I found her there lying down just now. I'd better get on with my work of watching.

[*Enter Periplectomenus from his house, in great anger.*]

PER. [*to himself*] By gad, these fellows here, these slaves of the soldier next door, take me for a woman, not a man! The way they impose on me! Is the girl that I'm entertaining to be mauled and mocked at against her will? A lady that's free and freeborn, too, who came here yesterday from Athens with my guest!

SCEL. [*overhearing*] Heavens, I'm ruined! He's striding straight towards me. I'm afraid that there's some terrible trouble in store for me, judging from the words of this old fellow.

PER. [*aside*] I'll approach him. [*To Sceledrus*] Look here, Sceledrus, you fount of iniquity! Did you trifle with my guest here in front of the house just now?

SCEL. Good neighbour, listen to me, please.

PER. I listen to you?

SCEL. I want to clear myself.

PER. What? Clear yourself, when you've done so serious and dreadful a deed? Just because you people are freebooters, do you think you have the freedom to do anything you want, you gallows bird?

SCEL. May I speak, sir?

PER. [*taking a deep breath*] Now, may all the gods and goddesses so love me if I don't have the chance to give you a long and continuous raking with rods, from morning till night, because you broke my gutters and my tiles when you were chasing a monkey as worthless as yourself, and because you spied upon my guest embracing and kissing his sweetheart in my house, and because you dared to accuse your master's mistress, a decent girl, with dreadful conduct and likewise accused me of horrible behaviour, and because you maltreated my guest in front of my house—if I don't have permission to apply the whip-penalty to you, I say, I'll fill your master with more disgrace than the sea has waves in a heavy storm!

SCEL. [abjectly] I'm sunk to such a state, Periplectomenus, that I don't know whether I ought to argue the matter with you; unless, if that girl isn't this one and this one isn't that one, you prefer that I apologise. In fact, even now, I don't know what I saw. That girl of yours is so like this one of ours—if she isn't the same one.

PER. Go in my house and look. Then you'll know.

SCEL. May I?

PER. Why, I order you to. Observe her at your leisure.

SCEL. I'll certainly do it. [He goes into the house of Periplectomenus.]

PER. [calling at Pyrgopolynices' door] Hey, Philocomasium! Quick! Speed over to our house; it's absolutely necessary! Then, when Sceledrus leaves, speed quickly back to your own house! [To himself] Damn it! I'm afraid that she'll make a muddle of it now. If he doesn't see the woman— [listening] The door's opening.

[Reenter Sceledrus.]

SCEL. Ye immortal gods! I don't think the gods themselves could make a woman more like another, and more the same, considering that she isn't the same.

PER. What now?

SCEL. [humbly] I deserve to be punished.

PER. Well? Is it Philocomasium?

SCEL. It is, but it isn't.

PER. Did you see that one?

SCEL. I saw her and the guest, hugging and kissing.

PER. Is it Philocomasium?

SCEL. I don't know.

PER. Do you want to know for certain?

SCEL. Of course.

PER. Go into your house, then. Quick! See whether that girl of yours is inside.

SCEL. All right. An excellent suggestion! I'll be back with you in a minute. [He goes into the house of Pyrgopolynices.]

PER. [to himself] Heavens! I've never seen a mortal more cleverly and more marvellously bamboozled! But here he is again.

[Reenter Sceledrus, completely convinced.]

SCEL. [kneeling before Periplectomenus] I beseech you, Periplectomenus, by immortals and mortals, by my folly and by your knees—

PER. Why do you beseech me?

SCEL. To pardon my ignorance and folly. I realise now at last that I've been stupid, senseless, insane. Why, Philocomasium is inside there.

PER. Well, now, you Knave of the Cross! Did you see them both?

SCEL. Yes, sir.

PER. I'd like to meet your master.

SCEL. Indeed, sir, I admit that I deserve dreadful punishment and I confess that I maltreated the girl that's visiting you. I thought, though, that she was my master's mistress, over whom my master, the soldier, made me guard. You can't draw two drops of water from the same well more like each other than are this girl of ours and that guest of yours. And I admit also that I looked down through the skylight into your house.

PER. Why shouldn't you admit what I saw you do? And there you saw my guests kissing each other, I suppose?

SCEL. Yes; why deny what I saw? But I believed it was Philocomasium.

PER. And did you think that I was so worthless a mortal that I would knowingly permit such an outstanding outrage done in my house to my neighbour, the soldier?[8]

SCEL. Now at last, since I understand the situation, I realise that I have acted foolishly; but I didn't mean to do wrong.

PER. It was a dishonourable deed, just the same. A slave ought to keep his eyes and his hands and his words under control.

SCEL. If after this day I so much as utter a word, even what I know for certain, just give

[8] Riley has an amusing note here: "The old gentleman must surely have changed colour when he said this."

TITUS MACCIUS PLAUTUS

me over to be tortured. I'll give myself up to you. Pardon me this time, I beg of you.

PER. I'll force my feelings to believe that you didn't mean to do it. I'll pardon you this time.

SCEL. And may the gods bless you for it!

PER. But damn it! If the gods are to love you, you'll hold your tongue; after this you'd better not know even what you do know, or see what you do see.

SCEL. Good advice! I'm going to follow it. [*Still worried*] Have I entreated you enough?

PER. Oh, get out!

SCEL. Nothing else you wish of me, is there?

PER. [*turning away*] Yes, that you don't know me.

SCEL. [*aside*] He's deceived me. How kind and considerate of him not to be angry! [*His suspicions increase.*] I know what he's going to do. As soon as the soldier comes home from the forum, I'm to be seized in the house. He and Palaestrio together have me up for sale; I sensed it some time ago and I'm sure of it. By

the Lord! I'll never take a bite from the bait in that basket today; I'll dash off somewhere and hide myself for a few days, until the turmoil dies down and their anger subsides. I've deserved enough punishment for a whole wicked nation. [*Changing his mind*] Nevertheless, whatever the outcome, I'll go home just the same.[9] [*When Periplectomenus' back is turned, he slips into the soldier's house.*]

PER. [*to himself*] He's gone away from here. By Jove! I'm certain that a stuck pig often has much more sense. The way he was hocus-pocussed out of seeing what he did see! Well, his eyes and ears and thoughts have fled to our side. So far everything has gone splendidly; and the wench played her part delightfully! I'll go back and join the senate; Palaestrio is now at my house, and Sceledrus is now away; we can have a full session of the senate now. I'll go inside; I don't want a distribution of the parts to be made while I'm absent.[10] [*He goes into his house.*]

Act Three

SCENE ONE

Enter Palaestrio from the house of Periplectomenus.

PAL. [*to Pleusicles within*] You folks stay inside for a while, Pleusicles; let me make my observations first, so that the council we want to hold won't be ambushed. [*To himself*] We need a good safe place now, where no enemy can despoil us of our plans. For a well-planned plot is ill-planned if it aids the enemy, and if it does aid the enemy, it naturally injures you. In fact, the well-planned plot is constantly being cribbed, if the place for the conference is chosen with too little care or caution. For if the enemy learn your plans, with your own plans they tie your tongue and bind your hands, and do to you the very same things you intended to do to them. So I'll scout around and make sure that no hunter with long-eared snares will come after our counsels from the right or the left. [*Looking around*] Good! A clear view to the very end of the street. I'll call them out. [*Call-*

ing at the door*] Hey! Periplectomenus! Pleusicles! Come on out!

[*Enter Periplectomenus and Pleusicles.*]

PER. Here we are, your humble servants!

PAL. [*smiling*] It's easy to give orders to good men. But I'd like to know if we're to carry on with the same plan we considered inside.

PER. It couldn't be more suitable to our purpose.

PAL. No, but what do you think, Pleusicles?

PLEUSICLES Why should I dislike what you like? What person is more after my own heart than you are?

PAL. Pleasantly and fittingly spoken!

PER. Bless me! That's the way he ought to speak.

PLEUS. But this wretched affair afflicts me, and

[9] This final statement is considered by many critics a later addition to account for Sceledrus' presence in the house in Act Three, Scene Two. Periplectomenus clearly believes that Sceledrus has gone away from the house of the soldier.

[10] The text is corrupt here.

bothers me, body and soul.

PER. What is it that bothers you? Tell me.

PLEUS. That I am casting on you, a man of your age, these youthful concerns that befit neither you nor your character; that, through your regard for me, you are striving with all your might to aid me in my love affair and doing such actions as men of your age are more accustomed to avoid than to engage in. I'm ashamed that I'm causing you this anxiety in your old age, sir.

PAL. You're a new kind of lover, if you're ashamed of anything you do! You're not in love, you're more a ghost of a lover than a live lover, Pleusicles.

PLEUS. But to distress a man of his age with my love affair?

PER. [*somewhat indignant*] What's this you say? Do I seem to you such a dreadful Death's-head? Mere coffin-stuffing? You think I've lived such a long life, eh? Really, now, I'm not over fifty-four. My eyes are keen, my feet are nimble, my hands are quick.

PAL. [*to Pleusicles*] He may have white hair, but as far as spirit is concerned he doesn't seem the least bit old. He has the very same disposition he was born with.

PLEUS. To be sure, I find it to be as you say, Palaestrio. His kindness towards me is quite that of a young man.

PER. [*delighted*] Well, my young friend, the more you make trial of me, the more you'll realise how well disposed I am towards your love affair.

PLEUS. Why learn what is already known?

PER. But I want you to experience it at first hand, without going elsewhere.[11] Unless a person has himself been in love, he can hardly know the nature of a lover; as far as love is concerned, I still have a bit of use and juice in my body; I haven't yet withered away from all pleasures and delights. Likewise I'll prove to be either a merry jester or a gracious guest, nor do I contradict others at the banquet. I duly desire not to be disagreeable to the guests, and I prefer to proceed with the proper part of my speech, and likewise to be silent in my turn, when

someone else is talking. In short, I'm not one of these spitting, hawking, snivelling fellows; I was born in Ephesus, not in Apulia; I'm not an Animulian.[12]

PAL. [*to Pleusicles*] Oh, what a gracious young-old man, if he has all the virtues he mentions! He was clearly reared amid the charms of Venus!

PER. And I'll prove to be even more charming than I've promised. I never meddle with another man's mistress at a party; I don't make a grab for the food or snatch up a cup out of turn; nor am I ever the one to start a quarrel over the wine; if anyone annoys me there, I go on home, I cut off the conversation.

PAL. Surely, sir, your nature abounds in charm.[13] Find me three men of such character, and I'll pay their weight in gold.

PLEUS. You won't find another man of that age more delightful in every way, and more a friend to his friend.

PER. [*enjoying their praise*] I'll make you admit that I'm still youthful in my ways; I'll show myself so rich in kindnesses to you in every respect. Do you need a severe, fiery lawyer? Here I am! Do you want one that's calm? You'll say that I'm calmer than the silent sea; I'll be gentler even than a western zephyr. And from this same source I'll produce for you a most jovial guest, or a peerless parasite, or the cleverest of caterers. And as for dancing, no wanton can whirl more persuasively than I. [*He tries a few dance steps.*]

PAL. [*to Pleusicles*] What would you wish added to these choice talents, if you had a choice?

PLEUS. That I could thank him for his services as he deserves, and you too; I realise that I'm an ample annoyance to both of you. [*To Periplectomenus*] And it grieves me that I'm the cause of so much expense.

PER. You're stupid! Whatever is expended on a wicked wife or an enemy, that's real expense; but what is spent on a good guest and a friend is gain, and whatever is spent on religious rites is pure profit for a wise man. Thanks to the gods, I have the money with which to entertain you in pleasant fashion. Eat, drink, enjoy your-

[11] The text is corrupt here.

[12] Animula was a small town in Apulia.

[13] The text is corrupt here.

TITUS MACCIUS PLAUTUS

self, indulge in gaiety; this is Liberty Hall, and I too have my liberty. I want to live as I wish. Thanks to the gods, I say, I'm wealthy, and I could have married a well-bred and well-dowered wife; but I have no wish to introduce a she-barker into my house.

PAL. Why not? It's a pleasant business to beget children.

PER. By Jove, to be keeping one's freedom—that's far more pleasant![14]

PAL. You're a man that can give good advice to yourself, as well as to others.

PER. [*reflecting*] Well, it's nice to marry a good wife—if there's a place on earth where you can find one. But am I to bring home a wife who'd never say this to me: "Buy me some wool, my dear husband, so that a soft, warm cloak can be made for you, and some nice heavy under-wear, to keep you from being cold this winter"? You'd never hear a wife talk that way; but before the cocks crow she'd wake me out of a sound sleep and say: "Give me some money, my dear husband, for a present to my mother on the matron's holiday; give me some money to make preserves; give me money to give to the sorceress at the Minerva-festival, and to the dream interpreter, the fortune teller, the sooth-sayer. It would be terrible for the woman who foretells your fate from your eyebrows to get nothing. And I can't decently avoid giving something to the laundress; and the cateress has long been grumbling at receiving nothing; and then too, the midwife has complained that she didn't receive enough. What? Won't you send something to the nurse who brings up the home-born slaves?" All these and many other similar extravagances of the women keep me from taking a wife, who would worry me with such words as these.

PAL. The gods show you favour, by heaven! If you once lose that liberty of yours, you'll not find it easy to restore it to its rightful place.

PLEUS. [*unconvinced*] And yet it's praiseworthy for a man of noble birth and great wealth to rear children as a memorial to his family and himself.

PER. But I have many relatives; what need have

[14] There is a play here between *liberos,* meaning children, and *liberum,* meaning a free person.

I of children? Now I live well and happily, as I wish and as I please. When I die I'll bequeath my property to my relatives, I'll share it among them. They'll be at my house, they'll look after me, they'll come to see how I am, whether I want anything. They arrive before dawn, they inquire if I had a good night's sleep; I'll have them in place of children to send me presents. They offer sacrifice, and give me a larger part of it than they give themselves; they lead me to the sacrificial feast; they invite me to their houses for lunch, for dinner. The one that's rendered me the least considers himself the most wretched. They compete with each other in giving me gifts, and I mutter to myself: "They're gaping after my property; but their competition is feeding and enriching me."

PAL. You provide for yourself and your life in a mighty good manner; if you're happy, that's as good as having twins and triplets.

PER. Gad! If I'd had children, I'd have suffered plenty of anxiety. I'd be tormented in mind immediately. If a fever chanced to fall upon my son, I'd expect him to die; if he got drunk and had a fall or tumbled off his horse, I'd be afraid he had broken his legs or cracked his skull.

PLEUS. It's right that riches and a long life be given to this man; he preserves his property, enjoys life, and is helpful to his friends.

PAL. Oh, a delightful person! So love me, ye gods and goddesses, 'twere right for the gods to provide that all mortals should not live according to the same principle. Just as a good market-inspector puts a price on the merchandise, marks up the price on perfect goods so they will sell as they deserve and lowers the owner's price on faulty goods in proportion to the flaws, so should the gods have allotted human life. The man of charming character should receive a long life, while the reprobates and rascals should quickly hurry off to Hades. If the gods had so provided, wicked men would be less numerous, and would do their dirty deeds with less boldness, and moreover, for all the good citizens, the cost of living would come down.

PER. [*reprovingly*] A man is silly and stupid to criticise the gods and to find fault with their decisions. And now it's necessary to put a stop to all this. I want to do some marketing, my friend, so that I can entertain you at home in the style that suits us both, in a kind and jolly fashion, with jolly things to eat.

PLEUS. I think I've already caused you quite enough expense. No guest can be entertained at the house of a friend without becoming a nuisance after a three days' visit; but when he stays for ten days in succession, he becomes an Iliad of disasters. Even if the master is willing to put up with it, the slaves grumble.

PER. I've trained my slaves to serve in my service, my friend, not to boss me or to give me orders. If what I like is disagreeable to them, well, they're rowing the boat at my command, and what they hate they'll have to do, whether they like it or not, to the threat of a thrashing. Now, as I planned, I'll proceed with the marketing.

PLEUS. Well, if you're determined to do so, buy within reason; don't go to great expense. Anything at all is enough for me.

PER. Why don't you drop that old-fashioned and antiquated talk? My friend, you're indulging now in the cheap talk of the common classes. Why, they always say, when they're seated and the dinner is set before them: "What need of going to all this expense just on our account? Heavens! You were insane; this would be enough for ten people." They find fault with what's provided for them—but they gobble it down, just the same.

PAL. [*grinning*] Jove, sir, that's exactly what they do! [*To Pleusicles*] How shrewd and clever he is!

PER. [*continuing*] But no matter how stupendous the servings, these same men never say: "Have that dish taken away; remove this platter; take away the ham, I don't care for it; away with that pork; this conger eel will be excellent cold; put it aside, take it away." You wouldn't hear a one of them insisting on this; but they hurl their upper halves over the table and grab for food.

PAL. How neatly a good man has described bad manners!

PER. I haven't told you a hundredth part of the things I could, if I only had the time.

PAL. [*relieved*] Well, then, we ought first to turn our thoughts to the business at hand. At attention, now, both of you! I need your assistance, Periplectomenus; for I've just thought of a delightful trick that will shear our long-haired soldier friend, and give Philocomasium's lover a chance to carry her off and keep her as his own.

PER. I'd like to hear the plan.

PAL. And I'd like to have that ring of yours.

PER. How will it be used?

PAL. When I have it, then I'll tell you the plan I've devised.

PER. Use it. [*Handing him the ring*] Here, take it.

PAL. You take from me in return the wiles that I've worked out.

PER. We're listening eagerly with attentive ears.

PAL. My master is a great rascal with women, such as, I'm sure, there never has been and never will be.

PER. I'm sure of that, too.

PAL. He states, too, that his beauty surpasses that of Alexander,[15] and that's why, he says, all the women in Ephesus keep chasing him.

PER. Heavens! There are many husbands who wish that this were the truth about him![16] But I understand perfectly that he's just as you say. And so, Palaestrio, make your words as brief as possible.

PAL. Can you locate for me some lovely lady, with her heart and breast packed full of cunning and trickery?

PER. Freeborn or a freedwoman?

PAL. It makes no difference, provided you furnish one who's out for profit, who supports her body with her bodily charms, whose wits are awake. I can't expect intelligence; no one of them has that.

PER. Do you want a swell girl, or one that hasn't yet swelled out?

PAL. Oh, fairly juicy; and just as charming and youthful as possible.

---

[15] Alexander was another name for Paris, son of Priam of Troy.

[16] Lindsay reads *nunc*, suggested by Acidalius. *Non*, the reading of the manuscript, seems preferable.

PER. [*reflecting*]   Well, there's a client of mine, a lovely young courtesan; but why do you need her?

PAL.   You're to take her home to your house, and then to bring her here all dressed up like a married woman, her hair coiled up high with ribbons; and she's to pretend to be your wife. That's the way you must coach her.

PLEUS.   I don't see what you're driving at.

PAL.   You will. [*To Periplectomenus*] Does the girl have a maid?

PER.   Yes; a right cunning one.

PAL.   I need her too. You give the girl and her maid these instructions: she's to pretend she's your wife and madly in love with this soldier, and that she gave this ring to her little maid, who gave it at once to me, for me to deliver to the soldier; as if I were the go-between in this matter.

PER.   I hear you. He's deafened me with his demands! If you please, I can use my ears . . .[17]

PAL.   [*somewhat subdued*]   I'll give it to him and say it's a present from your wife, given over to me to bring the two of them together. That's the sort of person he is; the poor fool will be eager for her; the rascal isn't interested in a single thing except adultery.

PER.   If you sent old Sol himself to hunt for them, he couldn't find two more charming ladies for this business than I can. Don't worry a bit.

PAL.   See to it, then. But we need them quickly. [*Periplectomenus departs*] And now, Pleusicles, listen to me.

PLEUS.   Yours to obey.

PAL.   When the soldier comes home, be sure you remember not to mention the name Philocomasium.

PLEUS.   What name should I mention?

PAL.   Dicea.

PLEUS.   Of course; the same name that was agreed upon formerly.

PAL.   Enough! Off with you!

PLEUS.   I'll remember. But I want to know what's the point of remembering it.

PAL.   Well, I'll tell you that when the occasion

warrants it. Meanwhile, just hush. As the old gentleman acts his part now, you can play your part soon after.

PLEUS.   I'm going inside, then. [*He goes into the house of Periplectomenus.*]

PAL.   [*calling after him*]   And be sure you carry out my instructions carefully.

SCENE TWO

PAL.   [*to himself*]   What a turmoil I'm creating, what machines I'm moving forward! I'll snatch the concubine away from the soldier this very day, provided my cohorts are properly drilled. And now I'll call out that fellow. [*Shouting at Pyrgopolynices' door*] Hey, Sceledrus! If you're not busy, come out here in front of the house! Palaestrio's calling you.

[*Enter Lurcio, somewhat unsteadily.*]

LURCIO   Sceledrus, he's—he's not at leisure.

PAL.   Why not?

LURCIO   He's taking a snorter in his sleep.

PAL.   What? Snorter?

LURCIO   Snoring, I meant to say. But snoring is just about the same as—as when you snort.

PAL.   Oho! And is Sceledrus asleep inside?

LURCIO   Not with his nose anyhow; he's making an awful noise with that.

PAL.   He grabbed a goblet on the sly, I guess, when he was putting some nard in the wine-flagon,[18] being the butler. But look here, you rascal! You're his under-butler, and—

LURCIO   What d'ye want?

PAL.   How did he happen to go to sleep?

LURCIO   With his eyes, I suppose.

PAL.   I didn't ask you that, you scamp. Come here! [*Lurcio obeys.*] You're a dead dog right now if I don't learn the truth. Did you draw wine for him?

LURCIO   No, I didn't.

PAL.   You deny it?

LURCIO   Damn it! Of course I—I deny it, for he told me not to admit it. And I really didn't draw off eight half-pints into a pitcher, and—and he really didn't drink it off hot for lunch, either.

PAL.   And you didn't drink anything?

---

[17] The text is corrupt here.

[18] The text is corrupt here.

LURCIO The gods damn me if I drank, if I could drink!

PAL. How's that?

LURCIO Why, because I guzzled it down; it was too hot, it burned my throat.

PAL. [*enviously*] Some people get gloriously drunk, while others swig vinegar and water. A nice, honest under-butler and butler the store-room's been entrusted to!

LURCIO By Jove, you'd be doing the same, if it had been entrusted to you. You're just envious now, because you can't follow our example.

PAL. Look here, now! Did he ever draw wine before this? Answer, you rascal. And so you won't be in the dark, I'll tell you this: if you tell any lies, Lurcio, there'll be a cross lurking for you.

LURCIO Is that so? Just so you can tattle what I've told, and then, when I'm ousted from my storeroom-saturation, you can get yourself another under-butler, if you get the butler's job for yourself.

PAL. Heavens! I won't do that. Come on, tell me frankly.

LURCIO To be sure, I never saw him draw— draw any wine. But this is how it was: he'd give me the order and then I'd draw it.

PAL. And that's why the wine casks were constantly standing on their heads there.

LURCIO No, indeed! That's not why the casks were tottering about. There was a little spot in the storeroom that was very slippery, and a two-pint jar stood there near the casks, and—and it kept getting itself filled up, ten times over. I saw it get full and then get empty. And when the jar went on a jag, then especially the casks began to totter.

PAL. Off with you! Get inside now! You're the ones on a jag in the storeroom. Damned if I won't bring master back from the forum!

LURCIO [*aside*] I'm ruined! Master will torture me, when he comes home and learns what's happened, because I didn't tell him. Damn it! I'll run off somewhere and postpone this punishment to another day. [*To the audience*] Don't tell him, I beg of you. [*He turns away.*]

PAL. Where are you going?

LURCIO I've been sent off somewhere; I'll be back here in a minute.

PAL. Who sent you?

LURCIO Philocomasium.

PAL. Go on, come back quickly.

LURCIO And if any punishment is parceled out, you can please just take my share during my absence. [*He departs.*]

PAL. [*to himself*] Now I understand what the girl's been up to. Since Sceledrus is asleep, she's sent this under-guard of hers into banishment, so that she could cross from her house to the one next door. That's fine. [*Looking down the street*] Why, Periplectomenus is bringing the woman I commissioned him to get, and a lovely figure she has! The gods are certainly giving us their aid! What a dignified garb and gait, not at all like a courtesan! The business at hand is shaping up successfully.

SCENE THREE

Enter Periplectomenus, accompanied by Acroteleutium and Milphidippa.

PER. I've explained the whole matter in detail to you at your house, Acroteleutium, and to you also, Milphidippa. Now, if you don't understand clearly our devices and deceptions, I want you to learn your lesson over again. If you do understand them, then we can talk about something else.

ACROTELEUTIUM It would be silly and stupid on my part, my dear patron, to work for another person or to promise my assistance there, if in the workshop I didn't know how to be wicked or deceitful.

PER. Well, it's a good thing to remind you.

ACR. Everyone realises what a good thing it is to remind a courtesan like me! Why, I had hardly heard the opening of your oration, when I told you myself how the soldier could be polished off.

PER. But no one is sufficiently smart, all by himself. In fact, I've often seen many people lose the road to good advice before they realised where it was.

ACR. If a woman has to do anything with wickedness and wiliness, she has an immortal memory for remembering forever; but if anything decent or honest has to be done, immediately they become forgetful and can't remember a thing.

PER. That's why I'm afraid you'll be forgetful; the two of you have to do both things; whatever mischief you girls do to the soldier will be a benefit to me.

ACR. As long as we do good without realising it, you needn't fear.

PER. You deserve a thousand punishments.

ACR. Hush! Don't fear; that's fitting for women even more worthless.

PER. [*gruffly*] It suits you, too. [*Approaching his house*] Follow me.

PAL. [*aside*] Why delay to go and meet them? [*He approaches.*] Delighted at your safe return! You come charmingly equipped [*indicating the girls*], by gad!

PER. You meet me at just the right time, Palaestrio. Here are the girls you wanted me to bring, and garbed as you wished.

PAL. Fine! You're my man, all right. [*Turning to Acroteleutium*] Palaestrio pays his respects to Acroteleutium.

ACR. [*to Periplectomenus*] Who is this fellow, please, that addresses me like an acquaintance?

PER. This is the man that drew up our plans.

ACR. Good day to you, architect.

PAL. And good day to you. But tell me, has this gentleman given you full instructions?

PER. I'm bringing them both thoroughly prepared.

PAL. I'd like to hear how well. [*To the girls*] I fear you might falter in something.

PER. I haven't added anything new of my own to your instructions.

ACR. You want your master, the soldier, to be tricked, of course?

PAL. You've said it.

ACR. Everything's arranged cleverly and skilfully, fittingly and delightfully.

PAL. And I want you to pretend to be this gentleman's wife.

ACR. So shall I be.

PAL. And to pretend that you've fallen in love with the soldier.

ACR. That's just what will happen.

PAL. And that the affair is being handled by me, as go-between, and by your maid.

ACR. You could be a grand fortuneteller, for you keep announcing what will come true.

PAL. And that your maid brought me this ring from you, for me to give to the soldier in your name.

ACR. You speak the truth.

PER. What need now of repeating all the things they remember?

ACR. It's better so. For consider this, my dear patron: when a shipbuilder is skilful and has laid down the keel properly to the very line, it's easy to build a ship, when everything is laid and set into place. Now this keel of ours has been skilfully laid and firmly placed; workmen and designers are here not untrained for the job. If we're not delayed by the timber-merchant[19] who's to furnish the necessary raw material— I have confidence in our talents for trickery— our ship will soon be ready.

PAL. You know my master, the soldier, I suppose?

ACR. A strange question! How could I help knowing that public plague, that boastful, frizzle-headed, perfume-reeking adulterer?

PAL. He doesn't know you, does he?

ACR. He's never seen me, so how could he know who I am?

PAL. Very pleasing, these words of yours! What we do, then, will be all the more delightful.

ACR. [*impatiently*] Can't you give me the fellow, and stop worrying about the rest? If I don't provide a delectable deception for him, just put all the blame on me.

PAL. Come, then; inside, all of you! Apply your cunning to this matter.

ACR. Just leave it to us.

PAL. All right, Periplectomenus; you take these girls inside now. I'll meet him in the forum and give him this ring and say it was given me by your wife who is madly in love with him. As soon as we come back from the forum, send this maid over to our house, as though she had been sent to him secretly.

PER. We'll do it; leave it to us.

PAL. You tend to it, then. I'll bring him back here well burdened with lies. [*He departs.*]

---

[19] The "timber-merchant" is, of course, the soldier who will supply the raw material for the deception.

PER. [*calling after him*] A pleasant walk, and success to your undertaking! [*To Acroteleutium*] Now, if I can manage this properly so that my guest this day can gain the soldier's concubine and take her off to Athens, if we can polish off this project today, what a gift I'll send to you!

ACR. Is the girl next door helping us?

PER. Most delightfully and obligingly.

Act Four

SCENE ONE

Enter Pyrgopolynices and Palaestrio from the forum.

PYRG. Well, it's a great pleasure to have your affairs progress successfully and as you wish. Today, for instance, I sent my parasite to King Seleucus to take to him the recruits I enrolled here; they can protect his kingdom while I take a vacation.

PAL. You should attend to your own business rather than that of Seleucus. There's a splendid new proposal that I'm commissioned to offer to you.

PYRG. Well then, I'll put everything else aside and turn my attention to you. Speak forth; my ears are at your disposal.

PAL. Look around and make sure that no one can overhear our conversation. I was ordered to handle this matter with great secrecy.

PYRG. [*looking about*] There's no one here.

PAL. [*handing him Periplectomenus' ring*] In the first place, I proffer you this pledge of her passion.

PYRG. [*puzzled*] What's this? Where does this come from?

PAL. From a charming and delightful lady, who loves you and wants to enjoy your beautiful beauty. And now her maid brought me this ring for me to give to you.

PYRG. [*examining the ring*] What about her? Is she freeborn, or some slave that has been freed?

PAL. Tut, tut! Would I have the nerve to be a messenger to you from a person once a slave,

ACR. I trust it will turn out so. When we add together all our artifices, I have no fear of being defeated at cunning deception.

PER. Let's go in, then, and consider our plans carefully; what has to be done we must do neatly and skilfully, so that we won't make any mistakes when the soldier comes.

ACR. You're the one delaying us.

[*They go into the house of Periplectomenus.*]

when you can't adequately meet the demands of all the freeborn women desirous of you?

PYRG. Married or unmarried?

PAL. Both married and unmarried.

PYRG. How is it possible for the same woman to be both married and unmarried?

PAL. Because she's a young woman married to an old man.

PYRG. Splendid!

PAL. She's a most agreeable and gracious lady.

PYRG. Don't lie, now.

PAL. Why, she's the one person worthy of being compared with you.

PYRG. God! What a beautiful creature she must be! But who is she?

PAL. The wife of Periplectomenus, the old fellow next door. She's just dying for you, sir, and she wants to leave him; she hates the old man. And now she asked me to beg and beseech you to give her permission and opportunity to love you.

PYRG. [*unable to conceal his eagerness*] Heavens! I certainly desire it, if she wants to.

PAL. Wants to? She longs for it!

PYRG. What shall we do with this concubine of mine here in the house?

PAL. Why not tell her to go away somewhere, wherever she pleases; I mean, her twin sister has come here to Ephesus and her mother too; they've come to take her away.

PYRG. Aha! What's that? Her mother has come to Ephesus?

PAL. That's the story from those who know.

PYRG. Mighty Mars! What a wonderful chance to get the wench out of the house!

TITUS MACCIUS PLAUTUS

PAL. Well, sir, do you want to do it in a nice way?

PYRG. Speak; give me your advice.

PAL. Do you want to get rid of her at once, and have her go gratefully?

PYRG. I'd like it.

PAL. Then this is what you ought to do. You have plenty of money; tell her to keep as a present the jewelry and trinkets you supplied her with, to leave your house, and go away wherever she wishes.

PYRG. I like your suggestion. But make sure that I don't let her go, and then have this new one change her mind.

PAL. Pooh! You're silly; why, she loves you like her own eyes.

PYRG. [*proudly*] Venus loves me.

PAL. Sh-h! Hush! The door's opening! Come over here out of sight. [*They step back. Enter Milphidippa from the house of Periplecto-menus.*] This is her packet-boat coming out here, her go-between.

PYRG. What do you mean—packet-boat?

PAL. It's her maid coming out of the house; she's the one that brought the ring I gave to you.

PYRG. She's a damned pretty wench.

PAL. She's only an ape and an owl in compari-son to her mistress. [*Milphidippa looks around.*] Do you see how she's hunting with her eyes and bird-catching with her ears?

SCENE TWO

MILPHIDIPPA [*aside, as she comes forward*] Here's the circus now in front of the house where my tricks must be performed. I'll pretend that I don't see them and don't know they're here yet.

PYRG. [*aside to Palaestrio*] Hush! Let's listen quietly to see if there's any mention of me.

MILPH. [*loudly*] Is there anyone around here who prefers to mind other people's business instead of his own, who wants to pry into my doings, the sort of person that doesn't have to earn his evening meal?[20] I'm afraid now that such men will hamper and hinder me some-where, if they come from their home while my mistress is on her way across here. Poor dear,

20 Such a person would have plenty of leisure to pry into the business of other people.

she's so eager to embrace him, and her heart's all in a flutter with love for him; she dotes on this man who's so charming and so handsome —the soldier Pyrgopolynices!

PYRG. [*aside to Palaestrio*] So this girl too is dying with love for me, eh? She praises my beauty. To be sure, her words need no cleanser.

PAL. [*to Pyrgopolynices*] How do you mean?

PYRG. Why, her words are clean-spoken and smartly polished.

PAL. Whenever she says anything about you, she has a smartly polished subject.

PYRG. Then too, her mistress is a very sleek and dainty wench. Gad, Palaestrio, I'm beginning to fancy her a bit already.

PAL. Before you've even set eyes on her?

PYRG. I believe you; isn't that the same as seeing her? Then too, though she is absent, this little packet-boat drives me to thoughts of love.

PAL. [*in alarm*] Heavens, sir! Don't you fall in love with this girl; she's engaged to me. If the mistress marries you today, I'm going to marry the maid immediately.

PYRG. Why delay, then, to speak to her?

PAL. [*advancing*] Follow me this way.

PYRG. I'm at your heels.

MILPH. Oh, I wish I could meet the man I came out to see!

PAL. [*to Milphidippa*] You shall. Your desire will be fulfilled. Be of good courage and have no fear. A certain man knows the whereabouts of the person you seek.

MILPH. [*pretending not to see them*] Whose voice have I heard here?

PAL. A partner in your councils and a sharer of your counsels.

MILPH. Gracious! Then what I'm concealing is not concealed.

PAL. No; it's both concealed and not concealed.

MILPH. How's that?

PAL. It's concealed from faithless fellows; but I'm your faithful friend.

MILPH. Give me the sign, if you are one of the initiated.

PAL. A certain woman loves a certain man.

MILPH. Goodness! Many women do that.

PAL. But not many give a gift from their own finger.

MILPH. Well, now I know you; now you've

smoothed out the slope for me. But is anyone here?

PAL. [*stepping forward*] Just as you please.

MILPH. Let me have you alone.

PAL. For a short or a long talk?

MILPH. Just a couple of words.

PAL. [*aside to Pyrgopolynices*] I'll be back to you in a minute.

PYRG. What about me? Am I to stand here a long time in this pointless fashion, charming and courageous as I am?

PAL. Be calm and stand still; it's your affair that I'm working on.

PYRG. [*with sarcasm*] It's your haste—that's killing me.

PAL. You have to feel your way gradually with this sort of baggage; you know that.

PYRG. All right; do as you think best.

PAL. [*aside*] This man's as stupid as a stone. [*Crossing to Milphidippa*] I'm at your service; what did you wish of me?

[*They withdraw beyond the soldier's hearing.*]

MILPH. How you want this Troy attacked, that's the plan I want to discuss with you.

PAL. Pretend that she's dying for him—

MILPH. I know that.

PAL. Refer to his beautiful face and figure and recall his courageous deeds.

MILPH. I'm all in readiness for that, as I showed you just now.

PAL. You manage the rest, pay attention, and take your cue from my words.

PYRG. [*calling to Palaestrio*] Give me some share in this business here today, won't you? [*Palaestrio returns to him.*] Now you're here at last.

PAL. [*to Pyrgopolynices*] Right here, sir. Command whatever you wish.

PYRG. What's that woman telling you?

PAL. She says that her poor mistress is suffering and in torment, and worn out with weeping, because she needs you and because she doesn't have you. That's why the maid has been sent here to you.

PYRG. Tell her to approach.

PAL. You know how you should act, don't you? Make yourself very disdainful, as though you didn't like the idea; shout at me for making you so common.

PYRG. I remember; I'll follow your advice.

PAL. Shall I call the woman, then, who's looking for you?

PYRG. Let her approach, if she wants anything.

PAL. [*to Milphidippa*] Approach, woman, if you want anything.

MILPH. [*to Pyrgopolynices*] Good day, handsome sir!

PYRG. [*aside*] Handsome? Why, she mentioned my surname. [*Aloud*] The gods give you whatever you wish!

MILPH. That permission to spend a lifetime with you—

PYRG. [*haughtily*] You're asking too much.

MILPH. I don't mean for myself; it's my mistress that's dying for you.

PYRG. [*proudly*] Many other women want the same thing, but they're not given the opportunity.

MILPH. Gracious me! I don't wonder that you set a high value on yourself—a man so priceless and so preeminent in beauty and bravery! Was there ever a man more worthy of being a god?

PAL. Heavens! He isn't human, in fact— [*aside*] for I'm sure there is more humanity in a vulture.

PYRG. [*aside*] Now I shall make myself important, since she praises me so. [*He struts about.*]

PAL. [*aside to Milphidippa*] Just look how the jackass struts about! [*To Pyrgopolynices*] But why don't you answer her? She's from the woman I mentioned to you just now.

PYRG. [*with assumed indifference*] From which one of them? So many chase after me; I can't remember them all.

MILPH. From the woman who robs her fingers and enriches yours. [*Pointing to the ring on the soldier's finger*] For this is the ring that I brought him from a woman who is eager for you, and he at once gave it to you.

PYRG What do you want now, woman? Tell me.

MILPH. That you don't scorn the lady who desires you, who now lives only in your life. Whether she is to exist or not depends on you alone.

PYRG. What does she wish, then?

MILPH. To talk to you and embrace you and enfold you in her arms. For unless you come

TITUS MACCIUS PLAUTUS

to her assistance, her heart will break. Oh, my Achilles! Come, do what I ask, save a charming woman with your charm; display your generous nature, O taker of cities, O slayer of kings!

PYRG.   Gad! What a nuisance this is! [*To Palaestrio*] How often have I told you, you rascal, not to promise my services to the common mob?

PAL.   [*concealing his laughter*]   Woman, do you hear that? I told you a while ago and now I tell you again: unless this boar gets his proper fee, he won't bestow his seed on every little sow.

MILPH.   He'll receive any price he demands.

PAL.   He needs a talent of golden Philips; he won't take less from anyone.

MILPH.   Goodness gracious! That's really very cheap!

PYRG.   There's never been any greed in my nature. I have enough wealth; in fact, I have more than a thousand pecks of gold coins.

PAL.   [*keeping a straight face*]   That's in addition to his treasures. And then of silver—why, he has mountains of it, not merely masses! Mount Aetna isn't even as high.

MILPH.   [*aside to Palaestrio*]   Heavenly day! What a liar!

PAL.   [*aside to Milphidippa*]   How am I doing?

MILPH.   Well, how am I? Wheedling him all right?

PAL.   Elegantly!

MILPH.   [*to Pyrgopolynices*]   Please now, send me back at once.

PAL.   Why don't you give her your answer, either that you will or you won't?

MILPH.   Yes, why torture the poor lady's heart, who has never done you any wrong?

PYRG.   [*yielding*]   Tell her to come out here to us. Say to her that I'll do what she wishes.

MILPH.   Now, sir, you're acting as you ought to act, since you want the woman who wants you—

PAL.   [*aside*]   Nothing half-baked about her brains!

MILPH.   And since you did not scorn my entreaty but permitted me to gain my request. [*Aside to Palaestrio*] Well? How am I doing?

PAL.   [*aside to Milphidippa*]   Jumping Jupiter! I just can't keep from laughing. Ha, ha, ha!

MILPH.   [*to Palaestrio*]   That's why I turned away from you.

PYRG.   Woman, you don't fully realise what a great honour I am paying that mistress of yours.

MILPH.   Oh, yes, I do, and I'll tell her.

PAL.   He could sell this favour to another woman for his weight in gold.

MILPH.   [*trying not to laugh*]   Gracious! I can believe that.

PAL.   Great warriors are born of those he makes pregnant, and his sons live eight hundred years.

MILPH.   [*aside to Palaestrio*]   Oh, you awful liar!

PYRG.   Actually, they live straight on for a thousand years, from one age to the next.

MILPH.   Bless me! How many years will this man live, when his sons live so long?

PYRG.   Woman, I was born on the day after Jupiter was born to Ops.

PAL.   And if he had been born a day ahead of Jupiter, this man would now be ruler of heaven.

MILPH.   [*aside to Palaestrio*]   Enough, enough, I beg of you! Let me leave you now, if I can, while I'm still alive.

PAL.   Why don't you go, then, since you have your answer?

MILPH.   [*to Pyrgopolynices*]   I'll go now and bring here the lady I'm acting for. Is there anything else you wish?

PYRG.   Yes, that I be no handsomer than I am. My beauty is such a bother to me.

PAL.   [*to Milphidippa*]   Why do you stand here now? Why don't you go?

MILPH.   I'm going.

PAL.   [*following Milphidippa, as she approaches the door*]   Yes, and listen, will you? Tell her with cunning and cleverness, so that her heart will leap with joy. [*In a lower tone*] Tell Philocomasium, if she's there, to cross over to our house; the soldier's here.

MILPH.   [*to Palaestrio*]   She's here with my mistress; they've been listening to our conversation on the sly.

PAL.   Excellent! From our conversation they will steer their course all the more cleverly.

MILPH.   You're delaying me; I'm going now.

PAL.   I'm neither delaying you nor touching you nor—I won't talk about that.

PYRG.   [*calling*]   Tell her to hasten out here. We'll give especial attention to this matter now. [*Milphidippa goes into the house of Periplectomenus.*]

SCENE THREE

PYRG. What do you advise me to do now with my concubine, Palaestrio? For I can't in any way let this new lady into my house before I get rid of her.

PAL. Why ask me what you're to do? I told you the most decent method of handling the matter. Let her keep all the jewelry and the garments that you fitted her out with; let her have them, keep them, carry them away. You can tell her it's an excellent time for her to go home. Say that her twin sister and her mother are here, and that she can have a happy trip home in their company.

PYRG. How do you know that they're here?

PAL. Because I saw her sister here with my own eyes.

PYRG. Did the sister meet her?

PAL. Yes, sir.

PYRG. She seemed like a fine wench, eh?

PAL. [*in disgust*] You want to get everything.

PYRG. Where did the sister say the mother was?

PAL. Sick abed in the ship with sore and swollen eyes; that's what the ship-captain who brought them told me; he's lodging here with the people next door. [*He indicates the house of Periplectomenus.*]

PYRG. Well, what about him? A fine, lusty fellow, eh?

PAL. [*still more disgusted*] Oh, get out, won't you, sir! A fine stallion for the mares you are! You chase after the males as much as the females. Come, sir; down to business!

PYRG. As to that advice of yours—I'd rather you talked over the matter with her yourself; you get along so well with her in your conversations.

PAL. How's that any better than for you to go and handle the matter yourself? You can say that it's necessary for you to marry; your relatives are begging you to, your friends are forcing you.

PYRG. You really think so?

PAL. Of course I do.

PYRG. I'll go in, then. Meanwhile you watch here in front of the house so that you can call me when that lady comes out.

PAL. You just tend to the business you're on.

PYRG. That's already tended to. If she won't go of her own free will, I'll drive her out forcibly.

PAL. Oh, don't do that; it would be much nicer to have her leave you with deep gratitude. And give her the things I mentioned; let her take away the jewelry and the clothing you furnished her with.

PYRG. I certainly want her to.

PAL. I think you'll prevail upon her without difficulty. But go on in; don't keep standing here.

PYRG. I obey your command. [*He goes into his house.*]

PAL. [*to the audience*] This wenching warrior doesn't seem to differ much, does he, from the way I described him to you a while ago? Now I need to have Acroteleutium appear, or her maid, or Pleusicles. [*Periplectomenus' door opens.*] Jupiter! How old Nick-of-Time aids me in every respect! I see the very ones I wanted, all coming out of the house next door.

SCENE FOUR

Enter Acroteleutium, Milphidippa, and Pleusicles from the house of Periplectomenus.

ACR. [*to her companions*] Follow me; at the same time make sure that there isn't anyone here to spy on us.

MILPH. Mercy, I don't see a soul, except the man we want to meet.

PAL. And I you.

MILPH. How goes it, architect of ours?

PAL. I the architect? Bah!

MILPH. What's the matter?

PAL. Why, in comparison with you, I'm not fit to drive a spike into a wall.

MILPH. Oh, come now!

PAL. Yes, you're a very fine and fluent rogue. [*To Acroteleutium*] How very cleverly she trimmed the soldier!

MILPH. But not enough yet.

PAL. Don't worry. The undertaking as a whole is shaping up nicely now. You just continue to give a helping hand, as you've done so far. The soldier has gone inside to beg his mistress to

TITUS MACCIUS PLAUTUS

leave him and to go off to Athens with her sister and mother.

PLEUS. Excellent! Superb!

PAL. Why, he's even presenting her with the jewelry and the clothing he furnished her with, to persuade her to leave. I advised him to do it.

PLEUS. [*confidently*] Her departure is certainly a simple matter, if she wants to go and he's eager to have her go.

PAL. Don't you know, sir, when you climb out of a deep well to the very top, that then the danger's greatest of falling back down again from the top? This business of ours is now at the top of the well; if the soldier gets suspicious, nothing can be carried off. That's why we have particular need of cunning now.

PLEUS. We have plenty of material at home for our purpose, I see: three women, you're the fourth, I'm fifth, and the old gentleman makes a sixth. With the talents that the six of us have for trickery, I'm sure, any city whatsoever can be captured by our cunning. Just give your assistance.

ACR. [*to Palaestrio*] That's why we've come, to learn what you wish.

PAL. Splendidly done! Now this is the task I command of you.

ACR. Commander, you'll gain your request, so far as I am able.

PAL. I want the soldier to be neatly, deftly, and delightfully deceived.

ACR. Gracious! What a pleasure your command is!

PAL. And you know how, don't you?

ACR. To be sure; I'm to pretend that I'm bursting with passion for him.

PAL. Just the thing.

ACR. And that because of this passion I've left my husband, being eager to marry him.

PAL. All correct. But there's this one additional point: you must say that this house [*indicating the house of Periplectomenus*] is part of your dowry, and that the old man left you after you divorced him. We don't want the soldier afraid to enter another man's house later on.

ACR. A clever bit of advice!

PAL. But when he comes out from the house, I want you to stand over there and pretend to despise your own beauty in comparison with his, and to be amazed at his excessive wealth; and at the same time praise to the skies his handsome figure, his charming manner, his beautiful face. Enough coaching?

ACR. I've got it. Will it be enough for you if I polish off my assignment so perfectly that you can't find a single fault in it?

PAL. Quite enough. [*Turning to Pleusicles*] Now, sir, here are my orders for you, in your turn. As soon as all this is finished and the lady here has gone inside, you be sure to join us here at once in the guise of a ship-captain. Have a broad-brimmed, dark-coloured hat, a woollen patch over your eyes, a dark-coloured cloak (since that's the seaman's colour) that's fastened over your left shoulder, with the right arm bared to the breast; be neat and trim. Pretend you're the master of the ship. All these things are in the old man's house, for he has fishermen among his slaves.

PLEUS. Well? Why don't you tell me what I'm to do when I get dressed up?

PAL. Come here and call for Philocomasium in her mother's name; tell her that if she's going to go to Athens she must go quickly with you to the harbour and she must have everything taken to the ship that she wants put on board; and that if she doesn't go you'll set sail, for the wind is favourable.

PLEUS. The picture's very pleasing. Proceed.

PAL. At once the soldier will urge her to go, to hurry, so as not to delay her mother.

PLEUS. It's wondrous wise you are!

PAL. I'll tell her to ask for me as an assistant to carry the luggage to the harbour. Then he'll order me to go with her to the harbour. And then—for this is my plan—immediately I'm straight off for Athens with you.

PLEUS. And when you get there, I won't let you be a slave for three days without giving you your freedom.

PAL. Go quickly now, and get on your garb.

PLEUS. Anything else?

PAL. Yes; remember the instructions.

PLEUS. I'm off. [*He goes into the house of Periplectomenus.*]

PAL. [*to the women*] You too be off inside at

once; I'm quite sure that the soldier will soon be coming out.

ACR. We honour your commands.

PAL. Come, come; off with you then. [*Acroteleutium and Milphidippa enter the house of Periplectomenus.*] And now look! The door's opening at just the right time. Out he comes in splendid spirits! He's gained his request. The poor fool, he's gaping after a phantom!

SCENE FIVE

Enter Pyrgopolynices from his house.

PYRG. I've gained from Philocomasium what I wished just as I wished it, on friendly and gracious terms.

PAL. How in the world am I to explain your long absence?

PYRG. I never realised before now how much that woman loved me.

PAL. How do you mean?

PYRG. How many words I had to say! What stubborn material she was! But finally I got what I wanted. I granted her, I gave her everything she wanted, everything she demanded. I even gave you to her as a gift.

PAL. What? Me too? How can I live without you?

PYRG. Come, cheer up! I'll free you from her. In fact, I tried in every way possible to persuade her to leave without taking you with her; but she wore me down.

PAL. [*pretending to resign himself*] I'll put my hopes in the gods and you. In the final analysis, however, although it is bitter to be deprived of so excellent a master as you, I can at least take pleasure in this—that, as a result of your own beauty and my efforts, there has come to you this affair with the woman next door, whom I am now winning over to you.

PYRG. Why say more? I'll give you liberty and wealth, if you finish this affair for me.

PAL. Finish it I shall, sir.

PYRG. But I'm so eager for her.

PAL. You must take it easy now; control your desires; don't be too anxious. Ah! There she is now! Coming out doors!

SCENE SIX

Enter Milphidippa and Acroteleutium from the house of Periplectomenus.

MILPH. [*aside to Acroteleutium*] Look, mistress! There's the soldier all ready for you.

ACR. [*to Milphidippa*] Where?

MILPH. To the left.

ACR. I see him.

MILPH. Look sideways, so that he won't know we see him.

ACR. I see him. Goodness! Now is the time for us bad girls to become worse.

MILPH. It's your turn to begin.

ACR. [*loudly, for the soldier's benefit*] Pray tell me, did you really meet him? [*In a lower tone*] Don't spare your voice; I want him to hear.

MILPH. Heavens! I even spoke with him, calmly too, as long as I wished, at my ease and my pleasure.

PYRG. [*aside to Palaestrio*] Do you hear what she says?

PAL. I do. How happy she is because she approached you!

ACR. Oh, what a lucky woman you are!

PYRG. [*aside to Palaestrio*] How everybody seems to love me!

PAL. You deserve it.

ACR. [*to Milphidippa*] Gracious me! 'Tis a miracle you mention—that you approached him and persuaded him. Why, they say that people approach him like a king, with letters and messengers.

MILPH. Really, though, I had great difficulty in approaching him and winning him over.

PAL. [*aside to Pyrgopolynices*] How great is your fame among women, sir!

PYRG. I must submit to it, since Venus so wishes.

ACR. [*loudly to Milphidippa*] I am grateful to Venus, and I beg and beseech her that I may win the man I love and desire, and that he may be kind to me and not refuse me what I want.

MILPH. I hope so, in spite of the fact that many women desire him; he scorns them all, he spurns them all, except you alone.

ACR. That's why I'm tormented with terror, because he is disdainful; I'm afraid that when he sees me his eyes will make him change his mind, and that so magnificent a mortal will immediately be scornful of my poor charms.

MILPH. He won't do that; just be free from anxiety.

PYRG. [aside] How she despises herself!

ACR. I fear that your praise exaggerated such beauty as I have.

MILPH. I saw to it that he wouldn't expect you to be as beautiful as you really are.

ACR. Ah me! If he is unwilling to marry me, I'll clasp his knees and beseech him to. If I can't prevail upon him, I'll seek some means of death; I just know that I cannot live without him.

PYRG. [aside to Palaestrio] I must prevent this woman's death, I see that. Shall I approach?

PAL. [to Pyrgopolynices] Not at all. You'll make yourself common if you hand yourself over to her unasked. Let her come to you of her own accord; let her do the seeking and courting and waiting. Do you want to lose that glorious reputation that you have? Please see to it that you don't. Why, I know well that it has never happened to any mortal except to two, yourself and Phaon of Lesbos,[21] to be so passionately loved by a woman.

ACR. Shall I go in, or will you call him out, my dear Milphidippa?

MILPH. Oh, no! Let's wait until someone comes out.

ACR. I just can't restrain myself from going in.

MILPH. The doors are closed.

ACR. Then I'll break them open.

MILPH. You're out of your senses.

ACR. If he has ever been in love, or if he has understanding equal to his beauty, he'll be merciful and forgive me for anything that I do through love for him.

PAL. [aside to Pyrgopolynices] Look, I beg of you! How the poor thing is perishing with passion!

PYRG. [languishing] It's beginning to be mutual.

PAL. Hush! Don't let her hear you.

MILPH. Why do you stand there stupefied? Why don't you knock?

21 The story is told that the poetess Sappho committed suicide when deserted by her lover Phaon.

ACR. Because the man I want is not inside.

MILPH. How do you know?

ACR. My sense of smell tells me; if he were inside, my nose would sense it from the odour.

PYRG. [aside to Palaestrio] She's a diviner. She's in love with me, and that's why Venus has given her powers of prophecy.

ACR. The man that I want to see is around here somewhere; I can certainly smell him.

PYRG. [aside to Palaestrio] Gad! This woman sees more with her nose than she does with her eyes.

PAL. [grinning] That's because she's blind with love, sir.

ACR. [catching sight of the soldier] Hold me up, I implore you!

MILPH. [supporting her] Why?

ACR. So that I won't fall.

MILPH. Why so?

ACR. Because I can't stand; my eyes make my senses falter.

MILPH. Heavens! Have you seen the soldier?

ACR. Yes.

MILPH. [pretending to look around] I don't see him. Where is he?

ACR. If you were in love, you would certainly see him.

MILPH. Gracious me! You don't love him a bit more than I would, ma'am, if I had your permission.

PAL. [aside to Pyrgopolynices] There's no doubt about it; all the women fall in love with you as soon as they see you.

PYRG. I don't know whether you've heard me mention this or not—but I'm the grandson of Venus.

ACR. [gazing at the soldier] My dear Milphidippa, go up to him, I beg of you; speak to him.

PYRG. [aside to Palaestrio] How she stands in awe of me!

PAL. She's coming towards us.

MILPH. [approaching them] I want the two of you.

PYRG. And we you.

MILPH. I have brought my mistress outside, as you requested.

PYRG. [coldly] So I see.

MILPH. Do tell her to come near you.

PYRG. [*haughtily*] Since you begged in her behalf, I have persuaded myself not to hate her, as I do other women.

MILPH. Heavens! She won't be able to say a word, if she comes near you. While she was looking at you, her eyes cut off her tongue.

PYRG The woman's ailment must be remedied, I see.

MILPH. What a quiver she's in! And how terror-stricken she was when she saw you!

PYRG. Well, armed warriors are the very same way. So don't wonder at a woman being afraid. But what is it that she wishes me to do?

MILPH. To go to her house. She longs to live with you and spend her whole life with you.

PYRG. What? I go to a woman that's married? Her husband would find me there.

MILPH. Why, for your sake she has turned her husband out of the house.

PYRG. How could she do that?

MILPH. The house is part of her dowry.

PYRG. Oh, really?

MILPH. Yes indeed, sir.

PYRG. Tell her to go home. I'll be there soon.

MILPH. Please don't keep her waiting; don't torture her poor mind.

PYRG. No, of course not. Go on in.

MILPH. We're going.

[*Milphidippa and the lovesick Acroteleutium go into the house of Periplectomenus.*]

PYRG. [*looking down the street*] But what do I see?

PAL. What do you see?

PYRG. Look! Somebody or other is coming this way in a sailor's outfit.

PAL. He's coming towards us; he obviously wants you. Why, it's the shipmaster.

PYRG. To be sure; coming to get her now.

PAL. I believe so.

SCENE SEVEN

Enter Pleusicles from the direction of the harbour.[22]

[22] Although Plautus does not so state, it is probable that Pleusicles left the house by a rear entrance in order to come from the direction of the harbour. Palaestrio, however, told the soldier in IV, iii that the

PLEUS. [*to himself*] If I didn't know that other men had in other ways done many shameful things on account of love, I'd have more scruples at going around here in this garb because of love. But since I've learned that many men have committed many disgraceful and wicked deeds as a result of their love affairs—I pass over how Achilles permitted his comrades to be slain.[23] [*Seeing Palaestrio and Pyrgopolynices*] But there's Palaestrio, standing with the soldier! Now I have to change my tune! [*Loudly*] Woman is assuredly the daughter of Delay herself! Any other delay, for instance, even though it's just as great, seems less than that which a woman causes. I suppose they act this way just from force of habit. Well, I'll summon this Philocomasium. [*Approaching the house of Pyrgopolynices*] I'll knock on the door. Hey! Is there anyone here?

PAL. [*stepping up to him*] Young man, what's the matter? What do you want? Why are you knocking?

PLEUS. I'm seeking Philocomasium; I come from her mother. If she intends to go, she must go now. She's delaying us all; we're anxious to set sail.

PYRG. [*stepping up*] Everything's been ready for a long time. Go, Palaestrio, get some assistants to help you take to the ship her jewelry, trinkets, clothing, all her precious things. Everything I gave her is packed; she can take it away.

PAL. I'm off. [*He goes into the soldier's house.*]

PLEUS. [*calling after him*] And hurry, damn it!

PYRG. He won't keep you waiting. [*Looking at the bandage over Pleusicles' eyes*] But what the devil is the matter with you? What happened to your eye?

PLEUS. [*pointing to his right eye, which is less bandaged*] Well, by Jove, I've got this eye.

PYRG. But I mean the left one.

PLEUS. I'll tell you: it's on account of a love

shipmaster was lodging with Periplectomenus, and it is possible that Pleusicles comes directly from the house.

[23] Achilles withdrew from the battle when his captive Briseis was taken by Agamemnon; Achilles' wrath on this occasion and its results are the theme of Homer's *Iliad*.

affair that I don't use this eye so much, confound it! If I'd kept away from love, I'd be able
to use this as much as the other. But these
people are delaying me too long.

PYRG.   Here they come out.

SCENE EIGHT

*Enter Palaestrio and Philocomasium from the
house of Pyrgopolynices.*

PAL.   [*to Philocomasium*]   When in the world
will you stop weeping, I want to know?

PHIL.   [*sobbing*]   How can I help weeping? I've
had such a happy life here, and—and now I'm
going away.

PAL.   [*pointing to Pleusicles*]   See! There's the
man who has come from your mother and
sister.

PHIL.   [*without interest*]   I see him.

PYRG.   Listen, Palaestrio, will you?

PAL.   What do you wish?

PYRG.   Go and order those things I gave her to
be brought out.
[*Palaestrio goes to the door and gives the orders
to the slaves.*]

PLEUS.   Good day, Philocomasium.

PHIL.   Good day to you, sir.

PLEUS.   Both your mother and your sister asked
me to give you their greetings.

PHIL.   I hope they're well.

PLEUS.   They beg you to come so that they can
set sail, while the breeze is favourable. They
would have come along with me, if your mother
had not been suffering from sore eyes.

PHIL.   I'll go. But I do it against my will; my
devotion to the soldier—

PLEUS.   I understand; you're sensible.

PYRG.   But she'd still be stupid today, if she
hadn't been spending her life with me.

PHIL.   That's just what tortures me, that I'm
being separated from such a man; why, you can
make anyone at all overflow with cleverness;
and I was so elated at heart when I was with
you. This distinction I see I must give up. [*She
sobs bitterly.*]

PYRG.   Ah! Don't cry.

PHIL.   I—I can't help it, when I look at you.

PYRG.   Be of good cheer.

PHIL.   No one but myself knows the anguish I
feel.

PAL.   Well, I don't at all wonder that you were
happy here, Philocomasium, and that his beauty,
his manners, his valour touched your heart with
tenderness; for, when I, a mere slave, look at
him, I weep that we are being parted. [*He turns
away, pretending to cry.*]

PHIL.   Please may I embrace you once before I
go?

PYRG.   You may.

PHIL.   [*embracing him*]   Oh, my darling! Oh, my
life!

PAL.   [*leading her to Pleusicles*]   Hold the woman, I beg of you, or she'll dash herself to the
ground.
[*Pleusicles holds her tenderly, as she pretends
to faint.*]

PYRG.   [*looking at them suspiciously*]   Hey! What
the devil does this mean?

PAL.   The poor girl has suddenly fallen into a
faint at the thought of leaving you.

PYRG.   Run inside and bring out some water.

PAL.   I don't want any water; I'd rather have her
rest a bit. Don't interfere, please, while she's
recovering.

PYRG.   [*watching Pleusicles and Philocomasium*]
These two have their heads too close together;
I don't like it. [*Pleusicles forgets himself and
kisses her.*] Sailor, get your lips away from her
lips; look out for trouble!

PLEUS.   I was trying to find out whether she was
breathing or not.

PYRG.   Then you should have used your ear.

PLEUS.   If you prefer, I'll let her go.

PYRG.   [*hastily*]   I don't want that. Keep holding
her.

PAL.   [*as a hint to the lovers*]   I'm unhappy.

PYRG.   [*to the slaves inside*]   Come out and bring
out here all the things I gave her.
[*Enter the slaves with the luggage.*]

PAL.   [*solemnly*]   And now, Household God, before I go, I bid you farewell! And all my fellow
slaves, both male and female, good-bye and a
happy life to you! And in your conversations I
hope that you will speak well of me, even
though I am absent. [*He pretends to weep.*]

PYRG. Come, come, Palaestrio! Cheer up!

PAL. Oh! Oh! I just can't keep from weeping at leaving you.

PYRG. Endure it calmly.

PAL. No one but myself knows the anguish I feel.

PHIL. [*pretending to regain consciousness*] But what's this? What has happened? What do I see? Greetings, O light of day!

PLEUS. Have you recovered now?

PHIL. [*looking at Pleusicles in feigned horror*] Heavens! What man have I embraced? I'm ruined! Am I in my senses? [*She sinks back again into Pleusicles' arms.*]

PLEUS. Have no fear— [*in a lower tone*] my darling!

PYRG. What does this mean?

PAL. The girl has just fainted away. [*Aside to Pleusicles*] I'm fearfully afraid that this business will become too public.
[*Philocomasium revives again.*]

PYRG. [*overhearing*] What's that you say?

PAL. I mean, sir, if all this stuff is carried through the city behind us; I fear that people may criticise you for it.

PYRG. I gave away my own property, not theirs; it's damned little I care for what they think. Come, go now with the blessings of the gods.

PAL. I mention this for your sake.

PYRG. I believe you.

PAL. And now good-bye, sir.

PYRG. Good-bye to you.

PAL. [*to the others*] You go on quickly; I'll follow you in a moment. I want a few words with my master. [*Philocomasium and Pleusicles depart, followed by the slaves with the luggage.*] I am most grateful to you for everything, sir, in spite of the fact that you have always considered other slaves more faithful than me to you. [*Pretending to weep*] If it were your wish, I should prefer to be your slave than another person's freedman.

PYRG. Be of good courage!

PAL. Ah me! When I consider how I must change my way of life, learn the ways of women and set aside the soldiers' ways!

PYRG. Come now, be a worthy fellow.

PAL. I can't now; I've lost all my desire.

PYRG. Go, follow them, don't delay!

PAL. [*tearfully*] Good-bye.

PYRG. Good-bye to you.

PAL. [*stopping*] If I happen to find myself a free man, I'll send you a message; remember, I beg of you, not to desert me.

PYRG. That's not the way I do things.

PAL. [*trying to keep a straight face*] And every now and then just consider how faithful I've been to you. If you do this, you'll know finally who is a good servant and who is a bad servant.

PYRG. I do know; I've often thought about it.

PAL. But you'll know it particularly today, even though you've realised it before this. Why, to-day you'll speak even more of my achievements, I'll guarantee.

PYRG. [*impressed*] I can hardly refrain from bidding you to stay.

PAL. [*in alarm*] Oh, don't do that, sir. People would say that you were deceitful and untruthful and faithless; and they would say that I was the only faithful slave you had. If I thought you could do it with honour, I'd urge you to; but it just can't be. Don't do it.

PYRG. Be off, then.

PAL. [*sadly*] I'll endure whatever happens.

PYRG. Well, good-bye.

PAL. [*apparently at the point of breaking down*] It's better to go quickly. [*He hastens off towards the harbour.*]

PYRG. [*calling after him*] Once more, good-bye. [*To himself*] Before this affair came up, I always thought he was the greatest rascal among the slaves; now I find that he is devoted to me. Now that I think it over, I've been very stupid to let him go. Well, I'll go in now to my beloved. [*He turns towards the door of Periplectomenus' house.*] But the door has made a noise, I perceive. [*He pauses.*]

SCENE NINE

Enter a Slave Boy from the house of Periplectomenus.

BOY [*to those within*] Don't be giving me orders; I remember my duty. I'll find him, no matter where he is. I'll track him down; I won't spare any labour.

PYRG. [aside] He's looking for me. I'll go to meet the lad.

BOY Oho! You're the person I'm looking for. Greetings to you, you most delightful man, abounding in opportuneness, the one mortal beloved beyond all others by the two deities.

PYRG. Which two?

BOY Mars and Venus.

PYRG. [approvingly] Smart boy!

BOY She begs you to come inside, she wants you, she desires you, she anxiously awaits you.

Act Five

Enter Periplectomenus from his house, followed by Cario and other slaves who are holding the struggling Pyrgopolynices.

PER. Drag him along! If he won't follow, pick him up and throw him out! Lift him up between heaven and earth! Tear him to pieces!

PYRG. Oh, God! Periplectomenus, I beg you to have mercy.

PER. You beg in vain. [To Cario] See that that knife of yours is well sharpened, Cario.

CARIO [testing his knife] Why, it's been anxious for a long time to rip open the abdomen of this adulterer, so that I can hang trinkets around his neck the way they hang from a baby's neck.

PYRG. [in terror] I'm killed!

PER. Not yet. You speak too soon.

CARIO [waving the knife] Can I fly at the man now?

PER. No. I want him clubbed with cudgels first.

CARIO With lots of them, I hope.[24]

PER. How did you dare to seduce another man's wife, you lecher?

PYRG. As the gods love me, she came to me of her own accord.

PER. He lies. Strike him!
[They raise their clubs.]

PYRG. Wait, while I explain.

PER. [to the slaves] Why do you hesitate?

PYRG. Won't you let me speak?

PER. Speak.

[24] One verse is lost at this point.

Do help the lovesick lady. Why do you stand there? Why don't you go inside?

PYRG. I'm going. [He enters the house of Periplectomenus.]

BOY [elated] Now he's entangled himself in the toils; the trap is all ready. The old man is at his post ready to plunge at this adulterer, who boasts of his beauty, who thinks that every woman that sees him falls in love with him. Everyone despises him, men and women both. Now I'll go in and join the uproar. I hear them shouting inside. [He returns to the house.]

PYRG. I was urged to come to her.

PER. But how did you dare? There, take that! [He strikes him, the slaves joining in.]

PYRG. Ow! Ow! I've had enough. Oh, heavens!

CARIO [eagerly] How soon am I to begin cutting?

PER. As soon as you wish. Spread the fellow apart; stretch him out.

PYRG. Oh, God! I beseech you, listen to me before he starts cutting.

PER. Speak.

PYRG. I had some justification; damn it, I thought she was divorced! That's what her maid, the go-between, told me.

PER. Swear that you won't injure a living soul because of this—that you've had a thrashing here today or that you will have a thrashing—if we send you away from here alive, you darling little grandson of Venus!

PYRG. I swear by Jupiter and Mars that I won't injure a soul because I've had a thrashing here today, and I think I deserved it. If I go away from here as a man,[25] I'm being well treated for my offence.

PER. And if you don't keep your word?

PYRG. Then may I always live unmanned.

CARIO [to Periplectomenus] Let's beat him once more; then I move we let him go.

PYRG. May the gods bless you forever, since you plead so well in my behalf.

[25] In this and the following verses, there is a play upon the two meanings of "testis," witness and genital gland.

CARIO Well, give us [*pointing to the slaves*] a mina of gold, then.

PYRG. What for?

CARIO So that we'll let you go away from here today with your manhood intact, you darling little grandson of Venus! Otherwise you shan't get away from here; don't deceive yourself about that.

PYRG. [*in haste*] You'll get it.

CARIO Now you show more sense. But don't count on your tunic and your cloak and your sword; you won't get them back.

A SLAVE Shall I hit him again, or are you going to let him beat it?

PYRG. I've been beaten to a jelly already. Please have mercy.

PER. [*to slaves*] Let him loose.

[*They do so.*]

PYRG. I am grateful to you.

PER. [*sternly*] If I ever catch you here again, you will lose your manhood.

PYRG. I accept your terms.

PER. Let's go inside, Cario.

[*Periplectomenus goes into his house, followed by Cario and the other slaves.*]

PYRG. [*looking down the street*] Well, I see my slaves! [*Enter Sceledrus and other slaves from the harbour*] Has Philocomasium departed already? Tell me.

SCEL. A long time ago.[26]

PYRG. Oh, damn it!

SCEL. You'd damn it still more, if you knew what I know. That fellow with the woollen patch over his eye was no sailor.

PYRG. Who was he, then?

SCEL. Philocomasium's lover.

PYRG. How do you know?

SCEL. I know, all right. Why, from the time they left the city gate, they never stopped kissing and hugging each other.

PYRG. What a confounded fool I am! I've been deceived; I see that now. That rogue of a fellow, Palaestrio! He's the one that lured me into this trap. [*Reflecting*] Well, I believe I've deserved it. If the same treatment were given to other adulterers, there would be fewer adulterers about; they would have greater fear of punishment, and less desire for such pursuits. [*To the slaves*] Let's go home. [*To the audience*] Give us your applause.

[26] Many editors assign the speeches of Sceledrus in this scene to an unnamed slave.

IN EVALUATING Plautine comedy, one must consider the nature of farce: its characteristics, its limitations, and its appeal.

That I admire not any comedy equally with tragedy, is, perhaps, from the sullenness of my humour; but that I detest those farces, which are now the most frequent entertainments of the stage, I am sure I have reason on my side. Comedy consists, though of low persons, yet of natural actions and characters; I mean such humours, adventures, and designs, as are to be found and met with in the world. Farce, on the other side, consists of forced humours, and unnatural events. Comedy presents us with the imperfections of human nature: Farce entertains us with what is monstrous and chimerical. The one causes laughter in those who can judge of men and manners, by the lively representation of their folly or corruption: the other produces the same effect in those who can judge of neither, and that only by its extravagancies. The first works on the judgment and fancy; the latter on the fancy only: there is more of satisfaction in the former kind of laughter, and in the latter more of scorn. But how it happens that an impossible adventure should cause our mirth, I cannot so easily imagine. Something there may be in the oddness of it, because on the stage it is the common effect of things unexpected to surprise us into a delight: and that is to be ascribed to the strange appetite, as I may call it, of the fancy. . . . In short, there is the same difference betwixt Farce and Comedy as betwixt an empiric and a true physician: both of them attain their ends, but what the one performs by hazard the other does by skill. And as the artist is often unsuccessful, while the mountebank succeeds, so farces more commonly take the people than comedies. For to write unnatural things is the most probable way of pleasing them who understand not Nature. [John Dryden, "Preface" to *An Evening's Love; or, The Mock Astrologer* (1671), *Dramatic Essays,* Everyman's Library, E. P. Dutton & Co., Inc., New York, n.d., p. 78.]

Now I, for one, at least, fail to see any reason why farce should be stamped with the stigma of illegitimacy. There are degrees in the drama, no doubt, and the highest places are reserved for tragedy and for comedy; but melodrama and burlesque and farce are all legitimate dramatic forms, and they have each an honorable pedigree. . . .

One of the phenomena of theatrical history is the scarcity of comedy and the prevalence of farce. There has been no time recorded in the annals of the English stage when the critics were not complaining of the dearth of real comedy, and denouncing the plethora of farces. . . . In fact, it is difficult to deny the frequent exactness of the epigram declaring that "a comedy is a farce by an author who is dead." . . .

Surely a form of art which can show as long a roll of masterpieces as farce is not despicable. Surely it deserves to be treated with the respect paid to the other forms of the drama. It is not as difficult, perhaps, as comedy, which depends on the clash of character and the sparkle of epigram; but it is not easy. It is an art with laws of its own. It is not burlesque, for one thing,

although it is akin to burlesque; and a marriage between the two is within the forbidden degrees.

Like true burlesque, as distinguished from mere extravaganza, farce demands the utmost seriousness in its conception and in its performance. Garrick declared that comedy was a serious thing—he would not have denied that farce is even more serious. Farce is negative towards burlesque and positive towards comedy; it repels the one and attracts the other. While farce and burlesque are abhorrent and cannot be joined to advantage, farce and comedy combine readily and melt one into the other in vague and imperceptible fluctuations. . . .

Farce bears much the same relation to comedy that melodrama does to tragedy. In farce and in melodrama there is a more summary psychology than in comedy and in tragedy. Events are of more importance than the persons to whom they happen. The author seeks to interest the spectator rather in things than in men and women; he relies more on the force of situation than on the development of character.

So farce may be defined as an ultra-logical comedy, in which everything is pushed to extremes, and the hero is the plaything of special providences. . . . And the moral of the play is not in the happy ending brought about arbitrarily and as the dramatist please; it resides rather in the hearty laughter which has cleared the air, and which is a boon in itself and a gift to be thankful for. Laughter is the great antiseptic; and it is quick to kill the germs of unwholesome sentimentality by which comedy is often attacked. [Brander Matthews, *Studies of the Stage,* Harper & Brothers, New York, 1894, pp. 206–214.]

Plautus's characters are types, but are these types grounded in reality or produced by the imagination after study of Greek models?

Having discovered that Greek culture was valuable, the Romans, being a practical people, proceeded at once to import it, wholesale, and in the original package. Their dramatists became adapters, taking the plots of the plays of Menander and of Menander's clever contemporaries, and transferring these into Latin, leaving the

scene in Athens, but inserting an abundance of local allusions to Roman manners. They kept the types of character which the Athenian dramatist had observed and which often had only rare counterparts in Rome; the braggart coward, for example, was a Greek and not a Roman,—the Greek had no stomach for fighting, whereas the

Roman had shortened his sword and enlarged his boundaries. As a result this Latin comic drama is singularly unreal. . . . [Brander Matthews, *The Development of the Drama,* Charles Scribner's Sons, New York, 1903, p. 97.]

Actually, Roman comedy is not in any significant way remote from Roman life. It is a safe guess that Roman censorship accounts more for the Greek names and the Greek settings in Plautus and Terence than does a servile veneration of Menander. . . . No scurrilous playwright dared make a Roman citizen ridiculous lest he fall under the Roman formula of condemnation "for diminishing the Majesty of the Republic." If comedy was to be fun, but not fun at the expense of Romans, the comedians very reasonably turned to foreign men and foreign parts. Yet these foreigners with the unmanageable Hellenic names walk in the Roman Forum, go to the Roman Capitol, worship the Roman household gods, and like all self-respecting Romans disdain the contemptible Greeks. . . .

Historical convention imagines the Romans an indomitable people, stern, steadfast, and serious beyond all others. It is disconcerting that almost our first literary records present the opposite view. The edifying picture of republican dignity and austerity undergoes a ludicrous distortion in Plautus. The senator appears not in toga and not exactly in undress, but as a feeble, furtive, henpecked dotard, secretly hot on the quest of his lost youth. . . . An equal favorite is the soldier, who appears not as the invincible fighting man drilled to the last degree of military precision, but a vain-glorious dolt duped and derided and humbled. He consciously subverts the public slogan, so Roman in quality, "It is sweet and seemly to die for one's country." Pyrgopolinices, for instance, has no intention of dying at all; he intends to live and taste the pleasures of civilian life, and having made his bed he purposes to lie in it and enjoy it. [Daniel C. Boughner, *The Braggart in Renaissance Comedy,* University of Minnesota Press, Minneapolis, 1954, pp. 7–10.]

Pure farce supposedly has no purpose beyond that of arousing unreflective laughter. Plautus, however, does not seem to limit himself to this attempt.

Behind the delightful laughter of this caricature, there is a serious satiric purpose. The asides of Artotrogus, the gibes of Palaestrio and Philocomasium, and the contempt of Pleusicles and Periplectomenus are in harmony with the spirit of the resentful civilians in Menander. This derisive aspect of the role is less striking than the Plautine hilarity, but is equally significant. It is emphasized by means of the disparity between the soldier's ostentatious manner of living and the boorishness of his character. In appearance he is a fop, strutting jauntily with military cloak and sword prominently displayed, and with the long and carefully dressed hair admired by the

girls; he is a curled and perfumed dandy. He exhibits the upstart's showy pride in the wealth he has amassed from soldiering, wealth he spends prodigally to maintain a position among the well-to-do Ephesian citizens. He lives sumptuously, attracts parasites by the excellence of his table, dresses gaudily, and lavishes costly presents on his favorites. His social betters, nevertheless, hate and deride him and treat him as a boor. The *miles gloriosus* in the hands of Plautus, therefore, becomes an apt vehicle for the satire of fashionable upstarts as well as braggart warriors. [Boughner, *op. cit.,* pp. 13–14.]

SIR DAVID LYNDSAY

1490–1555

Sir David Lyndsay was employed by James V, King of Scotland, first as an actor and musician, later in the post of Lyon King at Arms. By virtue of this latter position he was in charge of court entertainments. When the Satire of the Three Estates *was first performed in 1540, the King was in the audience. There were at least two other performances of the play during Lyndsay's lifetime: one in 1552, another in 1554. These versions differed from each other and from the original, which is not extant.*

Lyndsay's play is a Morality Play, appearing at the end of a tradition which had started near the beginning of the fifteenth century. It belongs to a class of these plays usually called full-scope moralities. Such plays characteristically included a number of themes and covered a relatively long period of time in the action; they sought comprehensiveness of treatment rather than intensity. The prolixity and the farcical elements of the Satire of the Three Estates *do not indicate a lack of serious intent; the moral earnestness of both author and audience is attested to by the length of performance, which in one instance at least ran nine hours.*

The Satire of the Three Estates

EDINBURGH FESTIVAL VERSION BY ROBERT KEMP

Characters

SPIRITUAL ESTATE *composed of Bishops, Abbots, Parsons, the Prioress*

TEMPORAL ESTATE *composed of Barons and Lords*

BURGESSES' ESTATE *composed of Burgesses and Merchants*

DILIGENCE *a herald*

KING HUMANITY

WANTONNESS *courtier of the King*

PLACEBO *courtier of the King*

SOLACE *courtier of the King*

LADY SENSUALITY

GOOD COUNSEL

FLATTERY *one of the Three Vices, sometimes disguised as Pardoner*

FALSEHOOD *one of the Three Vices*

DECEIT *one of the Three Vices*

VERITY *a Puritan maid*

CHASTITY

CORRECTION

CORRECTION'S VARLET

POOR MAN

JOHN THE COMMON-WEAL

FIRST SERGEANT

SECOND SERGEANT

HOMELINESS *maiden of Lady Sensuality*

DANGER *maiden of Lady Sensuality*

FUND-JENNET *a porter*

SOUTAR

SOUTAR'S WIFE

TAILOR

TAILOR'S WIFE

COMMON PEOPLE

Part One

There is a fanfare of trumpets and the members of the Three Estates of the Realm of Scotland enter singing. They are the Spirituality or Bishops, the Temporality or Barons, and the Burgesses, who are Merchants. They make their way on to the stage through the audience.

ESTATES [*sing*]

The Father, founder of faith and felicity,
That your fashion formèd to His similitude;
And His Son, our Saviour, shield in necessity,
That bought you from bane, ransomed on the Rood,

97

Re-pledging His prisoners with His heart-blood;
The Holy Ghost, governor and grounder of
    grace,
Of wisdom and welfare both fountain and flood,
Save you all that we see seated in this place,
And shield you from sin,
And with His Spirit you inspire
Till we have shown our desire!
Silence, Sovereigns, we require,
For now we begin!

[*During the singing Diligence, a herald, has entered. He addresses the audience.*]

DILIGENCE   People, attend to me, and hold you
    coy![1]
Here am I sent to you, a messenger,
From a noble and right redoubted Roy,[2]
The which has been absent this many a year,
Who bade me show to you, but[3] variance,
That he intends among you to compear,
With a triumphant awful ordinance,
With crown and sword and sceptre in his hand,
Tempered with mercy when penitence appears;
Howbeit that he long time has been sleepand,[4]
Where through misrule has reigned these many
    years
And innocents been brought upon their biers
By false reporters of this nation . . .
Though young oppressors of their elders leirs[5]
Be now well sure of reformation!
[*A fanfare.*]
And here by open proclamation,
I warn in name of his magnificence,
The Three Estatës of this nation,
That they compear with debtful diligence,
And to his grace make their obedience.
And first I warn the Spirituality,
And see the Burgesses spare not for expense,
But speed them here with Temporality!
[*As Diligence names them, Spirituality, Tempo-
rality, and the Merchants take their places.
Diligence turns to the audience again.*]
And I beseech you, famous auditors,
Convene into this congregation,
To be patient the space of certain hours,
Till you have heard our short narration.
Also we make you supplication

[1] Quiet.   [2] King.   [3] Without.
[4] Sleeping.   [5] Learn.

That no man take our words into disdain,
Howbeit you hear by lamentation,
The Common-Weal right piteously complain.
Prudent people, I pray you all,
Take no man grief in special;
For we shall speak in general,
For pastime and for play.
Therefore, till all our rhymes be rung,
And our mis-tonèd songs be sung,
Let every man keep well one tongue,
And every woman two!
[*A fanfare and march. Young King Humanity
enters with his train, chief among whom are
two light-hearted courtiers, Wantonness and
Placebo. The Estates sing "Salve, rex humani-
tatis." The King kneels before his throne.*]
KING   O Lord of lords, and King of kingës all,
Omnipotent of power, Prince but[6] peer
Eternal reigning in gloire celestial.
Unmade Maker, who, having no matter,
Made heaven and earth, fire, air and water
    clear,
Send me thy grace with peace perpetual,
That I may rule my realm to thy pleasure;
Then bring my soul to joy angelical.
I thee request, who rent was on the Rood,
Me to defend from deedës of defame,
That my people report of me but good,
And be my safeguard both from sin and shame,
I know my days endure but as a dream;
Therefore, O Lord, heartily I thee exhort
To give me grace to use my diadem
To thy pleasure and to my great comfort.
[*The King takes his seat on the throne.*]
WANTONNESS   My Sovereign Lord the Prince but
    peer,
Why do you make such dreary cheer?
Be blithe so long as you are here,
And pass time with pleasure:
For as long lives the merry man
As the sorry, for ought he can.
His bones full sore, sir, shall I ban[7]
That does you displeasure.
So long as Placebo and I
Remain into your company,
Your grace shall live right merrily,
Of this have you no doubt!

[6] Without.   [7] Curse.

SIR DAVID LYNDSAY

So long as you have us in cure,
Your grace, sir, shall want no pleasure:
Were Solace here, I you assure,
He would rejoice this rout!

PLACEBO   Good brother mine, where is Solace,
The mirror of all merriness?
I have great marvel, by the Mass,
He's tarrying so long.
Bide he away, we are but shent![8]
I wonder how he from us went.
I trow he has impediment
That let's him not to gang.

WANTONNESS   I left Solace, that same great loon,
Drinking into the borough's town—
It will cost him half-a-crown
Although he had no more!
Also he said he would go see
Fair Lady Sensuality,
The beryl of all beauty
And portraiture preclair.
[*Enter Solace, the third Courtier, running.*]

PLACEBO   By God, I see him at the last,
As he were chased running right fast;
He glares, even as he were aghast,
Or frightened by a ghost . . .
[*Solace, drunk, at first addresses the audience.*]

SOLACE   Wow! Who saw ever such a throng?
Methought some said I had gone wrong.
Had I help, I would sing a song
With a right merry noise!
I have such pleasure in my heart
That makes me sing the treble part—
Would some good fellow fill the quart?
That would my heart rejoice!
What is my name? Can ye not guess?
Sirs, know you not Sandy Solace?
They called my mother Bonny Bess
That dwelled between the Bows.
At twelve years old she learned to swyve,
Thankèd be thou, great god of life,
She made me fathers four or five—
But doubt, this is no mows![9]
And if I lie, sirs, ye may spier.[10]
But saw you not the King come here?
I am a sporter and play-fere[11]
To that young King.
He said he would, within short space,

To pass his time come to this place—
I pray to God to give him grace
And long to reign.

KING   My servant Solace, what made you tarry?
[*Solace suddenly sees him.*]

SOLACE   I wot not, sir, by sweet Saint Mary;
I have been in a fairy-fairy
Or else into a trance!
Sir, I have seen, I you assure,
The fairest earthly creature,
That ever was formèd by nature
And most for to advance.
To look on her is great delight
With lips so red and cheeks so white,
I would renounce all this world quite
To stand into her grace!
She is wanton and she is wise,
And clad she is in the new guise—
It would make all your flesh up-rise
To look upon her face.
Were I a king, it should be kend,
I would not spare on her to spend
And this same night for her to send
For my pleasure!
What rack of your prosperity,
If you want Sensuality?
I would not give a silly fly
For your treasure!

KING   Forsooth, my friends, I think you are not
wise,
To counsel me to break commandement
Directed by the Prince of Paradise;
Considering you know that mine intent
Is for to be to God obedient,
Who does forbid men to be lecherous.
Do I not so, perchance I shall repent.
Therefore I think your counsel odious.
The which you gave me till.[12]
Because I have been to this day
Tanquam tabula rasa
Ready for good and ill.

PLACEBO   Believe you that we will beguile you,
Or from your virtue we will wile you,
Or with our evil words defile you
Both into good and evil?
To take your grace's part we grant,
In all your deeds participant,

---

[8] Lost.   [9] No joke.   [10] Ask.   [11] Mate.   [12] To.

The Satire of the Three Estates   99

So that you be not a young saint
And then an old devil.

WANTONNESS Believe you, sir, that lechery be
sin?
No, trow not that! This is my reason why.
First at the Roman Court will you begin,
Which is the gleaming lamp of lechery,
Where cardinals and bishops generally
To love ladies they think a pleasant sport
And out of Rome have banished Chastity,
Who with our prelates can get no resort!

SOLACE Until you get a prudent queen,
I think your Majesty serene
Should have a lusty concubine
To play you with all:
For I know, by your quality,
You lack the gift of chastity.
Fall to, *in nomine Domini!*
For this is my counsel!
I speak, sir, under protestation
That none at me have indignation,
For all the prelates of this nation
For the most part,
They think no shame to have a whore
And some have three under their cure—
This to be true I'll you assure,
You shall hear afterward.
Sir, knew you all the matter through.
To play you would begin.
Ask at the monks of Balmerino
If lechery be sin!

PLACEBO Sir, send forth Sandy Solace,
Or else your minion Wantonness
And pray my Lady Prioress
The sooth to declare,
If it be sin to take a Katie
Or to live like a Bummilbaty.[13]
The Book says *"Omnia probate"*
And not for to spare!

[*Music. Lady Sensuality enters accompanied by
her maidens Homeliness and Danger, and by
Fund-Jennet, a porter. They take up their position at the end of the stage remote from the
King and his courtiers, who do not see them.*]

SENSUALITY Lovers awake! Behold the fiery
sphere,
Behold the natural daughter of Venus!

Behold, lovers, this lusty lady clear,
The fresh fountain of knightës amorous,
Replete with joys, douce and delicious.
Or who would make to Venus observance
In my mirthful chamber melodious?
There shall they find all pastime and pleasance.
Behold my head, behold my gay attire,
Behold my neck, lovesome and lily-white;
Behold my visage flaming as the fire,
Behold my paps, of portraiture perfite!
To look on me lovers have great delight;
Right so have all the kings of Christendom—
To them I have done pleasures infinite
And specially unto the Court of Rome.
One kiss of me were worth, in one morning,
A million of gold to knight or king.
And yet I am of nature so toward
I let no lover pass with a sore heart.
Of my name, would you know the verity?
Forsooth they call me Sensuality.
I hold it best now, ere we further gang,
To Dame Venus let us go sing a song.

HOMELINESS Madame, no tarrying
We shall fall to and sing.
Sister Danger, come near!

DANGER Sister, sing this song I may not,
Without the help of good Fund-Jennet,
Fund-Jennet, ho! Come take a part!

FUND-JENNET That shall I do with all my heart!
Sister, howbeit that I am hoarse,
I am content to hear a bass.
You two should love me as your life—
You know I learned you both to swyve
In my chamber, you know well where,
Since then the fiend a man you spare!

HOMELINESS Fund-Jennet, fie, you are to blame!
To speak foul words, think you not shame?

FUND-JENNET There are a hundred sitting by
That love japing as well as I,
Might they get in it privity—
But who begins the song, let's see!

[*They sing verses from the poem by Alexander
Montgomerie.*]

Hey, now the day daws,
The jolly cock crows,
Now shrouds the shaws[14]
Through Nature anon.

13 Booby.

14 Woods.

SIR DAVID LYNDSAY

The thissel-cock cries
On lovers that lies,
Now skailes[15] the skies,
The night is near gone.

The fields overflows
With gowans that grows
Where lilies like lowe[16] is,
As red as the roan;
The turtle that true is,
With notes that renews,
Her pearty pursues,
The night is near gone!

Now harts with their hinds
Conform to their kinds,
High tosses their tynds[17]
On ground where they groan,
Now hedge-hogs, with hares,
Aye passes in pairs,
Which duly declares
The night is near gone.

The season excels
Through sweetness that smells;
Now Cupid compels
Our hearts everyone,
On Venus who wakes
To muse on our maiks[18]
Then sing for their sakes
The night is near gone!

[*During the singing of the song the King and
his court see Sensuality and her party.*]

KING Up, Wantonness, thou sleeps too long!
Methought I heard a merry song.
I thee command in haste to gang,
See what yon mirth may mean!

WANTONNESS I trow, sir, by the Trinity,
Yon same is Sensuality,
If it be so, soon shall I see
That sovereign serene!

PLACEBO Sir, she is greatly to advance,
For she can both play and dance,
That perfect patron of pleasance,
A pearl of pulchritude!
Soft as the silk is her white lyre,[19]
Her hair is like the golden wire,
My heart burns in a flame of fire

¹⁵ Empties.   ¹⁶ Flame.   ¹⁷ Antlers.
¹⁸ Mates.   ¹⁹ Skin.

I swear you by the Rood.

SOLACE What say you, sir? Are you content
That she come here incontinent?
What 'vails your kingdom and your rent
And all your great treasure,
Without you have a merry life,
And cast aside all sturt and strife?
And so long as you lack a wife,
Fall to, and take your pleasure!

KING Forsooth, I wot not how it stands,
But since I heard of your tidings,
My body trembles, feet and hands,
And whiles is hot as fire!
I trow Cupido with his dart
Has wounded me out-through the heart;
My spirit will from my body part,
Get I not my desire!
Pass on, away, with diligence,
And bring her here to my presence!
Spare not for travel or expense,
I care not for no cost!
Pass on your way soon, Wantonness,
And take with you Sandy Solace,
And bring that Lady to this place,
Or else I am but lost!
Commend me to that sweetest thing,
Present her with this same rich ring,
And say I lie in languishing,
Except she make remede!
With sighing sore I am but shent[20]
Without she come incontinent
My heavy languor to relent
And save me now from deid![21]

WANTONNESS Doubt you not, sir, but we will get
her,
We shall be fiery for to fetch her,
But, faith, we would speed all the better,
Had I more than a plack![22]

SOLACE Sir! Let not sorrow in you sink,
But give us ducats for to drink
And we shall never sleep a wink
Till we have brought her back!
[*The King gives them a purse.*]

KING I pray you, speed you soon again!

WANTONNESS Yea, of this song, sir, we are fain!
We shall neither spare for wind nor rain
Till our day's work be done!

²⁰ Lost.   ²¹ Death.   ²² Halfpenny.

Farewell, for we are at the flight!
Placebo, rule our Roy aright—
We shall be here, man, ere midnight
Though we march with the moon!

[*A gay march. Solace and Wantonness make a detour of the stage and come to Sensuality and her court.*]

Pastime with pleasure and great prosperity
Be to you, Sovereign Sensuality!

SENSUALITY Sirs, you are welcome. Where go you? East or west?

WANTONNESS In faith, I trow we be at the farthest!

SENSUALITY What is your name? I pray, sir, declare!

WANTONNESS Marry, Wantonness, the King's secretair.

SENSUALITY What king is that, who has so gay a boy?

WANTONNESS Humanity, that rich redoubted Roy,
Who does commend him to you heartfully,
And sends you here a ring with a ruby,
In token that above all creature
He has chosen you to be his Paramour:
He bade me say that he will be but dead,
Without that you make hastily remede.

SENSUALITY How can I help him, though he should fore-fare?[23]
You know right well I'm no Mediciner.

SOLACE A kiss of your sweet mouth, in a morning,
To his sickness might be great comforting.
Also he makes you supplication
This night to make with him collation.

SENSUALITY I thank his grace of his benevolence!
Good sirs, I shall be ready out of hand.
In me there shall be found no negligence,
Both night and day, when his grace will demand.
Pass you before, and say I am command[24]
And think right long to have of him a sight.
And I to Venus make a faithful bond
That in his arms I think to lie all night.

WANTONNESS That shall be done . . . but yet ere I home pass,

[23] Perish.   [24] Coming.

Here I protest for Homeliness, your lass.

SENSUALITY She shall be at command, sir, when you will:
I trust she shall you find flinging your fill!

WANTONNESS Now hey for joy and mirth I dance!

[*Music, which accompanies the speech.*]

Take there a gay gamond[24a] of France!
Am I not worthy to advance
That am so good a page,
And that so speedily can run
To 'tice my master unto sin?
The fiend a penny he will win
Of this his marriage!

[*A dance, during which Wantonness and Placebo skip back to the King. On the way Wantonness pretends to hurt his leg.*]

WANTONNESS [*to audience*] I think this day to win great thank!
Hey, as a bridled cat I brank![25]
Alas, I have wrested[26] my shank . . .
Yet I gang, by St. Michael.
Which of my legs, sir, as you trow,
Was it that I did hurt even now?
But whereto should I ask at you—
I think they both are whole!

[*He turns to the King. The music ends.*]

Good morrow, Master, by the Mass!

KING Welcome, my minion Wantonness!
How hast thou sped on thy travel?

WANTONNESS Right well, by Him that harried hell!
Your errand is well done!

KING [*transported*] Then, Wantonness, full well is me!
Thou hast deserved both meat and fee,
By Him that made the moon!

[*Anxiously*]

There is one thing that I would spier . . .[27]
What shall I do when she comes here?
For I know not the craft perqueir[28]
Of lovers' gin;
Therefore at length you must me leir[29]
How to begin.

WANTONNESS To kiss her and clap her, sir, be not affeared!
She will not shrink though you kiss her a span

[24a] Caper.   [25] Prance.   [26] Sprained.
[27] Ask.   [28] By heart.   [29] Learn.

within the beard.
If you think she thinks shame, then hide the bairn's head
With her train, and tend her well, you wot what I mean!
Will you give me leave, sir, first to go to,
And I shall learn you the cues how to do?

KING God forbid, Wantonness, that I give you leave!
You are too perilous a page such practice to prove!

[*Wantonness sees Sensuality.*]

WANTONNESS Now, sir, prove as you please, I see her command![30]
Order you with gravity, we shall by you stand!

[*Music. The King and his courtiers prepare to welcome Sensuality. She apart first takes her vow to Venus, accompanied by music.*]

SENSUALITY O Venus goddess, unto thy celsitude
I give laud, gloire, honour and reverence,
Who granted me such perfect pulchritude,
That princes of my person have pleasance,
I make a vow, with humble observance,
That I will in thy temple visit thee
With sacrifice unto thy deity!

[*She turns towards the King.*]

And now my way I must advance
Until a prince of great puissance,
Who young men has in governance,
Rolling into his rage.
I am right glad, I you assure,
That potent prince to get in cure,
Who is of lustings the lure
And greatest of courage.

[*The music ends. A detour brings her at last to the King.*]

O potent prince, of pulchritude preclair,
God Cupido preserve your celsitude!
May the dame Venus keep your court from care,
As I would she should keep my own heart blood!

KING Welcome to me, peerless of pulchritude!
Welcome to me, thou sweeter than the amber,
Who may of all my dolour me denude!
Solace, convoy this lady to my chamber!

SENSUALITY I go this gait[31] with right good will.

30 Coming.   31 Way.

Sir Wantonness, tarry you still?
Let Homeliness the cup you fill
And bear you company!

[*Music, which continues till the departure of King and party.*]

HOMELINESS That shall I do without a doubt,
For he and I shall play cap-out!

WANTONNESS Now lady, let me have turn about,
Fill in for I am dry!
Your dame, by now, truly,
Has gotten upon her keel!
What rack though you and I
Go join the joust as well?

HOMELINESS Content I am with right good will,
Whenever you are ready,
All your pleasure to fulfill.

WANTONNESS Now well said, by our Lady!
I'll bear my master company,
As long as I endure!
If he be whisking wantonly,
We shall fling on the floor!

[*The King and his party go into the arbour at the top of the stage. As they disappear Good Counsel, a bearded figure, hobbles in and addresses the audience.*]

GOOD COUNSEL Consider, my sovereigns, I you beseech,
The cause most principal of my coming.
Princes or potestates are not worth a leek,
Be they not guided by my good governing.
There was never emperor, conqueror nor king,
Without my wisdom that might their weal advance.
My name is Good Counsel, without feigning;
Lords for lack of my law are brought to mischance.
And so, for conclusion,
Who guide them not by Good Counsel,
All in vain is their travail,
And finally fortune shall them fail,
And bring them to confusion.
And this I understand,
For I have my residence
With high princes of great puissance,
In England, Italy and France,
And many other land.
But out of Scotland, alas,
I have been banished long space—
That makes our guiders all lack grace,

And die before their day!
Because they lightly[32] Good Counsel,
Fortune turned on them her sail,
Which brought this realm to greatest bale[33]—
Who can the contrair say?
My lords, I came not here to lie;
Woes me for King Humanity,
O'erset with Sensuality
In his first beginning,
Through vicious counsel insolent!
So they may get riches or rent
To his welfare they take no tent,[34]
Nor what shall be the ending!
But would the King be guided yet with reason
And on mis-doers make punition,
Howbeit that I long time have been exiled
I trust in God my name shall yet be styled,
So till I see God send more of his grace,
I purpose to repose me in this place.
[*Good Counsel draws apart. Flattery, the first
of the Three Vices to appear, rushes in, dressed
in motley.*]

FLATTERY   Make room, sirs, ho! that I may run!
Lo, see how I am new come in,
Begaried[35] all with sundry hues!
Let be your din till I begin,
And I shall show you of my news!
Throughout all Christendom I have passed
And am come here now at the last,
Stormstayed on sea aye since Yule Day,
That we were fain to hew our mast,
Not half a mile beyond the May.[36]
But now among you I will remain,
I purpose never to sail again,
To put my life in chance of water.
Was never seen such wind and rain,
Nor of shipmen such clitter-clatter.
Some bade "Hail!" and some bade "Stand-by!"
"On starboard ho!" "A-luff fie, fie!"
Till all the ropes began to rattle,
Was never wight so fley't[37] as I,
When all the sails played brittle-brattle!
To see the waves, it was a wonder,
And wind, that rave the sails in sunder!
Now am I 'scaped from that affray;
What say you, sirs, am I not gay?
Know you not Flattery, your own fool,

That went to make this new array?
Was I not here with you at Yule?
Yes, by my faith, I think so well!
Where are my fellows that would not fail?
We should have come here for a cast!
Ho, Falsehood, ho!
[*Falsehood enters.*]
FALSEHOOD   We serve the Deil![38]
Who's that that cries for me so fast?
FLATTERY   Why, Falsehood, brother, know thou
    not me?
I am thy brother, Flattery!
FALSEHOOD   Now let me brace thee in my arms,
When friend meets friend, the heart aye warms!
[*They embrace.*]
FLATTERY   Where is Deceit, that limmer loon?[39]
FALSEHOOD   I left him drinking in the town,
He will be here incontinent.
FLATTERY   Now by the Holy Sacrament,
These tidings comfort all my heart!
He is right crafty as you ken,
And counsellor to the Merchant-men!
[*Enter Deceit.*]
DECEIT   Bon jour, brother, with all my heart,
Here am I come to take your part
Both into good and evil!
I met Good Counsel by the way,
Who put me in a felon fray[40]—
I give him to the devil!
How came you here, I pray you tell me!
FALSEHOOD   Marry, to seek King Humanity!
DECEIT   Now, by the good lady that me bare,
That same horse is my own mare!
Since we three seek yon noble King,
Let us devise some subtle thing!
Also I pray you as your brother,
That we, each one, be true to other.
I pray to God, nor I be hanged,
But I shall die ere you be wronged!
FALSEHOOD   What is thy counsel that we do?
DECEIT   Marry, sirs, this is my counsel, lo!
From time the King begins to stir him,
I dread Good Counsel may come near him,
And be we known to Lord Correction,
It will be our confusion.
Therefore, my dear brother, devise
To find some toy of the new guise.

---

[32] Disdain.   [33] Sorrow.   [34] Heed.
[35] Bedecked.   [36] May Island.   [37] Scared.

[38] Devil.   [39] Scoundrel.   [40] Fright.

FLATTERY   Marry, I shall find a thousand wiles.
  We must turn our clothes, and change our styles
  And so disguise us, that no man know us.
  Has no man clerk's clothing to lend us?
  And let us keep grave countenance,
  As we were new come out of France!

DECEIT   Now, by my soul, that is well devised!
  You'll see me soon right well disguised.

FALSEHOOD   And so shall I, man, by the Rood!
  Now, some good fellow, lend me a hood!
  [*The Three Vices disguise themselves in clothes from a bundle which Deceit has brought on.*]

DECEIT   Now am I busked, and who can spy?
  The devil stick me, if this be I!
  If this be I, or not, I cannot well say,
  Or has the Fiend of Fairy-folk borne me away?

FALSEHOOD   What say you of my gay garmoun?[41]

DECEIT   I say you look even like a loon.
  Now, brother Flattery, what do you?
  What kind of man shape you to be?

FLATTERY   Now, by my faith, my brother dear,
  I will go counterfeit a friar!

DECEIT   A friar? Whereto you cannot preach?

FLATTERY   What rack, if I can flatter and fleech?[42]
  Perchance I'll come to that honour,
  To be the King's confessor.
  Poor friars are free at any feast
  And marshalled aye among the best!
  [*Deceit has fetched a monk's cowl.*]

DECEIT   Here is thy gaining, all and some,
  That is a cowl of Tullilum!

FLATTERY   Who has a breviary to lend me?
  The fiend a soul, I trow, will ken me!
  [*The Bishop tosses down a breviary.*]

FALSEHOOD   We must do more yet, by St. James!
  For we must all three change our names.
  Christen me and I shall baptise thee.
  [*There follows a mock ceremony.*]

DECEIT   By God and thereabout may it be!
  How will you call me, I pray you tell!

FALSEHOOD   I wot not how to call mysel'!

DECEIT   But yet once name the bairn's name!

FALSEHOOD   Discretion, Discretion in God's name!

DECEIT   I need not now to care for thrift,
  But what shall be my Godbairn gift?

FALSEHOOD   I give you all the devils of hell!

DECEIT   No, brother, hold that to yoursel'!
  Now, sit down! Let me baptise thee!
  I wot not what thy name should be.

FALSEHOOD   But yet once name the bairn's name!

DECEIT   Sapience, Sapience, in God's name!

FLATTERY   Brother Deceit, come baptise me!

DECEIT   Then sit down lowly on thy knee!

FLATTERY   Now, brother, name the bairn's name.

DECEIT   Devotion in the devil's name.
  [*He splashes Flattery with water.*]

FLATTERY   The deil receive thee, lurdan loon![43]
  Thou has wet all my new shaven crown!

ALL   Devotion, Sapience, and Discretion—
  We three may rule this region.
  We shall find many crafty things
  For to beguile a hundred kings!

DECEIT   [*to Falsehood*]   For thou can right well crack and clatter,
  And I shall feign and
  [*to Flattery*]
                    thou shalt flatter

FLATTERY   But I would have, ere we departed,
  A drink to make us better hearted.

DECEIT   Well said, by Him that harried hell,
  I was even thinking that mysel'!
  [*While the Three Vices are drinking, the King appears leading Sensuality from the arbour.*]

KING   Now where is Placebo and Solace?
  Where is my minion Wantonness?
  Wantonness, ho! Come to me soon!
  [*Wantonness and Homeliness appear.*]

WANTONNESS   Why cried you, sir, till I had done?

KING   What were you doing, tell me that?

WANTONNESS   Marry, learning how my father me got!
  I wot not how it stands, but[44] doubt
  Methinks the world runs round about!

KING   And so think I, man, by my thrift!
  I see fifteen moons in the lift.[45]
  [*Solace, Placebo, and Danger appear.*]

SOLACE   Now show me, sir, I you exhort,
  How are you of your love content?
  Think you not this a merry sport?

KING   Yea, that I do in verament![46]

---

[41] Garment.   [42] Wheedle.

[43] Rogue.   [44] Without.   [45] Sky.   [46] Truth.

[*The King spies the Three Vices*.]
What bairns are yon upon the bent?
I did not see them all this day.

WANTONNESS   They will be here incontinent.
Stand still and hear what they will say.

[*The Three Vices come forward and salute the King*.]

VICES   Laud, honour, gloire, triumph and victory,
Be to your most excellent Majesty!

KING   You are welcome, good friends, by the
Rood!
Apparently you seem some men of good.
What are your names, tell me without delay!

DECEIT   Discretion, sir, is my name perfray.

KING   What is your name, sir, with the clippèd
crown?

FLATTERY   But doubt, my name is called Devotion.

KING   Welcome, Devotion, by Saint Jame!
Now, sirrah, tell what is your name?

FALSEHOOD   Marry, sir, they call me . . .what
call they me?
[*Aside*]
I wot not well, but if I lie!

KING   Can you not tell what is your name?

FALSEHOOD   I knew it when I came from home!

KING   What ails you cannot show it now?

FALSEHOOD [*confused*]   Marry, they call me Thin-
Drink, I trow!

KING   Thin-Drink, what kind of name is that?

DECEIT   Sapience, thou serves to bear a plate!
Methinks thou shows thee not well-witted.

FALSEHOOD   Sypiens, sir, Sypiens, marry now you
hit it!

[*Flattery brushes Falsehood aside*.]

FLATTERY   Sir, if you please to let me say,
That same is Sapientia!

FALSEHOOD   That same is it, by St. Michael!

KING   Why could thou not tell it thysel'?

FALSEHOOD   I pray your grace to pardon me.
And I shall show the verity—
I am so full of Sapience
That sometimes I will take a trance!

KING   Sapience should be a man of good.

FALSEHOOD   Sir, you may know that by my hood!

KING   Now have I Sapience and Discretion,
How can I fail to rule this region?
And Devotion to be my Confessor!
These three came in a happy hour.

[*To Falsehood*]
Here I make thee my secretar!
[*To Deceit*]
And thou shalt be my treasurer!
[*To Flattery*]
And thou shalt be my counsellor
In spiritual things, and confessor.

FLATTERY   I swear to you, sir, by St. Ann,
You never met a wiser man,
For many a craft, sir, do I can,
Were they well known.
I have no feel of flattery,
But fostered with philosophy,
A strong man in astronomy,
Which shall be soon shown!

FALSEHOOD   And I have great intelligence,
In quelling of the quintessence,
But to prove my experience,
Sir, lend me forty crowns!
To make multiplication,
And take my obligation—
If we make false narration,
Hold us for very loons!

DECEIT   Sir, I know by your physnomy,
You shall conquer, or else I lie,
Danskin,[47] Denmark and Almane,
Spitalfield and the Realm of Spain.
You shall have at your governance
Renfrew and the Realm of France,
Yea, Ru'glen and the Town of Rome,
Corstorphine and all Christendom.
Whereto, sir, by the Trinity,
You are a very A per se.

FLATTERY   Sir, when I dwelt in Italy,
I learned the craft of palmistry.
Show me the palm, sir, of your hand,
And I shall make you understand
If your grace be unfortunate
Or if you be predestinate.
[*The King shows his hand*.]
I see you will have fifteen queens
And fifteen score of concubines!
The Virgin Mary save your grace,
Saw ever man so white a face,
So great an arm, so fair a hand,
Or such a leg in all this land!
Were you in arms, I think no wonder,

[47] Dantzig.

Howbeit you struck down fifteen hundred.

KING You are right welcome, by the Rood!
You seem to be three men of good!
[*Good Counsel takes up a more prominent position.*]
But who is yon that stands so still?
Go spy and ask what is his will.
And if he yearns of my presence,
Bring him to me with diligence.
[*The Three Vices quickly confer.*]

FLATTERY I doubt full sore by God himsel'
That yon old carl be Good Counsel!
Get he once to the King's presence,
We three will get no audience!

DECEIT That matter I shall take on hand,
And say it is the King's command,
That he anon avoid this place,
And come not near the King his grace,
And that under the pain of treason!

FLATTERY Brother, I hold your counsel reason.
Now let us hear what he will say.
[*He addresses Good Counsel.*]
Old lyart[48] beard, good day, good day!

GOOD COUNSEL Good day again, sirs, by the Rood!
I pray God make you men of good.

DECEIT Pray not for us to Lord nor Lady,
For we are men of good already!
Sir, show to us what is your name.

GOOD COUNSEL Good Counsel they call me at home.

FALSEHOOD What sayest thou, carl, art thou Good Counsel?
Swift, pack thee hence, unhappy mortal!

GOOD COUNSEL I pray you, sirs, give me licence,
To come once to the King's presence
To speak but two words to his grace.

FLATTERY Quick, whoreson carl, devoid this place!

GOOD COUNSEL Brother, I know you well enough,
Howbeit you make it never so tough—
Flattery, Deceit and False-Report
That will not suffer to resort
Good Counsel to the King's presence.

DECEIT Swift, whoreson carl, go pack thee hence!
If ever thou come this gait[49] again,

[48] Hoary. [49] Way.

I vow to God thou shalt be slain!
[*They set upon Good Counsel and push him from the stage.*]

GOOD COUNSEL Since at this time I can get no presence,
Is no remede but take in patience.
But when youth-head has blown his wanton blast,
Then shall Good Counsel rule him at the last!
[*Good Counsel is chased out. The Three Vices return to the King.*]

KING What made you bide so long from my presence?
I think it long since you departed thence.
What was yon man, with a great bousteous beard?
Methought he made you all three very feared!

DECEIT It was a loathly lurdan loon,
Come to break booths into this town!
We have caused bind him to a pole
And send him to the Thieves' Hole.

KING Let him sit there with a mischance!
And let us go to our pastimes!

WANTONNESS Better go revel at the racket,
Or else go to the hurley-hacket,[50]
Or then to show our courtly courses,
Go see who best can run their horses!
[*As they make to move, Solace stops them.*]

SOLACE No, Sovereign, ere we further gang,
Let Sensuality sing a song.
[*The Ladies sing verses from a poem by Alexander Scott.*]

To love unlovèd is a pain,
For she that is my sovereign
Some wanton man so he has set her
That I can get no love again,
But breaks my heart, and nought the better!

When that I went with that sweet may
To dance, to sing, to sport and play,
And ofttimes in my arms to plait her
I do now mourn both night and day
And breaks my heart and nought the better!

What a poor glaikit[51] fool am I,
To slay myself with melancholy,
Since well I know I may not get her!
Or what should be the cause, and why
To break my heart and nought the better!

[50] A game. [51] Simple.

The Satire of the Three Estates

My heart, since thou may not her please,
Adieu! As good love comes as goes!
Go choose another and forget her!
God give him dolour and disease
That breaks their heart, and nought the better!
[*As the music ends, Verity enters, a Puritan
maid holding a Bible. She stands apart but
Flattery goes out to peer at her as she speaks.*]

VERITY If men of me would have intelligence,
Or know my name, they call me Verity.
Of Christës law I have experience,
And have o'er sailèd many a stormy sea.
Now I am seeking King Humanity;
For of his grace I have good esperance.
From time that he acquainted be with me,
His honour and high gloire I shall advance.
[*As Flattery returns Deceit greets him.*]

DECEIT Good day, Father, where have you
been?
Declare to us of your novelles.

FLATTERY There is now lighted on the green,
Dame Verity, by books and bells!
But come she to the King's presence,
There is no boot for us to bide!
Therefore I rede us, all go hence!

FALSEHOOD That will be not yet, by St. Bride!
But we shall either gang or ride
To Lords of Spirituality,
And make them trow yon bag of pride
Has spoken manifest heresy!
[*Here the Three Vices go to the Spirtual Estate.*]

FLATTERY O reverent fathers of the Spiritual
State,
We counsel you be wise and vigilant!
Dame Verity has lighted now of late,
And in her hand bearing the New Testament!
[*The Spiritual Estate confer in undertones for
a moment.*]

BISHOP I hold it best that we incontinent
Cause hold her fast into captivity,
Unto the third day of the Parliament
And then accuse her of heresy.
[*The Three Vices approach Verity.*]

FLATTERY What book is that, harlot, in thy hand?
[*He looks at it.*]
Out! Waylaway! This is the New Testament!
In English tongue, and printed in England!
Heresy, heresy! Fire, fire, incontinent!

VERITY Forsooth, my friend, you have a wrong
judgment,
For in this Book there is no heresy,
But our Christ's word, right douce and redo-
lent—
A springing well of sincere verity!

DECEIT Come on your way, for all your yellow
locks!
Your wanton words but[52] doubt you shall re-
pent!
This night you shall forfare[53] a pair of stocks,
And in the morn be brought to thole judgment.
[*Verity falls on her knees, not to the Vices but
to Heaven.*]

VERITY Get up, thou sleepest all too long, O
Lord,
And make some reasonable reformation
Of them that do tramp down Thy gracious
Word,
And have a deadly indignation
At them who make the true narration!

FLATTERY Sit down and take your rest
All night till it be day!
[*They put Verity in the stocks, and return to
Spirituality.*]

DECEIT My lord, we have with diligence,
Buckled up well yon blethering bard!

BISHOP I think you deserve good recompense.
Take these ten crowns for your reward!
[*Chastity enters intoning to herself a Latin
hymn.*]

CHASTITY How long shall this inconstant world
endure
That I should banished be so long, alas!
Few creatures, or none, take of me cure,
Which makes me many a night lie harbourless!

DILIGENCE Lady, I pray you show to me your
name!

CHASTITY Dame Chastity, banished without a
home!

DILIGENCE Then pass to ladies of religion,
Who make their vows to observe chastity.
Lo, where there sits a Prioress of renown
Among the rest of Spirituality.
[*Diligence points out the Prioress, who is one
of the members of the Spiritual Estate.*]

---

[52] Without.   [53] Endure.

CHASTITY   I grant yon lady has vowèd chastity,
For her profession thereto should accord.
She made that vow for an abbacy,
But not for Jesus Christ our Lord . . .
I shall observe your counsel if I may;
Come on, and hear what yon lady will say.
[*Diligence and Chastity approach the Prioress.*]
My prudent, lusty Lady Prioress,
Remember how you did vow chastity;
Madame, I pray you of your gentleness
That you would please to have of me pity
And this one might give me harboury!

PRIORESS   Pass hence, Madame, by Christ you
    come not here!
You are contrair to my complexion!
Go seek lodging from some old monk or friar,
Perchance they will be your protection.
Or to prelates make your progression
Who are obliged to you as well as I!
Dame Sensual has given direction
You to exclude out of my company!
[*Chastity now addresses the Spiritual Estate.*]

CHASTITY   Lords, I have passed through many
    uncouth shire,
But in this land I can get no lodging!
Of my name if you would have knowledging
Forsooth, my lords, they call me Chastity.
I you beseech of your graces benign,
Give me lodging this night for charity.

BISHOP   Pass on, Madame, we know you not!
Or by Him that the world has wrought,
Your coming shall be right dear bought,
If you make longer tarry!

ABBOT   But Doubt we will both live and die
With our love Sensuality;
We will have no more deal with thee
Than with the Queen of Faery.

PARSON   Pass home among the Nuns and dwell,
Who are of chastity the well—
I trust they will with book and bell
Receive you in their cloister!

CHASTITY   Sir, when I was the Nuns among,
Out of their dorter they me dang[54]
And would not let me bide so long
As say my Paternoster.
I see no grace therefore to get.

I hold it best, ere it be late,
For to go prove the temporal state
If they will me receive.
[*Chastity crosses to the Temporal Estate.*]
Good day, my lord Temporality,
And you, Merchant of gravity;
Full fain would I have harboury,
To lodge among the lave.[55]

LORD   Forsooth, we would be well content
To harbour you with good intent,
Were it not we have impediment—
For why? We two are married!

MERCHANT   But wist our wives that you were
    here,
They would make all this town in stir,
Therefore we rede you, run arear,
In dread you be miscarried!
[*Chastity now goes to the end of the stage where
the common people are watching. She ap-
proaches Soutar and Tailor, near whom are
Soutar's Wife and Tailor's Wife. A Soutar is
a shoemaker.*]

CHASTITY   You men of craft and great ingyne,[56]
Give me harboury for Christ his pine,
And win God's benison, and mine,
And help my hungry heart!

SOUTAR   Is this fair Lady Chastity?

TAILOR   Now welcome by the Trinity!
I think it were a great pity
That thou should lie thereout!

SOUTAR   Sit down, Madame, and take a drink,
And let no sorrow in you sink,
But let us play cap-out.
[*They entertain Chastity.*]

SOUTAR'S WIFE   What does the Soutar, my good-
    man?

TAILOR'S WIFE   Marry, fills the cup and tooms[57]
    the can
With a young maiden clad in white,
In whom the lurdan takes delight—
I trust, if I can reckon right,
She shapes to lodge with him all night!
Ere he come home, by God I trow
He will be drunken like a sow!

SOUTAR'S WIFE   This is a great despite, I think,
For to receive such a cow-clink!

[54] Beat.

[55] Rest.   [56] Ability.   [57] Empties.

What is your counsel that we do?

TAILOR'S WIFE Gossip, this is my counsel, lo!
Ding[58] you the one and I the other.

SOUTAR'S WIFE I am content, by God His Mother!
I think for me these whoreson smaiks[59]
Deserve right well to get their paiks!
[*They drive Chastity away*.]

TAILOR'S WIFE Go hence, harlot, how durst thou
be so bold
To lodge with our goodmen without licence?
I make a vow by Him that Judas sold,
This rock[60] of mine shall be thy recompense!

SOUTAR'S WIFE Show me thy name, duddron,[61]
with diligence!

CHASTITY Marry, Chastity is my name, by Saint
Blaise.

SOUTAR'S WIFE I pray God may He work on
thee vengeance
For I lovèd ne'er chastity all my days!
[*She pursues Chastity with her distaff, then the
Wives turn on their husbands*.]

SOUTAR'S WIFE I make a vow to Saint Crispin
I'll be revenged on that graceless groom.
And to begin the play, take there a flap!
[*She strikes the Soutar*.]

SOUTAR The fiend receive the hands that gave
me that!

SOUTAR'S WIFE What now, whoreson, begins thou
now to ban?[62]
Take there another upon thy peeled harn-pan![63]
[*To Tailor's Wife*] What now, gossip, wilt thou
not take my part?

TAILOR'S WIFE That shall I do, gossip, with all
my heart.
[*As the Wives chase their husbands off, Solace
catches sight of Chastity and speaks to the
King*.]

SOLACE Sovereign, get up and see a heavenly
sight,
A fair lady in white habilament!
She may be peer unto a king or knight,
Most like an angel by my judgment!
[*The King rises from among the ladies*.]

KING I shall go see that sight incontinent.
[*To Sensuality*]
Madame, behold if you have knowledging
Of yon lady, or what is her intent.

58 Strike. 59 Wretches. 60 Distaff.
61 Slut. 62 Curse. 63 Bald cranium.

Thereafter we shall turn but[64] tarrying.

SENSUALITY Sir, let me see what yon matter may
mean—
Perchance that I may know her by her face.
[*She looks more closely at Chastity*.]
But doubt, this is Dame Chastity, I ween!
Sir, I and she cannot bide in one place!
But if it be the pleasure of your grace,
That I remain into your company,
This woman right hastily make chase,
That she no more be seen in this country!

KING As ever you please, sweetheart, so shall it
be!
Dispose her as you think expedient.
Even as you list to let her live or die,
I will refer that thing to your judgment.

SENSUALITY I will that she be banishèd incontinent,
And never to come again in this country;
And if she does, but doubt she shall repent,
Also perchance a doleful death shall die!
Pass on, Sir Sapience and Discretion,
And banish her out of the King's presence!

DECEIT That shall we do, Madame, by God's
passion!
We shall do thy command with diligence.
And at your hands deserve good recompense.
Dame Chastity, come on, be not aghast!
We shall right soon upon your own expense
Into the stocks your bonny foot make fast!
[*The Vices place Chastity in the stocks beside
Verity*.]

CHASTITY Sister, alas, this is a care-full case,
That we with princes should be so abhorred!

VERITY Be blithe, sister, I trust within short
space,
That we shall be right honourably restored,
And with the King we shall be at concord,
For I heard tell Divine Correction
Is new landed, thanks be to Christ our Lord!
I wot he will be our protection!
[*A fanfare. Enter Correction's Varlet*.]

VARLET Sirs, stand back and hold you coy.[65]
I am the King Correction's boy,
Come here to dress his place!
See that you make obedience
Unto his noble excellence

64 Without. 65 Quiet.

From time you see his face!
He has made reformations
Out-through all Christian nations,
Where he finds great debates.
And so far as I understand,
He shall reform into this land
Even all the Three Estates.
For silence I protest
Both of Lord, Laird and Lady!
Now will I run but rest
And tell that all is ready!
[*Another fanfare. Exit Correction's Varlet. The Three Vices go into conference.*]

DECEIT   Brother, hear you yon proclamation?
I dread full sore of reformation,
Yon message makes me mangèd.[66]
What is your counsel, to me tell!
Remain we here, by God himsel',
We will be all three hangèd!

FLATTERY   I'll gang to Spirituality
And preach out-through his diosee,
Where I will be unknown,
Or keep me close in some cloister
With many a piteous Paternoster,
Till all their blasts be blown.

DECEIT   I'll be well treated, as you ken,
With my masters, the Merchant men,
Who can make small debate;
You know right few of them that thrives
Or can beguile the landward wives
Without their man Deceit.
Now, Falsehood, what shall be thy shift?

FALSEHOOD   No, care thou not, man, for my thrift!
Trows thou that I be daft?
No, I will live a lusty life
Withouten any sturt or strife,
Among the men of craft.

DECEIT   Falsehood, I would we made a bond—
Now, while the King is yet sleepand[67]
What rack to steal his box?

FALSEHOOD   Now, well said by the Sacrament!
I shall it steal incontinent,
Though it had twenty locks!
[*Falsehood steals the King's box.*]
Lo, here the box! Now let us go,
This may suffice for our rewards!

[66] Confounded.   [67] Sleeping.

DECEIT   Yea, that it may, man, by this day!
It may well make us landward lairds!
Now let us cast away our clothes,
In dread some follow on the chase!

FALSEHOOD   Right well devised, man, by Saint Blaise,
Would God we were out of this place!
[*Here they cast away their disguises.*]

DECEIT   Now, since there is no man to wrong us,
I pray you, brother, with my heart,
Let us go part this pelf among us,
Then hastily we shall depart!

FALSEHOOD   Trows thou to get as much as I?
That shalt thou not! I stole the box!
Thou did nothing but lookit by,
Aye lurking like a wily fox!
[*Deceit and Falsehood fight.*]

FALSEHOOD   Alas for ever my eye is out!

DECEIT   Upon thy craig[68] take there a clout!
[*Flattery has meantime stolen the box and runs out pursued by Deceit and Falsehood. Their flight is hastened by the fanfare and stately march to which enter Divine Correction and his train.*]

ESTATES   [*sing*]

Rex tremendae majestratis,
Juste judex ultionis,
Rex omnipotens gloriae.

CORRECTION   I am callèd Divine Correction.
Where I am not is no tranquillity!
By me traitors and tyrants are put down
Who think no shame of their iniquity.
What is a King? Nought but an officer,
To cause his lieges live in equity,
And under God to be a punisher
Of trespassers against His Majesty.
I am a judge, right potent and severe,
Come to do justice many a thousand mile.
I am so constant, both in peace and war,
No bribe or favour may my sight o'er-sile.[69]
[*Good Counsel enters and runs to greet his master.*]

GOOD COUNSEL   Welcome, my lord, welcome ten thousand times
To all the true men of this region!
Welcome for to correct all faults and crimes

[68] Throat.   [69] Obscure.

Among this cankered congregation!
Loose Chastity, I make supplication,
Put to freedom fair Lady Verity,
Who by unfaithful folk of this nation
Lies bound full fast into captivity!

CORRECTION   I marvel, Good Counsel, how that
    may be—
Are you not with the King familiar?

GOOD COUNSEL   That I am not, my lord, full woe
    is me,
But like a beggar am holden at the bar.

CORRECTION   Where lie yon ladies in captivity?
[*He turns to Verity and Chastity in the stocks.*]
How now, sisters, who has you so disguisèd?

VERITY   Unfaithful members of iniquity,
Despitefully, my lord, has us suppressèd.

CORRECTION   Go, put yon ladies to their liberty
Incontinent, and break down all the stocks!
But doubt, they are full dear welcome to me!
Make diligence! Methinks you do but mocks!
Speed hand, and spare not for to break the
    locks,
And tenderly to take them by the hand!
Had I them here, these knaves should ken my
    knocks,
That them oppressed and banished from this
    land!
[*Members of Correction's retinue release Verity
and Chastity. The Courtiers spy Correction.*]

WANTONNESS   Solace, knows thou not what I see?
A knight, or else a king thinks me,
Brother, what may this mean?

SOLACE   Whether that he be friend or foe,
Stand still and hear what he will say,
Such one I have not seen!

PLACEBO   I rede us, put upon the King,
And waken him out of his sleeping!
[*He rouses the King from the arms of Sen-
suality.*]
Sir, rise up and see an unco[70] thing!
Get up, you lie too long!

SENSUALITY   Put on your hood, John-fool! You
    rave!
How dare you be so pert, Sir Knave,
To touch the King? So Christ me save,
False whoreson, thou shalt hang!
[*Correction approaches the King.*]

CORRECTION   Get up, Sir King, you have sleepèd
    enough
Into the arms of Lady Sensual!
[*The King rises and faces him.*]
Remember how, into the time of Noë
For the foul stink and sin of lechery,
God by my wand did all the world destroy.
Sodom and Gommorra right so full rigorously
For that vile sin were burnt most cruelly.
Therefore I thee command incontinent
Banish from thee that whore Sensuality
Or beyond doubt rudely thou shalt repent!

KING   By whom have you so great authority?
Who does presume for to correct a King?
Know you not me, great King Humanity,
That in my region royally does reign?

CORRECTION   I have power great princes to down-
    thring[71]
That live contrair the Majesty Divine,
Against the truth who plainly do malign;
Repent they not, I put them to ruin!
I will begin at thee, who art the head,
And make on thee the first reformation,
Thy lieges then will follow thee indeed!
Swift, harlot, hence without dilation![72]

SENSUALITY   My lord, I make you supplication,
Give me licence to pass again to Rome!
Among the princes of that nation,
I let you know my fresh beauty will bloom!
Adieu, Sir King, I may no longer tarry!
Not that I care, as good love comes as goes!
I recommend you to the Queen of Faery—
I see you will be guided by my foes!
[*Sensuality and her retinue pass to the Estate
Spiritual.*]
My lordës of the Spiritual State,
Venus preserve you air[73] and late!
For I can make no more debate,
I am parted with your king,
And am banishèd this region,
By council of Correction.
Be ye not my protection,
I may seek my lodging!

BISHOP   Welcome, our days' darling!
Welcome with all our heart!
We without feigning
Shall plainly take your part!

---

[70] Strange.   [71] Overthrow.   [72] Delay.   [73] Early.

[*Sensuality, Homeliness, and Danger take their places with Bishop, Abbot, and Parson. Correction returns to the King.*]

CORRECTION   Since you are quit of Sensuality,
Receive into your service Good Counsel,
And right so this fair Lady Chastity,
Till you marry some Queen of blood royal.
Observe then chastity matrimonial.
Right so receive Verity by the hand . . .
Use their counsel, your fame shall never fall;
With them, therefore, make a perpetual bond!
[*The King receives Good Counsel, Chastity, and Verity.*]
Now, sir, attend to what I say,
Observe that same both night and day,
And never let them part you frae,[74]
Or else without a doubt,
Turn you to Sensuality,
To vicious life and ribaldry,
Out of your realm right shamefully,
You shall be rooted out!

KING   I am content to your counsel t'incline.
At your command shall be all that is mine.
[*Solemn music. He embraces Correction.*]

CORRECTION   I counsel you incontinent
To cause proclaim a Parliament
Of all the Three Estates,
That they be here with diligence
To make to you obedience
And then dress all debates!

KING   That shall be done, but[75] more demand.
Ho, Diligence, come here from hand
And take your information.
Go, warn the Spirituality,
Right so the Temporality,
By open proclamation,
In goodly haste for to appear
In their most honourable manner
To give us their counsels!
Who that is absent, to them show
That they shall under-lie the Law
And punished be that fails!

DILIGENCE   Sir, I shall both in borough and land,
With diligence do your command,
Upon my own expense.
Sir, I have served you all this year,
But I got never one dinner

Yet for my recompense!

KING   Pass on, and thou shalt be regarded
And for thy service well rewarded,
For why? With my consent,
Thou shalt have yearly for thy hire
The tithe mussels of the Ferry-mire
Confirmed in Parliament.

DILIGENCE   I will get riches through that rent
After the days of Doom,
When in the coal-pits of Tranent
Butter will grow on broom!
All night I had so great a drouth,[76]
I might not sleep a wink,
Ere I proclaim aught with my mouth,
But doubt I must have drink!
[*While Diligence refreshes himself Divine Correction tackles the Courtiers.*]

CORRECTION   Come here, Placebo and Solace,
With your companion Wantonness,
I know well your condition.
For enticing King Humanity
To receive Sensuality
You must suffer punition!

WANTONNESS   We grant, my Lord, we have done ill;
Therefore we put us in your will,
But we have been abused!

PLACEBO   For in good faith, sir, we believed
That lechery had no man grieved
Because it was so used!

SOLACE   Sir, we shall mend our condition
So you give us remission . . .
But give us leave to sing,
To dance, to play at chess and tables,
To read stories and merry fables
For pleasure of our King!

CORRECTION   See that you do no other crime!
You shall be pardoned at this time;
For why? As I suppose,
Princes may sometimes seek solace
With mirth and lawful merriness,
Their spirits to rejoice.
And right so hawking and hunting
Are honest pastimes for a king,
Into the time of peace;
And learn to run a heavy spear,
That he into the time of war

[74] From.   [75] Without.   [76] Thirst.

The Satire of the Three Estates   113

May follow at the chase!

KING Where is Sapience and Discretion?
And why comes not Devotion near?

VERITY They three were Flattery and Deceit,
And Falsehood, that unhappy loon,
Against us three that made debate,
And banished us from town to town.

CHASTITY They made us two fall in a swoon,
When they us lockèd in the stocks.
That dastard knave, Discretion,
Full thefteously did steal your box!

KING The Devil take them, since they are gone!
I make a vow to sweet Saint Fillan,
When I them find they'll bear their paiks.[77]
I see they have playèd me the glaiks![78]
Good Counsel, now show me the best,
How I shall keep my realm in rest.

GOOD COUNSEL The principal point, sir, of a
king's office,
Is for to do to every man justice,
And for to mix his justice with mercy,
Without rigour, favour or partiality.
Who guide them well, they win immortal fame;
Who the countrair, they get perpetual shame.
The Chronicles to know, I you exhort;

There shall you find both good and evil report;
For every prince, after his quality,
Though he be dead, his deeds shall never die!
Sir, if you please for to use my counsel,
Your fame and name shall be perpetual.
[*A fanfare.*]

DILIGENCE Hoyez, hoyez, hoyez!
At the command of King Humanity
I warn and charge all members of Parliament,
Both Spiritual State and Temporality,
That to his grace they be obedient
And speed them to the court, incontinent,
In good order, arrayèd royally.
Who is absent or inobedient,
The King's pleasure they shall under-lie!
[*To the audience*]
Also I make you exhortation,
Since you have heard the first part of our play,
Go, take a drink, and make collation;
Each man drink to his marrow, I you pray.
Tarry not long, it is late in the day.
Let some drink ale, and some drink claret wine;
By great doctors of physic I hear say
That mighty drink comforts the dull ingyne![79]
[*Music, a march. All go off.*]

Part Two

Fanfare. Diligence comes on to the empty stage as if to make a proclamation. Before he can do so, the Poor Man enters, addressing the audience.

POOR MAN Of your alms, good folk, for God's
love of heaven,
For I have motherless bairns either six or seven!
If you'll give me no good, for the love of Jesus,
Show me the right way to St. Andrews.

DILIGENCE Where have we gotten this goodly
companion?
Swift! Forth of the field, thou false, ragged
loon!
Officers, come chase this carl away,
Or deil a word you'll get more of our play!
[*The Poor Man climbs on to the King's throne.*]
Come down, or by God's crown, false loon I

shall slay thee!

POOR MAN Now swear by thy burnt shins, the
devil ding[80] them from you!

DILIGENCE Quick, beggar bogle, haste thee away,
Thou art over pert to spoil our play!

POOR MAN I will give for your play not a sow's
fart
For there is right little play at my hungry heart!

DILIGENCE What devil ails this crooked carl?

POOR MAN Marry, meikle sorrow!
I cannot get, though I gasp, to beg not or borrow.

DILIGENCE Where dwells thou, bankrupt, or what
is thine intent?

POOR MAN I dwell into Lothian, a mile from
Tranent.

DILIGENCE Where would thou be, carl? The

---

[77] Punishment.   [78] Deception.

[79] Intellect.   [80] Strike.

sooth to me show!

POOR MAN   Sir, even to St. Andrews, for to seek law.

DILIGENCE   For to seek law, in Edinburgh is the nearest way.

POOR MAN   Sir, I sought law there this many a dear day;

But I could get none at Session or Senate,

Therefore the meikle dumb devil drown all that menyie![81]

DILIGENCE   Show me thy matter, man, with all the circumstance,

How thou has happenèd on this unhappy chance.

POOR MAN   Good man, will you give me of your charity

And I shall declare you the black verity?

My father was an old man with grey hair

And was of age four score of years and more,

And Maud my mother was four score and fifteen;

And with my labour I did them both sustain.

We had a mare that carried salt and coal,

And every year she brought us home a foal.

We had three kye[82] that were both fat and fair,

None tidier hence to the town of Ayr.

My father was so weak of blood and bone,

That he died, wherefore my mother made great moan,

Then she died within a day or two,

And there began my poverty and woe.

Our good grey mare was grazing on the field

And our land's laird took her for his hire-yield.[83]

Our vicar took the best cow by the head

Incontinent, when my father was dead.

And when the vicar heard tell how that my mother

Was dead, from hand he took from me another.

Then Meg my wife did mourn both even and morrow

Till at the last she died for very sorrow.

And when the vicar heard tell my wife was dead,

The third cow he cleekèd[84] by the head.

Their hindmost clothes, that were of rapploch[85] grey,

The vicar made his clerk bear them away.

When all was gone I might make no debate,

But with my bairns passed for to beg my meat.

Now I have told you the black verity

How I am brought into this misery.

DILIGENCE   How did the Parson? Was he not thy good friend?

POOR MAN   The devil stick him, he cursed me for my teind[86]

And holds me yet under that same process

That caused me lack the Sacrament at Pace.[87]

In good faith, sir, though you would cut my throat,

I have no gear except one English groat

Which I propose to give a man of law.

DILIGENCE   Thou art the daftest fool that ever I saw!

Trows thou, man, by the law, to get remede

Of men of Church? No, never till thou be dead!

Be sure of priests thou wilt get no support.

POOR MAN   If that be true, the fiend receive the sort!

So, since I see I get no other grace,

I will lie down and rest me in this place.

[*He does so. Enter Pardoner, who is Flattery in his disguise.*]

PARDONER   Bona dies, bona dies!

Devout people, good day I say you,

Now tarry a little while I pray you

Till I be with you known!

Wot you well how I am named?

A noble man and undefamed,

If all the sooth were shown.

I am Sir Robert Rome-raker,

A perfect public pardoner

Admitted by the Pope.

Sirs, I shall show you, for my wage,

My pardons and my pilgrimage,

Which you shall see and grope.

I give to the devil with good intent

This woeful wicked New Testament,

With them that it translated.

Since laymen knew the verity,

Pardoners get no charity

Without that they debate it.

Deil fell the brain that has it wrought,

So fall them that the Book home brought,

[81] Pack.   [82] Cattle.   [83] A fine.
[84] Caught.   [85] Coarse cloth.

[86] Tithe.   [87] Easter.

Also I pray to the Rood
That Martin Luther, that false loon,
Black Bullenger and Melancthon
Had been smoored in their cude.[88]
By Him that bare the crown of thorn
I would Saint Paul had never been born,
Also I would his books
Were never read into the Kirk
But among friars into the mirk[89]
Or riven among the rooks!
My patent pardons you may see
Come from the Khan of Tartary
Well sealed with oyster shells.
Though you have no contrition
You shall have full remission
With help of books and bells.
Here is a relic, long and broad,
Of Finn MacColl[90] the right jaw blade
With teeth and all together.
Of Colin's cow here is a horn
For eating of MacConnel's corn
Was slain into Balquhidder.
Here is a cord both great and long,
Which hangèd Johnnie the Armstrong,
Of good hemp soft and sound.
Good holy people, I stand for'ard,
Whoever is hangèd with this cord
Needs never to be drowned!
Come win the pardon, now let see,
For meal, for malt or for money,
For cock, hen, goose, or grice![91]
Of relics here I have a hunder.
Why come you not? This is a wonder.
I trow you be not wise!
[*The Poor Man wakes up.*]

POOR MAN   What thing was yon that I heard
crack and cry?
I have been dreaming and drivelling of my kye!
With my right hand my whole body I sain,[92]
Saint Bride, Saint Bride, send me my kye again!
[*He sees the Pardoner.*]
I see standing yonder a holy man;
To make me help, let me see if I can!

PARDONER   Come win the pardon, and then I
shall thee sain!

POOR MAN   Will that pardon get me my kye
again?

[88] Smothered in their baptismal gown.
[89] Dark.   [90] A giant.   [91] Pig.   [92] Bless.

PARDONER   Carl, of thy kye I have nothing ado.
Come win my pardon, and kiss my relics too.
[*He blesses him with his relics.*]
Now loose thy purse, and lay down thy offering,
And thou shalt have my pardon even from hand.
Now win the pardon, limmer,[93] or thou art lost!

POOR MAN   My holy father, what will that pardon
cost?

PARDONER   Let see what money thou bearest in
thy bag.

POOR MAN   I have but one groat here bound into
a rag.

PARDONER   Hast thou no other money but one
groat?

POOR MAN   If I have more, sir, come and ripe
my coat!

PARDONER   Give me that groat, man, if thou hast
no more.

POOR MAN   With all my heart, master, lo, take it,
there!
Now let me see your pardon, with your leave.

PARDONER   A thousand year of pardons I thee
give!

POOR MAN   A thousand year? I will not live so
long.
Deliver me it, master, and let me gang!

PARDONER   A thousand year I lay upon thy head,
With *totiens quotiens;* now no longer plead.
Thou hast received thy pardon now already.

POOR MAN   But I can see nothing, sir, by our
Lady!

PARDONER   What craves the carl? Methinks thou
art not wise!

POOR MAN   I crave my groat, or else my merchandise!

PARDONER   I gave thee pardon for a thousand
year!

POOR MAN   How shall I get that pardon? Let me
hear!

PARDONER   Stand still, and I shall tell thee the
whole story!
When thou art dead and gone to Purgatory,
Being condemned to pain a thousand year,
Then shall thy pardon thee relieve but weir![94]
Now be content! You are a marvellous man!

POOR MAN   Shall I get nothing for my groat till
then?

[93] Rascal.   [94] Without doubt.

PARDONER That shalt thou not! I make it to you plain!

[*The Poor Man is now very angry.*]

POOR MAN No? Then, gossip, give me my groat again!

What say you, master? Call you this good reason,
That he should promise me a good pardon,
And here receive my money in this stead,
Then make to me no payment till I be dead?
When I am dead, I know full certainly
My silly soul will pass to Purgatory.
Declare me this! Now God nor Belial bind thee,
When I am there, curst carl, where shall I find thee?
Not into heaven, but rather into hell!
When thou art there, thou cannot help thysel'!

PARDONER Swift! Stand aback! I trow this man be mangit![95]

Thou gets not this groat, though thou should be hangèd!

POOR MAN Give me my groat, well bound into my clout!

Or by God's bread, Robin shall bear a rout!

[*He sets upon the Pardoner and chases him off.*]

DILIGENCE What kind of fooling is this all day?

Swift, smaiks,[96] out of the field, away!
Into a prison put them soon
Then hang them when the play is done!

[*A fanfare and a march. Enter the King, his Courtiers, Divine Correction, the Virtues. The music continues with the speech.*]

Famous people, attend, and you shall see
The Three Estates of this nation,
Come to the court with a strange gravity.
Therefore I make you supplication
Till you have heard our whole narration
To keep silence and be patient I pray you.
Howbeit we speak by adulation
We shall say nothing but the truth, I say you!

[*The Three Estates enter, led by their vices. They are walking backwards, Spirituality led by Flattery, Temporality by Deceit, and Burgesses by Falsehood.*]

WANTONNESS Now, broad benedicite!

What thing is yon that I see?
Look, Solace, my heart!

The Satire of the Three Estates

SOLACE Brother Wantonness, what thinks thou?

Yon are the Three Estates, I trow,
Going backwards!

WANTONNESS Backwards? Backwards? Out! Way-laway!

It is a great shame for them, I say,
Backward to gang.
I trow the King Correction
Must make a reformation,
Ere it be long!
Now let us go and tell the King!
Sir, we have seen a marvellous thing,
By our judgment!
The Three Estates of this region,
Are coming backwards, through this town,
To the Parliament!

KING Backward, backward, how may that be?

Make speed them hastily to me,
In dread that they go wrong!

PLACEBO Sir, I see them yonder coming,

They will be here even from hand,
As fast as they may gang!

GOOD COUNSEL Sir, hold you still and scare them not,

Till you perceive what be their thought,
And see what men them lead.
And let the King Correction
Make a sharp inquisition,
And mark them by the heads!

[*The Estates are singing a chorus made up from words from the following verses.*]

SPIRITUALITY

Gloire, honour, laud, triumph and victory,
Be to your mighty prudent excellence;
Here are we come, all the Estates Three,
Ready to make our due obedience,
At your command with humble observance,
As may pertain to Spirituality,
With counsel of the Temporality.

TEMPORALITY

Sir, you with mighty courage at command
Of your super-excellent Majesty,
Shall make service, both with our heart and hand,
And shall not dread in thy defence to die;
We are content, but doubt, that we may see
That noble, heavenly King Correction,

So he with mercy make punition.

BURGESSES

Sir, we are here your Burgesses and Merchants.
Thanks be to God that we may see your face,
Trusting we may now into divers lands
Convoy our gear with support of your grace;
For now, I trust, we shall get rest and peace,
When mis-doers are with your sword o'er-
    thrown,
Then may loyal merchants live upon their own.

[*The singing ends.*]

KING Welcome to me, my prudent lordës all,
You are my members, suppose I be your head:
Sit down that we may with your just counsel
Against mis-doers find sovereign remede.

CORRECTION My tender friends, I pray you with
  my heart,
Declare to me the thing that I would speir.[97]
What is the cause that you go all backward?
The verity thereof fain would I hear.

BISHOP Sovereign, we have gone so this many
  a year.
Howbeit you think we go undecently,
We think we go right wonder pleasantly.

DILIGENCE Sit down, my lords, into your proper
  places:
Then let the King consider all such cases.
Sit down, Sir Scribe, and sit down Deemster, too
And fence the Court as you were wont to do.
[*Music as The Estates take their places and all
present dispose themselves for a court of en-
quiry.*]

KING My prudent lordës of the Three Estates,
It is our will, above all other thing,
For to reform all those who make debates
Contrair the right, who daily do malign,
And they that do the Common-Weal down-
  thring.[98]
With help and counsel of King Correction,
It is our will for to make punishing,
And plain oppressors put to subjection.

BISHOP What thing is this, sir, that you have
  devised?
Sirs, you have need for to be well advised.
Be not hasty into your execution,
And be not o'er extreme in your punition.

[97] Ask.   [98] Overthrow.

And if you please to do, sir, as we say,
Postpone this Parliament to another day.
For why? The people of this region
Will not endure extreme correction!

CORRECTION Is this the part, my lords, that you
  will take
To make us supportation to correct?
It does appear that you are culpable,
That are not to correction applicable!
Swift, Diligence, go show it is our will,
That every man oppressed give in his bill.

DILIGENCE [*proclaims*] It is the King Correction's
  will
That every man oppressed give in his bill.
[*John the Common-Weal, a sturdy figure in
rags, rushes in.*]

JOHN Out of my way! For God's sake let me
  go!
Tell me again, good master, what you say.

DILIGENCE I warn all that be wrongeously of-
  fended,
Come and complain and they shall be amended.
What is thy name, fellow? That would I feel.

JOHN Forsooth, they call me John the Common-
  Weal.
Good master, I would ask at you one thing—
Where trust you I shall find yon new-made
  King?

DILIGENCE Come over, and I shall show thee to
  his grace.
[*He leads John to the King.*]

JOHN God's benison light in that lucky face!

KING Show me thy name, good man, I thee
  command.

JOHN Marry, John the Common-Weal of fair
  Scotland.
[*The King surveys John's rags.*]

KING The Common-Weal has been among his
  foes.

JOHN Yes, sir, that makes the Common-Weal
  want clothes!

KING What is the cause the Common-Weal is
  crookèd?

JOHN Because the Common-Weal has been
  o'er lookèd.

KING What makes thee look so with a dreary
  heart?

JOHN Because the Three Estates go all backward.

SIR DAVID LYNDSAY

KING   Sir Common-Weal, know you the limmers
    that them lead?

JOHN   Their canker colours, I know them by the
    heads!

As for our reverend fathers of Spirituality,

They are led by Flattery and careless Sensuality,

And as you see, Temporality has need of correction,

Who has long time been led by public oppression.

Lo, here is Falsehood, and Deceit well I ken,

Leaders of the Merchants and silly craftsmen.

What marvel though the Three Estates backward gang,

When such a vile company dwells them among,

Which has ruled this rout many dear days,

Which makes John the Common-Weal lack his
warm clothes?

Thou feignèd Flattery, the fiend fart in thy face!

When you were guider of the court we got
little grace!

My sovereign Lord Correction, I make you supplication,

Put these tried trickers from Christ's congregation!

CORRECTION   As you have devised, but doubt it
shall be done!

Come here, my sergeants, and do your debt
soon!

Put these three robbers into prison strong,

Howbeit you should hang them, you do them
no wrong!

FIRST SERGEANT   Sovereign lord, we shall obey
your commands.

Brother, upon these scoundrels lay on your
hands!

SECOND SERGEANT   Come here, gossip, come here,
come here!

Your reckless life you shall repent.

When were you wont to be so sweir?[99]

Stand still and be obedient!

[*The Sergeants hustle the Three Vices to the
stocks.*]

Put in your legs into the stocks,

For you had never meeter hose!

These stewats stink as they were brocks!

Now are you siccar,[100] I suppose!

[*They go to Correction.*]

My lord, we have done your commands.

Shall we put the ladies in captivity?

CORRECTION   Yea, hardly lay on them your hands!

Right so upon Sensuality.

[*Sensuality turns to the Bishop.*]

SENSUALITY   Adieu, my lord!

BISHOP   Adieu, my own sweet heart!

Now grief fall me that we two must part!

SENSUALITY   My lord, howbeit this parting does
me pain.

[*The sergeants chase Sensuality and her retinue
away to a place among the common people at
the foot of the stage.*]

LORD   My lords, you know the Three Estates,

For Common-Weal should make debates.

Let now among us be devised

Such acts as by good men be praised;

And for to save us from murmell,[101]

Soon, Diligence, fetch us Good Counsel!

For why? He is a man that knows

Both the Canon and the Civil Laws.

[*Diligence passes to Good Counsel.*]

DILIGENCE   Father, you must incontinent

Pass to the Lords of Parliament;

For why? They are determined all

To do nothing without counsel.

GOOD COUNSEL   My lords, God glad the company!

What is the cause you send for me?

MERCHANT   Sit down and give us your counsel,

How we shall slaik[102] the great murmell

Of poor people, that is well known

And as the Common-Weal has shown.

And as we know it is the King's will

That good remede be put theretill,

Sir Common-Weal, keep you the bar,

Let none except yourself come near!

[*John lays his hands on the Poor Man.*]

JOHN   You must let this poor creature

Support me for to keep the door.

I know his name full certainly,

He will complain as well as I.

GOOD COUNSEL   My worthy lords, since you have
ta'en on hand

Some reformation to make into this land,

And as you know it is the King his mind

Who to the Common-Weal has aye been kind,

<hr>

[99] Lazy.   [100] Sure.

[101] Complaint.   [102] Abate.

Though reive[103] and theft be stanched well
    enough,
Yet something more belongeth to the plough.
Now into peace you should provide for wars
And be sure of how many thousand spears
The King may be when he has ought to do;
For why, my lords, this is my reason, lo!
The husbandmen and commons they were wont
Go into battle foremost in the front.
But I have lost all my experience
Without you make some better diligence—
The Common-Weal must otherwise be styled
Or by my faith the King will be beguiled!
The poor commons daily as you may see
Decline down to extreme poverty
And are destroyed without God on them rue!

POOR MAN Sir, by God's bread, that tale is very
    true!
It is well known I had both neat and horse,
Now all my gear you see upon my corse.

CORRECTION Ere I depart I think to make an
    order!

JOHN I pray you, sir, begin first at the Border,
For how can we fend us against England,
When we can not, within our native land,
Destroy our own Scots, common traitor thieves,
Who to loyal labourers daily do mischief?
Were I a king, my lord, by God his wounds,
Who'er held common thieves within their
    bounds,
Where through that daily loyal men might be
    wronged,
Without remede these chieftains should be
    hanged!

LORD What other enemies hast thou let us ken?

JOHN Sir, I complain upon the idle men.
For why, sir, it is God's own bidding
All Christian men to work for their living.
This is against the strong beggars,
Fiddlers, pipers and pardoners,
These jugglers, jesters and idle couchers,[104]
These carriers and these quintessencers,
These bauble-bearers and these bards,
These sweir swingeours[105] with lords and lairds.
This is against these great fat friars,
Augustines, Carmelites and Cordelers,

---

103 Pillage. 104 Gamblers. 105 Idle rascals.

And all others that in cowls are clad,
Who labour not and are well fed—
I mean, not labouring spiritually,
Nor for their living corporally.
Lying in dens like idle dogs,
I them compare to well fed hogs!
I think they do themselves abuse,
Seeing that they the world refuse;
Having professed such poverty,
Then fly fast from necessity!

CORRECTION Whom upon more will you com-
    plain?

JOHN Marry, on more and more again!
For the poor man who with care cries
At the misuse of Law's assize.
A petty picking thief is hanged,
But he that all the world has wronged—
A cruel tyrant, a strong transgressor,
A common public plain oppressor—
By bribes may he obtain favours
Of treasures and compositors,
And through laws, consistorial,
Prolix, corrupt and perpetual,
The common people are so put under,
Though they be poor, it is no wonder!

CORRECTION Good John, I grant all that is true;
Your misfortune full sore I rue!
So, my lord Temporality,
I you command in time that ye
Expel oppression off your lands.
Also I say to you merchants,
If ever I find, by land or sea,
Deceit into your company,
Which is to Common-Weal contrair,
I vow to God I shall not spare!
My lords, what say you to this play?

LORD My sovereign lords, we will obey,
And take your part with heart and hand,
Whatever you please us to command.
But we beseech you, sovereign,
Of all our crimes that are by-gone,
To give us a remission,
And here we make to you condition
The Common-Weal for to defend,
From henceforth to our lives end!

CORRECTION On that condition I am content
To pardon you since you repent—
The Common-Weal take by the hand

And make with him perpetual band!

[*The Lords and the Burgesses receive John the Common-Weal.*]

John, have you any more debates
Against my lords, the Spiritual Estates?

JOHN   No, sir, I dare not speak the sooth—
Who plains on priests gets little ruth!

CORRECTION   Flyte[105a] on thy foe, fool, I desire thee,
So that you show but the verity!

JOHN   Gramercy, then I shall not spare,
First to complain on our vicar.
The poor cottar being like to die,
Having small infants two or three,
And has two kye [105b] withouten more,
The vicar must have one of them,
With the grey coat that haps[106] the bed,
Howbeit the wife be poorly clad!
And if the wife die on the morn,
Though all the bairns should be forlorn,
The other cow he cleeks[107] away,
With the poor coat of raploch grey.
Would God this custom were put down,
Which was never founded by reason!

LORD   Are all these tales true that thou tells?

POOR MAN   True, sir, the devil stick me else!
For by the Holy Trinity,
The same was practisèd on me!

[*John singles out the Parson.*]

JOHN   Our parson here he takes no other pyne
But to receive his teinds and spend them syne![108]

POOR MAN   Our bishops with their surplices of white,
They flow in riches royally and delight;
Like paradise are their palaces and places,
And lack no pleasure of the fairest faces!
No doubt I would think it a pleasant life
Aye when I list to part me from my wife
They take another of far greater beauty.
But ever alas, my lords, that may not be,
For I am bound, alas, in marriage,
But they like rams run rudely in their rage!

PARSON   Thou lies, false whoreson ragged loon!
There are no priests in all this town
That ever used such vicious crafts!

105a Rage.   105b Cattle.   106 Covers.
107 Catches.   108 Then.

BISHOP [*to Temporality*]   My lords, why do you thole[109] that lurdan loon
Of Churchmen to speak such detraction?
Yon villain puts me out of charity!

LORD   Why, my lord, says he aught but verity?
You cannot stop a poor man for to plain!

BISHOP   I will not suffer such words of yon villain!

POOR MAN   Then make give me my three fat kye again!

BISHOP   False carl, to speak to me stands thou not awe?

POOR MAN   The fiend receive them that first devised that law!
Within an hour after my dad was dead
The vicar had my cow hard by the head!

PARSON   False whoreson carl, I say that law is good,
Because it has been long our consuetude!

POOR MAN   When I am Pope, that law I shall put down!
It is a sore law for the poor common!

BISHOP   I make a vow these words thou shalt repent!

GOOD COUNSEL   I you require, my lords, be patient!
We came not here for disputations:
We came to make good reformations!

MERCHANT   My lords, conclude that all the temporal lands
Be set in feu to labourers with their hands,
With restrictions as shall be devised,
That they may live and not to be suppressed,
And when the King does make him for the war,
Let them be ready with harness, bow and spear!
And for myself, my lord, this I conclude.

GOOD COUNSEL   So say we all, your reason is so good!

JOHN   What do ye of the corpse-present and the cow?

BISHOP   We will want nothing that we have in use,
Kirtle nor cow, teind[110] lamb, teind grice[111] nor goose!

LORD   We shall decree here that the King his grace

109 Suffer.   110 Tithe.   111 Pig.

Shall write unto the Pope his Holiness.
With his consent, by proclamation,
Both corpse-present and cow we shall cry
down!

BISHOP To that, my lords, we plainly disassent!
Note that thereof I take an instrument!

LORD My lord, by Him that all the world has
wrought,
We care not whether you consent or not!
You are but one estate and we are two!
Et ubi maior pars ibi tota!

JOHN My lords, you have right prudently con-
cluded!
Attend now how the land is clean denuded
Of gold and silver that daily goes to Rome,
For bribes, more than the rest of Christendom.
Never a penny should go to Rome at all,
No more than did to Peter or to Paul!

MERCHANT We merchants, well I wot, within
our bounds
Have furnished priests ten hundred thousand
pounds
For their finance; none knows as well as we!
Therefore, my lords, devise some remedy!
Sir Simony has made with them a bond
The gold of weight they lead out of the land!

GOOD COUNSEL It is short time since any benefice
Was sped in Rome, except great bishopries.
But now for an unworthy vicarage.
A priest will run to Rome in pilgrimage.
A numbskull who was never at the school
Will run to Rome and keep a bishop's mule,
And then come home with many coloured
crack,
With a burden of benefices on his back—
Which is against the law, one man alone
For to possess more benefices than one.
So I conclude, my lords, and say for me
You should annul all this plurality!
Advise, my lords, what think you to conclude?

LORD Sir, by my faith, I think it very good
That from henceforth no priests shall pass to
Rome.
Because our substance they do still consume.
Also I think it best by my advice
That each priest should have but one benefice.

GOOD COUNSEL Mark well, my lords, there is no
benefice
Given to a man, but for a good office!

Who take office, and then they cannot use it,
Giver and taker, I say, are both abusèd.
A bishop's office is to be a preacher,
And of the Law of God a public teacher.

BISHOP Friend, where find ye that we should
preachers be?

GOOD COUNSEL Look what Saint Paul writes unto
Timothy.
Take there the Book; let see if you can spell!
[*He hands Bible to Bishop.*]

BISHOP I never read that, therefore read it
yoursel'!
[*Bishop casts it away.*]

MERCHANT Then before God, how can you be
excusèd,
To have an office and know not how to use it?
Wherefore were given you all the temporal
lands,
And all these tithes you have among your
hands?
They were given you for other causes, I ween,
Than mumble matins and keep your clothes
clean!
You say to the Apostles that you succeed,
But you show not that into word nor deed!

JOHN King James the First, Roy of this region,
Said David was a sore saint to the crown.
I hear men say that he was something blind,
That gave away more than he left behind.

ABBOT My lord Bishop, I marvel how that ye
Suffer this carl for to speak heresy!
For by my faith, my lord, will you take tent,[112]
Deserves he for to be burnt incontinent!
You cannot say but it is heresy
To speak against our law and liberty!
[*There is a great commotion. The Spiritual
Estates cry, "Burn him!" Correction intervenes
and addresses John.*]

CORRECTION Show forth your faith and feign it
not!
[*John pauses before saying his creed.*]

JOHN I believe in God that all has wrought,
And created every thing of naught;
And in his Son, our Lord Jesu,
Incarnate of the Virgin true;
Who under Pilate tholèd passion,
And died for our salvation;

112 Note.

122   SIR DAVID LYNDSAY

And on the third day rose again,
As Holy Scripture showeth plain.
Also, my Lord, it is well kennd,
How he did to the heaven ascend,
And set him down at the right hand
Of God the Father, I understand,
And shall come judge on Doomesday . . .
What will you more, sir, that I say?

CORRECTION   Show forth the rest: this is no
   game

JOHN   I trow Sanctam Ecclesiam. . . .
But not in their bishops nor their friars!

MERCHANT [*to Correction*]   I think, my lord, if
   good it so appears,
That the King's grace shall give no benefice
But to a preacher that can use that office.
The silly souls that are Christ Jesus' sheep
Should not be given to gourmand wolves to
   keep!
What is the cause of all the heresies
But the abusion of the prelacies?

LORD   We think your counsel is very good,
As you have said we all conclude!

POOR MAN   Oh, my lords, for the Holy Trinity,
Remember to reform the consistory!

PARSON   What cause thou, false robber, for to
   plain ye?

POOR MAN   Therein I happened among a greedy
   menyie![113]
I lent my gossip my mare to fetch home coals
And he her drowned into the quarry holes!
They gave me first a thing they call citandum,
Within eight days I got but libellandum,
Within a month I got ad opponendum,
In half a year I got interloquendum,
And then I got—how call you it?—ad replican-
   dum:
But I could never a word yet understand him!
But ere they came half way to concludendum
The fiend a plack[114] was left for to defend him.
Of pronunciation they made me wonder fain,
But I got never my good grey mare again!

LORD   My lords, we must reform the consistory
   laws,
Whose great defame above the heavens blows!
So that the King's honour we may advance,
We will conclude, as they have done in France.

Let spiritual matters pass to Spirituality,
And temporal matters to Temporality!

[*Verity and Chasity now press their complaint.*]

VERITY   My sovereign, I beseech your excellence,
Use justice on Spirituality,
The which to us has done great violence,
Because we did rehearse the verity;
They put us close into captivity,
So we remained into subjection,
Into languor and calamity
Till we were freed by King Correction.

CHASTITY   My lord, I have great cause for to
   complain,
I could get no lodging into this land;
The Spiritual State had me so at disdain.
With Dame Sensual they have made such a
   bond,
Among them all no friendship, sirs, I found:
And when I came the noble nuns among,
My lusty Lady Prioress from hand,
Out of her dorter dourly she me dang!

CORRECTION   What say you now, my Lady Prior-
   ess?
How have you used your office, can you guess?
What was the cause you refused harboury
To this young lusty Lady Chastity?

PRIORESS [*haughtily*]   I do my office after use
   and wont!
To your Parliament I will make no account!

[*First Sergeant steps forward and pulls her
from among the Spiritual Estates.*]

FIRST SERGEANT   Come on, my Lady Prioress,
We shall learn you to dance,
And that within a little space
A new pavane of France!

[*The Sergeants, in pulling her habit, haul it off
and show a gay dress underneath.*]

SECOND SERGEANT   Now brother, by the Mass,
By my judgment, I think
This holy Prioress
Is turnèd a cow-clink!

PRIORESS   I give my friends my malison,
That me compelled to be a nun,
And would not let me marry!
It was my friendes greediness
That made me be a Prioress,
Now heartily them I wary![115]

---

[113] Pack.   [114] Devil a halfpenny.

[115] Curse.

Howbeit the Nuns sing night and days,
Their heart wots not what their mouth says,
The sooth I you declare,
Making you intimation
To Christes congregation,
Nuns are not necessair!
But I shall do the best I can,
And marry some good honest man,
And brew good ale in tun!
Marriage, by my opinion,
It is better religion,
Than to be friar or nun!
[*Correction now turns to Flattery, who is in the stocks, still disguised as a friar.*]

CORRECTION Sergeant, I counsel you from hand,
Banish yon friar out of this land,
And that incontinent!
Yon flattering knave, without a fable
I think he is not profitable,
I know his false intent!

SERGEANT Come on, Sir friar, and be not fleyit,[116]
The King our master must be obeyed,
But you shall have no harm.
[*He takes Flattery out of the stocks.*]
If you would travel from town to town,
I think this hood and heavy gown
Will keep your wame[117] o'er warm!
[*He pulls off Flattery's habit, so that the motley is revealed.*]

GOOD COUNSEL Sir, by the Holy Trinity,
This same is feignèd Flattery,
I know him by his face!
Believing for to get promotion,
He said his name was Devotion,
And so beguiled your grace!

FLATTERY My lords, for God's sake, let not hang me
Howbeit these widdiefows[118] would wrong me!
I can make no debate
To win my meat at plough or harrows . . .
But I shall help to hang my marrows,
Both Falsehood and Deceit!

CORRECTION Then pass thy way and graith[119] the gallows!
Then help for to hang up thy fellows,

116 Frighted.   117 Belly.
118 Gallows worthy.   119 Rig.

Thou gets no other grace!
[*The gallows are brought in.*]

DECEIT Now Flattery, my old companion,
What does yon King Correction?
Knows thou not his intent?
Declare to us of thy nouvelles!

FLATTERY You'll all be hangèd, I see naught else,
And that incontinent!

DECEIT Now waylaway, will you cause hang us?
The deil brought yon curst King among us,
For meikle sturt and strife!

FLATTERY I had been put to death among you,
Were it not I took in hand to hang you,
And so I saved my life!

CORRECTION With the advice of King Humanity,
Here I determine with ripe advisement,
That all these prelates shall deprivèd be!

KING As you have said, but doubt it shall be!
[*The Courtiers lay hands on the Prelates.*]

WANTONNESS My lords, we pray you to be patient,
For we will do the King's commandement!

BISHOP I make a vow to God, if you us handle
You shall to hell be curst with book and candle!
[*The Spiritual Estate is despoiled.*]
We say the Kings were greater fools than we.
That us promoted to so great dignity!

ABBOT There is a thousand in the Church, but doubt,
Such fools as we, if they were well sought out!
Now brother, since it may no better be,
Let us go sup with Sensuality!
[*They go to Sensuality.*]

SENSUALITY Pass from us, fools, by Him that has us wrought,
You lodge not here, because I know you not!

GOOD COUNSEL [*to Correction*] Ere you depart, sir, off this region,
Give John the Common-Weal a gay garmoun![119a]
Because the Common-Weal has been o'er lookèd,
That is the cause that Common-Weal is crookèd.
With singular profit he has been so suppressed,

119a Garment.

That he is both cold, naked and disguised.

CORRECTION   As you have said, Father, I am
content,
Sergeants, give John a new habilament
Of satin, damask, or of the velvet fine
And give him place into our Parliament syne![119b]
[*Music. They clothe John gorgeously and re-
ceive him into Parliament.*]

ESTATES [*sing*]

Salve, res publica!

POOR MAN   I give you my broad benison,
That has given Common-Weal a gown,
But I beseech you, for All Hallows,
Cause hang Deceit and all his fellows,
And banish Flattery off the town,
For there was never such a loon!
[*The Sergeants take Deceit and Falsehood from
the stocks and lead them to the gallows.*]

FIRST SERGEANT   Come here, Deceit, my com-
panion!
Saw ever a man liker a loon
To hang upon a gallows?

DECEIT   This is enough to make me mangit![119c]
Grief fall me that I must be hanged!
Let me speak with my fellows!
I trow ill-fortune brought me here,
What meikle fiend made me so speedy?
Since it was said, it is seven year,
That I should wave into a widdy.[120]
I learned my masters to be greedy.
Adieu, for I see no remede.
Look what it is to be evil-deedy!

FIRST SERGEANT   Now in this halter slip thy head!
Stand still! Me thinks you draw aback!

DECEIT   Alas, master, you hurt my craig![121]

FIRST SERGEANT   It will hurt better, I would a
plack,
Right now when you hang on the knag![122]

DECEIT   Adieu, my masters, merchant men,
I have you servèd, as you ken
Truly, both air[123] and late!
I say to you, for conclusion,
I dread you go to confusion,
From time you lack Deceit,

I taught you merchants many a wile,
The upland wives for to beguile
Upon a market day;
And make them trust your stuff was good,
When it was rotten, by the Rood,
And swear it was not so!
I was aye whispering in your ear,
And taught you for to ban and swear
What your gear cost in France,
Howbeit the Devil a word was true!
Your craft if King Correction knew,
Would turn you to mischance!
I taught you wiles manifold—
To mix the new wine with the old,
That fashion was not folly!
To sell right dear and buy dirt-cheap,
And mix rye-meal among the soap,
And saffron with oyldolly.[124]
Forget no usury I pray you
More than the Vicar does the cow,
Or lords their double-mail.
Howbeit your ell-wand be too scant,
Or your pound-weight three ounces want,
Think that but little fail!
You young merchants may cry alas
For wanting of your wanted grace,
Yon curst King you may ban!
Had I lived but half a year,
I should have taught you crafts perqueir
To beguile wife and man!

SECOND SERGEANT   Come here, Falsehood, and
grace the gallows!
You must hang up among your fellows,
For your cankered condition!
Many a true man have you wronged,
Therefore but doubt you shall be hanged,
But[125] mercy or remission!

FALSEHOOD   Alas, must I be hangèd too?
What meikle devil is this ado?
How came I to this, cummer?[126]
My good masters, you craftsmen,
Want you Falsehood, full well I ken
You will all die for hunger.
Find me a Webster[127] that is loyal,
Or a Walker[128] that will not steal!
Their craftiness I ken.

119b Then.   119c Deranged.   120 Gallows.
121 Neck.   122 Gallows.   123 Early.

124 Olive oil.   125 Without.   126 Gossip.
127 Weaver.   128 Fuller.

The Satire of the Three Estates

Or a Miller that has no fault,
That will steal neither meal nor malt,
Hold them for holy men!
At our Fleshers take you no grief,
Though they blow lean mutton and beef,
That they seem fat and fair.
I taught Tailors in every town,
To shape five quarters in one gown,
To them I taught that lore!
Adieu, my masters, Wrights and Masons,
I need not teach you any lessons,
You know my craft perqueir!
Adieu, Blacksmiths and Loriners,[129]
Adieu, ye crafty Cordiners,
That sells the shoon o'er dear!
Among craftsmen it is a wonder,
To find ten loyal among a hunder,
The truth I to you tell!
Adieu, I may no longer tarry,
I must pass to the King of Fairy,
Or else straightway to hell!
Farewell, for I am to the widdy[130] wend!
For why? Falsehood made never better end.
[*Deceit and Falsehood are hanged, to a roll of drums.*]

FLATTERY Have I not 'scaped the gallows well?
Yea, that I have, by sweet Saint Gile,
For I had not been wrongit,

129 Saddlers.   130 Gallows.

Because deserved I, by All Hallows,
To have been marshalled with my fellows,
And high above them hanged!
I made far more faults than my mates,
I beguiled all the Three Estates,
With my hypocrisy.
Mark well! My mates the piper pay,
But Flattery slips clean away,
Of all the world I'm free!
[*Music.*]

DILIGENCE Famous people, heartily I you require
This little sport to take in patience.
We trust in God, if we live another year,
Where we have failed, we shall do diligence,
With more pleasure to make you recompense,
Because we have been some part tedious,
With matter rude, denude of eloquence,
Likewise, perchance, to some men odious.
Now let each man his way advance!
Let some go drink, and some go dance!
Minstrels, blow up a brawl of France!
Let see who hobbles best!
For I will run, incontinent,
To the tavern, ere ever I stent.[131]
I pray to God omnipotent,
To send you all good rest!
[*Music. A dance, followed by a march, during which exeunt omnes.*]

131 Stop.

ONE ELEMENT of the Morality Play which is likely to alienate modern audiences is its heavy dependence on allegory; our predispositions lead us to eschew, to tolerate, or to accept willingly its personified abstractions.

How could these old plays manage it to be so dry and tuneless, with human life in its richness and sweetness all about them? It must be because in these is committed the cardinal sin of literature,—the forsaking of the concrete for the abstract. The magnificent criminals, as always, go scot-free. Spenser and Bunyan range the world at will. But these petty offenders, the Morality authors, must feel the weight of our just indignation. They have bored us, their

gentle readers, who are not personified qualities nor any fashion of psychological figments, but human beings, living creatures, responding with sympathetic comprehension to Joseph, to Balaam, even to their asses [in the Miracle Plays], as we can never respond to Mundus and Studious Desire and Honest Recreation. The Moralities, as a rule, are successful only in failure. When the abstract blunders into the concrete, when the moral play clumsily slips over into

SIR DAVID LYNDSAY

human comedy or tragedy, it is possible to become interested. [Katharine Lee Bates, *The English Religious Drama*, The Macmillan Company, New York, 1893, p. 202.]

The morality was not, perhaps, quite such an arid type of drama as might be supposed, especially after the dramatists learnt, instead of leaving humanity as a dry bone of contention between the good and evil powers, to adopt a biographic mode of treatment, and thus to introduce the interest of growth and development. [E. K. Chambers, *The Medieval Stage*, Oxford University Press, New York, 1903, vol. 2, p. 201.]

The accepted premise beneath all such views [as that typical of the nineteenth century, in which drama suddenly became interesting with Marlowe's discoveries of dramatic "character"] is that with the Renaissance "interest in character," an old order passed, and abruptly. In dealing with the morality-play, the interlude, and the subsequent history-play we assume nearly the opposite. In the Morality—a field of reading for the most part admittedly and unrelievedly dull—we assume that we are already dealing with the making of Elizabethan patterns, and that that lends interest to medieval matters which might otherwise appear remote and dramatically dead. For what might be called "the Morality habit-of-mind" is a medieval heritage of the first importance to the understanding of the Elizabethan drama. . . .

To see Moralities only as the contest or warfare or duels of abstractions is indeed to make them "colourless": it is not to *see* them at all. As with the crudities of language in the Miracles, one must remember that these things were made to be *shown,* not read. . . . In the Morality it is easy to stick on the allegoric plane, oblivious to the original effect, viz. of real people "in modern dress" going through a complicated plot, the meaning of which was partly left for the audience to see.

It was this particular characteristic of the Morality which fathered the Elizabethan taste for seeking "applications": that is, morals and topic references together, preferably of course of a "confidential" sort. . . .

To our unromantic ancestors, didacticism was itself an attraction. The allegoric method had, however, far more subtle possibilities. It is easy to see how the contemporaneity of presentation made immediate room in the Morality for satire and social criticism; for something like the real-life scent is presented, *and* in a play whose business (if it has a moral) is *judging* the ways of the people it presents. . . .

But allegory can be of at least two distinct kinds. In one—which is the kind you immediately think of if allegory bores you—a prefabricated and preformulated code is naively demonstrated to be the right one, by an action predetermined to that end; and you may very reasonably object that life is not quite so simple as all that, nor the distinctions made by the code so infallibly distinct. But if one follows the development of the "allegorical tendency" from Roman to Roman Catholic civilization, as examined in C. S. Lewis's *Allegory of Love,* the personification of abstractions, to which the era of th*e Roman de la Rose,* the preachers and the Moralities seems so unreasonably addicted, appears in a very different light. It appears as nothing less than an instrument in the process of the evolution of self-awareness; and in that process the discovery of visualized (or visualizable) projections of mental events or states clearly played a major part. For some purposes the half-evanished Roman deities provided a "form" under which the mind could literally "see itself": as its own Mars (*Ira* or Anger) or Venus (*Voluptas*), or its own conflict as a war, a duel or a siege. This is approximately half-way between our modern capacity to think quite abstractly of abstracts ("desire" in "conflict" with "fear," or simply "conflict" as such) and the primitive limitation of being able only to "think" in terms of affecting or afflicting gods or spirits, each a pseudo-human superhuman. . . . The mitigated monotheism of a Christianity which (for untheological minds) starts with three gods and a goddess and includes steadily-increasing armies of sub-divinities—to say nothing of the hierarchies of the anti-gods—was very near to the paganism in which the separate divinities had come to be regarded as limited or localized and subjected to Fate or to a Jupiter whose functions

The Satire of the Three Estates

were not easy to distinguish from those of Fate. Simultaneously, the European mind becomes increasingly aware of the divided will: the *bellum intestinum* or war of the mind within itself, about which both Stoic and Christian use the same metaphors. . . . Here C. S. Lewis misses the interplay of "planes" when he complains of the absurd contradictions involved in presenting the *triumph* of Humility or the *vengeance* of Mercy. The battles or sieges with their crushings, revenges, and subsequent triumphs merely represent the *superiority,* on a moral and abstract plane, which the trial-by-arms allegorizes. The victory is only an image of a "betterness" in the mind, and unless a reference is evoked there, the morality fails of its moral effect. . . .

[An important point] is that made by T. S. Eliot in a brief but brilliant digression on allegory in his essay on Dante. Not thinking of allegoric drama at all, still less of pictures, he there remarks how allegory demands clear visual images, and that what we must consider is "the type of mind which by nature and *practice* tended to express itself in allegory." He adds: "Clear visual images are given much more intensity by having a meaning—we do not need to know what the meaning is, but in our awareness of the image we must be aware that the meaning is there too." . . . I take this to be relevant to the kind of allegory which became the common currency of the medieval world *because* it showed (made seeable) the mind to itself: *because* its "sensual and carnal emotion" was a picture-thinking, often in visions, deeper than what we commonly think of as "thought."

When it is effective, thinking or contemplation is itself visual: there is an intuitive apprehension of significances, rather than an intellectual decoding. Indeed, intellectual formulation may be difficult or impossible; or at least seems crude, tentative, and unsatisfying. We substitute a plotting of marks on a moral target for the jab and rip of the bullet.

I would not for a moment suggest that any Morality-play is capable of stirring that "certain carnal reverence." But that was, I believe, what they were meant to do. They appear towards the fag-end of the preaching-tradition, and much of their allegory is stereotype, lacking the vitality of the genuine *apprehensive* thing; so that whereas the Totentanz pictures, or Bruegel's engravings of the Deadly Sins, still give a taste of the original sting, the appeal of Moralities to their audiences, which apparently preferred them to miracle-plays, seems mysterious. Possibly one reason for it was that the authors were committed to the devising of a plot, the changes in which could not be foregone conclusions like those of a Bible-story. For the rest, there was the appeal of the "doubleness" of the action, which often involves seeing through the equivocation of appearances: as, for instance, in following the tricks of plausible vices, engaged by their rascality, but *morally* certain that the pot must go too often to the well, that pride goes before a fall, that fine feathers don't make fine birds—or some other such evergreen platitude. [A. P. Rossiter, *English Drama from Early Times to the Elizabethans,* Hutchinson's University Library, London, 1950, pp. 80–90.]

Lyndsay's play, written in a period of transition, reflects the intellectual milieu in its mixed tones and purposes as well as in its subject matter. Nevertheless, it belongs to the Morality type rather than to the more limited Interlude, and its links with earlier Moralities should not be ignored.

By the earlier sixteenth century the writing of plays was getting into the hands of the kind of educated layman who was produced by the grammar-schools. . . . We may find their fun crude; but where they touch the ethic of the

New Learning, or propagand naively for Education—still more when these themes get involved with the inky wars of the Reformation—it is an error to measure their importance only by aesthetic standards. The issues they debate

SIR DAVID LYNDSAY

are the foundations of the Elizabethan world and, in many ways, of our own. The old fideistic moulds were cracking, and in the dramatic confusion of the century between Medwall and Marlowe (c. 1493–1593) the play-of-abstractions is part of the struggle to establish new ones, to arrive at values applicable to the individual life, to man as subject in a state, and as member of a church no longer integrated in an authoritarian and indivisible Christendom.

Looked at this way, the dull or naive "educational" Moralities stand for the voice of the "new men"; the common-lawyers, financiers, civil servants (laymen or Erastian clergy), and schoolmasters who were coming to have a "stake in the country." The opposition of an "old" learning to the "New" leads logically to the state of things where Idleness, the vice in *The Marriage of Wit and Wisdom* (printed 1579) is a *priest*; but in an earlier stage, idleness and ignorance are pilloried simply as bars to sound learning, taken to be good in itself. The old model of the assault of the frailties on man-the-frail serves the new turns of propaganding for the New Learning, of teaching things which the New Learning thought important (e.g., geography and, later on, history), and of allegorizing "the struggle for knowledge" as an analogy to the old battle of the Soul against worldly temptations. The results often look to us as if written for the problem-children of backward actors who could only be taught "the play-way." [Rossiter, *op. cit.*, pp. 105–106.]

The Vice was becoming an established institution for the sake of diversion and as an end in itself. Low comicality was perhaps the most active agency in the degeneration of the morality play, so that the more serious and intellectual purposes of the moral interludes suffered; and yet, as we all know, the Elizabethan drama itself could stand an inordinate amount of buffoonery. The Renaissance had brought with it a new interest in the here and now and that in turn had replaced contemplation of the hereafter and the glorious history of the religious past. There was some change from the spiritual to the ethical, perhaps, and still more from the religious to the secular, but one must not urge on the sixteenth century too fast nor judge the people of the age solely by their most advanced thinkers. Controversy, political and religious, also diverted the morality from its main channel. . . . But *A Satire of the Three Estates* . . . in spite of its great variety of interests, is still a full-scope moral play that still devotes itself to the "commendation of vertew and the vituperation of vyce." [Hardin Craig, *English Religious Drama of the Middle Ages*, Oxford University Press, New York, 1955, pp. 380–381.]

There remains the question of the play's artistic achievement: whether, as a Morality Play, it is necessarily inept; or whether, because a Morality Play, it is only relatively successful; or whether it perhaps manages some aesthetic achievement in its own right and shares a certain significance in the development of English drama.

Even Lyndsay's *Satyre of the Thrie Estaitis*, estimable as it is for its earnest advocacy of reform in Church and state, is hardly attractive reading. . . . Lyndsay's dramatic satire is distinctly political, a keen and insistent, if not melodious, voice of the Scottish Reformation. King Humanity, after much wavering between the Virtues and the Vices, gives audience to the Three Estates and a Reform bill is presented. [Bates, *op. cit.*, p. 233.]

Sir David Lindsay's "Satire of the Three Estates" . . . is a poem which stands quite apart from the line of English stage progress by reason of its uncouth irregularity of form, and still more by its restriction to the Scots dialect and the social and political milieu of Edinburgh. Yet its imposing bulk and weight of thought, its boldness in meeting empirically the unsolved problems of histrionic presentation, and the neatness with which it offers commentary and contrast to such works as "Magnificence," "Respublica," "The Three Laws," and "King Johan," make it an important document in the history of even the southern British drama. . . .

It is necessary to turn back to "The Castle of Perseverance" to find in English drama any parallel to the tremendous scope of this play with its two hundred solid pages of verse, its equal appeal to the whole range of contemporary society from king to peasant, and that grand mediaeval leisureliness and simplicity which give it courage to attack the entire visible fabric of life from the highest problems of morality and government to the lowest reaches of profane wit. . . . The theatre is the "play-field" out of doors, the spectators make up the entire population, and the actors number at least forty. . . .

It is interesting to contrast the structure of this Scottish work with that of the only English moral plays of the century which at all approach it in length and satiric purpose—Skelton's "Magnificence" and Bale's "Three Laws." While Skelton, by sticking doggedly to the thin and inadequate frame of the interlude, has made his poem, however dull and over-weighted, a regular and, technically, even a rather admirable example of morality architecture; and while Bale introduces from classic act and scene division the support which he needed for his ambitious satire, Lindsay ignores equally the old and the new dramatic models, and wins attention by sheer force of intellect and unreasoned brilliance of execution. Independent farcical dialogues, or "interludes," as long and as non-moral as those of Heywood, are inserted at will in the intervals between the sections of a flagellation of ecclesiastical hypocrisy and greed more violent even than Bale's; and the long work wanders on with only a thin thread of story and with no observable law of growth. Yet "The Satire of the Three Estates" is a more readable play than either "Magnificence" or "The Three Laws." The very frankness of its irregularity disarms criticism and

piques the attention; and the photographic sincerity of all its pictures, whether of clownish turbulence or aristocratic vice, largely justifies the inclusion of each and goes far to keep the varied elements from clashing.

Lindsay had good reason to entitle his work as he did. It is as satire rather than as drama that it gains its effects; and it traces its literary ancestry, not through the sequence of the moral plays, but by way of the satiric dialogues of Dunbar, back to the art form of Langland. [C. F. Tucker Brooke, *The Tudor Drama*, Houghton Mifflin Company, Boston, 1911, pp. 88–92.]

From the medley of metres in the *Satire of the Three Estates* one must conclude that Sir David Lindsay was conscious of his prosodic materials almost to excess. Refinement is exquisite in the application of metres if not in the details of their construction. Nor is the verse bad: it is surprisingly better than that of nearly all other interludes, including those written by others of the learned professions. The various forms of poetry are used with a purpose and a method superior to that of the English playwrights—writers of interludes—who preceded and who followed him. Fifteen hundred and thirty-five was still early in the age of the interlude . . . and the *Satire* is in many ways its apogee. The ever-changing metres must have taxed the author considerably, for he knew he must nourish his behemoth on a variety of fare. It is difficult to praise this work too much, for its length set many obstacles; and that its verse continues always to be interesting in its manifold variations, each not only equal but superior to the work of contemporaries in the field, contributes to make it the bipartite *Faust* among interludes. Like Goethe, the similarly versatile Sir David was thoroughly awake to his versification, and he became a master of it. [J. E. Bernard, Jr., *The Prosody of the Tudor Interlude*, Yale Studies in English, vol. 90, Yale University Press, New Haven, Conn., 1939, pp. 76–77.]

One important thing about the "whole-life" Morality is that . . . it does provide an approximate first-idea of the kind of play which was later entitled "The Life and Death of X." . . .

In *Everyman* . . . it is obvious that [a single morality sequence] has been shaped to a unitary play of some 900 lines' length. . . . The tight-woven treatment of Holy Dying, where the way to salvation is allegorized as a journey on which Everyman finds the worth of Good-deed and the vanity of Good-fellowship, Kindred and Goods, may seem at first sight "seraphically free from taint of personality." But its grave concentration, no less than its earnestness on priesthood, are really the marks of an individual mind, not those of the Morality. It is quite untypical in far more besides the lack of Vices, devils, battery, squibs, and jocularities; and if for its time (*ante* 1495?) it is a highly artistic achievement, it must also be said that it is an artistic cul-de-sac. It could be repeated in the stronger words of a Marlowe or a Tourneur: it could not serve as germ for further growth.

With *The Castle of Perseverance* it is otherwise. It may—it does—demand a wealth of the virtue it names. Not one episode in its sprawling bulk is worthy to be set beside Everyman's "recognition" (*anagnorisis*) of God's "myghty messengere." Yet it has one great potentiality.

It is—what no previous play had been—a potential frame for a life-story: not of mankind as *Humanum Genus,* but the human-kind as revealed in One Man. . . .

Moreover, the *Castle* has a plotted action, and one concerned with a conflict whose result the audience must go on awaiting. . . .

The Morality-writer had to have a plot. His moral gave a point towards which his action must point, and in that way *débat* was slowly urged towards logic-of-events: which is true plot. For unless a "fable" *is* an argument, the structure is episodic and lacks true form. Here, in time, the "whole-life" kind of Morality was to lead to better things: through the handling of what at all events *purported* to be "real-life" stories by ordering them on a moral framework —or "frame-up," as you may prefer to call it . . . The Morality not only got at the dramatic essential of protracted conflict in a world of jarring wills, but also arrived at one of the simple formulae for play-making. It is put well enough by Dryden: "Tis the moral that directs the whole action of the play to one centre; and that action or fable is the example built upon the moral, which confirms the truth of it to our experience." [Rossiter, *op. cit.,* pp. 96–100.]

The Satire of the Three Estates

BEN JONSON

1572–1637

Jonson is so often associated with neoclassicism that it is easy to overemphasize this aspect of his work. The details of his life poorly support the picture of an arid classicist. Removed from Westminster School to be apprenticed in his stepfather's trade of bricklayer, Jonson received no university training. As a soldier in Flanders he killed a foe in single combat; later, in England, he killed an actor in a duel. He was jailed three times (once voluntarily). And his plays clearly reflect Jonson's knowledge of the boisterous London of his time. This is not to deny that Jonson was steeped in classical learning, although the accusation of "dryness" probably stems not so much from this characteristic as from his detachment and lack of sentiment. He approached the writing of drama as a serious social critic and conscientious artist, reacting against his contemporaries' romantic extravagance and slipshod carelessness in the handling of plot, character, and setting. He endeavored to observe the Unities, and his characters always remain close to the limited types of the Comedy of Humours. In writing satiric comedy, which was his forte, Jonson set himself the task of presenting, as he put it in the Prologue to Every Man In His Humour,

> *deeds and language, such as men do use;*
> *And persons such as Comedy would choose,*
> *When she would show an image of the times,*
> *And sport with human follies, not with crimes.*

Jonson was not always able to avoid crimes in his plays, but he succeeded admirably in furnishing an "image of the times." The Alchemist *(1610) is concerned with a favorite confidence game of the period, but the motives and techniques portrayed are sufficiently universal that it is not difficult to see in the play something very like the "scientific" swindles of only yesterday—or of today.*

ARGUMENT

T he sickness hot, a master quit, for fear,
H is house in town, and left one servant there;
E ase him corrupted, and gave means to know

A Cheater and his punk; who now brought low,
L eaving their narrow practice, were become
C ozeners at large; and only wanting some
H ouse to set up, with him they here contract,
E ach for a share, and all begin to act.
M uch company they draw, and much abuse,
I n casting figures, telling fortunes, news,
S elling of flies,[1] flat bawdry with the stone,
T ill it, and they, and all in fume are gone.

[1] Familiar spirits.

The Alchemist

A COMEDY IN FIVE ACTS

Characters

SUBTLE *the alchemist*

FACE *the house-keeper*

DOL COMMON *their colleague*

DAPPER *a lawyer's clerk*

DRUGGER *a tobacco-man*

LOVEWIT *master of the house*

SIR EPICURE MAMMON *a knight*

PERTINAX SURLY *a gamester*

TRIBULATION WHOLESOME *a pastor of Amsterdam*

ANANIAS *a deacon there*

KASTRIL *the angry boy*

DAME PLIANT *Kastril's sister, a widow*

NEIGHBOURS

OFFICERS, ATTENDANTS, AND OTHERS

The action of the play takes place in London.

Prologue

Fortune, that favours fools, these two short hours
We wish away, both for your sakes and ours,
Judging spectators; and desire, in place,
To th'author justice, to ourselves but grace.
Our scene is London, 'cause we would make known,
No country's mirth is better than our own:
No clime breeds better matter for your whore,
Bawd, squire, impostor, many persons more,
Whose manners, now called humours, feed the stage;
And which have still been subject for the rage
Or spleen of comic writers. Though this pen
Did never aim to grieve, but better men;
Howe'er the age he lives in doth endure
The vices that she breeds, above their cure.
But when the wholesome remedies are sweet,
And in their working gain and profit meet,
He hopes to find no spirit so much diseased,
But will with such fair correctives be pleased:
For here he doth not fear who can apply.
If there be any that will sit so nigh
Unto the stream, to look what it doth run,
They shall find things, they'd think or wish were done;
They are so natural follies, but so shown,
As even the doers may see, and yet not own.

Act One

SCENE ONE

A room in Lovewit's house. Enter Face, in a captain's uniform, with his sword drawn, and Subtle with a vial, quarrelling, and followed by Dol Common.

FACE Believe't, I will.

SUBTLE Thy worst. I fart at thee.

DOL Have you your wits? why gentlemen! for love—

FACE Sirrah, I'll strip you—

SUBTLE What to do? lick figs
Out at my—

FACE Rogue, rogue!—out of all your sleights.

DOL Nay, look ye, sovereign, general, are you madmen?

SUBTLE O, let the wild sheep loose. I'll gum your silks
With good strong water, an you come.

DOL Will you have
The neighbours hear you? will you betray all?
Hark! I hear somebody.

FACE Sirrah—

SUBTLE I shall mar
All that the tailor has made if you approach.

FACE You most notorious whelp, you insolent slave,
Dare you do this?

SUBTLE Yes, faith; yes, faith.

FACE Why, who
Am I, my mungrel, who am I?

SUBTLE I'll tell you,
Since you know not yourself.

FACE Speak lower, rogue.

SUBTLE Yes, you were once (time's not long past) the good,
Honest, plain, livery-three-pound-thrum, that kept
Your master's worship's house here in the Friers,
For the vacations—

FACE Will you be so loud?

SUBTLE Since, by my means, translated suburb-captain.

FACE By your means, doctor dog!

SUBTLE Within man's memory,
All this I speak of.

FACE Why, I pray you, have I
Been countenanced by you, or you by me?
Do but collect, sir, where I met you first.

SUBTLE I do not hear well.

FACE Not of this, I think it.
But I shall put you in mind, sir;—at Pie-corner,
Taking your meal of steam in, from cooks' stalls
Where, like the father of hunger, you did walk
Piteously costive, with your pinched-horn-nose,
And your complexion of the Roman wash,
Stuck full of black and melancholic worms,
Like powder-corns shot at the artillery-yard.

SUBTLE I wish you could advance your voice a little.

FACE When you went pinned up in the several rags
You had raked and picked from dunghills, before day;
Your feet in mouldy slippers, for your kibes;
A felt of rug, and a thin threaden cloak,
That scarce would cover your no buttocks—

SUBTLE So, sir!

FACE When all your alchemy, and your algebra,
Your minerals, vegetals, and animals,
Your conjuring, cozening, and your dozen of trades,
Could not relieve your corpse with so much linen
Would make you tinder, but to see a fire;
I gave you countenance, credit for your coals,
Your stills, your glasses, your materials;
Built you a furnace, drew you customers,
Advanced all your black arts; lent you, beside,
A house to practise in—

SUBTLE Your master's house!

FACE Where you have studied the more thriving skill
Of bawdry since.

SUBTLE Yes, in your master's house,
You and the rats here kept possession.
Make it not strange. I know you were one could keep
The buttery-hatch still locked, and save the chippings,

Sell the dole beer to aqua-vitæ men,
The which, together with your Christmas vails
At post-and-pair,[2] your letting out of counters,
Made you a pretty stock, some twenty marks,
And gave you credit to converse with cobwebs,
Here, since your mistress' death hath broke up
    house.

FACE You might talk softlier, rascal.

SUBTLE No, you scarab,
I'll thunder you in pieces: I will teach you
How to beware to tempt a Fury again
That carries tempest in his hand and voice.

FACE The place has made you valiant.

SUBTLE No, your clothes.—
Thou vermin, have I ta'en thee out of dung,
So poor, so wretched, when no living thing
Would keep thee company, but a spider, or
    worse?
Raised thee from brooms, and dust, and water-
    ing-pots,
Sublimed thee, and exalted thee, and fixed thee
In the third region, called our state of grace?
Wrought thee to spirit, to quintessence, with
    pains
Would twice have won me the philosopher's
    work?
Put thee in words and fashion, made thee fit
For more than ordinary fellowships?
Given thee thy oaths, thy quarrelling dimen-
    sions,
Thy rules to cheat at horse-race, cock-pit, cards,
Dice, or whatever gallant tincture else?
Made thee a second in mine own great art?
And have I this for thanks! Do you rebel,
Do you fly out in the projection?
Would you be gone now?

DOL Gentlemen, what mean you?
Will you mar all?

SUBTLE Slave, thou hadst had no name—

DOL Will you undo yourselves with civil war?

SUBTLE Never been known, past *equi clibanum*,
The heat of horse-dung, under ground, in
    cellars,
Or an ale-house darker than deaf John's; been
    lost
To all mankind, but laundresses and tapsters,
Had not I been.

2 A game of cards much played in the West of
England.

DOL Do you know who hears you, sovereign?

FACE Sirrah—

DOL Nay, general, I thought you were civil.

FACE I shall turn desperate, if you grow thus
    loud.

SUBTLE And hang thyself, I care not.

FACE Hang thee, collier.
And all thy pots and pans, in pictures, I will,
Since thou hast moved me—

DOL O, this will o'erthrow all.

FACE Write thee up bawd in Paul's, have all thy
    tricks
Of cozening with a hollow cole, dust, scrapings,
Searching for things lost, with a sieve and
    sheers,
Erecting figures in your rows of houses,
And taking in of shadows with a glass,
Told in red letters; and a face cut for thee,
Worse than Gamaliel Ratsey's.[3]

DOL Are you sound?
Have you your senses, masters?

FACE I will have
A book, but barely reckoning thy impostures,
Shall prove a true philosopher's stone to print-
    ers.

SUBTLE Away, you trencher-rascal!

FACE Out, you dog-leech!
The vomit of all prisons—

DOL Will you be
Your own destructions, gentlemen?

FACE Still spewed out
For lying too heavy on the basket.

SUBTLE Cheater!

FACE Bawd!

SUBTLE Cow-herd!

FACE Conjurer!

SUBTLE Cutpurse!

FACE Witch!

DOL O me!
We are ruined, lost! have you no more regard
To your reputations? where's your judgment?
    'slight,
Have yet some care of me, of your republic—

FACE Away, this brach! I'll bring thee, rogue,
    within
The statute of sorcery, tricesimo tertio
Of Harry the Eighth: ay, and perhaps thy neck

3 A notorious highwayman.

Within a noose, for laundring gold and barbing
it.

DOL [*snatches Face's sword*] You'll bring your head within a cockscomb, will you?
And you, sir, with your menstrue
[*She dashes Subtle's vial out of his hand.*]
—gather it up.
'Sdeath, you abominable pair of stinkards,
Leave off your barking, and grow one again,
Or, by the light that shines, I'll cut your throats.
I'll not be made a prey unto the marshal
For ne'er a snarling dog-bolt of you both.
Have you together cozened all this while,
And all the world, and shall it now be said,
You've made most courteous shift to cozen
yourselves?
[*To Face*]
You will accuse him! you will "bring him in
Within the statute!" Who shall take your word?
A whoreson, upstart, apocryphal captain,
Whom not a Puritan in Blackfriars will trust
So much as for a feather:
[*To Subtle*]
and you, too,
Will give the cause, forsooth! you will insult,
And claim a primacy in the divisions!
You must be chief! as if you only had
The powder to project with, and the work
Were not begun out of equality?
The venture tripartite? all things in common?
Without priority? 'Sdeath! you perpetual curs,
Fall to your couples again, and cozen kindly,
And heartily, and lovingly, as you should
And lose not the beginning of a term,
Or, by this hand, I shall grow factious too,
And take my part, and quit you.

FACE 'Tis his fault;
He ever murmurs, and objects his pains,
And says, the weight of all lies upon him.

SUBTLE Why, so it does.

DOL How does it? do not we
Sustain our parts?

SUBTLE Yes, but they are not equal.

DOL Why, if your part exceed to-day, I hope
Ours may to-morrow match it.

SUBTLE Ay, they *may*.

DOL May, murmuring mastiff! ay, and do. Death
on me!
Help me to throttle him.

[*Seizes Subtle by the throat.*]

SUBTLE Dorothy! Mistress Dorothy!
'Ods precious, I'll do anything. What do you
mean?

DOL Because o' your fermentation and cibation?

SUBTLE Not I, by heaven—

DOL [*to Face*] Your Sol and Luna—help me.

SUBTLE Would I were hanged then! I'll conform
myself.

DOL Will you, sir? do so then, and quickly:
swear.

SUBTLE What should I swear?

DOL To leave your faction, sir,
And labour kindly in the common work.

SUBTLE Let me not breathe if I meant aught
beside.
I only used those speeches as a spur
To him.

DOL I hope we need no spurs, sir. Do we?

FACE 'Slid, prove to-day who shall shark best.

SUBTLE Agreed.

DOL Yes, and work close and friendly.

SUBTLE 'Slight, the knot
Shall grow the stronger for this breach, with
me.

[*They shake hands.*]

DOL Why, so, my good baboons! Shall we go
make
A sort of sober, scurvy, precise neighbours,
That scarce have smiled twice since the king
came in,[4]
A feast of laughter at our follies? Rascals,
Would run themselves from breath, to see me
ride,
Or you t' have but a hole to thrust your heads
in,
For which you should pay ear-rent? No, agree.
And may Don Provost ride a feasting long,
In his old velvet jerkin and stained scarfs,
My noble sovereign, and worthy general,
Ere we contribute a new crewel garter
To his most worsted worship.

SUBTLE Royal Dol!
Spoken like Claridiana,[5] and thyself.

FACE For which at supper, thou shalt sit in
triumph,

[4] James succeeded to the throne in 1603, and this
was written in 1610.

[5] The heroine of the "Mirror of Knighthood."

And not be styled Dol Common, but Dol
  Proper,
Dol Singular: the longest cut at night,
Shall draw thee for his Dol Particular.
[*Bell rings without.*]
SUBTLE Who's that? one rings. To the window,
  Dol—
[*Exit Dol.*]
        Pray heaven,
The master do not trouble us this quarter.
FACE O, fear not him. While there dies one a
  week
O' the plague, he's safe, from thinking toward
  London:
Beside, he's busy at his hop-yards now;
I had a letter from him. If he do,
He'll send such word, for airing of the house,
As you shall have sufficient time to quit it:
Though we break up a fortnight, 'tis no matter.
[*Reenter Dol.*]
SUBTLE Who is it, Dol?
DOL A fine young quodling.
FACE O,
My lawyer's clerk, I lighted on last night,
In Holborn, at the Dagger. He would have
(I told you of him) a familiar,
To rifle with at horses, and win cups.
DOL O, let him in.
SUBTLE Stay. Who shall do't?
FACE Get you
Your robes on: I will meet him, as going out.
DOL And what shall I do?
FACE Not be seen; away!
[*Exit Dol.*]
Seem you very reserved.
SUBTLE Enough.
[*Exit.*]
FACE [*aloud and retiring*] God be wi' you, sir,
I pray you let him know that I was here:
His name is Dapper. I would gladly have staid
  but—
DAPPER [*within*] Captain, I am here.
FACE Who's that?—He's come, I think, doctor.
[*Enter Dapper.*]
Good faith, sir, I was going away.
DAPPER In truth,
I am very sorry, captain.
FACE But I thought
Sure I should meet you.

DAPPER Ay, I am very glad.
I had a scurvy writ or two to make
And I had lent my watch last night to one
That dines to-day at the sheriff's, and so was
  robbed
Of my pass-time.
[*Reenter Subtle in his velvet cap and gown.*]
Is this the cunning-man?
FACE This is his worship.
DAPPER Is he a doctor?
FACE Yes.
DAPPER And have you broke with him, captain?
FACE Ay.
DAPPER And how?
FACE Faith, he does make the matter, sir, so
  dainty,
I know not what to say.
DAPPER Not so, good captain.
FACE Would I were fairly rid of it, believe me.
DAPPER Nay, now you grieve me, sir. Why
  should you wish so?
I dare assure you, I'll not be ungrateful.
FACE I cannot think you will, sir. But the law
Is such a thing—and then he says, Read's
  matter
Falling so lately.
DAPPER Read! he was an ass,
And dealt, sir, with a fool.
FACE It was a clerk, sir.
DAPPER A clerk!
FACE Nay, hear me, sir, you know the law
Better, I think—
DAPPER I should, sir, and the danger:
You know, I showed the statute to you.
FACE You did so.
DAPPER And will I tell then! By this hand of
  flesh,
Would it might never write good courthand more,
If I discover. What do you think of me,
That I am a chiaus?
FACE What's that?
DAPPER The Turk was here.
As one would say, do you think I am a Turk?
FACE I'll tell the doctor so.
DAPPER Do, good sweet captain.
FACE Come, noble doctor, pray thee let's prevail,
This is the gentleman, and he is no chiaus.
SUBTLE Captain, I have returned you all my
  answer.

The Alchemist

I would do much, sir, for your love— But this
I neither may, nor can.

FACE   Tut, do not say so.
You deal now with a noble fellow, doctor,
One that will thank you richly; and he is no
      chiaus:
Let that, sir, move you.

SUBTLE   Pray you, forbear—

FACE   He has
Four angels here.

SUBTLE   You do me wrong, good sir.

FACE   Doctor, wherein? To tempt you with these
      spirits?

SUBTLE   To tempt my art and love, sir, to my
      peril.
'Fore heaven, I scarce can think you are my
      friend,
That so would draw me to apparent danger.

FACE   I draw you! a horse draw you, and a
      halter,
You, and your flies together—

DAPPER   Nay, good captain.

FACE   That knows no difference of men.

SUBTLE   Good words, sir.

FACE   Good deeds, sir, Doctor Dog's-meat.
      'Slight, I bring you
No cheating Clim o' the Cloughs, or Claribels,
That look as big as five-and-fifty, and flush;[6]
And spit out secrets like hot custard—

DAPPER   Captain!

FACE   Nor any melancholic underscribe,
Shall tell the vicar; but a special gentle,
That is the heir to forty marks a year,
Consorts with the small poets of the time,
Is the sole hope of his old grandmother;
That knows the law, and writes you six fair
      hands,
Is a fine clerk, and has his cyphering perfect,
Will take his oath o' the Greek Testament,
If need be, in his pocket; and can court
His mistress out of Ovid.

DAPPER   Nay, dear captain—

FACE   Did you not tell me so?

DAPPER   Yes; but I'd have you
Use master doctor with some more respect.

[6] Five-and-fifty was the highest number to stand
on at the old game of Primero. If a flush accompanied this, the hand swept the table.

FACE   Hang him, proud stag, with his broad vel-
      vet head!—
But for your sake, I'd choke ere I would change
An article of breath with such a puck-fist!
[Going]
Come, let's be gone.

SUBTLE   Pray you let me speak with you.

DAPPER   His worship calls you, captain.

FACE   I am sorry
I e'er embarked myself in such a business.

DAPPER   Nay, good sir; he did call you.

FACE   Will he take then?

SUBTLE   First, hear me—

FACE   Not a syllable, 'less you take.

SUBTLE   Pray you, sir—

FACE   Upon no terms but an *assumpsit*.

SUBTLE   Your humour must be law.
[He takes the four angels.]

FACE   Why now, sir, talk.
Now I dare hear you with mine honour. Speak.
So may this gentleman too.

SUBTLE   [offering to whisper to Face]   Why, sir—

FACE   No whispering.

SUBTLE   'Fore heaven, you do not apprehend the
      loss
You do yourself in this.

FACE   Wherein? for what?

SUBTLE   Marry, to be so importunate for one
That, when he has it, will undo you all:
He'll win up all the money in the town.

FACE   How?

SUBTLE   Yes, and blow up gamester after game-
      ster,
As they do crackers in a puppet-play.
If I do give him a familiar,
Give you him all you play for; never set him:
For he will have it.

FACE   You are mistaken, doctor.
Why, he does ask one but for cups and horses,
A rifling fly; none of your great familiars.

DAPPER   Yes, captain, I would have it for all
      games.

SUBTLE   I told you so.

FACE   [taking Dapper aside]   'Slight, that is a new
      business!
I understood you, a tame bird, to fly
Twice in a term, or so, on Friday nights,
When you had left the office, for a nag

Of forty or fifty shillings.

DAPPER Ay, 'tis true, sir;
But I do think now I shall leave the law,
And therefore—

FACE Why, this changes quite the case.
Do you think that I dare move him?

DAPPER If you please, sir;
All's one to him, I see.

FACE What! for that money?
I cannot with my conscience; nor should you
Make the request, methinks.

DAPPER No, sir, I mean
To add consideration.

FACE Why then, sir,
I'll try.
[*Goes to Subtle.*]
        Say that it were for all games, doctor?

SUBTLE I say then, not a mouth shall eat for
him
At any ordinary, but on the score;
That is a gaming mouth, conceive me.

FACE Indeed!

SUBTLE He'll draw you all the treasure of the
realm,
If it be set him.

FACE Speak you this from art?

SUBTLE Ay, sir, and reason too, the ground of
art.
He is of the only best complexion,
The queen of Fairy loves.

FACE What! is he?

SUBTLE Peace.
He'll overhear you. Sir, should she but see
him—

FACE What?

SUBTLE Do not you tell him.

FACE Will he win at cards too?

SUBTLE The spirits of dead Holland, living Isaac,
You'd swear, were in him; such a vigorous luck
As cannot be resisted. 'Slight, he'll put
Six of your gallants to a cloak, indeed.

FACE A strange success, that some man shall be
born to!

SUBTLE He hears you, man—

DAPPER Sir, I'll not be ingrateful.

FACE Faith, I have confidence in his good nature:
You hear, he says he will not be ingrateful.

SUBTLE Why, as you please; my venture follows
yours.

FACE Troth, do it, doctor; think him trusty, and
make him.
He may make us both happy in an hour;
Win some five thousand pound, and send us two
on't.

DAPPER Believe it, and I will, sir.

FACE And you shall, sir.
[*Takes him aside.*]
You have heard all?

DAPPER No, what was't? Nothing, I, sir.

FACE Nothing!

DAPPER A little, sir.

FACE Well, a rare star
Reigned at your birth.

DAPPER At mine, sir! No.

FACE The doctor
Swears that you are—

SUBTLE Nay, captain, you'll tell all now.

FACE Allied to the queen of Fairy.

DAPPER Who? that I am?
Believe it, no such matter—

FACE Yes, and that
You were born with a cawl on your head.

DAPPER Who says so?

FACE Come,
You know it well enough, though you dissemble
it.

DAPPER I' fac, I do not; you are mistaken.

FACE How!
Swear by your fac, and in a thing so known
Unto the doctor? how shall we, sir, trust you
In the other matter; can we ever think,
When you have won five or six thousand pound,
You'll send us shares in't by this rate?

DAPPER By Jove, sir,
I'll win ten thousand pound, and send you half.
I' fac's no oath.

SUBTLE No, no, he did but jest.

FACE Go to. Go thank the doctor: he's your
friend,
To take it so.

DAPPER I thank his worship.

FACE So!
Another angel.

DAPPER Must I?

FACE Must you! 'slight,

The Alchemist   141

What else is thanks? will you be trivial?—
  Doctor,

[*Dapper gives him the money.*]

When must he come for his familiar?

DAPPER Shall I not have it with me?

SUBTLE O, good sir!
There must be a world of ceremonies pass;
You must be bathed and fumigated first:
Besides, the queen of Fairy does not rise
Till it be noon.

FACE Not if she danced to-night.

SUBTLE And she must bless it.

FACE Did you never see
Her royal grace yet?

DAPPER Whom?

FACE Your aunt of Fairy?

SUBTLE Not since she kist him in the cradle,
  captain;
I can resolve you that.

FACE Well, see her grace,
Whate'er it cost you, for a thing that I know.
It will be somewhat hard to compass; but
However, see her. You are made, believe it,
If you can see her. Her grace is a lone woman,
And very rich; and if she takes a fancy,
She will do strange things. See her, at any hand.
'Slid, she may hap to leave you all she has:
It is the doctor's fear.

DAPPER How will't be done, then?

FACE Let me alone, take you no thought. Do you
But say to me, captain, I'll see her grace.

DAPPER "Captain, I'll see her grace."

FACE Enough.

[*Knocking within*]

SUBTLE Who's there?
Anon.—[*Aside to Face*] Conduct him forth by
  the back way.
Sir, against one o'clock prepare yourself;
Till when you must be fasting; only take
Three drops of vinegar in at your nose,
Two at your mouth, and one at either ear;
Then bathe your fingers' ends and wash your
  eyes,
To sharpen your five senses, and cry "hum"
Thrice, and then "buz" as often; and then come.
[*Exit.*]

FACE Can you remember this?

DAPPER I warrant you.

FACE Well then, away. It is but your bestowing

Some twenty nobles 'mong her grace's servants,
And put on a clean shirt: you do not know
What grace her grace may do you in clean
  linen.

[*Exeunt Face and Dapper.*]

SUBTLE [*within*] Come in? Good wives, I pray
  you forbear me now;
Troth, I can do you no good till afternoon—

[*Reenters, followed by Drugger.*]

What is your name, say you, Abel Drugger?

DRUGGER Yes, sir.

SUBTLE A seller of tobacco?

DRUGGER Yes, sir.

SUBTLE Umph!
Free of the grocers?

DRUGGER Ay, an't please you.

SUBTLE Well—
Your business, Abel?

DRUGGER This, an't please your worship;
I am a young beginner, and am building
Of a new shop, an't like your worship, just
At corner of a street:—Here is the plot on't—
And I would know by art, sir, of your worship,
Which way I should make my door, by necro-
  mancy,
And where my shelves; and which should be
  for boxes,
And which for pots. I would be glad to thrive,
  sir:
And I was wished to your worship by a gentle-
  man,
One Captain Face, that says you know men's
  planets,
And their good angels, and their bad.

SUBTLE I do,
If I do see them—

[*Reenter Face.*]

FACE What! my honest Abel?
Thou art well met here.

DRUGGER Troth, sir, I was speaking,
Just as your worship came here, of your wor-
  ship:
I pray you speak for me to master doctor.

FACE He shall do anything. Doctor, do you hear?
This is my friend, Abel, an honest fellow;
He lets me have good tobacco, and he does not
Sophisticate it with sack-lees or oil,
Nor washes it in muscadel and grains,
Nor buries it in gravel, under ground,

Wrapped up in greasy leather, or pissed clouts:
But keeps it in fine lily pots, that, opened,
Smell like conserve of roses, or French beans.
He has his maple block, his silver tongs,
Winchester pipes, and fire of juniper:
A neat, spruce, honest fellow, and no goldsmith.

SUBTLE He is a fortunate fellow, that I am sure on.

FACE Already, sir, have you found it? Lo thee, Abel!

SUBTLE And in right way toward riches—

FACE Sir!

SUBTLE This summer
He will be of the clothing of his company,
And next spring called to the scarlet; spend
what he can.

FACE What, and so little beard?

SUBTLE Sir, you must think,
He may have a receipt to make hair come:
But he'll be wise, preserve his youth, and fine
for't;
His fortune looks for him another way.

FACE 'Slid, doctor, how canst thou know this
so soon?
I am amused[7] at that.

SUBTLE By a rule, captain,
In metoposcopy, which I do work by;
A certain star in the forehead, which you see
not.
Your chestnut or your olive-coloured face
Does never fail: and your long ear doth prom-
ise.
I knew't, by certain spots, too, in his teeth,
And on the nail of his mercurial finger.

FACE Which finger's that?

SUBTLE His little finger. Look.
You were born upon a Wednesday?

DRUGGER Yes, indeed, sir.

SUBTLE The thumb, in chiromancy, we give
Venus;
The forefinger to Jove; the midst to Saturn;
The ring to Sol; the least to Mercury,
Who was the lord, sir, of his horoscope,
His house of life being Libra; which foreshowed
He should be a merchant, and should trade with
balance.

FACE Why, this is strange! Is it not, honest Nab?

SUBTLE There is a ship now coming from
Ormus,
That shall yield him such a commodity
Of drugs—
[*Pointing to the plan*]
            This is the west, and this the south?

DRUGGER Yes, sir.

SUBTLE And those are your two sides?

DRUGGER Ay, sir.

SUBTLE Make me your door then, south; your
broad side, west:
And on the east side of your shop, aloft,
Write Mathlai, Tarmiel, and Baraborat;
Upon the north part, Rael, Velel, Thiel.
They are the names of those Mercurial spirits
That do fright flies from boxes.

DRUGGER Yes, sir.

SUBTLE And
Beneath your threshold, bury me a loadstone
To draw in gallants that wears spurs: the rest,
They'll seem to follow.

FACE That's a secret, Nab!

SUBTLE And, on your stall, a puppet, with a vice
And a court-fucus, to call city-dames:
You shall deal much with minerals.

DRUGGER Sir, I have
At home, already—

SUBTLE Ay, I know you have arsenic,
Vitriol, sal-tartar, argaile, alkali,
Cinoper: I know all.—This fellow, captain,
Will come, in time, to be a great distiller,
And give a say—I will not say directly,
But very fair—at the philosopher's stone.

FACE Why, how now, Abel! is this true?

DRUGGER [*aside to Face*] Good captain,
What must I give?

FACE Nay, I'll not counsel thee.
Thou hear'st what wealth (he says, spend what
thou canst),
Thou'rt like to come to.

DRUGGER I would gi' him a crown.

FACE A crown! and toward such a fortune?
heart,
Thou shalt rather gi' him thy shop. No gold
about thee?

DRUGGER Yes, I have a portague,[8] I have kept
this half-year.

---

[7] Amazed.

[8] A gold coin worth about £3 12s.

FACE Out on thee, Nab! 'Slight, there was such
an offer—
Shalt keep't no longer, I'll give't him for thee.
Doctor,
Nab prays your worship to drink this, and
swears
He will appear more grateful, as your skill
Does raise him in the world.

DRUGGER I would entreat
Another favour of his worship.

FACE What is't, Nab?

DRUGGER But to look over, sir, my almanack,
And cross out my ill-days, that I may neither
Bargain, nor trust upon them.

FACE That he shall, Nab:
Leave it, it shall be done, 'gainst afternoon.

SUBTLE And a direction for his shelves.

FACE Now, Nab,
Art thou well pleased, Nab?

DRUGGER Thank, sir, both your worships.
[*Exit Drugger.*]

FACE Away.
Why, now, you smoaky persecutor of nature!
Now do you see, that something's to be done,
Beside your beech-coal, and your corsive waters,
Your crosslets, crucibles, and cucurbites?
You must have stuff brought home to you, to
work on:
And yet you think I am at no expense
In searching out these veins, then following
them,
Then trying them out. 'Fore God, my intelli-
gence
Costs me more money than my share oft comes
to,
In these rare works.

SUBTLE You are pleasant, sir.
[*Reenter Dol.*]

Act Two

SCENE ONE

*An outer room in Lovewit's house. Enter Sir
Epicure Mammon and Surly.*

MAMMON Come on, sir. Now you set your foot
on shore
In *Novo Orbe;* here's the rich Peru:

How now!
What says my dainty Dolkin?

DOL Yonder fish-wife
Will not away. And there's your giantess,
The bawd of Lambeth.

SUBTLE Heart, I cannot speak with them.

DOL Not afore night, I have told them in a
voice,
Thorough the trunk, like one of your familiars.
But I have spied Sir Epicure Mammon—

SUBTLE Where?

DOL Coming along, at far end of the lane,
Slow of his feet, but earnest of his tongue
To one that's with him.

SUBTLE Face, go you and shift.
[*Exit Face.*]
Dol, you must presently make ready too.

DOL Why, what's the matter?

SUBTLE O, I did look for him
With the sun's rising: marvel he could sleep.
This is the day I am to perfect for him
The magisterium, our great work, the stone;
And yield it, made, into his hands: of which
He has, this month, talked as he were possessed.
And now he's dealing pieces on't away.
Methinks I see him entering ordinaries,
Dispensing for the pox, and plaguy houses,
Reaching his dose, walking Moorfields for lepers,
And offering citizens' wives pomander-bracelets,
As his preservative, made of the elixir;
Searching the spittle, to make old bawds young;
And the highways, for beggars, to make rich:
I see no end of his labours. He will make
Nature ashamed of her long sleep: when art,
Who's but a step-dame, shall do more than she,
In her best love to mankind, ever could:
If his dream last, he'll turn the age to gold.
[*Exeunt.*]

And there within, sir, are the golden mines,
Great Solomon's Ophir! He was sailing to't,
Three years, but we have reached it in ten
months.
This is the day wherein, to all my friends,
I will pronounce the happy word, BE RICH;
THIS DAY YOU SHALL BE SPECTATISSIMI.

You shall no more deal with the hollow die,
Or the frail card. No more be at charge of
  keeping
The livery-punk for the young heir, that must
Seal, at all hours, in his shirt: no more,
If he deny, have him beaten to't, as he is
That brings him the commodity. No more
Shall thirst of satin, or the covetous hunger
Of velvet entrails for a rude-spun cloak,
To be displayed at Madam Augusta's, make
The sons of Sword and Hazard fall before
The golden calf, and on their knees, whole
  nights,
Commit idolatry with wine and trumpets:
Or go a feasting after drum and ensign.
No more of this. You shall start up young
  viceroys,
And have your punks and punketees, my Surly.
And unto thee I speak it first, BE RICH.
Where is my Subtle, there? Within, ho!

FACE [*within*] Sir, he'll come to you by and by.

MAMMON This is his fire-drake,
His Lungs, his Zephyrus, he that puffs his coals,
Till he firk nature up, in her own centre.
You are not faithful, sir. This night I'll change
All that is metal in my house to gold:
And, early in the morning, will I send
To all the plumbers and the pewterers,
And buy their tin and lead up; and to Lothbury
For all the copper.

SURLY What, and turn that, too?

MAMMON Yes, and I'll purchase Devonshire and
  Cornwall,
And make them perfect Indies! you admire
  now?

SURLY No, faith.

MAMMON But when you see th'effects of the
  Great Medicine,
Of which one part projected on a hundred
Of Mercury, or Venus, or the moon,
Shall turn it to as many of the sun;
Nay, to a thousand, so *ad infinitum:*
You will believe me.

SURLY Yes, when I see't, I will.
But if my eyes do cozen me so, and I
Giving them no occasion, sure I'll have
A whore shall piss them out next day.

MAMMON Ha! why?
Do you think I fable with you? I assure you,

He that has once the flower of the sun,
The perfect ruby, which we call elixir,
Not only can do that, but by its virtue,
Can confer honour, love, respect, long life;
Give safety, valour, yea, and victory,
To whom he will. In eight and twenty days,
I'll make an old man of fourscore, a child.

SURLY No doubt; he's that already.

MAMMON Nay, I mean,
Restore his years, renew him, like an eagle,
To the fifth age; make him get sons and daugh-
  ters,
Young giants; as our philosophers have done,
The ancient patriarchs, afore the flood,
But taking, once a week, on a knife's point,
The quantity of a grain of mustard of it;
Become stout Marses, and beget young Cupids.

SURLY The decayed vestals of Pict-hatch would
  thank you,
That keep the fire alive there.

MAMMON 'Tis the secret
Of nature naturized 'gainst all infections,
Cures all diseases coming of all causes;
A month's grief in a day, a year's in twelve;
And, of what age soever, in a month:
Past all the doses of your drugging doctors,
I'll undertake, withal, to fight the plague
Out of the kingdom in three months.

SURLY And I'll
Be bound, the players shall sing your praises
  then,
Without their poets.

MAMMON Sir, I'll do't. Meantime,
I'll give away so much unto my man,
Shall serve the whole city with preservative
Weekly; each house his dose, and at the rate—

SURLY As he that built the Water-work does
  with water?

MAMMON You are incredulous.

SURLY Faith, I have a humour,
I would not willingly be gulled. Your stone
Cannot transmute me.

MAMMON Pertinax [my] Surly,
Will you believe antiquity? records?
I'll show you a book where Moses and his
  sister,
And Solomon have written of the art;
Ay, and a treatise penned by Adam—

SURLY How!

MAMMON Of the philosopher's stone, and in High
Dutch.

SURLY Did Adam write, sir, in High Dutch?

MAMMON He did;
Which proves it was the primitive tongue.

SURLY What paper?

MAMMON On cedar board.

SURLY O that, indeed, they say,
Will last 'gainst worms.

MAMMON 'Tis like your Irish wood,
'Gainst cobwebs. I have a piece of Jason's fleece
too,
Which was no other than a book of alchemy,
Writ in large sheepskin, a good fat ram-vellum.
Such was Pythagoras' thigh, Pandora's tub,
And all that fable of Medea's charms,
The manner of our work; the bulls, our furnace,
Still breathing fire; our argent-vive, the dragon:
The dragon's teeth, mercury sublimate,
That keeps the whiteness, hardness, and the
biting;
And they are gathered into Jason's helm,
The alembic, and then sowed in Mars his field,
And thence sublimed so often, till they're fixed,
Both this, the Hesperian garden, Cadmus' story,
Jove's shower, the boon of Midas, Argus' eyes,
Boccace his Demogorgon, thousands more,
All abstract riddles of our stone.—
[*Enter Face, as a Servant.*]
                                How now!
Do we succeed? Is our day come? and holds it?

FACE The evening will set red upon you, sir;
You have colour for it, crimson: the red fer-
ment
Has done his office; three hours hence prepare
you
To see projection.

MAMMON Pertinax, my Surly.
Again I say to thee, aloud, "Be rich."
This day thou shalt have ingots; and to-morrow
Give lords th' affront.[9]—Is it, my Zephyrus,
right?
Blushes the bolt's-head?

FACE Like a wench with child, sir,
That were but now discovered to her master.

MAMMON Excellent witty Lungs!—my only care
is

[9] Meet and look them in the face.

Where to get stuff enough now, to project on;
This town will not half serve me.

FACE No, sir! buy
The covering off o' churches.

MAMMON That's true.

FACE Yes.
Let them stand bare, as do their auditory;
Or cap them new with shingles.

MAMMON No, good thatch:
Thatch will lie light upon the rafters, Lungs.—
Lungs, I will manumit thee from the furnace;
I will restore thee thy complexion, Puffe,
Lost in the embers; and repair this brain,
Hurt with the fume o' the metals.

FACE I have blown, sir,
Hard, for your worship; thrown by many a coal,
When 'twas not beech; weighed those I put in,
just
To keep your heat still even; these bleared eyes
Have waked to read your several colours, sir,
Of the pale citron, the green lion, the crow,
The peacock's tail, the plumed swan.

MAMMON And lastly,
Thou hast descried the flower, the *sanguis agni.*

FACE Yes, sir.

MAMMON Where's master?

FACE At his prayers, sir, he;
Good man, he's doing his devotions
For the success.

MAMMON Lungs, I will set a period
To all thy labours; thou shalt be the master
Of my seraglio.

FACE Good, sir.

MAMMON But do you hear?
I'll geld you, Lungs.

FACE Yes, sir.

MAMMON For I do mean
To have a list of wives and concubines
Equal with Solomon, who had the stone
Alike with me; and I will make me a back
With the elixir, that shall be as tough
As Hercules, to encounter fifty a night.—
Thou art sure thou saw'st it blood?

FACE Both blood and spirit, sir.

MAMMON I will have all my beds blown up, not
stuft:
Down is too hard: and then, mine oval room
Filled with such pictures as Tiberius took
From Elephantis, and dull Aretine

But coldly imitated. Then, my glasses
Cut in more subtle angles, to disperse
And multiply the figures, as I walk
Naked between my succubæ. My mists
I'll have of perfume, vapoured 'bout the room,
To lose our selves in; and my baths, like pits
To fall into; from whence we will come forth,
And roll us dry in gossamer and roses.—
Is it arrived at ruby?—Where I spy
A wealthy citizen, or [a] rich lawyer,
Have a sublimed pure wife, unto that fellow
I'll send a thousand pound to be my cuckold.

FACE   And I shall carry it?

MAMMON   No. I'll have no bawds
But fathers and mothers: they will do it best,
Best of all others. And my flatterers
Shall be the pure and gravest of divines,
That I can get for money. My mere fools,
Eloquent burgesses, and then my poets
The same that writ so subtly of the fart,
Whom I will entertain still for that subject.
The few that would give out themselves to be
Court and town-stallions, and, each-where, bely
Ladies who are known most innocent, for them,
Those will I beg, to make me eunuchs of:
And they shall fan me with ten estrich tails
A-piece, made in a plume to gather wind.
We will be brave, Puffe, now we have the
    med'cine.
My meat shall all come in, in Indian shells,
Dishes of agate set in gold, and studded
With emeralds, sapphires, hyacinths, and rubies.
The tongues of carps, dormice, and camels'
    heels,
Boiled in the spirit of sol, and dissolved pearl,
Apicius' diet, 'gainst the epilepsy:
And I will eat these broths with spoons of
    amber,
Headed with diamond and carbuncle.
My foot-boy shall eat pheasants, calvered sal-
    mons,
Knots, godwits, lampreys: I myself will have
The beards of barbels served, instead of salads;
Oiled mushrooms; and the swelling unctuous
    paps
Of a fat pregnant sow, newly cut off,
Drest with an exquisite and poignant sauce;
For which, I'll say unto my cook, "There's gold,
Go forth, and be a knight."

FACE   Sir, I'll go look
A little, how it heightens.
[Exit.]

MAMMON   Do.—My shirts
I'll have of taffeta-sarsnet, soft and light
As cobwebs; and for all my other raiment,
It shall be such as might provoke the Persian,
Were he to teach the world riot anew.
My gloves of fishes and birds' skins, perfumed
With gums of paradise, and Eastern air—

SURLY   And do you think to have the stone with
this?

MAMMON   No, I do think t'have all this with the
stone.

SURLY   Why, I have heard he must be *homo
frugi*,
A pious, holy, and religious man,
One free from mortal sin, a very virgin.

MAMMON   That makes it, sir; he is so: but I
buy it;
My venture brings it me. He, honest wretch,
A notable, superstitious, good soul,
Has worn his knees bare, and his slippers bald,
With prayer and fasting for it; and, sir, let him
Do it alone, for me, still. Here he comes.
Not a profane word afore him; 'tis poison.—
[*Enter Subtle.*]
Good morrow, father.

SUBTLE   Gentle son, good morrow,
And to your friend there. What is he, is with
you?

MAMMON   An heretic, that I did bring along,
In hope, sir, to convert him.

SUBTLE   Son, I doubt
You are covetous, that thus you meet your time
In the just point; prevent your day at morning.
This argues something worthy of a fear
Of importune and carnal appetite.
Take heed you do not cause the blessing leave
you,
With your ungoverned haste. I should be sorry
To see my labours, now even at perfection,
Got by long watching and large patience,
Not prosper where my love and zeal hath
placed them.
Which (heaven I call to witness, with your self,
To whom I have poured my thoughts) in all
my ends,
Have looked no way, but unto public good,

To pious uses, and dear charity,
Now grown a prodigy with men. Wherein
If you, my son, should now prevaricate,
And to your own particular lusts employ
So great and catholic a bliss, be sure
A curse will follow, yea, and overtake
Your subtle and most secret ways.

MAMMON   I know, sir;
You shall not need to fear me; I but come
To have you confute this gentleman.

SURLY   Who is,
Indeed, sir, somewhat costive of belief
Toward your stone; would not be gulled.

SUBTLE   Well, son,
All that I can convince him in, is this,
The WORK IS DONE, bright Sol is in his robe.
We have a medicine of the triple soul,
The glorified spirit. Thanks be to heaven,
And make us worthy of it!—Ulen Spiegel!

FACE [*within*]   Anon, sir.

SUBTLE   Look well to the register.
And let your heat still lessen by degrees,
To the aludels.

FACE [*within*]   Yes, sir.

SUBTLE   Did you look
O' the bolt's head yet?

FACE [*within*]   Which? on D, sir?

SUBTLE   Ay;
What's the complexion?

FACE [*within*]   Whitish.

SUBTLE   Infuse vinegar,
To draw his volatile substance and his tincture:
And let the water in glass E be filtered,
And put into the gripe's egg. Lute him well;
And leave him closed in balneo.

FACE [*within*]   I will, sir.

SURLY [*aside*]   What a brave language here is!
next to canting.

SUBTLE   I have another work you never saw,
son,
That three days since past the philosopher's
wheel,
In the lent heat of Athanor; and's become
Sulphur of Nature.

MAMMON   But 'tis for me?

SUBTLE   What need you?
You have enough in that is perfect.

MAMMON   O, but—

SUBTLE   Why, this is covetise!

MAMMON   No, I assure you,
I shall employ it all in pious uses,
Founding of colleges and grammar schools,
Marrying young virgins, building hospitals,
And now and then a church.
[*Reenter Face.*]

SUBTLE   How now!

FACE   Sir, please you,
Shall I not change the filter?

SUBTLE   Marry, yes;
And bring me the complexion of glass B.
[*Exit Face.*]

MAMMON   Have you another?

SUBTLE   Yes, son; were I assured
Your piety were firm, we would not want
The means to glorify it: but I hope the best.
I mean to tinct C in sand-heat to-morrow,
And give him imbibition.

MAMMON   Of white oil?

SUBTLE   No, sir, of red. F is come over the helm
too,
I thank my maker, in St. Mary's bath,
And shows *lac virginis*. Blessed be heaven!
I sent you of his fæces there calcined;
Out of that calx, I have won the salt of mercury.

MAMMON   By pouring on your rectified water?

SUBTLE   Yes, and reverberating in Athanor.
[*Reenter Face.*]
How now! what colour says it?

FACE   The ground black, sir.

MAMMON   That's your crow's head.

SURLY   Your cock's-comb's, is it not?

SUBTLE   No, 'tis not perfect. Would it were the
crow!
That work wants something.

SURLY [*aside*]   O, I looked for this.
The hay's[10] a pitching.

SUBTLE   Are you sure you loosed them
In their own menstrue?

FACE   Yes, sir, and then married them.
And put them in a bolt's-head nipped to diges-
tion,
According as you bade me, when I set
The liquor of Mars to circulation
In the same heat.

SUBTLE   The process then was right.

FACE   Yes, by the token, sir, the retort brake,

[10] A net for catching rabbits.

And what was saved was put into the pelican,
And signed with Hermes' seal.

SUBTLE   I think 'twas so.
We should have a new amalgama.

SURLY [*aside*]   O, this ferret
Is rank as any polecat.

SUBTLE   But I care not;
Let him e'en die; we have enough beside,
In embryon. H has his white shirt on?

FACE   Yes, sir,
He's ripe for inceration, he stands warm,
In his ash-fire. I would not you should let
Any die now, if I might counsel, sir,
For luck's sake to the rest: it is not good.

MAMMON   He says right.

SURLY [*aside*]   Ah, are you bolted?

FACE   Nay, I know't, sir,
I have seen the ill fortune. What is some three
   ounces
Of fresh materials?

MAMMON   Is't no more?

FACE   No more, sir,
Of gold, t'amalgame with some six of mercury.

MAMMON   Away, here's money. What will serve?

FACE   Ask him, sir.

MAMMON   How much?

SUBTLE   Give him nine pound; you may give him
   ten.

SURLY [*aside*]   Yes, twenty, and be cozened, do.

MAMMON   There 'tis.
[*Gives Face the money.*]

SUBTLE   This needs not; but that you will have
   it so.
To see conclusions of all: for two
Of our inferior works are at fixation,
A third is in ascension. Go your ways.
Have you set the oil of luna in kemia?

FACE   Yes, sir.

SUBTLE   And the philosopher's vinegar?

FACE   Ay.
[*Exit.*]

SURLY [*aside*]   We shall have a salad!

MAMMON   When do you make projection?

SUBTLE   Son, be not hasty, I exalt our med'cine,
By hanging him in *balneo vaporoso*.
And giving him solution; then congeal him;
And then dissolve him; then again congeal him;
For look, how oft I iterate the work,
So many times I add unto his virtue.

As if at first one ounce convert a hundred,
After his second loose, he'll turn a thousand;
His third solution, ten; his fourth, a hundred;
After his fifth, a thousand thousand ounces
Of any imperfect metal, into pure
Silver or gold, in all examinations,
As good as any of the natural mine.
Get you your stuff here against afternoon,
Your brass, your pewter, and your andirons.

MAMMON   Not those of iron?

SUBTLE   Yes, you may bring them too;
We'll change all metals.

SURLY   I believe you in that.

MAMMON   Then I may send my spits?

SUBTLE   Yes, and your racks.

SURLY   And dripping-pans, and pot-hangers, and
   hooks?
Shall he not?

SUBTLE   If he please.

SURLY   —To be an ass.

SUBTLE   How, sir!

MAMMON   This gentleman you must bear withal:
I told you he had no faith.

SURLY   And little hope, sir;
But much less charity, should I gull myself.

SUBTLE   Why, what have you observed, sir, in
   our art,
Seems so impossible?

SURLY   But your whole work, no more.
That you should hatch gold in a furnace, sir,
As they do eggs in Egypt!

SUBTLE   Sir, do you
Believe that eggs are hatched so?

SURLY   If I should?

SUBTLE   Why, I think that the greater miracle.
No egg but differs from a chicken more
Than metals in themselves.

SURLY   That cannot be.
The egg's ordained by nature to that end,
And is a chicken *in potentia*.

SUBTLE   The same we say of lead and other
   metals,
Which would be gold if they had time.

MAMMON   And that
Our art doth further.

SUBTLE   Ay, for 'twere absurd
To think that nature in the earth bred gold
Perfect in the instant: something went before.
There must be remote matter.

SURLY Ay, what is that?

SUBTLE Marry, we say—

MAMMON Ay, now it heats: stand, father,
Pound him to dust.

SUBTLE It is, of the one part,
A humid exhalation, which we call
Materia liquida, or the unctuous water;
On the one part, a certain crass and viscous
Portion of earth; both which, concorporate,
Do make the elementary matter of gold;
Which is not yet *propria materia*,
But common to all metals and all stones;
For, where it is forsaken of that moisture,
And hath more dryness, it becomes a stone:
Where it retains more of the humid fatness,
It turns to sulphur, or to quicksilver,
Who are the parents of all other metals.
Nor can this remote matter suddenly
Progress so from extreme unto extreme,
As to grow gold, and leap o'er all the means.
Nature doth first beget the imperfect, then
Proceeds she to the perfect. Of that airy
And oily water, mercury is engendered;
Sulphur of the fat and earthy part; the one,
Which is the last, supplying the place of male,
The other, of the female, in all metals.
Some do believe hermaphrodeity,
That both do act and suffer. But these two
Make the rest ductile, malleable, extensive.
And even in gold they are; for we do find
Seeds of them by our fire, and gold in them;
And can produce the species of each metal
More perfect thence, than nature doth in earth.
Beside, who doth not see in daily practice
Art can beget bees, hornets, beetles, wasps,
Out of the carcases and dung of creatures;
Yea, scorpions of an herb, being rightly placed?
And these are living creatures, far more perfect
And excellent than metals.

MAMMON Well said, father!
Nay, if he take you in hand, sir, with an argument,
He'll bray you in a mortar.

SURLY Pray you, sir, stay.
Rather than I'll be brayed, sir, I'll believe
That Alchemy is a pretty kind of game,
Somewhat like tricks o' the cards, to cheat a man
With charming.

SUBTLE Sir?

SURLY What else are all your terms,
Whereon no one of your writers 'grees with other?
Of your elixir, your *lac virginis*,
Your stone, your med'cine, and your chryso-sperme,
Your sal, your sulphur, and your mercury,
Your oil of height, your tree of life, your blood,
Your marchesite, your tutie, your magnesia,
Your toad, your crow, your dragon, and your panther;
Your sun, your moon, your firmament, your adrop,
Your lato, azoch, zernich, chibrit, heautarit,
And then your red man, and your white woman,
With all your broths, your menstrues, and materials
Of piss and egg-shells, women's terms, man's blood,
Hair o' the head, burnt clouts, chalk, merds, and clay,
Powder of bones, scalings of iron, glass,
And worlds of other strange ingredients,
Would burst a man to name?

SUBTLE And all these named,
Intending but one thing; which art our writers
Used to obscure their art.

MAMMON Sir, so I told him—
Because the simple idiot should not learn it,
And make it vulgar.

SUBTLE Was not all the knowledge
Of the Ægyptians writ in mystic symbols?
Speak not the scriptures oft in parables?
Are not the choicest fables of the poets,
That were the fountains and first springs of wisdom,
Wrapped in perplexed allegories?

MAMMON I urged that,
And cleared to him, that Sisyphus was damned
To roll the ceaseless stone, only because
He would have made OURS common.
[*Dol appears at the door.*]
Who is this?

SUBTLE 'Sprecious!—What do you mean? go in, good lady,
Let me entreat you
[*Dol retires.*]
Where's this varlet?

[*Reenter Face.*]

FACE   Sir.

SUBTLE   You very knave! do you use me thus?

FACE   Wherein, sir?

SUBTLE   Go in and see, you traitor. Go!

[*Exit Face.*]

MAMMON   Who is it, sir?

SUBTLE   Nothing, sir; nothing.

MAMMON   What's the matter, good sir?
I have not seen you thus distempered: who is't?

SUBTLE   All arts have still had, sir, their adver-
saries;
But ours the most ignorant.—

[*Reenter Face.*]
What now?

FACE   'Twas not my fault, sir; she would speak
with you.

SUBTLE   Would she, sir! Follow me.

[*Exit.*]

MAMMON   [*stopping him*] Stay, Lungs.

FACE   I dare not, sir.

MAMMON   Stay, man; what is she?

FACE   A lord's sister, sir.

MAMMON   How! pray thee, stay.

FACE   She's mad, sir, and sent hither—
He'll be mad too.—

MAMMON   I warrant thee.—
Why sent hither?

FACE   Sir, to be cured.

SUBTLE   [*within*] Why, rascal!

FACE   Lo you—Here, sir!

[*Exit.*]

MAMMON   'Fore God, a Bradamante, a brave
piece.

SURLY   Heart, this is a bawdy house! I will be
burnt else.

MAMMON   O, by this light, no: do not wrong
him. He's
Too scrupulous that way: it is his vice.
No, he's a rare physician, do him right,
An excellent Paracelsian, and has done
Strange cures with mineral physic. He deals all
With spirits, he; he will not hear a word
Of Galen, or his tedious recipes.—

[*Reenter Face.*]
How now, Lungs!

FACE   Softly, sir; speak softly. I meant
To have told your worship all. This must not
hear.

MAMMON   No, he will not be "gulled"; let him
alone.

FACE   You are very right, sir; she is a most rare
scholar,
And is gone mad with studying Broughton's
works.
If you but name a word touching the Hebrew,
She falls into her fit, and will discourse
So learnedly of genealogies,
As you would run mad too, to hear her, sir.

MAMMON   How might one do t'have conference
with her, Lungs?

FACE   O, divers have run mad upon the confer-
ence:
I do not know, sir. I am sent in haste
To fetch a vial.

SURLY   Be not gulled, Sir Mammon.

MAMMON   Wherein? pray ye, be patient.

SURLY   Yes, as you are.
And trust confederate knaves and bawds and
whores.

MAMMON   You are too foul, believe it.—Come
here, Ulen,
One word.

FACE   [*going*]   I dare not, in good faith.

MAMMON   Stay, knave.

FACE   He is extreme angry that you saw her, sir.

MAMMON   Drink that.

[*Gives him money.*]
                    What is she when she's out
of her fit?

FACE   O, the most affablest creature, sir! so
merry!
So pleasant! she'll mount you up, like quick-
silver,
Over the helm; and circulate like oil,
A very vegetal: discourse of state,
Of mathematics, bawdry, anything—

MAMMON   Is she no way accessible? no means,
No trick to give a man a taste of her—wit—
Or so?

SUBTLE   [*within*] Ulen!

FACE   I'll come to you again, sir.

[*Exit.*]

MAMMON   Surly, I did not think one of your
breeding
Would traduce personages of worth.

SURLY   Sir Epicure,
Your friend to use; yet still loth to be gulled:

I do not like your philosophical bawds.
Their stone is lechery enough to pay for,
Without this bait.

MAMMON 'Heart, you abuse yourself.
I know the lady, and her friends, and means,
The original of this disaster. Her brother
Has told me all.

SURLY And yet you never saw her
Till now!

MAMMON O yes, but I forgot. I have, believe it,
One of the treacherousest memories, I do think,
Of all mankind.

SURLY What call you her brother?

MAMMON My lord—
He will not have his name known, now I think
on't.

SURLY A very treacherous memory!

MAMMON On my faith—

SURLY Tut, if you have it not about you, pass it,
Till we meet next.

MAMMON Nay, by this hand, 'tis true.
He's one I honour, and my noble friend;
And I respect his house.

SURLY Heart! can it be
That a grave sir, a rich, that has no need,
A wise sir, too, at other times, should thus,
With his own oaths, and arguments, make hard
    means
To gull himself? And this be your elixir,
Your *lapis mineralis,* and your lunary,
Give me your honest trick yet at primero,
Or gleek; and take your *lutum sapientis,*
Your *menstruum simplex!* I'll have gold before
    you,
And with less danger of the quicksilver,
Or the hot sulphur.

[*Reenter Face.*]

FACE [*to Surly*] Here's one from Captain Face,
sir.
Desires you meet him in the Temple-church,
Some half-hour hence, and upon earnest business.

[*Whispers to Mammon.*]
Sir, if you please to quit us now; and come
Again within two hours, you shall have
My master busy examining o' the works;
And I will steal you in, unto the party,
That you may see her converse.—Sir, shall I
say

You'll meet the captain's worship?

SURLY Sir, I will.—

[*Walks aside.*]
But, by attorney, and to a second purpose.
Now, I am sure it is a bawdy-house;
I'll swear it, were the marshal here to thank
me:
The naming this commander doth confirm it.
Don Face! why, he's the most authentic dealer
In these commodities, the superintendent
To all the quainter traffickers in town!
He is the visitor, and does appoint
Who lies with whom, and at what hour; what
    price;
Which gown, and in what smock; what fall;
    what tire.
Him will I prove, by a third person, to find
The subtleties of this dark labyrinth:
Which if I do discover, dear Sir Mammon,
You'll give your poor friend leave, though no
    philosopher,
To laugh: for you that are, 'tis thought, shall
    weep.

FACE Sir, he does pray you'll not forget.

SURLY I will not, sir.
Sir Epicure, I shall leave you.

[*Exit.*]

MAMMON I follow you straight.

FACE But do so, good sir, to avoid suspicion.
This gentleman has a parlous head.

MAMMON But wilt thou, Ulen,
Be constant to thy promise?

FACE As my life, sir.

MAMMON And wilt thou insinuate what I am,
    and praise me,
And say I am a noble fellow?

FACE O, what else, sir.
And that you'll make her royal with the stone,
An empress; and yourself King of Bantam.

MAMMON Wilt thou do this?

FACE Will I, sir.

MAMMON Lungs, my Lungs!
I love thee.

FACE Send your stuff, sir, that my master
May busy himself about projection.

MAMMON Thou hast witched me, rogue: take,
go.

[*Gives him money.*]

FACE Your jack, and all, sir.

MAMMON Thou art a villain—I will send my jack,
And the weights too. Slave, I could bite thine ear,
Away, thou dost not care for me.

FACE Not I, sir!

MAMMON Come, I was born to make thee, my good weasel,
Set thee on a bench, and have thee twirl a chain
With the best lord's vermin of 'em all.

FACE Away, sir.

MAMMON A count, nay, a count palatine—

FACE Good sir, go.

MAMMON Shall not advance thee better: no, nor faster.

[*Exit. Reenter Subtle and Dol.*]

SUBTLE Has he bit? has he bit?

FACE And swallowed, too, my Subtle.
I have given him line, and now he plays, i' faith.

SUBTLE And shall we twitch him?

FACE Thorough both the gills.
A wench is a rare bait, with which a man
No sooner's taken, but he straight firks mad.

SUBTLE Dol, my Lord What'ts'hum's sister, you must now
Bear yourself *statelich*.

DOL O, let me alone.
I'll not forget my race, I warrant you.
I'll keep my distance, laugh and talk aloud;
Have all the tricks of a proud scurvy lady,
And be as rude as her woman.

FACE Well said, sanguine!

SUBTLE But will he send his andirons?

FACE His jack too.
And 's iron shoeing-horn; I have spoke to him. Well,
I must not lose my wary gamester yonder.

SUBTLE O, Monsieur Caution, that will not be gulled.

FACE Ay,
If I can strike a fine hook into him, now!—
The Temple-church, there I have cast mine angle.
Well, pray for me. I'll about it.

[*Knocking without.*]

SUBTLE What, more gudgeons!
Dol, scout, scout!

[*Dol goes to the window.*]
Stay, Face, you must go to the door;
'Pray God it be my anabaptist—Who is't, Dol?

DOL I know him not: he looks like a gold-end-man.

SUBTLE Ods so! 'tis he, he said he would send—
what call you him?
The sanctified elder, that should deal
For Mammon's jack and andirons. Let him in.
Stay, help me off, first, with my gown.

[*Exit Face with the gown.*]
Away,
Madam, to your withdrawing chamber.

[*Exit Dol.*]
Now,
In a new tune, new gesture, but old language.—
This fellow is sent from one negotiates with me
About the stone too; for the holy brethren
Of Amsterdam, the exiled saints; that hope
To raise their discipline by it. I must use him
In some strange fashion now, to make him admire me.

[*Enter Ananias. Aloud*]
Where is my drudge?

[*Reenter Face.*]

FACE Sir!

SUBTLE Take away the recipient,
And rectify your menstrue from the phlegma.
Then pour it on the Sol, in the cucurbite,
And let them macerate together.

FACE Yes, sir.
And save the ground?

SUBTLE No: *terra damnata*
Must not have entrance in the work.—Who are you?

ANANIAS A faithful brother, if it please you.

SUBTLE What's that?
A Lullianist? a Ripley? Filius artis?
Can you sublime and dulcify? calcine?
Know you the sapor pontic? sapor stiptic?
Or what is homogene, or heterogene?

ANANIAS I understand no heathen language, truly.

SUBTLE Heathen! you Knipper-doling? is Ars sacra,
Or chrysopœia, or spagyrica,
Or the pamphysic, or panarchic knowledge,
A heathen language?

The Alchemist   153

ANANIAS Heathen Greek, I take it.

SUBTLE How! heathen Greek?

ANANIAS All's heathen but the Hebrew.

SUBTLE Sirrah my varlet, stand you forth and speak to him,
Like a philosopher: answer, in the language.
Name the vexations, and the martyrizations
Of metals in the work.

FACE Sir, putrefaction,
Solution, ablution, sublimation,
Cohobation, calcination, ceration, and
Fixation.

SUBTLE This is heathen Greek, to you, now!—
And when comes vivification?

FACE After mortification.

SUBTLE What's cohobation?

FACE 'Tis the pouring on
Your *aqua regis,* and then drawing him off,
To the trine circle of the seven spheres.

SUBTLE What's the proper passion of metals?

FACE Malleation.

SUBTLE What's your *ultimum supplicium auri?*

FACE Antimonium.

SUBTLE This is heathen Greek to you!—And what's your mercury?

FACE A very fugitive, he will be gone, sir.

SUBTLE How know you him?

FACE By his viscosity,
His oleosity, and his suscitability.

SUBTLE How do you sublime him?

FACE With the calce of egg-shells,
White marble, talc.

SUBTLE Your magisterium now,
What's that?

FACE Shifting, sir, your elements,
Dry into cold, cold into moist, moist into hot,
Hot into dry.

SUBTLE This is heathen Greek to you still!
Your *lapis philosophicus?*

FACE 'Tis a stone,
And not a stone; a spirit, a soul, and a body:
Which if you do dissolve, it is dissolved.
If you coagulate, it is coagulated;
If you make it to fly, it flieth.

SUBTLE Enough.
[*Exit Face.*]
This is heathen Greek to you! What are you, Sir?

ANANIAS Please you, a servant of the exiled brethren,
That deal with widows' and with orphans' goods,
And make a just account unto the saints:
A deacon.

SUBTLE O, you are sent from Master Wholesome,
Your teacher?

ANANIAS From Tribulation Wholesome,
Our very zealous pastor.

SUBTLE Good! I have
Some orphans' goods to come here.

ANANIAS Of what kind, sir?

SUBTLE Pewter and brass, andirons and kitchenware;
Metals, that we must use our medicine on:
Wherein the brethren may have a penny-worth
For ready money.

ANANIAS Were the orphans' parents
Sincere professors?

SUBTLE Why do you ask?

ANANIAS Because
We then are to deal justly, and give, in truth,
Their utmost value.

SUBTLE 'Slid, you'd cozen else,
And if their parents were not of the faithful!—
I will not trust you, now I think on it,
Till I have talked with your pastor. Have you brought money
To buy more coals?

ANANIAS No, surely.

SUBTLE No! how so?

ANANIAS The brethren bid me say unto you, sir,
Surely, they will not venture any more
Till they may see projection.

SUBTLE How!

ANANIAS You have had,
For the instruments, as bricks, and lome, and glasses,
Already thirty pound; and for materials,
They say, some ninety more: and they have heard since,
That one, at Heidelberg, made it of an egg,
And a small paper of pin-dust.

SUBTLE What's your name?

ANANIAS My name is Ananias.

SUBTLE Out, the varlet

That cozened the apostles! Hence, away!
Flee, mischief! had your holy consistory
No name to send me, of another sound,
Than wicked Ananias? send your elders
Hither, to make atonement for you, quickly,
And give me satisfaction; or out goes
The fire; and down th' alembecs, and the furnace,
Piger Henricus, or what not. Thou wretch!
Both sericon and bufo shall be lost,
Tell them. All hope of rooting out the bishops,
Or the anti-Christian hierarchy shall perish,
If they stay threescore minutes: the aqueity,
Terreity, and sulphureity
Shall run together again, and all be annulled,
Thou wicked Ananias!
[*Exit Ananias.*]
               This will fetch 'em,
And make them haste towards their gulling more.
A man must deal like a rough nurse, and fright
Those that are froward, to an appetite.
[*Reenter Face in his uniform, followed by Drugger.*]

FACE He is busy with his spirits, but we'll upon him.

SUBTLE How now! what mates, what Baiards have we here?

FACE I told you he would be furious.—Sir, here's Nab
Has brought you another piece of gold to look on:
—We must appease him. Give it me,—and prays you,
You would devise—what is it, Nab?

DRUGGER A sign, sir.

FACE Ay, a good lucky one, a thriving sign, doctor.

SUBTLE I was devising now.

FACE 'Slight, do not say so,
He will repent he gave you any more—
What say you to his constellation, doctor,
The Balance?

SUBTLE No, that way is stale and common.
A townsman born in Taurus, gives the bull,
Or the bull's head: in Aries, the ram,
A poor-device! No, I will have his name

Formed in some mystic character; whose radii,
Striking the senses of the passers-by,
Shall, by a virtual influence, breed affections,
That may result upon the party owns it:
And thus—

FACE Nab!

SUBTLE He shall have *a bell*, that's *Abel;*
And by it standing one whose name is *Dee,*
In a *rug* gown, there's *D,* and *Rug,* that's *drug:*
And right anenst him a dog snarling *er;*
There's Drugger, Abel Drugger. That's his sign.
And here's now mystery and hieroglyphic!

FACE Abel, thou art made.

DRUGGER Sir, I do thank his worship.

FACE Six o' thy legs more will not do it, Nab.
He has brought you a pipe of tobacco, doctor.

DRUGGER Yes, sir;
I have another thing I would impart—

FACE Out with it, Nab.

DRUGGER Sir, there is lodged, hard by me,
A rich young widow—

FACE Good! a bona roba?

DRUGGER But nineteen at the most.

FACE Very good, Abel.

DRUGGER Marry, she's not in the fashion yet;
she wears
A hood, but it stands a cop.[11]

FACE No matter, Abel.

DRUGGER And I do now and then give her a fucus—

FACE What! dost thou deal, Nab?

SUBTLE I did tell you, captain.

DRUGGER And physic too, sometime, sir; for
which she trusts me
With all her mind. She's come up here of purpose
To learn the fashion.

FACE Good!—[*Aside*]—His match too!—On, Nab.

DRUGGER And she does strangely long to know her fortune.

FACE 'Ods lid, Nab, send her to the doctor, hither.

DRUGGER Yes, I have spoke to her of his worship already;
But she's afraid it will be blown abroad,

[11] Conical, terminating in a point.

And hurt her marriage.

FACE   Hurt it! 'tis the way
To heal it, if 'twere hurt; to make it more
Followed and sought. Nab, thou shalt tell her
   this.
She'll be more known, more talked of; and your
   widows
Are ne'er of any price till they be famous;
Their honour is their multitude of suitors:
Send her, it may be thy good fortune. What!
Thou dost not know?

DRUGGER   No, sir, she'll never marry
Under a knight: her brother has made a vow.

FACE   What! and dost thou despair, my little
   Nab,
Knowing what the doctor has set down for thee,
And seeing so many of the city dubbed?
One glass o' thy water, with a madam I know,
Will have it done, Nab: what's her brother, a
   knight?

DRUGGER   No, sir, a gentleman newly warm in
   his land, sir,
Scarce cold in his one and twenty, that does
   govern
His sister here; and is a man himself
Of some three thousand a year, and is come up
To learn to quarrel, and to live by his wits,
And will go down again, and die in the country.

FACE   How, to quarrel?

DRUGGER   Yes, sir, to carry quarrels,
As gallants do; to manage them by line.

FACE   'Slid, Nab, the doctor is the only man
In Christendom for him. He has made a table,
With mathematical demonstrations,
Touching the art of quarrels: he will give him
An instrument to quarrel by. Go, bring them
   both,
Him and his sister. And, for thee, with her
The doctor happ'ly may persuade. Go to:

'Shalt give his worship a new damask suit
Upon the premises.

SUBTLE   O, good captain!

FACE   He shall;
He is the honestest fellow, doctor. Stay not,
No offers; bring the damask, and the parties.

DRUGGER   I'll try my power, sir.

FACE   And thy will too, Nab.

SUBTLE   'Tis good tobacco, this! what is't an
   ounce?

FACE   He'll send you a pound, doctor.

SUBTLE   O no.

FACE   He will do't.
It is the goodest soul!—Abel, about it.
Thou shalt know more anon. Away, be gone.
[Exit Abel.]
A miserable rogue, and lives with cheese,
And has the worms. That was the cause, indeed,
Why he came now: he dealt with me in private,
To get a med'cine for them.

SUBTLE   And shall, sir. This works.

FACE   A wife, a wife for one of us, my dear
   Subtle!
We'll e'en draw lots, and he that fails, shall
   have
The more in goods, the other has in tail.

SUBTLE   Rather the less: for she may be so light
She may want grains.

FACE   Ay, or be such a burden,
A man would scarce endure her for the whole.

SUBTLE   Faith, best let's see her first, and then
   determine.

FACE   Content: but Dol must have no breath
   on't.

SUBTLE   Mum.
Away you, to your Surly yonder, catch him.

FACE   Pray God I have not staid too long.

SUBTLE   I fear it.
[Exeunt.]

Act Three

SCENE ONE

The lane before Lovewit's house. Enter Tribulation Wholesome and Ananias.

TRIBULATION   These chastisements are common
   to the saints,

And such rebukes we of the separation
Must bear with willing shoulders, as the trials
Sent forth to tempt our frailties.

ANANIAS   In pure zeal,
I do not like the man, he is a heathen,
And speaks the language of Canaan, truly.

TRIBULATION I think him a profane person indeed.

ANANIAS He bears
The visible mark of the beast in his forehead.
And for his stone, it is a work of darkness,
And with philosophy blinds the eyes of man.

TRIBULATION Good brother, we must bend unto all means,
That may give furtherance to the holy cause.

ANANIAS Which his cannot: the sanctified cause
Should have a sanctified course.

TRIBULATION Not always necessary:
The children of perdition are ofttimes
Made instruments even of the greatest works:
Beside, we should give somewhat to man's nature,
The place he lives in, still about the fire,
And fume of metals, that intoxicate
The brain of man, and make him prone to passion.
Where have you greater atheists than your cooks?
Or more profane, or choleric, than your glass-men?
More anti-Christian than your bell-founders?
What makes the devil so devilish, I would ask you,
Sathan, our common enemy, but his being
Perpetually about the fire, and boiling
Brimstone and arsenic? We must give, I say,
Unto the motives, and the stirrers up
Of humours in the blood. It may be so,
When as the work is done, the stone is made,
This heat of his may turn into a zeal,
And stand up for the beauteous discipline,
Against the menstruous cloth and rag of Rome.
We must await his calling, and the coming
Of the good spirit. You did fault, t'upbraid him
With the brethren's blessing of Heidelberg, weighing
What need we have to hasten on the work,
For the restoring of the silenced saints,
Which ne'er will be but by the philosopher's stone.
And so a learned elder, one of Scotland,
Assured me; *aurum potabile* being
The only med'cine, for the civil magistrate,
T'incline him to a feeling of the cause;
And must be daily used in the disease.

ANANIAS I have not edified more, truly, by man;
Not since the beautiful light first shone on me;
And I am sad my zeal hath so offended.

TRIBULATION Let us call on him then.

ANANIAS The motion's good,
And of the spirit; I will knock first.
[*Knocks.*]
                           Peace be
within!
[*The door is opened, and they enter.*]

SCENE TWO

A room in Lovewit's house. Enter Subtle, followed by Tribulation and Ananias.

SUBTLE O, are you come? 'twas time. Your three-score minutes
Were at last thread, you see; and down had gone
Furnus acediæ, turris circulatorius:
Lembec, bolt's-head, retort, and pelican
Had all been cinders. Wicked Ananias!
Art thou returned? nay, then it goes down yet.

TRIBULATION Sir, be appeased; he is come to humble
Himself in spirit, and to ask your patience,
If too much zeal hath carried him aside
From the due path.

SUBTLE Why, this doth qualify!

TRIBULATION The brethren had no purpose, verily,
To give you the least grievance: but are ready
To lend their willing hands to any project
The spirit and you direct.

SUBTLE This qualifies more!

TRIBULATION And for the orphans' goods, let them be valued.
Or what is needful else to the holy work,
It shall be numbered; here, by me, the saints
Throw down their purse before you.

SUBTLE This qualifies most!
Why, thus it should be, now you understand.
Have I discoursed so unto you of our stone,
And of the good that it shall bring your cause?
Showed you (beside the main of hiring forces
Abroad, drawing the Hollanders, your friends,
From the Indies, to serve you, with all their fleet)

That even the med'cinal use shall make you a faction,
And party in the realm? As, put the case,
That some great man in state, he have the gout,
Why, you but send three drops of your elixir,
You help him straight: there you have made a friend.
Another has the palsy or the dropsy,
He takes of your incombustible stuff,
He's young again: there you have made a friend.
A lady that is past the feat of body,
Though not of mind, and hath her face decayed
Beyond all cure of paintings, you restore,
With the oil of talc: there you have made a friend
And all her friends. A lord that is a leper,
A knight that has the bone-ache, or a squire
That hath both these, you make them smooth and sound,
With a bare fricace of your med'cine: still
You increase your friends.

TRIBULATION Ay, it is very pregnant.

SUBTLE And then the turning of this lawyer's pewter
To plate at Christmas—

ANANIAS Christ-tide, I pray you.

SUBTLE Yet, Ananias!

ANANIAS I have done.

SUBTLE Or changing
His parcel gilt to massy gold. You cannot
But raise your friends. Withal, to be of power
To pay an army in the field, to buy
The King of France out of his realms, or Spain
Out of his Indies. What can you not do
Against lords spiritual or temporal,
That shall oppone you?

TRIBULATION Verily, 'tis true.
We may be temporal lords ourselves, I take it.

SUBTLE You may be anything, and leave off to make
Long-winded exercises; or suck up
Your "ha!" and "hum!" in a tune. I not deny,
But such as are not graced in a state,
May, for their ends, be adverse in religion,
And get a tune to call the flock together:

For, to say sooth, a tune does much with women
And other phlegmatic people; it is your bell.

ANANIAS Bells are profane; a tune may be religious.

SUBTLE No warning with you! then farewell my patience.
'Slight, it shall down; I will not be thus tortured.

TRIBULATION I pray you, sir.

SUBTLE All shall perish. I have spoke it.

TRIBULATION Let me find grace, sir, in your eyes; the man
He stands corrected: neither did his zeal,
But as your self, allow a tune somewhere.
Which now, being tow'rd the stone, we shall not need.

SUBTLE No, nor your holy vizard, to win widows
To give you legacies; or make zealous wives
To rob their husbands for the common cause:
Nor take the start of bonds broke but one day,
And say they were forfeited by providence.
Nor shall you need o'er night to eat huge meals,
To celebrate your next day's fast the better;
The whilst the brethren and the sisters humbled,
Abate the stiffness of the flesh. Nor cast
Before your hungry hearers scrupulous bones;
As whether a Christian may hawk or hunt,
Or whether matrons of the holy assembly
May lay their hair out, or wear doublets,
Or have that idol starch about their linen.

ANANIAS It is indeed an idol.

TRIBULATION Mind him not, sir.
I do command thee, spirit of zeal, but trouble,
To peace within him! Pray you, sir, go on.

SUBTLE Nor shall you need to libel 'gainst the prelates,
And shorten so your ears against the hearing
Of the next wire-drawn grace. Nor of necessity
Rail against plays, to please the alderman
Whose daily custard you devour: nor lie
With zealous rage till you are hoarse. Not one
Of these so singular arts. Nor call yourselves
By names of Tribulation, Persecution,
Restraint, Long-patience, and such like, affected
By the whole family or wood of you,

Only for glory, and to catch the ear
Of the disciple.

TRIBULATION Truly, sir, they are
Ways that the godly brethren have invented,
For propagation of the glorious cause,
As very notable means, and whereby also
Themselves grow soon, and profitably, famous.

SUBTLE O, but the stone, all's idle to it! nothing!
The art of angels, nature's miracle,
The divine secret that doth fly in clouds
From east to west: and whose tradition
Is not from men, but spirits.

ANANIAS I hate traditions;
I do not trust them—

TRIBULATION Peace!

ANANIAS They are popish all.
I will not peace: I will not—

TRIBULATION Ananias!

ANANIAS Please the profane, to grieve the godly;
I may not.

SUBTLE Well, Ananias, thou shalt overcome.

TRIBULATION It is an ignorant zeal that haunts
him, sir:
But truly else a very faithful brother,
A botcher, and a man by revelation,
That hath a competent knowledge of the truth.

SUBTLE Has he a competent sum there in the
bag
To buy the goods within? I am made guardian,
And must, for charity and conscience' sake,
Now see the most be made for my poor
orphan;
Though I desire the brethren too good gainers:
There they are within. When you have viewed
and bought 'em,
And ta'en the inventory of what they are,
They are ready for projection; there's no more
To do: cast on the med'cine, so much silver
As there is tin there, so much gold as brass,
I'll give't you in by weight.

TRIBULATION But how long time,
Sir, must the saints expect yet?

SUBTLE Let me see,
How's the moon now? Eight, nine, ten days
hence,
He will be silver potate; then three days
Before he citronise. Some fifteen days,
The magisterium will be perfected.

ANANIAS About the second day of the third
week,
In the ninth month?

SUBTLE Yes, my good Ananias.

TRIBULATION What will the orphans' goods arise
to, think you?

SUBTLE Some hundred marks, as much as filled
three cars,
Unladen now: you'll make six millions of
them—
But I must have more coals laid in.

TRIBULATION How?

SUBTLE Another load,
And then we have finished. We must now in-
crease
Our fire to *ignis ardens,* we are past
Fimus equinus, balnei, cineris,
And all those lenter heats. If the holy purse
Should with this draught fall low, and that the
saints
Do need a present sum, I have a trick
To melt the pewter, you shall buy now instantly,
And with a tincture make you as good Dutch
dollars
As any are in Holland.

TRIBULATION Can you so?

SUBTLE Ay, and shall bide the third examination.

ANANIAS It will be joyful tidings to the brethren.

SUBTLE But you must carry it secret.

TRIBULATION Ay; but stay,
This act of coining, is it lawful?

ANANIAS Lawful!
We know no magistrate: or, if we did,
This is foreign coin.

SUBTLE It is no coining, sir.
It is but casting.

TRIBULATION Ha! you distinguish well:
Casting of money may be lawful.

ANANIAS 'Tis, sir.

TRIBULATION Truly, I take it so.

SUBTLE There is no scruple,
Sir, to be made of it; believe Ananias:
This case of conscience he is studied in.

TRIBULATION I'll make a question of it to the
brethren.

ANANIAS The brethren shall approve it lawful,
doubt not.

Where shall it be done?

[*Knocking without.*]

SUBTLE   For that we'll talk anon.
There's some to speak with me. Go in, I pray
    you,
And view the parcels. That's the inventory.
I'll come to you straight.

[*Exeunt Tribulation and Ananias.*]

            Who is it?—Face!
    appear.

[*Enter Face in his uniform.*]

How now! good prize?

FACE   Good pox! yond' costive cheater
Never came on.

SUBTLE   How then?

FACE   I have walked the round
Till now, and no such thing.

SUBTLE   And have you quit him?

FACE   Quit him! an hell would quit him too, he
    were happy.
'Slight! would you have me stalk like a mill-
    jade,
All day, for one that will not yield us grains?
I know him of old.

SUBTLE   Oh, but to have gulled him,
Had been a mastery.

FACE   Let him go, black boy!
And turn thee, that some fresh news may
    possess thee.
A noble count, a don of Spain, my dear
Delicious compeer, and my party-bawd,
Who is come hither private for his conscience,
And brought munition with him, six great
    slops,[12]
Bigger than three Dutch hoys, beside round
    trunks,[13]
Furnished with pistolets, and pieces of eight,
Will straight be here, my rogue, to have thy
    bath
(That is the colour), and to make his battery
Upon our Dol, our castle, our cinqueport,
Our Dover pier, our what thou wilt. Where is
    she?
She must prepare perfumes, delicate linen,
The bath in chief, a banquet, and her wit,
For she must milk his epididymis.
Where is the doxy?

[12] Large breeches or trousers worn by seamen.
[13] Trunk hose.

SUBTLE   I'll send her to thee:
And but despatch my brace of little John
    Leydens,
And come again myself.

FACE   Are they within then?

SUBTLE   Numbering the sum.

FACE   How much?

SUBTLE   A hundred marks, boy.

[*Exit.*]

FACE   Why, this is a lucky day. Ten pounds of
    Mammon!
Three of my clerk! a portague of my grocer!
This of the brethren! beside reversions,
And states to come in the widow, and my
    count!
My share to-day will not be bought for forty—

[*Enter Dol.*]

DOL   What?

FACE   Pounds, dainty Dorothy! art thou so near?

DOL   Yes; say, lord general, how fares our
    camp?

FACE   As with the few that had entrenched them-
    selves
Safe, by their discipline, against a world, Dol,
And laughed within those trenches, and grew
    fat
With thinking on the booties, Dol, brought in
Daily by their small parties. This dear hour,
A doughty don is taken with my Dol;
And thou mayst make his ransom what thou
    wilt
My Dousabel;[14] he shall be brought here fet-
    tered
With thy fair looks, before he sees thee; and
    thrown
In a down-bed, as dark as any dungeon;
Where thou shalt keep him waking with thy
    drum;
Thy drum, my Dol, thy drum; till he be tame
As the poor blackbirds were in the great frost,
Or bees are with a basin; and so hive him
In the swan-skin coverlid and cambric sheets,
Till he work honey and wax, my little God's-
    gift.

DOL   What is he, general?

FACE   An adalantado,
A grandee, girl. Was not my Dapper here yet?

[14] *Douce et belle.*

DOL No.

FACE Nor my Drugger?

DOL Neither.

FACE A pox on 'em,
They are so long a furnishing! such stinkards
Would not be seen upon these festive days.—
[Reenter Subtle.]
How now! have you done?

SUBTLE Done. They are gone: the sum
Is here in bank, my Face. I would we knew
Another chapman who would buy 'em outright.

FACE 'Slid, Nab shall do't against he have the
widow,
To furnish household.

SUBTLE Excellent, well thought on:
Pray God he come.

FACE I pray he keep away
Till our new business be o'erpast.

SUBTLE But, Face,
How camst thou by this secret don?

FACE A spirit
Brought me th'intelligence in a paper here,
As I was conjuring yonder in my circle
For Surly; I have my flies abroad. Your bath
Is famous, Subtle, by my means. Sweet Dol,
You must go tune your virginal, no losing
O' the least time: and, do you hear? good
action.
Firk, like a flounder; kiss, like a scallop, close;
And tickle him with thy mother tongue. His
great
Verdugoship has not a jot of language;
So much the easier to be cozened, my Dolly.
He will come here in a hired coach, obscure,
And our own coachman, whom I have sent as
guide,
No creature else.
[Knocking without.]
                    Who's that?

SUBTLE It is not he?
[Exit Dol.]

FACE O no, not yet this hour.
[Reenter Dol.]

SUBTLE Who is't?

DOL Dapper,
Your clerk.

FACE God's will then, queen of Fairy,
On with your tire;
[Exit Dol.]

and, doctor, with your robes.
Let's despatch him for God's sake.

SUBTLE 'Twill be long.

FACE I warrant you, take but the cues I give
you,
It shall be brief enough.
[Goes to the window.]
                    'Slight, here are more!
Abel, and I think the angry boy, the heir,
That fain would quarrel.

SUBTLE And the widow?

FACE No,
Not that I see. Away!
[Exit Subtle. Enter Dapper.]
                    O, sir, you are welcome.
The doctor is within a moving for you;
I have had the most ado to win him to it!—
He swears you'll be the darling of the dice:
He never heard her highness dote till now.
Your aunt has given you the most gracious
words
That can be thought on.

DAPPER Shall I see her grace?

FACE See her, and kiss her too.—
[Enter Abel, followed by Kastril.]
                    What, honest
Nab!
Hast brought the damask?

NAB No, sir; here's tobacco.

FACE 'Tis well done, Nab: thou'lt bring the
damask too?

DRUGGER Yes: here's the gentleman, captain,
Master Kastril,
I have brought to see the doctor.

FACE Where's the widow?

DRUGGER Sir, as he likes, his sister, he says,
shall come.

FACE O, is it so? good time. Is your name
Kastril, sir?

KASTRIL Ay, and the best of the Kastrils, I'd be
sorry else,
By fifteen hundred a year. Where is the doctor?
My mad tobacco-boy here tells me of one
That can do things: has he any skill?

FACE Wherein, sir?

KASTRIL To carry a business, manage a quarrel
fairly,
Upon fit terms.

FACE It seems, sir, you are but young

About the town, that can make that question.

KASTRIL   Sir, not so young but I have heard
   some speech
Of the angry boys, and seen them take tobacco;
And in his shop; and I can take it too.
And I would fain be one of 'em, and go down
And practise in the country.

FACE   Sir, for the duello,
The doctor, I assure you, shall inform you,
To the least shadow of a hair; and show you
An instrument he has of his own making,
Wherewith no sooner shall you make report
Of any quarrel, but he will take the height on't
Most instantly, and tell in what degree
Of safety it lies in, or mortality.
And how it may be borne, whether in a right
   line,
Or a half circle; or may else be cast
Into an angle blunt, if not acute:
And this he will demonstrate. And then, rules
To give and take the lie by.

KASTRIL   How! to take it?

FACE   Yes, in oblique he'll show you, or in circle;
But never in diameter.[15] The whole town
Study his theorems, and dispute them ordinarily
At the eating academies.

KASTRIL   But does he teach
Living by the wits too?

FACE   Anything whatever.
You cannot think that subtlety but he reads it.
He made me a captain. I was a stark pimp,
Just of your standing, 'fore I met with him;
It is not two months since. I'll tell you his
   method:
First, he will enter you at some ordinary.

KASTRIL   No, I'll not come there: you shall
   pardon me.

FACE   For why, sir?

KASTRIL   There's gaming there, and tricks.

FACE.   Why, would you be
A gallant, and not game?

KASTRIL   Ay, 'twill spend a man.

FACE   Spend you! it will repair you when you are
   spent,
How do they live by their wits there, that have
   vented
Six times your fortunes?

---

[15] The lie direct.

KASTRIL   What, three thousand a year!

FACE   Ay, forty thousand.

KASTRIL   Are there such?

FACE   Ay, sir,
And gallants yet. Here's a gentleman
Is born to nothing—
[*Points to Dapper.*]
                              forty marks a year
Which I count nothing:—he is to be initiated,
And have a fly of the doctor. He will win you
By unresistible luck, within this fortnight,
Enough to buy a barony. They will set him
Upmost, at the groom porters, all the Christ-
   mas:
And for the whole year through at every place
Where there is play, present him with the chair;
The best attendance, the best drink, sometimes
Two glasses of Canary, and pay nothing;
The purest linen and the sharpest knife,
The partridge next his trencher: and some-
   where
The dainty bed, in private, with the dainty.
You shall have your ordinaries bid for him,
As playhouses for a poet; and the master
Pray him aloud to name what dish he affects,
Which must be buttered shrimps: and those that
   drink
To no mouth else, will drink to his, as being
The goodly president mouth of all the board.

KASTRIL   Do you not gull one?

FACE   'Ods my life! do you think it?
You shall have a cast commander (can but get
In credit with a glover, or a spurrier,
For some two pair of either's ware aforehand),
Will, by most swift posts, dealing [but] with
   him,
Arrive at competent means to keep himself,
His punk, and naked boy, in excellent fashion,
And be admired for't.

KASTRIL   Will the doctor teach this?

FACE   He will do more, sir: when your land is
   gone,
As men of spirit hate to keep earth long
In a vacation, when small money is stirring,
And ordinaries suspended till the term,
He'll show a perspective, where on one side
You shall behold the faces and the persons
Of all sufficient young heirs in town,
Whose bonds are current for commodity;

On th'other side, the merchants' forms, and
others,
That without help of any second broker,
Who would expect a share, will trust such
parcels:
In the third square, the very street and sign
Where the commodity dwells, and does but
wait
To be delivered, be it pepper, soap,
Hops, or tobacco, oatmeal, wood, or cheeses.
All which you may so handle, to enjoy
To your own use, and never stand obliged.

KASTRIL I' faith! is he such a fellow?

FACE Why, Nab here knows him.
And then for making matches for rich widows,
Young gentlewomen, heirs, the fortunat'st man!
He's sent to, far and near, all over England,
To have his counsel, and to know their for-
tunes.

KASTRIL God's will, my suster shall see him.

FACE I'll tell you, sir,
What he did tell me of Nab. It's a strange
thing.—
By the way, you must eat no cheese, Nab, it
breeds melancholy,
And that same melancholy breeds worms; but
pass it:—
He told me, honest Nab here was ne'er at tav-
ern
But once in's life.

DRUGGER Truth, and no more I was not.

FACE And then he was so sick—

DRUGGER Could he tell you that too?

FACE How should I know it?

DRUGGER In troth, we had been a shooting,
And had a piece of fat ram-mutton to supper,
That lay so heavy o' my stomach—

FACE And he has no head
To bear any wine; for what with the noise of
the fiddlers,
And care of his shop, for he dares keep no
servants—

DRUGGER My head did so ache—

FACE And he was fain to be brought home,
The doctor told me: and then a good old
woman—

DRUGGER Yes, faith, she dwells in Seacoal-lane,
—did cure me,
With sodden ale, and pellitory of the wall

Cost me but twopence. I had another sickness
Was worse than that.

FACE Ay, that was with the grief
Thou took'st for being cessed at eighteenpence,
For the waterwork.

DRUGGER In truth, and it was like
T'have cost me almost my life.

FACE Thy hair went off?

DRUGGER Yes, sir; 'twas done for spite.

FACE Nay, so says the doctor.

KASTRIL Pray thee, tobacco-boy, go fetch my
suster;
I'll see this learned boy before I go;
And so shall she.

FACE Sir, he is busy now
But if you have a sister to fetch hither,
Perhaps your own pains may command her
sooner:
And he by that time will be free.

KASTRIL I go.
[*Exit.*]

FACE Drugger, she's thine: the damask!—
[*Exit Abel.*]

[*Aside*] Subtle
and I
Must wrestle for her.
Come on, Master Dap-
per,
You see how I turn clients here away,
To give your cause dispatch; have you per-
formed
The ceremonies were enjoined you?

DAPPER Yes, of the vinegar,
And the clean shirt.

FACE 'Tis well: that shirt may do you
More worship than you think. Your aunt's
a-fire,
But that she will not show it, t'have a sight of
you.
Have you provided for her grace's servants?

DAPPER Yes, here are six score Edward shillings.

FACE Good!

DAPPER And an old Harry's sovereign.

FACE Very good!

DAPPER And three James shillings, and an Elizabeth groat,
Just twenty nobles.

FACE O, you are too just.
I would you had had the other noble in Maries.

DAPPER I have some Philip and Maries.

FACE Ay, those same

Are best of all: where are they? Hark, the
   doctor.

*[Enter Subtle, disguised like a priest of Fairy,
with a stripe of cloth.]*

SUBTLE *[in a feigned voice]* Is yet her grace's
   cousin come?

FACE He is come.

SUBTLE And is he fasting?

FACE Yes.

SUBTLE And hath cried "hum"?

FACE Thrice you must answer.

DAPPER Thrice.

SUBTLE And as oft "buz"?

FACE If you have, say.

DAPPER I have.

SUBTLE Then, to her cuz,

Hoping that he hath vinegared his senses,
As he was bid, the Fairy queen dispenses,
By me, this robe, the petticoat of fortune;
Which that he straight put on, she doth impor-
   tune.
And though to fortune near be her petticoat,
Yet nearer is her smock, the queen doth note:
And therefore, even of that a piece she has sent,
Which, being a child, to wrap him in was rent;
And prays him for a scarf he now will wear it,
With as much love as then her grace did tear it,
About his eye

[They blind him with the rag.]

                       to show he is fortunate.

And, trusting unto her to make his state,
He'll throw away all worldly pelf about him;
Which that he will perform, she doth not doubt
   him.

FACE She need not doubt him, sir. Alas, he has
   nothing

But what he will part withal as willingly,
Upon her grace's word—throw away your
   purse—
As she would ask it:—handkerchiefs and all—

[He throws away, as they bid him.]

She cannot bid that thing but he'll obey.—
If you have a ring about you, cast it off,
Or a silver seal at your wrist; her grace will send
Her fairies here to search you, therefore deal
Directly with her highness: if they find

That you conceal a mite, you are undone.

DAPPER Truly, there's all.

FACE All what?

DAPPER My money; truly.

FACE Keep nothing that is transitory about you.

[Aside to Subtle] Bid Dol play music. Look,
   the elves are come

[Dol plays on the cittern within.]

To pinch you, if you tell not truth. Advise you.

[They pinch him.]

DAPPER O! I have a paper with a spur-ryal in't.

FACE *Ti, ti.*

They knew't, they say.

SUBTLE *Ti, ti, ti, ti.* He has more yet.

FACE *Ti, ti-ti-ti.*

[Aside to Subtle]

                       In the other pocket?

SUBTLE *Titi, titi, titi, titi, titi.*

They must pinch him or he will never confess,
   they say.

[They pinch him again.]

DAPPER O, O!

FACE Nay, pray you hold: he is her grace's
   nephew,

Ti, ti, ti? What care you? good faith, you shall
   care.—
Deal plainly, sir, and shame the fairies. Show
You are innocent.

DAPPER By this good light, I have nothing.

SUBTLE *Ti, ti, ti, ti, to, ta.* He does equivocate
   she says:

Ti, ti, do ti, ti ti do, ti da; and swears by the
   light when he is blinded.

DAPPER By this good *dark,* I have nothing but
   a half-crown

Of gold about my wrist, that my love gave me;
And a leaden heart I wore since she forsook me.

FACE I thought 'twas something. And would you
   incur

Your aunt's displeasure for these trifles? Come,
I had rather you had thrown away twenty half-
   crowns.

[Takes it off.]

You may wear your leaden heart still.—

[Enter Dol, hastily.]

                                        How
   now!

SUBTLE What news, Dol?

DOL Yonder's your knight, Sir Mammon.

FACE 'Ods lid, we never thought of him till now!
  Where is he?

DOL Here hard by: he is at the door.

SUBTLE And you are not ready now! Dol, get
  his suit.

[Exit Dol.]

He must not be sent back.

FACE O, by no means.
  What shall we do with this same puffin here,
  Now he's on the spit?

SUBTLE Why, lay him back awhile,
  With some device.

[Reenter Dol Common with Face's clothes.]

—Ti, ti, ti, ti, ti, ti, Would her grace speak with
  me?
I come.—Help, Dol!

[Knocking without.]

FACE [speaks through the keyhole] —Who's
  there? Sir Epicure,
My master's in the way. Please you to walk
Three or four turns, but till his back be turned,
And I am for you.—Quickly, Dol!

SUBTLE Her grace
Commends her kindly to you, Master Dapper.

DAPPER I long to see her grace.

SUBTLE She now is set
At dinner in her bed, and she has sent you
From her own private trencher, a dead mouse,
And a piece of gingerbread, to be merry withal,

And stay your stomach, lest you faint with fasting:
Yet if you could hold out till she saw you, she
  says,
It would be better for you.

FACE Sir, he shall
Hold out, an 'twere this two hours, for her high-
  ness;
I can assure you that. We will not lose
All we have done.—

SUBTLE He must not see, nor speak
To anybody, till then.

FACE For that we'll put, sir,
A stay in's mouth.

SUBTLE Of what?

FACE Of gingerbread.
Make you it fit. He that hath pleased her grace
Thus far, shall not now crinkle for a little.—
Gape, sir, and let him fit you.

[They thrust a gag of gingerbread in his mouth.]

SUBTLE Where shall we now bestow him?

DOL In the privy.

SUBTLE Come along, sir,
I must now show you Fortune's privy lodgings.

FACE Are they perfumed, and his bath ready?

SUBTLE All:
Only the fumigation's somewhat strong.

FACE [speaking through the keyhole] Sir Epicure,
  I am yours, sir, by and by.

[Exeunt with Dapper.]

Act Four

SCENE ONE

A room in Lovewit's house. Enter Face and
Mammon.

FACE O, sir, you are come in the only finest
  time.—

MAMMON Where's master?

FACE Now preparing for projection, sir.
  Your stuff will be all changed shortly.

MAMMON Into gold?

FACE To gold and silver, sir.

MAMMON Silver I care not for.

FACE Yes, sir, a little to give beggars.

MAMMON Where's the lady?

FACE At hand here. I have told her such brave
  things of you,
Touching your bounty and your noble spirit—

MAMMON Hast thou?

FACE As she is almost in her fit to see you.
  But, good sir, no divinity in your conference,
  For fear of putting her in a rage.—

MAMMON I warrant thee.

FACE Six men [sir] will not hold her down: and
  then,
If the old man should hear or see you—

MAMMON Fear not.

FACE The very house, sir, would run mad. You
  know it,

How scrupulous he is, and violent,
'Gainst the least act of sin. Physic or mathe-
matics,
Poetry, state, or bawdry, as I told you,
She will endure, and never startle; but
No word of controversy.

MAMMON   I am schooled, good Ulen.

FACE   And you must praise her house, remember
that,
And her nobility.

MAMMON   Let me alone:
No herald, no, nor antiquary, Lungs,
Shall do it better. Go.

FACE   [aside]   Why, this is yet
A kind of modern happiness, to have
Dol Common for a great lady.
[Exit.]

MAMMON   Now, Epicure,
Heighten thyself, talk to her all in gold;
Rain her as many showers as Jove did drops
Unto his Danäe; show the god a miser,
Compared with Mammon. What! the stone will
do't.
She shall feel gold, taste gold, hear gold, sleep
gold;
Nay, we will *concumbere* gold: I will be puis-
sant,
And mighty in my talk to her.—
[Reenter Face with Dol richly dressed.]
                              Here she comes.

FACE [aside]   To him, Dol, suckle him.—This is
the noble knight
I told your ladyship—

MAMMON   Madam, with your pardon,
I kiss your vesture.

DOL   Sir, I were uncivil
If I would suffer that: my lip to you, sir.

MAMMON   I hope my lord your brother be in
health, lady.

DOL   My lord my brother is, though I no lady,
sir.

FACE [aside]   Well said, my Guinea bird.

MAMMON   Right noble madam—

FACE [aside]   O, we shall have most fierce idolatry.

MAMMON   'Tis your prerogative.

DOL   Rather your courtesy.

MAMMON   Were there nought else t'enlarge your
virtues to me,

These answers speak your breeding and your
blood.

DOL   Blood we boast none, sir, a poor baron's
daughter.

MAMMON   Poor! and gat you? profane not. Had
your father
Slept all the happy remnant of his life
After that act, lien but there still, and panted,
He had done enough to make himself, his issue,
And his posterity noble.

DOL   Sir, although
We may be said to want the gilt and trappings,
The dress of honour, yet we strive to keep
The seeds and the materials.

MAMMON   I do see
The old ingredient, virtue, was not lost,
Nor the drug, money, used to make your com-
pound.
There is a strange nobility in your eye,
This lip, that chin! methinks you do resemble
One of the Austriac princes.

FACE   Very like!
[Aside]
Her father was an Irish costarmonger.

MAMMON   The house of Valois just had such a
nose,
And such a forehead yet the Medici
Of Florence boast.

DOL   Troth, and I have been likened
To all these princes.

FACE   I'll be sworn, I heard it.

MAMMON   I know not how! it is not any one,
But e'en the very choice of all their features.

FACE [aside]   I'll in, and laugh.
[Exit.]

MAMMON   A certain touch, or air,
That sparkles a divinity beyond
An earthly beauty!

DOL   O, you play the courtier.

MAMMON   Good lady, give me leave—

DOL   In faith, I may not,
To mock me, sir.

MAMMON   To burn in this sweet flame;
The phœnix never knew a nobler death.

DOL   Nay, now you court the courtier, and destroy
What you would build: this art, sir, in your
words,
Calls your whole faith in question.

MAMMON By my soul—

DOL Nay, oaths are made of the same air, sir.

MAMMON Nature
Never bestowed upon mortality
A more unblamed, a more harmonious feature;
She played the step-dame in all faces else:
Sweet madam, let me be particular—

DOL Particular, sir! I pray you know your distance.

MAMMON In no ill sense, sweet lady; but to ask
How your fair graces pass the hours? I see
You are lodged here, in the house of a rare man,
An excellent artist; but what's that to you?

DOL Yes, sir; I study here the mathematics,
And distillation.

MAMMON O, I cry your pardon.
He's a divine instructor! can extract
The souls of all things by his art; call all
The virtues, and the miracles of the sun,
Into a temperate furnace; teach dull nature
What her own forces are. A man, the emperor
Has courted above Kelly; sent his medals
And chains, to invite him.

DOL Ay, and for his physic, sir—

MAMMON Above the art of Æsculapius,
That drew the envy of the thunderer!
I know all this, and more.

DOL Troth, I am taken, sir,
Whole with these studies, that contemplate nature.

MAMMON It is a noble humour; but this form
Was not intended to so dark a use.
Had you been crooked, foul, of some coarse mould,
A cloister had done well; but such a feature
That might stand up the glory of a kingdom,
To live recluse! is a mere solœcism,
Though in a nunnery. It must not be.
I muse, my lord your brother will permit it:
You should spend half my land first, were I he.
Does not this diamond better on my finger
Than in the quarry?

DOL Yes.

MAMMON Why, you are like it.
You were created, lady, for the light.
Here, you shall wear it; take it, the first pledge
Of what I speak, to bind you to believe me.

DOL In chains of adamant?

MAMMON Yes, the strongest bands.

And take a secret too—here, by your side,
Doth stand this hour the happiest man in Europe.

DOL You are contented, sir?

MAMMON Nay, in true being,
The envy of princes and the fear of states.

DOL Say you so, Sir Epicure?

MAMMON Yes, and thou shalt prove it,
Daughter of honour. I have cast mine eye
Upon thy form, and I will rear this beauty
Above all styles.

DOL You mean no treason, sir?

MAMMON No, I will take away that jealousy.
I am the lord of the philosopher's stone,
And thou the lady.

DOL How, sir! have you that?

MAMMON I am the master of the mastery.
This day the good old wretch here o' the house
Has made it for us: now he's at projection.
Think therefore thy first wish now, let me hear it;
And it shall rain into thy lap, no shower,
But floods of gold, whole cataracts, a deluge,
To get a nation on thee.

DOL You are pleased, sir,
To work on the ambition of our sex.

MAMMON I am pleased the glory of her sex should know,
This nook here of the Friars is no climate
For her to live obscurely in, to learn
Physic and surgery, for the constable's wife
Of some odd hundred in Essex; but come forth,
And taste the air of palaces; eat, drink
The toils of empirics, and their boasted practice,
Tincture of pearl, and coral, gold, and amber;
Be seen at feasts and triumphs; have it asked
What miracle she is? set all the eyes
Of court a-fire, like a burning glass,
And work them into cinders, when the jewels
Of twenty states adorn thee, and the light
Strikes out the stars! that, when thy name is mentioned,
Queens may look pale; and we but showing our love,
Nero's Poppæa may be lost in story!
Thus will we have it.

DOL I could well consent, sir.
But in a monarchy, how will this be?
The prince will soon take notice, and both seize

You and your stone, it being a wealth unfit
For any private subject.

MAMMON If he knew it.

DOL Yourself do boast it, sir.

MAMMON To thee, my life.

DOL O, but beware, sir! you may come to end
The remnant of your days in a lothed prison,
By speaking of it.

MAMMON 'Tis no idle fear:
We'll therefore go withal, my girl, and live
In a free state, where we will eat our mullets,
Soused in high-country wines, sup pheasants'
  eggs
And have our cockles boiled in silver shells;
Our shrimps to swim again, as when they lived,
In a rare butter made of dolphins' milk,
Whose cream does look like opals; and with
  these
Delicate meats set ourselves high for pleasure,
And take us down again, and then renew
Our youth and strength with drinking the elixir,
And so enjoy a perpetuity
Of life and lust! And thou shalt have thy ward-
  robe
Richer than Nature's, still to change thyself,
And vary oftener, for thy pride, than she,
Or Art, her wise and almost-equal servant.
  [*Reenter Face*.]

FACE Sir, you are too loud. I hear you every
  word
Into the laboratory. Some fitter place;
The garden, or great chamber above. How like
  you her?

MAMMON Excellent! Lungs. There's for thee.
  [*Gives him money*.]

FACE But do you hear?
  Good sir, beware, no mention of the rabbins.

MAMMON We think not on 'em.
  [*Exeunt Mammon and Dol*.]

FACE O, it is well, sir.—Subtle!
  [*Enter Subtle*.]
  Dost thou not laugh?

SUBTLE Yes; are they gone?

FACE All's clear.

SUBTLE The widow is come.

FACE And your quarrelling disciple?

SUBTLE Ay.

FACE I must to my captainship again then.

SUBTLE Stay, bring them in first.

FACE So I meant. What is she?
  A bonnibel?

SUBTLE I know not.

FACE We'll draw lots:
  You'll stand to that?

SUBTLE What else?

FACE O, for a suit,
  To fall now like a curtain, flap!

SUBTLE To the door, man.

FACE You'll have the first kiss, 'cause I am not
  ready.
  [*Exit*.]

SUBTLE Yes, and perhaps hit you through both
  the nostrils.

FACE [*within*] Who would you speak with?

KASTRIL [*within*] Where's the captain?

FACE [*within*] Gone, sir.
  About some business.

KASTRIL [*within*] Gone!

FACE [*within*] He'll return straight.
  But, master doctor, his lieutenant, is here.
  [*Enter Kastril, followed by Dame Pliant*.]

SUBTLE Come near, my worshipful boy, my *terræ
  fili*,
  That is, my boy of land; make thy approaches:
  Welcome; I know thy lusts, and thy desires,
  And I will serve and satisfy them. Begin,
  Charge me from thence, or thence, or in this
  line;
  Here is my centre: ground thy quarrel.

KASTRIL You lie.

SUBTLE How, child of wrath and anger! the loud
  lie?
  For what, my sudden boy?

KASTRIL Nay, that look you to,
  I am aforehand.

SUBTLE O, this is no true grammar,
  And as ill logic! You must render causes, child,
  Your first and second intentions, know your
  canons
  And your divisions, moods, degrees, and differ-
  ences,
  Your predicaments, substance, and accident,
  Series extern and intern, with their causes,
  Efficient, material, formal, final,
  And have your elements perfect.

KASTRIL [*aside*] What is this!

BEN JONSON

The angry tongue he talks in?

SUBTLE That false precept,
Of being aforehand, has deceived a number,
And made them enter quarrels oftentimes
Before they were aware; and afterward,
Against their wills.

KASTRIL How must I do then, sir?

SUBTLE I cry this lady mercy: she should first
Have been saluted.

[*Kisses her.*]

                 I do call you lady,
Because you are to be one ere 't be long,
My soft and buxom widow.

KASTRIL Is she, i' faith?

SUBTLE Yes, or my art is an egregious liar.

KASTRIL How know you?

SUBTLE By inspection on her forehead,
And subtlety of her lip, which must be tasted
Often to make a judgment.

[*Kisses her again.*]

                'Slight, she melts
Like a myrobolane: here is yet a line,
In *rivo frontis,* tells me he is no knight.

DAME PLIANT What is he then, sir?

SUBTLE Let me see your hand.
O, your *linea fortunæ* makes it plain;
And stella here *in monte Veneris.*
But, most of all, *junctura annularis.*
He is a soldier, or a man of art, lady,
But shall have some great honour shortly.

DAME PLIANT Brother,
He's a rare man, believe me!

[*Reenter Face, in his uniform.*]

KASTRIL Hold your peace.
Here comes the t'other rare man.—'Save you,
   captain.

FACE Good Master Kastril! Is this your sister?

KASTRIL Ay, sir.
Please you to kiss her, and be proud to know
   her.

FACE I shall be proud to know you, lady.

[*Kisses her.*]

DAME PLIANT Brother,
He calls me lady too.

KASTRIL Ay, peace: I heard it.

[*Takes her aside.*]

FACE The count is come.

SUBTLE Where is he?

FACE At the door.

SUBTLE Why, you must entertain him.

FACE What will you do
With these the while?

SUBTLE Why, have them up, and show them
Some fustian book, or the dark glass.

FACE 'Fore God,
She is a delicate dabchick! I must have her.

[*Exit.*]

SUBTLE Must you! ay, if your fortune will, you
   must.—
Come, sir, the captain will come to us presently:
I'll have you to my chamber of demonstrations,
Where I will show you both the grammar and
   logic,
And rhetoric of quarrelling: my whole method
Drawn out in tables; and my instrument,
That hath the several scales upon't, shall make
   you
Able to quarrel at a straw's-breadth by moon-
   light.
And, lady, I'll have you look in a glass,
Some half an hour, but to clear your eyesight,
Against you see your fortune; which is greater
Than I may judge upon the sudden, trust me.

[*Exit, followed by Kastril and Dame Pliant. Reenter Face.*]

FACE Where are you, doctor?

SUBTLE [*within*] I'll come to you presently.

FACE I will have this same widow, now I have
   seen her,
On any composition.

[*Reenter Subtle.*]

SUBTLE What do you say?

FACE Have you disposed of them?

SUBTLE I have sent them up.

FACE Subtle, in troth, I needs must have this
   widow.

SUBTLE Is that the matter?

FACE Nay, but hear me.

SUBTLE Go to.
If you rebel once, Dol shall know it all:
Therefore be quiet, and obey your chance.

FACE Nay, thou art so violent now. Do but conceive,
Thou art old, and canst not serve—

SUBTLE Who cannot? I?
'Slight, I will serve her with thee, for a—

FACE Nay,
But understand: I'll give you composition.

SUBTLE I will not treat with thee; what! sell my fortune?
'Tis better than my birthright. Do not murmur:
Win her, and carry her. If you grumble, Dol
Knows it directly.

FACE Well, sir, I am silent.
Will you go help to fetch in Don in state?
[*Exit.*]

SUBTLE I follow you, sir.—We must keep Face in awe,
Or he will overlook us like a tyrant.

[*Reenter Face, introducing Surly disguised as a Spaniard.*]
Brain of a tailor! who comes here? Don John!

SURLY *Senores, beso las manos a vuestras mercedes.*

SUBTLE Would you had stooped a little, and kist our *anos!*

FACE Peace, Subtle.

SUBTLE Stab me; I shall never hold, man.
He looks in that deep ruff like a head in a platter,
Served in by a short cloak upon two trestles.

FACE Or what do you say to a collar of brawn, cut down
Beneath the souse, and wriggled with a knife?

SUBTLE 'Slud, he does look too fat to be a Spaniard.

FACE Perhaps some Fleming or some Hollander got him
In d'Alva's time; Count Egmont's bastard.

SUBTLE Don,
Your scurvy, yellow, Madrid face is welcome.

SURLY *Gratia.*

SUBTLE He speaks out of a fortification.
Pray God he have no squibs in those deep sets.[16]

SURLY *Por dios, senores, muy linda casa!*

SUBTLE What says he?

FACE Praises the house, I think;
I know no more but's action.

SUBTLE Yes, the *casa,*
My precious Diego will prove fair enough
To cozen you in. Do you mark? you shall
Be cozened, Diego.

---

[16] In the deep plaits of his *ruff.*

FACE Cozened, do you see,
My worthy Donzel, cozened.

SURLY *Entiendo.*

SUBTLE Do you intend it? so do we, dear Don.
Have you brought pistolets, or portagues,
My solemn Don? Dost thou feel any?

FACE [*feels his pockets*] Full.

SUBTLE You shall be emptied, Don, pumped and drawn
Dry, as they say.

FACE Milked, in troth, sweet Don.

SUBTLE See all the monsters; the great lion of all, Don.

SURLY *Con licencia, se puede ver a esta señora?*

SUBTLE What talks he now?

FACE Of the sennora.

SUBTLE O, Don,
This is the lioness, which you shall see
Also, my Don.

FACE 'Slid, Subtle, how shall we do?

SUBTLE For what?

FACE Why, Dol's employed, you know.

SUBTLE That's true.
'Fore heaven I know not: he must stay, that's all.

FACE Stay! that he must not by no means.

SUBTLE No! why?

FACE Unless you'll mar all. 'Slight, he will suspect it:
And then he will not pay not half so well.
This is a travelled punk-master, and does know
All the delays; a notable hot rascal.
And looks already rampant.

SUBTLE 'Sdeath, and Mammon
Must not be troubled.

FACE Mammon! In no case.

SUBTLE What shall we do then?

FACE Think: you must be sudden.

SURLY *Entiendo que la señora es tan hermosa,
que codicio tan verla, como la bien aventuranza de mi vida.*

FACE *Mi vida!* 'Slid, Subtle, he puts me in mind
o' the widow.
What dost thou say to draw her to it, ha!
And tell her 'tis her fortune? all our venture
Now lies upon't. It is but one man more,
Which of us chance to have her: and beside,
There is no maidenhead to be feared or lost.
What dost thou think on't, Subtle?

SUBTLE Who, I? why—

FACE The credit of our house too is engaged.

SUBTLE You made me an offer for my share
erewhile.

What wilt thou give me, 'i faith?

FACE O, by that light
I'll not buy now. You know your doom to me.
E'en take your lot, obey your chance, sir; win
her,
And wear her out, for me.

SUBTLE 'Slight, I'll not work her then.

FACE It is the common cause; therefore bethink
you.
Dol else must know it, as you said.

SUBTLE I care not.

SURLY Señores, porque se tarda tanto?

SUBTLE Faith, I am not fit, I am old.

FACE That's now no reason, sir.

SURLY Puede ser de hazer burla de mi amor?

FACE You hear the Don too? by this air I call,
And loose the hinges. Dol!

SUBTLE A plague of hell—

FACE Will you then do?

SUBTLE You are a terrible rogue!
I'll think of this: will you, sir, call the widow?

FACE Yes, and I'll take her too with all her
faults,
Now I do think on't better.

SUBTLE With all my heart, sir;
Am I discharged o' the lot?

FACE As you please.

SUBTLE Hands.
[They take hands.]

FACE Remember now, that upon any change,
You never claim her.

SUBTLE Much good joy and health to you, sir,
Marry a whore! fate, let me wed a witch first.

SURLY Por estas honradas barbas—

SUBTLE He swears by his beard.
Dispatch, and call the brother too.
[Exit Face.]

SURLY Tengo duda, señores, que no me hagan
alguna traycion.

SUBTLE How, issue on? yes, præsto, sennor.
Please you
Enthratha the chambratha, worthy don:
Where if you please the fates, in your bathada,
You shall be soaked, and stroked, and tubbed,
and rubbed,

And scrubbed, and fubbed, dear don, before
you go,
You shall in faith, my scurvy baboon don,
Be curried, clawed, and flawed, and tawed, in-
deed.
I will the heartlier go about it now,
And make the widow a punk so much the
sooner,
To be revenged on this impetuous Face:
The quickly doing of it is the grace.
[Exeunt Subtle and Surly.]

SCENE TWO

*Another room in the same house. Enter Face,
Kastril, and Dame Pliant.*

FACE Come, lady: I knew the doctor would not
leave
Till he had found the very nick of her fortune.

KASTRIL To be a countess, say you, a Spanish
countess, sir?

DAME PLIANT Why, is that better than an English
countess?

FACE Better! 'Slight, make you that a question,
lady?

KASTRIL Nay, she is a fool, captain, you must
pardon her.

FACE Ask from your courtier, to your inns-of-
court-man,
To your mere milliner; they will tell you all,
Your Spanish jennet is the best horse; your
Spanish
Stoup is the best garb; your Spanish beard
Is the best cut; your Spanish ruffs are the best
Wear; your Spanish pavin the best dance;
Your Spanish titillation in a glove
The best perfume: and for your Spanish pike,
And Spanish blade, let your poor captain
speak—
Here comes the doctor.
[Enter Subtle with a paper.]

SUBTLE My most honoured lady,
For so I am now to style you, having found
By this my scheme, you are to undergo
An honourable fortune very shortly.
What will you say now, if some—

FACE I have told her all, sir;
And her right worshipful brother here, that she
shall be

A countess; do not delay them, sir: a Spanish countess.

SUBTLE Still, my scarce-worshipful captain, you can keep
No secret! Well, since he has told you, madam,
Do you forgive him, and I do.

KASTRIL She shall do that, sir;
I'll look to it, 'tis my charge.

SUBTLE Well then: nought rests
But that she fit her love now to her fortune.

DAME PLIANT Truly I shall never brook a Spaniard.

SUBTLE No!

DAME PLIANT Never since eighty-eight,[17] could I abide them,
And that was some three years afore I was born, in truth.

SUBTLE Come, you must love him, or be miserable;
Choose which you will.

FACE By this good rush, persuade her,
She will cry strawberries else within this twelve month.

SUBTLE Nay, shads and mackerel, which is worse.

FACE Indeed, sir!

KASTRIL 'Ods lid, you shall love him, or I'll kick you.

DAME PLIANT Why,
I'll do as you will have me, brother.

KASTRIL Do,
Or by this hand I'll maul you.

FACE Nay, good sir,
Be not so fierce.

SUBTLE No, my enraged child;
She will be ruled. What, when she comes to taste
The pleasures of a countess! to be courted—

FACE And kissed, and ruffled!

SUBTLE Ay, behind the hangings.

FACE And then come forth in pomp!

SUBTLE And know her state!

FACE Of keeping all the idolaters of the chamber
Barer to her, than at their prayers!

SUBTLE Is served

17 Since 1588, the year of the "Invincible Armada."

Upon the knee!

FACE And has her pages, ushers,
Footmen, and coaches—

SUBTLE Her six mares—

FACE Nay, eight!

SUBTLE To hurry her through London, to the Exchange, Bethlem, the china-houses—

FACE Yes, and have
The citizens gape at her, and praise her tires,
And my lord's goose-turd bands, that ride with her!

KASTRIL Most brave! By this hand, you are not my suster
If you refuse.

DAME PLIANT I will not refuse, brother.

[*Enter Surly.*]

SURLY *Que es esto, señores, que no venga? Esta tardanza me mata!*

FACE It is the count come:
The doctor knew he would be here, by his art.

SUBTLE *En gallanta madama, Don! gallantissima!*

SURLY *Por todos los dioses, la mas acabada hermosura, que he visto enmi vada!*

FACE Is't not a gallant language that they speak?

KASTRIL An admirable language? Is't not French?

FACE No, Spanish, sir.

KASTRIL It goes like law French,
And that, they say, is the courtliest language.

FACE List, sir.

SURLY *El sol ha perdido su lumbre, con el esplandor que trae esta dama! Valgame dios!*

FACE He admires your sister.

KASTRIL Must not she make curt'sy?

SUBTLE 'Ods will, she must go to him, man, and kiss him!
It is the Spanish fashion, for the women
To make first court.

FACE 'Tis true he tells you, sir:
His art knows all.

SURLY *Porque no se acude?*

KASTRIL He speaks to her, I think.

FACE That he does, sir.

SURLY *Por el amor de dios, que es esto que se tarda?*

KASTRIL Nay, see: she will not understand him! gull,
Noddy.

DAME PLIANT What say you, brother?

KASTRIL Ass, my suster,
Go kuss him, as the cunning man would have
you;
I'll thrust a pin in your buttocks else.

FACE O no, sir.

SURLY *Señora mia, mi persona esta muy indigna
de allegar a tanta hermosura.*

FACE Does he not use her bravely?

KASTRIL Bravely, i' faith!

FACE Nay, he will use her better.

KASTRIL Do you think so?

SURLY *Señora, si sera servida, entremonos.*
[*Exit with Dame Pliant.*]

KASTRIL Where does he carry her?

FACE Into the garden, sir;
Take you no thought: I must interpret for her.

SUBTLE [*aside to Face*] Give Dol the word.
[*Exit Face.*]   Come,
my fierce child, advance,
We'll to our quarrelling lesson again.

KASTRIL Agreed.
I love a Spanish boy with all my heart.

SUBTLE Nay, and by this means, sir, you shall
be brother
To a great count.

KASTRIL Ay, I knew that at first,
This match will advance the house of the
Kastrils.

SUBTLE 'Pray God your sister prove but pliant!

KASTRIL Why,
Her name is so, by her other husband.

SUBTLE How!

KASTRIL The Widow Pliant. Knew you not that?

SUBTLE No, faith, sir;
Yet, by erection of her figure, I guess it.
Come, let's go practise.

KASTRIL Yes, but do you think, doctor,
I e'er shall quarrel well?

SUBTLE I warrant you.
[*Exeunt.*]

SCENE THREE

*Another room in the same house. Enter Dol
Common in her fit of raving, followed by Mammon.*

DOL *For after Alexander's death—*

MAMMON Good lady—

DOL *That Perdiccas and Antigonus were slain,
The two that stood, Seleuc and Ptolomee—*

MAMMON Madam—

DOL *Make up the two legs, and the fourth beast,
That was Gog-north and Egypt-south: which
after
Was called Grog-iron-leg and South-iron-leg.*

MAMMON Lady—

DOL *And then Gog-horned. So was Egypt, too.
Then Egypt-clay-leg, and Gog-clay-leg—*

MAMMON Sweet madam—

DOL *And last Gog-dust, and Egypt-dust, which
fall
In the last link of the fourth chain. And these
Be stars in story, which none see, or look at—*

MAMMON What shall I do?

DOL *For, as he says, except
We call the rabbins, and the heathen Greeks—*

MAMMON Dear lady—

DOL *To come from Salem, and from Athens,
And teach the people of Great Britain—*
[*Enter Face hastily, in his servant's dress.*]

FACE What's the matter, sir?

DOL *To speak the tongue of Eber and Favan—*

MAMMON O,
She's in her fit.

DOL *We shall know nothing—*

FACE Death, sir,
We are undone!

DOL *Where then a learned linguist
Shall see the ancient used communion
Of vowels and consonants—*

FACE My master will hear!

DOL *A wisdom, which Pythagoras held most
high—*

MAMMON Sweet honourable lady!

DOL *To comprise
All sounds of voices, in few marks of letters.*

FACE Nay, you must never hope to lay her now.
[*They all speak together.*]

DOL *And so we may arrive by Talmud skill,
And profane Greek, to raise the building up
Of Helen's house against the Ismaelite,
King of Thogarma, and his habergions
Brimstony, blue, and fiery; and the force
Of king Abaddon, and the beast of Cittim,
Which rabbi David Kimchi, Onkelos,
And Aben Ezra do interpret Rome.*

The Alchemist   *173*

FACE How did you put her into't?

MAMMON Alas, I talked
Of a fifth monarchy I would erect,
With the philosopher's stone, by chance, and she
Falls on the other four straight.

FACE Out of Broughton!
I told you so. 'Slid, stop her mouth.

MAMMON Is't best?

FACE She'll never leave else. If the old man hear her,
We are but fæces, ashes.

SUBTLE [*within*] What's to do there?

FACE O, we are lost! Now she hears him, she is quiet.

[*Enter Subtle: they run different ways.*]

MAMMON Where shall I hide me!

SUBTLE How! what sight is here?
Close deeds of darkness, and that shun the light!
Bring him again. Who is he? What, my son!
O, I have lived too long.

MAMMON Nay, good, dear father,
There was no unchaste purpose.

SUBTLE Not! and flee me,
When I come in?

MAMMON That was my error.

SUBTLE Error!
Guilt, guilt, my son: give it the right name. No marvel,
If I found check in your great work within,
When such affairs as these were managing!

MAMMON Why, have you so?

SUBTLE It has stood still this half hour:
And all the rest of our less works gone back.
Where is the instrument of wickedness,
My lewd false drudge?

MAMMON Nay, good sir, blame not him;
Believe me, 'twas against his will or knowledge:
I saw her by chance.

SUBTLE Will you commit more sin,
To excuse a varlet?

MAMMON By my hope, 'tis true, sir.

SUBTLE Nay, then I wonder less, if you, for whom
The blessing was prepared, would so tempt heaven,
And lose your fortunes.

MAMMON Why, sir?

SUBTLE This will retard

The work a month a least.

MAMMON Why, if it do,
What remedy? But think it not, good father:
Our purposes were honest.

SUBTLE As they were,
So the reward will prove—
[*A loud explosion within.*]
How now! ah me!
God and all saints be good to us.—
[*Reenter Face.*]
What's that?

FACE O, sir, we are defeated! all the works
Are flown *in fumo*, every glass is burst:
Furnace, and all rent down! as if a bolt
Of thunder had been driven through the house.
Retorts, receivers, pelicans, bolt-heads,
All struck in shivers!
[*Subtle falls down as in a swoon.*]
Help, good sir! alas,
Coldness and death invades him. Nay, Sir Mammon,
Do the fair offices of a man! you stand,
As you were readier to depart than he.
[*Knocking within.*]
Who's there? my lord her brother is come.

MAMMON Ha, Lungs!

FACE His coach is at the door. Avoid his sight,
For he's as furious as his sister's mad.

MAMMON Alas!

FACE My brain is quite undone with the fume, sir,
I ne'er must hope to be mine own man again.

MAMMON Is all lost, Lungs? will nothing be preserved
Of all our cost?

FACE Faith, very little, sir;
A peck of coals or so, which is cold comfort, sir.

MAMMON O, my voluptuous mind! I am justly punished.

FACE And so am I, sir.

MAMMON Cast from all hopes—

FACE Nay, certainties, sir.

MAMMON By mine own base affections.

SUBTLE [*seeming to come to himself*] O, the curst fruits of vice and lust!

MAMMON Good father,
It was my sin. Forgive it.

SUBTLE Hangs my roof

Over us still, and will not fall, O justice,
Upon us, for this wicked man!

FACE Nay, look, sir,
You grieve him now with staying in his sight:
Good sir, the nobleman will come too, and take you,
And that may breed a tragedy.

MAMMON I'll go.

FACE Ay, and repent at home, sir. It may be,
For some good penance you may have it yet;
A hundred pound to the box at Bethlem—

MAMMON Yes.

FACE For the restoring such as—have their wits.

MAMMON I'll do't.

FACE I'll send one to you to receive it.

MAMMON Do.
Is no projection left?

FACE All flown, or stinks, sir.

MAMMON Will nought be saved that's good for med'cine, think'st thou?

FACE I cannot tell, sir. There will be perhaps
Something about the scraping of the shards,
Will cure the itch,—
[aside]
                              though not your itch of
    mind, sir.
It shall be saved for you, and sent home. Good sir,
This way for fear the lord should meet you.
[Exit Mammon.]

SUBTLE [raising his head] Face!

FACE Ay.

SUBTLE Is he gone?

FACE Yes, and as heavily
As all the gold he hoped for were in's blood.
Let us be light though.

SUBTLE [leaping up] Ay, as balls, and bound
And hit our heads against the roof for joy:
There's so much of our care now cast away.

FACE Now to our don.

SUBTLE Yes, your young widow by this time
Is made a countess, Face; she has been in travail
Of a young heir for you.

FACE Good, sir.

SUBTLE Off with your case,
And greet her kindly, as a bridegroom should,
After these common hazards.

FACE Very well, sir.
Will you go fetch Don Diego off the while?

SUBTLE And fetch him over too, if you'll be pleased, sir:
Would Dol were in her place, to pick his pockets now!

FACE Why, you can do't as well, if you would set to't.
I pray you prove your virtue.

SUBTLE For your sake, sir.
[Exeunt.]

SCENE FOUR

Another room in the same house. Enter Surly and Dame Pliant.

SURLY Lady, you see into what hands you are fallen;
'Mongst what a nest of villains! and how near
Your honour was t'have catched a certain clap,
Through your credulity, had I but been
So punctually forward, as place, time,
And other circumstances would have made a man;
For you're a handsome woman; would you were wise too!
I am a gentleman come here disguised,
Only to find the knaveries of this citadel;
And where I might have wronged your honour, and have not,
I claim some interest in your love. You are,
They say, a widow, rich; and I'm a bachelor,
Worth nought: your fortunes may make me a man,
As mine have preserved you a woman. Think upon it,
And whether I have deserved you or no.

DAME PLIANT I will, sir.

SURLY And for these household-rogues, let me alone
To treat with them.
[Enter Subtle.]

SUBTLE How doth my noble Diego,
And my dear madam countess? hath the count
Been courteous, lady? liberal and open?
Donzel, methinks you look melancholic,
After your coitum, and scurvy: truly,
I do not like the dulness of your eye;
It hath a heavy cast, 'tis upsee Dutch,
And says you are a lumpish whore-master.

Be lighter, I will make your pockets so.
[*Attempts to pick them.*]

SURLY [*throws open his cloak*] Will you, don
bawd and pick-purse?
[*Strikes him down.*]
How now! reel you?
Stand up, sir, you shall find, since I am so
heavy,
I'll give you equal weight.

SUBTLE Help! murder!

SURLY No, sir,
There's no such thing intended: a good cart
And a clean whip shall ease you of that fear.
I am the Spanish don *that should be cozened,
Do you see, cozened!* Where's your Captain
Face,
That parcel-broker, and whole-bawd, all rascal?
[*Enter Face in his uniform.*]

FACE How, Surly!

SURLY O, make your approach, good captain.
I have found from whence your copper rings
and spoons
Come now, wherewith you cheat abroad in
taverns.
'Twas here you learned t'anoint your boot with
brimstone,
Then rub men's gold on't for a kind of touch,
And say 'twas naught, when you had changed
the colour,
That you might have't for nothing. And this
doctor,
Your sooty, smoky-bearded compeer, he
Will close you so much gold, in a bolt's-head,
And, on a turn, convey in the stead another
With sublimed mercury, that shall burst in the
heat,
And fly out all *in fumo!* Then weeps Mammon;
Then swoons his worship.
[*Face slips out.*]
Or, he is the Faustus,
That casteth figures and can conjure, cures
Plagues, piles, and pox, by the ephemerides,
And holds intelligence with all the bawds
And midwives of three shires: while you send
in—
Captain!—what! is he gone?—damsels with
child,
Wives that are barren, or the waiting-maid

With the green sickness.
[*Seizes Subtle as he is retiring.*]
—Nay, sir, you must
tarry,
Though he be scaped; and answer by the ears,
sir.
[*Reenter Face with Kastril.*]

FACE Why, now's the time, if ever you will
quarrel
Well, as they say, and be a true-born child:
The doctor and your sister both are abused.

KASTRIL Where is he? which is he? he is a slave,
Whate'er he is, and the son of a whore.—Are
you
The man, sir, I would know?

SURLY I should be loth, sir,
To confess so much.

KASTRIL Then you lie in your throat.

SURLY How!

FACE [*to Kastril*] A very errant rogue, sir, and
a cheater,
Employed here by another conjurer
That does not love the doctor, and would cross
him
If he knew how.

SURLY Sir, you are abused.

KASTRIL You lie:
And 'tis no matter.

FACE Well said, sir! He is
The impudent'st rascal—

SURLY You are indeed. Will you hear me, sir?

FACE By no means: bid him be gone.

KASTRIL Begone, sir, quickly.

SURLY This is strange!—Lady, do you inform
your brother.

FACE There is not such a foist in all the town,
The doctor had him presently; and finds yet
The Spanish count will come here.—
[*Aside*]
Bear up,
Subtle.

SUBTLE Yes, sir, he must appear within this
hour.

FACE And yet this rogue would come in a dis-
guise,
By the temptation of another spirit,
To trouble our art, though he could not hurt it!

KASTRIL Ay,

BEN JONSON

I know—
[*To his sister*]
            Away, you talk like a foolish mauther.

SURLY Sir, all is truth she says.

FACE Do not believe him, sir.
He is the lying'st swabber! Come your ways, sir.

SURLY You are valiant out of company!

KASTRIL Yes, how then, sir?
[*Enter Drugger with a piece of damask.*]

FACE Nay, here's an honest fellow too that knows him,
And all his tricks.
[*Aside to Drugger*]
            Make good what I say, Abel,
This cheater would have cozened thee o' the widow.
He owes this honest Drugger here seven pound,
He has had on him in twopenny'orths of tobacco.

DRUGGER Yes, sir.
And he has damned himself three terms to pay me.

FACE And what does he owe for lotium?

DRUGGER Thirty shillings, sir;
And for six syringes.

SURLY Hydra of villainy!

FACE Nay, sir, you must quarrel him out o' the house.

KASTRIL I will:
—Sir, if you get not out o' doors, you lie;
And you are a pimp.

SURLY Why, this is madness, sir,
Not valour in you; I must laugh at this.

KASTRIL It is my humour; you are a pimp and a trig.
And an *Amadis de Gaul,* or a Don Quixote.

DRUGGER Or a knight o' the curious coxcomb, do you see?
[*Enter Ananias.*]

ANANIAS Peace to the household!

KASTRIL I'll keep peace for no man,

ANANIAS Casting of dollars is concluded lawful.

KASTRIL Is he the constable?

SUBTLE Peace, Ananias.

FACE No, sir.

KASTRIL Then you are an otter, and a shad, a whit,
A very tim.

SURLY You'll hear me, sir?

KASTRIL I will not.

ANANIAS What is the motive?

SUBTLE Zeal in the young gentleman,
Against his Spanish slops.

ANANIAS They are profane,
Lewd, superstitious, and idolatrous breeches.

SURLY New rascals!

KASTRIL Will you be gone, sir?

ANANIAS Avoid, Sathan!
Thou art not of the light! That ruff of pride
About thy neck, betrays thee; and is the same
With that which the unclean birds, in seventy-
    seven,
Were seen to prank it with on divers coasts:
Thou look'st like antichrist, in that lewd hat.

SURLY I must give way.

KASTRIL Be gone, sir.

SURLY But I'll take
A course with you—

ANANIAS Depart, proud Spanish fiend!

SURLY Captain and doctor.

ANANIAS Child of perdition!

KASTRIL Hence, sir!—
[*Exit Surly.*]
Did I not quarrel bravely?

FACE Yes, indeed, sir.

KASTRIL Nay, an I give my mind to't, I shall do't.

FACE O, you must follow, sir, and threaten him tame:
He'll turn again else.

KASTRIL I'll re-turn him then.
[*Exit. Subtle takes Ananias aside.*]

FACE Drugger, this rogue prevented us, for thee:
We had determined that thou should'st have come
In a Spanish suit, and have carried her so; and he
A brokerly slave! goes, puts it on himself.
Hast brought the damask?

DRUGGER Yes, sir.

FACE Thou must borrow
A Spanish suit: hast thou no credit with the players?

DRUGGER Yes, sir; did you never see me play the Fool?

FACE I know not, Nab: [*aside*] thou shalt, if I
  can help it.—
Hieronimo's old cloak, ruff, and hat will serve;
I'll tell thee more when thou bring'st 'em.
[*Exit Drugger.*]
ANANIAS Sir, I know
The Spaniard hates the brethren, and hath spies
Upon their actions: and that this was one
I make no scruple.—But the holy synod
Have been in prayer and meditation for it;
And 'tis revealed no less to them than me,
That casting of money is most lawful.
SUBTLE True.
But here I cannot do it: if the house
Shou'd chance to be suspected, all would out,
And we be locked up in the Tower for ever,
To make gold there for the state, never come
  out;
And then are you defeated.
ANANIAS I will tell
This to the elders and the weaker brethren,
That the whole company of the separation
May join in humble prayer again.
SUBTLE And fasting.
ANANIAS Yea, for some fitter place. The peace
  of mind
Rest with these walls!
[*Exit.*]
SUBTLE Thanks, courteous Ananias.
FACE What did he come for?
SUBTLE About casting dollars,
  Presently, out of hand. And so I told him,
  A Spanish minister came here to spy,
  Against the faithful—
FACE I conceive. Come, Subtle,
  Thou art so down upon the least disaster!
  How wouldst thou ha' done, if I had not help't
  thee out?
SUBTLE I thank thee, Face, for the angry boy, i'
  faith.
FACE Who would have looked it should have
  been that rascal
Surly? He has dyed his beard and all. Well,
  sir,
Here's damask come to make you a suit.
SUBTLE Where's Drugger?
FACE He is gone to borrow me a Spanish habit;
  I'll be the count now.
SUBTLE But where's the widow?

FACE Within, with my lord's sister; Madam Dol
  Is entertaining her.
SUBTLE By your favour, Face.
  Now she is honest, I will stand again.
FACE You will not offer it?
SUBTLE Why?
FACE Stand to your word,
  Or—here comes Dol, she knows—
SUBTLE You are tyrannous still.
[*Enter Dol hastily.*]
FACE —Strict for my right.—How now, Dol!
  Hast [thou] told her,
The Spanish count will come?
DOL Yes; but another is come,
  You little looked for!
FACE Who is that?
DOL Your master;
  The master of the house.
SUBTLE How, Dol!
FACE She lies,
  This is some trick. Come, leave your quiblins,
  Dorothy.
DOL Look out and see.
[*Face goes to the window.*]
SUBTLE Art thou in earnest?
DOL 'Slight,
  Forty o' the neighbours are about him, talking.
FACE 'Tis he, by this good day.
DOL 'Twill prove ill day
  For some on us.
FACE We are undone, and taken.
DOL Lost, I'm afraid.
SUBTLE You said he would not come,
  While there died one a week within the liberties.
FACE No: 'twas within the walls.
SUBTLE Was't so! cry you mercy.
  I thought the liberties. What shall we do now,
  Face?
FACE Be silent: not a word, if he call or knock.
  I'll into mine old shape again and meet him,
  Of Jeremy, the butler. In the meantime,
  Do you two pack up all the goods and pur-
  chase.[18]
  That we can carry in the two trunks. I'll keep
  him
  Off for to-day, if I cannot longer: and then
  At night, I'll ship you both away to Ratcliff,

---

[18] A cant term for goods stolen.

Where we will meet to-morrow, and there we'll
  share.
Let Mammon's brass and pewter keep the cellar;
We'll have another time for that. But, Dol,
Prithee go heat a little water quickly;
Subtle must shave me: all my captain's beard

Must off, to make me appear smooth Jeremy.
You'll do it?
SUBTLE Yes, I'll shave you as well as I can.
FACE And not cut my throat, but trim me?
SUBTLE You shall see, sir.
[*Exeunt.*]

Act Five

SCENE ONE

Before Lovewit's door. Enter Lovewit, with several of the Neighbours.

LOVEWIT Has there been such resort, say you?
FIRST NEIGHBOUR Daily, sir.
SECOND NEIGHBOUR And nightly, too.
THIRD NEIGHBOUR Ay, some as brave as lords.
FOURTH NEIGHBOUR Ladies and gentlewomen.
FIFTH NEIGHBOUR Citizens' wives.
FIRST NEIGHBOUR And knights.
SIXTH NEIGHBOUR In coaches.
SECOND NEIGHBOUR Yes, and oyster-women.
FIRST NEIGHBOUR Beside other gallants.
THIRD NEIGHBOUR Sailors' wives.
FOURTH NEIGHBOUR Tobacco men.
FIFTH NEIGHBOUR Another Pimlico!
LOVEWIT What should my knave advance,
  To draw this company? he hung out no banners
  Of a strange calf with five legs to be seen,
  Or a huge lobster with six claws?
SIXTH NEIGHBOUR No, sir.
THIRD NEIGHBOUR We had gone in then, sir.
LOVEWIT He has no gift
  Of teaching in the nose that e'er I knew of.
  You saw no bills set up that promised cure
  Of agues, or the tooth-ache?
SECOND NEIGHBOUR No such thing, sir!
LOVEWIT Nor heard a drum struck for baboons
  or puppets?
FIFTH NEIGHBOUR Neither, sir.
LOVEWIT What device should he bring forth
  now?
  I love a teeming wit as I love my nourishment:
  'Pray God he have not kept such open house,
  That he hath sold my hangings, and my bed-
  ding!
  I left him nothing else. If he have eat them,
  A plague o' the moth, say I! Sure he has got

Some bawdy pictures to call all this ging;[19]
The friar and the nun; or the new motion
Of the knight's courser covering the parson's
  mare;
The boy of six year old with the great thing;
Or't may be, he has the fleas that run a tilt
Upon a table, or some dog to dance.
When saw you him?
FIRST NEIGHBOUR Who, sir, Jeremy?
SECOND NEIGHBOUR Jeremy butler?
We saw him not this month.
LOVEWIT How!
FOURTH NEIGHBOUR Not these five weeks, sir.
SIXTH NEIGHBOUR These six weeks at the least.
LOVEWIT You amaze me, neighbours!
FIFTH NEIGHBOUR Sure, if your worship know not
  where he is,
  He's slipt away.
SIXTH NEIGHBOUR Pray God he be not made
  away.
LOVEWIT Ha! it's no time to question, then.
[*Knocks at the door.*]
SIXTH NEIGHBOUR About
  Some three weeks since I heard a doleful cry,
  As I sat up a mending my wife's stockings.
LOVEWIT 'Tis strange that none will answer!
  Did'st thou hear
  A cry, sayst thou?
SIXTH NEIGHBOUR Yes, sir, like unto a man
  That had been strangled an hour, and could not
  speak.
SECOND NEIGHBOUR I heard it too, just this day
  three weeks, at two o'clock
Next morning.
LOVEWIT These be miracles, or you make them
  so!
  A man an hour strangled, and could not speak,

[19] Gang.

The Alchemist   **179**

And both you heard him cry?

THIRD NEIGHBOUR Yes, downward, sir.

LOVEWIT Thou art a wise fellow. Give me thy hand, I pray thee,
What trade art thou on?

THIRD NEIGHBOUR A smith, an't please your worship.

LOVEWIT A smith! then lend me thy help to get this door open.

THIRD NEIGHBOUR That I will presently, sir, but fetch my tools—

[*Exit.*]

FIRST NEIGHBOUR Sir, best to knock again afore you break it.

LOVEWIT [*knocks again*] I will.

[*Enter Face in his butler's livery.*]

FACE What mean you, sir?

FIRST, SECOND, FOURTH NEIGHBOURS Oh, here's Jeremy!

FACE Good sir, come from the door.

LOVEWIT Why, what's the matter?

FACE Yet farther, you are too near yet.

LOVEWIT In the name of wonder,
What means the fellow!

FACE The house, sir, has been visited.

LOVEWIT What, with the plague? stand thou then farther.

FACE No, sir,
I had it not.

LOVEWIT Who had it then? I left
None else but thee in the house.

FACE Yes, sir, my fellow,
The cat that kept the buttery, had it on her
A week before I spied it; but I got her
Conveyed away in the night: and so I shut
The house up for a month—

LOVEWIT How!

FACE Purposing then, sir,
To have burnt rose-vinegar, treacle, and tar,
And have made it sweet, that you should ne'er
have known it;
Because I knew the news would but afflict you, sir.

LOVEWIT Breathe less, and farther off! Why this is stranger:
The neighbours tell me all here that the doors
Have still been open—

FACE How, sir!

LOVEWIT Gallants, men and women,

And of all sorts tag-rag, been seen to flock here
In threaves,[20] these ten weeks, as to a second Hoksden,
In days of Pimlico and Eye-bright.

FACE Sir,
Their wisdoms will not say so.

LOVEWIT To-day they speak
Of coaches and gallants; one in a French hood
Went in, they tell me; and another was seen
In a velvet gown at the window: divers more
Pass in and out.

FACE They did pass through the doors then,
Or walls, I assure their eye-sights, and their spectacles;
For here, sir, are the keys, and here have been,
In this my pocket, now above twenty days:
And for before, I kept the fort alone there.
But that 'tis yet not deep in the afternoon,
I should believe my neighbours had seen double
Through the black pot, and made these apparitions!
For, on my faith to your worship, for these three weeks
And upwards, the door has not been opened.

LOVEWIT Strange!

FIRST NEIGHBOUR Good faith, I think I saw a coach.

SECOND NEIGHBOUR And I too,
I'd have been sworn.

LOVEWIT Do you but think it now?
And but one coach?

FOURTH NEIGHBOUR We cannot tell, sir: Jeremy
Is a very honest fellow.

FACE Did you see me at all?

FIRST NEIGHBOUR No; that we are sure on.

SECOND NEIGHBOUR I'll be sworn o' that.

LOVEWIT Fine rogues to have your testimonies built on!

[*Reenter Third Neighbour, with his tools.*]

THIRD NEIGHBOUR Is Jeremy come!

FIRST NEIGHBOUR O yes; you may leave your tools;
We were deceived, he says.

SECOND NEIGHBOUR He has had the keys;
And the door has been shut these three weeks.

SECOND NEIGHBOUR Like enough.

LOVEWIT Peace, and get hence, you changelings.

[20] In droves or heaps.

BEN JONSON

[*Enter Surly and Mammon.*]

FACE [*aside*] Surly come!
And Mammon made acquainted! they'll tell all.
How shall I beat them off? what shall I do?
Nothing's more wretched than a guilty con-
science.

SURLY No, sir, he was a great physician. This,
It was no bawdy-house, but a mere chancel!
You knew the lord and his sister.

MAMMON Nay, good Surly.—

SURLY The happy word, BE RICH—

MAMMON Play not the tyrant.—

SURLY *Should be to-day pronounced to all your
friends.*
And where be your andirons now? and your
brass pots,
That should have been golden flaggons, and
great wedges?

MAMMON Let me but breathe. What, they have
shut their doors,
Methinks!

SURLY Ay, now 'tis holiday with them.

MAMMON Rogues,
[*He and Surly knock.*]
Cozeners, impostors, bawds!

FACE What mean you, sir?

MAMMON To enter if we can.

FACE Another man's house!
Here is the owner, sir; turn you to him,
And speak your business.

MAMMON Are you, sir, the owner?

LOVEWIT Yes, sir.

MAMMON And are those knaves within your
cheaters!

LOVEWIT What knaves, what cheaters?

MAMMON Subtle and his Lungs.

FACE The gentleman is distracted, sir! No lungs,
Nor lights have been seen here these three
weeks, sir,
Within these doors, upon my word.

SURLY Your word,
Groom arrogant!

FACE Yes, sir, I am the housekeeper,
And know the keys have not been out of my
hands.

SURLY This is a new Face.

FACE You do mistake the house, sir:
What sign was't at?

SURLY You rascal! this is one

Of the confederacy. Come, let's get officers,
And force the door.

LOVEWIT Pray you stay, gentlemen.

SURLY No, sir, we'll come with warrant.

MAMMON Ay, and then
We shall have your doors open.
[*Exeunt Mammon and Surly.*]

LOVEWIT What means this?

FACE I cannot tell, sir.

FIRST NEIGHBOUR These are two of the gallants
That we do think we saw.

FACE Two of the fools!
You talk as idly as they. Good faith, sir,
I think the moon has crased 'em all. [*Aside*]—
O me,
The angry boy come too!
[*Enter Kastril.*]   He'll make a noise,
And ne'er away till he have betrayed us all.

KASTRIL [*knocking*] What, rogues, bawds, slaves,
you'll open the door, anon!
Punk, cockatrice, my suster! By this light
I'll fetch the marshal to you. You are a whore
To keep your castle—

FACE Who would you speak with, sir?

KASTRIL The bawdy doctor, and the cozening
captain,
And puss my suster.

LOVEWIT This is something, sure.

FACE Upon my trust, the doors were never open,
sir.

KASTRIL I have heard all their tricks told me
twice over,
By the fat knight and the lean gentleman.

LOVEWIT Here comes another.
[*Enter Ananias and Tribulation.*]

FACE [*aside*] Ananias too!
And his pastor!

TRIBULATION [*beating at the door*] The doors are
shut against us.

ANANIAS Come forth, you seed of sulphur, sons
of fire!
Your stench it is broke forth; abomination
Is in the house.

KASTRIL Ay, my suster's there.

ANANIAS The place,
It is become a cage of unclean birds.

KASTRIL Yes, I will fetch the scavenger, and the
constable.

TRIBULATION You shall do well.

ANANIAS   We'll join to weed them out.

KASTRIL   You will not come then, punk devise, my suster!

ANANIAS   Call her not sister; she's a harlot verily.

KASTRIL   I'll raise the street.

LOVEWIT   Good gentlemen, a word.

ANANIAS   Satan avoid, and hinder not our zeal!
[*Exeunt Ananias, Tribulation, and Kastril.*]

LOVEWIT   The world's turned Bethlem.

FACE   These are all broke loose,
Out of St. Katherine's, where they use to keep
The better sort of mad-folks.

FIRST NEIGHBOUR   All these persons
We saw go in and out here.

SECOND NEIGHBOUR   Yes, indeed, sir.

THIRD NEIGHBOUR   These were the parties.

FACE   Peace, you drunkards! Sir,
I wonder at it: please you to give me leave
To touch the door, I'll try an the lock be changed.

LOVEWIT   It amazes me!

FACE   [*goes to the door*]   Good faith, sir, I believe
There's no such thing: 'tis all *deceptio visus.*—
[*Aside*]
Would I could get him away.

DAPPER   [*within*]   Master captain! master doctor!

LOVEWIT   Who's that?

FACE   [*aside*]   Our clerk within, that I forgot!
I know not,
sir.

DAPPER   [*within*]   For God's sake, when will her grace be at leisure?

FACE   Ha!
Illusions, some spirit o' the air!—
[*Aside*]
His gag is
melted.
And now he sets out the throat.

DAPPER   [*within*]   I am almost stifled—

FACE   [*aside*]   Would you were altogether.

LOVEWIT   'Tis in the house.
Ha! list.

FACE   Believe it, sir, in the air.

LOVEWIT   Peace, you.

DAPPER   [*within*]   Mine aunt's grace does not use me well.

SUBTLE   [*within*]   You fool,

Peace, you'll mar all.

FACE   [*speaks through the keyhole, while Lovewit advances to the door unobserved*]   Or you will else, you rogue.

LOVEWIT   O, is it so? then you converse with spirits!—
Come, sir. No more of your tricks, good Jeremy.
The truth, the shortest way.

FACE   Dismiss this rabble, sir.—
[*Aside*]
What shall I do? I am catched.

LOVEWIT   Good neighbours,
I thank you all. You may depart.
[*Exeunt Neighbours.*]
—Come, sir,
You know that I am an indulgent master;
And therefore conceal nothing. What's your medicine,
To draw so many several sorts of wild fowl?

FACE   Sir, you were wont to affect mirth and wit—
But here's no place to talk on't in the street.
Give me but leave to make the best of my fortune,
And only pardon me the abuse of your house:
It's all I beg. I'll help you to a widow,
In recompense, that you shall give me thanks for,
Will make you seven years younger, and a rich one.
'Tis but your putting on a Spanish cloak:
I have her within. You need not fear the house:
It was not visited.

LOVEWIT   But by me, who came
Sooner than you expected.

FACE   It is true, sir.
'Pray you forgive me.

LOVEWIT   Well: let's see your widow.
[*Exeunt.*]

SCENE TWO

A room in the same house. Enter Subtle, leading in Dapper, with his eyes bound, as before.

SUBTLE   How! have you eaten your gag?

DAPPER   Yes, faith, it crumbled
Away in my mouth.

SUBTLE You have spoiled all then.

DAPPER No!
I hope my aunt of Fairy will forgive me.

SUBTLE Your aunt's a gracious lady; but in troth
You were to blame.

DAPPER The fume did overcome me,
And I did do't to stay my stomach. Pray you
So satisfy her grace.

[Enter Face in his uniform.]

Here comes the captain.

FACE How now! is his mouth down?

SUBTLE Ay, he has spoken!

FACE A pox, I heard him, and you too. He's
undone then.—
I have been fain to say, the house is haunted
With spirits, to keep churl back.

SUBTLE And hast thou done it?

FACE Sure, for this night.

SUBTLE Why, then triumph and sing
Of Face so famous, the precious king
Of present wits.

FACE Did you not hear the coil
About the door?

SUBTLE Yes, and I dwindled with it.

FACE Show him his aunt, and let him be dis-
patched:
I'll send her to you.

[Exit Face.]

SUBTLE Well, sir, your aunt her grace
Will give you audience presently, on my suit,
And the captain's word that you did not eat
your gag
In any contempt of her highness.

[Unbinds his eyes.]

DAPPER Not I, in troth, sir.

[Enter Dol Common like the queen of Fairy.]

SUBTLE Here she is come. Down o' your knees
and wriggle:
She has a stately presence.

[Dapper kneels and shuffles towards her.]

Good! Yet nearer,
And bid, God save you!

DAPPER Madam!

SUBTLE And your aunt.

DAPPER And my most gracious aunt, God save
your grace.

DOL Nephew, we thought to have been angry
with you;

But that sweet face of yours hath turned the
tide,
And made it flow with joy, that ebbed of love.
Arise, and touch our velvet gown.

SUBTLE The skirts,
And kiss 'em. So!

DOL Let me now stroke that head.
Much, nephew, shalt thou win, much shalt thou
spend;
Much shalt thou give away, much shalt thou
lend.

SUBTLE *[aside]* Ay, much! indeed.
Why do you not
thank her grace?

DAPPER I cannot speak for joy.

SUBTLE See, the kind wretch!
Your grace's kinsman right.

DOL Give me the bird.
Here is your fly in a purse, about your neck,
cousin;
Wear it, and feed it about this day sev'n-night
On your right wrist—

SUBTLE Open a vein with a pin.
And let it suck but once a week; till then,
You must not look on't.

DOL No: and, kinsman,
Bear yourself worthy of the blood you come on.

SUBTLE Her grace would have you eat no more
Woolsack pies,
No Dagger frumety.

DOL Nor break his fast
In Heaven and Hell.

SUBTLE She's with you everywhere!
Nor play with costarmongers, at mumchance,
tray-trip,
God-make-you-rich (whenas your aunt has done
it);
But keep
The gallant'st company, and the best games—

DAPPER Yes, sir.

SUBTLE Gleek and primero: and what you get,
be true to us.

DAPPER By this hand, I will.

SUBTLE You may bring's a thousand pound
Before to-morrow night, if but three thousand
Be stirring, an you will.

DAPPER I swear I will then.

SUBTLE Your fly will learn you all games.

FACE [*within*] Have you done there?

SUBTLE Your grace will command him no more duties?

DOL No:

But come, and see me often. I may chance
To leave him three or four hundred chests of treasure,
And some twelve thousand acres of fairy land,
If he game well and comely with good game-sters.

SUBTLE There's a kind aunt: kiss her departing part.—

But you must sell your forty mark a year now.

DAPPER Ay, sir, I mean.

SUBTLE Or, give't away; pox on't!

DAPPER I'll give't mine aunt: I'll go and fetch the writings.

[*Exit.*]

SUBTLE 'Tis well, away.

[*Reenter Face.*]

FACE Where's Subtle?

SUBTLE Here: what news?

FACE Drugger is at the door, go take his suit,
And bid him fetch a parson presently:
Say he shall marry the widow. Thou shalt spend
A hundred pound by the service!

[*Exit Subtle.*]

Now, Queen Dol,
Have you packed up all?

DOL Yes.

FACE And how do you like
The Lady Pliant?

DOL A good dull innocent.

[*Reenter Subtle.*]

SUBTLE Here's your Hieronimo's cloak and hat.

FACE Give me them.

SUBTLE And the ruff too?

FACE Yes; I'll come to you presently.

[*Exit.*]

SUBTLE Now he is gone about his project, Dol,
I told you of, for the widow.

DOL 'Tis direct
Against our articles.

SUBTLE Well, we will fit him, wench.
Hast thou gulled her of her jewels or her brace-lets?

DOL No; but I will do't.

SUBTLE Soon at night, my Dolly,

When we are shipped, and all our goods aboard,
Eastward for Ratcliff; we will turn our course
To Brainford, westward, if thou sayst the word,
And take our leaves of this o'erweening rascal,
This peremptory Face.

DOL Content, I'm weary of him.

SUBTLE Thou'st cause, when the slave will run a wiving, Dol,
Against the instrument that was drawn between us.

DOL I'll pluck his bird as bare as I can.

SUBTLE Yes, tell her
She must by any means address some present
To the cunning man, make him amend for wronging
His art with her suspicion; send a ring,
Or chain of pearl; she will be tortured else
Extremely in her sleep, say, and have strange things
Come to her. Wilt thou?

DOL Yes.

SUBTLE My fine flitter-mouse,
My bird o' the night! we'll tickle it at the Pigeons,
When we have all, and may unlock the trunks,
And say, this's mine, and thine; and thine, and mine.

[*They kiss. Reenter Face.*]

FACE What now! a billing?

SUBTLE Yes, a little exalted
In the good passage of our stock-affairs

FACE Drugger has brought his parson; take him in, Subtle,
And send Nab back again to wash his face.

SUBTLE I will: and shave himself?

[*Exit.*]

FACE If you can get him.

DOL You are hot upon it, Face, whate'er it is!

FACE A trick that Dol shall spend ten pound a month by.

[*Reenter Subtle.*]

Is he gone?

SUBTLE The chaplain waits you in the hall, sir.

FACE I'll go bestow him.

[*Exit.*]

DOL He'll now marry her instantly.

SUBTLE He cannot yet, he is not ready. Dear Dol,

Cozen her of all thou canst. To deceive him
Is no deceit, but justice, that would break
Such an inextricable tie as ours was.
DOL Let me alone to fit him.
[*Reenter Face.*]
FACE Come, my venturers,
You have packed up all? where be the trunks?
  bring forth.
SUBTLE Here.
FACE Let us see them. Where's the money?
SUBTLE Here.
In this.
FACE Mammon's ten pound; eight score before:
The brethren's money this. Drugger's and Dap-
  per's.
What paper's that?
DOL The jewel of the waiting maid's,
That stole it from her lady, to know certain—
FACE If she should have precedence of her mis-
  tress.
DOL Yes.
FACE What box is that?
SUBTLE The fish-wives' rings, I think,
And the ale-wives' single money. Is't not,
  Dol?
DOL Yes; and the whistle that the sailor's wife
Brought you to know an her husband were with
  Ward.
FACE We'll wet it to-morrow; and our silver
  beakers
And tavern cups. Where be the French petti-
  coats
And girdles and hangers?
SUBTLE Here, in the trunk,
And the bolts of lawn.
FACE Is Drugger's damask there,
And the tobacco?
SUBTLE Yes.
FACE Give me the keys.
DOL Why you the keys?
SUBTLE No matter, Dol; because
We shall not open them before he comes.
FACE 'Tis true, you shall not open them, indeed;
Nor have them forth, do you see? not forth,
  Dol.
DOL No!
FACE No, my smock-rampant. The right is, my
  master

Knows all, has pardoned me, and he will keep
  them;
Doctor, 'tis true—you look—for all your figures:
I sent for him, Indeed. Wherefore, good part-
  ners,
Both he and she be satisfied; for here
Determines the indenture tripartite
'Twixt Subtle, Dol, and Face. All I can do
Is to help you over the wall, o' the back-side,
Or lend you a sheet to save your velvet gown,
  Dol.
Here will be officers presently, bethink you
Of some course suddenly to 'scape the dock;
For thither you will come else.
[*Loud knocking*]
                                        Hark you,
  thunder.
SUBTLE You are a precious fiend!
OFFICER [*without*] Open the door.
FACE Dol, I am sorry for thee i' faith; but
  hear'st thou?
It shall go hard but I will place thee somewhere:
Thou shalt have my letter to Mistress Amo—
DOL Hang you!
FACE Or Madam Cæsarean.
DOL Pox upon you, rogue,
Would I had but time to beat thee!
FACE Subtle,
Let's know where you set up next; I will send
  you
A customer now and then, for old acquaintance:
What new course have you?
SUBTLE Rogue, I'll hang myself;
That I may walk a greater devil than thou,
And haunt thee in the flock-bed and the buttery.
[*Exeunt.*]

SCENE THREE

*An outer room in the same house. Enter Lovewit
in the Spanish dress, with the Parson. Loud
knocking at the door.*

LOVEWIT What do you mean, my masters?
MAMMON [*without*] Open your door,
Cheaters, bawds, conjurers.
OFFICER [*without*] Or we will break it open.
LOVEWIT What warrant have you?

OFFICER [*without*] Warrant enough, sir, doubt
not,
  If you'll not open it.
LOVEWIT Is there an officer there?
OFFICER [*without*] Yes, two or three for failing.
LOVEWIT Have but patience,
  And I will open it straight.
[*Enter Face, as butler.*]
FACE Sir, have you done?
  Is it a marriage? perfect?
LOVEWIT Yes, my brain.
FACE Off with your ruff and cloak then: be
  yourself, sir.
SURLY [*without*] Down with the door.
KASTRIL [*without*] 'Slight, ding it open.
LOVEWIT [*opening the door*] Hold,
  Hold, gentlemen, what means this violence?
[*Mammon, Surly, Kastril, Ananias, Tribulation,
and Officers rush in.*]
MAMMON Where is this collier?
SURLY And my Captain Face?
MAMMON These day owls.
SURLY That are birding in men's purses.
MAMMON Madam Suppository.
KASTRIL Doxy, my suster.
ANANIAS Locusts
  Of the foul pit.
TRIBULATION Profane as Bel and the Dragon.
ANANIAS Worse than the grasshoppers, or the
  lice of Egypt.
LOVEWIT Good gentlemen, hear me. Are you
  officers,
  And cannot stay this violence?
FIRST OFFICER Keep the peace.
LOVEWIT Gentlemen, what is the matter? whom
  do you seek?
MAMMON The chemical cozener.
SURLY And the captain pander.
KASTRIL The nun my suster.
MAMMON Madam Rabbi.
ANANIAS Scorpions.
  And caterpillars.
LOVEWIT Fewer at once, I pray you.
FIRST OFFICER One after another, gentlemen, I
  charge you,
  By virtue of my staff.
ANANIAS They are the vessels
  Of pride, lust, and the cart.

LOVEWIT Good zeal, lie still
A little while.
TRIBULATION Peace, Deacon Ananias.
LOVEWIT The house is mine here, and the doors
  are open;
  If there be any such persons as you seek for,
  Use your authority, search on o' God's name.
  I am but newly come to town, and finding
  This tumult 'bout my door, to tell you true,
  It somewhat mazed me; till my man here, fear-
  ing
  My more displeasure, told me he had done
  Somewhat an insolent part, let out my house
  (Belike presuming on my known aversion
  From any air o' the town while there was sick-
  ness),
  To a doctor and a captain: who, what they are
  Or where they be, he knows not.
MAMMON Are they gone?
LOVEWIT You may go in and search, sir.
[*Mammon, Ananias, and Tribulation go in.*]
                                        Here, I
  find
  The empty walls worse than I left them, smoked,
  A few cracked pots, and glasses, and a furnace;
  The ceiling filled with poesies of the candle,
  And madam with a dildo writ o' the walls:
  Only one gentlewoman I met here
  That is within, that said she was a widow—
KASTRIL Ay, that's my suster; I'll go thump her.
  Where is she?
[*Goes in.*]
LOVEWIT And should have married a Spanish
  count, but he,
  When he came to't, neglected her so grossly,
  That I, a widower, am gone through with her.
SURLY How! have I lost her then?
LOVEWIT Were you the don, sir?
  Good faith, now she does blame you extremely,
  and says
  You swore, and told her you had taken the
  pains
  To dye your beard, and umbre o'er your face,
  Borrowed a suit, and ruff, all for her love:
  And then did nothing. What an oversight,
  And want of putting forward, sir, was this!
  Well fare an old harquebusier yet,
  Could prime his powder, and give fire, and hit,

All in a twinkling!

[*Reenter Mammon.*]

MAMMON The whole nest are fled!

LOVEWIT What sort of birds were they?

MAMMON A kind of choughs,
Or thievish daws, sir, that have picked my purse
Of eight score and ten pounds within these five
    weeks,
Beside my first materials; and my goods,
That lie in the cellar, which I am glad they have
    left,
I may have home yet.

LOVEWIT Think you so, sir?

MAMMON Ay.

LOVEWIT By order of law, sir, but not otherwise.

MAMMON Not mine own stuff!

LOVEWIT Sir, I can take no knowledge
That they are yours, but by public means.
If you can bring certificate that you were gulled
    of them,
Or any formal writ out of a court,
That you did cozen yourself, I will not hold
    them.

MAMMON I'll rather lose them.

LOVEWIT That you shall not, sir,
By me, in troth: upon these terms, they are
    yours.
What, should they have been, sir, turned into
    gold, all?

MAMMON No.
I cannot tell—it may be they should—What
    then?

LOVEWIT What a great loss in hope have you
    sustained!

MAMMON Not I, the commonwealth has.

FACE Ay, he would have built
The city new; and made a ditch about it
Of silver, should have run with cream from
    Hogsden;
That every Sunday in Moorfields the younkers,
And tits and tom-boys should have fed on,
    gratis.

MAMMON I will go mount a turnip-cart, and
    preach
The end of the world within these two months.
    Surly,
What! in a dream?

SURLY Must I needs cheat myself,

With that same foolish vice of honesty!
Come, let us go and hearken out the rogues:
That Face I'll mark for mine, if e'er I meet him.

FACE If I can hear of him, sir, I'll bring you
    word
Unto your lodging; for in troth, they were
    strangers
To me, I thought them honest as myself, sir.

[*Exeunt Mammon and Surly. Reenter Ananias
and Tribulation.*]

TRIBULATION 'Tis well, the saints shall not lose
    all yet. Go
And get some carts—

LOVEWIT For what, my zealous friends?

ANANIAS To bear away the portion of the right-
    eous
Out of this den of thieves.

LOVEWIT What is that portion?

ANANIAS The goods, sometimes the orphans',
    that the brethren
Bought with their silver pence.

LOVEWIT What, those in the cellar,
The knight Sir Mammon claims?

ANANIAS I do defy
The wicked Mammon, so do all the brethren,
Thou profane man! I ask thee with what con-
    science
Thou canst advance that idol against us,
That have the seal? were not the shillings num-
    bered
That made the pounds; were not the pounds
    told out
Upon the second day of the fourth week,
In the eighth month, upon the table dormant,
The year of the last patience of the saints,
Six hundred and ten?

LOVEWIT Mine earnest vehement botcher,
And deacon also, I cannot dispute with you:
But if you get you not away the sooner,
I shall confute you with a cudgel.

ANANIAS Sir!

TRIBULATION Be patient, Ananias.

ANANIAS I am strong,
And will stand up, well girt, against a host
That threaten Gad in exile.

LOVEWIT I shall send you
To Amsterdam, to your cellar.

ANANIAS I will pray there,

Against thy house: may dogs defile thy walls,
And wasps and hornets breed beneath thy roof,
This seat of falsehood, and this cave of cozen-
age!

[*Exeunt Ananias and Tribulation. Enter Drugger.*]

LOVEWIT Another too?

DRUGGER Not I, sir, I am no brother.

LOVEWIT [*beats him*] Away, you Harry Nicholas!
do you talk?

[*Exit Drugger.*]

FACE No, this was Abel Drugger. Good sir,
go,

[*To the pastor*]

And satisfy him; tell him all is done:
He staid too long a washing of his face.
The doctor, he shall hear of him at Westchester;
And of the captain, tell him, at Yarmouth, or
Some good port-town else, lying for a wind.

[*Exit pastor.*]

If you can get off the angry child now, sir—

[*Enter Kastril, dragging in his sister.*]

KASTRIL Come on, you ewe, you have matched
most sweetly, have you not?
Did not I say, I would never have you tupped
But by a dubbed boy, to make you a lady-tom?
'Slight, you are a mammet! O, I could touse
you now.
Death, mun' you marry with a pox!

LOVEWIT You lie, boy!
As sound as you; and I'm aforehand with you.

KASTRIL Anon!

LOVEWIT Come, will you quarrel? I will feize[21]
you, sirrah;
Why do you not buckle to your tools?

KASTRIL Od's light,
This is a fine old boy as e'er I saw!

LOVEWIT What, do you change your copy now?
proceed,
Here stands my dove: stoop at her if you dare.

KASTRIL 'Slight, I must love him! I cannot
choose, i' faith,
An I should be hanged for't! Suster, I protest,

---

[21] Drive.

I honour thee for this match.

LOVEWIT O, do you so, sir?

KASTRIL Yes, and thou canst take tobacco and
drink, old boy,
I'll give her five hundred pound more to her
marriage,
Than her own state.

LOVEWIT Fill a pipe full, Jeremy.

FACE Yes; but go in and take it, sir.

LOVEWIT We will—
I will be ruled by thee in anything, Jeremy.

KASTRIL 'Slight, thou art not hide-bound, thou
art a jovy boy!
Come, let us in, I pray thee, and take our
whiffs.

LOVEWIT Whiff in with your sister, brother
boy.

[*Exeunt Kastril and Dame Pliant.*]
That master
That had received such happiness by a servant,
In such a widow, and with so much wealth,
Were very ungrateful, if he would not be
A little indulgent to that servant's wit,
And help his fortune, though with some small
strain
Of his own candour.

[*Advancing*]
Therefore, gentlemen,
And kind spectators, if I have outstript
An old man's gravity, or strict canon, think
What a young wife and a good brain may do;
Stretch age's truth sometimes, and crack it too.
Speak for thyself, knave.

FACE So I will, sir.

[*Advancing to the front of the stage*]
Gentlemen,
My part a little fell in this last scene,
Yet 'twas decorum. And though I am clean
Got off from Subtle, Surly, Mammon, Dol,
Hot Ananias, Dapper, Drugger, all
With whom I traded; yet I put myself
On you, that are my country: and this pelf,
Which I have got, if you do quit me, rests
To feast you often, and invite new guests.

[*Exeunt.*]

TO UNDERSTAND JONSON, and to avoid misunderstandings that are too easily incurred, it is important to consider the nature and significance of Humour Comedy in his work.

. . . when some peculiar quality
Doth so possess a man that it doth draw
All his affects, his spirits and his powers
In their confluctions all to run one way,
This may be truly said to be a humour.
[Ben Jonson, *Every Man Out of His Humour* (1599), Induction, ll. 105–109.]

By humour is meant some extravagant habit, passion, or affection, particular . . . to some one person, by the oddness of which, he is immediately distinguished from the rest of men; which being lively and naturally represented, most frequently begets that malicious pleasure in the audience which is testifield by laughter; as all things which are deviations from customs are ever the aptest to produce it: though by the way this laughter is only accidental, as the person represented is fantastic or bizarre; but pleasure is essential to it, as the imitation of what is natural. The description of these humours, drawn from the knowledge and observation of particular persons, was the peculiar genius and talent of Ben Jonson. [John Dryden, "An Essay of Dramatic Poesy" (1668), *Dramatic Essays,* Everyman's Library, E. P. Dutton & Co., Inc., New York, n.d., p. 44.]

In the first place, the presentation of certain selected humours throughout a long play involves the playwright . . . in one of two risks, either of making the characters too rigid or uniform in habit, puppet-like after the fashion of the personages in the old Morality, and dramatically unreal, or, in the consciousness of this danger, of striving to escape from it by exaggeration. Jonson was alert enough to see that the latter leads to unreality, and for this reason he protested against over-emphasis, especially of the "accidents" and frillings, and counselled a close attention to "life" as a corrective of artifice. In the second place, and as a corollary to what has just been said, characters thus fixed tend to become too simple. Even when the humour is not a plain study of a single folly, but a complex impression of several, with one slightly overtopping the rest, it is hard to sustain the combination throughout the action. The audience will make its own selection, and see the man who is not altogether "subtle" or "morose" as little else. This weakness reacts in a serious way by preventing any self-development in the characters. [G. Gregory Smith, *Ben Jonson,* St. Martin's Press, Inc., English Men of Letters Series, New York, 1919, pp. 86–87.]

His characters are and remain . . . simplified characters; but the simplification does not consist in the dominance of a particular humour or monomania. That is a very superficial account of it. The simplification consists largely in reduction of detail, in the seizing of aspects relevant to the relief of an emotional impulse which remains the same for that character, in making the character conform to a particular setting. This stripping is essential to the art, to which is also essential a flat distortion in the drawing; it is an art of caricature. . . . It is a great caricature, which is beautiful; and a great humour, which is serious. The "world" of Jonson is sufficiently large; it is a world of poetic imagination; it is sombre. He did not get the third dimension, but he was not trying to get it. [T. S. Eliot, "Ben Jonson" (1919), *Selected Essays,* Harcourt, Brace and Company, Inc., New York, 1932, p. 138.]

Another possible prejudice which requires close scrutiny concerns the effects of Jonson's "classicism" upon his art.

It is the possession of the qualities expressed by the epithet [classical] taken in its fuller sense which has given Jonson his importance in our literary perspective, and at the same time, and notwithstanding that to it much of the permanent value of his work as art is directly due, has reduced his claims to higher individual honour. . . . His devotion to the theory of the Humours blunts his interest, perhaps his powers, in the self-development of his characters; his views on plot and arrangement deprives his work, even when at its best, of its full range, and of a convincing liveliness of action; and, above all, his care to keep the spaniels of imagination and emotion on the leash tells heavily against him. . . . His love of rules has played havoc with his claim to be our master-realist; and his narrow realism has damned the larger hope of his art. . . .

If we say that Jonson was attracted to this [humour] theory of comedy by his classical instinct, we must dissociate ourselves from a popular misinterpretation. There is no denying the fact that Jonson has many things which suggest the method of the Latin masters, though the more closely we study him the more we seem to see the differences between him and his predecessors. But it is a strange critical error that the Jonsonian conception of the dramatic humours is only an English copying of the Plautine and Terentian types. . . . Jonson was attracted, as his Renaissance guides were, by the idea of balance, prevailing in physical and medical science. To restrain enthusiasm or "cure excess" is the first article of duty to the classicist: and Jonson and others in following this dictate of the literary conscience are not classicists in a derivative sense. [Smith, *op. cit.*, pp. 63–64, 85–86.]

Many were the wit-combats betwixt [Shakespeare] and Ben Jonson; which two I behold like a Spanish great galleon and an English man-of-war; Master Jonson (like the former) was built far higher in learning; solid, but slow, in his performances. Shakespeare, with the English man-of-war, lesser in bulk, but lighter in sailing, could turn with all tides, tack about, and take advantage of all winds, by the quickness of his wit and invention. [Thomas Fuller, "William Shakespeare," *The History of the Worthies of England, 1662.*]

We all know [Fuller's comparison]. But I think the past years have provided us with a still better image for Jonson. He reminds me irresistibly of a tank: a huge and cumbrous engine, crashing by its sheer weight through the complex hindrances offered by ill-digested learning, inordinate self-esteem and a rhetorical rather than a truly dramatic temperament. He is a ferocious satirist, a considerable, almost a great, poet, and a dramatist, not by innate vocation, but by external necessity. [William Archer, *The Old Drama and the New,* Small, Maynard and Co., Boston, 1923, p. 87.]

To the reader:

If thou beest more, thou art an understander, and then I trust thee. If thou art one that takest up, and but a Pretender, beware of what hands thou receivest thy commodity; for thou wert never more fair in the way to be cozened, than in this age, in Poetry, especially in Plays: wherein now the concupiscence of dances and of antics so reigneth, as to run away from nature, and be afraid of her, is the only point of art that tickles the spectators. But how out of purpose, and place, do I name art? When the professors are grown so obstinate contemners of it, and presumers on their own naturals, as they are deriders of all diligence that way, and, by simple mocking at the terms, when they understand not the things, think to get off wittily with their ignorance. Nay, they are esteemed the more learned, and sufficient for this, by the many, through their excellent vice of judgment. For they commend writers as they do fencers or wrestlers; who if they come in robustuously, and put for it with a great deal of violence, are received for the braver fellows: when many times their own rudeness is the cause of their disgrace, and a little touch of their adversary gives all that boisterous force the foil. I deny not but that these men, who always seek to do more than enough, may some time happen on some thing that is good and great; but very seldom; and when it comes it doth not recompense the rest of their ill. It sticks out perhaps, and is more eminent, because all is sordid and vile about it: as lights are more discerned in a thick darkness than a faint shadow. I speak not this out of a hope to do good to any man against his will; for I know if it were put to the question of theirs and mine, the worst would find more suffrages: because the most favour common errors. But I give thee this warning that there is a great difference between those that, to gain the opinion of copy, utter all they can, however unfitly; and those that use election and a mean. For it is only the disease of the unskilful to think rude things greater than polished: or scattered more numerous than composed. [Ben Jonson, *The Alchemist*, 1612 edition.]

Of all the dramatists of his time, Jonson is probably the one whom the present age would find the most sympathetic, if it knew him. There is a brutality, a lack of sentiment, a polished surface, a handling of large bold designs in brilliant colours, which ought to attract about three thousand people in London and elsewhere. At least, if we had a contemporary Jonson, it might be the Jonson who would arouse the enthusiasm of the intelligentsia. Though he is saturated in literature, he never sacrifices the theatrical qualities—theatrical in the most favourable sense—to literature or to the study of character. His work is a titanic show. [Eliot, *op. cit.*, pp. 138–139.]

The difficulty of explaining Jonson's characterization in terms of simple types appears in the examination of such a figure as Sir Epicure Mammon.

Supreme among the dupes is Sir Epicure Mammon. . . . Jonson presents this monster with a poetic licence whose only justification is that it succeeds. No city knight, with appetites so completely of the gullet and the groin, would ever have achieved the sumptuous fancies of which Sir Epicure is so gorgeously delivered. Jonson ransacked erotic Greece and sensual Rome in presenting this hyperbolical figure, thereby creating an effect which Charles Lamb found to be "equal to the greatest poetry." Sir Epicure Mammon epitomizes the common man, drunk with the prospect of illimitable wealth and the visions of a youth perpetual and immune. [John Palmer, *Ben Jonson*, Routledge & Kegan Paul, Ltd., London, 1934, pp. 185–186.]

[The study of Sir Epicure Mammon is] a literary *tour de force*, bodying forth a character which is not farcical, as some would hold, or burlesque, as with others, but dramatically true. Each dupe is agog for the philosopher's stone only because of the magnificence which the stone puts within his reach. . . . In no other character has Jonson turned what may be called the inconveniences of his dramatic style, his aggressive learning, his bookishness, his literary elaboration, to the simple universal purposes of comedy. [Smith, *op. cit.*, p. 115.]

The lechery of Sir Epicure is not quite so integral a part of him as it is of Subtle, Face, and Dol. He realizes, as the others do not, that lechery is a vice; the schemers in the alchemist's shop regard their immoral sexual relations as the natural order of things. [Helena Watts Baum, *The Satiric and the Didactic in Ben Jonson's Comedy,* University of North Carolina Press, Chapel Hill, N.C., 1947, p. 102.]

I think that Subtle and his colleagues recede into the background if the play is viewed in its correct perspective. It is Sir Epicure Mammon who is the important figure in *The Alchemist*. This is not prevented by his being the gull rather than the guller. . . . The way of life at which [he is] aiming is a wholesale "uninhibited" assertion of the self at the expense of all social and religious conventions. This assertion is manifested in two forms: firstly, the glorification of wealth, secondly, physical desire of somewhat gargantuan proportions. [D. J. Enright, "Crime and Punishment in Ben Jonson," *Scrutiny*, vol. 9, 1940, p. 236.]

Jonson was careful in shaping his plots, but the results of this labor are subject to disagreement and differences in interpretation. Is the plot of The Alchemist *quite simple or quite complex? Is the intrigue plot basic or superficial? What is the relationship between the movement of the plot and the tempo in the play?*

The steadfast and imperturbable skill of hand which has woven so many threads of incident, so many changes of intrigue, into so perfect and superb a pattern of incomparable art as dazzles and delights the reader of *The Alchemist* is unquestionably unique. . . . The manifold harmony of inventive combination and imaginative contrast—the multitudinous unity of various and concordant effects—the complexity and the simplicity of action and impression, which hardly allow the reader's mind to hesitate between enjoyment and astonishment, laughter and wonder, admiration and diversion—all the distinctive qualities which the alchemic cunning of the poet has fused together in the crucible of dramatic satire for the production of a flawless work of art, have given us the most perfect model of imaginative realism and satirical comedy that the world has ever seen. . . . [Algernon Charles Swinburne, *A Study of Ben Jonson*, Chatto & Windus, Ltd., London, 1889, pp. 36–37.]

The "perfect and superb pattern" which Swinburne so characteristically eulogized seems to have deceived many into identifying excellent construction with classical construction. Unity is achieved, but it is a "multitudinous unity of various and concordant effects." Scene changes take place only between Lovewit's house and the adjacent street; the duration of the action hardly exceeds that of the performance. But if Castelvetro believed that observance of the unities of time and place must usually produce unity of action, Jonson here proves him wrong. The "minor unities" became in Jonson's hands the handicaps which art sets itself in order to display its virtuosity in triumphing over their apparent limitations and in making them serve well a new master. Unity of place is made dynamic: a magnetized center which draws the attracted elements into a whirling centripetal force, spinning them into kaleidoscopic patterns. Unity of time is used to make inevitable the meeting of all the characters and the twining together of all the intrigues. [Freda L. Townsend, *Apologie for Bartholomew Fayre: The Art of Jonson's Comedies*, Modern Language Association of America, New York, 1947, pp. 68–69.]

When we approach [Jonson's] most famous works . . . we come upon one dominant characteristic of Elizabethan comedy which at once assigns it to a low stage in dramatic development. An enormous percentage of plays of the lighter sort deal with sheer rascality, usually assuming the form of imposture. . . . This characteristic hangs together with the fondness for disguise, and the readiness to believe in miraculously perfect transmogrifications. . . . It is evidently very easy to concoct some sort of a plot, if you start from an assumption of pure scoundrelism on one side and illimitable credulity on the other. But credulity in the characters, if carried beyond a reasonable pitch, demands a corresponding credulity in the audience. Elizabethan audiences, it would seem, were ungrudging in their response to this demand. They were childishly ready for any amount of make-believe. Modern audiences are more sophisticated. [Archer, *op. cit.*, pp. 82–83.]

Jonson employs immense dramatic skill: it is not so much skill in plot as skill in doing without a plot. . . . In . . . *The Alchemist* . . . the plot is enough to keep the players in motion; it is rather an "action" than a plot. The plot does not hold the play together; what holds the play together is a unity of inspiration that radiates into plot and personages alike. [Eliot, *op. cit.*, p. 134.]

The situations dealing with Dapper, Drugger, Sir Epicure Mammon, and Ananias are each handled separately and briefly and reach their climaxes independent of one another. Our interest alternates among them. Jonson uses a single dramaturgical technique for all of them: First an introduction, then an interval of neglect, finally the gulling. This duplication of action is a triumph of artifice; but it is not complicated. A simple situation is repeated five times. One must not mistake quantity for complexity. [Robert E. Knoll, "How to Read *The Alchemist*," *College English*, vol. 21, 1960, p. 458.]

The steadily increasing tempo of the play suggests to many readers nothing so much as the increasing concentration and tension of a series of helical spirals described by moving bodies where each curve of the helix is not only more closely wound than the last but more rapidly described. The action . . . begins in a leisurely way, the development being deliberately retarded by comic rhetoric. . . . Not until the second act, when the first two plots of Subtle and Face have been set on foot, is there any perceptible quickening. The third and fourth intrigues, brought about by their next two pieces of plotting, have joined the general movement by the middle of the act, the fifth enters in the second half and at the end we prepare for a sixth and a seventh. In the third act the complications begin and it is about this point that we realize, I think, how nearly symbolic or decorative and non-representative is the design. . . . Since it is of the essence of Subtle and Face's plots that the different intrigues they set on foot should be kept apart, it is equally of the essence of the whole design that we should continually anticipate collisions followed by collapse, that these should be avoided by a progressively narrow margin and that implicit in this should be the anticipation at each evasion of a subsequent still closer approach which will require a proportionally greater inventive effort on the part of the plotters if catastrophe is again to be avoided. It is this which, by the end of the third act, has made the helical action clear. In the fourth act a marked reversal of movement sets in and we begin to anticipate disaster rather than the success we have so far assumed. [Una Ellis-Fermor, *The Jacobean Drama*, 3d ed., rev., Methuen & Co., Ltd., London, 1953, pp. 44–46.]

The resolution has been criticized as artificial and lacking in moral force; it has been defended as proper, in various ways, to the spirit and meaning of the play.

He meant *The Alchemist* to serve as a lesson in morality and he emphasized in the Prologue the "wholesome remedies" and "fair correctives" that would be administered to the audience through his lines. But Jonson's delight in color and vitality overcame his theoretical insistence on classic morality, and the outrageous but ingenious Face emerges unscathed at the end of the play, his cheerful impudence intact. The moral of the play, if any, is that it is better to be a knave than a fool. Jonson had a strong moral sense and a gift for social indignation, but his heart was drawn towards liveliness and vigor even when he knew that by Renaissance standards they were both unclassical and undesirable. [Marchette Chute, *Ben Jonson of Westminster*, E. P. Dutton & Co., Inc., New York, 1953, p. 186.]

Lovewit's unexpected return to London creaks like a crane lowering a ponderous and desperate *deus ex machina*. He bears no warrant except as owner of the house, and his judgments sound thoroughly whimsical. He appears a more prosperous version of the knaves, and his habits in discourse link him to them. [See Lovewit's speech, page 179.] . . . Lovewit's early return, when many citizens are absent and the usual affairs of city business are suspended, seems [an] effort to encase the action within a private niche. Face gets the uneasy last words, which confess that the resolution lacks the full range of edifying judiciousness it might have, although he insists that this break does not offend the rules of decorum. The plea does not convince logically; it merely insists mysteriously that the author has written and therefore is right. [John J. Enck, *Jonson and the Comic Truth*, University of Wisconsin Press, Madison, Wis., 1957, p. 160.]

In Tragedy, where the actions and persons are great, and the crimes horrid, the laws of justice are more strictly observed; and examples of punishment to be made, to deter mankind from the pursuit of vice. . . . Thus Tragedy fulfills one great part of its institution; which is, by example, to instruct. But in Comedy it is not so; for the chief end of it is divertisement and delight: and that so much, that it is disputed . . . whether instruction be any part of its employment. At least I am sure it can be but its secondary end: for the business of the poet is to make you laugh. . . . This being then established, that the first end of Comedy is delight, and instruction only the second; it may reasonably be inferred, that Comedy is not so much obliged to the punishment of faults which it represents, as Tragedy. For the persons in Comedy are of a lower quality, the action is little, and the faults and vices are but the sallies of youth, and the frailties of human nature, and not premeditated crimes: such to which all men

are obnoxious, and not such as are attempted only by few, and those abandoned to all sense of virtue: such as move pity and commiseration, not detestation and horror: such, in short, as may be forgiven, not such as must of necessity be punished. [John Dryden, "Preface to 'An Evening's Love; or, The Mock Astrologer'" (1671), *Dramatic Essays, op. cit.*, p. 83.]

The withering humiliation of Subtle, as he and Dol escape, baffled and penniless, through the back window of their laboratory, is made more poignant by the parting sarcasms of the triumphant Face. . . . It is Subtle, not Face, the Alchemist, not his butler-confederate, who is the subject of the comedy, and the mark of its satire; and when the frauds and delusions of alchemy are finally paraded with ironical mockery by the incomparable rascal who had taken a chief part in them, we are entitled to say, with Face himself, that " 'twas decorum"; it is in keeping with the ends of comedy. [C. H. Herford and Percy Simpson, *Ben Jonson*, vol. 2, Oxford University Press, New York, 1925, pp. 108–109.]

The justice here is scarcely poetic. To some it may not seem punishment at all, but it is the only justice that many ironic comedies have. No one repents, no one reforms—not even, one suspects, Mammon, although, still extravagant, he claims that he will "preach/The end o' the world." The fools are fooled; the rascals get away. Yet all endure the most comic of all punishments: they remain themselves—a deadly retribution if one is a fool like Mammon or a rascal like Face. [Edward B. Partridge, *The Broken Compass*, Columbia University Press, New York, 1958, p. 156.]

The dramatic poetry of Jonson is not that of Shakespeare. But is it absolutely inferior or merely seeking to achieve different effects?

Subtle uses long and even preposterous rants to pound his victims into submission and belief. Dol engages in a similar debased eloquence when she assumes madness at the mention of Broughton's works. As literature such passages, if read

unimaginatively, are insipid. But the intention is evidently that Subtle shall talk so fast and furiously that his longest speeches will take only a few moments to deliver. His vehemence, not his sense, draws the simple flies into his web. Evidence of Jonson's eminently theatrical conception appears in the quarto, which prints certain speeches of Dol's mad scene in parallel columns. The speakers are to talk simultaneously. Most modern editions overlook this refinement, thus doing a great injustice to the playwright's art, concealing its theatrical effectiveness and its real vivacity. [Henry W. Wells, *Elizabethan and Jacobean Playwrights,* Columbia University Press, New York, 1939, pp. 202–203.]

[The play makes extensive use of slang and jargon, with the terms poured out in long lists which are sometimes positive, sometimes negative.] Nevertheless, this mastery of the catalogue is achieved at an expense ruinous to the other effects of language in the play. . . . In the opening quarrel the vituperations Face and Subtle throw at each other name dogs, qualities descriptive of the kind of snarling which flares forth frequently between the two men and later between them and their disgruntled customers. After this initial planting of the theme . . . figures rarely return to this metaphor. Other kinds of animal names recur in a sporadic fashion, as though Jonson had, at best, a passing interest in them. . . . Little phrases, hardly worth noting, use birds for terms of endearment. [Enck, *op. cit.,* p. 158.]

The imagery of *The Alchemist* is perfectly functional in several ways. First, it develops, as alchemy develops, beginning with base metals, such as a whore, a pander, and a quack, which it tries grandiloquently to transmute into finer beings—a Faery Queen, a precious king of present wits, and a divine instructor—finally ending, as the dream of the philosopher's stone ends, in a return to the state of base metals. The various vehicles which alchemize the base situation—the inflated epithets, the erotic allusions, the religious and commercial terms—ultimately show how thoroughly mean the situation is by bringing into the context the very standards by which it could be measured: the Christian and humanistic civilization of rational men. Against that immense background the three impostors and their commonwealth of fools play out their violent little actions contrasting sharply with the permanent values suggested by the imagery. . . .

The imagery is functional in another way. The images work on the same principle that the play as a whole and usually each scene work. They are extravagant, inflated, and ludicrous, because the tenors (gold, Dol, Mammon) are related to great vehicles (god, Queen, Jove). The monstrous gap that opens between the tenor that we know to be mean and the vehicle that we assume to be great, and the demand that we find some similarities between them to bridge that gap, outrages our sense of decency and decorum. That outrage, within the imagery, produces part of the comic tone of the play.

A third function of the imagery is to extend and develop the multiple references that alchemy had in actual life—especially the religious, medical, and commercial references. The alchemic process in this play has religious implications because the desire for gold is thought of as a sovereign remedy; it has sexual implications because the elixir is thought to have a sexual power; it has commercial implications because business terms are used in reference to the whole fraudulent practice. . . . In other words, the imagery suggests that, in the Alchemist's world, the acquisition of gold is a religion, a cure-all, a sexual experience, and a commercial enterprise. The world that opens before us, once we understand these multiple references of alchemy, is outrageously obscene, crude in metaphysic and vulgar in emotion. [Partridge, *op. cit.,* pp. 156–158.]

The charge against Jonson of an unsatisfying simplicity is not borne out by the apparent difficulty of deciding just what the central theme of The Alchemist *is.*

It would be foolish to deny that Ben had a robust mind. But does a single general idea emerge from his work? He was a vigorous satirist, scourging, by way of caricature, the follies of his age; but a thinker he was not. [Archer, *op. cit.*, pp. 125–126.]

The theme of this play is the power of illusion: like fairy gold, the treasure eludes all seekers, but the victims are enriched with potent gifts of imagination and hope: they are characters seen almost in the round. [M. C. Bradbrook, *The Growth and Structure of Elizabethan Comedy*, Chatto & Windus, Ltd., London, 1955, p. 146.]

In this comedy . . . Jonson treats lust in a markedly light manner. Part of the change is managed by increasing the tempo of the play, so that the spectator, amused by the antics of the rascals and their gulls, has no opportunity to meditate upon the evil of lust. . . . The lechery of Sir Epicure is reduced to an absurdity. He is vice-ridden; yet the emotion which he rouses is merely contemptuous amusement. Lust, overblown and rotten in Sir Epicure, is convincingly contrasted with lust in its ordinary, animal manifestations in Dol, Face, and Subtle. [Baum, *op. cit.*, p. 103.]

The Alchemist . . . is built on the double theme of lust and greed, and the whole play is constructed so as to isolate and magnify the central theme. [L. C. Knights, *Drama and Society in the Age of Jonson*, Chatto & Windus, Ltd., London, 1951, p. 207.]

Jonson's "attitude" is presented in his plays in different guises and in varying degrees of seriousness, but it is sufficiently clearly defined to be described with justification as his "theme."

This theme, what Jonson is concerned with in his drama, is what we may call "spiritual modesty," or the acknowledgement by the individual of his proper and ordained position in the universe. All the plays are "satire" in that they deal with persons from whom this acknowledgement, this modesty, is absent, and with the ambitions of these persons to exist in Brave New Worlds of some or other kind of Splendour, with their crime and their punishment. There is always this essential scheme of crime and punishment, and the crime is invariably of the same kind, though its gravity and the gravity of the punishment are hardly the same in any two plays. [Enright, *op. cit.*, p. 231.]

JOHN WEBSTER

c. 1580–a. 1635

*Almost nothing is known about Webster's life. The date of his birth
is conjectural, that of his death a mystery, even though Webster
wrote two plays which are generally considered among the best of
English Renaissance drama. Of course, a number of critics would
disagree with this estimate. "Tussaud laureate," George Bernard Shaw
dubbed him, and in the implications of that epithet are included most
of the objections to Webster's dramatic style. He has been accused
of sheer sensationalism, of presenting an artificial and lifeless
horror show to achieve the easy effect of shock upon a vulgar
audience. And yet, if we can judge by Webster's address "To the
Reader" prefatory to* The White Devil *(1612) and his Dedication
of* The Duchess of Malfi *(1614), the two plays upon which his fame
rests were not popular with their original audiences, the supposedly
crude group who are assumed to have demanded the violent and
sensational above all else. Most of the objections to Webster have
been raised by those who prefer a well-made play, and he
certainly does not provide that. But while he is often praised for the
sheer power of his dramatic poetry, he does not offer* only *poetry.
It is important to remember that this poetry is a part of the total
play; it does not exist in a vacuum. Webster is symptomatic of the
new age of doubt and insecurity which came near the beginning
of the seventeenth century. One of his foremost interests is in
probing abnormal psychological states at a time when the earlier,
simpler answers to riddles of human behavior were being rejected.
Whatever power his plays possess is related to the power, in lyric
verse, of his contemporary, Donne, who was also painfully aware of
a world in flux, with "all coherence gone."*

The Duchess of Malfi

Characters

FERDINAND *Duke of Calabria*

CARDINAL *his brother*

ANTONIO BOLOGNA *steward of the household to the Duchess*

DELIO *his friend*

DANIEL DE BOSOLA *gentleman of the horse to the Duchess*

CASTRUCHIO

MARQUIS OF PESCARA

COUNT MALATESTE

SILVIO, A LORD, OF MILAN ⎱ *gentlemen attending*
RODERIGO ⎰ *on the Duchess*

GRISOLAN

DOCTOR

DUCHESS OF MALFI *sister of Ferdinand and the Cardinal*

CARIOLA *her woman*

JULIA *Castruchio's wife, and the Cardinal's mistress*

OLD LADY

SEVERAL MADMEN, PILGRIMS, EXECUTIONERS, OFFICERS, ATTENDANTS, LADIES AND CHILDREN, etc.

The action of the play takes place in Amalfi, Rome, and Milan.

Act One

SCENE ONE

Amalfi, the Palace of the Duchess. Enter Antonio and Delio.

DELIO You are welcome to your country, dear
    Antonio;
  You have been long in France, and you return
  A very formal Frenchman in your habit:
  How do you like the French court?

ANTONIO   I admire it:

In seeking to reduce both state and people
To a fixed order, their judicious king
Begins at home; quits first his royal palace
Of flattering sycophants, of dissolute
And infamous persons,—which he sweetly
    terms
His master's masterpiece, the work of Heaven;
Considering duly that a prince's court
Is like a common fountain, whence should flow
Pure silver drops in general, but if't chance

Some cursed example poison't near the head,
Death and diseases through the whole land
  spread.
And what is't makes this blessed government
But a most provident council, who dare freely
Inform him the corruption of the times?
Though some o' th' court hold it presumption
To instruct princes what they ought to do,
It is a noble duty to inform them
What they ought to foresee.—Here comes
  Bosola,
[*Enter Bosola.*]
The only court-gall; yet I observe his railing
Is not for simple love of piety:
Indeed, he rails at those things which he wants;
Would be as lecherous, covetous, or proud,
Bloody, or envious, as any man,
If he had means to be so.—Here's the Cardinal.
[*Enter Cardinal.*]

BOSOLA I do haunt you still.

CARDINAL So.

BOSOLA I have done you better service than to
be slighted thus. Miserable age, where only the
reward of doing well is the doing of it!

CARDINAL You enforce your merit too much.

BOSOLA I fell into the galleys in your service;
where, for two years together, I wore two
towels instead of a shirt, with a knot on the
shoulder, after the fashion of a Roman mantle.
Slighted thus? I will thrive some way: blackbirds fatten best in hard weather; why not I
in these dog-days?

CARDINAL Would you could become honest!

BOSOLA With all your divinity do but direct me
the way to it. I have known many travel far
for it, and yet return as arrant knaves as they
went forth, because they carried themselves
always along with them. [*Exit Cardinal.*] Are
you gone? Some fellows, they say, are possessed with the devil, but this great fellow were
able to possess the greatest devil, and make
him worse.

ANTONIO He hath denied thee some suit?

BOSOLA He and his brother are like plum-trees
that grow crooked over standing-pools; they are
rich and o'er-laden with fruit, but none but
crows, 'pies, and caterpillars feed on them.
Could I be one of their flattering panders, I
would hang on their ears like a horseleech, till
I were full, and then drop off. I pray, leave
me. Who would rely upon these miserable de-
pendencies, in expectation to be advanced to-
morrow? what creature ever fed worse than
hoping Tantalus? nor ever died any man more
fearfully than he that hoped for a pardon.
There are rewards for hawks and dogs when
they have done us service; but for a soldier that
hazards his limbs in a battle, nothing but a kind
of geometry is his last supportation.

DELIO Geometry?

BOSOLA Aye, to hang in a fair pair of slings,
take his latter swing in the world upon an honorable pair of crutches, from hospital to hospital. Fare ye well, sir: and yet do not you scorn
us; for places in the court are but like beds in
the hospital, where this man's head lies at that
man's foot, and so lower and lower. [*Exit.*]

DELIO I knew this fellow seven years in the
  galleys
For a notorious murder; and 'twas thought
The Cardinal suborned it: he was released
By the French general, Gaston de Foix,
When he recovered Naples.

ANTONIO   'Tis great pity
He should be thus neglected: I have heard
He's very valiant. This foul melancholy
Will poison all his goodness; for, I'll tell you,
If too immoderate sleep be truly said
To be an inward rust unto the soul,
It then doth follow want of action
Breeds all black malcontents; and their close
  rearing,
Like moths in cloth, do hurt for want of wear-
  ing.

DELIO The presence 'gins to fill; you promised
  me
To make me the partaker of the natures
Of some of your great courtiers.

ANTONIO   The lord Car-
  dinal's
And other strangers' that are now in court?
I shall.—Here comes the great Calabrian duke.
[*Enter Ferdinand, Castruchio, Silvio, Roderigo,
Grisolan, and Attendants.*]

FERDINAND Who took the ring oftenest?[1]

SILVIO Antonio Bologna, my lord.

---

[1] In the tournament sport of tilting at the ring.

JOHN WEBSTER

FERDINAND Our sister duchess's great-master of her household? give him the jewel.—When shall we leave this sportive action, and fall to action indeed?

CASTRUCHIO Methinks, my lord, you should not desire to go to war in person.

FERDINAND Now for some gravity:—why, my lord?

CASTRUCHIO It is fitting a soldier arise to be a prince, but not necessary a prince descend to be a captain.

FERDINAND No?

CASTRUCHIO No, my lord; he were far better do it by a deputy.

FERDINAND Why should he not as well sleep or eat by a deputy? this might take idle, offensive, and base office from him, where as the other deprives him of honor.

CASTRUCHIO Believe my experience, that realm is never long in quiet where the ruler is a soldier.

FERDINAND Thou told'st me thy wife could not endure fighting.

CASTRUCHIO True, my lord.

FERDINAND And of a jest she broke of a captain she met full of wounds: I have forgot it.

CASTRUCHIO She told him, my lord, he was a pitiful fellow, to lie, like the children of Ismael, all in tents.[2]

FERDINAND Why, there's a wit were able to undo all the chirurgeons[3] o' the city; for although gallants should quarrel, and had drawn their weapons, and were ready to go to it, yet her persuasions would make them put up.

CASTRUCHIO That she would, my lord. How do you like my Spanish gennet?[4]

RODERIGO He is all fire.

FERDINAND I am of Pliny's opinion, I think he was begot by the wind; he runs as if he were ballast with quick-silver.[5]

SILVIO True, my lord, he reels from the tilt often.

[2] A play on words: *tents* also means rolls of bandage.
[3] Surgeons.
[4] Horse.
[5] In Pliny's *Natural History* was recorded an old belief that mares, impregnated by the west wind, give birth to extremely fleet foals with a life span of only three years.

RODERIGO AND GRISOLAN Ha, ha, ha!

FERDINAND Why do you laugh? methinks you that are courtiers should be my touchwood, take fire when I give fire; that is, laugh but when I laugh, were the subject never so witty.

CASTRUCHIO True, my lord: I myself have heard a very good jest and have scorned to seem to have so silly a wit as to understand it.

FERDINAND But I can laugh at your fool, my lord.

CASTRUCHIO He cannot speak, you know, but he makes faces: my lady cannot abide him.

FERDINAND No?

CASTRUCHIO Nor endure to be in merry company; for she says too much laughing, and too much company, fills her too full of the wrinkle.

FERDINAND I would, then, have a mathematical instrument made for her face, that she might not laugh out of compass.—I shall shortly visit you at Milan, Lord Silvio.

SILVIO Your grace shall arrive most welcome.

FERDINAND You are a good horseman, Antonio: you have excellent riders in France: what do you think of good horsemanship?

ANTONIO Nobly, my lord: as out of the Grecian horse issued many famous princes, so out of brave horsemanship arise the first sparks of growing resolution, that raise the mind to noble action.

FERDINAND You have bespoke it worthily.

SILVIO Your brother, the lord Cardinal, and sister duchess.

[*Enter Cardinal, Duchess, Cariola, and Julia.*]

CARDINAL Are the galleys come about?

GRISOLAN They are, my lord.

FERDINAND Here's the Lord Silvio is come to take his leave.

DELIO [*to Antonio*] Now, sir, your promise; What's that Cardinal?

I mean his temper? they say he's a brave fellow, Will play his five thousand crowns at tennis, dance,

Court ladies, and one that hath fought single combats.

ANTONIO Some such flashes superficially hang on him for form; but observe his inward character: he is a melancholy churchman; the spring in his face is nothing but the engendering of toads; where he is jealous of any man, he lays worse plots for them than ever was imposed on Hercules, for he strews in his way flatterers, panders, intelligencers, atheists, and a thousand such political monsters. He should have been Pope; but instead of coming to it by the primitive decency of the Church, he did bestow bribes so largely and so impudently as if he would have carried it away without Heaven's knowledge. Some good he hath done—

DELIO You have given too much of him. What's his brother?

ANTONIO The duke there? a most perverse and turbulent nature:
What appears in him mirth is merely outside;
If he laugh heartily, it is to laugh
All honesty out of fashion.

DELIO Twins?

ANTONIO In quality.
He speaks with others' tongues, and hears men's suits
With others' ears; will seem to sleep o' th' bench
Only to entrap offenders in their answers;
Dooms men to death by information;[6]
Rewards by hearsay.

DELIO Then the law to him
Is like a foul black cobweb to a spider,—
He makes it his dwelling and a prison
To entangle those shall feed him.

ANTONIO Most true:
He never pays debts unless they be shrewd turns.
And those he will confess that he doth owe.
Last, for his brother there, the Cardinal,
They that do flatter him most say oracles
Hang at his lips; and verily I believe them,
For the devil speaks in them.
But for their sister, the right noble duchess,
You never fixed your eye on three fair medals
Cast in one figure, of so different temper.
For her discourse, it is so full of rapture,
You only will begin then to be sorry
When she doth end her speech, and wish, in wonder,
She held it less vainglory to talk much,
Than your penance to hear her: whilst she speaks,

[6] Evidence from informers.

She throws upon a man so sweet a look,
That it were able to raise one to a galliard[7]
That lay in a dead palsy, and to dote
On that sweet countenance; but in that look
There speaketh so divine a continence
As cuts off all lascivious and vain hope.
Her days are practised in such noble virtue,
That sure her nights, nay, more, her very sleeps,
Are more in heaven than other ladies' shrifts.
Let all sweet ladies break their flattering glasses,
And dress themselves in her.

DELIO Fie, Antonio,
You play the wire-drawer with her commendations.[8]

ANTONIO I'll case the picture up: only thus much;
All her particular worth grows to this sum,—
She stains the time past, lights the time to come.

CARIOLA You must attend my lady in the gallery,
Some half an hour hence.

ANTONIO I shall.

[*Exeunt Antonio and Delio.*]

FERDINAND Sister, I have a suit to you.

DUCHESS To me, sir?

FERDINAND A gentleman here, Daniel de Bosola,
One that was in the galleys—

DUCHESS Yes, I know him.

FERDINAND A worthy fellow he is: pray, let me entreat for
The provisorship[9] of your horse.

DUCHESS Your knowledge of him
Commends him and prefers him.

FERDINAND Call him hither.

[*Exit Attendant.*]

We are now upon parting. Good Lord Silvio,
Do us commend to all our noble friends
At the leaguer.

SILVIO Sir, I shall.

DUCHESS You are for Milan?

SILVIO I am.

[7] A lively dance.
[8] Draw out her praises at great length.
[9] Office of purveyor.

JOHN WEBSTER

DUCHESS Bring the caroches.[10] We'll bring you down
To the heaven.

[*Exeunt all but Ferdinand and the Cardinal.*]

CARDINAL Be sure you entertain that Bosola
For your intelligence[11] I would not be seen in't;
And therefore many times I have slighted him
When he did court our furtherance, as this morning.

FERDINAND Antonio, the great-master of her household,
Had been far fitter.

CARDINAL You are deceived in him:
His nature is too honest for such business.—
He comes: I'll leave you.

[*Exit. Reenter Bosola.*]

BOSOLA I was lured to you.

FERDINAND My brother, here, the Cardinal could never
Abide you.

BOSOLA Never since he was in my debt.

FERDINAND Maybe some oblique character in your face
Made him suspect you.

BOSOLA Doth he study physiognomy?
There's no more credit to be given to th' face
Than to a sick man's urine, which some call
The physician's whore because she cozens him.
He did suspect me wrongfully.

FERDINAND For that
You must give great men leave to take their times.
Distrust doth cause us seldom be deceived:
You see the oft shaking of the cedar-tree
Fastens it more at root.

BOSOLA Yet, take heed;
For to suspect a friend unworthily
Instructs him the next way to suspect you,
And prompts him to deceive you.

FERDINAND [*giving him money*] There's gold.

BOSOLA So:
What follows? never rained such showers as these
Without thunderbolts i' th' tail of them: whose throat must I cut?

[10] Coaches.
[11] Spy service.

FERDINAND Your inclination to shed blood rides post
Before my occasion to use you. I give you that
To live i' th' court here, and observe the duchess;
To note all the particulars of her havior,
What suitors do solicit her for marriage,
And whom she best affects. She's a young widow:
I would not have her marry again.

BOSOLA No, sir?

FERDINAND Do not you ask the reason; but be satisfied
I say I would not.

BOSOLA It seems you would create me
One of your familiars.

FERDINAND Familiar? what's that?

BOSOLA Why, a very quaint invisible devil in flesh,
An intelligencer.

FERDINAND Such a kind of thriving thing
I would wish thee; and ere long thou may'st arrive
At a higher place by't.

BOSOLA Take your devils,
Which hell calls angels;[12] these cursed gifts would make
You a corrupter, me an impudent traitor;
And should I take these, they'd take me to hell.

FERDINAND Sir, I'll take nothing from you that I have given;
There is a place that I procured for you
This morning, the provisorship o' th' horse;
Have you heard on't?

BOSOLA No.

FERDINAND 'Tis yours: is't not worth thanks?

BOSOLA I would have you curse yourself now, that your bounty,
Which makes men truly noble, e'er should make me
A villain. Oh, that to avoid ingratitude
For the good deed you have done me, I must do

[12] Gold coins.

All the ill man can invent! Thus the devil
Candies all sins o'er; and what heaven terms
vile,
That names he complimental.

FERDINAND Be yourself;
Keep your old garb of melancholy; 'twill express
You envy those that stand above your reach,
Yet strive not to come near 'em: this will gain
Access to private lodgings, where yourself
May, like a politic dormouse—

BOSOLA As I have seen
some
Feed in a lord's dish, half asleep, not seeming
To listen to any talk; and yet these rogues
Have cut his throat in a dream. What's my
place?
The provisorship o' th' horse? say, then, my
corruption
Grew out of horse-dung: I am your creature.

FERDINAND Away!

BOSOLA Let good men, for good deeds, covet
good fame,
Since place and riches oft are bribes of shame:
Sometimes the devil doth preach.
[Exit Bosola.]
[Enter Duchess, Cardinal, and Cariola.]

CARDINAL We are to part from you; and your
own discretion
Must now be your director.

FERDINAND You are a widow:
You know already what man is; and therefore
Let not youth, high promotion, eloquence—

CARDINAL No,
Nor any thing without the addition, honor,
Sway your high blood.

FERDINAND Marry! they are most luxurious[13]
Will wed twice.

CARDINAL Oh, fie!

FERDINAND Their livers are more
spotted
Than Laban's sheep.[14]

DUCHESS Diamonds are of most
value,
They say, that have passed through most jew-
ellers' hands.

[13] Lecherous.
[14] Laban, father-in-law of Jacob, received all the
streaked and spotted sheep from the latter; see
Genesis XXX, 31-42.

FERDINAND Whores by that rule are precious.

DUCHESS Will you hear me?
I'll never marry.

CARDINAL So most widows say;
But commonly that motion lasts no longer
Than the turning of an hourglass: the funeral
sermon
And it end both together.

FERDINAND Now hear me:
You live in a rank pasture, here, i' th' court;
There is a kind of honeydew that's deadly;
'Twill poison your fame; look to't: be not cun-
ning;
For they whose faces do belie their hearts
Are witches ere they arrive at twenty years,
Aye, and give the devil suck.

DUCHESS This is terrible
good counsel.

FERDINAND Hypocrisy is woven of a fine small
thread,
Subtler than Vulcan's engine:[15] yet, believe't,
Your darkest actions, nay, your privat'st
thoughts,
Will come to light.

CARDINAL You may flatter yourself,
And take your own choice; privately be mar-
ried
Under the eaves of night—

FERDINAND Think'st the best
voyage
That e'er you made; like the irregular crab,
Which, though't goes backward, thinks that it
goes right
Because it goes its own way; but observe,
Such weddings may more properly be said
To be executed than celebrated.

CARDINAL The marriage
night
Is the entrance into some prison.

FERDINAND And those
joys,
Those lustful pleasures, are like heavy sleeps
Which do forerun man's mischief.

CARDINAL Fare you
well.
Wisdom begins at the end: remember it.
[Exit.]

[15] The invisible iron net in which he trapped his
wife, Venus, when she was with Mars.

DUCHESS I think this speech between you both was studied,
It came so roundly off.

FERDINAND You are my sister;
This was my father's poniard, do you see?
I'd be loath to see 't look rusty, 'cause 'twas his.
I would have you to give o'er these charge-able[16] revels:
A visor and a mask are whispering-rooms
That were never built for goodness;—fare ye well;—
And women like that part which, like the lamprey,
Hath never a bone in't.

DUCHESS Fie, sir!

FERDINAND Nay,
I mean the tongue; variety of courtship:
What cannot a neat knave with a smooth tale
Make a woman believe? Farewell, lusty widow.
[*Exit.*]

DUCHESS Shall this move me? If all my royal kindred
Lay in my way unto this marriage,
I'd make them my low footsteps: and even now,
Even in this hate, as men in some great battles,
By apprehending danger, have achieved
Almost impossible actions (I have heard soldiers say so),
So I through frights and threatenings will assay
This dangerous venture. Let old wives report
I winked[17] and chose a husband.—Cariola,
To thy known secrecy I have given up
More than my life—my fame.

CARIOLA Both shall be safe;
For I'll conceal this secret from the world
As warily as those that trade in poison
Keep poison from their children.

DUCHESS Thy protestation
Is ingenious[18] and hearty: I believe it.
Is Antonio come?

CARIOLA He attends you.

DUCHESS Good dear soul,
Leave me; but place thyself behind the arras,
Where thou mayst overhear us. Wish me good speed;
For I am going into a wilderness
Where I shall find nor path nor friendly clue
To be my guide.
[*Cariola goes behind the arras. Enter Antonio.*]
I sent for you: sit down;
Take pen and ink, and write: are you ready?

ANTONIO Yes.

DUCHESS What did I say?

ANTONIO That I should write somewhat.

DUCHESS Oh, I remember.
After these triumphs[19] and this large expense,
It's fit, like thrifty husbands,[20] we inquire
What's laid up for tomorrow.

ANTONIO So please your beauteous excellence.

DUCHESS Beauteous?
Indeed, I thank you: I look young for your sake;
You have ta'en my cares upon you.

ANTONIO I'll fetch your grace
The particulars of your revenue and expense.

DUCHESS Oh, you are an upright treasurer: but you mistook;
For when I said I meant to make inquiry
What's laid up for tomorrow, I did mean
What's laid up yonder for me.

ANTONIO Where?

DUCHESS In heaven.
I am making my will (as 'tis fit princes should,
In perfect memory), and, I pray, sir, tell me,
Were not one better make it smiling, thus,
Than in deep groans and terrible ghastly looks,
As if the gifts we parted with procured
That violent distraction?

ANTONIO Oh, much better.

DUCHESS If I had a husband now, this care were quit:
But I intend to make you overseer.
What good deed shall we first remember? Say.

ANTONIO Begin with that first good deed began i' th' world
After man's creation, the sacrament of marriage:

16 Costly.
17 Closed my eyes.
18 Ingenuous.

19 Festivities.
20 Housekeepers.

I'd have you first provide for a good husband;
Give him all.
DUCHESS   All?
ANTONIO   Yes, your excellent self.
DUCHESS   In a winding-sheet?
ANTONIO   In a couple.
DUCHESS   Saint
  Winfred,
That were a strange will!
ANTONIO   'Twere stranger if there were no will
  in you
To marry again.
DUCHESS   What do you think of mar-
  riage?
ANTONIO   I take't, as those that deny purgatory;
  It locally contains or Heaven or hell;
  There's no third place in 't.
DUCHESS   How do you affect
  it?
ANTONIO   My banishment, feeding my melan-
  choly,
  Would often reason thus.
DUCHESS   Pray, let's hear it.
ANTONIO   Say a man never marry, nor have
  children,
What takes that from him? only the bare name
Of being a father, or the weak delight
To see the little wanton ride a-cock-horse
Upon a painted stick, or hear him chatter
Like a taught starling.
DUCHESS   Fie, fie, what's all this?
One of your eyes is blood-shot; use my ring
  to 't,
They say 'tis very sovereign: 'twas my wedding-
  ring,
And I did vow never to part with it
But to my second husband.
ANTONIO   You have parted
  with it now.
DUCHESS   Yes, to help your eyesight.
ANTONIO   You have
  made me stark blind.
DUCHESS   How?
ANTONIO   There is a saucy and ambitious devil
  Is dancing in this circle.
DUCHESS   Remove him.
ANTONIO   How?
DUCHESS   There needs small conjuration, when
  your finger

May do it: thus; is it fit?
[*She puts the ring upon his finger: he kneels.*]
ANTONIO   What said you?
DUCHESS   Sir,
This goodly roof of yours is too low built;
I cannot stand upright in 't nor discourse,
Without I raise it higher: raise yourself;
Or, if you please, my hand to help you: so.
[*Raises him.*]
ANTONIO   Ambition, madam, is a great man's
  madness,
That is not kept in chains and close-pent rooms,
But in fair lightsome lodgings, and is girt
With the wild noise of prattling visitants,
Which makes it lunatic beyond all cure.
Conceive not I am so stupid but I aim
Whereto your favors tend: but he's a fool
That, being a-cold, would thrust his hands i'
  th' fire
To warm them.
DUCHESS   So, now the ground's broke,
You may discover what a wealthy mine
I make you lord of.
ANTONIO   O my unworthiness!
DUCHESS   You were ill to sell yourself:
This darkening of your worth is not like that
Which tradesmen use i' th' city; their false lights
Are to rid bad wares off: and I must tell you,
If you will know where breathes a complete
  man
(I speak it without flattery), turn your eyes,
And progress through yourself.
ANTONIO   Were there nor
  heaven
Nor hell, I should be honest: I have long served
  virtue,
And ne'er ta'en wages of her.
DUCHESS   Now she pays it.
The misery of us that are born great!
We are forced to woo, because none dare woo
  us;
And as a tyrant doubles with his words,
And fearfully equivocates, so we
Are forced to express our violent passions
In riddles and in dreams, and leave the path
Of simple virtue, which was never made
To seem the thing it is not. Go, go brag
You have left me heartless; mine is in your
  bosom:

206   JOHN WEBSTER

I hope 'twill multiply love there. You do tremble:
Make not your heart so dead a piece of flesh,
To fear more than to love me. Sir, be confident:
What is 't distracts you? This is flesh and blood, sir;
'Tis not the figure cut in alabaster
Kneels at my husband's tomb. Awake, awake, man!
I do here put off all vain ceremony,
And only do appear to you a young widow
That claims you for her husband, and, like a widow,
I use but half a blush in 't.

ANTONIO　　　　　Truth speak for me;
I will remain the constant sanctuary
Of your good name.

DUCHESS　　　　　I thank you, gentle love:
And 'cause you shall not come to me in debt,
Being now my steward, here upon your lips
I sign your *Quietus est.*[21] This you should have begged now:
I have seen children oft eat sweetmeats thus,
As fearful to devour them too soon.

ANTONIO　But for your brothers?

DUCHESS　　　　　Do not think of them:
All discord without this circumference
Is only to be pitied, and not feared:
Yet, should they know it, time will easily
Scatter the tempest.

ANTONIO　　　　　These words should be mine,
And all the parts you have spoke, if some part of it
Would not have savored flattery.

DUCHESS　　　　　Kneel.
[*Cariola comes from behind the arras.*]

ANTONIO　　　　　Ha!

DUCHESS　Be not amazed; this woman's of my counsel:
I have heard lawyers say, a contract in a chamber
Per verba [*de*] *presenti* is absolute marriage.[22]

---

[21] Acquittance of debt (an accountant's term).

[22] *Per . . . presenti:* using words in the present tense. In canon law, a marriage contract was valid if

---

[*She and Antonio kneel.*]
Bless, heaven, this sacred gordian,[23] which let violence
Never untwine!

ANTONIO　　　　　And may our sweet affections, like the spheres,
Be still in motion!

DUCHESS　　　　　Quickening, and make
The like soft music!

ANTONIO　　　　　That we may imitate the loving palms,
Best emblem of a peaceful marriage, that ne'er
Bore fruit, divided!

DUCHESS　　　　　What can the Church force more?

ANTONIO　That fortune may not know an accident,
Either of joy or sorrow, to divide
Our fixèd wishes!

DUCHESS　　　　　How can the Church build faster?[24]
We now are man and wife, and 'tis the Church
That must but echo this.—Maid, stand apart:
I now am blind.

ANTONIO　　　　　What's your conceit[25] in this?

DUCHESS　I would have you lead your fortune by the hand
Unto your marriage bed:
(You speak in me this, for we now are one:)
We'll only lie, and talk together, and plot
To appease my humorous[26] kindred; and if you please,
Like the old tale in 'Alexander and Lodowick,'
Lay a naked sword between us, keep us chaste.
Oh, let me shroud my blushes in your bosom,
Since 'tis the treasury of all my secrets!
[*Exeunt Duchess and Antonio.*]

CARIOLA　Whether the spirit of greatness or of woman
Reign most in her, I know not; but it shows
A fearful madness: I owe her much of pity.
[*Exit.*]

---

it was an immediate agreement rather than a plan for the future.

[23] The fabled knot, which could not be untied.

[24] More securely.

[25] Idea.

[26] Temperamental.

Act Two

SCENE ONE

The same. Enter Bosola and Castruchio.

BOSOLA You say you would fain be taken for an eminent courtier?[27]

CASTRUCHIO 'Tis the very main[28] of my ambition.

BOSOLA Let me see: you have a reasonable good face for 't already, and your nightcap expresses your ears sufficient largely.[29] I would have you learn to twirl the strings of your band[30] with a good grace, and in a set speech, at th' end of every sentence, to hum three or four times, or blow your nose till it smart again, to recover your memory. When you come to be a president in criminal causes, if you smile upon a prisoner, hang him, but if you frown upon him and threaten him, let him be sure to scape the gallows.

CASTRUCHIO I would be a very merry president.

BOSOLA Do not sup o' night; 'twill beget you an admirable wit.

CASTRUCHIO Rather it would make me have a good stomach to quarrel; for they say, your roaring boys[31] eat meat seldom, and that makes them so valiant. But how shall I know whether the people take me for an eminent fellow?

BOSOLA I will teach a trick to know it: give out you lie a-dying, and if you hear the common people curse you, be sure you are taken for one of the prime nightcaps. [*Enter an Old Lady.*] You come from painting now.

OLD LADY From what?

BOSOLA Why, from your scurvy face-physic. To behold thee not painted inclines somewhat near a miracle; these in thy face here were deep ruts and foul sloughs the last progress.[32] There was a lady in France that, having had the smallpox, flayed the skin off her face to make it more level; and whereas before she look'd like a nutmeg-grater, after she resembled an abortive hedgehog.

OLD LADY Do you call this painting?

BOSOLA No, no, but you call [it] careening of an old morphewed lady, to make her disembogue again: there's rough-cast phrase to your plastic.[33]

OLD LADY It seems you are well acquainted with my closet.

BOSOLA One would suspect it for a shop of witchcraft, to find in it the fat of serpents, spawn of snakes, Jews' spittle, and their young children's ordure; and all these for the face. I would sooner eat a dead pigeon taken from the soles of the feet of one sick of the plague than kiss one of you fasting. Here are two of you, whose sin of your youth is the very patrimony of the physician; makes him renew his foot-cloth with the spring, and change his high-priced courtesan with the fall of the leaf. I do wonder you do not loathe yourselves. Observe my meditation now.

What thing is in this outward form of man
To be beloved? We account it ominous,
If nature do produce a colt, or lamb,
A fawn, or goat, in any limb resembling
A man, and fly from 't as a prodigy:
Man stands amazed to see his deformity
In any other creature but himself.
But in our own flesh, though we bear diseases
Which have their true names only ta'en from
    beasts,—
As the most ulcerous wolf and swinish mea-
    sle,—[34]
Though we are eaten up of lice and worms,
And though continually we bear about us
A rotten and dead body, we delight
To hide it in rich tissue: all our fear,

---

[27] Member of a law court.

[28] Goal.

[29] Your lawyer's coif shows off your big ears.

[30] A lawyer wore a collar with a pair of bands or strips hanging down in front.

[31] Bullies.

[32] Royal procession.

[33] *Careening:* turning a boat on its side for repairs; *morphewed:* scaly-skinned; *disembogue:* put to sea; *rough-cast:* coarse plaster; *plastic:* modeling, primping.

[34] *Lupus* (Latin, *wolf*) is a medical term for ulcer; *measle* meant leprosy, popularly thought to be like a skin disease of swine.

Nay, all our terror, is lest our physician
Should put us in the ground to be made sweet.—
Your wife's gone to Rome: you two couple, and get you
To the wells at Lucca to recover your aches.
I have other work on foot.
[*Exeunt Castruchio and Old Lady.*]
                                    I observe our duchess
Is sick a-days, she pukes, her stomach seethes,
The fins of her eye-lids look most teeming blue,[35]
She wanes i' th' cheek, and waxes fat i' th' flank,
And, contrary to our Italian fashion,
Wears a loose-bodied gown: there's somewhat in 't.
I have a trick may chance discover it,
A pretty one; I have brought some apricots,
The first our spring yields.
[*Enter Antonio and Delio, talking together.*]
DELIO   And so long since married?
You amaze me.
ANTONIO   Let me seal your lips for ever:
For, did I think that anything but th' air
Could carry these words from you, I should wish
You had no breath at all.—Now, sir, in your contemplation?
You are studying to become a great wise fellow?
BOSOLA Oh, sir, the opinion of wisdom is a foul tetter[36] that runs all over a man's body: if simplicity direct us to have no evil, it directs us to a happy being; for the subtlest folly proceeds from the subtlest wisdom: let me be simply honest.
ANTONIO I do understand your inside.
BOSOLA   Do you so?
ANTONIO Because you would not seem to appear to th' world
Puffed up with your preferment, you continue
This out-of-fashion melancholy: leave it, leave it.
BOSOLA Give me leave to be honest in any

[35] The rims . . . look blue, like those of a pregnant woman.
[36] Eczema.

phrase, in any compliment whatsoever. Shall I confess myself to you? I look no higher than I can reach: they are the gods that must ride on winged horses. A lawyer's mule of a slow pace will both suit my disposition and business; for, mark me, when a man's mind rides faster than his horse can gallop, they quickly both tire.
ANTONIO You would look up to heaven, but I think
The devil, that rules i' th' air, stands in your light.
BOSOLA O, sir, you are lord of the ascendant,[37] chief man with the duchess; a duke was your cousin-german removed. Say you were lineally descended from King Pepin, or he himself, what of this? search the heads of the greatest rivers in the world, you shall find them but bubbles of water. Some would think the souls of princes were brought forth by some more weighty cause than those of meaner persons: they are deceived, there's the same hand to them; the like passions sway them; the same reason that makes a vicar go to law for a tithe-pig, and undo his neighbors, makes them spoil a whole province, and batter down goodly cities with the cannon.
[*Enter Duchess and Ladies.*]
DUCHESS Your arm, Antonio: do I not grow fat?
I am exceeding short-winded.—Bosola,
I would have you, sir, provide for me a litter;
Such a one as the Duchess of Florence rode in.
BOSOLA The duchess used one when she was great with child.
DUCHESS I think she did.—Come hither, mend my ruff;
Here, when?
Thou art such a tedious lady; and thy breath smells
Of lemon peels; would thou hadst done! Shall I swoon
Under thy fingers! I am so troubled
With the mother![38]
BOSOLA [*aside*] I fear, too much.
DUCHESS   I have heard you say

[37] Dominant force; a term from astrology.
[38] Hysteria, but with an obvious pun.

That the French courtiers wear their hats on
'fore
The king.

ANTONIO I have seen it.

DUCHESS In the presence?

ANTONIO Yes.

DUCHESS Why should not we bring up that
fashion? 'Tis
Ceremony more than duty that consists
In the removing of a piece of felt:
Be you the example to the rest o' th' court;
Put on your hat first.

ANTONIO You must pardon me:
I have seen, in colder countries than in France,
Nobles stand bare to th' prince; and the dis-
tinction
Methought showed reverently.

BOSOLA I have a present for your grace.

DUCHESS For
me, sir?

BOSOLA Apricots, madam.

DUCHESS O, sir, where are
they?
I have heard of none to-year.

BOSOLA [aside] Good; her color
rises.

DUCHESS Indeed, I thank you: they are won-
drous fair ones.
What an unskilful fellow is our gardener!
We shall have none this month.

BOSOLA Will not your
grace pare them?

DUCHESS No: they taste of musk, methink; indeed they do.

BOSOLA I know not: yet I wish your grace had
pared 'em.

DUCHESS Why?

BOSOLA I forgot to tell you, the knave
gardener,
Only to raise his profit by them the sooner,
Did ripen them in horse-dung.

DUCHESS O, you jest.—
You shall judge: pray taste one.

ANTONIO Indeed, madam,
I do not love the fruit.

DUCHESS Sir, you are loath
To rob us of our dainties: 'tis a delicate fruit;
They say they are restorative.

BOSOLA 'Tis a pretty art,
This grafting.

DUCHESS 'Tis so; a bettering of nature.

BOSOLA To make a pippin grow upon a crab,
A damson on a blackthorn.—
[Aside]
How greedily she
eats them!
A whirlwind strike off these bawd farthingales!
For, but for that and the loose-bodied gown,
I should have discovered apparently[39]
The young springal[40] cutting a caper in her
belly.

DUCHESS I thank you, Bosola: they were right
good ones,
If they do not make me sick.

ANTONIO How now, madam?

DUCHESS This green fruit and my stomach are
not friends:
How they swell me!

BOSOLA [aside] Nay, you are too much swelled
already.

DUCHESS O, I am in an extreme cold sweat!

BOSOLA I am
very sorry.

DUCHESS Lights to my chamber!—O good Antonio,
I fear I am undone!

DELIO Lights there, lights!
[Exeunt Duchess and Ladies. Exit, on the other
side, Bosola.]

ANTONIO O my most trusty Delio, we are lost!
I fear she's fallen in labor; and there's left
No time for her remove.

DELIO Have you prepared
Those ladies to attend her? and procured
That politic safe conveyance for the midwife
Your duchess plotted?

ANTONIO I have.

DELIO Make use, then,
of this forced occasion:
Give out that Bosola hath poisoned her
With these apricots; that will give some color
For her keeping close.

ANTONIO Fie, fie, the physicians
Will then flock to her.

39 Clearly.
40 Stripling.

DELIO   For that you may pretend
She'll use some prepared antidote of her own,
Lest the physicians should re-poison her.

ANTONIO I am lost in amazement: I know not
what to think on 't.

[*Exeunt.*]

SCENE TWO

The same. Enter Bosola.

BOSOLA So, so, there's no question but her tetchiness and most vulturous eating of the apricots are apparent signs of breeding. [*Enter an Old Lady.*] Now?

OLD LADY I am in haste, sir.

BOSOLA There was a young waiting-woman had a monstrous desire to see the glass-house—[41]

OLD LADY Nay, pray let me go.

BOSOLA And it was only to know what strange instrument it was should swell up a glass to the fashion of a woman's belly.

OLD LADY I will hear no more of the glass-house. You are still abusing women?

BOSOLA Who, I? no; only, by the way now and then, mention your frailties. The orange-tree bears ripe and green fruit and blossoms all together; and some of you give entertainment for pure love, but more for more precious reward. The lusty spring smells well; but drooping autumn tastes well. If we have the same golden showers that rained in the time of Jupiter the thunderer, you have the same Danaës still, to hold up their laps to receive them.[42] Didst thou never study the mathematics?

OLD LADY What's that, sir?

BOSOLA Why, to know the trick how to make a many lines meet in one center. Go, go, give your foster-daughters good counsel: tell them, that the devil takes delight to hang at a woman's girdle, like a false rusty watch, that she cannot discern how the time passes.

[41] A glass factory, located near the theater at which this play was first presented.

[42] Jupiter made love to Danaë in the form of a golden shower; Bosola makes of the latter a symbol of mercenary love.

[*Exit Old Lady. Enter Antonio, Delio, Roderigo, and Grisolan.*]

ANTONIO Shut up the court-gates.

RODERIGO   Why, sir? what's the danger?

ANTONIO Shut up the posterns presently, and call
All the officers o' th' court.

GRISOLAN   I shall instantly.

[*Exit.*]

ANTONIO Who keeps the key o' th' park gate?

RODERIGO   Forobosco.

ANTONIO Let him bring 't presently.

[*Reenter Grisolan with Servants.*]

FIRST SERVANT   O, gentlemen o' the court, the foulest treason!

BOSOLA [*aside*] If that these apricots should be poisoned now,
Without my knowledge!

FIRST SERVANT   There was taken even now
A Switzer in the duchess' bed chamber—

SECOND SERVANT   A Switzer?

FIRST SERVANT With a pistol in his great codpiece.

BOSOLA Ha, ha, ha!

FIRST SERVANT The cod-piece was the case for 't.

SECOND SERVANT   There was
A cunning traitor: who would have searched his cod-piece?

FIRST SERVANT True, if he had kept out of the ladies' chambers:
And all the molds of his buttons were leaden bullets.

SECOND SERVANT O wicked cannibal!
A fire-lock in 's cod-piece!

FIRST SERVANT   'Twas a French plot, Upon my life.

SECOND SERVANT To see what the devil can do!

ANTONIO Are all the officers here?

SERVANTS   We are.

ANTONIO   Gentlemen,
We have lost much plate you know; and but this evening
Jewels, to the value of four thousand ducats,
Are missing in the duchess' cabinet.

Are the gates shut?

SERVANTS Yes.

ANTONIO 'Tis the duchess'
pleasure
Each officer be locked into his chamber
Till the sun-rising; and to send the keys
Of all their chests and of their outward doors
Into her bed-chamber. She is very sick.

RODERIGO At her pleasure.

ANTONIO She entreats you take
't not ill:
The innocent shall be the more approved by it.

BOSOLA Gentleman o' th' wood-yard, where's
your Switzer now?

FIRST SERVANT By this hand, 'twas credibly reported by one o' th' black guard.[43]

[*Exeunt all except Antonio and Delio.*]

DELIO How fares it with the duchess?

ANTONIO She's
exposed
Unto the worst of torture, pain and fear.

DELIO Speak to her all happy comfort.

ANTONIO How I do play the fool with mine own
danger!
You are this night, dear friend, to post to
Rome:
My life lies in your service.

DELIO Do not doubt me.

ANTONIO O, 'tis far from me: and yet fear
presents me
Somewhat that looks like danger.

DELIO Believe it,
'Tis but the shadow of your fear, no more;
How superstitiously we mind our evils!
The throwing down salt, or crossing of a hare,
Bleeding at nose, the stumbling of a horse,
Or singing of a cricket, are of power
To daunt whole man in us. Sir, fare you well:
I wish you all the joys of a bless'd father:
And, for my faith, lay this unto your breast,—
Old friends, like old swords, still are trusted
best.

[*Exit. Enter Cariola.*]

CARIOLA Sir, you are the happy father of a
son:
Your wife commends him to you.

[43] Kitchen servants.

ANTONIO Blessèd com-
fort!—
For Heaven's sake tend her well: I'll presently
Go set a figure for 's nativity.[44]

[*Exeunt.*]

SCENE THREE

*Outside the same palace. Enter Bosola, with a
dark lantern.*

BOSOLA Sure I did hear a woman shriek: list,
ha!
And the sound came, if I received it right,
From the duchess' lodgings. There's some strat-
agem
In the confining all our courtiers
To their several wards: I must have part of it;
My intelligence will freeze else. List, again!
It may be 'twas the melancholy bird,
Best friend of silence and of solitariness,
The owl, that screamed so.—Ha! Antonio?

[*Enter Antonio with a candle, his sword
drawn.*]

ANTONIO I heard some noise.—Who's there?
what art thou? speak.

BOSOLA Antonio? put not your face nor body
To such a forced expression of fear:
I am Bosola, your friend.

ANTONIO Bosola!—
[*Aside*]
This mole does undermine me.—Heard you
not
A noise even now?

BOSOLA From whence?

ANTONIO From the
duchess' lodging.

BOSOLA Not I: did you?

ANTONIO I did, or else I dreamed.

BOSOLA Let's walk towards it.

ANTONIO No: it may be
'twas
But the rising of the wind.

BOSOLA Very likely.
Methinks 'tis very cold, and yet you sweat:
You look wildly.

[44] Cast his horoscope.

ANTONIO   I have been setting a figure
For the duchess' jewels.

BOSOLA   Ah, and how falls your
  question?
Do you find it radical?[45]

ANTONIO   What's that to you?
'Tis rather to be questioned what design,
When all men were commanded to their lodg-
  ings,
Makes you a night-walker.

BOSOLA   In sooth, I'll tell you:
Now all the court's asleep, I thought the devil
Had least to do here; I came to say my prayers;
And if it do offend you I do so,
You are a fine courtier.

ANTONIO [aside]   This fellow will undo me.—
You gave the duchess apricots to-day:
Pray Heaven they were not poisoned!

BOSOLA   Poisoned?
  A Spanish fig
For the imputation!

ANTONIO   Traitors are ever confident
Till they are discovered. There were jewels
  stol'n too:
In my conceit, none are to be suspected
More than yourself.

BOSOLA   You are a false steward.

ANTONIO   Saucy slave, I'll pull thee up by the
  roots.

BOSOLA   Maybe the ruin will crush you to pieces.

ANTONIO   You are an impudent snake indeed,
  sir:
Are you scarce warm, and do you show your
  sting?
You libel[46] well, sir.

BOSOLA   No, sir: copy it out,
And I will set my hand to't.

ANTONIO [aside]   My nose bleeds.
One that were superstitious would count
This ominous, when it merely comes by chance:
Two letters, that are wrought here for my
  name,
Are drowned in blood!
Mere accident.—For you, sir, I'll take order;
I' th' morn you shall be safe:—

⁴⁵ Fit to be decided; a term from astrology.
⁴⁶ To draw up formal charges, with a pun on the
other, more obvious meaning.

[Aside]
                                    'Tis that must
  color
Her lying-in: —sir, this door you pass not:
I do not hold it fit that you come near
The duchess' lodgings, till you have quit your-
  self.—
[Aside]
The great are like the base, nay, they are the
  same,
When they seek shameful ways to avoid shame.
[Exit.]

BOSOLA   Antonio hereabout did drop a paper:—
Some of your help, false friend.
[Opening his lantern]
                                    Oh, here it is.
What's here? a child's nativity calculated?
[Reads.] "The duchess was delivered of a son,
'tween the hours twelve and one in the night,
Anno. Dom. 1504,"—that's this year—"*decimo
nono Decembris*,"—that's this night,—"taken
according to the meridian of Malfi,"—that's
our duchess: happy discovery!—"The lord of
the first house being combust in the ascendant,
signifies short life; and Mars being in a human
sign, joined to the tail of the Dragon, in the
eighth house, doth threaten a violent death.
Caetera non scrutantur."[47]
Why, now 'tis most apparent: this precise[48]
  fellow
Is the duchess' bawd:—I have it to my wish!
This is a parcel of intelligency
Our courtiers were cased up for: it needs must
  follow
That I must be committed on pretense
Of poisoning her; which I'll endure, and laugh
  at.
If one could find the father now! but that
Time will discover. Old Castruchio
I' th' morning posts to Rome: by him I'll send
A letter that shall make her brothers' galls
O'erflow their livers. This was a thrifty way.
Though lust do mask in ne'er so strange dis-
  guise,
She's oft found witty, but is never wise.
[Exit.]

⁴⁷ Other things are not examined.
⁴⁸ Puritanical.

The Duchess of Malfi   213

SCENE FOUR

Rome. The palace of the Cardinal. Enter Cardinal and Julia.

CARDINAL Sit: thou art my best of wishes.
Prithee, tell me
What trick didst thou invent to come to Rome
Without thy husband.

JULIA   Why, my lord, I told him
I came to visit an old anchorite
Here for devotion.

CARDINAL   Thou art a witty false one,—
I mean, to him.

JULIA   You have prevailed with me
Beyond my strongest thoughts! I would not now
Find you inconstant.

CARDINAL   Do not put thyself
To such a voluntary torture, which proceeds
Out of your own guilt.

JULIA   How, my lord?

CARDINAL   You fear
My constancy, because you have approved[49]
Those giddy and wild turnings in yourself.

JULIA Did you e'er find them?

CARDINAL   Sooth, generally
for women;
A man might strive to make glass malleable,
Ere he should make them fixed.

JULIA   So, my lord.

CARDINAL We had need go borrow that fantas-
tic glass
Invented by Galileo the Florentine
To view another spacious world i' th' moon,
And look to find a constant woman there.

JULIA This is very well, my lord.

CARDINAL   Why do you
weep?
Are tears your justification? the self-same tears
Will fall into your husband's bosom, lady,
With a loud protestation that you love him
Above the world. Come, I'll love you wisely,
That's jealously; since I am very certain
You cannot make me cuckold.

JULIA   I'll go home
To my husband.

CARDINAL   You may thank me, lady,

I have taken you off your melancholy perch,
Bore you upon my fist, and showed you game,
And let you fly at it.—I pray thee, kiss me.—
When thou wast with thy husband, thou wast
watched
Like a tame elephant:—still you are to thank
me:—
Thou hadst only kisses from him and high feed-
ing;
But what delight was that? 'twas just like one
That hath a little fingering on the lute,
Yet cannot tune it:—still you are to thank me.

JULIA You told me of a piteous wound i' th'
heart
And a sick liver, when you wooed me first,
And spake like one in physic.[50]

CARDINAL   Who's that?—
[Enter Servant.]
Rest firm, for my affection to thee,
Lightning moves slow to 't.[51]

SERVANT   Madam, a gentleman,
That's come post from Malfi, desires to see you.

CARDINAL Let him enter: I'll withdraw.
[Exit.]

SERVANT   He says
Your husband, old Castruchio, is come to
Rome,
Most pitifully tir'd with riding post.
[Exit. Enter Delio.]

JULIA Signior Delio!
[Aside]
                    'Tis one of my old suitors.

DELIO I was bold to come and see you.

JULIA   Sir, you
are welcome.

DELIO Do you lie here?

JULIA   Sure, your own experi-
ence
Will satisfy you no: our Roman prelates
Do not keep lodging for ladies.

DELIO   Very well:
I have brought you no commendations from
your husband,
For I know none by him.

JULIA   I hear he's come to
Rome.

49 Experienced.

50 Under the care of a physician.
51 In comparison with it.

DELIO I never knew man and beast, of a horse
and a knight,
So weary of each other: if he had had a good
back,
He would have undertook to have borne his
horse,
His breech was so pitifully sore.

JULIA   Your laughter
Is my pity.

DELIO   Lady, I know not whether
You want money, but I have brought you some.

JULIA From my husband?

DELIO   No, from mine own
allowance.

JULIA I must hear the condition, ere I be bound
to take it.

DELIO Look on't, 'tis gold: hath it not a fine
color?

JULIA I have a bird more beautiful.

DELIO Try the sound on 't.

JULIA   A lute-string far ex-
ceeds it:
It hath no smell, like cassia or civet;
Nor is it physical,[52] though some fond[53] doctors
Persuade us seethe 't in cullises.[54] I'll tell you,
This is a creature bred by—
[*Reenter Servant.*]

SERVANT   Your husband's
come,
Hath delivered a letter to the Duke of Calabria
That, to my thinking, hath put him out of his
wits.
[*Exit.*]

JULIA Sir, you hear:
Pray, let me know your business and your suit
As briefly as can be.

DELIO With good speed: I would wish you,
At such time as you are non-resident
With your husband, my mistress.

JULIA Sir, I'll go ask my husband if I shall,
And straight return your answer.
[*Exit.*]

DELIO   Very fine!
Is this her wit, or honesty, that speaks thus?
I heard one say the duke was highly moved
With a letter sent from Malfi. I do fear

[52] Medicinal.
[53] Foolish.
[54] Strong broths, often prepared for the sick.

Antonio is betrayed: how fearfully
Shows his ambition now! unfortunate fortune!
They pass through whirlpools, and deep woes
do shun,
Who the event weigh ere the action's done.
[*Exit.*]

SCENE FIVE

*The same. Enter Cardinal and Ferdinand, with
a letter.*

FERDINAND I have this night digged up a man-
drake.[55]

CARDINAL Say you?

FERDINAND And I am grown mad with 't.

CARDINAL   What's
the prodigy?

FERDINAND Read there,—a sister damned: she's
loose i' th' hilts;
Grown a notorious strumpet.

CARDINAL   Speak lower.

FERDINAND   Lower?
Rogues do not whisper 't now, but seek to pub-
lish't
(As servants do the bounty of their lords)
Aloud; and with a covetous searching eye,
To mark who note them. O, confusion seize
her!
She hath had most cunning bawds to serve her
turn,
And more secure conveyances for lust
Than towns of garrison for service.

CARDINAL   Is 't possible?
Can this be certain?

FERDINAND   Rhubarb, O, for rhubarb
To purge this choler! here's the cursèd day
To prompt my memory; and here 't shall stick
Till of her bleeding heart I make a sponge
To wipe it out.

CARDINAL   Why do you make yourself
So wild a tempest?

FERDINAND   Would I could be one,
That I might toss her palace 'bout her ears,
Root up her goodly forests, blast her meads,

[55] A poisonous root, with forked human shape.
When dug up, it supposedly shrieked so horribly that
it drove the hearer mad.

And lay her general territory as waste
As she hath done her honors.

CARDINAL   Shall our blood,
The royal blood of Aragon and Castile,
Be thus attainted?

FERDINAND   Apply desperate physic:
We must not now use balsamum, but fire,
The smarting cupping-glass,[56] for that's the
    mean
To purge infected blood, such blood as hers.
There is a kind of pity in mine eye,—
I'll give it to my handkerchief; and now 'tis
    here,
I'll bequeath this to her bastard.

CARDINAL   What to do?

FERDINAND Why, to make soft lint for his
    mother's wounds,
When I have hewed her to pieces.

CARDINAL   Cursed crea-
    ture!
Unequal nature, to place women's hearts
So far upon the left side![57]

FERDINAND   Foolish men,
That e'er will trust their honor in a bark
Made of so slight weak bulrush as is woman,
Apt every minute to sink it!

CARDINAL Thus ignorance, when it hath pur-
    chased honor,
It cannot wield it.

FERDINAND   Methinks I see her laughing—
Excellent hyena! Talk to me somewhat, quickly,
Or my imagination will carry me
To see her in the shameful act of sin.

CARDINAL With whom?

FERDINAND   Happily[58] with some
    strong-thighed
    bargeman,
Or one o' the woodyard that can quoit the
    sledge[59]
Or toss the bar, or else some lovely squire
That carries coals up to her privy lodgings.

CARDINAL You fly beyond your reason.

FERDINAND   Go to,
    mistress!
'Tis not your whore's milk that shall quench

[56] Used for drawing blood.
[57] To make women so wrongheaded; cf. *sinister*.
[58] Perhaps.
[59] Throw the hammer.

my wild fire,
But your whore's blood.

CARDINAL How idly shows this rage, which car-
    ries you,
As men conveyed by witches through the air,
On violent whirlwinds! this intemperate noise
Fitly resembles deaf men's shrill discourse,
Who talk aloud, thinking all other men
To have their imperfection.

FERDINAND   Have not you
My palsy?

CARDINAL Yes, I can be angry, but
Without this rupture: there is not in nature
A thing that makes man so deformed, so
    beastly,
As doth intemperate anger. Chide yourself.
You have divers men who never yet expressed
Their strong desire of rest but by unrest,
By vexing of themselves. Come, put yourself
In tune.

FERDINAND So; I will only study to seem
The thing I am not. I could kill her now,
In you, or in myself; for I do think
It is some sin in us heaven doth revenge
By her.

CARDINAL Are you stark mad?

FERDINAND   I would have
    their bodies
Burnt in a coal-pit with the ventage stopped,
That their cursed smoke might not ascend to
    heaven;
Or dip the sheets they lie in in pitch or sulphur,
Wrap them in 't, and then light them like a
    match;
Or else to boil their bastard to a cullis,
And give 't his lecherous father to renew
The sin of his back.

CARDINAL   I'll leave you.

FERDINAND   Nay, I have
    done.
I am confident, had I been damned in hell,
And should have heard of this, it would have
    put me
Into a cold sweat. In, in; I'll go sleep.
Till I know who leaps my sister, I'll not stir:
That known, I'll find scorpions to string my
    whips,
And fix her in a general eclipse.

[*Exeunt.*]

JOHN WEBSTER

Act Three

SCENE ONE

Amalfi. The Palace of the Duchess. Enter Antonio and Delio.

ANTONIO Our noble friend, my most beloved
  Delio!
O, you have been a stranger long at court;
Came you along with the Lord Ferdinand?

DELIO I did, sir: and how fares your noble
  duchess?

ANTONIO Right fortunately well: she's an excellent
Feeder of pedigrees; since you last saw her,
She hath had two children more, a son and
  daughter.

DELIO Methinks 'twas yesterday: let me but
  wink,
And not behold your face, which to mine eye
Is somewhat leaner, verily I should dream
It were within this half-hour.

ANTONIO You have not been in law, friend
  Delio,
Nor in prison, nor a suitor at the court,
Nor begged the reversion of some great man's
  place,
Nor troubled with an old wife, which doth
  make
Your time so insensibly hasten.

DELIO   Pray, sir, tell me,
Hath not this news arrived yet to the ear
Of the lord cardinal?

ANTONIO   I fear it hath:
The Lord Ferdinand, that's newly come to
  court,
Doth bear himself right dangerously.

DELIO   Pray, why?

ANTONIO He is so quiet that he seems to sleep
The tempest out, as dormice do in winter:
Those houses that are haunted are most still
Till the devil be up.

DELIO   What say the common people?

ANTONIO The common rabble do directly say
She is a strumpet.

DELIO   And your graver heads
Which would be politic, what censure they?

ANTONIO They do observe I grow to infinite
  purchase,[60]
The left hand way, and all suppose the duchess
Would amend it, if she could; for, say they,
Great princes, though they grudge their officers
Should have such large and unconfinèd means
To get wealth under them, will not complain,
Lest thereby they should make them odious
Unto the people; for other obligation
Of love or marriage between her and me
They never dream of.

DELIO   The Lord Ferdinand
Is going to bed.

[Enter Duchess, Ferdinand, and Bosola.]

FERDINAND   I'll instantly to bed,
For I am weary.—I am to bespeak
A husband for you.

DUCHESS   For me, sir? pray, who is 't?

FERDINAND The great Count Malateste.

DUCHESS   Fie upon
  him!
A count? he 's a mere stick of sugar-candy;
You may look quite thorough him. When I
  choose
A husband, I will marry for your honor.

FERDINAND You shall do well in 't.—How is 't,
  worthy Antonio?

DUCHESS But, sir, I am to have private conference with you
About a scandalous report is spread
Touching mine honor.

FERDINAND   Let me be ever deaf to 't:
One of Pasquil's paper bullets,[61] court-calumny,
A pestilent air, which princes' palaces
Are seldom purged of. Yet, say that it were
  true,
I pour it in your bosom, my fixed love
Would strongly excuse, extenuate, nay, deny
Faults, were they apparent in you. Go, be safe
In your own innocency.

[60] Wealth.
[61] Lampoons. Pasquillo was a sharp-tongued Roman of the fifteenth century, whose name was given to a mutilated statue excavated in 1501. Every St. Mark's day the statue was dressed up and students affixed satires to it.

DUCHESS [*aside*]   O bless'd comfort!
This deadly air is purged.
[*Exeunt Duchess, Antonio, and Delio.*]
FERDINAND   Her guilt treads on
Hot-burning coulters.[62]—Now, Bosola,
How thrives our intelligence?
BOSOLA   Sir, uncertainly
'Tis rumored she hath had three bastards, but
By whom we may go read i' th' stars.
FERDINAND   Why, some
Hold opinion all things are written there.
BOSOLA   Yes, if we could find spectacles to read
   them.
I do suspect there hath been some sorcery
Used on the duchess.
FERDINAND   Sorcery? to what purpose?
BOSOLA   To make her dote on some desertless
   fellow
She shames to acknowledge.
FERDINAND   Can your faith
   give way
To think there 's power in potions or in charms,
To make us love whether we will or no?
BOSOLA   Most certainly.
FERDINAND   Away! these are mere gulleries, hor-
   rid things,
Invented by some cheating mountebanks
To abuse us. Do you think that herbs or charms
Can force the will? Some trials have been made
In this foolish practice, but the ingredients
Were lenitive poisons, such as are of force
To make the patient mad; and straight the
   witch
Swears by equivocation they are in love.
The witchcraft lies in her rank blood. This night
I will force confession from her. You told me
You had got, within these two days, a false key
Into her bed-chamber.
BOSOLA   I have.
FERDINAND   As I would wish.
BOSOLA   What do you intend to do?
FERDINAND   Can you
   guess?
BOSOLA   No.
FERDINAND   Do not ask, then:
He that can compass me, and know my drifts,

---

62 Plowshares.

May say he hath put a girdle 'bout the world,
And sounded all her quicksands.
BOSOLA   I do not
Think so.
FERDINAND   What do you think, then, pray?
BOSOLA   That
   you
Are your own chronicle too much, and grossly
Flatter yourself.
FERDINAND   Give me thy hand; I thank
   thee:
I never gave pension but to flatterers,
Till I entertained thee. Farewell.
That friend a great man's ruin strongly checks,
Who rails into his belief all his defects.
[*Exeunt.*]

SCENE TWO

*The bedchamber of the Duchess. Enter Duchess,
Antonio, and Cariola.*

DUCHESS   Bring me the casket hither, and the
   glass.—
You get no lodging here tonight, my lord.
ANTONIO   Indeed, I must persuade one.
DUCHESS   Very
   good:
I hope in time 'twill grow into a custom,
That noblemen shall come with cap and knee
To purchase a night's lodging of their wives.
ANTONIO   I must lie here.
DUCHESS   Must! you are a lord of
   misrule.
ANTONIO   Indeed, my rule is only in the night.
DUCHESS   To what use will you put me?
ANTONIO   We'll
   sleep together.
DUCHESS   Alas,
What pleasure can two lovers find in sleep!
CARIOLA   My lord, I lie with her often; and I
   know
She'll much disquiet you.
ANTONIO   See, you are com-
   plained of.
CARIOLA   For she's the sprawling'st bedfellow.
ANTONIO   I
   shall like her
The better for that.

CARIOLA Sir, shall I ask you a question?

ANTONIO O, I pray thee, Cariola.

CARIOLA Wherefore still, when you lie
With my lady, do you rise so early?

ANTONIO Laboring men
Count the clock oftenest, Cariola, are glad
When their task 's ended.

DUCHESS I'll stop your mouth.
[*Kisses him.*]

ANTONIO Nay, that's but one; Venus had two soft doves
To draw her chariot; I must have another—
[*She kisses him again.*]
When wilt thou marry, Cariola?

CARIOLA Never, my lord.

ANTONIO Oh, fie upon this single life! forgo it.
We read how Daphne, for her peevish flight,[63]
Became a fruitless bay-tree; Syrinx turned
To the pale empty reed; Anaxarete
Was frozen into marble: whereas those
Which married, or proved kind unto their friends,
Were by a gracious influence transshaped
Into the olive, pomegranate, mulberry,
Became flowers, precious stones, or eminent stars.

CARIOLA This is a vain poetry: but I pray you tell me,
If there were proposed me, wisdom, riches, and beauty,
In three several young men, which should I choose?

ANTONIO 'Tis a hard question: this was Paris' case,
And he was blind in 't, and there was great cause;
For how was 't possible he could judge right,
Having three amorous goddesses in view,
And they stark naked? 'twas a motion[64]
Were able to benight the apprehension
Of the severest counsellor of Europe.

---

[63] That is, for obstinately refusing Apollo. Syrinx was turned into a reed for rejecting Pan, and Anaxarete into a stone for rejecting Iphis.

[64] Spectacle.

Now I look on both your faces so well formed,
It puts me in mind of a question I would ask.

CARIOLA What is 't?

ANTONIO I do wonder why hard-favoured ladies,
For the most part, keep worse-favoured waiting women
To attend them, and cannot endure fair ones.

DUCHESS Oh, that's soon answered.
Did you ever in your life know an ill painter
Desire to have his dwelling next door to the shop
Of an excellent picture-maker? 'twould disgrace
His face-making, and undo him. I prithee,
When were we so merry?—My hair tangles.

ANTONIO Pray thee, Cariola, let 's steal forth the room,
And let her talk to herself: I have divers times
Served her the like, when she hath chafed extremely.
I love to see her angry. Softly, Cariola.
[*Exeunt Antonio and Cariola.*]

DUCHESS Doth not the color of my hair 'gin to change?
When I wax grey, I shall have all the court
Powder their hair with arras,[65] to be like me.
You have cause to love me; I entered you into my heart
Before you would vouchsafe to call for the keys.
[*Enter Ferdinand behind.*]
We shall one day have my brothers take you napping;
Methinks his presence, being now in court,
Should make you keep your own bed; but you'll say
Love mixed with fear is sweetest. I'll assure you,
You shall get no more children till my brothers
Consent to be your gossips.[66] Have you lost your tongue?
'Tis welcome:
For know, whether I am doomed to live or die,
I can do both like a prince.

FERDINAND Die, then, quickly!
[*Giving her a poniard*]

[65] White powder from iris root.
[66] Godparents to your children.

Virtue, where art thou hid? what hideous thing
Is it that doth eclipse thee?

DUCHESS   Pray, sir, hear me.

FERDINAND   Or is it true thou art but a bare
name,
And no essential thing?

DUCHESS   Sir,—

FERDINAND   Do not speak.

DUCHESS   No, sir: I will plant my soul in mine
ears, to hear you.

FERDINAND   O most imperfect light of human
reason,
That mak'st us so unhappy to foresee
What we can least prevent! Pursue thy wishes,
And glory in them: there 's in shame no com-
fort
But to be past all bounds and sense of shame.

DUCHESS   I pray, sir, hear me: I am married.

FERDINAND   So!

DUCHESS   Happily, not to your liking: but for
that,
Alas, your shears do come untimely now
To clip the bird's wings that's already flown!
Will you see my husband?

FERDINAND   Yes, if I could change
Eyes with a basilisk

DUCHESS   Sure, you came hither
By his confederacy.

FERDINAND   The howling of a wolf
Is music to thee,[67] screech-owl: prithee,
peace.—
Whate'er thou art that hast enjoyed my sister,
For I am sure thou hear'st me, for thine own
sake
Let me not know thee. I came hither prepared
To work thy discovery; yet am now persuaded
It would beget such violent effects
As would damn us both. I would not for ten
millions
I had beheld thee: therefore use all means
I never may have knowledge of thy name;
Enjoy thy lust still, and a wretched life,
On that condition.—And for thee, vile woman,
If thou do wish thy lecher may grow old
In thy embracements, I would have thee build
Such a room for him as our anchorites
To holier use inhabit. Let not the sun

---

[67] Compared to thee.

Shine on him till he 's dead; let dogs and mon-
keys
Only converse with him, and such dumb things
To whom nature denies use to sound his name;
Do not keep a paraquito, lest she learn it;
If thou do love him, cut out thine own tongue,
Lest it bewray him.

DUCHESS   Why might not I marry?
I have not gone about in this to create
Any new world or custom.

FERDINAND   Thou art undone;
And thou hast ta'en that massy sheet of lead
That hid thy husband's bones, and folded it
About my heart.

DUCHESS   Mine bleeds for 't.

FERDINAND   Thine? thy
heart?
What should I name 't unless a hollow bullet
Filled with unquenchable wildfire?

DUCHESS   You are in
this
Too strict; and were you not my princely
brother,
I would say, too wilful: my reputation
Is safe.

FERDINAND   Dost thou know what reputation is?
I'll tell thee,—to small purpose, since the in-
struction
Comes now too late.
Upon a time Reputation, Love, and Death,
Would travel o'er the world; and it was con-
cluded
That they should part, and take three several
ways.
Death told them, they should find him in great
battles,
Or cities plagued with plagues: Love gives them
counsel
To inquire for him 'mongst unambitious shep-
herds,
Where dowries were not talked of, and some-
times
'Mongst quiet kindred that had nothing left
By their dead parents: "Stay," quoth Reputa-
tion,
"Do not forsake me; for it is my nature,
If once I part from any man I meet,
I am never found again." And so for you:
You have shook hands with Reputation,

And made him invisible. So, fare you well:
I will never see you more.

DUCHESS   Why should only I,
Of all the other princes of the world,
Be cased up, like a holy relic? I have youth
And a little beauty.

FERDINAND   So you have some virgins
That are witches. I will never see thee more.
[*Exit. Reenter Antonio with a pistol, and Cariola.*]

DUCHESS   You saw this apparition?

ANTONIO   Yes: we are
Betrayed. How came he hither?—I should turn
This to thee, for that.
[*Points the pistol at Cariola.*]

CARIOLA   Pray, sir, do; and when
That you have cleft my heart, you shall read
there
Mine innocence.

DUCHESS   That gallery gave him entrance.

ANTONIO   I would this terrible thing would come
again,
That, standing on my guard, I might relate
My warrantable love.—
[*She shows the poniard.*]
                    Ha! what means this?

DUCHESS   He left this with me.

ANTONIO   And it seems did
wish
You would use it on yourself.

DUCHESS   His action seemed
To intend so much.

ANTONIO   This hath a handle to 't.
As well as a point: turn it towards him, and
So fasten the keen edge in his rank gall.
[*Knocking within.*]
How now! who knocks? more earthquakes?

DUCHESS   I
stand
As if a mine beneath my feet were ready
To be blown up.

CARIOLA   'Tis Bosola.

DUCHESS   Away!
O misery! methinks unjust actions
Should wear these masks and curtains, and not
we.
You must instantly part hence: I have fashioned it

Already.
[*Exit Antonio. Enter Bosola.*]

BOSOLA   The duke your brother is ta'en up in
a whirlwind,
Hath took horse, and 's rid post to Rome.

DUCHESS   So late?

BOSOLA   He told me, as he mounted into th'
saddle,
You were undone.

DUCHESS   Indeed, I am very near it.

BOSOLA   What's the
matter?

DUCHESS   Antonio, the master of our household,
Hath dealt so falsely with me in 's accounts:
My brother stood engaged with me for money
Ta'en up of certain Neapolitan Jews,[68]
And Antonio lets the bonds be forfeit.

BOSOLA   Strange!—
[*Aside*]
                    This is cunning.

DUCHESS   And hereupon
My brother's bills at Naples are protested
Against.—Call up our officers.

BOSOLA   I shall.
[*Exit. Reenter Antonio.*]

DUCHESS   The place that you must fly to is Ancona:
Hire a house there; I'll send after you
My treasure and my jewels. Our weak safety
Runs upon enginous wheels:[69] short syllables
Must stand for periods.[70] I must now accuse
you
Of such a feignèd crime as Tasso calls
Magnanima menzogna, a noble lie,
'Cause it must shield our honors.—Hark! they
are coming.
[*Reenter Bosola and Officers.*]

ANTONIO   Will your grace hear me?

DUCHESS   I have got well by you; you have
yielded me
A million of loss: I am like to inherit
The people's curses for your stewardship.
You had the trick in audit-time to be sick,

[68] "My brother furnished security for money which
I borrowed from Jews in Naples."
[69] Moves with swiftness and intricacy.
[70] Long sentences.

The Duchess of Malfi   221

Till I had signed your quietus; and that cured
  you
Without help of a doctor.—Gentlemen,
I would have this man be an example to you
  all;
So shall you hold my favor; I pray, let him;[71]
For h'as done that, alas, you would not think
  of,
And, because I intend to be rid of him,
I mean not to publish.—Use your fortune else-
  where.

ANTONIO   I am strongly armed to brook my over-
  throw;
As commonly men bear with a hard year,
I will not blame the cause on 't; but do think
The necessity of my malevolent star
Procures this, not her humor. O, the inconstant
And rotten ground of service! you may see,
'Tis even like him, that in a winter night,
Takes a long slumber o'er a dying fire,
A-loth to part from 't; yet parts thence as cold
As when he first sat down.

DUCHESS   We do confiscate,
Towards the satisfying of your accounts,
All that you have.

ANTONIO   I am all yours; and 'tis very
  fit
All mine should be so.

DUCHESS   So, sir, you have your
  pass.

ANTONIO   You may see, gentlemen, what 'tis to
  serve
A prince with body and soul.
[Exit.]

BOSOLA   Here's an example for extortion: what
  moisture is drawn out of the sea, when foul
  weather comes, pours down, and runs into the
  sea again.

DUCHESS   I would know what are your opinions
  of this Antonio.

SECOND OFFICER   He could not abide to see a
  pig's head gaping: I thought your grace would
  find him a Jew.

THIRD OFFICER   I would you had been his officer,
  for your own sake.

FOURTH OFFICER   You would have had more
  money.

71 Let him go.

FIRST OFFICER   He stopped his ears with black
  wool, and to those came to him for money
  said he was thick of hearing.

SECOND OFFICER   Some said he was an hermaph-
  rodite, for he could not abide a woman.

FOURTH OFFICER   How scurvy proud he would
  look when the treasury was full! Well, let him
  go!

FIRST OFFICER   Yes, and the chippings of the buttery fly after him, to scour his gold chain![72]

DUCHESS   Leave us. [Exeunt Officers.] What do
  you think of these?

BOSOLA   That these are rogues that in 's pros-
  perity,
But to have waited on his fortune, could have
  wished
His dirty stirrup riveted through their noses,
And followed after 's mule, like a bear in a
  ring;
Would have prostituted their daughters to his
  lust;
Made their first-born intelligencers; thought
  none happy
But such as were born under his blest planet,
And wore his livery: and do these lice drop off
  now?
Well, never look to have the like again:
He hath left a sort[73] of flattering rogues behind
  him;
Their doom must follow. Princes pay flatterers
In their own money: flatterers dissemble their
  vices,
And they dissemble their lies; that 's justice.
Alas, poor gentleman!

DUCHESS   Poor? he hath amply filled his coffers.

BOSOLA   Sure, he was too honest. Pluto, the god
  of riches,
When he's sent by Jupiter to any man,
He goes limping, to signify that wealth
That comes on God's name comes slowly; but
  when he's sent
On the devil's errand, he rides post and comes
  in by scuttles.[74]
Let me show you what a most unvalued jewel
You have in a wanton humor thrown away,

72 Chippings are bread crumbs; a gold chain was
the steward's badge of office.
73 Crowd.
74 Quick, running steps.

To bless the man shall find him. He was an
    excellent
Courtier and most faithful; a soldier that
    thought it
As beastly to know his own value too little
As devilish to acknowledge it too much.
Both his virtue and form deserved a far better
    fortune:
His discourse rather delighted to judge itself
    than show itself:
His breast was filled with all perfection,
And yet it seemed a private whispering-room,
It made so little noise of 't.

DUCHESS   But he was basely descended.

BOSOLA   Will you make yourself a mercenary
    herald,
Rather to examine men's pedigrees than virtues?
You shall want[75] him:
For know, an honest statesman to a prince
Is like a cedar planted by a spring;
The spring bathes the tree's root, the grateful
    tree
Rewards it with his shadow: you have not done
    so.
I would sooner swim to the Bermoothes[76] on
Two politicians' rotten bladders, tied
Together with an intelligencer's heart-string,
Than depend on so changeable a prince's favor.
Fare thee well, Antonio! since the malice of
    the world
Would needs down with thee, it cannot be said
    yet
That any ill happened unto thee,
Considering thy fall was accompanied with
    virtue.

DUCHESS   Oh, you render me excellent music!

BOSOLA   Say
you?

DUCHESS   This good one that you speak of is
    my husband.

BOSOLA   Do I not dream? can this ambitious age
Have so much goodness in 't as to prefer
A man merely for worth, without these shadows
Of wealth and painted honors? possible?

DUCHESS   I have had three children by him.

BOSOLA   For-
tunate lady!

[75] Miss.

[76] Bermudas.

For you have made your private nuptial bed
The humble and fair seminary[77] of peace.
No question but many an unbeneficed scholar
Shall pray for you for this deed, and rejoice
That some preferment in the world can yet
Arise from merit. The virgins of your land
That have no dowries shall hope your example
Will raise them to rich husbands. Should you
    want
Soldiers, 'twould make the very Turks and
    Moors
Turn Christians, and serve you for this act.
Last, the neglected poets of your time,
In honor of this trophy of a man,
Raised by that curious engine, your white hand,
Shall thank you, in your grave, for 't; and make
    that
More reverend than all the cabinets
Of living princes. For Antonio,
His fame shall likewise flow from many a pen.
When heralds shall want coats to sell to men.[78]

DUCHESS   As I taste comfort in this friendly
    speech,
So would I find concealment.

BOSOLA   Oh, the secret of my prince,
Which I will wear on th' inside of my heart!

DUCHESS   You shall take charge of all my coin
    and jewels,
And follow him; for he retires himself
To Ancona.

BOSOLA   So.

DUCHESS   Whither, within few days,
I mean to follow thee.

BOSOLA   Let me think:
I would wish your grace to feign a pilgrimage
To our Lady of Loretto, scarce seven leagues
From fair Ancona; so may you depart
Your country with more honor, and your flight
Will seem a princely progress, retaining
Your usual train about you.

DUCHESS   Sir, your direction
Shall lead me by the hand.

CARIOLA   In my opinion,
She were better progress to the baths at Lucca,
Or go visit the Spa in Germany;
For, if you will believe me, I do not like

[77] Seed-bed.

[78] *Want coats:* lack coats of arms. The sale of
honors was a common subject of satire.

The Duchess of Malfi   223

This jesting with religion, this feignèd
Pilgrimage.
DUCHESS   Thou art a superstitious fool:
Prepare us instantly for our departure.
Past sorrows, let us moderately lament them;
For those to come, seek wisely to prevent them.
[*Exeunt Duchess and Cariola.*]
BOSOLA   A politician is the devil's quilted anvil;
He fashions all sins on him, and the blows
Are never heard: he may work in a lady's
    chamber,
As here for proof. What rests but I reveal
All to my lord? Oh, this base quality[79]
Of intelligencer! why, every quality i' th' world
Prefers but gain or commendation:
Now for this act I am certain to be raised,
And men that paint weeds to the life are praised.
[*Exit.*]

SCENE THREE

*Rome. The Cardinal's Palace. Enter Cardinal,
Ferdinand, Malateste, Pescara, Silvio, and Delio.*

CARDINAL   Must we turn soldier, then?
MALATESTE   The em-
    peror
Hearing your worth that way, ere you attained
This reverend garment, joins you in commission
With the right fortunate soldier the Marquis of
    Pescara,
And the famous Lannoy.
CARDINAL   He that had the honor
Of taking the French king prisoner?
MALATESTE   The same.
Here's a plot drawn for a new fortification
At Naples.
[*They talk apart.*]
FERDINAND   This great Count Malateste, I per-
    ceive,
Hath got employment?
DELIO   No employment, my
    lord;
A marginal note in the muster-book, that he is
A voluntary lord.[80]
FERDINAND   He's no soldier?
DELIO   He has worn gunpowder in 's hollow
    tooth for the toothache.

[79] Profession.
[80] A volunteer.

SILVIO   He comes to the leaguer[81] with a full
    intent
To eat fresh beef and garlic, means to stay
Till the scent be gone, and straight return to
    court.
DELIO   He hath read all the late service[82]
As the city chronicle relates it;
And keeps two pewterers going, only to express
Battles in model.
SILVIO   Then he'll fight by the book.
DELIO   By the al-
    manac, I think,
To choose good days and shun the critical;
That's his mistress's scarf.
SILVIO   Yes, he protests
He would do much for that taffeta.
DELIO   I think he would run away from a battle,
To save it from taking prisoner.
SILVIO   He is horribly afraid
Gunpowder will spoil the perfume on 't.
DELIO   I saw a Dutchman break his pate once
For calling him pot-gun;[83] he made his head
Have a bore in 't like a musket.
SILVIO   I would he had made a touchhole to 't.
He is indeed a guarded sumpter-cloth,[84]
Only for the remove of the court.[85]
[*Enter Bosola. He talks apart with Ferdinand
and the Cardinal.*]
PESCARA   Bosola arrived? what should be the
    business?
Some falling-out amongst the cardinals.
These factions amongst great men, they are like
Foxes; when their heads are divided,
They carry fire in their tails, and all the country
About them goes to wrack for 't.[86]
SILVIO   What 's that
    Bosola?
DELIO   I knew him in Padua—a fantastical
scholar, like such who study to know how
many knots was in Hercules' club, of what
color Achilles' beard was, or whether Hector
were not troubled with the toothache. He hath

[81] The camp of a besieging army.
[82] Military operations.
[83] Popgun.
[84] Decorated horse cloth.
[85] The movement of the court from place to place.
[86] Samson tied jackals together by their tails to
fire the corn of the Philistines.

studied himself half blear-eyed to know the true symmetry of Caesar's nose by a shoeing-horn; and this he did to gain the name of a speculative man.

PESCARA Mark Prince Ferdinand:
A very salamander lives in 's eye,
To mock the eager violence of fire.

SILVIO That Cardinal hath made more bad faces with his oppression[87] than ever Michael Angelo made good ones: he lifts up 's nose, like a foul porpoise before a storm.

PESCARA The Lord Ferdinand laughs.

DELIO   Like a
deadly cannon that lightens
Ere it smokes.

PESCARA These are your true pangs of death,
The pangs of life, that struggle with great statesmen.

DELIO In such a deformed silence witches whisper
Their charms.

CARDINAL Doth she make religion her riding-hood
To keep her from the sun and tempest?

FERDINAND   That,
That damns her. Methinks her fault and beauty,
Blended together, show like leprosy,
The whiter, the fouler. I make it a question
Whether her beggarly brats were ever christened.

CARDINAL I will instantly solicit the state of Ancona
To have them banished.

FERDINAND   You are for Loretto?
I shall not be at your ceremony; fare you well.—
Write to the Duke of Malfi, my young nephew
She had by her first husband, and acquaint him
With 's mother's honesty.[88]

BOSOLA   I will.

FERDINAND   Antonio!
A slave that only smelled of ink and counters,
And never in 's life looked like a gentleman,
But in the audit-time.—Go, go presently.
Draw me out an hundred and fifty of our horse,
And meet me at the fort-bridge.
[*Exeunt.*]

[87] Show of emotion.
[88] Chastity.

SCENE FOUR

The shrine of Our Lady of Loretto. Enter Two Pilgrims.

FIRST PILGRIM I have not seen a goodlier shrine than this;
Yet I have visited many.

SECOND PILGRIM   The Cardinal of Aragon
Is this day to resign his cardinal's hat:
His sister duchess likewise is arrived
To pay her vow of pilgrimage. I expect
A noble ceremony.

FIRST PILGRIM   No question.
—They come.

Here the ceremony of the Cardinal's installment, in the habit of a soldier, performed in delivering up his cross, hat, robes, and ring, at the shrine, and investing him with sword, helmet, shield, and spurs; then Antonio, the Duchess, and their children, having presented themselves at the shrine, are, by a form of banishment in dumb-show expressed towards them by the Cardinal and the state of Ancona, banished: during all which ceremony, this ditty is sung, to very solemn music, by divers churchmen; then exeunt all except the Two Pilgrims.

Arms and honors deck thy story,
To thy fame's eternal glory!
Adverse fortune ever fly thee;
No disastrous fate come nigh thee!

I alone will sing thy praises,
Whom to honor virtue raises;
And thy study, that divine is,
Bent to martial discipline is.
Lay aside all those robes lie by thee;
Crown thy arts with arms, they'll beautify thee.

O worthy of worthiest name, adorned in this manner,
Lead bravely thy forces on under war's warlike banner!
O, mayst thou prove fortunate in all martial courses!
Guide thou still by skill in arts and forces!
Victory attend thee nigh, whilst fame sings loud thy powers;

Triumphant conquest crown thy head, and
blessings pour down showers![89]

FIRST PILGRIM   Here 's a strange turn of state!
who would have thought
So great a lady would have matched herself
Unto so mean a person? yet the Cardinal
Bears himself much too cruel.

SECOND PILGRIM   They are banished.

FIRST PILGRIM   But I would ask what power hath
this state
Of Ancona to determine of a free prince?

SECOND PILGRIM   They are a free state, sir, and
her brother showed
How that the Pope, fore-hearing of her loose-
ness,
Hath seized into th' protection of the Church
The dukedom which she held as dowager.

FIRST PILGRIM   But by what justice?

SECOND PILGRIM   Sure, I think
by none,
Only her brother's instigation.

FIRST PILGRIM   What was it with such violence
he took
Off from her finger?

SECOND PILGRIM   'Twas her wedding-ring;
Which he vowed shortly he would sacrifice
To his revenge.

FIRST PILGRIM   Alas, Antonio!
If that a man be thrust into a well,
No matter who sets hands to 't, his own weight
Will bring him sooner to th' bottom. Come, let's
hence.
Fortune makes this conclusion general,
All things do help th' unhappy man to fall.
[*Exeunt.*]

SCENE FIVE

*Near Loretto. Enter Duchess, Antonio, Children,
Cariola, and Servants.*

DUCHESS   Banished Ancona?

ANTONIO   Yes, you see what
power
Lightens in great men's breath.

DUCHESS   Is all our train

[89] A note in the 1623 edition reads: "The author
disclaims this ditty to be his."

Shrunk to this poor remainder?

ANTONIO   These poor
men,
Which have got little in your service, vow
To take your fortune: but your wiser bunt-
ings,[90]
Now they are fledged, are gone.

DUCHESS   They have done
wisely.
This puts me in mind of death: physicians thus,
With their hands full of money, use to give o'er
Their patients.

ANTONIO   Right the fashion of the world:
From decayed fortunes every flatterer shrinks;
Men cease to build where the foundation sinks.

DUCHESS   I had a very strange dream tonight.[91]

ANTONIO   What was 't?

DUCHESS   Methought I wore my coronet of state,
And on a sudden all the diamonds
Were changed to pearls.

ANTONIO   My interpretation
Is, you'll weep shortly; for to me the pearls
Do signify your tears.

DUCHESS   The birds that live
I' th' field on the wild benefit of nature
Live happier than we; for they may choose
their mates,
And carol their sweet pleasures to the spring.
[*Enter Bosola with a letter.*]

BOSOLA   You are happily o'erta'en.

DUCHESS   From my
brother?

BOSOLA   Yes, from the Lord Ferdinand your
brother
All love and safety.

DUCHESS   Thou dost blanch mischief,
Wouldst make it white. See, see, like to calm
weather
At sea before a tempest, false hearts speak fair
To those they intend most mischief.
[*Reads.*] "Send Antonio to me; I want his head
in a business."
A politic equivocation!
He doth not want your counsel, but your head;
That is, he cannot sleep till you be dead.
And here 's another pitfall that 's strewed o'er
With roses: mark it, 'tis a cunning one:

[90] Birds that follow the summer.
[91] Last night.

[*Reads.*] "I stand engaged for your husband for several debts at Naples: let not that trouble him; I had rather have his heart than his money":—

And I believe so too.

BOSOLA   What do you believe?

DUCHESS That he so much distrusts my husband's love,

He will by no means believe his heart is with him

Until he see it: the devil is not cunning

Enough to circumvent us in riddles.

BOSOLA Will you reject that noble and free league

Of amity and love which I present you?

DUCHESS Their league is like that of some politic kings,

Only to make themselves of strength and power

To be our after-ruin: tell them so.

BOSOLA And what from you?

ANTONIO   Thus tell him; I will not come.

BOSOLA And what of this?

[*Points to the letter.*]

ANTONIO   My brothers have dispersed

Bloodhounds abroad; which till I hear are muzzled,

No truce, though hatched with ne'er such politic skill,

Is safe, that hangs upon our enemies' will.

I'll not come at them.

BOSOLA   This proclaims your breeding:

Every small thing draws a base mind to fear,

As the adamant[92] draws iron. Fare you well, sir;

You shall shortly hear from 's.

[*Exit.*]

DUCHESS   I suspect some ambush:

Therefore by all my love I do conjure you

To take your eldest son, and fly towards Milan.

Let us not venture all this poor remainder

In one unlucky bottom.[93]

ANTONIO   You counsel safely.

Best of my life, farewell. Since we must part,

Heaven hath a hand in 't; but no otherwise

92 Magnet.

93 Bottom or hold of a ship.

Than as some curious artist takes in sunder

A clock or watch, when it is out of frame,

To bring 't in better order.

DUCHESS   I know not

Which is best, to see you dead, or part with you.

—Farewell, boy:

Thou art happy that thou hast not understanding

To know thy misery; for all our wit

And reading brings us to a truer sense

Of sorrow.—In the eternal church, sir,

I do hope we shall not part thus.

ANTONIO   O, be of comfort!

Make patience a noble fortitude,

And think not how unkindly we are used:

Man, like to cassia, is proved best, being bruised.

DUCHESS Must I, like to a slave-born Russian,

Account it praise to suffer tyranny?

And yet, O heaven, thy heavy hand is in 't!

I have seen my little boy oft scourge[94] his top,

An compared myself to 't: naught made me e'er

Go right but heaven's scourge-stick.

ANTONIO   Do not weep:

Heaven fashioned us of nothing, and we strive

To bring ourselves to nothing.—Farewell, Cariola,

And thy sweet armful.—If I do never see thee more,

Be a good mother to your little ones,

And save them from the tiger: fare you well.

DUCHESS Let me look upon you once more; for that

Speech came from a dying father.—Your kiss is colder

Than that I have seen an holy anchorite

Give to a dead man's skull.

ANTONIO My heart is turned to a heavy lump of lead,

With which I sound my danger: fare you well.

[*Exeunt Antonio and his son.*]

DUCHESS My laurel is all withered.

CARIOLA Look, madam, what a troop of armèd men

94 Whip with a string, to spin it.

The Duchess of Malfi   227

Make toward us.

DUCHESS   O, they are very welcome:
When Fortune's wheel is over-charged with princes,
The weight makes it move swift: I would have my ruin
Be sudden.

[Reenter Bosola masked, with a Guard.]
                        I am your adventure,[95] am I not?

BOSOLA   You are: you must see your husband no more.

DUCHESS   What devil art thou that counterfeits heaven's thunder?

BOSOLA   Is that terrible? I would have you tell me whether
Is that note worse that frights the silly birds
Out of the corn, or that which doth allure them
To the nets? you have hearkened to the last too much.

DUCHESS   O, misery! like to a rusty o'ercharged cannon,
Shall I never fly in pieces?—Come, to what prison?

BOSOLA   To none.

DUCHESS   Whither, then?

BOSOLA   To your
palace.

DUCHESS   I have heard
That Charon's boat serves to convey all o'er
The dismal lake, but brings none back again.

BOSOLA   Your brothers mean you safety and pity.

DUCHESS   Pity!
With such a pity men preserve alive
Pheasants and quails, when they are not fat enough
To be eaten.

BOSOLA   These are your children?

DUCHESS   Yes.

BOSOLA   Can they
prattle?

95 Quarry.

DUCHESS   No;
But I intend, since they were born accursed,
Curses shall be their first language.

BOSOLA   Fie, madam!
Forget this base, low fellow,—

DUCHESS   Were I a man,
I'd beat that counterfeit face[96] into thy other.

BOSOLA   One of no birth.

DUCHESS   Say that he was born
mean,
Man is most happy when 's own actions
Be arguments and examples of his virtue.

BOSOLA   A barren, beggarly virtue!

DUCHESS   I prithee, who is greatest? can you tell?
Sad tales befit my woe: I'll tell you one.
A salmon, as she swam unto the sea,
Met with a dogfish, who encounters her
With this rough language: "Why art thou so bold
To mix thyself with our high state of floods,
Being no eminent courtier, but one
That for the calmest and fresh time o' the year
Dost live in shallow rivers, rank'st thyself
With silly smelts and shrimps? and darest thou
Pass by our dog-ship without reverence?"
"O!" quoth the salmon, "sister, be at peace:
Thank Jupiter we both have passed the net!
Our value never can be truly known,
Till in the fisher's basket we be shown:
I' th' market then my price may be the higher,
Even when I am nearest to the cook and fire."
So to great men the moral may be stretchèd;
Men oft are valued high, when they're most wretched.—
But come, whither you please. I am armed 'gainst misery;
Bent to all sways of the oppressor's will:
There's no deep valley but near some great hill.
[Exeunt.]

96 Bosola is masked.

Act Four

SCENE ONE

Amalfi. The Palace of the Duchess. Enter Ferdinand and Bosola.

FERDINAND How doth our sister duchess bear herself
In her imprisonment?

BOSOLA   Nobly: I'll describe her.
She 's sad as one long used to 't, and she seems
Rather to welcome the end of misery
Than shun it; a behavior so noble
As gives a majesty to adversity:
You may discern the shape of loveliness
More perfect in her tears than in her smiles:
She will muse four hours together; and her silence,
Methinks, expresseth more than if she spake.

FERDINAND Her melancholy seems to be fortified
With a strange disdain.

BOSOLA   'Tis so; and this restraint,
Like English mastiffs that grow fierce with tying,
Makes her too passionately apprehend
Those pleasures she's kept from.

FERDINAND   Curse upon her!
I will no longer study in the book
Of another's heart. Inform her what I told you.
[*Exit. Enter Duchess.*]

BOSOLA All comfort to your grace!

DUCHESS   I will have none.
Pray thee, why dost thou wrap thy poisoned pills
In gold and sugar?

BOSOLA Your elder brother, the Lord Ferdinand,
Is come to visit you, and sends you word,
'Cause once he rashly made a solemn vow
Never to see you more, he comes i' th' night;
And prays you gently neither torch nor taper
Shine on your chamber: he will kiss your hand,
And reconcile himself; but for his vow
He dares not see you.

DUCHESS   At his pleasure.—Take
hence the lights.—
He 's come.

[*Enter Ferdinand.*]

FERDINAND Where are you?

DUCHESS   Here, sir.

FERDINAND   This darkness suits you well.

DUCHESS I would ask you pardon.

FERDINAND   You have it;
for I account it
The honorabl'st revenge, where I may kill,
To pardon.—Where are your cubs?

DUCHESS   Whom?

FERDINAND   Call
them your children;
For though our national law distinguish bastards
From true legitimate issue, compassionate nature
Makes them all equal.

DUCHESS   Do you visit me for this?
You violate a sacrament o' th' Church
Shall make you howl in hell for 't.

FERDINAND   It had been
well
Could you have lived thus always; for, indeed,
You were too much i' th' light:—but no more;
I come to seal my peace with you. Here 's a
hand
[*Gives her a dead man's hand.*]
To which you have vowed much love; the ring
upon 't
You gave.

DUCHESS I affectionately kiss it.

FERDINAND Pray, do, and bury the print of it in
your heart.
I will leave this ring with you for a love-token;
And the hand as sure as the ring; and do not
doubt
But you shall have the heart too: when you
need a friend,
Send it to him that owned it; you shall see
Whether he can aid you.

DUCHESS   You are very cold:
I fear you are not well after your travel.—
Ha! lights!—Oh, horrible!

FERDINAND   Let her have lights
enough.

[*Exit.*]

DUCHESS What witchcraft doth he practise, that he hath left
A dead man's hand here?

[*Here is discovered, behind a traverse,*[97] *the artificial figures of Antonio and his Children, appearing as if they were dead.*]

BOSOLA Look you, here 's the piece from which 'twas ta'en.
He doth present you this sad spectacle,
That, now you know directly they are dead,
Hereafter you may wisely cease to grieve
For that which cannot be recovered.

DUCHESS There is not between heaven and earth one wish
I stay for after this: it wastes me more
Than were 't my picture, fashioned out of wax,
Stuck with a magical needle, and then buried
In some foul dunghill; and yond 's an excellent property
For a tyrant, which I would account mercy.

BOSOLA   What 's that?

DUCHESS If they would bind me to that lifeless trunk,
And let me freeze to death.

BOSOLA   Come, you must live.

DUCHESS That 's the greatest torture souls feel in hell,
In hell, that they must live, and cannot die.
Portia, I'll new kindle thy coals again,
And revive the rare and almost dead example
Of a loving wife.[98]

BOSOLA   O, fie! despair? remember
You are a Christian.

DUCHESS   The Church enjoins fasting:
I'll starve myself to death.

BOSOLA   Leave this vain sorrow.
Things being at the worst begin to mend: the bee

[97] Curtain.

[98] After Brutus's death, his wife Portia, intent upon committing suicide in spite of the attempt of friends and relatives to prevent her from it, placed burning coals in her mouth, keeping it closed until she choked.

When he hath shot his sting into your hand, may then
Play with your eyelid.

DUCHESS   Good comfortable fellow,
Persuade a wretch that 's broke upon the wheel
To have all his bones new set; entreat him live
To be executed again. Who must dispatch me?
I account this world a tedious theatre,
For I do play a part in 't 'gainst my will.

BOSOLA Come, be of comfort; I will save your life.

DUCHESS Indeed,
I have not leisure to tend so small a business.

BOSOLA Now, by my life, I pity you.

DUCHESS   Thou art a fool, then,
To waste thy pity on a thing so wretched
As cannot pity itself. I am full of daggers.
Puff, let me blow these vipers from me.

[*Enter Servant.*]
What are you?

SERVANT   One that wishes you long life.

DUCHESS I would thou wert hanged for the horrible curse
Thou hast given me: I shall shortly grow one
Of the miracles of pity. I'll go pray;—
No, I'll go curse.

BOSOLA   O, fie!

DUCHESS   I could curse the stars—

BOSOLA O, fearful!

DUCHESS And those three smiling seasons of the year
Into a Russian winter: nay, the world
To its first chaos.

BOSOLA Look you, the stars shine still.

DUCHESS   O, but you must
Remember, my curse hath a great way to go.—
Plagues, that make lanes through largest families
Consume them!—

BOSOLA Fie, lady!

DUCHESS   Let them, like tyrants,
Never be remembered but for the ill they have done;
Let all the zealous prayers of mortified
Churchmen forget them!—

BOSOLA   O, uncharitable!

DUCHESS Let Heaven a little while cease crown-
  ing martyrs
To punish them!—
Go, howl them this, and say, I long to bleed:
It is some mercy when men kill with speed.
[*Exeunt Duchess and Servant. Reenter Fer-
dinand.*]

FERDINAND Excellent, as I would wish; she's
  plagued in art:
These presentations are but framed in wax
By the curious master in that quality,
Vincentio Lauriola, and she takes them
For true substantial bodies.

BOSOLA   Why do you do
  this?

FERDINAND To bring her to despair.

BOSOLA   'Faith, end
  here,
And go no farther in your cruelty:
Send her a penitential garment to put on
Next to her delicate skin, and furnish her
With beads and prayer-books.

FERDINAND   Damn her! that
  body of hers,
While that my blood ran pure in 't, was more
  worth
Than that which thou wouldst comfort, called
  a soul.
I will send her masks of common courtesans,
Have her meat served up by bawds and ruffians,
And, 'cause she'll needs be mad, I am resolved
To remove forth[99] the common hospital
All the mad-folk, and place them near her
  lodging;
There let them practise together, sing and dance,
And act their gambols to the full o' th' moon:
If she can sleep the better for it, let her.
Your work is almost ended.

BOSOLA   Must I see her again?

FERDINAND Yes.

BOSOLA   Never.

FERDINAND   You must.

BOSOLA   Never in
  mine own shape;
That's forfeited by my intelligence[100]
And this last cruel lie: when you send me next,

[99] Forth from.
[100] Acting as a spy.

The business shall be comfort.

FERDINAND   Very likely;
Thy pity is nothing of kin to thee. Antonio
Lurks about Milan: thou shalt shortly thither
To feed a fire as great as my revenge,
Which ne'er will slack till it have spent his fuel:
Intemperate agues make physicians cruel.
[*Exeunt.*]

SCENE TWO

The same. Enter Duchess and Cariola.

DUCHESS What hideous noise was that?

CARIOLA   'Tis the
  wild consort
Of madmen, lady, which your tyrant brother
Hath placed about your lodging: this tyranny,
I think, was never practised till this hour.

DUCHESS Indeed, I thank him: nothing but noise
  and folly
Can keep me in my right wits; whereas reason
And silence make me stark mad. Sit down;
Discourse to me some dismal tragedy.

CARIOLA O, 'twill increase your melancholy.

DUCHESS   Thou
  art deceived:
To hear of greater grief would lessen mine.
This is a prison?

CARIOLA   Yes, but you shall live
To shake this durance off.

DUCHESS   Thou art a fool:
The robin redbreast and the nightingale
Never live long in cages.

CARIOLA   Pray, dry your eyes.
What think you of, madam?

DUCHESS   Of nothing; when
  I muse thus,
I sleep.

CARIOLA Like a madman, with your eyes open?

DUCHESS Dost thou think we shall know one
  another in th' other world?

CARIOLA Yes, out of question.

DUCHESS   O, that it were
  possible
We might but hold some two days' conference
With the dead! From them I should learn some-
  what, I am sure,
I never shall know here. I'll tell thee a miracle;

I am not mad yet, to my cause of sorrow:
Th' heaven o'er my head seems made of molten
   brass,
The earth of flaming sulphur, yet I am not mad.
I am acquainted with sad misery
As the tanned galley-slave is with his oar;
Necessity makes me suffer constantly,
And custom makes it easy. Who do I look like
   now?

CARIOLA   Like to your picture in the gallery,
A deal of life in show, but none in practice;
Or rather like some reverend monument
Whose ruins are even pitied.

DUCHESS   Very proper;
And Fortune seems only to have her eyesight
To behold my tragedy.—
How now! what noise is that?
[*Enter Servant.*]

SERVANT   I am come to tell
you
Your brother hath intended you some sport.
A great physician, when the Pope was sick
Of a deep melancholy, presented him
With several sorts of madmen, which wild ob-
   ject
Being full of change and sport, forced him to
   laugh,
And so the imposthume[101] broke: the selfsame
   cure
The duke intends on you.

DUCHESS   Let them come in.

SERVANT   There 's a mad lawyer; and a secular
   priest;
A doctor that hath forfeited his wits
By jealousy; an astrologian
That in his works said such a day o' th' month
Should be the day of doom, and, failing of 't,
Ran mad; an English tailor crazed i' th' brain
With the study of new fashions; a gentleman-
   usher
Quite beside himself with care to keep in mind
The number of his lady's salutations
Or "How do you['s]" she employed him in each
   morning;
A farmer, too, an excellent knave in grain,[102]
Mad 'cause he was hindered transportation:[103]

101 Ulcer.
102 A pun: in the grain trade and in temperament.
103 Forbidden to export.

And let one broker[104] that 's mad loose to these,
You'd think the devil were among them.

DUCHESS   Sit, Cariola.—Let them loose when
   you please,
For I am chained to endure all your tyranny.
[*Enter Madmen.*]

MADMAN [*sings to a dismal kind of music*]

O, let us howl some heavy note,
Some deadly dogged howl,
Sounding as from the threatening throat
Of beasts and fatal fowl!
As ravens, screech-owls, bulls, and bears,
We'll bell, and bawl our parts,
Till irksome noise have cloyed your ears
And corrosived your hearts.
At last, whenas our quire wants breath,
Our bodies being blest,
We'll sing, like swans, to welcome death,
And die in love and rest.

FIRST MADMAN   Doom's-day not come yet? I'll
draw it nearer by a perspective,[105] or make a
glass that shall set all the world on fire upon
an instant. I cannot sleep; my pillow is stuffed
with a litter of porcupines.

SECOND MADMAN   Hell is a mere glass-house,
where the devils are continually blowing up
women's souls on hollow irons, and the fire
never goes out.

THIRD MADMAN   I will lie with every woman in
my parish the tenth night; I will tithe them
over like haycocks.

FOURTH MADMAN   Shall my pothecary out-go me
because I am a cuckold? I have found out his
roguery; he makes alum of his wife's urine, and
sells it to Puritans that have sore throats with
overstraining.[106]

FIRST MADMAN   I have skill in heraldry.

SECOND MADMAN   Hast?

FIRST MADMAN   You do give for your crest a
woodcock's head with the brains picked out on
't; you are a very ancient gentleman.

THIRD MADMAN   Greek is turned Turk: we are
only to be saved by the Helvetian translation.[107]

104 Pawnbroker.
105 Telescope.
106 From preaching.
107 The Genevan or "Breeches" Bible of 1560,
known for its strong Puritan bias.

JOHN WEBSTER

FIRST MADMAN Come on, sir, I will lay[108] the law to you.

SECOND MADMAN O, rather lay a corrosive: the law will eat to the bone.

THIRD MADMAN He that drinks but to satisfy nature is damned.

FOURTH MADMAN If I had my glass here, I would show a sight should make all the women here call me mad doctor.

FIRST MADMAN What's he? a rope-maker?[109]

SECOND MADMAN No, no, no, a snuffling knave that, while he shows the tombs, will have his hand in a wench's placket.[110]

THIRD MADMAN Woe to the caroche that brought home my wife from the masque at three o'clock in the morning! it had a large feather-bed in it.

FOURTH MADMAN I have pared the devil's nails forty times, roasted them in raven's eggs, and cured agues with them.

THIRD MADMAN Get me three hundred milchbats, to make possets to procure sleep.

FOURTH MADMAN All the college may throw their caps at me:
I have made a soap-boiler costive;[111] it was my masterpiece.

[*Here the dance, consisting of eight Madmen, with music answerable thereunto; after which Bosola, like an Old Man, enters.*]

DUCHESS Is he mad too?

SERVANT Pray, question him. I'll leave you.

[*Exeunt Servant and Madmen.*]

BOSOLA I am come to make thy tomb.

DUCHESS Ha! my tomb?
Thou speak'st as if I lay upon my death-bed,
Gasping for breath: dost thou perceive me sick?

BOSOLA Yes, and the more dangerously, since thy sickness
Is insensible.

DUCHESS Thou art not mad, sure: dost know me?

BOSOLA Yes.

DUCHESS Who am I?

---

[108] Expound.
[109] Rope makers were associated with hangmen.
[110] Opening in a petticoat.
[111] Soap was used for suppositories.

BOSOLA Thou art a box of worm-seed, at best but a salvatory of green mummy.[112] What's this flesh? a little crudded[113] milk, fantastical puff-paste. Our bodies are weaker than those paper-prisons boys use to keep flies in; more contemptible, since ours is to preserve earthworms. Didst thou ever see a lark in a cage? Such is the soul in the body: this world is like her little turf of grass, and the heaven o'er our heads, like her looking-glass, only gives us a miserable knowledge of the small compass of our prison.

DUCHESS Am not I thy duchess?

BOSOLA Thou art some great woman, sure, for riot begins to sit on thy forehead (clad in grey hairs) twenty years sooner than on a merry milk-maid's. Thou sleep'st worse than if a mouse should be forced to take up her lodging in a cat's ear: a little infant that breeds its teeth, should it lie with thee, would cry out, as if thou wert the more unquiet bed-fellow.

DUCHESS I am Duchess of Malfi still.

BOSOLA That makes thy sleeps so broken:
Glories, like glowworms, afar off shine bright,
But looked to near, have neither heat nor light.

DUCHESS Thou art very plain.

BOSOLA My trade is to flatter the dead, not the living; I am a tomb-maker.

DUCHESS And thou com'st to make my tomb?

BOSOLA Yes.

DUCHESS Let me be a little merry:—of what stuff wilt thou make it?

BOSOLA Nay, resolve me first, of what fashion?

DUCHESS Why, do we grow fantastical in our death-bed? do we affect fashion in the grave?

BOSOLA Most ambitiously. Princes' images on their tombs do not lie, as they were wont, seeming to pray up to heaven; but with their hands under their cheeks, as if they died of the toothache: they are not carved with their eyes fixed upon the stars; but as their minds were wholly bent upon the world, the selfsame way they seem to turn their faces.

DUCHESS Let me know fully therefore the effect Of this thy dismal preparation,

---

[112] *Salvatore of mummy* was an ointment box of dried flesh, which was widely used as medicine; but here the mummy is green, or undried.
[113] Curdled.

This talk fit for a charnel.

BOSOLA Now I shall:—

[*Enter Executioners, with a coffin, cords, and a bell.*]

Here is a present from your princely brothers;
And may it arrive welcome, for it brings
Last benefit, last sorrow.

DUCHESS Let me see it:
I have so much obedience in my blood,
I wish it in their veins to do them good.

BOSOLA This is your last presence-chamber.

CARIOLA O
my sweet lady!

DUCHESS Peace; it affrights not me.

BOSOLA I am the
common bellman,
That usually is sent to condemned persons
The night before they suffer.[114]

DUCHESS Even now
Thou said'st thou wast a tomb-maker.

BOSOLA 'Twas
to bring you
By degrees to mortification. Listen.

[*Rings his bell.*]

Hark, now every thing is still
The screech-owl and the whistler shrill
Call upon our dame aloud,
And bid her quickly don her shroud!
Much you had of land and rent:
Your length in clay's now competent:
A long war disturbed your mind;
Here your perfect peace is signed.
Of what is 't fools make such vain keeping?
Sin their conception, their birth weeping,
Their life a general mist of error,
Their death a hideous storm of terror.
Strew your hair with powders sweet,
Don clean linen, bathe your feet,
And (the foul fiend more to check)
A crucifix let bless your neck:
'Tis now full tide 'tween night and day;
End your groan, and come away.

CARIOLA Hence, villains, tyrants, murderers! alas!
What will you do with my lady?—Call for help.

[114] A bellman regularly exhorted to prayer condemned criminals in Newgate Prison, visiting them the night before the scheduled execution.

DUCHESS To whom? to our next neighbors? they are mad-folks.

BOSOLA Remove that noise.

DUCHESS Farewell, Cariola.
In my last will I have not much to give:
A many hungry guests have fed upon me;
Thine will be a poor reversion.[115]

CARIOLA I will die with her.

DUCHESS I pray thee, look thou giv'st my little boy
Some syrup for his cold, and let the girl
Say her prayers ere she sleep.

[*Cariola is forced out by the Executioners.*]
Now what you please:
What death?

BOSOLA Strangling;
Here are your executioners.

DUCHESS I forgive them:
The apoplexy, catarrh,[116] or cough o' th' lungs,
Would do as much as they do.

BOSOLA Doth not death fright you?

DUCHESS Who would be afraid on 't,
Knowing to meet such excellent company
In th' other world?

BOSOLA Yet, methinks,
The manner of your death should much afflict you:
This cord should terrify you.

DUCHESS Not a whit:
What would it pleasure me to have my throat cut
With diamonds? or to be smothered
With cassia? or to be shot to death with pearls?
I know death hath ten thousand several doors
For men to take their exits; and 'tis found
They go on such strange geometrical hinges,
You may open them both ways.—Any way, for heaven sake,
So I were out of your whispering. Tell my brothers
That I perceive death, now I am well awake,
Best gift is they can give or I can take.
I would fain put off my last woman's fault,
I'd not be tedious to you.

[115] Right of future possession.
[116] Cerebral hemorrhage.

FIRST EXECUTIONER   We are ready.

DUCHESS Dispose my breath how please you; but my body
Bestow upon my women, will you?

FIRST EXECUTIONER   Yes.

DUCHESS Pull, and pull strongly, for your able strength
Must pull down heaven upon me:—
Yet stay; heaven-gates are not so highly arched
As princes' palaces; they that enter there
Must go upon their knees.   [*Kneels.*]
Come, violent death
Serve for mandragora to make me sleep!—
Go tell my brothers, when I am laid out,
They then may feed in quiet.
[*They strangle her.*]

BOSOLA Where's the waiting woman? Fetch her: some other
Strangle the children.
[*Exeunt Executioners, some of whom return with Cariola.*]
Look you, there sleeps your mistress.

CARIOLA   O, you are damned
Perpetually for this! My turn is next,
Is 't not so ordered?

BOSOLA   Yes, and I am glad
You are so well prepared for 't.

CARIOLA   You are deceived, sir,
I am not prepared for 't, I will not die;
I will first come to my answer,[117] and know
How I have offended.

BOSOLA   Come, dispatch her.—
You kept her counsel; now you shall keep ours.

CARIOLA I will not die, I must not; I am contracted
To a young gentleman.

FIRST EXECUTIONER Here's your wedding ring.

CARIOLA Let me but speak with the duke; I'll discover
Treason to his person.

BOSOLA   Delays:—throttle her.

FIRST EXECUTIONER She bites and scratches.

CARIOLA   If you kill me now,

---

[117] Legal terminology: reply to a charge.

I am damned; I have not been at confession
This two years.

BOSOLA [*to Executioners*] When?

CARIOLA   I am quick with child.

BOSOLA   Why, then,
Your credit's saved.
[*They strangle Cariola.*]
        Bear her into th' next room;
Let this lie still.
[*Exeunt Executioners with the body of Cariola. Enter Ferdinand.*]

FERDINAND   Is she dead?

BOSOLA   She is what
You'd have her. But here begin your pity:
[*Shows the Children strangled.*]
Alas, how have these offended?

FERDINAND   The death
Of young wolves is never to be pitied.

BOSOLA   Fix
Your eye here.

FERDINAND   Constantly.

BOSOLA   Do you not weep?
Other sins only speak; murder shrieks out:
The element of water moistens the earth,
But blood flies upwards and bedews the heavens.

FERDINAND Cover her face; mine eyes dazzle: she died young.

BOSOLA I think not so; her infelicity
Seemed to have years too many.

FERDINAND   She and I were twins;
And should I die this instant, I had lived
Her time to a minute.

BOSOLA   It seems she was born first:
You have bloodily approved the ancient truth,
That kindred commonly do worse agree
Than remote strangers.

FERDINAND   Let me see her face
Again. Why didst not thou pity her? what
An excellent honest man mightst thou have been,
If thou hadst borne her to some sanctuary!
Or, bold in a good cause, opposed thyself,
With thy advancèd sword above thy head,
Between her innocence and my revenge!
I bade thee, when I was distracted of my wits,
Go kill my dearest friend, and thou hast done 't.

The Duchess of Malfi   235

For let me but examine well the cause:
What was the meanness of her match to me?
Only I must confess I had a hope,
Had she continu'd widow, to have gained
An infinite mass of treasure by her death:
And that was the main cause; her marriage,—
That drew a stream of gall quite through my
  heart.
For thee, as we observe in tragedies
That a good actor many times is cursed
For playing a villain's part, I hate thee for 't,
And, for my sake, say thou hast done much ill
  well.

BOSOLA Let me quicken your memory, for I
  perceive
You are falling into ingratitude: I challenge
The reward due to my service.

FERDINAND   I'll tell thee
What I'll give thee.

BOSOLA   Do.

FERDINAND   I'll give thee a pardon
For this murder.

BOSOLA   Ha!

FERDINAND   Yes, and 'tis
The largest bounty I can study to do thee.
By what authority didst thou execute
This bloody sentence?

BOSOLA   By yours.

FERDINAND   Mine? was I
  her judge?
Did any ceremonial form of law
Doom her to not-being? did a complete jury
Deliver her conviction up i' th' court?
Where shalt thou find this judgement regis-
  tered,
Unless in hell? See, like a bloody fool,
Thou'st forfeited thy life, and thou shalt die
  for 't.

BOSOLA The office of justice is perverted quite
When one thief hangs another. Who shall dare
To reveal this?

FERDINAND   O, I'll tell thee;
The wolf shall find her grave, and scrape it up,
Not to devour the corpse, but to discover
The horrid murder.

BOSOLA   You, not I, shall quake for 't.

FERDINAND Leave me.

BOSOLA   I will first receive my pension.

FERDINAND You are a villain.

BOSOLA   When your ingratitude
Is judge, I am so.

FERDINAND   O, horror, that not the fear
Of him which binds the devils can prescribe man
Obedience!—Never look upon me more.

BOSOLA Why, fare thee well.
Your brother and yourself are worthy men:
You have a pair of hearts are hollow graves,
Rotten, and rotting others; and your vengeance,
Like two chained bullets, still goes arm in arm:
You may be brothers; for treason, like the
  plague,
Doth take much in a blood.[118] I stand like one
That long hath ta'en a sweet and golden dream:
I am angry with myself, now that I wake.

FERDINAND Get thee into some unknown part
  o' th' world,
That I may never see thee.

BOSOLA   Let me know
Wherefore I should be thus neglected. Sir,
I served your tyranny, and rather strove
To satisfy yourself than all the world:
And though I loathed the evil, yet I loved
You that did counsel it; and rather sought
To appear a true servant than an honest man.

FERDINAND I'll go hunt the badger by owl-light:
'Tis a deed of darkness.

[*Exit.*]

BOSOLA He's much distracted. Off, my painted
  honor!
While with vain hopes our faculties we tire,
We seem to sweat in ice and freeze in fire.
What would I do, were this to do again?
I would not change my peace of conscience
For all the wealth of Europe.—She stirs; here's
  life:—
Return, fair soul, from darkness, and lead mine
Out of this sensible[119] hell:—she's warm, she
  breathes:—
Upon thy pale lips I will melt my heart,
To store them with fresh color.—Who's there!
Some cordial drink!—Alas! I dare not call:
So pity would destroy pity.—Her eye opes,
And heaven in it seems to ope, that late was
  shut,

[118] *Doth take . . . blood:* runs in families.
[119] Perceived by the senses.

236   JOHN WEBSTER

To take me up to mercy.

DUCHESS Antonio!

BOSOLA Yes, madam, he is living;
The dead bodies you saw were but feigned
statues:
He's reconciled to your brothers: the Pope hath
wrought
The atonement.

DUCHESS Mercy!

[*Dies.*]

BOSOLA O, she's gone again! there the cords of
life broke.
O, sacred innocence, that sweetly sleeps
On turtles'[120] feathers, whilst a guilty conscience
Is a black register wherein is writ
All our good deeds and bad, a perspective
That shows us hell! That we cannot be suffered

To do good when we have a mind to it!
This is manly sorrow; these tears, I am very
certain,
Never grew in my mother's milk: my estate
Is sunk below the degree of fear: where were
These penitent fountains while she was living?
O, they were frozen up! Here is a sight
As direful to my soul as is the sword
Unto a wretch hath slain his father. Come, I'll
bear thee
Hence, and execute thy last will; that's deliver
Thy body to the reverend dispose
Of some good women: that the cruel tyrant
Shall not deny me. Then I'll post to Milan,
Where somewhat I will speedily enact
Worth my dejection.

[*Exit with the body.*]

Act Five

SCENE ONE

Milan, a public place. Enter Antonio and Delio.

ANTONIO What think you of my hope of reconcilement
To the Aragonian brethren?

DELIO I misdoubt it;
For though they have sent their letters of safe-
conduct
For your repair to Milan, they appear
But nets to entrap you. The Marquis of Pes-
cara,
Under whom you hold certain land in cheat,[121]
Much 'gainst his noble nature hath been moved
To seize those lands; and some of his depend-
ants
Are at this instant making it their suit
To be invested in your revenues.
I cannot think they mean well to your life
That do deprive you of your means of life,
Your living.

ANTONIO You are still an heretic
To any safety I can shape myself.

DELIO Here comes the marquis: I will make
myself
Petitioner for some part of your land,

120 Turtledoves'.
121 Escheat; subject to forfeiture.

To know whither it is flying.

ANTONIO I pray do.

[*Withdraws. Enter Pescara.*]

DELIO Sir, I have a suit to you.

PESCARA To me?

DELIO An easy
one:
There is the citadel of Saint Bennet,
With some demesnes, of late in the possession
Of Antonio Bologna,—please you bestow them
on me.

PESCARA You are my friend; but this is such a
suit,
Nor fit for me to give, nor you to take.

DELIO No, sir?

PESCARA I will give you ample reason
for 't
Soon in private:—here's the Cardinal's mistress.

[*Enter Julia.*]

JULIA My lord, I am grown your poor peti-
tioner,
And should be an ill beggar, had I not
A great man's letter here, the Cardinal's,
To court you in my favor.

[*Gives a letter.*]

PESCARA He entreats for you
The citadel of Saint Bennet, that belonged
To the banishèd Bologna.

JULIA   Yes.

PESCARA   I could not
Have thought of a friend I could rather pleas-
   ure with it:
'Tis yours.

JULIA   Sir, I thank you; and he shall know
How doubly I am engaged both in your gift,
And speediness of giving, which makes your grant
The greater.
[*Exit.*]

ANTONIO [*aside*]   How they fortify themselves
   With my ruin!

DELIO   Sir, I am little bound to you.

PESCARA   Why?

DELIO   Because you denied this suit to me, and
   gave 't
To such a creature.

PESCARA   Do you know what it was?
It was Antonio's land; not forfeited
By course of law, but ravished from his throat
By the Cardinal's entreaty: it were not fit
I should bestow so main a piece of wrong
Upon my friend; 'tis a gratification
Only due to a strumpet, for it is injustice.
Shall I sprinkle the pure blood of innocents
To make those followers I call my friends
Look ruddier[122] upon me? I am glad
This land, ta'en from the owner by such wrong,
Returns again unto so foul an use
As salary for his lust. Learn, good Delio,
To ask noble things of me, and you shall find
I'll be a noble giver.

DELIO   You instruct me well.

ANTONIO [*aside*]   Why, here's a man now who
   would fright impudence
From sauciest beggars.

PESCARA   Prince Ferdinand's come
   to Milan,
Sick, as they give out, of an apoplexy;
But some say 'tis a frenzy: I am going
To visit him.
[*Exit.*]

ANTONIO   'Tis a noble old fellow.

DELIO   What course do you mean to take, Antonio?

ANTONIO   This night I mean to venture all my
   fortune,

Which is no more than a poor lingering life,
To the Cardinal's worst of malice: I have got
Private access to his chamber; and intend
To visit him about the mid of night,
As once his brother did our noble duchess.
It may be that the sudden apprehension
Of danger,—for I'll go in mine own shape,—
When he shall see it fraight[123] with love and
   duty,
May draw the poison out of him, and work
A friendly reconcilement: if it fail,
Yet it shall rid me of this infamous calling;
For better fall once than be ever falling.

DELIO   I'll second you in all danger; and, how-
   e'er,
My life keeps rank with yours.

ANTONIO   You are still my
   lovèd
And best friend.
[*Exeunt.*]

SCENE TWO

Milan, the Palace of the Cardinal and Ferdinand.
Enter Pescara and Doctor.

PESCARA   Now, doctor, may I visit your patient?

DOCTOR   If't please your lordship: but he's in-
   stantly
To take the air here in the gallery
By my direction.

PESCARA   Pray thee, what's his disease?

DOCTOR   A very pestilent disease, my lord,
They call lycanthropia.

PESCARA   What's that?
I need a dictionary to 't.

DOCTOR   I'll tell you.
In those that are possessed with 't there o'er-
   flows
Such melancholy humor they imagine
Themselves to be transformèd into wolves;
Steal forth to churchyards in the dead of night,
And dig dead bodies up: as two nights since
One met the duke 'bout midnight in a lane
Behind Saint Mark's Church, with the leg of a
   man
Upon his shoulder; and he howled fearfully;

---

122 More ardently.

123 Fraught.

Said he was a wolf, only the difference
Was, a wolf's skin was hairy on the outside,
His on the inside; bade them take their swords,
Rip up his flesh, and try: straight I was sent
     for,
And, having ministered to him, found his grace
Very well recovered.

PESCARA   I am glad on 't.

DOCTOR   Yet not without some
     fear
Of a relapse. If he grow to his fit again,
I'll go a nearer way to work with him
Than ever Paracelsus dreamed of; if
They'll give me leave, I'll buffet his madness
Out of him. Stand aside; he comes.

[*Enter Ferdinand, Cardinal, Malateste, and
Bosola.*]

FERDINAND   Leave me.

MALATESTE   Why doth your lordship love this
     solitariness?

FERDINAND   Eagles commonly fly alone: they are
     crows, daws, and starlings that flock together.
     Look, what's that follows me?

MALATESTE   Nothing, my lord.

FERDINAND   Yes.

MALATESTE   'Tis your shadow.

FERDINAND   Stay it; let it not haunt me.

MALATESTE   Impossible, if you move, and the
     sun shine.

FERDINAND   I will throttle it.

[*Throws himself on the ground.*]

MALATESTE   O, my lord, you are angry with
     nothing.

FERDINAND   You are a fool: how is 't possible I
     should catch my shadow, unless I fall upon 't?
     When I go to hell, I mean to carry a bribe; for,
     look you, good gifts evermore make way for
     the worst persons.

PESCARA   Rise, good my lord.

FERDINAND   I am studying the art of patience.

PESCARA   'Tis a noble virtue.

FERDINAND   To drive six snails before me from
     this town to Moscow; neither use goad nor
     whip to them, but let them take their own
     time;—the patient'st man i' th' world match me
     for an experiment;—and I'll crawl after like a
     sheep-biter.[124]

[124] A stealthy sheep-stealing dog; hence, a sneak
thief.

CARDINAL   Force him up.

[*They raise him.*]

FERDINAND   Use me well, you were best. What I
     have done, I have done: I'll confess nothing.

DOCTOR   Now let me come to him.—Are you
     mad, my lord? are you out of your princely
     wits?

FERDINAND   What's he?

PESCARA   Your doctor.

FERDINAND   Let me have his head sawed off, and
     his eyebrows filed more civil.

DOCTOR   I must do mad tricks with him, for
     that's the only way on 't.—I have brought
     your grace a salamander's skin to keep you
     from sunburning.

FERDINAND   I have cruel sore eyes.

DOCTOR   The white of a cockatrix's egg is pres-
     ent remedy.

FERDINAND   Let it be a new laid one, you were
     best.—Hide me from him: physicians are like
     kings,—they brook no contradiction.

DOCTOR   Now he begins to fear me: now let me
     alone with him.

CARDINAL   How now? put off your gown?

DOCTOR   Let me have some forty urinals filled
     with rosewater: he and I'll go pelt one another
     with them.—Now he begins to fear me.—Can
     you fetch a frisk,[125] sir?—Let him go, let him
     go, upon my peril: I find by his eye he stands
     in awe of me; I'll make him as tame as a dor-
     mouse.

FERDINAND   Can you fetch your frisks, sir?—I
     will stamp him into a cullis,[126] flay off his skin,
     to cover one of the anatomies[127] this rogue
     hath set i' th' cold yonder in Barber-Chirur-
     geon's-hall.[128]—Hence, hence! you are all of
     you like beasts for sacrifice: there's nothing left
     of you but tongue and belly, flattery and
     lechery. [*Exit.*]

PESCARA   Doctor, he did not fear you throughly.

DOCTOR   True;
I was somewhat too forward.

BOSOLA   Mercy upon me,

[125] Cut a caper.
[126] Broth which was often fed to the sick; in preparation, bones and flesh were bruised.
[127] Skeletons.
[128] The Barber Surgeons were granted annually the
bodies of four executed felons.

What a fatal judgement hath fallen upon this Ferdinand!

PESCARA Knows your grace what accident hath brought
Unto the prince this strange distraction?

CARDINAL [aside] I must feign somewhat.—Thus they say it grew.
You have heard it rumored, for these many years
None of our family dies but there is seen
The shape of an old woman, which is given
By tradition to us to have been murdered
By her nephews for her riches. Such a figure
One night, as the prince sat up late at 's book,
Appeared to him; when crying out for help,
The gentlemen of 's chamber found his grace
All on a cold sweat, altered much in face
And language: since which apparition,
He hath grown worse and worse, and I much fear
He cannot live.

BOSOLA Sir, I would speak with you.

PESCARA We'll leave your grace,
Wishing to the sick prince, our noble lord,
All health of mind and body.

CARDINAL You are most welcome.
[Exeunt Pescara, Malateste, and Doctor.]
Are you come? So.—
[Aside]
This fellow must not know
By any means I had intelligence
In our duchess' death; for, though I counselled it,
The full of all th' engagement seemed to grow
From Ferdinand.—Now, sir, how fares our sister?
I do not think but sorrow makes her look
Like to an oft-dyed garment: she shall now
Taste comfort from me. Why do you look so wildly?
O, the fortune of your master here the prince
Dejects you; but be you of happy comfort:
If you'll do one thing for me I'll entreat,
Though he had a cold tombstone o'er his bones,
I'd make you what you would be.

BOSOLA Anything;

Give it me in a breath, and let me fly to 't:
They that think long, small expedition win,
For musing much o' th' end cannot begin.
[Enter Julia.]

JULIA Sir, will you come in to supper?

CARDINAL I am busy;
Leave me.

JULIA [aside] What an excellent shape hath that fellow!
[Exit.]

CARDINAL 'Tis thus. Antonio lurks here in Milan:
Inquire him out, and kill him. While he lives,
Our sister cannot marry; and I have thought
Of an excellent match for her. Do this, and style me
Thy advancement.

BOSOLA But by what means shall I find him out?

CARDINAL There is a gentleman called Delio
Here in the camp, that hath been long approved
His loyal friend. Set eye upon that fellow;
Follow him to mass; maybe Antonio,
Although he do account religion
But a school-name, for fashion of the world
May accompany him; or else go inquire out
Delio's confessor, and see if you can bribe
Him to reveal it. There are a thousand ways
A man might find to trace him; as to know
What fellows haunt the Jews for taking up
Great sums of money, for sure he 's in want;
Or else to go to th' picture-makers, and learn
Who bought her picture lately: some of these
Happily may take.

BOSOLA Well, I'll not freeze i' th' business:
I would see that wretched thing, Antonio,
Above all sights i' th' world.

CARDINAL Do, and be happy.
[Exit.]

BOSOLA This fellow doth breed basilisks in 's eyes,
He's nothing else but murder; yet he seems
Not to have notice of the duchess' death.
'Tis his cunning: I must follow his example;
There cannot be a surer way to trace
Than that of an old fox.

[*Reenter Julia, with a pistol.*]

JULIA   So, sir, you are well met.

BOSOLA   How now?

JULIA   Nay, the doors are fast enough: Now, sir,
I will make you confess your treachery.

BOSOLA   Treachery?

JULIA   Yes,
Confess to me which of my women 'twas
You hired to put love-powder into my drink?

BOSOLA   Love-powder?

JULIA   Yes, when I was at Malfi.
Why should I fall in love with such a face else?
I have already suffered for thee so much pain,
The only remedy to do me good
Is to kill my longing.

BOSOLA   Sure, your pistol holds
Nothing but perfumes or kissing-comfits.[129]
Excellent lady! You have a pretty way on 't
To discover your longing. Come, come, I'll disarm you,
And arm[130] you thus: yet this is wondrous strange.

JULIA   Compare thy form and my eyes together, you'll find
My love no such great miracle. Now you'll say
I am wanton: this nice modesty in ladies
Is but a troublesome familiar[131] that haunts them.

BOSOLA   Know you me, I am a blunt soldier.

JULIA   The better:
Sure, there wants fire where there are no lively sparks
Of roughness.

BOSOLA   And I want compliment.

JULIA   Why, ignorance
In courtship cannot make you do amiss,
If you have a heart to do well.

BOSOLA   You are very fair.

JULIA   Nay, if you lay beauty to my charge,

129 Candies used to sweeten the breath.
130 Embrace.
131 Spirit.

I must plead unguilty.

BOSOLA   Your bright eyes carry
A quiver of darts in them sharper than sunbeams.

JULIA   You will mar me with commendation,
Put yourself to the charge of courting me,
Whereas now I woo you.

BOSOLA [*aside*]   I have it, I will work upon this creature.
—Let us grow most amorously familiar:
If the great Cardinal now should see me thus,
Would he not count me a villain?

JULIA   No; he might
Count me a wanton, not lay a scruple
Of offense on you; for if I see and steal
A diamond, the fault is not i' th' stone,
But in me the thief that purloins it. I am sudden
With you: we that are great women of pleasure
Use to cut off these uncertain wishes
And unquiet longings, and in an instant join
The sweet delight and the pretty excuse together.
Had you been i' th' street, under my chamber-window,
Even there I should have courted you.

BOSOLA   O, you are
An excellent lady!

JULIA   Bid me do somewhat for you
Presently, to express I love you.

BOSOLA   I will;
And if you love me, fail not to effect it.
The Cardinal is grown wondrous melancholy;
Demand the cause, let him not put you off
With feigned excuse; discover the main ground on 't.

JULIA   Why would you know this?

BOSOLA   I have depended on him,
And I hear that he is fallen in some disgrace
With the emperor: if he be, like the mice
That forsake falling houses, I would shift
To other dependence.

JULIA   You shall not need
Follow the wars: I'll be your maintenance.

BOSOLA   And I your loyal servant: but I cannot
Leave my calling.

The Duchess of Malfi

JULIA   Not leave an ungrateful
General for the love of a sweet lady?
You are like some cannot sleep in feather-beds,
But must have blocks for their pillows.

BOSOLA   Will
  you do this?

JULIA Cunningly.

BOSOLA Tomorrow I'll expect th' intelligence.

JULIA Tomorrow? get you into my cabinet;
You shall have it with you. Do not delay me,
No more than I do you: I am like one
That is condemned; I have my pardon prom-
  ised,
But I would see it sealed. Go, get you in:
You shall see me wind my tongue about his
  heart
Like a skein of silk.
[*Exit Bosola. Reenter Cardinal.*]

CARDINAL   Where are you?
[*Enter Servants.*]

SERVANTS   Here.

CARDINAL Let none, upon your lives, have con-
  ference
With the Prince Ferdinand, unless I know it.—
[*Aside*]
In this distraction he may reveal
The murder.
[*Exeunt Servants.*]
                    Yond's my lingering consumption:
I am weary of her, and by any means
Would be quit of.

JULIA   How now, my lord? what ails
  you?

CARDINAL Nothing.

JULIA   O, you are much altered:
  come, I must be
Your secretary,[132] and remove this lead
From off your bosom: what's the matter?

CARDINAL   I may
  not
Tell you.

JULIA Are you so far in love with sorrow
You cannot part with part of it? or think you
I cannot love your grace when you are sad
As well as merry? or do you suspect
I, that have been a secret to your heart

___
[132] Confidante.

These many winters, cannot be the same
Unto your tongue?

CARDINAL   Satisfy thy longing,—
The only way to make thee keep my counsel
Is, not to tell thee.

JULIA   Tell your echo this,
Or flatterers, that like echoes still report
What they hear though most imperfect, and not
  me;
For if that you be true unto yourself,
I'll know.

CARDINAL Will you rack me?

JULIA   No, judgement shall
Draw it from you: it is an equal fault,
To tell one's secrets unto all or none.

CARDINAL The first argues folly.

JULIA   But the last tyranny.

CARDINAL Very well: why, imagine I have com-
  mitted
Some secret deed which I desire the world
May never hear of.

JULIA   Therefore may not I know
  it?
You have concealed for me as great a sin
As adultery. Sir, never was occasion
For perfect trial of my constancy
Till now: sir, I beseech you—

CARDINAL   You'll repent it.

JULIA Never.

CARDINAL It hurries thee to ruin: I'll not tell
  thee.
Be well advised, and think what danger 'tis
To receive a prince's secrets: they that do,
Had need have their breasts hooped with ada-
  mant
To contain them. I pray thee, yet be satisfied;
Examine thine own frailty; 'tis more easy
To tie knots than unloose them: 'tis a secret
That, like a lingering poison, may chance lie
Spread in thy veins, and kill thee seven year
  hence.

JULIA Now you dally with me.

CARDINAL   No more; thou
  shalt know it.
By my appointment the great Duchess of Malfi
And two of her young children, four nights
  since,

Were strangled.

JULIA   O Heaven! sir, what have you
done!

CARDINAL   How now? how settles this? think you
your bosom
Will be a grave dark and obscure enough
For such a secret?

JULIA   You have undone yourself,
sir.

CARDINAL   Why?

JULIA   It lies not in me to conceal it.

CARDINAL   No?
Come, I will swear you to 't upon this book.

JULIA   Most religiously.

CARDINAL   Kiss it.
[*She kisses the book*.]
Now you shall
Never utter it; thy curiosity
Hath undone thee: thou'rt poisoned with that
book;
Because I knew thou couldst not keep my
counsel,
I have bound thee to 't by death.
[*Reenter Bosola*.]

BOSOLA   For pity sake,
Hold!

CARDINAL   Ha! Bosola?

JULIA   I forgive you
This equal piece of justice you have done;
For I betrayed your counsel to that fellow:
He overheard it; that was the cause I said
It lay not in me to conceal it.

BOSOLA   O foolish woman,
Couldst not thou have poisoned him?

JULIA   'Tis weak-
ness,
Too much to think what should have been
done. I go,
I know not whither.
[*Dies*.]

CARDINAL   Wherefore com'st thou
hither?

BOSOLA   That I might find a great man like
yourself,
Not out of his wits as the Lord Ferdinand,
To remember my service.

CARDINAL   I'll have thee hewed
in pieces.

BOSOLA   Make not yourself such a promise of
that life
Which is not yours to dispose of.

CARDINAL   Who placed
thee here?

BOSOLA   Her lust, as she intended.

CARDINAL   Very well:
Now you know me for your fellow-murderer.

BOSOLA   And wherefore should you lay fair mar-
ble colors[133]
Upon your rotten purposes to me?
Unless you imitate some that do plot great
treasons,
And when they have done, go hide themselves
i' th' graves
Of those were actors in 't?

CARDINAL   No more; there is
A fortune attends thee.

BOSOLA   Shall I go sue
To Fortune any longer? 'Tis the fool's
Pilgrimage.

CARDINAL   I have honors in store for thee.

BOSOLA   There are a many ways that conduct
to seeming
Honor, and some of them very dirty ones.

CARDINAL   Throw
To the devil thy melancholy. The fire burns
well:
What need we keep a stirring of't, and make
A greater smother? Thou wilt kill Antonio?

BOSOLA   Yes.

CARDINAL   Take up that body.

BOSOLA   I think I shall
Shortly grow the common bier for churchyards.

CARDINAL   I will allow thee some dozens of attendants
To aid thee in the murder.

BOSOLA   Oh, by no means. Physicians that apply
horse-leeches to any rank swelling use to cut
off their tails, that the blood may run through
them the faster: let me have no train when I
go to shed blood, lest it make me have a
greater when I ride to the gallows.

CARDINAL   Come to me after midnight, to help
to remove
That body to her own lodging: I'll give out

[133] *Lay . . . colors:* paint wood to make it look
like marble.

The Duchess of Malfi   243

She died o' th' plague; 'twill breed the less inquiry
After her death.

BOSOLA   Where's Castruchio her husband?

CARDINAL He's rode to Naples, to take possession
Of Antonio's citadel.

BOSOLA   Believe me, you have done
A very happy turn.

CARDINAL   Fail not to come:
There is the master-key of our lodgings; and by that
You may conceive what trust I plant in you.

BOSOLA You shall find me ready.
[*Exit Cardinal.*]
                                    O poor Antonio,
Though nothing be so needful to thy estate
As pity, yet I find nothing so dangerous;
I must look to my footing:
In such slippery ice-pavements men had need
To be frost-nailed well, they may break their necks else;
The precedent's here afore me. How this man
Bears up in blood! seems fearless! Why, 'tis well:
Security some men call the suburbs of hell,
Only a dead wall between. Well, good Antonio,
I'll seek thee out; and all my care shall be
To put thee into safety from the reach
Of these most cruel biters that have got
Some of thy blood already. It may be,
I'll join with thee in a most just revenge:
The weakest arm is strong enough that strikes
With the sword of justice. Still methinks the duchess
Haunts me.—There, there, 'tis nothing but my melancholy.
O Penitence, let me truly taste thy cup,
That throws men down only to raise them up!
[*Exit.*]

SCENE THREE

Milan, a fortification. Enter Antonio and Delio.

DELIO Yond's the Cardinal's window. This fortification
Grew from the ruins of an ancient abbey;
And to yond side o' th' river lies a wall,
Piece of a cloister, which in my opinion
Gives the best echo that you ever heard,
So hollow and so dismal, and withal
So plain in the distinction of our words,
That many have supposed it is a spirit
That answers.

ANTONIO   I do love these ancient ruins.
We never tread upon them but we set
Our foot upon some reverend history:
And, questionless, here in this open court,
Which now lies naked to the injuries
Of stormy weather, some men lie interred
Loved the church so well, and gave so largely to 't,
They thought it should have canopied their bones
Till doomsday; but all things have their end:
Churches and cities, which have diseases
Like to men, must have like death that we have.

ECHO *Like death that we have.*

DELIO Now the echo hath caught you.

ANTONIO   It groaned,
methought, and gave
A very deadly accent.

ECHO   *Deadly accent.*

DELIO I told you 'twas a pretty one: you may make it
A huntsman, or a falconer, a musician,
Or a thing of sorrow.

ECHO   *A thing of sorrow.*

ANTONIO Aye, sure, that suits it best.

ECHO   *That suits
it best.*

ANTONIO 'Tis very like my wife's voice.

ECHO   *Aye,
wife's voice.*

DELIO Come, let's walk further from 't. I would not have you
Go to th' Cardinal's tonight: do not.

ECHO   *Do not.*

DELIO Wisdom doth not more moderate wasting sorrow
Than time: take time for 't; be mindful of thy safety.

ECHO *Be mindful of thy safety.*

ANTONIO   Necessity compels me:
Make scrutiny throughout the passes of

Your own life, you'll find it impossible
To fly your fate.

ECHO   *O, fly your fate.*

DELIO   Hark!
The dead stones seem to have pity on you, and give you
Good counsel.

ANTONIO Echo, I will not talk with thee,
For thou art a dead thing.

ECHO   *Thou art a dead thing.*

ANTONIO My duchess is asleep now,
And her little ones, I hope sweetly: O Heaven,
Shall I never see her more?

ECHO   *Never see her more.*

ANTONIO I marked not one repetition of the echo
But that; and on the sudden a clear light
Presented me a face folded in sorrow.

DELIO Your fancy merely.

ANTONIO   Come, I'll be out of this ague,
For to live thus is not indeed to live;
It is a mockery and abuse of life:
I will not henceforth save myself by halves;
Lose all, or nothing.

DELIO   Your own virtue save you!
I'll fetch your eldest son, and second you:
It may be that the sight of his own blood
Spread in so sweet a figure may beget
The more compassion. However, fare you well.
Though in our miseries Fortune have a part,
Yet in our noble sufferings she hath none:
Contempt of pain, that we may call our own.
[*Exeunt.*]

SCENE FOUR

*Milan, the palace of the Cardinal and Ferdinand.
Enter Cardinal, Pescara, Malateste, Roderigo,
and Grisolan.*

CARDINAL You shall not watch tonight by the sick prince;
His grace is very well recovered.

MALATESTE Good my lord, suffer us.

CARDINAL   Oh, by no means;
The noise, and change of object in his eye,
Doth more distract him: I pray, all to bed;

And though you hear him in his violent fit,
Do not rise, I entreat you.

PESCARA   So, sir; we shall not.

CARDINAL Nay, I must have you promise upon your honors,
For I was enjoined to 't by himself; and he seemed
To urge it sensibly.[134]

PESCARA   Let our honors bind
This trifle.

CARDINAL Nor any of your followers.

MALATESTE   Neither.

CARDINAL It may be, to make trial of your promise,
When he's asleep, myself will rise and feign
Some of his mad tricks, and cry out for help,
And feign myself in danger.

MALATESTE   If your throat were cutting,
I'd not come at you, now I have protested against it.

CARDINAL Why, I thank you.

GRISOLAN   'Twas a foul storm tonight.

RODERIGO The Lord Ferdinand's chamber shook like an osier.

MALATESTE 'Twas nothing but pure kindness in the devil,
To rock his own child.
[*Exeunt all except the Cardinal.*]

CARDINAL The reason why I would not suffer these
About my brother, is, because at midnight
I may with better privacy convey
Julia's body to her own lodging. O, my conscience!
I would pray now; but the devil takes away my heart
For having any confidence in prayer.
About this hour I appointed Bosola
To fetch the body: when he hath served my turn,
He dies.
[*Exit. Enter Bosola.*]

BOSOLA Ha! 'twas the Cardinal's voice; I heard him name
Bosola and my death. Listen; I hear

[134] With strong feeling.

One's footing.

[*Enter Ferdinand.*]

FERDINAND   Strangling is a very quiet death.

BOSOLA [*aside*]   Nay, then, I see I must stand
upon my guard.

FERDINAND   What say to that? whisper softly; do
you agree to 't? So; it must be done i' th' dark:
the Cardinal would not for a thousand pounds
the doctor should see it.

BOSOLA   My death is plotted; here 's the consequence of murder.

We value not desert nor Christian breath,

When we know black deeds must be cured with
death.

[*Enter Antonio and Servant.*]

SERVANT   Here stay, sir, and be confident, I pray:
I'll fetch you a dark lantern.

[*Exit.*]

ANTONIO   Could I take him
At his prayers, there were hope of pardon.

BOSOLA   Fall
right, my sword!—

[*Stabs him.*]

I'll not give thee so much leisure as to pray.

ANTONIO   O, I am gone! Thou hast ended a long
suit
In a minute.

BOSOLA   What art thou?

ANTONIO   A most wretched
thing,
That only have thy benefit in death,
To appear myself.

[*Reenter Servant with a lantern.*]

SERVANT   Where are you, sir?

ANTONIO   Very near
my home.—Bosola?

SERVANT   O, misfortune!

BOSOLA   Smother thy pity, thou art dead else.—
Antonio?
The man I would have saved 'bove mine own
life!
We are merely the stars' tennis-balls, struck and
bandied
Which way please them.—O good Antonio,
I'll whisper one thing in thy dying ear
Shall make thy heart break quickly! thy fair
duchess
And two sweet children—

ANTONIO   Their very names

Kindle a little life in me.

BOSOLA   Are murdered.

ANTONIO   Some men have wished to die
At the hearing of sad tidings; I am glad
That I shall do 't in sadness:[135] I would not
now
Wish my wounds balmed nor healed, for I have
no use
To put my life to. In all our quest of greatness,
Like wanton boys, whose pastime is their care,
We follow after bubbles blown in th' air.
Pleasure of life, what is 't? only the good
Hours of an ague; merely a preparative
To rest, to endure vexation. I do not ask
The process[136] of my death; only commend me
To Delio.

BOSOLA   Break, heart!

ANTONIO   And let my son
Fly the courts of princes.

[*Dies.*]

BOSOLA   Thou seem'st
To have loved Antonio?

SERVANT   I brought him hither,
To have reconciled him to the Cardinal.

BOSOLA   I do not ask thee that.
Take him up, if thou tender thine own life,
And bear him where the lady Julia
Was wont to lodge.—Oh, my fate moves swift;
I have this Cardinal in the forge already;
Now I'll bring him to th' hammer. O direful
misprision![137]
I will not imitate things glorious,
No more than base; I'll be mine own exam-
ple.—
On, on, and look thou represent, for silence,
The thing thou bear'st.

[*Exeunt.*]

SCENE FIVE

The same. Enter Cardinal, with a book.

CARDINAL   I am puzzled in a question about
hell:
He says, in hell there's one material fire,
And yet it shall not burn all men alike.

---

[135] In reality.
[136] Account.
[137] Mistake.

Lay him by. How tedious is a guilty conscience!
When I look into the fishponds in my garden,
Methinks I see a thing armed with a rake,
That seems to strike at me.
[*Enter Bosola and Servant bearing Antonio's body.*]
                          Now, art thou come?
Thou look'st ghastly:
There sits in thy face some great determination
Mixed with some fear.

BOSOLA   Thus it lightens into
    action:
I am come to kill thee.

CARDINAL   Ha!—Help! our guard!

BOSOLA Thou art deceived; they are out of thy
    howling.

CARDINAL Hold; and I will faithfully divide
    Revenues with thee.

BOSOLA   Thy prayers and proffers
Are both unseasonable.

CARDINAL   Raise the watch!
We are betrayed!

BOSOLA   I have confined your flight:
I'll suffer your retreat to Julia's chamber,
But no further.

CARDINAL Help! we are betrayed!
[*Enter, above, Pescara, Malateste, Roderigo, and Grisolan.*]

MALATESTE Listen.

CARDINAL   My dukedom for rescue!

RODERIGO   Fie
    upon
His counterfeiting!

MALATESTE   Why, 'tis not the Cardinal.

RODERIGO Yes, yes, 'tis he: but I'll see him
    hanged
Ere I'll go down to him.

CARDINAL   Here's a plot upon me;
I am assaulted! I am lost, unless some rescue.

GRISOLAN He doth this pretty well; but it will
    not serve
To laugh me out of mine honor.

CARDINAL   The sword's at
    my throat!

RODERIGO You would not bawl so loud then.

MALATESTE   Come,
    come,
Let's go to bed: he told us thus much aforehand.

PESCARA He wished you should not come at
    him; but, believe 't,
The accent of the voice sounds not in jest:
I'll down to him, howsoever, and with engines
Force ope the doors.
[*Exit above.*]

RODERIGO   Let's follow him aloof,
And note how the Cardinal will laugh at him.
[*Exeunt, above, Malateste, Roderigo, and Grisolan.*]

BOSOLA There's for first,
[*Kills the Servant.*]
'Cause you shall not unbarricade the door
To let in rescue.

CARDINAL What cause hast thou to pursue my
    life?

BOSOLA Look there.

CARDINAL Antonio?

BOSOLA   Slain by my hand unwit-
    tingly.
Pray, and be sudden: when thou killed'st thy
    sister,
Thou took'st from Justice her most equal bal-
ance,
And left her naught but her sword.

CARDINAL   O, mercy!

BOSOLA Now, it seems thy greatness was only
    outward,
For thou fall'st faster of thyself than calamity
Can drive thee. I'll not waste longer time;
    there!
[*Stabs him.*]

CARDINAL Thou hast hurt me.

BOSOLA   Again!
[*Stabs him again.*]

CARDINAL   Shall I die
    like a leveret,[138]
Without any resistance?—Help, help, help!
I am slain!
[*Enter Ferdinand.*]

FERDINAND Th' alarum? give me a fresh horse;
Rally the vaunt-guard, or the day is lost.
Yield, yield! I give you the honor of arms,
Shake my sword over you; will you yield?

CARDINAL   Help
    me;
I am your brother!

[138] A hare in its first year.

The Duchess of Malfi   247

FERDINAND   The devil! My brother fight
Upon the adverse party?
[*He wounds the Cardinal, and, in the scuffle, gives Bosola his death-wound.*]
                                   There flies your ransom.
CARDINAL   O justice!
I suffer now for what hath former bin:
Sorrow is held the eldest child of sin.
FERDINAND   Now you're brave fellows. Caesar's fortune was harder than Pompey's; Caesar died in the arms of prosperity, Pompey at the feet of disgrace. You both died in the field. The pain's nothing: pain many times is taken away with the apprehension of greater, as the toothache with the sight of a barber that comes to pull it out: there's philosophy for you.
BOSOLA   Now my revenge is perfect.—Sink, thou main cause
[*Kills Ferdinand.*]
Of my undoing!—The last part of my life
Hath done me best service.
FERDINAND   Give me some wet hay; I am broken-winded.
I do account this world but a dog-kennel:
I will vault credit[139] and affect[140] high pleasures
Beyond death.
BOSOLA   He seems to come to himself,
Now he's so near the bottom.
FERDINAND   My sister, O my sister! there's the cause on 't.
Whether we fall by ambition, blood, or lust,
Like diamonds we are cut with our own dust.
[*Dies.*]
CARDINAL   Thou hast thy payment too.
BOSOLA   Yes, I hold my weary soul in my teeth.
'Tis ready to part from me. I do glory
That thou, which stood'st like a huge pyramid
Begun upon a large and ample base,
Shalt end in a little point, a kind of nothing.
[*Enter, below, Pescara, Malateste, Roderigo, and Grisolan.*]
PESCARA   How now, my lord?
MALATESTE   O sad disaster!
RODERIGO   How
Comes this?

139 Overleap expectation.
140 Aspire to.

BOSOLA   Revenge for the Duchess of Malfi murdered
By th' Aragonian brethren; for Antonio
Slain by this hand; for lustful Julia
Poisoned by this man; and lastly for myself,
That was an actor in the main of all,
Much 'gainst mine own good nature, yet i' th' end
Neglected.
PESCARA   How now, my lord?
CARDINAL   Look to my brother: he gave us these large wounds
As we were struggling here i' the rushes.[141]
And now,
I pray, let me be laid by and never thought of.
[*Dies.*]
PESCARA   How fatally, it seems, he did withstand
His own rescue!
MALATESTE   Thou wretched thing of blood,
How came Antonio by his death?
BOSOLA   In a mist;
I know not how: such a mistake as I
Have often seen in a play. O, I am gone!
We are only like dead walls or vaulted graves,
That, ruined, yield no echo. Fare you well.
It may be pain, but no harm, to me to die
In so good a quarrel. O, this gloomy world!
In what a shadow, or deep pit of darkness,
Doth, womanish and fearful, mankind live!
Let worthy minds ne'er stagger in distrust
To suffer death or shame for what is just:
Mine is another voyage.
[*Dies.*]
PESCARA   The noble Delio, as I came to the palace,
Told me of Antonio's being here, and showed me
A pretty gentleman, his son and heir.
[*Enter Delio and Antonio's son.*]
MALATESTE   O sir,
You come too late!
DELIO   I heard so, and was armed for 't
Ere I came. Let us make noble use
Of this great ruin; and join all our force
To establish this young hopeful gentleman

141 Used as floor coverings.

In 's mother's right. These wretched eminent
  things
Leave no more fame behind 'em, than should
  one
Fall in a frost, and leave his print in snow;
As soon as the sun shines, it ever melts,
Both form and matter. I have ever thought

Nature doth nothing so great for great men
  As when she's pleased to make them lords of
  truth:
Integrity of life is fame's best friend,
Which nobly, beyond death, shall crown the
  end.
[*Exeunt.*]

STRUCTURE—or lack of it—in The Duchess of Malfi *has been the play's most discussed feature. Webster is seemingly careless of motivation; negligent of the time element; inconsistent, even contradictory in details; and unsure of focus. His ability in design has been attacked as grossly inept, defended as merely unusual, and dismissed as irrelevant.*

[*The Duchess of Malfi*] is . . . in the first half a mere simple narrative of events, leading up to a long-continued and various hell in the second part. It is often discussed if the [plot of the play is] weak. Webster's method does not really take cognisance of a plot in the ordinary sense of the word. He is too atmospheric. It is like enquiring if there is bad drawing in a nocturne of Whistler's. [Rupert Brooke, *John Webster and the Elizabethan Drama*, Sidgwick & Jackson, Ltd., London, 1916, pp. 96–97.]

Among the snatches of real poetry in the dialogue, I hesitate to include the much admired speech of Ferdinand: "Cover her face: mine eyes dazzle: she died young." It is not difficult to hit upon sayings which shall pass for tightly dramatic simply because they are unforeseen and unlikely. I shall not, however, attempt to strike the balance between poetry and laboured rhetoric in the writing of the play: my point is that, as a work of dramatic architecture, it is about as bad as it can possibly be. The poet slavishly follows the straggling narrative of his original, where, if he knew the rudiments of his business, he ought to compress and concentrate; and where he departs from his original, it is to invent crude and arbitrary horrors which would

be hooted or laughed off the stage if a melodramatist of today dared to offer them to his public. [William Archer, *The Old Drama and the New,* Small, Maynard and Co., Boston, 1923, p. 61.]

To William Archer . . . Webster is a morbid being, something of a poet, but dramatically quite incompetent. Let us first consider how far this charge of incompetence is really justified by Webster's plots. For it is, I think, quite possible to underrate even his stage-craft until we learn to look at his tragedies as his audience saw them —less as wholes than as a series of great situations. Webster cannot give his plays a close-knit logical unity; he is often childishly irrelevant; and his characters are sometimes wildly inconsistent from scene to scene. That was the fashion of his day. But his work remains more than a mere chaos of dramatic fragments, and he is a highly successful playwright in his own Gothic style. . . . Like some great ragged thundercloud he piles up slowly to overshadow his world with the sinister yellow darkness that he loves; the atmosphere grows stifling; and then comes the sudden glare before which the situation lies revealed in all its vivid nakedness, with an intensity of black and white that calm daylight could never have given. [F. L. Lucas, "General Introduction," *The Complete Works of John Webster,* vol. 1, Chatto & Windus, Ltd., London, 1927, pp. 20–21.]

Here then we enter Webster's kingdom; the interplay of thought, the meeting of mind and mind in the double and simultaneous expression of action and reflection. The true plot of his play is not the events which proceed upon the surface and are flung off, as it were, as a casual expression, but the progress of the minds of the central figures toward deeper and deeper self-knowledge, the approach to the impenetrable mystery of fate perceived in the moments of intensest suffering and action, which are also the moments of clearest insight. [U. M. Ellis-Fermor, *The Jacobean Drama,* 3d ed., rev., Methuen & Co., Ltd., London, 1953, p. 176.]

The pattern of Websterian tragedy is this. The hideous norms of the world are mortality and oppression. An individual struggles to escape the laws of the norm, is caught, falls back, and is reabsorbed in the general level. This pattern of aberrational struggle and defeat continually recurs. It is a law of man's nature and his world. Thus the most individualistic action becomes horribly typical. [Travis Bogard, *The Tragic Satire of John Webster,* University of California Press, Berkeley, Calif., 1955, p. 43.]

It is Webster's limitation that, like certain others of his fellow dramatists, he fell back at times on the easy shorthand of theatrical effectiveness to carry him over difficulties in the solution of the technical problems which stood in his way. We do not have to make a virtue of his failures; at the same time we have also to bear in mind that tidiness and logic of design is more to be expected in the case of a play like, say, *The Silver Box* than of *The Duchess of Malfi.* [Moody E. Prior, *The Language of Tragedy,* Columbia University Press, New York, 1947, p. 132.]

A structural problem of particular importance is posed by the last act. The solution of this problem is intimately connected with questions of theme and meaning in the play.

The interest of the play is over [with Act 4]; for Antonio is admittedly a shadowy character as to whose fate we are very indifferent; and though we are willing enough to see Ferdinand, the Cardinal and Bosola punished, we could quite well dispense with that gratification. Webster, however, is not the man to leave any of his dramatis personae alive if he can help it; so he gives us a fifth act in which five more persons are killed off. [Archer, *op. cit.,* p. 60.]

The fifth act has repeatedly been criticized as an anti-climactic cluttering of the stage with corpses. It is true that with the death of the Duchess in the fourth act a light goes out of the play. The heroic story has been told. But the satiric story, the revelation of the real condition of man's world, has not been completed. The fifth act with its frightening development of the theme of death is essential to the picture of the tragic world.

The fourth act shows the destruction of good by evil and the way in which humanity can assert its integrity even in defeat. The fifth act shows what happens in a world where good is dead and integrity is absent. [Bogard, *op. cit.,* p. 140.]

Because the play is called *The Duchess of Malfi,* she has been looked on as its key figure; and her creator has been censured for continuing the play for another act after her death. But though she is the heroine in the sense that she is the chief object of our sympathies, she does not provide the chief motive force in the action; nor is it, in her relation to that action, that the theme of the play is to be found. This theme, as always with Webster, is the act of sin and its consequences. Till these consequences are followed out to their final conclusion, the dramatist's intention is not made plain. Moreover the central figure, as far as that action is concerned, is the man who murders her; the man who has elected, against the promptings of his better self, to be the devil's agent in the drama. [David Cecil, *Poets and Story-Tellers*, The Macmillan Company, New York, 1949, p. 39.]

Webster's characters appear to some as individuals, to others as types. Attitudes vary also on the relationship between character and action.

Though the popular conception of [Webster] is rather one of immense gloom and perpetual preoccupation with death, his power lies almost more in the intense, sometimes horrible, vigour of some of his scenes, and his uncanny probing to the depths of the heart. In his characters you see the instincts at work jerking and actuating them, and emotions pouring out irregularly, unconsciously, in floods or spurts and jets, driven outward from within, as you sometimes do in real people. [Brooke, *op. cit.*, p. 123.]

Websterian tragedy can be fully comprehended only when it is understood that development of character, in the sense that Shakespeare's heroes change and grow, is not a central element. If Shakespeare's tragedy be conceived as a vortex, centering the moral universe in the suffering soul of an individual, then Webster's may be likened to a framed general action, like a stage panorama, which makes its most significant revelations through the presentation of man's relations to man. . . . Shakespearian tragedy is individual, with a suggested generality of application; Websterian tragedy is broadly social, with individuals serving as normative examples of Webster's conception of life. [Bogard, *op. cit.*, p. 39.]

His purpose seems to be to create, as rapidly as is consistent with fullness and depth, a pic-

ture of the world in which his characters move; a world created of their thoughts and of the deeds which are the outcome of their thoughts. Any process which will quickly make us free of this country is fitting for his purpose, whether dramatic revelation or repeated analysis of one character by the others; any process that will bring us quickly to knowledge of and intimacy with these people, so that we may understand, as with a lifetime's familiarity, the field of the mind in which each moves. From this point of view, the first act is often given over to this induction; by the end of it we see the characters his people present to the world and something also of the underlying character guessed at sometimes by the others, known with a greater or less degree of consciousness by themselves, and by the dramatist profoundly and subtly understood. [Ellis-Fermor, *op. cit.*, p. 175.]

The people in . . . *The Duchess of Malfi* become representative rather than individual and are viewed in terms of their outward aspects rather than their inner natures. Once their fundamental identities are established, their course of action, rebellious, oppressive, or merely yielding, becomes more important than their motives. It is the fight, not the character of the fighter, that reveals most about the tragic structure of the world. [Bogard, *op. cit.*, p. 43.]

In their attempts to explain or resolve Bosola's apparent inconsistencies, critics have approached the character both through types from which it develops and through its supposed functions in the play.

[Webster's tool-villains] . . . represent two incongruous, incompatible rôles,—malcontent and tool-villain. . . . Now one rôle is uppermost, now the other, now villain, now moralist, without any ethical or psychological coherence between the two, without even an effort for such coherence in the shape of a contention of motives.

For motives they, as conventional figures, have none. As tool-villains it is their part, for all their fine ideas, implicitly to obey their master; as malcontents, to meditate gloomily and rail and flout. . . .

Yet in Bosola Webster tried, perhaps, to connect the two alien rôles, to intimate by Bosola's scruples—once at hiring out to Ferdinand and once in the middle of his work—and by his later repentance and vengeance, the contention of two natures within him. But that is mere plastering and patchwork. Only at these moments does Webster deal with the motives of Bosola. . . . Really, he is . . . a dramaturgic puppet, a fine sort of stage property. [E. E. Stoll, *John Webster,* Alfred Mudge and Son, Boston, 1905, pp. 124–126.]

Despite all his activity in the play, [Bosola] is less a character than a chorus. We cannot put his features together and make a living man out of them. He is simply a creature out of the night, the very dust grown self-conscious, death with a human heart. [Clifford Leech, *John Webster: A Critical Study,* Hogarth Press, Ltd., London, 1951, pp. 88–89.]

Bosola sees himself as a Machiavellian . . . but it is a reflective Machiavellian, a man philosophizing upon "policy" itself. To the court, however, he presents not quite this character, but that of the conventional melancholy villain, despising a world that has despised him; a disguise that is penetrated by the astute Antonio,

who at the same time makes us aware of a third Bosola, the one who, underlying both of these, gradually emerges, to the point of self recognition, as the play goes on:

> ANTONIO You would looke up to Heaven, but I thinke
> The Divell, that rules i' th' aire, stands in your light [Act 2, Scene 1].

[Ellis-Fermor, *op. cit.,* p. 178.]

With respect to his own tragedy, Bosola's emergence may be described as follows: as a kind of cynical act of rebellion against an evil universe, he pursues an evil course himself, rationalizing it in terms of gratitude and devotion to Ferdinand. He learns, through observing the suffering of the Duchess and through his other experiences, the virtue of her passiveness and a somewhat more masculine, active concept, which is that even in an evil universe one must remain virtuous—true to himself: one must *be* himself. This, in Malraux's famous phrase, is *la condition humaine;* and this is one of the facts which give tragic significance to human life. So Bosola seems to suggest, in his dying words [Act 5, Scene 5]. [C. G. Thayer, "The Ambiguity of Bosola," *Studies in Philology,* vol. 54, 1957, p. 171.]

What may appear to be development in Bosola, from a thing of evil to a man filled with remorse, is in fact no more than a return to what he essentially is. He is the example of a man who has lost integrity of life. He has put aside his essential nature, forfeiting his "own shape" in order to serve Ferdinand, and in so doing has been false to himself. Only in the end, when the Duchess is dead, does his integrity reassert itself. But it is then too late for redemption. [Bogard, *op. cit.,* pp. 78–79.]

The weakness and implausibility of Ferdinand's stated motives contrast strangely with his intensity of emotion.

There is not the smallest reason why [the brothers] should object to their sister's making an open and honourable marriage. Towards the end of the play, this thought seems to strike Ferdinand, and he tells us that . . .

> he had a hope,
> Had she continued widow, to have gained
> An infinite mass of treasure by her death.

but it is hard to guess how this can be, seeing that the Duchess has a surviving son by her first marriage. [Archer, *op. cit.*, p. 53.]

Even if Archer's objection . . . is set aside, Ferdinand's statement still fails to explain his savagery toward the Duchess. [Prior, *op. cit.*, p. 123.]

We should note, indeed, that Webster puts the whole weight of the persecution on him. Certainly in Act I, scene i the Cardinal joins him in forbidding their sister to marry again, it is the Cardinal who procures her banishment from Ancona, and it is made abundantly clear that the Cardinal is privy to her death. But when the two men appear together there is no question which is the more deeply moved. . . . It is Ferdinand who controls the slow tormenting and execution in Act IV. It is Ferdinand who suffers lycanthropy when his sister is dead. [Leech, *op. cit.*, pp. 99–100.]

Ferdinand alone misstates the events of the play in accord with the rankness that lies within

him; the others, however foul themselves, perceive their relative position more clearly and there is no such complex reversal of values in the imagery which they employ. The imagery is in the case of the Duke clearly an important— rather an essential means in the presentation of a complex and difficult psychological case, and to disregard it is to come short of understanding the character. [Prior, *op. cit.*, p. 124.]

As the action of [the] play progresses, it often appears that . . . the Duchess [is] oppressed not so much by individuals, feeling personal hatreds, desire for revenge, and lust to kill, as by representatives of destructive instincts in human nature, momentarily abstracted from personal motivation. In very real ways, Webster keeps death, disease, insanity, and other forces which destroy men's bodies and souls before the minds of the audience. [Bogard, *op. cit.*, p. 50.]

If the action of the play is to be comprehensible, we must assume in Ferdinand an incestuous passion of which he is not fully aware. . . . [His stated hope to have enriched himself by her death is] inconsistent with the reference in the play to the Duchess's son by her first husband; either, then, Webster wished here to emphasize Ferdinand's uncertainty about his own motives, or the dramatist was himself not fully conscious of the springs of action in his play. . . . But, whether or not Webster knew it, he drew Ferdinand as a man who could not rid himself of his sister's image. [Leech, *op. cit.*, pp. 100–101.]

Despite her general attractiveness, the Duchess has not impressed all critics as being completely guiltless.

The Duchess had the innocence of abundant life in a sick and melancholy society, where the fact that she has "youth and a little beauty" is precisely why she is hated. She reminds us too that one of the essential characteristics of inno-

cence in the martyr is an unwillingness to die. When Bosola comes to murder her he makes elaborate attempts to put her half in love with easeful death and to suggest that death is really a deliverance. The attempt is motivated by a grimly controlled pity, and is roughly the equivalent of the vinegar sponge in the Passion. When the Duchess, her back to the wall, says "I am the Duchess of Malfi still," "still" having its full weight of "always," we understand how it is that even after her death her invisible presence continues to be the most vital character in the play. [Northrop Frye, *Anatomy of Criticism,* Princeton University Press, Princeton, N. J., 1957, pp. 219–220.]

Yet we must recognise that her wooing and her marriage with Antonio constitute an overturning of a social code: she defies the responsibilities of "degree," both as a woman in speaking first and as a Duchess in marrying beneath her. . . . The Duchess is both over-ambitious in her overtures to Antonio and careless of her Duchy's good.

Moreover, she was a widow, and in the seventeenth century the woman who re-married did not escape criticism. . . .

But indeed the more we consider the Duchess, the more hints of guilt seem to appear. There is even a strange parallel between the wooing scene, where the Duchess hides Cariola behind the arras and then launches into the declaration of her love, and the scene in Act V, Scene II where Julia, the rank whore, proclaims her passion for Bosola and then hides him in her cabinet while she extorts a confession of guilt from the Cardinal: in both cases, a woman's frank avowal; in both, a hidden witness; in both, a woman's triumph leading to her destruction. It is difficult to resist the idea that Julia is meant to provide a comment on the behaviour of the Duchess: they are sisters, Webster hints, in their passions and in their consequent actions. There is, too, an independence of mind, a note of challenge, in the Duchess's references to religion. . . . This

[hint of irreligion] is to be joined with the Duchess's cursing in Act IV, Scene I.

> I could curse the Starres. . . .
> And those three smyling seasons of the
>   yeere
> Into a Russian winter: nay the world
> To its first Chaos.

Her provocation has been dreadful, but this longing for the first chaos links her with many characters in Elizabethan and Jacobean drama whose ambitions are thwarted and who would in anger overturn the hierarchies of "degree." . . . Here Webster shows us a woman at odds with life itself. So too her clinging to her own identity as the one thing, the one value, left in a world gone fantastically evil—"I am Duchesse of *Malfy* still." . . . There is a grandeur in the egoism, but its implications are essentially anarchic. [Leech, *op. cit.,* pp. 69–77.]

The spirit of greatness or the spirit of woman: the spirit of implacable defiance of the worst of fate or the spirit of submission; the spirit of courage or the spirit of fear; of integrity or death. These are the forces which are brought into sharp conflict within Webster's heroine. It is the spirit of woman which will threaten to destroy her integrity. Through her womanish fears, evil will cause her to betray her greatness and bring her, possessed of a "fearful madness," to the verge of the destructive escape insanity provides. . . .

Only at the last can she disperse the mist of terror which has prevented her dignified acceptance of her fate. The spirit of greatness mounts high in her. . . . The Duchess, firm in her resolve, and fixing her faith in heaven, goes quietly to her death. [Bogard, *op. cit.,* pp. 65, 78.]

While some critics have found no coherent meaning in Webster's play, others have suggested a variety of meanings.

Indeed, so much was [imagining encounters between persons Webster's] deepest and most individual concern that the separate scene and its implications could be at odds with other parts

of the play. There is no confusion when we see the Duchess as neglectful of duty and yet the focus of our strongest sympathy and our admiration: those things can cohere in this play. . . .

But there is, I think, an element of imperfect resolution in the Duchess of Malfi, in that we are not at any one time made simultaneously conscious of the separate strands in the pattern. In fact, Webster's mind and attention do seem divided. The play includes a not very successfully handled tragedy of Ferdinand; at times it approaches (never, I think, quite reaches) the condition of the emblem-writing, with suffering goodness exhibited to our view; at other times the frailty of the Duchess is underlined and explored; and at the end we are offered, somewhat carelessly, the notion that the Cardinal and Ferdinand have been mere intruders on a normality which will be restored in the person of the young Duke. . . . In *The Duchess* we are pulled successively in different directions, and on the completion of our reading we are likely to feel we have the task of constructing a whole of which Webster has given us the separate parts. [Clifford Leech, "An Addendum on Webster's Duchess," *Philological Quarterly*, vol. 27, 1958, p. 256.]

[Webster] brings his people, by the most careful preparation, to the position in which, if ever, a man should see absolute reality—and before them is only "a mist." It is for him as for a later dramatist [Ibsen in *Peer Gynt*], this negation, this quality of nothingness, this empty, boundless, indefinable grey mist that is the final horror, the symbol of ignorance, of the infinite empty space in which man hovers, the material and the spiritual world both in different terms unreal. [Ellis-Fermor, *op. cit.*, pp. 172–173.]

His vision is a moral one. Webster sees life as a struggle between right and wrong. Or rather between good and evil. Here we come to one of the key facts about him. He was a child of his age; the age of the Reformation: and he conceived morality in religious terms. An act to him was wrong, not because it interfered with the happiness of man in this world, but because it was a sin; a breach of the eternal laws established by the God who created man. Moreover it was a voluntary breach. Here again he reveals himself the child of a Christian society. Men to him are not the helpless sport of an indifferent fate as they were to the Greeks. Possessed of free will, his villains sin deliberately. These evil voluntary acts are the cause of human tragedy. Indeed his subject matter may be summed up as a study of the working of sin in the world. [Cecil, *op. cit.*, pp. 29–30.]

In Webster's world there is no justice, no law, either of God or man, to mete out punishment for evil and reward for good. Death itself is not justice but the normal course of events, the culmination of spiritual and physical decay. Honor and revenge do not signify in the end, for, whether the death be violent or natural, it is always a working out through men of forces larger than man. Evil and good are dragged down together in death, just as they are meshed together in life. The only triumph comes when, even in the moment of defeat, an individual is roused to assert his own integrity of life. This is not a question of virtue and vice. In Webster's tragic world, characters are significant not because of their morality but because of their struggle. Some lose their identities in the forces of evil. Some die in the attempt to preserve the good. But ultimately it is the struggling ones, the splendid fighters for self, who matter. [Bogard, *op. cit.*, p. 79.]

MOLIÈRE

(Jean Baptiste Poquelin)

1622–1673

Jean Baptiste Poquelin was the son of a prosperous upholsterer who became attached to the French Court and was consequently able to send his son to one of the best schools in Paris: the Collège de Clermont, a private school run by the Jesuit order. Here Jean Baptiste was introduced to Roman comedy and to acting by performing in Latin plays written by the faculty. When it became necessary to choose a career he began the study of law, but abandoned this pursuit after only one semester and joined a theatrical company. It was at this time that he took the name Molière, possibly to avoid embarrassing his father, since actors were not considered quite respectable. After a brief, unsuccessful attempt to survive in Paris, in 1644 the company, with Molière heading it, set out to tour the provinces, playing a repertory consisting mainly of farces. During this period Molière encountered Italian theatrical companies, and the influence of the commedia dell' arte *was added to the earlier one of Roman comedy. Probably to enhance his company's chances for success, Molière now turned to the writing of comedy; his first important work,* The Blunderer, *was written in 1655. This play, like other early ones of Molière, was farce, but shortly after the company scored a success in the Court of Louis XIV in 1658 he began writing social comedy with* The Affected Ladies. *Most of Molière's plays are a mixture of farce and social satire, for he sought to entertain while provoking "thoughtful laughter."* Le Misanthrope *(1666) makes use*

of character types but contains less action than do most of
Molière's plays. In addition, the thought is more complex and
ambiguous than is customary in Molière. It was perhaps for this
reason that it was at best only moderately successful when first
performed.

The Misanthrope

DONE INTO ENGLISH VERSE BY RICHARD WILBUR

Characters

ALCESTE *in love with Célimène*

PHILINTE *Alceste's friend*

ORONTE *in love with Célimène*

CÉLIMÈNE *Alceste's beloved*

ELIANTE *Célimène's cousin*

ARSINOÉ *a friend of Célimène*

ACASTE, CLITANDRE *marquesses*

BASQUE *Célimène's servant*

A GUARD *of the Marshalsea*

DUBOIS *Alceste's valet*

The scene throughout is in Célimène's house at Paris.

Act One

SCENE ONE

Philinte, Alceste.

PHILINTE Now, what's got into you?

ALCESTE [*seated*] Kindly leave me alone.

PHILINTE Come, come, what is it? This lugubrious tone . . .

ALCESTE Leave me, I said; you spoil my solitude.

PHILINTE Oh, listen to me, now, and don't be rude.

ALCESTE I choose to be rude, Sir, and to be hard of hearing.

PHILINTE These ugly moods of yours are not endearing;
Friends though we are, I really must insist . . .

ALCESTE [*abruptly rising*] Friends? Friends, you say? Well, cross me off your list.
I've been your friend till now, as you well know;
But after what I saw a moment ago
I tell you flatly that our ways must part.
I wish no place in a dishonest heart.

PHILINTE Why, what have I done, Alceste? Is this quite just?

ALCESTE My God, you ought to die of self-disgust.
I call your conduct inexcusable, Sir,
And every man of honor will concur.
I see you almost hug a man to death,
Exclaim for joy until you're out of breath,

259

And supplement these loving demonstrations
With endless offers, vows, and protestations;
Then when I ask you "Who was that?" I find
That you can barely bring his name to mind!
Once the man's back is turned, you cease to
    love him,
And speak with absolute indifference of him!
By God, I say it's base and scandalous
To falsify the heart's affections thus;
If I caught myself behaving in such a way,
I'd hang myself for shame, without delay.

PHILINTE It hardly seems a hanging matter to
    me;
I hope that you will take it graciously
If I extend myself a slight reprieve,
And live a little longer, by your leave.

ALCESTE How dare you joke about a crime so
    grave?

PHILINTE What crime? How else are people to
    behave?

ALCESTE I'd have them be sincere, and never
    part
With any word that isn't from the heart.

PHILINTE When someone greets us with a show
    of pleasure,
It's but polite to give him equal measure,
Return his love the best that we know how,
And trade him offer for offer, vow for vow.

ALCESTE No, no, this formula you'd have me
    follow,
However fashionable, is false and hollow,
And I despise the frenzied operations
Of all these barterers of protestations,
These lavishers of meaningless embraces,
These utterers of obliging commonplaces,
Who court and flatter everyone on earth
And praise the fool no less than the man of
    worth.
Should you rejoice that someone fondles you,
Offers his love and service, swears to be true,
And fills your ears with praises of your name,
When to the first damned fop he'll say the
    same?
No, no: no self-respecting heart would dream
Of prizing so promiscuous an esteem;
However high the praise, there's nothing worse
Than sharing honors with the universe
Esteem is founded on comparison:
To honor all men is to honor none.

Since you embrace this indiscriminate vice,
Your friendship comes at far too cheap a price;
I spurn the easy tribute of a heart
Which will not set the worthy man apart:
I choose, Sir, to be chosen; and in fine,
The friend of mankind is no friend of mine.

PHILINTE But in polite society, custom decrees
That we show certain outward courtesies. . . .

ALCESTE Ah, no! we should condemn with all
    our force
Such false and artificial intercourse.
Let men behave like men; let them display
Their inmost hearts in everything they say;
Let the heart speak, and let our sentiments
Not mask themselves in silly compliments.

PHILINTE In certain cases it would be uncouth
And most absurd to speak the naked truth;
With all respect for your exalted notions,
It's often best to veil one's true emotions.
Wouldn't the social fabric come undone
If we were wholly frank with everyone?
Suppose you met with someone you couldn't
    bear;
Would you inform him of it then and there?

ALCESTE Yes.

PHILINTE   Then you'd tell old Emilie it's
    pathetic
The way she daubs her features with cosmetic
And plays the gay coquette at sixty-four?

ALCESTE I would.

PHILINTE And you'd call Dorilas a bore,
And tell him every ear at court is lame
From hearing him brag about his noble name?

ALCESTE Precisely.

PHILINTE   Ah, you're joking.

ALCESTE   *Au con-
    traire:*
In this regard there's none I'd choose to spare.
All are corrupt; there's nothing to be seen
In court or town but aggravates my spleen.
I fall into deep gloom and melancholy
When I survey the scene of human folly,
Finding on every hand base flattery,
Injustice, fraud, self-interest, treachery. . . .
Ah, it's too much; mankind has grown so base,
I mean to break with the whole human race.

PHILINTE This philosophic rage is a bit extreme;
You've no idea how comical you seem;
Indeed, we're like those brothers in the play

Called *School for Husbands*,[1] one of whom was prey . . .

ALCESTE   Enough now! None of your stupid similes.

PHILINTE   Then let's have no more tirades, if you please.
The world won't change, whatever you say or do;
And since plain speaking means so much to you,
I'll tell you plainly that by being frank
You've earned the reputation of a crank,
And that you're thought ridiculous when you rage
And rant against the manners of the age.

ALCESTE   So much the better; just what I wish to hear.
No news could be more grateful to my ear.
All men are so detestable in my eyes,
I should be sorry if they thought me wise.

PHILINTE   Your hatred's very sweeping, is it not?

ALCESTE   Quite right: I hate the whole degraded lot.

PHILINTE   Must all poor human creatures be embraced,
Without distinction, by your vast distaste?
Even in these bad times, there are surely a few . . .

ALCESTE   No, I include all men in one dim view:
Some men I hate for being rogues; the others
I hate because they treat the rogues like brothers,
And, lacking a virtuous scorn for what is vile,
Receive the villain with a complaisant smile.
Notice how tolerant people choose to be
Toward that bold rascal who's at law with me.
His social polish can't conceal his nature;
One sees at once that he's a treacherous creature;
No one could possibly be taken in
By those soft speeches and that sugary grin.
The whole world knows the shady means by which
The low-brow's grown so powerful and rich,
And risen to a rank so bright and high
That virtue can but blush, and merit sigh.
Whenever his name comes up in conversation,
None will defend his wretched reputation;

¹ Another highly popular comedy by Molière (1661).

Call him knave, liar, scoundrel, and all the rest,
Each head will nod, and no one will protest.
And yet his smirk is seen in every house,
He's greeted everywhere with smiles and bows,
And when there's any honor that can be got
By pulling strings, he'll get it, like as not.
My God! It chills my heart to see the ways
Men come to terms with evil nowadays;
Sometimes, I swear, I'm moved to flee and find
Some desert land unfouled by humankind.

PHILINTE   Come, let's forget the follies of the times
And pardon mankind for its petty crimes;
Let's have an end of rantings and of railings,
And show some leniency toward human failings.
This world requires a pliant rectitude;
Too stern a virtue makes one stiff and rude;
Good sense views all extremes with detestation,
And bids us to be noble in moderation.
The rigid virtues of the ancient days
Are not for us; they jar with all our ways
And ask of us too lofty a perfection.
Wise men accept their times without objection,
And there's no greater folly, if you ask me,
Than trying to reform society.
Like you, I see each day a hundred and one
Unhandsome deeds that might be better done,
But still, for all the faults that meet my view,
I'm never known to storm and rave like you.
I take men as they are, or let them be,
And teach my soul to bear their frailty;
And whether in court or town, whatever the scene,
My phlegm's as philosophic as your spleen.

ALCESTE   This phlegm which you so eloquently commend,
Does nothing ever rile it up, my friend?
Suppose some man you trust should treacherously
Conspire to rob you of your property,
And do his best to wreck your reputation?
Wouldn't you feel a certain indignation?

PHILINTE   Why, no. These faults of which you so complain
Are part of human nature, I maintain,
And it's no more a matter for disgust
That men are knavish, selfish and unjust,
Than that the vulture dines upon the dead,
And wolves are furious, and apes ill-bred.

ALCESTE Shall I see myself betrayed, robbed, torn to bits,

And not . . . oh, let's be still and rest our wits.

Enough of reasoning, now. I've had my fill.

PHILINTE Indeed, you would do well, Sir, to be still.

Rage less at your opponent, and give some thought

To how you'll win this lawsuit that he's brought.

ALCESTE I assure you I'll do nothing of the sort.

PHILINTE Then who will plead your case before the court?

ALCESTE Reason and right and justice will plead for me.

PHILINTE Oh, Lord. What judges do you plan to see?

ALCESTE Why, none. The justice of my cause is clear.

PHILINTE Of course, man; but there's politics to fear. . . .

ALCESTE No, I refuse to lift a hand. That's flat.

I'm either right, or wrong.

PHILINTE Don't count on that.

ALCESTE No, I'll do nothing.

PHILINTE Your enemy's influence

Is great, you know. . . .

ALCESTE That makes no difference.

PHILINTE It will; you'll see.

ALCESTE Must honor bow to guile?

If so, I shall be proud to lose the trial.

PHILINTE Oh, really . . .

ALCESTE I'll discover by this case

Whether or not men are sufficiently base

And impudent and villainous and perverse

To do me wrong before the universe.

PHILINTE What a man!

ALCESTE Oh, I could wish, whatever the cost,

Just for the beauty of it, that my trial were lost.

PHILINTE If people heard you talking so, Alceste,

They'd split their sides. Your name would be a jest.

ALCESTE So much the worse for jesters.

PHILINTE May I enquire

Whether this rectitude you so admire,

And these hard virtues you're enamored of

Are qualities of the lady whom you love?

It much surprises me that you, who seem

To view mankind with furious disesteem,

Have yet found something to enchant your eyes

Amidst a species which you so despise.

And what is more amazing, I'm afraid,

Is the most curious choice your heart has made.

The honest Eliante is fond of you,

Arsinoé, the prude, admires you too;

And yet your spirit's been perversely led

To choose the flighty Célimène instead,

Whose brittle malice and coquettish ways

So typify the manners of our days.

How is it that the traits you most abhor

Are bearable in this lady you adore?

Are you so blind with love that you can't find them?

Or do you contrive, in her case, not to mind them?

ALCESTE My love for that young widow's not the kind

That can't perceive defects; no, I'm not blind.

I see her faults, despite my ardent love,

And all I see I fervently reprove.

And yet I'm weak; for all her falsity,

That woman knows the art of pleasing me,

And though I never cease complaining of her,

I swear I cannot manage not to love her.

Her charm outweighs her faults; I can but aim

To cleanse her spirit in my love's pure flame.

PHILINTE That's no small task; I wish you all success.

You think then that she loves you?

ALCESTE Heavens, yes!

I wouldn't love her did she not love me.

PHILINTE Well, if her taste for you is plain to see,

Why do these rivals cause you such despair?

ALCESTE True love, Sir, is possessive, and cannot bear

To share with all the world. I'm here today

To tell her she must send that mob away.

PHILINTE If I were you, and had your choice to make,

Eliante, her cousin, would be the one I'd take;
That honest heart, which cares for you alone,
Would harmonize far better with your own.

ALCESTE True, true: each day my reason tells
me so;
But reason doesn't rule in love, you know.

PHILINTE I fear some bitter sorrow is in store;
This love . . .

SCENE TWO

Oronte, Alceste, Philinte.

ORONTE [*to Alceste*] The servants told me at
the door
That Eliante and Célimène were out,
But when I heard, dear Sir, that you were
about,
I came to say, without exaggeration,
That I hold you in the vastest admiration,
And that it's always been my dearest desire
To be the friend of one I so admire.
I hope to see my love of merit requited,
And you and I in friendship's bond united.
I'm sure you won't refuse—if I may be frank—
A friend of my devotedness—and rank.
[*During this speech, Alceste is abstracted, and
seems unaware that he is being spoken to. He
only breaks off his reverie when Oronte speaks.*]
It was for you, if you please, that my words
were intended.

ALCESTE For me, Sir?

ORONTE   Yes, for you. You're not
offended?

ALCESTE By no means. But this much surprises
me. . . .
The honor comes most unexpectedly. . . .

ORONTE My high regard should not astonish
you;
The whole world feels the same. It is your due.

ALCESTE Sir . . .

ORONTE   Why, in all the state there
isn't one
Can match your merits; they shine, Sir, like the
sun.

ALCESTE Sir . . .

ORONTE   You are higher in my estima-
tion
Than all that's most illustrious in the nation.

ALCESTE Sir . . .

ORONTE   If I lie, may heaven strike me
dead!
To show you that I mean what I have said,
Permit me, Sir, to embrace you most sincerely,
And swear that I will prize our friendship
dearly.
Give me your hand. And now, Sir, if you
choose,
We'll make our vows.

ALCESTE   Sir . . .

ORONTE   What! You refuse?

ALCESTE Sir, it's a very great honor you extend:
But friendship is a sacred thing, my friend;
It would be profanation to bestow
The name of friend on one you hardly know.
All parts are better played when well-rehearsed;
Let's put off friendship, and get acquainted
first.
We may discover it would be unwise
To try to make our natures harmonize.

ORONTE By heaven! You're sagacious to the
core;
This speech has made me admire you even
more.
Let time, then, bring us closer day by day;
Meanwhile, I shall be yours in every way.
If, for example, there should be anything
You wish at court, I'll mention it to the King.
I have his ear, of course; it's quite well known
That I am much in favor with the throne.
In short, I am your servant. And now, dear
friend,
Since you have such fine judgment, I intend
To please you, if I can, with a small sonnet
I wrote not long ago. Please comment on it,
And tell me whether I ought to publish it.

ALCESTE You must excuse me, Sir; I'm hardly
fit
To judge such matters.

ORONTE   Why not?

ALCESTE   I am, I fear,
Inclined to be unfashionably sincere.

ORONTE Just what I ask; I'd take no satisfaction
In anything but your sincere reaction.
I beg you not to dream of being kind.

ALCESTE Since you desire it, Sir, I'll speak my
mind.

ORONTE *Sonnet.* It's a sonnet. . . . *Hope* . . .
the poem's addressed
To a lady who wakened hopes within my breast.
Hope . . . this is not the pompous sort of
thing.
Just modest little verses, with a tender ring.

ALCESTE Well, we shall see.

ORONTE   *Hope* . . . I'm anxious to hear
Whether the style seems properly smooth and
clear,
And whether the choice of words is good or
bad.

ALCESTE We'll see, we'll see.

ORONTE   Perhaps I ought to
add
That it took me only a quarter-hour to write it.

ALCESTE The time's irrelevant, Sir: kindly recite
it.

ORONTE [*reading*] *Hope comforts us awhile, 'tis
true,*
Lulling our cares with careless laughter,
And yet such joy is full of rue,
My Phyllis, if nothing follows after.

PHILINTE I'm charmed by this already; the style's
delightful.

ALCESTE [*sotto voce, to Philinte*] How can you
say that? Why, the thing is frightful.

ORONTE *Your fair face smiled on me awhile,*
But was it kindness so to enchant me?
'Twould have been fairer not to smile,
If hope was all you meant to grant me.

PHILINTE What a clever thought! How handsomely you phrase it!

ALCESTE [*sotto voce, to Philinte*] You know the
thing is trash. How dare you praise it?

ORONTE *If it's to be my passion's fate*
Thus everlastingly to wait,
Then death will come to set me free:
For death is fairer than the fair;
Phyllis, to hope is to despair
When one must hope eternally.

PHILINTE The close is exquisite—full of feeling
and grace.

ALCESTE [*sotto voce, aside*] Oh, blast the close;
you'd better close your face
Before you send your lying soul to hell.

PHILINTE I can't remember a poem I've liked
so well.

ALCESTE [*sotto voce, aside*] Good Lord!

ORONTE [*to Philinte*]   I fear
you're flattering me a bit.

PHILINTE Oh, no!

ALCESTE [*sotto voce, aside*] What else d'you
call it, you hypocrite?

ORONTE [*to Alceste*] But you, Sir, keep your
promise now: don't shrink
From telling me sincerely what you think.

ALCESTE Sir, these are delicate matters; we all
desire
To be told that we've the true poetic fire.
But once, to one whose name I shall not men-
tion,
I said, regarding some verse of his invention,
That gentlemen should rigorously control
That itch to write which often afflicts the soul;
That one should curb the heady inclination
To publicize one's little avocation;
And that in showing off one's works of art
One often plays a very clownish part.

ORONTE Are you suggesting in a devious way
That I ought not . . .

ALCESTE   Oh, that I do not say.
Further, I told him that no fault is worse
Than that of writing frigid, lifeless verse,
And that the merest whisper of such a shame
Suffices to destroy a man's good name.

ORONTE D'you mean to say my sonnet's dull
and trite?

ALCESTE I don't say that. But I went on to cite
Numerous cases of once-respected men
Who came to grief by taking up the pen.

ORONTE And am I like them? Do I write so
poorly?

ALCESTE I don't say that. But I told this person,
"Surely
You're under no necessity to compose;
Why you should wish to publish, heaven
knows.
There's no excuse for printing tedious rot
Unless one writes for bread, as you do not.
Resist temptation, then, I beg of you;
Conceal your pastimes from the public view;
And don't give up, on any provocation,
Your present high and courtly reputation,
To purchase at a greedy printer's shop
The name of silly author and scribbling fop."
These were the points I tried to make him see.

ORONTE I sense that they are also aimed at me;
But now—about my sonnet—I'd like to be told . . .
ALCESTE Frankly, that sonnet should be pigeon-holed.
You've chosen the worst models to imitate.
The style's unnatural. Let me illustrate:
For example, *Your fair face smiled on me awhile,*
Followed by, *'Twould have been fairer not to smile!*
Or this: *such joy is full of rue;*
Or this: *For death is fairer than the fair;*
Or, *Phyllis, to hope is to despair*
When one must hope eternally!
This artificial style, that's all the fashion,
Has neither taste, nor honesty, nor passion;
It's nothing but a sort of wordy play,
And nature never spoke in such a way.
What, in this shallow age, is not debased?
Our fathers, though less refined, had better taste;
I'd barter all that men admire today
For one old love-song I shall try to say:

If the King had given me for my own
Paris, his citadel,
And I for that must leave alone
Her whom I love so well,
I'd say then to the Crown,
Take back your glittering town;
My darling is more fair, I swear,
My darling is more fair.

The rhyme's not rich, the style is rough and old,
But don't you see that it's the purest gold
Beside the tinsel nonsense now preferred,
And that there's passion in its every word?

If the King had given me for my own
Paris, his citadel,
And I for that must leave alone
Her whom I love so well,
I'd say then to the Crown,
Take back your glittering town;
My darling is more fair, I swear,
My darling is more fair.

There speaks a loving heart.

[*To Philinte*]
You're laughing, eh?
Laugh on, my precious wit. Whatever you say,
I hold that song's worth all the bibelots
That people hail today with "ah's" and "oh's."
ORONTE And I maintain my sonnet's very good.
ALCESTE It's not at all surprising that you should.
You have your reasons; permit me to have mine
For thinking that you cannot write a line.
ORONTE Others have praised my sonnet to the skies.
ALCESTE I lack their art of telling pleasant lies.
ORONTE You seem to think you've got no end of wit.
ALCESTE To praise your verse, I'd need still more of it.
ORONTE I'm not in need of your approval, Sir.
ALCESTE That's good; you couldn't have it if you were.
ORONTE Come now, I'll lend you the subject of my sonnet;
I'd like to see you try to improve upon it.
ALCESTE I might, by chance, write something just as shoddy;
But then I wouldn't show it to everybody.
ORONTE You're most opinionated and conceited.
ALCESTE Go find your flatterers, and be better treated.
ORONTE Look here, my little fellow, pray watch your tone.
ALCESTE My great big fellow, you'd better watch your own.
PHILINTE [*stepping between them*] Oh, please, please, gentlemen! This will never do.
ORONTE The fault is mine, and I leave the field to you.
I am your servant, Sir, in every way.
ALCESTE And I, Sir, am your most abject valet.

SCENE THREE
Philinte, Alceste.

PHILINTE Well, as you see, sincerity in excess
Can get you into a very pretty mess;
Oronte was hungry for appreciation. . . .

The Misanthrope

ALCESTE Don't speak to me.
PHILINTE   What?
ALCESTE   No more conversation.
PHILINTE Really, now . . .
ALCESTE   Leave me alone.
PHILINTE   If
I . . .
ALCESTE Out of my sight!

PHILINTE But what . . .
ALCESTE   I won't listen.
PHILINTE   But . . .
ALCESTE Silence!
PHILINTE   Now, is it polite . . .
ALCESTE By heaven, I've had enough. Don't follow me.
PHILINTE Ah, you're just joking. I'll keep you company.

Act Two

SCENE ONE

Alceste, Célimène.

ALCESTE Shall I speak plainly, Madam? I confess
Your conduct gives me infinite distress,
And my resentment's grown too hot to smother.
Soon, I foresee, we'll break with one another.
If I said otherwise, I should deceive you;
Sooner or later, I shall be forced to leave you,
And if I swore that we shall never part,
I should misread the omens of my heart.
CÉLIMÈNE You kindly saw me home, it would appear,
So as to pour invectives in my ear.
ALCESTE I've no desire to quarrel. But I deplore
Your inability to shut the door
On all these suitors who beset you so.
There's what annoys me, if you care to know.
CÉLIMÈNE Is it my fault that all these men pursue me?
Am I to blame if they're attracted to me?
And when they gently beg an audience,
Ought I to take a stick and drive them hence?
ALCESTE Madam, there's no necessity for a stick;
A less responsive heart would do the trick.
Of your attractiveness I don't complain;
But those your charms attract, you then detain
By a most melting and receptive manner,
And so enlist their hearts beneath your banner.
It's the agreeable hopes which you excite
That keep these lovers round you day and night;
Were they less liberally smiled upon,
That sighing troop would very soon be gone.

But tell me, Madam, why it is that lately
This man Clitandre interests you so greatly?
Because of what high merits do you deem
Him worthy of the honor of your esteem?
Is it that your admiring glances linger
On the splendidly long nail of his little finger?
Or do you share the general deep respect
For the blond wig he chooses to affect?
Are you in love with his embroidered hose?
Do you adore his ribbons and his bows?
Or is it that this paragon bewitches
Your tasteful eye with his vast German breeches?
Perhaps his giggle, or his falsetto voice,
Makes him the latest gallant of your choice?
CÉLIMÈNE You're much mistaken to resent him so.
Why I put up with him you surely know:
My lawsuit's very shortly to be tried,
And I must have his influence on my side.
ALCESTE Then lose your lawsuit, Madam, or let it drop;
Don't torture me by humoring such a fop.
CÉLIMÈNE You're jealous of the whole world, Sir.
ALCESTE That's true.
Since the whole world is well-received by you.
CÉLIMÈNE That my good nature is so unconfined
Should serve to pacify your jealous mind;
Were I to smile on one, and scorn the rest,
Then you might have some cause to be distressed.
ALCESTE Well, if I mustn't be jealous, tell me, then,
Just how I'm better treated than other men.

CÉLIMÈNE You know you have my love. Will that not do?

ALCESTE What proof have I that what you say is true?

CÉLIMÈNE I would expect, Sir, that my having said it
Might give the statement a sufficient credit.

ALCESTE But how can I be sure that you don't tell
The selfsame thing to other men as well?

CÉLIMÈNE What a gallant speech! How flattering to me!
What a sweet creature you make me out to be!
Well then, to save you from the pangs of doubt,
All that I've said I hereby cancel out;
Now, none but yourself shall make a monkey of you:
Are you content?

ALCESTE   Why, why am I doomed to love you?
I swear that I shall bless the blissful hour
When this poor heart's no longer in your power!
I make no secret of it: I've done my best
To exorcise this passion from my breast;
But thus far all in vain; it will not go;
It's for my sins that I must love you so.

CÉLIMÈNE Your love for me is matchless, Sir; that's clear.

ALCESTE Indeed, in all the world it has no peer;
Words can't describe the nature of my passion,
And no man ever loved in such a fashion.

CÉLIMÈNE Yes, it's a brand-new fashion, I agree:
You show your love by castigating me,
And all your speeches are enraged and rude.
I've never been so furiously wooed.

ALCESTE Yet you could calm that fury, if you chose.
Come, shall we bring our quarrels to a close?
Let's speak with open hearts, then, and begin . . .

SCENE TWO

Célimène, Alceste, Basque.

CÉLIMÈNE What is it?

BASQUE   Acaste is here.

CÉLIMÈNE   Well, send him in.

SCENE THREE

Célimène, Alceste.

ALCESTE What! Shall we never be alone at all?
You're always ready to receive a call,
And you can't bear, for ten ticks of the clock,
Not to keep open house for all who knock.

CÉLIMÈNE I couldn't refuse him: he'd be most put out.

ALCESTE Surely that's not worth worrying about.

CÉLIMÈNE Acaste would never forgive me if he guessed
That I consider him a dreadful pest.

ALCESTE If he's a pest, why bother with him then?

CÉLIMÈNE Heavens! One can't antagonize such men;
Why, they're the chartered gossips of the court,
And have a say in things of every sort.
One must receive them, and be full of charm;
They're no great help, but they can do you harm,
And though your influence be ever so great,
They're hardly the best people to alienate.

ALCESTE I see, dear lady, that you could make a case
For putting up with the whole human race;
These friendships that you calculate so nicely . . .

SCENE FOUR

Alceste, Célimène, Basque.

BASQUE Madam, Clitandre is here as well.

ALCESTE   Precisely.

CÉLIMÈNE Where are you going?

ALCESTE   Elsewhere.

CÉLIMÈNE   Stay.

ALCESTE   No, no.

CÉLIMÈNE Stay, Sir.

ALCESTE   I can't.

CÉLIMÈNE   I wish it.

ALCESTE   No, I must go.
I beg you, Madam, not to press the matter;

You know I have no taste for idle chatter.

CÉLIMÈNE Stay: I command you.

ALCESTE   No, I cannot
stay.

CÉLIMÈNE Very well; you have my leave to go
away.

SCENE FIVE

*Eliante, Philinte, Acaste, Clitandre, Alceste,
Célimène, Basque.*

ELIANTE [*to Célimène*] The Marquesses have
kindly come to call.
Were they announced?

CÉLIMÈNE   Yes. Basque, bring
chairs for all.
[*Basque provides the chairs, and exits. To Alceste*]
You haven't gone?

ALCESTE   No; and I shan't depart
Till you decide who's foremost in your heart.

CÉLIMÈNE Oh, hush.

ALCESTE   It's time to choose; take
them, or me.

CÉLIMÈNE You're mad.

ALCESTE   I'm not, as you shall
shortly see.

CÉLIMÈNE Oh?

ALCESTE   You'll decide.

CÉLIMÈNE   You're joking now,
dear friend.

ALCESTE No, no; you'll choose; my patience is
at an end.

CLITANDRE Madam, I come from court, where
poor Cléonte
Behaved like a perfect fool, as is his wont.
Has he no friend to counsel him, I wonder,
And teach him less unerringly to blunder?

CÉLIMÈNE It's true, the man's a most accom-
plished dunce;
His gauche behavior strikes the eye at once;
And every time one sees him, on my word,
His manner's grown a trifle more absurd.

ACASTE Speaking of dunces, I've just now con-
versed
With old Damon, who's one of the very worst;
I stood a lifetime in the broiling sun

Before his dreary monologue was done.

CÉLIMÈNE Oh, he's a wondrous talker, and has
the power
To tell you nothing hour after hour:
If, by mistake, he ever came to the point,
The shock would put his jawbone out of joint.

ELIANTE [*to Philinte*] The conversation takes its
usual turn,
And all our dear friends' ears will shortly burn.

CLITANDRE Timante's a character, Madam.

CÉLIMÈNE   Isn't
he, though?
A man of mystery from top to toe,
Who moves about in a romantic mist
On secret missions which do not exist.
His talk is full of eyebrows and grimaces;
How tired one gets of his momentous faces;
He's always whispering something confidential
Which turns out to be quite inconsequential;
Nothing's too slight for him to mystify;
He even whispers when he says "good-by."

ACASTE Tell us about Géralde.

CÉLIMÈNE   That tiresome ass.
He mixes only with the titled class,
And fawns on dukes and princes, and is bored
With anyone who's not at least a lord.
The man's obsessed with rank, and his dis-
courses
Are all of hounds and carriages and horses;
He uses Christian names with all the great,
And the word "Milord," with him, is out of
date.

CLITANDRE He's very taken with Bélise, I hear.

CÉLIMÈNE She is the dreariest company, poor
dear.
Whenever she comes to call, I grope about
To find some topic which will draw her out,
But, owing to her dry and faint replies,
The conversation wilts, and droops, and dies.
In vain one hopes to animate her face
By mentioning the ultimate commonplace;
But sun or shower, even hail or frost
Are matters she can instantly exhaust.
Meanwhile her visit, painful though it is,
Drags on and on through mute eternities,
And though you ask the time, and yawn, and
yawn,
She sits there like a stone and won't be gone.

ACASTE Now for Adraste.

CÉLIMÈNE   Oh, that conceited elf
Has a gigantic passion for himself;
He rails against the court, and cannot bear it
That none will recognize his hidden merit;
All honors given to others give offense
To his imaginary excellence.

CLITANDRE   What about young Cléon? His house,
    they say,
Is full of the best society, night and day.

CÉLIMÈNE   His cook has made him popular, not
    he:
It's Cléon's table that people come to see.

ELIANTE   He gives a splendid dinner, you must
    admit.

CÉLIMÈNE   But must he serve himself along with
    it?
For my taste, he's a most insipid dish
Whose presence sours the wine and spoils the
    fish.

PHILINTE   Damas, his uncle, is admired no end.
What's your opinion, Madam?

CÉLIMÈNE   Why, he's my
    friend.

PHILINTE   He seems a decent fellow, and rather
    clever.

CÉLIMÈNE   He works too hard at cleverness,
    however.
I hate to see him sweat and struggle so
To fill his conversation with bons mots.
Since he's decided to become a wit
His taste's so pure that nothing pleases it;
He scolds at all the latest books and plays,
Thinking that wit must never stoop to praise,
That finding fault's a sign of intellect,
That all appreciation is abject,
And that by damning everything in sight
One shows oneself in a distinguished light.
He's scornful even of our conversations:
Their trivial nature sorely tries his patience;
He folds his arms, and stands above the battle,
And listens sadly to our childish prattle.

ACASTE   Wonderful, Madam! You've hit him off
    precisely.

CLITANDRE   No one can sketch a character so
    nicely.

ALCESTE   How bravely, Sirs, you cut and thrust
    at all
These absent fools, till one by one they fall:
But let one come in sight, and you'll at once

Embrace the man you lately called a dunce,
Telling him in a tone sincere and fervent
How proud you are to be his humble servant.

CLITANDRE   Why pick on us? Madame's been
    speaking, Sir,
And you should quarrel, if you must, with her.

ALCESTE   No, no, by God, the fault is yours,
    because
You lead her on with laughter and applause,
And make her think that she's the more de-
    lightful
The more her talk is scandalous and spiteful.
Oh, she would stoop to malice far, far less
If no such claque approved her cleverness.
It's flatterers like you whose foolish praise
Nourishes all the vices of these days.

PHILINTE   But why protest when someone ridi-
    cules
Those you'd condemn, yourself, as knaves or
    fools?

CÉLIMÈNE   Why, Sir? Because he loves to make
    a fuss.
You don't expect him to agree with us,
When there's an opportunity to express
His heaven-sent spirit of contrariness?
What other people think, he can't abide;
Whatever they say, he's on the other side;
He lives in deadly terror of agreeing;
'Twould make him seem an ordinary being.
Indeed, he's so in love with contradiction,
He'll turn against his most profound conviction
And with a furious eloquence deplore it,
If only someone else is speaking for it.

ALCESTE   Go on, dear lady, mock me as you
    please;
You have your audience in ecstasies.

PHILINTE   But what she says is true: you have a
    way
Of bridling at whatever people say;
Whether they praise or blame, your angry spirit
Is equally unsatisfied to hear it.

ALCESTE   Men, Sir, are always wrong, and that's
    the reason
That righteous anger's never out of season;
All that I hear in all their conversation
Is flattering praise or reckless condemnation.

CÉLIMÈNE   But . . .

ALCESTE   No, no, Madam, I am forced
    to state

The Misanthrope

That you have pleasures which I deprecate,
And that these others, here, are much to blame
For nourishing the faults which are your shame.
CLITANDRE I shan't defend myself, Sir; but I
     vow
I'd thought this lady faultless until now.
ACASTE I see her charms and graces, which are
     many;
But as for faults, I've never noticed any.
ALCESTE I see them, Sir; and rather than ignore
     them,
I strenuously criticize her for them.
The more one loves, the more one should ob-
     ject
To every blemish, every least defect.
Were I this lady, I would soon get rid
Of lovers who approved of all I did,
And by their slack indulgence and applause
Endorsed my follies and excused my flaws.
CÉLIMÈNE If all hearts beat according to your
     measure,
The dawn of love would be the end of pleasure;
And love would find its perfect consummation
In ecstasies of rage and reprobation.
ELIANTE Love, as a rule, affects men otherwise,
And lovers rarely love to criticize.
They see their lady as a charming blur,
And find all things commendable in her.
If she has any blemish, fault, or shame,
They will redeem it by a pleasing name.
The pale-faced lady's lily-white, perforce;
The swarthy one's a sweet brunette, of course;
The spindly lady has a slender grace;
The fat one has a most majestic pace;
The plain one, with her dress in disarray,
They classify as *beauté négligée;*
The hulking one's a goddess in their eyes,
The dwarf, a concentrate of Paradise;
The haughty lady has a noble mind;
The mean one's witty, and the dull one's kind;
The chatterbox has liveliness and verve,
The mute one has a virtuous reserve.
So lovers manage, in their passion's cause,
To love their ladies even for their flaws.
ALCESTE But I still say . . .
CÉLIMÈNE   I think it would be
     nice
To stroll around the gallery once or twice.
What! You're not going, Sirs?

CLITANDRE AND ACASTE   No, Madam, no.
ALCESTE You seem to be in terror lest they go.
Do what you will, Sirs; leave, or linger on,
But I shan't go till after you are gone.
ACASTE I'm free to linger, unless I should per-
     ceive
Madame is tired, and wishes me to leave.
CLITANDRE And as for me, I needn't go today
Until the hour of the King's *coucher.*
CÉLIMÈNE [*to Alceste*] You're joking, surely?
ALCESTE   Not
     in the least; we'll see
Whether you'd rather part with them, or me.

SCENE SIX

*Alceste, Célimène, Eliante, Acaste, Philinte, Cli-
tandre, Basque.*

BASQUE [*to Alceste*] Sir, there's a fellow here
     who bids me state
That he must see you, and that it can't wait.
ALCESTE Tell him that I have no such pressing
     affairs.
BASQUE It's a long tailcoat that this fellow
     wears,
With gold all over.
CÉLIMÈNE [*to Alceste*] You'd best go down and
     see.
Or—have him enter.

SCENE SEVEN

*Alceste, Célimène, Eliante, Acaste, Philinte, Cli-
tandre, Guard.*

ALCESTE [*confronting the Guard*] Well, what do
     you want with me?
Come in, Sir.
GUARD   I've a word, Sir, for your ear.
ALCESTE Speak it aloud, Sir; I shall strive to
     hear.
GUARD The Marshals have instructed me to say
You must report to them without delay.
ALCESTE Who? Me, Sir?
GUARD   Yes, Sir; you.
ALCESTE   But what
     do they want?
PHILINTE [*to Alceste*] To scotch your silly quar-
     rel with Oronte.

CÉLIMÈNE [*to Philinte*]   What quarrel?

PHILINTE   Oronte and
he have fallen out
Over some verse he spoke his mind about;
The Marshals wish to arbitrate the matter.

ALCESTE   Never shall I equivocate or flatter!

PHILINTE   You'd best obey their summons; come,
   let's go.

ALCESTE   How can they mend our quarrel, I'd
   like to know?
Am I to make a cowardly retraction,
And praise those jingles to his satisfaction?
I'll not recant; I've judged that sonnet rightly.
It's bad.

PHILINTE   But you might say so more politely.
   . . .

ALCESTE   I'll not back down; his verses make me
   sick.

PHILINTE   If only you could be more politic!
But come, let's go.

ALCESTE   I'll go, but I won't unsay
A single word.

PHILINTE   Well, let's be on our way.

ALCESTE   Till I am ordered by my lord the King
To praise that poem, I shall say the thing
Is scandalous, by God, and that the poet
Ought to be hanged for having the nerve to
   show it.

[*To Clitandre and Acaste, who are laughing*]
By heaven, Sirs, I really didn't know
That I was being humorous.

CÉLIMÈNE   Go, Sir, go;
Settle your business.

ALCESTE   I shall, and when I'm
   through,
I shall return to settle things with you.

Act Three

SCENE ONE

Clitandre, Acaste.

CLITANDRE   Dear Marquess, how contented you
   appear;
All things delight you, nothing mars your cheer.
Can you, in perfect honesty, declare
That you've a right to be so debonair?

ACASTE   By Jove, when I survey myself, I find
No cause whatever for distress of mind.
I'm young and rich; I can in modesty
Lay claim to an exalted pedigree;
And owing to my name and my condition
I shall not want for honors and position.
Then as to courage, that most precious trait,
I seem to have it, as was proved of late
Upon the field of honor, where my bearing,
They say, was very cool and rather daring.
I've wit, of course; and taste in such perfection
That I can judge without the least reflection,
And at the theater, which is my delight,
Can make or break a play on opening night,
And lead the crowd in hisses or bravos,
And generally be known as one who knows.
I'm clever, handsome, gracefully polite;
My waist is small, my teeth are strong and
   white;

As for my dress, the world's astonished eyes
Assure me that I bear away the prize.
I find myself in favor everywhere,
Honored by men, and worshipped by the fair;
And since these things are so, it seems to me
I'm justified in my complacency.

CLITANDRE   Well, if so many ladies hold you
   dear,
Why do you press a hopeless courtship here?

ACASTE   Hopeless, you say? I'm not the sort of
   fool
That likes his ladies difficult and cool.
Men who are awkward, shy, and peasantish
May pine for heartless beauties, if they wish,
Grovel before them, bear their cruelties,
Woo them with tears and sighs and bended
   knees,
And hope by dogged faithfulness to gain
What their poor merits never could obtain.
For men like me, however, it makes no sense
To love on trust, and foot the whole expense.
Whatever any lady's merits be,
I think, thank God, that I'm as choice as she;
That if my heart is kind enough to burn
For her, she owes me something in return;
And that in any proper love affair
The partners must invest an equal share

CLITANDRE You think, then, that our hostess favors you?

ACASTE I've reason to believe that that is true.

CLITANDRE How did you come to such a mad conclusion?
You're blind, dear fellow. This is sheer delusion.

ACASTE All right, then: I'm deluded and I'm blind.

CLITANDRE Whatever put the notion in your mind?

ACASTE Delusion.

CLITANDRE What persuades you that you're right?

ACASTE I'm blind.

CLITANDRE But have you any proofs to cite?

ACASTE I tell you I'm deluded.

CLITANDRE Have you, then,
Received some secret pledge from Célimène?

ACASTE Oh, no: she scorns me.

CLITANDRE Tell me the truth, I beg.

ACASTE She just can't bear me.

CLITANDRE Ah, don't pull my leg.
Tell me what hope she's given you, I pray.

ACASTE I'm hopeless, and it's you who win the day.
She hates me thoroughly, and I'm so vexed
I mean to hang myself on Tuesday next.

CLITANDRE Dear Marquess, let us have an armistice
And make a treaty. What do you say to this?
If ever one of us can plainly prove
That Célimène encourages his love,
The other must abandon hope, and yield,
And leave him in possession of the field.

ACASTE Now, there's a bargain that appeals to me;
With all my heart, dear Marquess, I agree
But hush.

SCENE TWO

Célimène, Acaste, Clitandre.

CÉLIMÈNE Still here?

CLITANDRE 'Twas love that stayed our feet.

CÉLIMÈNE I think I heard a carriage in the street.
Whose is it? D'you know?

SCENE THREE

Célimène, Acaste, Clitandre, Basque.

BASQUE Arsinoé is here, *Madame.*

CÉLIMÈNE Arsinoé, you say? Oh, dear.

BASQUE Eliante is entertaining her below.

CÉLIMÈNE What brings the creature here, I'd like to know?

ACASTE They say she's dreadfully prudish, but in fact
I think her piety . . .

CÉLIMÈNE It's all an act.
At heart she's worldly, and her poor success
In snaring men explains her prudishness.
It breaks her heart to see the beaux and gallants
Engrossed by other women's charms and talents,
And so she's always in a jealous rage
Against the faulty standards of the age.
She lets the world believe that she's a prude
To justify her loveless solitude,
And strives to put a brand of moral shame
On all the graces that she cannot claim.
But still she'd love a lover; and Alceste
Appears to be the one she'd love the best.
His visits here are poison to her pride;
She seems to think I've lured him from her side;
And everywhere, at court or in the town,
The spiteful, envious woman runs me down.
In short, she's just as stupid as can be,
Vicious and arrogant in the last degree,
And . . .

SCENE FOUR

Arsinoé, Célimène, Clitandre, Acaste.

CÉLIMÈNE Ah! What happy chance has brought you here?
I've thought about you ever so much, my dear.

ARSINOÉ I've come to tell you something you should know.

CÉLIMÈNE How good of you to think of doing so!

[*Clitandre and Acaste go out, laughing.*]

SCENE FIVE

Arsinoé, Célimène.

ARSINOÉ It's just as well those gentlemen didn't tarry.

CÉLIMÈNE Shall we sit down?

ARSINOÉ That won't be necessary.
Madam, the flame of friendship ought to burn
Brightest in matters of the most concern,
And as there's nothing which concerns us more
Than honor, I have hastened to your door
To bring you, as your friend, some information
About the status of your reputation.
I visited, last night, some virtuous folk,
And, quite by chance, it was of you they spoke;
There was, I fear, no tendency to praise
Your light behavior and your dashing ways.
The quantity of gentlemen you see
And your by now notorious coquetry
Were both so vehemently criticized
By everyone, that I was much surprised.
Of course, I needn't tell you where I stood;
I came to your defense as best I could,
Assured them you were harmless, and declared
Your soul was absolutely unimpaired.
But there are some things, you must realize,
One can't excuse, however hard one tries,
And I was forced at last into conceding
That your behavior, Madam, is misleading,
That it makes a bad impression, giving rise
To ugly gossip and obscene surmise,
And that if you were more *overtly* good,
You wouldn't be so much misunderstood.
Not that I think you've been unchaste—no! no!
The saints preserve me from a thought so low!
But mere good conscience never did suffice:
One must avoid the outward show of vice.
Madam, you're too intelligent, I'm sure,
To think my motives anything but pure
In offering you this counsel—which I do
Out of a zealous interest in you.

CÉLIMÈNE Madam, I haven't taken you amiss;
I'm very much obliged to you for this;
And I'll at once discharge the obligation
By telling you about *your* reputation.
You've been so friendly as to let me know
What certain people say of me, and so
I mean to follow your benign example
By offering you a somewhat similar sample.
The other day, I went to an affair
And found some most distinguished people there
Discussing piety, both false and true.
The conversation soon came round to you.
Alas! Your prudery and bustling zeal
Appeared to have a very slight appeal.
Your affectation of a grave demeanor,
Your endless talk of virtue and of honor,
The aptitude of your suspicious mind
For finding sin where there is none to find,
Your towering self-esteem, that pitying face
With which you contemplate the human race,
Your sermonizings and your sharp aspersions
On people's pure and innocent diversions—
All these were mentioned, Madam, and, in fact,
Were roundly and concertedly attacked.
"What good," they said, "are all these outward shows,
When everything belies her pious pose?
She prays incessantly; but then, they say,
She beats her maids and cheats them of their pay;
She shows her zeal in every holy place,
But still she's vain enough to paint her face;
She holds that naked statues are immoral,
But with a naked *man* she'd have no quarrel."
Of course, I said to everybody there
That they were being viciously unfair;
But still they were disposed to criticize you,
And all agreed that someone should advise you
To leave the morals of the world alone,
And worry rather more about your own.
They felt that one's self-knowledge should be great
Before one thinks of setting others straight;
That one should learn the art of living well
Before one threatens other men with hell,
And that the Church is best equipped, no doubt,
To guide our souls and root our vices out.
Madam, you're too intelligent, I'm sure,
To think my motives anything but pure
In offering you this counsel—which I do

The Misanthrope

Out of a zealous interest in you.

ARSINOÉ I dared not hope for gratitude, but I
Did not expect so acid a reply;
I judge, since you've been so extremely tart,
That my good counsel pierced you to the heart.

CÉLIMÈNE Far from it, Madam. Indeed, it seems
   to me
We ought to trade advice more frequently.
One's vision of oneself is so defective
That it would be an excellent corrective.
If you are willing, Madam, let's arrange
Shortly to have another frank exchange
In which we'll tell each other, *entre nous,*
What you've heard tell of me, and I of you.

ARSINOÉ Oh, people never censure you, my
   dear;
It's me they criticize. Or so I hear.

CÉLIMÈNE Madam, I think we either blame or
   praise
According to our taste and length of days.
There is a time of life for coquetry,
And there's a season, too, for prudery.
When all one's charms are gone, it is, I'm sure,
Good strategy to be devout and pure:
It makes one seem a little less forsaken.
Some day, perhaps, I'll take the road you've
   taken:
Time brings all things. But I have time aplenty,
And see no cause to be a prude at twenty.

ARSINOÉ You give your age in such a gloating
   tone
That one would think I was an ancient crone;
We're not so far apart, in sober truth,
That you can mock me with a boast of youth!
Madam, you baffle me, I wish I knew
What moves you to provoke me as you do.

CÉLIMÈNE For my part, Madam, I should like
   to know
Why you abuse me everywhere you go.
Is it my fault, dear lady, that your hand
Is not, alas, in very great demand?
If men admire me, if they pay me court
And daily make me offers of the sort
You'd dearly love to have them make to you,
How can I help it? What would you have me do?
If what you want is lovers, please feel free
To take as many as you can from me.

ARSINOÉ Oh, come. D'you think the world is
   losing sleep

Over that flock of lovers which you keep,
Or that we find it difficult to guess
What price you pay for their devotedness?
Surely you don't expect us to suppose
Mere merit could attract so many beaux?
It's not your virtue that they're dazzled by;
Nor is it virtuous love for which they sigh.
You're fooling no one, Madam; the world's not
   blind;
There's many a lady heaven has designed
To call men's noblest, tenderest feelings out,
Who has no lovers dogging her about;
From which it's plain that lovers nowadays
Must be acquired in bold and shameless ways,
And only pay one court for such reward
As modesty and virtue can't afford.
Then don't be quite so puffed up, if you please,
About your tawdry little victories;
Try, if you can, to be a shade less vain,
And treat the world with somewhat less disdain.
If one were envious of your amours,
One soon could have a following like yours;
Lovers are no great trouble to collect
If one prefers them to one's self-respect.

CÉLIMÈNE Collect them then, my dear; I'd love
   to see
You demonstrate that charming theory;
Who knows, you might . . .

ARSINOÉ   Now, Madam,
   that will do;
It's time to end this trying interview.
My coach is late in coming to your door,
Or I'd have taken leave of you before.

CÉLIMÈNE Oh, please don't feel that you must
   rush away;
I'd be delighted, Madam, if you'd stay.
However, lest my conversation bore you,
Let me provide some better company for you;
This gentleman, who comes most apropos,
Will please you more than I could do, I know.

SCENE SIX

Alceste, Célimène, Arsinoé.

CÉLIMÈNE Alceste, I have a little note to write
   Which simply must go out before tonight;
   Please entertain *Madame;* I'm sure that she
   Will overlook my incivility.

SCENE SEVEN

Alceste, Arsinoé.

ARSINOÉ Well, Sir, our hostess graciously contrives
For us to chat until my coach arrives;
And I shall be forever in her debt
For granting me this little tête-à-tête.
We women very rightly give our hearts
To men of noble character and parts,
And your especial merits, dear Alceste,
Have roused the deepest sympathy in my breast.
Oh, how I wish they had sufficient sense
At court, to recognize your excellence!
They wrong you greatly, Sir. How it must hurt you
Never to be rewarded for your virtue!

ALCESTE Why, Madam, what cause have I to feel aggrieved?
What great and brilliant thing have I achieved?
What service have I rendered to the King
That I should look to him for anything?

ARSINOÉ Not everyone who's honored by the State
Has done great services. A man must wait
Till time and fortune offer him the chance.
Your merit, Sir, is obvious at a glance,
And . . .

ALCESTE Ah, forget my merit; I'm not neglected.
The court, I think, can hardly be expected
To mine men's souls for merit, and unearth
Our hidden virtues and our secret worth.

ARSINOÉ *Some* virtues, though, are far too bright to hide;
Yours are acknowledged, Sir, on every side.
Indeed, I've heard you warmly praised of late
By persons of considerable weight.

ALCESTE This fawning age has praise for everyone,
And all distinctions, Madam, are undone.
All things have equal honor nowadays,
And no one should be gratified by praise.
To be admired, one only need exist,
And every lackey's on the honors list.

ARSINOÉ I only wish, Sir, that you had your eye
On some position at court, however high;
You'd only have to hint at such a notion
For me to set the proper wheels in motion;
I've certain friendships I'd be glad to use
To get you any office you might choose.

ALCESTE Madam, I fear that any such ambition
Is wholly foreign to my disposition.
The soul God gave me isn't of the sort
That prospers in the weather of a court.
It's all too obvious that I don't possess
The virtues necessary for success.
My one great talent is for speaking plain;
I've never learned to flatter or to feign;
And anyone so stupidly sincere
Had best not seek a courtier's career.
Outside the court, I know, one must dispense
With honors, privilege, and influence;
But still one gains the right, foregoing these,
Not to be tortured by the wish to please.
One needn't live in dread of snubs and slights,
Nor praise the verse that every idiot writes,
Nor humor silly Marquesses, nor bestow
Politic sighs on Madam So-and-So.

ARSINOÉ Forget the court, then; let the matter rest.
But I've another cause to be distressed
About your present situation, Sir.
It's to your love affair that I refer.
She whom you love, and who pretends to love you,
Is, I regret to say, unworthy of you.

ALCESTE Why, Madam! Can you seriously intend
To make so grave a charge against your friend?

ARSINOÉ Alas, I must. I've stood aside too long
And let that lady do you grievous wrong;
But now my debt to conscience shall be paid:
I tell you that your love has been betrayed.

ALCESTE I thank you, Madam; you're extremely kind.
Such words are soothing to a lover's mind.

ARSINOÉ Yes, though she *is* my friend, I say again
You're very much too good for Célimène.
She's wantonly misled you from the start.

ALCESTE You may be right; who knows another's heart?
But ask yourself if it's the part of charity
To shake my soul with doubts of her sincerity.

ARSINOÉ Well, if you'd rather be a dupe than doubt her,

That's your affair. I'll say no more about her.

ALCESTE Madam, you know that doubt and vague suspicion
Are painful to a man in my position;
It's most unkind to worry me this way
Unless you've some real proof of what you say.

ARSINOÉ Sir, say no more: all doubt shall be removed,
And all that I've been saying shall be proved.
You've only to escort me home, and there
We'll look into the heart of this affair.
I've ocular evidence which will persuade you
Beyond a doubt, that Célimène's betrayed you.
Then, if you're saddened by that revelation,
Perhaps I can provide some consolation.

Act Four

SCENE ONE

Eliante, Philinte.

PHILINTE Madam, he acted like a stubborn child;
I thought they never would be reconciled;
In vain we reasoned, threatened, and appealed;
He stood his ground and simply would not yield.
The Marshals, I feel sure, have never heard
An argument so splendidly absurd.
"No, gentlemen," said he, "I'll not retract.
His verse is bad: extremely bad, in fact.
Surely it does the man no harm to know it.
Does it disgrace him, not to be a poet?
A gentleman may be respected still,
Whether he writes a sonnet well or ill.
That I dislike his verse should not offend him;
In all that touches honor, I commend him;
He's noble, brave, and virtuous—but I fear
He can't in truth be called a sonneteer.
I'll gladly praise his wardrobe; I'll endorse
His dancing, or the way he sits a horse;
But, gentlemen, I cannot praise his rhyme.
In fact, it ought to be a capital crime
For anyone so sadly unendowed
To write a sonnet, and read the thing aloud."
At length he fell into a gentler mood
And, striking a concessive attitude,
He paid Oronte the following courtesies:
"Sir, I regret that I'm so hard to please,
And I'm profoundly sorry that your lyric
Failed to provoke me to a panegyric."
After these curious words, the two embraced,
And then the hearing was adjourned—in haste.

ELIANTE His conduct has been very singular lately;
Still, I confess that I respect him greatly.
The honesty in which he takes such pride
Has—to my mind—its noble, heroic side.
In this false age, such candor seems outrageous;
But I could wish that it were more contagious.

PHILINTE What most intrigues me in our friend Alceste
Is the grand passion that rages in his breast.
The sullen humors he's compounded of
Should not, I think, dispose his heart to love;
But since they do, it puzzles me still more
That he should choose your cousin to adore.

ELIANTE It does, indeed, belie the theory
That love is born of gentle sympathy,
And that the tender passion must be based
On sweet accords of temper and of taste.

PHILINTE Does she return his love, do you suppose?

ELIANTE Ah, that's a difficult question, Sir. Who knows?
How can we judge the truth of her devotion?
Her heart's a stranger to its own emotion.
Sometimes it thinks it loves, when no love's there;
At other times it loves quite unaware.

PHILINTE I rather think Alceste is in for more
Distress and sorrow than he's bargained for;
Were he of my mind, Madam, his affection
Would turn in quite a different direction,
And we would see him more responsive to
The kind regard which he receives from you.

ELIANTE Sir, I believe in frankness, and I'm inclined,
In matters of the heart, to speak my mind.
I don't oppose his love for her; indeed,
I hope with all my heart that he'll succeed,

And were it in my power, I'd rejoice
In giving him the lady of his choice.
But if, as happens frequently enough
In love affairs, he meets with a rebuff—
If Célimène should grant some rival's suit—
I'd gladly play the role of substitute;
Nor would his tender speeches please me less
Because they'd once been made without success.

PHILINTE Well, Madam, as for me, I don't oppose
Your hopes in this affair; and heaven knows
That in my conversations with the man
I plead your cause as often as I can.
But if those two should marry, and so remove
All chance that he will offer you his love,
Then I'll declare my own, and hope to see
Your gracious favor pass from him to me.
In short, should you be cheated of Alceste,
I'd be most happy to be second best.

ELIANTE Philinte, you're teasing.

PHILINTE   Ah, Madam, never fear;
No words of mine were ever so sincere,
And I shall live in fretful expectation
Till I can make a fuller declaration.

SCENE TWO

Alceste, Eliante, Philinte.

ALCESTE Avenge me, Madam! I must have satisfaction,
Or this great wrong will drive me to distraction!

ELIANTE Why, what's the matter? What's upset you so?

ALCESTE Madam, I've had a mortal, mortal blow.
If Chaos repossessed the universe,
I swear I'd not be shaken any worse.
I'm ruined. . . . I can say no more. . . . My soul . . .

ELIANTE Do try, Sir, to regain your self-control.

ALCESTE Just heaven! Why were so much beauty and grace
Bestowed on one so vicious and so base?

ELIANTE Once more, Sir, tell us . . .

ALCESTE   My world has gone to wrack;

I'm—I'm betrayed; she's stabbed me in the back:
Yes, Célimène (who would have thought it of her?)
Is false to me, and has another lover.

ELIANTE Are you quite certain? Can you prove these things?

PHILINTE Lovers are prey to wild imaginings
And jealous fancies. No doubt there's some mistake. . . .

ALCESTE Mind your own business, Sir, for heaven's sake.

[To Eliante]

Madam, I have the proof that you demand
Here in my pocket, penned by her own hand.
Yes, all the shameful evidence one could want
Lies in this letter written to Oronte—
Oronte! whom I felt sure she couldn't love,
And hardly bothered to be jealous of.

PHILINTE Still, in a letter, appearances may deceive;
This may not be so bad as you believe.

ALCESTE Once more I beg you, Sir, to let me be;
Tend to your own affairs; leave mine to me.

ELIANTE Compose yourself; this anguish that you feel . . .

ALCESTE Is something, Madam, you alone can heal.
My outraged heart, beside itself with grief,
Appeals to you for comfort and relief,
Avenge me on your cousin, whose unjust
And faithless nature has deceived my trust;
Avenge a crime your pure soul must detest.

ELIANTE But how, Sir?

ALCESTE   Madam, this heart within my breast
Is yours; pray take it; redeem my heart from her,
And so avenge me on my torturer.
Let her be punished by the fond emotion,
The ardent love, the bottomless devotion,
The faithful worship which this heart of mine
Will offer up to yours as to a shrine.

ELIANTE You have my sympathy, Sir, in all you suffer;
Nor do I scorn the noble heart you offer;
But I suspect you'll soon be mollified,

And this desire for vengeance will subside.
When some beloved hand has done us wrong
We thirst for retribution—but not for long;
However dark the deed that she's committed,
A lovely culprit's very soon acquitted.
Nothing's so stormy as an injured lover,
And yet no storm so quickly passes over.

ALCESTE   No, Madam, no—this is no lovers' spat;
I'll not forgive her; it's gone too far for that;
My mind's made up; I'll kill myself before
I waste my hopes upon her any more.
Ah, here she is. My wrath intensifies.
I shall confront her with her tricks and lies,
And crush her utterly, and bring you then
A heart no longer slave to Célimène.

SCENE THREE

Célimène, Alceste.

ALCESTE   [*aside*]   Sweet heaven, help me to control my passion.

CÉLIMÈNE   [*aside*]   Oh, Lord.
[*To Alceste*]

                                    Why stand there
staring in that fashion?
And what d'you mean by those dramatic sighs,
And that malignant glitter in your eyes?

ALCESTE   I mean that sins which cause the blood to freeze
Look innocent beside your treacheries;
That nothing Hell's or Heaven's wrath could do
Ever produced so bad a thing as you.

CÉLIMÈNE   Your compliments were always sweet and pretty.

ALCESTE   Madam, it's not the moment to be witty.
No, blush and hang your head: you've ample reason,
Since I've the fullest evidence of your treason.
Ah, this is what my sad heart prophesied;
Now all my anxious fears are verified;
My dark suspicion and my gloomy doubt
Divined the truth, and now the truth is out.
For all your trickery, I was not deceived;
It was my bitter stars that I believed.
But don't imagine that you'll go scot-free;
You shan't misuse me with impunity.

I know that love's irrational and blind;
I know the heart's not subject to the mind,
And can't be reasoned into beating faster;
I know each soul is free to choose its master;
Therefore had you but spoken from the heart,
Rejecting my attentions from the start,
I'd have no grievance, or at any rate
I could complain of nothing but my fate.
Ah, but so falsely to encourage me—
That was a treason and a treachery
For which you cannot suffer too severely,
And you shall pay for that behavior dearly.
Yes, now I have no pity, not a shred;
My temper's out of hand; I've lost my head;
Shocked by the knowledge of your double-dealings,
My reason can't restrain my savage feelings;
A righteous wrath deprives me of my senses,
And I won't answer for the consequences.

CÉLIMÈNE   What does this outburst mean? Will you please explain?
Have you, by any chance, gone quite insane?

ALCESTE   Yes, yes, I went insane the day I fell
A victim to your black and fatal spell,
Thinking to meet with some sincerity
Among the treacherous charms that beckoned me.

CÉLIMÈNE   Pooh. Of what treachery can you complain?

ALCESTE   How sly you are, how cleverly you feign!
But you'll not victimize me any more.
Look: here's a document you've seen before.
This evidence, which I acquired today,
Leaves you, I think, without a thing to say.

CÉLIMÈNE   Is this what sent you into such a fit?

ALCESTE   You should be blushing at the sight of it.

CÉLIMÈNE   Ought I to blush? I truly don't see why.

ALCESTE   Ah, now you're being bold as well as sly;
Since there's no signature, perhaps you'll claim . . .

CÉLIMÈNE   I wrote it, whether or not it bears my name.

ALCESTE   And you can view with equanimity
This proof of your disloyalty to me!

CÉLIMÈNE Oh, don't be so outrageous and extreme.

ALCESTE You take this matter lightly, it would
seem.
Was it no wrong to me, no shame to you,
That you should send Oronte this billet-doux?

CÉLIMÈNE Oronte! Who said it was for him?

ALCESTE   Why, those
Who brought me this example of your prose.
But what's the difference? If you wrote the
letter
To someone else, it pleases me no better.
My grievance and your guilt remain the same.

CÉLIMÈNE But need you rage, and need I blush
for shame,
If this was written to a *woman* friend?

ALCESTE Ah! Most ingenious. I'm impressed no
end;
And after that incredible evasion
Your guilt is clear. I need no more persuasion.
How dare you try so clumsy a deception?
D'you think I'm wholly wanting in perception?
Come, come, let's see how brazenly you'll try
To bolster up so palpable a lie:
Kindly construe this ardent closing section
As nothing more than sisterly affection!
Here, let me read it. Tell me, if you dare to,
That this is for a woman . . .

CÉLIMÈNE   I don't care to.
What right have you to badger and berate me,
And so highhandedly interrogate me?

ALCESTE Now, don't be angry; all I ask of you
Is that you justify a phrase or two . . .

CÉLIMÈNE No, I shall not. I utterly refuse,
And you may take those phrases as you choose.

ALCESTE Just show me how this letter could be
meant
For a woman's eyes, and I shall be content.

CÉLIMÈNE No, no, it's for Oronte; you're per-
fectly right.
I welcome his attentions with delight,
I prize his character and his intellect,
And everything is just as you suspect.
Come, do your worst now; give your rage free
rein;
But kindly cease to bicker and complain.

ALCESTE [*aside*] Good God! Could anything
be more inhuman?

Was ever a heart so mangled by a woman?
When I complain of how she has betrayed me,
She bridles, and commences to upbraid me!
She tries my tortured patience to the limit;
She won't deny her guilt; she glories in it!
And yet my heart's too faint and cowardly
To break these chains of passion, and be free,
To scorn her as it should, and rise above
This unrewarded, mad, and bitter love.
[*To Célimène*]
Ah, traitress, in how confident a fashion
You take advantage of my helpless passion,
And use my weakness for your faithless charms
To make me once again throw down my arms!
But do at least deny this black transgression;
Take back that mocking and perverse confes-
sion;
Defend this letter and your innocence,
And I, poor fool, will aid in your defense.
Pretend, pretend, that you are just and true,
And I shall make myself believe in you.

CÉLIMÈNE Oh, stop it. Don't be such a jealous
dunce,
Or I shall leave off loving you at once.
Just why should I *pretend?* What could impel
me
To stoop so low as that? And kindly tell me
Why, if I loved another, I shouldn't merely
Inform you of it, simply and sincerely!
I've told you where you stand, and that admis-
sion
Should altogether clear me of suspicion;
After so generous a guarantee,
What right have you to harbor doubts of me?
Since women are (from natural reticence)
Reluctant to declare their sentiments,
And since the honor of our sex requires
That we conceal our amorous desires,
Ought any man for whom such laws are broken
To question what the oracle has spoken?
Should he not rather feel an obligation
To trust that most obliging declaration?
Enough, now. Your suspicions quite disgust
me;
Why should I love a man who doesn't trust me?
I cannot understand why I continue,
Fool that I am, to take an interest in you.
I ought to choose a man less prone to doubt,

And give you something to be vexed about.

ALCESTE Ah, what a poor enchanted fool I am;
These gentle words, no doubt, were all a sham;
But destiny requires me to entrust
My happiness to you, and so I must.
I'll love you to the bitter end, and see
How false and treacherous you dare to be.

CÉLIMÈNE No, you don't really love me as you ought.

ALCESTE I love you more than can be said or thought;
Indeed, I wish you were in such distress
That I might show my deep devotedness.
Yes, I could wish that you were wretchedly poor,
Unloved, uncherished, utterly obscure;
That fate had set you down upon the earth
Without possessions, rank, or gentle birth;
Then, by the offer of my heart, I might
Repair the great injustice of your plight;
I'd raise you from the dust, and proudly prove
The purity and vastness of my love.

CÉLIMÈNE This is a strange benevolence indeed!
God grant that I may never be in need. . . .
Ah, here's Monsieur Dubois, in quaint disguise.

SCENE FOUR

Célimène, Alceste, Dubois.

ALCESTE Well, why this costume? Why those frightened eyes?
What ails you?

DUBOIS Well, Sir, things are most mysterious.

ALCESTE What do you mean?

DUBOIS I fear they're very serious.

ALCESTE What?

DUBOIS Shall I speak more loudly?

ALCESTE Yes; speak out.

DUBOIS Isn't there someone here, Sir?

ALCESTE Speak, you lout!
Stop wasting time.

DUBOIS Sir, we must slip away.

ALCESTE How's that?

DUBOIS We must decamp without delay.

ALCESTE Explain yourself.

DUBOIS I tell you we must fly.

ALCESTE What for?

DUBOIS We mustn't pause to say good-by.

ALCESTE Now what d'you mean by all of this, you clown?

DUBOIS I mean, Sir, that we've got to leave this town.

ALCESTE I'll tear you limb from limb and joint from joint
If you don't come more quickly to the point.

DUBOIS Well, Sir, today a man in a black suit,
Who wore a black and ugly scowl to boot,
Left us a document scrawled in such a hand
As even Satan couldn't understand
It bears upon your lawsuit, I don't doubt;
But all Hell's devils couldn't make it out.

ALCESTE Well, well, go on. What then? I fail to see
How this event obliges us to flee.

DUBOIS Well, Sir: an hour later, hardly more,
A gentleman who's often called before
Came looking for you in an anxious way.
Not finding you, he asked me to convey
(Knowing I could be trusted with the same)
The following message. . . . Now, what *was* his name?

ALCESTE Forget his name, you idiot. What did he say?

DUBOIS Well, it was one of your friends, Sir, anyway.
He warned you to begone, and he suggested
That if you stay, you may well be arrested.

ALCESTE What? Nothing more specific? Think, man, think!

DUBOIS No, Sir. He had me bring him pen and ink,
And dashed you off a letter which, I'm sure,
Will render things distinctly less obscure.

ALCESTE Well—let me have it!

CÉLIMÈNE What *is* this all about?

ALCESTE God knows; but I have hopes of finding out.
How long am I to wait, you blitherer?

DUBOIS [*after a protracted search for the letter*]
  I must have left it on your table, Sir.

ALCESTE I ought to . . .

CÉLIMÈNE   No, no, keep your self-
  control;

Act Five

SCENE ONE

Alceste, Philinte.

ALCESTE No, it's too much. My mind's made up,
  I tell you.

PHILINTE Why should this blow, however hard,
  compel you . . .

ALCESTE No, no don't waste your breath in ar-
  gument;
Nothing you say will alter my intent;
This age is vile, and I've made up my mind
To have no further commerce with mankind.
Did not truth, honor, decency, and the laws
Oppose my enemy and approve my cause?
My claims were justified in all men's sight;
I put my trust in equity and right;
Yet, to my horror and the world's disgrace,
Justice is mocked, and I have lost my case!
A scoundrel whose dishonesty is notorious
Emerges from another lie victorious!
Honor and right condone his brazen fraud,
While rectitude and decency applaud!
Before his smirking face, the truth stands
  charmed,
And virtue conquered, and the law disarmed!
His crime is sanctioned by a court decree!
And not content with what he's done to me,
The dog now seeks to ruin me by stating
That I composed a book now circulating,
A book so wholly criminal and vicious
That even to speak its title is seditious!
Meanwhile Oronte, my rival, lends his credit
To the same libelous tale, and helps to spread
  it!
Oronte! a man of honor and of rank,
With whom I've been entirely fair and frank;
Who sought me out and forced me, willy-nilly,
To judge some verse I found extremely silly;
And who, because I properly refused

Go find out what's behind his rigmarole.

ALCESTE It seems that fate, no matter what I do,
Has sworn that I may not converse with you;
But, Madam, pray permit your faithful lover
To try once more before the day is over.

To flatter him, or see the truth abused,
Abets my enemy in a rotten slander!
There's the reward of honesty and candor!
The man will hate me to the end of time
For failing to commend his wretched rhyme!
And not this man alone, but all humanity
Do what they do from interest and vanity;
They prate of honor, truth, and righteousness,
But lie, betray, and swindle nonetheless.
Come then: man's villainy is too much to bear;
Let's leave this jungle and this jackal's lair.
Yes! treacherous and savage race of men,
You shall not look upon my face again.

PHILINTE Oh, don't rush into exile prematurely;
Things aren't as dreadful as you make them,
  surely.
It's rather obvious, since you're still at large,
That people don't believe your enemy's charge.
Indeed, his tale's so patently untrue
That it may do more harm to him than you.

ALCESTE Nothing could do that scoundrel any
  harm:
His frank corruption is his greatest charm,
And, far from hurting him, a further shame
Would only serve to magnify his name.

PHILINTE In any case, his bald prevarication
Has done no injury to your reputation,
And you may feel secure in that regard.
As for your lawsuit, it should not be hard
To have the case reopened, and contest
This judgment. . . .

ALCESTE   No, no, let the verdict
  rest.
Whatever cruel penalty it may bring,
I wouldn't have it changed for anything.
It shows the times' injustice with such clarity
That I shall pass it down to our posterity
As a great proof and signal demonstration
Of the black wickedness of this generation.

It may cost twenty thousand francs; but I
Shall pay their twenty thousand, and gain
  thereby
The right to storm and rage at human evil,
And send the race of mankind to the devil.

PHILINTE Listen to me. . . .

ALCESTE   Why? What can
  you possibly say?
Don't argue, Sir; your labor's thrown away.
Do you propose to offer lame excuses
For men's behavior and the times' abuses?

PHILINTE No, all you say I'll readily concede:
This is a low, conniving age indeed;
Nothing but trickery prospers nowadays,
And people ought to mend their shabby ways.
Yes, man's a beastly creature; but must we
  then
Abandon the society of men?
Here in the world, each human frailty
Provides occasion for philosophy,
And that is virtue's noblest exercise;
If honesty shone forth from all men's eyes,
If every heart were frank and kind and just,
What could our virtues do but gather dust
(Since their employment is to help us bear
The villainies of men without despair)?
A heart well-armed with virtue can endure. . . .

ALCESTE Sir, you're a matchless reasoner, to be
  sure;
Your words are fine and full of cogency;
But don't waste time and eloquence on me.
My reason bids me go, for my own good.
My tongue won't lie and flatter as it should;
God knows what frankness it might next com-
  mit,
And what I'd suffer on account of it.
Pray let me wait for Célimène's return
In peace and quiet. I shall shortly learn,
By her response to what I have in view,
Whether her love for me is feigned or true.

PHILINTE Till then, let's visit Eliante upstairs.

ALCESTE No, I am too weighed down with som-
  ber cares.
Go to her, do; and leave me with my gloom
Here in the darkened corner of this room.

PHILINTE Why, that's no sort of company, my
  friend;
I'll see if Eliante will not descend.

SCENE TWO

Célimène, Oronte, Alceste.

ORONTE Yes, Madam, if you wish me to remain
Your true and ardent lover, you must deign
To give me some more positive assurance.
All this suspense is quite beyond endurance.
If your heart shares the sweet desires of mine,
Show me as much by some convincing sign;
And here's the sign I urgently suggest;
That you no longer tolerate Alceste,
But sacrifice him to my love, and sever
All your relations with the man forever.

CÉLIMÈNE Why do you suddenly dislike him so?
You praised him to the skies not long ago.

ORONTE Madam, that's not the point. I'm here
  to find
Which way your tender feelings are inclined.
Choose, if you please, between Alceste and me,
And I shall stay or go accordingly.

ALCESTE [*emerging from the corner*] Yes, Mad-
  am, choose; this gentleman's demand
Is wholly just, and I support his stand.
I too am true and ardent; I too am here
To ask you that you make your feelings clear.
No more delays, now; no equivocation;
The time has come to make your declaration.

ORONTE Sir, I've no wish in any way to be
An obstacle to your felicity.

ALCESTE Sir, I've no wish to share her heart
  with you;
That may sound jealous, but at least it's true.

ORONTE If, weighing us, she leans in your direction . . .

ALCESTE If she regards you with the least affection . . .

ORONTE I swear I'll yield her to you there and
  then.

ALCESTE I swear I'll never see her face again.

ORONTE Now, Madam, tell us what we've come
  to hear.

ALCESTE Madam, speak openly and have no
  fear.

ORONTE Just say which one is to remain your
  lover.

ALCESTE Just name one name, and it will all be
  over.

ORONTE What! Is it possible that you're undecided?

ALCESTE What! Can your feelings possibly be
divided?

CÉLIMÈNE Enough: this inquisition's gone too
far:
How utterly unreasonable you are!
Not that I couldn't make the choice with ease;
My heart has no conflicting sympathies;
I know full well which one of you I favor,
And you'd not see me hesitate or waver.
But how can you expect me to reveal
So cruelly and bluntly what I feel?
I think it altogether too unpleasant
To choose between two men when both are
present;
One's heart has means more subtle and more
kind
Of letting its affections be divined,
Nor need one be uncharitably plain
To let a lover know he loves in vain.

ORONTE No, no, speak plainly; I for one can
stand it.
I beg you to be frank.

ALCESTE   And I demand it.
The simple truth is what I wish to know,
And there's no need for softening the blow.
You've made an art of pleasing everyone,
But now your days of coquetry are done:
You have no choice now, Madam, but to
choose,
For I'll know what to think if you refuse;
I'll take your silence for a clear admission
That I'm entitled to my worst suspicion.

ORONTE I thank you for this ultimatum, Sir,
And I may say I heartily concur.

CÉLIMÈNE Really, this foolishness is very wear-
ing:
Must you be so unjust and overbearing?
Haven't I told you why I must demur?
Ah, here's Eliante; I'll put the case to her.

SCENE THREE

Eliante, Philinte, Célimène, Oronte, Alceste.

CÉLIMÈNE Cousin, I'm being persecuted here
By these two persons, who, it would appear,

Will not be satisfied till I confess
Which one I love the more, and which the less,
And tell the latter to his face that he
Is henceforth banished from my company.
Tell me, has ever such a thing been done?

ELIANTE You'd best not turn to me; I'm not the
one
To back you in a matter of this kind:
I'm all for those who frankly speak their mind.

ORONTE Madam, you'll search in vain for a de-
fender.

ALCESTE You're beaten, Madam, and may as
well surrender.

ORONTE Speak, speak, you must; and end this
awful strain.

ALCESTE Or don't, and your position will be
plain.

ORONTE A single word will close this painful
scene.

ALCESTE But if you're silent, I'll know what you
mean.

SCENE FOUR

*Arsinoé, Célimène, Eliante, Alceste, Philinte,
Acaste, Clitandre, Oronte.*

ACASTE [*to Célimène*] Madam, with all due deference, we two
Have come to pick a little bone with you.

CLITANDRE [*to Oronte and Alceste*] I'm glad
you're present, Sirs; as you'll soon learn,
Our business here is also your concern.

ARSINOÉ [*to Célimène*] Madam, I visit you so
soon again
Only because of these two gentlemen,
Who came to me indignant and aggrieved
About a crime too base to be believed.
Knowing your virtue, having such confidence
in it,
I couldn't think you guilty for a minute,
In spite of all their telling evidence;
And, rising above our little difference,
I've hastened here in friendship's name to see
You clear yourself of this great calumny.

ACASTE Yes, Madam, let us see with what composure
You'll manage to respond to this disclosure.

The Misanthrope   283

You lately sent Clitandre this tender note.

CLITANDRE   And this one, for Acaste, you also
  wrote.

ACASTE [*to Oronte and Alceste*]   You'll recognize
  this writing, Sirs, I think;
The lady is so free with pen and ink
That you must know it all too well, I fear.
But listen: this is something you should hear.

"How absurd you are to condemn my light-
heartedness in society, and to accuse me of
being happiest in the company of others. Nothing could be more unjust; and if you do not
come to me instantly and beg pardon for saying
such a thing, I shall never forgive you as long
as I live. Our big bumbling friend the Viscount . . ."

What a shame that he's not here.

"Our big bumbling friend the Viscount, whose
name stands first in your complaint, is hardly
a man to my taste; and ever since the day I
watched him spend three-quarters of an hour
spitting into a well, so as to make circles in the
water, I have been unable to think highly of
him. As for the little Marquess . . ."

In all modesty, gentlemen, that is I.

"As for the little Marquess, who sat squeezing
my hand for such a long while yesterday, I find
him in all respects the most trifling creature
alive; and the only things of value about him
are his cape and his sword. As for the man with
the green ribbons . . ."

[*To Alceste*]
It's your turn now, Sir.

"As for the man with the green ribbons, he
amuses me now and then with his bluntness
and his bearish ill-humor; but there are many
times indeed when I think him the greatest bore
in the world. And as for the sonneteer . . ."

[*To Oronte*]
Here's your helping.

"And as for the sonneteer, who has taken it
into his head to be witty, and insists on being

an author in the teeth of opinion, I simply
cannot be bothered to listen to him, and his
prose wearies me quite as much as his poetry.
Be assured that I am not always so well-
entertained as you suppose; that I long for
your company, more than I dare to say, at all
these entertainments to which people drag me;
and that the presence of those one loves is the
true and perfect seasoning to all one's pleasures."

CLITANDRE   And now for me.

"Clitandre, whom you mention, and who so
pesters me with his saccharine speeches, is the
last man on earth for whom I could feel any
affection. He is quite mad to suppose that I
love him, and so are you, to doubt that you
are loved. Do come to your senses; exchange
your suppositions for his; and visit me as often
as possible, to help me bear the annoyance of
his unwelcome attentions."

It's a sweet character that these letters show,
And what to call it, Madam, you well know.
Enough. We're off to make the world ac-
  quainted
With this sublime self-portrait that you've
  painted.

ACASTE   Madam, I'll make you no farewell ora-
  tion;
No, you're not worthy of my indignation.
Far choicer hearts than yours, as you'll dis-
  cover,
Would like this little Marquess for a lover.

SCENE FIVE

*Célimène, Eliante, Arsinoé, Alceste, Oronte,
Philinte.*

ORONTE   So! After all those loving letters you
  wrote,
You turn on me like this, and cut my throat!
And your dissembling, faithless heart, I find,
Has pledged itself by turns to all mankind!
How blind I've been! But now I clearly see;
I thank you, Madam, for enlightening me.
My heart is mine once more, and I'm content;

The loss of it shall be your punishment.
[*To Alceste*]
Sir, she is yours; I'll seek no more to stand
Between your wishes and this lady's hand.

SCENE SIX

Célimène, Eliante, Arsinoé, Alceste, Philinte.

ARSINOÉ [*to Célimène*] Madam, I'm forced to speak. I'm far too stirred
To keep my counsel, after what I've heard.
I'm shocked and staggered by your want of morals.
It's not my way to mix in others' quarrels;
But really, when this fine and noble spirit,
This man of honor and surpassing merit,
Laid down the offering of his heart before you,
How *could* you . . .
ALCESTE Madam, permit me, I implore you,
To represent myself in this debate.
Don't bother, please, to be my advocate.
My heart, in any case, could not afford
To give your services their due reward;
And if I chose, for consolation's sake,
Some other lady, 'twould not be you I'd take.
ARSINOÉ What makes you think you could, Sir?
And how dare you
Imply that I've been trying to ensnare you?
If you can for a moment entertain
Such flattering fancies, you're extremely vain.
I'm not so interested as you suppose
In Célimène's discarded gigolos.
Get rid of that absurd illusion, do.
Women like me are not for such as you.
Stay with this creature, to whom you're so attached;
I've never seen two people better matched.

SCENE SEVEN

Célimène, Eliante, Alceste, Philinte.

ALCESTE [*to Célimène*] Well, I've been still throughout this exposé,
Till everyone but me has said his say.
Come, have I shown sufficient self-restraint?
And may I now . . .

CÉLIMÈNE Yes, make your just complaint.
Reproach me freely, call me what you will;
You've every right to say I've used you ill.
I've wronged you, I confess it; and in my shame
I'll make no effort to escape the blame.
The anger of those others I could despise;
My guilt toward you I sadly recognize.
Your wrath is wholly justified, I fear;
I know how culpable I must appear,
I know all things bespeak my treachery,
And that, in short, you've grounds for hating me.
Do so; I give you leave.
ALCESTE Ah, traitress—how,
How should I cease to love you, even now?
Though mind and will were passionately bent
On hating you, my heart would not consent.
[*To Eliante and Philinte*]
Be witness to my madness, both of you;
See what infatuation drives one to;
But wait; my folly's only just begun,
And I shall prove to you before I'm done
How strange the human heart is, and how far
From rational we sorry creatures are.
[*To Célimène*]
Woman, I'm willing to forget your shame,
And clothe your treacheries in a sweeter name;
I'll call them youthful errors, instead of crimes,
And lay the blame on these corrupting times.
My one condition is that you agree
To share my chosen fate, and fly with me
To that wild, trackless, solitary place
In which I shall forget the human race.
Only by such a course can you atone
For those atrocious letters; by that alone
Can you remove my present horror of you,
And make it possible for me to love you.
CÉLIMÈNE What! *I* renounce the world at my young age,
And die of boredom in some hermitage?
ALCESTE Ah, if you really loved me as you ought,
You wouldn't give the world a moment's thought;
Must you have me, and all the world beside?
CÉLIMÈNE Alas, at twenty one is terrified

Of solitude. I fear I lack the force
And depth of soul to take so stern a course.
But if my hand in marriage will content you,
Why, there's a plan which I might well consent
  to,
And . . .

ALCESTE   No. I detest you now. I could excuse
Everything else, but since you thus refuse
To love me wholly, as a wife should do,
And see the world in me, as I in you,
Go! I reject your hand, and disenthrall
My heart from your enchantments, once for all.

SCENE EIGHT

Eliante, Alceste, Philinte.

ALCESTE [*to Eliante*]   Madam, your virtuous
  beauty has no peer;
Of all this world, you only are sincere;
I've long esteemed you highly, as you know;
Permit me ever to esteem you so,
And if I do not now request your hand,
Forgive me, Madam, and try to understand.

I feel unworthy of it; I sense that fate
Does not intend me for the married state,
That I should do you wrong by offering you
My shattered heart's unhappy residue,
And that in short . . .

ELIANTE   Your argument's well
  taken:
Nor need you fear that I shall feel forsaken.
Were I to offer him this hand of mine,
Your friend Philinte, I think, would not decline.

PHILINTE   Ah, Madam, that's my heart's most
  cherished goal,
For which I'd gladly give my life and soul.

ALCESTE [*to Eliante and Philinte*]   May you be
  true to all you now profess,
And so deserve unending happiness.
Meanwhile, betrayed and wronged in every-
  thing,
I'll flee this bitter world where vice is king,
And seek some spot unpeopled and apart
Where I'll be free to have an honest heart.

PHILINTE   Come, Madam, let's do everything we
  can
To change the mind of this unhappy man.

*LE MISANTHROPE is unquestionably concerned with manners;
but what is the relative importance of manners and character,
of society and the individual, in the play? And how limited is the
society with which it deals?*

More than any of his other comedies, *Le Misanthrope* portrays high Parisian society. Molière is not dealing, as some of his admirers would lead us to suppose, with society in general, for he presents only one class and neglects family relations, religious, political, and economic conditions, etc. But his picture of *la société mondaine* is remarkably large and impressive. We see seventeenth-century upper-class society in its amusements, its relation to the court, its interest in conversation, law-suits, dueling, gossip, portraiture, costume, poetry, and love making. . . . Moreover, Molière exposes the superficiality and falsity of this society and raises

the question whether it is better to tolerate it or to leave it. [Henry Carrington Lancaster, *A History of French Dramatic Literature in the Seventeenth Century*, Johns Hopkins Press, Baltimore, 1936, Part III, vol. 2, p. 657.]

In the great comedies, with which [Molière] took the most pains, a picture of manners unrolls in which the condition of the characters tends to be lost from sight. In the *Misanthrope*, the greatest of them all, a certain familiarity with the period and the language is required in reading the play, to realize that these persons are great ladies and gentlemen, adorned by the prestige that opinion attaches to great names, and separated by a gulf from the "bonne bourgeoisie." . . . Do not scenes like that of mutual criticism between Célimène and Arsinoé give the impression that the difference between these great ladies and a pair of fishwives is more a matter of manners than of fineness of feeling? . . . The characters of the *Misanthrope* are not primarily the dukes, marquises, viscountesses, which their counterparts in reality would have been, but are compromisers, coquettes, prudes, fops, asses, and misanthropists. Of course their idleness marks these people as members of that society in which . . . good manners could be developed to their highest perfection because no one had anything else to do. . . . The portrait gallery of Célimène contains perhaps figures especially appropriate to her circle, yet [these types] are not to be found exclusively among the best people.

In other words, Molière gives a picture of society in which character is shown as more important than station in the relations of men with each other. Society appears more comic when people are regarded as varieties of the *genus homo* than when they are considered as occupants of this or that position or bearers of this or that title. His comedy is more a comedy of character than a comedy of manners, more a picture of universal humanity than a picture of contemporary society. [Percy Addison Chapman, *The Spirit of Molière: An Interpretation,* ed. Jean-Albert Bédé, Princeton University Press, Princeton, N.J., 1940, pp. 239–240.]

"He did not set out to write a comedy full of incidents," said Visé in a commentary which is believed to have been published with Molière's approval, "but simply a play in which he could speak against the manners of the age."

There is one striking difference between the *Misanthrope* and Molière's other plays. He does not confine himself to the study of the psychology of an individual seen against the background of a stable society. His irony is turned on society as well as on Alceste, and the play ends . . . not with the restoration of order, but with something that is very like a mark of interrogation. [Martin Turnell, *The Classical Moment: Studies*

of Corneille, Molière and Racine, Hamish Hamilton, Ltd., London, 1947, p. 92.]

[Alceste] exhibits . . . all the stigmata of the comic figure, but in an entirely novel way. Whereas the comic figure had been cut off from the world by his unreason, Alceste is cut off from it by his reasonableness and his goodness— qualities that he has in excess, to be sure, but for their excess society is at least as much to blame as his own make-up.

> I want straightforwardness and upright dealing
> And no word said except from honest feeling.

In those lines you have a virtuous temper on a reasoned basis, only the reasoning has no congruity with such comic reasoning as shapes the social order at which he lashes out. And here is a major new departure. Social comedy is invariably an analysis of individuality, and the comic figure is invariably an individual; but he is an absurd individual, not for a moment capable of maintaining his position. Here, on the contrary, is a ridiculous person triple-armored in reason, occupying positions defensible by logic; a completely integrated, self-contained individual who stands or falls by an interpretation of himself that flatly contradicts the comic interpretation.

> My word, good sirs, I never thought to find
> Myself so ludicrous.

It is in such challenges that we must read the riddle of the Misanthrope—the valiant fighter who begins by proclaiming to Philinte: "So much the worse for anyone that laughs!" However devoid of the comic perception, he is perfectly aware that he can become an object of ridicule; and he means to prove that a man can rise to withstanding the comic spirit and nullifying it, and that goodness is more powerful than society. [Ramon Fernandez, *Molière: The Man Seen through the Plays,* trans. Wilson Follet, Hill and Wang, Inc., New York, 1958, pp. 155–156.]

Few critics would call Alceste a completely comic figure; but fewer still would claim for him completely sympathetic and even tragic nobility. There is little agreement, indeed, on which of his traits are foolish and which admirable.

Alceste is comic in his lack of a sense of proportion, in the violence of his indignation over small matters, in his indifference to the *moeurs* of a *salon,* in the manner in which he upbraids the woman he loves, in the fact that he seems himself to be devoid of a sense of humor, but at the same time his uncompromising honesty wins our admiration, and the intensity of his passion, our sympathy. He has dreamed of an ideal world in which the truth is the only goal. This aim he follows as far as we can see him, without regard for his own fortunes or the feelings of his fellows. [Lancaster, *op. cit.*, pp. 658–659.]

The truth is, the comic character may, strictly speaking, be quite in accord with stern morality. All it has to do is to bring itself into accord with society. The character of Alceste is that of a thoroughly honest man. But then he is unsociable, and, on that very account, ludicrous. A flexible vice may not be so easy to ridicule as a rigid virtue. It is *rigidity* that society eyes with suspicion. Consequently, it is the rigidity of Alceste that makes us laugh, though here rigidity stands for honesty. The man who withdraws into himself is liable to ridicule, because the comic is largely made up of this very withdrawal. This accounts for the comic being so frequently dependent on the manners or ideas, or, to put it bluntly, on the prejudices, of a society. [Henri Bergson, "Laughter" (1900), *Comedy*, Doubleday & Company, Inc., New York, 1956, p. 150. Introduction and Appendix by Wylie Sypher.]

Alceste ends up by deciding to shun the world of men. But what is this world? It is made up mostly of sham, of pretentiousness, of injustice, of malice. It is a world of selfishness and of lies, in which bad poets are praised, in which influence and not equity controls the administration of justice . . . in which externals are taken as sure indications of true merit, and where characters as well as hearts may be used as matter for game regardless of the consequence. It is a world in which one says what one does not mean and in which nothing is worse than silence unless it be sincerity. Worst of all it is a world which pities a virtuous man. This is the world as seen not merely through the eyes of Alceste, but as seen by Molière, for all of what I have mentioned actually emerges in the play. And so in a sense the tables are turned. Instead of the usual ridiculous character attempting to operate in a sane and natural world, we have in Alceste a *simply logical* individual unable to operate in a world of completely distorted values. [E. B. O. Borgerhoff, *The Freedom of French Classicism,* Princeton University Press, Princeton, N.J., 1950, pp. 156–157.]

Society—or the comic intelligence—reflects a person's own likeness back to him. Alceste will have none of this distorting mirror; it makes him close both his eyes and his fists. But he thereby quite ceases to see himself and hence to examine himself. His reasonableness and his goodness had had no props outside himself, and he is therefore no longer able to distinguish their dictates from those of his own ego. His idiosyncrasies appear to him as revelations vouchsafed by reason, his fits of temper as righteous inspirations. . . .

It is possible for an individual, instead of shutting his eyes, to muster enough strength to shatter the mirror that a given society is, in order to put another in its place. It will always be averred after the fact that a society can be transformed when its rules penalize or outrage men's best attributes. But there remains, deep within and inexpugnable, the inconsistency that the person once self-deceived detects in his behavior; and what manner of revolution is to extirpate that? The Misanthrope recognizes this contradiction in himself, and his "undying" hatred and his flight into the wilderness are partly dictated by disappointment in himself—major facts too often overlooked. In other words, Alceste becomes transformed; even in his own eyes he is not the man at the end that he was at the beginning; and when he gives up the struggle he is overthrown as much by his own verdict as by society's.

The story of Alceste is primarily the story of a will power that goes bankrupt. Note how, in the early acts, he expresses himself persistently and vehemently in the language of volition: "I want people to be straightforward," "I mean to get angry." He seems to have no doubt that a man can regulate his behavior according to his will, and this belief curiously increases the severity of his judgments of people. This vigorous man, this vehicle of an unacknowledged reasonableness, is contending for something more than mere reasonableness: he is trying to wrest Célimène away from a world of depravities, and he battles as he does because he possesses self-confidence, and he has self-confidence because he believes that he is loved. . . . He bets on his will; over and above that he lives on advances against a capital fund of heroism that he takes for granted. The different parts notch into one another; on Alceste's behavior in relation to Célimène depends the justification of his attitude throughout the play. But there ensues Célimène's betrayal, followed by an appalling reversal on the part of Alceste. Here is the moment for him to be the man he thinks he is. First, then, in a gesture of magnificent rage he lays down the law to his emotions by offering his heart to Éliante. Enter Célimène. She displays sham feeling; she quibbles frivolously; she calculates the odds; she flings taunts; she is first evasive and then arrogant; in short, she does everything that would tend to harden Alceste's determination. But what do the dictates of the will amount to now? . . .

Alceste's frustration culminates in the closing scene . . . Here he is no longer the same person, not only because he is suffering torments through his love, but also because his love has just shown him his kinship with the monsters of that pit in which the vices hold sway—a discovery that he owes to his perception of what in him lies and to his loss of trust in his own will power. And in the final terms proposed by Alceste and rejected by Célimène do we not descry a half conscious expedient for recovering the conviction that his life makes sense? a sort of tacit license that he confers on himself to resume the language of volition and the appearance of complying with it? [Fernandez, *op. cit.*, pp. 156–158.]

. . . Alceste's violence leads to a state of hysteria—Molière's word for it is *emportement* —in which the actual world is transformed into a comic nightmare, reminding us a little oddly of a Disney cartoon. The nightmare is in Alceste's mind, and the contrast between his distorted outlook and unreasonable behaviour and the humdrum world in which he lives makes him at once a comic and a moving figure. Our response . . . to the whole play, is a balance between two impulses which superficially appear to exclude one another—the impulse to laugh at Alceste's absurdity and the impulse to pity the obvious waste of his gifts. The art of the comic writer depends on preserving this nice balance between two apparently contradictory emotions, on the continual switch from one set of feelings to another and back again without ever allowing the balance to tip over to the extremes of tragedy or farce. . . . Alceste reaches the point at which reason totters, but he . . . will retreat into the world of words and harmless denunciation. It is not the least of the dramatist's achievements that he establishes this feeling of confidence in his audience and convinces us that it will be so.

It is the failure to understand this that has led to many of the attempts to turn *The Misanthrope* into a tragedy. Fernandez, for example, has suggested that in the course of the play Alceste's character undergoes a radical change and that the man who departs for the "desert" as the curtain falls is no longer the same man as the fiery reformer of Act I. The change is supposed to lie in the collapse of the will. It is an entertaining theory, but I can find no evidence for it in the text of the play. It is true that Alceste is always using expressions of great determination . . . but . . . there is no real volition behind the words which are a sort of smoke screen used to hide a complete absence of determination.

The Alceste of Act V is identical with the Alceste of Act I. His *physical* exile is the logical outcome of the *psychological* exile—the retreat into a private world—which is studied with such profound insight in the course of the play. [Turnell, *op. cit.*, pp. 101–102.]

In satire, one or more characters usually represent the norm—the social and moral standard which the satirist regards as correct. In The Misanthrope *the norm has been found in Philinte, in Eliante, even in Alceste, and in a combination of characters.*

Affection for Alceste is apt to turn writers against Philinte, or, when one of them condemns the former, he exalts the latter, but there is no evidence that either was a spokesman for Molière, or that he regarded either as a villain. Philinte is, of course, excessive in his praises and declares that he is no more disturbed by the trickery, injustice, and selfishness of mankind than he is to see "*Des singes malfaisants, et des loups speins de rage.*" But he shows great forbearance in dealing with Alceste and he must have had certain virtues in order to win his friendship and the hand of Éliante, even though he may not have been cut, like Alceste, from the cloth of which martyrs and autocrats are made. Like him, Éliante accepts the universe, but she does not flatter as he sometimes does, nor does she renounce society, though she admires Alceste and is for those who speak their thoughts. [Lancaster, *op. cit.*, pp. 659–660.]

In *The Misanthrope* . . . Philinte is the sensible person in whose view Alceste's bumptious plain-speaking is absurd in one direction and Oronte's obsequiousness absurd in the other. Similarly Éliante stands between Célimène's flirtatiousness and Arsinoé's prudery. . . .

The sensible man of Molière is the exact opposite of the romantic hero developed in the drama of the next century. To Rousseau, the prophet of romanticism, Philinte, who conformed to social usage, was therefore a despicable hypocrite; and Alceste, who rebelled at white lies, was therefore noble. In Molière's view, on the contrary, to conform in small things was to restrict one's freedom in nonessentials for the sake of greater freedom in essentials. [Alan Reynolds Thompson, *The Anatomy of Drama*, University of California Press, Berkeley, Calif., 1942, p. 214.]

Although Philinte is certainly Molière's spokesman in many places and certainly helps to provide the background of reason and sanity which contributes largely to the poise of the play, his role is a shifting one. We do not feel . . . that the whole of the play is behind his words, and the explanation is to be found in Éliante's observations on Alceste in Act IV, Scene I . . .

Éliante is the only wholly sympathetic character in the play. It would not be accurate to say that she represents Molière's own point of view more completely than Philinte, but her role is of the first importance. In *The Misanthrope* . . . Molière felt the need of two spokesmen. . . . Éliante qualifies the role of Philinte and it is this that gives the play a mellowness which is unique in Molière's work. For Éliante's words display a fresh attitude towards the comic hero. . . . Alceste awakens the sympathies of the audience to a degree which is exceptional in seventeenth-century and indeed in all comedy.

Éliante minimizes Alceste's peculiarities and by placing the emphasis on his "rare virtue" she corrects Philinte. [Turnell, *op. cit.*, pp. 104–105.]

Who then represents Molière? Éliante, Alceste, or Philinte? I believe that it is impossible to say, unless they all do. And if that is so then we are faced with all sorts of contradictions. And it seems to me that these contradictions are there and are not removable. The world is as it is, Molière seems to say, with a great many objectionable features. One has to accept them. It is useless to attempt to correct them, and if one tries, one only makes one's self ridiculous, and yet . . . [Borgerhoff, *op. cit.*, p. 159.]

The dénouement of the play is unusual for comedy, and is often dismissed as unsatisfactory. Attempts to explain it deal with the nature of the problem which Molière set for himself and with the sort of solution which it demanded.

And so all the easy philosophy of moderation really breaks down and we are left with what is actually a rather heartless situation. Éliante, the sincere person who loves, or at least could love Alceste, too easily takes Philinte as second choice, while Alceste, who desperately wishes to love sincerely a sincere person, has to leave because he feels himself unworthy of the woman he ought to love, and because he feels that the woman he loves is unworthy of him. All of this is in the dénouement and the play has to be ended of course. But precisely, there could be no satisfactory end, because there is no humanly satisfactory general solution to the problem of human behavior. And in this play Molière put himself in a position where the morality was reduced to that problem. . . .

With all the laughter and the simplicity and the balance then, Molière leaves us with a question mark, because he had himself the sense to see the satisfaction in excess, and the limitations of reasonableness. [Borgerhoff, *op. cit.*, pp. 159–160.]

At the close of the play society, in the persons of Célimène and her retainers, leaves by one exit and Alceste abandons society by another, leaving an empty stage. . . .

In *The Misanthrope*, more than in any of the other plays, the *honnête homme* is a symbolical figure and Molière is particularly careful to avoid the appearance of imposing a solution. The most that he does is to suggest that a blending of the virtues of Philinte and Éliante may have some bearing on the complicated situation which he has created. In no other play does he reveal such variety and complexity of feelings, but in no other does he show such reluctance to judge the individual or so marked a tendency to call in question all accepted standards and formulas. It is a masterly exploration of the motives behind social behaviour; feelings are tracked down, as surely as in Racine, to the moment of their formation; but judgment on them is suspended. There is in truth no formal ending to the play. The catharsis lies in the clarifying of our feelings, in the perception that social adjustment is a personal matter where in the last resort no facile slogan or philosophical system can help us; and the "message," if we must have one, is that we must have the courage to create our own "order," whatever the cost, instead of yielding to the temptation of an easy escape. [Turnell, *op. cit.*, pp. 119–120.]

JEAN RACINE

1639–1699

*A chart of the influences that helped to shape Racine's thought
and dramatic technique must include most of the major figures of
the seventeenth century in France: the critic and legislator of French
classicism, Boileau; the poet and maker of fables, La Fontaine;
the playwrights Corneille and Molière; almost all who were
associated with Port-Royal, the convent and school where the
austere doctrines of Jansenism were formulated and practised;
even Mme. de Maintenon, the second wife of Louis XIV, at
whose request Racine wrote his last two plays, the Biblical
dramas* Esther (*1689*) *and* Athaliah (*1691*). *Racine was a student
at Port-Royal, where he was sent by his Jansenist grandmother
after his parents died. At the school, he was soaked in Greek
and Latin literature as well as severe theological doctrines
stressing the weakness of the human will. He began his dramatic
career as a mere imitator of Corneille, but by his third play,*
Andromache (*1667*), *written on the model of Euripides, he was
considered by many an incomparably gifted writer of tragedy.
He triumphed over the attempts of friends of Corneille, among
them Molière, to bring about his downfall. After the success of*
Berenice *in the same season* (*1670*) *that Corneille offered a
play based on exactly the same passage in Suetonius, his position
was unassailable. His other plays, even the satire on the law
courts,* Les Plaideurs (The Litigants) *1668, are still absorbing
to the reader. But none so dazzles the emotions or offers such a
good case for the prescribed structure of the classical drama
as* Phaedra (*1677*). *Its perfections make all the more regrettable
Racine's subsequent retirement from the theater, complete except
for the two plays he was persuaded to write by Mme. de Maintenon.*

Phaedra

TRANSLATED BY KENNETH MUIR

Characters

THESEUS *King of Athens*

PHAEDRA *his wife*

HIPPOLYTUS *son of Theseus and Antiope*

ARICIA *Princess of the blood royal of Athens*

THERAMENES *tutor to Hippolytus*

ŒNONE *nurse and confidante of Phaedra*

ISMENE *confidante of Aricia*

PANOPE *woman of Phaedra's suite*

GUARDS

The action of the play takes place in Troezen.

Act One

SCENE ONE

Hippolytus and Theramenes.

HIPPOLYTUS It is decided, dear Theramenes.
I'm leaving now, and cutting short my stay
In pleasant Troezen. In my state of doubt
I blush at my own sloth. Six months and more
My father has been absent, yet I stay
Still ignorant of his fate, not even knowing
In what part of the world he hides his head.

THERAMENES Where will you seek him then? I
 have already,
My lord, to satisfy your natural fears,
Crossed the Corinthian sea, and asked for
 Theseus
Upon those distant shores where Acheron
Is lost among the dead. I went to Elidos
And sailed from Tenaros upon the sea
Where Icarus once fell. By what new hope,
Or in what lucky region will you find
His footprints now? Who knows, indeed, who
 knows
Whether it is the King your father's will,
That we should try to probe the mystery
Of his long absence? While we are afraid,
Even for his life, that hero, unperturbed,
Screening from us his latest love exploit,
May just be waiting till a woman . . .

HIPPOLYTUS   Stop,
Dear Theramenes; respect the King
Who has outgrown the headstrong faults of
 youth.

No such unworthy obstacle detains him.
Phaedra has conquered his inconstancy,
And fears no rival now. In seeking him,
I do my duty, and thereby escape
A place I dare not stay in.

THERAMENES   Since when, my lord,
Have you been frightened of the peaceful place
You used to love in childhood? You once pre-
    ferred it
To the noisy pomp of Athens and the court.
What danger, or rather, should I say, what
    grief
Drives you away?

HIPPOLYTUS   Alas, that happy time
Is now no more. For everything has changed
Since to these shores the gods despatched the
    Queen,
The daughter of Minos and of Pasiphaë.

THERAMENES   I know the cause indeed; for Phae-
    dra here
Vexes and wounds your sight—a dangerous
Stepmother, who had scarce set eyes on you
Ere she procured your exile. But her hatred
Is either vanished, or at least relaxed.
Besides, what perils can you undergo
From a dying woman, one who seeks to die?
Phaedra, who will not speak about her illness,
Tired of herself and even of the sunshine,
Is scarcely hatching plots against you.

HIPPOLYTUS   No:
Her vain hostility is not my fear.
In leaving her, I flee another foe:
I flee—I will admit it—young Aricia,
Last of a fatal race that has conspired
Against us.

THERAMENES   What? Do you yourself, my lord,
Persecute her? The Pallantids' lovely sister
Was not involved in her treacherous brothers'
    plots.
And should you hate her innocent charms?

HIPPOLYTUS   If I
Did hate her, I would not be fleeing.

THERAMENES   My lord,
May I explain your flight? Is it that you
No longer are that proud Hippolytus,
Relentless enemy of the laws of love,
And of a yoke to which your father bowed
So many times? Does Venus whom your pride
So long has slighted wish to justify

The amorous Theseus? While, like the rest of
    mortals,
You're forced to cense her altars? Are you in
    love,
My lord?

HIPPOLYTUS   What do you dare to ask, my friend?
You have known my heart since it began to
    beat,
And can you ask me to repudiate
My former proud, disdainful sentiments?
I sucked the pride which so amazes you
From an Amazonian mother; and when I
    reached
A riper age, and knew myself, I gloried
In what I was. Then in your friendly zeal
You told me all my father's history.
My soul, attentive to your voice, was thrilled
To hear the tale of his heroic deeds—
Consoling mortals for Alcides' absence,
By slaying monsters, putting brigands down,
Procrustes, Cercyon, Sciron, and Sinis,
The scattered bones of the giant of Epidaurus,
Crete reeking with the Minotaur's foul blood.
But when you told of deeds less glorious,
The way his faith was pledged a hundred times—
Helen of Sparta stolen from her kin,
Salamis witness of Periboea's tears,
And many more, whose names he has forgotten,
Of credulous women by his love deceived:
Ariadne on her rocky isle
Telling her wrongs; and Phaedra at the last,
Kidnapped, but under better auspices;
You know how listening to the sorry tale
I begged you cut it short, and would have been
Happy to blot out from my memory
The worser half of the tale. And shall I now
Be bound so ignominiously by the gods?
My base affections, unlike those of Theseus,
Can claim no heap of honors as excuse,
And so deserve more scorn. As I have slain
No monster yet, I have not earned the right
So to transgress; and if my pride must melt,
Should I have chosen for my conqueror
Aricia? Surely my wandering senses
Should have recalled that we are kept apart
By an eternal obstacle. My father
Holds her in reprobation, and forbids her
Ever to marry: of a guilty stem
He fears a shoot, and wishes to entomb

With her the memory of her brothers' name.
Under his tutelage until she dies,
Never for her shall Hymen's fires be lit.
Should I support her rights against a father
Incensed against her, give example to
Temerity, and let my youth embark
Upon a wild sca? . . .

THERAMENES   If your hour is come,
My lord, heaven cares not for our reasons.
  Theseus,
Wishing to shut your eyes, has opened them.
His hatred, rousing a rebellious flame,
Lends a new luster to his enemy.
But, after all, why fear an honest love?
If it is sweet, why should you not dare taste it?
Why will you trust a shy or sullen scruple?
Or fear to walk where Hercules once trod?
What spirits has not Venus tamed? And where
Would you be, you who fight against her, if
Antiope, always to her laws opposed,
Had not with modest ardor burned for Theseus?
But why do you affect a haughty speech?
Confess that all is changed: and for some days
You're seen less often, proud and solitary,
Racing the chariot on the shore, or skilled
In the art of Neptune, making the wild steeds
Obedient to the bit. The forest echoes
Less often to our shouts. Your eyes are heavy,
Charged with a secret passion. There is no
  doubt:
You love, you burn; you perish from an illness
Which you conceal. And are you now in love
With charming Aricia?

HIPPOLYTUS   Theramenes,
I'm setting off in quest of my lost father.

THERAMENES   Won't you see Phaedra, my lord,
  before you go?

HIPPOLYTUS   So I intend; and you may tell her so.
I'll see her—since my duty thus ordains.
But what's the new misfortune which disturbs
Her dear Œnone?

SCENE TWO

Enter Œnone.

ŒNONE   Alas! my lord, what trouble
Can equal mine? The Queen has nearly reached
Her fatal term. In vain both night and day

I've watched beside her. She's dying of a sick-
  ness
She hides from me; and in her spirit reigns
Continual disorder. Restless affliction
Now drags her from her bed to see once more
The light of day; and her deep grief demands
That all should keep away. She's coming now.

HIPPOLYTUS   It is enough. I'll leave this place to
  her,
And not offend her with my hated face.
[*Exeunt Hippolytus and Theramenes.*]

SCENE THREE

Enter Phaedra.

PHAEDRA   Let's go no further, dear Œnone, stay.
I've reached the limit of my strength; my eyes
Are blinded by the daylight, and my knees
Give way beneath me.
[*She sits.*]

ŒNONE   O all-powerful Gods,
May all our tears appease you!

PHAEDRA   How these vain
Adornments, how these veils, now weigh me
  down.
What busy hand, in tying all these knots,
Has taken care to gather on my brow
This heavy load of hair? Now all afflicts me,
Hurts me, and conspires to hurt me.

ŒNONE   How
Her wishes seem now to destroy each other!
Madam, it was yourself, with your own hands,
Who dressed and decked your hair, wishing to
  show
Yourself, and see once more the light of day.
But now you see it, ready to hide yourself,
You hate the day you sought.

PHAEDRA   O shining Sun,
Author of my sad race, thou of whom my
  mother
Boasted herself the daughter, who blush perhaps
At these my sufferings, I see you now
For the last time.

ŒNONE   What! have you not lost
That cruel desire? And shall I see you still
Renouncing life and making of your death
The dreadful preparations?

PHAEDRA   Oh that I were seated

In the forest shade, where through a cloud of dust
I could behold a chariot racing by!

ŒNONE   What, madam?

PHAEDRA   Fool! Where am I?
What have I said?
Where have my wits been wandering? I have lost them.
The gods have robbed me of them. I blush, Œnone.
I let you see too much my shameful sorrows,
And, spite of me, my eyes are filled with tears.

ŒNONE   If you must blush, blush rather at your silence
Which but augments your griefs. Deaf to our pleading,
Rebellious to our care, and without pity,
Do you wish to end your days? What madness now
Stops them in mid-career? What spell or poison
Has drained their source? Three nights have come and gone
Since sleep last entered in your eyes; three days
Have chased the darkness since you took some food.
What frightful scheme are you attempting now?
For you insult the gods who gave you life,
Betray the husband to whom your faith is given,
Betray your hapless children whom you throw
Under a rigorous yoke. Think that one day
Will snatch their mother from them, and give up
Their hopes to the stranger's son, to that proud foe
Of you, and of your blood, the Amazon's son,
Hippolytus.

PHAEDRA   Ah Gods!

ŒNONE   Does this reproach—?

PHAEDRA   Wretch! What name has issued from your mouth?

ŒNONE   You are right to be angry: I like to see you tremble
At that ill-omened name. Then live! Both love and duty
Reanimate you. Live. Do not let the son
Of the Scythian, crushing your children with his rule,
Command the noblest blood of Greece and heaven.

But don't delay: each moment threatens life.
Repair your weakened strength, while yet life's torch
Can be rekindled.

PHAEDRA   I have too much prolonged
Its guilty span.

ŒNONE   What! are you torn apart
By some remorse? What crime could have produced
Such agony? Your hands were never stained
With innocent blood.

PHAEDRA   Thanks to the gods, my hands
Are guiltless still. But would to heaven my heart
Were innocent as they!

ŒNONE   What frightful scheme
Have you conceived to terrify your heart?

PHAEDRA   I have said enough. Spare me the rest.
I die
Because I cannot such confession make.

ŒNONE   Die then; and keep inhuman silence still.
But seek another hand to close your eyes.
Although there but remains a feeble flame
In you, my soul will journey to the dead
Before you, since there are a thousand ways
By which we can go thither—mine the shortest.
Cruel! When have I betrayed your confidence?
Think, that my arms received you at your birth,
For you I've left my country and my children.
Is this the price of my fidelity?

PHAEDRA   What fruit can come from so much violence?
You would be horror-struck if I should tell you.

ŒNONE   What will you say to me more horrible
Than seeing you expire before my eyes?

PHAEDRA   But when you know my crime and the dread fate
That crushes me, I shall die just the same,
And die more guilty.

ŒNONE   Madam, by all the tears
That I have shed for you, by your weak knees
That I embrace now, free my mind from doubt.

PHAEDRA   You wish it: rise.

ŒNONE   Speak: I am listening.

PHAEDRA   What shall I say? And where shall I begin?

ŒNONE   Cease to insult me by these needless fears.

PHAEDRA O hate of Venus and her fatal wrath!
Love led my mother into desperate ways.

ŒNONE Forget them, madam. Let an eternal silence
Hide their remembrance.

PHAEDRA   My sister, Ariadne,
Stricken with love, upon a desolate coast
Despairing died.

ŒNONE   What are you doing, madam?
What mortal spite enkindles you today
Against your nearest . . . ?

PHAEDRA   Since Venus so ordains,
Last and most wretched of my tragic race,
I too shall perish.

ŒNONE   Are you then in love?

PHAEDRA All of love's frenzies I endure.

ŒNONE   For whom?

PHAEDRA You're going to hear the last extreme of horror.
I love . . . I shudder at the fatal name . . .
I love . . .

ŒNONE Whom do you love?

PHAEDRA   You know the son
Of the Amazon—the prince I've harshly used.

ŒNONE Hippolytus! Great Gods!

PHAEDRA   'Tis you have named him
Not I.

ŒNONE O righteous heaven! The blood in my veins
Is turned to ice. O crime! O hapless race!
Disastrous voyage! O unlucky coast!
Why did we travel to your perilous shores?

PHAEDRA My evil comes from a more distant place.
Scarce had I wedded Theseus and established
My happiness, it seemed, I saw in Athens
My haughty foe. I saw him—blushed and blanched
To see him—and my soul was all distraught.
My eyes were blinded, and I could not speak.
I felt my body freeze and burn; I knew
The terrible fires of Venus, the tortures fated
To one whom she pursues. I hoped to avert them
By my assiduous prayers. I built for her
A temple, and took pains to adorn its walls.
Myself surrounded by the sacrifices,

I sought for my lost reason in their entrails.
Weak remedies of love incurable!
In vain upon the altars I burnt incense;
My lips implored the goddess, but I worshipped
Only Hippolytus; and seeing him
Each day even at the altar's foot
I offered all to the god I dared not name.
I shunned him everywhere. O heavy weight
Of misery! My eyes beheld the son
In the father's countenance. At length I dared
To rebel against myself. I spurred my spirit
To persecute him, striving thus to banish
The enemy I worshipped by assuming
A stepmother's proverbial cruelty.
I clamored for his exile till my cries
Tore my dear enemy from his father's arms.
I breathed again, Œnone. In his absence
My calmer days flowed by in innocence,
Compliant to my husband, while my griefs
Lay hidden. I bore him children. But in vain
Were all precautions, for Fate intervened.
Brought by my husband to Troezen, once more
I saw the enemy I had sent away.
My keen wound bled again—it is no more
A passion hidden in my veins, but now
It's Venus fastened on her helpless prey.
I have a just abhorrence of my crime;
I hate my life, abominate my lust;
Longing by death to rescue my good name
And hide my black love from the light of day.
Your tears have conquered me. I have confessed
All my dark secret; and I won't regret it
If you respect now my approaching death,
And do not wound me with unjust reproofs,
Or with vain remedies keep alive within me
The last faint spark of life.

SCENE FOUR

Enter Panope.

PANOPE   I would prefer
To hide these tidings from you, madam, but
I must reveal them. Death has robbed you now
Or your unconquerable husband, and
It is known to all but you.

ŒNONE   What do you say?

PANOPE That the mistaken Queen in vain demands

Theseus' return from heaven; and that from ships
  Arrived in port, Hippolytus, his son,
  Has just heard of his death.
PHAEDRA   Heaven!
PANOPE   For the choice
  Of ruler, Athens is divided. Some
  Vote for the Prince, your son, and others, madam,
  Forgetting the laws of the State, dare give their voices
  To the son of the stranger. It is even said
  An insolent faction has designed to place
  Aricia on the throne. I thought you should
  Be warned about this danger. Hippolytus
  It ready to depart, and it is feared,
  If he becomes involved in this new storm,
  Lest he draw to him all the fickle mob.
ŒNONE No more, Panope. The Queen has heard you,
  And won't neglect your warning.
[*Exit Panope.*]

SCENE FIVE

ŒNONE   I had ceased,
  Madam, to urge that you should live. Indeed,
  I thought that I should follow you to the grave;
  I had no further voice to change your mind.
  But this new blow imposes other laws.

Act Two

SCENE ONE

Aricia and Ismene.

ARICIA Hippolytus asks to see me in this place?
  Hippolytus seeks me here to say good-by?
  Ismene, is it true? You are not mistaken?
ISMENE It is the first result of Theseus' death.
  Madam, prepare yourself to see the hearts
  Scattered by Theseus fly from every side
  Towards you. Aricia at last is mistress
  Of her fate, and soon will see the whole of Greece
  Submit to her.
ARICIA   It's not a false report?

Your fortune shows a different face; the King
  Is now no more, and his place must be filled.
  His death has left you with a son to whom
  You have a duty; slave if he loses you,
  A king if you live. On whom in his misfortune
  Do you wish that he should lean? His tears will have
  No hand but yours to wipe them; and his cries,
  Borne even to the gods, would then incense
  His ancestors against his mother. Live.
  You have no longer reason to reproach
  Yourself; your love becomes a usual love;
  Theseus in dying cuts the sacred knots
  Which made the crime and horror of your passion.
  Hippolytus becomes less terrible to you,
  And you can see him without guiltiness.
  Perhaps, convinced of your aversion, he
  Is going to lead the rebels. Undeceive him,
  Appease his spirit. King of these happy shores,
  Troezen is his portion; but he knows
  That the laws give your son the lofty ramparts
  Minerva builded. Both of you, indeed,
  Have a true enemy. Unite together
  To combat Aricia.
PHAEDRA   To your advice
  I let myself be drawn. Well, let me live,
  If I can be restored to life; and if
  My love for a son can in this grievous moment
  Reanimate the rest of my weak spirits.

Do I cease to be a slave, and have no foe?
ISMENE No, madam, the gods are now no more against you,
  And Theseus has rejoined your brothers' shades.
ARICIA Is it known what caused his death?
ISMENE They spread
  An unbelievable tale of it. It is said
  That stealing a new love this faithless husband
  Was swallowed by the waves. It is even said—
  A widespread rumor this—that he descended
  To Hades with Peirithous, and saw
  Cocytus and the gloomy banks, and living
  Appeared to the infernal shades, but then
  Could not emerge from those sad regions,

And cross the bourn from which there's no
  return.
ARICIA Shall I believe a man before his hour
Can enter the dark dwelling of the dead?
What spell could draw him to those fearsome
  coasts?
ISMENE Theseus is dead, madam, and you alone
Have doubts of it. Athens is mourning for it,
Troezen, informed of it, acknowledges
Hippolytus as King; and Phaedra, here
In this palace, trembling for her son, now seeks
The advice of anxious friends.
ARICIA   Do you believe
Hippolytus, less cruel than his father,
Will make my chains less heavy, sympathize
With my misfortunes?
ISMENE   Madam, I do believe it.
ARICIA But do you really know that heartless
  man?
By what fond hope do you think he'll pity me?
In me alone respect a sex he scorns?
You've seen how he avoids me, seeks those
  places
Where I am not.
ISMENE   I know all that is said
About his coldness. But I've seen when near you
This proud Hippolytus; and in seeing him,
The rumor of his pride has doubly whetted
My curiosity. His actual presence
Seemed not to correspond. At your first glances
I've seen him get confused. His eyes, which
  wished
Vainly to shun you, could not leave your face.
The name of lover would offend his heart,
But yet he has a lover's tender eyes,
If not his words.
ARICIA   How my heart, dear Ismene,
Drinks in a speech which may have little basis.
Is it believable to you who know me
That the sad plaything of a pitiless fate,
Whose heart is fed on bitterness and tears,
Should be acquainted with the trivial griefs
Of love? The remnant of the blood of a king,
Erechtheus, the noble son of Earth,
Alone I have escaped war's ravages.
I've lost six brothers in the flower of youth—
Hope of a famous house!—all reaped by the
  sword.
The moistened earth regretfully drank the blood

Of the offspring of Erechtheus. You know
How since their death a cruel law was made,
Forbidding Greeks to breathe a lover's sighs
For me. It is feared the sister's reckless flames
May kindle once again her brothers' ashes.
But you know well with what disdainful eye
I looked upon a conqueror's suspicions;
And how, opposed to love, I often thanked
The unjust Theseus whose convenient harshness
Aided my scorn. But then my eyes had not
Beheld his son. Not that by eyes alone
Basely enchanted, I love his beauty and charm,
Gifts with which nature wishes to honor him,
And which he scorns, or seems unconscious of;
I love in him his nobler wealth, his father's
  virtues,
Without his faults. I love—I do confess it—
That generous pride that never yet has bowed
Beneath the amorous yoke. Phaedra took pride
In Theseus' practiced sighs. But as for me,
I am more proud, and shun the easy glory
Of gaining homage that a thousand others
Have had before me, and of penetrating
A heart completely open. But to bend
A heart inflexible, to make a soul
Insensible to love feel all its pain,
To enchain a captive by his bonds amazed,
In vain rebellion against the pleasing yoke,
That's what I wish; and that is what provokes
  me.
It's easier to disarm Hercules
Than Prince Hippolytus; and conquests soon
And often made will bring less glory to
The victor's eyes. But, dear Ismene, how
Unwise I am! for I shall be resisted
Only too much; and you perhaps will hear me
Lament the pride that I admire today.
If he would love! With what extreme delight
Would I make him . . .
ISMENE   You'll hear him now,
  himself.
He comes to you.

SCENE TWO

Enter Hippolytus.

HIPPOLYTUS Madam, before I leave,
I thought that I should tell you of your fate.
My father lives no more. My apprehension

Presaged the reasons of his too long absence;
And death alone, stopping his famous deeds,
Could hide him for so long within this world.
The gods have yielded to the Fates at last
The friend and the successor of Alcides.
I think your hatred, allowing him his virtues,
Will hear without regret what is his due.
One hope allays my deadly sorrow now.
From your strict tutelage I'll deliver you,
Revoke the laws whose rigor I've deplored.
Do what you will. Dispose of your own heart,
And in this Troezen, my heritage,
Which has forthwith accepted me as King,
I leave you as free, nay freer, than myself.

ARICIA   Temper your generosity, my lord,
For its excess embarrasses me. So
To honor my disgrace will put me—more
Than you think—under the harsh laws from
  which
You would exempt me.

HIPPOLYTUS   Athens, undecided
In the choice of a successor, speaks of you,
Names me and the Queen's son.

ARICIA   Me, my lord?

HIPPOLYTUS   I know, without self-flattery, that a
  law
Seems to reject me. Greece reproaches me
With an alien mother. But if my brother were
My only rival, over him I have
Some veritable claims that I would save
Out of the law's caprice. Another bridle,
More lawful, checks my boldness. I yield to you,
Or rather give you back what is your own,
A scepter which your ancestors received
From the most famous man that ever lived;
Adoption placed it in Ægeus' hands;
Athens protected and enlarged by Theseus
Joyfully recognized so good a king,
And left in oblivion your luckless brothers.
Now Athens calls you back within her walls;
With a long quarrel she has groaned enough;
Enough her fields have reeked with blood of
  thine.
Troezen obeys me; and the plains of Crete
Offer to Phaedra's son a rich domain.
Attica is yours, and I am going
On your behalf to reunite the suffrages
We share between us.

ARICIA   Astonished and confused
At all I hear, I am afraid . . . afraid
A dream abuses me. Am I awake?
Can I believe in such a plan? What god,
My lord, what god has put it in your breast?
How justly is your glory spread abroad
In every place! And how the truth surpasses
Your fame! You would betray yourself for me?
Would it not be enough for you to refrain
From hating me? And to prevent your soul
So long from this hostility . . .

HIPPOLYTUS   I hate you
Madam? However they depict my pride,
Do you think it bore a monster? What settled
  hate,
What savage manners could, in seeing you,
Not become milder? Could I have resisted
The charm that . . .

ARICIA   What, my lord?

HIPPOLYTUS   I've gone
  too far.
I see that reason yields to violence.
Since I've begun to speak, I must continue.
I must inform you, madam, of a secret
My heart no longer can contain. You see
Before you a lamentable prince, a type
Of headstrong pride. I, rebel against love,
For long have scorned its captives. I deplored
The shipwreck of weak mortals, and proposed
To contemplate the tempests from the shore.
But now enslaved under the common law,
I see myself transported. In a moment
My mad audacity has been subdued.
My proud soul is at last enslaved. For nearly
Six months, ashamed and desperate, and wear-
  ing
The marks of torture, against you, against
  myself,
Vainly I strove. Present I fled from you,
Absent I sought you. In the midst of forests
Your image followed me; the light of day,
The shadows of the night, brought to my eyes
The charms I shunned, and everything con-
  spired
To make the rebel Hippolytus your captive.
Now for all fruit of my superfluous cares,
I seek but do not find myself. My bow, my
  spears,

My chariot call to me in vain. No more
Do I remember Neptune's lessons; the woods
Now echo to my groans. My idle steeds
Have now forgot my voice. Perhaps the tale
Of love so wild will make you, as you listen,
Blush for your work. What an uncouth recital
Of a heart that's offered you. What a strange
    captive
For bonds so beautiful! But to your eyes
The offering should be the richer for it;
Remember that I speak an alien tongue,
And don't reject vows that are ill expressed,
Vows that without you I had never formed.

SCENE THREE

Enter Theramenes.

THERAMENES My lord, the Queen is coming. I
    come before
To tell you that she seeks you.
HIPPOLYTUS   Me?
THERAMENES   I don't
    know why.
But she has sent to ask for you. She wishes
To speak with you before you go.
HIPPOLYTUS   Phaedra!
What shall I say to her? And what can she
Expect . . .
ARICIA   My lord, you can't refuse to hear
    her.
Though you are sure of her hostility,
You ought to have some pity for her tears.
HIPPOLYTUS Yet you are going. And I depart,
    not knowing
Whether I have offended by my words
The charms that I adore. I do not know
Whether this heart I leave now in your
    hands . . .
ARICIA Go, Prince, pursue your generous de-
    signs;
Put tributary Athens in my power.
And all those gifts that you have wished to
    make me,
I accept. But yet that Empire, great and glori-
    ous,
Is not to me the richest of your gifts.
[*Exeunt Aricia and Ismene.*]

SCENE FOUR

HIPPOLYTUS Friend, is all ready? But the Queen
    approaches.
Go, see that all's prepared for our departure.
Run, give the signal, and return at once
To free me from a vexing interview.
[*Exit Theramenes.*]

SCENE FIVE

Enter Phaedra and Œnone.

PHAEDRA He's here: my blood retreats towards
    my heart,
And I forget what I had meant to say.
ŒNONE Think of a son whose sole hope lies in
    you.
PHAEDRA It is said that your immediate de-
    parture
Is sundering us, my lord. I come to wed
My tears unto your griefs; and to explain
My anxious fears to you. My son is now
Without a father; and the day is near
Which of my death will make him witness too.
His youth is threatened by a thousand foes,
And you alone can arm against them—but
Secret remorse is fretting in my soul.
I fear you're deaf to his cries, and that you'll
    wreak
On him your wrath against an odious mother.
HIPPOLYTUS Madam, I do not harbor such base
    feelings.
PHAEDRA Although you hate me, I shall not com-
    plain,
My lord: for you have seen me bent to harm
    you.
You could not read the tables of my heart.
I've taken care to invite your enmity,
And could not bear your presence where I
    dwelt.
In public, and in private, your known foe,
I've wished the seas to part us, and even for-
    bidden
The mention of your name within my hearing.
But if one measures punishment by the offense,
If only hatred can attract your hate,
Never was woman who deserved more pity,

My lord, and less deserved your enmity.

HIPPOLYTUS A mother jealous for her children's rights
Seldom forgives her stepson. I know it, madam.
Nagging suspicions are the commonest fruits
Of second marriage; and another wife
Would have disliked me just the same; and I
Might well have had to swallow greater wrongs.

PHAEDRA Ah, my lord! Heaven—I dare avow it now—
Has made me an exception to that rule.
And what a different care perplexes me
And eats me up.

HIPPOLYTUS   Madam, it is not time
To grieve. Perhaps your husband is alive.
Heaven to our tears may grant his swift return.
Neptune, his tutelary god, protects him,
To whom my father never prayed in vain.

PHAEDRA None has beheld the marches of the dead
A second time, my lord. Since he has seen
Those dismal shores, you hope in vain some god
Will send him back. The greedy Acheron
Never lets go its prey. What do I say?
He is not dead since he still lives in you.
Ever before my eyes I see my husband.
I see him, speak with him, and my heart still . . .
I'm wandering, my lord. My foolish feelings,
In spite of me, declare themselves.

HIPPOLYTUS   I see
Love's wonderful effects. Dead though he is,
Theseus is always present to your eyes:
Your soul is ever burning with your love.

PHAEDRA Yes, Prince, I pine and burn for Theseus.
I love him, not as when he visited
The underworld, a fickle lover, bent
To stain great Pluto's bed, but faithful, proud,
Attractive, young, and even a little shy,
Charming all hearts, an image of the gods,
Or even as you are now. He had your bearing,
Your eyes, your speech; and such a modesty
Made flush his face when over the Cretan waves
He came and turned the hearts of Minos' daughters.

What were you doing then? Why without you
Did he assemble there the flower of Greece?
And why were you too young to sail with him
Unto our shores? For then you would have slain
The Minotaur, despite the devious ways
Of his vast lair: my sister, to redeem you
From your confusion, with the fateful thread
Would have armed your hand—but no, for I myself,
Inspired by love, would have forestalled her plan.
It would have been me, Prince; by timely aid,
I would have led you through the labyrinth.
How many cares that charming head of yours
Would then have cost me! I would not have trusted
To that weak thread alone, but walked before you,
Companion in the peril which you chose:
And going down into the labyrinth,
Phaedra would have returned with you, or else
Been lost with you.

HIPPOLYTUS   O Gods! What do I hear?
Do you forget that Theseus is my father,
And you his wife?

PHAEDRA   By what do you judge that I
Have done so, Prince? Would I forget my honor?

HIPPOLYTUS Forgive me, madam. I admit, with blushing,
I misinterpreted an innocent speech.
I am ashamed to stay within your sight;
I'm going. . . .

PHAEDRA   Ah! cruel! You've understood too well.
I've said enough to save you from mistaking.
Know Phaedra, then, and all her madness. Yes,
I love; but do not think that I condone it,
Or think it innocent; nor that I ever
With base complaisance added to the poison
Of my mad passion. Hapless victim of
Celestial vengeance, I abhor myself
More than you can. The gods are witnesses—
Those gods who kindled in my breast the flame
Fatal to all my blood, whose cruel boast
Was to seduce a weak and mortal heart.
Recall what's past. I did not flee from you,

Hardhearted man, I drove you away. I wished
To seem to you both hateful and inhuman.
To resist you better I aroused your hatred.
But what have profited my useless pains?
You loathed me more: I did not love you less;
And your misfortunes lent you further charms.
I've languished, shriveled in the flames, in tears.
Your eyes will tell you so—if for a moment
Your eyes could look at me. What am I saying?
Think you that this confession I have made
Was voluntary? I trembled for a son
I did not dare betray and came to beg you
No more to hate him—futile schemes devised
By a heart too full of what it loves. Alas!
I could only speak to you about yourself.
Avenge yourself; punish an odious love,
Son worthy of a noble father, free
The universe of a monster who offends you.
Theseus' widow dares to love Hippolytus!
Believe me, Prince,
This dreadful monster would not seek to flee.
There is my heart: there you should aim your
    blow.
I feel it now, eager to expiate
Its sin, advanced towards your arm. Strike.
Or if you think it unworthy of your blows,
Your hatred envying me a death so sweet,
Or if you think your hand with blood too vile
Would be imbrued, lend me your sword in-
    stead.
Give it me.
[*She takes sword.*]

ŒNONE What are you doing, madam?
O righteous Gods! But someone's coming.
    Leave
These hateful testimonies. Come inside,
And flee a certain shame.
[*Exeunt Œnone and Phaedra.*]

Act Three

SCENE ONE

Phaedra and Œnone.

PHAEDRA O! that the honors which are brought
    to me
Were paid elsewhere! Why do you urge me so?

SCENE SIX

Enter Theramenes.

THERAMENES Is it Phaedra who flees,
Or rather is led away? O why, my lord,
These marks of sorrow? I see you without
    sword,
Speechless and pale.

HIPPOLYTUS Theramenes, let's flee,
I am amazed, and cannot without horror
Behold myself. Phaedra . . . but no, great
    Gods!
In deep oblivion may this horrid secret
Remain entombed!

THERAMENES If you would now depart,
The sails are ready. But Athens has decided.
Her chiefs have taken the votes of all the tribes.
Your brother wins, and Phaedra gets her way.

HIPPOLYTUS Phaedra?

THERAMENES A herald, bearing Athens'
    will,
Comes to remit the reins of government
Into her hands. Her son is King, my lord.

HIPPOLYTUS O Gods, who know her heart, is it
    her virtue
That thus you recompense?

THERAMENES There is, however,
A muffled rumor that the King's alive.
It is said that in Epirus he's appeared.
But I, who sought him there, I know too
    well . . .

HIPPOLYTUS No matter. Let us listen to every-
    thing,
And neglect nothing. Examine this report
And trace it to its source. If it should prove
Unfounded, let's depart. Whatever the cost,
Let's put the scepter into worthy hands.

Can you wish me to be seen? What do you
    come with
To flatter my desolation? Hide me rather.
Not only have I spoken; but my frenzy
Is noised abroad. I've said those things which
    ought

Phaedra

Never to be heard. O heavens! The way he
listened!
By devious means he somehow failed to grasp
What I was saying—then he recoiled. His
blush
Doubled my shame. Why did you turn aside
The death I sought? Did he turn pale with
fear
When with his sword I sought my breast, or
seek
To snatch it from me? Since my hands had
touched it
But once, it was made horrible in his eyes,
And would profane his hands.

ŒNONE   Thus in your
woes
Lamenting to yourself, you feed a flame
That ought to be put out. Would it not be bet-
ter,
Worthy the blood of Minos, in nobler cares
To seek your peace? To spite a heartless man
Who had recourse to flight, assume the con-
duct
Of affairs, and reign.

PHAEDRA   I reign? To place the State
Under my law, when reason reigns no longer
Over myself; when I have abdicated
From the empire of my senses; when beneath
A yoke of shame I scarcely breathe; when I
Am dying.

ŒNONE   Fly.

PHAEDRA   I cannot leave him.

ŒNONE   You dared
To banish him, and dare not shun him now?

PHAEDRA   Too late. He knows of my mad pas-
sion.
I've crossed the bounds of rigid modesty,
Declared my shame before my conqueror's
eyes,
And hope has slipped perforce into my heart.
It was you who rallied my declining strength,
When my departing soul was on my lips,
And by your flattering counsels knew the way
To bring me back to life. You made me glimpse
How I could love him.

ŒNONE   To save you from your
ills,
Guilty or innocent, what would I not

Have done? But if an insult ever touched you,
Can you forget his haughty scorn? And how
With cruel eyes his obstinate rigor let you
Lie prostrate at his feet. How his fierce pride
Rendered him odious! If only Phaedra
Had seen him, at that moment, with my eyes!

PHAEDRA   Œnone, he may leave this native pride
Which wounds you. Nurtured in the pathless
woods,
He has their roughness. Hardened by savage
laws,
He hears love spoken of for the first time;
Perhaps it was surprise that caused his silence;
Perhaps my pleas had too much violence.

ŒNONE.   Remember a barbarian gave him birth.

PHAEDRA   Although a Scythian and barbarian,
She yet has loved.

ŒNONE   He has for all our sex
A deadly hatred.

PHAEDRA   So I shall not see him
Prefer a rival. All your counsels now
Are out of season. Serve my passion, Œnone,
And not my reason. He opposes now
To love a heart impenetrable; let us
Discover some more vulnerable place.
The charms of ruling have appeared to touch
him.
Athens attracts him; he has not been able
To hide it. His ships have turned their prows;
their sails
Flap in the wind. Find this ambitious youth,
Œnone; make the royal crown to glitter
Before his eyes. Let him wear upon his brow
The sacred diadem. I only wish
The honor of his love, and yield to him
The power I cannot keep. He will instruct
My son in the art of ruling, who may perhaps
Regard him as a father. Both son and mother
I put under his power. Try every means
To bend him; he will listen to your speech
More readily than to mine. Urge, weep, and
moan.
Paint Phaedra dying; do not blush to use
The tone of a suppliant. I will approve
Of all you do. You are my only hope.
I await your coming to decide my fate.
[*Exit Œnone.*]

SCENE TWO

PHAEDRA O thou who seest the shame to which
  I've come,
Venus implacable, am I confounded
Enough for thee? Thou canst not further urge
Thy cruelty; thy victory is complete.
O cruel! If thou wishest another triumph
Attack an enemy who is more rebellious.
Hippolytus flees thee; and, thy wrath defying,
Has never to thy altars bowed the knee.
Thy name appears to shock his haughty ears.
Goddess, avenge thyself. Thy cause is mine.
O let him love! Œnone is returned.
I am detested then. He would not hear you?

SCENE THREE

Enter Œnone.

ŒNONE Madam, you must repress the very
  thought
Of your vain passion, and recall again
Your former virtue. The King that we thought
  dead
Will soon appear before your eyes. Theseus
Is come. The people rush to see him. I went,
At your command, to seek Hippolytus,
When I heard a thousand shouts . . .
PHAEDRA   My hus-
  band lives,
Œnone. It is enough. I have confessed
A love which foully wrongs him. Theseus lives.
I wish to know no more.
ŒNONE   What?
PHAEDRA   I foretold it,
But you would not believe it. Your tears pre-
  vailed
Over my shame. I would have died today
Worthy of tears. I followed your advice—
I die dishonored.
ŒNONE   Die?
PHAEDRA   O righteous heaven!
What have I done today? My husband's coming,
And his son with him. I shall see the witness
Of my adulterous passion watch how boldly
I greet his father—my heart still full of sighs
To which he would not listen, and my eyes

Still moist with tears he scorned. Do you sup-
  pose
That he, so sensitive to Theseus' honor,
Will hide the fires that burn me—and betray
His father and his king? Could he contain
The horror I inspire? He would keep silence
In vain. I know my perfidies, Œnone;
I am not one of those who in their crimes
Enjoy a tranquil peace, and know the art
To keep their countenance without a blush.
I know my madness: I recall it all.
I think already that these walls, these arches,
Are going to speak; they but await my husband
Before they utter forth my crimes. Die, then.
My death will free me from a crowd of horrors.
Is it a great mischance to cease to live?
Death has no terrors for the unfortunate.
I only fear the name I leave behind me.
A dreadful heritage for my poor children!
The blood of Jupiter should puff up their cour-
  age,
With a just pride; but yet a mother's crime
Will be a heavy burden. One day, I fear,
A speech—too true!—will cast it in their teeth
They had a guilty mother; and I fear
That crushed by such a hateful load, they'll
  never
Dare raise their eyes.
ŒNONE   It is true. I pity them.
Never was fear more justified than yours.
But why expose them to such insults? Why
Against yourself give evidence? All would be
  lost.
It will be said that guilty Phaedra fled
The terrible sight of husband she betrayed.
Hippolytus will rejoice that by your death
You corroborate his tale. What could I say
To your accuser? Face to face with him
I shall be easy to confound, and see him
Rejoicing in his triumph, while he tells
Your shame to all who listen. Rather let
Fire from heaven consume me! But tell me true
Is he still dear to you? And with what eyes
Do you behold this insolent prince?
PHAEDRA   I see him
Even as a monster hideous to my eyes.
ŒNONE Why yield him then a total victory?
You fear him, madam. Dare to accuse him first

Of the crime that he will charge you with today.
Who will contradict you? Everything
Speaks against him—his sword by lucky chance
Left in your hands, your present sore distress,
Your former sorrow, his father long ago
Warned by your outcries, and his actual exile
Obtained by you yourself.

PHAEDRA   How should I dare
Oppress and slander innocence?

ŒNONE   My zeal
Only requires your silence. Like you I shrink
From such an action. You would find me
  readier
To face a thousand deaths; but since I'd lose
  you
Without this painful remedy, and your life
For me is of such value that all else
Must yield to it, I'll speak. And Theseus,
  angered
By what I tell him, will restrict his vengeance
To his son's exile. When he punishes,
A father is always father, satisfied
With a light penalty. But even if
His guiltless blood is spilt, your threatened
  honor
Is yet too valuable to be exposed.
Whatever it demands, you must submit,
Madam. And to save your threatened honor
All must be sacrificed, including virtue.
Someone is coming. I see Theseus.

PHAEDRA   Ah!
I see Hippolytus. In his haughty eyes
I see my ruin written. Do what you will,
I resign myself to you. In my disorder,
I can do nothing for myself.

SCENE FOUR

Enter Theseus, Hippolytus, and Theramenes.

THESEUS   Now Fortune,
Madam, no longer frowns, and in your
  arms . . .

PHAEDRA Stay, Theseus. Do not profane the love
  you feel.
I am not worthy of your sweet caresses.
You are insulted. Fortune has not spared
Your wife during your absence. I am unworthy

To please you, or approach you; and hence-
  forward
I ought to think only of where to hide.
[*Exeunt Phaedra and Œnone.*]

SCENE FIVE

THESEUS What is the reason for this strange
  reception?

HIPPOLYTUS Phaedra alone the mystery can ex-
  plain.
But if my ardent prayers can move your heart,
Permit me not to see her any more.
And let Hippolytus disappear forever
From places where she dwells.

THESEUS   Leave me, my
  son?

HIPPOLYTUS I sought her not: you brought her
  to these shores,
And when you left entrusted to the banks
Of Troezen, Aricia and the Queen,
I was instructed to look after them.
But what can now delay me? In my youth
I showed enough my prowess in the forests
Against unworthy foes; and could I not,
Escaping an ignoble idleness,
In blood more glorious stain my spears? Before
You reached my present age, already
More than one tyrant, more than one grim
  monster
Had felt your mighty strength; already you,
Chastiser of insolence, had secured the shores
Of the two seas; the private traveler feared
Outrage no more; and Hercules could rest
From his long labors, hearing of your deeds.
But I, an unknown son of famous sire,
Am even further from my mother's deeds!
Suffer my courage to be used at last;
And if some monster has escaped your arm,
Let me then lay the honorable skin
Before your feet; or by the lasting memory
Of a fine death perpetuate the days
So nobly ended, and prove to all the world
I was your son.

THESEUS   What do I now behold?
What horror makes my frightened family
Flee from my sight? If I return so feared,
So little wanted, why, heaven, from my prison

Did you release me? I had one friend alone;
Imprudently he wished to steal the wife
Of the King of Epirus. I aided, with regret,
His amorous designs; but angry fate
Blinded us both. The King surprised me there,
Defenseless, weaponless. I saw Peirithous,
Sad object of my tears, by this barbarian
Given to cruel monsters whom he fed
With blood of luckless mortals. He shut me up
In dismal caverns underground that neighbored
The empire of the shades. After six months
The gods again looked on me. I deceived
The eyes of those who guarded me. I cleansed
The world of a perfidious enemy;
To his own monsters he became a prey.
And when with joy I approach the dearest
   things
Now left me by the gods—what do I say?—
When to itself my soul returns and takes its
   fill
Of that dear sight, for welcome I receive
A shuddering fear and horror. All flee; all
   shrink
From my embraces. And I feel the terror
That I inspire. I'd like to be again
In the prisons of Epirus. Speak. Phaedra com-
   plains
That I am wronged. Who has betrayed me?
Why

Have I not been avenged? Has Greece, to
   whom
So many times my arms proved useful, now
Granted asylum to a criminal?
You do not answer! Is my son, my own son,
Leagued with my enemies? Let us go in.
I cannot stay in doubt that overwhelms me.
Let me know both the offense and the offender.
Let Phaedra tell the cause of her distress.
[Exit Theseus.]

SCENE SIX

HIPPOLYTUS Where did that speech, which petri-
   fied me, tend?
Does Phaedra, still a prey to her mad passion,
Wish to accuse, and so destroy, herself?
What will the King say? What destructive
   poison
Is scattered over all his house by love.
And I, full of a love he will detest,
How different from the man that he remembers!
What black presentiments affright me now!
But innocence has nought to fear. Let's go:
Seek by what happy art I can awaken
My father's tenderness—speak of a love
That he may wish to crush, though all his
   power
Will not be able to drive it from my heart.

Act Four

SCENE ONE

Theseus and Œnone.

THESEUS What do I hear? A traitor, a rash
   traitor,
To plot this outrage to his father's honor?
How harshly, Destiny, dost thou pursue me!
I know not where I'm going, nor what I am!
O tenderness and bounty ill repaid!
Audacious projects! evil thought! To reach
The goal of his black passion he sought the aid
Of violence. I recognize the sword—
The instrument of his rage—with which I
   armed him
For nobler purposes. All the ties of blood

Could not restrain him! And Phaedra hesitated
To punish him! Her silence spared the villain!
ŒNONE She rather spared a pitiable father.
Being ashamed of a violent lover's scheme
And of the wicked fire caught from her eyes,
Phaedra desired to die; her murderous hand
Would have put out the pure light of her eyes.
I saw her raise her arm. I ran to stop her.
Alone I tried to save her for your love,
And, mourning for her troubles and your fears,
I have unwillingly interpreted
The tears you saw.
THESEUS   The villain! He was not
   able
To stop himself from turning pale. I saw him

Tremble with fear when he encountered me.
I was astonished at his lack of joy;
His cold embraces froze my tenderness.
But was this guilty passion which devours him
Already manifest in Athens?

ŒNONE   My lord,
Recall the Queen's complaints. A criminal love
Was cause of all her hatred.

THESEUS   And did this passion
Kindle again at Troezen?

ŒNONE   Oh my lord,
I have told you all that passed. Too long the
  Queen
Has in her mortal grief been left alone;
So let me leave, and hasten to her side.
[*Exit Œnone.*]

SCENE TWO

Enter Hippolytus.

THESEUS   Ah! here he is. Great Gods! What eye,
  as mine,
Would not have been deceived? Why should
  the brow
Of a profane adulterer shine with virtue?
And should one not by certain signs perceive
The heart of villainous men?

HIPPOLYTUS   May I inquire,
My lord, what dismal cloud is on your face?
Dare you confide in me?

THESEUS   Villain! Do you then
  dare
To show yourself before me? Monster, whom
Too long the thunder's spared, vile brigand,
Of whom I purged the earth, as I believed,
After the transport of a horrible love
Has brought your lust even to your father's
  bed,
You show your hostile head! You would appear
In places full of your own infamy,
And do not seek, under an unknown sky
A country which my name has not yet reached.
Flee, traitor! Do not come to brave my hatred,
Or try a rage that I can scarcely hold.
I have enough opprobrium that I caused
The birth of such a criminal, without

Your shameful death should come to soil the
  glory
Of all my noble deeds. Flee! If you do not wish
A sudden death to add you to the villains
This hand has punished, take good care that
  never
The star that lights us see you in this place
Set a rash foot. Fly, I say; and hasten
To purge my territories forever from
Your horrible aspect. And thou, O Neptune!
If formerly my courage cleansed your shores
Of infamous assassins, remember now,
That for reward of all my happy efforts,
Thou promisedst to grant one prayer of mine.
In the long rigors of a cruel prison
I did not once implore thy immortal power;
Niggardly of the help that I expected,
I saved my prayers for greater needs. Today
I do implore thee. Avenge a wretched father!
This traitor I abandon to thy wrath.
In his own blood stifle his shameless lusts.
And by thy furies I shall recognize
Thy favors.

HIPPOLYTUS   Does Phaedra charge Hippolytus
With love incestuous? Such an excess of horror
Renders me speechless. So many sudden blows
Crush me at once, they take away my words
And choke my utterance.

THESEUS   Traitor, you thought
Phaedra would bury in a cowardly silence
Your brutal conduct. You should not have left
The sword which in her hands has helped to
  damn you.
Or rather, piling up your perfidy,
You should have bought her silence with her
  life.

HIPPOLYTUS   With this black falsehood right-
  eously incensed,
I would now speak the truth; but I suppress
A secret that would touch you too. Approve
The respect which seals my lips; and, without
  wishing
To augment your griefs, I urge you to examine
My life. Remember who I am. Small crimes
Always precede the great. Whoever crosses
The bounds of law may violate at last
The holiest rights. There are degrees of crime
Just as of virtue—never innocence

Changes to utter license at one stroke.
One day alone is not enough to turn
A good man to a treacherous murderer,
Still less to incest. Suckled at the breast
Of a chaste heroine, I have not belied
The fountain of her blood. Pitheus, thought
To be the wisest of all men, did deign
To instruct me. I do not wish to give
Too favorable a picture of myself;
But if some virtue's fallen to my share,
My lord, I think that I have clearly shown
My hatred of the crimes imputed to me.
By this Hippolytus is known in Greece.
I've pushed my virtue to the edge of harshness.
My moral inflexibility is known.
The day's not purer than my inmost heart,
And people wish Hippolytus could be smitten
By some profane love. . . .

THESEUS   Yes, it is that same
  pride
Which now condemns you. I see the hateful
  cause
Of your frigidity. Phaedra alone
Charmed your lascivious eyes; your soul, indif-
  ferent
To every other object, disdained to burn
With innocent flames.

HIPPOLYTUS   No, father, this my
  heart—
I cannot hide it longer—has not disdained
To burn with virtuous love. I do confess
My veritable offense. I love. I love
('Tis true) despite your prohibition, sir.
Aricia to her laws holds me enslaved.
The daughter of Pallas has overcome your son.
I worship her; rebellious to your orders
I can neither sigh nor burn, except for her.

THESEUS   You love her? Heavens! But no, the
  artifice
Is gross. You feign yourself a criminal
To justify yourself.

HIPPOLYTUS   For six months now,
My lord, I shunned her, but I loved. I came
Trembling to tell you. Can nothing disabuse
  you?
Or by what terrible oath can I convince you?
By earth, and heaven, and by the whole of
  nature . . .

THESEUS   Rogues always have recourse to per-
  jury.
Cease, cease, and spare me further useless
  speech,
If your feigned virtue has no other aid.

HIPPOLYTUS   Although to you it may seem false
  and cunning,
Phaedra, within her heart, will be more just.

THESEUS   Ah! how your impudence excites my
  wrath!

HIPPOLYTUS   How long my exile? What the place
  prescribed?

THESEUS   Even if you should go beyond the
  pillars
Of Hercules, I still would be too near you.

HIPPOLYTUS   Charged with this hideous crime, I
  should not have
One friend to plead for me when you desert me.

THESEUS   Go seek for friends who morbidly ap-
  plaud
Adultery and incest, ungrateful traitors,
Dishonorable and lawless, fit protectors
Of such a villain.

HIPPOLYTUS   You speak to me once more
Of incest and adultery. I hold
My peace. Yet Phaedra's mother . . . Phaedra
  springs
From a race, as you well know, my lord, more
  filled
With horrors than mine is.

THESEUS   What! will your rage
Lose all restraint before me? For the last time,
Out of my sight! Go, traitor. Do not wait
For a wrathful father to have you driven out
With infamy.

[*Exit Hippolytus.*]

SCENE THREE

THESEUS   O wretched man, you run
To inevitable destruction. Neptune, feared
Even by the gods themselves, has given his
  word,
And he'll perform it. An avenging god
Pursues you, and you'll not escape. I loved you,
And feel that notwithstanding your offense
My heart is yearning for you in advance.
But it was you who forced me to condemn you.

Was ever father more outraged than I?
Just gods, you see the grief that overwhelms me.
How could I father such a guilty child?

SCENE FOUR

Enter Phaedra.

PHAEDRA   My lord, I come to you with fearful
  heart.
I overheard your wrathful voice, and tremble
Lest your dire threats should have a prompt
  result.
If there is still time, spare your child, your
  blood.
I dare to implore you. Save me from the horror
Of hearing his blood cry. O do not cause me
The everlasting grief of spilling it
By a father's hand.
THESEUS   No, madam, in my own
  blood
My hand has not been steeped. But none the
  less
He's not escaped me. An immortal hand
Is charged with his destruction. Neptune him-
  self
Owes it to me, and you will be avenged.
PHAEDRA   Neptune owes it to you! Your wrathful
  prayers . . .
THESEUS   What! do you fear now lest they should
  be answered?
Rather join yours unto my lawful prayers.
Recount to me his crimes in all their vileness;
Heat up my anger which is too restrained,
Too slow. For you are not acquainted yet
With all his crimes. His mad attempt against
  you
Has led to further wrongs. Your mouth, he says,
Is full of lies; and he maintains, his heart
And faith are given to Aricia—that he loves
  her.
PHAEDRA   What, my lord?
THESEUS   That's what he said,
  but I
Knew how to take this frivolous pretense.
Let's hope from Neptune a swift stroke of jus-
  tice.
I'm going myself to pray before his altar,
To accomplish his immortal vows with speed.
[*Exit Theseus.*]

SCENE FIVE

PHAEDRA   He's gone. What news has beaten on
  my ears!
What half-extinguished fire within my breast
Revives! What thunderbolt! What dreadful news!
I flew, with all my heart, to save his son,
Breaking away from the restraining arms
Of terrified Œnone; to my remorse
I yielded. And who knows how far it would
Have carried me? Perhaps to accuse myself;
Perhaps, if my voice had failed not, the dread
  truth
Might have escaped me. . . . Hippolytus feels
  love,
But not for me. Aricia has his heart!
Aricia has his faith! Gods! When the ingrate,
Pitiless to my pleading, armed himself
With eye so proud and brow so stern, I thought
His heart to love would be forever closed,
Invulnerable to all my sex; and yet
Another has bent his will; and in his eyes
Another has found favor. Perhaps he has
A heart that's easily touched. I am alone
The object of his scorn. And I undertook
The task of his defense!

SCENE SIX

Enter Œnone.

PHAEDRA   Do you know
Œnone, what I have just learnt?
ŒNONE   No, madam.
But trembling I have come to you, and pale,
Aware of your intentions; and I feared
A madness which might well be fatal to you.
PHAEDRA   Would you believe it, Œnone? I have
  a rival.
ŒNONE   What?
PHAEDRA   Hippolytus is in love. I cannot doubt it.
That savage enemy no one could conquer
Whom pleading and respect would both annoy,
The tiger I encountered but with fear,
Has recognized a conqueror at least.
Aricia has found the way to his heart.
ŒNONE   Aricia?
PHAEDRA   O pain I never knew before!
To what new torment am I now reserved!

All I have suffered, all my frenzied fears,
My passion's fury and its fierce remorse,
The unbearable insult of his cruel repulse,
Shadowed but feebly what I now endure.
They love each other. By what potent spell
Have I been hoodwinked? How have they met?
  Since when?
And where? You must have known: why did
  you hide it?
Could you not tell me of their furtive love?
Were they not often seen to speak together,
To seek each other? Did they go to hide
Deep in the woods? But they, alas, could meet
With perfect freedom. Heaven itself approved
Their innocent desires. They could pursue
Their amorous purposes without remorse,
And every day, for them, broke clear and calm!
While I, sad castaway of Nature, hid
From day and light. Death is the only god
I dared invoke; and I waited him,
Feeding on gall and steeped in tears, but yet
I did not dare (so closely I was watched)
To weep my fill. I tasted that sour pleasure
In fear and trembling; and with brow serene
Disguising my distress, I was deprived
Too often of my tears.

ŒNONE   But their vain loves
Will bear no fruit, for they will meet no more.

PHAEDRA   Forever and forever they will love.
At the moment when I speak—ah! deadly
  thought!—
They brave the fury of a maddened lover.
Despite the exile which will sunder them,
They vow eternal faith. I cannot bear
A joy which is an outrage to me. Œnone,
Take pity on my jealous rage. That girl
Must be destroyed; the anger of my husband
Against her hateful blood must be aroused
To no light penalty. The sister's crime
Exceeds the brothers'. In my jealous fury
I wish to urge him . . . But what am I doing?
Where has my reason fled? I jealous? I
To beg of Theseus? My husband is not dead,
And I am still aflame. For whom? Each word
Makes my hair stand on end. My crimes already
Have overflowed the measure. Both at once
I breathe the stench of incest and deceit.
My murderous hands, all apt for vengeance,
  burn

To plunge in innocent blood! Wretch! And I
  live!
And I endure the sight of sacred Phoebus
From whom I am derived. My ancestor
Is sire and master of the gods; and heaven,
Nay all the universe, is teeming now
With my forbears. Where then can I hide?
Flee to eternal night. What do I say?
For there my father holds the fatal urn,
Put by the Fates in his stern hands, 'tis said.
Minos in Hades judges the pale ghosts.
Ah, how his shade will tremble when his eyes
Behold his daughter there, confessing sins—
Crimes yet unknown in hell! What wilt thou
  say,
Father, to see this hideous spectacle?
Methinks I now behold the dreadful urn
Fall from thy hand! Methinks I see thee search
For some new punishment, thyself become
The torturer of thine own blood. Forgive:
A cruel god has doomed thy family.
Behold his vengeance in thy daughter's lust.
But yet, alas, never has my sad heart
Once plucked the fruit of the atrocious crime
Whose shame pursues me. Dogged by miseries
To the last gasp, in torture, I render up
A life I long to lose.

ŒNONE   Repel, madam,
An unreal terror! Behold with other eyes
A venial fault. You love. One's destiny
Cannot be overcome, and you were drawn
By a fatal spell. Is it a prodigy
Unknown before amongst us? And has love
Conquered no other hearts than yours alone?
Frailty is but too natural to us all.
You are a mortal—bow to mortals' lot.
The yoke that you bewail is nothing new:
The gods themselves—the dwellers on Olym-
  pus—
Who scare us from such crimes, have before
  now
Been scorched with lawless fires.

PHAEDRA   What do I hear?
What counsels do you dare to give me now?
Would you thus poison me until the end?
Wretch! Thus you ruined me; and when I fled
You brought me back. It was your pleading
Made me forget my duty. When I avoided
Hippolytus, it was you who made me see him.

Phaedra   *313*

What have you done? Why has your wicked mouth
Blackened his honor? Perhaps he will be slain,
The father's impious prayer to Neptune answered.
No longer will I hearken to you. Go,
Thou execrable monster, go and leave me
To my unhappy fate. May the just gods
Reward thee with a punishment to fright

Those who by servile arts feed princes' vices,
Urging them down the path they wish to take,
And smoothing it before them—base flatterers,
The most pernicious gift the angry heavens
Can give to kings.

[*Exit Phaedra.*]

ŒNONE   Ah! Gods! to do her service
I have done all, left all. And I receive
This for reward. I get but my deserts.

Act Five

SCENE ONE

Hippolytus and Aricia.

ARICIA How in this mortal danger can you still
Keep silence, and thus leave a loving father
In error? If you scorn my pleading tears,
And easily consent no more to see me,
Go, separate yourself from sad Aricia:
But yet, before you leave, preserve your life;
Defend your honor from a vile reproach,
And force your father to revoke his prayers.
There is still time. Why, by what caprice,
Do you leave the field thus free to your accuser?
Enlighten Theseus.

HIPPOLYTUS   What have I not said?
Should I reveal the soiling of his bed?
Should I, by telling a too truthful tale,
Make flush my father's brow? For you alone
Have pierced the hateful mystery. My heart
Can be unbosomed only to the gods
And you. I could not hide from you—by this
Judge if I love you—all I would conceal
Even from myself. But yet remember, madam,
Under what seal I have revealed it to you.
Forget, if you are able, what I've said,
And may you never open your chaste lips
To tell of this affair. Let us rely
Upon the justice of the gods, for they
Are much concerned to justify me; and Phaedra
Sooner or later punished for her crime
Cannot avoid deserved ignominy.
That's all I ask of you. I permit all else
To my unbounded anger. Leave the serfdom
To which you are reduced, and follow me.

Dare to accompany my flight, Aricia.
Dare to come with me; snatch yourself away
From this unholy place, where virtue breathes
A poisoned air. To hide your disappearance,
Profit from the confusion that is caused
By my disgrace. I can assure the means
For your departure. All your guards are mine,
Powerful upholders of our cause. Argos
Holds out its arms to us, and Sparta calls us.
Let's bear our righteous cries to mutual friends;
And suffer not that Phaedra by our ruin
Should drive us from the throne, and to her son
Promise your spoil and mine. The chance is good;
We must embrace it. . . . What fear now restrains you?
You seem uncertain. Your interest alone
Inspires me to this boldness. When I am
Ablaze, what freezes you? Are you afraid
To tread with me the paths of exile?

ARICIA   Alas!
How dear, my lord, would such an exile be!
Tied to your fate, with what delight would I
Live, by the rest of mortals quite forgotten!
But since I'm not united by such ties,
Can I, with honor, flee with you? I know
That without blemish I can free myself
From Theseus' hands—it would not be to leave
The bosom of my family—and flight
Is lawful if we flee from tyrants. But,
My lord, you love me, and my startled honor . . .

HIPPOLYTUS No, no, I've too much care of your renown.
A nobler plan has brought me in your presence:

Flee from your enemies, and follow me,
Your husband. Free in our misfortunes, since
Heaven has ordained it so, our troth depends
Upon ourselves alone. Hymen need not
Be ringed with torches. At the gates of Troezen,
Among the tombs, the ancient sepulchers
Of the princes of my line, is a holy temple
Dreadful to perjurers. 'Tis there that mortals
Dare not make empty vows, lest they receive
Swift punishment; and, fearing there to meet
Inevitable death, the lie has not
A sterner bridle. There, if you will trust me,
We will confirm the solemn oath, and take
To witness it the god who's worshipped there,
Praying that he will act as father to us.
I'll call to witness the most sacred gods,
The chaste Diana, Juno the august,
And all the gods who, witnessing my love,
Will guarantee my holy promises.

ARICIA The King is coming. Fly, Prince; leave
    at once.
I will remain a moment, to conceal
My own departure. Go, but leave with me
Some faithful guide to lead my timid steps
To where you wait for me.
[*Exit Hippolytus.*]

SCENE TWO

Enter Theseus and Ismene.

THESEUS [*aside*]   O Gods! enlighten
My troubled heart, and deign to show the truth
That I am seeking here.

ARICIA [*to Ismene*]   Remember all,
My dear Ismene, and prepare for flight.
[*Exit Ismene.*]

SCENE THREE

THESEUS You change your color, and seem
    speechless, madam.
What was Hippolytus doing here?

ARICIA   My lord,
To bid me an eternal farewell.

THESEUS   Your eyes
Have learnt to conquer that rebellious spirit,
And his first sighs were your accomplishment.

ARICIA My lord, I cannot hide the truth from
    you.
He's not inherited your unjust hate;
He does not treat me as a criminal.

THESEUS I see. He vows you an eternal love.
Do not rely on his inconstant heart,
For he would swear as much to others.

ARICIA   He,
My lord?

THESEUS You ought to have made him less in-
    constant.
How can you bear this horrible division
Of his affections?

ARICIA   And how do you endure
That a horrible tale should smirch a blameless
    life?
Have you so little knowledge of his heart?
Do you discriminate so ill, my lord,
'Twixt crime and innocence? Must a hateful
    cloud
Conceal his virtue from your eyes alone,
Which brightly shines for others? It is wrong
To give him up to lying tongues. Cease now:
Repent your murderous prayers. Fear lest the
    heavens
Should bear you so much hatred as to grant
What you implored. For often in their wrath
They take our proffered victims; and their gifts
Are but the punishments of our own crimes.

THESEUS No. You wish in vain to hide his out-
    rage.
You're blinded by your love. I put my trust
In sure and irreproachable witnesses:
I've seen, I've seen a stream of genuine tears.

ARICIA Take care, my lord. Your hands invin-
    cible
Have freed mankind of monsters without num-
    ber,
But all are not destroyed, and you have left
One still alive. . . . Your son, my lord, forbids
    me
To tell you more. And knowing the respect
He wishes to retain for you, I would
Afflict him sorely if I dared to speak.
I imitate his modesty, and flee
Out of your presence, lest I should be forced
To break my silence.
[*Exit Aricia.*]

SCENE FOUR

THESEUS   What is in her mind?
What does it hide, this speech of hers, begun
So many times, and always interrupted?
Would they distract me with an empty feint?
Have they agreed together to torture me?
But I myself, in spite of my stern rigor,
What plaintive voice within my heart cried out?
I am afflicted by a secret pity,
And stand amazed. Let me a second time
Interrogate Œnone. I want to have
A clearer picture of the crime. Guards,
Send for Œnone. Let her come alone.

SCENE FIVE

Enter Panope.

PANOPE   My lord, I know not what the Queen is
    planning,
But yet I fear her violent distress.
Mortal despair is painted on her face,
Marked with Death's pallor. Œnone, from her
    presence
Driven away with shame, has thrown herself
Into the deep sea: it is not known why
She took her desperate action; and the waves
Have hidden her forever.
THESEUS   What do I hear?
PANOPE   The Queen has not been calmed by this
    dread deed.
Distress still grows within her doubtful soul.
Sometimes, to ease her secret griefs, she takes
Her children, bathing them with tears,
And then, renouncing her maternal love,
She suddenly repels them with her hand.
Then here and there she walks irresolute,
Her wandering eyes no longer knowing us.
Thrice she has written; then, with change of
    mind,
Thrice she has torn the letter she began.
Deign to see her, my lord, and try to help her.
THESEUS   O heavens! Œnone dead! and Phaedra
    now
Desires to die. Recall my son. Let him
Defend himself. Let him come and speak with
    me.

I'm ready to hear him. O Neptune, do not
    hasten
Thy deadly blessings. I would now prefer
That they should never be fulfilled. Perhaps
I have believed unfaithful witnesses
And raised too soon towards thee my cruel
    hands.
By what despair now will my prayers be fol-
    lowed!
[*Exit Panope.*]

SCENE SIX

Enter Theramenes.

THESEUS   Theramenes, is it you? What have you
    done
With Hippolytus? I entrusted him to you
From a tender age. But what has caused these
    tears
I see you shedding. What is my son doing?
THERAMENES   O tardy and superfluous cares, vain
    love!
Hippolytus is no more.
THESEUS   O Gods!
THERAMENES   I have seen
The most lovable of mortals die, and I must
    add,
My lord, the least guilty.
THESEUS   My son is dead?
When I hold out my arms to him, the gods
Have hastened his destruction. What dread blow
Has snatched him from me? What sudden thun-
    derclap?
THERAMENES   Scarce had we passed the gates of
    Troezen,
He rode upon his chariot; his sad guards,
Around him ranged, were silent as their lord.
Brooding, he followed the Mycenæ road,
And loosely held the reins. His splendid steeds,
Which once with noble zeal obeyed his voice,
Now with dejected eye and lowered head
Seemed to adapt themselves to his sad thoughts.
Then suddenly from out the waves there came
A dreadful cry which broke the silent air
And from the bosom of the earth a voice
With dreadful groans replied. Our blood was
    frozen,

Even to our hearts. The manes of the listening steeds
Stood up. Then on the liquid plain arose
A watery mountain which appeared to boil.
The wave approached, then broke, and vomited
Among the foamy seas a raging monster:
His huge head armed with menacing horns, his body
Covered with yellow scales, half-bull, half-dragon,
With his croup curved in involuted folds.
The seashore trembled with his bellowing;
The sky with horror saw that savage monster;
The earth was moved, the air infected with it;
The sea which brought it started back amazed.
Everyone fled; seeing all courage vain,
They sought asylum in a neighboring temple.
Hippolytus alone, a worthy son
Of a heroic father, stopped his horses,
Seized his javelins, approached the monster,
And, with a dart, thrown with unerring aim,
Wounded it in the flank. With rage and pain,
The monster leapt, and at the horses' feet
Fell roaring, rolled itself, and offered them
Its flaming mouth, which covered them with fire,
And blood and smoke. Then terror seized them; deaf,
This time, nor voice nor bridle did they know.
Their master spent himself in useless efforts;
Their bits were reddened with a bloody foam.
'Tis said, that in this terrible confusion
A god was seen who spurred their dusty flanks.
Fear hurtled them across the rocks. The axle
Screeched and snapped. The bold Hippolytus
Saw all his chariot shiver into splinters;
And tangled in the reins, he fell. Excuse
My grief. That cruel sight will be for me
An everlasting source of tears. I've seen,
My lord, I've seen your most unlucky son
Dragged by the horses which his hands had fed.
He tried to check them; but, frightened by his voice,
They ran; and soon his body was a single wound.
The plain resounded with our grievous cries.
At last they slackened speed; they stopped not far
From those old tombs where his royal ancestors
Are the cold relics. There I ran, in tears,
And his guard followed me. A trail of blood
Showed us the way. The rocks were stained with it.
The loathsome brambles carried bloodstained scraps
Of hair torn from his head. I reached him, called
To him; he stretched his hand to me, and opened
His dying eyes, then closed them suddenly.
"The heavens," said he, "now snatch my guiltless life.
Look after Aricia when I am dead.
Dear friend, if my father one day learns the truth,
And weeps the tragic ending of a son
Falsely accused, in order to appease
My blood and plaintive ghost, tell him to treat
His captive kindly, to give her . . ." At this word
The hero died and left within my arms
Only a corpse, disfigured, where the wrath
Of the gods had triumphed, one which his father's eyes
Would fail to recognize.

THESEUS   My son! dear hope
Now taken from me! Inexorable gods,
Too well indeed you have fulfilled your word!
To what remorse my life is now reserved!

THERAMENES Then gentle Aricia arrived; she came,
My lord, escaping from your wrath, to take him
Before the gods as husband. She approached.
She saw the red and reeking grass; she saw
(What an object for a lover's eyes!)
Hippolytus lying there a shapeless mass.
A while she wished to doubt of her disaster
And failed to recognize the man she loved.
She saw Hippolytus—and asked for him still.
At last too sure that he was lying there,
She with a mournful look reproached the gods;
Cold, moaning, almost lifeless, she fell down
At her lover's feet. Ismene was beside her;
Ismene, weeping, brought her back to life,
Or rather, back to grief. And I have come,
Hating the light, to tell you the last wish
Of a dead hero; and discharge, my lord,
The unhappy task his dying heart reposed
Upon me. But I see his mortal foe
Approaching.

Phaedra

SCENE SEVEN

Enter Phaedra, Panope, and Guards.

THESEUS   Well, you triumph, and my son
Is lifeless. Ah! how I have cause to fear!
A cruel suspicion, excusing him, alarms me.
But, madam, he is dead. Receive your victim,
Joy in his death, whether unjust or lawful.
I'll let my eyes forever be abused,
Believe him criminal, since you accuse him.
His death alone gives matter for my tears
Without my seeking harsh enlightenment,
Which could not bring him back, and might
    increase
The sum of my misfortunes. Let me, far from
    you,
Far from this coast flee from the bloody image
Of my rent son. Perplexed and persecuted
By deadly memories, I would banish me
From the whole world. Everything seems to rise
Against my injustice. Even my very fame
Augments my punishment. Less known of men,
I could the better hide. I hate the honors
The gods bestow upon me; and I'm going
To mourn their murderous favors, and no more
Tire them with useless prayers. Whate'er they
    granted,
Would never compensate me for the loss
Of what they've taken away.

PHAEDRA   No, Theseus.
I must break an unjust silence; to your son
Restore his innocence. He was not guilty.

THESEUS   Unhappy father! It was by your word
That I condemned him. Cruel! do you think
That you can be excused . . . ?

PHAEDRA   My time is
    precious.
Hear me, Theseus. It was I myself
Who cast upon your chaste and modest son
Unholy and incestuous eyes. The heavens
Put in my breast that fatal spark—the rest
Was undertaken by the vile Œnone.
She trembled lest Hippolytus should disclose
A passion he abhorred. The traitress then,
Relying on my utter weakness, hastened
To accuse him to your face. She's punished for
it.
Fleeing my wrath she sought amidst the waves
Too soft a punishment. The sword by now
Would have cut short my life, had I not left
Virtue suspected. Baring my remorse
Before you, I wished to take a slower road
To the house of Death. I have taken—I have
    made
Course through my burning veins a deadly
    poison
Medea brought to Athens. Already the venom
Has reached my dying heart, and thrown upon
    it
An unimagined cold. Already I see,
As through a mist, the sky above, the husband
My presence outrages; and Death, that robs
My eyes of clearness, to the day they soil
Restores its purity.

PANOPE   She is dying, my lord.

THESEUS   Oh! that the memory of her black
    deed
Could perish with her! Of my error now
Only too well enlightened, let us go
To mix the blood of my unhappy son
With tears; to embrace the little that remains
Of that dear son, and expiate the madness
Of my detested prayer; to render him
The honors that he has too much deserved;
And, the better to appease his angry spirit,
Despite her family's plotting, from today
I'll hold Aricia as my own true child.

TRAGEDY IN RACINE is theological. It is more than the war between the spirit and the flesh; it is the dramatist's shattering conviction that sexual love must lead to disaster.

"A scene in Corneille," wrote Giraudoux, "is an official rendezvous where one comes to discuss in hopes of a settlement. In Racine, it is the explanation which closes for the time a series of negotiations between wild beasts"; and a few pages later he speaks of Racine's characters confronting one another "on a footing of awful equality, of physical and moral nudity." The morality of Racine's world is the morality of the jungle, but the violence is intensified and not diminished by the characters' exceptional powers of insight, their extremely sensitive consciousness of their most intimate feelings which belonged to a people of whom the poet constantly uses the word *sensible*. [Martin Turnell, *The Classical Moment; Studies of Corneille, Molière and Racine*, Hamish Hamilton, Ltd., London, 1947, pp. 180–181.]

Racine had become so obsessed by the Jansenist sense of the inherent sinfulness of sexual love that even Hippolytus's love for Aricia is described as *un fol amour*, as an aberration of his *sens égarés*. It leads to disaster as surely as Phaedra's incestuous passion, but to assume that he is destroyed merely because he abandons the role assigned to him by tradition is to underrate the subtlety of Racine's interpretation. The view underlying the play is that once a "limit" has been passed, once weakness or wickedness has entered into the human heart, it can never be cast out again and nothing can stop its ravages. This is felt strongly by Phaedra and Hippolytus, who both realize too late that the limit has been passed. . . . This applies to the "innocent" as well as to the "guilty." Hippolytus is described more than once as *l'insensible Hippolyte,* and it is precisely his "insensibility" which provides the best protection against the consequences of the furious passions which are unleashed among those who surround him. The stoic ideal, however, is a negative one and Hippolytus is fully conscious of its inadequacy. As soon as his father

is reported to be dead, he moves away from it towards something more positive and more human. His feelings for Aricia lead to a relaxation of his father's prohibition against her marrying and when he tells her:

> Greece reproaches me
> With an alien mother. But if my brother were
> My only rival, over him I have
> Some veritable claims that I would save
> Out of the law's caprice.

—there is a distinction between *droits* and *lois,* between natural human "rights" and inhuman "laws." The distinction is a vital one and it is apparent in all Racine's work. In his earlier plays he had exposed the hollowness of an order which had ceased to be a true order and had degenerated into mere "legalism," into the external observance of empty formulas. In *Phaedra* the criticism becomes more searching. The dilemma lies in the fact that though "laws" are incapable of providing a constructive solution of the problems which confronted Racine's contemporaries, they were the only barrier against anarchy. Once a "law," however capricious, was set aside, the way was open to confusion and disorder. This is brought home by the tragic accents of Phaedra's declaration:

> I reign? To place the State
> Under my law, when reason reigns no longer
> Over myself; when I have abdicated
> From the empire of my senses; when beneath
> A yoke of shame I scarcely breathe . . .

The choice lies between legalism and disaster, between an "insensibility," which excludes natural "rights," and a "shameful yoke." In a tragic world the person who desires no more than his natural rights follows the road to destruction. Theseus forbade Aricia to marry because she came of contaminated "blood." Hippolytus's relaxation of his father's prohibition is tantamount to an infringement of "law" which at once involves him in the intrigues that are going on in his entourage. The maxim, as always in Racine, is that there is not and indeed cannot be a middle course which offers security and honor. [*Ibid.*, pp. 193–194.]

In all Racine's plays, reason is powerless to resist the swirls of passion. Phaedra's attempt to shift the blame for her downfall on to the gods is the purest Jansenist doctrine and it shows the weaknesses of that line as a guide to living. At the same time, it does nothing to mitigate its votaries' sense of guilt. The honesty and lucidity with which Phaedra faces the implications of her conduct and her recognition of the code which she has outraged are characteristic of seventeenth-century literature.

The movement of the play is essentially a destructive movement. The human personality is shattered by its own passions and the play closes with its total dislocation. The false report of Theseus's death raises Phaedra's hopes for a moment; in spite of her rebuff by Hippolytus, she is led on by the thought that her love is no longer illicit and may be satisfied. The violence of passion is increased by the simultaneous discovery that Theseus is living and that Hippolytus is in love with Aricia. The terrible clarity with which these discoveries are registered in Phaedra's mind throw a good deal of light on the tragic process. [*Ibid.*, pp. 207–208.]

In nearly all Racine's plays, passion leads logically to death; but in *Phaedra* the connection between passion and death is much closer and much more complex. The connection is underlined by the incest *motif*. *Phaedra* appears to be the only play in which the theme of incest is introduced, but it would be more accurate to say that it is the only play in which it is *openly* introduced. For, as Jean Giraudoux once suggested, the passions in all Racine's plays are surrounded by an atmosphere of incest. He also made another interesting suggestion. He suggested that in Racine passion is always *contagious,* and the point is worth developing. In the other plays the principal character suffers from a fatal passion which infects those who surround him or her, so that each of them develops the same passion for a third person. Orestes infects Hermione who becomes infatuated with Pyrrhus who in turn is infatuated with Andromache. Roxane infects Bajazet who falls in love with Atalide. Phaedra infects the "insensible" Hippolytus who becomes desperately in love with Aricia. [*Ibid.*, p. 213.]

Racine's characters see themselves with a terrible intensity,
see themselves always in the past. Georges Poulet's analysis is useful
for an understanding not only of Phaedra *but of all of Racine.*

The *feeling of self* in the Racinian being: it is that of a man who falls over a precipice, is terrified, and yet looks at himself in a detached and extraordinarily lucid fashion, as if his future death were already accomplished, and he saw himself *in the past.*

The Racinian tragedy is an action *in the past.* We see it less in its actuality, in its immediacy, in the palpable shock of it, than in the reflective thought and in the affective echo it produces afterward, mediately and almost indirectly, in its victims and spectators. At the moment in which we have become conscious of it, it has already taken place. It fulminates, like the lightning one recognizes only when it is gone and has become part of the past. In that respect, the tragedy of Racine differs from all other tragedy, which by its nature renders the action in a time that is progressive, that is in the course of being. Here, it is a time realized that engages us, and the action which confronts us, being in each of its consecutive parts an action which has just taken place and which in each instant is only just past, it seems that we are witnessing the process by which things in the last analysis become "fatal" in our eyes and force us to recognize that indeed they could not have happened otherwise. The Racinian fatality is characterized by this *retardation* of thought upon action, which paints the latter the color of unchangeable lead, and which brings it about that each past contingency, even if it be only one second past, becomes as necessary as the most general law. The Racinian fatality is the "What have I said!" of Phaedra. It is the fatality of irreversibility. [Georges Poulet, *Studies in Human Time*, Johns Hopkins Press, Baltimore, 1956, p. 123.]

I know my frenzies, I recall them all.
[*Phaedra*, Act 3, Scene 3.]

There is no light more intense or more cruel than that projected by the self-awareness of Racinian characters. The reflective consciousness which leads them to the discovery of their own being, reveals to them not only the kind of being they are, but the kind of continuity or progression in time which has more and more made them become what they are. The particular lucidity they bring to this knowledge reaches as far as their past extends. It makes rise up in their course and development all the thoughts and actions which have issued from their very depths to bring them to the extreme situation into which they are thrown and of which they become aware. It even goes back further and seems to search the original shadows for a primary principle, a prenatal tendency, which, from before their existence, contained its germ and waited to enfold it in frenzies and passions. Thus the tragic consciousness is here found invested with the power of contemplating itself through the whole field of its duration: it everywhere recognizes itself as monstrously similar. [*Ibid.*, p. 124.]

"Racine," says Thierry Maulnier, "goes straight to what is hardest and purest in life and death,—in destiny." How is it that one can speak of the *purity* of Racinian destiny, since nothing is less pure or more horrible than the successive visages it seems to present? "What wilt thou say, my father, of this horrible spectacle?" [*Phaedra*, Act 4, Scene 6.]

Let us be careful, however, not to confound with destiny the *horrible spectacle* which makes the consciousness of Phaedra, like the shade of Minos, shudder; for it is the spectacle offered to Phaedra by Phaedra, the light under which she sees herself in the horrible and incessant revolutions of the life of her senses: "I feel my whole body shiver and burn"; experience of the self by the self, situated in the contact and contrast of the successive moments, but which immediately another presence replaces:

I recognized Venus and her terrible fires,
Inevitable torments of a blood she pursues.
[*Phaedra*, Act 1, Scene 3.]

[*Ibid.*, pp. 125–126.]

Whatever may be one's response to the other characters in Phaedra, *one is inevitably fascinated by Phaedra herself. She is not alone responsible for her acts. She may be more sinned against than sinning.*

The character of Phaedra, as we have already suggested, was the product of a long secretion of feeling and of experience in writing for the theatre. She is a woman "in the August of her life," married to a roving and absent husband, the mother of a child old enough to be considered as the next King of Athens. It is impossible to assign an exact age to her. It varies according to the ideas of the period, the producer, the actress. The Champmeslé was about thirty-five when she created the part, but this means little since she continued to play it for twenty years. In the next century, Adrienne Lecouvreur played it triumphantly as a young actress of twenty-five. Mlle Clairon, still more daring, made her debut in it at eighteen. Rachel, in the nineteenth century, essayed it at the age of twenty-three, though the Phaedra of her middle years was considered better. At the other end of the scale, many contemporary playgoers will have mixed memories of Sarah Bernhardt presenting scenes from Phaedra at the age of seventy. All that can be deduced from the text is that Phaedra is a mature woman, full of experience and disillusion, but also capable of an irresistible infatuation which torments and wastes her. [Geoffrey Brereton, *Jean Racine, a Critical Biography,* Cassell & Co., Ltd., London, 1951, pp. 221–222.]

Phaedra is at least half innocent and it is this, combined with the inevitability of her wrongdoing, which lifts the part so high among tragic roles and presents almost inexhaustible subtleties of interpretation to the great actress. As Racine himself pointed out, "she is involved, by her destiny and by the anger of the gods, in an unlawful passion by which she is the first to be horrified. She makes every effort to overcome it. She prefers to pine and die rather than to declare it to anyone; and when she is forced to reveal it, she speaks of it with a confusion which shows plainly that her crime is rather a punishment of the gods than an effect of her own will."

But Phaedra has to accomplish one act which goes beyond blind passion. In denouncing the innocent Hippolytus to his father Theseus, she acts with a certain premeditation. The malice of her accusation is attenuated by the desperate state of her mind when she makes it; after it has been made she repents and intends to withdraw it, but is silenced by the shock of learning that Hippolytus loves Aricia. He has spurned her not because of his youthful chastity, but because he prefers her "rival." Yet these attenuations are not enough. In spite of them, Phaedra might still appear odious to an audience which is not, while in the theatre, in a position to weigh with care the psychological circumstances surrounding the act, but sees chiefly the act and its consequences. Racine therefore seeks to remove the most obvious blame from Phaedra by laying it on the nurse, Oenone. It is Oenone who suggests the accusation to her mistress, Oenone who makes it to Theseus with her mistress's passive consent. . . .

From psychological stupidity springs misplaced external activity and from such activity springs disaster: such is the lesson of Oenone. This gross, well-intentioned, bustling character does not rate as an evil genius, since she cannot compose but only mistranslate. She is not a second Narcisse, who was pernicious with intent. She is, however, the willing servant of the evil which lies *in posse* in Phaedra's emotions, waiting for some interpreter bold enough and fool enough to define it as a policy. . . . She is actuated throughout by loyalty to her mistress and when at length Phaedra turns upon her and curses her for meddling, she employs the heroic logic of the simple-hearted and goes out to kill herself. In other theatres at other periods she might well be the heroine of a play, but not in seventeenth-century tragedy. [*Ibid.,* pp. 225–227.]

Phaedra illustrates even better [than *Athaliah*] Racine's genius for approaching a union of incompatibles. Here, too, he tries to fuse Greek Tragedy with Christian doctrine, but this time using a pagan and not a Biblical theme. Although Euripides' *Hippolytus* is his chief model, the character of his heroine is drawn from Jansenism. The voice is the voice of Phaedra, but the thoughts are the thoughts of Port-Royal. When Phaedra speaks of Venus, the pagan goddess becomes the demon of Original Sin:

> It is no more
> A passion hidden in my veins, but now
> It's Venus fastened on her helpless prey.
> I have a just abhorrence of my crime;
> I hate my life, abominate my lust. . . .

A more subtle creation than Athaliah, Phaedra is pagan and Christian together. Conscious of sin, she cannot avoid it, a victim at once of Greek fate and Jansenist predestination.

But can Racine combine in his audience the feelings appropriate to Greek Tragedy and those appropriate to Original Sin? He says in his Preface that the intention of the play is to show up vice and make us hate it. Phaedra would not be a great tragic character if our reaction were hatred. No doubt the malevolence theory of tragic pleasure, held by Rousseau and Emile

Faguet, would allow Racine to say that our aesthetic satisfaction is bound up with hate of this damned soul in torment. Mr. F. L. Lucas compares Rousseau with those early Fathers who included among celestial pleasures the spectacle, *du paradis,* of the torments of hell. Whatever one may think of such a theatre in the after-life, we fortunately know that Racine's views of the mundane theatre in Athens and Paris were rather different. In the Preface to *Phaedra,* he says that the true purpose of Tragedy is not to divert but to instruct, and that the pursuit of such an aim might reconcile the religious to this form of profane drama. He also says, following Aristotle, that the tragic hero should have qualities exciting compassion and terror, and he explains why he thinks that the character of Phaedra satisfies Aristotle's rules:

> Phaedra is neither completely guilty nor completely innocent. She is involved by her destiny, and by the anger of the gods, in an illegitimate passion, which she more than anyone regards with horror. She does all she can to overcome it. . . . Her crime is a punishment from the gods rather than an act of will.

In that case, one may well ask how on earth Phaedra can be regarded as a sinner, or her fate as just. If her *crime* is a "punishment" from the gods, justice is indeed a blind goddess. In the death of Hippolytus, divine justice appears even more unjust. In order that Hippolytus's death should not cause "more indignation than pity," says Racine, he has made Hippolytus subject to *"quelque faiblesse"* (our old friend

hamartia), which would "make him a little guilty towards his father." The *faiblesse* is Hippolytus's love for a girl related to his father's enemies. For this, he is torn to pieces by a sea monster. As Racine says, "the smallest faults are severely punished" in his play. This is the moral instruction that is to reconcile tragic drama with religion. It reminds me of the late Mr. J. S. Smart's description of the doctrine of Gervinus, that in Shakespeare's eyes any fault is punishable by death. Macbeth murders a king; he must die. Desdemona shocks her father by marrying a blackamoor; she must die. Juliet imprudently allows herself to fall in love at first sight; she must die. "Compared with this procedure, the Bloody Assize was humane," comments Mr. Smart:

> If a man were brought before a criminal court, accused of stealing a box of matches, duly convicted of stealing a box of matches, and then sentenced to penal servitude for life, the public mind would be outraged: such a penalty would seem to show a deeper guilt in the judge than in the culprit.

I do not know that the fate of Racine's Hippolytus stirs either indignation or pity, for the character is a dramatic failure. But in his portrayal of Phaedra, Racine undoubtedly reaches tragic sublimity. And like Lear, Phaedra is more sinned against than sinning. How could Racine suppose that the morality of his play would commend itself to the religious? [D. D. Raphael, *The Paradox of Tragedy,* Indiana University Press, Bloomington, Ind., 1960, pp. 63–66.]

Racine owes much of the structure of his play, at least in the bare outlines, to his classical sources. To say that much is not, of course, in any way to disparage his achievement.

Phaedra is perhaps Racine's masterpiece; it is certainly the highest achievement of French classical tragedy. . . .

The Greek legend of Phaedra and Hippolytus was the subject of the *Hippolytus* of Euripides,

of the *Phaedra* of Seneca, and of several French dramas prior to [Racine's] *Phaedra.* Racine was indebted to these last for only a few minor touches. Euripides was his chief source, from which he derived the general outlines of his play and of the characters of Phaedra, Theseus, and the Nurse, and some phases of the character of Hippolytus. He followed Seneca, however, in making Phaedra herself declare her love to Hippolytus and in making the Nurse originate the slander against him, which is lent color of truth by his loss of his sword (whereas in Euripides it is the Nurse who, unknown to Phaedra, informs Hippolytus of the Queen's passion for him, and it is Phaedra who, when the shame of this exposure and of his abusive words drives her to suicide, leaves in death a letter accusing him of having dishonored her); as in Seneca, the absence of Theseus at the beginning of the play is identified with that hero's fabled expedition to Hades, and Phaedra believes him dead; again as in Seneca, she survives Hippolytus and in a dying confession clears him of all blame. But Racine's borrowings from his classical models are not limited to characterization and turns of plot; he at times imitates their scenes, as to both development and language. [Lacy Lockert, *Studies in French-Classical Tragedy,* Vanderbilt University Press, Nashville, Tenn., 1958, pp. 388–389.]

Racine offers insights not only into the nature of classical tragedy but also into the life of his own time.

The more perfect a work is the deeper are the characteristics portrayed in it. We might extract from Racine the whole system of the monarchical sentiments of our seventeenth century,—the portrait of the king, of the queen, of the children of France, of noble courtiers, ladies of honor, and prelates; all the dominant ideas of the time,—feudal fidelity, chivalric honor, servility of the ante-chamber, the decorum of the palace, the devotion of servants and subjects, the perfection of manners, the sway and tyranny of propriety, the natural and artificial niceties of language, of the heart, of Christianity and of morality; in short, the habits and sentiments which make up the principal traits of the ancient regime. [H. Taine, *The Ideal in Art,* Holt and Williams, New York, 1868, p. 69.]

We read Racine in English, but we should not altogether forget the power of his language (and if one has any sense of the French one should try out such lines as those quoted below).

The two most musical lines Racine ever wrote always seem to me two lines out of *Phaedra:*

Ariane ma soeur, de quel amour blessée
Vous mourûtes au bords où vous fûtes laissée.

It is said that when Rachel spoke these two lines on the stage for the first time the effect was so tremendous that Alfred de Musset fainted in his box. The effect was very great when Sarah Bernhardt used to say them. I once heard an extremely cosmopolitan critic, who disliked Racine, say that he thought the two circumflexed *u*'s were hideous; of course if that is your impression the lines would sound hideous, but those who admire these lines admire them because of the long repeated stress on the *u,* and the muted *e*'s at the end of the lines. Modern French poets have made great capital out of the long *u*'s. One poet (Arthur Rimbaud) went so far as to say that every vowel in French had a special colour; and that the letter *u* was green. [Maurice Baring, *Have You Anything to Declare?* Alfred A. Knopf, Inc., New York, 1937, p. 115.]

The richness of Racine is of a piece with the Greek drama. Jean-Louis Barrault suggests how much of that richness can be revealed to a sensitive actor-producer.

Racine is perhaps the greatest and certainly the most musical of all our French poets. How elegantly he hides his power behind an alexandrine!

For me *Phaedra* opened the door on to the whole of Racine.

He is the most alive thing in the world, for since his death he has enjoyed the sacred privilege of living for us at each and every stage of his career. You and I call ourselves mortals probably because we die every day; what we were yesterday is dead, what we shall be tomorrow is still unborn. But Racine has lived again for us throughout these 250 years—wholly and simultaneously: the child playing in the gardens of Port Royal, the novice pirouetting to Uzès, the young man in revolt against his masters, the dramatic author living his season in hell, the mature man who has become the King's docile

historiographer, the strict father writing severe letters to his son, and finally the aged poet singing the praises of the Lord among the girls at Saint-Cyr.

It is a multiple Racine that Racine offers us, for he is composed of as many characters as he put into his tragedies—characters that did not always agree with each other; so he offers us too as many conflicts as he had to wage with himself, within himself.

The spirit at war with the flesh, the flesh at war with the spirit—that is the eternal conflict. Baudelaire said later: "In every man, at every moment, there are two simultaneous postulations, one towards God and the other towards Satan. The desire to mount the scale confronted by the delights of descent." [Jean-Louis Barrault, *Reflections on the Theatre*, Barrie and Rockliff, London, 1949, p. 105.]

The final word is the author's: Racine's Preface *explains much about sources and intentions, although it certainly does not proscribe critical speculation about the nature of this particular tragedy or of tragedy in general.*

Here is another tragedy of which the subject is taken from Euripides. Although I have followed a slightly different road from that author's for the conduct of the action, I have not scrupled to enrich my play with all that seemed to me most striking in his. While I owe only the single idea of the character of Phaedra to him, I could say that I owe to him that which I could reasonably show on the stage. I am not surprised that this character had so great a success in the time of Euripides, and that it has also succeeded so well in our century, since it has all the qualities which Aristotle demanded in the heroes of a tragedy, and which are proper to excite pity and terror. Indeed, Phaedra is neither entirely guilty, nor entirely innocent; she is involved, by her fate

and the wrath of the gods, in an unlawful passion, of which she is the first to feel horror; she makes every effort to overcome it; she prefers to let herself die rather than to confess it to anyone; and when she is forced to discover it, she speaks of it with a confusion that makes plain that her crime is rather a punishment of the gods than a movement of her will.

I have even taken care to render her a little less odious than she is in the tragedies of the ancients, where she resolves of herself to accuse Hippolytus. I thought that the calumny was too base and evil to put into the mouth of a princess who elsewhere displays such noble and virtuous sentiments. This baseness appeared to me more suitable to a nurse, who could have more servile inclinations, and who nevertheless undertakes this false accusation only to save the life and honor of her mistress. Phaedra consents to it only because she is in such agitation that she is beside herself; and she comes a moment after in the action to justify innocence and declare the truth.

Hippolytus is accused, in Euripides and Seneca, of having actually violated his stepmother: *vim corpus tulit*. But he is here accused of only having had the intention. I wished to spare Theseus a confusion which would have rendered him less agreeable to the audience.

With regard to the character of Hippolytus, I have noticed among the ancients that Euripides is reproached for having represented him as a philosopher exempt of all imperfection: which made the death of the young prince cause much more indignation than pity. I thought I should give him some weakness which would make him a little guilty towards his father, without however taking away from him any of the greatness of soul with which he spares Phaedra's honor and lets himself be oppressed without accusing her. I call weakness the passion which he feels, against his will, for Aricia, who is the daughter and the sister of mortal enemies of his father.

This Aricia is not a character of my invention. Virgil says that Hippolytus married her, and had a son by her, after Æsculapius had brought him back to life. And I have also read in some authors that Hippolytus had wedded and brought to Italy a young Athenian of high birth, called Aricia, and who had given her name to a small Italian town.

I mention these authorities because I have very scrupulously set myself to follow the fable. I have even followed the story of Theseus as given in Plutarch.

It is in this historian that I have found that what gave occasion to believe that Theseus descended into the underworld to rescue Proserpine was a journey that the prince had made in Epirus towards the source of the Acheron, at the home of a king whose wife Peirithous wishes to bear off, and who took Theseus prisoner after slaying Peirithous. So I have tried to keep the verisimilitude of the story, without losing anything of the ornaments of the fable, which is an abundant storehouse of poetical imagery; and the rumor of Theseus' death, based on this fabulous voyage, gives an opportunity to Phaedra to make a declaration of love which becomes one of the principal causes of her misfortune, and which she would never have dared to make so long as she believed that her husband was alive.

For the rest, I dare not yet assert that this play is indeed the best of my tragedies. I leave it to readers and to time to decide its true value. What I can assert is that I have not made one where virtue is put in a more favorable light than in this one; the least faults are severely punished; the very thought of a crime is regarded with as much horror as the crime itself; the weaknesses of love are shown as true weaknesses; the passions are displayed only to show all the disorder of which they are the cause; and vice is everywhere depicted in colors which make the deformity recognized and hated. That is properly the end which every man who works for the public should propose to himself; and it is that which the first tragic poets kept in sight above everything. Their theatre was a school where virtue was not less well taught than in the schools of the philosophers. So Aristotle was willing to give rules for the dramatic poem; and Socrates, the wisest of philosophers, did not disdain to set his hand to the tragedies of Euripides. It could be wished that our works were as solid and as full of useful instructions as those of these poets. That would perhaps be a means of reconciling tragedy with numerous people, celebrated for their piety and for their doctrine, who have condemned it in recent times, and who would doubtless judge it more favorably if the authors thought as much about instructing their audiences as about diverting them, and if they followed in this respect the true function of tragedy.

WILLIAM CONGREVE

1670–1729

The son of an army officer, Congreve was born in Yorkshire and educated in Ireland. Not until 1690 did he arrive in London. The following year he took up the study of law, perhaps as an excuse for remaining in the city. His first play, The Old Bachelor, *was produced in 1693 and was an immediate success. His fifth and last,* The Way of the World, *appeared in 1700 and proved a disappointing failure. In later years Congreve insisted on being thought of as a gentleman rather than a writer, a preference sometimes ascribed to bitterness over the reception accorded his best play.* The Way of the World *is the ultimate flowering, after the Restoration, of the Restoration comedy of manners inaugurated by Sir George Etherege in 1668. Comedy of this sort assumes the standard of a fashionable society; it stresses the importance of urbanity, grace, intelligence, and conversational brilliance. But Congreve's play is not limited to the superficialities, however clever and amusing, of coterie drama. He himself objected in his dedication of the play, with some asperity, to those who "come with expectation to laugh out the last act of a play, and are better entertained with two or three unseasonable jests, than with the artful solution of the* fable." *He had, he said, sought to avoid portraying fools so gross that "they should rather disturb than divert the well-natured and reflecting part of an audience." Instead he had designed characters "which should appear ridiculous, not so much through a natural folly (which is incorrigible, and therefore not proper for the stage) as through an affected wit; a wit, which at the same time that it is affected, is also false." His audience missed his subtleties; "this play had been acted two or three days, before some of these hasty judges could find the leisure to distinguish betwixt the character of a Witwoud and a Truewit."*

The Way of the World

Characters

FAINALL *in love with Mrs. Marwood*

MIRABELL *in love with Mrs. Millamant*

WITWOUD, PETULANT *followers of Mrs. Millamant*

SIR WILFULL WITWOUD *half-brother to Witwoud, and nephew to Lady Wishfort*

WAITWELL *servant to Mirabell*

LADY WISHFORT *enemy to Mirabell, for having falsely pretended love to her*

MRS. MILLAMANT *a fine lady, niece to Lady Wishfort, who loves Mirabell*

MRS. MARWOOD *friend to Fainall, and likes Mirabell*

MRS. FAINALL *daughter to Lady Wishfort, and wife to Fainall, formerly friend to Mirabell*

FOIBLE *woman to Lady Wishfort*

MINCING *woman to Mrs. Millamant*

BETTY *waiting-maid at a chocolate house*

PEG *maid to Lady Wishfort*

COACHMEN, DANCERS, FOOTMEN, AND ATTENDANTS

The action of the play takes place in London.

Prologue

FAINALL Of those few fools who with ill stars are cursed,
Sure scribbling fools, called poets, fare the worst:
For they're a sort of fools which Fortune makes,
And after she has made 'em fools, forsakes.
With Nature's oafs 'tis quite a different case,
For Fortune favors all her idiot-race.
In her own nest the cuckoo-eggs we find,
O'er which she broods to hatch the changeling-kind.[1]

No portion for her own she has to spare,
So much she dotes on her adopted care.

Poets are bubbles,[2] by the town drawn in,
Suffered at first some trifling stakes to win;
But what unequal hazards do they run!
Each time they write they venture all they've won:
The squire that's buttered[3] still, is sure to be undone.
This author heretofore has found your favor,
But pleads no merit from his past behavior.

[1] The cuckoo lays its eggs in the nests of other birds. "Changeling" means both (*a*) a child exchanged for another in infancy, and (*b*) an idiot.

[2] Dupes, easily cheated.

[3] Persuaded to increase his bets progressively.

329

To build on that might prove a vain presumption,
Should grants, to poets made, admit resumption;
And in Parnassus he must lose his seat
If that be found a forfeited estate.

He owns with toil he wrought the following scenes;
But, if they're naught, ne'er spare him for his pains.
Damn him the more: have no commiseration
For dullness on mature deliberation.
He swears he'll not resent one hissed-off scene;
Nor, like those peevish wits, his play maintain,
Who, to assert their sense, your taste arraign.

Some plot we think he has, and some new thought;
Some humor too, no farce—but that's a fault.
Satire, he thinks, you ought not to expect;
For so reformed a town who dares correct?
To please, this time, has been his sole pretence;
He'll not instruct, lest it should give offence.

Should he by chance a knave or fool expose,
That hurts none here; sure here are none of those.
In short, our play shall (with your leave to show it)
Give you one instance of a passive poet,
Who to your judgments yields all resignation;
So save or damn, after your own discretion.

Act One

SCENE ONE

A chocolate house. Mirabell and Fainall, rising from cards, Betty waiting.

MIRABELL   You are a fortunate man, Mr. Fainall!

FAINALL   Have we done?

MIRABELL   What you please. I'll play on to entertain you.

FAINALL   No, I'll give you your revenge another time, when you are not so indifferent; you are thinking of something else now, and play too negligently. The coldness of a losing gamester lessens the pleasure of the winner. I'd no more play with a man that slighted his ill fortune than I'd make love to a woman who undervalued the loss of her reputation.

MIRABELL   You have a taste extremely delicate, and are for refining on your pleasures.

FAINALL   Prithee, why so reserved? Something has put you out of humor.

MIRABELL   Not at all. I happen to be grave today, and you are gay; that's all.

FAINALL   Confess, Millamant and you quarrelled last night after I left you. My fair cousin has some humors that would tempt the patience of a stoic. What, some coxcomb came in, and was well received by her, while you were by?

MIRABELL   Witwoud and Petulant; and what was worse, her aunt, your wife's mother, my evil

genius; or to sum up all in her own name, my old Lady Wishfort came in.

FAINALL   Oh, there it is then! She has a lasting passion for you, and with reason.—What, then my wife was there?

MIRABELL   Yes, and Mrs. Marwood, and three or four more, whom I never saw before. Seeing me, they all put on their grave faces, whispered one another; then complained aloud of the vapors;[4] and after fell into a profound silence.

FAINALL   They had a mind to be rid of you.

MIRABELL   For which reason I resolved not to stir. At last the good old lady broke through her painful taciturnity with an invective against long visits. I would not have understood her, but Millamant joining in the argument, I rose, and with a constrained smile, told her I thought nothing was so easy as to know when a visit began to be troublesome. She reddened, and I withdrew without expecting her reply.

FAINALL   You were to blame to resent what she spoke only in compliance with her aunt.

MIRABELL   She is more mistress of herself than to be under the necessity of such a resignation.

FAINALL   What! though half her fortune depends upon her marrying with my lady's approbation?

MIRABELL   I was then in such a humor, that I

---

[4] Fits of melancholy; the blues.

should have been better pleased if she had been less discreet.

FAINALL Now I remember, I wonder not they were weary of you. Last night was one of their cabal nights. They have 'em three times a week, and meet by turns at one another's apartments, where they come together like the coroner's inquest, to sit upon the murdered reputations of the week. You and I are excluded; and it was once proposed that all the male sex should be excepted; but somebody moved that, to avoid scandal, there might be one man of the community; upon which motion Witwoud and Petulant were enrolled members.

MIRABELL And who may have been the foundress of this sect? My Lady Wishfort, I warrant, who publishes her detestation of mankind; and full of the vigour of fifty-five, declares for a friend and ratafia;[5] and let posterity shift for itself, she'll breed no more.

FAINALL The discovery of your sham addresses to her, to conceal your love to her niece, has provoked this separation; had you dissembled better, things might have continued in the state of nature.

MIRABELL I did as much as man could, with any reasonable conscience; I proceeded to the very last act of flattery with her, and was guilty of a song in her commendation. Nay, I got a friend to put her into a lampoon and compliment her with the imputation of an affair with a young fellow, which I carried so far that I told her the malicious town took notice that she was grown fat of a sudden; and when she lay in of a dropsy, persuaded her she was reported to be in labor. The devil's in't, if an old woman is to be flattered further, unless a man should endeavor downright personally to debauch her; and that my virtue forbade me. But for the discovery of this amour I am indebted to your friend, or your wife's friend, Mrs. Marwood.

FAINALL What should provoke her to be your enemy unless she has made you advances which you have slighted? Women do not easily forgive omissions of this nature.

MIRABELL She was always civil to me till of late. I confess I am not one of those coxcombs who

are apt to interpret a woman's good manners to her prejudice, and think that she who does not refuse 'em everything, can refuse 'em nothing.

FAINALL You are a gallant man, Mirabell; and though you may have cruelty enough not to satisfy a lady's longing, you have too much generosity not to be tender of her honor. Yet you speak with an indifference which seems to be affected and confesses you are conscious of a negligence.

MIRABELL You pursue the argument with a distrust that seems to be unaffected and confesses you are conscious of a concern for which the lady is more indebted to you than is your wife.

FAINALL Fy, fy, friend! if you grow censorious I must leave you. I'll look upon the gamesters in the next room.

MIRABELL Who are they?

FAINALL Petulant and Witwoud. [*To Betty*] Bring me some chocolate. [*Exit.*]

MIRABELL Betty, what says your clock?

BETTY Turned of the last canonical hour,[6] sir. [*Exit.*]

MIRABELL How pertinently the jade answers me! [*Looking on his watch*] Ha! almost one o'clock! Oh, y'are come! [*Enter Footman.*] Well, is the grand affair over? You have been something tedious.

FOOTMAN Sir, there's such coupling at Pancras that they stand behind one another, as 'twere in a country dance. Ours was the last couple to lead up; and no hopes appearing of dispatch; besides, the parson growing hoarse, we were afraid his lungs would have failed before it came to our turn; so we drove round to Duke's place; and there they were riveted in a trice.

MIRABELL So, so, you are sure they are married?

FOOTMAN Married and bedded, sir; I am witness.

MIRABELL Have you the certificate?

FOOTMAN Here it is, sir.

MIRABELL Has the tailor brought Waitwell's clothes home, and the new liveries?

FOOTMAN Yes, sir.

[6] Hours when legal marriages might be performed generally. At St. Pancras Church and St. James Church at Duke's Place, both referred to below, marriages could be performed without banns or special licenses.

[5] A cordial.

MIRABELL   That's well. Do you go home again, d'ye hear, and adjourn the consummation till further orders. Bid Waitwell shake his ears, and Dame Partlet[7] rustle up her feathers and meet me at one o'clock by Rosamond's Pond,[8] that I may see her before she returns to her lady; and as you tender your ears be secret.

[*Exit Footman. Enter Fainall, followed shortly by Betty.*]

FAINALL   Joy of your success, Mirabell; you look pleased.

MIRABELL   Ay; I have been engaged in a matter of some sort of mirth, which is not yet ripe for discovery. I am glad this is not a cabal night. I wonder, Fainall, that you who are married and of consequence should be discreet, will suffer your wife to be of such a party.

FAINALL   Faith, I am not jealous. Besides, most who are engaged are women and relations; and for the men, they are of a kind too contemptible to give scandal.

MIRABELL   I am of another opinion. The greater the coxcomb, always the more the scandal: for a woman who is not a fool can have but one reason for associating with a man who is one.

FAINALL   Are you jealous as often as you see Witwoud entertained by Millamant?

MIRABELL   Of her understanding I am, if not of her person.

FAINALL   You do her wrong; for, to give her her due, she has wit.

MIRABELL   She has beauty enough to make any man think so; and complaisance enough not to contradict him who shall tell her so.

FAINALL   For a passionate lover, methinks you are a man somewhat too discerning in the failings of your mistress.

MIRABELL   And for a discerning man, somewhat too passionate a lover; for I like her with all her faults; nay, like her for her faults. Her follies are so natural, or so artful, that they become her; and those affectations which in another woman would be odious serve but to make her more agreeable. I'll tell thee, Fainall, she once used me with that insolence, that in revenge I took her to pieces; sifted her, and

7 A hen, wife of Chanticleer in the story of the cock and the fox.

8 In St. James's Park.

separated her failings; I studied 'em, and got 'em by rote. The catalogue was so large that I was not without hopes one day or other to hate her heartily: to which end I so used myself to think of 'em, that at length, contrary to my design and expectation, they gave me every hour less and less disturbance; till in a few days it became habitual to me to remember 'em without being displeased. They are now grown as familiar to me as my own frailties; and in all probability, in a little time longer I shall like 'em as well.

FAINALL   Marry her, marry her! be half as well acquainted with her charms as you are with her defects, and my life on't, you are your own man again.

MIRABELL   Say you so?

FAINALL   Ay, ay, I have experience: I have a wife, and so forth.

[*Enter Messenger.*]

MESSENGER   Is one Squire Witwoud here?

BETTY   Yes, what's your business?

MESSENGER   I have a letter for him from his brother Sir Wilfull, which I am charged to deliver into his own hands.

BETTY   He's in the next room, friend—that way.

[*Exit Messenger.*]

MIRABELL   What, is the chief of that noble family in town—Sir Wilfull Witwoud?

FAINALL   He is expected today. Do you know him?

MIRABELL   I have seen him. He promises to be an extraordinary person. I think you have the honor to be related to him.

FAINALL   Yes; he is half brother to this Witwoud by a former wife, who was sister to my Lady Wishfort, my wife's mother. If you marry Millamant, you must call cousins too.

MIRABELL   I had rather be his relation than his acquaintance.

FAINALL   He comes to town in order to equip himself for travel.

MIRABELL   For travel! why, the man that I mean is above forty.

FAINALL   No matter for that; 'tis for the honor of England, that all Europe should know we have blockheads of all ages.

MIRABELL   I wonder there is not an act of Parliament to save the credit of the nation, and pro-

WILLIAM CONGREVE

hibit the exportation of fools.

FAINALL By no means; 'tis better as 'tis. 'Tis better to trade with a little loss than to be quite eaten up with being overstocked.

MIRABELL Pray, are the follies of this knight-errant and those of the squire his brother anything related?

FAINALL Not at all; Witwoud grows by the knight, like a medlar[9] grafted on a crab. One will melt in your mouth, and t'other set your teeth on edge; one is all pulp, and the other all core.

MIRABELL So one will be rotten before he be ripe, and the other will be rotten without ever being ripe at all.

FAINALL Sir Wilfull is an odd mixture of bashfulness and obstinacy. But when he's drunk he's as loving as the monster in *The Tempest*,[10] and much after the same manner. To give t'other his due, he has something of good-nature, and does not always want wit.

MIRABELL Not always: but as often as his memory fails him, and his commonplace[11] of comparisons. He is a fool with a good memory and some few scraps of other folks' wit. He is one whose conversation can never be approved; yet it is now and then to be endured. He has indeed one good quality, he is not exceptious; for he so passionately affects the reputation of understanding raillery that he will construe an affront into a jest; and call downright rudeness and ill language, satire, and fire.

FAINALL If you have a mind to finish his picture, you have an opportunity to do it at full length. Behold the original!

[*Enter Witwoud.*]

WITWOUD Afford me your compassion, my dears! pity me, Fainall! Mirabell, pity me!

MIRABELL I do from my soul.

FAINALL Why, what's the matter?

WITWOUD No letters for me, Betty?

BETTY Did not a messenger bring you one but now, sir?

WITWOUD Ay, but no other?

BETTY No, sir.

WITWOUD That's hard, that's very hard.—A messenger! a mule, a beast of burden! he has brought me a letter from the fool my brother, as heavy as a panegyric in a funeral sermon, or a copy of commendatory verses from one poet to another: and what's worse, 'tis as sure a forerunner of the author as an epistle dedicatory.

MIRABELL A fool, and your brother, Witwoud!

WITWOUD Ay, ay, my half-brother. My half-brother he is, no nearer upon honor.

MIRABELL Then 'tis possible he may be but half a fool.

WITWOUD Good, good, Mirabell, *le drôle!*[12] good, good; hang him, don't let's talk of him.—Fainall, how does your lady? Gad, I say anything in the world to get this fellow out of my head. I beg pardon that I should ask a man of pleasure and the town a question at once so foreign and domestic. But I talk like an old maid at a marriage; I don't know what I say. But she's the best woman in the world.

FAINALL 'Tis well you don't know what you say, or else your commendation would go near to make me either vain or jealous.

WITWOUD No man in town lives well with a wife but Fainall.—Your judgment, Mirabell.

MIRABELL You had better step and ask his wife, if you would be credibly informed.

WITWOUD Mirabell?

MIRABELL Ay.

WITWOUD My dear, I ask ten thousand pardons —gad, I have forgot what I was going to say to you!

MIRABELL I thank you heartily, heartily.

WITWOUD No, but prithee excuse me—my memory is such a memory.

MIRABELL Have a care of such apologies, Witwoud; for I never knew a fool but he affected to complain, either of the spleen or his memory.

FAINALL What have you done with Petulant?

WITWOUD He's reckoning his money—my money it was. I have no luck today.

FAINALL You may allow him to win of you at

---

[9] A soft fruit resembling a crab apple. It becomes edible only after it has begun to decay.

[10] Caliban, in Act 2, Scene 2.

[11] Memorable quotations were recorded in a commonplace book, often for later appropriation and use.

[12] The witty one.

play, for you are sure to be too hard for him at repartee. Since you monopolise the wit that is between you, the fortune must be his of course.

MIRABELL I don't find that Petulant confesses the superiority of wit to be your talent, Witwoud.

WITWOUD Come, come, you are malicious now, and would breed debates. Petulant's my friend, and a very honest fellow, and a very pretty fellow, and has a smattering—faith and troth, a pretty deal of an odd sort of a small wit. Nay, I'll do him justice. I'm his friend, I won't wrong him neither. And if he had any judgment in the world, he would not be altogether contemptible. Come, come, don't detract from the merits of my friend.

FAINALL You don't take your friend to be overnicely bred?

WITWOUD No, no, hang him, the rogue has no manners at all, that I must own—no more breeding than a bum-baily,[13] that I grant you—'tis pity, faith; the fellow has fire and life.

MIRABELL What, courage?

WITWOUD Hum, faith I don't know as to that, I can't say as to that—yes, faith, in a controversy, he'll contradict anybody.

MIRABELL Though 'twere a man whom he feared, or a woman whom he loved?

WITWOUD Well, well, he does not always think before he speaks—we have all our failings. You are too hard upon him, you are, faith. Let me excuse him—I can defend most of his faults, except one or two. One he has, that's the truth on't; if he were my brother, I could not acquit him—that, indeed, I could wish were otherwise.

MIRABELL Ay, marry, what's that, Witwoud?

WITWOUD Oh, pardon me!—expose the infirmities of my friend!—No, my dear, excuse me there.

FAINALL What! I warrant he's unsincere, or 'tis some such trifle.

WITWOUD No, no; what if he be? 'Tis no matter for that, his wit will excuse that. A wit should no more be sincere than a woman constant; one argues a decay of parts,[14] as t'other of beauty.

MIRABELL Maybe you think him too positive?

13 A low order of bailiff.
14 Talents.

WITWOUD No, no, his being positive is an incentive to argument, and keeps up conversation.

FAINALL Too illiterate?

WITWOUD That! that's his happiness—his want of learning gives him the more opportunities to show his natural parts.

MIRABELL He wants words?

WITWOUD Ay: but I like him for that now; for his want of words gives me the pleasure very often to explain his meaning.

FAINALL He's impudent?

WITWOUD No, that's not it.

MIRABELL Vain?

WITWOUD No.

MIRABELL What! he speaks unseasonable truths sometimes, because he has not wit enough to invent an evasion?

WITWOUD Truths! ha! ha! ha! no, no; since you will have it,—I mean, he never speaks truth at all—that's all. He will lie like a chambermaid, or a woman of quality's porter. Now that is a fault.

[*Enter Coachman.*]

COACHMAN Is Master Petulant here, mistress?

BETTY Yes.

COACHMAN Three gentlewomen in a coach would speak with him.

FAINALL Oh brave Petulant! three!

BETTY I'll tell him.

COACHMAN You must bring two dishes of chocolate and a glass of cinnamon-water.

[*Exeunt Betty and Coachman.*]

WITWOUD That should be for two fasting strumpets and a bawd troubled with wind. Now you may know what the three are.

MIRABELL You are very free with your friend's acquaintance.

WITWOUD Ay, ay, friendship without freedom is as dull as love without enjoyment or wine without toasting. But to tell you a secret, these are trulls whom he allows coach-hire, and something more, by the week, to call on him once a day at public places.

MIRABELL How!

WITWOUD You shall see he won't go to 'em, because there's no more company here to take notice of him. Why this is nothing to what he used to do—before he found out this way, I have known him call for himself.

FAINALL Call for himself! what dost thou mean?

WITWOUD Mean! why he would slip out of this chocolate house, just when you had been talking to him—as soon as your back was turned —whip he was gone!—then trip to his lodging, clap on a hood and scarf and a mask, slap into a hackney-coach, and drive hither to the door again in a trice, where he would send in for himself; that I mean, call for himself, wait for himself; nay, and what's more, not finding himself, sometimes leave a letter for himself.

MIRABELL I confess this is something extraordinary.—I believe he waits for himself now, he is so long a-coming: Oh! I ask his pardon.

[*Enter Petulant and Betty.*]

BETTY Sir, the coach stays.

PETULANT Well, well—I come. 'Sbud,[15] a man had as good be a professed midwife as a professed whoremaster, at this rate! to be knocked up and raised at all hours, and in all places. Pox on 'em, I won't come!—D'ye hear, tell 'em I won't come—let 'em snivel and cry their hearts out.

FAINALL You are very cruel, Petulant.

PETULANT All's one, let it pass—I have a humor to be cruel.

MIRABELL I hope they are not persons of condition that you use at this rate.

PETULANT Condition! condition's a dried fig, if I am not in humor!—By this hand, if they were your—a—a—your what-d'ye-call-'ems themselves, they must wait or rub off,[16] if I want appetite.

MIRABELL What-d'ye-call-'ems! what are they, Witwoud?

WITWOUD Empresses, my dear—by your what-d'ye-call-'ems he means sultana queens.

PETULANT Ay, Roxolanas.[17]

MIRABELL Cry you mercy!

FAINALL Witwoud says they are—

PETULANT What does he say th'are?

WITWOUD I? fine ladies, I say.

PETULANT Pass on, Witwoud.—Hark'ee, by this light his relations—two co-heiresses his cousins,

15 A contraction of " 'sbodikins," meaning "God's dear body."

16 Go away.

17 Roxolana was the wife of Solyman, the Turkish sultan in Davenant's *The Siege of Rhodes.*

and an old aunt who loves caterwauling better than a conventicle.

WITWOUD Ha! ha! ha! I had a mind to see how the rogue would come off.—Ha! ha! ha! gad, I can't be angry with him if he had said they were my mother and my sisters.

MIRABELL No!

WITWOUD No; the rogue's wit and readiness of invention charm me. Dear Petulant!

BETTY They are gone, sir, in great anger.

PETULANT Enough, let 'em trundle. Anger helps complexion, saves paint.

FAINALL This continence is all dissembled; this is in order to have something to brag of the next time he makes court to Millamant and swear he has abandoned the whole sex for her sake.

MIRABELL Have you not left off your impudent pretensions there yet? I shall cut your throat some time or other, Petulant, about that business.

PETULANT Ay, ay, let that pass—there are other throats to be cut.

MIRABELL Meaning mine, sir?

PETULANT Not I—I mean nobody—I know nothing. But there are uncles and nephews in the world—and they may be rivals—what then! All's one for that.

MIRABELL How! hark'ee, Petulant, come hither —explain, or I shall call your interpreter.

PETULANT Explain! I know nothing. Why, you have an uncle, have you not, lately come to town, and lodges by my Lady Wishfort's?

MIRABELL True.

PETULANT Why, that's enough—you and he are not friends; and if he should marry and have a child you may be disinherited, ha?

MIRABELL Where hast thou stumbled upon all this truth?

PETULANT All's one for that; why, then, say I know something.

MIRABELL Come, thou art an honest fellow, Petulant, and shalt make love to my mistress; thou sha't, faith. What hast thou heard of my uncle?

PETULANT I? Nothing, I. If throats are to be cut, let swords clash! snug's the word, I shrug and am silent.

MIRABELL Oh, raillery, raillery! Come, I know

The Way of the World

thou art in the woman's secrets. What, you're a cabalist; I know you stayed at Millamant's last night after I went. Was there any mention made of my uncle or me? Tell me. If thou hadst but good-nature equal to thy wit, Petulant, Tony Witwoud, who is now thy competitor in fame, would show as dim by thee as a dead whiting's eye by a pearl of orient; he would no more be seen by thee, than Mercury is by the sun. Come, I'm sure thou wo't tell me.

PETULANT If I do, will you grant me common sense then for the future?

MIRABELL Faith, I'll do what I can for thee, and I'll pray that Heaven may grant it thee in the meantime.

PETULANT Well, hark'ee.

[*Mirabell and Petulant talk apart.*]

FAINALL Petulant and you both will find Mirabell as warm a rival as a lover.

WITWOUD Pshaw! pshaw! that she laughs at Petulant is plain. And for my part, but that it is almost a fashion to admire her, I should—hark'ee—to tell you a secret, but let it go no further—between friends, I shall never break my heart for her.

FAINALL How!

WITWOUD She's handsome; but she's a sort of an uncertain woman.

FAINALL I thought you had died for her.

WITWOUD Umh—no—

FAINALL She has wit.

WITWOUD 'Tis what she will hardly allow anybody else. Now, demme, I should hate that, if she were as handsome as Cleopatra. Mirabell is not so sure of her as he thinks for.

FAINALL Why do you think so?

WITWOUD We stayed pretty late there last night, and heard something of an uncle to Mirabell, who is lately come to town—and is between him and the best part of his estate. Mirabell and he are at some distance, as my Lady Wishfort has been told; and you know she hates Mirabell worse than a Quaker hates a parrot, or than a fishmonger hates a hard frost. Whether this uncle has seen Mrs. Millamant or not, I cannot say, but there were items of such a treaty being in embryo; and if it should come to life, poor Mirabell would be in some sort unfortunately fobbed,[18] i'faith.

FAINALL 'Tis impossible Millamant should hearken to it.

WITWOUD Faith, my dear, I can't tell; she's a woman, and a kind of humorist.[19]

MIRABELL [*talking apart with Petulant*] And this is the sum of what you could collect last night?

PETULANT The quintessence. Maybe Witwoud knows more, he stayed longer. Besides, they never mind him; they say anything before him.

MIRABELL I thought you had been the greatest favorite.

PETULANT Ay, *tête-à-tête,* but not in public, because I make remarks.

MIRABELL You do?

PETULANT Ay, ay; pox, I'm malicious, man! Now he's soft you know; they are not in awe of him —the fellow's well-bred; he's what you call a what-d'ye-call-'em, a fine gentleman—but he's silly withal.

MIRABELL I thank you. I know as much as my curiosity requires. Fainall, are you for the Mall?[20]

FAINALL Ay, I'll take a turn before dinner.

WITWOUD Ay, we'll all walk in the Park; the ladies talked of being there.

MIRABELL I thought you were obliged to watch for your brother Sir Wilfull's arrival.

WITWOUD No, no; he comes to his aunt's, my Lady Wishfort. Pox on him! I shall be troubled with him too; what shall I do with the fool?

PETULANT Beg him for his estate, that I may beg you afterwards: and so have but one trouble with you both.

WITWOUD Oh rare Petulant! Thou art as quick as fire in a frosty morning. Thou shalt to the Mall with us, and we'll be very severe.

PETULANT Enough! I'm in a humor to be severe.

MIRABELL Are you? Pray then walk by yourselves: let not us be accessory to your putting the ladies out of countenance with your senseless ribaldry, which you roar out aloud as often as they pass by you; and when you have made a handsome woman blush, then you think you have been severe.

PETULANT What, what! then let 'em either show

---

[18] Cheated.
[19] Given to humours; a whimsical person.
[20] In St. James's Park.

WILLIAM CONGREVE

their innocence by not understanding what they hear, or else show their discretion by not hearing what they would not be thought to understand.

MIRABELL But hast thou then sense enough to know that thou oughtest to be most ashamed thyself, when thou hast put another out of countenance?

PETULANT Not I, by this hand!—I always take

blushing either for a sign of guilt or ill breeding.

MIRABELL I confess you ought to think so. You are in the right, that you may plead the error of your judgment in defence of your practice.
Where modesty's ill manners, 'tis but fit
That impudence and malice pass for wit.
[*Exeunt.*]

Act Two

SCENE ONE

St. James's Park. Mrs. Fainall and Mrs. Marwood.

MRS. FAINALL Ay, ay, dear Marwood, if we will be happy, we must find the means in ourselves and among ourselves. Men are ever in extremes: either doting or averse. While they are lovers, if they have fire and sense, their jealousies are insupportable; and when they cease to love (we ought to think at least) they loath; they look upon us with horror and distaste; they meet us like the ghosts of what we were, and as such, fly from us.

MRS. MARWOOD True, 'tis an unhappy circumstance of life, that love should ever die before us; and that the man so often should outlive the lover. But say what you will, 'tis better to be left than never to have been loved. To pass our youth in dull indifference, to refuse the sweets of life because they once must leave us, is as preposterous as to wish to have been born old because we one day must be old. For my part, my youth may wear and waste, but it shall never rust in my possession.

MRS. FAINALL Then it seems you dissemble an aversion to mankind only in compliance to my mother's humor?

MRS. MARWOOD Certainly. To be free; I have no taste of those insipid dry discourses with which our sex of force must entertain themselves apart from men. We may affect endearments to each other, profess eternal friendships, and seem to dote like lovers; but 'tis not in our natures long to persevere. Love will resume his

empire in our breasts; and every heart, or soon or late, receive and re-admit him as its lawful tyrant.

MRS. FAINALL Bless me, how have I been deceived! why you profess a libertine.

MRS. MARWOOD You see my friendship by my freedom. Come, be as sincere, acknowledge that your sentiments agree with mine.

MRS. FAINALL Never!

MRS. MARWOOD You hate mankind?

MRS. FAINALL Heartily, inveterately.

MRS. MARWOOD Your husband?

MRS. FAINALL Most transcendently; ay, though I say it, meritoriously.

MRS. MARWOOD Give me your hand upon it.

MRS. FAINALL There.

MRS. MARWOOD I join with you; what I have said has been to try you.

MRS. FAINALL It is possible? dost thou hate those vipers, men?

MRS. MARWOOD I have done hating 'em, and am now come to despise 'em; the next thing I have to do is eternally to forget 'em.

MRS. FAINALL There spoke the spirit of an Amazon, a Penthesilea![21]

MRS. MARWOOD And yet I am thinking sometimes to carry my aversion further.

MRS. FAINALL How?

MRS. MARWOOD Faith, by marrying; if I could but find one that loved me very well, and would be thoroughly sensible of ill usage, I think I should do myself the violence of undergoing the ceremony.

[21] Queen of the Amazons who fought with Achilles.

The Way of the World

337

MRS. FAINALL You would not make him a cuckold?[22]

MRS. MARWOOD No; but I'd make him believe I did and that's as bad.

MRS. FAINALL Why had not you as good do it?

MRS. MARWOOD Oh! if he should ever discover it, he would then know the worst and be out of his pain; but I would have him ever to continue upon the rack of fear and jealousy.

MRS. FAINALL Ingenious mischief! would thou wert married to Mirabell.

MRS. MARWOOD Would I were!

MRS. FAINALL You change color.

MRS. MARWOOD Because I hate him.

MRS. FAINALL So do I; but I can hear him named. But what reason have you to hate him in particular?

MRS. MARWOOD I never loved him; he is, and always was, insufferably proud.

MRS. FAINALL By the reason you give for your aversion, one would think it dissembled; for you have laid a fault to his charge of which his enemies must acquit him.

MRS. MARWOOD Oh! then it seems you are one of his favorable enemies! Methinks you look a little pale—and now you flush again.

MRS. FAINALL Do I? I think I am a little sick o' the sudden.

MRS. MARWOOD What ails you?

MRS. FAINALL My husband. Don't you see him? He turned short upon me unawares, and has almost overcome me.

[*Enter Fainall and Mirabell.*]

MRS. MARWOOD Ha! ha! ha! he comes opportunely for you.

MRS. FAINALL For you, for he has brought Mirabell with him.

FAINALL My dear!

MRS. FAINALL My soul!

FAINALL You don't look well today, child.

MRS. FAINALL D'ye think so?

MIRABELL He is the only man that does, madam.

MRS. FAINALL The only man that would tell me so at least; and the only man from whom I could hear it without mortification.

FAINALL Oh my dear, I am satisfied of your tenderness; I know you cannot resent anything

22 A husband whose wife has been unfaithful to him. His symbol was horns, referred to later.

from me, especially what is an effect of my concern.

MRS. FAINALL Mr. Mirabell, my mother interrupted you in a pleasant relation last night; I would fain hear it out.

MIRABELL The persons concerned in that affair have yet a tolerable reputation. I am afraid Mr. Fainall will be censorious.

MRS. FAINALL He has a humor more prevailing than his curiosity, and will willingly dispense with the hearing of one scandalous story, to avoid giving an occasion to make another by being seen to walk with his wife. This way, Mr. Mirabell, and I dare promise you will oblige us both.

[*Exeunt Mrs. Fainall and Mirabell.*]

FAINALL Excellent creature! Well, sure if I should live to be rid of my wife, I should be a miserable man.

MRS. MARWOOD Ay?

FAINALL For having only that one hope, the accomplishment of it, of consequence, must put an end to all my hopes; and what a wretch is he who must survive his hopes! Nothing remains when that day comes, but to sit down and weep like Alexander when he wanted other worlds to conquer.

MRS. MARWOOD Will you not follow 'em?

FAINALL Faith, I think not.

MRS. MARWOOD Pray let us; I have a reason.

FAINALL You are not jealous?

MRS. MARWOOD Of whom?

FAINALL Of Mirabell.

MRS. MARWOOD If I am, is it consistent with my love to you that I am tender of your honor?

FAINALL You would intimate, then, as if there were a fellow-feeling between my wife and him.

MRS. MARWOOD I think she does not hate him to that degree she would be thought.

FAINALL But he, I fear, is too insensible.

MRS. MARWOOD It may be you are deceived.

FAINALL It may be so. I do now begin to apprehend it.

MRS. MARWOOD What?

FAINALL That I have been deceived, madam, and you are false.

MRS. MARWOOD That I am false! what mean you?

WILLIAM CONGREVE

FAINALL To let you know I see through all your little arts.—Come, you both love him; and both have equally dissembled your aversion. Your mutual jealousies of one another had made you clash till you have both struck fire. I have seen the warm confession reddening on your cheeks and sparkling from your eyes.

MRS. MARWOOD You do me wrong.

FAINALL I do not. 'Twas for my ease to oversee and wilfully neglect the gross advances made him by my wife; that by permitting her to be engaged, I might continue unsuspected in my pleasures and take you oftener to my arms in full security. But could you think, because the nodding husband would not wake, that e'er the watchful lover slept?

MRS. MARWOOD And wherewithal can you reproach me?

FAINALL With infidelity, with loving another, with love of Mirabell.

MRS. MARWOOD 'Tis false! I challenge you to show an instance that can confirm your groundless accusation. I hate him.

FAINALL And wherefore do you hate him? He is insensible and your resentment follows his neglect. An instance! the injuries you have done him are a proof: your interposing in his love. What cause had you to make discoveries of his pretended passion? to undeceive the credulous aunt, and be the officious obstacle of his match with Millamant?

MRS. MARWOOD My obligations to my lady urged me. I had professed a friendship to her and could not see her easy nature so abused by that dissembler.

FAINALL What, was it conscience then? Professed a friendship! O the pious friendships of the female sex!

MRS. MARWOOD More tender, more sincere, and more enduring, than all the vain and empty vows of men, whether professing love to us, or mutual faith to one another.

FAINALL Ha! ha! ha! you are my wife's friend too.

MRS. MARWOOD Shame and ingratitude! do you reproach me? you, you upbraid me? Have I been false to her, through strict fidelity to you, and sacrificed my friendship to keep my love inviolate? And have you the baseness to charge me with the guilt, unmindful of the merit? To you it should be meritorious, that I have been vicious: and do you reflect that guilt upon me which should lie buried in your bosom?

FAINALL You misinterpret my reproof. I meant but to remind you of the slight account you once could make of strictest ties when set in competition with your love to me.

MRS. MARWOOD 'Tis false; you urged it with deliberate malice! 'twas spoken in scorn, and I never will forgive it.

FAINALL Your guilt, not your resentment, begets your rage. If yet you loved, you could forgive a jealousy; but you are stung to find you are discovered.

MRS. MARWOOD It shall be all discovered. You too shall be discovered; be sure you shall. I can but be exposed.—If I do it myself I shall prevent your baseness.

FAINALL Why, what will you do?

MRS. MARWOOD Disclose it to your wife; own what has passed between us.

FAINALL Frenzy!

MRS. MARWOOD By all my wrongs I'll do't!—I'll publish to the world the injuries you have done me, both in my fame and fortune! With both I trusted you, you bankrupt in honor, as indigent of wealth.

FAINALL Your fame I have preserved. Your fortune has been bestowed as the prodigality of your love would have it, in pleasures which we both have shared. Yet, had not you been false, I had ere this repaid it—'tis true. Had you permitted Mirabell with Millamant to have stolen their marriage, my lady had been incensed beyond all means of reconcilement: Millamant had forfeited the moiety of her fortune, which then would have descended to my wife—and wherefore did I marry, but to make lawful prize of a rich widow's wealth, and squander it on love and you?

MRS. MARWOOD Deceit and frivolous pretence!

FAINALL Death, am I not married? What's pretence? Am I not imprisoned, fettered? Have I not a wife? nay a wife that was a widow, a young widow, a handsome widow; and would be again a widow, but that I have a heart of proof, and something of a constitution to bustle through the ways of wedlock and this world!

Will you yet be reconciled to truth and me?

MRS. MARWOOD Impossible. Truth and you are inconsistent; I hate you and shall for ever.

FAINALL For loving you?

MRS. MARWOOD I loathe the name of love after such usage; and next to the guilt with which you would asperse me, I scorn you most. Farewell!

FAINALL Nay, we must not part thus.

MRS. MARWOOD Let me go.

FAINALL Come, I'm sorry.

MRS. MARWOOD I care not—let me go—break my hands, do—I'd leave 'em to get loose.

FAINALL I would not hurt you for the world. Have I no other hold to keep you here?

MRS. MARWOOD Well, I have deserved it all.

FAINALL You know I love you.

MRS. MARWOOD Poor dissembling!—Oh, that—well, it is not yet—

FAINALL What? what is it not? what is it not yet? It is not yet too late—

MRS. MARWOOD No, it is not yet too late—I have that comfort.

FAINALL It is, to love another.

MRS. MARWOOD But not to loathe, detest, abhor mankind, myself, and the whole treacherous world.

FAINALL Nay, this is extravagance.—Come I ask your pardon—no tears—I was to blame, I could not love you and be easy in my doubts. Pray forbear—I believe you; I'm convinced I've done you wrong; and any way, every way will make amends. I'll hate my wife yet more, damn her! I'll part with her, rob her of all she's worth, and we'll retire somewhere, anywhere, to another world. I'll marry thee—be pacified.— 'Sdeath, they come. Hide your face, your tears —you have a mask, wear it a moment. This way, this way—be persuaded.

[*Exeunt. Enter Mirabell and Mrs. Fainall.*]

MRS. FAINALL They are here yet.

MIRABELL They are turning into the other walk.

MRS. FAINALL While I only hated my husband, I could bear to see him; but since I have despised him, he's too offensive.

MIRABELL Oh, you should hate with prudence.

MRS. FAINALL Yes, for I have loved with indiscretion.

MIRABELL You should have just so much disgust for your husband as may be sufficient to make you relish your lover.

MRS. FAINALL You have been the cause that I have loved without bounds, and would you set limits to that aversion of which you have been the occasion? Why did you make me marry this man?

MIRABELL Why do we daily commit disagreeable and dangerous actions? To save that idol, reputation. If the familiarities of our loves had produced that consequence of which you were apprehensive, where could you have fixed a father's name with credit, but on a husband? I knew Fainall to be a man lavish of his morals, an interested and professing friend, a false and designing lover; yet one on whose wit and outward fair behavior have gained a reputation with the town enough to make that woman stand excused who has suffered herself to be won by his addresses. A better man ought not to have been sacrificed to the occasion; a worse had not answered to the purpose. When you are weary of him you know your remedy.

MRS. FAINALL I ought to stand in some degree of credit with you, Mirabell.

MIRABELL In justice to you, I have made you privy to my whole design, and put it in your power to ruin or advance my fortune.

MRS. FAINALL Whom have you instructed to represent your pretended uncle?

MIRABELL Waitwell, my servant.

MRS. FAINALL He is an humble servant[23] to Foible, my mother's woman, and may win her to your interest.

MIRABELL Care is taken for that—she is won and worn by this time. They were married this morning.

MRS. FAINALL Who?

MIRABELL Waitwell and Foible. I would not tempt my servant to betray me by trusting him too far. If your mother, in hopes to ruin me, should consent to marry my pretended uncle, he might, like Mosca in *The Fox*,[24] stand upon terms; so I made him sure beforehand.

MRS. FAINALL So if my poor mother is caught in

[23] Suitor.

[24] In Ben Jonson's play, the clever servant gets the advantage over his master, Volpone.

a contract, you will discover the imposture betimes; and release her by producing a certificate of her gallant's former marriage?

MIRABELL Yes, upon condition that she consent to my marriage with her niece, and surrender the moiety of her fortune in her possession.

MRS. FAINALL She talked last night of endeavoring at a match between Millamant and your uncle.

MIRABELL That was by Foible's direction and my instruction, that she might seem to carry it more privately.

MRS. FAINALL Well, I have an opinion of your success; for I believe my lady will do anything to get a husband; and when she has this, which you have provided for her, I suppose she will submit to anything to get rid of him.

MIRABELL Yes, I think the good lady would marry anything that resembled a man, though 'twere no more than what a butler could pinch out of a napkin.

MRS. FAINALL Female frailty! we must all come to it, if we live to be old, and feel the craving of a false appetite when the true is decayed.

MIRABELL An old woman's appetite is depraved like that of a girl—'tis the green sickness of a second childhood; and, like the faint offer of a latter spring, serves but to usher in the fall, and withers in an affected bloom.

MRS. FAINALL Here's your mistress.

[*Enter Mrs. Millamant, Witwoud, and Mincing.*]

MIRABELL Here she comes, i'faith, full sail, with her fan spread and her streamers out, and a shoal of fools for tenders. Ha, no, I cry her mercy!

MRS. FAINALL I see but one poor empty sculler, and he tows her woman after him.

MIRABELL [*to Mrs. Millamant*] You seem to be unattended, madam—you used to have the *beau monde* throng after you; and a flock of gay fine perukes hovering round you.

WITWOUD Like moths about a candle.—I had like to have lost my comparison for want of breath.

MRS. MILLAMANT Oh, I have denied myself airs today. I have walked as fast through the crowd—

WITWOUD As a favorite just disgraced; and with as few followers.

MRS. MILLAMANT Dear Mr. Witwoud, truce with your similitudes; for I'm as sick of 'em—

WITWOUD As a physician of a good air.—I cannot help it, madam, though 'tis against myself.

MRS. MILLAMANT Yet, again! Mincing, stand between me and his wit.

WITWOUD Do, Mrs. Mincing, like a screen before a great fire.—I confess I do blaze today, I am too bright.

MRS. FAINALL But, dear Millamant, why were you so long?

MRS. MILLAMANT Long! Lord, have I not made violent haste? I have asked every living thing I met for you; I have inquired after you, as after a new fashion.

WITWOUD Madam, truce with your similitudes.—No, you met her husband, and did not ask him for her.

MRS. MILLAMANT By your leave, Witwoud, that were like inquiring after an old fashion, to ask a husband for his wife.

WITWOUD Hum, a hit! a hit! a palpable hit! I confess it.

MRS. FAINALL You were dressed before I came abroad.

MRS. MILLAMANT Ay, that's true.—Oh, but then I had— Mincing, what had I? Why was I so long?

MINCING O mem, your la'ship stayed to peruse a packet of letters.

MRS. MILLAMANT Oh, ay, letters—I had letters—I am persecuted with letters—I hate letters—Nobody knows how to write letters, and yet one has 'em, one does not know why. They serve one to pin up one's hair.

WITWOUD Is that the way? Pray, madam, do you pin up your hair with all your letters? I find I must keep copies.

MRS. MILLAMANT Only with those in verse, Mr. Witwoud, I never pin up my hair with prose. I think I tried once, Mincing.

MINCING O mem, I shall never forget it.

MRS. MILLAMANT Ay, poor Mincing tift[25] and tift all the morning.

MINCING Till I had the cramp in my fingers, I'll vow, mem; and all to no purpose. But when your la'ship pins it up with poetry it sits so

[25] Arranged.

pleasant the next day as anything, and is so pure and so crips.

WITWOUD Indeed, so *crips?*

MINCING You're such a critic, Mr. Witwoud.

MRS. MILLAMANT Mirabell, did you take exceptions last night? Oh, ay, and went away.—Now I think on't I'm angry—no, now I think on't I'm pleased—for I believe I gave you some pain.

MIRABELL Does that please you?

MRS. MILLAMANT Infinitely; I love to give pain.

MIRABELL You would affect a cruelty which is not your nature; your true vanity is in the power of pleasing.

MRS. MILLAMANT Oh, I ask you pardon for that —one's cruelty is one's power; and when one parts with one's cruelty, one parts with one's power; and when one has parted with that, I fancy one's old and ugly.

MIRABELL Ay, ay, suffer your cruelty to ruin the object of your power, to destroy your lover— and then how vain, how lost a thing you'll be! Nay, 'tis true: you are no longer handsome when you've lost your lover; your beauty dies upon the instant; for beauty is the lover's gift. 'Tis he bestows your charms—your glass is all a cheat. The ugly and the old, whom the looking-glass mortifies, yet after commendation can be flattered by it, and discover beauties in it; for that reflects our praises, rather than your face.

MRS. MILLAMANT O the vanity of these men!— Fainall, d'ye hear him? If they did not commend us, we were not handsome! Now you must know they could not commend one, if one was not handsome. Beauty the lover's gift!—Lord, what is a lover, that it can give? Why, one makes lovers as fast as one pleases, and they live as long as one pleases, and they die as soon as one pleases; and then, if one pleases, one makes more.

WITWOUD Very pretty. Why, you make no more of making of lovers, madam, than of making so many card-matches.

MRS. MILLAMANT One no more owes one's beauty to a lover, than one's wit to an echo. They can but reflect what we look and say: vain empty things if we are silent or unseen, and want a being.

MIRABELL Yet to those two vain empty things you owe the two greatest pleasures of your life.

MRS. MILLAMANT How so?

MIRABELL To your lover you owe the pleasure of hearing yourselves praised; and to an echo the pleasure of hearing yourselves talk.

WITWOUD But I know a lady that loves talking so incessantly, she won't give an echo fair play; she has that everlasting rotation of tongue, that an echo must wait till she dies, before it can catch her last words.

MRS. MILLAMANT O fiction!—Fainall, let us leave these men.

MIRABELL [*aside to Mrs. Fainall*] Draw off Witwoud.

MRS. FAINALL Immediately.—I have a word or two for Mr. Witwoud.

[*Exeunt Mrs. Fainall and Witwoud.*]

MIRABELL I would beg a little private audience too.—You had the tyranny to deny me last night; though you knew I came to impart a secret to you that concerned my love.

MRS. MILLAMANT You saw I was engaged.

MIRABELL Unkind! You had the leisure to entertain a herd of fools; things who visit you from their excessive idleness; bestowing on your easiness that time which is the incumbrance of their lives. How can you find delight in such society? It is impossible they should admire you, they are not capable: or if they were, it should be to you as a mortification; for sure to please a fool is some degree of folly.

MRS. MILLAMANT I please myself—besides, sometimes to converse with fools is for my health.

MIRABELL Your health! is there a worse disease than the conversation of fools?

MRS. MILLAMANT Yes, the vapors; fools are physic for it, next to assafœtida.

MIRABELL You are not in a course of fools?

MRS. MILLAMANT Mirabell, if you persist in this offensive freedom, you'll displease me.—I think I must resolve, after all, not to have you: we shan't agree.

MIRABELL Not in our physic, it may be.

MRS. MILLAMANT And yet our distemper, in all likelihood, will be the same; for we shall be sick of one another. I shan't endure to be reprimanded nor instructed; 'tis so dull to act always by advice, and so tedious to be told of one's faults—I can't bear it. Well, I won't have you,

Mirabell—I'm resolved—I think—you may go. —Ha! ha! ha! what would you give, that you could help loving me?

MIRABELL I would give something that you did not know I could not help it.

MRS. MILLAMANT Come, don't look grave then. Well, what do you say to me?

MIRABELL I say that a man may as soon make a friend by his wit, or a fortune by his honesty, as win a woman by plain-dealing and sincerity.

MRS. MILLAMANT Sententious Mirabell! Prithee, don't look with that violent and inflexible wise face, like Solomon at the dividing of the child in an old tapestry hanging.

MIRABELL You are merry, madam, but I would persuade you for a moment to be serious.

MRS. MILLAMANT What, with that face? no, if you keep your countenance, 'tis impossible I should hold mine. Well, after all, there is something very moving in a love-sick face. Ha! ha! ha!—well, I won't laugh, don't be peevish— Heigho! now I'll be melancholy, as melancholy as a watch-light.[26] Well, Mirabell, if ever you will win me, woo me now.—Nay, if you are so tedious, fare you well—I see they are walking away.

MIRABELL Can you not find in the variety of your disposition one moment—

MRS. MILLAMANT To hear you tell me Foible's married, and your plot like to speed? No.

MIRABELL But how came you to know it?

MRS. MILLAMANT Without the help of the devil, you can't imagine—unless she should tell me herself. Which of the two it may have been I will leave you to consider; and when you have done thinking of that, think of me. [*Exit.*]

MIRABELL I have something more.—Gone!— Think of you? to think of a whirlwind, though 'twere in a whirlwind, were a case of more steady contemplation; a very tranquility of mind and mansion. A fellow that lives in a windmill has not a more whimsical dwelling than the heart of a man that is lodged in a woman. There is no point of the compass to which they cannot turn, and by which they are not turned; and by one as well as another. For motion, not method, is their occupation. To know this, and yet con-

tinue to be in love, is to be made wise from the dictates of reason, and yet persevere to play the fool by the force of instinct.—Oh, here come my pair of turtles!—What, billing so sweetly! is not Valentine's day over with you yet? [*Enter Waitwell and Foible.*] Sirrah Waitwell, why sure you think you were married for your own recreation, and not for my conveniency.

WAITWELL Your pardon, sir. With submission, we have indeed been solacing in lawful delights; but still with an eye to business, sir. I have instructed her as well as I could. If she can take your directions as readily as my instructions, sir, your affairs are in a prosperous way.

MIRABELL Give you joy, Mrs. Foible.

FOIBLE O 'las, sir, I'm so ashamed!—I'm afraid my lady has been in a thousand inquietudes for me. But I protest, sir, I made as much haste as I could.

WAITWELL That she did indeed, sir. It was my fault that she did not make more.

MIRABELL That I believe.

FOIBLE But I told my lady as you instructed me, sir, that I had a prospect of seeing Sir Rowland, your uncle; and that I would put her ladyship's picture in my pocket to show him; which I'll be sure to say has made him so enamored of her beauty that he burns with impatience to lie at her ladyship's feet and worship the original.

MIRABELL Excellent Foible! Matrimony has made you eloquent in love.

WAITWELL I think she has profited, sir, I think so.

FOIBLE You have seen Madam Millamant, sir?

MIRABELL Yes.

FOIBLE I told her, sir, because I did not know that you might find an opportunity; she had so much company last night.

MIRABELL Your diligence will merit more—in the meantime— [*Gives money.*]

FOIBLE O dear, sir, your humble servant!

WAITWELL Spouse!

MIRABELL Stand off, sir, not a penny!—Go on and prosper, Foible—the lease shall be made good and the farm stocked, if we succeed.

FOIBLE I don't question your generosity, sir: and you need not doubt of success. If you have no

---

[26] Small candle used as a night light.

more commands, sir, I'll be gone; I'm sure my lady is at her toilet, and can't dress till I come —[*looking out*] Oh, dear, I'm sure that was Mrs. Marwood that went by in a mask! If she has seen me with you I'm sure she'll tell my lady. I'll make haste home and prevent her. Your servant, sir.—B'w'y, Waitwell. [*Exit.*]

WAITWELL Sir Rowland, if you please.—The jade's so pert upon her preferment she forgets herself.

MIRABELL Come, sir, will you endeavor to forget yourself, and transform into Sir Rowland?

WAITWELL Why, sir, it will be impossible I should remember myself.—Married, knighted, and attended all in one day! 'Tis enough to make any man forget himself. The difficulty will be how to recover my acquaintance and familiarity with my former self, and fall from my transformation to a reformation into Waitwell. Nay, I shan't be quite the same Waitwell neither; for now, I remember me, I'm married and can't be my own man again.

Ay there's my grief; that's the sad change of life,
To lose my title, and yet keep my wife.

[*Exeunt.*]

Act Three

SCENE ONE

A room in Lady Wishfort's house. Lady Wishfort at her toilet, Peg waiting.

LADY WISHFORT Merciful! No news of Foible yet?

PEG No, madam.

LADY WISHFORT I have no more patience.—If I have not fretted myself till I am pale again, there's no veracity in me! Fetch me the red—the red, do you hear, sweetheart?—An arrant ash-color, as I am a person! Look you how this wench stirs! Why dost thou not fetch me a little red? didst thou not hear me, Mopus?[27]

PEG The red ratafia does your ladyship mean, or the cherry-brandy?

LADY WISHFORT Ratafia, fool! No, fool. Not the ratafia, fool—grant me patience!—I mean the Spanish paper,[28] idiot—complexion, darling. Paint! paint! paint! dost thou understand that, changeling, dangling thy hands like bobbins before thee? Why dost thou not stir, puppet? thou wooden thing upon wires!

PEG Lord, madam, your ladyship is so impatient!—I cannot come at the paint, madam; Mrs. Foible has locked it up and carried the key with her.

LADY WISHFORT A pox take you both!—fetch me the cherry-brandy then. [*Exit Peg.*] I'm as pale

27 Mope, dull one.
28 A cosmetic preparation.

and as faint, I look like Mrs. Qualmsick, the curate's wife, that's always breeding.—Wench, come, come, wench, what art thou doing? sipping, tasting?—Save thee, dost thou not know the bottle?

[*Reenter Peg with a bottle and china cup.*]

PEG Madam, I was looking for a cup.

LADY WISHFORT A cup, save thee! and what a cup hast thou brought!—Dost thou take me for a fairy, to drink out of an acorn? Why didst thou not bring thy thimble? Hast thou ne'er a brass thimble clinking in thy pocket with a bit of nutmeg?—I warrant thee. Come, fill, fill!—So—again.—[*Knocking at the door.*] See who that is.—Set down the bottle first—here, here, under the table.—What, wouldst thou go with the bottle in thy hand, like a tapster? As I am a person, this wench has lived in an inn upon the road before she came to me, like Maritornes the Asturian in *Don Quixote!*—No Foible yet?

PEG No, madam; Mrs. Marwood.

LADY WISHFORT Oh, Marwood; let her come in. —Come in, good Marwood.

[*Enter Mrs. Marwood.*]

MRS. MARWOOD I'm surprised to find your ladyship in dishabille at this time of day.

LADY WISHFORT Foible's a lost thing—has been abroad since morning, and never heard of since.

MRS. MARWOOD I saw her but once, as I came masked through the park, in conference with Mirabell.

LADY WISHFORT With Mirabell!—You call my blood into my face, with mentioning that traitor. She durst not have the confidence! I sent her to negotiate an affair in which, if I'm detected, I'm undone. If that wheedling villain has wrought upon Foible to detect me, I'm ruined. O my dear friend, I'm a wretch of wretches if I'm detected.

MRS. MARWOOD Oh madam, you cannot suspect Mrs. Foible's integrity!

LADY WISHFORT Oh, he carries poison in his tongue that would corrupt integrity itself! If she has given him an opportunity, she has as good as put her integrity into his hands. Ah, dear Marwood, what's integrity to an opportunity?—Hark! I hear her!—dear friend, retire into my closet, that I may examine her with more freedom.—You'll pardon me, dear friend; I can make bold with you.—There are books over the chimney.—Quarles and Prynne, and *The Short View of the Stage*, with Bunyan's works, to entertain you—[*to Peg*] Go, you thing, and send her in.

[*Exeunt Mrs. Marwood and Peg. Enter Foible.*]

LADY WISHFORT O Foible, where hast thou been? what hast thou been doing?

FOIBLE Madam, I have seen the party.

LADY WISHFORT But what hast thou done?

FOIBLE Nay, 'tis your ladyship has done, and are to do; I have only promised. But a man so enamored—so transported!—Well, here it is, all that is left; all that is not kissed away.—Well, if worshipping of pictures be a sin—poor Sir Rowland, I say.

LADY WISHFORT The miniature has been counted like—but hast thou not betrayed me, Foible? Hast thou not detected me to that faithless Mirabell?—What hadst thou to do with him in the Park? Answer me, has he got nothing out of thee?

FOIBLE [*aside*] So the devil has been beforehand with me. What shall I say?—[*Aloud*] Alas, madam, could I help it, if I met that confident thing? Was I in fault? If you had heard how he used me, and all upon your ladyship's account, I'm sure you would not suspect my fidelity. Nay, if that had been the worst, I could have borne; but he had a fling at your ladyship too; and then I could not hold, but i'faith I gave him his own.

LADY WISHFORT Me? what did the filthy fellow say?

FOIBLE O madam! 'tis a shame to say what he said—with his taunts and his fleers, tossing up his nose. Humph! (says he) what, you are hatching some plot (says he), you are so early abroad, or catering (says he), ferreting some disbanded officer, I warrant.—Half-pay is but thin subsistence (says he)—well, what pension does your lady propose? Let me see (says he), what, she must come down pretty deep now, she's superannuated (says he) and—

LADY WISHFORT Odds my life, I'll have him, I'll have him murdered! I'll have him poisoned! Where does he eat?—I'll marry a drawer to have him poisoned in his wine. I'll send for Robin from Locket's[29] immediately.

FOIBLE Poison him! poisoning's too good for him. Starve him, madam, starve him; marry Sir Rowland, and get him disinherited. Oh you would bless yourself to hear what he said!

LADY WISHFORT A villain! superannuated!

FOIBLE Humph (says he), I hear you are laying designs against me too (says he), and Mrs. Millamant is to marry my uncle (he does not suspect a word of your ladyship); but (says he) I'll fit you for that (says he); I'll hamper you for that (says he); you and your old frippery too (says he); I'll handle you—

LADY WISHFORT Audacious villain! handle me; would he durst!—Frippery! old frippery! was there ever such a foul-mouthed fellow? I'll be married tomorrow; I'll be contracted tonight.

FOIBLE The sooner the better, madam.

LADY WISHFORT Will Sir Rowland be here, sayest thou? When, Foible?

FOIBLE Incontinently, madam. No new sheriff's wife expects the return of her husband after knighthood with that impatience in which Sir Rowland burns for the dear hour of kissing your ladyship's hand after dinner.

LADY WISHFORT Frippery! superannuated frippery! I'll frippery the villain; I'll reduce him to frippery and rags! a tatterdemalion! I hope to

[29] "Robin" was a generic name for a tapster; Locket's was a fashionable tavern.

see him hung with tatters, like a Long-lane penthouse[30] or a gibbet thief. A slander-mouthed railer! I warrant the spendthrift prodigal's in debt as much as the million lottery, or the whole court upon a birthday. I'll spoil his credit with his tailor. Yes, he shall have my niece with her fortune, he shall.

FOIBLE He! I hope to see him lodge in Ludgate[31] first, and angle into Blackfriars for brass farthings with an old mitten.

LADY WISHFORT Ay, dear Foible; thank thee for that, dear Foible. He has put me all out of patience. I shall never recompose my features to receive Sir Rowland with any economy of face. This wretch has fretted me that I am absolutely decayed. Look, Foible.

FOIBLE Your ladyship has frowned a little too rashly, indeed, madam. There are some cracks discernible in the white varnish.

LADY WISHFORT Let me see the glass.—Cracks, sayest thou?—why, I am arrantly flayed—I look like an old peeled wall. Thou must repair me, Foible, before Sir Rowland comes, or I shall never keep up to my picture.

FOIBLE I warrant you, madam, a little art once made your picture like you; and now a little of the same art must make you like your picture. Your picture must sit for you, madam.

LADY WISHFORT But art thou sure Sir Rowland will not fail to come? Or will he not fail when he does come? Will he be importunate, Foible, and push? For if he should not be importunate, I shall never break decorums—I shall die with confusion, if I am forced to advance.—Oh, no, I can never advance!—I shall swoon if he should expect advances. No, I hope Sir Rowland is better bred than to put a lady to the necessity of breaking her forms. I won't be too coy, neither.—I won't give him despair—but a little disdain is not amiss; a little scorn is alluring.

FOIBLE A little scorn becomes your ladyship.

LADY WISHFORT Yes, but tenderness becomes me best—a sort of dyingness—you see that picture has a sort of a—ha, Foible? a swimmingness in

the eye—yes, I'll look so—my niece affects it; but she wants features. Is Sir Rowland handsome? Let my toilet be removed—I'll dress above. I'll receive Sir Rowland here: Is he handsome? Don't answer me. I won't know: I'll be surprised, I'll be taken by surprise.

FOIBLE By storm, madam. Sir Rowland's a brisk man.

LADY WISHFORT Is he! O then he'll importune, if he's a brisk man. I shall save decorums if Sir Rowland importunes. I have a mortal terror at the apprehension of offending against decorums. Oh, I'm glad he's a brisk man. Let my things be removed, good Foible.

[Exit Lady Wishfort. Enter Mrs. Fainall.]

MRS. FAINALL O Foible. I have been in a fright, lest I should come too late! That devil Marwood saw you in the Park with Mirabell, and I'm afraid will discover it to my lady.

FOIBLE Discover what, madam!

MRS. FAINALL Nay, nay, put not on that strange face. I am privy to the whole design, and know that Waitwell, to whom thou wert this morning married, is to personate Mirabell's uncle, and as such, winning my lady, to involve her in those difficulties from which Mirabell only must release her, by his making his conditions to have my cousin and her fortune left to her own disposal.

FOIBLE O dear madam, I beg your pardon. It was not my confidence in your ladyship that was deficient; but I thought the former good correspondence between your ladyship and Mr. Mirabell might have hindered his communicating this secret.

MRS. FAINALL Dear Foible, forget that.

FOIBLE O dear madam, Mr. Mirabell is such a sweet, winning gentleman—but your ladyship is the pattern of generosity.—Sweet lady, to be so good! Mr. Mirabell cannot choose but be grateful. I find your ladyship has his heart still. Now, madam, I can safely tell your ladyship our success: Mrs. Marwood had told my lady; but I warrant I managed myself. I turned it all for the better. I told my lady that Mr. Mirabell railed at her; I laid horrid things to his charge, I'll vow; and my lady is so incensed that she'll be contracted to Sir Rowland tonight, she says;

[30] A stall where old clothes were sold.

[31] A debtors' prison. The inmates lowered receptacles for charity from passers-by.

I warrant I worked her up, that he may have her for asking for, as they say of a Welsh maidenhead.

MRS. FAINALL O rare Foible!

FOIBLE I beg your ladyship to acquaint Mr. Mirabell of his success. I would be seen as little as possible to speak to him—besides, I believe Madam Marwood watches me.—She has a month's mind,[32] but I know Mr. Mirabell can't abide her.—[Calls] John! Remove my lady's toilet.—Madam, your servant: my lady is so impatient I fear she'll come for me if I stay.

MRS. FAINALL I'll go with you up the back-stairs, lest I should meet her.

[Exeunt. Enter Mrs. Marwood.]

MRS. MARWOOD Indeed, Mrs. Engine, is it thus with you? are you become a go-between of this importance? yes, I shall watch you. Why this wench is the *passe-partout,* a very master-key to everybody's strong-box. My friend Fainall, have you carried it so swimmingly? I thought there was something in it; but it seems 'tis over with you. Your loathing is not from a want of appetite, then, but from a surfeit. Else you could never be so cool to fall from a principal to be an assistant; to procure for him! a pattern of generosity, that, I confess. Well, Mr. Fainall, you have met with your match.—O man, man! woman, woman! the devil's an ass: if I were a painter, I would draw him like an idiot, a driveller with a bib and bells. Man should have his head and horns, and woman the rest of him. Poor simple fiend!—"Madam Marwood has a month's mind, but he can't abide her."—'Twere better for him you had not been his confessor in that affair, without you could have kept his counsel closer. I shall not prove another pattern of generosity; he has not obliged me to that with those excesses of himself! and now I'll have none of him. Here comes the good lady, panting ripe; with a heart full of hope, and a head full of care, like any chemist upon the day of projection.[33]

[Enter Lady Wishfort.]

32 Strong desire.
33 When the alchemist attempted to transmute base metal into gold.

LADY WISHFORT O dear, Marwood, what shall I say for this rude forgetfulness?—but my dear friend is all goodness.

MRS. MARWOOD No apologies, dear madam; I have been very well entertained.

LADY WISHFORT As I'm a person, I am in a very chaos to think I should so forget myself:—but I have such an olio of affairs, really I know not what to do.—[Calls] Foible!—I expect my nephew, Sir Wilfull, every moment too.—Why, Foible!—He means to travel for improvement.

MRS. MARWOOD Methinks Sir Wilfull should rather think of marrying than travelling at his years. I hear he is turned of forty.

LADY WISHFORT Oh, he's in less danger of being spoiled by his travels—I am against my nephew's marrying too young. It will be time enough when he comes back, and has acquired discretion to choose for himself.

MRS. MARWOOD Methinks Mrs. Millamant and he would make a very fit match. He may travel afterwards. 'Tis a thing very usual with young gentlemen.

LADY WISHFORT I promise you I have thought on't—and since 'tis your judgment, I'll think on't again. I assure you I will; I value your judgment extremely. On my word, I'll propose it.

[Enter Foible.]

LADY WISHFORT Come, come, Foible—I had forgot my nephew will be here before dinner—I must make haste.

FOIBLE Mr. Witwoud and Mr. Petulant are come to dine with your ladyship.

LADY WISHFORT O dear, I can't appear till I'm dressed.—Dear Marwood, shall I be free with you again, and beg you to entertain 'em? I'll make all imaginable haste. Dear friend, excuse me.

[Exeunt Lady Wishfort and Foible. Enter Mrs. Millamant and Mincing.]

MRS. MILLAMANT Sure never anything was so unbred as that odious man!—Marwood, your servant.

MRS. MARWOOD You have a color; what's the matter?

MRS. MILLAMANT That horrid fellow, Petulant, has provoked me into a flame: I have broken my fan.—Mincing, lend me yours. Is not all the powder out of my hair?

MRS. MARWOOD No. What has he done?

MRS. MILLAMANT Nay, he has done nothing; he has only talked—nay, he has said nothing neither; but he has contradicted everything that has been said. For my part, I thought Witwoud and he would have quarrelled.

MINCING I vow, mem, I thought once they would have fit.

MRS. MILLAMANT Well, 'tis a lamentable thing, I swear, that one has not the liberty of choosing one's acquaintance as one does one's clothes.

MRS. MARWOOD If we had that liberty, we should be as weary of one set of acquaintance, though never so good, as we are of one suit though never so fine. A fool and a doily stuff[34] would now and then find days of grace, and be worn for variety.

MRS. MILLAMANT I could consent to wear 'em, if they would wear alike; but fools never wear out —they are such *drap de Berri*[35] things! Without one could give 'em to one's chambermaid after a day or two.

MRS. MARWOOD 'Twere better so indeed. Or what think you of the playhouse? A fine, gay, glossy fool should be given there, like a new masking habit, after the masquerade is over and we have done with the disguise. For a fool's visit is always a disguise; and never admitted by a woman of wit, but to blind her affair with a lover of sense. If you would but appear barefaced now, and own Mirabell, you might as easily put off Petulant and Witwoud as your hood and scarf. And indeed, 'tis time, for the town has found it; the secret is grown too big for the pretence. 'Tis like Mrs. Primly's great belly; she may lace it down before, but it burnishes on her hips. Indeed, Millamant, you can no more conceal it than my Lady Strammel can her face; that goodly face, which in defiance of her Rhenish wine tea,[36] will not be comprehended in a mask.

MRS. MILLAMANT I'll take my death, Marwood,

34 A cheap woolen cloth.

35 Heavy, durable woolens imported from France.

36 Supposed to be good for both the figure and the complexion.

you are more censorious than a decayed beauty or a discarded toast.—Mincing, tell the men they may come up.—My aunt is not dressing here; their folly is less provoking than your malice. [*Exit Mincing.*] The town has found it! What has it found? That Mirabell loves me is no more a secret than it is a secret that you discovered it to my aunt, or than the reason why you discovered it is a secret.

MRS. MARWOOD You are nettled.

MRS. MILLAMANT You are mistaken. Ridiculous!

MRS. MARWOOD Indeed, my dear, you'll tear another fan, if you don't mitigate those violent airs.

MRS. MILLAMANT O silly! ha! ha! ha! I could laugh immoderately. Poor Mirabell! his constancy to me has quite destroyed his complaisance for all the world beside. I swear, I never enjoined it him to be so coy. If I had the vanity to think he would obey me, I would command him to show more gallantry—'tis hardly well-bred to be so particular on one hand, and so insensible on the other. But I despair to prevail, and so let him follow his own way. Ha! ha! ha! pardon me, dear creature, I must laugh, ha! ha! ha! though I grant you 'tis a little barbarous, ha! ha! ha!

MRS. MARWOOD What pity 'tis so much fine raillery and delivered with so significant gesture, should be so unhappily directed to miscarry!

MRS. MILLAMANT Ha! dear creature, I ask your pardon—I swear I did not mind you.

MRS. MARWOOD Mr. Mirabell and you both may think it a thing impossible, when I shall tell him by telling you—

MRS. MILLAMANT O dear, what? for it is the same thing if I hear it—ha! ha! ha!

MRS. MARWOOD That I detest him, hate him, madam.

MRS. MILLAMANT O madam, why so do I—and yet the creature loves me—ha! ha! ha! How can one forbear laughing to think of it.—I am a sibyl if I am not amazed to think what he can see in me. I'll take my death, I think you are handsomer—and within a year or two as young —if you could but stay for me, I should overtake you, but that cannot be.—Well, that thought makes me melancholic.—Now, I'll be sad.

MRS. MARWOOD Your merry note may be changed sooner than you think.

MRS. MILLAMANT D'ye say so? Then I'm resolved I'll have a song to keep up my spirits.

[*Enter Mincing.*]

MINCING The gentlemen stay but to comb, madam, and will wait on you.

MRS. MILLAMANT Desire Mrs._____ that is in the next room to sing the song I would have learned yesterday.—You shall hear it, madam—not that there's any great matter in it—but 'tis agreeable to my humor.

[*Enter a lady, who sings the following song, then exit.*]

Love's but the frailty of the mind,
When 'tis not with ambition joined;
A sickly flame, which, if not fed, expires,
And feeding, wastes in self-consuming fires.

'Tis not to wound a wanton boy
Or amorous youth, that gives the joy;
But 'tis the glory to have pierced a swain,
For whom inferior beauties sighed in vain.

Then I alone the conquest prize,
When I insult a rival's eyes:
If there's delight in love, 'tis when I see
That heart, which others bleed for, bleed for me.

[*Enter Petulant and Witwoud.*]

MRS. MILLAMANT Is your animosity composed, gentlemen?

WITWOUD Raillery, raillery, madam; we have no animosity—we hit off a little wit now and then, but no animosity. The falling out of wits is like the falling out of lovers: we agree in the main, like treble and bass.—Ha, Petulant?

PETULANT Ay, in the main—but when I have a humor to contradict—

WITWOUD Ay, when he has a humor to contradict, then I contradict too. What, I know my cue. Then we contradict one another like two battledores; for contradictions beget one another like Jews.

PETULANT If he says black's black—if I have a humor to say 'tis blue—let that pass—all's one

for that. If I have a humor to prove it, it must be granted.

WITWOUD Not positively must—but it may—it may.

PETULANT Yes, it positively must, upon proof positive.

WITWOUD Ay, upon proof positive it must; but upon proof presumptive it only may.—That's a logical distinction now, madam.

MRS. MARWOOD I perceive your debates are of importance and very learnedly handled.

PETULANT Importance is one thing, and learning's another; but a debate's a debate, that I assert.

WITWOUD Petulant's an enemy to learning; he relies altogether on his parts.

PETULANT No, I'm no enemy to learning; it hurts not me.

MRS. MARWOOD That's a sign indeed it's no enemy to you.

PETULANT No, no, it's no enemy to anybody but them that have it.

MRS. MILLAMANT Well, an illiterate man's my aversion. I wonder at the impudence of any illiterate man to offer to make love.

WITWOUD That I confess I wonder at too.

MRS. MILLAMANT Ah! to marry an ignorant that can hardly read or write!

PETULANT Why should a man be any further from being married, though he can't read, than he is from being hanged? The ordinary's[37] paid for setting the psalm, and the parish priest for reading the ceremony. And for the rest which is to follow in both cases, a man may do it without book—so all's one for that.

MRS. MILLAMANT D'ye hear the creature?—Lord, here's company, I'll be gone.

[*Exeunt Mrs. Millamant and Mincing. Enter Sir Wilfull Witwoud in a riding dress, followed by Footman.*]

WITWOUD In the name of Bartlemew and his fair,[38] what have we here?

MRS. MARWOOD 'Tis your brother, I fancy. Don't you know him?

WITWOUD Not I.—Yes, I think it is he—I've al-

[37] The prison chaplain, who read a psalm before an execution.

[38] The annual Bartholomew Fair in Smithfield.

most forgot him; I have not seen him since the Revolution.[39]

FOOTMAN [*to Sir Wilfull*]   Sir, my lady's dressing. Here's company; if you please to walk in, in the mean time.

SIR WILFULL   Dressing! what, it's but morning here, I warrant, with you in London; we should count it towards afternoon in our parts, down in Shropshire.—Why, then, belike, my aunt han't dined yet, ha, friend?

FOOTMAN   Your aunt, sir?

SIR WILFULL   My aunt, sir! yes, my aunt, sir, and your lady, sir; your lady is my aunt, sir.—Why, what dost thou not know me, friend? why then send somebody hither that does. How long hast thou lived with thy lady, fellow, ha?

FOOTMAN   A week, sir; longer than anybody in the house, except my lady's woman.

SIR WILFULL   Why then belike thou dost not know thy lady, if thou seest her—ha, friend?

FOOTMAN   Why, truly, sir, I cannot safely swear to her face in a morning, before she is dressed. 'Tis like I may give a shrewd guess at her by this time.

SIR WILFULL   Well, prithee try what thou canst do; if thou canst not guess, inquire her out, dost hear, fellow? and tell her, her nephew, Sir Wilfull Witwoud, is in the house.

FOOTMAN   I shall, sir.

SIR WILFULL   Hold ye; hear me, friend; a word with you in your ear; prithee who are these gallants?

FOOTMAN   Really, sir, I can't tell; here come so many here, 'tis hard to know 'em all. [*Exit.*]

SIR WILFULL   Oons, this fellow knows less than a starling; I don't think a' knows his own name.

MRS. MARWOOD   Mr. Witwoud, your brother is not behindhand in forgetfulness—I fancy he has forgot you too.

WITWOUD   I hope so—the devil take him that remembers first, I say.

SIR WILFULL   Save you, gentlemen and lady!

MRS. MARWOOD   For shame, Mr. Witwoud; why don't you speak to him?—And you, sir.

WITWOUD   Petulant, speak.

PETULANT   And you, sir.

[39] The Revolution of 1688, when James II was dethroned.

SIR WILFULL   No offence, I hope. [*Salutes[40] Mrs. Marwood.*]

MRS. MARWOOD   No, sure, sir.

WITWOUD   This is a vile dog, I see that already. No offense! ha! ha! ha! To him; to him, Petulant, smoke him.[41]

PETULANT   It seems as if you had come a journey, sir; hem, hem [*surveying him round*].

SIR WILFULL   Very likely, sir, that it may seem so.

PETULANT   No offence, I hope, sir.

WITWOUD   Smoke the boots, the boots; Petulant, the boots: ha! ha! ha!

SIR WILFULL   May be not, sir; thereafter, as 'tis meant, sir.

PETULANT   Sir, I presume upon the information of your boots.

SIR WILFULL   Why, 'tis like you may, sir: if you are not satisfied with the information of my boots, sir, if you will step to the stable, you may inquire further of my horse, sir.

PETULANT   Your horse, sir! your horse is an ass, sir!

SIR WILFULL   Do you speak by way of offence, sir?

MRS. MARWOOD   The gentleman's merry, that's all sir.—[*Aside*] 'Slife, we shall have a quarrel betwixt an horse and an ass before they find one another out.—[*Aloud*] You must not take anything amiss from your friends, sir. You are among your friends here, though it may be you don't know it.—If I am not mistaken, you are Sir Wilfull Witwoud.

SIR WILFULL   Right, lady; I am Sir Wilfull Witwoud, so I write myself; no offence to anybody, I hope; and nephew to the Lady Wishfort of this mansion.

MRS. MARWOOD   Don't you know this gentleman, sir?

SIR WILFULL   Hum! what, sure 'tis not—yea by'r Lady, but 'tis—s'heart, I know not whether 'tis or no—yea, but 'tis, by the Wrekin.[42] Brother Anthony! what, Tony, i'faith! what, dost thou not know me? By'r Lady, nor I thee, thou art so becravated, and so beperiwigged.—'Sheart,

[40] Kisses.
[41] Make fun of him.
[42] A hill in Shropshire.

WILLIAM CONGREVE

why dost not speak? art thou overjoyed?

WITWOUD Odso, brother, is it you? your servant, brother.

SIR WILFULL Your servant! why yours, sir. Your servant again—'Sheart, and your friend and servant to that—and a—and a—flap-dragon for your service, sir! and a hare's foot and a hare's scut for your service, sir! an you be so cold and so courtly.

WITWOUD No offence, I hope, brother.

SIR WILFULL 'Sheart, sir, but there is, and much offence!—A pox, is this your Inns o' Court[43] breeding, not to know your friends and your relations, your elders and your betters?

WITWOUD Why, brother Wilfull of Salop,[44] you may be as short as a Shrewsbury-cake,[45] if you please. But I tell you 'tis not modish to know relations in town: you think you're in the country, where great lubberly brothers slabber and kiss one another when they meet, like a call of sergeants[46]—'tis not the fashion here; 'tis not indeed, dear brother.

SIR WILFULL The fashion's a fool; and you're a fop, dear brother. 'Sheart, I've suspected this— by'r Lady, I conjectured you were a fop, since you began to change the style of your letters, and write on a scrap of paper gilt round the edges, no bigger than a *subpœna*. I might expect this when you left off, "Honored brother," and "hoping you are in good health," and so forth —to begin with a "Rat me, knight, I'm so sick of a last night's debauch"—'ods heart, and then tell a familiar tale of a cock and a bull, and a whore and a bottle, and so conclude.—You could write news before you were out of your time,[47] when you lived with honest Pumple Nose, the attorney of Furnival's Inn—you could entreat to be remembered then to your friends round the Wrekin. We could have gazettes, then, and Dawks's Letter, and the Weekly Bill,[48] till of late days.

PETULANT 'Slife, Witwoud, were you ever an attorney's clerk? of the family of the Furnivals? Ha! ha! ha!

WITWOUD Ay, ay, but that was but for a while: not long, not long. Pshaw! I was not in my own power then; an orphan, and this fellow was my guardian. Ay, ay, I was glad to consent to that man to come to London: he had the disposal of me then. If I had not agreed to that, I might have been bound 'prentice to a felt-maker in Shrewsbury; this fellow would have bound me to a maker of felts.

SIR WILFULL 'Sheart, and better than to be bound to a maker of fops; where, I suppose, you have served your time; and now you may set up for yourself.

MRS. MARWOOD You intend to travel, sir, I am informed.

SIR WILFULL Belike I may, madam. I may chance to sail upon the salt seas, if my mind hold.

PETULANT And the wind serve.

SIR WILFULL Serve or not serve, I shan't ask licence of you, sir; nor the weathercock your companion: I direct my discourse to the lady, sir.—'Tis like my aunt may have told you, madam—yes, I have settled my concerns, I may say now, and am minded to see foreign parts. If an' how that the peace holds, whereby that is, taxes abate.

MRS. MARWOOD I thought you had designed for France at all adventures.

SIR WILFULL I can't tell that; 'tis like I may, and 'tis like I may not. I am somewhat dainty in making a resolution—because when I make it I keep it. I don't stand shill I, shall I, then; if I say't, I'll do't. But I have thoughts to tarry a small matter in town, to learn somewhat of your lingo first, before I cross the seas. I'd gladly have a spice of your French, as they say, whereby to hold discourse in foreign countries.

MRS. MARWOOD Here's an academy in town for that use.

---

[43] The four societies in which lawyers were trained; Furnival's Inn, mentioned below, was one of them.

[44] Shropshire.

[45] A rich, sweet biscuit.

[46] The comparison is to the mutual congratulations of a group of lawyers who have all been raised to a particular rank at the same time.

[47] Before he had completed his apprenticeship for the law.

[48] Dawks's News-letter was a weekly news summary; the Weekly Bill was a mortality list.

SIR WILFULL   There is? 'Tis like there may.

MRS. MARWOOD   No doubt you will return very much improved.

WITWOUD   Yes, refined, like a Dutch skipper from a whale-fishing.

[*Enter Lady Wishfort and Fainall.*]

LADY WISHFORT   Nephew, you are welcome.

SIR WILFULL   Aunt, your servant.

FAINALL   Sir Wilfull, your most faithful servant.

SIR WILFULL   Cousin Fainall, give me your hand.

LADY WISHFORT   Cousin Witwoud, your servant; Mr. Petulant, your servant; nephew, you are welcome again. Will you drink anything after your journey, nephew, before you eat? Dinner's almost ready.

SIR WILFULL   I'm very well, I thank you, aunt—however, I thank you for your courteous offer. 'Sheart, I was afraid you would have been in the fashion too, and have remembered to have forgot your relations. Here's your cousin Tony; belike, I mayn't call him brother, for fear of offence.

LADY WISHFORT   Oh, he's a rallier, nephew—my cousin's a wit: and your great wits always rally their best friends to choose. When you have been abroad, nephew, you'll understand raillery better.

[*Fainall and Mrs. Marwood talk apart.*]

SIR WILFULL   Why then, let him hold his tongue in the mean time, and rail when that day comes.

[*Enter Mincing.*]

MINCING   Mem, I am come to acquaint your la'ship that dinner is impatient.

SIR WILFULL   Impatient! why then belike it won't stay till I pull off my boots.—Sweetheart, can you help me to a pair of slippers?—My man's with his horses, I warrant.

LADY WISHFORT   Fy, fy, nephew! you would not pull off your boots here?—Go down into the hall—dinner shall stay for you.—My nephew's a little unbred, you'll pardon him, madam.—Gentlemen, will you walk?—Marwood—

MRS. MARWOOD   I'll follow you, madam—before Sir Wilfull is ready.

[*Exeunt all but Mrs. Marwood and Fainall.*]

FAINALL   Why then, Foible's a bawd, an arrant, rank, match-making bawd. And I, it seems, am a husband, a rank husband; and my wife's a very errant, rank wife—all in the way of the world. 'Sdeath, to be a cuckold by anticipation, a cuckold in embryo! sure I was born with budding antlers, like a young satyr, or a citizen's child.[49] 'Sdeath! to be outwitted—to be out-jilted—out-matrimonied!—If I had kept my speed like a stag, 'twere somewhat—but to crawl after, with my horns, like a snail, and be outstripped by my wife—'tis scurvy wedlock.

MRS. MARWOOD   Then shake it off; you have often wished for an opportunity to part—and now you have it. But first prevent their plot—the half of Millamant's fortune is too considerable to be parted with to a foe, to Mirabell.

FAINALL   Damn him! that had been mine—had you not made that fond discovery—that had been forfeited, had they been married. My wife had added lustre to my horns by that increase of fortune; I could have worn 'em tipped with gold, though my forehead had been furnished like a deputy-lieutenant's hall.[50]

MRS. MARWOOD   They may prove a cap of maintenance[51] to you still, if you can away with your wife. And she's no worse than when you had her—I dare swear she had given up her game before she was married.

FAINALL   Hum! that may be. She might throw up her cards, but I'll be hanged if she did not put pam in her pocket.[52]

MRS. MARWOOD   You married her to keep you; and if you can contrive to have her keep you better than you expected, why should you not keep her longer than you intended?

FAINALL   The means, the means!

MRS. MARWOOD   Discover to my lady your wife's conduct; threaten to part with her!—my lady loves her, and will come to any composition to save her reputation. Take the opportunity of breaking it just upon the discovery of this imposture. My lady will be enraged beyond bounds, and sacrifice niece, and fortune, and

[49] Allusions to two stock jokes. One is to the horns of the cuckold, the other to the supposedly numerous seductions of citizens' wives by courtiers.

[50] With numerous sets of antlers.

[51] In heraldry, a symbol of high office; it sometimes had two points.

[52] The jack of clubs, highest card in the fashionable game of loo.

all, at that conjuncture. And let me alone to keep her warm; if she should flag in her part, I will not fail to prompt her.

FAINALL Faith, this has an appearance.

MRS. MARWOOD I'm sorry I hinted to my lady to endeavor a match between Millamant and Sir Wilfull; that may be an obstacle.

FAINALL Oh, for that matter, leave me to manage him: I'll disable him for that; he will drink like a Dane; after dinner I'll set his hand in.[53]

MRS. MARWOOD Well, how do you stand affected towards your lady?

FAINALL Why, faith, I'm thinking of it.—Let me see—I am married already, so that's over. My wife has played the jade with me—well, that's over too. I never loved her, or if I had, why that would have been over too by this time. Jealous of her I cannot be, for I am certain; so there's an end of jealousy: Weary of her I am, and shall be—no, there's no end of that— no, no, that were too much to hope. Thus far concerning my repose; now for my reputation. As to my own, I married not for it, so that's out of the question; and as to my part in my wife's—why, she had parted with hers before; so bringing none to me, she can take none from me. 'Tis against all rule of play, that I should lose to one who has not wherewithal to stake.

MRS. MARWOOD Besides, you forget, marriage is honorable.

FAINALL Hum, faith, and that's well thought on; marriage is honorable as you say; and if so, wherefore should cuckoldom be a discredit, being derived from so honorable a root?

MRS. MARWOOD Nay, I know not; if the root be honorable, why not the branches?

FAINALL So, so, why this point's clear—well, how do we proceed?

MRS. MARWOOD I will contrive a letter which shall be delivered to my lady at the time when that rascal who is to act Sir Rowland is with her. It shall come as from an unknown hand— for the less I appear to know of the truth, the better I can play the incendiary. Besides, I would not have Foible provoked if I could help it—because you know she knows some passages—nay, I expect all will come out. But let the mine be sprung first, and then I care not if I am discovered.

FAINALL If the worst come to the worst—I'll turn my wife to grass. I have already a deed of settlement of the best part of her estate which I wheedled out of her; and that you shall partake at least.

MRS. MARWOOD I hope you are convinced that I hate Mirabell now; you'll be no more jealous?

FAINALL Jealous! no—by this kiss—let husbands be jealous; but let the lover still believe; or if he doubt, let it be only to endear his pleasure, and prepare the joy that follows when he proves his mistress true. But let husbands' doubts convert to endless jealousy; or if they have belief, let it corrupt to superstition and blind credulity. I am single, and will herd no more with 'em. True, I wear the badge, but I'll disown the order. And since I take my leave of 'em, I care not if I leave 'em a common motto to their common crest:—

All husbands must or pain or shame endure;
The wise too jealous are, fools too secure.
[*Exeunt.*]

Act Four

SCENE ONE

A room in Lady Wishfort's house. Lady Wishfort and Foible.

LADY WISHFORT Is Sir Rowland coming, sayest thou, Foible? and are things in order?

FOIBLE Yes, madam, I have put wax lights in the sconces, and placed the footmen in a row in the hall, in their best liveries, and the coachman and postillion to fill up the equipage.

LADY WISHFORT Have you pulvilled[54] the coachman and postillion, that they may not stink of the stable when Sir Rowland comes by?

FOIBLE Yes, madam.

[53] Start him playing the game.

[54] Sprinkled with scented powder.

LADY WISHFORT And are the dancers and the music ready, that he may be entertained in all points with correspondence to his passion?

FOIBLE All is ready, madam.

LADY WISHFORT And—well—and how do I look, Foible?

FOIBLE Most killing well, madam.

LADY WISHFORT Well, and how shall I receive him? in what figure shall I give his heart the first impression? There is a great deal in the first impression. Shall I sit?—no, I won't sit —I'll walk—ay, I'll walk from the door upon his entrance; and then turn full upon him—no, that will be too sudden. I'll lie—ay, I'll lie down—I'll receive him in my little dressing-room, there's a couch—yes, yes, I'll give the first impression on a couch.—I won't lie neither, but loll and lean upon one elbow with one foot a little dangling off, jogging in a thoughtful way—yes—and then as soon as he appears, start, ay, start and be surprised, and rise to meet him in a pretty disorder—yes— Oh, nothing is more alluring than a levee[55] from a couch, in some confusion—it shows the foot to advantage, and furnishes with blushes, and recomposing airs beyond comparison. Hark! there's a coach.

FOIBLE 'Tis he, madam.

LADY WISHFORT O dear!—Has my nephew made his addresses to Millamant? I ordered him.

FOIBLE Sir Wilfull is set in to drinking, madam, in the parlor.

LADY WISHFORT Odds my life, I'll send him to her. Call her down, Foible; bring her hither. I'll send him as I go—when they are together, then come to me, Foible, that I may not be too long alone with Sir Rowland.

[*Exit. Enter Mrs. Millamant and Mrs. Fainall.*]

FOIBLE Madam, I stayed here to tell your lady-ship that Mr. Mirabell has waited this half-hour for an opportunity to talk with you: though my lady's orders were to leave you and Sir Wilfull together. Shall I tell Mr. Mirabell that you are at leisure?

MRS. MILLAMANT No—what would the dear man have? I am thoughtful, and would amuse my-self—bid him come another time.

---

55 Rising.

"There never yet was woman made
  Nor shall but to be cursed."[56]

[*Repeating, and walking about*] That's hard.

MRS. FAINALL You are very fond of Sir John Suckling today, Millamant, and the poets.

MRS. MILLAMANT Heh? Ay, and filthy verses—so I am.

FOIBLE Sir Wilfull is coming, madam. Shall I send Mr. Mirabell away?

MRS. MILLAMANT Ay, if you please, Foible, send him away—or send him hither—just as you will, dear Foible. I think I'll see him—shall I? ay, let the wretch come.

[*Exit Foible.*]

"Thyrsis, a youth of the inspired train."[57]

[*Repeating*] Dear Fainall, entertain Sir Wilfull —thou hast philosophy to undergo a fool, thou art married and hast patience—I would confer with my own thoughts.

MRS. FAINALL I am obliged to you that you would make me your proxy in this affair, but I have business of my own.

[*Enter Sir Wilfull.*]

MRS. FAINALL O Sir Wilfull, you are come at the critical instant. There's your mistress up to the ears in love and contemplation; pursue your point now or never.

SIR WILFULL Yes; my aunt will have it so—I would gladly have been encouraged with a bottle or two, because I'm somewhat wary at first before I am acquainted [*while Millamant walks about repeating to herself*].—But I hope, after a time, I shall break my mind—that is, upon further acquaintance—so for the present, cousin, I'll take my leave—if so be you'll be so kind to make my excuse, I'll return to my company—

MRS. FAINALL O fy, Sir Wilfull! what, you must not be daunted.

SIR WILFULL Daunted! no, that's not it; it is not so much for that—for if so be that I set on't, I'll do't. But only for the present, 'tis sufficient till further acquaintance, that's all—your serv-ant.

MRS. FAINALL Nay, I'll swear you shall never lose so favorable an opportunity if I can help

---

56 Quoted from Sir John Suckling.

57 From Edmund Waller, "The Story of Phoebus and Daphne, Applied."

WILLIAM CONGREVE

it. I'll leave you together, and lock the door. [*Exit.*]

SIR WILFULL Nay, nay, cousin—I have forgot my gloves—what d'ye do?—'Sheart, a'has locked the door indeed, I think—nay, Cousin Fainall, open the door—pshaw, what a vixen trick is this?—Nay, now a'has seen me too.—Cousin, I made bold to pass through as it were—I think this door's enchanted!

MRS. MILLAMANT [*repeating*]

"I prithee spare me, gentle boy,
Press me no more for that slight toy."[58]

SIR WILFULL Anan?[59] Cousin, your servant.

MRS. MILLAMANT [*repeating*]

"That foolish trifle of a heart."
Sir Wilfull!

SIR WILFULL Yes—your servant. No offence, I hope, cousin.

MRS. MILLAMANT [*repeating*]

"I swear it will not do its part,
  Though thou dost thine, employest thy power and art."

Natural, easy Suckling!

SIR WILFULL Anan? Suckling! no such suckling neither, cousin, nor stripling: I thank Heaven, I'm no minor.

MRS. MILLAMANT Ah, rustic, ruder than Gothic!

SIR WILFULL Well, well, I shall understand your lingo one of these days, cousin; in the meanwhile I must answer in plain English.

MRS. MILLAMANT Have you any business with me, Sir Wilfull?

SIR WILFULL Not at present, cousin—yes, I made bold to see, to come and know if that how you were disposed to fetch a walk this evening; if so be that I might not be troublesome, I would have sought a walk with you.

MRS. MILLAMANT A walk! what then?

SIR WILFULL Nay, nothing—only for the walk's sake, that's all.

MRS. MILLAMANT I nauseate walking; 'tis a country diversion; I loathe the country, and everything that relates to it.

SIR WILFULL Indeed! ha! look ye, look ye, you do? Nay, 'tis like you may—here are choice of pastimes here in town, as plays and the like; that must be confessed indeed.

[58] From a song by Sir John Suckling.
[59] What's that?

The Way of the World

MRS. MILLAMANT *Ah l'étourdie!*[60] I hate the town too.

SIR WILFULL Dear heart, that's much—ha! that you should hate 'em both! ha! 'tis like you may; there are some can't relish the town, and others can't away with the country—'tis like you may be one of those, cousin.

MRS. MILLAMANT Ha! ha! ha! yes, 'tis like I may.—You have nothing further to say to me?

SIR WILFULL Not at present, cousin.—'Tis like when I have an opportunity to be more private—I may break my mind in some measure—I conjecture you partly guess—however, that's as time shall try—but spare to speak and spare to speed, as they say.

MRS. MILLAMANT If it is of no great importance, Sir Wilfull, you will oblige me to leave me; I have just now a little business—

SIR WILFULL Enough, enough, cousin: yes, yes, all a case—when you're disposed. Now's as well as another time, and another time as well as now. All's one for that—yes, yes, if your concerns call you, there's no haste; it will keep cold, as they say. Cousin, your servant—I think this door's locked.

MRS. MILLAMANT You may go this way, sir.

SIR WILFULL Your servant; then with your leave I'll return to my company. [*Exit.*]

MRS. MILLAMANT Ay, ay; ha! ha! ha!

"Like Phœbus sung the no less amorous boy."[61]

[*Enter Mirabell.*]

MIRABELL "Like Daphne she, as lovely and as coy."

Do you lock yourself up from me, to make my search more curious? or is this pretty artifice contrived to signify that here the chase must end, and my pursuits be crowned? For you can fly no further.

MRS. MILLAMANT Vanity! no—I'll fly, and be followed to the last moment. Though I am upon the very verge of matrimony, I expect you should solicit me as much as if I were wavering at the grate of a monastery, with one foot over the threshold. I'll be solicited

[60] The giddy (town), with a pun on *l'étourdi,* "the fool."
[61] The third line from the poem by Edmund Waller, "The Story of Phoebus and Daphne, Applied," cited earlier. Mirabell adds the fourth.

355

to the very last, nay, and afterwards.

MIRABELL What, after the last?

MRS. MILLAMANT Oh, I should think I was poor and had nothing to bestow, if I were reduced to an inglorious ease and freed from the agreeable fatigues of solicitation.

MIRABELL But do not you know that when favors are conferred upon instant and tedious solicitation, that they diminish in their value, and that both the giver loses the grace, and the receiver lessens his pleasure?

MRS. MILLAMANT It may be in things of common application; but never sure in love. Oh, I hate a lover that can dare to think he draws a moment's air, independent of the bounty of his mistress. There is not so impudent a thing in nature as the saucy look of an assured man, confident of success. The pedantic arrogance of a very husband has not so pragmatical an air. Ah! I'll never marry, unless I am first made sure of my will and pleasure.

MIRABELL Would you have 'em both before marriage? or will you be contented with the first now, and stay for the other till after grace?

MRS. MILLAMANT Ah! don't be impertinent.—My dear liberty, shall I leave thee? my faithful solitude, my darling contemplation, must I bid you then adieu? Ay-h adieu—my morning thoughts, agreeable wakings, indolent slumbers, all ye *douceurs,* ye *sommeils du matin,*[62] *adieu?*—I can't do't, 'tis more than impossible —positively, Mirabell, I'll lie abed in a morning as long as I please.

MIRABELL Then I'll get up in a morning as early as I please.

MRS. MILLAMANT Ah! idle creature, get up when you will—and d'ye hear, I won't be called names after I'm married; positively I won't be called names.

MIRABELL Names!

MRS. MILLAMANT Ay, as wife, spouse, my dear, joy, jewel, love, sweetheart, and the rest of that nauseous cant, in which men and their wives are so fulsomely familiar—I shall never bear that. Good Mirabell, don't let us be familiar or fond, nor kiss before folks, like my

62 Sweet indulgences, morning slumbers.

Lady Fadler and Sir Francis; nor go to Hyde Park together the first Sunday in a new chariot, to provoke eyes and whispers, and then never to be seen there together again; as if we were proud of one another the first week, and ashamed of one another ever after. Let us never visit together; nor go to a play together; but let us be very strange and well-bred. Let us be as strange as if we had been married a great while; and as well-bred as if we were not married at all.

MIRABELL Have you any more conditions to offer? Hitherto your demands are pretty reasonable.

MRS. MILLAMANT Trifles!—As liberty to pay and receive visits to and from whom I please; to write and receive letters, without interrogatories or wry faces on your part; to wear what I please; and choose conversation with regard only to my own taste; to have no obligation upon me to converse with wits that I don't like, because they are your acquaintance: or to be intimate with fools, because they may be your relations. Come to dinner when I please; dine in my dressing-room when I'm out of humor, without giving a reason. To have my closet inviolate; to be sole empress of my tea-table, which you must never presume to approach without first asking leave. And lastly, wherever I am, you shall always knock at the door before you come in. These articles subscribed, if I continue to endure you a little longer, I may by degrees dwindle into a wife.

MIRABELL Your bill of fare is something advanced in this latter account.—Well, have I liberty to offer conditions—that when you are dwindled into a wife, I may not be beyond measure enlarged into a husband?

MRS. MILLAMANT You have free leave; propose your utmost; speak and spare not.

MIRABELL I thank you.—*Imprimis*[63] then, I covenant, that your acquaintance be general; that you admit no sworn confidant or intimate of your own sex; no she-friend to screen her affairs under your countenance, and tempt you to make trial of a mutual secrecy. No decoy-duck to wheedle you a fop-scrambling[64] to the

63 Legal terminology: "first of all."
64 Chasing a fop.

play in a mask—then bring you home in a pretended fright, when you think you shall be found out—and rail at me for missing the play, and disappointing the frolic which you had, to pick me up and prove my constancy.

MRS. MILLAMANT Detestable *imprimis!* I go to the play in a mask!

MIRABELL *Item,* I article, that you continue to like your own face, as long as I shall: and while it passes current with me, that you endeavor not to new-coin it. To which end, together with all vizards[65] for the day, I prohibit all masks for the night, made of oiled-skins, and I know not what—hogs' bones, hares' gall, pig-water, and the marrow of a roasted cat. In short, I forbid all commerce with the gentlewoman in What-d'ye-call-it Court. *Item,* I shut my doors against all bawds with baskets, and pennyworths of muslin, china, fans, atlases,[66] etc.—*Item,* when you shall be breeding—

MRS. MILLAMANT Ah! name it not.

MIRABELL Which may be presumed, with a blessing on our endeavors—

MRS. MILLAMANT Odious endeavors!

MIRABELL I denounce against all strait lacing, squeezing for a shape, till you mould my boy's head like a sugar-loaf, and instead of a man child, make me father to a crooked billet. Lastly, to the dominion of the tea-table I submit—but with proviso, that you exceed not in your province; but restrain yourself to native and simple tea-table drinks, as tea, chocolate, and coffee; as likewise to genuine and authorised tea-table talk—such as mending of fashions, spoiling reputations, railing at absent friends, and so forth—but that on no account you encroach upon the men's prerogative, and presume to drink healths, or toast fellows; for prevention of which I banish all foreign forces, all auxiliaries to the tea-table, as orange-brandy, all aniseed, cinnamon, citron, and Barbadoes waters, together with ratafia, and the most noble spirit of clary[67]—but for cowslip wine, poppy water, and all dormitives, those I allow.—These provisos admitted, in other things I may prove a tractable and complying husband.

[65] Masks.
[66] Atlas is a variety of satin.
[67] These were all strongly alcoholic beverages.

MRS. MILLAMANT O horrid provisos! filthy strong-waters! I toast fellows! odious men! I hate your odious provisos.

MIRABELL Then we are agreed! shall I kiss your hand upon the contract? And here comes one to be a witness to the sealing of the deed. [*Enter Mrs. Fainall.*]

MRS. MILLAMANT Fainall, what shall I do? shall I have him? I think I must have him.

MRS. FAINALL Ay, ay, take him, take him, what should you do?

MRS. MILLAMANT Well then—I'll take my death, I'm in a horrid fright—Fainall, I shall never say it—well—I think—I'll endure you.

MRS. FAINALL Fy! fy! have him, have him, and tell him so in plain terms; for I am sure you have a mind to him.

MRS. MILLAMANT Are you? I think I have—and the horrid man looks as if he thought so too— well, you ridiculous thing you, I'll have you —I won't be kissed, nor I won't be thanked— here kiss my hand though.—So, hold your tongue now; don't say a word.

MRS. FAINALL Mirabell, there's a necessity for your obedience;—you have neither time to talk nor stay. My mother is coming; and in my conscience if she should see you, would fall into fits, and maybe not recover time enough to return to Sir Rowland, who, as Foible tells me, is in a fair way to succeed. Therefore spare your ecstasies for another occasion, and slip down the back-stairs, where Foible waits to consult you.

MRS. MILLAMANT Ay, go, go. In the meantime I suppose you have said something to please me.

MIRABELL I am all obedience. [*Exit.*]

MRS. FAINALL Yonder Sir Wilfull's drunk, and so noisy that my mother has been forced to leave Sir Rowland to appease him; but he answers her only with singing and drinking— what they may have done by this time I know not; but Petulant and he were upon quarrelling as I came by.

MRS. MILLAMANT Well, if Mirabell should not make a good husband, I am a lost thing,—for I find I love him violently.

MRS. FAINALL So it seems; for you mind not what's said to you.—If you doubt him, you had best take up with Sir Wilfull.

MRS. MILLAMANT How can you name that super-annuated lubber? foh!

[*Enter Witwoud.*]

MRS. FAINALL So, is the fray made up, that you have left 'em?

WITWOUD Left 'em? I could stay no longer—I have laughed like ten christ'nings—I am tipsy with laughing—if I had stayed any longer I should have burst,—I must have been let out and pieced in the sides like an unsized camlet.[68]—Yes, yes, the fray is composed; my lady came in like a *nolle prosequi*,[69] and stopped the proceedings.

MRS. MILLAMANT What was the dispute?

WITWOUD That's the jest; there was no dispute. They could neither of 'em speak for rage, and so fell a sputtering at one another like two roasting apples.

[*Enter Petulant, drunk.*]

WITWOUD Now, Petulant, all's over, all's well. Gad, my head begins to whim it about—why dost thou not speak? thou art both as drunk and as mute as a fish.

PETULANT Look you, Mrs. Millamant—if you can love me, dear nymph—say it—and that's the conclusion—pass on, or pass off—that's all.

WITWOUD Thou hast uttered volumes, folios, in less than *decimo sexto*,[70] my dear Lacedemonian.[71] Sirrah Petulant, thou are an epitomiser of words.

PETULANT Witwoud—you are an annihilator of sense.

WITWOUD Thou art a retailer of phrases; and dost deal in remnants of remnants, like a maker of pincushions—thou art in truth (metaphorically speaking) a speaker of shorthand.

PETULANT Thou art (without a figure) just one-half of an ass, and Baldwin[72] yonder, thy half-brother, is the rest.—A Gemini[73] of asses split would make just four of you.

WITWOUD Thou dost bite, my dear mustard-seed; kiss me for that.

PETULANT Stand off!—I'll kiss no more males— I have kissed your twin yonder in a humor of reconciliation, till he [*hiccups*] rises upon my stomach like a radish.

MRS. MILLAMANT Eh! filthy creature! what was the quarrel?

PETULANT There was no quarrel—there might have been a quarrel.

WITWOUD If there had been words enow between 'em to have expressed provocation, they had gone together by the ears like a pair of castanets.

PETULANT You were the quarrel.

MRS. MILLAMANT Me!

PETULANT If I have a humor to quarrel, I can make less matters conclude premises.—If you are not handsome, what then, if I have a humor to prove it? If I shall have my reward, say so; if not, fight for your face the next time yourself—I'll go sleep.

WITWOUD Do; wrap thyself up like a wood-louse, and dream revenge—and hear me, if thou canst learn to write by to-morrow morning, pen me a challenge.—I'll carry it for thee.

PETULANT Carry your mistress's monkey a spider!—Go flea dogs, and read romances!—I'll go to bed to my maid. [*Exit.*]

MRS. FAINALL He's horridly drunk.—How came you all in this pickle?

WITWOUD A plot! a plot! to get rid of the knight —your husband's advice; but he sneaked off.

[*Enter Sir Wilfull drunk, and Lady Wishfort.*]

LADY WISHFORT Out upon't, out upon't! At years of discretion, and comport yourself at this rantipole[74] rate!

SIR WILFULL No offence, aunt.

LADY WISHFORT Offence! as I'm a person, I'm ashamed of you—foh! how you stink of wine! D'ye think my niece will ever endure such a Borachio! you're an absolute Borachio.[75]

SIR WILFULL Borachio?

LADY WISHFORT At a time when you should commence an amour, and put you best foot foremost—

SIR WILFULL 'Sheart, an you grutch me your

---

68 Cloth made of Angora or camel's hair; *"unsized"* means that it has not yet been sized or stiffened.

69 Legal terminology: "unwilling to prosecute."

70 A very small size for a book (sixteenmo).

71 Lacedemonians or Spartans were noted for terseness of speech.

72 The ass in *Reynard the Fox.*

73 The twins in the zodiac.

74 Boisterous.

75 Drunkard.

WILLIAM CONGREVE

liquor, make a bill—give me more drink, and take my purse—
[*Sings*]

Prithee fill me the glass,
Till it laughs in my face,
With ale that is potent and mellow;
He that whines for a lass,
Is an ignorant ass,
For a bumper has not its fellow.

But if you would have me marry my cousin—say the word, and I'll do't—Wilfull will do't, that's the word—Wilfull will do't, that's my crest—my motto I have forgot.

LADY WISHFORT My nephew's a little overtaken, cousin—but 'tis with drinking your health.—O' my word you are obliged to him.

SIR WILFULL *In vino veritas,*[76] aunt.—If I drunk your health today, cousin—I am a Borachio. But if you have a mind to be married, say the word, and send for the piper; Wilfull will do't. If not, dust it away, and let's have t'other round.—Tony!—Odds heart, where's Tony!—Tony's an honest fellow; but he spits after a bumper, and that's a fault.—
[*Sings*]

We'll drink, and we'll never ha' done, boys,
Put the glass then around with the sun, boys,
Let Apollo's example invite us;
For he's drunk every night,
And that makes him so bright,
That he's able next morning to light us.

The sun's a good pimple,[77] an honest soaker; he has a cellar at your Antipodes. If I travel, aunt, I touch at your Antipodes.—Your Antipodes are a good, rascally sort of topsy-turvy fellows: If I had a bumper, I'd stand upon my head and drink a health to 'em—A match or no match, cousin with the hard name?—Aunt, Wilfull will do't. If she has her maidenhead, let her look to't; if she has not, let her keep her own counsel in the meantime, and cry out at the nine months' end.

MRS. MILLAMANT Your pardon, madam, I can stay no longer—Sir Wilfull grows very power-

ful. Eh! how he smells! I shall be overcome if I stay.—Come, cousin.
[*Exeunt Mrs. Millamant and Mrs. Fainall.*]

LADY WISHFORT Smells! he would poison a tallow-chandler and his family! Beastly creature, I know not what to do with him!—Travel, quotha! aye, travel, travel, get thee gone, get thee gone; get thee but far enough, to the Saracens, or the Tartars, or the Turks!—for thou art not fit to live in a Christian commonwealth, thou beastly pagan!

SIR WILFULL Turks, no; no Turks, aunt: your Turks are infidels, and believe not in the grape. Your Mahometan, your Mussulman, is a dry stinkard—no offence, aunt. My map says that your Turk is not so honest a man as your Christian. I cannot find by the map that your Mufti is orthodox—whereby it is a plain case that orthodox is a hard word, aunt, and [*hiccups*] Greek for claret.—
[*Sings*]

To drink is a Christian diversion,
Unknown to the Turk or the Persian:
Let Mahometan fools
Live by heathenish rules,
And be damned over tea-cups and coffee.
But let British lads sing,
Crown a health to the king,
And a fig for your sultan and sophy![78]

Ah Tony!
[*Enter Foible, who whispers to Lady Wishfort.*]

LADY WISHFORT [*aside to Foible*] Sir Rowland impatient? Good lack! what shall I do with this beastly tumbril?—[*Aloud.*] Go lie down and sleep, you sot!—or, as I'm a person, I'll have you bastinadoed with broomsticks.—Call up the wenches.
[*Exit Foible.*]

SIR WILFULL Ahey! wenches, where are the wenches?

LADY WISHFORT Dear Cousin Witwoud, get him away, and you will bind me to you inviolably. I have an affair of moment that invades me with some precipitation—you will oblige me to all futurity.

WITWOUD Come, knight.—Pox on him, I don't

[76] "There is truth in wine."
[77] Boon companion.

[78] The shah of Persia.

know what to say to him.—Will you go to a cock-match?

SIR WILFULL With a wench, Tony! Is she a shakebag, sirrah? Let me bite your cheek for that.

WITWOUD Horrible! he has a breath like a bagpipe! Ay, ay; come, will you march, my Salopian?

SIR WILFULL Lead on, little Tony—I'll follow thee, my Anthony, my Tantony. Sirrah, thou shalt be my Tantony, and I'll be thy pig.[79]

And a fig for your sultan and sophy.

[Exeunt Sir Wilfull, singing, and Witwoud.]

LADY WISHFORT This will never do. It will never make a match—at least before he has been abroad.

[Enter Waitwell, disguised as Sir Rowland.]

LADY WISHFORT Dear Sir Rowland, I am confounded with confusion at the retrospection of my own rudeness!—I have more pardons to ask than the pope distributes in the year of jubilee. But I hope, where there is likely to be so near an alliance, we may unbend the severity of decorums and dispense with a little ceremony.

WAITWELL My impatience, madam, is the effect of my transport; and till I have the possession of your adorable person, I am tantalised on the rack; and do but hang, madam, on the tenter of expectation.

LADY WISHFORT You have an excess of gallantry, Sir Rowland, and press things to a conclusion with a most prevailing vehemence.—But a day or two for decency of marriage—

WAITWELL For decency of funeral, madam! The delay will break my heart—or, if that should fail, I shall be poisoned. My nephew will get an inkling of my designs, and poison me—and I would willingly starve him before I die—I would gladly go out of the world with that satisfaction.—That would be some comfort to me, if I could but live so long as to be revenged on that unnatural viper!

LADY WISHFORT Is he so unnatural, say you? Truly I would contribute much both to the saving of your life, and the accomplishment of your revenge. Not that I respect myself, though he has been a perfidious wretch to me.

WAITWELL Perfidious to you!

LADY WISHFORT O Sir Rowland, the hours he has died away at my feet, the tears that he has shed, the oaths that he has sworn, the palpitations that he has felt, the trances and the tremblings, the ardors and the ecstasies, the kneelings and the risings, the heart-heavings and the hand-gripings, the pangs and the pathetic regards of his protesting eyes! Oh, no memory can register!

WAITWELL What, my rival! is the rebel my rival? —a' dies!

LADY WISHFORT No, don't kill him at once, Sir Rowland, starve him gradually, inch by inch.

WAITWELL I'll do't. In three weeks he shall be barefoot; in a month out at knees with begging an alms.—He shall starve upward and upward, till he has nothing living but his head, and then go out in a stink like a candle's end upon a save-all.[80]

LADY WISHFORT Well, Sir Rowland, you have the way—you are no novice in the labyrinth of love—you have the clue. But as I am a person, Sir Rowland, you must not attribute my yielding to any sinister appetite, or indigestion of widowhood; nor impute my complacency to any lethargy of continence. I hope you do not think me prone to any iteration of nuptials—

WAITWELL Far be it from me—

LADY WISHFORT If you do, I protest I must recede—or think that I have made a prostitution of decorums; but in the vehemence of compassion, and to save the life of a person of so much importance—

WAITWELL I esteem it so.

LADY WISHFORT Or else you wrong my condescension.

WAITWELL I do not, I do not!

LADY WISHFORT Indeed you do.

WAITWELL I do not, fair shrine of virtue!

LADY WISHFORT If you think the least scruple of carnality was an ingredient—

WAITWELL Dear madam, no. You are all camphor and frankincense, all chastity and odor.

[79] St. Anthony was the patron saint of swineherds.

[80] A device for holding a candle so that it will burn to the end.

WILLIAM CONGREVE

LADY WISHFORT Or that—
[*Enter Foible.*]

FOIBLE Madam, the dancers are ready; and there's one with a letter who must deliver it into your own hands.

LADY WISHFORT Sir Rowland, will you give me leave? Think favorably, judge candidly, and conclude you have found a person who would suffer racks in honor's cause, dear Sir Rowland, and will wait on you incessantly. [*Exit.*]

WAITWELL Fy, fy!—What a slavery have I undergone! Spouse, hast thou any cordial? I want spirits.

FOIBLE What a washy rogue art thou, to pant thus for a quarter of an hour's lying and swearing to a fine lady!

WAITWELL Oh, she is the antidote to desire! Spouse, thou wilt fare the worse for't—I shall have no appetite to iteration of nuptials this eight-and-forty hours.—By this hand I'd rather be a chairman in the dog-days—than act Sir Rowland till this time tomorrow!

[*Reenter Lady Wishfort, with a letter.*]

LADY WISHFORT Call in the dancers.—Sir Rowland, we'll sit, if you please, and see the entertainment. [*A dance.*] Now, with your permission, Sir Rowland, I will peruse my letter. —I would open it in your presence, because I would not make you uneasy. If it should make you uneasy, I would burn it. Speak, if it does —but you may see the superscription is like a woman's hand.

FOIBLE [*aside to Waitwell*] By Heaven! Mrs. Marwood's, I know it.—My heart aches—get it from her.

WAITWELL A woman's hand! no, madam, that's no woman's hand. I see that already. That's somebody whose throat must be cut.

LADY WISHFORT Nay, Sir Rowland, since you give me a proof of your passion by your jealousy, I promise you I'll make a return by a frank communication.—You shall see it—we'll open it together—look you here.—[*Reads*] "Madam, though unknown to you"—Look you here, 'tis from nobody that I know—"I have that honor for your character, that I think myself obliged to let you know you are abused. He who pretends to be Sir Rowland, is a cheat and a rascal."—Oh, heavens! what's this?

FOIBLE [*aside*] Unfortunate! all's ruined!

WAITWELL How, how, let me see, let me see!— [*Reads*] "A rascal, and disguised and suborned for that imposture,"—O villainy! O villainy!— "by the contrivance of—"

LADY WISHFORT I shall faint, I shall die, oh!

FOIBLE [*aside to Waitwell*] Say 'tis your nephew's hand—quickly, his plot, swear it, swear it!

WAITWELL Here's a villain! madam, don't you perceive it, don't you see it?

LADY WISHFORT Too well, too well! I have seen too much.

WAITWELL I told you at first I knew the hand.— A woman's hand! The rascal writes a sort of a large hand; your Roman hand—I saw there was a throat to be cut presently. If he were my son, as he is my nephew, I'd pistol him!

FOIBLE O treachery!—But are you sure, Sir Rowland, it is his writing?

WAITWELL Sure! am I here? do I live? do I love this pearl of India? I have twenty letters in my pocket from him in the same character.

LADY WISHFORT How!

FOIBLE O what luck it is, Sir Rowland, that you were present at this juncture! This was the business that brought Mr. Mirabell disguised to Madam Millamant this afternoon. I thought something was contriving when he stole by me and would have hid his face.

LADY WISHFORT How, how!—I heard the villain was in the house indeed; and now I remember, my niece went away abruptly when Sir Wilfull was to have made his addresses.

FOIBLE Then, then, madam, Mr. Mirabell waited for her in her chamber! but I would not tell your ladyship to discompose you when you were to receive Sir Rowland.

WAITWELL Enough, his date is short.

FOIBLE No, good Sir Rowland, don't incur the law.

WAITWELL Law! I care not for law. I can but die, and 'tis in a good cause.—My lady shall be satisfied of my truth and innocence, though it cost me my life.

LADY WISHFORT No, dear Sir Rowland, don't fight; if you should be killed I must never show my face; or hanged—Oh, consider my reputation, Sir Rowland!—No, you shan't fight— I'll go in and examine my niece; I'll make her confess. I conjure you, Sir Rowland, by all your love, not to fight.

WAITWELL I am charmed, madam; I obey. But some proof you must let me give you; I'll go for a black box which contains the writings of my whole estate, and deliver that into your hands.

LADY WISHFORT Ay, dear Sir Rowland, that will be some comfort; bring the black box.

WAITWELL And may I presume to bring a contract to be signed this night? may I hope so far?

LADY WISHFORT Bring what you will; but come alive, pray come alive. Oh, this is a happy discovery!

WAITWELL Dead or alive I'll come—and married we will be in spite of treachery; ay, and get an heir that shall defeat the last remaining glimpse of hope in my abandoned nephew. Come, my buxom widow:

Ere long you shall substantial proofs receive,
That I'm an errant knight—

FOIBLE [*aside*]   Or arrant knave.
[*Exeunt.*]

Act Five

SCENE ONE

A room in Lady Wishfort's house. Lady Wishfort and Foible.

LADY WISHFORT Out of my house, out of my house, thou viper! thou serpent, that I have fostered! thou bosom traitress, that I raised from nothing!—Begone! begone! begone!—go! go!—That I took from washing of old gauze and weaving of dead hair,[81] with a bleak blue nose over a chafing-dish of starved embers, and dining behind a traverse rag, in a shop no bigger than a birdcage!—Go, go! starve again, do, do!

FOIBLE Dear madam, I'll beg pardon on my knees.

LADY WISHFORT Away! out! out!—Go, set up for yourself again!—Do, drive a trade, do, with your three-pennyworth of small ware, flaunting upon a packthread, under a brandyseller's bulk,[82] or against a dead wall by a balladmonger! Go, hang out an old Frisoneer gorget,[83] with a yard of yellow colberteen again. Do; an old gnawed mask, two rows of pins, and a child's fiddle; a glass necklace with the beads broken, and a quilted nightcap with one ear. Go, go, drive a trade!—These were your commodities, you treacherous trull! This was the merchandise you dealt in when I took you into my house, placed you next myself, and

made you governante of my whole family! You have forgot this, have you, now you have feathered your nest?

FOIBLE No, no, dear madam. Do but hear me; have but a moment's patience, I'll confess all. Mr. Mirabell seduced me; I am not the first that he has wheedled with his dissembling tongue; your ladyship's own wisdom has been deluded by him; then how should I, a poor ignorant, defend myself? O madam, if you knew but what he promised me, and how he assured me your ladyship should come to no damage!—Or else the wealth of the Indies should not have bribed me to conspire against so good, so sweet, so kind a lady as you have been to me.

LADY WISHFORT No damage! What, to betray me, and marry me to a cast-servingman! to make me a receptacle, an hospital for a decayed pimp! No damage! O thou frontless impudence, more than a big-bellied actress!

FOIBLE Pray, do but hear me, madam; he could not marry you ladyship, madam.—No, indeed, his marriage was to have been void in law, for he was married to me first, to secure your ladyship. He could not have bedded your ladyship; for if he had consummated with your ladyship, he must have run the risk of the law, and been put upon his clergy.[84]—Yes, indeed, I inquired of the law in that case before I would meddle or make.

81 Making wigs.

82 Stall.

83 A woolen collar. Colberteen is a cheap, coarse lace.

84 Required to prove his ability to read in order to escape the death penalty.

LADY WISHFORT   What, then. I have been your property, have I? I have been convenient to you, it seems!—While you were catering for Mirabell, I have been broker for you! What, have you made a passive bawd of me?—This exceeds all precedent; I am brought to fine uses, to become a botcher of second-hand marriages between Abigails and Andrews![85]—I'll couple you!—Yes, I'll baste you together, you and your Philanderer! I'll Duke's Place you, as I am a person! Your turtle is in custody already: you shall coo in the same cage if there be a constable or warrant in the parish. [*Exit.*]

FOIBLE   Oh, that ever I was born! Oh, that I was ever married!—A bride!—ay, I shall be a Bridewell-bride.[86]—Oh!
[*Enter Mrs. Fainall.*]

MRS. FAINALL   Poor Foible, what's the matter?

FOIBLE   O madam, my lady's gone for a constable. I shall be had to a justice and put to Bridewell to beat hemp. Poor Waitwell's gone to prison already.

MRS. FAINALL   Have a good heart, Foible; Mirabell's gone to give security for him. This is all Marwood's and my husband's doing.

FOIBLE   Yes, yes; I know it, madam. She was in my lady's closet, and overheard all that you said to me before dinner. She sent the letter to my lady; and that missing effect, Mr. Fainall laid this plot to arrest Waitwell when he pretended to go for the papers; and in the meantime Mrs. Marwood declared all to my lady.

MRS. FAINALL   Was there no mention made of me in the letter? My mother does not suspect my being in the confederacy? I fancy Marwood has not told her, though she has told my husband.

FOIBLE   Yes, madam; but my lady did not see that part; we stifled the letter before she read so far—Has that mischievous devil told Mr. Fainall of your ladyship then?

MRS. FAINALL   Ay, all's out—my affair with Mirabell—everything discovered. This is the last day of our living together, that's my comfort.

FOIBLE   Indeed, madam; and so 'tis a comfort if

[85] Generic names for servants.
[86] Bridewell was a prison.

you knew all—he has been even with your ladyship, which I could have told you long enough since, but I love to keep peace and quietness by my goodwill. I had rather bring friends together than set 'em at distance. But Mrs. Marwood and he are nearer related than ever their parents thought for.

MRS. FAINALL   Sayest thou so, Foible? canst thou prove this?

FOIBLE   I can take my oath of it, madam; so can Mrs. Mincing. We have had many a fair word from Madam Marwood, to conceal something that passed in our chamber one evening when you were at Hyde Park; and we were thought to have gone a-walking, but we went up unawares—though we were sworn to secrecy too. Madam Marwood took a book and swore us upon it, but it was but a book of poems. So long as it was not a Bible-oath, we may break it with a safe conscience.

MRS. FAINALL   This discovery is the most opportune thing I could wish.—Now, Mincing!
[*Enter Mincing.*]

MINCING   My lady would speak with Mrs. Foible, mem. Mr. Mirabell is with her; he has set your spouse at liberty, Mrs. Foible, and would have you hide yourself in my lady's closet till my old lady's anger is abated. Oh, my old lady is in a perilous passion at something Mr. Fainall has said; he swears, and my old lady cries. There's a fearful hurricane, I vow. He says, mem, how that he'll have my lady's fortune made over to him, or he'll be divorced.

MRS. FAINALL   Does your lady or Mirabell know that?

MINCING   Yes, mem; they have sent me to see if Sir Wilfull be sober, and to bring him to them. My lady is resolved to have him, I think, rather than lose such a vast sum as six thousand pounds.—O come, Mrs. Foible, I hear my old lady.

MRS. FAINALL   Foible, you must tell Mincing that she must prepare to vouch when I call her.

FOIBLE   Yes, yes, madam.

MINCING   O yes, mem, I'll vouch anything for your ladyship's service, be what it will.
[*Exeunt Mincing and Foible. Enter Lady Wishfort and Mrs. Marwood.*]

LADY WISHFORT   O my dear friend, how can I

enumerate the benefits that I had received from your goodness! To you I owe the timely discovery of the false vows of Mirabell; to you I owe the detection of the imposter Sir Rowland. And now you are become an intercessor with my son-in-law, to save the honor of my house and compound for the frailties of my daughter. Well, friend, you are enough to reconcile me to the bad world, or else I would retire to deserts and solitudes, and feed harmless sheep by groves and purling streams. Dear Marwood, let us leave the world, and retire by ourselves and be shepherdesses.

MRS. MARWOOD   Let us first dispatch the affair in hand, madam. We shall have leisure to think of retirement afterwards. Here is one who is concerned in the treaty.

LADY WISHFORT   Oh, daughter, daughter! is it possible thou shouldst be my child, bone of my bone, and flesh of my flesh, and, as I may say, another me, and yet transgress the most minute particle of severe virtue? Is it possible you should lean aside to iniquity, who have been cast in the direct mould of virtue? I have not only been a mould but a pattern for you, and a model for you, after you were brought into the world.

MRS. FAINALL   I don't understand your ladyship.

LADY WISHFORT   Not understand! Why, have you not been naught?[87] have you not been sophisticated? Not understand! here I am ruined to compound for your caprices and your cuckoldoms. I must pawn my plate and my jewels, and ruin my niece, and all little enough—

MRS. FAINALL   I am wronged and abused, and so are you. 'Tis a false accusation, as false as hell, as false as your friend there, aye, or your friend's friend, my false husband.

MRS. MARWOOD   My friend, Mrs. Fainall! your husband my friend! what do you mean?

MRS. FAINALL   I know what I mean, madam, and so do you; and so shall the world at a time convenient.

MRS. MARWOOD   I am sorry to see you so passionate, madam. More temper would look more like innocence. But I have done. I am sorry my zeal to serve your ladyship and

family should admit of misconstruction, or make me liable to affronts. You will pardon me, madam, if I meddle no more with an affair in which I am not personally concerned.

LADY WISHFORT   O dear friend, I am so ashamed that you should meet with such returns!—[To Mrs. Fainall] You ought to ask pardon on your knees, ungrateful creature! she deserves more from you than all your life can accomplish.—[To Mrs. Marwood] Oh, don't leave me destitute in this perplexity!—no, stick to me, my good genius.

MRS. FAINALL   I tell you, madam, you are abused. —Stick to you! ay, like a leech, to suck your best blood—she'll drop off when she's full. Madam, you shan't pawn a bodkin, nor part with a brass counter, in composition for me. I defy 'em all. Let 'em prove their aspersions; I know my own innocence, and dare stand a trial. [Exit.]

LADY WISHFORT   Why, if she should be innocent, if she should be wronged after all, ha?—I don't know what to think—and I promise you her education has been unexceptionable—I may say it; for I chiefly made it my own care to initiate her very infancy in the rudiments of virtue, and to impress upon her tender years a young odium and aversion to the very sight of men. Ay, friend, she would ha' shrieked if she had but seen a man till she was in her teens. As I am a person 'tis true—she was never suffered to play with a male child, though but in coats; nay, her very babies[88] were of the feminine gender. Oh, she never looked a man in the face but her own father, or the chaplain, and him we made a shift to put upon her for a woman, by the help of his long garments and his sleek face, till she was going in her fifteen.

MRS. MARWOOD   'Twas much she should be deceived so long.

LADY WISHFORT   I warrant you, or she would never have borne to have been catechised by him; and have heard his long lectures against singing and dancing, and such debaucheries; and going to filthy plays, and profane music-meetings, where the lewd trebles squeak noth-

---

[87] Naughty. "Sophisticated" means "corrupted."

[88] Dolls.

WILLIAM CONGREVE

ing but bawdy, and the basses roar blasphemy. Oh, she would have swooned at the sight or name of an obscene play-book!—and can I think, after all this, that my daughter can be naught? What, a whore? and thought it excommunication to set her foot within the door of a playhouse! O dear friend, I can't believe it, no, no! as she says, let him prove it, let him prove it.

MRS. MARWOOD   Prove it, madam! What, and have your name prostituted in a public court! yours and your daughter's reputation worried at the bar by a pack of bawling lawyers! To be ushered in with an "Oyez" of scandal; and have your case opened by an old fumbling lecher in a quoif like a man-midwife; to bring your daughter's infamy to light; to be a theme for legal punsters and quibblers by the statute; and become a jest against a rule of court, where there is no precedent for a jest in any record—not even in Doomsday Book; to discompose the gravity of the bench, and provoke naughty interrogatories in more naughty law Latin; while the good judge, tickled with the proceeding, simpers under a grey beard, and fidgets off and on his cushion as if he had swallowed cantharides, or sat upon cowitch![89]—

LADY WISHFORT   Oh, 'tis very hard!

MRS. MARWOOD   And then to have my young revellers of the Temple take notes, like 'prentices at a conventicle; and after, talk it over again in commons, or before drawers in an eating-house.[90]

LADY WISHFORT   Worse and worse!

MRS. MARWOOD   Nay, this is nothing; if it would end here 'twere well. But it must, after this, be consigned by the shorthand writers to the public press; and from thence be transferred to the hands, nay into the throats and lungs of hawkers, with voices more licentious than the loud flounderman's or the woman that cries grey peas. And this you must hear till you are

[89] Cowhage, a plant with pods which cause intolerable itching.

[90] Law students would be required to take notes like apprentices being catechized by their puritanical masters, then would talk it over in the school dining hall or before the waiters in a tavern.

stunned; nay, you must hear nothing else for some days.

LADY WISHFORT   Oh, 'tis insupportable! No, no, dear friend, make it up, make it up; ay, ay, I'll compound. I'll give up all, myself and my all, my niece and her all—anything, everything for composition.

MRS. MARWOOD   Nay, madam, I advise nothing, I only lay before you, as a friend, the inconveniences which perhaps you have overseen. Here comes Mr. Fainall; if he will be satisfied to huddle up all in silence, I shall be glad. You must think I would rather congratulate than condole with you.

[Enter Fainall.]

LADY WISHFORT   Ay, ay, I do not doubt it, dear Marwood; no, no, I do not doubt it.

FAINALL   Well, madam, I have suffered myself to be overcome by the importunity of this lady, your friend; and am content you shall enjoy your own proper estate during life, on condition you oblige yourself never to marry, under such penalty as I think convenient.

LADY WISHFORT   Never to marry!

FAINALL   No more Sir Rowlands; the next imposture may not be so timely detected.

MRS. MARWOOD   That condition, I dare answer, my lady will consent to without difficulty; she has already but too much experienced the perfidiousness of men.—Besides, madam, when we retire to our pastoral solitude we shall bid adieu to all other thoughts.

LADY WISHFORT   Ay, that's true; but in case of necessity, as of health, or some such emergency——

FAINALL   Oh, if you are prescribed marriage, you shall be considered; I will only reserve to myself the power to choose for you. If your physic be wholesome, it matters not who is your apothecary. Next, my wife shall settle on me the remainder of her fortune not made over already; and for her maintenance depend entirely on my discretion.

LADY WISHFORT   This is most inhumanly savage; exceeding the barbarity of a Muscovite husband.

FAINALL   I learned it from his Czarish majesty's retinue, in a winter evening's conference over brandy and pepper, amongst other secrets of matrimony and policy as they are at present practised in the northern hemisphere. But this must be agreed unto, and that positively. Lastly, I will be endowed, in right of my wife, with that six thousand pounds which is the moiety of Mrs. Millamant's fortune in your possession; and which she has forfeited (as will appear by the last will and testament of your deceased husband, Sir Jonathan Wishfort) by her disobedience in contracting herself against your consent or knowledge; and by refusing the offered match with Sir Wilfull Witwoud, which you, like a careful aunt, had provided for her.

LADY WISHFORT My nephew was *non compos*,[91] and could not make his addresses.

FAINALL I come to make demands—I'll hear no objections.

LADY WISHFORT You will grant me time to consider?

FAINALL Yes, while the instrument is drawing, to which you must set your hand till more sufficient deeds can be perfected: which I will take care shall be done with all possible speed. In the meantime I'll go for the said instrument, and till my return you may balance this matter in your own discretion. [*Exit.*]

LADY WISHFORT This insolence is beyond all precedent, all parallel; must I be subject to this merciless villain?

MRS. MARWOOD 'Tis severe indeed, madam, that you should smart for your daughter's wantonness.

LADY WISHFORT 'Twas against my consent that she married this barbarian, but she would have him, though her year was not out.—Ah! her first husband, my son Languish, would not have carried it thus. Well, that was my choice, this is hers: she is matched now with a witness. —I shall be mad!—Dear friend, is there no comfort for me? must I live to be confiscated at this rebel-rate?—Here come two more of my Egyptian plagues too.

[*Enter Mrs. Millamant and Sir Wilfull Witwoud.*]

SIR WILFULL Aunt, your servant.

LADY WISHFORT Out, caterpillar, call not me aunt! I know thee not!

SIR WILFULL I confess I have been a little in disguise, as they say.—'Sheart, and I'm sorry for't. What would you have? I hope I have committed no offence, aunt—and if I did I am willing to make satisfaction; and what can a man say fairer? If I have broke anything I'll pay for't, an it cost a pound. And so let that content for what's past, and make no more words. For what's to come, to pleasure you I'm willing to marry my cousin. So pray let's all be friends; she and I are agreed upon the matter before a witness.

LADY WISHFORT How's this, dear niece? have I any comfort? can this be true?

MRS. MILLAMANT I am content to be a sacrifice to your repose, madam; and to convince you that I had no hand in the plot, as you were misinformed. I have laid my commands on Mirabell to come in person, and be a witness that I give my hand to the flower of knighthood: and for the contract that passed between Mirabell and me, I have obliged him to make a resignation of it in your ladyship's presence. He is without, and waits your leave for admittance.

LADY WISHFORT Well, I'll swear I am something revived at this testimony of your obedience; but I cannot admit that traitor. I fear I cannot fortify myself to support his appearance. He is as terrible to me as a Gorgon; if I see him I fear I shall turn to stone, and petrify incessantly.

MRS. MILLAMANT If you disoblige him, he may resent your refusal and insist upon the contract still. Then 'tis the last time he will be offensive to you.

LADY WISHFORT Are you sure it will be the last time?—If I were sure of that—shall I never see him again?

MRS. MILLAMANT Sir Wilfull, you and he are to travel together, are you not?

SIR WILFULL 'Sheart, the gentleman's a civil gentleman, aunt; let him come in. Why, we are sworn brothers and fellow-travellers.—We are to be Pylades and Orestes,[92] he and I.—He is to be my interpreter in foreign parts. He has been overseas once already; and with proviso

---

[91] "Not in his right mind."

[92] From Greek legend: types of faithful friends.

WILLIAM CONGREVE

that I marry my cousin, will cross 'em once again only to bear me company.—'Sheart, I'll call him in—an I set on't once, he shall come in; and see who'll hinder him. [*Exit.*]

MRS. MARWOOD [*aside*] This is precious fooling, if it would pass; but I'll know the bottom of it.

LADY WISHFORT O dear Marwood, you are not going.

MRS. MARWOOD Not far, madam; I'll return immediately.

[*Exit. Enter Sir Wilfull and Mirabell.*]

SIR WILFULL Look up, man, I'll stand by you; 'sbud an she do frown, she can't kill you;—besides—harkee, she dare not frown desperately, because her face is none of her own. 'Sheart, an she should, her forehead would wrinkle like the coat of a cream-cheese; but mum for that, fellow-traveller.

MIRABELL If a deep sense of the many injuries I have offered to so good a lady, with a sincere remorse, and a hearty contrition, can but obtain the least glance of compassion, I am too happy. Ah, madam, there was a time!—but let it be forgotten—I confess I have deservedly forfeited the high place I once held of sighing at your feet. Nay, kill me not, by turning from me in disdain. I come not to plead for favor —nay, not for pardon; I am a suppliant only for your pity—I am going where I never shall behold you more—

SIR WILFULL How, fellow-traveller! you shall go by yourself then.

MIRABELL Let me be pitied first, and afterwards forgotten.—I ask no more.

SIR WILFULL By'r Lady, a very reasonable request, and will cost you nothing, aunt! Come, come, forgive and forget, aunt; why you must, an you are a Christian.

MIRABELL Consider, madam, in reality, you could not receive much prejudice. It was an innocent device; though I confess it had a face of guiltiness, it was at most an artifice which love contrived—and errors which love produces have even been accounted venial. At least think it is punishment enough that I have lost what in my heart I hold most dear, that to your cruel indignation I have offered up this beauty, and with her my peace and quiet; nay, all my hopes of future comfort.

SIR WILFULL An he does not move me, would I may never be o' the quorum!—an it were not as good a deed as to drink, to give her to him again, I would I might never take shipping!— Aunt, if you don't forgive quickly, I shall melt, I can tell you that. My contract went no farther than a little mouth-glue,[93] and that's hardly dry—one doleful sigh more from my fellow-traveller, and 'tis dissolved.

LADY WISHFORT Well, nephew, upon your account—Ah, he has a false insinuating tongue! —Well, sir, I will stifle my just resentment at my nephew's request. I will endeavor what I can to forget, but on proviso that you resign the contract with my niece immediately.

MIRABELL It is in writing, and with papers of concern; but I have sent my servant for it, and will deliver it to you, with all acknowledgements for your transcendent goodness.

LADY WISHFORT [*aside*] Oh, he has witchcraft in his eyes and tongue!—When I did not see him, I could have bribed a villain to his assassination; but his appearance rakes the embers which have so long lain smothered in my breast.

[*Enter Fainall and Mrs. Marwood.*]

FAINALL Your date of deliberation, madam, is expired. Here is the instrument; are you prepared to sign?

LADY WISHFORT If I were prepared, I am not impowered. My niece exerts a lawful claim, having matched herself by my direction to Sir Wilfull.

FAINALL That sham is too gross to pass on me —though 'tis imposed on you, madam.

MRS. MILLAMANT Sir, I have given my consent.

MIRABELL And, sir, I have resigned my pretensions.

SIR WILFULL And, sir, I assert my right and will maintain it in defiance of you, sir, and of your instrument. 'Sheart, an you talk of an instrument, sir, I have an old fox[94] by my thigh shall hack your instrument of ram vellum[95] to shreds, sir!—it shall not be sufficient for a

---

[93] Saliva.

[94] Sword.

[95] Legal documents written on sheepskin or parchment.

mittimus[96] or a tailor's measure. Therefore withdraw your instrument, sir, or by'r Lady, I shall draw mine.

LADY WISHFORT Hold, nephew, hold!

MRS. MILLAMANT Good Sir Wilfull, respite your valor.

FAINALL Indeed! Are you provided of your guard, with your single beef-eater there? But I'm prepared for you, and insist upon my first proposal. You shall submit your own estate to my management, and absolutely make over my wife's to my sole use, as pursuant to the purport and tenor of this other covenant.—I suppose, madam, your consent is not requisite in this case; nor, Mr. Mirabell, your resignation; nor, Sir Wilfull, your right.—You may draw your fox if you please, sir, and make a bear-garden flourish somewhere else; for here it will not avail. This, my Lady Wishfort, must be subscribed, or your darling daughter's turned adrift, like a leaky hulk, to sink or swim, as she and the current of this lewd town can agree.

LADY WISHFORT Is there no means, no remedy to stop my ruin? Ungrateful wretch! dost thou not owe thy being, thy subsistence, to my daughter's fortune?

FAINALL I'll answer you when I have the rest of it in my possession.

MIRABELL But that you would not accept of a remedy from my hands—I own I have not deserved you should owe any obligation to me; or else perhaps I could advise—

LADY WISHFORT Oh, what? to save me and my child from ruin, from want, I'll forgive all that's past; nay, I'll consent to anything to come, to be delivered from this tyranny.

MIRABELL Aye, madam; but that is too late; my reward is intercepted. You have disposed of her who only could have made me a compensation for all my services; but be it as it may, I am resolved I'll serve you! you shall not be wronged in this savage manner.

LADY WISHFORT How! Dear Mr. Mirabell, can you be so generous at last! But it is not possible. Harkee, I'll break my nephew's match;

[96] Warrant.

you shall have my niece yet, and all her fortune, if you can but save me from this imminent danger.

MIRABELL Will you? I'll take you at your word. I ask no more. I must have leave for two criminals to appear.

LADY WISHFORT Aye, aye, anybody, anybody!

MIRABELL Foible is one, and a penitent.

[*Enter Mrs. Fainall, Foible, and Mincing.*]

MRS. MARWOOD [*to Fainall*] O my shame! [*Mirabell and Lady Wishfort go to Mrs. Fainall and Foible.*] These corrupt things are brought hither to expose me.

FAINALL If it must all come out, why let 'em know it; 'tis but the way of the world. That shall not urge me to relinquish or abate one tittle of my terms; no, I will insist the more.

FOIBLE Yes, indeed, madam. I'll take my Bible oath of it.

MINCING And so will I, mem.

LADY WISHFORT O Marwood, Marwood, art thou false? my friend deceive me! hast thou been a wicked accomplice with that profligate man?

MRS. MARWOOD Have you so much ingratitude and injustice to give credit against your friend, to the aspersions of two such mercenary trulls?

MINCING Mercenary, mem? I scorn your words. 'Tis true we found you and Mr. Fainall in the blue garret; by the same token, you swore us to secrecy upon Messalina's[97] poems. Mercenary! No, if we would have been mercenary, we should have held our tongues; you would have bribed us sufficiently.

FAINALL Go, you are an insignificant thing!—Well, what are you the better for this; is this Mr. Mirabell's expedient? I'll be put off no longer.—You, thing that was a wife, shall smart for this! I will not leave thee wherewithall to hide thy shame; your body shall be naked as your reputation.

MRS. FAINALL I despise you, and defy your malice—you have aspersed me wrongfully—I have proved your falsehood—go, you and your treacherous—I will not name it, but starve together—perish!

[97] Messalina was a notorious Roman Empress; but this is probably Mincing's mispronunciation of "Miscellaneous."

FAINALL Not while you are worth a groat, indeed, my dear.—Madam, I'll be fooled no longer.

LADY WISHFORT Ah, Mr. Mirabell, this is small comfort, the detection of this affair.

MIRABELL Oh, in good time—your leave for the other offender and penitent to appear, madam. [*Enter Waitwell with a box of writings.*]

LADY WISHFORT O Sir Rowland!—Well, rascal!

WAITWELL What your ladyship pleases. I have brought the black box at last, madam.

MIRABELL Give it me.—Madam, you remember your promise?

LADY WISHFORT Ay, dear sir.

MIRABELL Where are the gentlemen?

WAITWELL At hand, sir, rubbing their eyes—just risen from sleep.

FAINALL 'Sdeath, what's this to me? I'll not wait your private concerns.

[*Enter Petulant and Witwoud.*]

PETULANT How now? What's the matter? whose hand's out?

WITWOUD Heyday! what, are you all got together like players at the end of the last act?

MIRABELL You may remember, gentlemen, I once requested your hands as witnesses to a certain parchment.

WITWOUD Ay, I do, my hand I remember—Petulant set his mark.

MIRABELL You wrong him; his name is fairly written, as shall appear.—[*Undoing the box*] You do not remember, gentlemen, anything of what that parchment contained?

WITWOUD No.

PETULANT Not I; I writ, I read nothing.

MIRABELL Very well, now you shall know.—Madam, your promise.

LADY WISHFORT Ay, ay, sir, upon my honor.

MIRABELL Mr. Fainall, it is now time that you should know that your lady, while she was at her own disposal, and before you had by your insinuations wheedled her out of a pretended settlement of the greatest part of her fortune—

FAINALL Sir! pretended!

MIRABELL Yes, sir, I say that this lady while a widow, having, it seems, received some cautions respecting your inconstancy and tyranny of temper, which from her own partial opinion and fondness of you she could never have suspected—she did, I say, by the wholesome advice of friends, and of sages learned in the laws of this land, deliver this same as her act and deed to me in trust, and to the uses within mentioned. You may read if you please [*holding out the parchment*]—though perhaps what is written on the back may serve your occasions.

FAINALL Very likely, sir, what's here?—Damnation! [*Reads*] "A deed of conveyance of the whole estate real of Arabella Languish, widow, in trust to Edward Mirabell."—Confusion!

MIRABELL Even so, sir; 'tis the *Way of the World,* sir, of the widows of the world. I suppose this deed may bear an elder date than what you have obtained from your lady?

FAINALL Perfidious fiend! then thus I'll be revenged. [*Offers to run at Mrs. Fainall.*]

SIR WILFULL Hold, sir! now you make your bear-garden flourish somewhere else, sir.

FAINALL Mirabell, you shall hear of this, sir, be sure you shall.—Let me pass, oaf! [*Exit.*]

MRS. FAINALL Madam, you seem to stifle your resentment; you had better give it vent.

MRS. MARWOOD Yes, it shall have vent—and to your confusion; or I'll perish in the attempt. [*Exit.*]

LADY WISHFORT O daughter, daughter! 'tis plain thou hast inherited thy mother's prudence.

MRS. FAINALL Thank Mr. Mirabell, a cautious friend, to whose advice all is owing.

LADY WISHFORT Well, Mr. Mirabell, you have kept your promise—and I must perform mine. —First, I pardon, for your sake, Sir Rowland there, and Foible. The next thing is to break the matter to my nephew—and how to do that—

MIRABELL For that, madam, give yourself no trouble; let me have your consent. Sir Wilfull is my friend; he has had compassion upon lovers, and generously engaged a volunteer in this action for our service; and now designs to prosecute his travels.

SIR WILFULL 'Sheart, aunt, I have no mind to marry. My cousin's a fine lady, and the gentleman loves her, and she loves him, and they deserve one another; my resolution is to see foreign parts—I have set on't—and when I'm set on't I must do't. And if these two gentlemen would travel too, I think they may be spared.

PETULANT For my part, I say little—I think things are best off or on.

WITWOUD I'gad, I understand nothing of the matter; I'm in a maze yet, like a dog in a dancing-school.

LADY WISHFORT Well, sir, take her, and with her all the joy I can give you.

MRS. MILLAMANT Why does not the man take me? Would you have me give myself to you over again?

MIRABELL Ay, and over and over again [*kissing her hand*]; I would have you as often as possibly I can. Well, Heaven grant I love you not too well; that's all my fear.

SIR WILFULL 'Sheart, you'll have time enough to toy after you're married; or if you will toy now, let us have a dance in the mean time, that we who are not lovers may have some other employment besides looking on.

MIRABELL With all my heart, dear Sir Wilfull.

What shall we do for music?

FOIBLE O sir, some that were provided for Sir Rowland's entertainment are yet within call. [*A dance.*]

LADY WISHFORT As I am a person, I can hold out no longer;—I have wasted my spirits so today already, but I am ready to sink under the fatigue; and I cannot but have some fears upon me yet, that my son Fainall will pursue some desperate course.

MIRABELL Madam, disquiet not yourself on that account; to my knowledge his circumstances are such he must of force comply. For my part, I will contribute all that in me lies to a reunion; in the mean time, [*to Mrs. Fainall*] madam, let me before these witnesses restore to you this deed of trust; it may be a means, well-managed, to make you live easily together.

From hence let those be warned who mean
  to wed;
Lest mutual falsehood stain the bridal bed;
For each deceiver to his cost may find,
That marriage-frauds too oft are paid in kind.
[*Exeunt.*]

Epilogue

MRS. MILLAMANT After our Epilogue this crowd
  dismisses,
I'm thinking how this play'll be pulled to
  pieces.
But pray consider, ere you doom its fall,
How hard a thing 'twould be to please you all.
There are some critics so with spleen diseased,
They scarcely come inclining to be pleased:
And sure he must have more than mortal skill,
Who pleases any one against his will.
Then, all bad poets we are sure are foes,
And how their number's swelled, the town well
  knows:
In shoals I've marked 'em judging in the pit;
Though they're on no pretence for judgment fit,
But that they have been damned for want of wit.
Since when, they by their own offences taught,
Set up for spies on plays and finding fault.
Others there are whose malice we'd prevent;
Such who watch plays with scurrilous intent
To mark out who by characters are meant.
And though no perfect likeness they can trace,

Yet each pretends to know the copied face.
Those with false glosses feed their own ill-
  nature,
And turn to libel what was meant a satire.
May such malicious fops this fortune find,
To think themselves alone the fools designed!
If any are so arrogantly vain,
To think they singly can support a scene,
And furnish fool enough to entertain.
For well the learn'd and the judicious know
That satire scorns to stoop so meanly low
As any one abstracted fop to show.
For, as when painters form a matchless face,
They from each fair one catch some different
  grace;
And shining features in one portrait blend,
To which no single beauty must pretend;
So poets oft do in one piece expose
Whole *belles assemblées*[98] of coquettes and
  beaux.

[98] Polite gatherings.

THE PLOT of The Way of the World *has borne much of the blame for the play's initial lack of success; but those who dislike the plot are not agreed upon whether it moves too little or too much.*

The Way of the World is the best-written, the most dazzling, the most intellectually accomplished of all English comedies, perhaps of all the comedies of the world. But it has the defects of the very qualities which make it so brilliant. A perfect comedy does not sparkle so much, is not so exquisitely written, because it needs to advance, to develop. . . . The beginning of the third act, the description of Mirabell's feelings in the opening scene, and many other parts of *The Way of the World,* are not to be turned over, but to be re-read until the psychological subtlety of the sentiment, the perfume of the delicately chosen phrases, the music of the sentences, have produced their full effect upon the nerves. But, meanwhile, what of the action? The reader dies of a rose in aromatic pain, but the spectator fidgets in his stall, and wishes that the actors and actresses would be doing something. In no play of Congreve's is the literature so consummate, in none is the human interest in movement and surprise so utterly neglected, as in *The Way of the World.* . . . We have

slow, elaborate dialogue, spread out like some beautiful endless tapestry, and no action whatever. [Edmund Gosse, *Life of William Congreve,* Walter Scott, London, 1888, pp. 135–136.]

The comedy has plot, but it is obscure and teasingly intricate. Much of the action is narrated rather than dramatized. It is not unfolded progressively, but in compact bits separated by long stretches of dialogue justified only by its brilliance . . . all of the principal characters are related or about to become so. This device gives an artificial unity to the group, but keeping the relationship clear imposes unnecessary strain upon the attention of the audience. The scintillating dialogue and restless energy of the characters attract attention to themselves and away from the plot, but to convince oneself that the comedy has intricate plot one should try to narrate it in as few words as possible. [D. Crane Taylor, *William Congreve,* Oxford University Press, New York, 1931, p. 147.]

It is possible to admit a weakness of plot, while dismissing such weakness as unimportant.

As a matter of fact, whatever concessions [*The Way of the World*] makes to the mere mechanics of playwriting only do it harm, only enforce on the play one or two inferior characters and an ending that is stock and even stagy.

Almost every talented writer who sets about writing plays must be often plagued by the dilemma of writing for the theater or writing for himself. There are times when he virtually cannot do both. This is not a matter of "integrity," but of working in a medium that to be effective must quite literally achieve *effects*—something vivid or startling, carefully planted or staged. Stagecraft, to an extent not found in the craft of

other arts, is tricks. And the playwright is always menaced by dangers from both sides, by the Scylla of flatness, by the Charybdis of falsity. The artless method leads all too often to boredom, the artful method inspires disbelief.

Moreover, in the case of high comedy—of *The Misanthrope* or *The Way of the World*—we tend to deal (as mere realism does not) with the scarcely amendable faults and contradictions of human nature, with life as a process rather than as something that forges a plot. We are to understand that the conflict between an Alceste and a Célimène is unresolvable, and that the way of the world is no passing fashion, but an eternal fact. Action, in the realistic or dramatic sense, is not only a little too crude for high comedy; it is really a little irrelevant. There is too much awareness involved; and rather than the struggle against defeat that we find in drama, high com-edy has a skepticism that is very nearly defeatism. [Louis Kronenberger, *The Thread of Laughter*, Alfred A. Knopf, Inc., New York, 1952, pp. 140–141.]

The plot also has its earnest defenders. One defense analyzes the plot as a conflict over legacies.

The plot is primarily a struggle between two pairs of adulterers for the control of three legacies; the initial intrigue based on the Sir Rowland hoax; the counterintrigue on an exposure of the identity of Sir Rowland, a threatened divorce to avenge adultery, and a series of extortions to requite cuckoldry. The plot does not gyrate continually about Mirabell and Millamant; instead it evolves out of the hopes and fears of the four adulterers as they scheme to snare the ambivalent Lady Wishfort into an irrevocable disposal of the legacies. Unless this group of five is regarded as the center of the action, the entire play lacks unity; and neither the zany courtships nor the proviso scene of the fourth act are integrated with the aftermath of adultery theme. Moreover, the increased tempo and heightened suspense of the fifth act—emanating from Fainall's attempted extortion, his wife's denial of the unchastity charge, and Lady Wishfort's bewildered ambivalence—seem forced and melodramatic; and above all, the surprise rising from producing the valid deed of conveyance will seem merely a meretricious excrescence instead of an "artful solution of the *fable*." [Paul and Miriam Mueschke, *A New View of Congreve's Way of the World*, University of Michigan Press, Ann Arbor, Mich., 1958, p. 11.]

Another defense is concerned primarily with the organic purposes of the plot's seeming intricacy.

The supposed complexity of the plot, as we shall see, is intended to be confusing; the confusion is an essential part of the dramatic impact. In part the complication comes from the standard Restoration convention about intrigue. That is, as long as there is an inconsistency between appearances and emotions, power is given to the person who knows this inconsistency. The power ceases if the inconsistency ceases, if there are no secrets left to be discovered. More important, the plot becomes complex because Congreve deals out the secrets of the play so slowly, so gradually, that they assume an intricacy far beyond that of the actual situation.

Within this complicating convention, Congreve . . . makes four points: (1) he compares and contrasts two kinds of reality, emotional and dynastic; (2) he builds two actions, unraveling and emancipating; (3) he develops and evaluates his characters in terms of their relation to these two actions and these two kinds of reality; (4) finally, he unifies his material around a single Romantic idea.

The Way of the World deals with a typical family situation—a fight for the control of an estate. Presiding over the family at the beginning of the play is the absurd Lady Wishfort who holds in a "Cabal," a gossip club, her daughter Mrs. Fainall and her niece Millamant. She controls all of Mrs. Fainall's estate and part of Millamant's as well. As the plot thickens, a contest develops as to who shall get these estates from Lady Wishfort: Mr. Fainall or . . . Mirabell.

So far, so simple. But Congreve seems to complicate these fairly straightforward family relations. . . . To an audience, however, only two facts emerge: that Mrs. Fainall is Lady

WILLIAM CONGREVE

Wishfort's daughter and that Lady Wishfort has control over Millamant's estate. The other relationships, particularly the confusion of Witwouds, serve only to create the impression of a welter of consanguinity. Congreve is confusing his audience gratuitously, and we must infer he has some reason for doing so.

He does the same thing with the emotional relations that he does with the family structure. Behind the already complicated dynastic relations lie even more complicated emotional affairs. . . .

The discrepancy between the family structure and the emotional structure plays into the Restoration convention about intrigue: a discrepancy between appearances (the overt family relations) and "nature" (the hidden emotional facts) gives power to the man who knows the discrepancy. At the beginning of the play, Mirabell is trying to set up such a situation. . . . Finally . . . Mirabell wins the contest by knowing the ultimate discrepancy between appearance and nature. He produces a deed by Mrs. Fainall conveying all her estate to him as her trustee; she made it when she was a widow . . . and it therefore predates any deed Fainall could now obtain. These various deeds at the end of the play combine and fuse the two kinds of reality, dynastic and emotional, from which the play is built.

Congreve, even though the plot is complicated enough, makes it seem even more complicated. There are certain hidden facts—we could call them quanta of knowledge—and a large part of the so-called complexity simply involves revealing these facts, slowly unraveling the appearances which cover them over. There are only four such quanta in the play: Marwood's desire for Mirabell, Marwood's relationship with Fainall, Mirabell's past affair with Mrs. Fainall, and Mirabell's plot with his disguised servant. But Congreve gives the impression of far greater complexity by measuring out each secret slowly, person by person, until the final complete revelation. . . .

Congreve has unduly complicated both kinds of relationship, dynastic and emotional, and in both cases some of the complications are not essential to the plot. We must look for the reason. The confusion which is the prevailing atmosphere of the play becomes almost a kind of symbol for one of the points Congreve wants to make. That is, the confusion asks the question that underlies almost every facet of the play: What is the true interaction between these two kinds of relationships? . . . The technique is much the same as that in T. S. Eliot's *The Confidential Clerk,* where emotional and dynastic relations proliferate in the same way to define two kinds of reality and test their relative "realness." As it develops, *The Way of the World* does just exactly that. . . .

The unraveling with its final clue, the deed, suggests the relation between the two complex realities of family and emotional ties: that the "real" reality is the inward, emotional nature; this reality is a changing flux that gives birth to a more stable framework of overt social facts (dynastic relations); when, for whatever reason, these social facts are not true reflections of the underlying emotional relations (Mrs. Fainall's marriage, the projected "marriage" of Lady Wishfort to Mirabell's servant, and the like) a situation of power results in favor of one who knows the inconsistency; the antidote to such situations is to create an overt, social situation which will truly reflect the underlying realities. This interplay between two kinds of reality leads, naturally enough, to two kinds of action in the play. The first—I will call it the *unraveling*—peels off bit by bit the surface appearances to get at the real facts of emotion underneath. The second, which I will call the *emancipating,* sets up a new social structure based on those underlying emotional realities.

In the unraveling action the final deed is the final fact, the heart of the whole situation hidden in a mysterious black box. Just as Mirabell's contract with Millamant suggests an ideal of balance between the social and personal aspects of marriage, so this deed represents a fusion of the social and personal aspects of the entire dramatic situation. The deed is effective in law as a result of Mrs. Fainall's social and dynastic status: only as a widow could she make a valid conveyance of her property. Yet the deed formalized a hidden emotional situation. The deed is effective because it destroys the very *res* of

Fainall's actions; his motive is brought out into the open and dealt with directly as motive. In all these respects, this deed contrasts with the deed Fainall attempts to get from Lady Wishfort, which is based on an opposition of social and emotional situations. . . . Fainall's deed is an abortive attempt to make social pressure permanently dislocate emotions, to create a retrograde movement in which the fear of scandal separates Mirabell and Millamant. In the nature of things it fails. . . .

The deed is thus not only the most hidden secret in the unraveling action; it is also one of the foundation posts for the new social structure evolved in the emancipating action. In that slow emancipation, by the end of the play, all of the characters who are dependent on Lady Wishfort are freed. [Norman N. Holland, *The First Modern Comedies: The Significance of Etherege, Wycherley and Congreve*, Harvard University Press, Cambridge, Mass., 1959, pp. 176–182.]

The ambiguous title hints at the problems of morality and meaning in the play. A common interpretation sees Congreve, with most Restoration dramatists, as amoral at best, distinguished from his fellows only in possessing more ability and more detachment.

Life is accepted and observed—not as a problem, but a pageant. . . . Microcosm and macrocosm are justified in that they are plain to the senses. The whole duty of man is to talk, when he can, like Mirabell. The cheerful wickedness of Etherege has given place to a more rounded and systematic iniquity; Congreve's characters are epicures in pleasure, exquisites in villainy. Their morality is as smoothly asserted in conduct and precept as the philosophy of Pope, which confines the universe in a couplet, and dismisses its ruler in an epigram. . . . Congreve's theme is often but simple wickedness, empty of pleasure or lust. There is an equable finality about the morality of *The Way of the World*—a dead level of conscience against which is vividly thrown a brilliant variety of manners and habits. It is a final assertion of that noble laziness of mind which began with Etherege, in accepting and enjoying the vicissitudes of fortune, and ended, with Congreve, in despising them. Congreve seems ever to be passing his creatures in review with faint, expressive smiles of disdain. [John Palmer, *The Comedy of Manners*, G. Bell & Sons, Ltd., London, 1913, pp. 191–192.]

A somewhat more positive view finds a morality suggested through the play's tone.

The play is well named; its concern is not with this person's folly or that one's vice, but with all leisure-class society, its incentives of pleasure, its temptations to betray or misbehave. But if what we are watching is in one sense the way of the great world, where courteous words hide treacherous hearts, there is something else to be observed: not simply how self-indulgent or inconstant these people are, but how foiled and frustrated. They cannot, many of them, have what they want in the way of a husband or lover; they dare not believe in friendship or hope for love. They are trapped by the baseness of their own view of life and by the very selfishness of their own desires. Even in suffering they cannot find salvation, for they do not know how to suffer; their reaction, on feeling pain, is to try to inflict it elsewhere. Having shaken our heads in disapproval of them, we must at the last shake our heads more sadly, in dismay.

There is no need for others to moralize about them: they themselves point the moral all too vividly.

This is something apprehended in the midst of the spin and sparkle of language and wit. . . . It is a question of tone; the teaching of the play, so far as it does teach, is in the tone; Congreve is not only too good an artist to try to teach more overtly, he is perhaps too skeptical and baffled and—if you choose—superficial a philosopher to know how. He was, one supposes, the perfect worldling, with far too much taste and sensibility to acquiesce cynically in what he saw of life, and yet with too strong and pessimistic a sense of the way of the world—and too great an affinity for it—ever to protest very much. . . . We must look elsewhere for writers with more severe and positive values, for writers who aspire beyond tone to something like vision; but *The Way of the World* yet furnishes, in its own esthetic fashion, a sense of the melancholy in life, the awful hell of life. No tone could be more civilized than Congreve's, yet no story suggests how little being civilized avails. [Kronenberger, *op. cit.*, pp. 137–138.]

Other critics find in the play moral meanings which are more prominent, more complex, and more closely connected with plot and character.

In *The Way of the World* life is regarded not as a pageant but as a sequence of integrated experiences in which the present in invariably conditioned by the past and foreshadows the future. . . .

This brittle world of leisure and sophistication, like the Roman world upon which it is modeled, is rooted in inherited wealth. To remain in this coterie, wealth is essential; and throughout this comedy all the intrigue and counter-intrigue of the adulterers center on retaining or obtaining legacies. Congreve's protest against the way of the world is that of a man of reflective judgment who sees that happiness and the dignity of life are sacrificed to an exaggerated care for the means of living, to predatory legacy seeking, to false values, to the slavery of some ruling passion or appetite, to intellectual brilliance tarnished by moral weakness.

Congreve is not an apologist for, but rather a satirist of the way of the world. He castigates vice on two moral levels by contrasting the punishment of a pair of transgressors on the way to reformation with that of a pair on the way to degradation. Since the rake, the adulteress, the cast mistress, and the cuckold are astute, they are aware of their own social and emotional predicaments; consequently the play and interplay of their emotions and motives take on a deeper and subtler ethical significance. Unlike those buoyant comedies based on the initial stages of illicit intrigue, *The Way of the World* reveals the deceit and dissension rife in the final stages of adulterous intimacy; consequently the spirit of these scenes is not that of avid expectation but rather of sated disillusionment. The effect of adultery on the integration or disintegration of character is stressed; the transgressors by their conscious response to situations engendered by vicious conduct are ultimately either restored to integrity or branded with infamy. [Mueschke, *op. cit.*, pp. 12–13.]

A recurrent problem in Restoration comedy . . . was how to establish and convey an impression of a mean between the plain dealer and the double-dealer. . . . Congreve's solution in his last comedy was to depict the *savoir-faire* of the truewit as a norm, midway between the gratuitous asperity of the plain dealer and the calculated hypocrisy of the double-dealer. Since the excess of asperity leads to folly, the excess of hypocrisy, to knavery, neither plain dealer nor double-dealer is a suitable norm for realistic comedy; indeed, only the truewit is sufficiently balanced and resourceful to cope with those peculiarities of behavior which set one man too far apart from his fellows for the well-being of either. The approved mores, in this comedy, depend on a policy of laissez faire for those capable of self-direction, one of coercion for those incapable of self-discipline; the truewit, as an accredited representative of the group, restrains wayward egos from expanding beyond the predetermined limits regarded as socially and morally acceptable. After the distinction between the truewit and a witwoud is clarified, the nature of the norm determined, and the relation of corrigibility to the regeneration-degeneration motif understood, this conclusion, surprising though it may seem, emerges: the ethos of Congreve's most mature and reflective comedy is essentially conventional; it is the morality of the golden mean. [*Ibid.*, pp. 66–67.]

The world has two ways: the flux of emotions in time and the build-up and breakdown of discrepancies between nature and social appearances. Social forms build up until they become rigid, separate entities no longer connected to emotional realities and then break down—Mrs. Fainall's marriage, for example, or Marwood's friendship with Lady Wishfort.

The ways of the world, then, are cyclic. The play assumes two kinds of reality, public appearance (typified by family relations) and an inner, personal nature (typified by emotions). One "way" is that there is an organic flux of both inward and outward natures. Passions are quickly born, grow, and die. From them grow more slowly the outer, social relations of people (marriages and "breeding"), which in turn define and limit future passions. The other way is that there is and ought to be a difference (with Congreve, not necessarily a contradiction) between these two kinds of reality; one must retain a decorum and balance between them (as exemplified by the match between Mirabell and Millamant). Too much of a difference (Mrs. Fainall's marriage or her husband's blackmail) results in a situation where the social fact exerts undue restraint on the emotional. Too little difference leads to the absurdities of Sir Wilfull's behavior. [Holland, *op. cit.*, pp. 194–195.]

HENRIK IBSEN

1828–1906

Ibsen's impact upon the drama of the nineteenth century was shattering. After his plays had made the rounds of the great theaters and acting companies, the artificialities and exaggerations of the romantic drama could no longer dominate the stage, and the contrivances of the well-made play were no longer very convincing. Ibsen constructed his remarkable career in waves. Most of his early and least consequential plays were historical in theme and tended to be melodramatic in tone. Then came the two poetic dramas, Brand *(1865) and* Peer Gynt *(1867), both written in Rome, both large in scale and filled with the kind of probing exploration of character that fired a whole generation of theatergoers and playwrights. He was admired not only as a dramatic poet but as a moral teacher. The result, some years after his death, was a certain aversion to his work on the part of many, who found moral pronouncements all through Ibsen's plays, whether the playwright had placed them there or not, and therefore almost entirely missed Ibsen's subtlety of judgment or utter unwillingness to make any judgment at all. For as Bernard Shaw was quick to point out, far from being a self-righteous preacher, Ibsen was an unmasker of preachers and reformers, especially those who were full of their own virtue. The bite that accompanies Ibsen's exposures makes up for the dated elements in his social dramas,* The Pillars of Society, A Doll's House, Ghosts, *and* An Enemy of the People. *These four plays, written from 1875 to 1882, make up the third wave of Ibsen's plays. The fourth and last consists of great symbolic dramas, reaching from* The Wild Duck *(1884) and* Rosmersholm *(1886) to* John Gabriel Borkman *(1896) and* When We Dead Awaken *(1899). For such plays no generalization will do. Only the closest of readings, with full awareness that there must be some loss in translation from the Norwegian, can do them justice.*

Rosmersholm

A PLAY IN FOUR ACTS
TRANSLATED BY EVA LE GALLIENNE

Characters

JOHANNES ROSMER *owner of Rosmersholm; a former clergyman*

REBEKKA WEST *a member of the household*

PROFESSOR KROLL *Rosmer's brother-in-law*

ULRIK BRENDEL

PEDER MORTENSGAARD[1]

MRS. HELSETH *housekeeper at Rosmersholm*

[1] For stage purposes, often *Peter.*

The action takes place at Rosmersholm, an old estate in the neighborhood of a small town on a fjord on the west coast of Norway.

Act One

Sitting-room at Rosmersholm; spacious, old fashioned, and comfortable. In front, on the right, a stove decked with fresh birch branches and wild flowers. Farther back, on the same side, a door. In the back wall, folding doors opening into the hall. To the left, a window, and before it a stand with flowers and plants. Beside the stove a table with a sofa and easy chairs. On the walls, old and more recent portraits of clergymen, officers, and government officials in uniform. The window is open; so are the door into the hall and the house door beyond. Outside can be seen an avenue of fine old trees, leading up to the house. It is a summer evening, after sunset.

Rebekka West is sitting in an easy chair by the window, and crocheting a large white woolen shawl, which is nearly finished. She now and then looks out expectantly through the leaves of the plants. Mrs. Helseth presently enters.

MRS. HELSETH I suppose I had better start laying the table for supper, Miss?

REBEKKA Yes, do. Mr. Rosmer should be back in a few minutes.

MRS. HELSETH Aren't you sitting in a draught there, Miss?

REBEKKA Yes, there is a little draught. You might just close the window.

[*Mrs. Helseth shuts the door into the hall, and then comes to the window.*]

MRS. HELSETH [*about to shut the window, looks out*] Isn't that Mr. Rosmer out there now?

REBEKKA [*hastily*] Where? [*Rises.*] Yes, so it is. [*Stands behind the curtain.*] Stand back a little. Don't let him see us.

MRS. HELSETH [*draws back from window*] You see, Miss?—He's beginning to use the path by the mill again.

REBEKKA He used it the day before yesterday too. [*Peeps out between the curtains and the windowframe.*] But I wonder whether—

MRS. HELSETH Will he bring himself to cross the foot-bridge, do you think?

REBEKKA That's just what I want to see. [*After a pause.*] No, he's turning back. Today, again! He's going by the upper road. [*Leaves the window.*] A long way round.

MRS. HELSETH Well—Good Lord!—you can't blame him for not wanting to cross that bridge, Miss. When you think of what happened there—

REBEKKA [*folding up her work*] They certainly cling to their dead at Rosmersholm.

MRS. HELSETH Do you know what *I* think, Miss? I think it's the dead that cling to Rosmersholm.

REBEKKA [*looks at her*] How do you mean—the dead?

MRS. HELSETH It's as if they kept trying to come back; as if they couldn't quite free themselves from those they've left behind.

REBEKKA What an idea! What put that into your head?

MRS. HELSETH That would account for the White Horse, you see.

REBEKKA What is all this about a white horse, Mrs. Helseth?

MRS. HELSETH It's no use talking to you about it, Miss; you don't believe such things.

REBEKKA Do *you* believe them?

MRS. HELSETH [*goes and shuts the window*] You'd only make fun of me, Miss. [*Looks out.*] Look! Isn't that Mr. Rosmer on the path again—?

REBEKKA [*looks out*] Let me see. [*Goes to the window.*] No. Why—it's Professor Kroll!

MRS. HELSETH Yes, so it is.

REBEKKA What a funny thing! He seems to be coming here.

MRS. HELSETH He makes no bones about going over the foot-bridge—even if she was his own sister! Well, I suppose I'd better lay the table, Miss.

[*She goes out. Rebekka stands at the window for a short time; then smiles and nods to someone outside. It begins to grow dark.*]

REBEKKA [*goes to the door*] Oh, Mrs. Helseth! You'd better prepare a little something extra; something the Professor's specially fond of.

MRS. HELSETH [*outside*] Very well, Miss; I'll see to it.

REBEKKA [*opens the door to the hall*] Well—what a surprise! Welcome, my dear Professor!

KROLL [*in the hall, laying down his stick*] Many thanks. I hope I'm not disturbing you?

REBEKKA You! How can you say such things!

KROLL [*comes in*] Charming as ever! [*Looks around.*] Is Rosmer up in his room?

REBEKKA No, he's out for a walk. He's been gone a bit longer than usual; but he's sure to be here any minute. [*Indicating the sofa.*] Won't you sit down till he comes?

KROLL [*laying down his hat*] Many thanks. [*Sits down and looks about him.*] What nice things you've done to the old place! It's all so cheerful—flowers everywhere!

REBEKKA Mr. Rosmer's very fond of flowers.

KROLL And you are too, I suppose.

REBEKKA Yes, I am; I find them very soothing. We had to do without them though—until quite recently.

KROLL [*nods sadly*] I know; on account of poor Beata. Their scent seemed to overpower her.

REBEKKA Their colors, too. They upset her terribly.

KROLL Yes, I remember. [*In a lighter tone.*] Well—how are things going out here?

REBEKKA Oh, quietly and peacefully as usual; the days slip by—one day just like the last. But what about you? I hope Mrs. Kroll is well?

KROLL Oh, my dear Miss West, I'd rather not talk about my affairs. In family life one has to expect complications—especially in times like these.

REBEKKA [*sits in an armchair by the sofa*] You

haven't been to see us once, all during the holidays. Why haven't you? Tell me.

KROLL I didn't want to make a nuisance of myself.

REBEKKA I can't tell you how we've missed you—

KROLL Besides—I've been away—

REBEKKA But only for a couple of weeks. I hear you've been attending a lot of meetings— You've been going in for politics—?

KROLL [*nods*] Yes, what do you say to that? Who would ever have thought I'd become a political firebrand in my old age?

REBEKKA [*smiling*] Well, you have always been a bit of a firebrand, Professor Kroll.

KROLL In private life, perhaps—for my own amusement. But this is a serious matter. Do you ever read any of these radical newspapers, by any chance?

REBEKKA I must admit, my dear Professor, that I—

KROLL As far as you you're concerned, my dear Miss West, there's no reason why you shouldn't—

REBEKKA No, that's what I feel. I like to know what's going on—to keep up with the times—

KROLL Certainly. And one naturally doesn't expect a woman to take an active part in this controversy—one might almost call it a civil war —that is raging all about us. Then you're no doubt familiar with the disgraceful way these gentlemen of "the people" have seen fit to treat me? The infamous abuse they've dared to heap upon me?

REBEKKA I must say you gave as good as you got!

KROLL I did indeed. And I'm proud of it. Now that I've tasted blood they'll soon find out I'm not the man to turn the other cheek—[*Breaks off.*] But why should we discuss this painful subject?

REBEKKA No, dear Professor, don't let us talk about it.

KROLL I'd rather talk about you; how are you getting on at Rosmersholm, now that our poor Beata—?

REBEKKA Thank you, well enough. It seems so empty here without her; one can't help feeling

very sad—we miss her in so many ways. But, apart from that—

KROLL Do you plan to go on staying here?— permanently, I mean?

REBEKKA I really haven't given it much thought. I've grown so accustomed to this place— It's almost as if I, too, belonged here.

KROLL But you *do!* You *do* belong here!

REBEKKA And as long as Mr. Rosmer needs me —as long as I can be of any help or comfort to him—I feel I should remain.

KROLL [*looks at her much moved*] It's a very wonderful thing, Miss West, for a woman to give up the best years of her life to others, as you have.

REBEKKA What else had I to live for?

KROLL Your devotion to your foster-father was admirable. It must have been very hard for you; half-paralyzed and unreasonable as he was—

REBEKKA You mustn't think Dr. West was always so unreasonable—at least, not during the first years in Finmark. It was those terrible sea voyages that undermined his health. It wasn't until afterwards, when we moved down here—those last two years before his death— that things became so difficult.

KROLL And presumably the years that followed were more difficult still—

REBEKKA How can you say that! I was devoted to Beata—poor darling! She had such need of tenderness and care.

KROLL How kind you are to speak of her with so much understanding.

REBEKKA [*moves a little nearer*] Dear Professor, you reassure me! You couldn't say that with such sincerity if you had any resentment in your heart towards me.

KROLL Resentment! Why should you think that?

REBEKKA Well, mightn't it be natural that you should resent a stranger presiding over things at Rosmersholm?

KROLL What on earth—!

REBEKKA But you have no such feeling, have you? [*Takes his hand.*] Thank you, my dear Professor; many, many thanks!

KROLL What on earth put that into your head?

REBEKKA You've been to see us so seldom lately

—I began to be a little frightened.

KROLL Then you were totally mistaken, my dear Miss West. And, after all, things haven't really changed; you were in full charge here long before poor Beata died.

REBEKKA Yes—but that was only a kind of stewardship on her behalf—

KROLL All the same—for my part, Miss West— I should be only too happy to see you— But perhaps I shouldn't mention such a thing.

REBEKKA What do you mean?

KROLL I'd be only too happy to see you take poor Beata's place.

REBEKKA I have the only place I want, Professor.

KROLL For all practical purposes, yes; but not as far as—

REBEKKA [interrupting gravely] Shame on you, Professor Kroll. You shouldn't joke about such things!

KROLL I dare say our good Rosmer feels he's had more than enough of married life. But still—

REBEKKA Don't be so absurd, Professor!

KROLL But still—tell me—how old are you now, Miss West?—if you'll forgive the question!

REBEKKA I'm ashamed to admit, Professor, I'm past twenty-nine—I'm in my thirtieth year.

KROLL And Rosmer—how old is he? Let me see: he is five years younger than I am, so that would make him forty-three. That seems to me most suitable.

REBEKKA [rises] No doubt—yes; very suitable indeed! You'll stay for supper, won't you?

KROLL Yes, thank you; I'd like to very much. There's a matter I must discuss with Rosmer. And from now on, Miss West, I shall resume my former practice of coming out more often; We can't have you getting your head full of foolish notions!

REBEKKA Yes—do that! I wish you would! [Shakes both his hands.] Again—many thanks! How kind and good you are!

KROLL [gruffly] Am I? That's not what I hear at home!

[Johannes Rosmer enters by the door on the right.]

REBEKKA Mr. Rosmer! Just look who's here!

ROSMER Mrs. Helseth told me. [Professor Kroll has risen; Rosmer takes his hand; with quiet emotion] Welcome back to this house, my dear Kroll. [Lays his hands on Kroll's shoulders and looks into his eyes.] My dear, dear friend! I was certain things would straighten out between us.

KROLL My dear fellow—don't tell me you've been imagining things too?

REBEKKA [to Rosmer] Isn't it wonderful, Rosmer? It was all imagination!

ROSMER Is that really true? Then what made you stay away from me?

KROLL [gravely, in a low voice] I didn't want to be a constant reminder of those unhappy years —and of poor Beata's tragic death.

ROSMER How good of you! But then—you always were considerate. Still—it wasn't necessary to stay away on that account— Let's sit here on the sofa. [They sit down.] No, I assure you, the thought of Beata isn't painful to me. She seems so close to us. We speak of her every day.

KROLL Do you really?

REBEKKA [lighting the lamp] Yes, indeed we do.

ROSMER It's natural enough. We were both so devoted to her. And Rebek—Miss West and I did everything in our power to help her.— We're confident of that; there's no room for self-reproach. That's why we can think of her with a sense of peace—a quiet tenderness.

KROLL What splendid people you are! That settles it—I shall come out and see you every single day!

REBEKKA [seats herself in an arm-chair] Be sure and keep your word!

ROSMER [with some hesitation] You know—I regret even this short interruption in our friendship. Ever since we've known each other you've been my chief adviser—since my student days, in fact.

KROLL Yes—I've always been proud of it. But is there anything in particular—?

ROSMER There are a number of things I'm most anxious to discuss with you. I'd like to talk to you quite frankly—heart to heart.

REBEKKA It would do you good, wouldn't it, Mr. Rosmer? It must be such a comfort—between old friends—

KROLL And I've a great deal to discuss with

you. You know, of course, I've begun to take an active part in politics?

ROSMER I know. How did that come about?

KROLL I was forced into it—I had no choice. It's no longer possible to stand by idly looking on. Now that the radical party has, so unfortunately, come into power, it is high time that something was done about it. I have persuaded some of our friends in town to band together —to take some constructive action. I tell you it is high time!

REBEKKA [*with a faint smile*] Perhaps, it might even be a little late?

KROLL Oh, unquestionably, we should have stemmed the tide long ago—that would have been far better! But who could possibly foresee what was to happen? Not I, certainly! [*Rises and walks up and down.*] But I can tell you my eyes are open now. You'd never believe it— but this seditious element has actually gained a foothold in the school!

ROSMER The school? You surely don't mean *your* school?

KROLL Yes, I tell you! What do you say to that? And it has come to my knowledge that for the past six months the senior boys—a considerable number of them at any rate—have been members of a secret society and subscribe to Mortensgaard's paper.

REBEKKA What! *The Beacon?*

KROLL Yes; nice mental sustenance for future government officials, is it not? But the most distressing thing is that it's the most gifted students who have taken part in this conspiracy against me. The only ones who seem to have kept away from it are the dunces—at the bottom of the class.

REBEKKA Does this really affect you so very deeply, Professor Kroll?

KROLL Does it affect me? To see the work of a lifetime thwarted and undermined? [*Lower*] Still—all this might be endurable, perhaps. There's something worse, however. [*Looks around.*] You're sure no one can hear us?

REBEKKA No, no; of course not.

KROLL Then, listen to this: the spirit of revolt has actually crept into my own house—into my own quiet home; the harmony of my family life has been utterly destroyed.

ROSMER [*rises*] What do you mean? Into your home—!

REBEKKA [*goes over to the professor*] What can have happened, dear Professor?

KROLL You wouldn't believe it, would you, that my own children—? In short—I find that Lauritz is the ringleader of this conspiracy; and my daughter Hilda has embroidered a red portfolio to keep *The Beacon* in.

ROSMER —Your own home? It seems impossible!

KROLL Yes—doesn't it? The very home of duty and obedience—where, at my insistence, order and decency have always reigned supreme—

REBEKKA How does your wife take all this?

KROLL That's the most astonishing thing about it. My wife, who has always shared my opinion on all subjects—has undeviatingly upheld my principles—seems inclined to take the children's point of view in this affair. She tells me I'm to blame—that I'm too harsh with them. Yet, surely there are times when discipline— Well, you see how my house is divided against itself. I naturally say as little about it as possible. Such things are best kept quiet. [*Wanders about the room.*] Ah, well, well, well. [*Stands at window with hands behind his back and looks out.*]

REBEKKA [*comes up close to Rosmer, and says rapidly and in a low voice, so that the professor does not hear her*] Tell him!

ROSMER [*also in a low voice*] Not this evening.

REBEKKA [*as before*] Yes! Tell him *now!* [*Goes to the table and busies herself with the lamp.*]

KROLL [*comes forward*] Well, my dear Rosmer, now you know how the spirit of the times has cast its shadow over me—over my domestic as well as my official life. I could hardly be expected not to resist this dangerous and destructive force—this anarchy. I shall fight it with every weapon I can lay my hands on. I shall fight it by word and deed.

ROSMER What do you expect to gain by that?

KROLL I shall at least have done my duty as a citizen. And I hold it the duty of every right-thinking man with an atom of patriotism to do likewise. This was my main reason for wanting to talk to you this evening.

ROSMER But, my dear Kroll, how do you

mean—? How could I possibly—?

KROLL You must stand by your old friends. You must join our ranks—march with us to battle!

REBEKKA Professor Kroll, you know how Mr. Rosmer dislikes that sort of thing.

KROLL Then he must get over his dislike. You've let yourself get out of touch with things, Rosmer. You bury yourself away out here, delving into the past, absorbed in your genealogical research—oh, far be it from me to scoff at such things—but this is no time to indulge in these pursuits. You have no conception of what is happening throughout the country. There is scarcely an established principle that hasn't been attacked; the whole order of Society is threatened! It will be a colossal task to set things right again.

ROSMER Yes—I quite agree. But that sort of work isn't at all in my line.

REBEKKA Besides, I think Mr. Rosmer has gradually acquired a wider view on life.

KROLL [*with surprise*] A wider view?

REBEKKA Well—freer, if you like; less prejudiced.

KROLL What does this mean? Rosmer, you are surely not so weak as to be taken in by any temporary advantage these anarchists have won?

ROSMER As you know, I've very little understanding of politics, dear Kroll. But it does seem clear that in the past few years, men have at last begun to think for themselves— as individuals.

KROLL And you immediately assume this to be to their advantage? You are mistaken, I assure you. I don't think you quite realize what these ideas are, that the radicals are spreading among the people—not only in the city, but out here in the country too. You should make some inquiries! You'd find them based on the brand of wisdom proclaimed in the pages of *The Beacon*.

REBEKKA Yes; Mortensgaard certainly has great influence.

KROLL It's inconceivable! A man with such a record—who was dismissed from his position as schoolteacher on moral grounds—to set himself up as a leader of the people! And he succeeds too! He actually succeeds! He is about to enlarge his paper, I understand. He's on the lookout for a capable assistant.

REBEKKA I'm surprised you and your friends don't start a paper of your own.

KROLL That is precisely what we intend to do. Only today we purchased the *County News*. Financial backing is no problem to us, of course, but—[*Turns to Rosmer.*] and now I come to the real purpose of my visit.—Where are we to find an editor? That is the vital question. Tell me, Rosmer—don't you feel it your duty, for the good of the cause, to undertake this task?

ROSMER [*almost in consternation*] I!

REBEKKA You can't be serious!

KROLL I can well understand your dislike of public meetings, and all that they imply. But this position would enable you to keep in the background—or rather—

ROSMER No, no!— Please don't ask me to do this.

KROLL I'd have no objection to trying my own hand at it. But that's out of the question—I'm burdened with too many duties as it is; while you have ample leisure—there's nothing to prevent you from undertaking it. We'd naturally give you all the help we could.

ROSMER I can't do it, Kroll. I'm not suited to it.

KROLL That's what you said when your father procured you the ministry here—

ROSMER And I was right. That's why I resigned it.

KROLL If you're as good an editor as you were a clergyman, we shan't complain!

ROSMER Once and for all, my dear Kroll, I cannot do it.

KROLL Well—but you'll lend us your name, at any rate?

ROSMER My name?

KROLL Yes, the mere name, Johannes Rosmer, will be a great help to the paper. We are all of us looked upon as hopeless reactionaries. I believe I myself am supposed to be a desperate fanatic! This will make it difficult for us to reach the people—poor misguided wretches that they are! You, on the other hand, have always kept aloof. Everyone knows and appreciates your integrity, your humanity, your fine mind and unimpeachable honor. Then, too,

HENRIK IBSEN

you are esteemed and respected as a former clergyman. And think of what the name "Rosmer" stands for in this part of the country!

ROSMER No doubt—

KROLL [pointing to the portraits on the walls] Rosmers of Rosmersholm—clergymen and soldiers, high-ranking officials; worthy, honorable gentlemen all!—A family that for nearly two centuries has held its place as the first in the district. [Lays his hand on Rosmer's shoulder.] You owe it to yourself, Rosmer, to all the traditions of your race, to defend those things that have always been held most precious in our society. [Turns round.] Don't you agree with me, Miss West?

REBEKKA [laughing softly, as if to herself] I'm afraid it all strikes me as utterly ludicrous—

KROLL Ludicrous?

REBEKKA Yes, ludicrous. I think I'd better tell you—

ROSMER [quickly] No, no—don't! Not just now!

KROLL [looks from one to the other] But, my dear friends, what does this mean—? [Interrupting himself] H'm!
[Mrs. Helseth appears in doorway.]

MRS. HELSETH There's a man at the kitchen-door; he says he wants to see you, Sir.

ROSMER [relieved] Well—show him in.

MRS. HELSETH In here, Sir?

ROSMER Yes, of course.

MRS. HELSETH But he doesn't look like the sort you'd bring into the drawing room.

REBEKKA What does he look like, Mrs. Helseth?

MRS. HELSETH He's not much to look at, Miss, and that's a fact.

ROSMER Did he give his name?

MRS. HELSETH I think he said he was called Hekman—or something of the sort.

ROSMER I know no one of that name.

MRS. HELSETH And then he said something about Uldrik, too.

ROSMER [in surprise] Ulrik Hetman! Was that it?

MRS. HELSETH That's it—Hetman.

KROLL I seem to have heard that name—

REBEKKA It's the name that strange man used to write under—

ROSMER [to Kroll] It's Ulrik Brendel's pen name.

KROLL Quite right! That scoundrel Brendel!

REBEKKA He's still alive, then.

ROSMER I heard he had joined a troupe of actors.

KROLL When I last heard of him, he was in the workhouse.

ROSMER Ask him to come in, Mrs. Helseth.

MRS. HELSETH Very well. [She goes out.]

KROLL You're not going to let a man like that into your house?

ROSMER He was once my tutor.

KROLL I know. And I know too that he filled your head with a lot of revolutionary notions and that your father showed him the door—with a horsewhip.

ROSMER [with a touch of bitterness] Yes. Father was a martinet at home as well as in his regiment.

KROLL You should be forever grateful to him for that, my dear Rosmer. Well!
[Mrs. Helseth opens the door on the right for Ulrik Brendel, and then withdraws, shutting the door behind him. He is a handsome man, with gray hair and beard; somewhat gaunt but active and well set up. He is dressed like a common tramp: threadbare frock-coat; worn-out shoes; no shirt visible. He wears an old pair of black gloves, and carries a soft, greasy felt hat under his arm, and a walking-stick in his hand.]

BRENDEL [hesitates at first, then goes quickly up to Kroll, and holds out his hand] Good evening, Johannes!

KROLL I beg your pardon—

BRENDEL I'll be bound you never expected to see me again! And within these hated walls, too?

KROLL I beg your pardon—[Pointing] Over there—

BRENDEL [turns] Oh, of course! There you are! Johannes—my own beloved boy—!

ROSMER [takes his hand] My dear old teacher.

BRENDEL I couldn't pass by Rosmersholm without paying you a flying visit—in spite of certain memories!

ROSMER You are heartily welcome here now—I assure you.

BRENDEL And who is this charming lady—? [Bows.] Mrs. Rosmer, no doubt.

ROSMER Miss West.

BRENDEL A near relation, I expect. And yonder stranger—? A brother of the cloth, I see.

ROSMER Professor Kroll.

BRENDEL Kroll? Kroll? Wait a bit— Weren't you a student of philology in your young days?

KROLL Of course I was.

BRENDEL Why, *Donnerwetter*—then I must have known you!

KROLL I beg your pardon.

BRENDEL Of course! You were—

KROLL I beg your pardon—

BRENDEL Yes! You were one of those paragons of virtue that got me kicked out of the Debating Club!

KROLL It's very possible. But I acknowledge no closer acquaintance.

BRENDEL Well, well! *Nach Belieben, Herr Doktor*. It's all one to me. Ulrik Brendel remains Ulrik Brendel just the same!

REBEKKA I suppose you're on your way to town, Mr. Brendel?

BRENDEL You have hit it, most charming lady. At certain intervals, I am constrained to strike a blow for existence. It goes against the grain; but—*enfin*—imperious necessity—

ROSMER Oh, but my dear Mr. Brendel, mayn't I be allowed to help you? In one way or another, I am sure—

BRENDEL To propose such a thing to me! You surely wouldn't wish to desecrate our friendship? Never, my dear Johannes; never!

ROSMER But what do you plan to do in town? I'm afraid you won't find it easy to—

BRENDEL Leave that to me, my boy. The die is cast. You see before you a man about to embark on a great campaign—greater and more intensive than all my previous excursions put together. [*To Kroll*] May I be so bold as to ask the *Herr Professor*—*unter uns*—have you such a thing as a reasonably clean, respectable and commodious Assembly Hall in your esteemed city?

KROLL There is the Workers Union Hall—that is the largest.

BRENDEL And has the *Herr Professor* any official influence in this, no doubt worthy, organization?

KROLL I have nothing whatever to do with it.

REBEKKA [*to Brendel*] You should apply to Peder Mortensgaard.

BRENDEL Pardon, Madame—what sort of an idiot is he?

ROSMER What makes you suppose that he's an idiot?

BRENDEL The name has such a distinctly plebeian sound.

KROLL I never expected *that* answer.

BRENDEL However, I will conquer my reluctance; there's no alternative. When a man finds himself at a turning point in his career, as I do—so be it. I will get in touch with this person—open direct negotiations with him—

ROSMER Are you really at a turning point in your career—in all seriousness?

BRENDEL Doesn't my own boy know that wherever I am and whatever I do, it's always in all seriousness? I'm about to put on a new man—to discard this modest reserve I have hitherto maintained.

ROSMER How so?

BRENDEL I intend to take hold of life with a strong hand.—Go forward. Mount upward. We live in a tempestuous, an equinoctial age— I am about to lay my mite on the altar of Emancipation.

KROLL So, you too—?

BRENDEL [*to them all*] Is the public in these parts at all familiar with my infrequent writings?

KROLL No; I must honestly admit that—

REBEKKA I've read some of them. My foster-father had them in his library.

BRENDEL Then you wasted your time, fair lady. They're all so much trash, let me tell you.

REBEKKA Indeed?

BRENDEL Those that you've read, yes. My really significant works no man or woman knows. No one—except myself.

REBEKKA Why is that?

BRENDEL For the simple reason that I have never written them.

ROSMER But my dear Mr. Brendel—

BRENDEL You know I've always been a bit of a sybarite, my dear Johannes; a *Feinschmecker*. I like to enjoy things in solitude; then I enjoy them doubly—tenfold. Glorious dreams come to me—intoxicating thoughts—bold, lofty, unique ideas, that carry me aloft on powerful pinions; these I transform into poems, visions, pictures—all in the abstract, you understand.

ROSMER Yes, yes.

BRENDEL The joys, the ecstasy I have reveled in, Johannes! The mysterious bliss of creation—in the abstract, as I said before. I have been showered with applause, gratitude and fame; I have been crowned with laurel-wreaths; all these tributes I have garnered with joyous, tremulous hands. In my secret imaginings I have been satiated with delight—with a rapture so intense, so intoxicating—

KROLL H'm.

ROSMER But you've never written down any of these things?

BRENDEL Not a word. The vulgar business of writing has always nauseated me—filled me with disgust. Besides, why should I profane my own ideals, when I can enjoy them by myself in all their purity? But now they must be offered up. I assure you I feel as a mother must when she delivers her young daughters into their bridegrooms' arms. Nevertheless—they must be offered up—offered upon the altar of Freedom. I will start with a series of carefully planned lectures—all over the country—

REBEKKA [with animation] How splendid of you, Mr. Brendel! You'll be giving the most precious thing you have.

ROSMER The only thing.

REBEKKA [looking significantly at Rosmer] There aren't many people who'd do that—who'd have the courage to do that!

ROSMER [returning the look] Who knows?

BRENDEL I see my audience is touched. That puts new heart into me—strengthens my will. So now I will proceed to action. Just one thing more. [To the professor] Tell me, Herr Preceptor—is there a Temperance Society in town? A Total Abstinence Society? But of course there must be!

KROLL I am the president, at your service.

BRENDEL Of course! One only has to look at you! Then—be prepared! I may come and join up for a week or so.

KROLL I beg your pardon—we do not accept members by the week.

BRENDEL A la bonne heure, Herr Pedagogue.

Ulrik Brendel has never been one to force his way into such societies. [Turns.] But I dare not prolong my stay in this house, so rich in memories. I must get to town and select a suitable lodging. There is a decent hotel in the place, I hope.

REBEKKA You'll have a hot drink before you go?

BRENDEL What sort of a hot drink, gracious lady?

REBEKKA A cup of tea, or—

BRENDEL I thank my bountiful hostess—but I dislike taking advantage of private hospitality. [Waves his hand.] Farewell, gentlefolk all! [Goes toward door but turns again.] Oh, I almost forgot, Johannes—Pastor Rosmer—would you do your former teacher a favor, for old time's sake?

ROSMER I should be delighted.

BRENDEL Then, could you lend me a dress shirt —just for a day or two?

ROSMER Is that all?

BRENDEL You see, I happen to be traveling on foot—just for the time being. They're sending my trunk after me.

ROSMER I see. But are you sure there's nothing else?

BRENDEL Yes—come to think of it—if you could spare me a light overcoat—

ROSMER Of course I can.

BRENDEL And perhaps a respectable pair of shoes as well—?

ROSMER I'll see to it. As soon as we know your address, we'll send them off to you.

BRENDEL I wouldn't dream of putting you to so much trouble! Give me the bagatelles now—I'll take them with me.

ROSMER Very well. Just come upstairs with me.

REBEKKA No, let me go. Mrs. Helseth and I will see to it.

BRENDEL I could never allow this distinguished lady—!

REBEKKA Oh, nonsense, Mr. Brendel! Come along. [She goes out.]

ROSMER [detaining him] There must be something else I can do for you?

BRENDEL No; I can't think of a thing. But, of course—damnation take it! It just occurred to me; I wonder if you happen to have eight crowns on you, Johannes?

ROSMER Let me see. [*Opens his purse.*] Here are two ten-crown notes.

BRENDEL Never mind—they'll do. I can always get change in town. Meanwhile—many thanks! Don't forget—that was two tens you lent me. Good night, my own dear boy. Good night, honored Sir!

[*Goes out right. Rosmer takes leave of him, and shuts the door behind him.*]

KROLL Merciful Heaven!—so this is that Ulrik Brendel people once expected such great things of.

ROSMER [*quietly*] At least he's had the courage to live life in his own way. It seems to me that's something to his credit.

KROLL What do you mean? A life like his! Don't tell me he still has the power to influence you?

ROSMER Far from it. My mind is quite clear now, on all points.

KROLL I wish I could believe that, Rosmer. You're easily swayed, you know.

ROSMER Sit down. I've got to talk to you.

KROLL Very well.

[*They seat themselves on the sofa.*]

ROSMER [*after a slight pause*] Our life here must strike you as very comfortable and pleasant.

KROLL Yes, indeed; it's comfortable and pleasant now—and peaceful, too. You have found a home, Rosmer—and I have lost one.

ROSMER My dear friend, don't say that. The wound will heal in time.

KROLL Never. The sting can never be removed. Things can never be the same.

ROSMER Now listen to me, Kroll. We have been close friends for a great many years. Does it seem to you conceivable that anything could ever break our friendship?

KROLL I can think of nothing that could ever come between us. What makes you ask that question?

ROSMER I ask it because I know how intolerant you are of any opposition to your way of seeing things.

KROLL That may be; but you and I have always agreed—at least on essentials.

ROSMER [*in a low voice*] I'm afraid that's no longer true.

KROLL [*tries to jump up*] What's that you say?

ROSMER [*holds him back*] No, please sit still!

KROLL What does this mean? I don't understand you. Explain yourself.

ROSMER It's as though my spirit had grown young again. I see things now with different eyes—with *youthful* eyes, Kroll; that's why I no longer agree with you, but with—

KROLL With whom? Tell me!

ROSMER With your children.

KROLL With my children?

ROSMER With Lauritz and Hilda—yes.

KROLL [*bows his head*] A traitor! Johannes Rosmer a traitor!

ROSMER I should have been happy—completely happy—in being what you call a traitor! But the thought of you saddened me. I knew it would be a great grief to you.

KROLL I shall never get over it, Rosmer. [*Looks gloomily at him.*] That you should be willing to share in this work of destruction—bring ruin on our unhappy country!

ROSMER I intend to work for Freedom.

KROLL Oh, yes—I know! That's what these false prophets call it—that's what their wretched followers call it too. But what sort of freedom can come from Anarchy, I ask you? From this spirit of evil that is spreading poison throughout our entire society?

ROSMER I'm not wedded to this spirit of evil, as you call it, and I belong to neither party. I want to bring men together regardless of which side they may be on. I want them to unite for the common good. I intend to devote my whole life and all my strength to this one end: the creation of a true democracy.

KROLL Haven't we democracy enough already! It's my opinion that we are all of us rapidly being dragged down into the mud where, hitherto, only the common people have seemed to prosper.

ROSMER For that very reason I have faith in the true purpose of Democracy.

KROLL What purpose?

ROSMER That of giving all men a sense of their own nobility.

KROLL All men—!

ROSMER As many as possible, at any rate.

KROLL By what means, may I ask?

ROSMER By freeing their thoughts and purifying their aims.

KROLL You're a dreamer, Rosmer. And you think *you* can do this?

ROSMER No, my dear friend; but I can at least open their eyes. They must do it for themselves.

KROLL And you think they can?

ROSMER Yes.

KROLL By their own strength?

ROSMER It must be by their own strength. There is no other.

KROLL [*rises*] A strange way for a clergyman to talk!

ROSMER I am no longer a clergyman.

KROLL But what about your faith? The faith you were brought up in?

ROSMER I no longer believe in it.

KROLL You no longer—!

ROSMER I've given it up. I *had* to give it up, Kroll.

KROLL I see. I suppose one thing leads to another. So this was why you resigned your position in the church?

ROSMER Yes. When it finally dawned on me that this was no temporary aberration—but, rather, a deep conviction that I neither could nor would shake off—then I left the church.

KROLL To think that all this time, we, your friends, had no suspicion of what was going on inside you. Rosmer, Rosmer, how could you bring yourself to hide the truth from us!

ROSMER I felt it concerned no one but myself. And I didn't want to cause you and my other friends unnecessary grief. I intended to go on living here just as before, quietly, serenely, happily. Reading, studying; steeping myself in all the books that had hitherto been closed to me. I wanted to become thoroughly familiar with this great world of truth and freedom that was suddenly revealed to me.

KROLL Every word proves what you are—a traitor! But why did you change your mind? What made you decide to admit your guilt? And why just now?

ROSMER You yourself forced me to it, Kroll.

KROLL *I* did?

ROSMER I was shocked to hear of your violence on the platform; to read your bitter speeches; the scurrilous attacks, the cruel, contemptuous scorn you heaped on your opponents. How could *you* be like that, Kroll? Then I realized I had an imperative duty to perform. Men are becoming evil in this struggle. We must get back to peace, and joy and mutual understanding. That's why I've made up my mind to declare my beliefs openly—to try my strength. Couldn't you—on your side—join in this work, and help me?

KROLL Never! I shall never make peace with the destroyers of society.

ROSMER Then if we must fight, let us, at least, use honorable weapons.

KROLL Any man who goes against my fundamental principles I shall refuse to recognize; nor do I owe him any consideration.

ROSMER Does that include me, as well?

KROLL It is you who have broken with me, Rosmer; our friendship is at an end.

ROSMER You *can't* mean that?

KROLL Not *mean* it! This is an end to all your former friendships; now you must take the consequences.

[*Rebekka West enters, and opens the door wide.*]

REBEKKA He's gone. He is on his way to his great sacrifice! And now we can go to supper. Come, Professor.

KROLL [*takes up his hat*] Good night, Miss West. I have nothing more to do here.

REBEKKA [*eagerly*] What does he mean? [*Shuts the door and comes forward.*] Did you tell him?

ROSMER Yes. He knows now.

KROLL We shan't let you go, Rosmer. You'll come back to us again.

ROSMER I shall never go back to your opinions.

KROLL Time will tell. You are not a man to stand alone.

ROSMER But I shan't be alone; there are two of us to share the loneliness.

KROLL You mean—? [*A suspicion crosses his face.*] I see! Just what Beata said—!

ROSMER Beata—?

KROLL [*shaking off the thought*] No, no, forgive me; that was vile.

ROSMER Why? What do you mean?

KROLL Never mind! Forgive me! Good-bye. [*Goes toward door.*]

ROSMER [*follows him*] Kroll! Our friendship can't end like this. I'll come and see you tomorrow.

KROLL [*in the hall, turns*] You shall never set foot in my house again.

[*Takes up his stick and goes out. Rosmer stands for a moment in the doorway; then shuts the door and walks up to the table.*]

ROSMER It can't be helped, Rebekka. We'll face it together—like the loyal friends we are.

REBEKKA What do you suppose he meant by "that was vile"?

ROSMER Don't give it a thought, my dear. He himself didn't believe what he was saying. I'll go and talk to him tomorrow. Good night.

REBEKKA Are you going up already, just as usual? I thought perhaps—after what had happened—

ROSMER No—I'll go up, as usual. I can't tell you how relieved I feel now that it's over. You see—I'm quite calm about it all, Rebekka dear. And you must take it calmly too. Good night.

REBEKKA Good night, dear Rosmer; sleep well! [*Rosmer goes out by the hall door, and his steps are heard ascending the staircase; Rebekka goes and pulls a bell-rope. Shortly after, Mrs. Helseth enters.*]

REBEKKA You might as well clear the table, Mrs. Helseth. Mr. Rosmer doesn't care for anything, and Professor Kroll's gone home.

MRS. HELSETH Gone home? Is anything the matter with him?

REBEKKA [*takes up work*] He said he felt a storm coming on—

MRS. HELSETH That's queer. There's not a cloud in the sky this evening.

REBEKKA I hope he won't run into that White Horse. I've a feeling the ghosts may be quite busy for a while.

MRS. HELSETH Good gracious, Miss! Don't say such dreadful things.

REBEKKA Well, well—who knows?

MRS. HELSETH [*softly*] You mean you think someone's going to be taken from us, Miss?

REBEKKA Of course not! Why should I think that? But there are all sorts of white horses in this world, Mrs. Helseth— Well, good night. I'm going to my room.

MRS. HELSETH Good night, Miss.

[*Rebekka goes out with her work.*]

MRS. HELSETH [*turns the lamp down, shaking her head and muttering to herself*] Lord, Lord! That Miss West! What queer things she does say!

Act Two

Johannes Rosmer's study. Entrance door on the left. At the back, a doorway with a curtain drawn aside, leading into Rosmer's bedroom. On the right a window, and in front of it a writing table covered with books and papers. Bookshelves and bookcases round the room. The furniture is simple. On the left, an old-fashioned sofa, with a table in front of it.

Johannes Rosmer, in a smoking-jacket, is sitting in a high-backed chair at the writing table. He is cutting and turning over the leaves of a pamphlet, and reading a little here and there. There is a knock at the door.

ROSMER [*without moving*] Come in.

REBEKKA [*enters; she is wearing a dressing-gown*] Good morning.

ROSMER [*turning the leaves of the pamphlet*] Good morning, dear. Is there anything you want?

REBEKKA I just wanted to know if you had slept well.

ROSMER Yes, I had a good restful night—no dreams; what about you?

REBEKKA I slept well; at least toward morning—

ROSMER I don't know when I've ever felt so light-hearted! It was good to get that off my chest at last.

REBEKKA You should have done it long ago.

ROSMER I can't imagine why I was such a coward.

REBEKKA Well, it wasn't exactly cowardice—

ROSMER Oh yes, it was; it was partly cowardice, at any rate—I realize that now.

REBEKKA That makes it all the braver. [*Sits on a chair at writing table close to him.*] Rosmer, I want to tell you something I did last night— I hope you won't object—

ROSMER Object? You know I never—

REBEKKA You may think it was unwise of me—

ROSMER Well—tell me.

REBEKKA I gave Ulrik Brendel a note to Mortensgaard, before he left.

ROSMER [*a little doubtful*] Did you, Rebekka? What did you say?

REBEKKA I told him he'd be doing you a favor if he were to keep an eye on Brendel; help him in any way he could.

ROSMER Oh, you shouldn't have done that, dear. I'm afraid it will do more harm than good. And Mortensgaard is not the sort of man I choose to have dealings with. You know all about that former unpleasantness between us.

REBEKKA But wouldn't it be as well to be on good terms with him again?

ROSMER I? With Mortensgaard? What for?

REBEKKA I thought it might be to your advantage—now that your old friends have turned against you.

ROSMER [*looks at her and shakes his head*] You surely don't believe that Kroll or any of the others would try to take revenge on me? That they'd ever think of—?

REBEKKA You never know what people will do in the first heat of anger. After the way the Professor took it—it seemed to me—

ROSMER You should know him better than that. Kroll is a thoroughly honorable man. I'll go in and see him after lunch. I'd like to talk to all of them. You'll see—things will come out all right.

[*Mrs. Helseth appears at door.*]

REBEKKA [*rises*] What is it, Mrs. Helseth?

MRS. HELSETH Professor Kroll is downstairs in the hall.

ROSMER [*rises hastily*] Kroll!

REBEKKA The Professor! Fancy!

MRS. HELSETH He wants to know if he may come up and talk to Mr. Rosmer.

ROSMER [*to Rebekka*] What did I tell you?—of course he may. [*Goes to door and calls downstairs.*] Come up, dear friend! I am delighted to see you.

[*Rosmer holds the door open for him; Mrs. Helseth exits. Rebekka closes the curtain to the alcove and tidies up here and there. Enter Kroll, hat in hand.*]

ROSMER [*with quiet emotion*] I was sure we hadn't said good-bye for good.

KROLL I see things in quite a different light today.

ROSMER I was sure you would, Kroll; now that you've had time to think things over—

KROLL You misunderstand me. [*Lays his hat on table beside sofa.*] It is of the utmost importance that I speak to you, alone.

ROSMER But, why shouldn't Miss West—?

REBEKKA No, no, Mr. Rosmer. I'll go.

KROLL [*looks at her from head to foot*] I must ask Miss West's pardon for coming at such an early hour—for taking her unawares, before she has had time to—

REBEKKA [*surprised*] How do you mean? Do you see anything wrong in my wearing a dressing gown about the house?

KROLL Heaven forbid! Who am I to know what now may be customary at Rosmersholm?

ROSMER Why, Kroll—you are not yourself today!

REBEKKA My respects, Professor Kroll! [*Goes out.*]

KROLL With your permission—[*Sits.*]

ROSMER Yes, do sit down, let's talk things over amicably. [*Sits opposite the professor.*]

KROLL I haven't closed my eyes since yesterday. All night long I lay there turning things over in my mind.

ROSMER And what have you to say today?

KROLL It will be a long story, Rosmer. As a kind of preliminary—let me give you news of Ulrik Brendel.

ROSMER Has he called on you?

KROLL No. He took up quarters in a disreputable tavern, in the lowest possible company. There he started drinking and playing host to the others till his money ran out. In the end he turned on them; abused them as a pack of thieves and blackguards—in which he was undoubtedly quite right—whereupon they beat him up and pitched him into the gutter.

ROSMER So he's incorrigible, after all.

KROLL He had pawned the overcoat, but I hear that has been redeemed for him. Can you guess by whom?

ROSMER By you, perhaps?

KROLL No. By the noble Mr. Mortensgaard.

ROSMER Indeed!

KROLL Yes. It seems Mr. Brendel's first visit was to the "plebeian idiot."

ROSMER That was a lucky thing for him.

KROLL To be sure it was. [*Leans across the table towards Rosmer.*] This brings me to a matter I feel it my duty to warn you about, for our old —or rather for our former—friendship's sake.

ROSMER What matter, my dear Kroll?

KROLL I warn you: there are things going on behind your back in this house.

ROSMER What makes you think that? Is it Reb —is it Miss West you're referring to?

KROLL Precisely. Oh, it's not surprising. All this time she's been given such a free hand here. But still—

ROSMER You're quite mistaken in this, Kroll. She and I are completely honest with each other—on all subjects.

KROLL Then has she informed you that she has started a correspondence with the editor of *The Beacon?*

ROSMER You mean those few words she gave to Ulrik Brendel?

KROLL Oh, so you know about it. And you mean to say that you approve of her associating with this cheap journalist—this scandal-monger who never ceases to hold me up to ridicule?

ROSMER My dear Kroll, I don't suppose it occurred to her to look at it from that angle. And, besides, she's a free agent—just as I am.

KROLL I see. It's all part of this new line of conduct, I presume. Miss West undoubtedly shares your present point of view?

ROSMER Yes, she does. We've worked towards it together—in loyal friendship.

KROLL [*looks at him and slowly shakes his head*] You're a blind, deluded man, Rosmer!

ROSMER I? Why should you call me that?

KROLL Because I dare not—*will* not think the worst. No, no! Let me finish! You really do value my friendship, don't you, Rosmer? And my respect?

ROSMER Surely that question should require no answer.

KROLL Very well. But there are other questions that do require an answer—a full explanation on your part. Are you willing to submit to a sort of cross-examination—?

ROSMER Cross-examination?

KROLL Yes. Will you allow me to inquire frankly into various matters that it may pain you to be reminded of? You see—this apostasy of yours—this emancipation, as you prefer to call it—is bound up with many other things that for your own sake you must explain to me.

ROSMER Ask me anything you like, my dear Kroll. I have nothing to hide.

KROLL Then tell me—what do you think was the real—the basic—reason for Beata's suicide?

ROSMER Have you doubts on that score? You can hardly expect to find a reasonable explanation for the actions of a poor demented invalid.

KROLL But are you quite certain Beata was completely irresponsible? Remember, the doctors were by no means convinced of that.

ROSMER If the doctors had ever seen her as I so often saw her—day after day, night after night—they would have had no doubts.

KROLL I had no doubts either, then.

ROSMER No, unfortunately there wasn't the slightest room for doubt. Those paroxysms of morbid passion she was seized with! How could I respond to them—they appalled me; I told you all about it at the time. And then the constant reproaches she heaped upon herself in those last years; without basis—without reason.

KROLL After she found out she could never have children; yes—I know.

ROSMER She suffered untold agonies of mind—tormented herself incessantly—over something entirely out of her control. No normal human being would behave like that.

KROLL Tell me—do you remember having any books in the house at that time, dealing with marital relations? From the so-called modern point of view, I mean?

ROSMER   Yes—I believe Miss West once lent me such a book; she inherited Dr. West's library, you know. But, my dear Kroll, you don't suppose for a moment we were careless enough to let it fall into poor Beata's hands? I give you my solemn word, we were both entirely blameless in this matter. It was her own sick brain that drove Beata to the verge of madness.

KROLL   I can tell you one thing, at any rate: Beata—poor, tormented creature that she was—put an end to her own life in order to bring happiness to yours; to set you free to live—after your own heart.

ROSMER   [starts half up from chair]   What do you mean by that?

KROLL   Listen to me quietly, Rosmer! I must speak about it now. Not long before she died she came to see me twice and poured out all her sorrow and despair.

ROSMER   On this same subject?

KROLL   No. The first time she kept insisting you were about to break with the Faith—to leave the church.

ROSMER   [eagerly]   That's quite impossible—utterly impossible! You're mistaken, I assure you!

KROLL   What makes you think that?

ROSMER   Because as long as Beata lived I'd come to no decision. I was in a turmoil—that is true—wrestling with doubts; but I never said a word to anyone; I fought it out alone and in the utmost secrecy. I don't think even Rebekka—

KROLL   Rebekka?

ROSMER   Well—Miss West then; I call her Rebekka for convenience' sake.

KROLL   So I have noticed.

ROSMER   It's quite inconceivable that Beata could ever have suspected such a thing. And if she had, why didn't she mention it to me? She never did—she never said a single word.

KROLL   Poor thing—she begged and implored me to talk to you.

ROSMER   Why didn't you, then?

KROLL   Because I thought she was unbalanced! I took that for granted at the time. To accuse a man like you of such a thing! The second time she came—it was about a month later—

she seemed much calmer. But just as she was leaving, she turned to me and said: "It won't be long now before the White Horse appears at Rosmersholm."

ROSMER   The White Horse, yes—she often spoke of that.

KROLL   I tried to steer her away from such sad thoughts—but she continued: "I haven't long to live. Rosmer must marry Rebekka at once."

ROSMER   [almost speechless]   What are you saying? I marry—?

KROLL   That was a Thursday afternoon.— The following Saturday evening she threw herself from the bridge into the mill-race.

ROSMER   And you never warned us—!

KROLL   You know she was always saying she hadn't long to live.

ROSMER   I know; but still—you should have warned us!

KROLL   I thought of it, but by then it was too late.

ROSMER   But after it happened—why didn't you? Why haven't you told me this before?

KROLL   I didn't want to add to your grief—what good would it have done? In any case, at the time I took everything she said for the hysterical ravings of an unsound mind. Until yesterday evening I believed that firmly—

ROSMER   And now?

KROLL   Didn't Beata see quite clearly when she declared you were about to desert the faith you were brought up in?

ROSMER   [looks fixedly straight before him]   That I cannot understand! It's quite incomprehensible—

KROLL   Incomprehensible or not—there it is. And now—what about her other accusation, Rosmer? How much truth is there in that?

ROSMER   Was that an accusation?

KROLL   Perhaps you did not notice the way she worded it. She had to go, she said—why?— Well? Answer me!

ROSMER   So that I might marry Rebekka—

KROLL   That is not exactly the way she put it. Beata expressed it differently. She said: "I haven't long to live; Johannes must marry Rebekka at once."

ROSMER   [looks at him for a moment; then rises]   Now I understand you, Kroll!

KROLL Well? And what is your answer?

ROSMER [*still quiet and self-restrained*] To something so unheard of—? The only right answer would be to show you the door.

KROLL [*rises*] Well and good.

ROSMER [*stands in front of him*] Wait a minute, Kroll! For well over a year—ever since Beata left us—Rebekka West and I have lived here alone at Rosmersholm. All that time you have been aware of Beata's accusation against us. Yet I've never noticed the slightest sign of disapproval on your part.

KROLL Until yesterday evening I had no idea you were an atheist; and that the woman sharing your home was a free-thinker.

ROSMER I see. You don't believe there can be purity of mind among free-thinkers? You don't believe there's such a thing as an instinctive sense of morality?

KROLL I have no great faith in any morality that is not founded on the teachings of the church.

ROSMER And does this apply to Rebekka and me as well? To our relationship?

KROLL Consideration for you cannot alter my opinion that there is very little separation between free-thought and—

ROSMER And?

KROLL Free love—since you force me to put it into words.

ROSMER [*in a low voice*] Aren't you ashamed to say such a thing to me! You, who have known me since I was a boy?

KROLL All the more reason for me to say it. I know how easily you are influenced by those around you. And this Rebekka of yours—well, this Miss West then—what do we really know about her? Next to nothing! In short, Rosmer —I refuse to give you up. I urge you to try and save yourself while there's still time.

ROSMER In what way—save myself?

[*Mrs. Helseth peeps in at the door.*]

ROSMER What do you want?

MRS. HELSETH I'm to ask Miss West to come downstairs.

ROSMER Miss West is not up here.

MRS. HELSETH Isn't she? [*Looks around room.*] That's strange. [*Goes.*]

ROSMER You were saying—

KROLL Listen to me. What went on here in secret while Beata was alive—what may be going on here now, I shall inquire into no further. Your marriage was a most unhappy one; that may serve to excuse you, to some extent—

ROSMER How little you really know me—!

KROLL Don't interrupt me. What I mean is this: if your relationship with Miss West is to continue, at least keep your new opinions, your tragic fall from faith—for which she is undoubtedly to blame—keep these things to yourself! No! Let me speak! Let me speak! If the worst comes to the worst then for heaven's sake, think and believe and do whatever you like, but be discreet about it. It's a purely personal matter! It's not necessary to shout it from the house-tops.

ROSMER Perhaps not. But it is necessary for me to free myself from a false and ambiguous position.

KROLL It's your duty to uphold the traditions of your race, Rosmer! Remember that! For countless generations Rosmersholm has been a stronghold of discipline and order—of all those precious things that are most revered and highly respected in our Society. The whole district has always taken its stamp from Rosmersholm. It would cause the most deplorable, the most irreparable confusion, if it became known that you of all people had broken away from what might be called the Rosmer Way of Life.

ROSMER That's not the way I see things, Kroll. It seems to me my duty is to spread a little light and happiness here, where former Rosmers spread only gloom and despotism.

KROLL [*looks at him sternly*] That indeed would be a worthy mission for the last of the Rosmers to perform! No. Leave such things alone—they are not for you. You were born to live the quiet life of a scholar.

ROSMER Perhaps. But all the same, I feel compelled to take part in the present crisis.

KROLL You realize it will mean a life and death struggle with all your former friends?

ROSMER [*quietly*] I can't believe they are all as fanatical as you.

KROLL You are a simple-hearted soul, Rosmer; a naïve soul. You have no conception of the powerful storm that will sweep over you. [*Mrs. Helseth looks in at the door.*]

MRS. HELSETH Miss West would like to know—

ROSMER What is it?

MRS. HELSETH There's a man downstairs who wants a few words with you, Sir.

ROSMER Is it the one who was here yesterday?

MRS. HELSETH No; it's that Mortensgaard.

ROSMER Mortensgaard!

KROLL Aha! I see. So it's already come to this!

ROSMER Why should he want to see me? Why didn't you send him away?

MRS. HELSETH Miss West told me to ask if he might come upstairs a minute.

ROSMER Tell him I'm busy—

KROLL [*to Mrs. Helseth*] No! No! By all means let him come up, Mrs. Helseth. [*Mrs. Helseth goes; Kroll takes up hat.*] I shall leave the field to him—for the moment. But the main battle has yet to be fought.

ROSMER I give you my word of honor, Kroll— I have nothing whatever to do with Mortensgaard.

KROLL I no longer believe anything you say, Rosmer. I can no longer take your word on any subject. It's war to the death now. We shall make every effort to disarm you.

ROSMER That you should have sunk so low, Kroll!

KROLL You dare say that to me! A man who—! Remember Beata?

ROSMER Are you going to harp on that again?

KROLL No. I shall leave you to solve the mystery of Beata's death after your own conscience— if you still possess anything of the sort.

[*Peder Mortensgaard enters slowly and quietly by the door left. He is a small, wiry man with thin reddish hair and beard.*]

KROLL [*with a look of hatred*] I never thought I'd live to see *The Beacon* burning at Rosmersholm! [*Buttons his coat.*] That settles it! I no longer have any doubt which course to take.

MORTENSGAARD [*deferentially*] *The Beacon* may always be relied upon to light the Professor home.

KROLL Yes; your good will has been apparent for some time. There is, to be sure, a commandment about bearing false witness against your neighbor—

MORTENSGAARD There is no need for Professor Kroll to teach me the commandments.

KROLL Not even the seventh?

ROSMER Kroll—!

MORTENSGAARD Were that necessary, it would surely be the Pastor's business.

KROLL [*with covert sarcasm*] The Pastor's? Oh, of course! Pastor Rosmer is unquestionably the man for that.— Good luck to your conference, gentlemen! [*Goes out, slams door behind him.*]

ROSMER [*keeps eyes fixed on closed door and says to himself*] So be it, then. [*Turns.*] Now, Mr. Mortensgaard; what brings you here?

MORTENSGAARD I really came to see Miss West. I wanted to thank her for the nice note she sent me yesterday.

ROSMER Yes, I know she wrote to you. Did you get a chance to talk to her?

MORTENSGAARD Yes, for a little while. [*With a faint smile*] I understand there has been a certain change of views at Rosmersholm.

ROSMER Yes. My views have changed on many subjects. On all subjects, perhaps.

MORTENSGAARD So Miss West told me. She suggested that I come up and talk things over with you.

ROSMER Talk what over, Mr. Mortensgaard?

MORTENSGAARD I should like to make an announcement in *The Beacon*. May I say that your views have changed, and that you are now ready to support the cause of progress—the cause of Freedom?

ROSMER Announce it, by all means. In fact I urge you to do so.

MORTENSGAARD It will be in tomorrow morning. It will cause quite a sensation: Pastor Rosmer of Rosmersholm stands ready to guide people toward the Light—in this sense too.

ROSMER I don't quite understand you.

MORTENSGAARD It's always a good thing for us to gain the approval of men like you—men well-known for their strict Christian principles; the moral support it gives our Cause is much needed—and invaluable.

ROSMER [*with some surprise*] Then, you don't know—? Didn't Miss West tell you about that, too?

MORTENSGAARD About what, Pastor Rosmer? Miss West seemed in a great hurry; she said I'd better come upstairs and hear the rest from you.

ROSMER I'd better tell you myself, then. You see—I've freed myself in every way: I no longer have any connection with the church, or with its doctrines; they no longer concern me in the least.

MORTENSGAARD [looks at him in amazement] What! if the skies were to fall I couldn't be more—! Pastor Rosmer! Is this true?

ROSMER Yes. So, you see—I am now in full accord with you. In this too I share the opinions you have held for many years. And this too you may announce tomorrow in The Beacon.

MORTENSGAARD No. Forgive me, my dear Pastor, but I don't think it would be wise to touch on that side of the question.

ROSMER How do you mean?

MORTENSGAARD Not at first—at all events.

ROSMER I don't quite understand—

MORTENSGAARD Let me explain; you naturally don't know the circumstances as well as I do. Since you've come over to the cause of freedom —and I gather from Miss West you intend to take an active part in the Progressive movement—I presume you would wish to help the cause to the fullest possible extent.

ROSMER Yes, I'm most anxious to do so.

MORTENSGAARD Then I think I should point out, that if your defection from the church is publicly announced, it will prove a serious handicap to you from the start.

ROSMER You think so?

MORTENSGAARD Undoubtedly. You could accomplish very little—particularly in this part of the country. We've a great many free-thinkers in our ranks already—too many, I was about to say. What the party lacks is the Christian element, Pastor Rosmer—something that commands respect. That is our greatest need. So— in matters that do not directly concern the general public—it would seem wiser to be discreet. That's my opinion, at any rate.

ROSMER In other words, if I make known my break with the church, you dare not have anything to do with me?

MORTENSGAARD [shaking his head] I shouldn't

like to risk it, Pastor Rosmer. In recent years I have made it a point never to lend support to anything or anyone antagonistic to the church.

ROSMER Have you, yourself, returned to the fold, then?

MORTENSGAARD That is a purely personal matter.

ROSMER So that's it. Now I understand you.

MORTENSGAARD You should understand, Pastor Rosmer, that my hands are tied more than most people's.

ROSMER How so?

MORTENSGAARD I am a marked man, you should know that.

ROSMER Indeed?

MORTENSGAARD A marked man, yes. Surely you've not forgotten? You were mainly responsible for that.

ROSMER If I'd seen things then as I do now, I should have shown more understanding.

MORTENSGAARD I dare say, but it's too late now. You branded me for good—branded me for life—I don't suppose you quite realize what that means. You soon may, though.

ROSMER I?

MORTENSGAARD Yes. You surely don't think Professor Kroll and his set will ever forgive a desertion like yours? They say the County News will be most sanguinary in future. You may find yourself a marked man, too.

ROSMER They can't possibly harm me in personal matters, Mr. Mortensgaard. My private life has always been beyond reproach.

MORTENSGAARD [with a sly smile] That's a bold statement, Mr. Rosmer.

ROSMER Perhaps, but I feel I have the right to make it.

MORTENSGAARD Even if you were to examine your own conduct as thoroughly as you once examined mine?

ROSMER Your tone is very curious. What are you hinting at? Anything definite?

MORTENSGAARD Yes, quite definite. It's only a little thing. But it could prove quite nasty, if the wrong people were to get wind of it.

ROSMER Then be good enough to tell me what it is.

MORTENSGAARD Can't you guess that for yourself?

ROSMER Certainly not. I've no idea.

MORTENSGAARD Then I suppose I'd better tell you. I have a rather curious letter in my possession—one that was written here at Rosmersholm.

ROSMER Miss West's letter, you mean? Is there anything curious about that?

MORTENSGAARD No, there's nothing curious about that one. But I once received another letter from this house.

ROSMER Was that from Miss West too?

MORTENSGAARD No, Pastor Rosmer.

ROSMER From whom do you mean then? Tell me!

MORTENSGAARD From the late Mrs. Rosmer.

ROSMER From my wife! You received a letter from my wife?

MORTENSGAARD Yes, I did.

ROSMER When?

MORTENSGAARD Not long before Mrs. Rosmer died—about a year and a half ago, perhaps. That is the letter I find curious.

ROSMER I suppose you know my wife's mind was affected at that time.

MORTENSGAARD Yes, I know many people thought so. But the letter gave no indication of anything like that. No—when I called the letter "curious," I meant it in quite a different sense.

ROSMER What on earth could my poor wife have written to you about?

MORTENSGAARD She begins by saying something to the effect that she is living in great fear and anguish. There are so many malicious people in this neighborhood, she writes, whose only thought is to do you every possible harm.

ROSMER Me?

MORTENSGAARD That's what she says. Then comes the most curious part of all. Shall I go on?

ROSMER Of course! By all means.

MORTENSGAARD Your late wife then begs me to be magnanimous. She knows, she says, that it was you who had me dismissed from my position as a teacher and she humbly implores me not to take revenge.

ROSMER What did she mean? In what way take revenge?

MORTENSGAARD She says in the letter, that if I should hear scandalous rumors about certain things at Rosmersholm, I must discount them; that they are slanders spread by evil-minded people to do you injury.

ROSMER Is all this in the letter?

MORTENSGAARD You're welcome to read it yourself, Pastor Rosmer, at your convenience.

ROSMER But I don't understand—! What scandalous rumors could she have been referring to?

MORTENSGAARD First that you had deserted the Faith. She denied this absolutely—then. And next—h'm—

ROSMER Well?

MORTENSGAARD Next she writes—and this is rather confused—that to her knowledge there has been no breach of morals at Rosmersholm; that she has never been wronged in any way. And if rumors of that sort should reach me, she begs me to say nothing of the matter in *The Beacon*.

ROSMER No name is mentioned?

MORTENSGAARD None.

ROSMER Who brought you this letter?

MORTENSGAARD I promised not to say. It was brought to me one evening, after dark.

ROSMER If you had made inquiries at the time, you would have found out that my poor wife was not fully responsible for her actions.

MORTENSGAARD I did make inquiries, Pastor Rosmer. But that was not the impression I received.

ROSMER Indeed? And what made you choose this particular moment to tell me about this letter?

MORTENSGAARD I felt I should warn you to be exceedingly cautious, Pastor Rosmer.

ROSMER In my personal life, you mean?

MORTENSGAARD Yes; you're no longer entirely your own master. Remember—you've ceased to be a neutral.

ROSMER Then you are quite convinced I have something to conceal?

MORTENSGAARD There's no reason why a man of liberal views shouldn't be able to live his life to the full—live it exactly as he chooses; however I repeat, this is a time for caution. If certain rumors were to get about concerning you —rumors that might offend current prejudices, shall we say?—the whole Liberal Movement might be seriously affected. Good-bye, Pastor Rosmer.

ROSMER Good-bye.

MORTENSGAARD I'll go straight back to the office. This is important news; I'll have it in *The Beacon* by tomorrow.

ROSMER Be sure to include everything.

MORTENSGAARD Don't worry! I shall include everything that respectable people need to know.

[*He bows and goes out. Rosmer remains standing in doorway while he goes down the stairs. The outer door is heard to close.*]

ROSMER [*in doorway, calls softly*] Rebekka, Re —h'm. [*Aloud*] Mrs. Helseth—isn't Miss West down there?

MRS. HELSETH [*from the hall below*] No; she's not here, Sir.

[*The curtain in the background is drawn aside. Rebekka appears in doorway*.]

REBEKKA Rosmer!

ROSMER [*turns*] Rebekka! What are you doing there? Have you been in my room all the time?

REBEKKA [*goes up to him*] Yes, Rosmer. I was listening.

ROSMER How could you do such a thing, Rebekka!

REBEKKA I had to. He was so disgusting when he said that about my dressing-gown—

ROSMER Then you were in there when Kroll—?

REBEKKA Yes, I had to know what he meant by all those things he said—

ROSMER I would have told you.

REBEKKA You'd scarcely have told me everything. And certainly not in his words.

ROSMER You heard the whole conversation, then?

REBEKKA Most of it, I think. I had to go downstairs a moment when Mortensgaard came.

ROSMER Then you came up again?

REBEKKA Don't be angry with me; please, Rosmer, dear!

ROSMER You're perfectly free to do whatever seems right to you, you know that. What do you make of it all, Rebekka—? Oh, I don't

know when I've ever needed you as much as I do now!

REBEKKA After all, we knew this would have to come some day; we've been prepared for it.

ROSMER But, not for this.

REBEKKA Why not for this?

ROSMER I knew of course that sooner or later our friendship would be misunderstood— would be dragged down into the mud. Not by Kroll—I never expected that of him—but by all those others; those coarse-grained, insensitive people who are blind to everything but evil. I had good reason to guard our relationship so jealously. It was a dangerous secret.

REBEKKA Why should we care what all those people think! We know we've done no wrong.

ROSMER No wrong, you say? I? Yes, until today I was convinced of that. But now, Rebekka—?

REBEKKA What?

ROSMER How am I to explain Beata's dreadful accusation?

REBEKKA [*vehemently*] Don't talk about Beata. — Don't *think* about Beata any more! You were just beginning to escape from her—she's dead!

ROSMER After what I've heard, she seems in a ghastly sort of way to be alive again.

REBEKKA Not that, Rosmer! Please—not that!

ROSMER Yes, I tell you. Somehow we must get to the bottom of it all. How could she possibly have misinterpreted things in such a hideous way?

REBEKKA She was on the verge of madness! Surely you're not beginning to doubt that?

ROSMER That's just it—I no longer feel quite sure; besides—even if she was—

REBEKKA Even if she was—?

ROSMER I mean—if her sick mind was on the borderline, what was it that gave the final impetus—that drove her to actual madness?

REBEKKA What possible good can it do, to torment yourself with questions that have no answers?

ROSMER I cannot help it, Rebekka. Much as I'd like to, I can't shake off these doubts.

REBEKKA Don't you see how dangerous it is to keep on dwelling on this one morbid subject?

ROSMER [*walks about restlessly in thought*] I must have given myself away somehow. She must have noticed how much happier I was after you came to live with us.

REBEKKA Well—even if she did—?

ROSMER She must have noticed how many things we had in common; how we were drawn together by our interest in the same books—in all the new ideas and theories. Yet I can't understand it! I was so careful to spare her feelings. I went out of my way, it seems to me, to keep her from knowing just how many interests we shared. Isn't that so, Rebekka?

REBEKKA Yes, it is.

ROSMER And you did the same. Yet in spite of that—! Oh, it's awful to think of! All that time she must have been watching us, observing us, noticing everything in silence; and her morbid love of me made her see it all in a false light.

REBEKKA [*clenching her hands*] I should never have come to Rosmersholm!

ROSMER The agony she must have gone through in silence! The sordid images her sick brain must have conjured up! Did she never say anything to you? Give any indication of her feelings, that might have warned you?

REBEKKA [*as if startled*] Do you think I'd have stayed here a moment longer if she had?

ROSMER No, no, of course not.— Oh, how she must have struggled, Rebekka—and all alone! To be so desperate, and quite alone! And then, the final triumph—the heartbreaking, silent accusation—of the mill-race. [*Throws himself into the chair by the writing-table, puts his elbows on the table and buries his face in his hands.*]

REBEKKA [*approaches him cautiously from behind*] Tell me something, Rosmer. If it were in your power to call Beata back—to you—to Rosmersholm—would you do it?

ROSMER How do I know what I would do, or wouldn't do? I can't tear my thoughts away from this one thing—this one irrevocable thing.

REBEKKA You were just beginning to live, Rosmer. You *had* begun to live. You had freed yourself—in every way. You were feeling so buoyant, so happy—

ROSMER It's true—I was. And now, to have to face all this!

REBEKKA [*behind him, rests her arms on the back of his chair*] We were so happy sitting downstairs in the old room together, in the twilight —don't you remember? Talking over our new plans; helping one another to see life with new eyes. You wanted to take part in life, at last—to be really *alive* in life—you used to say. You wanted to go from house to house spreading the word of freedom, winning over men's hearts and minds, awakening in them a sense of the nobility of life—of their *own* nobility; you wanted to create a noble race of men—

ROSMER Noble—and happy, yes.

REBEKKA Yes—happy, too.

ROSMER For minds are ennobled through happiness, Rebekka.

REBEKKA Don't you think—through suffering, too. Great suffering, I mean?

ROSMER Yes; if one can live through it, conquer it, and go beyond it.

REBEKKA That's what *you* must do.

ROSMER [*shakes his head gloomily*] I shall never quite get over this. There'll always be a doubt —a question in my mind. I'll never again experience the joy that fills life with such sweetness.

REBEKKA [*bends over his chair-back and says more softly*] What joy do you mean, Rosmer?

ROSMER [*looking up at her*] Peaceful joy.— The confidence of innocence.

REBEKKA [*recoils a step*] Ah! Innocence; yes. [*A short pause.*]

ROSMER [*with elbow on table, leaning his head on his hand, and looking straight before him*] And how cleverly she worked the whole thing out. How systematically she put it all together! First she began to doubt the soundness of my faith.— At that time how could she have suspected that? But she did suspect it; and later she became convinced of it. And then, of course, it was easy enough for her to believe in the possibility of all the rest. [*Sits up in his chair and runs his hands through his hair.*] All these wild imaginings! I shall never get rid of them. I feel it. I know it. Suddenly, at any moment, they'll come sweeping through my

mind—bringing back the thought of the dead.

REBEKKA Like the White Horse of Rosmersholm.

ROSMER Yes—just like that. Sweeping through the darkness—through the silence.

REBEKKA And because of this wretched hallucination, you'd be willing to give up being alive in life!

ROSMER It's hard—it's hard, Rebekka. But I have no choice. How can I ever recover from all this?

REBEKKA [*behind his chair*] You must take up new interests; you must enter into new relationships—

ROSMER [*surprised, looks up*] New relationships?

REBEKKA Yes—with the world at large. You must live, work, *act*—instead of sitting here brooding over insoluble enigmas.

ROSMER [*rises*] New relationships? [*Walks across the floor, stops at the door and then comes back.*] One question occurs to me, Rebekka; has it never occurred to you?

REBEKKA [*scarcely breathing*] Tell me—what it is.

ROSMER What future is there for our relationship—after today?

REBEKKA I believe our friendship will endure—in spite of everything.

ROSMER That's not quite what I meant. The thing that first brought us together and that unites us so closely—our faith in the possibility of a pure comradeship between a man and a woman—

REBEKKA What of that—?

ROSMER A relationship such as ours, I mean—shouldn't that presuppose a happy, peaceful life—?

REBEKKA Well—?

ROSMER But the life I face is one of struggle, unrest and violent agitation. For I intend to live my life, Rebekka! I will not be crushed by these gloomy speculations. I refuse to have a way of life imposed upon me, either by the living or by—anyone else.

REBEKKA No! That must not happen, Rosmer. You must be free in every way!

ROSMER Then—can you guess my thoughts? Can you guess them, Rebekka? There's only one way that I can free myself—rid myself of these haunting memories—this loathsome, tragic past.

REBEKKA What way is that?

ROSMER It must be stamped out, and replaced by something alive and real—

REBEKKA [*groping for the chair-back*] Alive and real—? You mean—?

ROSMER [*comes nearer*] If I were to ask you—? Oh, Rebekka! Will you be my wife?

REBEKKA [*for a moment, speechless, then cries out with joy*] Your wife! Your—! I!

ROSMER Yes, let us truly belong to one another—let us be as one. The empty place must remain empty no longer.

REBEKKA I—take Beata's place—?

ROSMER Then it will be as though she'd never been.

REBEKKA [*softly, trembling*] You believe that, Rosmer?

ROSMER It must be so! It must! I refuse to live my life chained to a corpse; help me to free myself, Rebekka! Together we will conquer all memories of the past; in freedom, in joy, in passion. You shall be to me my first, my only, wife.

REBEKKA [*with self-control*] You must never speak of this again! I can never be your wife.

ROSMER Never! You mean—you could never come to love me? But we love each other already, Rebekka! Our friendship has already turned to love.

REBEKKA [*puts her hands over her ears as if in terror*] No, no! Don't talk like that! Don't say such things!

ROSMER [*seizes her arm*] But it has! Our relationship is full of promise. You must feel that too—you must, Rebekka!

REBEKKA [*once more firm and calm*] Listen to me. If you speak of this again—I shall go away from Rosmersholm. I mean it.

ROSMER You! Go away! But that's impossible.

REBEKKA It's still more impossible that I should ever be your wife. I can't be. I can never marry you.

ROSMER [*looks at her in surprise*] You *can't* be? You say that so strangely. Why can't you be?

REBEKKA [*seizes both his hands*] For your sake,

as well as mine—don't ask me why. [*Lets go his hands.*] Don't ask me, Rosmer. [*Goes towards door.*]

ROSMER From now on I shall never cease to ask that question—why?

REBEKKA [*turns and looks at him*] Then it's all over.

ROSMER Between us, you mean?

REBEKKA Yes.

ROSMER It will never be over between us; and you will never go away from Rosmersholm.

REBEKKA [*with her hand on the door handle*] Perhaps not. But if you ask that question again, it will be over all the same.

ROSMER How do you mean?

REBEKKA Because then I shall go, the way Beata went. I've warned you, Rosmer—

ROSMER Rebekka—?

REBEKKA [*in the doorway, nods slowly*] I've warned you. [*She goes out.*]

ROSMER [*stares thunderstruck at the door, and says to himself*] What does this mean?

Act Three

The sitting-room at Rosmersholm. The window and the hall door are open. A bright sunny morning. Rebekka West, dressed as in the first act, stands at the window, watering and arranging the flowers. Her crochet work lies in the arm-chair. Mrs. Helseth moves about the room, dusting the furniture with a feather duster.

REBEKKA [*after a short silence*] It's strange that Mr. Rosmer should stay upstairs so late today.

MRS. HELSETH He often does. He'll be down soon, I expect.

REBEKKA Have you seen him yet this morning?

MRS. HELSETH I caught a glimpse of him when I took his coffee up; he was in his bedroom, dressing.

REBEKKA He didn't seem to feel well yesterday, that's why I asked.

MRS. HELSETH No; he didn't look well. I was wondering if there was anything wrong between him and his brother-in-law.

REBEKKA What do you think it could be?

MRS. HELSETH I really couldn't say. Perhaps it's that Mortensgaard that's made trouble between them.

REBEKKA It's possible. Do you know anything about this Peder Mortensgaard?

MRS. HELSETH No indeed, Miss. How could you think that? A person like him!

REBEKKA You mean because of that newspaper of his?

MRS. HELSETH Not just because of that; but you must have heard about him, Miss. He had a child by a married woman whose husband had deserted her.

REBEKKA Yes, I've heard it mentioned. But that must have been long before I came here.

MRS. HELSETH Lord, yes! He was quite young at the time; and she should have known better. He wanted to marry her too; but of course that was impossible. He paid dearly for it, they say. But he's gone up in the world since then. Plenty of people run after him now.

REBEKKA Yes, I hear most of the poor people go to him when they're in any trouble.

MRS. HELSETH Oh, not just the poor people, Miss. There've been others too—

REBEKKA [*looks at her furtively*] Really?

MRS. HELSETH [*by the sofa, dusting away vigorously*] Oh, yes, Miss. Perhaps the very last people you'd ever dream of.

REBEKKA [*busy with the flowers*] That's just one of your ideas, Mrs. Helseth. You can't be sure about a thing like that.

MRS. HELSETH That's what you think, Miss. But I am sure all the same. I may as well tell you— I once took a letter to Mortensgaard myself.

REBEKKA [*turning*] *You* did?

MRS. HELSETH Yes indeed I did. And what's more, that letter was written here at Rosmersholm.

REBEKKA Really, Mrs. Helseth?

MRS. HELSETH Yes indeed, Miss. And it was written on fine note paper, too; and sealed with fine red sealing wax.

REBEKKA And you were asked to deliver it?

Then, my dear Mrs. Helseth, it's not very hard to guess who wrote it.

MRS. HELSETH Well?

REBEKKA It was poor Mrs. Rosmer, I suppose—

MRS. HELSETH I never said so, Miss.

REBEKKA What was in the letter? But, of course, you couldn't very well know that.

MRS. HELSETH Suppose I did know, all the same?

REBEKKA You mean she told you?

MRS. HELSETH No, not exactly. But after Mortensgaard had read it, he began asking me questions—kept on and on at me; it wasn't hard to guess what it was all about.

REBEKKA What do you think it was? Dear, darling Mrs. Helseth, do tell me!

MRS. HELSETH Certainly not, Miss. Not for the world!

REBEKKA But surely you can tell *me!* After all, we're such good friends.

MRS. HELSETH The good Lord preserve me from telling you anything about that, Miss. No! All I can say is that it was a horrible thing they'd got the poor sick lady to believe.

REBEKKA Who got her to believe it?

MRS. HELSETH Wicked people, Miss West. Wicked people.

REBEKKA Wicked—?

MRS. HELSETH Yes, and I say it again; real wicked people!

REBEKKA Who do you suppose it could have been?

MRS. HELSETH Oh, I know well enough what I think. But Lord forbid I should say anything. To be sure, there's a certain lady in town who —hm!

REBEKKA You mean Mrs. Kroll, don't you?

MRS. HELSETH She's a fine one, she is, with her airs and graces! She was always on her high horse with me. And I don't think she's ever had any too much love for you, either.

REBEKKA Do you think Mrs. Rosmer was in her right mind when she wrote that letter?

MRS. HELSETH A person's mind is a queer thing, Miss; not *clear* out of her mind, I wouldn't say.

REBEKKA She seemed to go all to pieces when she found out she could never have children; that's when she first showed signs of madness.

MRS. HELSETH Yes, that was a dreadful blow to her, poor lady.

REBEKKA [*takes up her crochet work and sits in the chair by the window*] Still—it may have been the best thing for Mr. Rosmer.

MRS. HELSETH What, Miss?

REBEKKA That there were no children. Don't you think so?

MRS. HELSETH I don't quite know what to say to that.

REBEKKA I think it was. He could never have put up with a house full of children; they'd have disturbed him with their crying.

MRS. HELSETH But children don't cry at Rosmersholm, Miss.

REBEKKA [*looks at her*] Don't cry?

MRS. HELSETH No. As long as people can remember, children have never been known to cry in this house.

REBEKKA How very strange.

MRS. HELSETH Yes, isn't it? It runs in the family. And then there's another strange thing. When they grow up, they never laugh. Never—as long as they live.

REBEKKA Why, how queer—

MRS. HELSETH Do you ever remember hearing or seeing Pastor Rosmer laugh, Miss?

REBEKKA No—I don't believe I ever have, come to think of it. You're right, Mrs. Helseth. But then nobody laughs much in this part of the country, it seems to me.

MRS. HELSETH No, they don't. It began at Rosmersholm, they say. And I suppose it spread round about, like one of those contagions.

REBEKKA You're a very wise woman, Mrs. Helseth.

MRS. HELSETH Don't you go making fun of me, Miss! [*Listens.*] Hush—here's the Pastor coming down. He doesn't like to see me dusting. [*She goes out. Johannes Rosmer, with hat and stick in his hand, enters from the hall.*]

ROSMER Good morning, Rebekka.

REBEKKA Good morning, dear. [*A moment after—crocheting*] Are you going out?

ROSMER Yes.

REBEKKA It's such beautiful weather.

ROSMER You didn't come in to see me this morning.

REBEKKA No, I didn't. Not today.

ROSMER Aren't you going to in the future?

REBEKKA I don't know yet, dear.

ROSMER Has anything come for me?

REBEKKA The *County News* came, yes.

ROSMER The *County News*?

REBEKKA There it is—on the table.

ROSMER [*puts down his hat and cane*] Is there anything in it—?

REBEKKA Yes.

ROSMER Why didn't you send it up?

REBEKKA I thought you'd see it soon enough.

ROSMER Indeed? [*Takes the paper and reads, standing by the table.*] Good heavens! ". . . We feel it our duty to issue a solemn warning against unprincipled renegades." [*Looks at her.*] They call me a renegade, Rebekka.

REBEKKA They mention no names.

ROSMER It's obvious enough. [*Reads on.*] "Men who secretly betray the cause of righteousness . . ." "Brazen Judases who seize the opportunity to proclaim their apostasy as soon as they feel it will work to their advantage."— ". . . wanton defamation of a name honored through generations."—". . . in expectation of suitable rewards from the party momentarily in power." [*Lays down the paper on the table.*] How dare they—? Men who have known me intimately for years! They know there's not a word of truth in all this—they themselves can't possibly believe it.— Yet they write it all the same.

REBEKKA That's not all of it.

ROSMER [*takes up the paper again*] "Inexperience and lack of judgment the only excuse"— "pernicious influence—possibly extending to certain matters which, for the present, we prefer not to make public." [*Looks at her.*] What do they mean by that?

REBEKKA It is aimed at me—obviously.

ROSMER [*lays down the paper*] It's an outrage— the work of thoroughly dishonorable men.

REBEKKA Yes, I don't think they need throw stones at Mortensgaard!

ROSMER [*walks about the room*] This has got to stop. If this kind of thing continues, all that is best in human nature will be destroyed. It must be stopped. It must! If only I could find some way to bring a little light into all this hideous darkness—how happy I should be!

REBEKKA [*rises*] Yes, that would be a cause worth living for!

ROSMER If I could only make them see themselves! Make them repent and feel ashamed! If I could only make them see that they must work together for the common good—in charity and tolerance!

REBEKKA Try it, Rosmer, try! You could do it— I *know* you could!

ROSMER I believe it might be possible. And then—how glorious life would be! Instead of all this hideous discord—universal aspiration. A common goal. Each man in his own way contributing his best to further progress and enlightenment. Happiness for all—through all. [*Happens to look out of the window, shudders and says sadly*] But it could never come through me, Rebekka.

REBEKKA Why not through you?

ROSMER Nor could I ever have a share in it.

REBEKKA Stop doubting yourself, Rosmer!

ROSMER There can be no happiness where there is guilt.

REBEKKA [*looks straight before her*] Stop talking about guilt—!

ROSMER You know nothing about guilt, Rebekka. But I—

REBEKKA You least of all.

ROSMER [*points out the window*] The mill-race.

REBEKKA Oh, Rosmer—!

[*Mrs. Helseth looks in at the door.*]

MRS. HELSETH Miss West!

REBEKKA Not just now, Mrs. Helseth—presently!

MRS. HELSETH Just one word, Miss.

[*Rebekka goes to the door. Mrs. Helseth tells her something. They whisper together for a few moments. Mrs. Helseth nods and goes out.*]

ROSMER [*uneasily*] Was it anything for me?

REBEKKA No, just household matters. Why don't you go out into the fresh air, dear Rosmer. Take a good, long walk.

ROSMER [*takes up his hat*] Very well. Let's go together.

REBEKKA I can't just now. You go alone. Throw off these gloomy thoughts. Promise me that.

ROSMER I'm afraid I'll never be able to do that.

REBEKKA But this is a mere delusion, Rosmer! You must not let it gain a hold on you—

ROSMER It's no mere delusion. I brooded over it all night. Perhaps Beata was right after all.

REBEKKA In what?

ROSMER When she suspected me of being in love with you.

REBEKKA Ah! I see.

ROSMER [*lays his hat on the table*] I keep asking myself—weren't we deceiving ourselves when we called our feeling friendship?

REBEKKA Should we have called it—?

ROSMER Love—? Yes. Even while Beata was alive, it was always you I thought of—you I longed for. It was with you that I found peace and happiness. Thinking back—it seems to me we fell in love from the very first—as two children might; sweetly, mysteriously—untroubled by dreams of passion or desire. Don't you think that's true, Rebekka? Tell me.

REBEKKA [*struggling with herself*] I don't know what to answer.

ROSMER And we imagined this communion was merely friendship, when all the time it was a spiritual marriage. That is why I say I'm guilty. I had no right to it. No right—for Beata's sake.

REBEKKA No right to happiness? Is that what you believe, Rosmer?

ROSMER She watched us with the eyes of love—and judged us accordingly. What else could she have done? That judgment was inevitable.

REBEKKA But since she was wrong, why should you blame yourself?

ROSMER She killed herself for love of me. That fact remains. I shall never get over that, Rebekka.

REBEKKA You *must* get over it. You've devoted your life to a great cause—you must think only of that.

ROSMER [*shakes his head*] It can never be accomplished. Not by me. Not now that I know.

REBEKKA Why not by you?

ROSMER Because no victory was ever truly won by guilty men.

REBEKKA [*vehemently*] Oh, all these doubts, these fears, these scruples! They're all ancestral relics come to haunt you. It's like this myth about the dead returning in the shape of galloping white horses—it's all part of the same thing!

ROSMER That may be so—but if I can't escape these things, what difference does it make? And what I say is true, Rebekka; only a happy man —a blameless man—can bring a cause to lasting victory.

REBEKKA Does happiness mean so much to you, Rosmer?

ROSMER —Yes, it does.

REBEKKA And yet you don't know how to laugh!

ROSMER In spite of that, I have a great capacity for happiness.

REBEKKA You must go for your walk now, dear. A good long walk. Do you hear? There—here is your hat. And here is your stick.

ROSMER [*takes them from her*] Thanks. You're sure you won't come with me?

REBEKKA No, I can't just now.

ROSMER Very well; you're always with me, anyhow.

[*He goes out by the entrance door. Rebekka waits a moment, cautiously watching his departure from behind the open door; then she goes to the door on right.*]

REBEKKA [*opens the door and says in a low tone*] Mrs. Helseth! You may show him in, now.

[*Goes toward the window; a moment after, Professor Kroll enters. He bows silently and formally, and keeps his hat in his hand.*]

KROLL Has he gone?

REBEKKA Yes.

KROLL Does he usually stay out for some time?

REBEKKA Yes, usually. But one can't count on him today. So if you prefer not to see him—

KROLL No; it's you I want to see; and quite alone.

REBEKKA Then we had better not waste time. Sit down, Professor.

[*Sits in the easy chair by window; Kroll sits on chair beside her.*]

KROLL I don't suppose you quite realize, Miss West, how deeply this change in Johannes Rosmer has affected me.

REBEKKA We expected that would be so—at first.

KROLL Only at first?

REBEKKA Rosmer was so confident that sooner or later you would join him.

KROLL I?

REBEKKA Yes, you—and all his other friends as well.

KROLL There you see! That only goes to show

how faulty his judgment has become, where men and practical matters are concerned.

REBEKKA Well, after all—since he's chosen to be free—to stand completely on his own—

KROLL But wait—you see, I don't believe that for a moment.

REBEKKA Oh. Then what do you believe?

KROLL I believe *you* are at the bottom of it all.

REBEKKA Your wife put that into your head, Professor.

KROLL Never mind who put it into my head; the fact remains that I have a strong suspicion —an exceedingly strong suspicion—the more I think things over, and piece together what I know of your behavior ever since you came here.

REBEKKA [*looks at him*] I seem to recall a time when you felt an exceedingly strong faith in me, dear Professor. I might almost call it a *warm* faith.

KROLL [*in a subdued voice*] Whom could you not bewitch, if you set your mind to it?

REBEKKA You think I set my mind to—?

KROLL Yes, I do. I'm no longer such a fool as to imagine you had any feelings in the matter. You simply wanted to worm your way in here —to become firmly entrenched at Rosmersholm; and I was to help you do it. I see through your little game quite clearly now.

REBEKKA You seem to forget that it was Beata who begged and implored me to come and live out here.

KROLL Yes, when you had bewitched her too. For surely one could never call her feeling for you friendship? It was worship—idolatry. It developed into a kind of—I don't know what to call it—a kind of frenzied passion.—Yes, that's the only word for it.

REBEKKA Be so good as to remember your sister's condition. So far as I am concerned, I don't think anyone can accuse me of being hysterical.

KROLL No, that's true enough; and that makes you doubly dangerous to those you wish to get into your power. It's easy enough for you; you weigh each action with cold deliberation and accurately calculate each consequence; you're able to do this because you have no heart.

REBEKKA Are you so sure of that?

KROLL Yes; now I'm quite convinced of it. Otherwise how could you have lived here year after year pursuing your aim so ruthlessly? Well —you've succeeded in your purpose; you've gained full power over him and over everything around him. And in order to do this, you didn't hesitate to rob him of his happiness.

REBEKKA That is not true. I did no such thing— you, yourself, did that!

KROLL *I* did!

REBEKKA Yes, when you led him to imagine he was responsible for Beata's tragic death.

KROLL Has that really affected him so deeply?

REBEKKA Well, naturally. A mind as sensitive as his—

KROLL I thought a so-called emancipated man would be above such scruples— But I'm not surprised—in fact I anticipated something of the sort. Look at his ancestors—these men that stare out at us from all these portraits; the heritage they've handed down to him in an unbroken line through generations is not so easily discounted.

REBEKKA [*looks down thoughtfully*] It's true; Johannes Rosmer's family roots go deep.

KROLL Yes, and you should have taken that into account; especially if you had any real affection for him. But such a thing would be difficult for you to grasp. Your background is so entirely different.

REBEKKA What do you mean by background?

KROLL I am speaking of your origin—your family background, Miss West.

REBEKKA Oh, I see! It's true I come of very humble people; but still—

KROLL I am not referring to rank or social position. I was thinking of your moral background.

REBEKKA Moral—? In what sense?

KROLL The circumstances of your birth.

REBEKKA What do you mean by that?

KROLL I mention it only because I feel it accounts for your whole conduct.

REBEKKA I don't understand this. I demand an explanation!

KROLL I shouldn't have thought an explanation would be necessary. If you didn't know the facts, doesn't it seem rather odd that you should have let Dr. West adopt you?

REBEKKA [*rises*] Ah! Now I understand.

KROLL —and that you should have taken his name? Your mother's name was Gamvik.

REBEKKA [*walks across the room*] My father's name was Gamvik, Professor Kroll.

KROLL Your mother's work must have kept her in constant touch with the doctor of the district—

REBEKKA Yes, it did.

KROLL And at your mother's death he immediately adopts you and takes you to live with him. He treats you with the greatest harshness, yet you make no attempt to get away. You're well aware that he won't leave you a penny— actually, all he left you was a trunk full of books—and yet you stay on; you put up with him and nurse him to the end.

REBEKKA [*stands by the table, looking scornfully at him*] And because I did all this, you assume there must be something improper—something immoral about my birth?

KROLL I believe your care of him was the result of involuntary filial instinct. As a matter of fact I attribute your entire conduct to the circumstances of your birth.

REBEKKA [*vehemently*] But there is not a word of truth in what you say! And I can prove it! Dr. West didn't come to Finmark till after I was born.

KROLL I beg your pardon, Miss West, I've made inquiries. He was there the year before.

REBEKKA You're wrong! You're utterly wrong, I tell you!

KROLL The day before yesterday you told me yourself that you were twenty-nine—in your thirtieth year, you said.

REBEKKA Really! Did I say that?

KROLL Yes, you did. And I calculate from that—

REBEKKA Stop! You needn't. You might as well know—I'm a year older than I say I am.

KROLL [*smiles incredulously*] Indeed! You surprise me! What motive have you for that?

REBEKKA After I'd passed twenty-five I felt I was getting a little old for an unmarried woman, so I began to lie about my age.

KROLL I should have thought an emancipated woman like you would be above such conventions!

REBEKKA I know it was absurd and idiotic of me—but there you are! It's one of those silly ideas one clings to in spite of oneself.

KROLL Be that as it may; but that still does not refute my theory; for Dr. West paid a brief visit to Finmark the year before his appointment there.

REBEKKA [*with a vehement outburst*] That's not true!

KROLL Not true, Miss West?

REBEKKA No. My mother never mentioned such a thing.

KROLL She didn't—eh?

REBEKKA No, never. Nor Dr. West either; he never said a word about it.

KROLL Mightn't that have been because they both had good reason to wish to skip a year, just as you have done? Perhaps it runs in the family, Miss West.

REBEKKA [*walks about clenching and wringing her hands*] What you say is quite impossible. You simply want to trick me into believing it! But it's not true—it can't be true! It can't! It can't—!

KROLL [*rises*] My dear Miss West—why in Heaven's name are you so upset about it? You quite terrify me! What am I to think—to believe—?

REBEKKA Nothing! You must think and believe nothing.

KROLL Then you really must explain this agitation. Why should this matter—this possibility —affect you in this way?

REBEKKA [*controlling herself*] It is perfectly simple, Professor Kroll. I don't choose to be considered illegitimate.

KROLL I see! Well—I suppose I shall have to be satisfied with that explanation—at least for the time being. But then, am I to conclude that you still have certain prejudices on this point too?

REBEKKA Yes, I suppose I have.

KROLL I don't think this so-called Emancipation of yours goes very deep! You've steeped yourself in a lot of new ideas and new opinions. You've picked up a lot of theories out of books

—theories that claim to overthrow certain irrefutable and unassailable principles—principles that form the bulwark of our Society. But this has been no more than a superficial, intellectual exercise, Miss West. It has never really been absorbed into your bloodstream.

REBEKKA [*thoughtfully*] Perhaps you are right.

KROLL Just put yourself to the test—you'll see! And if this is true of you, how much truer must it be of Johannes Rosmer. For him all this is sheer, unmitigated madness—it's running blindfold to destruction! Do you suppose a man of his sensitive retiring nature could bear to be an outcast—to be persecuted by all his former friends—exposed to ruthless attacks from all the best elements in the community? Of course not! He's not the man to endure that.

REBEKKA He must endure it! It's too late for him to turn back now.

KROLL No, it's not too late—not by any means; it's still possible to hush the matter up—or it can be attributed to a mere temporary aberration, however deplorable. But one thing is essential.

REBEKKA What might that be?

KROLL You must persuade him to legalize this relationship, Miss West.

REBEKKA His relationship with me?

KROLL Yes. You must insist on his doing that.

REBEKKA You still cling to the belief that our relationship requires to be legalized, as you call it?

KROLL I prefer not to examine the situation too closely. But I seem to have noticed that the usual cause for lightly disregarding the so-called conventions is—

REBEKKA A relationship between man and woman, you mean?

KROLL Frankly—yes. That is my opinion.

REBEKKA [*wanders across the room and looks out the window*] I might almost say—I wish you were right, Professor Kroll.

KROLL What do you mean? You say that very strangely.

REBEKKA Oh, never mind—don't let's discuss it any more. Listen! Here he comes.

KROLL So soon! I must go, then.

REBEKKA [*goes towards him*] No—please stay.

There's something I want you to hear.

KROLL Not just now. I don't think I could bear to see him.

REBEKKA Please—I beg you! You'll regret it later, if you don't. It's the last time I shall ever ask anything of you.

KROLL [*looks at her in surprise and puts down his hat*] Very well, Miss West—if you insist. [*A short silence. Then Johannes Rosmer enters from the hall.*]

ROSMER [*sees the professor and stops in the doorway*] What! You here!

REBEKKA He would have preferred not to meet you, dearest.

KROLL [*involuntarily*] "Dearest"!

REBEKKA Yes, Professor; Rosmer and I sometimes call each other "dearest." That's another result of our relationship.

KROLL Was this what you wanted me to hear?

REBEKKA That—and a good deal more.

ROSMER [*comes forward*] What is the purpose of this visit?

KROLL I wanted to make one last effort to stop you—to win you back.

ROSMER [*points to the newspaper*] After what's printed there?

KROLL I did not write it.

ROSMER Did you take any steps to prevent it?

KROLL I should not have felt justified in doing that. It was not in my power, in any case.

REBEKKA [*tears the paper into shreds, crushes up the pieces and throws them behind the stove*] There! Now it's out of sight; let it be out of mind, too. There'll be no more of that sort of thing, Rosmer.

KROLL If you use your influence, you can make sure of that!

REBEKKA Come and sit down, Rosmer. Let's all sit down. I'm going to tell you everything.

ROSMER [*seats himself mechanically*] What has come over you, Rebekka? Why this peculiar calm? What is it?

REBEKKA It's the calm of decision. [*Seats herself.*] Sit down—you too, Professor.
[*Kroll seats himself.*]

ROSMER Decision? What decision?

REBEKKA I've come to a decision, Rosmer. I'm going to give you back what to you makes life worth living: your confidence of innocence.

ROSMER What are you talking about!

REBEKKA Just listen to me—then you'll know.

ROSMER Well?

REBEKKA When I first came here from Finmark —with Dr. West—I felt as if a great, new, wonderful world was opening up before me. Dr. West had taught me many things—in fact, all the scattered knowledge I had of life in those days, I'd learned from him. [*With a struggle and in a scarcely audible voice*] And then—

KROLL And then?

ROSMER But, Rebekka—I already know all this.

REBEKKA [*mastering herself*] Yes, of course; I suppose you do.

KROLL [*looks hard at her*] Perhaps I had better go.

REBEKKA No, stay where you are, Professor. [*To Rosmer*] So, you see—I wanted to be a part of this new world; I wanted to belong to it—to share in all these new ideas. One day Professor Kroll was telling me of the great influence Ulrik Brendel had over you, when you were still a boy; I suddenly thought it might be possible for me to carry on his work.

ROSMER You came here with a hidden purpose—?

REBEKKA I wanted us to join hands and work for this new Freedom; we were to be in the very front ranks and march on side by side; Forward—always forward. But I soon found there was a gloomy, insurmountable barrier standing in your way.

ROSMER Barrier? What barrier?

REBEKKA I knew there could be no freedom for you unless you could break loose—get out into the clear bright sunshine. I saw you pining away here; defeated—stultified by your disastrous marriage.

ROSMER You've never before spoken of my marriage in such terms.

REBEKKA No—I did not dare; I didn't want to frighten you.

KROLL [*nods to Rosmer*] Do you hear that?

REBEKKA [*goes on*] I could see where your salvation lay—your only salvation. And so I set to work.

ROSMER Set to work? How?

KROLL Do you mean by that—?

REBEKKA Yes, Rosmer.—[*Rises.*] No! Stay where you are! You too, Professor Kroll. Now you must know the truth. It wasn't you, Rosmer. You are entirely innocent. It was *I* who worked on Beata and deliberately lured her into madness.

ROSMER [*springs up*] Rebekka!

KROLL [*rises from sofa*] —into madness!

REBEKKA Yes, the madness that led her to the mill-race. That is the truth. Now you know all about it.

ROSMER [*as if stunned*] I don't understand.— What is it she's saying? I don't understand a word—!

KROLL But I'm beginning to.

ROSMER But what did you do? What could you possibly have said to her? There was nothing to tell—absolutely nothing!

REBEKKA She was given to understand that you were gradually working yourself free from all your former beliefs and prejudices.

ROSMER Yes, but that was not true at the time.

REBEKKA I knew it soon would be.

KROLL [*nods to Rosmer*] Aha!

ROSMER Well? And what else? I must know everything.

REBEKKA Shortly after that—I begged and implored her to let me go away from Rosmersholm.

ROSMER What made you want to go—then?

REBEKKA I didn't want to. I wanted to stay here. But I led her to believe it would be wisest for me to go—for all our sakes—before it was too late. I hinted that if I were to remain here, something—anything—might happen.

ROSMER You actually did all this!

REBEKKA Yes, Rosmer.

ROSMER So that is what you meant by "setting to work"!

REBEKKA [*in a broken voice*] That's what I meant—yes.

ROSMER [*after a pause*] Have you confessed everything now, Rebekka?

REBEKKA Yes.

KROLL No, not quite.

REBEKKA [*looks at him in fear*] What more could there be?

KROLL Didn't you finally persuade Beata that it was necessary—not merely that it would be wisest—but that it was definitely necessary for you to go away as soon as possible—for yours and Rosmer's sake? Well? Didn't you?

REBEKKA [*low and indistinctly*] I may have.— Yes, perhaps.

ROSMER [*sinks into armchair by window*] And she was deceived by all these lies! Poor, wretched, bewildered little thing—she actually believed them; firmly believed them! [*Looks up at Rebekka.*] Oh! Why didn't she come to me! But she didn't—she never said a word. You persuaded her not to, didn't you, Rebekka? I see it in your face.

REBEKKA She had become obsessed by the fact that she was childless—and never could have children; because of that she felt she had no right here. She was convinced it was her duty to efface herself—her duty to you, I mean.

ROSMER And you did nothing to dissuade her from that thought?

REBEKKA No.

KROLL Perhaps you confirmed her in it? Answer me! Didn't you?

REBEKKA I dare say that's how she understood it.

ROSMER She always gave way to you in everything; you dominated her completely. And then —she *did* efface herself! [*Springs up.*] How could you play this horrible game, Rebekka?

REBEKKA I had to choose between your life and hers.

KROLL [*severely and impressively*] What right had you to make such a choice!

REBEKKA [*vehemently*] You seem to think I acted with shrewd deliberation—that I was cold and calm about it all; but I was a very different person then. And, anyway—most people's minds are divided, it seems to me. I wanted Beata out of the way—somehow; but at the same time it never occurred to me that the thing would really happen. A voice inside me kept crying out "Stop! No further!"—but I couldn't resist the impulse to go on. And I went on—step by step—in spite of myself. I thought: a little further—just a little further; a tiny step more—and then another; I couldn't stop! And suddenly—there it was! That's the way these things happen, you see.
[*A short silence.*]

ROSMER [*to Rebekka*] What will become of you now? After this?

REBEKKA I don't know. It doesn't greatly matter.

KROLL Not a single word of remorse! I dare say you feel none?

REBEKKA [*coldly putting aside his question*] You must excuse me, Professor Kroll—that concerns no one but myself. I shall deal with that in my own way.

KROLL [*to Rosmer*] So this is the woman you've been sharing your life with—in the closest intimacy! [*Looks round at the portraits.*] I wonder what all these good souls would say, if they could see us now!

ROSMER Are you going back to town?

KROLL [*takes up his hat*] Yes. The sooner, the better.

ROSMER [*does the same*] Then I'll go with you.

KROLL You will! There—you see! I was sure we hadn't really lost you.

ROSMER Come, Kroll! Let us go.
[*Both go out through the hall without looking at Rebekka. After a moment Rebekka goes cautiously to the window and looks out through the flowers.*]

REBEKKA [*speaks to herself under her breath*] And still he won't venture over the bridge— he's taking the upper-road again. He never will cross by the mill-race. Never. [*Leaves the window.*] Ah, well!
[*Goes and pulls bell-rope—a moment after, Mrs. Helseth enters.*]

MRS. HELSETH Yes, Miss?

REBEKKA Mrs. Helseth, would you be so kind as to have my trunk brought down from the attic?

MRS. HELSETH Your trunk, Miss?

REBEKKA Yes, you know, the brown sealskin trunk.

MRS. HELSETH I know the one, Miss. Are you going on a journey?

REBEKKA Yes, Mrs. Helseth—I'm going on a journey.

MRS. HELSETH You mean—at once?

REBEKKA As soon as I've packed.

MRS. HELSETH Well—I must say! You'll be back soon, won't you, Miss?

REBEKKA I'm never coming back, Mrs. Helseth.

MRS. HELSETH *Never,* Miss! But how shall we manage at Rosmersholm without you? And just when the poor master was beginning to be happy and comfortable, too!

REBEKKA I had a bad fright today, Mrs. Helseth.

MRS. HELSETH Good gracious, Miss! How?

REBEKKA I thought I caught a glimpse of the White Horses.

MRS. HELSETH The White Horses! In broad daylight!

REBEKKA I expect they're around both day and night—the White Horses of Rosmersholm. [*With a change of tone*] And now—would you see to the trunk, Mrs. Helseth?

MRS. HELSETH Yes, of course, Miss; the trunk. [*They both go out by the door right.*]

Act Four

The sitting-room at Rosmersholm. Late evening. A lighted lamp, with a lamp-shade, on the table. Rebekka West stands by the table, packing some small articles in a handbag. Her cloak, hat and the white crocheted shawl are hanging over the back of the sofa.

Mrs. Helseth enters from the door right.

MRS. HELSETH [*speaks in a low voice and appears ill at ease*] All your things are down now, Miss. They're in the kitchen hallway.

REBEKKA Thank you. You've ordered the carriage?

MRS. HELSETH Yes. What time will you want it, Miss? The coachman wants to know.

REBEKKA About eleven o'clock, I should think. The steamer sails at midnight.

MRS. HELSETH [*hesitates a little*] But what about Mr. Rosmer? Supposing he's not back by then?

REBEKKA I'll have to leave all the same. If I don't see him, say I'll write to him—a long letter, tell him.

MRS HELSETH Letters may be all very well—but, poor Miss West— Don't you think you should try and have another talk with him?

REBEKKA Perhaps. And yet—perhaps I'd better not.

MRS. HELSETH To think I should live to see this! I certainly never thought a thing like this would happen!

REBEKKA What *did* you think then, Mrs. Helseth?

MRS. HELSETH I thought Pastor Rosmer would be more dependable.

REBEKKA Dependable?

MRS. HELSETH That's what I said, Miss.

REBEKKA But, my dear Mrs. Helseth, what do you mean by that?

MRS. HELSETH I mean what's right and proper, Miss. He shouldn't be allowed to get out of it like this.

REBEKKA [*looks at her*] Listen to me, Mrs. Helseth—I want you to be quite honest with me; why do you think I am going away?

MRS. HELSETH I suppose it can't be helped, Miss. But it's not right of Pastor Rosmer all the same. There was some excuse for Mortensgaard; her husband was still alive, you see—so they couldn't marry, however much they wanted to. But in Pastor Rosmer's case—!

REBEKKA [*with a faint smile*] Did you actually believe such a thing of Pastor Rosmer and me?

MRS. HELSETH No, never, Miss! That is, I mean —not until today.

REBEKKA And what made you change your mind?

MRS. HELSETH I'm told the papers are saying dreadful things about the Pastor—

REBEKKA Aha!

MRS. HELSETH I wouldn't put anything past a man who would take up Mortensgaard's religion!

REBEKKA I see. But what about me? What have you to say of me?

MRS. HELSETH Lord bless me, Miss—I can't think you're to blame. We're all of us human—and it's not easy for a single woman to be always on her guard.

REBEKKA That is very true, Mrs. Helseth.— We are all of us human.— Did you hear something?

MRS. HELSETH [*in a low voice*] I thought—I do believe he's coming, Miss.

REBEKKA [*starts*] In that case—? [*Resolutely*] Well—so be it.

[*Rosmer enters from hall.*]

ROSMER [*sees handbag, etc.—turns to Rebekka and asks*] What does this mean?

REBEKKA I am going.

ROSMER At once?

REBEKKA Yes. [*To Mrs. Helseth*] Eleven o'clock, then.

MRS. HELSETH Very well, Miss. [*Goes out by the door right.*]

ROSMER [*after a short pause*] Where are you going, Rebekka?

REBEKKA North; by the steamer.

ROSMER Why North?

REBEKKA That's where I came from.

ROSMER What do you plan to do?

REBEKKA I don't know. I just want to put an end to the whole business.

ROSMER Put an end to it?

REBEKKA Rosmersholm has crushed me.

ROSMER [*his attention aroused*] How can you say that?

REBEKKA Crushed me utterly—completely. When I came here I had a healthy, fearless spirit—but I've had to bow before an alien law. I no longer have the courage to face anything.

ROSMER Why not? What law do you mean?

REBEKKA Don't let's talk about it, Rosmer. What happened between you and Kroll?

ROSMER We have made peace.

REBEKKA I see. So that is how it ended.

ROSMER All our old friends were gathered at his house. They convinced me that the kind of work I had in mind was not for me. And anyway—the rehabilitation of mankind—! How hopeless it all seems! I shall give up all thought of that.

REBEKKA Perhaps it's for the best.

ROSMER Have you come to think that too?

REBEKKA These past few days I've come to think it; yes.

ROSMER You're lying.

REBEKKA Lying—!

ROSMER Yes, you're lying. You never really had faith in me. You never really believed I would succeed.

REBEKKA I believed we might succeed together.

ROSMER That's not true, either. You believed yourself destined for great things; you believed you could use me as an instrument—as a means

to serve your ends. That's what you believed.

REBEKKA Listen to me, Rosmer—

ROSMER [*seats himself listlessly on the sofa*] Oh, what is the use? I know the truth now. I've been nothing but clay in your hands.

REBEKKA You *must* listen to me, Rosmer. We must talk this thing through. It'll be the last time we'll ever talk together. [*Sits in chair close to sofa.*] I was going to write you all about it —once I'd got away—but perhaps it's best that I should tell you now.

ROSMER Have you still more to confess?

REBEKKA Yes. The most vital thing of all.

ROSMER Vital—?

REBEKKA Something you've never suspected for a moment—and yet it's the key to all the rest.

ROSMER [*shakes his head*] I don't understand.

REBEKKA It is true that I did everything to worm my way in here—I had a feeling it would be to my advantage whichever way things went.

ROSMER And you succeeded in your purpose.

REBEKKA In those days I believe I could have succeeded in absolutely anything—my spirit was still free and fearless then. I had no scruples; no personal ties stood in my way. Then I began to be possessed by the thing that was to crush me—the thing that broke my spirit and warped my life forever.

ROSMER Why can't you speak plainly?

REBEKKA I became possessed by a wild, uncontrollable passion, Rosmer—

ROSMER Passion? You—! For what? For whom?

REBEKKA For you.

ROSMER [*tries to spring up*] What—?

REBEKKA [*stops him*] No—stay where you are! Let me go on.

ROSMER You mean to tell me you loved me— in that way?

REBEKKA At that time I called it love. Yes, I thought it was love, then. But now I know it wasn't. It was what I just said: a wild, uncontrollable passion.

ROSMER [*with difficulty*] Can this be true, Rebekka? Is it possible that you're really speaking of *yourself*?

REBEKKA It's hard for you to believe it of me, isn't it?

ROSMER So this was the cause—this was the reason—that you "set to work" as you call it?

REBEKKA It swept over me like a storm at sea—like one of those winter-storms we have up in the North. It seizes hold of you and carries you off with it—wherever it will. Resistance is impossible.

ROSMER And you let this storm carry poor Beata to her death.

REBEKKA Yes. It was a death-struggle between us at that time, you see.

ROSMER You were certainly the strongest; stronger than Beata and me together.

REBEKKA I knew you well enough to realize that I had no hope of reaching you until you were a free man—not only in spirit, but in fact.

ROSMER But I don't understand you, Rebekka. You—your whole conduct—is incomprehensible to me. I am free now—both in spirit and in fact. You have reached the very goal you aimed at from the first. And yet—in spite of that—

REBEKKA I have never been further from my goal than I am now.

ROSMER And yet in spite of that, I say—yesterday when I asked you, begged you, to be my wife—you cried out, as if in terror, that that could never be!

REBEKKA I cried out in despair, Rosmer.

ROSMER But why?

REBEKKA Because Rosmersholm has robbed me of my strength. My spirit that was once so fearless has become warped and crippled here —as though its wings had been clipped. I no longer have any daring, Rosmer—I've lost the power of action.

ROSMER How did this happen to you?

REBEKKA Through living with you.

ROSMER But how? How?

REBEKKA When I found myself alone with you —and you began to be yourself again—

ROSMER Yes, yes?

REBEKKA —for you were never quite yourself while Beata was alive—

ROSMER No—I'm afraid that's true.

REBEKKA Then I was able to live here with you in peace, in solitude; you confided your thoughts to me without reserve; I became aware af your slightest mood—of all the tenderness and delicacy of your nature; and gradually—little by little—a great change came over me. At first it was almost imperceptible—but it grew and grew—until at last it dominated my whole being.

ROSMER What *is* all this, Rebekka!

REBEKKA And all that other thing—that evil, sensual thing—seemed to fade into the distance. All violent passion subsided—conquered by silence. My mind was filled with peace. My spirit became still; it was like the stillness on one of our northern birdcliffs under the midnight sun.

ROSMER Tell me more about this, Rebekka. Everything you know about it—tell me!

REBEKKA There's not much more to tell. Only this: I knew then that love had come to me; real love—love that asks nothing for itself— that is content with life together—just as we have known it.

ROSMER If I'd only had an inkling of all this—!

REBEKKA It's perhaps best as it is. Yesterday when you asked me to be your wife—I cried out with joy—

ROSMER Yes, you did, didn't you, Rebekka? It sounded so to me.

REBEKKA For a moment—yes! For a moment I forgot myself! It was my former fearless spirit trying to assert itself—struggling for freedom. But it no longer has any power—no power to endure.

ROSMER How do you account for this change in you?

REBEKKA My will has become infected by the Rosmer view on life—your view on life at any rate.

ROSMER Infected?

REBEKKA Yes! It has grown weak and sickly. It's become a slave to laws that it despised before. Living with you, Rosmer, has exalted and purified my spirit—

ROSMER How I wish I could believe that, Rebekka—!

REBEKKA You *can* believe it. The Rosmer view on life exalts—but—but—!

ROSMER Well?

REBEKKA —it kills happiness!

ROSMER You really think that?

REBEKKA I know it does, for me.

ROSMER How can you be so sure? If I were to ask you again, now, Rebekka—if I were to beg you—to entreat you—

REBEKKA My dearest—you must never speak of this again! There's something—in my past—that makes it quite impossible!

ROSMER Something beyond what you've already told me?

REBEKKA Yes. It has to do with something else —something quite different.

ROSMER I've sometimes thought—isn't it strange, Rebekka?—I've sometimes thought I knew.

REBEKKA And yet—? In spite of that—?

ROSMER I never really believed it. I used to speculate on it sometimes—play with it—in my thoughts—

REBEKKA I'll tell you about it—if you want me to—

ROSMER No—not a word! Whatever it may be —I can forget it.

REBEKKA But I can't, you see.

ROSMER Rebekka—!

REBEKKA That's what's so dreadful, Rosmer! Happiness is here; I've only to stretch out my hand to seize it. But now I've changed, and this—thing in my past, stands in the way.

ROSMER Your past is dead, Rebekka. It can no longer touch you—it no longer has any claim on you, as you are now.

REBEKKA You know those are just phrases! What about innocence? Can I ever find that again?

ROSMER [*wearily*] Innocence—!

REBEKKA Innocence, yes. Happiness and joy cannot exist without it—you said that yourself, Rosmer. That was the truth you wanted to instill in those noble men you dreamed of—

ROSMER Don't remind me of that, Rebekka. It was an immature dream, a nebulous fancy— I no longer believe in it myself. Nobility cannot be imposed upon us from without.

REBEKKA [*quietly*] Not even by love, Rosmer? Quiet, unselfish love?

ROSMER [*thoughtfully*] Yes—what a great power that could be! How glorious—if only it existed! But does it? If I were only sure—if I could only convince myself of that.

REBEKKA You don't believe me, Rosmer?

ROSMER How can I believe you fully—when I think of all these incredible things you've concealed from me for years? And now—this new approach—how do I know what secret purpose lies behind it? Is there something you wish to gain by it? Be honest with me! You know I'll do anything in my power to give you what you want.

REBEKKA [*wringing her hands*] Oh these doubts —these morbid doubts! Rosmer, Rosmer!

ROSMER I know! But what can I do? I'll never be able to get rid of them. How can I ever be quite certain of your love?

REBEKKA But you must know in your heart how truly changed I am—and that this change has come to me through you—because of you!

ROSMER I no longer believe in my power to change others, Rebekka. I no longer believe in myself in any way. I have no faith in myself, and I have no faith in you.

REBEKKA [*looks at him sadly*] How will you be able to endure life, Rosmer?

ROSMER I don't know. I can't imagine how. I don't think I will be able to endure it. I can think of nothing in this world worth living for.

REBEKKA Still—life renews itself continually. Let's cling to it, Rosmer. We shall leave it soon enough.

ROSMER [*jumps up restlessly*] Then give me back my faith. My faith in your love, Rebekka! My faith in you! Give me proof! I must have proof!

REBEKKA Proof! How can I give you proof?

ROSMER You must! I can't endure this desolation—this dreadful emptiness—this—this—
[*A loud knock at the hall door.*]

REBEKKA [*starts from her chair*] What was that?
[*The door opens. Ulrik Brendel enters. He wears a dress shirt, a black coat and a good pair of high shoes, with his trousers tucked into them. Otherwise he is dressed as in the first act. He looks excited.*]

ROSMER Oh—it's you, Mr. Brendel!

BRENDEL Johannes, my boy—hail and farewell!

ROSMER Where are you going so late at night?

BRENDEL Downhill.

ROSMER How do you mean?

BRENDEL I am going home, beloved pupil. I am homesick for the great Nothingness.

ROSMER Something has happened to you, Mr. Brendel; what is it?

BRENDEL So, you notice the change in me, eh?

I'm not surprised! When last I entered these halls, I was a prosperous man—full of self-confidence—

ROSMER I don't quite understand—

BRENDEL But tonight you see me a deposed monarch, squatting on the ash-heap that was once my palace.

ROSMER If there's anything I can do to help you—

BRENDEL You have managed to retain your good child-like heart, Johannes. Could you oblige me with a loan?

ROSMER Of course! Gladly.

BRENDEL Could you spare me an ideal or two?

ROSMER What did you say?

BRENDEL A couple of cast-off ideals? You'd be doing a good deed, I assure you. For I'm broke, my boy. Cleaned out. Stripped.

REBEKKA Didn't you give your lecture, Mr. Brendel?

BRENDEL No, entrancing lady. Only think! Just as I stood there ready to empty my horn of plenty, I made the painful discovery that I was bankrupt.

REBEKKA But what about all those unwritten works of yours?

BRENDEL I've sat for twenty-five years like a miser on his money-bags. And yesterday—when I went to open them, intending to pour forth the treasure—I found there was none! The Teeth of Time had ground it into dust. It all amounted to *nichts* and nothing!

ROSMER Are you quite sure of that?

BRENDEL There is no room for doubt, my boy. The President convinced me.

ROSMER The President?

BRENDEL Well—his Excellency, then. *Ganz nach Belieben.*

ROSMER But whom do you mean?

BRENDEL Peder Mortensgaard, of course.

ROSMER What!

BRENDEL [*mysteriously*] Hush! Peder Mortensgaard is Lord and Master of the Future. Never have I stood in a more august presence. Peder Mortensgaard has divine power; he is omnipotent; he can do anything he wills!

ROSMER You don't really believe that!

BRENDEL Yes, my boy! For Peder Mortensgaard never *wills* more than he can do. Peder Mor-

tensgaard is capable of living without ideals. And that, you see, is the secret of action and success. It is the sum of worldly wisdom. *Basta!*

ROSMER [*in a low voice*] I understand now why you're leaving poorer than you came.

BRENDEL *Bien!* So just take a *Beispiel* from your old teacher. Throw out everything he tried to impress upon your mind. Don't build your house on shifting sand. And be wary—be very sure—before you build too many hopes on this charming creature who fills your life with sweetness.

REBEKKA Is that meant for me?

BRENDEL Yes, my fascinating mermaid.

REBEKKA Why shouldn't he build hopes on me?

BRENDEL [*comes a step nearer*] It seems my former pupil has chosen to fight for a great cause.

REBEKKA Well—?

BRENDEL His Victory is certain, but—remember this—on one irrevocable condition.

REBEKKA What condition?

BRENDEL [*taking her gently by the wrist*] That the woman who loves him, will gladly go out into the kitchen and hack off her sweet, rosy, little finger—here—right at the middle joint. Item: that the aforesaid loving woman will—with equal gladness—chop off her incomparable, exquisite, left ear. [*Lets her go, and turns to Rosmer.*] Farewell, my victorious Johannes.

ROSMER Are you going now? In the dark? In the middle of the night?

BRENDEL The dark is best. Peace be with you. [*He goes. There is a short silence in the room.*]

REBEKKA [*breathes heavily*] It's so close in here—it's stifling! [*Goes to the window, opens it, and remains standing by it.*]

ROSMER [*sits down in arm-chair by stove*] There's nothing else to do, Rebekka—I see that now. You'll have to go away.

REBEKKA Yes, I see no choice.

ROSMER Let's make the most of these last moments. Come over here and sit with me.

REBEKKA [*goes and sits on the sofa*] What have you to say to me, Rosmer?

ROSMER First I want to tell you this; you needn't have any anxiety about your future.

REBEKKA [*smiles*] Ha—my future!

ROSMER I took care of that long ago. Whatever

happens, you will be looked after.

REBEKKA You thought of that too—my dearest!

ROSMER I should think you'd have known that.

REBEKKA It's a long time since I've concerned myself with things of that sort.

ROSMER I suppose you thought things could never change between us.

REBEKKA Yes, I did.

ROSMER So did I. But if I were to go—

REBEKKA You will live longer than I will, Rosmer—

ROSMER This wretched life of mine! At least I have the power to end it when I choose.

REBEKKA What do you mean? You'd never think of—?

ROSMER Would that be so strange? I've allowed myself to be defeated—miserably, ignominiously defeated. I turned my back on the work I had to do; I surrendered—gave up the fight before it had actually begun!

REBEKKA You must take it up again, Rosmer! You'll win—you'll see! You have the power to change men's spirits; to fill their minds with hope and aspiration—to bring nobility into their lives. Try! Don't give up the fight!

ROSMER I no longer have faith, Rebekka!

REBEKKA But you've already proved your power. You've changed my spirit. As long as I live I can never go back to being what I was.

ROSMER If I could only believe that.

REBEKKA [*pressing her hands together*] Oh, Rosmer! Do you know of nothing—nothing, that could make you believe that?

ROSMER [*starts as if in fear*] Don't ask me that, Rebekka! This must go no further. Don't say another word!

REBEKKA But it must go further! Tell me! Do you know of anything that could remove this doubt? I can think of nothing.

ROSMER It's best that you shouldn't—best for us both.

REBEKKA No! I won't be put off with that. Do you know of anything that would absolve me in your eyes? If you do—I have the right to know it.

ROSMER [*as if impelled against his will to speak*] Very well—let's see. You say you're filled with a great love—a pure, transcendent love. That through me your spirit has been changed—your life transformed. Is this really true, Rebekka? You're sure of that? Shall we put it to the test?

REBEKKA I am ready to do that.

ROSMER At any time?

REBEKKA Now, if you like. The sooner the better.

ROSMER Then would you be willing, Rebekka—now—this evening—for my sake—to— [*Breaks off.*] Oh—no, no!

REBEKKA Yes, Rosmer—yes! Tell me, and you'll see!

ROSMER Have you the courage to—are you willing to—gladly, as Ulrik Brendel said—for my sake, now tonight—gladly—to go the same way Beata went?

REBEKKA [*rises slowly from the sofa; almost voiceless*] Rosmer!

ROSMER That question will go on haunting me after you're gone; I shan't be able to get away from it. Over and over again I shall come back to it. I can picture it so clearly: You're standing out on the bridge, right in the very center. Now you're leaning far out over the railing, as though hypnotized by the rushing stream below. But then—you turn away. You dare not do—what she did.

REBEKKA And supposing I *did* dare? Dared to do it—gladly? What then?

ROSMER I should *have* to believe you then. My faith would be restored to me; faith in my vision of life—faith in my power to make men see that vision.

REBEKKA [*takes up her shawl slowly, and puts it over her head; says with composure*] You shall have your faith again.

ROSMER Have you the courage, have you the will—to do this, Rebekka?

REBEKKA You'll know that tomorrow—or later—when they find my body.

ROSMER [*puts his hand to his forehead*] There's a ghastly fascination about this—

REBEKKA For I don't want to be left down there—any longer than necessary. You must see that they find me.

ROSMER [*springs up*] This is sheer madness! Go—or stay, if you will! I'll believe anything you tell me—just as I always have.

REBEKKA These are just words, Rosmer! This time, there can be no escape in cowardice. After today—how can you ever believe in me again?

ROSMER But I don't want to see you fail, Rebekka.

REBEKKA I shall not fail.

ROSMER You won't be able to help it. You'd never have the courage Beata had.

REBEKKA Don't you think so?

ROSMER No—never. You're not like Beata. You're not under the spell of madness.

REBEKKA No. But I've fallen under another spell—the spell of Rosmersholm; and now I know that if I've sinned, then I must pay the penalty.

ROSMER [*looks at her fixedly*] Is that what you've come to believe, Rebekka?

REBEKKA Yes.

ROSMER [*with resolution*] Well, I still believe that man is a free spirit. There is no judge above us; we must each judge ourselves.

REBEKKA [*misunderstanding him*] That's true, too. My going will save what's best in you.

ROSMER There's nothing left in me to save.

REBEKKA Oh, yes there is! But as for me—I should be nothing but a kind of sea-troll, clinging to the ship on which you must sail forward —pulling it back. I must go overboard. Why should I stay on in this world dragging out a stunted life? Pondering and brooding over a happiness that my past forbids me to enjoy? No—I must get out of the game.

ROSMER If you go—then I go with you.

REBEKKA [*smiles almost imperceptibly, looks at him, and says more softly*] Yes, you come too —you shall be witness—

ROSMER I will go with you, I say.

REBEKKA As far as the bridge, yes. You know you never dare set foot on it.

ROSMER You've noticed that?

REBEKKA [*sadly and brokenly*] Yes; that's how I knew my love was hopeless.

ROSMER I lay my hand upon your head, Rebekka—and take you in marriage as my true wife.

REBEKKA [*takes both his hands, and bows her head towards his breast*] Thank you, Rosmer. [*Lets him go.*] Now I can go—gladly!

ROSMER Man and wife should go together.

REBEKKA Only as far as the bridge, Rosmer.

ROSMER Out onto the bridge too; I have the courage now. However far you go—I shall go with you.

REBEKKA Are you quite certain, Rosmer? Is this the best way for you?

ROSMER I'm quite certain it's the only way.

REBEKKA What if you were deceiving yourself? Supposing this were only a delusion— One of those White Horses that prey on Rosmersholm?

ROSMER It may be so. The White Horses! We Rosmers can never escape them!

REBEKKA Then stay, Rosmer!

ROSMER The husband belongs with his wife, as the wife with her husband.

REBEKKA Tell me this first: Is it you who go with me? Or is it I who go with you?

ROSMER We shall never know the answer to that question, Rebekka.

REBEKKA I should so like to know—

ROSMER We go together, Rebekka. I with you, and you with me.

REBEKKA Yes—I believe that's true—

ROSMER For now we two are *one*.

REBEKKA Yes, now we are *one*. Come! Let us go—gladly! [*They go out hand in hand through the hall, and are seen to turn to the left. The door remains open. The room stands empty for a little while. Then the door to the right is opened by Mrs. Helseth.*]

MRS. HELSETH Miss West—the carriage is— [*Looks around.*] No one here? They must have gone out together—at this time of night too! [*Goes out into hall, looks round, and comes in again.*] They're not out on the bench. Ah, well —[*Goes to the window and looks out.*] Lord bless me! What's that white thing out there—! It's them—out on the bridge, and in each other's arms! [*Shrieks aloud.*] Ah! Over the railing— both of them—down into the mill-race! Help! Help! [*Her knees tremble; she leans on the chair-back, shaking all over; she can scarcely get the words out.*] No! No one can help them now. It's the dead wife—the dead wife has taken them.

MANY SUMMARIES of Ibsen's dramatic method have been attempted: he is, after all, the founding father of the modern theater. Shaw's, in 1913, is famous. J. W. McFarlane's, made in 1960, adds a desirable note of mystery to the earlier judgment.

The drama was born of old from the union of two desires: the desire to have a dance and the desire to hear a story. The dance became a rant: the story became a situation. When Ibsen began to make plays, the art of the dramatist had shrunk into the art of contriving a situation. And it was held that the stranger the situation, the better the play. Ibsen saw that, on the contrary, the more familiar the situation, the more interesting the play. Shakespear had put ourselves on the stage but not our situations. Our uncles seldom murder our fathers, and cannot legally marry our mothers; we do not meet witches; our kings are not as a rule stabbed and succeeded by their stabbers; and when we raise money by bills we do not promise to pay pounds of our flesh. Ibsen supplies the want left by Shakespear. He gives us not only ourselves, but ourselves in our own situations. The things that happen to his stage figures are things that happen to us. One consequence is that his plays are much more important to us than Shakespear's. Another is that they are capable both of hurting us cruelly and of filling us with excited hopes of escape from idealistic tyrannies, and with visions of intenser life in the future. [Bernard Shaw, *The Quintessence of Ibsenism* (1913), Hill and Wang, Inc., New York, 1957, p. 182.]

The new technique is new only on the modern stage. It has been used by preachers and orators ever since speech was invented. It is the technique of playing upon the human conscience; and it has been practised by the playwright whenever the playwright has been capable of it. Rhetoric, irony, argument, paradox, epigram, parable, the rearrangement of haphazard facts into orderly and intelligent situations: these are both the oldest and the newest arts of the drama; and your plot construction and art of preparation are only the tricks of theatrical talent and the shifts of moral sterility, not the weapons of dramatic genius. In the theatre of Ibsen we are not flattered spectators killing an idle hour with an ingenious and amusing entertainment: we are "guilty creatures sitting at a play"; and the technique of pastime is no more applicable than at a murder trial.

The technical novelties of the Ibsen and post-Ibsen plays are, then: first, the introduction of the discussion and its development until it so overspreads and interpenetrates the action that it finally assimilates it, making play and discussion practically identical; and, second, as a consequence of making the spectators themselves the persons of the drama, and the incidents of their own lives its incidents, the disuse of the old stage tricks by which audiences had to be induced to take an interest in unreal people and improbable circumstances, and the substitution of a forensic technique of recrimination, disillusion, and penetration through ideals to the truth, with a free use of all the rhetorical and lyrical arts of the orator, the preacher, the pleader, and the rhapsodist. [*Ibid.*, p. 184.]

To ask for the essence of Ibsen, still more for the quintessence of Ibsenism, is to formulate a wholly misleading question; there is nothing to be got by boiling down, there is no extract of wisdom that would allow us to regard his drama as a linctus for the ills of mankind. If one must have an analogy, one might be a little nearer the truth by asking for the root of Ibsen; for just as the root of (say) 9 is not 3 but that more ambiguous entity mathematicians call ±3, so the root of Ibsen's view of life, however positively he may at times seem to express himself, conveys the impression of being similarly "plus or minus." The separate bits may not add up very satisfactorily, but they function.

The problem is then what sort of questions the modern Ibsenite should ask. One notices that in an age when literature gave itself to the business of debate, Ibsen himself waited for question time and cast his dramas in an interrogative mould. "I do but ask," he was fond of saying to those who sought enlightenment from him about the meaning of his works, "my call is not to answer." His dramas are those of one who understood the strategy of the contrived question and the shrewd supplementary, who knew how much more could be achieved by implication and insinuation and by the manner and timing of the asking than by the mere forcing of some answer. Perhaps his critics could learn from his example and acknowledge that there is room for an approach to Ibsen that questions the questions we ask of him rather than competes for answers. He offers a problem in delicate handling in which the matter of whether questions can be found to yield definite answers is subordinate to that of finding a genuinely Ibsenite question with the rightly provocative degree of obliquity. [J. W. McFarlane, *Ibsen and the Tempo of Norwegian Literature*, Oxford University Press, New York, 1960, pp. 67–68.]

Many sensitive critics have insisted that it is only in the theatre that Ibsen should properly be judged. It is not good, they suggest, to go trudging down long avenues of reference every time Ibsen points his finger; there is, in the theatre, no time for digression, the pace has to be maintained. This was the view of James Joyce, whose early enthusiasm for Ibsen led him to teach himself Norwegian, the better to read the plays, who in March 1901 in his newly acquired foreign tongue wrote to Ibsen a very moving letter of homage and admiration, and who in an enthusiastic article on *When We Dead Awaken* in the *Fortnightly Review* of April 1900 claimed that "appreciation, hearkening, is the only true criticism":

If any plays demand a stage they are the plays of Ibsen. . . . They are so packed with thought. At some chance expression, the mind is tortured with some question, and in a flash long reaches of life are opened up in vista, yet the vision is momentary unless we stay to ponder it. It is just to prevent excessive pondering that Ibsen requires to be acted.

The real answer seems to be therefore that there is no answer; or rather that there is an infinity of answers too stark and stiff to fit anywhere but where they touch—which makes the modern Ibsenites' search for enlightenment a matter not of discovering some single secret truth but of rejecting a multiplicity of explanations which under scrutiny turn out to be inadmissible. Not even the precise ambiguity of the paradox nor the ambiguous precision of the "symbol" serve in the last resort to break down the complex unity of his art; he is irreducible. [*Ibid.*, p. 72.]

The philosophical struggle in Rosmersholm *is between paganism and Christianity. It can be discussed different ways, as H. J. Weigand and Bernard Shaw demonstrate; it must be discussed, even if it cannot be resolved, or rather, even if Ibsen refuses to bring it to a conclusion.*

Behind the Rosmer-Rebecca tragedy loom the great outlines of a conflict with the solution of which Ibsen wrestled again and again. Once more the issue of paganism versus Christianity, egoism versus altruism, assertion of self versus renunciation of self, is fought out. . . .

Finmarken, the ancient stronghold of paganism, the country which, together with Finland,

the Norseman's imagination to this day peoples with witches and demons, is the home of the modern [pagan superwoman] Rebecca West. Her free pagan spirit disciplined by the schooling of modern science, she sets foot in Rosmersholm,[1] the Northern citadel of the Christian faith. From

[1] A fictitious locality, of course.

the first she sets out craftily, systematically, to instill her view of life into the pliable Rosmer. She seems to succeed; for, as she had foreseen, his inherited beliefs are not proof against the attacks levelled against them by modern science. But then, when victory seemed already assured, her onward march came to a sudden halt. Rosmer's intellectual fortifications had fallen, but Rebecca had failed to reckon sufficiently with that part of his inheritance which, penetrating below the surface of ideas intellectually entertained, had become rooted in his very instincts: the morality of altruism. In Rosmer's Christian conscience Rebecca encountered an obstacle against which her intellectual weapons were of no avail. Unable to make further progress, she gradually slipped back, losing the advantage of the initiative.

And now it became the turn of Christianity, defeated in its intellectual outer works, but firmly entrenched in the central fastness of its ethics, to score its victories. Through the innate nobility of Rosmer's instincts Rebecca's amoralistic will is weakened, infected and, in the end, utterly broken. . . .

Rebecca not only acknowledges her defeat but submits unresistingly to a law which she feels to the end as foreign to her inmost nature. She tells Rosmer that she is a living proof of the fact that his view of life ennobles.

And yet, this victory of Christianity is, at best, incomplete. The law of sin and expiation is the law of Rebecca's beloved. Her acceptance of it it but the corollary of the fact that she has ceased to exist as a personality independent of her lover. Like its other victims, Christianity has broken her, but in contrast to them, she is a willing victim, marching unbound to the altar of the god who demanded her sacrifice.

It was not Ibsen's intention to stage a mystery play "ad maiorem dei gloriam." What made him return again and again to the typical conflict of paganism versus Christianity was not the desire to see one of them crushed: it was his yearning to effect a reconciliation between them. His own self was torn by their conflict. . . .

In reading the results of this experiment, the mystic and the skeptic in Ibsen come to a parting of the ways. The mystic would fain make himself believe that in the presence of death, the universal solvent, an actual fusion of two souls had occurred; that the barriers of individuation have melted away; that two polar opposites have been reconciled. He pins his faith on a miracle transcending reason.

But the skeptic, who has traced out every step in Rebecca's development on the basis of naturalistic psychology, makes his reservations. He refuses to believe in a mystical fusion of personalities. Rosmer has not been transformed, he points out; it is Rebecca who has made an unconditional surrender.

And the poet, mystic and skeptic in one, having performed his experiment before our eyes, is unwilling and unable to set his hand to an unequivocal report on his findings. [H. J. Weigand, *The Modern Ibsen*, Dutton Everyman Paperback, New York, 1960, pp. 205–208.]

What is really driving Rosmer is the superstition of expiation by sacrifice. He sees that when Rebecca goes into the millstream he must go too. And he speaks his real mind in the words, "There is no judge over us: therefore we must do justice upon ourselves." But the woman's soul is free of this to the end; for when she says, "I am under the power of the Rosmersholm view of life *now*. What I have sinned it is fit I should expiate," we feel in that speech a protest against the Rosmersholm view of life: the view that denied her right to live and be happy from the first, and now at the end, even in denying its God, exacts her life as a vain blood-offering for its own blindness. The woman has the higher light: she goes to her death out of fellowship with the man who is driven thither by the superstition which has destroyed his will. [Shaw, *op. cit.*, p. 105.]

The technical mastery of Rosmersholm *deserves careful attention. It is demonstrated not only in the extraordinary balance or symmetry of the play but in a variety of small details.*

Rosmersholm . . . is Ibsen's most perfectly balanced work. Architecturally, he never produced anything so harmonious: it is his most Sophoclean play. He was himself on the verge of a great reconciliation. . . . He was no longer the wounded wild duck, flying south to the coasts of the sun; he was turning again to his own people and knitting up his life with theirs.

Rosmersholm is the most clearly located of all the plays; the old manor house at Molde can be identified as the scene. Rebekke comes from Finmark, in farthest northern Norway, that desolate region of the polar night and the midnight sun.[1]

Rosmer and Rebekke are figures of heroic magnitude set in a scene isolated and haunted. The feeling of remoteness, of all other life being far distant, the silence and circumscribed self-sufficiency of the homestead belongs to Norway, a land of great distances and far-scattered dwellings. Life at Rosmersholm is cut off from life elsewhere, and in this isolation the rule of the dead is strengthened. The power of the dead Rosmers, the sense of their presence and of the presence of the dead wife, springs from that Norse inheritance of the supernatural which Ibsen had already drawn on in *Brand, Peer Gynt,* and *Ghosts.* Here it is not the trolls of the mountains but the spirits of the homestead which haunt the minds of the living. The sense of a ghostly world impinging on humanity has persisted in Norse literature from the time of the Eddas to the latest poems of the day—Nordahl Grieg wrote of the war dead as "ghosts looming through minds of new men."

Such a spiritual climate breeds heroic character but breeds it for a tragic destiny. The primitive horror of the old housekeeper—

[1] She describes the passion that swept over her as like one of the storms that sweep the northern seas; and the peace of her love for Rosmer as like the silence of the bird-cliffs under the midnight sun. Rebekke is essentially of North Norway. . . .

No one can help them now. . . . the dead wife has taken them.

sums up, in the last line of the play, all the living force of these dark powers.

The organization is superb. All Ibsen's technical achievements since *A Doll's House* are summed up in this play. The use of implication, including what came to be called his "retrospective method"; scenic suggestion; the forging of a chain of tiny events to give scale to the great crises. Some of the earlier drafts contain what appear in the light of the finished play to be fantastic details—in one, Rebekke is Rosmer's wife, in another she is governess to his two daughters; and from the shock of these incongruities can be estimated the justness of the "selected events."

The play has an exact symmetry: the first half deals with Rosmer, and the second with Rebekke: Act I with his present, Act II with his past, Act III with Rebekke's past and Act IV with her present. But the story of the two is one story, as they recognize at the end. "Man and wife shall go together . . . for now we two are one." [M. C. Bradbrook, *Ibsen, the Norwegian,* Chatto & Windus, Ltd., London, 1948, pp. 109–111.]

Out of the family situation, in which Ibsen himself had been involved and which had been so disastrous for his happiness in after life, developed the fixed pattern of family relationships we see in his plays, a pattern which is repeated and repeated again and again until it no longer represents a danger to him. . . . The theme of illegitimacy occurs often, a subject which may have obsessed Ibsen himself. It plays a part in *Lady Inger,* in *Ghosts,* in *The Wild Duck,* in *Rosmersholm* and in *Little Eyolf.* Incest also is a salient feature of *Ghosts, Rosmersholm* and *Little Eyolf.*

It is this pathological element which inspires the themes and situations and characters of many

HENRIK IBSEN

of Ibsen's plays. In his early work it is mostly suppressed and given the form of ideas, but in the later plays ideas and reality go side by side, and gradually the ideas begin to recede into the background. In his young days he had hoped to free himself of his obsessions by talking of man's vocation, the true marriage, truth and freedom and the realization of the individual, but with *The Wild Duck* and *Rosmersholm* these ideas are subordinated to the fate of the individuals themselves, which is directed by irrational impulses over which the mind no longer has control. It is now that the family situation is portrayed as belonging no more to the realms of philosophy and ideas but to those of pure human relationships. It is now that Ibsen for the first time can portray the family situation without symbolical circumlocution. [P. F. D. Tennant, *Ibsen's Dramatic Technique,* Bowes & Bowes, Ltd., London, 1948, pp. 25–26.]

The most characteristic feature of Ibsen's technique of exposition is . . . his use of what may be called the retrospective method, a technique employed by Sophocles, by Racine and to a certain extent by Hebbel. That is to say, he prefers to begin his tragedy just before the catastrophe and to make the dialogue unravel the preceding events in retrospect, instead of presenting the actual events in succession on the stage. This type of exposition concentrates the action into a very small space of time, in conformity with the realistic desire to observe the unities. It is also, as it happens, a type of exposition favoured by the traditional fate-tragedy, the dramatic conflict in all cases being between past and present, the sins of the past contrasting violently with the calm atmosphere of the present and swiftly destroying the idyll as retribution approaches. The dramatic contrast between the beginnings and endings of Ibsen's plays is dependent for its effect on this type of exposition. In *Pillars of Society* the false atmosphere of calm at the sewing party is dispersed as the past is revealed step by step and brings about the fall of the self-righteous consul. In *Ghosts* the play opens with Regine watering flowers, in *Rosmersholm* Rebekka is arranging flowers in the morning-room as the curtain rises,

and in *Hedda Gabler* Aunt Julia arrives in the first scene to greet the young married couple with a bouquet. Nothing could however be more characteristic of Ibsen than the endings of these plays, Osvald going mad, Rebekka and Rosmer throwing themselves into the mill-race, and Hedda shooting herself. [*Ibid.,* p. 91.]

Ibsen . . . develops the stage whisper to complete realism, that is, the whisper which is neither heard by characters on the stage nor by the audience. This again loads the atmosphere with suspense though it is a matter for the actor to give it its full dramatic significance.

In *Rosmersholm* Rebekka is talking to Rosmer, and Madam Helseth asks to speak to her. Rebekka asks her to wait, but she insists on a few words. Then the directions are as follows: "Rebekka goes to the door. Madam Helseth gives her a message. They whisper together. Madam Helseth gives a nod and goes out." Rosmer then asks agitatedly, "Was it anything for me?" Rebekka replies, "No, it was only about household matters. Now you ought to go and take a walk in the fresh air, Rosmer. You ought to take a really long walk." Only after a long conversation does he finally go. When he has gone out Rebekka calls for Madam Helseth and Rektor Kroll is shown in. [*Ibid.,* pp. 106–107.]

Ibsen, as a dramatist, is neither primarily a thinker nor a psychologist; he is an illusionist and artist, and as such, his contribution to the theatre is a lasting one. The illusion is brought home by the apparent moral sincerity behind it. Ibsen's moral indignation could slur over many psychological weaknesses and his dramatic technique was able to create illusion by freely using the borrowed trappings of contemporary thought. John Stuart Mill's utilitarianism, Kierkegaard's rectitudinitis, the Darwinist jargon of heredity, natural selection and the influence of environment, combined with Old Testament and Lutheran doctrines of sin and retribution, produce in the nonconformist conscience of the strait-laced Ibsen an honest conviction of morality being synonymous with happiness, of truth and individual freedom being the greatest good, and of divine wrath visiting punishment in the form of disease, degeneration or a sickly conscience on all those, who for material interests, fail to follow the path of righteousness and the vocation to which they have been called. This highly romantic ideal is given an illusion of stark reality by the dramatic technique with which it is presented. It is this technique of Ibsen's which deluded his contemporaries into accepting him as a thinker. It is the same technique which for posterity has marked him as a dramatist of the first order. [*Ibid.*, p. 120.]

AUGUST STRINDBERG

1849–1912

*The scope and depth of Strindberg's several dramatic methods are
still being discovered, as new performances and closer readings
reveal elements in the Swedish dramatist's imagination that were
hardly even suspected by his first audiences and interpreters. One
sees now that even his self-avowed naturalistic plays, such as* The
Father *(1887) and* Miss Julie *(1888), were very far from the
deterministic texture and bare-boned simplifications of naturalism.
It is hard to miss, even in those violent plays, the motions of
self-examination, which grow and grow over dozens of plays until
they become the great structuring elements of the trilogy* To
Damascus *(1898 and 1904), and* A Dream Play *(1902),* The Dance
of Death *(1902), and* The Ghost Sonata *(1907). Strindberg
seems always to have been moving in the direction of the
drama of interiority and to have been willing to use any
novelty of technique which would bring him (and his audiences)
more deeply inside the dark mystery at the center of his
characters. He early relinquished the obvious trappings of character,
such as physical deformity or a catchphrase of the "Barkis is
willin' " kind, in the famous scornful preface to* Miss Julie. *More
and more he looked, as he put it in the introductory note to*
A Dream Play, *"to imitate the disjointed but apparently logical
form of a dream. Anything at all may happen. Everything is
possible. . . . Time and space do not exist. . . ." The imagination is
freed to reach as far as it can—into the true, the false, the
conventional, the absurd. The Swedish playwright wanted the*

fullest possible experience of the human condition for himself and, in so far as the theater could provide means flexible and fertile enough, for his audiences. He had sought the philosopher's stone: his hands were permanently stained from his experiments in alchemy. He found instead some considerable psychological truths and the dramatic methods with which to express them.

The Dance of Death

TRANSLATED BY C. D. LOCOCK

Characters

EDGAR *captain in the garrison artillery*

ALICE *his wife, formerly an actress*

KURT *quarantine officer*

JENNY

AN OLD WOMAN

ALLAN *Kurt's son*

JUDITH *Edgar's daughter*

THE LIEUTENANT

A SENTRY

The action takes place inside a fort on an island off the coast of Sweden, sometime in the 1890's.

Part One

The interior of a circular fort of grey stone. In the background two large gates with glass doors, showing a sea-coast with batteries and the sea. On each side of the gateway a window with flower-pots and bird-cages. To the right of the door a cottage piano; further down the stage a sewing-table and two armchairs. To the left, in the middle of the stage, a writing-table with telegraph apparatus: further forward a what-not containing photographs, and close to it a couch. Against the wall a sideboard. A lamp hangs from the ceiling. On the wall by the piano hang two large laurel-wreaths with ribbons, one on each side of the portrait of a woman in theatrical costume. By the door a hat-stand on which accoutrements, swords, etc., are hanging; near it a chiffonier. To the left of the door hangs a mercurial barometer.

It is a warm autumn evening. The fortress gates are open, and one can see an artilleryman on sentry duty out by the shore battery. He wears a kind of busby, and his sword glitters now and then in the red glow of the setting sun. The sea is dark and still.

The Captain is sitting in the arm-chair to the left of the sewing-table, fingering a cigar which has gone out. He is wearing an undress uniform, rather the worse for wear, with riding-boots and spurs. Looks tired and bored. Alice is sitting in the arm-chair on the right, doing nothing. Looks tired and expectant.

425

CAPTAIN Won't you play to me a little?

ALICE [*indifferently, but not pettishly*] What shall I play?

CAPTAIN Whatever *you* like!

ALICE You don't like my repertoire!

CAPTAIN Nor you mine!

ALICE [*evasively*] Do you want the doors left open?

CAPTAIN If you wish it!

ALICE We'll leave them then. . . . [*A pause*] Why aren't you smoking?

CAPTAIN I'm beginning to find strong tobacco rather too much for me.

ALICE [*almost in a friendly tone*] Smoke something milder then! Why, it's your only joy, as you call it.

CAPTAIN Joy! What may that be?

ALICE Don't ask me! I know as little about it as you do! . . . Won't you have your whisky now?

CAPTAIN I'll wait a little! . . . What have you got for supper?

ALICE How should I know? Ask Kristin!

CAPTAIN Oughtn't mackerel to be in soon? Why, it's autumn now!

ALICE Yes, it's autumn!

CAPTAIN Outside and in! But apart from the cold, outside and in, that comes with autumn, a broiled mackerel, with a slice of lemon, and a glass of white Burgundy is not altogether to be despised!

ALICE You're getting quite eloquent!

CAPTAIN Is there any Burgundy left in the cellar?

ALICE I'm not aware that we've *had* any cellar these last five years. . . .

CAPTAIN You never do know anything. However, we *must* get in a supply for our silver wedding. . . .

ALICE Do you really mean to celebrate that?

CAPTAIN Naturally!

ALICE It would be more natural to hide our misery, our twenty-five years of misery. . . .

CAPTAIN Yes, dear Alice, it has been misery, but rather jolly too, now and then! One must make use of what little time there is: after that comes the end!

ALICE Is it the end? If only it were!

CAPTAIN It *is* the end! Just enough left to wheel out on a barrow and put on a garden bed!

ALICE And all that trouble for the sake of a garden bed!

CAPTAIN Yes, that's how it is; *I* didn't arrange it!

ALICE All that trouble! [*A pause*] Have you had your letters?

CAPTAIN Yes!

ALICE Was the butcher's bill among them?

CAPTAIN Yes!

ALICE How much was it?

CAPTAIN [*takes a paper out of his pocket and puts on his glasses, but takes them off again at once*] Read it yourself! I can't see now. . . .

ALICE What's wrong with your eyes?

CAPTAIN Don't know!

ALICE Old age.

CAPTAIN What nonsense! Me!

ALICE Yes, not me!

CAPTAIN Hm!

ALICE [*looks at the bill*] Can you pay this?

CAPTAIN Yes! but not at the moment!

ALICE Later on of course! In a year, when you're retired with a small pension and it's too late! Later on, when you get ill again. . . .

CAPTAIN Ill? I have never been ill: just a little out of sorts once. I shall live another twenty years yet!

ALICE The doctor thought otherwise!

CAPTAIN The doctor!

ALICE Yes: who else would be likely to know anything about an illness?

CAPTAIN I haven't any illness, and never have had. Nor shall I. I shall go off bang! like an old soldier!

ALICE Talking of the doctor, you know they're having a party there this evening.

CAPTAIN [*agitated*] Yes, and what of it? We're not invited because we don't associate with the doctor's family, and we don't do so because we don't want to—because I despise the pair of them. Rabble, that's what they are!

ALICE That's what you say about everybody!

CAPTAIN Because everybody *is* rabble!

ALICE Except you!

CAPTAIN Yes, because I have behaved decently in all circumstances. That's why I'm not rabble! [*A pause*]

ALICE Would you like to play cards?

CAPTAIN All right!

ALICE [takes a pack of cards from the sewing-table drawer and begins to shuffle] Just fancy, they're having the band at the Doctor's for a private entertainment!

CAPTAIN [angrily] That's because he truckles to the Colonel in the town! truckles—that's what it is!— If one could only do that!

ALICE [dealing] At one time I was a friend of Gerda's, but she played me false. . . .

CAPTAIN They're all false, the whole lot of them! . . . What's that trump over there?

ALICE Take your glasses!

CAPTAIN They're no use! . . . Well, well!

ALICE Spades are trumps!

CAPTAIN [disappointed] Spades? . . .

ALICE [leads] Well, however that may be, so far as the new officers' wives are concerned we're on the black list in any case!

CAPTAIN [plays and takes the trick] What does that matter? We never give any parties, so it won't be noticed! I can put up with being alone . . . I have always been so!

ALICE And I too! But the children! the children are growing up without any companionship!

CAPTAIN They must find that for themselves in the town! . . . That was my trick! Any trumps left?

ALICE Just one!—That was mine!

CAPTAIN Six and eight are fifteen. . . .

ALICE Fourteen, fourteen!

CAPTAIN Six and eight makes me fourteen. . . . I seem to have forgotten how to count! And two is sixteen. . . . [Yawns.] Your deal!

ALICE You're tired!

CAPTAIN [dealing] Not in the least!

ALICE [listening to sounds outside] One can hear the band even here! [A pause] Do you think Kurt was asked there?

CAPTAIN He arrived this morning, so I expect he has found time to get out his dress clothes, though not to call on us!

ALICE Quarantine officer! Is there to be a quarantine station here?

CAPTAIN Yes! . . .

ALICE After all, he is my cousin—we once had the same name. . . .

CAPTAIN No great honour in that!

ALICE Look here, now! . . . [Sharply] Leave my family alone, and I'll leave yours!

CAPTAIN All right, all right! Must we start that all over again?

ALICE Is the quarantine officer a doctor?

CAPTAIN Oh, dear no! Merely a sort of civilian manager or book-keeper. Kurt, as you know, was never anything!

ALICE He was a poor sort of creature. . . .

CAPTAIN Who has cost me a lot of money. . . . And the way he left his wife and children—simply infamous!

ALICE Don't be too hard on him, Edgar!

CAPTAIN Yes, that's what he was! . . . I wonder what he's been doing since in America! Well, I can't say I'm longing for him! But he was a nice sort of fellow, and I used to like arguing with him.

ALICE Because he was so accommodating. . . .

CAPTAIN [loftily] Accommodating or not, he was at least a man one could talk to. . . . On this island here there isn't one single person who can understand what I say. . . . It's a society of idiots. . . .

ALICE It's curious, isn't it, Kurt's coming just in time for our silver wedding—whether we celebrate it or not?

CAPTAIN Why curious? . . . Oh yes, I see! It was he who brought us together—got you married—so they said!

ALICE Well, didn't he!

CAPTAIN Of course he did! . . . Just an idea of his. . . . Well, you can judge for yourself!

ALICE A thoughtless whim. . . .

CAPTAIN For which we've had to pay—not he!

ALICE Yes, only think if I'd still been on the stage! All my friends are celebrities now!

CAPTAIN [getting up] Quite so, quite so! . . . Well, I'll have my whisky now! [Goes to the sideboard and mixes a drink, which he takes standing.] There ought to be a rail here to put one's feet on; then one could imagine oneself in Copenhagen, in the American bar!

ALICE We must have a rail made, if only to remind us of Copenhagen. After all that was the best time we ever had!

CAPTAIN [drinks eagerly] Yes. Do you remember Nimb's navarin aux pommes? [Smacks his lips.]

ALICE No, but I remember the concerts at the Tivoli!

CAPTAIN You've got such exalted tastes, you have!

ALICE You ought to be proud of having a wife with good taste!

CAPTAIN So I am!

ALICE Sometimes, when you want to show her off!

CAPTAIN [drinking] They must be dancing at the Doctor's . . . I can hear the bass tubas' three-four time: pom—pom-pom!

ALICE I can hear the whole tune of the "Alcazar Waltz." Ah well, it wasn't yesterday—the last time I danced a waltz!

CAPTAIN Could you still manage it?

ALICE Still?

CAPTAIN Ye-es! I should have thought you were past dancing now—both of us!

ALICE But I'm ten years younger than you!

CAPTAIN In that case we must be the same age: the lady is always supposed to be ten years younger!

ALICE For shame! Why you're an old man: I am still in my best years!

CAPTAIN Oh yes, I know you can be charming enough to other people—when you give your mind to it.

ALICE Shall we have the lamp lighted now?

CAPTAIN If you like!

ALICE Will you ring then?

[The Captain goes wearily to the writing-table and rings the bell. Enter Jenny from the right.]

CAPTAIN Would you be so kind as to light the lamps, Jenny?

ALICE [sharply] Light the hanging lamp!

JENNY Yes, ma'am. [Lights the lamp while the Captain watches her.]

ALICE [curtly] Have you cleaned the chimney properly?

JENNY Rather!

ALICE Do you call that a proper answer?

CAPTAIN Now, now—

ALICE [to Jenny] Leave the room! I will light the lamp myself. I suppose that's the only thing to do!

JENNY [going] I think so too!

ALICE [getting up] Go!

JENNY [stopping] I wonder what you'd say if I did go, ma'am!

[Alice says nothing. Jenny goes out. The Captain comes forward and lights the lamp.]

ALICE [uneasily] Do you think she'll leave?

CAPTAIN Shouldn't be surprised! If so, we're in a nice mess!

ALICE It's your fault. You spoil them!

CAPTAIN Not at all! You can see how polite they always are to me!

ALICE That's because you cringe to them! The fact is you cringe to all your inferiors, because, despot as you are, you have a slavish nature.

CAPTAIN Oh, come!

ALICE Yes, you cringe to your men and your NCO's, but you can't get on with your equals or your superiors.

CAPTAIN Ouf!

ALICE That's the way with all tyrants! . . . Do you think she'll leave?

CAPTAIN Yes, unless you go out and speak nicely to her!

ALICE I?

CAPTAIN If I did, you'd say I was flirting with the maids!

ALICE Only think—if she does go! I should have to do all the work, the same as last time, and ruin my hands!

CAPTAIN That's not the worst! If Jenny goes, Kristin goes too, and we shall never get a servant to come to the island again! The mate on the steamboat scares away all the new arrivals who come to apply for the place. . . . If he forgets, then my corporals see to it!

ALICE Yes, your corporals! whom I have to feed in my kitchen, because you don't dare show them the door. . . .

CAPTAIN No; if I did, they'd leave too as soon as their time was up . . . then we'd have to shut up the gun-shop!

ALICE Well, we shall be ruined!

CAPTAIN That's why the officers are thinking of asking His Majesty for a maintenance subsidy. . . .

ALICE Who for?

CAPTAIN For the corporals!

ALICE [laughing] You're too mad!

CAPTAIN Yes, let me hear you laugh a little! I may need it.

ALICE I shall soon have forgotten how to laugh. . . .

CAPTAIN [lighting his cigar] That's a thing one

should never forget . . . life is tedious enough anyhow!

ALICE It is certainly not amusing! . . . Do you care to play any more?

CAPTAIN No, it tires me.

[*A pause*]

ALICE You know it does somehow annoy me to think that my cousin, the new quarantine officer's first visit should be to our enemies!

CAPTAIN Hardly worth talking about, is it?

ALICE Well, but did you see in the papers that he was put down in the list of arrivals as of independent means? He must have come into some money!

CAPTAIN Of independent means! Oho! A rich relation! Certainly the first in this family!

ALICE In your family, yes! There've been plenty in mine.

CAPTAIN If he has money he's probably stuck-up; but *I'll* keep him in check! and he shan't get a chance of seeing my cards!

[*Clicking from the telegraph receiver*]

ALICE Who is it?

CAPTAIN [*without moving*] Quiet—one moment!

ALICE Why don't you go and see?

CAPTAIN I can hear: I can hear what they're saying! It's the children! [*Goes to the apparatus and taps out a reply. After that the receiver goes on clicking for a time and then the Captain replies again.*]

ALICE Well?

CAPTAIN One moment! [*Switches off.*] It's the children, at the guard-house in the town. Judith isn't well again and is staying away from school.

ALICE Again! what else did they say?

CAPTAIN Money, of course!

ALICE Why need Judith be in such a hurry? It would be quite soon enough if she took her examination next year!

CAPTAIN Tell her so and see what good it does!

ALICE You ought to tell her!

CAPTAIN How many times haven't I told her! But you know quite well, children do what they like!

ALICE In this house at any rate! . . . [*The Captain yawns.*] Must you yawn in the presence of your wife?

CAPTAIN What is one to do? . . . Don't you notice how we say the same things every blessed day? When you came out just now with your good old retort, "In this house at any rate," I ought to have replied with my ancient "It's not *my* house only." But since I have already given this answer five hundred times, I yawn instead. So you can take my yawn to mean either that I can't be bothered to answer or "You are right, my angel," or "Now let's stop!"

ALICE You're very amiable this evening!

CAPTAIN Isn't it nearly time for supper?

ALICE Did you know they had ordered supper from the Grand Hotel for the Doctor's party?

CAPTAIN No! Then they'll be having ptarmigan. [*Smacks his lips.*] Ptarmigan, you know, is the finest bird there is, but to roast it with pork-fat is sheer barbarism. . . .

ALICE Ugh! Talking about food!

CAPTAIN About wine then? I wonder what those barbarians would have with their ptarmigan?

ALICE Shall I play to you?

CAPTAIN [*seats himself at the writing-table*] The last resource! Yes, if you'll leave out your funeral marches and dirges . . . they sound like music with a purpose. I keep on interpolating—"See how unhappy I am! miaow, miaow!" Or "See what a terrible husband I have! Pom, pom, pom! Oh, if he would only die soon! Bangs from the joyful drums, fanfares: ending up with the 'Alcazar Waltz'! 'Champagne Galop'!" Apropos of champagne, there must be at least two bottles left. Shall we have them up and pretend we've got a party?

ALICE No, that we won't! They're mine—a present to me personally!

CAPTAIN You are always economical!

ALICE And you're always stingy, to your wife at any rate!

CAPTAIN Then I don't know what to suggest. Would you like to see me dance?

ALICE No, thank you! You are past dancing, I fancy.

CAPTAIN You ought to have some woman friend to stay with you!

ALICE Thanks! you ought to have some man to stay with you!

CAPTAIN Thanks! we have tried that—and agreed

that it was a complete failure! As an experiment it was interesting: the moment we had another person in the house we became quite happy . . . to begin with . . .

ALICE   But afterwards!

CAPTAIN   Oh, don't talk of it!

[*Knocking heard at the door, left.*]

ALICE   Who can it be, so late as this?

CAPTAIN   Jenny doesn't usually knock.

ALICE   Go and open the door, and don't call out "Come in!" It sounds like a workshop!

CAPTAIN   [*going towards the door, left*] You don't like workshops!

[*Another knock.*]

ALICE   Do open the door!

CAPTAIN   [*opens the door and takes a visiting-card which is handed to him*] It's Kristin.—Has Jenny left? [*To Alice, since the answer is not heard by the audience*] Jenny has left!

ALICE   Then I've to be a servant-girl again!

CAPTAIN   And I the man!

ALICE   Couldn't we get one of your men to help in the kitchen?

CAPTAIN   Not in these days!

ALICE   But surely it couldn't be Jenny, sending in her card like that?

CAPTAIN   [*examines the card through his glasses and then hands it to Alice*] You read it—I can't!

ALICE   [*looks at the card*] Kurt! it's Kurt! Go out and bring him in!

CAPTAIN   [*goes out left*] Kurt! well, this *is* delightful!

[*Alice arranges her hair and seems to come to life again.*]

CAPTAIN   [*comes in from the left with Kurt*] Here he is—the old traitor! Welcome, old man! I'd like to hug you!

ALICE   [*going towards Kurt*] Delighted to see you, Kurt!

KURT   Thank you! . . . It's a long time since we met!

CAPTAIN   What is it? fifteen years! And we've grown old. . . .

ALICE   Oh, Kurt looks just the same to me.

CAPTAIN   Sit down, sit down!—And first of all —the programme! any engagement for this evening?

KURT   I've been asked to the Doctor's, but I didn't promise to go!

ALICE   Then you must stay with your relations!

KURT   That seems the natural thing to do, but the Doctor is my superior in a way, and there'll be trouble afterwards!

CAPTAIN   What nonsense! I've never been afraid of my superiors. . . .

KURT   Afraid or not—the trouble's there all the same!

CAPTAIN   I am master on this island! Keep behind me and nobody will dare touch you!

ALICE   Do be quiet, Edgar! [*Takes Kurt by the hand.*] Masters and superiors or not, you stay here with us. That's the right and proper thing to do!

KURT   All right then!—Especially as I think I'm welcome.

CAPTAIN   And why shouldn't you be? Surely there's no ill-feeling. . . . [*Kurt cannot conceal a certain embarrassment.*] What could there be? You used to be a bit of a rascal: but you were young and I have forgotten that! I'm not one to cherish old grudges!

[*Alice looks annoyed. All three sit down at the sewing-table.*]

ALICE   Well, you've been about the world a bit?

KURT   Yes, and now I find myself back again with you. . . .

CAPTAIN   Whom you married off twenty-five years ago.

KURT   Oh, hardly that! but that doesn't matter. I'm glad to see you have stuck together for twenty-five years. . . .

CAPTAIN   Yes, we've worried along! at times things have been rather so-so: still, as you say, we've stuck together. And Alice has had nothing to complain of: plenty of everything and heaps of money. I daresay you don't know I'm a famous author, writer of textbooks. . . .

KURT   Yes, I remember, when we went our different ways, you'd just published a manual on rifle-shooting that sold well. Is it still used in the military schools?

CAPTAIN   It's still to be found there, and keeps its place as number one, though they've tried to shelve it in favour of an inferior one . . . which is certainly in use now, though utterly worthless!

[*Embarrassing silence.*]

KURT   You've been travelling abroad, I hear.

ALICE   Yes, we've been to Copenhagen five times —just fancy!

CAPTAIN   Yes, you see when I took Alice away from the theatre . . .

ALICE   Took me?

CAPTAIN   Yes, took you as a wife should be taken. . . .

ALICE   How brave you have grown!

CAPTAIN   But afterwards, as I never heard the last about my ruining her brilliant career—hm! . . . I had to make up for it by promising to take my wife to Copenhagen. . . . And this I have kept to—honourably! Five times we've been there! Five! [*Holding up the fingers of his left hand.*] Have you been to Copenhagen?

KURT   [*smiling*]   No, I've mostly been in America. . . .

CAPTAIN   America? Isn't that rather an outlandish sort of place?

KURT   [*embarrassed*]   Well, it isn't Copenhagen!

ALICE   Have you—heard anything—from your children?

KURT   No!

ALICE   Forgive me, dear friend, but it really was rather inconsiderate to leave them like that. . . .

KURT   I didn't leave them: the Court gave them to the mother. . . .

CAPTAIN   We won't talk about that now! I think you were lucky to get out of that mess!

KURT   [*to Alice*]   How are your children?

ALICE   Quite well, thank you! They're at school in the town and will soon be grown up!

CAPTAIN   Yes, they're smart little kids; the boy has a marvellous brain—marvellous! He's going to join the General Staff. . . .

ALICE   If they will have him!

CAPTAIN   Have him? Why, he's got the makings of a War Minister!

KURT   Talking of other things—there's going to be a quarantine station here: plague, cholera and that sort of thing. The Doctor will be my superior, as you know. What sort of man is he?

CAPTAIN   Man? He isn't a man at all! He's a brainless scoundrel!

KURT   [*to Alice*]   Very unpleasant for me!

ALICE   Not quite so bad as Edgar makes out: still I can't deny that he doesn't attract me. . . .

CAPTAIN   A scoundrel, that's what he is! and that's what the rest of them are too—the Customs Surveyor, the Postmaster, the telephone girl, the chemist, the pilot . . . what is it they call him . . . the Master Pilot—scoundrels, all of them; and that's why I don't associate with them!

KURT   Are you on bad terms with the whole lot of them?

CAPTAIN   The whole lot!

ALICE   Yes, it's quite true—one can't associate with such people!

CAPTAIN   It's just as if all the tyrants in the country had been sent to this island to be kept in custody!

ALICE   [*ironically*]   Precisely so!

CAPTAIN   [*good-humouredly*]   Hm! is that meant for me? I am no tyrant—at any rate not in my own house!

ALICE   You take care not to try *that* on!

CAPTAIN   [*to Kurt*]   You mustn't pay any attention to her! I am a most agreeable husband, and the old girl's the best wife in the world!

ALICE   Will you have anything to drink, Kurt?

KURT   No, thank you—not now!

CAPTAIN   Have you become . . .

KURT   A little moderate—that's all!

CAPTAIN   Is that American?

KURT   Yes!

CAPTAIN   No moderation for me! I'd as soon have none at all! A man ought to be able to manage his bottle!

KURT   Coming back to our neighbours on the island here—my position will put me in touch with everybody. . . . It won't be by any means plain sailing; one gets drawn into people's intrigues, however little one wants it.

ALICE   You take up with them—you'll come back to us in the end! Your true friends are here!

KURT   Don't you find it rather dreadful—being alone in the midst of enemies?

ALICE   It isn't very pleasant!

CAPTAIN   It isn't dreadful at all! All my life I have had nothing but enemies, and they have helped me rather than hurt me! On my deathbed I shall be able to say, "I owe no man anything, I have never got anything for nothing, and every scrap that I own I have had to fight for."

The Dance of Death

ALICE   Yes, Edgar's path has not been strewn with roses. . . .

CAPTAIN   With thorns and stones, flints . . . but a man's own strength! do you know what that is?

KURT   [*simply*]   Yes, I learnt to see its insufficiency ten years ago!

CAPTAIN   You must be a poor sort of creature then!

ALICE   [*to the Captain*]   Edgar!

CAPTAIN   Yes, he must be a poor creature if he has no strength of his own! No doubt it's true that when the machine stops working there is nothing left but a barrow-load to throw over the garden beds; but so long as the machine holds together, the thing is to kick and to fight, with hand and with foot, so long as the gear holds! That's my philosophy!

KURT   [*smiling*]   You do say funny things!

CAPTAIN   But you don't believe it is so?

KURT   No, I certainly don't!

CAPTAIN   No, but it is so all the same!

During the last scene the wind has begun to blow, and now one of the doors in the background slams to.

CAPTAIN   [*getting up*]   It's beginning to blow! I could feel it coming on! [*Goes to shut the doors and taps the barometer.*]

ALICE   [*to Kurt*]   You'll stay to supper, won't you?

KURT   Thank you!

ALICE   It will have to be something quite simple: our housemaid has left.

KURT   Oh, it's sure to be all right!

ALICE   You are so modest in your requirements, my dear Kurt!

CAPTAIN   [*at the barometer*]   If you could only see how the glass is falling! I felt it in my bones!

ALICE   [*aside, to Kurt*]   He's nervous!

CAPTAIN   We ought to have supper soon!

ALICE   [*getting up*]   I'm just going to see about it now! You two can sit here and have your talk; [*aside, to Kurt*] but don't contradict him or he'll lose his temper. And don't ask why he never became a major!
[*Kurt nods assent. Alice goes towards the door, right.*]

CAPTAIN   [*sits down at the sewing-table with Kurt*]   See that we have something nice, old girl!

ALICE   Give me some money and you shall have it!

CAPTAIN   Always money! [*Alice goes out. To Kurt*] Money, money, money! All day long I go about with a purse, till I fancy in the end that I *am* a purse! Do you know the feeling?

KURT   Oh, rather! the only difference being that I imagined I was a pocket-book!

CAPTAIN   Ha-ha! so you know the brand then! Those women! Ha-ha! And you yourself got hold of one of the right sort!

KURT   [*patiently*]   All that can be buried, now!

CAPTAIN   A regular jewel, she was! . . . Then there's myself. I have got at least—in spite of everything—a good woman! For she *is* straight, in spite of everything!

KURT   [*smiling good-naturedly*]   In spite of everything!

CAPTAIN   Don't laugh now!

KURT   [*as before*]   In spite of everything!

CAPTAIN   Yes, she's been a faithful wife . . . a splendid mother, splendid! . . . But [*with a glance towards the door, right*] she's got the devil of a temper. You know there have been times when I have cursed you for saddling me with her!

KURT   [*good-humouredly*]   But I never did that! Listen, man . . .

CAPTAIN   Tcha! you talk nonsense! You forget everything that's unpleasant to remember! Now don't mind me: I'm accustomed to commanding and storming at people, you see; but you know me, so you won't get angry.

KURT   Not a bit! But I didn't get you a wife! Quite the reverse!

CAPTAIN   [*not allowing his flow of language to be checked*]   Don't you think life's a queer thing anyhow?

KURT   Well, I suppose it is!

CAPTAIN   And then growing old! Not pleasant, but it *is* interesting! Well, I haven't old age to complain of, but it's just *beginning* to make itself felt! All the people one knows die off, and one feels so lonely!

KURT   Happy the man who has a wife to grow old with!

CAPTAIN   Happy? yes, there is happiness in that;

AUGUST STRINDBERG

for one's children leave one too! You should never have left yours!

KURT I didn't: they were taken from me. . . .

CAPTAIN Now you mustn't get angry when I say . . .

KURT But it *wasn't* so. . . .

CAPTAIN Well, anyhow it's forgotten. But you *are* lonely!

KURT One gets used to anything, my dear fellow!

CAPTAIN Could one . . . could one get used to . . . to being quite alone then?

KURT Well, look at me!

CAPTAIN What have you been doing these fifteen years?

KURT What a question! These fifteen years!

CAPTAIN They say you have come into some money and are a rich man!

KURT Rich—well hardly!

CAPTAIN I wasn't thinking of borrowing. . . .

KURT If you were, I should be quite ready. . . .

CAPTAIN It's awfully good of you, but I have my own banking account. You see in this household [*glancing towards the door, right*]—nothing must be wanting. The day I run short of money—off she goes!

KURT Oh, surely not!

CAPTAIN Not? But I know it!—Can you believe it?—She always watches for the times when I *am* short of money, just for the pleasure of convincing me that I don't provide for my family!

KURT But I thought you said you had a large income.

CAPTAIN Certainly I have a large income . . . but it's not enough.

KURT Then it's not large, in the ordinary sense. . . .

CAPTAIN Life is queer, and we are too! [*Clicking on the telegraph receiver*]

KURT What's that?

CAPTAIN Only the time-signal.

KURT Haven't you got a telephone?

CAPTAIN Yes, in the kitchen. But we use the telegraph: the telephone girls repeat everything we say.

KURT Social life out here by the sea must be awful.

CAPTAIN It's simply horrible! All life is horrible!

And you, who believe in a sequel, do you think there will be peace afterwards?

KURT I suppose there will be fighting and storms there too!

CAPTAIN There too! If there *is* any "there"! Rather annihilation!

KURT Are you sure that annihilation would come without pain?

CAPTAIN I shall die bang! And without pain!

KURT You know that, do you?

CAPTAIN Yes, I know that!

KURT You don't seem to be satisfied with your life?

CAPTAIN Satisfied? The day I die—then I shall be satisfied!

KURT [*getting up*] You don't know that! . . . But tell me: what are you two doing in this house? What is happening here? there's a smell like poisonous wallpaper—one feels sick the moment one comes in! I would rather go, if I hadn't promised Alice to stay. There's a dead body under the floor. There is hatred—one can hardly breathe. [*The Captain falls in a heap and stares vacantly.*] What's the matter with you? Edgar! [*The Captain does not move. Kurt slaps him on the shoulder.*] Edgar!

CAPTAIN [*recovering his senses*] Did you say anything? [*Looks round.*] I thought it was Alice! . . . Oh, it's you?—Now . . . [*relapses into apathy again*].

KURT This is terrible! [*Goes and opens door, right.*] Alice!

ALICE [*comes out, wearing a kitchen apron*] What is it?

KURT I don't know! look at him!

ALICE [*calmly*] He is absent-minded like that sometimes! . . . I'll play to him—then he'll wake up!

KURT *No*, don't! don't. . . . Let me try! . . . Can he hear? Can he see?

ALICE Neither hear nor see just now!

KURT And you say that so calmly! Alice, what are you two doing in this house?

ALICE Ask him . . . there!

KURT Him there? . . . Why, it's your husband!

ALICE To me he is a stranger—the same stranger that he was twenty-five years ago! I know nothing about this man . . . except that . . .

KURT Stop! he may hear you!

ALICE He can hear nothing now.

[*A bugle call is heard outside.*]

CAPTAIN [*springs to his feet and seizes his sword and cap*] Excuse me! I must just go and inspect the sentries! [*Goes out through the doorway in the background.*]

KURT Is he ill?

ALICE I don't know!

KURT Is he out of his mind?

ALICE I don't know!

KURT Does he drink?

ALICE More boasting about it than actual drinking!

KURT Sit down and talk; but calmly and truthfully!

ALICE [*sitting down*] What am I to say?—That I have lived in this tower for a lifetime, imprisoned, guarded by a man I have always hated —whom I now hate so utterly that, the day he died, I should laugh aloud!

KURT Why did you never separate?

ALICE You may well ask! Twice we broke off our engagement; since then there has not been a day that we didn't try to separate . . . but we are welded together and cannot get free! Once we *were* separated—in our own home— for five years! Now only death can part us. We know that, and that is why we wait for him as our deliverer!

KURT Why are you both so lonely?

ALICE Because he isolates me! First of all he uprooted my brothers and sisters from the house—"uprooting" is his own word for it— then my girl friends and others. . . .

KURT But *his* relations? You have uprooted them?

ALICE Yes; for after robbing me of my honour and my good name, they almost robbed me of my life.—In the end I had to keep up communication with the outside world and other human beings by means of that telegraph there —you see the telephone-girls used to spy on us. I taught myself how to use it. He knows nothing about this, and you mustn't tell him, or he'll kill me.

KURT Terrible! terrible! . . . But why does he blame *me* for your marriage?—Let me tell you how it was! . . . Edgar was my friend when we were boys. He fell in love with you at first sight. Then he came to me and asked me to act as intermediary. I said at once, "No!" Moreover, knowing your cruel and tyrannical disposition, my dear Alice, I warned him . . . and when he became importunate I sent him to get hold of your brother to plead for him.

ALICE I believe what you say; but he has deceived himself so all these years that you'll never get the idea out of his head now!

KURT Well, let him lay the blame on me then, if that relieves his sufferings.

ALICE That's really too much. . . .

KURT I am so used to . . . but what really does hurt me is the injustice of accusing me of deserting my children. . . .

ALICE That is his nature. He says anything that suits him, and then he believes it. But he seems to be fond of you—chiefly because you don't contradict him. . . . Now try not to be tired of us! I really think you have come at a fortunate moment for us: I regard your coming simply as a godsend! . . . Kurt! you mustn't get tired of us! We really are the most unhappy creatures in the whole world! [*Weeps.*]

KURT One marriage I have seen at close quarters, and that was dreadful! But this is almost worse!

ALICE Do you think so?

KURT Yes!

ALICE Whose fault is it?

KURT Alice! the moment you cease asking whose fault it is, you will find relief. Try to regard it as a fact, a trial that must be borne. . . .

ALICE That I can't do—it's too much! [*Gets up.*] It's past all cure!

KURT You poor creatures! Do you know why you hate each other?

ALICE No: ours is the most unreasoning hatred —without cause, without object, but also without end. And why do you think he is most afraid of death? Why, because he's afraid I shall marry again!

KURT Then he loves you!

ALICE Probably! But that doesn't stop him from hating me!

KURT [*as if to himself*] They call that love-hate,

and it comes from the abyss! . . . Does he like your playing to him?

ALICE Yes, but only hideous tunes—like that horrible "Entry of the Boyars." When he hears that, he becomes possessed and wants to dance.

KURT Dances, does he?

ALICE Yes, he's quite funny at times!

KURT One thing more—pardon my asking!— where are the children?

ALICE Perhaps you don't know that two of them are dead?

KURT Have you been through that too?

ALICE What is there that I have not been through?

KURT But the other two?

ALICE In the town. It was impossible they should live at home: he set them against me. . . .

KURT And you set them against him.

ALICE Of course. So it came to forming parties, canvassing and bribery . . . and then, so as not to ruin them utterly, we parted from them! What should have been a bond of union became the cause of disunion: the blessing of a home became its curse. . . . Yes, sometimes I think we belong to an accursed race!

KURT After the Fall—why yes, I suppose we do!

ALICE [*sharply, with a venomous look*] What fall?

KURT Our first parents'!

ALICE Oh, I thought you meant something else! [*Embarrassed silence*]

ALICE [*folding her hands*] Kurt! you are my kinsman, the friend of my childhood! I have not always treated you as I should! Now I have got my punishment, and you your revenge!

KURT Not revenge! there is no question of that! Don't talk of it!

ALICE Do you remember one Sunday when you were engaged? I had asked you to dinner. . . .

KURT Hush!

ALICE I must speak—have pity on me! . . . And when you came, you found us out and had to go home again!

KURT You'd been asked out yourselves: is it worth talking about?

ALICE Kurt! when I asked you to supper just now I thought we had something left in the larder! [*Hides her face in her hands.*] And there is nothing—not even a piece of bread! [*Weeps.*]

KURT Poor, poor Alice!

ALICE But when *he* comes in and wants something to eat, and finds there's nothing, he'll be furious! You've never seen him furious! . . . O God, what humiliation!

KURT Let me go out and get something.

ALICE There's nothing to be got on the island!

KURT Not on my account, but for his sake and yours. . . . Let me think of something, something. . . . We must turn the whole thing into a joke when he comes back. . . . I'll suggest that we have a drink, and meanwhile I'll think of something. . . . Get him into a good temper, play to him—any little thing will do! Sit down at the piano and be ready!

ALICE Look at my hands; do you call them fit to play with? I have to clean the brass and wipe glasses, light the fires and do the rooms. . . .

KURT But you've got two servants!

ALICE We have to say that, because he's an officer . . . but the servants are continually leaving, and sometimes we have none at all— usually in fact. How shall I get out of this— this supper? . . . oh, if only the house would catch fire!

KURT Hush, Alice, hush!

ALICE Or the sea rise and sweep us away!

KURT No, no, I cannot listen to you!

ALICE What will he say, what will he say? . . . Don't go, Kurt! don't leave me!

KURT No, my poor friend, I *won't* go!

ALICE Ah, but when you *have* gone . . .

KURT Has he ever struck you?

ALICE Me? oh, no! He knows I would have left him if he had! One must keep some sort of pride!

[*From outside is heard:* "Halt! Who goes there?"—"A friend!"]

KURT [*getting up*] Is that him?

ALICE [*frightened*] Yes, it's him!

[*A pause*]

KURT What on earth shall we do?

ALICE I don't know, I don't know!

CAPTAIN [*enters from the back, cheerfully*] Ah! here we are! free at last! . . . Well, has she managed to get in her complaints? Isn't hers a wretched life—what?

KURT What's the weather like outside?

CAPTAIN Half a gale! . . . [*Facetiously, setting one of the outer doors ajar*] Sir Bluebeard and the young maiden in the tower; and outside marches the sentry with drawn sword, keeping watch over the beautiful maiden. . . . And then come the brothers, but the sentry's on guard—look! one, two, one, two! a fine sentry! Look at him! Meli-tam-tam-ta, melita-lia-lay! Shall we dance the sword dance? Kurt ought to see that!

KURT No, have the "Entry of the Boyars" instead!

CAPTAIN So you know that, do you? Alice in the kitchen apron, come and play! Come, I say! [*Alice goes reluctantly to the piano. Pinching her arm*] I know you've been maligning me!

ALICE I?

[*Kurt turns away. Alice plays the "Entrance March." The Captain goes through a kind of Hungarian dance behind the writing-table, jingling his spurs. Then he sinks down on the floor, without being noticed by Kurt or Alice, who plays the piece through to the end.*]

ALICE [*without turning round*] Shall we have it over again? [*Silence. Turns round and sees the Captain lying senseless on the floor, hidden from the audience by the writing-table.*] Oh Heavens! [*She remains standing, with arms crossed over her breast, and gives a sigh as of thankfulness and relief.*]

KURT [*turns round and goes quickly to the Captain*] What is it? what is it?

ALICE [*in a state of great tension*] Is he dead?

KURT I don't know! come and help me!

ALICE [*without moving*] I couldn't touch him! . . . Is he dead?

KURT No, he's alive!

[*Alice sighs. Kurt stays by the Captain, who has got up and is being helped into a chair.*]

CAPTAIN What was it? [*Silence*] What was it?

KURT Why, you fell down!

CAPTAIN Did anything happen?

KURT You fell on the floor. How do you feel now?

CAPTAIN I? It was nothing at all! I don't know

of anything! What are you both standing and gaping at?

KURT You are ill.

CAPTAIN Nonsense! Go on playing, Alice! . . . Ah, now it's coming back again! [*Clasps his head.*]

ALICE Now you see! You *are* ill!

CAPTAIN Don't shriek! It's only a giddy attack!

KURT We must have a doctor!—I'll go and telephone! . . .

CAPTAIN I won't have a doctor!

KURT You must! For our own sakes we must call him in—otherwise we shall be held responsible!

CAPTAIN I'll turn him out if he comes! I'll shoot him down! . . . Ah, there it is again! [*Clasps his head.*]

KURT [*goes towards the door, right*] Now I am going to telephone! [*Goes out.*] [*Alice takes off her apron.*]

CAPTAIN Will you give me a glass of water?

ALICE I suppose I must! [*Gives him a glass of water.*]

CAPTAIN How amiable!

ALICE Are you ill?

CAPTAIN Pray forgive me for not being quite well!

ALICE Will you look after yourself then?

CAPTAIN You probably wouldn't care to!

ALICE That you can be sure of!

CAPTAIN The hour is come for which you have waited so long.

ALICE Yes, the hour you believed would never come!

CAPTAIN Don't be angry with me!

KURT [*coming in from the right*] It's too bad. . . .

ALICE What did he say?

KURT Rang off, without another word!

ALICE [*to the Captain*] Now we see the result of your boundless arrogance!

CAPTAIN I think I'm getting worse! . . . try and get a doctor from the town!

ALICE [*goes to the telegraph*] I must do it by telegraph then!

CAPTAIN [*half rising, in astonishment*] Can—you—telegraph?

ALICE [*telegraphing*] I can!

CAPTAIN Really? Go on then! . . . What a deceitful woman! [*To Kurt*] Come and sit by me! [*Kurt does so.*] Hold my hand! I sit here and keep falling—can you imagine it?—down something—an extraordinary feeling!

KURT Have you had this sort of attack before?

CAPTAIN Never! . . .

KURT While you're waiting for an answer from the town I'll go and have a talk with the Doctor. Has he attended you before?

CAPTAIN He has!

KURT Then he knows your constitution! [*Goes to the left.*]

ALICE The answer won't take long. It is kind of you, Kurt! but come back soon!

KURT As soon as I can! [*Goes out.*]

CAPTAIN He's a good fellow, Kurt! And how he's changed!

ALICE Yes, and for the better! I'm sorry for him, though, being mixed up with our wretched affairs just at this time of all times!

CAPTAIN Good luck for us, though! . . . I wonder how things really are with him! Did you notice that he wouldn't talk about his own affairs?

ALICE I noticed it, but I don't think anyone asked him!

CAPTAIN Think of it—his life! and ours! I wonder if all men's lives are like that!

ALICE Very likely—though they don't talk about it as we do!

CAPTAIN I've sometimes thought that misery attracts misery, and that those who are happy shun unhappiness. That is why we never see anything but misery!

ALICE Have you ever known any happy people?

CAPTAIN Let me think! . . . No! . . . Yes—the Ekmarks!

ALICE How can you say that? Why, she had an operation last year. . . .

CAPTAIN So she did! Well, then I don't know . . . yes, the von Kraffts!

ALICE Yes, the whole family lived an idyllic life: well off, respected, nice children, suitable marriages, everything all right till they were fifty. Then that cousin of theirs went and committed a crime—prison and all that! And that was the end of their peace. The family name

was dragged through the mire in all the papers. . . . The "Krafft murder" made it impossible for that highly respected family to show their faces out of doors; the children had to be taken away from school. . . . Oh, God!

CAPTAIN I wonder what's the matter with me!

ALICE What do you think?

CAPTAIN Heart, or head! I feel as if my soul wanted to fly away and dissolve into a cloud of smoke.

ALICE Are you hungry?

CAPTAIN Yes: what about supper?

ALICE [*walks about uneasily*] I'll ask Jenny.

CAPTAIN But she's left!

ALICE Oh, so she has!

CAPTAIN Ring for Kristin; I want some fresh water!

ALICE [*rings*] Suppose . . . ! [*Rings again.*] She doesn't hear!

CAPTAIN Go and see about it! . . . Suppose she has left too!

ALICE [*goes and opens door, left*] Good heavens! here's her box in the passage, ready packed!

CAPTAIN Then she's gone!

ALICE This is hell! [*Bursts into tears, falls on her knees, and lays her head on a chair, sobbing.*]

CAPTAIN And everything at once! . . . And of course Kurt comes just in time to see what a mess we're in! If there is one humiliation left, let it come now—now!

ALICE Do you know what I think? Kurt has gone and isn't coming back!

CAPTAIN I can quite believe it of him!

ALICE Yes, we are accursed! . . .

CAPTAIN What do you mean?

ALICE Don't you see how everybody shuns us?

CAPTAIN What do I care? [*Clicking on the receiver*] There's the answer! Quiet! I can hear it! . . . Nobody has time! Excuses—the rabble!

ALICE That's what you get for despising your doctors, and not paying their bills!

CAPTAIN That is not the fact!

ALICE Even when you could, you wouldn't pay, because you looked down on their work, just as you looked down on mine and everybody else's! . . . They won't come! And the telephone is cut off, because you didn't think that worth anything either! Nothing is worth anything, except your rifles and guns!

CAPTAIN Don't stand there chattering. . . .

ALICE Everything comes back to us!

CAPTAIN What a superstition! that's the sort of thing old women say!

ALICE Well, you'll see! Do you know that we owe Kristin six months' wages?

CAPTAIN Well, she's stolen that amount!

ALICE Besides that, I have had to borrow from her!

CAPTAIN I can believe that of you!

ALICE How ungrateful you are! You know I borrowed it for the children's journey to town!

CAPTAIN A nice way of coming back—Kurt's was! A scoundrel, like the rest of them! And a coward! Didn't dare say he'd had enough of it, —that it was more amusing at the Doctor's ball! Probably expected a rotten supper here! . . . Just like the villain!

KURT [*comes in quickly, left*] Well, my dear Edgar, here it is! The Doctor knows your heart inside and out. . . .

CAPTAIN Heart?

KURT Yes; for a long time there has been a chalky deposit in your heart. . . .

CAPTAIN Stony heart?

KURT And . . .

CAPTAIN Is it dangerous?

KURT Yes—that is to say . . .

CAPTAIN It *is* dangerous!

KURT Yes!

CAPTAIN Fatal?

KURT You will have to be very careful! In the first place, no cigars! [*The Captain throws away his cigar.*] Secondly, no whisky! . . . And then, to bed!

CAPTAIN [*frightened*] No, *that* I will not do! No bed for me! That means the end! That means never getting up again! I shall sleep on the couch to-night. What else did he say?

KURT He was very nice—would come at once if you called him.

CAPTAIN Nice was he—the hypocrite! I won't see him! . . . Am I allowed to eat then?

KURT Not to-night! And the next few days only milk!

CAPTAIN Milk! I can't bear the taste of it!

KURT Well, you'll soon learn to!

CAPTAIN No, I'm too old to learn! [*Clasps his head.*] Ah, now it's come again! [*Remains seated, staring.*]

ALICE [*to Kurt*] What did the doctor say?

KURT Said he *may* die!

ALICE Thank God!

KURT Take care, Alice, take care! . . . And now go and fetch a pillow and a rug: I'm going to put him to bed here on the couch! Then I'll sit on the chair here, all night!

ALICE And I?

KURT You go to bed. The sight of you seems to make him worse!

ALICE Give your orders—I'll obey! you mean well by us both! [*Goes out left.*]

KURT By you both—mark that! I take no side in party squabbles! [*Takes the water-bottle and goes out to the right.*]

The wind is heard blowing outside. Then the background door blows open, and an Old Woman of poor and unpleasant appearance peeps in.

CAPTAIN [*wakes, sits up and looks about him*] Ah, so they have deserted me, the scoundrels! [*Catches sight of the Old Woman and is frightened.*] Who is it? what do you want?

OLD WOMAN I just wanted to shut the door, kind sir!

CAPTAIN But why? why should you?

OLD WOMAN Because it blew open just as I went by.

CAPTAIN You meant to steal, did you?

OLD WOMAN Not much here worth taking—so Kristin said!

CAPTAIN Kristin!

OLD WOMAN Good night, sir! Sleep well! [*Shuts the door and goes. Alice comes in from the left with pillows and a rug.*]

CAPTAIN Who was that at the door? Was there anybody?

ALICE Yes, it was old Maja from the workhouse going by.

CAPTAIN Are you sure?

ALICE Are you frightened?

CAPTAIN I, frightened? Oh, dear no!

ALICE As you don't want to go to bed you can lie down here.

CAPTAIN [*goes and lies on the couch*] I'll sleep

here. [*Tries to take Alice's hand, but she draws it away. Kurt comes in with the water-bottle.*] Kurt! don't leave me!

KURT I'm going to stay with you all night! Alice is going to bed!

CAPTAIN Good night then, Alice!

ALICE [*to Kurt*] Good night, Kurt!

KURT Good night! [*Gets a chair and sits down by the Captain's couch.*] Won't you take your boots off?

CAPTAIN No, a soldier should always be prepared!

KURT Are you expecting a battle then?

CAPTAIN Perhaps! [*Sits up on the couch.*] Kurt! you're the only human being I've ever laid my soul bare to! Now listen to one thing! If I should die to-night . . . take care of my children!

KURT I will!

CAPTAIN Thank you! I rely on you!

KURT Can you explain why you rely on me?

CAPTAIN We have not been friends—for friendship I don't believe in, and our families were born enemies and have always been at war. . . .

KURT And yet you rely on me?

CAPTAIN Yes! and I don't know why! [*Silence.*] Do you think I'm going to die?

KURT Like everybody else! No exception will be made in your case!

CAPTAIN Are you being sarcastic?

KURT Yes! . . . Are you afraid of death? The wheelbarrow and the garden bed!

CAPTAIN Suppose that were not the end!

KURT Many think so!

CAPTAIN And afterwards?

KURT Nothing but surprises, I imagine!

CAPTAIN But one knows nothing for certain.

KURT No, that's just it, that's why one has to be ready for everything.

CAPTAIN You're not so childish, I suppose, as to believe in hell?

KURT Don't you believe in it—you who are actually in it?

CAPTAIN That is merely a metaphor!

KURT You have painted yours so vividly that all thought of metaphors, poetical or not, is excluded! [*Silence*]

CAPTAIN If you only knew what agonies I'm suffering!

KURT Of the body?

CAPTAIN No, not of the body!

KURT Then it must be of the spirit. There is no other alternative.

[*A pause*]

CAPTAIN [*sitting up on the couch*] I don't want to die!

KURT Just now you wanted annihilation!

CAPTAIN Yes, if it be painless.

KURT But that, we know, it is not!

CAPTAIN Is this annihilation then?

KURT The beginning of it!

CAPTAIN Good night!

KURT Good night!

The same setting, but the lamp is just going out. Through the windows and the glass panes of the doors in the background a cloudy morning is visible. The sea is rough. Sentry by the battery as before. The Captain is lying on the couch asleep. Kurt sits on a chair near him, looking pale and worn out from watching.

ALICE [*coming in from the left*] Is he asleep?

KURT Yes, ever since what should have been sunrise.

ALICE What sort of night did he have?

KURT He got some sleep now and then, but he would talk so much.

ALICE What about?

KURT He kept on arguing about religion like a schoolboy, and at the same time claimed to have solved the riddles of the universe! Finally, towards dawn, he discovered the immortality of the soul!

ALICE To his own glory!

KURT Quite so! . . . He is really the most arrogant person I have ever met. "*I* exist: therefore there is a God!"

ALICE You've realized that! . . . Look at those boots! With them he would have trampled the earth flat, if he'd been allowed! With them he has trampled down other people's fields and gardens; with them he has trampled on other people's toes and on my own head! . . . Tiger, your bullet has got you now!

KURT He might have been a comic figure, were he not so tragic! After all there are elements of greatness in all his petty meanness! Can't you find a single kind word to say for him?

ALICE [*sits down*] Yes, as long as he doesn't hear! One word of praise makes him mad with conceit!

KURT He can't hear anything: he's had morphia.

ALICE Edgar was brought up in poverty—one of many brothers and sisters. While still quite young he had to support his family by giving lessons, since his father was a scamp—or worse. No doubt it's hard on a young man to have to give up all the pleasures of youth in order to slave for a swarm of ungrateful children whom he hasn't brought into the world. I was a little girl when I saw him as a young man, going about in the winter without an overcoat, with the thermometer showing forty degrees of frost—his little sisters wore woolly coats. . . . It was fine, and I admired him, though his ugliness repelled me. He is unusually ugly, isn't he?

KURT Yes, and his ugliness at times has something repulsive about it. I noticed it particularly when we were not on good terms; and then, when we were not together, his image grew and took on horrible shapes and sizes, so that he literally haunted me!

ALICE Think of me then! . . . However, his earlier years as an officer were no doubt a martyrdom. But he got help now and then from rich people. He never will admit that, and he's taken whatever he's been able to get as a tribute due to him, and without a word of thanks!

KURT We were going to speak well of him!

ALICE After he's dead—yes! . . . Well! . . . That's all I can remember!

KURT Have you found him malicious?

ALICE Yes—and yet he can be both kind and easily moved!—As an enemy he's simply horrible!

KURT Why did he never become a major?

ALICE You ought to be able to guess that! They didn't want to have a man over them who'd been a tyrant when he was under them! But you must never let him see you know anything about that! He himself says that he didn't want to be major. . . . Did he mention the children at all?

KURT Yes, he was longing for Judith!

ALICE So I should think. And do you know what Judith is? His own image, whom he has trained to attack me! Only think—my own daughter . . . has raised her hand against me!

KURT Oh, that is too terrible!

ALICE Hush! he's moving! Supposing he heard us! . . . He's so cunning too!

KURT He really is waking up!

ALICE Doesn't he look like an ogre? I'm terrified of him!

[*Silence*]

CAPTAIN [*stirs, wakes, sits up and looks round*] It's morning! at last! . . .

KURT How do you feel now?

CAPTAIN Bad!

KURT Would you like to see a doctor?

CAPTAIN No . . . I want to see Judith! My child!

KURT Wouldn't it be as well to set your house in order before, or—shall I say—in case anything should happen?

CAPTAIN What do you mean? What could happen?

KURT What may happen to us all!

CAPTAIN Oh, nonsense! I shan't die so easily as all that, I tell you! Don't congratulate yourself too soon, Alice!

KURT Think of your children! make your will, so that at least your wife may keep the furniture!

CAPTAIN Is she to get my property while I'm still alive?

KURT No; but if anything happens she oughtn't to be turned out into the street! One who has tidied, dusted and polished these things for twenty-five years ought to have some right to keep them. May I send for the solicitor?

CAPTAIN No!

KURT You are a cruel man—more cruel even than I thought!

CAPTAIN Here it is again! [*Falls back on the couch unconscious.*]

ALICE [*going out to the right*] There's somebody in the kitchen: I must go!

KURT Yes, go! There's not much to be done here!

[*Alice goes out.*]

CAPTAIN [*recovering consciousness*] Well, Kurt, how are you going to manage about your quarantine station here?

KURT Oh, that'll be all right!

CAPTAIN No, I'm commander on this island, so you'll have to deal with me! Don't forget that!

KURT Have you ever seen a quarantine station?

CAPTAIN Have I? Yes, before you were born! And I'll give you one piece of advice—don't put your disinfecting chambers too near the shore.

KURT My idea was to try and get as near the water . . .

CAPTAIN That shows how much you know about your business! Why, water is the element of the bacilli—their life element!

KURT But the salt water of the sea is needed for washing away impurities!

CAPTAIN Idiot! . . . Well now, as soon as you are settled in, you must fetch your children to live with you.

KURT Do you suppose they'll let themselves be fetched?

CAPTAIN Of course, if you're anything of a man! It would make a good impression on the neighbourhood if they could see you fulfilling your duties in that point too. . . .

KURT I have always fulfilled my duties in that point!

CAPTAIN [*raising his voice*] In that point which is your weakest!

KURT Haven't I told you . . .

CAPTAIN [*takes no notice*] For one doesn't desert one's children like that. . . .

KURT Oh, go on!

CAPTAIN I am a relative of yours—an elder relative, and as such I think I have a right to tell you the truth, even if it is unpalatable. . . . You mustn't take it amiss. . . .

KURT Are you hungry?

CAPTAIN Yes, I am! . . .

KURT Would you like something light?

CAPTAIN No, something solid.

KURT If so you're done for!

CAPTAIN Isn't it enough for a man to be ill, without starving too?

KURT That's what it comes to!

CAPTAIN And no drink, and no smoke! Such a life's hardly worth living!

KURT Death requires sacrifices—or he comes at once!

ALICE [*enters with some bouquets, telegrams and letters*] These are for you! [*Throws the flowers on the writing-table.*]

CAPTAIN [*flattered*] For me! . . . Let me see them! . . .

ALICE Oh, they're only from the NCO's, the band, and the corporals!

CAPTAIN You are jealous!

ALICE Oh no! If they were laurel wreaths . . . it might be another matter. But those you could never get!

CAPTAIN Hm! . . . Here's a wire from the Colonel . . . you read it, Kurt! . . . The Colonel's a gentleman anyhow, though he is a bit of an idiot! . . . And here's another from . . . let me see! Why, it's from Judith! . . . Kindly wire her to come by the next boat! . . . And here . . . yes!—one is not quite without one's friends after all! It's good of them to think of a sick man, a man of merits above his rank, without fear and without reproach!

ALICE I don't understand! do they congratulate you on being ill?

CAPTAIN Hyena!

ALICE [*to Kurt*] Yes, we had a doctor here who was so detested that when he left the island they gave a banquet—not in his honour, in honour of his departure!

CAPTAIN Put the flowers in vases. . . . You can't call me credulous—and of course everybody is rabble—but, by Jove, this simple homage really is genuine . . . it can't be anything but genuine!

ALICE Idiot!

KURT [*reading a telegram*] Judith says she can't come because the boat's delayed owing to the gale!

CAPTAIN Is that all?

KURT No-o!—there's a postscript!

CAPTAIN Out with it!

KURT Well, she begs Daddy not to drink so much!

CAPTAIN Impudence! . . . That's what children are! . . . That's my one beloved daughter . . . my Judith . . . my idol!

ALICE And image!

CAPTAIN Such is life and its purest joys! Good God!

ALICE Now you're beginning to reap what

you've sown! You set her against her mother, and now she turns against her father! Don't tell me there is no God!

CAPTAIN [*to Kurt*]   What does the Colonel say?

KURT   He gives you leave of absence—nothing more!

CAPTAIN   Leave of absence? But I never asked for any!

ALICE   No, but I did!

CAPTAIN   I don't accept it!

ALICE   Your deputy is already appointed!

CAPTAIN   That doesn't affect *me!*

ALICE   You see, Kurt! here is a man for whom laws do not exist, no constitution is valid, no human order is prescribed. . . . He stands above everything and everybody: the universe is created for his own private use: the sun and moon pursue their courses to bear his praises to the stars. Such is my husband! this insignificant captain, who never could manage to be major: whose bumptiousness makes him all men's laughing-stock, while he imagines that he is feared: this wretched creature who is afraid of the dark and puts his faith in barometers:— and all this coupled with and ending in the grand climax—a barrowful of manure—and that not of the first quality!

CAPTAIN [*fanning himself with a bouquet in a self-satisfied way, without paying any attention to Alice*]   Have you asked Kurt to breakfast?

ALICE   No!

CAPTAIN   Then see at once about two—two nice Chateaubriand steaks.

ALICE   Two?

CAPTAIN   I'm going to have one myself!

ALICE   But there are three of us here!

CAPTAIN   Oh, you're having some too? All right, get three then!

ALICE   Where am I to get them? Last night you asked Kurt to supper and there wasn't a crust of bread in the house. Kurt has had to keep watch all night on an empty stomach: he's had no coffee because there wasn't any, and because our credit is gone!

CAPTAIN   She's angry with me for not dying yesterday!

ALICE   No; for not dying twenty-five years ago: for not dying before I was born!

CAPTAIN [*to Kurt*]   Hark to her! . . . That's the result of your match-making, my dear Kurt! Our marriage wasn't made in heaven—that's a certainty! [*Alice and Kurt look at each other meaningly. The Captain gets up and goes towards the door.*] However, say what you will, I'm going on duty now! [*Puts on an old-fashioned busby, fastens on his sword and puts on his cloak.*] If anyone calls for me they'll find me at the battery! [*Alice and Kurt try to stop him, but in vain.*] Out of my way! [*Goes out.*]

ALICE   Yes, go! you always go, always turn your back when the fight becomes too hot for you! always leave your wife to cover your retreat, you bottle-hero, you boaster, you arch-liar! Curses on you!

KURT   It's a fathomless abyss!

ALICE   Yes, and you don't know all yet!

KURT   Is there more then?

ALICE   But I feel ashamed. . . .

KURT   Where is he off to now? And how does he get the strength?

ALICE   You may well ask that! He's going down now to see the NCO's and thank them for the flowers . . . and then he'll eat and drink with them! and abuse his fellow-officers! . . . If you only knew how often he's been threatened with dismissal! Only sympathy for his family has saved him! And he fondly imagines it is fear of his superiority! And the poor officers' wives, who have put in a good word for us—he hates and abuses!

KURT   I must tell you that I applied for the post here in order to find peace by the sea. . . . I knew nothing of your affairs. . . .

ALICE   Poor Kurt! . . . How will you get anything to eat?

KURT   Oh, I shall go to the Doctor's. But what about you? Do let me see after things for you.

ALICE   So long as he doesn't get to know. If he did, he would kill me!

KURT [*looking out of the window*]   Look! there he is on the rampart, out in the storm!

ALICE   I'm sorry for him—that he's what he is!

KURT   I'm sorry for you both! . . . What can be done?

ALICE   I don't know! . . . A batch of bills

came, too, which he didn't see! . . .

KURT It may be an advantage sometimes *not* to see things!

ALICE [*at the window*] He has unbuttoned his cloak, for the wind to blow on his breast! So now he does want to die!

KURT I don't think he does. Just now, when he felt his life slipping away, he grabbed hold of mine; began to busy himself with my affairs, as if he wanted to creep into me and live my life!

ALICE That is exactly his vampire nature . . . to seize hold of other people's fates, to suck interest out of their lives, to order and arrange for them, since his own life is absolutely without interest for him. And remember, Kurt! Never let him into your family life! never let him get to know your friends—or he'll take them away from you and make them his own! . . . He's a regular wizard in that way! . . . If he met your children you'd soon find them *his* most intimate friends: he would advise them and bring them up to suit his own ideas—above all, in *opposition* to your wishes!

KURT Alice! Wasn't it he who took my children away from me—when I was divorced?

ALICE Since that's all over now—yes, it was he!

KURT I had suspected it—but I never knew! It was he!

ALICE When you sent my husband as peace-maker to your wife—relying on him absolutely—he started a flirtation with her, and showed her the trick how to get hold of the children!

KURT O God! . . . God in heaven!

ALICE There you have another side of him! [*Silence*]

KURT Do you know, last night, when he thought he was going to die . . . he . . . made me promise to look after his children!

ALICE But you don't want to take your revenge on my children?

KURT By keeping my promise? Yes! I shall look after your children, and his!

ALICE That is the greatest revenge you could take: there's nothing he hates so much as generosity!

KURT So I may consider myself revenged—without taking revenge!

ALICE I love revenge as I love justice, and I rejoice to see evil get its punishment!

KURT You've got no further than that?

ALICE Nor ever shall! The day I forgave or loved an enemy I should be a hypocrite!

KURT Alice, it may be a duty not to say everything, not to see everything! It is called forbearance, and that we all need!

ALICE Not I! My life lies open and clear: I have always played the game.

KURT That's saying a good deal!

ALICE No, it's not saying enough! What I have suffered, undeservedly, for the sake of this man whom I never loved . . .

KURT Why did you marry him then?

ALICE You might tell *me* that! Because he took me! Seduced me! I don't know! And then I longed to climb social heights . . .

KURT And you deserted your art!

ALICE My despised art!—But he cheated me, you know! He held out prospects of a happy life . . . a beautiful home; and all I found was debts . . . the only gold was on his uniform, and even that wasn't gold! He cheated me!

KURT Wait a little! When a young man falls in love he sees the future in a hopeful light . . . one must forgive him if his hopes are not always realized! I have the same deceit on my own conscience, but I don't regard myself as a cheat! . . . What are you looking at on the rampart out there?

ALICE I'm looking to see if he hasn't fallen down.

KURT And has he?

ALICE No, worse luck! He cheats me all the time!

KURT Then I'll go and see the doctor and the lawyer!

ALICE [*seats herself at the window*] Yes, go, dear Kurt! I'll sit here and wait. And I have learnt how to wait!

INTERVAL

The same setting, by daylight. The Sentry is marching by the battery as before. Alice is sitting in the arm-chair, right. Her hair is grey.

KURT [*comes in left after knocking*] Good morning, Alice!

ALICE   Good morning, my friend! Sit down!

KURT   [*sits down in arm-chair, left*]   The boat's just coming in.

ALICE   Then I know what's in store for us, if he's on it!

KURT   He is: I caught sight of the glitter of his helmet. . . . What's he been doing in the town?

ALICE   It's easy to work that out. He was in parade dress—so he must have gone to see the Colonel. He had on his best gloves—so he was paying calls.

KURT   Did you notice how quiet he was yesterday? Since he gave up drinking and became temperate he has become a different man—calm, reserved, considerate. . . .

ALICE   I know. If that man had always kept sober he would have been a terror to mankind. Perhaps it's lucky for mankind that he made himself ridiculous and harmless with his whisky!

KURT   The Spirit of the Bottle has chastised him! . . . But have you noticed how, since death set his mark on him, he has gained a dignity which ennobles him? Perhaps his newly awakened idea of immortality has given him another conception of life.

ALICE   You deceive yourself! he is conjuring up evil! And don't believe what he says: he lies deliberately, and he knows the art of intrigue as no one else. . . .

KURT   [*looking at Alice*]   Alice! what's this? Your hair has turned grey these last two nights!

ALICE   No, my friend: it's been like that for years. It's simply that I've stopped darkening it, since my husband is as good as dead! Twenty-five years in a prison! Did you know this place was a prison in the old days?

KURT   A prison! Yes, the walls look like that!

ALICE   And my complexion! Even the children took on the prison colour in here!

KURT   It isn't easy to imagine little children prattling within these walls!

ALICE   It wasn't often they did prattle either! The two who died perished from want of light!

KURT   What do you think's coming next?

ALICE   The decisive blow against *us*! I saw a well-known gleam in his eye when you read out Judith's telegram. It ought, of course, to have fallen on her; but she, as you know, always gets

off scot-free; so his hatred struck at you!

KURT   What do you think he's aiming at in my case?

ALICE   It's not easy to say: but he possesses an incredible talent—it may be just luck—for nosing out other people's secrets. . . . And did you notice how, the whole of yesterday, he seemed to be living in your quarantine station: how he sucked an interest in life from your being: how he ate your children alive? . . . A man-eater, you see! I know him! His own life is going, or is gone. . . .

KURT   I've got that impression too—that he's already on the other side. His face seems to be phosphorescent, as if he were undergoing dissolution. . . . His eyes flame like will-o'-the-wisps over graves or swamps. . . . Ah, here he comes! Tell me—have you thought of the possibility that he might be jealous?

ALICE   No, he's too conceited for that! "Show me the man I need be jealous of!" Those were his own words!

KURT   So much the better! even his faults have their advantages! . . . Anyhow, shall I get up and go to meet him?

ALICE   No, don't be too polite, or he'll think you're being treacherous! And as soon as he begins to lie, pretend to believe him! I can easily translate his lies and get at the truth, with the help of my dictionary! . . . I have a presentiment of something dreadful. . . . But, Kurt! don't lose your self-control! . . . My one advantage through our long struggle has been that I have always been temperate, and so kept my wits about me. . . . His whisky always handicapped him! . . . Now we shall see!

[*The Captain comes in from the left, in parade dress, helmet, cloak and white gloves. Calm, dignified, but pale and hollow-eyed. Comes forward with tottering steps and sits at the right of the stage, some way from Alice and Kurt, with his helmet and cloak still on. During the following conversation he keeps his sword between his knees.*]

CAPTAIN   Good morning!—Excuse my sitting down like this, but I'm rather tired!

ALICE AND KURT   Good morning!

ALICE   How are you now?

CAPTAIN   Splendid! Just a little tired! . . .

ALICE What news from the town?

CAPTAIN Oh, all sorts! Among other things I went to see the doctor, and he said it was nothing: that if I took care of myself, I might live another twenty years!

ALICE [to Kurt] Now he's lying! [To the Captain] That was good news, dear!

CAPTAIN It was! [Silence, during which the Captain looks at Alice and Kurt, as if he wanted them to say something.]

ALICE [to Kurt] Don't say a word! Let him speak first: then he'll show his hand!

CAPTAIN [to Alice] Did you say anything?

ALICE No, nothing!

CAPTAIN [slowly] Now, Kurt!

ALICE [to Kurt] There! Now he's coming out!

CAPTAIN I—I was in the town, as you know. [Kurt nods assent.] And—er—I made the acquaintance—among others—of a young cadet [drawlingly] in the artillery! [Pause, during which Kurt seems uneasy] As . . . we are short of cadets here, I arranged with the Colonel to let him come here. This ought to please you—you especially—when I tell you—that—it was—your own son!

ALICE [to Kurt] The vampire! Now you see!

KURT In ordinary circumstances that ought to please a father; in my case it is merely painful!

CAPTAIN I don't understand!

KURT There is no need that you should: it is enough that I don't wish it!

CAPTAIN Oh, you think so! . . . In that case let me tell you that the young man has been ordered to report here, and that from this moment he takes his orders from me!

KURT Then I shall make him apply to be transferred to another regiment!

CAPTAIN That you can't do, since you've no rights over your son!

KURT Have I not?

CAPTAIN No: the Court gave them to the mother!

KURT Then I shall put myself in communication with the mother!

CAPTAIN No need for that!

KURT No need?

CAPTAIN No: I have already done so! Ha! [Kurt rises but sinks back again.]

ALICE [to Kurt] Now he must die!

KURT He is a man-eater!

CAPTAIN So much for that! [To Alice and Kurt, directly] Did you two say anything?

ALICE No: is your hearing bad?

CAPTAIN It is, rather! . . . But if you'll come nearer I'll tell you something between ourselves!

ALICE There is no necessity! Besides, a witness may be advantageous for both parties!

CAPTAIN You're right there! It's always a good thing to have a witness! . . . But first of all—have you got the will ready?

ALICE [handing him a document] The solicitor drew it up himself!

CAPTAIN In your favour! . . . good! [Reads the document and then tears it carefully into strips, which he throws on the floor.] So much for that! Ha!

ALICE [to Kurt] Did you ever see such a man?

KURT He isn't a man!

CAPTAIN Now, Alice! this is what I want to say to you! . . .

ALICE [uneasily] Please go on!

CAPTAIN [calmly, as before] In consideration of your long-expressed desire to terminate the miserable life which has resulted from our unfortunate marriage, and on account of the entire lack of feeling with which you have treated your husband and children, and on account of the negligence which you have displayed in the management of our domestic economy—I have this day, while I was in town, filed an application for divorce with the Borough Court!

ALICE Indeed? and the grounds?

CAPTAIN Apart from the grounds already mentioned I have others which are purely personal! For instance, since it has been ascertained that I may live for another twenty years, I am thinking of changing this unfortunate union for one that suits me better—in other words, unite my destiny with that of some woman who, together with devotion to her husband, may also bring into the household youth and—may I say?—a little beauty!

ALICE [takes off her ring and throws it at the Captain] As you please!

CAPTAIN [picks up the ring and puts it in his waistcoat pocket] She throws away her ring!

The Dance of Death

445

Will the witness be so good as to note that?

ALICE [*rises, in great agitation*] So you intend to throw me out and put another woman into my house?

CAPTAIN Tcha!

ALICE Very well! then we'll have some plain speaking! . . . Cousin Kurt, that man has been guilty of an attempt to murder his wife!

KURT Attempt to murder?

ALICE Yes! he pushed me into the water!

CAPTAIN Without witnesses!

ALICE He lies! Judith saw it!

CAPTAIN What difference does that make?

ALICE She can give evidence!

CAPTAIN No, she cannot! she says she saw nothing!

ALICE You've taught the child to lie!

CAPTAIN There was no need: you had already taught her!

ALICE Did you meet Judith?

CAPTAIN Tcha!

ALICE O God! O God!

CAPTAIN The fortress has surrendered! the enemy is given ten minutes for evacuation under safe-conduct! [*Places his watch on the table.*] Ten minutes; watch on the table! [*Remains standing, with his hand on his heart.*]

ALICE [*goes up to the Captain and seizes his arm*] What is it?

CAPTAIN I don't know!

ALICE Do you want anything—will you have something to drink?

CAPTAIN Whisky? No! I don't want to die! You! . . . [*Straightens himself.*] Don't touch me! . . . Ten minutes, or the garrison will be hewn down! [*Draws his sword.*] Ten minutes! [*Goes out at back.*]

KURT Who is this man?

ALICE He's a demon—not a man!

KURT What does he want with my son?

ALICE He wants him as a hostage, so as to have you under his thumb: he wants to isolate you from the authorities of the island. . . . Did you know that people here call this island "Little Hell"?

KURT No, I never heard that! . . . Alice, you are the first woman who ever aroused my pity: all others have seemed to me to deserve their fate!

ALICE Don't desert me now! Don't go away from me—he beats me . . . he has beaten me for the last twenty-five years . . . before the children too . . . he has pushed me into the sea . . .

KURT After that I am against him absolutely! When I came here it was without malice—not one thought of his former slanders and attempts to humiliate me! I forgave him even when you told me he was the man who separated me from my children . . . for he was ill and dying. . . . But now that he wants to rob me of my son, he must die—he, or I!

ALICE Good! No surrender of the fortress! Rather blow it up, and him with it, into the air, even if we have to go too! I have the powder ready!

KURT When I came here I bore no malice; when I felt that your hatred was infecting me I wanted to go; but now I feel irresistibly called on to hate this man—as I have hated evil itself! . . . What are we to do?

ALICE He has taught me the tactics! Drum up his enemies and seek out allies!

KURT To think that he should have discovered my wife! Why didn't those two meet ages ago? What a tussle there would have been—earthquaking!

ALICE But now those two souls have met . . . and they must be separated! I have an idea where his vulnerable point lies . . . I have long suspected it. . . .

KURT Who is his dearest foe on the island?

ALICE The Quartermaster!

KURT Is he an honest fellow?

ALICE He is; and he knows what I . . . I know it too . . . he knows what the Sergeant-major and the Captain have been up to!

KURT Been up to? Do you mean . . . ?

ALICE Embezzlements!

KURT That's too appalling! No, I'd rather not be mixed up with that sort of thing!

ALICE Ha, ha! You can't hit an enemy?

KURT There was a time when I could: but I can't any longer!

ALICE Why not?

KURT Because I have discovered . . . that justice is done in any case!

ALICE And you'll wait for that! Meanwhile

you'll have lost your son! Look at my grey hair. . . . Yes, and feel how thick it is still! . . . He intends to marry again . . . and then I am free—to do the same!—I am free! And in ten minutes he will be under arrest down below, down there [*stamping on the floor*]—down there! . . . and I shall dance upon his head, I shall dance the "Boyars' Entry March." . . . [*Goes through a few steps with her hands at her waist.*] . . . Ha, ha, ha, ha! And then I'll play the piano for him to listen to! [*Bangs the notes.*] Ha! the tower is opening its gates, and the sentry with the drawn sword will be guarding—not me, but him . . . meli-tam-tam-ta, melita-lia-lay! Him, him, him shall he guard!

KURT [*who has been watching her with an intoxicated look*] Alice, are you a devil too?

ALICE [*jumps up on a chair and pulls down the laurel wreaths*] These shall go with me when the garrison marches forth! . . . triumphal laurels! and fluttering ribbons! A little dusty, but eternally green—like my own youth! I am not old, Kurt!

KURT [*his eyes shining*] You're a devil!

ALICE In Little Hell! . . . Look here! I'll make myself tidy . . . [*Takes her hair down.*] . . . dress in two minutes . . . go to the Quartermaster in another two . . . and then, up goes the fort sky-high!

KURT [*as before*] You are a devil!

ALICE That's what you always said, when we were children! Do you remember when we were children and got engaged? Ha-ha! You were shy of course. . . .

KURT [*seriously*] Alice!

ALICE Yes, you were! and it suited you. You know there are coarse women who like shy men, and . . . they say there are shy men who like coarse women! . . . You did like me just a little then, didn't you?

KURT I don't know where I am!

ALICE With an actress whose manners are free —but, all the same, an excellent woman. Yes, yes! But now I'm free, free, free! . . . Turn your back while I change my blouse!

[*Alice unbuttons her blouse. Kurt rushes up to her, seizes her in his arms, lifts her high in the air and bites her throat so that she screams.*

Then he hurls her on to the couch and rushes out to the left.]

The same setting, evening. Through the background windows the Sentry by the battery is seen throughout. The laurel wreaths are hanging over the arm of a chair. The hanging lamp is lit. Soft music.

The Captain, pale and hollow-eyed, his hair streaked with grey, in an undress uniform the worse for wear and riding-boots, is seated at the writing-table playing patience. He is wearing his glasses. After the raising of the curtain the entr'acte music continues until the next character appears. The Captain continues his game, but starts suddenly now and then, looking up and listening anxiously.

He seems unable to get the game to come out, becomes impatient and mixes up the cards. Then he goes to the window, left, opens it and throws out the pack. The window remains open, rattling on its hinges. He goes to the sideboard, becomes frightened at the noise made by the window, and turns round to see what it is. Takes out three square, dark-coloured whisky-bottles, examines them carefully, and throws them out of the window. Takes out some cigar-boxes, sniffs at one, and throws them out of the window.

After that he takes off his glasses, wipes them, and puts them on to see how they suit him. Then he throws them out of the window, stumbles along among the furniture as if he cannot see properly, and lights a six-light candelabrum on the chiffonier. Catches sight of the laurel wreaths, picks them up and goes towards the window, but turns back again. Takes the piano-cover and folds it carefully round the wreaths, taking some pins from the writing-table to fasten the corners, and puts them all together on a chair. Goes to the piano, bangs with his fists on the keys, locks the key-board and throws the key out of the window. Then he lights the candles on the piano. Goes to the what-not, takes his wife's portrait, looks at it and tears it to pieces, which he throws on the floor. The window rattles on its hinges and he becomes frightened again.

The Dance of Death

Then, as soon as he has become calm, he takes up the portraits of his son and daughter, kisses them hastily and thrusts them into his breast-pocket. All the rest of the portraits he sweeps down with his elbow and kicks into a heap.

Then he sits down wearily at the writing-table and puts his hand to his heart. Lights the candle on the table and sighs; stares into vacancy as if he saw unpleasant visions. . . . Gets up and goes to the chiffonier, opens the lid and takes out a packet of letters tied up with blue silk, and throws them into the stove. Closes the chiffonier. The telegraph receiver gives a single click and then stops. The Captain shrinks back in mortal terror and remains standing, with his hand on his heart, listening. Hearing nothing more from the receiver he listens in the direction of the door, left. Goes and opens it, takes one step through and comes back with a cat on his arm, stroking its back. Then he goes out to the right, and the music ceases.

Alice comes in at the back; she is dressed for walking, with darkened hair, hat and gloves. Looks round, surprised at the number of lights. Kurt comes in from the left, looking nervous.

ALICE   It looks like Christmas Eve in here!
KURT   Well?
ALICE [*holds out her hand for him to kiss*]   Say "Thank you!" [*Kurt kisses her hand reluctantly.*] Six witnesses—four of them solid as rock! The report has been made and the answer is coming here by telegram—here in the very heart of the fortress!
KURT   Oh, is it?
ALICE   Don't say "Oh, is it?" Say "Thank you!"
KURT   Why has he lighted so many candles?
ALICE   Because he's afraid of the dark of course! . . . Look at the telegraph-key! Doesn't it look like the handle of a coffee-mill?—I grind, and I grind, and the beans crack, as if one were pulling out teeth. . . .
KURT   What *has* he been doing here?
ALICE   It looks as if he intended to move! Down below there—that's where you'll move to!
KURT   Alice, don't talk like that! To me it is distressing. . . . He was my friend when I was young; many a time when I was in difficulties

he showed me kindness. . . . I'm sorry for him!
ALICE   Then what about me, who have done no wrong and have had to sacrifice my career to this monster?
KURT   That career of yours? Was it so very brilliant?
ALICE [*mad with rage*]   What's that you say? Don't you know who I am, what I have been?
KURT   There, there!
ALICE   Are *you* beginning too—already?
KURT   Already?
[*Alice flings her arms round Kurt's neck and kisses him. Kurt seizes her arms and bites her in the neck so that she screams.*]
ALICE   Biting me!
KURT [*beside himself*]   Yes, I want to bite your throat and suck your blood like a lynx! You've roused the wild beast in me that for years I've been trying to kill by means of renunciation and self-torture. I came here thinking myself a shade better than you two, but now I am the the vilest of all! Since I have come to see you in all your hideous nakedness: since passion has darkened my sense of sight—I have come to know the full power of evil; the ugly becomes beautiful: the good becomes ugly and feeble! . . . Come here, and I'll choke you . . . with a kiss! [*Embraces her.*]
ALICE [*showing her left hand*]   Look at the marks of the fetters which you have broken. I was a slave and am set free!
KURT   But I'm going to bind you. . . .
ALICE   You?
KURT   I!
ALICE   For one moment I thought you were . . .
KURT   Religious?
ALICE   Yes, you held forth about the Fall. . . .
KURT   Did I?
ALICE   And I thought you had come here to preach. . . .
KURT   You thought that? . . . In an hour we shall be in the town! Then you shall see what I am. . . .
ALICE   And we'll go to the theatre this evening and show ourselves! If I run away, the shame will be his: you see that, don't you?
KURT   I am beginning to see: imprisonment is not enough. . . .

ALICE No, that is not enough! there must be shame too!

KURT A curious world! You commit a shameful act, and he has to bear the shame!

ALICE Since the world is so stupid!

KURT It's as if these prison walls had drunk in all the evil qualities of the criminals within them: one has only to breathe here to become infected! You were thinking of the theatre and supper, I suppose! I was thinking of my son!

ALICE [strikes him on the mouth with her glove] You old fossil! [Kurt raises his hand to box her ears. Alice shrinks back.] Tout beau!

KURT Forgive me!

ALICE On your knees then! [Kurt falls to his knees.] On your face! [Kurt touches the floor with his forehead.] Kiss my foot! [Kurt kisses her foot.] And never do that sort of thing again! . . . Up!

KURT [getting up] Where have I come to? Where am I?

ALICE You know that!

KURT [looking round with horror] I almost think . . .

CAPTAIN [comes in from the right, looking miserable and leaning on a stick] Can I have a talk with you, Kurt? Alone?

ALICE About that safe-conduct?

CAPTAIN [seats himself at the sewing-table] Would you be so kind as to sit with me a little, Kurt? And, Alice, will you grant us one moment's . . . peace?

ALICE What's all this? New signals!—[To Kurt] Do sit down!—[Kurt sits down unwillingly.]—and hearken to the words of old age and wisdom! . . . If a telegram comes give me a call! [Goes out to the left.]

CAPTAIN [with dignity, after a pause] Can you understand a human destiny like mine, like ours?

KURT No more than I can understand my own!

CAPTAIN What then is the meaning of all this jumble?

KURT In my better moments I have thought that the meaning was simply this: that we should be unable to discern the meaning and yet bend ourselves.

CAPTAIN Bend! Without a fixed point outside me I can never bend myself!

KURT Quite correct: but as a mathematician you ought to be able to look for that unknown point, seeing that several known ones are given. . . .

CAPTAIN I have looked for it and—I have not found it!

KURT Then you must have made some mistake. Begin all over again!

CAPTAIN Yes, I'll begin all over again! . . . Tell me! Where did you learn this resignation of yours?

KURT I have none left. Don't over-estimate me!

CAPTAIN As you may have noticed, my interpretation of the art of living has been—elimination! That is, cancel and pass on! Early in life I made for myself a sack, into which I stuffed my humiliations; when it was full, I threw it into the sea!—I doubt if any human being has suffered so many humiliations as I. But when I cancelled them and passed on, they ceased to exist!

KURT I've noticed how you've created in your imagination both your life and your environment!

CAPTAIN How else could I have borne life? how could I have held out? [Presses his hand to his heart.]

KURT How are you now?

CAPTAIN Bad! [A pause] Then there comes a moment when the capacity for creating, as you call it, ceases. And then the reality stands out in all its nakedness! . . . It's terrible! [He is speaking now in the tearful voice of an old man, his lower jaw drooping.] Look here, my dear friend! [Controls himself and speaks in his ordinary voice.] Forgive me! . . . When I saw the Doctor in the town just now—[the tearful voice again] he said I was a broken man . . . [in his ordinary voice] and that I couldn't live long!

KURT He told you that?

CAPTAIN [tearful voice] Yes, that's what he said!

KURT The other wasn't true then?

CAPTAIN What? Oh . . . no, that wasn't true! [A pause]

KURT And wasn't the other thing true either?

CAPTAIN What, my dear fellow?

KURT About my son being ordered to report here as a cadet!

CAPTAIN I've never heard a word about that!

KURT You know, your talent for cancelling your own misdeeds is unbounded!

CAPTAIN My good fellow, I don't understand what you mean!

KURT In that case you're done for!

CAPTAIN Yes, there isn't much left!

KURT Tell me now! Perhaps you never petitioned for that divorce which would bring your wife into such disgrace?

CAPTAIN Divorce? No, I never heard of it!

KURT [*getting up*] Then will you admit that you've been lying?

CAPTAIN My friend uses such strong language. We all need forbearance!

KURT You have discovered that?

CAPTAIN [*firmly, in a clear voice*] Yes, I have discovered that! . . . So forgive me, Kurt! Forgive everything!

KURT Spoken like a man!—But I have nothing to forgive! Moreover, I am not the man you think I am—not now! Least of all, one worthy to receive your confessions!

CAPTAIN [*in a clear voice*] Life was so strange! So contrary, so malevolent, ever since my childhood . . . and mankind so malevolent that I became so too. . . . [*Kurt walks about uneasily and looks at the telegraph apparatus.*] What are you looking at?

KURT Can one shut off a thing like that?

CAPTAIN Not very well!

KURT [*with increasing alarm*] Who is Sergeant-major Östberg?

CAPTAIN He's an honest fellow—rather an eye to the main chance of course!

KURT And who's the Quartermaster?

CAPTAIN He's my enemy, I expect, but I've nothing against him.

KURT [*looking out of the window at a lantern which is moving about*] What are they doing with a lantern out by the battery?

CAPTAIN Is there a lantern there?

KURT Yes, and people moving about!

CAPTAIN Probably it's what we call a fatigue-party!

KURT What's that?

CAPTAIN A few men and a corporal! Probably some poor fellow's going to be locked up!

KURT Ah!

[*A pause*]

CAPTAIN Now that you know Alice, what do you think of her?

KURT I can hardly tell . . . I don't understand people at all! She's as inexplicable to me as you are—as I am myself! You see I'm getting to the age when wisdom admits, "I know nothing: I understand nothing!" But when I see a thing done I like to know the motive. . . . Why did you push her into the water?

CAPTAIN I don't know! It simply occurred to me, quite naturally, while she was standing on the pier, that she ought to go in.

KURT Have you never regretted it?

CAPTAIN Never!

KURT That's very strange!

CAPTAIN It certainly is! So strange that I can't believe it was I that behaved in such a vulgar way!

KURT Hasn't it ever occurred to you she might take her revenge?

CAPTAIN That, I think, she has done in full; and I find it equally natural!

KURT How did you arrive so quickly at this cynical resignation?

CAPTAIN Since I looked death in the face, life has shown itself to me from another point of view. . . . Tell me! If you had to judge between Alice and me, which would you say was in the right?

KURT Neither! But both of you would have my utmost sympathy—you perhaps a little more than she!

CAPTAIN Give me your hand, Kurt!

KURT [*gives him his hand and lays the other on the Captain's shoulder*] Dear old fellow!

ALICE [*enters left, now carrying a parasol*] Dear me, how intimate! friendship for ever! . . . Hasn't the telegram come?

KURT [*coldly*] No!

ALICE This delay makes me impatient, and when I get impatient I hurry things up! . . . Look, Kurt! now for the final bullet! now we'll bring him down! . . . First of all, I load—I know all about the rifle-manual, I do! That famous rifle-manual which never ran to 5,000 copies! . . . And then I take aim [*taking aim with her parasol*]—fire! And how's the new wife? the young, the fair, the unknown? You don't know!

But I know how my lover is! [*Throws her arms round Kurt's neck and kisses him. He pushes her away.*] He's quite well, though still a little shy! . . . You miserable creature! I never loved you! Too conceited to be jealous, you could not see how I was fooling you just now! [*The Captain draws his sword and rushes at her to strike her, but hits only the furniture.*] Help, help!

[*Kurt does not stir.*]

CAPTAIN [*falls, with the sword in his hand*] Judith, avenge me!

ALICE   Hurrah! he's dead!

[*Kurt retires towards door at back.*]

CAPTAIN [*rising*]   Not yet! [*Sheathes his sword: goes and sits in arm-chair by the sewing-table.*] Judith! Judith!

ALICE [*going towards Kurt*]   I'm coming now— with you!

KURT [*thrusting her from him so that she falls on her knees*]   Go back to the abyss from whence you came!—Good-bye for ever! [*Goes towards door.*]

CAPTAIN   Don't leave me, Kurt: she'll kill me!

ALICE   Kurt! don't desert me! don't desert us!

KURT   Good-bye! [*Goes.*]

ALICE [*changing her attitude*]   What a wretch! There's a friend for you!

CAPTAIN [*gently*]   Forgive me, Alice! and come here! Come quickly!

ALICE [*turning towards him*]   That's the most miserable wretch and hypocrite I've ever met! —You *are* a man, anyhow!

CAPTAIN   Alice, listen! I can't live much longer!

ALICE   Oh!

CAPTAIN   The doctor told me!

ALICE   Then all the rest was untrue?

CAPTAIN   Yes!

ALICE [*beside herself*]   Oh, what have I done? . . .

CAPTAIN   There's a remedy for everything!

ALICE   Ah, but this is past all cure!

CAPTAIN   Nothing is past all cure, if only one cancels it, and passes on!

ALICE   But the telegram! The telegram!

CAPTAIN   What telegram?

ALICE [*on her knees beside the Captain*]   Are we outcasts? Must it be? I have sprung a mine under myself—under both of us! Why did you have to tell lies? And why need that man come

and tempt me? . . . We are lost! All might have been cured, all forgiven, through your high-mindedness!

CAPTAIN   What is there that cannot be forgiven? What have I not forgiven you?

ALICE   You are right . . . but there can be no remedy!

CAPTAIN   I know your talent for inventing evil, but I cannot guess . . .

ALICE   Oh, if I could only find a way out! If only I could! Then I should take care of you . . . I should love you, Edgar!

CAPTAIN   Listen to that! Where am I?

ALICE   Do you think no one can help us? . . . No—no mortal could do that!

CAPTAIN   Who could then?

ALICE [*looking straight into his eyes*]   I don't know! . . . Oh, and what is to become of the children, with a dishonoured name . . .?

CAPTAIN   Have you dishonoured that name?

ALICE   Not I! Not I! . . . And they'll have to leave school! And when they go out into the world they'll be lonely, as we are lonely, and evil as we are! Then you didn't meet Judith either—I gather now?

CAPTAIN   No! but cancel that!

[*Clicking in telegraph apparatus. Alice starts up.*]

ALICE [*screams out*]   Now, at last, ruin is upon us! [*To the Captain*] Don't listen to it!

CAPTAIN [*calmly*]   I won't listen, dear child: calm yourself!

ALICE [*standing by the instrument on tiptoe to see out of the window*]   Don't listen! Don't listen!

CAPTAIN [*stopping up his ears*]   I'm stopping my ears, Lisa, my child!

ALICE [*on her knees with outstretched hands*]   God help us!—the fatigue-party is coming! [*Weeping bitterly*] God in heaven! [*She seems to move her lips as if in silent prayer. The instrument goes on clicking for a while, and a long strip of paper comes out. Then silence again. She gets up, tears off the paper strip and reads it to herself. Then she raises her eyes to heaven, goes up to the Captain and kisses his forehead.*] It's over! It was nothing! [*Sits down in the other chair, takes out her handkerchief and bursts into tears.*]

The Dance of Death

CAPTAIN What are these secrets of yours?

ALICE Don't ask me! it's all over now!

CAPTAIN As you like, child!

ALICE You wouldn't have said that three days ago! What has done it?

CAPTAIN Well, dear, when I fell down that first time I passed over for a while to the other side of the grave. I have forgotten what I saw there, but the impression remains!

ALICE What was it?

CAPTAIN The hope—of something better!

ALICE Something better?

CAPTAIN Yes! That this could be the true life I have never really believed . . . this life is death—or worse!

ALICE And we . . .

CAPTAIN Were probably set here to torment each other . . . so it seems!

ALICE Have we tormented each other enough?

CAPTAIN Yes, so I believe! And played sad havoc! [*Looks round.*] . . . Shall we put our house in order? And clean up everything?

ALICE [*getting up*] Yes, if it's possible.

CAPTAIN [*looking about the room*] It can't be done in a day—it certainly can't!

ALICE In two then!—Many days!

CAPTAIN Let's hope so! . . . [*A pause.*] So you didn't manage to get free this time! But then you didn't get me locked up either! [*Alice looks astonished.*] Yes, I knew you wanted to have me in prison, but I cancel that! . . . I don't suppose that's the worst thing you've done. . . . [*Alice is speechless.*] Moreover, I was not guilty of that embezzlement!

ALICE And now the idea is that I should be your nurse?

CAPTAIN If you will!

ALICE What else is there for me to do?

CAPTAIN I don't know!

ALICE [*sits down, listless and despairing*] These must be the eternal torments! Is there no end to them?

CAPTAIN Yes, if we wait patiently! Perhaps when death comes, life begins.

ALICE If only it were so!

[*A pause*]

CAPTAIN You think Kurt was a hypocrite?

ALICE Certainly I do!

CAPTAIN I don't! But all who come near us become evil, and go their ways. . . . Kurt was weak, and evil is strong! [*A pause.*] How commonplace life is now! Once we fought—now we merely shake our fists!—I'm almost sure that, three months from now, we shall be having our silver wedding . . . with Kurt for our best man . . . and the Doctor and Gerda among the guests . . . the Quartermaster to propose the toast, and the Sergeant-major to lead the cheering! The Colonel will invite himself, if I know him!—Yes, you may laugh! But do you remember Adolph's silver wedding —that fellow in the Rifles? When the bride had to wear the ring on her right hand because the bridegroom, in a tender moment, had chopped off her left ring-finger with a bill-hook. [*Alice holds her handkerchief to her mouth to stop herself from laughing.*] Are you crying? No, I do believe you're laughing!—Yes, child! We weep in part and we laugh in part! Which is the more fitting—well, don't ask me! . . . I saw the other day in the papers about a man who had been divorced seven times— consequently married seven times—who finally ran off in his ninety-ninth year and re-married his first wife! That's what love is! . . . Whether life is serious or only a jest I cannot say! It may be that it is most painful when it is a jest, and that when serious it is really most pleasant and peaceful. . . . But the moment one learns at last to be serious, some one comes and turns it into a jest! Kurt, for example! . . . Shall we have our silver wedding? [*Alice is silent.*] Do say "yes"—they'll laugh at us, but what does that matter? We'll laugh too, or keep serious—just as it suits us!

ALICE So be it, then!

CAPTAIN [*seriously*] Silver wedding be it then! [*Gets up.*] Cancel, and pass on!—well then, let's pass on!

Part Two

The action takes place in a house on the island during the following summer.

An oval-shaped drawing-room in white and gold. The wall at the back is broken by some French windows standing open. Through these is seen the garden terrace outside, with stone balustrade and light-blue faïence pots containing petunias and scarlet pelargoniums. This terrace is a public promenade. In the background is seen the shore battery with an artilleryman on sentry duty. In the distance the open sea.

The drawing-room contains on the left a gilded sofa, table and chairs: on the right a grand piano, a writing-table and a fireplace. In the foreground an American easy chair. By the writing-table is a copper standard lamp with a table attached to it. On the walls are several old oil-paintings.

Allan is sitting at the writing-table doing sums. Judith comes in through the French window. She is in summer dress, short skirt, hair in plaits. She holds her hat in one hand and a tennis-racket in the other. She stops in the doorway. Allan rises, serious and respectful.

JUDITH [*seriously, but in a friendly tone*] Why don't you come and play tennis?

ALLAN [*shyly, struggling with his emotion*] I'm so busy. . . .

JUDITH Didn't you see I put my bike pointing *towards* the oak, and not the other way?

ALLAN Yes, I saw!

JUDITH Well, and what does that mean?

ALLAN It means . . . that you want me to come and play tennis . . . but my work . . . I've got some problems to do . . . and your father's a very strict teacher. . . .

JUDITH Do you like him?

ALLAN Yes, I do! He takes such an interest in all his pupils. . . .

JUDITH He takes an interest in everybody and everything.—Are you coming?

ALLAN You know well enough I'd like to: but I oughtn't to!

JUDITH I'll get leave from Daddy!

ALLAN No, don't do that! It'll only lead to a lot of talk!

JUDITH Don't you think I can *manage* him? He wants what I want!

ALLAN I suppose that's because you're so hard! —That's why!

JUDITH You ought to be hard too!

ALLAN I don't belong to the wolf family!

JUDITH Then you must be a sheep!

ALLAN I'd rather be that!

JUDITH Tell me why you won't come and play?

ALLAN You know why.

JUDITH Tell me all the same! . . . The Lieutenant . . .

ALLAN Yes, you don't care one pin about me, but you can't enjoy yourself with the Lieutenant unless I'm there too, so that you can see me being tortured!

JUDITH Am I so cruel? I never knew that!

ALLAN Well, you know now!

JUDITH I must reform then. I don't want to be cruel; I don't want *you* to think I'm bad.

ALLAN You only say that to be able to tyrannize over me! I'm already your slave, but you aren't content with that. The slave must be tortured and thrown to wild beasts! . . . You've got that other fellow in your clutches already, so what do you want me for? You go your way and I'll go mine!

JUDITH Are you ordering me to go? [*Allan does not answer.*] Very well, I'll go then!—Being cousins we shall have to meet occasionally, but I shan't trouble you! [*Allan sits at the table and goes on with his sums. Judith, instead of going, comes forward and gradually approaches the table where Allan is sitting.*] Don't be afraid—I'm just going . . . I only wanted to see what sort of place the quarantine officer's got. [*Looks round.*] White and gold!—Bechstein grand!—hoo!—We're still in the fort-tower since Dad got pensioned, the same old tower Mummy's been in twenty-five years. . . . And we're only there on sufferance! You are rich, you . . .

ALLAN [*calmly*] We aren't rich!

JUDITH So you say, but you're always so nicely dressed. For that matter, whatever you wear

The Dance of Death

always seems to suit you! . . . Do you hear what I say? [*Comes nearer.*]

ALLAN [*submissively*] Yes, I hear.

JUDITH How can you hear when you sit there doing sums or whatever it is?

ALLAN I don't hear with my eyes!

JUDITH Your eyes! . . . By the way, have you ever looked at them in a glass?

ALLAN Oh, get away!

JUDITH You despise me, do you?

ALLAN My dear girl, I'm not thinking about you at all!

JUDITH [*coming nearer*] Archimedes, sitting at his sums, when the soldier comes and cuts him down! [*Mixes up his papers with her racket.*]

ALLAN Leave my papers alone!

JUDITH That's what Archimedes said too! . . . I suppose you've got some curious idea in your head: you think I can't live without you!

ALLAN Why can't you leave me in peace?

JUDITH Be polite and I'll help you with your exam. . . .

ALLAN You?

JUDITH Yes; I know the examiners. . . .

ALLAN [*severely*] What do you mean?

JUDITH Don't you know one ought to get the examiners on one's side?

ALLAN Do you mean your father and the Lieutenant?

JUDITH And the Colonel!

ALLAN You mean that under your protection I shouldn't have to work?

JUDITH You're a bad translator . . .

ALLAN Of a bad original . . .

JUDITH You ought to be ashamed of yourself!

ALLAN So I am, and of you too! I'm ashamed of having listened to you! . . . Why don't you go?

JUDITH Because I know how much you value my company.—Yes, you always manage to pass under my window! You've always got something to do in the town that makes you take the same boat as I do! You can't go for a sail without having me to look after the foresail for you!

ALLAN [*shyly*] Young girls shouldn't say that sort of thing!

JUDITH Do you mean to say I'm a child?

ALLAN Sometimes you're a good child, and sometimes a bad woman! You seem to have picked *me* out to be your sheep.

JUDITH You are a sheep: that's why I'm going to protect you!

ALLAN [*getting up*] The wolf makes a jolly poor shepherd! . . . You want to eat me . . . that's the idea, I suppose! You want to pawn your pretty eyes so as to get hold of my head.

JUDITH Oh, have you been looking at my eyes? I shouldn't have thought you had the pluck! [*Allan gathers up his papers and starts to go out to the right. Judith places herself before the door.*]

ALLAN Get out of my way, or . . .

JUDITH Or what?

ALLAN If only you were a boy! Bah! But you're a girl!

JUDITH Yes?

ALLAN If you'd had one spark of pride you'd have gone; I as good as turned you out!

JUDITH I'll pay you back for that!

ALLAN I'm sure you will!

JUDITH [*furious, going out at the back*] I'll—pay—you—back—for that! [*Goes out.*]

KURT [*coming in from the left*] Where are you off to, Allan?

ALLAN Oh, is that you?

KURT Who was it went off in such a hurry—making the bushes shake like that?

ALLAN Judith.

KURT A trifle hot-headed, but a nice girl!

ALLAN Any girl who is ill-natured and coarse is always said to be a nice girl!

KURT You shouldn't be so hard on people, Allan! . . . Aren't you satisfied with your new relations?

ALLAN I like Uncle Edgar. . . .

KURT Yes, he has many good points. . . . And then your other teachers? The Lieutenant for example?

ALLAN He's so variable! sometimes I fancy he's got some grudge against me.

KURT Oh, no! . . . You're always having "fancies" about people. Don't brood, but do the correct thing; mind your own business, and let other people mind theirs!

ALLAN So I do; but they won't leave me in peace! They drag one in . . . just like the cuttle-fish down by the jetty . . . they don't bite, but they stir up an eddy that sucks. . . .

KURT [*in a friendly tone*] You seem to be inclined to melancholy! Don't you get on all right here with me? Is there anything you miss?

ALLAN I've never had such a good time, but . . . there's something here that chokes me!

KURT Here by the sea? Don't you like the sea?

ALLAN Yes, the open sea! But on the shore there's goose-grass, cuttle-fish, jelly-fish, and sea-nettles or whatever they're called!

KURT You shouldn't stay indoors so much! Go out and play tennis!

ALLAN That doesn't amuse me!

KURT I see: you're angry with Judith!

ALLAN Judith?

KURT You're so particular about your fellow-creatures! One shouldn't be that; it leads to loneliness.

ALLAN I'm not particular, but . . . I feel as if I were at the bottom of a wood-pile . . . and had to wait my turn to get into the fire . . . it weighs me down so—all that's above me. . . .

KURT Wait till your turn comes! The pile keeps on getting smaller. . . .

ALLAN Yes, but so slowly, oh, so slowly! . . . And meanwhile I lie there and grow mouldy!

KURT It is not pleasant to be young! And yet people envy you!

ALLAN Do they? Would you change with me?

KURT No, thank you!

ALLAN Do you know what's the worst of all? It's to sit still and keep quiet while one's elders are talking nonsense. . . . I'm certain I know more about a thing than they do . . . and yet I have to keep silence! Oh, of course I don't count you as one of the old ones!

KURT Why not?

ALLAN Perhaps because we've only just got to know each other . . .

KURT And because . . . you then formed another opinion of me!

ALLAN Yes!

KURT I imagine that, during the years we were separated, you didn't always feel very friendly towards me?

ALLAN No!

KURT Did you ever see my photograph?

ALLAN Only one—and that was very unflattering!

KURT And old-looking?

ALLAN Yes!

KURT Ten years ago my hair turned grey in a single night . . . it has since got right again of itself. . . . Let's talk about something else! . . . Ah, here comes your Aunt! my cousin! How do you like her?

ALLAN I'd rather not say!

KURT Then I won't ask!

ALICE [*comes in, dressed in a very light summer walking dress with parasol*] Good morning, Kurt! [*Gives him a look signifying that Allan is to go.*]

KURT [*to Allan*] You'd better go, Allan!
[*Allan goes out to the right. Alice sits on the sofa left, Kurt on a chair near her.*]

ALICE [*confused*] He's coming in a minute, so you needn't feel embarrassed!

KURT Why should I?

ALICE With your strict ideas . . .

KURT As regards myself, yes!

ALICE Quite so! . . . I forgot myself once when I saw in you the liberator, but you kept your presence of mind . . . and so we have a right to forget . . . what has never been!

KURT Forget it then!

ALICE Still . . . I don't think *he* has forgotten. . . .

KURT You mean that night when he fell down from a heart attack . . . and you began to exult too soon, thinking he was dead?

ALICE Yes! . . . Since then he has recovered; but when he stopped drinking he learnt how to keep silent, and now he's terrible. He's up to something that I can't understand. . . .

KURT Alice, your husband is a harmless fool. He shows me nothing but kindness . . .

ALICE Beware of his kindnesses! I know them!

KURT Oh, I say . . .

ALICE So he's hoodwinked you too! . . . Can't you see the danger? Don't you notice the traps?

KURT No!

ALICE Then your doom is sealed!

KURT Oh, heavens!

ALICE Fancy my sitting here watching ruin creeping towards you like a cat. . . . I point to it, but you can't see it!

KURT Allan, with his unspoilt vision, can't see it either. As a matter of fact he sees only

The Dance of Death

Judith. That, I think, ought to be a certain guarantee of friendly relations.

ALICE Do you know Judith?

KURT A coquettish little thing, with pigtails down her back, and skirts a bit too short. . . .

ALICE Exactly! But I saw her in a long skirt the other day . . . looking quite the young lady . . . not so very young either when she had her hair up!

KURT She's a bit precocious, I admit!

ALICE And she's playing with Allan!

KURT That's all right, so long as it is play.

ALICE Oh, it *is*, is it? . . . And now, in a minute or two, Edgar will be here. He'll sit in your arm-chair—he loves it so passionately he could steal it.

KURT He can have it!

ALICE Let him sit over there, and we'll stay here. And when he talks—he's always very chatty in the morning—when he talks about trivial matters, I'll translate them for you! . . .

KURT Oh, you're too clever, far too clever, my dear Alice! What could I have to fear, so long as I look after my quarantine properly and behave myself in other respects?

ALICE You believe in justice and honour and all that sort of thing.

KURT Yes; and experience has taught me that belief. Once I believed the opposite. . . . It cost me dear!

ALICE Now he's coming! . . .

KURT I've never seen you frightened before!

ALICE My courage was merely ignorance of the danger!

KURT The danger? . . . You'll begin to frighten me soon!

ALICE Oh, if only I could! . . . There!

[*The Captain comes in at the back, in civilian dress, black frock-coat, military cap, and silver-handled stick. He greets them with a nod, and goes and sits in the arm-chair.*]

ALICE [*to Kurt*] Let him speak first!

CAPTAIN This is a splendid chair you've got here, my dear Kurt! Simply splendid!

KURT You may have it with pleasure, if you'll accept it!

CAPTAIN I didn't mean . . .

KURT No, but *I* do! Surely you've given *me* enough things . . .

CAPTAIN [*volubly*] Oh, nonsense! . . . And sitting here I get a view of the whole island, all the public walks, all the people on their verandas, all the ships upon the sea, going out and coming in. . . . You really have hit on the very best bit of the island—which certainly is *not* an Island of the Blest. What do you say, Alice? . . . Yes, they call it "Little Hell," and here Kurt has built himself a Paradise: no Eve, of course: for when she came, Paradise was at an end! By the way, do you know this place was once a royal hunting lodge?

KURT So I've heard!

CAPTAIN You live royally, you do! But, if I may say so, you have to thank me for that!

ALICE [*to Kurt*] There now! he wants to steal you!

KURT I have a good many things to thank you for!

CAPTAIN Oh, nonsense!—By the way, did you get those cases of wine?

KURT Yes!

CAPTAIN And you're satisfied?

KURT Perfectly! you can tell your dealer so, with my compliments!

CAPTAIN His things are always first-rate . . .

ALICE [*to Kurt*] At second-rate prices; and you have to pay the difference. . . .

CAPTAIN What did you say, Alice?

ALICE I? Nothing!

CAPTAIN Yes: when this quarantine station was established, I intended to apply for the post myself . . . and with that object I made a study of quarantine systems.

ALICE [*to Kurt*] That's a lie!

CAPTAIN [*bragging*] The antiquated ideas held by the Board on disinfection methods were not shared by me! *I* was on the side of the Neptunists—so called because they lay stress on the use of water . . .

KURT Excuse me! I certainly remember it was I who preached water, and you fire, on that occasion.

CAPTAIN I? What nonsense!

ALICE [*aloud*] Yes, I remember that too!

CAPTAIN Do you?

KURT I remember it all the more . . .

CAPTAIN [*cutting him short*] Well, it may be so, but it makes no difference! [*Raising his voice*]

However . . . we have now reached a point where a new state of affairs—[*to Kurt, who tries to interrupt*] Be quiet, please!—has come to pass . . . and the quarantine system is on the point of taking a giant's stride forward.

KURT By the way, do you know who writes those silly articles in the paper?

CAPTAIN [*getting red*] No, I don't; but why do you call them silly?

ALICE [*to Kurt*] Look out! He wrote them himself!

KURT [*to Alice*] He did? . . . [*To the Captain*] Not very intelligent then?

CAPTAIN You're hardly the one to judge of that!

ALICE Are you going to quarrel?

KURT Oh no!

CAPTAIN It's difficult to keep peace on the island, but we ought to set a good example. . . .

KURT Yes; and can you explain this to me? When I came here I made friends at once with all the officials; with the lawyer especially I became on intimate terms—as intimate as one can be at our time of life. Well, after a time—it was just after you got well again—they all began, one man after another, to show me the cold shoulder, and yesterday the lawyer cut me on the public promenade. I can't tell you how hurt I felt! [*The Captain remains silent.*] Have *you* noticed any ill-feeling towards yourself?

CAPTAIN No; quite the contrary!

ALICE [*to Kurt*] Don't you see he's stolen your friends?

KURT [*to the Captain*] I wondered whether it could have anything to do with that new issue which I refused to subscribe to!

CAPTAIN Oh, no! But can you tell me why you wouldn't subscribe?

KURT Because I'd already put my little savings into your soda factory! Also because a new issue shows there's something wrong with the original shares.

CAPTAIN [*preoccupied*] That's a splendid lamp you've got! Where on earth did you get it?

KURT In the town of course.

ALICE [*to Kurt*] You keep an eye on your lamp!

KURT [*to the Captain*] You mustn't think I'm ungrateful or distrustful, Edgar.

CAPTAIN No, but it doesn't show much confidence, your wanting to back out of a thing which you helped to start.

KURT My dear fellow, ordinary prudence tells a man to save himself and what is his before it's too late!

CAPTAIN Save? Is there any danger afoot? Is anyone thinking of robbing you?

KURT Why put it so crudely?

CAPTAIN Weren't you pleased when I helped you to invest your money at six per cent?

KURT Yes, I was even grateful!

CAPTAIN You're not grateful—it's not your nature: but that's not your fault!

ALICE [*to Kurt*] Just listen to him!

KURT No doubt my nature is full of imperfections, and my struggle against them has not been very successful: still I do recognize obligations. . . .

CAPTAIN Show it then! [*Stretches out his hand to pick up a newspaper.*] Ah, what have we here . . . an announcement! [*Reads.*] Death of the Sanitary Commissioner!

ALICE [*to Kurt*] He's speculating in the corpse already!

CAPTAIN [*as if to himself*] This will involve certain . . . changes . . .

KURT In what respect?

CAPTAIN [*getting up*] That remains to be seen!

ALICE [*to the Captain*] Where are you going?

CAPTAIN I think I must go into the town! . . . [*Catches sight of an envelope on the writing-table, picks it up abstractedly as it were, reads the address, and puts it back.*] Forgive my absent-mindedness!

KURT No harm done!

CAPTAIN There's Allan's geometry-set! Where is the boy?

KURT Out, playing with the girls.

CAPTAIN That great boy? I don't like it! And Judith oughtn't to be running about like that. . . . You'd better keep an eye on your young gentleman, and I'll look after my young lady! [*Passes the piano and strikes a few notes.*] Splendid tone—this instrument! A Steinbech, isn't it?

KURT A Bechstein!

CAPTAIN Yes, you're well off, you are! You ought to thank me for bringing you here!

ALICE [*to Kurt*] That's a lie! he tried to keep you away!

CAPTAIN Well, good-bye for the present! I'm taking the next boat! [*Goes out, examining the pictures on the walls.*]

ALICE Well?

KURT Well?

ALICE At present I don't understand his plans. But—tell me one thing! That envelope he looked at—who was the letter from?

KURT I'm ashamed to say—it was my one secret!

ALICE And *that* he scented out! He's a wizard, you see, as I told you before! . . . Is there anything printed on the envelope?

KURT Yes, the words "Electors' Association."

ALICE Then he's guessed your secret. You want to get into Parliament, I gather! And now you'll have the pleasure of seeing *him* there instead!

KURT Has he ever thought of it?

ALICE No, but he's thinking of it now! I read that in his face while he was looking at the envelope.

KURT Is that why he's going into the town?

ALICE No: he decided on that when he saw the obituary notice!

KURT What does he expect to gain by the Commissioner's death?

ALICE You may well ask! . . . Perhaps the man was an enemy who stood in the way of his schemes!

KURT If he is as terrible as you say, there may be some reason to fear him!

ALICE Didn't you see how he wanted to steal you away, to tie your hands by alleging obligations which don't exist? For instance, he never got you the post: on the contrary, he tried to keep you out of it! He's a man-stealer, an insect, a wood-worm, burrowing inside you, till one day you'll be as hollow as a rotten pine-tree. . . . He hates you, though he's bound to you by the memories of youthful friendship. . . .

KURT How ingenious you become when you hate!

ALICE And stupid, when one loves! Blind and stupid!

KURT No, no! Don't say that!

ALICE Do you know what's meant by a vampire? . . . Why, it's a dead man's soul, seeking a body to live in as a parasite. Edgar is dead, ever since he fell down that time! He has no interests of his own, no personality, no initia-

tive. But if he can only manage to get hold of some human being, he twines himself round him, throws out his suckers, and begins to grow and blossom. Now he's clinging on to you!

KURT If he gets too near, I'll shake him off!

ALICE Try shaking off a burr—then you'll see! . . . Now, do you know why he doesn't want Judith and Allan to play together?

KURT I suppose he's anxious about their feelings!

ALICE Not in the least! . . . He wants to marry Judith to . . . the Colonel!

KURT [*shocked*] That old widower?

ALICE Yes!

KURT Horrible! . . . And Judith?

ALICE If she could get the General, who is eighty, she'd take him, so as to snub the Colonel, who is sixty. Snubbing, you see— that's her object in life! To trample and to snub—there you have the watchword of *that* family!

KURT Judith like that? That fair, proud and glorious young damsel!

ALICE Oh, we know all about that! . . . May I sit here and write a letter?

KURT [*tidying the writing-table*] Please do!

ALICE [*takes off her gloves and sits at the writing-table*] Now I'll try my hand at the art of war! I failed once, when I meant to slay my dragon! But now I've learnt something of the business!

KURT Are you aware that one's supposed to load before firing?

ALICE Yes, and with ball-cartridges too!

[*Kurt withdraws to the right, Alice ponders and writes. Allan rushes in without seeing Alice, and throws himself face downwards on the sofa, sobbing into a lace handkerchief.*]

ALICE [*watches him for a moment, then gets up and goes towards the sofa; speaks gently*] Allan! [*Allan sits up, embarrassed, and hides the handkerchief behind his back; Alice in a gentle, womanly manner, and with real emotion*] You mustn't be afraid of me, Allan! I'm not likely to hurt you. . . . What is the matter?— Are you ill?

ALLAN Yes!

ALICE In what way?

ALLAN I don't know!

ALICE Have you got a headache?

ALLAN No-o!

ALICE In your chest? frightful pain?

ALLAN Yes! Ye-es!

ALICE Pain—pain as if your heart were melting away! Something that drags, and drags . . .

ALLAN How do you know?

ALICE And then you want to die—you wish you were dead, and everything is so hard. And you think only of one thing, always the same . . . one person, always the same . . . but if two are thinking of the same person, then grief weighs heavily—on one of them. . . . [*Allan forgets himself and fingers the handkerchief.*] That is the illness no one can cure . . . you can't eat, you don't want to drink, only to weep, and such bitter tears . . . and you like to be in the woods, so that nobody can see you, for that is the kind of grief people laugh at . . . cruel people! Ugh! . . . What do you want of her? Nothing! You don't want to kiss her lips, for you think you'd die if you did. You feel as if death were approaching when your thoughts fly to her! And it is death, dear, the death which gives life. But that you won't understand just yet!

A scent of violets! it must be hers! [*Goes up to Allan and takes the handkerchief gently away.*] Yes, it's she, she everywhere, she only! Oh, oh, oh! [*Allan sees no help for it, and hides his face on her breast.*] Poor boy! Poor boy! Oh, how it hurts, how it hurts! [*Dries his tears with the handkerchief.*] There, there, there! Cry! That's right—cry it out! That eases the heart! . . . But now, Allan, get up and be a man—otherwise she won't look at you, she, the cruel one, who is *not* cruel!

Has she been tormenting you . . . with the Lieutenant? Look here, my child! you must make friends with the Lieutenant, so that you two can have talks about her! That usually gives a little relief too!

ALLAN I don't want to look at the Lieutenant!

ALICE Look here, little boy! It won't be long before the Lieutenant looks you up so as to have a talk about her! You see . . . [*Allan looks up, with a ray of hope.*] Well? Shall I be nice and tell you? [*Allan bows his head.*] He's just as unhappy as you are!

ALLAN [*joyfully*] No?

ALICE Oh but he is! And he wants somebody to open his heart to when Judith hurts him. You seem to be happy already!

ALLAN Doesn't she want the Lieutenant?

ALICE Nor you either, dear boy! What she wants is the Colonel! [*Allan becomes depressed again.*] Raining again, is it?—Well, the handkerchief you can't have! Judith's careful of her belongings and likes her dozen complete! [*Allan looks disappointed.*] Yes, you see, that's what Judith is! . . . Now sit down there while I write another letter; then you can take a message for me! [*Goes to the table and writes.*]

LIEUTENANT [*comes in at the back with a melancholy air, but without any comic effect; does not notice Alice, but goes straight towards Allan*] Cadet! [*Allan gets up and stands at attention.*] Please don't get up!

[*Alice watches them. The Lieutenant goes up to Allan and sits down beside him. Sighs, produces a handkerchief like the other one, and wipes his forehead. Allan looks greedily at the handkerchief. The Lieutenant looks sadly at Allan. Alice coughs. The Lieutenant springs to attention.*]

ALICE Please don't get up!

LIEUTENANT I beg your pardon, madam!

ALICE Don't mention it! . . . Do sit down and have a talk with the cadet! He's feeling rather lonely on the island here! [*Goes on writing.*]

LIEUTENANT [*speaking to Allan in a low tone, embarrassed*] Frightfully hot, what?

ALLAN Very!

LIEUTENANT Finished the sixth book yet?

ALLAN Just got to the last proposition.

LIEUTENANT Bit of a teaser, that! [*Silence*] Have you . . . [*seeking for words*] been playing tennis to-day?

ALLAN No; too hot in the sun!

LIEUTENANT [*in despair, but without being comic*] Yes, it's frightfully hot to-day!

ALLAN [*in a whisper*] Yes, frightfully!
[*Silence*]

LIEUTENANT Have you . . . been out sailing to-day?

ALLAN No, I couldn't get anyone to look after the foresail!

LIEUTENANT Could you . . . trust *me* to look after it?

ALLAN [*respectfully as before*] That would be too great an honour, Lieutenant!

LIEUTENANT Oh, not at all! . . . Do you think . . . there'll be a nice breeze to-day, say about noon? That's the only time I'm free!

ALLAN [*slyly*] The wind always drops about noon, and . . . that's the time Miss Judith has her lesson. . . .

LIEUTENANT [*depressed*] Oh, yes, yes! Hm! Do you think that . . .

ALICE Would either of you young gentlemen care to take a note for me? [*Allan and the Lieutenant regard each other suspiciously.*] To Judith! . . . [*Allan and the Lieutenant spring to their feet and hasten towards Alice, but with a certain dignity intended to conceal their emotions.*] Both of you? Well, it's all the more sure to be delivered! [*Hands the letter to the Lieutenant.*] . . . Now, Lieutenant, may I have that handkerchief? My daughter is careful about her washing! She's got a touch of meanness in her character. . . . Give me the handkerchief! . . . I don't want to laugh at you, but you mustn't make yourselves ridiculous, unnecessarily. Moreover, the Colonel doesn't like the part of Othello! [*Takes the handkerchief.*] Now, young men, be off, and try to hide your feelings as best you can!

[*The Lieutenant bows and goes, closely followed by Allan.*]

ALICE [*calls out*] Allan!

ALLAN [*stopping reluctantly in the doorway*] Yes, Aunt!

ALICE Stay here! Unless you want to do yourself more harm than you can stand!

ALLAN But he's going!

ALICE Let him be singed! You take care of yourself!

ALLAN I don't want to take care of myself!

ALICE Then you'll be crying later on! And I shall have the trouble of consoling you!

ALLAN I'd rather go!

ALICE Go then! But if you come back, young madcap, I shall have the right to laugh at you! [*Allan runs after the Lieutenant. Alice goes on writing.*]

KURT [*coming in*] Alice, I've had an anonymous letter which is worrying me!

ALICE Have you noticed how, since he stopped wearing his uniform, Edgar has become another man? I should never have believed a coat could make so much difference!

KURT You didn't answer my question!

ALICE It wasn't a question! It was a piece of information! What are you afraid of?

KURT Everything!

ALICE He went into the town! His journeys to town always result in something dreadful!

KURT I can take no steps, though; I don't know from what quarter the attack will begin!

ALICE [*folding up her letter*] We'll see whether I've guessed that! . . .

KURT Will you help me then?

ALICE Yes! . . . But no further than my interests permit! Mine—that is to say, my children's!

KURT I understand! . . . Listen! How quiet everything is, in nature, on the sea, everywhere!

ALICE But beyond the silence I hear voices . . . murmurs, cries!

KURT Hush! I hear something too! . . . No, it was only the sea-gulls!

ALICE *I* hear something else! . . . And now I'm going to the post . . . with this letter!

The same setting. Allan is sitting at the writing-table, working. Judith is standing in the doorway, wearing a tennis hat and carrying the handle-bar of a bicycle.

JUDITH May I borrow your spanner?

ALLAN [*without looking up*] No, you mayn't.

JUDITH Now you're being rude, the moment I begin running after you!

ALLAN [*not snappily*] I'm being nothing at all: I merely ask to be left in peace!

JUDITH [*coming forward*] Allan!

ALLAN Well, what is it?

JUDITH You mustn't be angry with me!

ALLAN I'm not!

JUDITH Shake hands then!

ALLAN [*gently*] I don't want to shake hands, but I'm not angry! . . . What is it you really want with me?

JUDITH You are so stupid!

ALLAN Very likely!

JUDITH You think I'm cruel and nothing else!

ALLAN No, I know you're nice too! You *can* be nice!

JUDITH Well, it isn't my fault . . . that . . . you and the Lieutenant go and cry in the woods. What do you cry for? Tell me! [*Allan is embarrassed.*] Tell me now! . . . I never cry. And how is it you two are such friends now? . . . What do you talk about when you're walking arm in arm? [*Allan is at a loss for a reply.*] Allan! you shall soon see who I am, and that I can strike a blow for anyone I care about! . . . And one piece of advice I will give you . . . though I don't want to tell tales! . . . Be prepared!

ALLAN For what?

JUDITH For trouble!

ALLAN Where from?

JUDITH From where you least expect it!

ALLAN I'm fairly well used to disagreeable things: I haven't had a particularly pleasant life. What's coming now?

JUDITH [*thoughtfully*] You poor boy! . . . Give me your hand! [*Allan gives her his hand.*] Look at me! . . . Don't you dare to look at me? [*Allan hurries out to the left in order to conceal his emotion.*]

LIEUTENANT [*coming in at back*] I beg your pardon! I thought the cadet . . .

JUDITH Lieutenant! Will you be my friend and confidant!

LIEUTENANT If you will honour me . . .

JUDITH Yes! . . . Just one word! Don't desert Allan when misfortune comes!

LIEUTENANT What misfortune?

JUDITH You'll see soon—perhaps to-day! . . . Do you like Allan?

LIEUTENANT That young fellow is my best pupil; I esteem him personally too on account of his strength of character. . . . Yes, life has moments when one needs—[*emphatically*] strength to bear, to endure, in one word—to suffer.

JUDITH That was more than one word! . . . However, you like Allan!

LIEUTENANT Yes!

JUDITH Go and see him and make friends with him. . . .

LIEUTENANT That's what I came for—that and nothing else! I had no other object in my call!

JUDITH I never dreamt of anything of the sort —the sort of thing you mean! . . . Allan went out that way [*pointing left*].

LIEUTENANT [*reluctantly going out to the left*] Very well . . . I'll do it!

JUDITH Yes, please do!

ALICE [*coming in at the back*] What are you doing here?

JUDITH I wanted to borrow a spanner!

ALICE Will you listen to me for a moment?

JUDITH Of course I will! [*Alice sits down on the sofa. Judith remains standing.*] But say quickly whatever you have to say. I don't like long lectures.

ALICE Lectures? . . . Very well! put up your hair and wear a long skirt.

JUDITH Why?

ALICE Because you're no longer a child! And you're too young to have to make yourself out younger than you are!

JUDITH What does that mean?

ALICE That you're of marriageable age! And that your way of dressing shocks people!

JUDITH All right, I'll do it!

ALICE You understand then?

JUDITH Oh, yes!

ALICE And we're agreed?

JUDITH Entirely!

ALICE On all points!

JUDITH Even the sorest!

ALICE Will you at the same time stop playing— with Allan?

JUDITH It's to be serious then?

ALICE Yes!

JUDITH Then we may as well start at once. [*She has put down the handle-bar, and now lets down her bicycle-skirt and twists her hair into a knot, fastening it with a hairpin which she takes out of her mother's hair.*]

ALICE It isn't usual to dress in other people's drawing-rooms!

JUDITH Do I look all right? . . . Now I'm ready! Come now who dares!

ALICE You look decent now anyway! . . . And now leave Allan in peace!

JUDITH I don't understand what you mean.

ALICE Don't you see he's miserable. . . .

JUDITH Yes, I think I've noticed it; but I don't know why. *I'm* not miserable!

ALICE That's your strength! But wait a little . . . ah, yes! one day you'll get to know what it means! . . . Now go home, and don't forget

. . . that you're wearing a long skirt.

JUDITH Does one have to walk differently then?

ALICE Try!

JUDITH [*tries to walk like a grown-up lady*] Oh! I've got chains on my feet! I'm all entangled! I can't run now!

ALICE Yes, child: now begins the walk, along the dreary road toward the unknown, which one knows beforehand, and yet must pretend not to know! . . . Shorter steps, and slower, much slower! Children's shoes must go, Judith: you must have boots now!—You don't remember giving up socks and having shoes; but I do!

JUDITH I'll never be able to stand this!

ALICE And yet you must! You must!

JUDITH [*goes up to her mother and kisses her lightly on the cheek; then goes out in a dignified manner like a lady, but forgets to take the handle-bar*] Good-bye!

KURT [*coming in from the right*] Here already!

ALICE Yes!

KURT Is *he* back?

ALICE Yes!

KURT What did he look like?

ALICE In full dress!—so he's been calling on the Colonel. Two orders on his breast.

KURT Two?—I knew he was to get the Order of the Sword on retirement. What's the other?

ALICE I don't understand these things: it was a white cross inside a red one.

KURT It must be Portuguese! . . . Let me think!—Ah!—didn't his articles in the paper treat of quarantine stations in Portuguese harbours?

ALICE Yes—so far as I remember!

KURT And he's never been in Portugal?

ALICE Never!

KURT And I have!

ALICE Why do you give yourself away so? He hears everything, and his memory is wonderful!

KURT Don't you think Judith got this distinction for him?

ALICE Well really! . . . There are limits. . . . [*Gets up.*] And you have passed them!

KURT Must we quarrel then?

ALICE That depends on you! Don't meddle with my interests!

KURT If they cross mine, I have to meddle with

them, however lightly. . . . There he comes!

ALICE Now it's going to happen!

KURT What—is going to happen?

ALICE We shall see!

KURT I hope it comes to a direct attack; this state of siege has got on my nerves! I haven't a friend left on the whole island!

ALICE Hush! quick! . . . You sit this side . . . he'll take the arm-chair of course: then I can prompt you!

CAPTAIN [*comes in at the back, in full dress uniform, wearing the Order of the Sword and the Portuguese Order of Christ*] Good morning! —So this is the meeting-place!

ALICE You're tired! Sit down! [*Contrary to expectation the Captain sits on the sofa, left.*] Make yourself comfortable!

CAPTAIN This is all right!—You're too kind!

ALICE [*to Kurt*] Be careful! He suspects us!

CAPTAIN [*angrily*] What's that you said?

ALICE [*to Kurt*] He's probably been drinking.

CAPTAIN [*rudely*] No, he has not! [*Silence*] Well? . . . How have you been amusing yourselves?

ALICE And you?

CAPTAIN Are you looking at my orders?

ALICE No-o!

CAPTAIN So I imagine. You're jealous.—Usually one congratulates a person on the distinctions conferred on him!

ALICE Please accept our congratulations!

CAPTAIN We get this sort of thing instead of the laurel wreaths they give to actresses!

ALICE That's one for the wreaths on the fortress walls at home . . .

CAPTAIN Which your brother gave you . . .

ALICE Oh, be quiet, do!

CAPTAIN And before which I have had to bow down for twenty-five years . . . and which have taken me twenty-five years to unmask!

ALICE Have you met my brother?

CAPTAIN Good heavens, yes! [*Alice is crushed. Silence*] Well, Kurt! You're not saying much, are you?

KURT I am waiting!

CAPTAIN Well now! I suppose you've heard the great news?

KURT No!

CAPTAIN Well, I don't like having to be the one to tell you. . . .

KURT Out with it!

CAPTAIN The soda-factory has gone to smash!

KURT Very unpleasant news!—and how does it affect you?

CAPTAIN Not at all badly: I sold out in time!

KURT That was wise of you!

CAPTAIN But how about you?

KURT Bad!

CAPTAIN It's your own fault! You ought to have sold out in time, or taken up new shares.

KURT I should merely have lost them as well.

CAPTAIN Not at all! If you had subscribed, the company would have kept on its legs.

KURT Not the company—the directors! I regarded that new subscription as a collection for their benefit!

CAPTAIN Can that idea save you? That's the question!

KURT No; I've got to give up everything!

CAPTAIN Everything!

KURT Even my house, the furniture!

CAPTAIN But this is terrible!

KURT I've been through worse!

[*Silence*]

CAPTAIN That's what happens when amateurs will go and speculate.

KURT You surprise me. You know that if I hadn't subscribed I should have been boycotted. . . . "More work for the coast population, toilers of the sea, inexhaustible capital, inexhaustible as the ocean . . . philanthropy and national profit" . . . that's what you wrote, and had printed! . . . And now you call it speculation!

CAPTAIN [*undisturbed*] What are you thinking of doing now?

KURT I suppose I must have an auction!

CAPTAIN A very wise decision!

KURT What do you mean?

CAPTAIN What I said! . . . You see—[*slowly*] there will be certain changes here . . .

KURT Here on the island?

CAPTAIN Yes! . . . For instance . . . your official residence will be exchanged for a simpler one.

KURT I see!

CAPTAIN Yes, the intention is to have the quarantine station on the further side of the island, close to the sea!

KURT My original idea!

CAPTAIN [*dryly*] I know nothing about that. . . . I am not acquainted with your ideas on the subject! . . . However—it's an excellent excuse for getting rid of your furniture at once; then it's more likely to pass by unnoticed—I mean the scandal!

KURT What?

CAPTAIN The scandal! [*Working himself up*] It *is* a scandal to come to a new place and at once get involved in financial difficulties. It's unpleasant for your relations . . . for them in particular!

KURT Particularly for me—I should have thought!

CAPTAIN I'll tell you one thing, my dear Kurt: if you hadn't had me at your side in this affair, you'd have lost your job.

KURT That too!

CAPTAIN You find it a little difficult to keep things in order! . . . There have been complaints about your work!

KURT Justifiable complaints?

CAPTAIN Tcha! After all—in spite of your other admirable qualities—you are—a slacker!— Don't interrupt me! You're a terrible slacker!

KURT How curious!

CAPTAIN However! The change we spoke of will probably take place almost immediately! And I wanted to advise you to have the auction at once, or to try to sell privately.

KURT Privately? Where could I find a buyer here?

CAPTAIN I suppose you don't mean that I'm to go and settle in among your furniture? That would make a fine story—[*jerkily*] hm!—especially if one . . . thinks of what happened . . . once upon a time . . .

KURT What was that?—Do you mean what *didn't* happen?

CAPTAIN [*turning round*] How quiet you are, Alice! what's the matter, old girl? You're not in very good form!

ALICE I'm just thinking . . .

CAPTAIN O Lord! Thinking, are you? But you'll

have to think quickly, correctly, and clearly, if it's to do any good!—Now then! one, two, three—think! Ha-ha! You can't do it! . . . Very well, then I'll have a shot! . . . Where's Judith?

ALICE Oh, somewhere about!

CAPTAIN Where's Allan? [*Alice says nothing.*] Where's the Lieutenant? [*Alice says nothing.*] Now, Kurt! What are you thinking of doing with Allan now?

KURT Doing with him?

CAPTAIN Yes; you can't afford to keep him in the artillery, can you?

KURT Perhaps not!

CAPTAIN You must try and get him into some cheap infantry regiment—up in Norrland or somewhere.

KURT Norrland?

CAPTAIN Yes! or suppose you let him go in for something practical, right away!—If I were in your place I'd put him into an office! . . . Why not? [*Kurt says nothing.*] In these enlightened days! Tcha! . . . Alice is so *unusually* silent! . . . Yes, my children, this is the swinging see-saw of life: now one's up, looking bravely round: and now one's down, and then one comes up again! and so on! So much for that! Yes! . . . [*To Alice*] Did you say anything? [*Alice shakes her head.*] We may expect visitors here in a few days!

ALICE Were you speaking to me?

CAPTAIN We may expect visitors in a few days! distinguished visitors!

ALICE Well, who?

CAPTAIN Aha! so you're interested! . . . Now you can sit down and guess who's coming; and between your guesses you can read this letter, once again! [*Gives her an opened letter.*]

ALICE My letter? Opened? Back from the post-office?

CAPTAIN [*getting up*] Yes: in my capacity as head of the family, and your guardian, I watch over the family's most sacred interests, and cut short with an iron hand every attempt to loosen family ties by means of a criminal correspondence! Tcha! [*Alice is crushed.*] I'm not dead, I tell you; but don't get angry just at the moment when I'm trying to raise us all from an unde-

served humiliation—undeserved at any rate on my part!

ALICE Judith! Judith!

CAPTAIN And Holofernes?—Will that be me? Bah! [*Goes out at back.*]

KURT Who is this man?

ALICE I don't know!

KURT We're beaten!

ALICE Yes . . . without a doubt!

KURT As for me, he has gnawed me through and through; but so cunningly that I can't accuse him in any way.

ALICE Accuse? Why, you're under an obligation to him!

KURT Does he know what he's doing?

ALICE No, I don't believe he does. He follows his nature and instincts, and just now he seems to be in favour where good and bad luck are dealt out.

KURT I suppose it's the Colonel who's coming here.

ALICE Probably! And that's why Allan must go!

KURT You agree to that?

ALICE Oh, yes!

KURT Then our ways part!

ALICE [*preparing to go*] For a little while! . . . But we'll meet again!

KURT Presumably!

ALICE And do you know where?

KURT Here!

ALICE You realize that?

KURT That's simple! *He* takes the house and buys the furniture!

ALICE I think so too! But don't desert me!

KURT Not for a little thing like that!

ALICE Good afternoon! [*Goes out.*]

KURT Good afternoon!

The same setting, but a cloudy day and rain outside. Alice and Kurt come in at the back, with umbrellas and raincoats.

ALICE So I've got you here! . . . Kurt, I can't be cruel enough to welcome you to your own house. . . .

KURT Oh, why not? I've gone through three distraints . . . and worse than that . . . *I* don't mind!

ALICE Did *he* summon you here?

KURT It was a formal summons, but I don't understand on what grounds!

ALICE Why, he's not your superior?

KURT No, but he's set himself up as a king on this island! And if anyone resists him, he's only got to mention the Colonel's name, and they all bow down at once!—By the way, is it to-day the Colonel comes?

ALICE He's expected—but I don't know anything for certain! Do sit down!

KURT [*sitting down*] Everything's the same here!

ALICE Don't think about it!—Don't tear open the wound!

KURT Wound? It only seems to me a little strange! Strange as the man himself!—Do you know, when I made his acquaintance as a young man I fled from him . . . but he was after me. Flattered me, offered me his services and put me under obligations. . . . I renewed my efforts to escape, but in vain. . . . Now I'm his slave!

ALICE Yes, and why? It's he who's indebted to you, while you are the debtor!

KURT After my ruin he offered to help Allan with his examination. . . .

ALICE That will cost you dear! . . . Does your candidacy for Parliament still hold good?

KURT Yes; and so far as I can see there's nothing in my way!

[*Silence*]

ALICE Is Allan really leaving to-day?

KURT Yes—if I can't prevent it!

ALICE That was a short-lived happiness!

KURT Short, like everything but life itself; that is terribly long!

ALICE It is indeed! . . . Won't you come and wait in the morning-room? Even if it doesn't hurt you, it hurts me—these surroundings.

KURT If *you* wish it!

ALICE I'm ashamed—I could die of shame . . . but I can't alter things!

KURT Let's go then! Just as you like!

ALICE There's somebody coming too!

[*They go out to the left. The Captain and Allan come in at the back, both in uniform, wearing cloaks.*]

CAPTAIN Sit down here, my boy: I want to have a talk with you! [*Sits in the arm-chair. Allan sits on the chair, left.*] It's raining to-day, or I should enjoy myself sitting here looking at the sea. [*Silence*] Well?—So you don't want to go?

ALLAN I don't like leaving my father!

CAPTAIN Oh, your father! He's rather an unfortunate man! [*Silence*] And parents seldom understand what's best for their children! That is to say—there are exceptions of course! Hm! Tell me, Allan! do you have any dealings with your mother?

ALLAN Yes, she writes occasionally!

CAPTAIN You know she's your guardian?

ALLAN Oh, yes!

CAPTAIN Now, Allan! Did you know your mother had given me full power to act on her behalf?

ALLAN No, I didn't know that!

CAPTAIN You know it now, then! And that is why all discussion about your career is ended! . . . So you'll go to Norrland?

ALLAN But I haven't got the money.

CAPTAIN I've seen to that!

ALLAN Then all I can do is to thank you, Uncle!

CAPTAIN You're grateful, you are! It's not everybody that is! Hm! . . . [*Raising his voice*] The Colonel . . . you know the Colonel?

ALLAN [*embarrassed*] No, I don't.

CAPTAIN [*accenting each syllable*] The—Col-onel is my particular friend—[*more quickly*] as perhaps you know! Hm! The Colonel has been kind enough to take an interest in my family, including my wife's relations. The Colonel, through his intervention, has been able to supply the money needed for the completion of your course!—Now you know your obligations, and your father's obligations, to the Colonel! . . . Do I make myself clear? [*Allan inclines his head.*] Now go and pack your things! The money will be handed to you on the gangway! Well, good-bye, my boy! [*Holds out one finger.*] Good-bye! [*Gets up and goes out to the right. Allan, alone, stands looking sadly about the room.*]

JUDITH [*comes in at the back, with hooded cloak and umbrella; in other respects she is beautifully dressed, wears a long skirt and has her hair up*] Is that you, Allan?

ALLAN [*turns round and examines Judith care-*

fully] Is that *you*, Judith?

JUDITH You don't recognize me? But where have you been all this time? . . . What are you looking at?—My long skirt . . . and my hair . . . you've never seen that before! . . .

ALLAN Well!

JUDITH Do I look like a married woman? [*Allan turns away; seriously*] What are you doing here?

ALLAN I've been saying good-bye!

JUDITH What! Are you—leaving?

ALLAN I'm transferred to Norrland.

JUDITH [*dumbfounded*] To Norrland?—When do you start?

ALLAN To-day!

JUDITH Whose idea is that?

ALLAN Your father's!

JUDITH So I should have thought! [*Walks up and down, stamping her feet.*] I wish you hadn't got to go to-day!

ALLAN So as to meet the Colonel!

JUDITH What do you know about the Colonel? . . . Is it certain you're going?

ALLAN I've no choice in the matter! And now I want to go myself.

[*Silence*]

JUDITH Why do you want to go now?

ALLAN I want to get away! Out, into the world!

JUDITH It's too cramped here! Yes, I understand, Allan: it is unbearable!—People speculate—in soda, and in human beings! [*Silence; with genuine feeling*] Allan! I have always been, as you know, one of those lucky people who cannot suffer: but now—I'm beginning to know what it is!

ALLAN You are?

JUDITH Yes!—now I'm beginning! [*She presses both hands to her breast.*] Oh, what agony! Oh! . . .

ALLAN What is it?

JUDITH I don't know!—I'm being suffocated! I think I'm dying!

ALLAN Judith!

JUDITH [*screaming*] Oh! . . . Is *this* how it feels? Is this . . . oh, poor boys!

ALLAN I should jeer at you, if I were as cruel as you are!

JUDITH I'm not cruel, but I didn't know better! . . . You mustn't go!

ALLAN I have to!

JUDITH Go then! . . . But give me something to remember you by!

ALLAN What have I to give you?

JUDITH [*with deep and genuine feeling*] You! . . . No, I *cannot* live through this! [*Cries aloud, clasping her breast.*] The pain, the pain . . . what have you done to me? . . . I don't want to live any longer!—Allan! Don't go, not alone! We'll go out together, and we'll take the little cutter, the little white one—and we'll sail out to sea; we'll make fast the sheet—there's a glorious breeze—and so we'll sail on till we go down—right out there, far away, where there's no goose-grass and no jelly-fish!—Shall we? Answer me!—But we ought to have washed the sails yesterday—they ought to be quite white—I want to see white in that hour—and then you shall swim, with your arm round me till you're tired—and then we'll sink. . . . [*Turns round.*] That'll be fine! Far finer than being miserable here and smuggling letters which Daddy opens and scoffs at! Allan! [*She seizes him by the arms and shakes him.*] Do you hear me?

ALLAN [*who has been watching her with shining eyes*] Judith! Judith! why didn't you say all this before?

JUDITH Why, I didn't know! how could I say what I didn't know?

ALLAN And now I've got to leave you! . . . But, I suppose it's the best and the only way! I can't compete with a man . . . who . . .

JUDITH Don't talk about the Colonel!

ALLAN Isn't it true?

JUDITH It's true—and it's untrue!

ALLAN Can't you make it quite untrue?

JUDITH Yes, it shall be so now! Within an hour!

ALLAN Will you keep your word! I can wait, and endure, and work . . . Judith!

JUDITH Don't go yet!—How long shall I have to wait?

ALLAN A year!

JUDITH [*overjoyed*] One? I'll wait a thousand years: and if you don't come, then I'll turn the vault of heaven upside down till the sun rises in the west. . . . Hush! Somebody's coming! —Allan, we must part. . . . Hush!—Take me in your arms! [*They embrace.*] But you mustn't kiss me! [*Turns her head away.*] There! go now! —go!

[*Allan goes towards back and puts on his cloak. Then they rush into each other's arms, so that Judith disappears beneath the cloak, and they kiss for one moment. Allan rushes out. Judith throws herself face downward on the sofa and sobs. Allan returns and falls on his knees by the sofa.*]

ALLAN No, I can't go! I can't leave you—not now, not now!

JUDITH [*getting up*] If you only knew how beautiful you are now! If you could only see yourself!

ALLAN No, no! A man can't be beautiful! But you, Judith! You—that you! . . . Oh, I know when you're nice you seem like another Judith . . . my own! . . . But if you deceive me now, I shall die!

JUDITH I think I shall die anyhow! . . . Oh, if I could only die now, this moment, while I'm so happy! . . .

ALLAN Somebody's coming!

JUDITH Let them come! I'm afraid of nothing in the whole world—not now! But I wish you could take me under your cloak. [*She pretends to hide under his cloak.*] Then I'd fly with you to Norrland. What shall we do in Norrland? Join the Light Infantry . . . the sort that wear feathers in their caps . . . they look fine and will suit you splendidly. [*Plays with his hair. Allan kisses the tips of her fingers—one after the other, and then her boots.*] What are you doing, you silly boy? You'll get your lips all black! [*Gets up hastily.*] . . . And then I shan't be able to kiss you when you go! . . . Come, and I'll go with you!

ALLAN No, I should be put under arrest!

JUDITH I'll go with you there too!

ALLAN They wouldn't let you! . . . Now we must part!

JUDITH I shall swim after the steamer . . . and then you'll jump in and rescue me, and it'll get into the paper, and then we can be engaged! Shall we do that?

ALLAN You can still make jokes, can you?

JUDITH There's always time for tears! . . . Say "good-bye" now! . . .

[*They rush into each other's arms; then Allan*

withdraws *through the door at back, which remains open, and they embrace outside in the rain.*]

ALLAN The rain's pouring down on you, Judith!

JUDITH As if I cared!

[*They tear themselves away from each other. Allan goes: Judith remains standing in the rain and wind, which plays havoc with her hair and clothes while she waves her handkerchief. Then she rushes into the room again and throws herself on the sofa, her face buried in her hands.*]

ALICE [*comes in and goes up to Judith*] What's this? . . . Are you ill?—Get up and let me have a look at you! [*Judith gets up. Alice looks at her carefully.*] You're not ill! . . . But I'm not going to console *you!* [*Goes out to the right.*]

[*The Lieutenant comes in at the back.*]

JUDITH [*gets up and puts on her hooded cloak*] Will you come to the telegraph office with me?

LIEUTENANT If I can be of any service . . . but I don't think it's quite proper!

JUDITH So much the better! I want you to compromise me—but without any illusions! . . . You go first!

[*They go out at the back. The Captain and Alice come in from the right, the Captain in undress uniform.*]

CAPTAIN [*sitting in the arm-chair*] Let him in! [*Alice goes and opens door on the left and then sits down on the sofa.*]

KURT [*coming in from the left*] You wish to speak to me?

CAPTAIN [*in a friendly but rather patronizing tone*] Yes, I have several important things to tell you!—Sit down!

KURT [*sits on chair left*] I am all ears!

CAPTAIN Very well then! . . . [*Bombastically*] You are aware that our quarantine system has been going to rack and ruin for nearly a century . . . hm!

ALICE [*to Kurt*] Hark to the candidate speaking!

CAPTAIN But—with the unprecedented development which we see nowadays in . . .

ALICE [*to Kurt*] Means of communication of course!

CAPTAIN . . . In all possible respects, the Government has been considering a policy of ex-

The Dance of Death

467

pansion. With that object the Health Commissioners have appointed Inspectors—and!

ALICE [*to Kurt*] He's giving dictation . . .

CAPTAIN . . . You may as well hear it now as later! I have been appointed an Inspector of Quarantines!

[*Silence*]

KURT I congratulate you—and pay my respects at the same time!

CAPTAIN In consideration of the ties of kinship which exist between us our personal relations will remain unaltered! However, to change the subject, your son Allan has, at my request, been transferred to an infantry regiment in Norrland!

KURT But I won't have that!

CAPTAIN Your wishes in the matter are subordinate to those of the mother . . . and since the mother has given me full power to decide, I have come to the above-mentioned decision!

KURT I admire you!

CAPTAIN Is that all you feel at the very moment when you're about to part from your son? Have you no other purely human feelings?

KURT You mean I ought to be suffering?

CAPTAIN Yes!

KURT It would please you if I suffered. You want me to be able to suffer!

CAPTAIN Are you really capable of suffering? I was ill once—you were present . . . and I can only remember that your face showed unfeigned pleasure!

ALICE That is not true! Kurt sat up with you all night, and soothed you when your pangs of conscience became unendurable . . . but when you recovered you were ungrateful . . .

CAPTAIN [*pretending not to hear her*] Allan accordingly must leave us!

KURT Who will provide the money?

CAPTAIN That I have already done: that is to say, we—a syndicate who have interested ourselves in the young man's future!

KURT A syndicate!

CAPTAIN Yes!—And to make sure that it's all right you may have a look at these lists. [*Hands him some papers.*]

KURT Lists? [*Reads the papers.*] Why, they're begging lists!

CAPTAIN Call them what you please!

KURT Have you been begging on behalf of my son?

CAPTAIN Ungrateful again!—An ungrateful person is the heaviest burden the earth bears!

KURT Socially then I am dead! . . . And my candidacy is done for! . . .

CAPTAIN What candidacy!

KURT Why, for Parliament!

CAPTAIN Surely you never dreamt of anything of that sort! . . . Particularly as you might have guessed that I, as the older resident, intended to offer my own services, which you appear to have under-estimated!

KURT Oh, well! So that's finished too!

CAPTAIN It doesn't seem to affect you much!

KURT You have taken everything now! Is there anything more you want?

CAPTAIN Have you anything more? And have you anything to reproach me with? Think carefully—have you anything to reproach me with?

[*Silence*]

KURT Strictly speaking—nothing! Everything has been done correctly and lawfully, as between honest citizens in everyday life! . . .

CAPTAIN You speak with a resignation which I should call cynical. But your whole nature, my dear Kurt, has a cynical bent, and there are moments when I might be tempted to share Alice's opinion of you—that you are a hypocrite, a hypocrite of the first rank!

KURT [*calmly*] Is that Alice's opinion?

ALICE [*to Kurt*] It was, once! But is so no longer; for to bear what you have borne takes sheer heroism, or—something else!

CAPTAIN I think the discussion may now be regarded as closed. Kurt, you'd better go and say "good-bye" to Allan; he sails by the next boat!

KURT [*getting up*] So soon? . . . Well, I've been through worse than this!

CAPTAIN Yes, you say that so often that I'm beginning to wonder what you really were up to in America.

KURT What I was up to? Why, I had misfortunes! And to meet with misfortune is the incontestable right of every human being.

CAPTAIN [*sharply*] There are misfortunes of our own making: were they of that kind?

KURT Isn't that a question of conscience?

CAPTAIN [*curtly*] Have *you* a conscience?

KURT There are wolves, and there are sheep. Men don't count it an honour to be a sheep! Still I'd rather be that than a wolf!

CAPTAIN You don't recognize the old truth, that every man is the architect of his own fortune?

KURT Is that true?

CAPTAIN And you don't know that a man's own strength . . .

KURT Oh, I know all about that, ever since the night when *your* own strength deserted you and left you lying on the floor!

CAPTAIN [*raising his voice*] A deserving man like your humble servant—yes, look at me—I have fought for fifty years—against a world of foes; but at last I've won the game, through perseverance, through loyalty, through energy and—through integrity!

ALICE You should leave that for other people to say!

CAPTAIN Other people won't say it, because they're jealous!—However, we're expecting visitors! My daughter Judith is meeting her fiancé to-day. . . . Where is Judith?

ALICE She's out!

CAPTAIN In the rain? . . . Send for her!

KURT Perhaps I may go now?

CAPTAIN No, stay! . . . Is Judith dressed? Decently?

ALICE Oh, fairly. . . . Did the Colonel say for certain he was coming?

CAPTAIN [*getting up*] Yes: that is to say, he's going to pay us a surprise visit as they call it! . . . And I'm expecting a telegram from him —any moment!—[*Going out to the right*] I'll be back in a minute!

ALICE There you have the man! Is he a human being?

KURT Last time you asked me that, I answered, no! Now I believe he's the commonest type of them that possess the earth . . . perhaps we are a little like that too? making use of our fellow-creatures and of favourable opportunities!

ALICE He has eaten you, and yours, alive . . . and you stick up for him?

KURT I've been through worse. . . . But this man-eater has left my soul untouched—that he could not devour!

ALICE What "worse" have you been through?

KURT Do *you* ask that? . . .

ALICE Are you being rude?

KURT No, I don't want to be, and for that reason . . . don't ask me again!

CAPTAIN [*coming in from the right*] The telegram was there, you see!—Kindly read it, Alice: my sight is so bad! . . . [*Sits pompously in the arm-chair.*] . . . Read it!—You needn't go, Kurt! [*Alice reads it rapidly to herself; she looks confused.*] We-ell? Aren't you pleased? [*Alice does not speak, but fixes her eyes on the Captain; he continues, ironically.*] Who is it from?

ALICE It's from the Colonel!

CAPTAIN [*delighted*] I thought so! . . . And what does the Colonel say?

ALICE This is what he says: "On account of Miss Judith's impertinent telephone message I regard our relations as broken off—for good!" [*Looks fixedly at the Captain.*]

CAPTAIN Once more, if you please!

ALICE [*reading quickly*] "On account of Miss Judith's impertinent telephone message I regard our relations as broken off—for good!"

CAPTAIN [*turning pale*] It's Judith!

ALICE And there is Holofernes!

CAPTAIN What are you then?

ALICE That you will soon find out!

CAPTAIN This is your doing!

ALICE No!

CAPTAIN [*beside himself*] This is your doing!

ALICE No! [*The Captain tries to get up and draw his sword, but falls back from an apoplectic stroke.*] Now you've got it!

CAPTAIN [*in an old man's tearful voice*] Don't be angry with me! I am so ill!

ALICE Are you? I'm glad to hear it! . . .

KURT Let's carry him to bed!

ALICE No, I won't touch him! [*Rings the bell.*]

CAPTAIN [*as before*] You mustn't be angry with me! [*To Kurt*] Think of my children!

KURT This is too sublime! I'm to look after his children when he's stolen mine!

ALICE What self-deception!

CAPTAIN Think of my children! [*Goes on mumbling unintelligibly.*] Blu-blu-blu.

ALICE At last that tongue is stayed!—It can brag no more, lie no more, wound no more!—

The Dance of Death

You, Kurt, who believe in God, thank Him on my behalf! Thank Him for freeing me from the tower, from the wolf, from the vampire!

KURT No, Alice! don't say that!

ALICE [*with her face close to the Captain's*] Where now is your own strength? What? And your energy? [*The Captain, speechless, spits in her face.*] So you can still spit venom, you viper! Then I'll tear the tongue from your throat! [*Strikes him on the ear.*] The head is off, but it still goes red! . . . O Judith, glorious girl, whom I bore like vengeance beneath my heart! You, you have set us free, all of us!— If you've any more heads, hydra, we'll take them too! [*Pulls his beard.*] To think that there is justice on earth! Sometimes I dreamt it, but I never believed it! Kurt, ask God to forgive me for misjudging Him! Oh, there *is* justice! Then I, too, will become a sheep! Tell Him that, Kurt! A little success is good for us; it's adversity that turns us into wolves!

[*The Lieutenant comes in at the back.*]

ALICE The Captain has had a stroke. Please help us to wheel out the chair!

LIEUTENANT Madam! . . .

ALICE What is it?

LIEUTENANT Well, Miss Judith . . .

ALICE Help us here first! you can tell us about Judith afterwards! [*The Lieutenant wheels the chair out to the right.*] Out with the carcass! Out with him, and throw open the doors! The place must be aired! [*Throws open the doors in the background. It has cleared up outside.*] Ouf! . . .

KURT Are you going to desert him?

ALICE One does desert a stranded vessel: the crew save their lives! . . . It isn't my business to lay out a rotting beast! Skinners and scavengers can look after him! A garden bed is too nice a thing to get such a barrow-load of filth! . . . Now I'm going to have a bath and clean off all this dirt, if I ever can be clean again! [*Judith is seen out on the balustrade, bareheaded, waving her handkerchief towards the sea.*]

KURT [*going towards door at back*] Who is that? Judith! [*Calls out*] Judith!

JUDITH [*comes in, crying out*] He's gone!

KURT Who?

JUDITH Allan's gone!

KURT Without saying "good-bye"?

JUDITH *We* said good-bye: and he sent you his love, Uncle!

ALICE Oh, that's how it was?

JUDITH [*throwing herself into Kurt's arms*] He's gone!

KURT He'll come back, dear!

ALICE Or we'll follow him!

KURT [*pointing to door right*] And leave him? —The world . . .

ALICE The world! Bah! . . . Judith, come and kiss me! [*Judith goes up to Alice, who kisses her on the forehead.*] Do you want to go after him?

JUDITH Need you ask?

ALICE But your father is ill.

JUDITH What does that matter?

ALICE That's my Judith!—Oh, Judith, how I love you!

JUDITH Besides, Daddy isn't mean . . . and he doesn't like being fussed over! There's some style about Daddy, whatever you say!

ALICE In a way—yes!

JUDITH And I fancy he isn't exactly longing for me—since that telephone business! . . . And why should he want to saddle me with an old fellow like that? No! Allan, Allan! [*Throws herself into Kurt's arms.*] I want to go to Allan! [*Tears herself free and runs out to wave. Kurt follows her and waves too.*]

ALICE How strange that flowers should grow out of filth!

[*The Lieutenant comes in from the right.*]

ALICE Well?

LIEUTENANT Yes; Miss Judith . . .

ALICE Is it so sweet to feel the letters of her name caressing your lips that you forget the dying man?

LIEUTENANT Well, but she said . . .

ALICE She?—Call her Judith rather than that! —But first of all, what's happening in there?

LIEUTENANT Oh, there! . . . It's all over!

ALICE All over?—O God, I thank Thee on my behalf and that of all mankind, that Thou hast freed us from this evil! . . . Give me your arm! I want to go out and breathe.—Breathe! [*The Lieutenant offers his arm; checking herself*] Did he say anything before he died?

AUGUST STRINDBERG

LIEUTENANT Miss Judith's father said a few words!

ALICE What did he say?

LIEUTENANT He said, "Forgive them, for they know not what they do."

ALICE Incredible!

LIEUTENANT Yes, Miss Judith's father was a good and noble man.

ALICE Kurt!

[*Kurt comes in at the back.*]

ALICE It's over!

KURT Ah! . . .

ALICE Do you know what his last words were? No, you couldn't. "Forgive them, for they know not what they do." . . .

KURT Can you translate that?

ALICE I suppose he meant that *he'd* always done right, and died as one who had been wronged by life.

KURT I suppose there'll be a nice funeral sermon!

ALICE And heaps of wreaths—from the NCO's!

KURT Yes!

ALICE A year ago he said something of this kind: "It looks as if life for us were some colossal jest!"

KURT Do you think he jested with us when he was dying?

ALICE No! . . . But now that he's dead I feel a strange desire to speak well of him!

KURT Let's do so then!

LIEUTENANT Miss Judith's father was a good and noble man!

ALICE [*to Kurt*] You hear that?

KURT "They know not what they do!" How often I've asked you if he knew what he was doing! And you thought he didn't! Come then —forgive him!

ALICE Riddles! riddles! . . . But just think of it—peace in the house now! The wonderful peace of death! Wonderful as that solemn restlessness when a child comes into the world! I can hear the silence . . . and I see on the floor the marks of the chair which carried him away.—I feel that my own life is ended now, and that I am on the road to dissolution! . . . It's strange, you know, but the Lieutenant's simple words—and he is a simple soul—pursue me still; but now I see a new meaning in them. My husband, my youth's beloved—yes, you laugh?—he *was* a good and noble man—in spite of everything!

KURT In spite of everything? And a brave man too—what a fight for his own existence and his family's!

ALICE What worries! what humiliations! Which he cancelled—so as to be able to pass on!

KURT He was one who had been *passed over!* That means much! Go in, Alice!

ALICE No! I can't do it! While we were talking here, the image of him as he was in his youth rose up before me. I saw him—I see him—now, just as he was when he was twenty! . . . I must have loved that man!

KURT And hated!

ALICE *And* hated! . . . Peace be with him! [*Goes towards the door on the right, and pauses there, with folded hands.*]

FEW THEMES are as enduring in Strindberg's plays as misogyny, the hatred of women. Attack Strindberg or defend him—attack women or defend them—the subject makes uncommonly absorbing reading in the plays or the writing about them.

Strindberg has been labelled a misogynist by many of his biographers. I cannot subscribe to this evaluation; and in her commentaries to [the] revealing letters of August Strindberg, Harriet Bosse likewise refutes this presumption. That label has been given him by critics who fail to realize that in most of his plays Strindberg delineated his characters objectively and logically, making both the husband and the wife share the blame for their inability to live together harmoniously. This is perhaps especially evident in one of his most devastating marital

The Dance of Death

tragedies, *The Dance of Death*. Both Edgar and Alice suffer from grievous faults and are a constant source of irritation and outrage to each other. They therefore mutually bring about the horror that besets their conjugal union. Furthermore, Strindberg wrote about life as he saw it and as he had experienced it; and his experiences had been largely on the seamy side. It is true that his characters were not everyday types: they are often endowed with particular peculiarities and abnormalities, yet not so abnormal and rare that they are not to be found in our society, both of a past era and of today. Our divorce courts and our newspapers bear witness to that. The monotonous chores and tasks of everyday life, the succession of national conflicts and wars and the threat of impending ones are contributing causes for much of the contradictory behavior and the aberrant, neurotic confusion in the minds of many in our world today. [Arvid Paulson, (ed. and transl.), *Letters of Strindberg to Harriet Bosse,* Thomas Nelson & Sons, New York, 1959, p. vii.]

It cannot be said that Strindberg, even at his fiercest, is harder on women than Dickens. No doubt his case against them is far more complete, because he does not shirk the specifically sexual factors in it. But this really softens it. . . . The general impression that Strindberg's women are the revenge of a furious woman-hater for his domestic failures, whilst Dickens is a genial idealist (he had little better luck domestically, by the way), is produced solely by

Dickens either making fun of the affair or believing that women are born so and must be admitted to the fellowship of the Holy Ghost on a feminine instead of a human basis; whilst Strindberg takes womanliness with deadly seriousness as an evil not to be submitted to for a moment without vehement protest and demand for quite practicable reform. [Bernard Shaw, *The Quintessence of Ibsenism*, Hill and Wang, Inc., New York, 1957, pp. 163–165.]

An Ibsenite actor has to present a man at war with himself. A Strindbergian actor is at war with someone else, often his wife. His emotions come right out of him with no interference whatsoever and fly like bullets at the enemy. It is quite a different pattern, and calls for quite a different sort of performance, a Dionysiac performance. . . .

Sometimes, Strindberg is content to give us raw chunks of life. As we see *The Dance of Death* we think "How real how real how real" and then? We are reminded of our own marital quarrels; Strindberg gets his finger on the sore and leaves it there. *The Dance of Death* is in two long parts. If, as is usually the case, only the first is performed, we have the impression of incompleteness. We have received a two-hour sample of marital misery, remarkable for its intensity and concentration, yet shocking in its monotony, its monomania. We have heard a single note endlessly extended, a prolonged shriek. [Eric Bentley, *In Search of Theater,* Vintage Books, New York, 1954, p. 127.]

Hatred provides the theme and the texture for The Dance of Death.
*It also offers Strindberg every opportunity for theatrical virtuosity,
for the use of music, for "tragic vehemence."*

When Strindberg found that Ibsen had already used the *Danse Macabre* in *John Gabriel Borkman,* he took *The Entry of the Boyars* as the tune for his own *Dance of Death.* He concentrated his sense of life's malevolence in the stone turret of an island fortress that had once been a prison. The walls were impregnated with hatred, the atmosphere poisoned all who breathed

it. Once more the theme was married hatred and married misery, and Strindberg conjured up the savage skill of his Naturalist plays to draw a loathsome wife and, this time, a still more evil and treacherous husband. He composed this awful figure, this larger-than-life vampire Captain, who destroyed the peace of all about him as he staggered from one death throe to the next, from caricatures of many men including Geijer-stam, and over them all he poured his own despair. "Life was so alien, so contrary, so cruel, right from my childhood, and people were so cruel that I became so too." And into Kurt, the Quarantine Master, returned after fifteen years abroad, divorced and robbed of his children, who first tried to save the doomed couple and then was infected himself with their poison, Strindberg slipped another of his selves—sensuous, well-meaning, weak. [Elizabeth Sprigge, *The Strange Life of August Strindberg*, The Macmillan Company, New York, 1949, p. 192.]

The Dance of Death [is] a dissection in Strindberg's expert manner of the 'eighties of the love-hate relationship between man and woman. The apparently ceaseless tormenting of each other by the Captain and Alice, his wife, becomes to Strindberg a symbol of life itself. The first part ends on the note of death bringing release: "Perhaps, when death comes, life will begin," says the Captain after his stroke. In the second part the Captain suffers another and fatal stroke, and in grotesque triumph Alice has his corpse carried out; then she begins to recall her dead husband as he had been in his youth, and to think of him in a forgiving spirit. It is to be noted that here, on the whole, Strindberg, contrary to his usual practice, condemns the man rather than the woman. *The Dance of Death* provides further evidence of . . . the coexistence in Strindberg's work, at one and the same time, of various literary manners.

Strindberg introduces a lyrical *motif* into the embittered domesticity of *The Dance of Death,* with the relationship between Judith, the young daughter, and Allan. [B. M. E. Mortensen and B. W. Downs, *Strindberg,* Cambridge University Press, New York, 1949, pp. 134–135.]

Perhaps it is . . . tragic vehemence which strikes the English reader most forcibly, and repels him, unless or until he can adjust himself to the values implied. Partly it is Strindberg's own sharpness of response and his fierce vitality that explain the vehemence, partly one may conclude that his aggressive emphasis on certain ideas betrays and underlines his inward doubts,

both of himself and his beliefs, so that the overtones in the abuse and the slam of the banged door on the stage are the author's own anguished whispers and subdued searchings of the heart. The tragic tone, however, so the reader will argue, remains; but this charge of unduly tragic outlook can be levelled against much of Scandinavian literature as a whole, more specifically against Norwegian and Swedish literature. Strindberg is not "gloomier" than many other Northern authors. The German, so often apparently humourless himself, does not reject foreign literature on the score of "gloom." No doubt this explains the easy success in Germany, many years ago, of some of Strindberg's worse efforts. Yet there is, one may think, implicit in the German acceptance an underrating or ignoring of Strindberg's own peculiar humour and sense of irony, which are there for the English reader to find and enjoy, though so often distorted or obscured by clumsy translations (Strindberg's language at the best of times almost defies rendering into English). Because Strindberg's sense of humour is not an English one, that does not mean that it has not a positive, Swedish, character, a fact which holds good for many other Swedish writers as well. The *snaps*-drinking lumberjack of Northern Sweden, up against the rigours and monotony of the endless snow-covered forests, must of necessity develop a different kind of humour from that of the beer-swilling yokels of Shakespeare's Warwickshire. . . .

Certain Swedish critics of Strindberg, of whom Heidenstam was really the first, have called him a barbarian, and have dwelt on his savage strength and uncontrolled moods. This interpretation deliberately leaves out of account the hypersensitve temperament and in many ways sophisticated responses of the author, a sophistication which is often revealed in irony, and thus rejects what to many of his readers must be his greatest fascination—the combination of primitive, dynamic vitality and poetic imagination with a subtle awareness of all the discordant and conflicting claims of life, as they arise in modern society. Strindberg does not, like his much better known contemporary Ibsen, busy himself with projecting contemporary social problems *qua* social problems on the stage. One may say that his canvas would have been a more varied one if he had done so, yet, through this, his plays, even if more abstract, are less dependent on matters of merely topical interest. Like Ibsen, on the other hand, Strindberg was intent on stripping the mask from hypocrisy: and against the faultless workmanship and extraordinarily intelligent, though sometimes over-schematic, art of the Norwegian, his most positive quality is clearly revealed by contrast; that most positive quality is his fluidity. [*Ibid.*, pp. 221–223.]

BERNARD SHAW

1856–1950

The subtitle of Man and Superman, *"A Comedy and a Philosophy,"
describes almost all the plays of George Bernard Shaw.
Each of his dramas has its moments of high comedy. Each
presents some segment of Shavian philosophy—that is, when
it does not try to communicate Shaw's wisdom in its entirety.
Everything he ever wrote had some element of the tract or the
pamphlet about it. It was hard for him to avoid special pleading
in the music, art, and drama criticism that he wrote after he moved
to London from Dublin at the age of 20, even if it was only that
people who coughed in concert halls should be taken outside and
their "ailment" treated by "gently passing a warm steam-roller
over their chests." His career as a critic, Socialist pamphleteer,
and novelist lasted for some sixteen years, until his first play,*
Widowers' Houses, *was produced at the end of 1892. In January
of that year he wrote to the actress Florence Farr, "You are wrong
to scorn farcical comedy. It is by jingling the bell of a jester's cap
that I, like Heine, have made people listen to me. All genuinely
intellectual work is humorous." In the same letter he confessed—
with no great persuasion needed to make him do so—that he was
of the first of the two orders of genius, not a "mere monster
produced by the accidental excess of some faculty—musical,
muscular, sexual even," but rather the kind "produced by the
breed throwing forward to the godlike man. . . ." Thus the texture
and the terms of Shavian drama: the establishment of a comic
tone through which the doctrine of the Life Force could be most*

persuasively articulated. Shaw explained the Life Force to a lecture audience in 1912: "Your purpose in life is simply to help on the purpose of the universe. By higher and higher organization man must become superman, and superman super-superman, and so on." And so on through an extraordinary number of successful plays—Arms and the Man, Candida, Caesar and Cleopatra, Man and Superman, Major Barbara, The Doctor's Dilemma, Getting Married, Heartbreak House, Back to Methuselah, *and* Saint Joan, *just to name an even number. It is an incomparable record for quality and quantity in the modern theater, as the length of his years, 94, is without equal among great playwrights. "I cannot remember any period in my life when I could help inventing people and scenes," Shaw wrote at the beginning of his career to another playwright. And shortly after, he expressed something like his creed in another letter, this one to the actress Ellen Terry: "Never stagnate. Life is a constant becoming: all stages lead to the beginning of others." As is frequently true with dramatists of this skill, Shaw's own words explain him best.*

Man and Superman

A COMEDY AND A PHILOSOPHY

Characters

JOHN TANNER [*also* DON JUAN TENORIO]

ANN WHITEFIELD [*also* THE OLD WOMAN, DOÑA ANA]

ROEBUCK RAMSDEN [*also* THE STATUE, DOÑA ANA'S FATHER]

OCTAVIUS ROBINSON

VIOLET ROBINSON

HECTOR MALONE

MENDOZA [*also* THE DEVIL]

HENRY STRAKER, *also* TANNER'S CHAUFFEUR

MRS. WHITEFIELD

HECTOR MALONE, SR.

MISS RAMSDEN

MAID

BRIGANDS *Social-Democrats, anarchists, and others*

SOLDIERS

The action takes place in England and Spain, in a London study, a carriage drive in the park of a country house near Richmond, outside a cave in the Sierra Nevada mountains, and in the garden of a villa in Granada. The time, in the early years of this century.

Act One

Roebuck Ramsden is in his study, opening the morning's letters. The study, handsomely and solidly furnished, proclaims the man of means. Not a speck of dust is visible: it is clear that there are at least two housemaids and a parlor-maid downstairs, and a housekeeper upstairs who does not let them spare elbow-grease. Even the top of Roebuck's head is polished: on a sunshiny day he could heliograph his orders to distant camps by merely nodding. In no other respect, however, does he suggest the military man. It is in active civil life that men get his broad air of importance, his dignified expectation of deference, his determinate mouth disarmed and refined since the hour of his success by the withdrawal of opposition and the concession of comfort and precedence and power. He is more than a highly respectable man: he is marked out as a president of highly respectable men, a chairman among directors, an alderman among coun-

cillors, a mayor among aldermen. *Four tufts of iron-grey hair, which will soon be as white as isinglass, and are in other respects not at all unlike it, grow in two symmetrical pairs above his ears and at the angles of his spreading jaws. He wears a black frock coat, a white waistcoat (it is bright spring weather), and trousers, neither black nor perceptibly blue, of one of those indefinitely mixed hues which the modern clothier has produced to harmonize with the religions of respectable men. He has not been out of doors yet today; so he still wears his slippers, his boots being ready for him on the hearthrug. Surmising that he has no valet, and seeing that he has no secretary with a shorthand notebook and a typewriter, one meditates on how little our great burgess domesticity has been disturbed by new fashions and methods, or by the enterprise of the railway and hotel companies which sell you a Saturday to Monday of life at Folkestone as a real gentleman for two guineas, first class fares both ways included.*

How old is Roebuck? The question is important on the threshold of a drama of ideas; for under such circumstances everything depends on whether his adolescence belonged to the sixties or to the eighties. He was born, as a matter of fact, in 1839, and was a Unitarian and Free Trader from his boyhood, and an Evolutionist from the publication of the Origin of Species. *Consequently he has always classed himself as an advanced thinker and fearlessly outspoken reformer.*

*Sitting at his writing table, he has on his right the windows giving on Portland Place. Through these, as through a proscenium, the curious spectator may contemplate his profile as well as the blinds will permit. On his left is the inner wall, with a stately bookcase, and the door not quite in the middle, but somewhat further from him. Against the wall opposite him are two busts on pillars: one, to his left, of John Bright; the other, to his right, of Mr Herbert Spencer. Between them hangs an engraved portrait of Richard Cobden, enlarged photographs of Martineau, Huxley, and George Eliot; autotypes of allegories by Mr G. F. Watts (for Roebuck believes in the fine arts with all the earnestness of a man who does not understand them), and an impres-*sion of Dupont's engraving of Delaroche's Beaux Arts hemicycle, representing the great men of all ages. On the wall behind him, above the mantelshelf, is a family portrait of impenetrable obscurity.*

A chair stands near the writing table for the convenience of business visitors. Two other chairs are against the wall between the busts.

A parlormaid enters with a visitor's card. Roebuck takes it, and nods, pleased. Evidently a welcome caller.

RAMSDEN Show him in.
[*The parlormaid goes out and returns with the visitor.*]
MAID Mr Robinson.

Mr Robinson is really an uncommonly nice looking young fellow. He must, one thinks, be the jeune premier; for it is not in reason to suppose that a second such attractive male figure should appear in one story. The slim, shapely frame, the elegant suit of new mourning, the small head and regular features, the pretty little moustache, the frank clear eyes, the wholesome bloom on the youthful complexion, the well-brushed glossy hair, not curly, but of fine texture and good dark color, the arch of good nature in the eyebrows, the erect forehead and neatly pointed chin, all announce the man who will love and suffer later on. And that he will not do so without sympathy is guaranteed by an engaging sincerity and eager modest serviceableness which stamp him as a man of amiable nature. The moment he appears, Ramsden's face expands into fatherly liking and welcome, an expression which drops into one of decorous grief as the young man approaches him with sorrow in his face as well as in his black clothes. Ramsden seems to know the nature of the bereavement. As the visitor advances silently to the writing table, the old man rises and shakes his hand across it without a word: a long, affectionate shake which tells the story of a recent sorrow common to both.

RAMSDEN [*concluding the handshake and cheering up*] Well, well, Octavius, it's the common lot.

BERNARD SHAW

We must all face it some day. Sit down. [*Octavius takes the visitor's chair. Ramsden replaces himself in his own.*]

OCTAVIUS Yes: we must face it, Mr Ramsden. But I owed him a great deal. He did everything for me that my father could have done if he had lived.

RAMSDEN He had no son of his own, you see.

OCTAVIUS But he had daughters; and yet he was as good to my sister as to me. And his death was so sudden! I always intended to thank him —to let him know that I had not taken all his care of me as a matter of course, as any boy takes his father's care. But I waited for an opportunity; and now he is dead—dropped without a moment's warning. He will never know what I felt. [*He takes out his handkerchief and cries unaffectedly.*]

RAMSDEN How do we know that, Octavius? He may know it: we cannot tell. Come! Dont grieve. [*Octavius masters himself and puts up his handkerchief.*] Thats right. Now let me tell you something to console you. The last time I saw him—it was in this very room—he said to me: "Tavy is a generous lad and the soul of honor; and when I see how little consideration other men get from their sons, I realize how much better than a son he's been to me." There! Doesnt that do you good?

OCTAVIUS Mr Ramsden: he used to say to me that he had met only one man in the world who was the soul of honor, and that was Roebuck Ramsden.

RAMSDEN Oh, that was his partiality: we were very old friends, you know. But there was something else he used to say about you. I wonder whether I ought to tell you or not!

OCTAVIUS You know best.

RAMSDEN It was something about his daughter.

OCTAVIUS [*eagerly*] About Ann! Oh, do tell me that, Mr Ramsden.

RAMSDEN Well, he said he was glad, after all, you were not his son, because he thought that someday Annie and you—[*Octavius blushes vividly.*] Well, perhaps I shouldnt have told you. But he was in earnest.

OCTAVIUS Oh, if only I thought I had a chance! You know, Mr Ramsden, I dont care about money or about what people call position; and

I cant bring myself to take an interest in the business of struggling for them. Well, Ann has a most exquisite nature; but she is so accustomed to be in the thick of that sort of thing that she thinks a man's character incomplete if he is not ambitious. She knows that if she married me she would have to reason herself out of being ashamed of me for not being a big success of some kind.

RAMSDEN [*getting up and planting himself with his back to the fireplace*] Nonsense, my boy, nonsense! Youre too modest. What does she know about the real value of men at her age? [*More seriously*] Besides, she's a wonderfully dutiful girl. Her father's wish would be sacred to her. Do you know that since she grew up to years of discretion, I dont believe she has ever once given her own wish as a reason for doing anything or not doing it. It's always "Father wishes me to," or "Mother wouldnt like it." It's really almost a fault in her. I have often told her she must learn to think for herself.

OCTAVIUS [*shaking his head*] I couldnt ask her to marry me because her father wished it, Mr Ramsden.

RAMSDEN Well, perhaps not. No: of course not. I see that. No: you certainly couldnt. But when you win her on your own merits, it will be a great happiness to her to fulfil her father's desire as well as her own. Eh? Come! Youll ask her, wont you?

OCTAVIUS [*with sad gaiety*] At all events I promise you I shall never ask anyone else.

RAMSDEN Oh, you shant need to. She'll accept you, my boy—although [*here he suddenly becomes very serious indeed*] you have one great drawback.

OCTAVIUS [*anxiously*] What drawback is that, Mr Ramsden? I should rather say which of my many drawbacks?

RAMSDEN I'll tell you, Octavius. [*He takes from the table a book bound in red cloth.*] I have in my hand a copy of the most infamous, the most scandalous, the most mischievous, the most blackguardly book that ever escaped burning at the hands of the common hangman. I have not read it: I would not soil my mind with such filth; but I have read what the papers say of it. The title is quite enough for me. [*He reads it.*]

The Revolutionist's Handbook and Pocket Companion, by John Tanner, M.I.R.C., Member of the Idle Rich Class.

OCTAVIUS [*smiling*] But Jack—

RAMSDEN [*testily*] For goodness' sake, dont call him Jack under my roof. [*He throws the book violently down on the table; then, somewhat relieved, he comes past the table to Octavius, and addresses him at close quarters with impressive gravity.*] Now, Octavius, I know that my dead friend was right when he said you were a generous lad. I know that this man was your schoolfellow, and that you feel bound to stand by him because there was a boyish friendship between you. But I ask you to consider the altered circumstances. You were treated as a son in my friend's house. You lived there; and your friends could not be turned from the door. This man Tanner was in and out there on your account almost from his childhood. He addresses Annie by her Christian name as freely as you do. Well, while her father was alive, that was her father's business, not mine. This man Tanner was only a boy to him: his opinions were something to be laughed at, like a man's hat on a child's head. But now Tanner is a grown man and Annie a grown woman. And her father is gone. We dont as yet know the exact terms of his will; but he often talked it over with me; and I have no more doubt than I have that youre sitting there that the will appoints me Annie's trustee and guardian. [*Forcibly*] Now I tell you, once for all, I cant and I wont have Annie placed in such a position that she must, out of regard for you, suffer the intimacy of this fellow Tanner. It's not fair: it's not right: it's not kind. What are you going to do about it?

OCTAVIUS But Ann herself has told Jack that whatever his opinions are, he will always be welcome because he knew her dear father.

RAMSDEN [*out of patience*] That girl's mad about her duty to her parents. [*He starts off like a goaded ox in the direction of John Bright, in whose expression there is no sympathy for him; as he speaks he fumes down to Herbert Spencer, who receives him still more coldly.*] Excuse me, Octavius; but there are limits to social toleration. You know that I am not a bigoted or prejudiced man. You know that I am plain Roebuck Ramsden when other men who have done less have got handles to their names, because I have stood for equality and liberty of conscience while they were truckling to the Church and to the aristocracy. Whitefield and I lost chance after chance through our advanced opinions. But I draw the line at Anarchism and Free Love and that sort of thing. If I am to be Annie's guardian, she will have to learn that she has a duty to me. I wont have it: I will not have it. She must forbid John Tanner the house; and so must you.

[*The parlormaid returns.*]

OCTAVIUS But—

RAMSDEN [*calling his attention to the servant*] Ssh! Well?

THE MAID Mr Tanner wishes to see you, sir.

RAMSDEN Mr Tanner!

OCTAVIUS Jack!

RAMSDEN How dare Mr Tanner call on me! Say I cannot see him.

OCTAVIUS [*hurt*] I am sorry you are turning my friend from your door like that.

THE MAID [*calmly*] He's not at the door, sir. He's upstairs in the drawing room with Miss Ramsden. He came with Mrs Whitefield and Miss Ann and Miss Robinson, sir.

[*Ramsden's feelings are beyond words.*]

OCTAVIUS [*grinning*] Thats very like Jack, Mr Ramsden. You must see him, even if it's only to turn him out.

RAMSDEN [*hammering out his words with suppressed fury*] Go upstairs and ask Mr Tanner to be good enough to step down here. [*The parlormaid goes out; and Ramsden returns to the fireplace, as to a fortified position.*] I must say that of all the confounded pieces of impertinence—well, if these are Anarchist manners, I hope you like them. And Annie with him! Annie! A—[*he chokes*].

OCTAVIUS Yes: thats what surprises me. He's so desperately afraid of Ann. There must be something the matter.

Mr John Tanner suddenly opens the door and enters. He is too young to be described simply as a big man with a beard. But it is already plain that middle life will find him in that category.

He has still some of the slimness of youth; but youthfulness is not the effect he aims at: his frock coat would befit a prime minister; and a certain high-chested carriage of the shoulders, a lofty pose of the head, and the Olympian majesty with which a mane, or rather a huge wisp, of hazel-colored hair is thrown back from an imposing brow, suggest Jupiter rather than Apollo. He is prodigiously fluent of speech, restless, excitable (mark the snorting nostril and the restless blue eye, just the thirty-secondth of an inch too wide open), possibly a little mad. He is carefully dressed, not from the vanity that cannot resist finery, but from a sense of the importance of everything he does which leads him to make as much of paying a call as other men do of getting married or laying a foundation stone. A sensitive, susceptible, exaggerative, earnest man: a megalomaniac, who would be lost without a sense of humor.

Just at present the sense of humor is in abeyance. To say that he is excited is nothing: all his moods are phases of excitement. He is now in the panic-stricken phase; and he walks straight up to Ramsden as if with the fixed intention of shooting him on his own hearthrug. But what he pulls from his breast pocket is not a pistol, but a foolscap document which he thrusts under the indignant nose of Ramsden.

TANNER [*exclaims*] Ramsden: do you know what that is?

RAMSDEN [*loftily*] No, sir.

TANNER It's a copy of Whitefield's will. Ann got it this morning.

RAMSDEN When you say Ann, you mean, I presume, Miss Whitefield.

TANNER I mean our Ann, your Ann, Tavy's Ann, and now, Heaven help me, my Ann!

OCTAVIUS [*rising, very pale*] What do you mean?

TANNER Mean! [*He holds up the will.*] Do you know who is appointed Ann's guardian by this will?

RAMSDEN [*coolly*] I believe I am.

TANNER You! You and I, man. I! I!! I!!! Both of us! [*He flings the will down on the writing table.*]

RAMSDEN You! Impossible.

TANNER It's only too hideously true. [*He throws himself into Octavius's chair.*] Ramsden: get me out of it somehow. You dont know Ann as well as I do. She'll commit every crime a respectable woman can; and she'll justify every one of them by saying that it was the wish of her guardians. She'll put everything on us; and we shall have no more control over her than a couple of mice over a cat.

OCTAVIUS Jack: I wish you wouldnt talk like that about Ann.

TANNER This chap's in love with her: thats another complication. Well, she'll either jilt him and say I didnt approve of him, or marry him and say you ordered her to. I tell you, this is the most staggering blow that has ever fallen on a man of my age and temperament.

RAMSDEN Let me see that will, sir. [*He goes to the writing table and picks it up.*] I cannot believe that my old friend Whitefield would have shown such a want of confidence in me as to associate me with—[*His countenance falls as he reads.*]

TANNER It's all my own doing: thats the horrible irony of it. He told me one day that you were to be Ann's guardian; and like a fool I began arguing with him about the folly of leaving a young woman under the control of an old man with obsolete ideas.

RAMSDEN [*stupended*] My ideas obsolete!!!!!!!

TANNER Totally. I had just finished an essay called "Down with Government by the Greyhaired"; and I was full of arguments and illustrations. I said the proper thing was to combine the experience of an old hand with the vitality of a young one. Hang me if he didnt take me at my word and alter his will—it's dated only a fortnight after that conversation—appointing me as joint guardian with you!

RAMSDEN [*pale and determined*] I shall refuse to act.

TANNER Whats the good of that? Ive been refusing all the way from Richmond; but Ann keeps on saying that of course she's only an orphan; and that she cant expect the people who were glad to come to the house in her father's time to trouble much about her now. Thats the latest game. An orphan! It's like hearing an ironclad talk about being at the mercy of the wind and waves.

OCTAVIUS This is not fair, Jack. She is an orphan. And you ought to stand by her.

TANNER Stand by her! What danger is she in? She has the law on her side; she has popular sentiment on her side; she has plenty of money and no conscience. All she wants with me is to load up all her moral responsibilities on me, and do as she likes at the expense of my character. I cant control her; and she can compromise me as much as she likes. I might as well be her husband.

RAMSDEN You can refuse to accept the guardianship. *I* shall certainly refuse to hold it jointly with you.

TANNER Yes; and what will she say to that? What does she say to it? Just that her father's wishes are sacred to her, and that she shall always look up to me as her guardian whether I care to face the responsibility or not. Refuse! You might as well refuse to accept the embraces of a boa constrictor when once it gets round your neck.

OCTAVIUS This sort of talk is not kind to me, Jack.

TANNER [*rising and going to Octavius to console him, but still lamenting*] If he wanted a young guardian, why didnt he appoint Tavy?

RAMSDEN Ah! why indeed?

OCTAVIUS I will tell you. He sounded me about it; but I refused the trust because I loved her. I had no right to let myself be forced on her as a guardian by her father. He spoke to her about it; and she said I was right. You know I love her, Mr Ramsden; and Jack knows it too. If Jack loved a woman, I would not compare her to a boa constrictor in his presence, however much I might dislike her. [*He sits down between the busts and turns his face to the wall.*]

RAMSDEN I do not believe that Whitefield was in his right senses when he made that will. You have admitted that he made it under your influence.

TANNER You ought to be pretty well obliged to me for my influence. He leaves you two thousand five hundred for your trouble. He leaves Tavy a dowry for his sister and five thousand for himself.

OCTAVIUS [*his tears flowing afresh*] Oh, I cant take it. He was too good to us.

TANNER You wont get it, my boy, if Ramsden upsets the will.

RAMSDEN Ha! I see. You have got me in a cleft stick.

TANNER He leaves me nothing but the charge of Ann's morals, on the ground that I have already more money than is good for me. That shows that he had his wits about him, doesnt it?

RAMSDEN [*grimly*] I admit that.

OCTAVIUS [*rising and coming from his refuge by the wall*] Mr Ramsden: I think you are prejudiced against Jack. He is a man of honor, and incapable of abusing—

TANNER Dont, Tavy: you'll make me ill. I am not a man of honor: I am a man struck down by a dead hand. Tavy: you must marry her after all and take her off my hands. And I had set my heart on saving you from her!

OCTAVIUS Oh, Jack, you talk of saving me from my highest happiness.

TANNER Yes, a lifetime of happiness. If it were only the first half hour's happiness, Tavy, I would buy it for you with my last penny. But a lifetime of happiness! No man alive could bear it: it would be hell on earth.

RAMSDEN [*violently*] Stuff, sir. Talk sense; or else go and waste someone else's time: I have something better to do than listen to your fooleries. [*He positively kicks his way to his table and resumes his seat.*]

TANNER You hear him, Tavy! Not an idea in his head later than eighteen sixty. We cant leave Ann with no other guardian to turn to.

RAMSDEN I am proud of your contempt for my character and opinions, sir. Your own are set forth in that book, I believe.

TANNER [*eagerly going to the table*] What! Youve got my book! What do you think of it?

RAMSDEN Do you suppose I would read such a book, sir?

TANNER Then why did you buy it?

RAMSDEN I did not buy it, sir. It has been sent me by some foolish lady who seems to admire your views. I was about to dispose of it when Octavius interrupted me. I shall do so now, with your permission. [*He throws the book into the waste-paper basket with such vehemence* *that Tanner recoils under the impression that it is being thrown at his head.*]

TANNER You have no more manners than I have myself. However, that saves ceremony between us. [*He sits down again.*] What do you intend to do about this will?

OCTAVIUS May I make a suggestion?

RAMSDEN Certainly, Octavius.

OCTAVIUS Arnt we forgetting that Ann herself may have some wishes in this matter?

RAMSDEN I quite intend that Annie's wishes shall be consulted in every reasonable way. But she is only a woman, and a young and inexperienced woman at that.

TANNER Ramsden: I begin to pity you.

RAMSDEN [*hotly*] I dont want to know how you feel towards me, Mr Tanner.

TANNER Ann will do just exactly what she likes. And whats more, she'll force us to advise her to do it; and she'll put the blame on us if it turns out badly. So, as Tavy is longing to see her—

OCTAVIUS [*shyly*] I am not, Jack.

TANNER You lie, Tavy: you are. So lets have her down from the drawing room and ask her what she intends us to do. Off with you, Tavy, and fetch her. [*Tavy turns to go.*] And dont be long; for the strained relations between myself and Ramsden will make the interval rather painful.

[*Ramsden compresses his lips, but says nothing.*]

OCTAVIUS Never mind him, Mr Ramsden. He's not serious. [*He goes out.*]

RAMSDEN [*very deliberately*] Mr Tanner: you are the most impudent person I have ever met.

TANNER [*seriously*] I know it, Ramsden. Yet even I cannot wholly conquer shame. We live in an atmosphere of shame. We are ashamed of everything that is real about us; ashamed of ourselves, of our relatives, of our incomes, of our accents, of our opinions, of our experience, just as we are ashamed of our naked skins. Good Lord, my dear Ramsden, we are ashamed to walk, ashamed to ride in an omnibus, ashamed to hire a hansom instead of keeping a carriage, ashamed of keeping one horse instead of two and a groom-gardener instead of a coachman and footman. The more things a

man is ashamed of, the more respectable he is. Why, youre ashamed to buy my book, ashamed to read it: the only thing youre not ashamed of is to judge me for it without having read it; and even that only means that youre ashamed to have heterodox opinions. Look at the effect I produce because my fairy godmother withheld from me this gift of shame. I have every possible virtue that a man can have except—

RAMSDEN I am glad you think so well of yourself.

TANNER All you mean by that is that you think I ought to be ashamed of talking about my virtues. You dont mean that I havnt got them: you know perfectly well that I am as sober and honest a citizen as yourself, as truthful personally, and much more truthful politically and morally.

RAMSDEN [*touched on his most sensitive point*] I deny that. I will not allow you or any man to treat me as if I were a mere member of the British public. I detest its prejudices; I scorn its narrowness; I demand the right to think for myself. You pose as an advanced man. Let me tell you that I was an advanced man before you were born.

TANNER I knew it was a long time ago.

RAMSDEN I am as advanced as ever I was. I defy you to prove that I have ever hauled down the flag. I am more advanced than ever I was. I grow more advanced every day.

TANNER More advanced in years, Polonius.

RAMSDEN Polonius! So you are Hamlet, I suppose.

TANNER No: I am only the most impudent person youve ever met. Thats your notion of a thoroughly bad character. When you want to give me a piece of your mind, you ask yourself, as a just and upright man, what is the worst you can fairly say of me. Thief, liar, forger, adulterer, perjurer, glutton, drunkard? Not one of these names fit me. You have to fall back on my deficiency in shame. Well, I admit it. I even congratulate myself; for if I were ashamed of my real self, I should cut as stupid a figure as any of the rest of you. Cultivate a little impudence, Ramsden; and you will become quite a remarkable man.

RAMSDEN I have no—

Man and Superman

TANNER You have no desire for that sort of notoriety. Bless you, I knew that answer would come as well as I know that a box of matches will come out of an automatic machine when I put a penny in the slot: you would be ashamed to say anything else.

The crushing retort for which Mr Ramsden has been visibly collecting his forces is lost forever; for at this point Octavius returns with Miss Ann Whitefield and her mother; and Ramsden springs up and hurries to the door to receive them. Whether Ann is good-looking or not depends upon your taste; also and perhaps chiefly on your age and sex. To Octavius she is an enchantingly beautiful woman, in whose presence the world becomes transfigured, and the puny limits of individual consciousness are suddenly made infinite by a mystic memory of the whole life of the race to its beginnings in the east, or even back to the paradise from which it fell. She is to him the reality of romance, the inner good sense of nonsense, the unveiling of his eyes, the freeing of his soul, the abolition of time, place, and circumstance, the etherealization of his blood into rapturous rivers of the very water of life itself, the revelation of all the mysteries and the sanctification of all the dogmas. To her mother she is, to put it as moderately as possible, nothing whatever of the kind. Not that Octavius's admiration is in any way ridiculous or discreditable. Ann is a well formed creature, as far as that goes; and she is perfectly ladylike, graceful, and comely, with ensnaring eyes and hair. Besides, instead of making herself an eyesore, like her mother, she has devised a mourning costume of black and violet silk which does honor to her late father and reveals the family tradition of brave unconventionality by which Ramsden sets such store.

But all this is beside the point as an explanation of Ann's charm. Turn up her nose, give a cast to her eye, replace her black and violet confection by the apron and feathers of a flower girl, strike all the aitches out of her speech, and Ann would still make men dream. Vitality is as common as humanity; but, like humanity, it sometimes rises to genius; and Ann is one of the vital geniuses. Not at all, if you please, an oversexed person: that is a vital defect, not a true excess. She is a perfectly respectable, perfectly self-controlled woman, and looks it; though her pose is fashionably frank and impulsive. She inspires confidence as a person who will do nothing she does not mean to do; also some fear, perhaps, as a woman who will probably do everything she means to do without taking more account of other people than may be necessary and what she calls right. In short, what the weaker of her own sex sometimes call a cat.

Nothing can be more decorous than her entry and her reception by Ramsden, whom she kisses. The late Mr Whitefield would be gratified almost to impatience by the long faces of the men (except Tanner, who is fidgety), the silent handgrasps, the sympathetic placing of chairs, the sniffing of the widow, and the liquid eye of the daughter, whose heart, apparently, will not let her control her tongue to speech. Ramsden and Octavius take the two chairs from the wall, and place them for the two ladies; but Ann comes to Tanner and takes his chair, which he offers with a brusque gesture, subsequently relieving his irritation by sitting down on the corner of the writing table with studied indecorum. Octavius gives Mrs Whitefield a chair next Ann, and himself takes the vacant one which Ramsden has placed under the nose of the effigy of Mr Herbert Spencer.

Mrs Whitefield, by the way, is a little woman, whose faded flaxen hair looks like straw on an egg. She has an expression of muddled shrewdness, a squeak of protest in her voice, and an odd air of continually elbowing away some larger person who is crushing her into a corner. One guesses her as one of those women who are conscious of being treated as silly and negligible, and who, without having strength enough to assert themselves effectually, at any rate never submit to their fate. There is a touch of chivalry in Octavius's scrupulous attention to her, even whilst his whole soul is absorbed by Ann.

Ramsden goes solemnly back to his magisterial seat at the writing table, ignoring Tanner, and opens the proceedings.

BERNARD SHAW

RAMSDEN   I am sorry, Annie, to force business on you at a sad time like the present. But your poor dear father's will has raised a very serious question. You have read it, I believe? [*Ann assents with a nod and a catch of her breath, too much affected to speak.*] I must say I am surprised to find Mr Tanner named as joint guardian and trustee with myself of you and Rhoda. [*A pause. They all look portentous; but have nothing to say. Ramsden, a little ruffled by the lack of any response, continues*] I dont know that I can consent to act under such conditions. Mr Tanner has, I understand, some objection also; but I do not profess to understand its nature: he will no doubt speak for himself. But we are agreed that we can decide nothing until we know your views. I am afraid I shall have to ask you to choose between my sole guardianship and that of Mr Tanner; for I fear it is impossible for us to undertake a joint arrangement.

ANN   [*in a low musical voice*]   Mamma—

MRS WHITEFIELD   [*hastily*]   Now, Ann, I do beg you not to put it on me. I have no opinion on the subject; and if I had, it would probably not be attended to. I am quite content with whatever you three think best.

[*Tanner turns his head and looks fixedly at Ramsden, who angrily refuses to receive this mute communication.*]

ANN   [*resuming in the same gentle voice, ignoring her mother's bad taste*]   Mamma knows that she is not strong enough to bear the whole responsibility for me and Rhoda without some help and advice. Rhoda must have a guardian; and though I am older, I do not think any young unmarried woman should be left quite to her own guidance. I hope you agree with me, Granny?

TANNER   [*starting*]   Granny! Do you intend to call your guardians Granny?

ANN   Dont be foolish, Jack. Mr Ramsden has always been Grandpapa Roebuck to me: I am Granny's Annie; and he is Annie's Granny. I christened him so when I first learned to speak.

RAMSDEN   [*sarcastically*]   I hope you are satisfied, Mr Tanner. Go on, Annie: I quite agree with you.

ANN   Well, if I am to have a guardian, can I set aside anybody whom my dear father appointed for me?

RAMSDEN   [*biting his lip*]   You approve of your father's choice, then?

ANN   It is not for me to approve or disapprove. I accept it. My father loved me and knew best what was good for me.

RAMSDEN   Of course I understand your feeling, Annie. It is what I should have expected of you; and it does you credit. But it does not settle the question so completely as you think. Let me put a case to you. Suppose you were to discover that I had been guilty of some disgraceful action—that I was not the man your poor dear father took me for! Would you still consider it right that I should be Rhoda's guardian?

ANN   I cant imagine you doing anything disgraceful, Granny.

TANNER   [*to Ramsden*]   You havnt done anything of the sort, have you?

RAMSDEN   [*indignantly*]   No, sir.

MRS WHITEFIELD   [*placidly*]   Well, then, why suppose it?

ANN   You see, Granny, Mamma would not like me to suppose it.

RAMSDEN   [*much perplexed*]   You are both so full of natural and affectionate feeling in these family matters that it is very hard to put the situation fairly before you.

TANNER   Besides, my friend, you are not putting the situation fairly before them.

RAMSDEN   [*sulkily*]   Put it yourself, then.

TANNER   I will. Ann: Ramsden thinks I am not fit to be your guardian; and I quite agree with him. He considers that if your father had read my book, he wouldnt have appointed me. That book is the disgraceful action he has been talking about. He thinks it's your duty for Rhoda's sake to ask him to act alone and to make me withdraw. Say the word; and I will.

ANN   But I havnt read your book, Jack.

TANNER   [*diving at the waste-paper basket and fishing the book out for her*]   Then read it at once and decide.

RAMSDEN   [*vehemently*]   If I am to be your guardian, I positively forbid you to read that book, Annie. [*He smites the table with his fist and rises.*]

Man and Superman

ANN Of course not if you dont wish it. [*She puts the book on the table.*]

TANNER If one guardian is to forbid you to read the other guardian's book, how are we to settle it? Suppose I order you to read it! What about your duty to me?

ANN [*gently*] I am sure you would never purposely force me into a painful dilemma, Jack.

RAMSDEN [*irritably*] Yes, yes, Annie: this is all very well, and, as I said, quite natural and becoming. But you must make a choice one way or the other. We are as much in a dilemma as you.

ANN I feel that I am too young, too inexperienced, to decide. My father's wishes are sacred to me.

MRS WHITEFIELD If you two men wont carry them out I must say it is rather hard that you should put the responsibility on Ann. It seems to me that people are always putting things on other people in this world.

RAMSDEN I am sorry you take it in that way.

ANN [*touchingly*] Do you refuse to accept me as your ward, Granny?

RAMSDEN No: I never said that. I greatly object to act with Mr Tanner: thats all.

MRS WHITEFIELD Why? Whats the matter with poor Jack?

TANNER My views are too advanced for him.

RAMSDEN [*indignantly*] They are not. I deny it.

ANN Of course not. What nonsense! Nobody is more advanced than Granny. I am sure it is Jack himself who has made all the difficulty. Come, Jack! be kind to me in my sorrow. You dont refuse to accept me as your ward, do you?

TANNER [*gloomily*] No. I let myself in for it; so I suppose I must face it. [*He turns away to the bookcase, and stands there, moodily studying the titles of the volumes.*]

ANN [*rising and expanding with subdued but gushing delight*] Then we are all agreed; and my dear father's will is to be carried out. You dont know what a joy that is to me and to my mother! [*She goes to Ramsden and presses both his hands, saying*] And I shall have my dear Granny to help and advise me. [*She casts a glance at Tanner over her shoulder.*] And Jack the Giant Killer. [*She goes past her mother to Octavius.*] And Jack's inseparable friend Ricky-

ticky-tavy. [*He blushes and looks inexpressibly foolish.*]

MRS WHITEFIELD [*rising and shaking her widow's weeds straight*] Now that you are Ann's guardian, Mr Ramsden, I wish you would speak to her about her habit of giving people nicknames. They cant be expected to like it. [*She moves towards the door.*]

ANN How can you say such a thing, Mamma! [*Glowing with affectionate remorse*] Oh, I wonder can you be right! Have I been inconsiderate? [*She turns to Octavius, who is sitting astride his chair with his elbows on the back of it. Putting her hand on his forehead she turns his face up suddenly.*] Do you want to be treated like a grown-up man? Must I call you Mr Robinson in future?

OCTAVIUS [*earnestly*] Oh please call me Ricky-ticky-tavy. "Mr Robinson" would hurt me cruelly. [*She laughs and pats his cheek with her finger; then comes back to Ramsden.*]

ANN You know I'm beginning to think that Granny is rather a piece of impertinence. But I never dreamt of its hurting you.

RAMSDEN [*breezily, as he pats her affectionately on the back*] My dear Annie, nonsense. I insist on Granny. I wont answer to any other name than Annie's Granny.

ANN [*gratefully*] You all spoil me, except Jack.

TANNER [*over his shoulder, from the bookcase*] I think you ought to call me Mr Tanner.

ANN [*gently*] No you dont, Jack. Thats like the things you say on purpose to shock people: those who know you pay no attention to them. But, if you like, I'll call you after your famous ancestor Don Juan.

RAMSDEN Don Juan!

ANN [*innocently*] Oh, is there any harm in it? I didnt know. Then I certainly wont call you that. May I call you Jack until I can think of something else?

TANNER Oh, for Heaven's sake dont try to invent anything worse. I capitulate. I consent to Jack. I embrace Jack. Here endeth my first and last attempt to assert my authority.

ANN You see, Mamma, they all really like to have pet names.

MRS WHITEFIELD Well, I think you might at least drop them until we are out of mourning.

486   BERNARD SHAW

ANN [*reproachfully, stricken to the soul*] Oh, how could you remind me, Mother? [*She hastily leaves the room to conceal her emotion.*]

MRS WHITEFIELD Of course. My fault as usual! [*She follows Ann.*]

TANNER [*coming from the bookcase*] Ramsden: we're beaten—smashed—nonentitized, like her mother.

RAMSDEN Stuff, sir. [*He follows Mrs Whitefield out of the room.*]

TANNER [*left alone with Octavius, stares whimsically at him*] Tavy: do you want to count for something in the world?

OCTAVIUS I want to count for something as a poet: I want to write a great play.

TANNER With Ann as the heroine?

OCTAVIUS Yes: I confess it.

TANNER Take care, Tavy. The play with Ann as the heroine is all right; but if youre not very careful, by Heaven she'll marry you.

OCTAVIUS [*sighing*] No such luck, Jack!

TANNER Why, man, your head is in the lioness's mouth: you are half swallowed already—in three bites—Bite One, Ricky; Bite Two, Ticky; Bite Three, Tavy; and down you go.

OCTAVIUS She is the same to everybody, Jack: you know her ways.

TANNER Yes: she breaks everybody's back with the stroke of her paw; but the question is, which of us will she eat? My own opinion is that she means to eat you.

OCTAVIUS [*rising, pettishly*] It's horrible to talk like that about her when she is upstairs crying for her father. But I do so want her to eat me that I can bear your brutalities because they give me hope.

TANNER Tavy: thats the devilish side of a woman's fascination: she makes you will your own destruction.

OCTAVIUS But it's not destruction: it's fulfilment.

TANNER Yes, of her purpose; and that purpose is neither her happiness nor yours, but Nature's. Vitality in a woman is a blind fury of creation. She sacrifices herself to it: do you think she will hesitate to sacrifice you?

OCTAVIUS Why, it is just because she is self-sacrificing that she will not sacrifice those she loves.

TANNER That is the profoundest of mistakes, Tavy. It is the self-sacrificing women that sacrifice others most recklessly. Because they are unselfish, they are kind in little things. Because they have a purpose which is not their own purpose, but that of the whole universe, a man is nothing to them but an instrument of that purpose.

OCTAVIUS Dont be ungenerous, Jack. They take the tenderest care of us.

TANNER Yes, as a soldier takes care of his rifle or a musician of his violin. But do they allow us any purpose of freedom of our own? Will they lend us to one another? Can the strongest man escape from them when once he is appropriated? They tremble when we are in danger, and weep when we die; but the tears are not for us, but for a father wasted, a son's breeding thrown away. They accuse us of treating them as a mere means to our pleasure; but how can so feeble and transient a folly as a man's selfish pleasure enslave a woman as the whole purpose of Nature embodied in a woman can enslave a man?

OCTAVIUS What matter, if the slavery makes us happy?

TANNER No matter at all if you have no purpose of your own, and are, like most men, a mere breadwinner. But you, Tavy, are an artist: that is, you have a purpose as absorbing and as unscrupulous as a woman's purpose.

OCTAVIUS Not unscrupulous.

TANNER Quite unscrupulous. The true artist will let his wife starve, his children go barefoot, his mother drudge for his living at seventy, sooner than work at anything but his art. To women he is half vivisector, half vampire. He gets into intimate relations with them to study them, to strip the mask of convention from them, to surprise their inmost secrets, knowing that they have the power to rouse his deepest creative energies, to rescue him from his cold reason, to make him see visions and dream dreams, to inspire him, as he calls it. He persuades women that they may do this for their own purpose whilst he really means them to do it for his. He steals the mother's milk and blackens it to make printer's ink to scoff at her and glorify ideal women with. He pretends to spare her the pangs of child-bearing so that he may have for himself the tenderness and fostering that belong of right to her children. Since marriage began, the great artist has been known as a bad husband. But he is worse: he is a child-robber, a blood-sucker, a hypocrite, and a cheat. Perish the race and wither a thousand women if only the sacrifice of them enable him to act Hamlet better, to paint a finer picture, to write a deeper poem, a greater play, a profounder philosophy! For mark you, Tavy, the artist's work is to show us ourselves as we really are. Our minds are nothing but this knowledge of ourselves; and he who adds a jot to such knowledge creates new mind as surely as any woman creates new men. In the rage of that creation he is as ruthless as the woman, as dangerous to her as she to him, and as horribly fascinating. Of all human struggles there is none so treacherous and remorseless as the struggle between the artist man and the mother woman. Which shall use up the other? that is the issue between them. And it is all the deadlier because, in your romanticist cant, they love one another.

OCTAVIUS Even if it were so—and I dont admit it for a moment—it is out of the deadliest struggles that we get the noblest characters.

TANNER Remember that the next time you meet a grizzly bear or a Bengal tiger, Tavy.

OCTAVIUS I meant where there is love, Jack.

TANNER Oh, the tiger will love you. There is no love sincerer than the love of food. I think Ann loves you that way: she patted your cheek as if it were a nicely underdone chop.

OCTAVIUS You know, Jack, I should have to run away from you if I did not make it a fixed rule not to mind anything you say. You come out with perfectly revolting things sometimes.

[*Ramsden returns, followed by Ann. They come in quickly, with their former leisurely air of decorous grief changed to one of genuine concern, and, on Ramsden's part, of worry. He comes between the two men, intending to address Octavius, but pulls himself up abruptly as he sees Tanner.*]

RAMSDEN I hardly expected to find you still here, Mr Tanner.

TANNER Am I in the way? Good morning, fellow guardian. [*He goes towards the door.*]

ANN Stop, Jack. Granny: he must know, sooner or later.

RAMSDEN Octavius: I have a very serious piece of news for you. It is of the most private and delicate nature—of the most painful nature too, I am sorry to say. Do you wish Mr Tanner to be present whilst I explain?

OCTAVIUS [*turning pale*] I have no secrets from Jack.

RAMSDEN Before you decide that finally, let me say that the news concerns your sister, and that it is terrible news.

OCTAVIUS Violet! What has happened? Is she—dead?

RAMSDEN I am not sure that it is not even worse than that.

OCTAVIUS Is she badly hurt? Has there been an accident?

RAMSDEN No: nothing of that sort.

TANNER Ann: will you have the common humanity to tell us what the matter is?

ANN [*half whispering*] I cant. Violet has done something dreadful. We shall have to get her away somewhere. [*She flutters to the writing table and sits in Ramsden's chair, leaving the three men to fight it out between them.*]

OCTAVIUS [*enlightened*] Is that what you meant, Mr Ramsden?

RAMSDEN Yes. [*Octavius sinks upon a chair, crushed.*] I am afraid there is no doubt that Violet did not really go to Eastbourne three weeks ago when we thought she was with the Parry Whitefields. And she called on a strange doctor yesterday with a wedding ring on her finger. Mrs Parry Whitefield met her there by chance; and so the whole thing came out.

OCTAVIUS [*rising with his fists clenched*] Who is the scoundrel?

ANN She wont tell us.

OCTAVIUS [*collapsing into the chair again*] What a frightful thing!

TANNER [*with angry sarcasm*] Dreadful. Appalling. Worse than death, as Ramsden says. [*He comes to Octavius.*] What would you not give, Tavy, to turn it into a railway accident, with all her bones broken, or something equally respectable and deserving of sympathy?

OCTAVIUS Dont be brutal, Jack.

TANNER Brutal! Good Heavens, man, what are you crying for? Here is a woman we all supposed to be making bad water-color sketches, practising Grieg and Brahms, gadding about to concerts and parties, wasting her life and her money. We suddenly learn that she has turned from these sillinesses to the fulfilment of her highest purpose and greatest function—to increase, multiply, and replenish the earth. And instead of admiring her courage and rejoicing in her instinct; instead of crowning the completed womanhood and raising the triumphal strain of "Unto us a child is born: unto us a son is given," here you are—you who have been as merry as grigs in your mourning for the dead —all pulling long faces and looking as ashamed and disgraced as if the girl had committed the vilest of crimes.

RAMSDEN [*roaring with rage*] I will not have these abominations uttered in my house. [*He smites the writing table with his fist.*]

TANNER Look here: if you insult me again I'll take you at your word and leave your house. Ann: where is Violet now?

ANN Why? Are you going to her?

TANNER Of course I am going to her. She wants help; she wants money; she wants respect and congratulation; she wants every chance for her child. She does not seem likely to get it from you: she shall from me. Where is she?

ANN Don't be so headstrong, Jack. She's upstairs.

TANNER What! Under Ramsden's sacred roof! Go and do your miserable duty, Ramsden. Hunt her out into the street. Cleanse your threshold from her contamination. Vindicate the purity of your English home. I'll go for a cab.

ANN [*alarmed*] Oh, Granny, you mustnt do that.

OCTAVIUS [*broken-heartedly, rising*] I'll take her away, Mr Ramsden. She had no right to come to your house.

RAMSDEN [*indignantly*] But I am only too anxious to help her. [*Turning on Tanner*] How dare you, sir, impute such monstrous intentions to me? I protest against it. I am ready to put down my last penny to save her from being driven to run to you for protection.

TANNER [*subsiding*] It's all right, then. He's not going to act up to his principles. It's agreed that we all stand by Violet.

OCTAVIUS But who is the man? He can make reparation by marrying her; and he shall, or he shall answer for it to me.

RAMSDEN He shall, Octavius. There you speak like a man.

TANNER Then you dont think him a scoundrel, after all?

OCTAVIUS Not a scoundrel! He is a heartless scoundrel.

RAMSDEN A damned scoundrel. I beg your pardon, Annie; but I can say no less.

TANNER So we are to marry your sister to a damned scoundrel by way of reforming her character? On my soul, I think you are mad.

ANN Dont be absurd, Jack. Of course you are quite right, Tavy; but we dont know who he is: Violet wont tell us.

TANNER What on earth does it matter who he is? He's done his part; and Violet must do the rest.

RAMSDEN [*beside himself*] Stuff! lunacy! There is a rascal in our midst, a libertine, a villain worse than a murderer; and we are not to learn who he is! In our ignorance we are to shake him by the hand; to introduce him into our homes; to trust our daughters with him; to—to—

ANN [*coaxingly*] There, Granny, dont talk so loud. It's most shocking: we must all admit that; but if Violet wont tell us, what can we do? Nothing. Simply nothing.

RAMSDEN Humph! I'm not so sure of that. If any man has paid Violet any special attention, we can easily find that out. If there is any man of notoriously loose principles among us—

TANNER Ahem!

RAMSDEN [*raising his voice*] Yes, sir, I repeat, if there is any man of notoriously loose principles among us—

TANNER Or any man notoriously lacking in self-control.

RAMSDEN [*aghast*] Do you dare to suggest that *I* am capable of such an act?

TANNER My dear Ramsden, this is an act of of which every man is capable. That is what comes of getting at cross purposes with Nature. The suspicion you have just flung at me clings to us all. It's a sort of mud that sticks to the judge's ermine or the cardinal's robe as fast as to the rags of the tramp. Come, Tavy! dont look so bewildered: it might have been me: it might have been Ramsden; just as it might have been anybody. If it had, what could we do but lie and protest—as Ramsden is going to protest.

RAMSDEN [*choking*] I—I—I—

TANNER Guilt itself could not stammer more confusedly. And yet you know perfectly well he's innocent, Tavy.

RAMSDEN [*exhausted*] I am glad you admit that, sir. I admit, myself, that there is an element of truth in what you say, grossly as you may distort it to gratify your malicious humor. I hope, Octavius, no suspicion of me is possible in your mind.

OCTAVIUS Of you! No, not for a moment.

TANNER [*drily*] I think he suspects me just a little.

OCTAVIUS Jack: you couldnt—you wouldnt—

TANNER Why not?

OCTAVIUS [*appalled*] Why not!

TANNER Oh, well, I'll tell you why not. First, you would feel bound to quarrel with me. Second, Violet doesnt like me. Third, if I had the honor of being the father of Violet's child, I should boast of it instead of denying it. So be easy: our friendship is not in danger.

OCTAVIUS I should have put away the suspicion with horror if only you would think and feel naturally about it. I beg your pardon.

TANNER My pardon! Nonsense! And now lets sit down and have a family council. [*He sits down. The rest follow his example, more or less under protest.*] Violet is going to do the State a service; consequently she must be packed abroad like a criminal until it's over. Whats happening upstairs?

ANN Violet is in the housekeeper's room—by herself, of course.

TANNER Why not in the drawing room?

ANN Dont be absurd, Jack. Miss Ramsden is in the drawing room with my mother, considering what to do.

TANNER Oh! the housekeeper's room is the penitentiary, I suppose; and the prisoner is waiting to be brought before her judges. The old cats!

ANN Oh, Jack!

RAMSDEN You are at present a guest beneath the roof of one of the old cats, sir. My sister is the mistress of this house.

TANNER She would put me in the housekeeper's room, too, if she dared, Ramsden. However, I withdraw cats. Cats would have more sense. Ann: as your guardian, I order you to go to Violet at once and be particularly kind to her.

ANN I have seen her, Jack. And I am sorry to say I am afraid she is going to be rather obstinate about going abroad. I think Tavy ought to speak to her about it.

OCTAVIUS How can I speak to her about such a thing? [*He breaks down.*]

ANN Dont break down, Ricky. Try to bear it for all our sakes.

RAMSDEN Life is not all plays and poems, Octavius. Come! Face it like a man.

TANNER [*chafing again*] Poor dear brother! Poor dear friends of the family! Poor dear Tabbies and Grimalkins! Poor dear everybody except the woman who is going to risk her life to create another life! Tavy: dont you be a selfish ass. Away with you and talk to Violet; and bring her down here if she cares to come. [*Octavius rises.*] Tell her we'll stand by her.

RAMSDEN [*rising*] No, sir—

TANNER [*rising also and interrupting him*] Oh, we understand: it's against your conscience; but still youll do it.

OCTAVIUS I assure you all, on my word, I never meant to be selfish. It's so hard to know what to do when one wishes earnestly to do right.

TANNER My dear Tavy, your pious English habit of regarding the world as a moral gymnasium built expressly to strengthen your character in, occasionally leads you to think about your own confounded principles when you should be thinking about other people's necessities. The need of the present hour is a happy mother and a healthy baby. Bend your energies on that; and you will see your way clearly enough.

[*Octavius, much perplexed, goes out.*]

RAMSDEN [*facing Tanner impressively*] And Morality, sir? What is to become of that?

TANNER Meaning a weeping Magdalen and an

innocent child branded with her shame. Not in our circle, thank you. Morality can go to its father the devil.

RAMSDEN I thought so, sir. Morality sent to the devil to please our libertines, male and female. That is to be the future of England, is it?

TANNER Oh, England will survive your disapproval. Meanwhile, I understand that you agree with me as to the practical course we are to take?

RAMSDEN Not in your spirit, sir. Not for your reasons.

TANNER You can explain that if anybody calls you to account, here or hereafter. [*He turns away and plants himself in front of Mr Herbert Spencer, at whom he stares gloomily*.]

ANN [*rising and coming to Ramsden*] Granny: hadnt you better go up to the drawing room and tell them what we intend to do?

RAMSDEN [*looking pointedly at Tanner*] I hardly like to leave you alone with this gentleman. Will you not come with me?

ANN Miss Ramsden would not like to speak about it before me, Granny. I ought not to be present.

RAMSDEN You are right: I should have thought of that. You are a good girl, Annie.

[*He pats her on the shoulder. She looks up at him with beaming eyes; and he goes out, much moved. Having disposed of him, she looks at Tanner. His back being turned to her, she gives a moment's attention to her personal appearance, then softly goes to him and speaks almost into his ear.*]

ANN Jack, [*he turns with a start*] are you glad that you are my guardian? You dont mind being made responsible for me, I hope.

TANNER The latest addition to your collection of scapegoats, eh?

ANN Oh, that stupid old joke of yours about me! Do please drop it. Why do you say things that you know must pain me? I do my best to please you, Jack: I suppose I may tell you so now that you are my guardian. You will make me so unhappy if you refuse to be friends with me.

TANNER [*studying her as gloomily as he studied the bust*] You need not go begging for my regard. How unreal our moral judgments are!

You seem to me to have absolutely no conscience—only hypocrisy; and you cant see the difference—yet there is a sort of fascination about you. I always attend to you, somehow. I should miss you if I lost you.

ANN [*tranquilly slipping her arm into his and walking about with him*] But isnt that only natural, Jack? We have known each other since we were children. Do you remember—

TANNER [*abruptly breaking loose*] Stop! I remember everything.

ANN Oh, I daresay we were often very silly; but—

TANNER I wont have it, Ann. I am no more that schoolboy now than I am the dotard of ninety I shall grow into if I live long enough. It is over: let me forget it.

ANN Wasn't it a happy time? [*She attempts to take his arm again.*]

TANNER Sit down and behave yourself. [*He makes her sit down in the chair next the writing table.*] No doubt it was a happy time for you. You were a good girl and never compromised yourself. And yet the wickedest child that ever was slapped could hardly have had a better time. I can understand the success with which you bullied the other girls: your virtue imposed on them. But tell me this: did you ever know a good boy?

ANN Of course. All boys are foolish sometimes; but Tavy was always a really good boy.

TANNER [*struck by this*] Yes: youre right. For some reason you never tempted Tavy.

ANN Tempted! Jack!

TANNER Yes, my dear Lady Mephistopheles, tempted. You were insatiably curious as to what a boy might be capable of, and diabolically clever at getting through his guard and surprising his inmost secrets.

ANN What nonsense! All because you used to tell me long stories of the wicked things you had done—silly boy's tricks! And you call such things inmost secrets! Boys' secrets are just like men's; and you know what they are!

TANNER [*obstinately*] No, I dont. What are they, pray?

ANN Why, the things they tell everybody, of course.

TANNER Now I swear I told you things I told no

one else. You lured me into a compact by which we were to have no secrets from one another. We were to tell one another everything. I didnt notice that you never told me anything.

ANN You didnt want to talk about me, Jack. You wanted to talk about yourself.

TANNER Ah, true, horribly true. But what a devil of a child you must have been to know that weakness and to play on it for the satisfaction of your own curiosity! I wanted to brag to you, to make myself interesting. And I found myself doing all sorts of mischievous things simply to have something to tell you about. I fought with boys I didnt hate; I lied about things I might just as well have told the truth about; I stole things I didnt want; I kissed little girls I didnt care for. It was all bravado: passionless and therefore unreal.

ANN I never told of you, Jack.

TANNER No; but if you had wanted to stop me you would have told of me. You wanted me to go on.

ANN [*flashing out*] Oh, thats not true: it's not true, Jack. I never wanted you to do those dull, disappointing, brutal, stupid, vulgar things. I always hoped that it would be something really heroic at last. [*Recovering herself*] Excuse me, Jack; but the things you did were never a bit like the things I wanted you to do. They often gave me great uneasiness; but I could not tell of you and get you into trouble. And you were only a boy. I knew you would grow out of them. Perhaps I was wrong.

TANNER [*sardonically*] Do not give way to remorse, Ann. At least nineteen twentieths of the exploits I confessed to you were pure lies. I soon noticed that you didnt like the true stories.

ANN Of course I knew that some of the things couldnt have happened. But—

TANNER You are going to remind me that some of the most disgraceful ones did.

ANN [*fondly, to his great terror*] I dont want to remind you of anything. But I knew the people they happened to, and heard about them.

TANNER Yes; but even the true stories were touched up for telling. A sensitive boy's humiliations may be very good fun for ordinary thickskinned grown-ups; but to the boy himself they are so acute, so ignominious, that he cannot confess them—cannot but deny them passionately. However, perhaps it was as well for me that I romanced a bit; for, on the one occasion when I told you the truth, you threatened to tell of me.

ANN Oh, never. Never once.

TANNER Yes, you did. Do you remember a dark-eyed girl named Rachel Rosetree? [*Ann's brows contract for an instant involuntarily.*] I got up a love affair with her; and we met one night in the garden and walked about very uncomfortably with our arms round one another, and kissed at parting, and were most conscientiously romantic. If that love affair had gone on, it would have bored me to death; but it didnt go on; for the next thing that happened was that Rachel cut me because she found out that I had told you. How did she find it out? From you. You went to her and held the guilty secret over her head, leading her a life of abject terror and humiliation by threatening to tell on her.

ANN And a very good thing for her, too. It was my duty to stop her misconduct; and she is thankful to me for it now.

TANNER Is she?

ANN She ought to be, at all events.

TANNER It was not your duty to stop my misconduct, I suppose.

ANN I did stop it by stopping her.

TANNER Are you sure of that? You stopped my telling you about my adventures; but how do you know that you stopped the adventures?

ANN Do you mean to say that you went on in the same way with other girls?

TANNER No. I had enough of that sort of romantic tomfoolery with Rachel.

ANN [*unconvinced*] Then why did you break off our confidences and become quite strange to me?

TANNER [*enigmatically*] It happened just then that I got something that I wanted to keep all to myself instead of sharing it with you.

ANN I am sure I shouldnt have asked for any of it if you had grudged it.

TANNER It wasnt a box of sweets, Ann. It was

something youd never have let me call my own.

ANN [*incredulously*] What?

TANNER My soul.

ANN Oh, do be sensible, Jack. You know youre talking nonsense.

TANNER The most solemn earnest, Ann. You didnt notice at that time that you were getting a soul too. But you were. It was not for nothing that you suddenly found you had a moral duty to chastise and reform Rachel. Up to that time you had traded pretty extensively in being a good child; but you had never set up a sense of duty to others. Well, I set one up too. Up to that time I had played the boy buccaneer with no more conscience than a fox in a poultry farm. But now I began to have scruples, to feel obligations, to find that veracity and honor were no longer goody-goody expressions in the mouths of grown-up people, but compelling principle in myself.

ANN [*quietly*] Yes, I suppose youre right. You were beginning to be a man, and I to be a woman.

TANNER Are you sure it was not that we were beginning to be something more? What does the beginning of manhood and womanhood mean in most people's mouths? You know: it means the beginning of love. But love began long before that for me. Love played its part in the earliest dreams and follies and romances I can remember—may I say the earliest follies and romances we can remember?—though we did not understand it at the time. No: the change that came to me was the birth in me of moral passion; and I declare that according to my experience moral passion is the only real passion.

ANN All passions ought to be moral, Jack.

TANNER Ought! Do you think that anything is strong enough to impose oughts on a passion except a stronger passion still?

ANN Our moral sense controls passion, Jack. Dont be stupid.

TANNER Our moral sense! And is that not a passion? Is the devil to have all the passions as well as all the good tunes? If it were not a passion—if it were not the mightiest of the passions,

all the other passions would sweep it away like a leaf before a hurricane. It is the birth of that passion that turns a child into a man.

ANN There are other passions, Jack. Very strong ones.

TANNER All the other passions were in me before; but they were idle and aimless—mere childish greediness and cruelties, curiosities and fancies, habits and superstitions, grotesque and ridiculous to the mature intelligence. When they suddenly began to shine like newly lit flames it was by no light of their own, but by the radiance of the dawning moral passion. That passion dignified them, gave them conscience and meaning, found them a mob of appetites and organized them into an army of purposes and principles. My soul was born of that passion.

ANN I noticed that you got more sense. You were a dreadfully destructive boy before that.

TANNER Destructive! Stuff! I was only mischievous.

ANN Oh, Jack, you were very destructive. You ruined all the young fir trees by chopping off their leaders with a wooden sword. You broke all the cucumber frames with your catapult. You set fire to the common: the police arrested Tavy for it because he ran away when he couldnt stop you. You—

TANNER Pooh! Pooh! Pooh! These were battles, bombardments, stratagems to save our scalps from the red Indians. You have no imagination, Ann. I am ten times more destructive now than I was then. The moral passion has taken my destructiveness in hand and directed it to moral ends. I have become a reformer, and, like all reformers, an iconoclast. I no longer break cucumber frames and burn gorse bushes: I shatter creeds and demolish idols.

ANN [*bored*] I am afraid I am too feminine to see any sense in destruction. Destruction can only destroy.

TANNER Yes. That is why it is so useful. Construction cumbers the ground with institutions made by busybodies. Destruction clears it and gives us breathing space and liberty.

ANN It's no use, Jack. No woman will agree with you there.

TANNER Thats because you confuse construction and destruction with creation and murder. Theyre quite different: I adore creation and abhor murder. Yes: I adore it in tree and flower, in bird and beast, even in you. [*A flash of interest and delight suddenly chases the growing perplexity and boredom from her face.*] It was the creative instinct that led you to attach me to you by bonds that have left their mark on me to this day. Yes, Ann: the old childish compact between us was an unconscious love compact—

ANN Jack!

TANNER Oh, dont be alarmed—

ANN I am not alarmed.

TANNER [*whimsically*] Then you ought to be: where are your principles?

ANN Jack: are you serious or are you not?

TANNER Do you mean about the moral passion?

ANN No, no: the other one. [*Confused.*] Oh! you are so silly: one never knows how to take you.

TANNER You must take me quite seriously. I am your guardian; and it is my duty to improve your mind.

ANN The love compact is over, then, is it? I suppose you grew tired of me?

TANNER No; but the moral passion made our childish relations impossible. A jealous sense of my new individuality arose in me—

ANN You hated to be treated as a boy any longer. Poor Jack!

TANNER Yes, because to be treated as a boy was to be taken on the old footing. I had become a new person; and those who knew the old person laughed at me. The only man who behaved sensibly was my tailor: he took my measure anew every time he saw me, whilst all the rest went on with their old measurements and expected them to fit me.

ANN You became frightfully self-conscious.

TANNER When you go to heaven, Ann, you will be frightfully conscious of your wings for the first year or so. When you meet your relatives there, and they persist in treating you as if you were still a mortal, you will not be able to bear them. You will try to get into a circle which has never known you except as an angel.

ANN So it was only your vanity that made you run away from us after all?

TANNER Yes, only my vanity, as you call it.

ANN You need not have kept away from me on that account.

TANNER From you above all others. You fought harder than anybody against my emancipation.

ANN [*earnestly*] Oh, how wrong you are! I would have done anything for you.

TANNER Anything except let me get loose from you. Even then you had acquired by instinct that damnable woman's trick of heaping obligations on a man, of placing yourself so entirely and helplessly at his mercy that at last he dare not take a step without running to you for leave. I know a poor wretch whose one desire in life is to run away from his wife. She prevents him by threatening to throw herself in front of the engine of the train he leaves her in. That is what all women do. If we try to go where you do not want us to go there is no law to prevent us; but when we take the first step your breasts are under our foot as it descends: your bodies are under our wheels as we start. No woman shall ever enslave me in that way.

ANN But, Jack, you cannot get through life without considering other people a little.

TANNER Ay; but what other people? It is this consideration of other people—or rather this cowardly fear of them which we call consideration—that makes us the sentimental slaves we are. To consider you, as you call it, is to substitute your will for my own. How if it be a baser will than mine? Are women taught better than men or worse? Are mobs of voters taught better than statesmen or worse? Worse, of course, in both cases. And then what sort of world are you going to get, with its public men considering its voting mobs, and its private men considering their wives? What does Church and State mean nowadays? The Woman and the Ratepayer.

ANN [*placidly*] I am so glad you understand politics, Jack: it will be most useful to you if you go into parliament. [*He collapses like a pricked bladder.*] But I am sorry you thought my influence a bad one.

TANNER I dont say it was a bad one. But bad or good, I didnt choose to be cut to your measure. And I wont be cut to it.

ANN Nobody wants you to, Jack. I assure you

—really on my word—I dont mind your queer opinions one little bit. You know we have all been brought up to have advanced opinions. Why do you persist in thinking me so narrow minded?

TANNER   Thats the danger of it. I know you dont mind, because youve found out that it doesnt matter. The boa constrictor doesnt mind the opinions of a stag one little bit when once she has got her coils round it.

ANN   [rising in sudden enlightenment]   O-o-o-o-oh! now I understand why you warned Tavy that I am a boa constrictor. Granny told me. [She laughs and throws her boa round his neck.] Doesnt it feel nice and soft, Jack?

TANNER   [in the toils]   You scandalous woman, will you throw away even your hypocrisy?

ANN   I am never hypocritical with you, Jack. Are you angry? [She withdraws the boa and throws it on a chair.] Perhaps I shouldnt have done that.

TANNER   [contemptuously]   Pooh, prudery! Why should you not, if it amuses you?

ANN   [shyly]   Well, because—because I suppose what you really meant by the boa constrictor was this [she puts her arms round his neck].

TANNER   [staring at her]   Magnificent audacity! [She laughs and pats his cheeks.] Now just to think that if I mentioned this episode not a soul would believe me except the people who would cut me for telling, whilst if you accused me of it nobody would believe my denial!

ANN   [taking her arms away with perfect dignity] You are incorrigible, Jack. But you should not jest about our affection for one another. Nobody could possibly misundersand it. You do not misundersand it, I hope.

TANNER   My blood interprets for me, Ann. Poor Ricky Ticky Tavy!

ANN   [looking quickly at him as if this were a new light]   Surely you are not so absurd as to be jealous of Tavy.

TANNER   Jealous! Why should I be? But I dont wonder at your grip on him. I feel the coils tightening round my very self, though you are only playing with me.

ANN   Do you think I have designs on Tavy?

TANNER   I know you have.

ANN   [earnestly]   Take care, Jack. You may make Tavy very unhappy if you mislead him about me.

TANNER   Never fear: he will not escape you.

ANN   I wonder are you really a clever man!

TANNER   Why this sudden misgiving on the subject?

ANN   You seem to understand all the things I dont understand; but you are a perfect baby in the things I do understand.

TANNER   I understand how Tavy feels for you, Ann: you may depend on that, at all events.

ANN   And you think you understand how I feel for Tavy, dont you?

TANNER   I know only too well what is going to happen to poor Tavy.

ANN   I should laugh at you, Jack, if it were not for poor Papa's death. Mind! Tavy will be very unhappy.

TANNER   Yes; but he wont know it, poor devil. He is a thousand times too good for you. Thats why he is going to make the mistake of his life about you.

ANN   I think men make more mistakes by being too clever than by being too good. [She sits down, with a trace of contempt for the whole male sex in the elegant carriage of her shoulders.]

TANNER   Oh, I know you dont care very much about Tavy. But there is always one who kisses and one who only allows the kiss. Tavy will kiss; and you will only turn the cheek. And you will throw him over if anybody better turns up.

ANN   [offended]   You have no right to say such things, Jack. They are not true, and not delicate. If you and Tavy choose to be stupid about me, that is not my fault.

TANNER   [remorsefully]   Forgive my brutalities, Ann. They are levelled at this wicked world, not at you. [She looks up at him, pleased and forgiving. He becomes cautious at once.] All the same, I wish Ramsden would come back. I never feel safe with you: there is a devilish charm—or no: not a charm, a subtle interest. [She laughs.]—Just so: you know it; and you triumph in it. Openly and shamelessly triumph in it!

ANN   What a shocking flirt you are, Jack!

TANNER   A flirt!! I!!!

ANN   Yes, a flirt. You are always abusing and offending people; but you never really mean to let go your hold of them.

TANNER   I will ring the bell. This conversation has already gone further than I intended.

[*Ramsden and Octavius come back with Miss Ramsden, a hard-headed old maiden lady in a plain brown silk gown, with enough rings, chains, and brooches to show that her plainness of dress is a matter of principle, not of poverty. She comes into the room very determinedly: the two men, perplexed and downcast, following her. Ann rises and goes eagerly to meet her. Tanner retreats to the wall between the busts and pretends to study the pictures. Ramsden goes to his table as usual; and Octavius clings to the neighborhood of Tanner.*]

MISS RAMSDEN   [*almost pushing Ann aside as she comes to Mrs Whitefield's chair and plants herself there resolutely*]   I wash my hands of the whole affair.

OCTAVIUS   [*very wretched*]   I know you wish me to take Violet away, Miss Ramsden. I will. [*He turns irresolutely to the door.*]

RAMSDEN   No, no—

MISS RAMSDEN   What is the use of saying no, Roebuck? Octavius knows that I would not turn any truly contrite and repentant woman from your doors. But when a woman is not only wicked, but intends to go on being wicked, she and I part company.

ANN   Oh, Miss Ramsden, what do you mean? What has Violet said?

RAMSDEN   Violet is certainly very obstinate. She wont leave London. I dont understand her.

MISS RAMSDEN   I do. It's as plain as the nose on your face, Roebuck, that she wont go because she doesnt want to be separated from this man, whoever he is.

ANN   Oh, surely, surely! Octavius: did you speak to her?

OCTAVIUS   She wont tell us anything. She wont make any arrangement until she has consulted somebody. It cant be anybody else than the scoundrel who has betrayed her.

TANNER   [*to Octavius*]   Well, let her consult him. He will be glad enough to have her sent abroad. Where is the difficulty?

MISS RAMSDEN   [*taking the answer out of Octa-vius's mouth*]   The difficulty, Mr Jack, is that when I offered to help her I didnt offer to become her accomplice in her wickedness. She either pledges her word never to see that man again, or else she finds some new friends; and the sooner the better.

[*The parlormaid appears at the door. Ann hastily resumes her seat, and looks as unconcerned as possible. Octavius instinctively imitates her.*]

MAID   The cab is at the door, maam.

MISS RAMSDEN   What cab?

MAID   For Miss Robinson.

MISS RAMSDEN   Oh! [*Recovering herself*] All right. [*The maid withdraws.*] She has sent for a cab.

TANNER   *I* wanted to send for that cab half an hour ago.

MISS RAMSDEN   I am glad she understands the position she has placed herself in.

RAMSDEN   I dont like her going away in this fashion, Susan. We had better not do anything harsh.

OCTAVIUS   No: thank you again and again; but Miss Ramsden is quite right. Violet cannot expect to stay.

ANN   Hadnt you better go with her, Tavy?

OCTAVIUS   She wont have me.

MISS RAMSDEN   Of course she wont. She's going straight to that man.

TANNER   As a natural result of her virtuous reception here.

RAMSDEN   [*much troubled*]   There, Susan! You hear! and theres some truth in it. I wish you could reconcile it with your principles to be a little patient with this poor girl. She's very young and theres a time for everything.

MISS RAMSDEN   Oh, she will get all the sympathy she wants from the men. I'm surprised at you, Roebuck.

TANNER   So am I, Ramsden, most favorably.

Violet appears at the door. She is as impenitent and self-possessed a young lady as one would desire to see among the best behaved of her sex. Her small head and tiny resolute mouth and chin; her haughty crispness of speech and trimness of carriage; the ruthless elegance of her equipment, which includes a very smart hat with a dead bird in it, mark a personality which is as formidable as it is exquisitely pretty. She is not a siren, like Ann: admiration comes to her without any compulsion or even interest on her part; besides, there is some fun in Ann, but in this woman none, perhaps no mercy either: if anything restrains her, it is intelligence and pride, not compassion. Her voice might be the voice of a schoolmistress addressing a class of girls who had disgraced themselves as she proceeds with complete composure and some disgust to say what she has come to say.

VIOLET I have only looked in to tell Miss Ramsden that she will find her birthday present to me, the filagree bracelet, in the housekeeper's room.

TANNER Do come in, Violet; and talk to us sensibly.

VIOLET Thank you: I have had quite enough of the family conversation this morning. So has your mother, Ann: she has gone home crying. But at all events, I have found out what some of my pretended friends are worth. Goodbye.

TANNER No, no: one moment. I have something to say which I beg you to hear. [*She looks at him without the slightest curiosity, but waits, apparently as much to finish getting her glove on as to hear what he has to say.*] I am altogether on your side in this matter. I congratulate you, with the sincerest respect, on having the courage to do what you have done. You are entirely in the right; and the family is entirely in the wrong.

[*Sensation. Ann and Miss Ramsden rise and turn towards the two. Violet, more surprised than any of the others, forgets her glove, and comes forward into the middle of the room, both puzzled and displeased. Octavius alone does not move nor raise his head: he is overwhelmed with shame.*]

ANN [*pleading to Tanner to be sensible*] Jack!

MISS RAMSDEN [*outraged*] Well, I must say!

VIOLET [*sharply to Tanner*] Who told you?

TANNER Why, Ramsden and Tavy of course. Why should they not?

VIOLET But they dont know.

TANNER Dont know what?

VIOLET They dont know that I am in the right, I mean.

TANNER Oh, they know it in their hearts, though they think themselves bound to blame you by their silly superstitions about morality and propriety and so forth. But I know, and the whole world really knows, though it dare not say so, that you were right to follow your instinct; that vitality and bravery are the greatest qualities a woman can have, and motherhood her solemn initiation into womanhood; and that the fact of your not being legally married matters not one scrap either to your own worth or to our real regard for you.

VIOLET [*flushing with indignation*] Oh! You think me a wicked woman, like the rest. You think I have not only been vile, but that I share your abominable opinions. Miss Ramsden: I have borne your hard words because I knew you would be sorry for them when you found out the truth. But I wont bear such a horrible insult as to be complimented by Jack on being one of the wretches of whom he approves. I have kept my marriage a secret for my husband's sake. But now I claim my right as a married woman not to be insulted.

OCTAVIUS [*raising his head with inexpressible relief*] You are married!

VIOLET Yes; and I think you might have guessed it. What business had you all to take it for granted that I had no right to wear my wedding ring? Not one of you even asked me: I cannot forget that.

TANNER [*in ruins*] I am utterly crushed. I meant well. I apologize—abjectly apologize.

VIOLET I hope you will be more careful in future about the things you say. Of course one does not take them seriously; but they are very disagreeable, and rather in bad taste, I think.

TANNER [*bowing to the storm*] I have no defence: I shall know better in future than to take any woman's part. We have all disgraced ourselves in your eyes, I am afraid, except Ann. She befriended you. For Ann's sake, forgive us.

VIOLET Yes: Ann has been kind; but then Ann knew.

TANNER [*with a desperate gesture*] Oh!!! Unfathomable deceit! Double crossed!

MISS RAMSDEN [*stiffly*] And who, pray, is the

gentleman who does not acknowledge his wife?

VIOLET [*promptly*] That is my business, Miss Ramsden, and not yours. I have my reasons for keeping my marriage a secret for the present.

RAMSDEN All I can say is that we are extremely sorry, Violet. I am shocked to think of how we have treated you.

OCTAVIUS [*awkwardly*] I beg your pardon, Violet. I can say no more.

MISS RAMSDEN [*still loth to surrender*] Of course what you say puts a very different complexion on the matter. All the same, I owe it to myself—

VIOLET [*cutting her short*] You owe me an apology, Miss Ramsden: thats what you owe both to yourself and to me. If you were a married woman you would not like sitting in the housekeeper's room and being treated like a naughty child by young girls and old ladies without any serious duties and responsibilities.

TANNER Dont hit us when we're down, Violet. We seem to have made fools of ourselves; but really it was you who made fools of us.

VIOLET It was no business of yours, Jack, in any case.

TANNER No business of mine! Why, Ramsden as good as accused me of being the unknown gentleman.

[*Ramsden makes a frantic demonstration; but Violet's cool keen anger extinguishes it.*]

VIOLET You! Oh, how infamous! How abominable! How disgracefully you have all been talking about me! If my husband knew it he would never let me speak to any of you again. [*To Ramsden*] I think you might have spared me that, at least.

RAMSDEN But I assure you I never—at least it is a monstrous perversion of something I said that—

MISS RAMSDEN You neednt apologize, Roebuck. She brought it all on herself. It is for her to apologize for having deceived us.

VIOLET I can make allowances for you, Miss Ramsden: you cannot understand how I feel on this subject, though I should have expected rather better taste from people of greater experience. However, I quite feel that you have placed yourselves in a very painful position; and the most truly considerate thing for me to do is to go at once. Good morning. [*She goes, leaving them staring.*]

MISS RAMSDEN Well, I must say!

RAMSDEN [*plaintively*] I dont think she is quite fair to us.

TANNER You must cower before the wedding ring like the rest of us, Ramsden. The cup of our ignominy is full.

Act Two

On the carriage drive in the park of a country house near Richmond an open touring car has broken down. It stands in front of a clump of trees round which the drive sweeps to the house, which is partly visible through them: indeed Tanner, standing in the drive with his back to us, could get an unobstructed view of the west corner of the house on his left were he not far too much interested in a pair of supine legs in dungaree overalls which protrude from beneath the machine. He is watching them intently with bent back and hands supported on his knees. His leathern overcoat and peaked cap proclaim him one of the dismounted passengers.

LEGS Aha! I got him.

TANNER All right now?

LEGS Aw rawt nah.

Tanner stoops and takes the legs by the ankles, drawing their owner forth like a wheelbarrow, walking on his hands, with a hammer in his mouth. He is a young man in a neat suit of blue serge, clean shaven, dark eyed, square fingered, with short well brushed black hair and rather irregular sceptically turned eyebrows. When he is manipulating the car his movements are swift and sudden, yet attentive and deliberate. With Tanner and Tanner's friends his manner is not in the least deferential, but cool and reticent, keeping them quite effectually at a distance whilst giving them no excuse for complaining of him. Nevertheless he has a vigilant eye on them always, and that, too, rather cynically, like a man who knows the world well from its seamy side. He speaks slowly and with a touch of sarcasm; and as he does not at all affect the gentleman in his speech, it may be inferred that his smart appearance is a mark of respect to himself and his own class, not to that which employs him.

He now gets into the car to stow away his tools and divest himself of his overalls. Tanner takes off his leathern overcoat and pitches it into the car with a sigh of relief, glad to be rid of it. The chauffeur, noting this, tosses his head contemptuously, and surveys his employer sardonically.

CHAUFFEUR Had enough of it, eh?

TANNER I may as well walk to the house and stretch my legs and calm my nerves a little. [*Looking at his watch*] I suppose you know that we have come from Hyde Park Corner to Richmond in twenty-one minutes.

CHAUFFEUR I'd ha done it under fifteen if I'd had a clear road all the way.

TANNER Why do you do it? Is it for love of sport or for the fun of terrifying your unfortunate employer?

CHAUFFEUR What are you afraid of?

TANNER The police, and breaking my neck.

CHAUFFEUR Well, if you like easy going, you can take a bus, you know. It's cheaper. You pay me to save your time and give you the value of what you paid for the car. [*He sits down calmly.*]

TANNER I am the slave of that car and of you too. I dream of the accursed thing at night.

CHAUFFEUR Youll get over that all right. If youre going up to the house, may I ask how long youre going to stay? Because if you mean to put in the whole morning in there talking to the ladies, I'll put the car in the garage and make myself agreeable with a view to lunching here. If not, I'll keep the car on the go about here till you come.

TANNER Better wait here. We shant be long. Theres a young American gentleman, a Mr Malone, who is driving Mr Robinson down in his new American steam car.

CHAUFFEUR [*springing up and coming hastily out of the car to Tanner*] American steam car! Wot! Racin us dahn from London!

TANNER Perhaps theyre here already.

CHAUFFEUR If I'd known it! [*With deep reproach*] Why didnt you tell me, Mr Tanner?

TANNER Because Ive been told that this car is capable of eighty-four miles an hour; and I already know what you are capable of when there is a rival car on the road. No, Henry: there are things it is not good for you to know; and this was one of them. However, cheer up: we are going to have a day after your own heart. The American is to take Mr Robinson and his sister and Miss Whitefield. We are to take Miss Rhoda.

CHAUFFEUR [*consoled, and musing on another matter*] Thats Miss Whitefield's sister, isnt it?

TANNER Yes.

CHAUFFEUR And Miss Whitefield herself is goin in the other car? Not with you?

TANNER Why the devil should she come with me? Mr Robinson will be in the other car. [*The Chauffeur looks at Tanner with cool incredulity, and turns to the car, whistling a popular air softly to himself. Tanner, a little annoyed, is about to pursue the subject, when he hears the footsteps of Octavius on the gravel. Octavius is coming from the house, dressed for motoring, but without his overcoat.*] Weve lost the race, thank Heaven: heres Mr Robinson. Well, Tavy, is the steam car a success?

OCTAVIUS I think so. We came from Hyde Park Corner here in seventeen minutes. [*The Chauffeur, furious, kicks the car with a groan of vexation.*] How long were you?

TANNER Oh, about three quarters of an hour or so.

CHAUFFEUR [*remonstrating*] Now, now, Mr Tanner, come now! We could ha done it easy under fifteen.

TANNER By the way, let me introduce you. Mr Octavius Robinson: Mr Enry Straker.

STRAKER Pleased to meet you, sir. Mr Tanner is gittin at you with is Enry Straker, you know. You call it Henery. But I dont mind, bless you!

TANNER You think it's simply bad taste in me to chaff him, Tavy. But youre wrong. This man takes more trouble to drop his aitches than ever his father did to pick them up. It's a mark of caste to him. I have never met anybody more swollen with the pride of class than Enry is.

STRAKER   Easy, easy! A little moderation, Mr Tanner.

TANNER   A little moderation, Tavy, you observe. You would tell me to draw it mild. But this chap has been educated. Whats more, he knows that we havnt. What was that Board School of yours, Straker?

STRAKER   Sherbrooke Road.

TANNER   Sherbrooke Road! Would any of us say "Rugby," "Harrow," "Eton," in that tone of intellectual snobbery? Sherbrooke Road is a place where boys learn something: Eton is a boy farm where we are sent because we are nuisances at home, and because in after life, whenever a Duke is mentioned, we can claim him as an old school-fellow.

STRAKER   You dont know nothing about it, Mr Tanner. It's not the Board School that does it: it's the Polytechnic.

TANNER   His university, Octavius. Not Oxford, Cambridge, Durham, Dublin, or Glasgow. Not even those Nonconformist holes in Wales. No, Tavy. Regent Street! Chelsea! The Borough!— I dont know half their confounded names: these are his universities, not mere shops for selling class limitations like ours. You despise Oxford, Enry, dont you?

STRAKER   No, I dont. Very nice sort of place, Oxford, I should think, for people that like that sort of place. They teach you to be a gentleman there. In the Polytechnic they teach you to be an engineer or such like. See?

TANNER   Sarcasm, Tavy, sarcasm! Oh, if you could only see into Enry's soul, the depth of his contempt for a gentleman, the arrogance of his pride in being an engineer, would appal you. He positively likes the car to break down because it brings out my gentlemanly helplessness and his workmanlike skill and resource.

STRAKER   Never you mind him, Mr Robinson. He likes to talk. We know him, dont we?

OCTAVIUS   [earnestly]   But theres a great truth at the bottom of what he says. I believe most intensely in the dignity of labor.

STRAKER   [unimpressed]   Thats because you never done any, Mr Robinson. My business is to do away with labor. Youll get more out of me and a machine than you will out of twenty laborers, and not so much to drink either.

TANNER   For Heaven's sake, Tavy, dont start him on political economy. He knows all about it; and we dont. Youre only a poetic Socialist, Tavy: he's a scientific one.

STRAKER   [unperturbed]   Yes. Well, this conversation is very improvin; but Ive got to look after the car; and you two want to talk about your ladies. I know. [He pretends to busy himself about the car, but presently saunters off to indulge in a cigaret.]

TANNER   Thats a very momentous social phenomenon.

OCTAVIUS   What is?

TANNER   Straker is. Here have we literary and cultured persons been for years setting up a cry of the New Woman whenever some unusually old fashioned female came along, and never noticing the advent of the New Man. Straker's the New Man.

OCTAVIUS   I see nothing new about him, except your way of chaffing him. But I dont want to talk about him just now. I want to speak to you about Ann.

TANNER   Straker knew even that. He learnt it at the Polytechnic, probably. Well, what about Ann? Have you proposed to her?

OCTAVIUS [self-reproachfully]   I was brute enough to do so last night.

TANNER   Brute enough! What do you mean?

OCTAVIUS   [dithyrambically]   Jack: we men are all coarse: we never understand how exquisite a woman's sensibilities are. How could I have done such a thing!

TANNER   Done what, you maudlin idiot?

OCTAVIUS   Yes, I am an idiot. Jack: if you had heard her voice! If you had seen her tears! I have lain awake all night thinking of them. If she had reproached me, I could have borne it better.

TANNER   Tears! Thats dangerous. What did she say?

OCTAVIUS   She asked me how she could think of anything now but her dear father. She stifled a sob—[he breaks down].

BERNARD SHAW

TANNER [*patting him on the back*] Bear it like a man, Tavy, even if you feel it like an ass. It's the old game: she's not tired of playing with you yet.

OCTAVIUS [*impatiently*] Oh, dont be a fool, Jack. Do you suppose this eternal shallow cynicism of yours has any real bearing on a nature like hers?

TANNER Hm! Did she say anything else?

OCTAVIUS Yes; and that is why I expose myself and her to your ridicule by telling you what passed.

TANNER [*remorsefully*] No, dear Tavy, not ridicule, on my honor! However, no matter. Go on.

OCTAVIUS Her sense of duty is so devout, so perfect, so—

TANNER Yes: I know. Go on.

OCTAVIUS You see, under this new arrangement, you and Ramsden are her guardians; and she considers that all her duty to her father is now transferred to you. She said she thought I ought to have spoken to you both in the first instance. Of course she is right; but somehow it seems rather absurd that I am to come to you and formally ask to be received as a suitor for your ward's hand.

TANNER I am glad that love has not totally extinguished your sense of humor, Tavy.

OCTAVIUS That answer wont satisfy her.

TANNER My official answer, is obviously: Bless you, my children: may you be happy!

OCTAVIUS I wish you would stop playing the fool about this. If it is not serious to you, it is to me, and to her.

TANNER You know very well that she is as free to choose as you are.

OCTAVIUS She does not think so.

TANNER Oh, doesnt she just! However, say what you want me to do?

OCTAVIUS I want you to tell her sincerely and earnestly what you think about me. I want you to tell her that you can trust her to me—that is, if you feel you can.

TANNER I have no doubt that I can trust her to you. What worries me is the idea of trusting you to her. Have you read Maeterlinck's book about the bee?

OCTAVIUS [*keeping his temper with difficulty*] I am not discussing literature at present.

TANNER Be just a little patient with me. *I* am not discussing literature: the book about the bee is natural history. It's an awful lesson to mankind. You think that you are Ann's suitor; that you are the pursuer and she the pursued; that it is your part to woo, to persuade, to prevail, to overcome. Fool: it is you who are the pursued, the marked down quarry, the destined prey. You need not sit looking longingly at the bait through the wires of the trap: the door is open, and will remain so until it shuts behind you for ever.

OCTAVIUS I wish I could believe that, vilely as you put it.

TANNER Why, man, what other work has she in life but to get a husband? It is a woman's business to get married as soon as possible, and a man's to keep unmarried as long as he can. You have your poems and your tragedies to work at: Ann has nothing.

OCTAVIUS I cannot write without inspiration. And nobody can give me that except Ann.

TANNER Well, hadnt you better get it from her at a safe distance? Petrarch didnt see half as much of Laura, nor Dante of Beatrice, as you see of Ann now; and yet they wrote first-rate poetry—at least so I'm told. They never exposed their idolatry to the test of domestic familiarity; and it lasted them to their graves. Marry Ann; and at the end of a week youll find no more inspiration in her than in a plate of muffins.

OCTAVIUS You think I shall tire of her!

TANNER Not at all: you dont get tired of muffins. But you dont find inspiration in them; and you wont in her when she ceases to be a poet's dream and becomes a solid eleven stone wife. Youll be forced to dream about somebody else; and then there will be a row.

OCTAVIUS This sort of talk is no use, Jack. You dont understand. You have never been in love.

TANNER I! I have never been out of it. Why, I am in love even with Ann. But I am neither the slave of love nor its dupe. Go to the bee, thou poet: consider her ways and be wise. By Heaven, Tavy, if women could do without our work, and we ate their children's bread instead of making it, they would kill us as the spider kills her mate or as the bees kill the drone.

And they would be right if we were good for nothing but love.

OCTAVIUS   Ah, if we were only good enough for Love! There is nothing like Love: there is nothing else but Love: without it the world would be a dream of sordid horror.

TANNER   And this—this is the man who asks me to give him the hand of my ward! Tavy: I believe we were changed in our cradles, and that you are the real descendant of Don Juan.

OCTAVIUS   I beg you not to say anything like that to Ann.

TANNER   Dont be afraid. She has marked you for her own; and nothing will stop her now. You are doomed. [*Straker comes back with a newspaper.*] Here comes the New Man, demoralizing himself with a halfpenny paper as usual.

STRAKER   Now would you believe it, Mr Robinson, when we're out motoring we take in two papers: the *Times* for him, the *Leader* or the *Echo* for me. And do you think I ever see my paper? Not much. He grabs the *Leader* and leaves me to stodge myself with his *Times*.

OCTAVIUS   Are there no winners in the *Times*?

TANNER   Enry dont old with bettin, Tavy. Motor records are his weakness. Whats the latest?

STRAKER   Paris to Biskra at forty miles an hour average, not countin the Mediterranean.

TANNER   How many killed?

STRAKER   Two silly sheep. What does it matter? Sheep dont cost such a lot: they were glad to ave the price without the trouble o sellin em to the butcher. All the same, d'y'see, therell be a clamor agin it presently; and then the French Government'll stop it; an our chance'll be gone, see? Thats what makes me fairly mad: Mr Tanner wont do a good run while he can.

TANNER   Tavy: do you remember my uncle James?

OCTAVIUS   Yes. Why?

TANNER   Uncle James had a first rate cook: he couldnt digest anything except what she cooked. Well, the poor man was shy and hated society. But his cook was proud of her skill, and wanted to serve up dinners to princes and ambassadors. To prevent her from leaving him, that poor old man had to give a big dinner twice a month, and suffer agonies of awkwardness. Now here am I; and here is this chap Enry Straker, the New Man. I loathe travelling; but I rather like Enry. He cares for nothing but tearing along in a leather coat and goggles, with two inches of dust all over him, at sixty miles an hour and the risk of his life and mine. Except, of course, when he is lying on his back in the mud under the machine trying to find out where it has given way. Well, if I dont give him a thousand mile run at least once a fortnight I shall lose him. He will give me the sack and go to some American millionaire; and I shall have to put up with a nice respectful groom-gardener-amateur, who will touch his hat and know his place. I am Enry's slave, just as Uncle James was his cook's slave.

STRAKER   [*exasperated*]   Garn! I wish I had a car that would go as fast as you can talk, Mr Tanner. What I say is that you lose money by a motor car unless you keep it workin. Might as well ave a pram and a nussmaid to wheel you out in it as that car and me if you dont git the last inch out of us both.

TANNER   [*soothingly*]   All right, Henry, all right. We'll go out for half an hour presently.

STRAKER   [*in disgust*]   Arf an ahr! [*He returns to his machine; seats himself in it; and turns up a fresh page of his paper in search of more news.*]

OCTAVIUS   Oh, that reminds me. I have a note for you from Rhoda. [*He gives Tanner a note.*]

TANNER   [*opening it*]   I rather think Rhoda is heading for a row with Ann. As a rule there is only one person an English girl hates more than she hates her eldest sister; and thats her mother. But Rhoda positively prefers her mother to Ann. She—[*indignantly*] oh, I say!

OCTAVIUS   Whats the matter?

TANNER   Rhoda was to have come with me for a ride in the motor car. She says Ann has forbidden her to go out with me.

[*Straker suddenly begins whistling his favourite air with remarkable deliberation. Surprised by this burst of larklike melody, and jarred by a sardonic note in its cheerfulness, they turn and look inquiringly at him. But he is busy with his paper; and nothing comes of their movement.*]

OCTAVIUS   [*recovering himself*]   Does she give any reason?

BERNARD SHAW

TANNER   Reason! An insult is not a reason. Ann forbids her to be alone with me on any occasion. Says I am not a fit person for a young girl to be with. What do you think of your paragon now?

OCTAVIUS   You must remember that she has a very heavy responsibility now that her father is dead. Mrs Whitefield is too weak to control Rhoda.

TANNER   [*staring at him*]   In short, you agree with Ann.

OCTAVIUS   No; but I think I understand her. You must admit that your views are hardly suited for the formation of a young girl's mind and character.

TANNER   I admit nothing of the sort. I admit that the formation of a young lady's mind and character usually consists in telling her lies; but I object to the particular lie that I am in the habit of abusing the confidence of girls.

OCTAVIUS   Ann doesnt say that, Jack.

TANNER   What else does she mean?

STRAKER   [*catching sight of Ann coming from the house*]   Miss Whitefield, gentlemen. [*He dismounts and strolls away down the avenue with the air of a man who knows he is no longer wanted.*]

ANN   [*coming between Octavius and Tanner*]   Good morning, Jack. I have come to tell you that poor Rhoda has got one of her headaches and cannot go out with you today in the car. It is a cruel disappointment to her, poor child!

TANNER   What do you say now, Tavy?

OCTAVIUS   Surely you cannot misunderstand, Jack. Ann is showing you the kindest consideration, even at the cost of deceiving you.

ANN   What do you mean?

TANNER   Would you like to cure Rhoda's headache, Ann?

ANN   Of course.

TANNER   Then tell her what you said just now; and add that you arrived about two minutes after I had received her letter and read it.

ANN   Rhoda has written to you!

TANNER   With full particulars.

OCTAVIUS   Never mind him, Ann. You were right —quite right. Ann was only doing her duty, Jack; and you know it. Doing it in the kindest way, too.

ANN   [*going to Octavius*]   How kind you are, Tavy! How helpful! How well you understand! [*Octavius beams.*]

TANNER   Ay: tighten the coils. You love her, Tavy, dont you?

OCTAVIUS   She knows I do.

ANN   Hush. For shame, Tavy!

TANNER   Oh, I give you leave. I am your guardian; and I commit you to Tavy's care for the next hour. I am off for a turn in the car.

ANN   No, Jack. I must speak to you about Rhoda. Ricky: will you go back to the house and entertain your American friend? He's rather on Mamma's hands so early in the morning. She wants to finish her housekeeping.

OCTAVIUS   I fly, dearest Ann. [*He kisses her hand.*]

ANN   [*tenderly*]   Ricky Ticky Tavy! [*He looks at her with an eloquent blush, and runs off.*]

TANNER   [*bluntly*]   Now look here, Ann. This time youve landed yourself; and if Tavy were not in love with you past all salvation he'd have found out what an incorrigible liar you are.

ANN   You misunderstand, Jack. I didnt dare tell Tavy the truth.

TANNER   No: your daring is generally in the opposite direction. What the devil do you mean by telling Rhoda that I am too vicious to associate with her? How can I ever have any human or decent relations with her again, now that you have poisoned her mind in that abominable way?

ANN   I know you are incapable of behaving badly—

TANNER   Then why did you lie to her?

ANN   I had to.

TANNER   Had to!

ANN   Mother made me.

TANNER   [*his eye flashing*]   Ha! I might have known it. The mother! Always the mother!

ANN   It was that dreadful book of yours. You know how timid mother is. All timid women are conventional: We must be conventional, Jack, or we are so cruelly, so vilely misunderstood. Even you, who are a man, cannot say what you think without being misunderstood and vilified—yes: I admit it: I have had to vilify you. Do you want to have poor Rhoda misunderstood and vilified in the same way? Would it be right for mother to let her expose herself to such treatment before she is old enough to judge for herself?

TANNER In short, the way to avoid misunderstanding is for everybody to lie and slander and insinuate and pretend as hard as they can. That is what obeying your mother comes to.

ANN I love my mother, Jack.

TANNER [*working himself up into a sociological rage*] Is that any reason why you are not to call your soul your own? Oh, I protest against this vile abjection of youth to age! Look at fashionable society as you know it. What does it pretend to be? An exquisite dance of nymphs. What is it? A horrible procession of wretched girls, each in the claws of a cynical, cunning, avaricious, disillusioned, ignorantly experienced, foul-minded old woman whom she calls mother, and whose duty it is to corrupt her mind and sell her to the highest bidder. Why do these unhappy slaves marry anybody, however old and vile, sooner than not marry at all? Because marriage is their only means of escape from these decrepit fiends who hide their selfish ambitions, their jealous hatreds of the young rivals who have supplanted them, under the mask of maternal duty and family affection. Such things are abominable: the voice of nature proclaims for the daughter a father's care and for the son a mother's. The law for father and son and mother and daughter is not the law of love: it is the law of revolution, of emancipation, of final supersession of the old and worn-out by the young and capable. I tell you, the first duty of manhood and womanhood is a Declaration of Independence: the man who pleads his father's authority is no man: the woman who pleads her mother's authority is unfit to bear citizens to a free people.

ANN [*watching him with quiet curiosity*] I suppose you will go in seriously for politics some day, Jack.

TANNER [*heavily let down*] Eh? What? Wh—? [*Collecting his scattered wits*] What has that got to do with what I have been saying?

ANN You talk so well.

TANNER Talk! Talk! It means nothing to you but talk. Well, go back to your mother, and help her to poison Rhoda's imagination as she has poisoned yours. It is the tame elephants who enjoy capturing the wild ones.

ANN I am getting on. Yesterday I was a boa constrictor: today I am an elephant.

TANNER Yes. So pack your trunk and begone: I have no more to say to you.

ANN You are so utterly unreasonable and impracticable. What can I do?

TANNER Do! Break your chains. Go your way according to your own conscience and not according to your mother's. Get your mind clean and vigorous; and learn to enjoy a fast ride in a motor car instead of seeing nothing in it but an excuse for a detestable intrigue. Come with me to Marseilles and across to Algiers and Biskra at sixty miles an hour. Come right down to the Cape if you like. That will be a Declaration of Independence with a vengeance. You can write a book about it afterwards. That will finish your mother and make a woman of you.

ANN [*thoughtfully*] I dont think there would be any harm in that, Jack. You are my guardian: you stand in my father's place, by his own wish. Nobody could say a word against our travelling together. It would be delightful: thank you a thousand times, Jack. I'll come.

TANNER [*aghast*] Youll come!!!

ANN Of course.

TANNER But—[*he stops, utterly appalled; then resumes feebly*] No: look here, Ann: if theres no harm in it theres no point in doing it.

ANN How absurd you are! You dont want to compromise me, do you?

TANNER Yes: thats the whole sense of my proposal.

ANN You are talking the greatest nonsense; and you know it. You would never do anything to hurt me.

TANNER Well, if you dont want to be compromised, dont come.

ANN [*with simple earnestness*] Yes, I will come, Jack, since you wish it. You are my guardian; and I think we ought to see more of one another and come to know one another better. [*Gratefully*] It's very thoughtful and very kind of you, Jack, to offer me this lovely holiday, especially after what I said about Rhoda. You really are good—much better than you think. When do we start?

TANNER But—

The conversation is interrupted by the arrival of Mrs Whitefield from the house. She is accompanied by the American gentleman, and followed by Ramsden and Octavius.

Hector Malone is an Eastern American; but he is not at all ashamed of his nationality. This makes English people of fashion think well of him, as of a young fellow who is manly enough to confess to an obvious disadvantage without any attempt to conceal or extenuate it. They feel that he ought not to be made to suffer for what is clearly not his fault, and make a point of being specially kind to him. His chivalrous manners to women, and his elevated moral sentiments, being both gratuitous and unusual, strike them as perhaps a little unfortunate; and though they find his vein of easy humor rather amusing when it has ceased to puzzle them (as it does at first), they have had to make him understand that he really must not tell anecdotes unless they are strictly personal and scandalous, and also that oratory is an accomplishment which belongs to a cruder stage of civilization than that in which his migration has landed him. On these points Hector is not quite convinced: he still thinks that the British are apt to make merits of their stupidities, and to represent their various incapacities as points of good breeding. English life seems to him to suffer from a lack of edifying rhetoric (which he calls moral tone); English behavior to show a want of respect for womanhood; English pronunciation to fail very vulgarly in tackling such words as "world," "girl," "bird," etc.; English society to be plain spoken to an extent which stretches occasionally to intolerable coarseness; and English intercourse to need enlivening by games and stories and other pastimes; so he does not feel called upon to acquire these defects after taking great pains to cultivate himself in a first rate manner before venturing across the Atlantic. To this culture he finds English people either totally indifferent, as they very commonly are to all culture, or else politely evasive, the truth being that Hector's culture is nothing but a state of saturation with our literary exports of thirty years ago, reimported by him to be unpacked at a moment's notice and hurled at the head of English literature, science, and art at every conversational opportunity. The dismay set up by these sallies encourages him in his belief that he is helping to educate England. When he finds people chattering harmlessly about Anatole France and Nietzsche, he devastates them with Matthew Arnold, "The Autocrat of the Breakfast Table," and even Macaulay; and as he is devoutly religious at bottom, he first leads the unwary, by humorous irreverence, to leave popular theology out of account in discussing moral questions with him, and then scatters them in confusion by demanding whether the carrying out of his ideals of conduct was not the manifest object of God Almighty in creating honest men and pure women. The engaging freshness of his personality and the dumbfoundering staleness of his culture make it extremely difficult to decide whether he is worth knowing; for whilst his company is undeniably pleasant and enlivening, there is intellectually nothing new to be got out of him, especially as he despises politics, and is careful not to talk commercial shop, in which department he is probably much in advance of his English capitalist friends. He gets on best with romantic Christians of the amoristic sect: hence the friendship which has sprung up between him and Octavius.

In appearance Hector is a neatly built young man of twenty-four, with a short, smartly trimmed black beard, clear, well shaped eyes, and an ingratiating vivacity of expression. He is, from the fashionable point of view, faultlessly dressed. As he comes along the drive from the house with Mrs Whitefield he is sedulously making himself agreeable and entertaining, and thereby placing on her slender wit a burden it is unable to bear. An Englishman would let her alone, accepting boredom and indifference as their common lot; and the poor lady wants to be either let alone or let prattle about the things that interest her.

Ramsden strolls over to inspect the motor car. Octavius joins Hector.

ANN [*pouncing on her mother joyously*] Oh, Mamma, who do you think! Jack is going to take me to Nice in his motor car. Isn't it lovely? I am the happiest person in London.

TANNER [*desperately*] Mrs Whitefield objects. I am sure she objects. Doesnt she, Ramsden?

RAMSDEN I should think it very likely indeed.

ANN You dont object, do you, Mother?

MRS WHITEFIELD *I* object! Why should I? I think it will do you good, Ann. [*Trotting over to Tanner*] I meant to ask you to take Rhoda out for a run occasionally: she is too much in the house; but it will do when you come back.

TANNER Abyss beneath abyss of perfidy!

ANN [*hastily, to distract attention from this outburst*] Oh, I forgot: you have not met Mr Malone. Mr Tanner, my guardian: Mr Hector Malone.

HECTOR Pleased to meet you, Mr Tanner. I should like to suggest an extension of the travelling party to Nice, if I may.

ANN Oh, we're all coming. Thats understood, isnt it?

HECTOR I also am the mawdest possessor of a motor car. If Miss Rawbnsn will allow me the privilege of taking her, my car is at her service.

OCTAVIUS Violet!

[*General constraint.*]

ANN [*subduedly*] Come, Mother: we must leave them to talk over the arrangements. I must see to my travelling kit.

[*Mrs Whitefield looks bewildered; but Ann draws her discreetly away; and they disappear round the corner towards the house.*]

HECTOR I think I may go so far as to say that I can depend on Miss Rawbnsn's consent.

[*Continued embarrassment.*]

OCTAVIUS I'm afraid we must leave Violet behind. There are circumstances which make it impossible for her to come on such an expedition.

HECTOR [*amused and not at all convinced*] Too American, eh? Must the young lady have a chaperone?

OCTAVIUS It's not that, Malone—at least not altogether.

HECTOR Indeed! May I ask what other objection applies?

TANNER [*impatiently*] Oh, tell him, tell him. We shall never be able to keep the secret unless everybody knows what it is. Mr Malone: if you go to Nice with Violet, you go with another man's wife. She is married.

HECTOR [*thunderstruck*] You dont tell me so!

TANNER We do. In confidence.

RAMSDEN [*with an air of importance, lest Malone should suspect a misalliance*] Her marriage has not yet been made known: she desires that it shall not be mentioned for the present.

HECTOR I shall respect the lady's wishes. Would it be indiscreet to ask who her husband is, in case I should have an opportunity of cawnsulting him about this trip?

TANNER We dont know who he is.

HECTOR [*retiring into his shell in a very marked manner*] In that case, I have no more to say. [*They become more embarrassed than ever.*]

OCTAVIUS You must think this very strange.

HECTOR A little singular. Pardn mee for saying so.

RAMSDEN [*half apologetic, half huffy*] The young lady was married secretly; and her husband has forbidden her, it seems, to declare his name. It is only right to tell you, since you are interested in Miss—er—in Violet.

OCTAVIUS [*sympathetically*] I hope this is not a disappointment to you.

HECTOR [*softened, coming out of his shell again*] Well: it is a blow. I can hardly understand how a man can leave his wife in such a position. Surely it's not custoMary. It's not manly. It's not considerate.

OCTAVIUS We feel that, as you may imagine, pretty deeply.

RAMSDEN [*testily*] It is some young fool who has not enough experience to know what mystifications of this kind lead to.

HECTOR [*with strong symptoms of moral repugnance*] I hope so. A man need be very young and pretty foolish too to be excused for such conduct. You take a very lenient view, Mr Ramsden. Too lenient to my mind. Surely marriage should ennoble a man.

TANNER [*sardonically*] Ha!

HECTOR Am I to gather from that cachination

506

that you dont agree with me, Mr Tanner?

TANNER [*drily*] Get married and try. You may find it delightful for a while: you certainly wont find it ennobling. The greatest common measure of a man and a woman is not necessarily greater than the man's single measure.

HECTOR Well, we think in America that a woman's morl number is higher than a man's, and that the purer nature of a woman lifts a man right out of himself, and makes him better than he was.

OCTAVIUS [*with conviction*] So it does.

TANNER No wonder American women prefer to live in Europe! It's more comfortable than standing all their lives on an altar to be worshipped. Anyhow, Violet's husband has not been ennobled. So whats to be done?

HECTOR [*shaking his head*] I cant dismiss that man's cawnduct as lightly as you do, Mr Tanner. However, I'll say no more. Whoever he is, he's Miss Rawbnsn's husband; and I should be glad for her sake to think better of him.

OCTAVIUS [*touched; for he divines a secret sorrow*] I'm very sorry, Malone. Very sorry.

HECTOR [*gratefully*] Youre a good fellow, Rawbnsn. Thank you.

TANNER Talk about something else. Violet's coming from the house.

HECTOR I should esteem it a very great favor, gentlemen, if you would take the opportunity to let me have a few words with the lady alone. I shall have to cry off this trip; and it's rather a dullicate—

RAMSDEN [*glad to escape*] Say no more. Come, Tanner. Come, Tavy.

[*He strolls away into the park with Octavius and Tanner, past the motor car. Violet comes down the avenue to Hector.*]

VIOLET Are they looking?

HECTOR No.

[*She kisses him.*]

VIOLET Have you been telling lies for my sake?

HECTOR Lying! Lying hardly describes it. I overdo it. I get carried away in an ecstasy of mendacity. Violet: I wish youd let me own up.

VIOLET [*instantly becoming serious and resolute*] No, no, Hector: you promised me not to.

HECTOR I'll keep my prawmis until you release me from it. But I feel mean, lying to those men, and denying my wife.

VIOLET I wish your father were not so unreasonable. Just dastardly.

HECTOR He's not unreasonable. He's right from his point of view. He has a prejudice against the English middle class.

VIOLET It's too ridiculous. You know how I dislike saying such things to you, Hector; but if I were to—oh, well, no matter.

HECTOR I know. If you were to marry the son of an English manufacturer of awffice furniture, your friends would consider it a misalliance. And here's my silly old dad, who is the biggest awffice furniture man in the world, would shew me the door for marrying the most perfect lady in England merely because she has no handle to her name. Of course it's just absurd. But I tell you, Violet, I don't like deceiving him. I feel as if I was stealing his money. Why wont you let me own up?

VIOLET We cant afford it. You can be as romantic as you please about love, Hector, but you mustnt be romantic about money.

HECTOR [*divided between his uxoriousness and his habitual elevation of moral sentiment*] Thats very English. [*Appealing to her impulsively*] Violet: dad's bound to find us out someday.

VIOLET Oh yes, later on of course. But dont lets go over this every time we meet, dear. You promised—

HECTOR All right, all right, I—

VIOLET [*not to be silenced*] It is I and not you who suffer by this concealment; and as to facing a struggle and poverty and all that sort of thing I simply will not do it. It's too silly.

HECTOR You shall not. I'll sort of borrow the money from my dad until I get on my own feet; and then I can own up and pay up at the same time.

VIOLET [*alarmed and indignant*] Do you mean to work? Do you want to spoil our marriage?

HECTOR Well, I dont mean to let marriage spoil my character. Your friend Mr Tanner has got the laugh on me a bit already about that; and—

VIOLET The beast! I hate Jack Tanner.

HECTOR [*magnanimously*] Oh, he's all right: he only needs the love of a good woman to ennoble him. Besides, he's proposed a motoring trip to Nice; and I'm going to take you.

VIOLET How jolly!

HECTOR Yes; but how are we going to manage? You see, theyve warned me off going with you, so to speak. Theyve told me in cawnfidnce that youre married. Thats just the most overwhelming cawnfidnce Ive ever been honored with.

[*Tanner returns with Straker, who goes to his car.*]

TANNER Your car is a great success, Mr Malone. Your engineer is showing it off to Mr Ramsden.

HECTOR [*eagerly—forgetting himself*] Lets come, Vi.

VIOLET [*coldly, warning him with her eyes*] I beg your pardon, Mr Malone: I did not quite catch—

HECTOR [*recollecting himself*] I ask to be allowed the pleasure of showing you my little American steam car, Miss Rawbnsn.

VIOLET I shall be very pleased.

[*They go off together down the avenue.*]

TANNER About this trip, Straker.

STRAKER [*preoccupied with the car*] Yes?

TANNER Miss Whitefield is supposed to be coming with me.

STRAKER So I gather.

TANNER Mr Robinson is to be one of the party.

STRAKER Yes.

TANNER Well, if you can manage so as to be a good deal occupied with me, and leave Mr Robinson a good deal occupied with Miss Whitefield, he will be deeply grateful to you.

STRAKER [*looking round at him*] Evidently.

TANNER "Evidently"! Your grandfather would have simply winked.

STRAKER My grandfather would have touched his at.

TANNER And I should have given your good nice respectful grandfather a sovereign.

STRAKER Five shillins, more likely. [*He leaves the car and approaches Tanner.*] What about the lady's views?

TANNER She is just as willing to be left to Mr Robinson as Mr Robinson is to be left to her. [*Straker looks at his principal with cool scepticism; then turns to the car whistling his favorite air.*] Stop that aggravating noise. What do you mean by it? [*Straker calmly resumes the melody and finishes it. Tanner politely hears it out before he again addresses Straker, this time with elaborate seriousness.*] Enry: I have ever been a warm advocate of the spread of music among the masses; but I object to your obliging the company whenever Miss Whitefield's name is mentioned. You did it this morning, too.

STRAKER [*obstinately*] It's not a bit o use. Mr Robinson may as well give it up first as last.

TANNER Why?

STRAKER Garn! You know why. Course it's not my business; but you neednt start kiddin me about it.

TANNER I am not kidding. I dont know why.

STRAKER [*cheerfully sulky*] Oh, very well. All right. It aint my business.

TANNER [*impressively*] I trust, Enry, that, as between employer and engineer, I shall always know how to keep my proper distance, and not intrude my private affairs on you. Even our business arrangements are subject to the approval of your Trade Union. But dont abuse your advantages. Let me remind you that Voltaire said that what was too silly to be said could be sung.

STRAKER It wasnt Voltaire: it was Bow Mar Shay.

TANNER I stand corrected: Beaumarchais of course. Now you seem to think that what is too delicate to be said can be whistled. Unfortunately your whistling, though melodious, is unintelligible. Come! theres nobody listening: neither my genteel relatives nor the secretary of your confounded Union. As man to man, Enry, why do you think that my friend has no chance with Miss Whitefield?

STRAKER Cause she's arter summun else.

TANNER Bosh! who else?

STRAKER You.

TANNER Me!!!

STRAKER Mean to tell me you didnt know? Oh, come, Mr Tanner!

TANNER [*in fierce earnest*] Are you playing the fool, or do you mean it?

STRAKER [*with a flash of temper*] I'm not playin no fool. [*More coolly*] Why, it's as plain as the nose on your face. If you aint spotted that, you dont know much about these sort of things. [*Serene again*] Ex-cuse me, you know, Mr Tanner; but you asked me as man to man; and

I told you as man to man.

TANNER [*wildly appealing to the heavens*] Then I—I am the bee, the spider, the marked down victim, the destined prey.

STRAKER I dunno about the bee and the spider. But the marked down victim, thats what you are and no mistake; and a jolly good job for you, too, I should say.

TANNER [*momentously*] Henry Straker: the golden moment of your life has arrived.

STRAKER What d'y'mean?

TANNER That record to Biskra.

STRAKER [*eagerly*] Yes?

TANNER Break it.

STRAKER [*rising to the height of his destiny*] D'y'mean it?

TANNER I do.

STRAKER When?

TANNER Now. Is that machine ready to start?

STRAKER [*quailing*] But you cant—

TANNER [*cutting him short by getting into the car*] Off we go. First to the bank for money; then to my rooms for my kit; then to your rooms for your kit; then break the record from London to Dover or Folkestone; then across the Channel and away like mad to Marseilles, Gibraltar, Genoa, any port from which we can sail to a Mahometan country where men are protected from women.

STRAKER Garn! youre kiddin.

TANNER [*resolutely*] Stay behind then. If you wont come I'll do it alone. [*He starts the motor.*]

STRAKER [*running after him*] Here! Mister! Arf a mo! Steady on! [*He scrambles in as the car plunges forward.*]

Act Three

Evening in the Sierra Nevada. Rolling slopes of brown with olive trees instead of apple trees in the cultivated patches, and occasional prickly pears instead of gorse and bracken in the wilds. Higher up, tall stone peaks and precipices, all handsome and distinguished. No wild nature here: rather a most aristocratic mountain landscape made by a fastidious artist-creator. No vulgar profusion of vegetation: even a touch of aridity in the frequent patches of stones: Spanish magnificence and Spanish economy everywhere.

Not very far north of a spot at which the high road over one of the passes crosses a tunnel on the railway from Malaga to Granada is one of the mountain amphitheatres of the Sierra. Looking at it from the wide end of the horse-shoe, one sees, a little to the right, in the face of the cliff, a romantic cave which is really an abandoned quarry, and towards the left, a little hill, commanding a view of the road, which skirts the amphitheatre on the left, maintaining its higher level on embankments and an occasional stone arch. On the hill, watching the road, is a man who is either a Spaniard or a Scotchman. Probably a Spaniard, since he wears the dress of a Spanish goatherd and seems at home in the

Sierra Nevada, but very like a Scotchman for all that. In the hollow, on the slope leading to the quarry-cave, are about a dozen men who, as they recline at their ease round a heap of smouldering white ashes of dead leaf and brushwood, have an air of being conscious of themselves as picturesque scoundrels honoring the Sierra by using it as an effective pictorial background. As a matter of artistic fact they are not picturesque; and the mountains tolerate them as lions tolerate lice. An English policeman or Poor Law Guardian would recognize them as a selected band of tramps and ablebodied paupers.

This description of them is not wholly contemptuous. Whoever has intelligently observed the tramp, or visited the ablebodied ward of a workhouse, will admit that our social failures are not all drunkards and weaklings. Some of them are men who do not fit the class they were born into. Precisely the same qualities that make the educated gentleman an artist may make an uneducated manual laborer an ablebodied pauper. There are men who fall helplessly into the workhouse because they are good for nothing; but there are also men who are there because they are strongminded enough to disregard the social convention (obviously not a disinterested one on the part of the ratepayer) which bids a man live by heavy and badly paid drudgery when he has the alternative of walking into the workhouse, announcing himself as a destitute person, and legally compelling the Guardians to feed, clothe, and house him better than he could feed, clothe, and house himself without great exertion. When a man who is born a poet refuses a stool in a stockbroker's office and starves in a garret, sponging on a poor landlady or on his friends and relatives sooner than work against his grain; or when a lady, because she is a lady, will face any extremity of parasitic dependence rather than take a situation as cook or parlormaid, we make large allowances for them. To such allowances the ablebodied pauper and his nomadic variant the tramp are equally entitled.

Further, the imaginative man, if his life is to be tolerable to him, must have leisure to tell himself stories and a position which lends itself to imaginative decoration. The ranks of unskilled labor offer no such positions. We misuse our laborers horribly; and when a man refuses to be misused, we have no right to say that he is refusing honest work. Let us be frank in this matter before we go on with our play; so that we may enjoy it without hypocrisy. If we were reasoning, far-sighted people, four fifths of us would go straight to the Guardians for relief, and knock the whole social system to pieces with most beneficial reconstructive results. The reason we do not do this is because we work like bees or ants, by instinct or habit, not reasoning about the matter at all. Therefore when a man comes along who can and does reason, and who, applying the Kantian test to his conduct, can truly say to us, "If everybody did as I do, the world would be compelled to reform itself industrially, and abolish slavery and squalor, which exist only because everybody does as you do," let us honor that man and seriously consider the advisability of following his example. Such a man is the ablebodied, ableminded pauper. Were he a gentleman doing his best to get a pension or a sinecure instead of sweeping a crossing, nobody would blame him for deciding that so long as the alternative lies between living mainly at the expense of the community and allowing the community to live mainly at his, it would be folly to accept what is to him personally the greater of the two evils.

We may therefore contemplate the tramps of the Sierra without prejudice, admitting cheerfully that our objects—briefly, to be gentlemen of fortune—are much the same as theirs, and the difference in our position and methods merely accidental. One or two of them, perhaps, it would be wiser to kill without malice in a friendly and frank manner; for there are bipeds, just as there are quadrupeds, who are too dangerous to be left unchained and unmuzzled; and these cannot fairly expect to have other men's lives wasted in the work of watching them. But as society has not the courage to kill them and, when it catches them, simply wreaks on them some superstitious expiatory rites of torture and degradation and then lets them loose with heightened qualifications for mischief, it is just as well that they are at large in the Sierra, and in the hands of a chief who looks as if he might possibly, on provocation, order them to be shot.

This chief, seated in the centre of the group on a squared block of stone from the quarry, is a tall strong man, with a striking cockatoo nose, glossy black hair, pointed beard, upturned moustache, and a Mephistophelean affectation which is fairly imposing, perhaps because the scenery admits of a larger swagger than Piccadilly, perhaps because of a certain sentimentality in the man which gives him that touch of grace which alone can excuse deliberate picturesqueness. His eyes and mouth are by no means rascally; he has a fine voice and a ready wit; and whether he is really the strongest man in the party or not, he looks it. He is certainly the best fed, the best dressed, and the best trained. The fact that he speaks English is not unexpected, in spite of the Spanish landscape; for, with the exception of one man who might be guessed as a bullfighter ruined by drink and one unmistakeable Frenchman, they are all cockney or American; therefore, in a land of cloaks and sombreros, they mostly wear seedy overcoats, woollen mufflers, hard hemispherical hats, and dirty brown gloves. Only a very few dress after their leader, whose

BERNARD SHAW

broad sombrero with a cock's feather in the band and voluminous cloak descending to his high boots are as un-English as possible. None of them are armed; and the ungloved ones keep their hands in their pockets because it is their national belief that it must be dangerously cold in the open air with the night coming on. (It is as warm an evening as any reasonable man could desire.)

Except the bullfighting inebriate there is only one person in the company who looks more than, say, thirty-three. He is a small man with reddish whiskers, weak eyes, and the anxious look of a small tradesman in difficulties. He wears the only tall hat visible: it shines in the sunset with the sticky glow of some sixpenny patent hat reviver, often applied and constantly tending to produce a worse state of the original surface than the ruin it was applied to remedy. He has a collar and cuffs of celluloid; and his brown Chesterfield overcoat, with velvet collar is still presentable. He is preeminently the respectable man of the party, and is certainly over forty, possibly over fifty. He is the corner man on the leader's right, opposite three men in scarlet ties on his left. One of these three is the Frenchman. Of the remaining two, who are both English, one is argumentative, solemn, and obstinate; the other rowdy and mischievous.

The chief, with a magnificent fling of the end of his cloak across his left shoulder, rises to address them. The applause which greets him shows that he is a favorite orator.

CHIEF Friends and fellow brigands. I have a proposal to make to this meeting. We have now spent three evenings in discussing the question "Have Anarchists or Social-Democrats the most personal courage?" We have gone into the principles of Anarchism and Social-Democracy at great length. The cause of Anarchy has been ably represented by our one Anarchist, who doesnt know what Anarchism means—
[Laughter]

ANARCHIST [rising] A point of order, Mendoza—

MENDOZA [forcibly] No, by thunder: your last point of order took half an hour. Besides, Anarchists dont believe in order.

ANARCHIST [mild, polite but persistent: he is, in fact, the respectable looking elderly man in the celluloid collar and cuffs] That is a vulgar error. I can prove—

MENDOZA Order, order.

THE OTHERS [shouting] Order, order. Sit down. Chair! Shut up.
[The Anarchist is suppressed.]

MENDOZA On the other hand we have three Social-Democrats among us. They are not on speaking terms; and they have put before us three distinct and incompatible views of Social-Democracy.
[The three men in scarlet ties protest in unison.]

FIRST SOCIAL-DEMOCRAT Mr Chairman, I protest. A personal explanation.

SECOND SOCIAL-DEMOCRAT It's a lie. I never said so. Be fair, Mendoza.

THIRD SOCIAL-DEMOCRAT Je demande la parole. C'est absolument faux. C'est faux! faux!! faux!!! Assas-s-s-s-sin!!!!!!

MENDOZA Order, order.

THE OTHERS Order, order, order! Chair!
[The Social-Democrats are suppressed.]

MENDOZA Now, we tolerate all opinions here. But after all, comrades, the vast majority of us are neither Anarchists nor Socialists, but gentlemen and Christians.

THE MAJORITY [shouting assent] Hear, hear! So we are. Right.

ROWDY SOCIAL-DEMOCRAT [smarting under suppression] You ain't no Christian. Youre a Sheeny, you are.

MENDOZA [with crushing magnanimity] My friend: I am an exception to all rules. It is true that I have the honor to be a Jew; and when the Zionists need a leader to reassemble our race on its historic soil of Palestine, Mendoza will not be the last to volunteer. [Sympathetic applause—"Hear, hear," etc.] But I am not a slave to any superstition. I have swallowed all the formulas, even that of Socialism; though, in a sense, once a Socialist, always a Socialist.

SOCIAL-DEMOCRATS Hear, hear!

MENDOZA But I am well aware that the ordinary man—even the ordinary brigand, who can scarcely be called an ordinary man ["Hear, hear!"]—is not a philosopher. Common sense is good enough for him; and in our business affairs common sense is good enough for me. Well, what is our business here in the Sierra Nevada, chosen by the Moors as the fairest spot in Spain? Is it to discuss abstruse questions of political economy? No: it is to hold up motor cars and secure a more equitable distribution of wealth.

SULKY SOCIAL-DEMOCRAT All made by labor, mind you.

MENDOZA [*urbanely*] Undoubtedly. All made by labor, and on its way to be squandered by wealthy vagabonds in the dens of vice that disfigure the sunny shores of the Mediterranean. We intercept that wealth. We restore it to circulation among the class that produced it and that chiefly needs it: the working class. We do this at the risk of our lives and liberties, by the exercise of the virtues of courage, endurance, foresight, and abstinence—especially abstinence. I myself have eaten nothing but prickly pears and broiled rabbit for three days.

SULKY SOCIAL-DEMOCRAT [*stubbornly*] No more aint we.

MENDOZA [*indignantly*] Have I taken more than my share?

SULKY SOCIAL-DEMOCRAT [*unmoved*] Why should you?

ANARCHIST Why should he not? To each according to his needs: from each according to his means.

FRENCHMAN [*shaking his fist at the Anarchist*] Fumiste!

MENDOZA [*diplomatically*] I agree with both of you.

GENUINELY ENGLISH BRIGANDS Hear, hear! Bravo Mendoza!

MENDOZA What I say is, let us treat one another as gentlemen, and strive to excel in personal courage only when we take the field.

ROWDY SOCIAL-DEMOCRAT [*derisively*] Shikespear. [*A whistle comes from the goatherd on the hill. He springs up and points excitedly forward along the road to the north.*]

GOATHERD Automobile! Automobile! [*He rushes down the hill and joins the rest, who all scramble to their feet.*]

MENDOZA [*in ringing tones*] To arms! Who has the gun?

SULKY SOCIAL-DEMOCRAT [*handing a rifle to Mendoza*] Here.

MENDOZA Have the nails been strewn in the road?

ROWDY SOCIAL-DEMOCRAT Two ahnces of em.

MENDOZA Good! [*To the Frenchman*] With me, Duval. If the nails fail, puncture their tires with a bullet.

[*He gives the rifle to Duval, who follows him up the hill. Mendoza produces an opera glass. The others hurry across to the road and disappear to the north.*]

MENDOZA [*on the hill, using his glass*] Two only, a capitalist and his chauffeur. They look English.

DUVAL Angliche! Aoh yess. Cochons! [*Handling the rifle*] Faut tirer, n'est-ce-pas?

MENDOZA No: the nails have gone home. Their tire is down: they stop.

DUVAL [*shouting to the others*] Fondez sur eux, nom de Dieu!

MENDOZA [*rebuking his excitement*] Du calme, Duval: keep your hair on. They take it quietly. Let us descend and receive them.

[*Mendoza descends, passing behind the fire and coming forward, whilst Tanner and Straker, in their motoring goggles, leather coats, and caps, are led in from the road by the brigands.*]

TANNER Is this the gentleman you describe as your boss? Does he speak English?

ROWDY SOCIAL-DEMOCRAT Course e daz. Y' downt suppowz we Hinglishmen luts ahrselves be bossed by a bloomin Spenniard, do you?

MENDOZA [*with dignity*] Allow me to introduce myself: Mendoza, President of the League of the Sierra! [*Posing loftily*] I am a brigand: I live by robbing the rich.

TANNER [*promptly*] I am a gentleman: I live by robbing the poor. Shake hands.

ENGLISH SOCIAL-DEMOCRATS Hear, hear!

[*General laughter and good humour. Tanner and Mendoza shake hands. The Brigands drop into their former places.*]

STRAKER Ere! where do I come in?

TANNER [*introducing*] My friend and chauffeur.

SULKY SOCIAL-DEMOCRAT [*suspiciously*] Well, which is he?—friend or show-foor? It makes all the difference, you know.

MENDOZA [*explaining*] We should expect ransom for a friend. A professional chauffeur is free of the mountains. He even takes a trifling percentage of his principal's ransom if he will honor us by accepting it.

STRAKER I see. Just to encourage me to come this way again. Well, I'll think about it.

DUVAL [*impulsively rushing across to Straker*] Mon frère! [*He embraces him rapturously and kisses him on both cheek.*]

STRAKER [*disgusted*] Ere, git aht: dont be silly. Who are you, pray?

DUVAL Duval: Social-Democrat.

STRAKER Oh, youre a Social-Democrat, are you?

ANARCHIST He means that he has sold out to the parliamentary humbugs and the bourgeoisie. Compromise! That is his faith.

DUVAL [*furiously*] I understand what he say. He say Bourgeois. He say Compromise. Jamais de la vie! Misérable menteur—

STRAKER See here, Captain Mendoza, ah mach o this sort o thing do you put up with here? Are we avin a pleasure trip in the mountains, or are we at a Socialist meetin?

THE MAJORITY Hear, hear! Shut up. Chuck it. Sit down.

[*The Social-Democrats and the Anarchist are hustled into the background. Straker, after superintending this proceeding with satisfaction, places himself on Mendoza's left, Tanner being on his right.*]

MENDOZA Can we offer you anything? Broiled rabbit and prickly pears—

TANNER Thank you: we have dined.

MENDOZA [*to his followers*] Gentlemen: business is over for the day. Go as you please until morning.

[*The Brigands disperse into groups lazily. Some go into the cave. Others sit down or lie down to sleep in the open. A few produce a pack of cards and move off towards the road; for it is now starlight, and they know that motor cars have lamps which can be turned to account for lighting a card party.*]

STRAKER [*calling after them*] Dont none of you go fooling with that car, d'ye hear?

MENDOZA No fear, Monsieur le Chauffeur. The first one we captured cured us of that.

STRAKER [*interested*] What did it do?

MENDOZA It carried three brave comrades of ours, who did not know how to stop it, into Granada, and capsized them opposite the police station. Since then we never touch one without sending for the chauffeur. Shall we chat at our ease?

TANNER By all means.

[*Tanner, Mendoza, and Straker sit down on the turf by the fire. Mendoza delicately waives his presidential dignity, of which the right to sit on the squared stone block is the appanage, by sitting on the ground like his guests, and using the stone only as a support for his back.*]

MENDOZA It is the custom in Spain always to put off business until tomorrow. In fact, you have arrived out of office hours. However, if you would prefer to settle the question of ransom at once, I am at your service.

TANNER Tomorrow will do for me. I am rich enough to pay anything in reason.

MENDOZA [*respectfully, much struck by this admission*] You are a remarkable man, sir. Our guests usually describe themselves as miserably poor.

TANNER Pooh! Miserably poor people dont own motor cars.

MENDOZA Precisely what we say to them.

TANNER Treat us well: we shall not prove ungrateful.

STRAKER No prickly pears and broiled rabbits, you know. Dont tell me you cant do us a bit better than that if you like.

MENDOZA Wine, kids, milk, cheese, and bread can be procured for ready money.

STRAKER [*graciously*] Now youre talkin.

TANNER Are you all Socialists here, may I ask?

MENDOZA [*repudiating this humiliating misconception*] Oh no, no, no: nothing of the kind, I assure you. We naturally have modern views as to the injustice of the existing distribution of wealth: otherwise we should lose our self-respect. But nothing that you could take exception to, except two or three faddists.

TANNER I had no intention of suggesting anything discreditable. In fact, I am a bit of a Socialist myself.

STRAKER [*drily*] Most rich men are, I notice.

MENDOZA Quite so. It has reached us, I admit. It is in the air of the century.

STRAKER Socialism must be lookin up a bit if

your chaps are taking to it.

MENDOZA That is true, sir. A movement which is confined to philosophers and honest men can never exercise any real political influence: there are too few of them. Until a movement shows itself capable of spreading among brigands, it can never hope for a political majority.

TANNER But are your brigands any less honest than ordinary citizens?

MENDOZA Sir: I will be frank with you. Brigandage is abnormal. Abnormal professions attract two classes: those who are not good enough for ordinary bourgeois life and those who are too good for it. We are dregs and scum, sir: the dregs very filthy, the scum very superior.

STRAKER Take care! Some o the dregs'll hear you.

MENDOZA It does not matter: each brigand thinks himself scum, and likes to hear the others called dregs.

TANNER Come! you are a wit. [*Mendoza inclines his head, flattered.*] May one ask you a blunt question?

MENDOZA As blunt as you please.

TANNER How does it pay a man of your talent to shepherd such a flock as this on broiled rabbit and prickly pears? I have seen men less gifted, and I'll swear less honest, supping at the Savoy on foie gras and champagne.

MENDOZA Pooh! they have all had their turn at the broiled rabbit, just as I shall have my turn at the Savoy. Indeed, I have had a turn there already—as waiter.

TANNER A waiter! You astonish me!

MENDOZA [*reflectively*] Yes: I, Mendoza of the Sierra, was a waiter. Hence, perhaps, my cosmopolitanism. [*With sudden intensity*] Shall I tell you the story of my life?

STRAKER [*apprehensively*] If it aint too long, old chap—

TANNER [*interrupting him*] Tsh-sh: you are a Philistine, Henry: you have no romance in you. [*To Mendoza*] You interest me extremely, President. Never mind Henry: he can go to sleep.

MENDOZA The woman I loved—

STRAKER Oh, this is a love story, is it? Right you are. Go on: I was only afraid you were going to talk about yourself.

MENDOZA Myself! I have thrown myself away for her sake: that is why I am here. No matter: I count the world well lost for her. She had, I pledge you my word, the most magnificent head of hair I ever saw. She had humour; she had intellect; she could cook to perfection; and her highly strung temperament made her uncertain, incalculable, variable, capricious, cruel, in a word, enchanting.

STRAKER A six shillin novel sort o woman, all but the cookin. Er name was Lady Gladys Plantagenet, wasnt it?

MENDOZA No, sir: she was not an earl's daughter. Photography, reproduced by the half-tone process, has made me familiar with the appearance of the daughters of the English peerage; and I can honestly say that I would have sold the lot, faces, dowries, clothes, titles, and all, for a smile from this woman. Yet she was a woman of the people, a worker: otherwise—let me reciprocate your bluntness—I should have scorned her.

TANNER Very properly. And did she respond to your love?

MENDOZA Should I be here if she did? She objected to marry a Jew.

TANNER On religious grounds?

MENDOZA No: she was a freethinker. She said that every Jew considers in his heart that English people are dirty in their habits.

TANNER [*surprised*] Dirty!

MENDOZA It showed her extraordinary knowledge of the world; for it is undoubtedly true. Our elaborate sanitary code makes us unduly contemptuous of the Gentile.

TANNER Did you ever hear that, Henry?

STRAKER Ive heard my sister say so. She was cook in a Jewish family once.

MENDOZA I could not deny it; neither could I eradicate the impression it made on her mind. I could have got round any other objection; but no woman can stand a suspicion of indelicacy as to her person. My entreaties were in vain: she always retorted that she wasn't good enough for me, and recommended me to marry an accursed barmaid named Rebecca Lazarus, whom I loathed. I talked of suicide: she offered me a packet of beetle poison to do it with. I hinted at murder: she went into hysterics! and as I am a living man I went to America so that she might sleep without dreaming that I was stealing upstairs to cut her throat. In America I went out west and fell in with a man who was wanted by the police for holding up trains. It was he who had the idea of holding up motor cars in the South of Europe: a welcome idea to a desperate and disappointed man. He gave me some valuable introductions to capitalists of the right sort. I formed a syndicate; and the present enterprise is the result. I became leader, as the Jew always becomes leader, by his brains and imagination. But with all my pride of race I would give everything I possess to be an Englishman. I am like a boy: I cut her name on the trees and her initials on the sod. When I am alone I lie down and tear my wretched hair and cry Louisa—

STRAKER [*startled*] Louisa!

MENDOZA It is her name—Louisa—Louisa Straker—

TANNER Straker!

STRAKER [*scrambling up on his knees most indignantly*] Look here: Louisa Straker is my sister, see? Wot do you mean by gassin about her like this? Wotshe go to do with you?

MENDOZA A dramatic coincidence! You are Enry her favorite brother!

STRAKER Oo are you callin Enry? What call have you to take a liberty with my name or with hers? For two pins I'd punch your fat edd, so I would.

MENDOZA [*with grandiose calm*] If I let you do it, will you promise to brag of it afterwards to her? She will be reminded of her Mendoza: that is all I desire.

TANNER This is genuine devotion, Henry. You should respect it.

STRAKER [*fiercely*] Funk, more likely.

MENDOZA [*springing to his feet*] Funk! Young man: I come of a famous family of fighters; and as your sister well knows, you would have as much chance against me as a perambulator against your motor car.

STRAKER [*secretly daunted, but rising from his knees with an air of reckless pugnacity*] I aint afraid of you. With your Louisa! Louisa! Miss Straker is good enough for you, I should think.

MENDOZA I wish you could persuade her to think so.

STRAKER [*exasperated*] Here—

TANNER [*rising quickly and interposing*] Oh come, Henry: even if you could fight the President you cant fight the whole League of the Sierra. Sit down again and be friendly. A cat may look at a king; and even a President of brigands may look at your sister. All this family pride is really very old fashioned.

STRAKER [*subdued, but grumbling*] Let him look at her. But wot does he mean by making out that she ever looked at im? [*Reluctantly resuming his couch on the turf*] Ear him talk, one ud think she was keepin company with him. [*He turns his back on them and composes himself to sleep.*]

MENDOZA [*to Tanner, becoming more confidential as he finds himself virtually alone with a sympathetic listener in the still starlight of the mountains; for all the rest are asleep by this time*] It was just so with her, sir. Her intellect reached forward into the twentieth century: her social prejudices and family affections reached back into the dark ages. Ah, sir, how the words of Shakespear seem to fit every crisis in our emotions!

I loved Louisa: forty thousand brothers
Could not with all their quantity of love
Make up my sum.

And so on. I forget the rest. Call it madness if you will—infatuation. I am an able man, a strong man: in ten years I should have owned a first-class hotel. I met her; and—you see!— I am a brigand, an outcast. Even Shakespear cannot do justice to what I feel for Louisa. Let me read you some lines that I have written about her myself. However slight their literary merit may be, they express what I feel better than any casual words can. [*He produces a packet of hotel bills scrawled with manuscript, and kneels at the fire to decipher them, poking it with a stick to make it glow.*]

TANNER [*slapping him rudely on the shoulder*] Put them in the fire, President.

MENDOZA [*startled*] Eh?

TANNER You are sacrificing your career to a monomania.

MENDOZA I know it.

TANNER No you dont. No man would commit such a crime against himself if he really knew what he was doing. How can you look round at these august hills, look up at this divine sky, taste this finely tempered air, and then talk like a literary hack on a second floor in Bloomsbury?

MENDOZA [*shaking his head*] The Sierra is no better than Bloomsbury when once the novelty has worn off. Besides, these mountains make you dream of women—of women with magnificent hair.

TANNER Of Louisa, in short. They will not make me dream of women, my friend: I am heart-whole.

MENDOZA Do not boast until morning, sir. This is a strange country for dreams.

TANNER Well, we shall see. Goodnight.

[*He lies down and composes himself to sleep. Mendoza, with a sigh, follows his example; and for a few moments there is peace in the Sierra.*]

MENDOZA [*sits up suddenly and says pleadingly to Tanner*] Just allow me to read a few lines before you go to sleep. I should really like your opinion of them.

TANNER [*drowsily*] Go on. I am listening.

MENDOZA I saw thee first in Whitsun week
Louisa, Louisa—

TANNER [*rousing himself*] My dear President, Louisa is a very pretty name; but it really doesnt rhyme well to Whitsun week.

MENDOZA Of course not. Louisa is not the rhyme, but the refrain.

TANNER [*subsiding*] Ah, the refrain. I beg your pardon. Go on.

MENDOZA Perhaps you do not care for that one: I think you will like this better.

[*He recites, in rich soft tones, and in slow time*]

Louisa, I love thee.
I love thee, Louisa.
Louisa, Louisa, Louisa, I love thee.
One name and one phrase make my music, Louisa.
Louisa, Louisa, Louisa, I love thee.
Mendoza thy lover,
Thy lover, Mendoza,
Mendoza adoringly lives for Louisa.

Theres nothing but that in the world for Mendoza.
Louisa, Louisa, Mendoza adores thee.

[*Affected.*] There is no merit in producing beautiful lines upon such a name. Louisa is an exquisite name, is it not?
[*Tanner, all but asleep, responds with a faint groan.*]

MENDOZA O wert thou, Louisa,
The wife of Mendoza,
Mendoza's Louisa, Louisa Mendoza,
How blest were the life of Louisa's Mendoza!
How painless his longing of love for Louisa!

That is real poetry—from the heart—from the heart of hearts. Dont you think it will move her? [*No answer. Resignedly*] Asleep, as usual. Doggrel to all the world: heavenly music to me! Idiot that I am to wear my heart on my sleeve! [*He composes himself to sleep, murmuring*] Louisa, I love thee; I love thee, Louisa; Louisa, Louisa, Louisa, I—

Straker snores; rolls over on his side; and relapses into sleep. Stillness settles on the Sierra; and the darkness deepens. The fire has again buried itself in white ash and ceased to glow. The peaks shew unfathomably dark against the starry firmament; but now the stars dim and vanish; and the sky seems to steal away out of the universe. Instead of the Sierra there is nothing: omnipresent nothing. No sky, no peaks, no light, no sound, no time nor space, utter void. Then somewhere the beginning of a pallor, and with it a faint throbbing buzz as of a ghostly violoncello palpitating on the same note endlessly. A couple of ghostly violins presently take advantage of this bass

and therewith the pallor reveals a man in the void, an incorporated but visible man, seated, absurdly enough, on nothing. For a moment he

BERNARD SHAW

raises his head as the music passes him by. Then, with a heavy sigh, he droops in utter dejection; and the violins, discouraged, retrace their melody in despair and at last give it up, extinguished by wailings from uncanny wind instruments, thus:—

It is all very odd. One recognizes the Mozartian strain; and on this hint, and by the aid of certain sparkles of violet light in the pallor, the man's costume explains itself as that of a Spanish nobleman of the fifteenth or sixteenth century. Don Juan, of course; but where? Why? How? Besides, in the brief lifting of his face, now hidden by his hat brim, there was a curious suggestion of Tanner. A more critical, fastidious, handsome face, paler and colder, without Tanner's impetuous credulity and enthusiasm, and without a touch of his modern plutocratic vulgarity, but still a resemblance, even an identity. The name too: Don Juan Tenorio, John Tanner. Where on earth—or elsewhere—have we got to from the twentieth century and the Sierra?

Another pallor in the void, this time not violet, but a disagreeable smoky yellow. With it, the whisper of a ghostly clarionet turning this tune into infinite sadness:

The yellowish pallor moves: there is an old crone wandering in the void, bent and toothless; draped, as well as one can guess, in the coarse brown frock of some religious order. She wanders and wanders in her slow hopeless way, much as a wasp flies in its rapid busy way, until she blunders against the thing she seeks: companionship. With a sob of relief the poor old creature clutches at the presence of the man and addresses him in her dry unlovely voice, which can still express pride and resolution as well as suffering.

OLD WOMAN Excuse me; but I am so lonely; and this place is so awful.

DON JUAN A new comer?

OLD WOMAN Yes: I suppose I died this morning. I confessed; I had extreme unction; I was in bed with my family about me and my eyes fixed on the cross. Then it grew dark; and when the light came back it was this light by which I walk seeing nothing. I have wandered for hours in horrible loneliness.

DON JUAN [*sighing*] Ah! you have not yet lost the sense of time. One soon does, in eternity.

OLD WOMAN Where are we?

DON JUAN In hell.

OLD WOMAN [*proudly*] Hell! I in hell! How dare you?

DON JUAN [*unimpressed*] Why not, Señora?

OLD WOMAN You do not know to whom you are speaking. I am a lady, and a faithful daughter of the Church.

DON JUAN I do not doubt it.

OLD WOMAN But how then can I be in hell? Purgatory, perhaps: I have not been perfect: who has? But hell! Oh, you are lying.

DON JUAN Hell, Señora, I assure you; hell at its best: that is, its most solitary—though perhaps you would prefer company.

OLD WOMAN But I have sincerely repented; I have confessed—

DON JUAN How much?

OLD WOMAN More sins than I really committed. I loved confession.

DON JUAN Ah, that is perhaps as bad as confessing too little. At all events, Señora, whether by oversight or intention, you are certainly damned, like myself; and there is nothing for it now but to make the best of it.

OLD WOMAN [*indignantly*] Oh! and I might have been so much wickeder! All my good deeds wasted! It is unjust.

DON JUAN No: you were fully and clearly warned. For your bad deeds, vicarious atonement, mercy without justice. For your good deeds, justice without mercy. We have many good people here.

OLD WOMAN Were you a good man?

DON JUAN I was a murderer.

OLD WOMAN A murderer! Oh, how dare they send me to herd with murderers! I was not as

Man and Superman

bad as that: I was a good woman. There is some mistake: where can I have it set right?

DON JUAN I do not know whether mistakes can be corrected here. Probably they will not admit a mistake even if they have made one.

OLD WOMAN But whom can I ask?

DON JUAN I should ask the Devil, Señora: he understands the ways of this place, which is more than I ever could.

OLD WOMAN The Devil! *I* speak to the Devil!

DON JUAN In hell, Señora, the Devil is the leader of the best society.

OLD WOMAN I tell you, wretch, I know I am not in hell.

DON JUAN How do you know?

OLD WOMAN Because I feel no pain.

DON JUAN Oh, then there is no mistake: you are intentionally damned.

OLD WOMAN Why do you say that?

DON JUAN Because hell, Señora, is a place for the wicked. The wicked are quite comfortable in it: it was made for them. You tell me you feel no pain. I conclude you are one of those for whom hell exists.

OLD WOMAN Do you feel no pain?

DON JUAN I am not one of the wicked, Señora; therefore it bores me, bores me beyond description, beyond belief.

OLD WOMAN Not one of the wicked! You said you were a murderer.

DON JUAN Only a duel. I ran my sword through an old man who was trying to run his through me.

OLD WOMAN If you were a gentleman, that was not a murder.

DON JUAN The old man called it murder, because he was, he said, defending his daughter's honor. By this he means that because I foolishly fell in love with her and told her so, she screamed; and he tried to assassinate me after calling me insulting names.

OLD WOMAN You were like all men. Libertines and murderers all, all, all!

DON JUAN And yet we meet here, dear lady.

OLD WOMAN Listen to me. My father was slain by just such a wretch as you, in just such a duel, for just such a cause. I screamed: it was my duty. My father drew on my assailant: his honor demanded it. He fell: that was the reward of honor. I am here: in hell, you tell me: that is the reward of duty. Is there justice in heaven?

DON JUAN No; but there is justice in hell: heaven is far above such idle human personalities. You will be welcome in hell, Señora. Hell is the home of honor, duty, justice, and the rest of the seven deadly virtues. All the wickedness on earth is done in their name: where else but in hell should they have their reward? Have I not told you that the truly damned are those who are happy in hell?

OLD WOMAN And are you happy here?

DON JUAN [*springing to his feet*] No; and that is the enigma on which I ponder in darkness. Why am I here? I, who repudiated all duty, trampled honor underfoot, and laughed at justice!

OLD WOMAN Oh, what do I care why you are here? Why am *I* here? I, who sacrificed all my inclinations to womanly virtue and propriety!

DON JUAN Patience, lady: you will be perfectly happy and at home here. As saith the poet, "Hell is a city much like Seville."

OLD WOMAN Happy! here! where I am nothing! where I am nobody!

DON JUAN Not at all: you are a lady; and wherever ladies are is hell. Do not be surprised or terrified: you will find everything here that a lady can desire, including devils who will serve you from sheer love of servitude, and magnify your importance for the sake of dignifying their service—the best of servants.

OLD WOMAN My servants will be devils.

DON JUAN Have you ever had servants who were not devils?

OLD WOMAN Never: they were devils, perfect devils, all of them. But that is only a manner of speaking. I thought you meant that my servants here would be real devils.

DON JUAN No more real devils than you will be a real lady. Nothing is real here. That is the horror of damnation.

OLD WOMAN Oh, this is all madness. This is worse than fire and the worm.

DON JUAN For you, perhaps, there are consolations. For instance: how old were you when you changed from time to eternity?

OLD WOMAN Do not ask me how old I was—as if I were a thing of the past. I am seventy-seven.

DON JUAN A ripe age, Señora. But in hell old age is not tolerated. It is too real. Here we worship Love and Beauty. Our souls being entirely damned, we cultivate our hearts. As a lady of seventy-seven, you would not have a single acquaintance in hell.

OLD WOMAN How can I help my age, man?

DON JUAN You forget that you have left your age behind you in the realm of time. You are no more seventy-seven than you are seven or seventeen or twenty-seven.

OLD WOMAN Nonsense!

DON JUAN Consider, Señora: was not this true even when you lived on earth? When you were seventy, were you really older underneath your wrinkles and your grey hairs than when you were thirty?

OLD WOMAN No, younger: at thirty I was a fool. But of what use is it to feel younger and look older?

DON JUAN You see, Señora, the look was only an illusion. Your wrinkles lied, just as the plump smooth skin of many a stupid girl of seventeen, with heavy spirits and decrepit ideas, lies about her age! Well, here we have no bodies: we see each other as bodies only because we learnt to think about one another under that aspect when we were alive; and we still think in that way, knowing no other. But we can appear to one another at what age we choose. You have but to will any of your old looks back, and back they will come.

OLD WOMAN It cannot be true.

DON JUAN Try.

OLD WOMAN *Seventeen!*

DON JUAN *Stop.* Before you decide, I had better tell you that these things are a matter of fashion. Occasionally we have a rage for seventeen; but it does not last long. Just at present the fashionable age is forty—or say thirty-seven; but there are signs of a change. If you were at all good-looking at twenty-seven, I should suggest your trying that, and setting a new fashion.

OLD WOMAN I do not believe a word you are saying. However, twenty-seven be it. [*Whisk!*

the Old Woman becomes a young one, magnificently attired, and so handsome that in the radiance into which her dull yellow halo has suddenly lightened one might almost mistake her for Ann Whitefield.]

DON JUAN Doña Ana de Ulloa!

ANA What? You know me!

DON JUAN And you forget me!

ANA I cannot see your face. [*He raises his hat.*] Don Juan Tenorio! Monster! You who slew my father! Even here you pursue me.

DON JUAN I protest I do not pursue you. [*Going*] Allow me to withdraw.

ANA [*seizing his arm*] You shall not leave me alone in this dreadful place.

DON JUAN Provided my staying be not interpreted as pursuit.

ANA [*releasing him*] You may well wonder how I can endure your presence. My dear, dear father!

DON JUAN Would you like to see him?

ANA My father here!!!

DON JUAN No: he is in heaven.

ANA I knew it. My noble father! He is looking down on us now. What must he feel to see his daughter in this place, and in conversation with his murderer!

DON JUAN By the way, if we should meet him—

ANA How can we meet him? He is in heaven.

DON JUAN He condescends to look in upon us here from time to time. Heaven bores him. So let me warn you that if you meet him he will be mortally offended if you speak of me as his murderer! He maintains that he was a much better swordsman than I, and that if his foot had not slipped he would have killed me. No doubt he is right: I was not a good fencer. I never dispute the point; so we are excellent friends.

ANA It is no dishonor to a soldier to be proud of his skill in arms.

DON JUAN You would rather not meet him, probably.

ANA How dare you say that?

DON JUAN Oh, that is the usual feeling here. You may remember that on earth—though of course we never confessed it—the death of anyone we knew, even those we liked best, was always mingled with a certain satisfaction at being finally done with them.

ANA   Monster! Never, never.

DON JUAN [*placidly*] I see you recognize the feeling. Yes: a funeral was always a festivity in black, especially the funeral of a relative. At all events, family ties are rarely kept up here. Your father is quite accustomed to this: he will not expect any devotion from you.

ANA   Wretch: I wore mourning for him all my life.

DON JUAN Yes: it became you. But a life of mourning is one thing: an eternity of it quite another. Besides, here you are as dead as he. Can anything be more ridiculous than one dead person mourning for another? Do not look shocked, my dear Ana; and do not be alarmed: there is plenty of humbug in hell (indeed there is hardly anything else); but the humbug of death and age and change is dropped because here we are all dead and all eternal. You will pick up our ways soon.

ANA   And will all the men call me their dear Ana?

DON JUAN No. That was a slip of the tongue. I beg your pardon.

ANA [*almost tenderly*] Juan: did you really love me when you behaved so disgracefully to me?

DON JUAN [*impatiently*] Oh, I beg you not to begin talking about love. Here they talk of nothing else but love: its beauty, its holiness, its spirituality, its devil knows what!—Excuse me; but it does so bore me. They dont know what theyre talking about: I do. They think they have achieved the perfection of love because they have no bodies. Sheer imaginative debauchery! Faugh!

ANA   Has even death failed to refine your soul, Juan? Has the terrible judgment of which my father's statue was the minister taught you no reverence?

DON JUAN How is that very flattering statue, by the way? Does it still come to supper with naughty people and cast them into this bottomless pit?

ANA   It has been a great expense to me. The boys in the monastery school would not let it alone: the mischievous ones broke it; and the studious ones wrote their names on it. Three new noses in two years, and fingers without end. I had to leave it to its fate at last; and now I fear it is shockingly mutilated. My poor father!

DON JUAN Listen! [*Two great chords rolling on syncopated waves of sound break forth—D minor and its dominant: a sound of dreadful joy to all musicians.*] Ha! Mozart's statue music. It is your father. You had better disappear until I prepare him. [*She vanishes.*]

From the void comes a living statue of white marble, designed to represent a majestic old man. But he waives his majesty with infinite grace; walks with a feather-like step; and makes every wrinkle in his war worn visage brim over with holiday joyousness. To his sculptor he owes a perfectly trained figure, which he carries erect and trim; and the ends of his moustache curl up, elastic as watchsprings, giving him an air which, but for its Spanish dignity, would be called jaunty. He is on the pleasantest terms with Don Juan. His voice, save for a much more distinguished intonation, is so like the voice of Roebuck Ramsden that it calls attention to the fact that they are not unlike one another in spite of their very different fashions of shaving.

DON JUAN Ah, here you are, my friend. Why dont you learn to sing the splendid music Mozart has written for you?

STATUE Unluckily he has written it for a bass voice. Mine is a counter tenor. Well: have you repented yet?

DON JUAN I have too much consideration for you to repent, Don Gonzalo. If I did, you would have no excuse for coming from heaven to argue with me.

STATUE True. Remain obdurate, my boy. I wish I had killed you, as I should have done but for an accident. Then I should have come here; and you would have had a statue and a reputation for piety to live up to. Any news?

DON JUAN Yes: your daughter is dead.

STATUE [*puzzled*] My daughter? [*Recollecting*] Oh! the one you were taken with. Let me see:

what was her name?

DON JUAN Ana.

STATUE To be sure: Ana. A goodlooking girl, if I recollect aright. Have you warned Whatshisname? Her husband.

DON JUAN My friend Ottavio? No: I have not seen him since Ana arrived.

[*Ana comes indignantly to light.*]

ANA What does this mean? Ottavio here and your friend! And you, father, have forgotten my name. You are indeed turned to stone.

STATUE My dear: I am so much more admired in marble than I ever was in my own person that I have retained the shape the sculptor gave me. He was one of the first men of his day: you must acknowledge that.

ANA Father! Vanity! Personal vanity! From you!

STATUE Ah, you outlived that weakness, my daughter: you must be nearly eighty by this time. I was cut off (by an accident) in my sixty-fourth year, and am considerably your junior in consequence. Besides, my child, in this place, what our libertine friend here would call the farce of parental wisdom is dropped. Regard me, I beg, as a fellow creature, not as a father.

ANA You speak as this villain speaks.

STATUE Juan is a sound thinker, Ana. A bad fencer, but a sound thinker.

ANA [*horror creeping upon her*] I begin to understand. These are devils, mocking me. I had better pray.

STATUE [*consoling her*] No, no, no, my child: do not pray. If you do, you will throw away the main advantage of this place. Written over the gate here are the words "Leave every hope behind, ye who enter." Only think what a relief that is! For what is hope? A form of moral responsibility. Here there is no hope, and consequently no duty, no work, nothing to be gained by praying, nothing to be lost by doing what you like. Hell, in short, is a place where you have nothing to do but amuse yourself. [*Don Juan sighs deeply.*] You sigh, friend Juan; but if you dwelt in heaven, as I do, you would realize your advantages.

DON JUAN You are in good spirits today, Com-

mander. You are positively brilliant. What is the matter?

STATUE I have come to a momentous decision, my boy. But first, where is our friend the Devil? I must consult him in the matter. And Ana would like to make his acquaintance, no doubt.

ANA You are preparing some torment for me.

DON JUAN All that is superstition, Ana. Reassure yourself. Remember: the devil is not so black as he is painted.

STATUE Let us give him a call.

At the wave of the Statue's hand the great chords roll out again; but this time Mozart's music gets grotesquely adulterated with Gounod's. A scarlet halo begins to glow; and into it the Devil rises, very Mephistophelean, and not at all unlike Mendoza, though not so interesting. He looks older; is getting prematurely bald; and, in spite of an effusion of good-nature and friendliness, is peevish and sensitive when his advances are not reciprocated. He does not inspire much confidence in his powers of hard work or endurance, and is, on the whole, a disagreeably self-indulgent looking person; but he is clever and plausible, though perceptibly less well bred than the two other men, and enormously less vital than the woman.

DEVIL [*heartily*] Have I the pleasure of again receiving a visit from the illustrious Commander of Calatrava? [*Coldly*] Don Juan, your servant. [*Politely*] And a strange lady? My respects, Señora.

ANA Are you—

DEVIL [*bowing*] Lucifer, at your service.

ANA I shall go mad.

DEVIL [*gallantly*] Ah, Señora, do not be anxious. You come to us from earth, full of the prejudices and terrors of that priest-ridden place. You have heard me ill spoken of; and yet, believe me, I have hosts of friends there.

ANA Yes: you reign in their hearts.

DEVIL [*shaking his head*] You flatter me, Señora; but you are mistaken. It is true that the world cannot get on without me; but it never gives me credit for that: in its heart it mistrusts and hates me. Its sympathies are all with misery, with poverty, with starvation of the body, and of the heart. I call on it to sympathize with joy, with love, with happiness, with beauty—

DON JUAN [*nauseated*] Excuse me: I am going. You know I cannot stand this.

DEVIL [*angrily*] Yes: I know that you are no friend of mine.

STATUE What harm is he doing you, Juan? It seems to me that he was talking excellent sense when you interrupted him.

DEVIL [*warmly patting the Statue's hand*] Thank you, my friend: thank you. You have always understood me: he has always disparaged and avoided me.

DON JUAN I have treated you with perfect courtesy.

DEVIL Courtesy! What is courtesy? I care nothing for mere courtesy. Give me warmth of heart, true sincerity, the bond of sympathy with love and joy—

DON JUAN You are making me ill.

DEVIL There! [*Appealing to the Statue*] You hear, sir! Oh, by what irony of fate was this cold selfish egotist sent to my kingdom, and you taken to the icy mansions of the sky!

STATUE I can't complain. I was a hypocrite; and it served me right to be sent to heaven.

DEVIL Why, sir, do you not join us, and leave a sphere for which your temperament is too sympathetic, your heart too warm, your capacity for enjoyment too generous?

STATUE I have this day resolved to do so. In future, excellent Son of the Morning, I am yours. I have left heaven for ever.

DEVIL [*again touching the marble hand*] Ah, what an honor! What a triumph for our cause! Thank you, thank you. And now, my friend— I may call you so at last—could you not persuade him to take the place you have left vacant above?

STATUE [*shaking his head*] I cannot conscientiously recommend anybody with whom I am on friendly terms to deliberately make himself dull and uncomfortable.

DEVIL Of course not; but are you sure he would be uncomfortable? Of course you know best: you brought him here originally; and we had the greatest hopes of him. His sentiments were in the best taste of our best people. You re-

member how he sang? [*He begins to sing in a nasal operatic baritone, tremulous from an eternity of misuse in the French manner*]

Vivan le femmine!
Viva il buon vino!

STATUE [*taking up the tune an octave higher in his counter tenor*]

Sostegno e gloria
D'umanità.

DEVIL Precisely. Well, he never sings for us now.

DON JUAN Do you complain of that? Hell is full of musical amateurs: music is the brandy of the damned. May not one lost soul be permitted to abstain?

DEVIL You dare blaspheme against the sublimest of the arts!

DON JUAN [*with cold disgust*] You talk like a hysterical woman fawning on a fiddler.

DEVIL I am not angry. I merely pity you. You have no soul; and you are unconscious of all that you lose. Now you, Señor Commander, are a born musician. How well you sing! Mozart would be delighted if he were still here; but he moped and went to heaven. Curious how these clever men, whom you would have supposed born to be popular here, have turned out social failures, like Don Juan!

DON JUAN I am really very sorry to be a social failure.

DEVIL Not that we dont admire your intellect, you know. We do. But I look at the matter from your own point of view. You dont get on with us. The place doesnt suit you. The truth is, you have—I wont say no heart; for we know that beneath all your affected cynicism you have a warm one—

DON JUAN [*shrinking*] Dont, please dont.

DEVIL [*nettled*] Well, youve no capacity for enjoyment. Will that satisfy you?

DON JUAN It is a somewhat less insufferable form of cant than the other. But if youll allow me, I'll take refuge, as usual, in solitude.

DEVIL Why not take refuge in heaven? Thats the proper place for you. [*To Ana*] Come, Señora! Could you not persuade him for his own good to try change of air?

ANA But can he go to heaven if he wants to?

DEVIL Whats to prevent him?

ANA Can anybody—can *I* go to heaven if I want to?

DEVIL [*rather contemptuously*] Certainly, if your taste lies that way.

ANA But why doesnt everybody go to heaven, then?

STATUE [*chuckling*] *I* can tell you that, my dear. It's because heaven is the most angelically dull place in all creation: thats why.

DEVIL His excellency the Commander puts it with military bluntness; but the strain of living in heaven is intolerable. There is a notion that I was turned out of it; but as a matter of fact nothing could have induced me to stay there. I simply left it and organized this place.

STATUE I dont wonder at it. Nobody could stand an eternity in heaven.

DEVIL Oh, it suits some people. Let us be just, Commander: it is a question of temperament. I dont admire the heavenly temperament: I dont understand it: I dont know that I particularly want to understand it; but it takes all sorts to make a universe. There is no accounting for tastes: there are people who like it. I think Don Juan would like it.

DON JUAN But—pardon my frankness—could you really go back there if you desired to; or are the grapes sour?

DEVIL Back there! I often go back there. Have you never read the book of Job? Have you any canonical authority for assuming that there is any barrier between our circle and the other one?

ANA But surely there is a great gulf fixed.

DEVIL Dear lady: a parable must not be taken literally. The gulf is the difference between the angelic and the diabolic temperament. What more impassable gulf could you have? Think of what you have seen on earth. There is no physical gulf between the philosopher's class room and the bull ring; but the bull fighters do not come to the class room for all that. Have you ever been in the country where I have the largest following? England. There they have great racecourses, and also concert rooms where they play the classical compositions of His Excellency's friend Mozart. Those who go to the racecourses can stay away from them and go to the classical concerts instead if they like: there is no law against it; for Englishmen never will be slaves: they are free to do whatever the Government and public opinion allow them to do. And the classical concert is admitted to be a higher, more cultivated, poetic, intellectual, ennobling place than the racecourse. But do the lovers of racing desert their sport and flock to the concert room? Not they. They would suffer there all the weariness the Commander has suffered in heaven. There is the great gulf of the parable between the two places. A mere physical gulf they could bridge; or at least I could bridge it for them (the earth is full of Devil's Bridges); but the gulf of dislike is impassable and eternal. And that is the only gulf that separates my friends here from those who are invidiously called the blest.

ANA I shall go to heaven at once.

STATUE My child: one word of warning first. Let me complete my friend Lucifer's similitude of the classical concert. At every one of these concerts in England you will find rows of weary people who are there, not because they really like classical music, but because they think they ought to like it. Well, there is the same thing in heaven. A number of people sit there in glory, not because they are happy, but because they think they owe it to their position to be in heaven. They are almost all English.

DEVIL Yes: the Southerners give it up and join me just as you have done. But the English really do not seem to know when they are thoroughly miserable. An Englishman thinks he is moral when he is only uncomfortable.

STATUE In short, my daughter, if you go to heaven without being naturally qualified for it, you will not enjoy yourself there.

ANA And who dares say that I am not naturally qualified for it? The most distinguished princes of the Church have never questioned it. I owe it to myself to leave this place at once.

DEVIL [*offended*] As you please, Señora. I should have expected better taste from you.

ANA Father: I shall expect you to come with me. You cannot stay here. What will people say?

STATUE People! Why, the best people are here —princes of the Church and all. So few go to heaven, and so many come here that the blest, once called a heavenly host, are a continually dwindling minority. The saints, the fathers, the elect of long ago are the cranks, the faddists, the outsiders of today.

DEVIL   It is true. From the beginning of my career I knew that I should win in the long run by sheer weight of public opinion, in spite of the long campaign of misrepresentation and calumny against me. At the bottom the universe is a constitutional one; and with such a majority as mine I cannot be kept permanently out of office.

DON JUAN   I think, Ana, you had better stay here.

ANA [jealously]   You do not want me to go with you.

DON JUAN   Surely you do not want to enter heaven in the company of a reprobate like me.

ANA   All souls are equally precious. You repent, do you not?

DON JUAN   My dear Ana, you are silly. Do you suppose heaven is like earth, where people persuade themselves that what is done can be undone by repentance; that what is spoken can be unspoken by withdrawing it; that what is true can be annihilated by a general agreement to give it the lie? No: heaven is the home of the masters of reality: that is why I am going thither.

ANA   Thank you: I am going to heaven for happiness. I have had quite enough of reality on earth.

DON JUAN   Then you must stay here; for hell is the home of the unreal and of the seekers for happiness. It is the only refuge from heaven, which is, as I tell you, the home of the masters of reality, and from earth, which is the home of the slaves of reality. The earth is a nursery in which men and women play at being heroes and heroines, saints and sinners; but they are dragged down from their fool's paradise by their bodies: hunger and cold and thirst, age and decay and disease, death above all, make them slaves of reality: thrice a day meals must be eaten and digested: thrice a century a new generation must be engendered: ages of faith, of romance, and of science are all driven at last to have but one prayer "Make me a healthy

animal." But here you escape this tyranny of the flesh; for here you are not an animal at all: you are a ghost, an appearance, an illusion, a convention, deathless, ageless: in a word, bodiless. There are no social questions here, no political questions, no religious questions, best of all, perhaps, no sanitary questions. Here you call your appearance beauty, your emotions love, your sentiments heroism, your aspirations virtue, just as you did on earth; but here there are no hard facts to contradict you, no ironic contrast of your needs with your pretensions, no human comedy, nothing but a perpetual romance, a universal melodrama. As our German friend put it in his poem, "the poetically nonsensical here is good sense; and the Eternal Feminine draws us ever upward and on"—without getting us a step farther. And yet you want to leave this paradise!

ANA   But if hell be so beautiful as this, how glorious must heaven be!

[The Devil, the Statue, and Don Juan all begin to speak at once in violent protest; then stop, abashed.]

DON JUAN   I beg your pardon.

DEVIL   Not at all. I interrupted you.

STATUE   You were going to say something.

DON JUAN   After you, gentlemen.

DEVIL [to Don Juan]   You have been so eloquent on the advantages of my dominions that I leave you to do equal justice to the drawbacks of the alternative establishment.

DON JUAN   In heaven, as I picture it, dear lady, you live and work instead of playing and pretending. You face things as they are; you escape nothing but glamor; and your steadfastness and your peril are your glory. If the play still goes on here and on earth, and all the world is a stage, heaven is at least behind the scenes. But heaven cannot be described by metaphor. Thither I shall go presently, because there I hope to escape at last from lies and from the tedious, vulgar pursuit of happiness, to spend my eons in contemplation—

STATUE   Ugh!

DON JUAN   Señor Commander: I do not blame your disgust: a picture gallery is a dull place for a blind man. But even as you enjoy the contemplation of such romantic mirages as beauty

BERNARD SHAW

and pleasure; so would I enjoy the contemplation of that which interests me above all things: namely, Life: the force that ever strives to attain greater power of contemplating itself. What made this brain of mine, do you think? Not the need to move my limbs; for a rat with half my brain moves as well as I. Not merely the need to do, but the need to know what I do, lest in my blind efforts to live I should be slaying myself.

STATUE You would have slain yourself in your blind efforts to fence but for my foot slipping, my friend.

DON JUAN Audacious ribald: your laughter will finish in hideous boredom before morning.

STATUE Ha ha! Do you remember how I frightened you when I said something like that to you from my pedestal in Seville? It sounds rather flat without my trombones.

DON JUAN They tell me it generally sounds flat with them, Commander.

ANA Oh, do not interrupt with these frivolities, father. Is there nothing in heaven but contemplation, Juan?

DON JUAN In the heaven I seek, no other joy. But there is the work of helping Life in its struggle upward. Think of how it wastes and scatters itself, how it raises up obstacles to itself and destroys itself in its ignorance and blindness. It needs a brain, this irresistible force, lest in its ignorance it should resist itself. "What a piece of work is man!" says the poet. Yes; but what a blunderer! Here is the highest miracle of organization yet attained by life, the most intensely alive thing that exists, the most conscious of all the organisms; and yet, how wretched are his brains! Stupidity made sordid and cruel by the realities learnt from toil and poverty: Imagination resolved to starve sooner than face these realities, piling up illusions to hide them, and calling itself cleverness, genius! And each accusing the other of its own defect: Stupidity accusing Imagination of folly, and Imagination accusing Stupidity of ignorance: whereas, alas! Stupidity has all the knowledge, and Imagination all the intelligence.

DEVIL And a pretty kettle of fish they make of it between them. Did I not say, when I was arranging that affair of Faust's, that all Man's reason has done for him is to make him beastlier than any beast. One splendid body is worth the brains of a hundred dyspeptic, flatulent philosophers.

DON JUAN You forget that brainless magnificence of body has been tried. Things immeasurably greater than Man in every respect but brain have existed and perished. The megatherium, the ichthyosaurus have paced the earth with seven-league steps and hidden the day with cloud vast wings. Where are they now? Fossils in museums, and so few and imperfect at that, that a knuckle bone or a tooth of one of them is prized beyond the lives of a thousand soldiers. These things lived and wanted to live; but for lack of brains they did not know how to carry out their purpose, and so destroyed themselves.

DEVIL And is Man any the less destroying himself for all this boasted brain of his? Have you walked up and down upon the earth lately? I have; and I have examined Man's wonderful inventions. And I tell you that in the arts of life Man invents nothing; but in the arts of death he outdoes Nature herself, and produces by chemistry and machinery all the slaughter of plague, pestilence, and famine. The peasant I tempt today eats and drinks what was eaten and drunk by the peasants of ten thousand years ago; and the house he lives in has not altered as much in a thousand centuries as the fashion of a lady's bonnet in a score of weeks. But when he goes out to slay, he carries a marvel of mechanism that lets loose at the touch of his finger all the hidden molecular energies, and leaves the javelin, the arrow, the blowpipe of his fathers far behind. In the arts of peace Man is a bungler. I have seen his cotton factories and the like, with machinery that a greedy dog could have invented if it had wanted money instead of food. I know his clumsy typewriters and bungling locomotives and tedious bicycles: they are toys compared to the Maxim gun, the submarine torpedo boat. There is nothing in Man's industrial machinery but his greed and sloth: his heart is in his weapons. This marvellous force of life of which you boast is a force of Death: Man measures his strength by his destructiveness. What is his religion? An excuse for hating me. What is his law? An excuse for hanging you. What is his morality? Gentility! an excuse for consuming without producing. What is his art? An excuse for gloating over pictures of slaughter. What are his politics? Either the worship of a despot because a despot can kill, or parliamentary cock-fighting. I spent an evening lately in a certain celebrated legislature, and heard the pot lecturing the kettle for its blackness, and ministers answering questions. When I left I chalked up on the door the old nursery saying "Ask no questions and you will be told no lies." I bought a sixpenny family magazine, and found it full of pictures of young men shooting and stabbing one another. I saw a man die: he was a London bricklayer's laborer with seven children. He left seventeen pounds club money; and his wife spent it all on his funeral and went into the workhouse with the children next day. She would not have spent sevenpence on her children's schooling: the law had to force her to let them be taught gratuitously; but on death she spent all she had. Their imagination glows, their energies rise up at the idea of death, these people: they love it; and the more horrible it is the more they enjoy it. Hell is a place far above their comprehension: they derive their notion of it from two of the greatest fools that ever lived, an Italian and and Englishman. The Italian described it as a place of mud, frost, filth, fire, and venomous serpents: all torture. This ass, when he was not lying about me, was maundering about some woman whom he saw once in the street. The Englishman described me as being expelled from heaven by cannons and gunpowder; and to this day every Briton believes that the whole of his silly story is in the Bible. What else he says I do not know; for it is all in a long poem which neither I nor anyone else ever succeeded in wading through. It is the same in everything. The highest form of literature is the tragedy, a play in which everybody is murdered at the end. In the old chronicles you read of earthquakes and pestilences, and are told that these showed the power and majesty of God and the littleness of Man. Nowadays the chronicles describe battles. In a battle two bodies of men shoot at one another with bullets and explosive shells until one body runs away, when the others chase the fugitives on horseback and cut them to pieces as they fly. And this, the chronicle concludes, shows the greatness and majesty of empires, and the littleness of the vanquished. Over such battles the people run about the streets yelling with delight, and egg their Governments on to spend hundreds of millions of money in the slaughter, whilst the strongest Ministers dare not spend an extra penny in the pound against the poverty and pestilence through which they themselves daily walk. I could give you a thousand instances; but they all come to the same thing: the power that governs the earth is not the power of Life but of Death; and the inner need that has served Life to the effort of organising itself into the human being is not the need for higher life but for a more efficient engine of destruction. The plague, the famine, the earthquake, the tempest were too spasmodic in their action; the tiger and crocodile were too easily satiated and not cruel enough: something more constantly, more ruthlessly, more ingeniously destructive was needed; and that something was Man, the inventor of the rack, the stake, the gallows, the electric chair; of sword and gun and poison gas: above all, of justice, duty, patriotism, and all the other isms by which even those who are clever enough to be humanely disposed are persuaded to become the most destructive of all the destroyers.

DON JUAN Pshaw! All this is old. Your weak side, my diabolic friend, is that you have always been a gull: you take Man at his own valuation. Nothing would flatter him more than your opinion of him. He loves to think of himself as bold and bad. He is neither one nor the other: he is only a coward. Call him tyrant, murderer, pirate, bully; and he will adore you, and swagger about with the consciousness of having the blood of the old sea kings in his veins. Call him liar and thief; and he will only take an action against you for libel. But call him coward; and he will go mad with rage: he will face death to outface that stinging truth. Man gives every reason for his conduct save one, every excuse for his crimes save one, every plea for his safety save one; and that one is his coward-

BERNARD SHAW

ice. Yet all his civilization is founded on his cowardice, on his abject tameness, which he calls his respectability. There are limits to what a mule or an ass will stand; but Man will suffer himself to be degraded until his vileness becomes so loathsome to his oppressors that they themselves are forced to reform it.

DEVIL Precisely. And these are the creatures in whom you discover what you call a Life Force!

DON JUAN Yes; for now comes the most surprising part of the whole business.

STATUE What's that?

DON JUAN Why, that you can make any of these cowards brave by simply putting an idea into his head.

STATUE Stuff! As an old soldier I admit the cowardice: it's as universal as sea sickness, and matters just as little. But that about putting an idea into a man's head is stuff and nonsense. In a battle all you need to make you fight is a little hot blood and the knowledge that it's more dangerous to lose than to win.

DON JUAN That is perhaps why battles are so useless. But men never really overcome fear until they imagine they are fighting to further a universal purpose—fighting for an idea, as they call it. Why was the Crusader braver than the pirate? Because he fought, not for himself, but for the Cross. What force was it that met him with a valor as reckless as his own? The force of men who fought, not for themselves, but for Islam. They took Spain from us, though we were fighting for our very hearths and homes; but when we, too, fought for that mighty idea, a Catholic Church, we swept them back to Africa.

DEVIL [*ironically*] What! You a Catholic, Señor Don Juan! A devotee! My congratulations.

STATUE [*seriously*] Come, come! As a soldier, I can listen to nothing against the Church.

DON JUAN Have no fear, Commander: this idea of a Catholic Church will survive Islam, will survive the Cross, will survive even that vulgar pageant of incompetent schoolboyish gladiators which you call the Army.

STATUE Juan: you will force me to call you to account for this.

DON JUAN Useless: I cannot fence. Every idea for which Man will die will be a Catholic idea.

When the Spaniard learns at last that he is no better than the Saracen, and his prophet no better than Mahomet, he will arise, more Catholic than ever, and die on a barricade across the filthy slum he starves in, for a universal liberty and equality.

STATUE Bosh!

DON JUAN What you call bosh is the only thing men dare die for. Later on, Liberty will not be Catholic enough: men will die for human perfection, to which they will sacrifice all their liberty gladly.

DEVIL Ay: they will never be at a loss for an excuse for killing one another.

DON JUAN What of that? It is not death that matters, but the fear of death. It is not killing and dying that degrades us, but base living and accepting the wages and profits of degradation. Better ten dead men than one live slave or his master. Men shall yet rise up, father against son and brother against brother, and kill one another for the great Catholic idea of abolishing slavery.

DEVIL Yes, when the Liberty and Equality of which you prate shall have made free white Christians cheaper in the labor market than black heathen slaves sold by auction at the block.

DON JUAN Never fear! The white laborer shall have his turn too. But I am not now defending the illusory forms the great ideas take. I am giving you examples of the fact that this creature Man, who in his own selfish affairs is a coward to the backbone, will fight for an idea like a hero. He may be abject as a citizen; but he is dangerous as a fanatic. He can only be enslaved whilst he is spiritually weak enough to listen to reason. I tell you, gentlemen, if you can show a man a piece of what he now calls God's work to do, and what he will later on call by many new names, you can make him entirely reckless of the consequences to himself personally.

ANA Yes: he shirks all his responsibilities and leaves his wife to grapple with them.

STATUE Well said, daughter. Do not let him talk you out of your common sense.

DEVIL Alas! Señor Commander, now that we have got on to the subject of Woman, he will talk more than ever. However, I confess it is for me the one supremely interesting subject.

DON JUAN To a woman, Señor, man's duties and responsibilities begin and end with the task of getting bread for her children. To her, Man is only a means to the end of getting children and rearing them.

ANA Is that your idea of a woman's mind? I call it cynical and disgusting animalism.

DON JUAN Pardon me, Ana: I said nothing about a woman's whole mind. I spoke of her view of Man as a separate sex. It is no more cynical than her view of herself as above all things a Mother. Sexually, Woman is Nature's contrivance for perpetuating its highest achievement. Sexually, Man is Woman's contrivance for fulfilling Nature's behest in the most economical way. She knows by instinct that far back in the evolutionary process she invented him, differentiated him, created him in order to produce something better than the single-sexed process can produce. Whilst he fulfils the purpose for which she made him, he is welcome to his dreams, his follies, his ideals, his heroisms, provided that the keystone of them all is the worship of Woman, of motherhood, of the family, of the hearth. But how rash and dangerous it was to invent a separate creature whose sole function was her own impregnation! For mark what has happened. First Man has multiplied on her hands until there are as many men as women; so that she has been unable to employ for her purposes more than a fraction of the immense energy she has left at his disposal by saving him the exhausting labor of gestation. This superfluous energy has gone to his brain and to his muscle. He has become too strong to be controlled by her bodily, and too imaginative and mentally vigorous to be content with mere self-reproduction. He has created civilization without consulting her, taking her domestic labor for granted as the foundation of it.

ANA That is true, at all events.

DEVIL Yes; and this civilization! What is it, after all?

DON JUAN After all, an excellent peg to hang your cynical commonplaces on; but before all, it is an attempt on Man's part to make himself something more than the mere instrument of Woman's purpose. So far, the result of Life's continual effort, not only to maintain itself, but to achieve higher and higher organization and completer self-consciousness, is only, at best, a doubtful campaign between its forces and those of Death and Degeneration. The battles in this campaign are mere blunders, mostly won, like actual military battles, in spite of the commanders.

STATUE That is a dig at me. No matter: go on, go on.

DON JUAN It is a dig at a much higher power than you, Commander. Still, you must have noticed in your profession that even a stupid general can win battles when the enemy's general is a little stupider.

STATUE [*very seriously*] Most true, Juan, most true. Some donkeys have amazing luck.

DON JUAN Well, the Life Force is stupid; but it is not so stupid as the forces of Death and Degeneration. Besides, these are in its pay all the time. And so life wins, after a fashion. What mere copiousness of fecundity can supply and mere greed preserve, we possess. The survival of whatever form of civilization can produce the best rifle and the best fed rifleman is assured.

DEVIL Exactly! the survival, not of the most effective means of Life but of the most effective means of Death. You always come back to my point, in spite of your wrigglings and evasions and sophistries, not to mention the intolerable length of your speeches.

DON JUAN Oh, come! who began making long speeches? However, if I overtax your intellect, you can leave us and seek the society of love and beauty and the rest of your favorite boredoms.

DEVIL [*much offended*] This is not fair, Don Juan, and not civil. I am also on the intellectual plane. Nobody can appreciate it more than I do. I am arguing fairly with you, and, I think, successfully refuting you. Let us go on for another hour if you like.

DON JUAN Good: let us.

STATUE Not that I see any prospect of your coming to any point in particular, Juan. Still, since in this place, instead of merely killing time

BERNARD SHAW

we have to kill eternity, go ahead by all means.

DON JUAN [*somewhat impatiently*] My point, you marble-headed old masterpiece, is only a step ahead of you. Are we agreed that Life is a force which has made innumerable experiments in organizing itself; that the mammoth and the man, the mouse and the megatherium, the flies and the fleas and the Fathers of the Church, are all more or less successful attempts to build up that raw force into higher and higher individuals, the ideal individual being omnipotent, omniscient, infallible, and withal completely, unilludedly self-conscious: in short, a god?

DEVIL I agree, for the sake of argument.

STATUE I agree, for the sake of avoiding argument.

ANA I most emphatically disagree as regards the Fathers of the Church; and I must beg you not to drag them into the argument.

DON JUAN I did so purely for the sake of alliteration, Ana; and I shall make no further allusion to them. And now, since we are, with that exception, agreed so far, will you not agree with me further that Life has not measured the success of its attempts at godhead by the beauty or bodily perfection of the result, since in both these respects the birds, as our friend Aristophanes long ago pointed out, are so extraordinarily superior, with their power of flight and their lovely plumage and, may I add, the touching poetry of their loves and nestings, that it is inconceivable that Life, having once produced them, should, if love and beauty were her object, start off on another line and labor at the clumsy elephant and the hideous ape, whose grandchildren we are?

ANA Aristophanes was a heathen; and you, Juan, I am afraid, are very little better.

DEVIL You conclude, then, that Life was driving at clumsiness and ugliness?

DON JUAN No, perverse devil that you are, a thousand times no. Life was driving at brains —at its darling object: an organ by which it can attain not only self-consciousness but self-understanding.

STATUE This is metaphysics, Juan. Why the devil should—[*to the Devil*] I beg your pardon—

DEVIL Pray dont mention it. I have always regarded the use of my name to secure additional emphasis as a high compliment to me. It is quite at your service, Commander.

STATUE Thank you: thats very good of you. Even in heaven, I never quite got out of my old military habits of speech. What I was going to ask Juan was why Life should bother itself about getting a brain. Why should it want to understand itself? Why not be content to enjoy itself?

DON JUAN Without a brain, Commander, you would enjoy yourself without knowing it, and so lose all the fun.

STATUE True, most true. But I am quite content with brain enough to know that I'm enjoying myself. I dont want to understand why. In fact, I'd rather not. My experience is that one's pleasures dont bear thinking about.

DON JUAN That is why intellect is so unpopular. But to Life, the force behind the Man, intellect is a necessity, because without it he blunders into death. Just as Life, after ages of struggle, evolved that wonderful bodily organ the eye, so that the living organism could see where it was going and what was coming to help or threaten it, and thus avoid a thousand dangers that formerly slew it, so it is evolving today a mind's eye that shall see, not the physical world, but the purpose of life, and thereby enable the individual to work for that purpose instead of thwarting and baffling it by setting up shortsighted personal aims as at present. Even as it is, only one sort of man has ever been happy, has ever been universally respected among all the conflicts of interests and illusions.

STATUE You mean the military man.

DON JUAN Commander: I do not mean the military man. When the military man approaches, the world locks up its spoons and packs off its womankind. No: I sing not arms and the hero, but the philosophic man: he who seeks in contemplation to discover the inner will of the world, in invention to discover the means of fulfilling that will, and in action to do that will by the so-discovered means. Of all other sorts of men I declare myself tired. They are tedious failures. When I was on earth, professors of all sorts prowled round me feeling for an unhealthy spot in me on which they could fasten. The doctors of medicine bade me consider what I must do to save my body, and offered me quack cures for imaginary diseases. I replied that I was not a hypochondriac; so they called me Ignoramus and went their way. The doctors of divinity bade me consider what I must do to save my soul; but I was not a spiritual hypochondriac any more than a bodily one, and would not trouble myself about that either; so they called me Atheist and went their way. After them came the politician, who said there was only one purpose in nature, and that was to get him into parliament. I told him I did not care whether he got into parliament or not; so he called me Mugwump and went his way. Then came the romantic man, the Artist, with his love songs and his paintings and his poems; and with him I had great delight for many years, and some profit; for I cultivated my senses for his sake; and his songs taught me to hear better, his paintings to see better, and his poems to feel more deeply. But he led me at last into the worship of Woman.

ANA Juan.

DON JUAN Yes: I came to believe that in her voice was all the music of the song, in her face all the beauty of the painting, and in her soul all the emotion of the poem.

ANA And you were disappointed, I suppose. Well, was it her fault that you attributed all these perfections to her?

DON JUAN Yes, partly. For with a wonderful instinctive cunning, she kept silent and allowed me to glorify her: to mistake my own visions, thoughts, and feelings for hers. Now my friend the romantic man was often too poor or too timid to approach those women who were beautiful or refined enough to seem to realize his ideal; and so he went to his grave believing in his dream. But I was more favored by nature and circumstance. I was of noble birth and rich; and when my person did not please, my conversation flattered, though I generally found myself fortunate in both.

STATUE Coxcomb!

DON JUAN Yes; but even my coxcombry pleased. Well, I found that when I had touched a woman's imagination, she would allow me to persuade myself that she loved me; but when my suit was granted she never said "I am happy; my love is satisfied": she always said first, "At last, the barriers are down," and second, "When will you come again?"

ANA That is exactly what men say.

DON JUAN I protest I never said it. But all women say it. Well, these two speeches always alarmed me; for the first meant that the lady's impulse had been solely to throw down my fortifications and gain my citadel; and the second openly announced that henceforth she regarded me as her property, and counted my time as already wholly at her disposal.

DEVIL That is where your want of heart came in.

STATUE [*shaking his head*] You shouldn't repeat what a woman says, Juan.

ANA [*severely*] It should be sacred to you.

STATUE Still, they certainly do say it. I never minded the barriers; but there was always a slight shock about the other, unless one was very hard hit indeed.

DON JUAN Then the lady, who had been happy and idle enough before, became anxious, preoccupied with me, always intriguing, conspiring, pursuing, watching, waiting, bent wholly on making sure of her prey: I being the prey, you understand. Now this was not what I had bargained for. It may have been very proper and very natural; but it was not music, painting, poetry, and joy incarnated in a beautiful woman. I ran away from it. I ran away from it very often: in fact I became famous for running away from it.

ANA Infamous, you mean.

DON JUAN I did not run away from you. Do you blame me for running away from the others?

ANA Nonsense, man. You are talking to a woman of seventy-seven now. If you had had the chance, you would have run away from me too—if I had let you. You would not have found it so easy with me as with some of the others. If men will not be faithful to their home and their duties, they must be made to be. I daresay you all want to marry lovely incarnations of music and painting and poetry. Well, you cant have them, because they dont exist. If flesh and blood is not good enough for you, you must go without: thats all. Women have to put up with flesh-and-blood husbands —and little enough of that too, sometimes; and you will have to put up with flesh-and-blood wives. [*The Devil looks dubious. The Statue makes a wry face.*] I see you dont like that, any of you; but it's true, for all that; so if you dont like it you can lump it.

DON JUAN My dear lady, you have put my whole case against romance into a few sentences. That is just why I turned my back on the romantic man with the artist nature, as he called his infatuation. I thanked him for teaching me to use my eyes and ears; but I told him that his beauty worshipping and happiness hunting and woman idealizing was not worth a dump as a philosophy of life; so he called me Philistine and went his way.

ANA It seems that Woman taught you something, too, with all her defects.

DON JUAN She did more: she interpreted all the other teaching for me. Ah, my friends, when the barriers were down for the first time, what an astounding illumination! I had been prepared for infatuation, for intoxication, for all the illusions of love's young dream; and lo! never was my perception clearer, nor my criticism more ruthless. The most jealous rival of my mistress never saw every blemish in her more keenly than I. I was not duped: I took her without chloroform.

ANA But you did take her.

DON JUAN That was the revelation. Up to that moment I had never lost the sense of being my own master; never consciously taken a single step until my reason had examined and approved it. I had come to believe that I was a purely rational creature: a thinker! I said, with the foolish philosopher, "I think; therefore I am." It was Woman who taught me to say "I am; therefore I think." And also "I would think more; therefore I must be more."

STATUE This is extremely abstract and metaphysical, Juan. If you would stick to the concrete and put your discoveries in the form of entertaining anecdotes about your adventures with women, your conversation would be easier to follow.

DON JUAN Bah! What need I add? Do you not understand that when I stood face to face with Woman, every fibre in my clear critical brain warned me to spare her and save myself. My morals said "No." My conscience said "No." My chivalry and pity for her said "No." My prudent regard for myself said "No." My ear, practised on a thousand songs and symphonies; my eye, exercised on a thousand paintings; tore her voice, her features, her color to shreds. I caught all those tell-tale resemblances to her father and mother by which I knew what she would be like in thirty years' time. I noted the gleam of gold from a dead tooth in the laughing mouth: I made curious observations of the strange odors of the chemistry of the nerves. The visions of my romantic reveries, in which I had trod the plains of heaven with a deathless, ageless creature of coral and ivory, deserted me in that supreme hour. I remembered them and desperately strove to recover their illusion; but they now seemed the emptiest of inventions: my judgement was not to be corrupted: my brain still said "No" on every issue. And whilst I was in the act of framing my excuse to the lady, Life seized me and threw me into her arms as a sailor throws a scrap of fish into the mouth of a seabird.

STATUE You might as well have gone without thinking such a lot about it, Juan. You are like all the clever men: you have more brains than is good for you.

DEVIL And were you not the happier for the experience, Señor Don Juan?

DON JUAN The happier, no: the wiser, yes. That moment introduced me for the first time to myself, and, through myself, to the world. I saw then how useless it is to attempt to impose conditions on the irresistible force of Life: to preach prudence, careful selection, virtue, honor, chastity—

ANA Don Juan: a word against chastity is an insult to me.

DON JUAN I say nothing against your chastity, Señora, since it took the form of a husband and twelve children. What more could you have done had you been the most abandoned of women?

ANA I could have had twelve husbands and no children: thats what I could have done, Juan.

And let me tell you that that would have made all the difference to the earth which I replenished.

STATUE Bravo Ana! Juan: you are floored, quelled, annihilated.

DON JUAN No: for though that difference is the true essential difference—Doña Ana has, I admit, gone straight to the real point—yet it is not a difference of love or chastity, or even constancy; for twelve children by twelve different husbands would have replenished the earth perhaps more effectively. Suppose my friend Ottavio had died when you were thirty, you would never have remained a widow: you were too beautiful. Suppose the successor of Ottavio had died when you were forty, you would still have been irresistible; and a woman who marries twice marries three times if she becomes free to do so. Twelve lawful children borne by one highly respectable lady to three different fathers is not impossible nor condemned by public opinion. That such a lady may be more law abiding than the poor girl whom we used to spurn into the gutter for bearing one unlawful infant is no doubt true; but dare you say she is less self-indulgent?

ANA She is more virtuous: that is enough for me.

DON JUAN In that case, what is virtue but the Trade Unionism of the married? Let us face the facts, dear Ana. The Life Force respects marriage only because marriage is a contrivance of its own to secure the greatest number of children and the closest care of them. For honor, chastity, and all the rest of your moral figments it cares not a rap. Marriage is the most licentious of human institutions—

ANA Juan!

STATUE [*protesting*] Really!—

DON JUAN [*determinedly*] I say the most licentious of human institutions: that is the secret of its popularity. And a woman seeking a husband is the most unscrupulous of all the beasts of prey. The confusion of marriage with morality has done more to destroy the conscience of the human race than any other single error. Come, Ana! Do not look shocked: you know better than any of us that marriage is a man-trap baited with simulated accomplishments and delusive idealizations. When your sainted mother, by dint of scoldings and punishments, forced you to learn how to play half a dozen pieces on the spinet—which she hated as much as you did—had she any other purpose than to delude your suitors into the belief that your husband would have in his home an angel who would fill it with melody, or at least play him to sleep after dinner? You married my friend Ottavio: well, did you ever open the spinet from the hour when the Church united him to you?

ANA You are a fool, Juan. A young married woman has something else to do than sit at the spinet without any support for her back; so she gets out of the habit of playing.

DON JUAN Not if she loves music. No: believe me, she only throws away the bait when the bird is in the net.

ANA [*bitterly*] And men, I suppose, never throw off the mask when their bird is in the net. The husband never becomes negligent, selfish, brutal —oh, never!

DON JUAN What do these recriminations prove, Ana? Only that the hero is as gross an imposture as the heroine.

ANA It is all nonsense: most marriages are perfectly comfortable.

DON JUAN "Perfectly" is a strong expression, Ana. What you mean is that sensible people make the best of one another. Send me to the galleys and chain me to the felon whose number happens to be next before mine; and I must accept the inevitable and make the best of the companionship. Many such companionships, they tell me, are touchingly affectionate; and most are at least tolerably friendly. But that does not make a chain a desirable ornament nor the galleys an abode of bliss. Those who talk most about the blessings of marriage and the constancy of its vows are the very people who declare that if the chain were broken and the prisoners left free to choose, the whole social fabric would fly asunder. You cannot have the argument both ways. If the prisoner is happy, why lock him in? If he is not, why pretend that he is?

ANA At all events, let me take an old woman's privilege again, and tell you flatly that marriage peoples the world and debauchery does not.

DON JUAN How if a time come when this shall cease to be true? Do you not know that where there is a will there is a way? that whatever Man really wishes to do he will finally discover a means of doing? Well, you have done your best, you virtuous ladies, and others of your way of thinking, to bend Man's mind wholly towards honorable love as the highest good, and to understand by honorable love romance and beauty and happiness in the possession of beautiful, refined, delicate, affectionate women. You have taught women to value their own youth, health, shapeliness, and refinement above all things. Well, what place have squalling babies and household cares in this exquisite paradise of the senses and emotions? Is it not the inevitable end of it all that the human will shall say to the human brain: "Invent me a means by which I can have love, beauty, romance, emotion, passion, without their wretched penalties, their expenses, their worries, their trials, their illnesses and agonies and risks of death, their retinue of servants and nurses and doctors and schoolmasters."

DEVIL All this, Señor Don Juan, is realized here in my realm.

DON JUAN Yes, at the cost of death. Man will not take it at that price: he demands the romantic delights of your hell whilst he is still on earth. Well, the means will be found: the brain will not fail when the will is in earnest. The day is coming when great nations will find their numbers dwindling from census to census; when the six roomed villa will rise in price above the family mansion; when the viciously reckless poor and the stupidly pious rich will delay the extinction of the race only by degrading it; whilst the boldly prudent, the thriftily selfish and ambitious, the imaginative and poetic, the lovers of money and solid comfort, the worshippers of success, of art, and of love, will all oppose to the Force of Life the device of sterility.

STATUE That is all very eloquent, my young friend; but if you had lived to Ana's age, or even to mine, you would have learned that the people who get rid of the fear of poverty and children and all the other family troubles, and devote themselves to having a good time of it,

only leave their minds free for the fear of old age and ugliness and impotence and death. The childless laborer is more tormented by his wife's idleness and her constant demands for amusement and distraction than he could be by twenty children; and his wife is more wretched than he. I have had my share of vanity; for as a young man I was admired by women; and as a statue I am praised by art critics. But I confess that had I found nothing to do in the world but wallow in these delights I should have cut my throat. When I married Ana's mother—or perhaps, to be strictly correct, I should rather say when I at last gave in and allowed Ana's mother to marry me—I knew that I was planting thorns in my pillow, and that marriage for me, a swaggering young officer thitherto unvanquished, meant defeat and capture.

ANA [*scandalized*] Father!

STATUE I am sorry to shock you, my love; but since Juan has stripped every rag of decency from the discussion I may as well tell the frozen truth.

ANA Hmf! I suppose I was one of the thorns.

STATUE By no means: you were often a rose. You see, your mother had most of the trouble you gave.

DON JUAN Then may I ask, Commander, why you have left heaven to come here and wallow, as you express it, in sentimental beatitudes which you confess would once have driven you to cut your throat?

STATUE [*struck by this*] Egad, thats true.

DEVIL [*alarmed*] What! You are going back from your word! [*To Don Juan*] And all your philosophizing has been nothing but a mask for proselytizing! [*To the Statue*] Have you forgotten already the hideous dullness from which I am offering you a refuge here? [*To Don Juan*] And does your demonstration of the approaching sterilization and extinction of mankind lead to anything better than making the most of those pleasures of art and love which you yourself admit refined you, elevated you, developed you?

DON JUAN I never demonstrated the extinction of mankind. Life cannot will its own extinction either in its blind amorphous state or in any of the forms into which it has organized itself. I had not finished when His Excellency interrupted me.

STATUE I begin to doubt whether you ever will finish, my friend. You are extremely fond of hearing yourself talk.

DON JUAN True; but since you have endured so much, you may as well endure to the end. Long before this sterilization which I described becomes more than a clearly foreseen possibility, the reaction will begin. The great central purpose of breeding the race: ay, breeding it to heights now deemed superhuman: that purpose which is now hidden in a mephitic cloud of love and romance and prudery and fastidiousness, will break through into clear sunlight as a purpose no longer to be confused with the gratification of personal fancies, the impossible realization of boys' and girls' dreams of bliss, or the need of older people for companionship or money. The plain-spoken marriage services of the vernacular Churches will no longer be abbreviated and half suppressed as indelicate. The sober decency, earnestness, and authority of their declaration of the real purpose of marriage will be honored and accepted, whilst their romantic vowings and pledgings and until-death-do-us-partings and the like will be expunged as unbearable frivolities. Do my sex the justice to admit, Señora, that we have always recognized that the sex relation is not a personal or friendly relation at all.

ANA Not a personal or friendly relation! What relation is more personal? more sacred? more holy?

DON JUAN Sacred and holy, if you like, Ana, but not personally friendly. Your relation to God is sacred and holy: dare you call it personally friendly? In the sex relation the universal creative energy, of which the parties are both the helpless agents, overrides and sweeps away all personal considerations, and dispenses with all personal relations. The pair may be utter strangers to one another, speaking different languages, different in race and color, in age and disposition, with no bond between them but a possibility of that fecundity for the sake of which the Life Force throws them into one another's arms at the exchange of a glance. Do

we not recognize this by allowing marriages to be made by parents without consulting the woman? Have you not often expressed your disgust at the immorality of the English nation, in which women and men of noble birth become acquainted and court each other like peasants? And how much does even the peasant know of his bride or she of him before he engages himself? Why, you would not make a man your lawyer or your family doctor on so slight an acquaintance as you would fall in love with and marry him!

ANA Yes, Juan: we know the libertine's philosophy. Always ignore the consequences to the woman.

DON JUAN The consequences, yes: they justify her fierce grip of the man. But surely you do not call that attachment a sentimental one. As well call the policeman's attachment to his prisoner a love relation.

ANA You see you have to confess that marriage is necessary, though, according to you, love is the slightest of all human relations.

DON JUAN How do you know that it is not the greatest of all human relations? far too great to be a personal matter. Could your father have served his country if he had refused to kill any enemy of Spain unless he personally hated him? Can a woman serve her country if she refuses to marry any man she does not personally love? You know it is not so: the woman of noble birth marries as the man of noble birth fights, on political and family grounds, not on personal ones.

STATUE [*impressed*] A very clever point that, Juan: I must think it over. You are really full of ideas. How did you come to think of this one?

DON JUAN I learnt it by experience. When I was on earth, and made those proposals to ladies which, though universally condemned, have made me so interesting a hero of legend, I was not infrequently met in some such way as this. The lady would say that she would countenance my advances, provided they were honorable. On inquiring what that proviso meant, I found that it meant that I proposed to get possession of her property if she had any, or to undertake her support for life if she had not;

BERNARD SHAW

that I desired her continual companionship, counsel, and conversation to the end of my days, and would take a most solemn oath to be always enraptured by them: above all, that I would turn my back on all other women for ever for her sake. I did not object to these conditions because they were exorbitant and inhuman: it was their extraordinary irrelevance that prostrated me. I invariably replied with perfect frankness that I had never dreamt of any of these things; that unless the lady's character and intellect were equal or superior to my own, her conversation must degrade and her counsel mislead me; that her constant companionship might, for all I knew, become intolerably tedious to me; that I could not answer for my feelings for a week in advance, much less to the end of my life; that to cut me off from all natural and unconstrained intercourse with half my fellow-creatures would narrow and warp me if I submitted to it, and, if not, would bring me under the curse of clandestinity; that, finally, my proposals to her were wholly unconnected with any of these matters, and were the outcome of a perfectly simple impulse of my manhood towards her womanhood.

ANA You mean that it was an immoral impulse.

DON JUAN Nature, my dear lady, is what you call immoral. I blush for it; but I cannot help it. Nature is a pandar, Time a wrecker, and Death a murderer. I have always preferred to stand up to those facts and build institutions on their recognition. You prefer to propitiate the three devils by proclaiming their chastity, their thrift, and their loving kindness; and to base your institutions on their flatteries. Is it any wonder that the institutions do not work smoothly?

STATUE What used the ladies to say, Juan?

DON JUAN Oh, come! Confidence for confidence. First tell me what you used to say to the ladies.

STATUE I! Oh, I swore that I would be faithful to the death; that I should die if they refused me; that no woman could ever be to me what she was—

ANA She! Who?

STATUE Whoever it happened to be at the time, my dear. I had certain things I always said. One of them was that even when I was eighty, one white hair of the woman I loved would make me tremble more than the thickest gold tress from the most beautiful young head. Another was that I could not bear the thought of anyone else being the mother of my children.

DON JUAN [revolted] You old rascal!

STATUE [stoutly] Not a bit; for I really believed it with all my soul at the moment. I had a heart: not like you. And it was this sincerity that made me successful.

DON JUAN Sincerity! To be fool enough to believe a ramping, stamping, thumping lie: that is what you call sincerity! To be so greedy for a woman that you deceive yourself in your eagerness to deceive her: sincerity, you call it!

STATUE Oh, damn your sophistries! I was a man in love, not a lawyer. And the women loved me for it, bless them!

DON JUAN They made you think so. What will you say when I tell you that though I played the lawyer so callously, they made me think so too? I also had my moments of infatuation in which I gushed nonsense and believed it. Sometimes the desire to give pleasure by saying beautiful things so rose in me on the flood of emotion that I said them recklessly. At other times I argued against myself with a devilish coldness that drew tears. But I found it just as hard to escape when I was cruel as when I was kind. When the lady's instinct was set on me, there was nothing for it but lifelong servitude or flight.

ANA You dare boast, before me and my father, that every woman found you irresistible.

DON JUAN Am I boasting? It seems to me that I cut the most pitiable of figures. Besides, I said "when the lady's instinct was set on me." It was not always so; and then, heavens! what transports of virtuous indignation! what overwhelming defiance to the dastardly seducer! what scenes of Imogen and Iachimo!

ANA I made no scenes. I simply called my father.

DON JUAN And he came, sword in hand, to vindicate outraged honor and morality by murdering me.

STATUE Murdering! What do you mean? Did I kill you or did you kill me?

DON JUAN Which of us was the better fencer?

STATUE I was.

DON JUAN Of course you were. And yet you, the hero of those scandalous adventures you have just been relating to us, you had the effrontery to pose as the avenger of outraged morality and condemn me to death! You would have slain me but for an accident.

STATUE I was expected to, Juan. That is how things were arranged on earth. I was not a social reformer; and I always did what it was customary for a gentleman to do.

DON JUAN That may account for your attacking me, but not for the revolting hypocrisy of your subsequent proceedings as a statue.

STATUE That all came of my going to heaven.

DEVIL I still fail to see, Señor Don Juan, that these episodes in your earthly career and in that of the Señor Commander in any way discredit my view of life. Here, I repeat, you have all that you sought without anything that you shrank from.

DON JUAN On the contrary, here I have everything that disappointed me without anything that I have not already tried and found wanting. I tell you that as long as I can conceive something better than myself I cannot be easy unless I am striving to bring it into existence or clearing the way for it. That is the law of my life. That is the working within me of Life's incessant aspiration to higher organization, wider, deeper, intenser self-consciousness, and clearer self-understanding. It was the supremacy of this purpose that reduced love for me to the mere pleasure of a moment, art for me to the mere schooling of my faculties, religion for me to a mere excuse for laziness, since it had set up a God who looked at the world and saw that it was good, against the instinct in me that looked through my eyes at the world and saw that it could be improved. I tell you that in the pursuit of my own pleasure, my own health, my own fortune, I have never known happiness. It was not love for Woman that delivered me into her hands: it was fatigue, exhaustion. When I was a child, and bruised my head against a stone, I ran to the nearest woman and cried away my pain against her apron. When I grew up, and bruised my soul against the brutalities and stupidities with which I had to strive, I did again just what I had done as a child. I have enjoyed, too, my rests, my recuperations, my breathing times, my very prostrations after strife; but rather would I be dragged through all the circles of the foolish Italian's Inferno than through the pleasures of Europe. That is what has made this place of eternal pleasures so deadly to me. It is the absence of this instinct in you that makes you that strange monster called a Devil. It is the success with which you have diverted the attention of men from their real purpose, which in one degree or another is the same as mine, to yours, that has earned you the name of The Tempter. It is the fact that they are doing your will, or rather drifting with your want of will, instead of doing their own, that makes them the uncomfortable, false, restless, artificial, petulant, wretched creatures they are.

DEVIL [*mortified*] Señor Don Juan: you are uncivil to my friends.

DON JUAN Pooh! Why should I be civil to them or to you? In this Palace of Lies a truth or two will not hurt you. Your friends are all the dullest dogs I know. They are not beautiful: they are only decorated. They are not clean: they are only shaved and starched. They are not dignified: they are only fashionably dressed. They are not educated: they are only college passmen. They are not religious: they are only pewrenters. They are not moral: they are only conventional. They are not virtuous: they are only cowardly. They are not even vicious: they are only "frail." They are not artistic: they are only lascivious. They are not prosperous: they are only rich. They are not loyal, they are only servile; not dutiful, only sheepish; not public spirited, only patriotic; not courageous, only quarrelsome; not determined, only obstinate; not masterful, only domineering; not self-controlled, only obtuse; not self-respecting, only vain; not kind, only sentimental; not social, only gregarious; not considerate, only polite; not intelligent, only opinionated; not progressive, only factious; not imaginative, only superstitious; not just, only vindictive; not generous, only propitiatory; not disciplined, only cowed; and not truthful at all: liars every one of them, to the very backbone of their souls.

STATUE Your flow of words is simply amazing, Juan. How I wish I could have talked like that to my soldiers.

DEVIL It is mere talk, though. It has all been said before; but what change has it ever made? What notice has the world ever taken of it?

DON JUAN Yes, it is mere talk. But why is it mere talk? Because, my friend, beauty, purity, respectability, religion, morality, art, patriotism, bravery, and the rest are nothing but words which I or anyone else can turn inside out like a glove. Were they realities, you would have to plead guilty to my indictment; but fortunately for your self-respect, my diabolical friend, they are not realities. As you say, they are mere words, useful for duping barbarians into adopting civilization, or the civilized poor into submitting to be robbed and enslaved. That is the family secret of the governing caste; and if we who are of that caste aimed at more Life for the world instead of at more power and luxury for our miserable selves, that secret would make us great. Now, since I, being a nobleman, am in the secret too, think how tedious to me must be your unending cant about all these moralistic figments, and how squalidly disastrous your sacrifice of your lives to them! If you even believed in your moral game enough to play it fairly, it would be interesting to watch; but you dont: you cheat at every trick; and if your opponent outcheats you, you upset the table and try to murder him.

DEVIL On earth there may be some truth in this, because the people are uneducated and cannot appreciate my religion of love and beauty; but here—

DON JUAN Oh yes: I know. Here there is nothing but love and beauty. Ugh! it is like sitting for all eternity at the first act of a fashionable play, before the complications begin. Never in my worst moments of superstitious terror on earth did I dream that hell was so horrible. I live, like a hairdresser, in the continual contemplation of beauty, toying with silken tresses. I breathe an atmosphere of sweetness, like a confectioner's shopboy. Commander: are there any beautiful women in heaven?

STATUE None. Absolutely none. All dowdies. Not two pennorth of jewelry among a dozen of them. They might be men of fifty.

DON JUAN I am impatient to get there. Is the word beauty ever mentioned; and are there any artistic people?

STATUE I give you my word they wont admire a fine statue even when it walks past them.

DON JUAN I go.

DEVIL Don Juan: shall I be frank with you?

DON JUAN Were you not so before?

DEVIL As far as I went, yes. But I will now go further, and confess to you that men get tired of everything, of heaven no less than of hell; and that all history is nothing but a record of the oscillations of the world between these two extremes. An epoch is but a swing of the pendulum; and each generation thinks the world is progressing because it is always moving. But when you are as old as I am; when you have a thousand times wearied of heaven, like myself and the Commander, and a thousand times wearied of hell, as you are wearied now, you will no longer imagine that every swing from heaven to hell is an emancipation, every swing from hell to heaven an evolution. Where you now see reform, progress, fulfilment of upward tendency, continual ascent by Man on the stepping stones of his dead selves to higher things, you will see nothing but an infinite comedy of illusion. You will discover the profound truth of the saying of my friend Koheleth, that there is nothing new under the sun. Vanitas vanitatum—

DON JUAN [*out of all patience*] By Heaven, this is worse than your cant about love and beauty. Clever dolt that you are, is a man no better than a worm, or a dog than a wolf, because he gets tired of everything? Shall he give up eating because he destroys his appetite in the act of gratifying it? Is a field idle when it is fallow? Can the Commander expand his hellish energy here without accumulating heavenly energy for his next term of blessedness? Granted that the great Life Force has hit on the device of the clockmaker's pendulum, and uses the earth for its bob; that the history of each oscillation, which seems so novel to us the actors, is but the history of the last oscillation repeated; nay more, that in the unthinkable infinitude of time the sun throws off the earth and catches it again a thousand times as a circus rider throws up a ball, and that our agelong epochs are but the moments between the toss and the catch, has the colossal mechanism no purpose?

DEVIL   None, my friend. You think, because you have a purpose, Nature must have one. You might as well expect it to have fingers and toes because you have them.

DON JUAN   But I should not have them if they served no purpose. And I, my friend, am as much a part of Nature as my own finger is a part of me. If my finger is the organ by which I grasp the sword and the mandoline, my brain is the organ by which Nature strives to understand itself. My dog's brain serves only my dog's purposes; but my own brain labors at a knowledge which does nothing for me personally but make my body bitter to me and my decay and death a calamity. Were I not possessed with a purpose beyond my own I had better be a ploughman than a philosopher; for the ploughman lives as long as the philosopher, eats more, sleeps better, and rejoices in the wife of his bosom with less misgiving. This is because the philosopher is in the grip of the Life Force. This Life Force says to him "I have done a thousand wonderful things unconsciously by merely willing to live and following the line of least resistance: now I want to know myself and my destination, and choose my path; so I have made a special brain—a philosopher's brain—to grasp this knowledge for me as the husbandman's hand grasps the plough for me. And this," says the Life Force to the philosopher, "must thou strive to do for me until thou diest, when I will make another brain and another philosopher to carry on the work."

DEVIL   What is the use of knowing?

DON JUAN   Why, to be able to choose the line of greatest advantage instead of yielding in the direction of the least resistance. Does a ship sail to its destination no better than a log drifts nowhither? The philosopher is Nature's pilot. And there you have our difference: to be in hell is to drift: to be in heaven is to steer.

DEVIL   On the rocks, most likely.

DON JUAN   Pooh! Which ship goes oftenest on the rocks or to the bottom? the drifting ship or the ship with a pilot on board?

DEVIL   Well, well, go your way, Señor Don Juan. I prefer to be my own master and not the tool of any blundering universal force. I know that beauty is good to look at; that music is good to hear; that love is good to feel; and that they are all good to think about and talk about. I know that to be well exercised in these sensations, emotions, and studies is to be a refined and cultivated being. Whatever they may say of me in churches on earth, I know that it is universally admitted in good society that the Prince of Darkness is a gentleman; and that is enough for me. As to your Life Force, which you think irresistible, it is the most resistible thing in the world for a person of any character. But if you are naturally vulgar and credulous, as all reformers are, it will thrust you first into religion, where you will sprinkle water on babies to save their souls from me; then it will drive you from religion into science, where you will snatch the babies from the water sprinkling and inoculate them with disease to save them from catching it accidentally; then you will take to politics, where you will become the catspaw of corrupt functionaries and the henchman of ambitious humbugs; and the end will be despair and decrepitude, broken nerve and shattered hopes, vain regrets for that worst and silliest of wastes and sacrifices, the waste and sacrifice of the power of enjoyment: in a word, the punishment of the fool who pursues the better before he has secured the good.

DON JUAN   But at least I shall not be bored. The service of the Life Force has that advantage, at all events. So fare you well, Señor Satan.

DEVIL   [*amiably*]   Fare you well, Don Juan. I shall often think of our interesting chats about things in general. I wish you every happiness: heaven, as I said before, suits some people. But if you should change your mind, do not forget that the gates are always open here to the repentant prodigal. If you feel at any time that warmth of heart, sincere unforced affection, innocent enjoyment, and warm, breathing, palpitating reality—

DON JUAN   Why not say flesh and blood at once, though we have left those two greasy commonplaces behind us?

DEVIL   [*angrily*]   You throw my friendly farewell

BERNARD SHAW

back in my teeth, then, Don Juan?

DON JUAN By no means. But though there is much to be learnt from a cynical devil, I really cannot stand a sentimental one. Señor Commander: you know the way to the frontier of hell and heaven. Be good enough to direct me.

STATUE Oh, the frontier is only the difference between two ways of looking at things. Any road will take you across it if you really want to get there.

DON JUAN Good. [*Saluting Doña Ana*] Señora: your servant.

ANA But I am going with you.

DON JUAN I can find my own way to heaven, Ana; not yours. [*He vanishes.*]

ANA How annoying!

STATUE [*calling after him*] Bon voyage, Juan! [*He wafts a final blast of his great rolling chords after him as a parting salute. A faint echo of the first ghostly melody comes back in acknowledgment.*] Ah! there he goes. [*Puffing a long breath out through his lips*] Whew! How he does talk! They'll never stand it in heaven.

DEVIL [*gloomily*] His going is a political defeat. I cannot keep these Life Worshippers: they all go. This is the greatest loss I have had since that Dutch painter went: a fellow who would paint a hag of seventy with as much enjoyment as a Venus of twenty.

STATUE I remember: he came to heaven. Rembrandt.

DEVIL Ay, Rembrandt. There is something unnatural about these fellows. Do not listen to their gospel, Señor Commander: it is dangerous. Beware of the pursuit of the Superhuman: it leads to an indiscriminate contempt for the Human. To a man, horses and dogs and cats are mere species, outside the moral world. Well, to the Superman, men and women are a mere species too, also outside the moral world. This Don Juan was kind to women and courteous to men as your daughter here was kind to her pet cats and dogs; but such kindness is a denial of the exclusively human character of the soul.

STATUE And who the deuce is the Superman?

DEVIL Oh, the latest fashion among the Life Force fanatics. Did you not meet in heaven, among the new arrivals, that German Polish madman? What was his name? Nietzsche?

STATUE Never heard of him.

DEVIL Well, he came here first, before he recovered his wits. I had some hopes of him; but he was a confirmed Life Force worshipper. It was he who raked up the Superman, who is as old as Prometheus; and the twentieth century will run after this newest of the old crazes when it gets tired of the world, the flesh, and your humble servant.

STATUE Superman is a good cry; and a good cry is half the battle. I should like to see this Nietzsche.

DEVIL Unfortunately he met Wagner here, and had a quarrel with him.

STATUE Quite right, too. Mozart for me!

DEVIL Oh, it was not about music. Wagner once drifted into Life Force worship, and invented a Superman called Siegfried. But he came to his senses afterwards. So when they met here, Nietzsche denounced him as a renegade; and Wagner wrote a pamphlet to prove that Nietzsche was a Jew; and it ended in Nietzsche's going to heaven in a huff. And a good riddance too. And now, my friend, let us hasten to my palace and celebrate your arrival with a grand musical service.

STATUE With pleasure: youre most kind.

DEVIL This way, Commander. We go down the old trap. [*He places himself on the grave trap.*]

STATUE Good. [*Reflectively*] All the same, the Superman is a fine conception. There is something statuesque about it. [*He places himself on the grave trap beside the Devil. It begins to descend slowly. Red glow from the abyss.*] Ah, this reminds me of old times.

DEVIL And me also.

ANA Stop!

[*The trap stops.*]

DEVIL You, Señora, cannot come this way. You will have an apotheosis. But you will be at the palace before us.

ANA That is not what I stopped you for. Tell me: where can I find the Superman?

DEVIL He is not yet created, Señora.

STATUE And never will be, probably. Let us proceed: the red fire will make me sneeze. [*They descend.*]

ANA Not yet created! Then my work is not yet done. [*Crossing herself devoutly*] I believe in the Life to Come. [*Crying to the universe*] A father! a father for the Superman!

She vanishes into the void; and again there is nothing: all existence seems suspended infinitely. Then, vaguely, there is a live human voice crying somewhere. One sees, with a shock, a mountain peak shewing faintly against a lighter background. The sky has returned from afar; and we suddenly remember where we were. The cry becomes distinct and urgent: it says "Automobile, automobile." The complete reality comes back with a rush: in a moment it is full morning in the Sierra; and the brigands are scrambling to their feet and making for the road as the goatherd runs down from the hill, warning them of the approach of another motor. Tanner and Mendoza rise amazedly and stare at one another with scattered wits. Straker sits up to yawn for a moment before he gets on his feet, making it a point of honor not to show any undue interest in the excitement of the bandits. Mendoza gives a quick look to see that his followers are attending to the alarm; then exchanges a private word with Tanner.

MENDOZA Did you dream?

TANNER Damnably. Did you?

MENDOZA Yes. I forget what. You were in it.

TANNER So were you. Amazing!

MENDOZA I warned you. [*A shot is heard from the road.*] Dolts! they will play with that gun. [*The brigands come running back scared.*] Who fired that shot? [*To Duval*] Was it you?

DUVAL [*breathless*] I have not shoot. Dey shoot first.

ANARCHIST I told you to begin by abolishing the State. Now we are all lost.

ROWDY SOCIAL-DEMOCRAT [*stampeding across the amphitheatre*] Run, everybody.

MENDOZA [*collaring him; throwing him on his back; and drawing a knife*] I stab the man who stirs. [*He blocks the way. The stampede is checked.*] What has happened?

SULKY SOCIAL-DEMOCRAT A motor—

ANARCHIST Three men—

DUVAL Deux femmes—

MENDOZA Three men and two women! Why have you not brought them here? Are you afraid of them?

ROWDY ONE [*getting up*] Thyve a hescort. Ow, de-ooh luts ook it, Mendowza.

SULKY ONE Two armored cars full o soldiers at the ed o the valley.

ANARCHIST The shot was fired in the air. It was a signal.

[*Straker whistles his favorite air, which falls on the ears of the brigands like a funeral march.*]

TANNER It is not an escort, but an expedition to capture you. We were advised to wait for it; but I was in a hurry.

ROWDY ONE [*in an agony of apprehension*] And ow my good Lord, ere we are, wytin for em! Luts tike to the mahntns.

MENDOZA Idiot, what do you know about the mountains? Are you a Spaniard? You would be given up by the first shepherd you met. Besides, we are already within range of their rifles.

ROWDY ONE But—

MENDOZA Silence. Leave this to me. [*To Tanner*] Comrade: you will not betray us.

STRAKER Oo are you callin comrade?

MENDOZA Last night the advantage was with me. The robber of the poor was at the mercy of the robber of the rich. You offered your hand: I took it.

TANNER I bring no charge against you, comrade. We have spent a pleasant evening with you: that is all.

STRAKER I gev my and to nobody, see?

MENDOZA [*turning on him impressively*] Young man: if I am tried, I shall plead guilty, and explain what drove me from England, home, and duty. Do you wish to have the respectable name of Straker dragged through the mud of a Spanish criminal court? The police will search me. They will find Louisa's portrait. It will be published in the illustrated papers. You blench. It will be your doing, remember.

STRAKER [*with baffled rage*] I dont care about the court. It's avin our name mixed up with yours that I object to, you blackmailin swine, you.

MENDOZA Language unworthy of Louisa's brother! But no matter: you are muzzled: that is enough for us.

BERNARD SHAW

[*He turns to face his own men, who back uneasily across the amphitheatre towards the cave to take refuge behind him, as a fresh party, muffled for motoring, comes from the road in riotous spirits. Ann, who makes straight for Tanner, comes first; then Violet, helped over the rough ground by Hector holding her right hand and Ramsden her left. Mendoza goes to his presidential block and seats himself calmly with his rank and file grouped behind him, and his staff, consisting of Duval and the Anarchist on his right and the two Social-Democrats on his left, supporting him in flank.*]

ANN   It's Jack!

TANNER   Caught!

HECTOR   Why, certainly it is. I said it was you, Tanner. Weve just been stopped by a puncture: the road is full of nails.

VIOLET   What are you doing here with all these men?

ANN   Why did you leave us without a word of warning?

HECTOR   I wawnt that bunch of roses, Miss Whitefield. [*To Tanner*] When we found you were gone, Miss Whitefield bet me a bunch of roses my car would not overtake yours before you reached Monte Carlo.

TANNER   But this is not the road to Monte Carlo.

HECTOR   No matter. Miss Whitefield tracked you at every stopping place: she is a regular Sherlock Holmes.

TANNER   The Life Force! I am lost.

OCTAVIUS   [*bounding gaily down from the road into the amphitheatre, and coming between Tanner and Straker*] I am so glad you are safe, old chap. We were afraid you had been captured by brigands.

RAMSDEN   [*who has been staring at Mendoza*] I seem to remember the face of your friend here. [*Mendoza rises politely and advances with a smile between Ann and Ramsden.*]

HECTOR   Why, so do I.

OCTAVIUS   I know you perfectly well, sir; but I cant think where I have met you.

MENDOZA   [*to Violet*] Do you remember me, madam?

VIOLET   Oh, quite well; but I am so stupid about names.

MENDOZA   It was at the Savoy Hotel. [*To Hector*] You sir, used to come with this lady [*indicating Violet*] to lunch. [*To Octavius*] You, sir, often brought this lady [*indicating Ann*] and her mother to dinner on your way to the Lyceum Theatre. [*To Ramsden*] You, sir, used to come to supper, with [*dropping his voice to a confidential but perfectly audible whisper*] several different ladies.

RAMSDEN   [*angrily*]   Well, what is that to you, pray?

OCTAVIUS   Why, Violet, I thought you hardly knew one another before this trip, you and Malone!

VIOLET   [*vexed*]   I suppose this person was the manager.

MENDOZA   The waiter, madam. I have a grateful recollection of you all. I gathered from the bountiful way in which you treated me that you all enjoyed your visits very much.

VIOLET   What impertinence! [*She turns her back on him, and goes up the hill with Hector.*]

RAMSDEN   That will do, my friend. You do not expect these ladies to treat you as an acquaintance, I suppose, because you have waited on them at table.

MENDOZA   Pardon me: it was you who claimed my acquaintance. The ladies followed your example. However, this display of the unfortunate manners of your class closes the incident. For the future, you will please address me with the respect due to a stranger and fellow traveller. [*He turns haughtily away and resumes his presidential seat.*]

TANNER   There! I have found one man on my journey capable of reasonable conversation; and you all instinctively insult him. Even the New Man is as bad as any of you. Enry: you have behaved just like a miserable gentleman.

STRAKER   Gentleman! Not me.

RAMSDEN   Really, Tanner, this tone—

ANN   Dont mind him, Granny: you ought to know him by this time.

[*She takes his arm and coaxes him away to the hill to join Violet and Hector. Octavius follows her, doglike.*]

VIOLET   [*calling from the hill*]   Here are the soldiers. They are getting out of their motors.

Man and Superman

DUVAL [*panicstricken*] Oh, nom de Dieu!

ANARCHIST Fools: the State is about to crush you because you spared it at the prompting of the political hangers-on of the bourgeoisie.

SULKY SOCIAL-DEMOCRAT [*argumentative to the last*] On the contrary, only by capturing the State machine—

ANARCHIST It is going to capture you.

ROWDY SOCIAL-DEMOCRAT [*his anguish culminating*] Ow, chack it. Wot are we ere for? Wot are we wytin for?

MENDOZA [*between his teeth*] Go on. Talk politics, you idiots: nothing sounds more respectable. Keep it up. I tell you.

[*The soldiers line the road, commanding the* amphitheatre *with their rifles. The brigands, struggling with an overwhelming impulse to hide behind one another, look as unconcerned as they can. Mendoza rises superbly, with undaunted front. The officer in command steps down from the road into the amphitheatre; looks hard at the brigands; and then inquiringly at Tanner.*]

OFFICER Who are these men, Señor Ingles?

TANNER My escort.

[*Mendoza, with a Mephistophelean smile, bows profoundly. An irrepressible grin runs from face to face among the brigands. They touch their hats, except the Anarchist, who defies the State with folded arms.*]

Act Four

The garden of a villa in Granada. Whoever wishes to know what it is like must go to Granada to see. One may prosaically specify a group of hills dotted with villas, the Alhambra on the top of one of the hills, and a considerable town in the valley, approached by dusty white roads in which the children, no matter what they are doing or thinking about, automatically whine for halfpence and reach out little clutching brown palms for them; but there is nothing in this description except the Alhambra, the begging, and the color of the roads, that does not fit Surrey as well as Spain. The difference is that the Surrey hills are comparatively small and ugly, and should properly be called the Surrey Protuberances; but these Spanish hills are of mountain stock: the amenity which conceals their size does not compromise their dignity.

This particular garden is on a hill opposite the Alhambra; and the villa is as expensive and pretentious as a villa must be if it is to be let furnished by the week to opulent American and English visitors. If we stand on the lawn at the foot of the garden and look uphill, our horizon is the stone balustrade of a flagged platform on the edge of infinite space at the top of the hill. Between us and this platform is a flower garden with a circular basin and fountain in the centre, surrounded by geometrical flower beds, gravel paths, and clipped yew trees in the genteelest order. The garden is higher than our lawn; so we reach it by a few steps in the middle of its embankment. The platform is higher again than the garden, from which we mount a couple more steps to look over the balustrade at a fine view of the town up the valley and of the hills that stretch away beyond it to where, in the remotest distance, they become mountains. On our left is the villa, accessible by steps from the left hand corner of the garden. Returning from the platform through the garden and down again to the lawn (a movement which leaves the villa behind us on our right) we find evidence of literary interests on the part of the tenants in the fact that there is no tennis net nor set of croquet hoops, but, on our left, a little iron garden table with books on it, mostly yellow-backed, and a chair beside it. A chair on the right has also a couple of open books upon it. There are no newspapers, a circumstance which, with the absence of games, might lead an intelligent spectator to the most far reaching conclusions as to the sort of people who live in the villa. Such speculations are checked, however, on this delightfully fine afternoon, by the appearance at a little gate in a paling on our left, of Henry Straker in his professional costume. He opens the gate for an elderly gentleman, and follows him on to the lawn.

542 BERNARD SHAW

The elderly gentleman defies the Spanish sun in a black frock coat, tall silk hat, trousers in which narrow stripes of dark grey and lilac blend into a highly respectable color, and a black necktie tied into a bow over spotless linen. Probably therefore a man whose social position needs constant and scrupulous affirmation without regard to climate: one who would dress thus for the middle of the Sahara or the top of Mont Blanc. And since he has not the stamp of the class which accepts as its life-mission the advertizing and maintenance of first rate tailoring and millinery, he looks vulgar in his finery, though in a working dress of any kind he would look dignified enough. He is a bullet cheeked man with a red complexion, stubby hair, smallish eyes, a hard mouth that folds down at the corners, and a dogged chin. The looseness of skin that comes with age has attacked his throat and the laps of his cheeks; but he is still hard as an apple above the mouth; so that the upper half of his face looks younger than the lower. He has the self-confidence of one who has made money, and something of the truculence of one who has made it in a brutalizing struggle, his civility having under it a perceptible menace that he has other methods in reserve if necessary. Withal, a man to be rather pitied when he is not to be feared; for there is something pathetic about him at times, as if the huge commercial machine which has worked him into his frock coat had allowed him very little of his own way and left his affections hungry and baffled. At the first word that falls from him it is clear that he is an Irishman whose native intonation has clung to him through many changes of place and rank. One can only guess that the original material of his speech was perhaps the surly Kerry brogue; but the degradation of speech that occurs in London, Glasgow, Dublin, and big cities generally has been at work on it so long that nobody but an arrant cockney would dream of calling it a brogue now; for its music is almost gone, though its surliness is still perceptible. Straker, being a very obvious cockney, inspires him with implacable contempt, as a stupid Englishman who cannot even speak his own language properly. Straker, on the other hand, regards the old gentleman's accent as a joke thoughtfully provided by Providence expressly for the amusement of the British race, and treats him normally with the indulgence due to an inferior and unlucky species, but occasionally with indignant alarm when the old gentleman shows signs of intending his Irish nonsense to be taken seriously.

STRAKER   I'll go tell the young lady. She said youd prefer to stay here. [He turns to go up through the garden to the villa.]

IRISHMAN [who had been looking round him with lively curiosity]   The young lady? Thats Miss Violet, eh?

STRAKER [stopping on the steps with sudden suspicion]   Well, you know, dont you?

IRISHMAN   Do I?

STRAKER [his temper rising]   Well, do you or dont you?

IRISHMAN   What business is that of yours? [Straker, now highly indignant, comes back from the steps and confronts the visitor.]

STRAKER   I'll tell you what business it is of mine. Miss Robinson—

IRISHMAN [interrupting]   Oh, her name is Robinson, is it? Thank you.

STRAKER   Why, you dont know even her name?

IRISHMAN   Yes I do, now that youve told me.

STRAKER [after a moment of stupefaction at the old man's readiness in repartee]   Look here: what do you mean by gittin into my car and lettin me bring you here if youre not the person I took that note to?

IRISHMAN   Who else did you take it to, pray?

STRAKER   I took it to Mr Ector Malone, at Miss Robinson's request, see? Miss Robinson is not my principal: I took it to oblige her. I know Mr Malone; and he aint you, not by a long chalk. At the hotel they told me that your name is Ector Malone—

MALONE   Hector Malone.

STRAKER [with calm superiority]   Hector in your own country: thats what comes o livin in provincial places like Ireland and America. Over here youre Ector: if you avnt noticed it before, you soon will.

[The growing strain of the conversation is here relieved by Violet, who has sallied from the *villa and through the garden to the steps, which she now descends, coming very opportunely between Malone and Straker.*]

VIOLET [*to Straker*] Did you take my message?

STRAKER Yes, miss. I took it to the hotel and sent it up, expecting to see young Mr Malone. Then out walks this gent, and says it's all right and he'll come with me. So as the hotel people said he was Mr Ector Malone, I fetched him. And now he goes back on what he said. But if he isnt the gentleman you meant, say the word: it's easy enough to fetch him back again.

MALONE I should esteem it a great favor if I might have a short conversation with you, madam. I am Hector's father, as this bright Britisher would have guessed in the course of another hour or so.

STRAKER [*coolly defiant*] No, not in another year or so. When weve ad you as long to polish up as weve ad im, perhaps youll begin to look a little bit up to is mark. At present you fall a long way short. Youve got too many aitches, for one thing. [*To Violet, amiably*] All right, Miss: you want to talk to him: I shant intrude. [*He nods affably to Malone and goes out through the little gate in the paling.*]

VIOLET [*very civilly*] I am so sorry, Mr Malone, if that man has been rude to you. But what can we do? He is our chauffeur.

MALONE Your hwat?

VIOLET The driver of our automobile. He can drive a motor car at seventy miles an hour, and mend it when it breaks down. We are dependent on our motor cars; and our motor cars are dependent on him; so of course we are dependent on him.

MALONE Ive noticed, madam, that every thousand dollars an Englishman gets seems to add one to the number of people he's dependent on. However, you neednt apologize for your man: I made him talk on purpose. By doing so I learnt that youre staying here in Grannida with a party of English, including my son Hector.

VIOLET [*conversationally*] Yes. We intended to go to Nice; but we had to follow a rather eccentric member of our party who started first and came here. Wont you sit down? [*She clears the nearest chair of the two books on it.*]

MALONE [*impressed by this attention*] Thank you. [*He sits down, examining her curiously as she goes to the iron table to put down the books. She turns to him again.*] Miss Robinson, I believe?

VIOLET [*sitting down*] Yes.

MALONE [*taking a letter from his pocket*] Your note to Hector runs as follows. [*Violet is unable to repress a start. He pauses quietly to take out and put on his spectacles, which have gold rims.*] "Dearest: they have all gone to the Alhambra for the afternoon. I have shammed headache and have the garden all to myself. Jump into Jack's motor: Straker will rattle you here in a jiffy. Quick, quick, quick. Your loving Violet." [*He looks at her, but by this time she has recovered, and meets his spectacles with perfect composure; he continues slowly*] Now I dont know on hwat terms young people associate in English society; but in America that note would be considered to imply a very considerable degree of affectionate intimacy between the parties.

VIOLET Yes: I know your son very well, Mr Malone. Have you any objection?

MALONE [*somewhat taken aback*] No, no objection exactly. Provided it is understood that my son is altogether dependent on me, and that I have to be consulted in any important step he may propose to take.

VIOLET I am sure you would not be unreasonable with him, Mr Malone.

MALONE I hope not, Miss Robinson; but at your age you might think many things unreasonable that dont seem so to me.

VIOLET [*with a little shrug*] Oh, well, I suppose theres no use our playing at cross purposes, Mr Malone. Hector wants to marry me.

MALONE I inferred from your note that he might. Well, Miss Robinson, he is his own master; but if he marries you he shall not have a rap from me. [*He takes off his spectacles and pockets them with the note.*]

VIOLET [*with some severity*] That is not very complimentary to me, Mr Malone.

MALONE I say nothing against you, Miss Robinson: I daresay you are an amiable and excellent young lady. But I have other views for Hector.

VIOLET Hector may not have other views for himself, Mr Malone.

MALONE Possibly not. Then he does without me: thats all. I daresay you are prepared for that. When a young lady writes to a young man to come to her quick, quick, quick, money seems nothing and love seems everything.

VIOLET [*sharply*] I beg your pardon, Mr Malone: I do not think anything so foolish. Hector must have money.

MALONE [*staggered*] Oh, very well, very well. No doubt he can work for it.

VIOLET What is the use of having money if you have to work for it? [*She rises impatiently*.] It's all nonsense, Mr Malone: you must enable your son to keep up his position. It is his right.

MALONE [*grimly*] I should not advise you to marry him on the strength of that right, Miss Robinson.

[*Violet, who has almost lost her temper, controls herself with an effort; unclenches her fingers; and resumes her seat with studied tranquility and reasonableness.*]

VIOLET What objection have you to me, pray? My social position is as good as Hector's, to say the least. He admits it.

MALONE [*shrewdly*] You tell him so from time to time, eh? Hector's social position in England, Miss Robinson, is just what I choose to buy for him. I have made him a fair offer. Let him pick out the most historic house, castle, or abbey that England contains. The very day he tells me he wants it for a wife worthy of its traditions, I buy it for him, and give him the means of keeping it up.

VIOLET What do you mean by a wife worthy of its traditions? Cannot any well bred woman keep such a house for him?

MALONE No: she must be born to it.

VIOLET Hector was not born to it, was he?

MALONE His granmother was a barefooted Irish girl that nursed me by a turf fire. Let him marry another such, and I will not stint her marriage portion. Let him raise himself socially with my money or raise somebody else: so long as there is a social profit somewhere, I'll regard my expenditure as justified. But there must be a profit for someone. A marriage with you would leave things just where they are.

VIOLET Many of my relations would object very much to my marrying the grandson of a common woman, Mr Malone. That may be prejudice; but so is your desire to have him marry a title prejudice.

MALONE [*rising, and approaching her with a scrutiny in which there is a good deal of reluctant respect*] You seem a pretty straightforward downright sort of a young woman.

VIOLET I do not see why I should be made miserably poor because I cannot make profits for you. Why do you want to make Hector unhappy?

MALONE He will get over it all right enough. Men thrive better on disappointments in love than on disappointments in money. I daresay you think that sordid; but I know what I'm talking about. Me father died of starvation in Ireland in the black 47. Maybe youve heard of it.

VIOLET The Famine?

MALONE [*with smouldering passion*] No, the starvation. When a country is full o food, and exporting it, there can be no famine. Me father was starved dead; and I was starved out to America in me mother's arms. English rule drove me and mine out of Ireland. Well, you can keep Ireland. Me and me like are coming back to buy England; and we'll buy the best of it. I want no middle class properties and no middle class women for Hector. Thats straightforward, isnt it, like yourself?

VIOLET [*icily pitying his sentimentality*] Really, Mr Malone, I am astonished to hear a man of your age and good sense talking in that romantic way. Do you suppose English noblemen will sell their places to you for the asking?

MALONE I have the refusal of two of the oldest family mansions in England. One historic owner cant afford to keep all the rooms dusted: the other cant afford the death duties. What do you say now?

VIOLET Of course it is very scandalous; but surely you know that the Government will sooner or later put a stop to all these Socialistic attacks on property.

MALONE [*grinning*]   D'y'think theyll be able to get that done before I buy the house—or rather the abbey? Theyre both abbeys.

VIOLET [*putting that aside rather impatiently*] Oh, well, let us talk sense. Mr Malone. You must feel that we havent been talking sense so far.

MALONE   I cant say I do. I mean all I say.

VIOLET   Then you dont know Hector as I do. He is romantic and faddy—he gets it from you, I fancy—and he wants a certain sort of a wife to take care of him. Not a faddy sort of person, you know.

MALONE   Somebody like you, perhaps?

VIOLET [*quietly*]   Well, yes. But you cannot very well ask me to undertake this with absolutely no means of keeping up his position.

MALONE [*alarmed*]   Stop a bit, stop a bit. Where are we getting to? I'm not aware that I'm asking you to undertake anything.

VIOLET   Of course, Mr Malone, you can make it very difficult for me to speak to you if you choose to misunderstand me.

MALONE [*half bewildered*]   I dont wish to take any unfair advantage; but we seem to have got off the straight track somehow.

[*Straker, with the air of a man who has been making haste, opens the little gate, and admits Hector, who, snorting with indignation, comes upon the lawn, and is making for his father when Violet, greatly dismayed, springs up and intercepts him. Straker does not wait; at least he does not remain visibly within earshot.*]

VIOLET   Oh, how unlucky! Now please, Hector, say nothing. Go away until I have finished speaking to your father.

HECTOR [*inexorably*]   No, Violet: I mean to have this thing out, right away. [*He puts her aside; passes her by; and faces his father, whose cheeks darken as his Irish blood begins to simmer.*] Dad: youve not played this hand straight.

MALONE   Hwat d'y'mean?

HECTOR   Youve opened a letter addressed to me. Youve impersonated me and stolen a march on this lady. Thats disawnerable.

MALONE [*threateningly*]   Now you take care what

youre saying, Hector. Take care, I tell you.

HECTOR   I have taken care. I am taking care. I'm taking care of my honor and my position in English society.

MALONE [*hotly*]   Your position has been got by my money: do you know that?

HECTOR   Well, youve just spoiled it all by opening that letter. A letter from an English lady, not addressed to you—a cawnfidential letter! a dullicate letter! a private letter! opened by my father! Thats a sort of thing a man cant struggle against in England. The sooner we go back together the better. [*He appeals mutely to the heavens to witness the shame and anguish of two outcasts.*]

VIOLET [*snubbing him with an instinctive dislike for scene making*]   Dont be unreasonable, Hector. It was quite natural for Mr Malone to open my letter: his name was on the envelope.

MALONE   There! Youve no common sense, Hector. I thank you, Miss Robinson.

HECTOR   I thank you, too. It's very kind of you. My father knows no better.

MALONE [*furiously clenching his fists*]   Hector—

HECTOR [*with undaunted moral force*]   Oh, it's no use hectoring me. A private letter's a private letter, dad: you cant get over that.

MALONE [*raising his voice*]   I wont be talked back to by you, d'y'hear?

VIOLET   Ssh! please, please. Here they all come. [*Father and son, checked, glare mutely at one another as Tanner comes in through the little gate with Ramsden, followed by Octavius and Ann.*]

VIOLET   Back already!

TANNER   The Alhambra is not open this afternoon.

VIOLET   What a sell!

[*Tanner passes on, and presently finds himself between Hector and a strange elder, both apparently on the verge of personal combat. He looks from one to the other for an explanation. They sulkily avoid his eye, and nurse their wrath in silence.*]

RAMSDEN   Is it wise for you to be out in the sunshine with such a headache, Violet?

TANNER   Have you recovered too, Malone?

VIOLET   Oh, I forgot. We have not all met before. Mr Malone: wont you introduce your father?

HECTOR [with Roman firmness] No, I will not. He is no father of mine.

MALONE [very angry] You disown your dad before your English friends, do you?

VIOLET Oh, please dont make a scene.

[Ann and Octavius, lingering near the gate, exchange an astonished glance, and discreetly withdraw up the steps to the garden, where they can enjoy the disturbance without intruding. On their way to the steps Ann sends a little grimace of mute sympathy to Violet, who is standing with her back to the little table, looking on in helpless annoyance as her husband soars to higher and higher moral eminences without the least regard to the old man's millions.]

HECTOR I'm very sorry, Miss Rawbnsn; but I'm contending for a principle. I am a son, and I hope, a dutiful one; but before everything I'm a Mahn!!! And when dad treats my private letters as his own, and takes it on himself to say that I shant marry you if I am happy and fortunate enough to gain your consent, then I just snap my fingers and go my own way.

TANNER Marry Violet!

RAMSDEN Are you in your senses?

TANNER Do you forget what we told you?

HECTOR [recklessly] I dont care what you told me.

RAMSDEN [scandalized] Tut tut, sir! Monstrous! [He flings away toward the gate, his elbows quivering with indignation.]

TANNER Another madman! These men in love should be locked up. [He flings away towards the gate, his elbows towards the garden; but Malone, taking offence in a new direction, follows him and compels him, by the aggressiveness of his tone, to stop.]

MALONE I dont understand this. Is Hector not good enough for this lady, pray?

TANNER My dear sir, the lady is married already. Hector knows it; and yet he persists in his infatuation. Take him home and lock him up.

MALONE [bitterly] So this is the highborn social tone I've spoilt be me ignorant, uncultivated behavior! Makin love to a married woman!

[He comes angrily between Hector and Violet, and almost bawls into Hector's left ear] Youve picked up that habit of the British aristocracy, have you?

HECTOR Thats all right. Dont you trouble yourself about that. I'll answer for the morality of what I'm doing.

TANNER [coming forward to Hector's right hand with flashing eyes] Well said, Malone! You also see that mere marriage laws are not morality! I agree with you; but unfortunately Violet does not.

MALONE I take leave to doubt that, sir. [Turning on Violet] Let me tell you, Mrs Robinson, or whatever your right name is, you had no right to send that letter to my son when you were the wife of another man.

HECTOR [outraged] This is the last straw. Dad: you have insulted my wife.

MALONE Your wife!

TANNER You the missing husband! Another moral impostor! [He smites his brow, and collapses into Malone's chair.]

MALONE Youve married without my consent!

RAMSDEN You have deliberately humbugged us, sir!

HECTOR Here: I have had just enough of being badgered. Violet and I are married: thats the long and the short of it. Now what have you got to say—any of you?

MALONE I know what Ive got to say. She's married a beggar.

HECTOR No: she's married a Worker. [His American pronunciation imparts an overwhelming intensity to this simple and unpopular word.] I start to earn my own living this very afternoon.

MALONE [sneering angrily] Yes: youre very plucky now, because you got your remittance from me yesterday or this morning, I reckon. Waitl it's spent. You wont be so full of cheek then.

HECTOR [producing a letter from his pocketbook] Here it is [thrusting it on his father]. Now you just take your remittance and yourself out of my life. I'm done with remittances; and I'm done with you. I dont sell the privilege of insulting my wife for a thousand dollars.

MALONE [*deeply wounded and full of concern*] Hector: you dont know what poverty is.

HECTOR [*fervidly*] Well, I wawnt to know what it is. I wawnt'be a Mahn. Violet: you come along with me, to your own home: I'll see you through.

OCTAVIUS [*jumping down from the garden to the lawn and running to Hector's left hand*] I hope youll shake hands with me before you go, Hector. I admire and respect you more than I can say. [*He is affected almost to tears as they shake hands.*]

VIOLET [*also almost in tears, but of vexation*] Oh, dont be an idiot, Tavy. Hector's about as fit to become a workman as you are.

TANNER [*rising from his chair on the other side of Hector*] Never fear: theres no question of his becoming a navvy, Mrs Malone. [*To Hector*] Theres really no difficulty about capital to start with. Treat me as a friend: draw on me.

OCTAVIUS [*impulsively*] Or on me.

MALONE [*with fierce jealousy*] Who wants your durty money? Who should he draw on but his own father? [*Tanner and Octavius recoil, Octavius rather hurt, Tanner consoled by the solution of the money difficulty. Violet looks up hopefully.*] Hector: dont be rash, my boy. I'm sorry for what I said: I never meant to insult Violet: I take it all back. She's just the wife you want: there!

HECTOR [*patting him on the shoulder*] Well, thats all right, dad. Say no more: we're friends again. Only, I take no money from anybody.

MALONE [*pleading abjectly*] Dont be hard on me, Hector. I'd rather you quarrelled and took the money than made friends and starved. You dont know what the world is: I do.

HECTOR No, no, NO. Thats fixed: thats not going to change. [*He passes his father inexorably by, and goes to Violet.*] Come, Mrs Malone: youve got to move to the hotel with me, and take your proper place before the world.

VIOLET But I must go in, dear, and tell Davis to pack. Wont you go on and make them give you a room overlooking the garden for me? I'll join you in half an hour.

HECTOR Very well. Youll dine with us, Dad, wont you?

MALONE [*eager to conciliate him*] Yes, yes.

HECTOR See you all later.

[*He waves his hand to Ann, who has now been joined by Tanner, Octavius, and Ramsden in the garden, and goes out through the little gate, leaving his father and Violet together on the lawn.*]

MALONE Youll try to bring him to his senses, Violet: I know you will.

VIOLET I had no idea he could be so headstrong. If he goes on like that, what can I do?

MALONE Dont be discurridged: domestic pressure may be slow; but it's sure. Youll wear him down. Promise me you will.

VIOLET I will do my best. Of course I think it's the greatest nonsense deliberately making us poor like that.

MALONE Of course it is.

VIOLET [*after a moment's reflection*] You had better give me the remittance. He will want it for his hotel bill. I'll see whether I can induce him to accept it. Not now, of course, but presently.

MALONE [*eagerly*] Yes, yes, yes: thats just the thing. [*He hands her the thousand dollar bill, and adds cunningly*] Y'understand that this is only a bachelor allowance.

VIOLET [*coolly*] Oh, quite. [*She takes it.*] Thank you. By the way, Mr Malone, those two houses you mentioned—the abbeys.

MALONE Yes?

VIOLET Dont take one of them until Ive seen it. One never knows what may be wrong with these places.

MALONE I wont. I'll do nothing without consulting you, never fear.

VIOLET [*politely, but without a ray of gratitude*] Thanks: that will be much the best way.

[*She goes calmly back to the villa, escorted obsequiously by Malone to the upper end of the garden.*]

TANNER [*drawing Ramsden's attention to Malone's cringing attitude as he takes leave of Violet*] And that poor devil is a billionaire! one of the master spirits of the age! Led in a string like a pug dog by the first girl who takes the trouble to despise him! I wonder will it ever come to that with me. [*He comes down to the lawn.*]

RAMSDEN [*following him*] The sooner the better for you.

MALONE [slapping his hands as he returns through the garden] Thatll be a grand woman for Hector. I wouldnt exchange her for ten duchesses. [He descends to the lawn and comes between Tanner and Ramsden.]

RAMSDEN [very civil to the billionaire] It's an unexpected pleasure to find you in this corner of the world, Mr Malone. Have you come to buy up the Alhambra?

MALONE Well, I dont say I mightnt. I think I could do better with it than the Spanish government. But thats not what I came about. To tell you the truth, about a month ago I overheard a deal between two men over a bundle of shares. They differed about the price: they were young and greedy, and didnt know that if the shares were worth what was bid for them they must be worth what was asked, the margin being too small to be of any account, you see. To amuse meself, I cut in and bought the shares. Well, to this day I havnt found out what the business is. The office is in this town; and the name is Mendoza, Limited. Now whether Mendoza's a mine, or a steamboat line, or a bank, or a patent article—

TANNER He's a man. I know him: his principles are thoroughly commercial. Let us take you round the town in our motor, Mr Malone, and call on him on the way.

MALONE If youll be so kind, yes. And may I ask who—

TANNER Mr Roebuck Ramsden, a very old friend of your daughter-in-law.

MALONE Happy to meet you, Mr Ramsden.

RAMSDEN Thank you. Mr Tanner is also one of our circle.

MALONE Glad to know you also, Mr Tanner.

TANNER Thanks. [Malone and Ramsden go out very amicably through the little gate. Tanner calls to Octavius, who is wandering in the garden with Ann] Tavy! [Tavy comes to the steps, Tanner whispers loudly to him] Violet's father-in-law is a financier of brigands.

[Tanner hurries away to overtake Malone and Ramsden. Ann strolls to the steps with an idle impulse to torment Octavius.]

ANN Wont you go with them, Tavy?

OCTAVIUS [tears suddenly flushing his eyes] You cut me to the heart, Ann, by wanting me to go.

[He comes down on the lawn to hide his face from her. She follows him caressingly.]

ANN Poor Ricky Ticky Tavy! Poor heart!

OCTAVIUS It belongs to you, Ann. Forgive me: I must speak of it. I love you. You know I love you.

ANN What's the good, Tavy? You know that my mother is determined that I shall marry Jack.

OCTAVIUS [amazed] Jack!

ANN It seems absurd, doesn't it?

OCTAVIUS [with growing resentment] Do you mean to say that Jack has been playing with me all this time? That he has been urging me not to marry you because he intends to marry you himself?

ANN [alarmed] No, no: you mustnt lead him to believe that I said that. I dont for a moment think that Jack knows his own mind. But it's clear from my father's will that he wished me to marry Jack. And my mother is set on it.

OCTAVIUS But you are not bound to sacrifice yourself always to the wishes of your parents.

ANN My father loved me. My mother loves me. Surely their wishes are a better guide than my own selfishness.

OCTAVIUS Oh, I know how unselfish you are, Ann. But believe me—though I know I am speaking in my own interest—there is another side to this question. Is it fair to Jack to marry him if you do not love him? Is it fair to destroy my happiness as well as your own if you can bring yourself to love me?

ANN [looking at him with a faint impulse of pity] Tavy, my dear, you are a nice creature—a good boy.

OCTAVIUS [humiliated] Is that all?

ANN [mischievously in spite of her pity] Thats a great deal, I assure you. You would always worship the ground I trod on, wouldn't you?

OCTAVIUS I do. It sounds ridiculous; but it's no exaggeration. I do; and I always shall.

ANN Always is a long word, Tavy. You see, I shall have to live up always to your idea of my divinity; and I dont think I could do that if we were married. But if I marry Jack, youll never be disillusioned—at least not until I grow too old.

OCTAVIUS I too shall grow old, Ann. And when

I am eighty, one white hair of the woman I love will make me tremble more than the thickest gold tress from the most beautiful young head.

ANN [*quite touched*] Oh, thats poetry, Tavy, real poetry. It gives me that strange sudden sense of an echo from a former existence which always seems to me such a striking proof that we have immortal souls.

OCTAVIUS Do you believe that it is true?

ANN Tavy: if it is to come true, you must lose me as well as love me.

OCTAVIUS Oh! [*He hastily sits down at the little table and covers his face with his hands.*]

ANN [*with conviction*] Tavy: I wouldnt for worlds destroy your illusions. I can neither take you nor let you go. I can see exactly what will suit you. You must be a sentimental old bachelor for my sake.

OCTAVIUS [*desperately*] Ann: I'll kill myself.

ANN Oh no, you wont: that wouldn't be kind. You wont have a bad time. You will be very nice to women; and you will go a good deal to the opera. A broken heart is a very pleasant complaint for a man in London if he has a comfortable income.

OCTAVIUS [*considerably cooled, but believing that he is only recovering his self-control*] I know you mean to be kind, Ann. Jack has persuaded you that cynicism is a good tonic for me. [*He rises with quiet dignity.*]

ANN [*studying him slyly*] You see, I'm disillusionizing you already. Thats what I dread.

OCTAVIUS You do not dread disillusionizing Jack.

ANN [*her face lighting up with mischievous ecstasy—whispering*] I cant: he has no illusions about me. I shall surprise Jack the other way. Getting over an unfavorable impression is ever so much easier than living up to an ideal. Oh, I shall enrapture Jack sometimes!

OCTAVIUS [*resuming the calm phase of despair, and beginning to enjoy his broken heart and delicate attitude without knowing it*] I dont doubt that. You will enrapture him always. And he—the fool!—thinks you would make him wretched.

ANN Yes: thats the difficulty, so far.

OCTAVIUS [*heroically*[Shall *I* tell him that you love him?

ANN [*quickly*] Oh no: he'd run away again.

OCTAVIUS [*shocked*] Ann: would you marry an unwilling man?

ANN What a queer creature you are, Tavy! Theres no such creature as a willing man when you really go for him. [*She laughs naughtily.*] I'm shocking you, I suppose. But you know you are really getting a sort of satisfaction already in being out of danger yourself.

OCTAVIUS [*startled*] Satisfaction! [*Reproachfully*] You say that to me!

ANN Well, if it were really agony, would you ask for more of it?

OCTAVIUS Have I asked for more of it?

ANN You have offered to tell Jack that I love him. Thats self-sacrifice, I suppose; but there must be some satisfaction in it. Perhaps it's because youre a poet. You are like the bird that presses its breast against the sharp thorn to make itself sing.

OCTAVIUS It's quite simple. I love you; and I want you to be happy. You dont love me; so I cant make you happy myself; but I can help another man to do it.

ANN Yes: it seems quite simple. But I doubt if we ever know why we do things. The only really simple thing is to go straight for what you want and grab it. I suppose I dont love you, Tavy; but sometimes I feel as if I should like to make a man of you somehow. You are very foolish about women.

OCTAVIUS [*almost coldly*] I am content to be what I am in that respect.

ANN Then you must keep away from them, and only dream about them. I wouldnt marry you for worlds, Tavy.

OCTAVIUS I have no hope, Ann: I accept my ill luck. But I dont think you quite know how much it hurts.

ANN You are so softhearted! It's queer that you should be so different from Violet. Violet's as hard as nails.

OCTAVIUS Oh no. I am sure Violet is thoroughly womanly at heart.

ANN [*with some impatience*] Why do you say that? Is it unwomanly to be thoughtful and businesslike and sensible? Do you want Violet to be an idiot—or something worse, like me?

OCTAVIUS Something worse—like you! What do

you mean, Ann?

ANN Oh well, I dont mean that, of course. But I have a great respect for Violet. She gets her own way always.

OCTAVIUS [*sighing*] So do you.

ANN Yes; but somehow she gets it without coaxing—without having to make people sentimental about her.

OCTAVIUS [*with brotherly callousness*] Nobody could get very sentimental about Violet, I think, pretty as she is.

ANN Oh yes they could, if she made them.

OCTAVIUS But surely no really nice woman would deliberately practice on men's instincts in that way.

ANN [*throwing up her hands*] Oh, Tavy, Tavy, Ricky Ticky Tavy, heaven help the woman who marries you!

OCTAVIUS [*his passion reviving at the name*] Oh why, why, why do you say that? Dont torment me. I dont understand.

ANN Suppose she were to tell fibs and lay snares for men?

OCTAVIUS Do you think *I* would marry such a woman—I, who have known and loved you?

ANN Hm! Well, at all events, she wouldn't let you if she were wise. So thats settled. And now I cant talk any more. Say you forgive me, and that the subject is closed.

OCTAVIUS I have nothing to forgive; and the subject is closed. And if the wound is open, at least you shall never see it bleed.

ANN Poetic to the last, Tavy. Goodbye, dear.

[*She pats his cheek; has an impulse to kiss him and then another impulse of distaste which prevents her; finally runs away through the garden and into the villa. Octavius again takes refuge at the table, bowing his head on his arms and sobbing softly. Mrs Whitefield, who has been pottering round the Granada shops and has a net full of little parcels in her hand, comes in through the gate and sees him.*]

MRS WHITEFIELD [*running to him and lifting his head*] Whats the matter, Tavy? Are you ill?

OCTAVIUS No, nothing, nothing.

MRS WHITEFIELD [*still holding his head, anxiously*] But youre crying. Is it about Violet's marriage?

OCTAVIUS No, no. Who told you about Violet?

MRS WHITEFIELD [*restoring the head to its owner*]

I met Roebuck and that awful old Irishman. Are you sure youre not ill? Whats the matter?

OCTAVIUS [*affectionately*] It's nothing. Only a man's broken heart. Doesnt that sound ridiculous?

MRS WHITEFIELD But what is it all about? Has Ann been doing anything to you?

OCTAVIUS It's not Ann's fault. And dont think for a moment that I blame you.

MRS WHITEFIELD [*startled*] For what?

OCTAVIUS [*pressing her hand consolingly*] For nothing. I said I didnt blame you.

MRS WHITEFIELD But I havnt done anything. Whats the matter?

OCTAVIUS [*smiling sadly*] Cant you guess? I daresay you are right to prefer Jack to me as a husband for Ann; but I love Ann; and it hurts rather. [*He rises and moves away from her towards the middle of the lawn.*]

MRS WHITEFIELD [*following him hastily*] Does Ann say that I want her to marry Jack?

OCTAVIUS Yes: she has told me.

MRS WHITEFIELD [*thoughtfully*] Then I'm very sorry for you, Tavy. It's only her way of saying she wants to marry Jack. Little she cares what *I* say or what *I* want!

OCTAVIUS But she would not say it unless she believed it. Surely you dont suspect Ann of— of deceit!!

MRS WHITEFIELD Well, never mind, Tavy. I dont know which is best for a young man: to know too little, like you, or too much, like Jack.

[*Tanner returns.*]

TANNER Well, Ive disposed of old Malone. Ive introduced him to Mendoza, Limited; and left the two brigands together to talk it out. Hullo, Tavy! anything wrong?

OCTAVIUS I must go wash my face, I see. [*To Mrs Whitefield*] Tell him what you wish. [*To Tanner*] You may take it from me, Jack, that Ann approves of it.

TANNER [*puzzled by his manner*] Approves of what?

OCTAVIUS Of what Mrs Whitefield wishes. [*He goes his way with sad dignity to the villa.*]

TANNER [*to Mrs Whitefield*] This is very mysterious. What is it you wish? It shall be done, whatever it is.

MRS WHITEFIELD [*with snivelling gratitude*]

Thank you, Jack. [*She sits down. Tanner brings the other chair from the table and sits close to her with his elbows on his knees, giving her his whole attention.*] I dont know why it is that other people's children are so nice to me, and that my own have so little consideration for me. It's no wonder I dont seem able to care for Ann and Rhoda as I do for you and Tavy and Violet. It's a very queer world. It used to be so straightforward and simple; and now nobody seems to think and feel as they ought. Nothing has been right since that speech that Professor Tyndall made at Belfast.

TANNER Yes: life is more complicated than we used to think. But what am I to do for you?

MRS WHITEFIELD Thats just what I want to tell you. Of course youll marry Ann whether I like it or not—

TANNER [*starting*] It seems to me that I shall presently be married to Ann whether I like it myself or not.

MRS WHITEFIELD [*peacefully*] Oh, very likely you will: you know what she is when she has set her mind on anything. But dont put it on me: thats all I ask. Tavy has just let out that she's been saying that I am making her marry you; and the poor boy is breaking his heart about it; for he is in love with her himself, though what he sees in her so wonderful, goodness knows: *I* dont. It's no use telling Tavy that Ann puts things into people's heads by telling them that I want them when the thought of them never crossed my mind. It only sets Tavy against me. But you know better than that. So if you marry her, dont put the blame on me.

TANNER [*emphatically*] I havnt the slightest intention of marrying her.

MRS WHITEFIELD [*slyly*] She'd suit you better than Tavy. She'd meet her match in you, Jack. I'd like to see her meet her match.

TANNER No man is a match for a woman, except with a poker and a pair of hobnailed boots. Not always even then. Anyhow, *I* cant take the poker to her. I should be a mere slave.

MRS WHITEFIELD No: she's afraid of you. At all events, you would tell her the truth about herself. She wouldnt be able to slip out of it as she does with me.

TANNER Everybody would call me a brute if I told Ann the truth about herself in terms of her own moral code. To begin with, Ann says things that are not strictly true.

MRS WHITEFIELD I'm glad somebody sees she is not an angel.

TANNER In short—to put it as a husband would put it when exasperated to the point of speaking out—she is a liar. And since she has plunged Tavy head over ears in love with her without any intention of marrying him, she is a coquette, according to the standard definition of a coquette as a woman who rouses passions she has no intention of gratifying. And as she has now reduced you to the point of being willing to sacrifice me at the altar for the mere satisfaction of getting me to call her a liar to her face, I may conclude that she is a bully as well. She cant bully men as she bullies women; so she habitually and unscrupulously uses her personal fascination to make men give her whatever she wants. That makes her almost something for which I know no polite name.

MRS WHITEFIELD [*in mild expostulation*] Well, you cant expect perfection, Jack.

TANNER I dont. But what annoys me is that Ann does. I know perfectly well that all this about her being a liar and a bully and a coquette and so forth is a trumped-up moral indictment which might be brought against anybody. We all lie; we all bully as much as we dare; we all bid for admiration without the least intention of earning it; we all get as much rent as we can out of our powers of fascination. If Ann would admit this I shouldnt quarrel with her. But she wont. If she has children she'll take advantage of their telling lies to amuse herself by whacking them. If another woman makes eyes at me, she'll refuse to know a coquette. She will do just what she likes herself whilst insisting on everybody else doing what the conventional code prescribes. In short, I can stand everything except her confounded hypocrisy. Thats what beats me.

MRS WHITEFIELD [*carried away by the relief of hearing her own opinion so eloquently expressed*] Oh, she is a hypocrite. She is: she is. Isnt she?

TANNER Then why do you want to marry me to her?

MRS WHITEFIELD [*querulously*] There now! Put it on me, of course. I never thought of it until Tavy told me she said I did. But, you know, I'm very fond of Tavy: he's a sort of son to me; and I dont want him to be trampled on and made wretched.

TANNER Whereas I dont matter, I suppose.

MRS WHITEFIELD Oh, you are different, somehow: you are able to take care of yourself. Youd serve her out. And anyhow, she must marry somebody.

TANNER Aha! there speaks the life instinct. You detest her; but you feel that you must get her married.

MRS WHITEFIELD [*rising, shocked*] Do you mean that I detest my own daughter! Surely you dont believe me to be so wicked and unnatural as that, merely because I see her faults.

TANNER [*cynically*] You love her, then?

MRS WHITEFIELD Why, of course I do. What queer things you say, Jack! We cant help loving our own blood relations.

TANNER Well, perhaps it saves unpleasantness to say so. But for my part, I suspect that the tables of consanguinity have a natural basis in a natural repugnance. [*He rises.*]

MRS WHITEFIELD You shouldnt say things like that, Jack. I hope you wont tell Ann that I have been speaking to you. I only wanted to set myself right with you and Tavy. I couldnt sit mumchance and have everything put on me.

TANNER [*politely*] Quite so.

MRS WHITEFIELD [*dissatisfied*] And now Ive only made matters worse. Tavy's angry with me because I dont worship Ann. And when it's been put into my head that Ann ought to marry you, what can I say except that it would serve her right?

TANNER Thank you.

MRS WHITEFIELD Now dont be silly and twist what I say into something I dont mean. I ought to have fair play—

[*Ann comes from the villa, followed presently by Violet, who is dressed for driving.*]

ANN [*coming to her mother's right hand with threatening suavity*] Well, Mamma darling, you seem to be having a delightful chat with Jack. We can hear you all over the place.

MRS WHITEFIELD [*appalled*] Have you overheard—

TANNER Never fear: Ann is only—well, we were discussing that habit of hers just now. She hasnt heard a word.

MRS WHITEFIELD [*stoutly*] I dont care whether she has or not: I have a right to say what I please.

VIOLET [*arriving on the lawn and coming between Mrs Whitefield and Tanner*] Ive come to say goodbye. I'm off for my honeymoon.

MRS WHITEFIELD [*crying*] Oh, dont say that, Violet. And no wedding, no breakfast, no clothes, nor anything.

VIOLET [*petting*] It wont be for long.

MRS WHITEFIELD Dont let him take you to America. Promise me that you wont.

VIOLET [*very decidedly*] I should think not, indeed. Dont cry, dear: I'm only going to the hotel.

MRS WHITEFIELD But going in that dress, with your luggage, makes one realize—[*she chokes, and then breaks out again*] how I wish you were my daughter, Violet!

VIOLET [*soothing her*] There, there: so I am. Ann will be jealous.

MRS WHITEFIELD Ann doesnt care a bit for me.

ANN Fie, Mother! Come, now: you mustnt cry any more: you know Violet doesnt like it.

[*Mrs Whitefield dries her eyes, and subsides.*]

VIOLET Goodbye, Jack.

TANNER Goodbye, Violet.

VIOLET The sooner you get married too, the better. You will be much less misunderstood.

TANNER [*restively*] I quite expect to get married in the course of the afternoon. You all seem to have set your minds on it.

VIOLET You might do worse. [*To Mrs Whitefield: putting her arm round her*] Let me take you to the hotel with me: the drive will do you good. Come in and get a wrap. [*She takes her towards the villa.*]

MRS WHITEFIELD [*as they go up through the garden*] I dont know what I shall do when you are gone, with no one but Ann in the house; and she always occupied with the men! It's not to be expected that your husband will care to be bothered with an old woman like me. Oh, you neednt tell me: politeness is all very well; but I know what people think—[*She talks herself and Violet out of sight and hearing. Ann, alone with Tanner, watches him and waits. He makes an irresolute movement towards the gate; but some magnetism in her draws him to her, a broken man.*]

ANN Violet is quite right. You ought to get married.

TANNER [*explosively*] Ann: I will not marry you. Do you hear? I wont, wont, wont, wont, WONT marry you.

ANN [*placidly*] Well, nobody axd you, sir she said, sir she said, sir she said. So thats settled.

TANNER Yes, nobody has asked me; but everybody treats the thing as settled. It's in the air. When we meet, the others go away on absurd pretexts to leave us alone together. Ramsden no longer scowls at me: his eye beams, as if he were already giving you away to me in church. Tavy refers me to your mother and gives me his blessing. Straker openly treats you as his future employer: it was he who first told me of it.

ANN Was that why you ran away?

TANNER Yes, only to be stopped by a lovesick brigand and run down like a truant schoolboy.

ANN Well, if you dont want to be married, you neednt be. [*She turns away from him and sits down, much at her ease.*]

TANNER [*following her*] Does any man want to be hanged? Yet men let themselves be hanged, without a struggle for life, though they could at least give the chaplain a black eye. We do the world's will, not our own. I have a frightful feeling that I shall let myself be married because it is the world's will that you should have a husband.

ANN I daresay I shall, someday.

TANNER But why me? me of all men! Marriage is to me apostasy, profanation of the sanctuary of my soul, violation of my manhood, sale of my birthright, shameful surrender, ignominious capitulation, acceptance of defeat. I shall decay like a thing that has served its purpose and is done with; I shall change from a man with a future to a man with a past; I shall see in the greasy eyes of all the other husbands their relief at the arrival of a new prisoner to share their ignominy. The young men will scorn me as one who has sold out: to the women I, who have always been an enigma and a possibility, shall be merely somebody else's property—and damaged goods at that: a secondhand man at best.

ANN Well, your wife can put on a cap and make herself ugly to keep you in countenance, like my grandmother.

TANNER So that she may make her triumph more insolent by publicly throwing away the bait the moment the trap snaps on the victim!

ANN After all, though, what difference would it make? Beauty is all very well at first sight; but who ever looks at it when it has been in the house three days? I thought our pictures very lovely when papa bought them; but I havnt looked at them for years. You never bother about my looks: you are too well used to me. I might be the umbrella stand.

TANNER You lie, you vampire: you lie.

ANN Flatterer. Why are you trying to fascinate me, Jack, if you dont want to marry me?

TANNER The Life Force. I am in the grip of the Life Force.

ANN I dont understand in the least: it sounds like the Life Guards.

TANNER Why dont you marry Tavy? He is willing. Can you not be satisfied unless your prey struggles?

ANN [*turning to him as if to let him into a secret*] Tavy will never marry. Havnt you noticed that that sort of man never marries?

TANNER What! a man who idolizes women! who sees nothing in nature but romantic scenery for love duets! Tavy, the chivalrous, the faithful, the tenderhearted and true! Tavy never marry! Why, he was born to be swept up by the first pair of blue eyes he meets in the street.

ANN Yes, I know. All the same, Jack, men like that always live in comfortable bachelor lodgings with broken hearts, and are adored by their landladies, and never get married. Men like you always get married.

TANNER [*smiting his brow*] How frightfully, horribly true! It has been staring me in the face all my life; and I never saw it before.

ANN Oh, it's the same with women. The poetic

temperament's a very nice temperament, very amiable, very harmless and poetic, I daresay; but it's an old maid's temperament.

TANNER Barren. The Life Force passes it by.

ANN If thats what you mean by the Life Force, yes.

TANNER You dont care for Tavy?

ANN [*looking round carefully to make sure that Tavy is not within earshot*] No.

TANNER And you do care for me?

ANN [*rising quietly and shaking her finger at him*] Now, Jack! Behave yourself.

TANNER Infamous, abandoned woman! Devil!

ANN Boa-constrictor! Elephant!

TANNER Hypocrite!

ANN [*softly*] I must be, for my future husband's sake.

TANNER For mine! [*Correcting himself savagely*] I mean for his.

ANN [*ignoring the correction*] Yes, for yours. You had better marry what you call a hypocrite, Jack. Women who are not hypocrites go about in rational dress and are insulted and get into all sorts of hot water. And then their husbands get dragged in too, and live in continual dread of fresh complications. Wouldnt you prefer a wife you could depend on?

TANNER No: a thousand times no: hot water is the revolutionist's element. You clean men as you clean milkpails, by scalding them.

ANN Cold water has its uses too. It's healthy.

TANNER [*despairingly*] Oh, you are witty: at the supreme moment the Life Force endows you with every quality. Well, I too can be a hypocrite. Your father's will appointed me your guardian, not your suitor. I shall be faithful to my trust.

ANN [*in low siren tones*] He asked me who I would have as my guardian before he made that will. I chose you!

TANNER The will is yours then! The trap was laid from the beginning.

ANN [*concentrating all her magic*] From the beginning—from our childhood—for both of us—by the Life Force.

TANNER I will not marry you. I will not marry you.

ANN Oh, you will, you will.

TANNER I tell you, no, no, no.

ANN I tell you, yes, yes, yes.

TANNER No.

ANN [*coaxing — imploring — almost exhausted*] Yes. Before it is too late for repentance. Yes.

TANNER [*struck by the echo from the past*] When did all this happen to me before? Are we two dreaming?

ANN [*suddenly losing her courage, with an anguish that she does not conceal*] No. We are awake; and you have said no: that is all.

TANNER [*brutally*] Well?

ANN Well, I made a mistake: you do not love me.

TANNER [*seizing her in his arms*] It is false. I love you. The Life Force enchants me. I have the whole world in my arms when I clasp you. But I am fighting for my freedom, for my honor, for my self, one and indivisible.

ANN Your happiness will be worth them all.

TANNER You would sell freedom and honor and self for happiness?

ANN It will not be all happiness for me. Perhaps death.

TANNER [*groaning*] Oh, that clutch holds and hurts. What have you grasped in me? Is there a father's heart as well as a mother's?

ANN Take care, Jack: if anyone comes while we are like this, you will have to marry me.

TANNER If we two stood now on the edge of a precipice, I would hold you tight and jump.

ANN [*panting, failing more and more under the strain*] Jack: let me go. I have dared so frightfully—it is lasting longer than I thought. Let me go: I cant bear it.

TANNER Nor I. Let it kill us.

ANN Yes: I dont care. I am at the end of my forces. I dont care. I think I am going to faint. [*At this moment Violet and Octavius come from the villa with Mrs Whitefield, who is wrapped up for driving. Simultaneously Malone and Ramsden, followed by Mendoza and Straker, come in through the little gate in the paling. Tanner shamefacedly releases Ann, who raises her hand giddily to her forehead.*]

MALONE Take care. Something's the matter with the lady.

RAMSDEN What does this mean?

VIOLET [*running between Ann and Tanner*] Are you ill?

ANN [*reeling, with a supreme effort*] I have promised to marry Jack.

[*She swoons. Violet kneels by her and chafes her hand. Tanner runs round to her other hand, and tries to lift her head. Octavius goes to Violet's assistance, but does not know what to do. Mrs Whitefield hurries back into the villa. Octavius, Malone, and Ramsden run to Ann and crowd round her, stooping to assist. Straker coolly comes to Ann's feet, and Mendoza to her head, both upright and self-possessed.*]

STRAKER Now then, ladies and gentlemen: she dont want a crowd round her: she wants air— all the air she can git. If you please, gents— [*Malone and Ramsden allow him to drive them gently past Ann and up the lawn towards the garden, where Octavius, who has already become conscious of his uselessness, joins them. Straker, following them up, pauses for a moment to instruct Tanner.*] Dont lift er ed, Mr Tanner: let it go flat so's the blood can run back into it.

MENDOZA He's right, Mr Tanner. Trust to the air of the Sierra. [*He withdraws delicately to the garden steps.*]

TANNER [*rising*] I yield to your superior knowledge of physiology, Henry.

[*He withdraws to the corner of the lawn; and Octavius immediately hurries down to him.*]

OCTAVIUS [*aside to Tanner, grasping his hand*] Jack: be very happy.

TANNER [*aside to Tavy*] I never asked her. It is a trap for me.

[*He goes up the lawn towards the garden. Octavius remains petrified.*]

MENDOZA [*intercepting Mrs Whitefield, who comes from the villa with a glass of brandy*] What is this, madam? [*He takes it from her.*]

MRS WHITEFIELD A little brandy.

MENDOZA The worst thing you could give her. Allow me. [*He swallows it.*] Trust to the air of the Sierra, madam.

[*For a moment the men all forget Ann and stare at Mendoza.*]

ANN [*in Violet's ear, clutching her round the neck*] Violet: did Jack say anything when I fainted?

VIOLET No.

ANN Ah! [*With a sigh of intense relief she relapses.*]

MRS WHITEFIELD Oh, she's fainted again.

[*They are about to rush back to her; but Mendoza stops them with a warning gesture.*]

ANN [*supine*] No, I havent. I'm quite happy.

TANNER [*suddenly walking determinedly to her, and snatching her hand from Violet to feel her pulse*] Why, her pulse is positively bounding. Come! get up. What nonsense! Up with you. [*He hauls her up summarily.*]

ANN Yes: I feel strong enough now. But you very nearly killed me, Jack, for all that.

MALONE A rough wooer, eh? Theyre the best sort, Miss Whitefield. I congratulate Mr Tanner; and I hope to meet you and him as frequent guests at the abbey.

ANN Thank you. [*She goes past Malone to Octavius.*] Ricky Ticky Tavy: congratulate me. [*Aside to him*] I want to make you cry for the last time.

OCTAVIUS [*steadfastly*] No more tears. I am happy in your happiness. And I believe in you in spite of everything.

RAMSDEN [*coming between Malone and Tanner*] You are a happy man, Jack Tanner. I envy you.

MENDOZA [*advances between Violet and Tanner*] Sir: there are two tragedies in life. One is to lose your heart's desire. The other is to gain it. Mine and yours, sir.

TANNER Mr Mendoza: I have no heart's desires. Ramsden: it is very easy for you to call me a happy man: you are only a spectator. I am one of the principals; and I know better. Ann: stop tempting Tavy, and come back to me.

ANN [*complying*] You are absurd, Jack. [*She takes his offered arm.*]

TANNER [*continuing*] I solemnly say that I am not a happy man. Ann looks happy; but she is only triumphant, successful, victorious. That is not happiness, but the price for which the strong sell their happiness. What we have both done this afternoon is to renounce happiness, renounce freedom, renounce tranquillity, above all, renounce the romantic possibilities of an unknown future for the cares of a household and a family. I beg that no man may seize the occasion to get half drunk and utter imbecile speeches and coarse pleasantries at my expense. We propose to furnish our own house according to our own taste; and I hereby give notice that the seven or eight travelling clocks, the four or five dressing cases, the carvers and fish slices, the copies of Patmore's *Angel in the House* in extra morocco, and the other articles you are preparing to heap upon us, will be instantly sold, and the proceeds devoted to circulating free copies of the *Revolutionist's Handbook.* The wedding will take place three days after our return to England, by special licence, at the office of the district superintendent registrar, in the presence of my solicitor and his clerk, who, like his clients, will be in ordinary walking dress—

VIOLET [*with intense conviction*] You are a brute, Jack.

ANN [*looking at him with fond pride and caressing his arm*] Never mind her, dear. Go on talking.

TANNER Talking!

[*Universal laughter.*]

SHAW USED HIS COMEDIES to explicate the core of his philosophical faith, his belief in the Life Force. Any serious analysis of his thought must begin with this—a task not at all difficult to undertake since the faith is embedded in such joyous comic fables.

The doctrine of the Life Force has formed the basis of some of Shaw's finest comedies from *Man and Superman* (1903) to *Back to Methuselah* (1921). Quite simply, it is his phrase for Creative Evolution, the progressive development of the species from unicellular organisms to man. Shaw sees purpose in each step of the slow evolutionary process, and he sees great hope for the future development of the race, since we have already produced Supermen (like John Tanner) who have mastered the use of the highest product of evolution, the human brain.

Tanner, in *Man and Superman,* like the Brothers Barnabas of *Back to Methuselah,* is an unyielding opponent of the social order, which can survive only by refusing to change. The opposition of the Superman, who realizes that the species must develop or die, and his society thus becomes a major comic theme and one which Shaw has exploited with all his own vitalism, optimism, and flair for the dramatic. [Alan S. Downer, *The British Drama,* Appleton-Century-Crofts, Inc., New York, 1950, p. 309.]

Shaw's philosophy has far reaches. It extends in one direction into romanticism, in another into pragmatism. And always, it is expressed in a rich rhetoric which takes full account of every ideology, even one opposed to Shaw's own.

Shaw's romanticism, which is also Ibsen's, is more highly developed philosophically than the romanticism of the first generation. Philosophically one should look for its affiliations less with "mysticism" or "materialism"—the two systems commonly associated with Shaw and Ibsen—than with the pragmatic pluralism of William James. The attitudes of pragmatic pluralism are part and parcel of Shaw's art as well as of his thought. Nowhere in dogmatic communist writing does one have a sense of dialectic as keenly as in a Shavian play. Shaw's mind is well stocked, as everyone knows, and he is famous for the number of things he can mention on one page; but all this would mean nothing if he could not marshal his facts ironically. The chief mark of Shavian prose is its use of ironic antithesis and juxtaposition. Contrary to what one expects from a propagandist, Shaw not only shows the liberal's sense of the other man's point of view, he has a sense of every conceivable point of view, and can pack all the points of view into one long sentence, which climbs by parallelisms and antitheses to a climax, and then sinks with the finality of a conqueror to a conclusion which Shaw will not allow you to evade. In its course the Shavian sentence, still more the Shavian paragraph, looks in all possible directions. For Shaw sees the world as what James called a multiverse, and that is unusual in a satirist, who is customarily something of a monomaniac.

It is a fact of curious interest that William James, who thought Shaw "a great power as a concrete moralist," hit upon one of the essentials of Shaw, to wit, "the way he brings home to the *eyes,* as it were, the difference between 'convention' and 'conscience.'" Such a statement would often be the cue for a discussion of Shaw as puritan and protestant. There is more to it than that. The difference between convention and conscience is certainly a moral matter, but

Shaw is a *concrete* moralist, a master of parable, who has worked out for the presentation of his protestant pragmatist morality a new dramaturgy. Shaw is one of the few artists who in political, moral, and social territory is not a mere expropriator; his grasp of political, moral, and social forces is really professional. But he is a genuine dramatist in that he brings his matter home to the eyes, which is something that neither the historian nor the sociologist, the poet or the novelist, need do. All these bring visions before the mind's eye; none, except the dramatist, has literally to unfold his vision before the physical eye. Appreciators of Shaw's dialogue have explained to us what Shaw has done for the ear; those who appreciate his dramaturgy know that he addressed himself also to the eye, not indeed in giving separate attention to the eye by way of spectacle, but in fusing the elements into the one kinetic picture which is stage production. William James's statement that Shaw's genius is much more important than his philosophy is true, if by it we understand that genius is a synthesizing power which obliterates barriers between thought and technique and gives evidence of both in a particular mode of presentation. The Shavian mode is drama. [Eric Bentley, *The Playwright As Thinker,* Meridian Books, Inc., New York, 1957, pp. 125–126.]

Shavian comedy is a complicated art. It owes much to Ibsen, at least by inversion. It springs, as Ronald Peacock shows, from the closest study of the dramatic art and owes much to other comic playwrights.

Within the limits of the art of comedy he has displayed a striking originality in two principal directions; first in the point of view he adopts for his critical attack, and secondly in his adaptation of comedy to the naturalist technique.

Regarding the first point, Shaw conforms to tradition in the sense that you must have a fixed point from which to work, to launch your criticism. In Molière, for instance, the established position is generally interpreted as the rule of the golden mean of reason. Shaw is also devoted to reason. But whilst Molière takes his fixed

point from the general experience of men as rational and social beings, Shaw takes his from a rational philosophy of his own. Hence he inverts the usual method. Instead of isolating the unreasonable character, he isolates the reasonable one. Molière gives us a series of characters who offend our idea of rational behaviour: Harpagon, Alceste, Arnolphe, Argan, Tartuffe are examples. Shaw, on the other hand, gives us a series that illustrates his own idea of rational behaviour: Dudgeon, Caesar, Tanner, Dubedat, Undershaft, Shotover, Magnus, Joan, and so on

—all characters with a head, with their eye on the point, piercing illusions and grasping reality.

The difference is accounted for by a difference of interest. Molière—and we can say Jonson too—feeding on the thought of the Renaissance, was interested in a conception of man; Shaw, under the influence of the thought of the late nineteenth century, in a conception of society. His main attack being on society, his transformation of traditional comic method is brilliant. Taking an unconventional character, a person with a gift of insight and freedom, he impinges it upon a group of conventional social animals, and the impact reveals at every turn stock notions and reactions, prejudices and dishonesties, in short the illusionary, the unreal, the irrational. Molière exposes one character in turn; Shaw the social herd, all together. And these characters of his are most certainly dramatic conceptions, because they create, by being what they are, startling situations. [Ronald Peacock, *The Poet in the Theatre,* Hill and Wang, Inc., New York, 1960, pp. 88–89.]

The second point about the mutual relations between Shaw's personal aim and the dramatic form concerns the realist convention in which he works. His comedy flowing from his criticism of society, he needs for his purposes the ordinary social milieu, with the sort of crisis that arises from typical bourgeois circumstances. In this milieu he lets his unconventional characters challenge the creatures of habit by word and action, and the rest follows. His material is that of all bourgeois drama since the middle of the nineteenth century, more particularly since Ibsen. One of the things he admired most in the latter was the way he made his audience feel that what they saw on the stage was what went on in their own homes. The direct attack is of the essence of Shaw's intention. His method in fact is to give us a comic version of Ibsen's principal theme, the rebel against society, the true man against the false. Ibsen being swayed on the whole by the Germanic seriousness, by some deep-seated emotional need for tragic crisis, his subjects and treatments were generally the reverse of comic. . . .

These are the two principal features of Shaw's work which make a mutual relationship between him and his form clear. Our first impulse is to say: this is not comedy as it ought to be. Our second is to justify it as the proper mode for Shaw's idea. With our third impulse we look more closely at work that seems to owe no obligation except to its own law, its own subject-matter, and we discover that it does owe something to its genre, to its predecessors, to pre-existent authorities. It illustrates a continuity, not a break. Shaw adheres first to the principle that comedy must have a fixed vantage-point, though he transforms it to suit his own purpose. He retains, too, the prerogatives and tricks of comedy, without, however, the necessity of being chained to them. He also keeps to stock types for comic purposes, but his new social philosophy gives him a new set of types. Even in incidentals he can follow well-worn grooves of the art; the Straker-Tanner relationship in *Man and Superman* rests on the conventional master-valet set-up, given a completely new vitality from the new social background. And his second great obligation is to the dramatic developments that immediately preceded him and in which he was caught up. He uses the natural probable situation of bourgeois life, public or domestic, that focuses a problem of social behaviour. And he acknowledges the debt by originality of treatment; that is, he gives us what no one else gave and Ibsen had only hinted at, comedy. [*Ibid.*, pp. 91–93.]

There may still be disagreement about the quality of Man and Superman, *although today its high rank in Shaw's theater is not often challenged. One instructive way to examine its reputed merits and demerits is to look at appraisals more or less contemporary with the play itself. Max Beerbohm speaks for the admirers (though he does not accept the play's point of view) in one of the best of his pieces for the London* Saturday Review, *James Huneker for the less enthusiastic in the course of an essay called* "The Quintessence of Shaw."

The name of this play's hero is John Tanner, corrupted from Don Juan Tenorio, of whom its bearer is supposed to be the lineal descendant and modern equivalent. But here we have merely one of the devices whereby Mr. Shaw seeks to catch the ear that he desires to box. Did not the end justify the means, Mr. Shaw's natural honesty would have compelled him to christen his hero Joseph or Anthony. For he utterly flouts the possibility of a Don Juan. Gazing out on the world, he beholds a tremendous battle of sex raging. But it is the Sabine ladies who, more muscular than even Rubens made them, are snatching and shouldering away from out the newly-arisen walls the shrieking gentlemen of Rome. It is the fauns who scud coyly, on tremulous hoofs, through the woodland, not daring a backward-glance at rude and dogged nymphs who are gaining on them every moment. Of course, this sight is an hallucination. There are, it is true, women who take the initiative, and men who shrink from following them. There are, and always have been. Such beings are no new discovery, though their existence is stupidly ignored by the average modern dramatist. But they are notable exceptions to the rule of Nature. True, again, that in civilised society marriage is more important and desirable to a woman than to a man. "All women," said one of Disraeli's characters, "ought to be married, and no men." The epigram sums up John Tanner's attitude towards life even more wittily than anything that has been put into his mouth by Mr. Shaw. John Tanner, pursued and finally bound in matrimony by Miss Ann Whitefield, supplies an excellent motive for a comedy of manners. But to that kind of comedy Mr. Shaw will not stoop—not wittingly, at least. From John Tanner he deduces a general law. For him, John Tanner is Man, and Ann Whitefield is Woman—nothing less. He has fallen into the error—a strange error for a man with his views—of confusing the natural sex-instinct with the desire for marriage. Because

women desire marriage more strongly than men, therefore, in his opinion, the sex-instinct is communicated from woman to man. I need not labour the point that this conclusion is opposite to the obvious truth of all ages and all countries. Man is the dominant animal. It was unjust of Nature not to make the two sexes equal. Mr. Shaw hates injustice, and so, partly to redress the balance by robbing Man of conscious superiority, and partly to lull himself into peace of mind, he projects as real that visionary world of flitting fauns and brutal Sabines. Idealist, he insists that things are as they would be if he had his way. His characters come from out of his own yearning heart. Only, we can find no corner for them in ours. We can no more be charmed by them than we can believe in them. Ann Whitefield is a minx. John Tanner is a prig. Prig versus Minx, with the gloves off, and Prig floored in every round—there you have Mr. Shaw's customary formula for drama; and he works it out duly in "Man and Superman." The main difference between this play and the others is that the minx and the prig are conscious not merely of their intellects, but of "the Life Force." Of this they regard themselves, with comparative modesty, as the automatic instruments. They are wrong. The Life Force could find no use for them. They are not human enough, not alive enough. That is the main drawback for a dramatist who does not love raw life; he cannot create living characters.

And yet it is on such characters as John and Ann that Mr. Shaw founds his hopes for the future of humanity. If we are very good, we *may* be given the Superman. If we are very scientific, and keep a sharp look out on our instincts, and use them just as our intellects shall prescribe, we *may* produce a race worthy to walk this fair earth. That is the hope with which we are to buoy ourselves up. It is a forlorn one. Man may, in the course of aeons, evolve into something better than now he is. But the process will be

560

not less unconscious than long. Reason and instinct have an inveterate habit of cancelling each other. If the world were governed by reason, it would not long be inhabited. Life is a muddle. It seems a brilliant muddle, if you are an optimist; a dull one, if you aren't; but in neither case can you deny that it is the muddlers who keep it going. The thinkers cannot help it at all. They are detached from "the Life Force." If they could turn their fellow-creatures into thinkers like themselves, all would be up. Fortunately, or unfortunately, they have not that power. The course of history has often been turned by sentiment, but by thought never. The thinkers are but valuable ornaments. A safe place is assigned to them on the world's mantelpiece, while humanity basks and blinks stupidly on the hearth, warming itself in the glow of the Life Force.

On that mantelpiece Mr. Shaw deserves a place of honor. He is a very brilliant ornament. And never have his ornamental qualities shone more brightly than in this latest book. Never has he thought more clearly or more wrongly, and never has he displayed better his genius for dialectic, and never has his humor gushed forth in such sudden natural torrents. This is his masterpiece, so far. Treasure it as the most complete expression of the most distinct personality in current literature. Treasure it, too, as a work of specific art, in line with your Plato and Lucian and Landor. [Max Beerbohm, *A Selection from Around Theatres,* Anchor edition, Doubleday & Company, Inc., New York, 1960, pp. 156–158.]

Some day in the far future, let us hope, when the spirit of Bernard Shaw shall have been gathered to the gods, his popular vogue may be an established fact. Audiences may flock to sip wit, philosophy, and humour before the footlights of the Shaw theatre; but unless the assemblage be largely composed of Shaw *replicas,* of overmen and overwomen ("oversouls," not altogether in the Emersonian sense), it is difficult to picture any other variety listening to *Man and Superman.* For one thing, it is not a play to be played, though it may be read with delight bordering on despair. A deeper reason exists for its hopelessness—it is such a violent attack on what might be called the Shaw superstructure, that his warm-

est enemies and chilliest admirers will wonder what it is all about. Even William Archer, one of the latter, confessed his disappointment.

Man and Superman—odious title—is Shaw's new attempt at a *Wild Duck,* formerly one of Ibsen's most puzzling productions. Shaw mocks Shaw as Ibsen sneered at Ibsen. This method of viewing the obverse of your own medal—George Meredith would say the back of the human slate —is certainly a revelation of mood-versatility, though a disquieting one to the man in the street. It does not seem to be playing fair in the game. Sometimes it is not. With Ibsen it was; he wished to have his fling at the Ibsenite, and he had it. Shaw-like one is tempted to exclaim, Aha! drums and trumpets again, even if the cart be repainted. (*Vide* his earlier prefaces.)

The book is dedicated to Mr. Arthur Bingham Walkley, who once wrote of his friend, "Mr. Bernard Shaw fails as a dramatist because he is always trying to prove something." In the end it is Shaw the man who is more interesting than his plays,—all the characters are so many,— Shaw's winking at one through the printed dialogue. [James Huneker, *Iconoclasts: A Book of Dramatists,* Charles Scribner's Sons, New York, 1905, pp. 256–257.]

A lengthy parabasis, written in genuine Shavian, shows us hell, the Devil, Don Juan, and Anna of Mozartean fame. At least the talk here is as brilliant as is commonly supposed to prevail in the nether regions. *Inter alia,* we read that marriage is the most licentious of human institutions—hence its popularity. Even the Devil is shocked. "The confusion of marriage with morality has done more to destroy the conscience of the human race than any other single error." "Beauty, purity, respectability, religion, art, patriotism, bravery, and the rest are nothing but words which I or any one else can turn inside out like a glove," continues this relentless rake and transformed preacher. Too true; but the seamy side as exhibited by Don Juan Shaw is not so convincing as in Nietzsche's transvaluation of all values. "They are mere words, useful for duping barbarians into adopting civilization, or the civilized poor into submitting to be robbed and enslaved."

Admitted, keen dissector of contemporary ills; but how about your play? In effect the author says: "To the devil with all art and plays, my play with the rest! What I wish to do is to tell you how to run the universe; and for this I will, if necessary, erect my pulpit in hell!"

After this what more can be said? The play peters out; there is talk, talk, talk. Ann calls the poetic temperament "the old maid's temperament"; the brigand chief sententiously remarks: "There are two tragedies in life: one is not to get your heart's desire; the other is to get it"— which sounds as if wrenched from a page of Chamfort or Rivarol; and Ann concludes with "Go on talking, Tanner, talking!" It is the epitaph of the piece, dear little misshapen, still-born comedy. Well may Mr. Shaw write "universal laughter" at the end. Yet I am willing to wager that some critics will be in tears at this exhibition of perverse waste and clever impotency. [*Ibid.*, pp. 262–264.]

Shaw is at least as good a critic of Shaw as he is of Ibsen, Strindberg, and others. Nobody could make out a better case for the point of view expressed in Man *and* Superman *than he does here in a passage from the Epistle Dedicatory to Arthur Bingham Walkley.*

The pretence that women do not take the initiative is part of the farce. Why, the whole world is strewn with snares, traps, gins, and pitfalls for the capture of men by women. Give women the vote, and in five years there will be a crushing tax on bachelors. Men, on the other hand, attach penalties to marriage, depriving women of property, of the franchise, of the free use of their limbs, of that ancient symbol of immortality, the right to make oneself at home in the house of God by taking off the hat, of everything that he can force Woman to dispense with without compelling himself to dispense with her. All in vain. Woman must marry because the race must perish without her travail: if the risk of death and the certainty of pain, danger, and unutterable discomforts cannot deter her, slavery and swaddled ankles will not. And yet we assume that the force that carries women through all these perils and hardships, stops abashed before the primnesses of our behavior for young ladies. It is assumed that the woman must wait, motionless, until she is wooed. Nay, she often does wait motionless. That is how the spider waits for the fly. But the spider spins her web. And if the fly, like my hero, shews a strength that promises to extricate him, how swiftly does she abandon her pretence of passiveness, and openly fling coil after coil about him until he is secured for ever!

If the really impressive books and other artworks of the world were produced by ordinary men, they would express more fear of women's pursuit than love of their illusory beauty. But ordinary men cannot produce really impressive art-works. Those who can are men of genius: that is, men selected by Nature to carry on the work of building up an intellectual consciousness of her own instinctive purpose. Accordingly, we observe in the man of genius all the unscrupulousness and all the "self-sacrifice" (the two things are the same) of Woman. He will risk the stake and the cross; starve, when necessary, in a garret all his life; study women and live on their work and care as Darwin studied worms and lived upon sheep; work his nerves into rags without payment, a sublime altruist in his disregard of himself, an atrocious egotist in his disregard of others. Here Woman meets a purpose as impersonal, as irresistible as her own; and the clash is sometimes tragic. When it is complicated by the genius being a woman, then the game is one for a king of critics: your George Sand becomes a mother to gain experience for the novelist and to develop her, and gobbles up men of genius, Chopins, Mussets and the like, as mere hors d'œuvres.

I state the extreme case, of course; but what is true of the great man who incarnates the philosophic consciousness of Life and the woman who incarnates its fecundity, is true in some degree of all geniuses and all women. Hence it is that the world's books get written, its pictures painted, its statues modelled, its symphonies composed, by people who are free from the otherwise universal dominion of the tyranny of sex. Which leads us to the conclusion, astonishing to the vulgar, that art, instead of being before all things the expression of the normal sexual situation, is really the only department in which sex is a superseded and secondary power, with its consciousness so confused and its purpose so perverted, that its ideas are mere fantasy to common men. Whether the artist becomes poet or philosopher, moralist or founder of a religion, his sexual doctrine is nothing but a barren special pleading for pleasure, excitement, and knowledge when he is young, and for contemplative tranquillity when he is old and satiated.

ANTON CHEKHOV

1860–1904

Chekhov's own life was as entertaining, as implausible, as wildly funny, and as poignant as any of his plays. He was often humiliated as a child by the beatings his autocratic father—who ran a grocery store in a little town in the south of Russia—administered to himself and to his brothers and to the people who worked for him. He was a Russian-speaking student in a Greek school. He was left behind by the family as a kind of guarantee for his father's debts when, after the grocery store fell into bankruptcy, the Chekhovs made their way to Moscow. When Anton finally arrived in Moscow, he found his family, sometimes joined by a female cousin and a dog, all sleeping on one huge mattress on the floor. He wrote many of the vignettes, anecdotes, and perfectly formed short stories which made him his first large reputation, sitting at the dining-room table, with friends and relatives and every kind of object crowding the space in which he was left to put words on paper. Nothing was too slight or too casual for a Chekhov story. Every aspect of reality could be teased into the shape of a narrative, brief or extended, with an open or a concealed point, or none at all besides the facts of the chronicle themselves, however few, however fragile. His first plays were like his stories, character sketches. They were given theatrical vitality by the addition of just the right gesture or grimace, just the correct touch of vaudeville humor. Those touches never left his drama. None of his full-length plays, no matter how somber or solemn at any given juncture, is without its inspired comic moments. There is compassion in his plays, surely, especially for those who are frustrated—*frustrated as husbands and wives* (Ivanov); *frustrated as writers and actors* (The Sea Gull); *frustrated in their efforts to do something, anything, of consequence* (Uncle Vanya); *frustrated in their yearning to enlarge their lives, to move from a small town to Moscow* (Three Sisters); *frustrated in their attempts to keep alive an outmoded and fast decaying way of life* (The Cherry Orchard). *There is compassion, but no single point of view, certainly not a tragic or a political one. "I fear those who read between the lines trying to find a definite trend of thought," Chekhov wrote. "I am neither liberal nor conservative, nor gradualist, nor ascetic, nor indifferentist. I should like to be an independent artist—and that is all." He was a doctor of medicine —though he rarely practiced that profession. He was a consumptive. He was a writer. And "sacrosanct" to him, as a result of all these things, were "the human body, health, reason, talent, inspiration, love, and absolute freedom."*

The Cherry Orchard

TRANSLATED BY CONSTANCE GARNETT

Characters

MADAME RANYEVSKY, LYUBOV ANDREYEVNA, *the owner of the Cherry Orchard*

ANYA *her daughter, aged seventeen*

VARYA *her adopted daughter, aged twenty-four*

GAYEV, LEONID ANDREYEVITCH *brother of Madame Ranyevsky*

LOPAKHIN, YERMOLAY ALEXEYEVITCH *a merchant*

TROFIMOV, PYOTR SERGEYEVITCH *a student*

SEMYONOV-PISHTCHIK *a landowner*

CHARLOTTA IVANOVNA *a governess*

YEPIKHODOV, SEMYON PANTALEYEVITCH *a clerk*

DUNYASHA *a maid*

FIRS *an old valet, aged eighty-seven*

YASHA *a young valet*

A VAGRANT

THE STATION MASTER

A POST-OFFICE CLERK

VISITORS, SERVANTS

The action takes place on the estate of Madame Ranyevsky.

Act One

A room, which has always been called the nursery. One of the doors leads into Anya's room. Dawn, sun rises during the scene. May, the cherry trees in flower, but it is cold in the garden with the frost of early morning. Windows closed. Enter Dunyasha with a candle and Lopakhin with a book in his hand.

LOPAKHIN The train's in, thank God. What time is it?

DUNYASHA Nearly two o'clock. [*Puts out the candle.*] It's daylight already.

LOPAKHIN The train's late! Two hours, at least. [*Yawns and stretches.*] I'm a pretty one; what a fool I've been. Came here on purpose to meet them at the station and dropped asleep. . . . Dozed off as I sat in the chair. It's annoying. . . . You might have waked me.

DUNYASHA I thought you had gone. [*Listens.*] There, I do believe they're coming!

LOPAKHIN [*listens*] No, what with the luggage and one thing and another . . . [*A pause*]. Lyubov Andreyevna has been abroad five years; I don't know what she is like now. . . . She's

567

a splendid woman. A good-natured, kind-hearted woman. I remember when I was a lad of fifteen, my poor father—he used to keep a little shop here in the village in those days—gave me a punch in the face with his fist and made my nose bleed. We were in the yard here—I forget what we'd come about—he had had a drop. Lyubov Andreyevna—I can see her now—she was a slim young girl then—took me to wash my face, and then brought me into this very room, into the nursery. "Don't cry, little peasant," says she, "it will be well in time for your wedding day." . . . [*A pause*] Little peasant . . . my father was a peasant, it's true, but here am I in a white waistcoat and brown shoes, like a pig in a bun shop. Yes, I'm a rich man, but for all my money, come to think, a peasant I was, and a peasant I am. [*Turns over the pages of the book.*] I've been reading this book and I can't make head or tail of it. I fell asleep over it.

[*A pause*]

DUNYASHA The dogs have been awake all night, they feel that the mistress is coming.

LOPAKHIN Why, what's the matter with you, Dunyasha?

DUNYASHA My hands are all of a tremble. I feel as though I should faint.

LOPAKHIN You're a spoilt soft creature, Dunyasha. And dressed like a lady too, and your hair done up. That's not the thing. One must know one's place.

[*Enter Yepikhodov with a nosegay; he wears a pea-jacket and highly polished creaking top-boots; he drops the nosegay as he comes in.*]

YEPIKHODOV [*picking up the nosegay*] Here! The gardener's sent this, says you're to put it in the dining-room [*giving Dunyasha the nosegay*].

LOPAKHIN And bring me some kvass.

DUNYASHA I will. [*Goes out.*]

YEPIKHODOV It's chilly this morning, three degrees of frost, though the cherries are all in flower. I can't say much for our climate. [*Sighs.*] I can't. Our climate is not often propitious to the occasion. Yermolay Alexeyevitch, permit me to call your attention to the fact that I purchased myself a pair of boots the day before yesterday, and they creak, I venture to assure you, so that there's no tolerating them. What ought I to grease them with?

LOPAKHIN Oh, shut up! Don't bother me.

YEPIKHODOV Every day some misfortune befalls me. I don't complain. I'm used to it, and I wear a smiling face.

[*Dunyasha comes in, hands Lopakhin the kvass.*]

YEPIKHODOV I am going. [*Stumbles against a chair, which falls over; as though triumphant*] There! There you see now, excuse the expression, an accident like that among others. . . . It's positively remarkable. [*Goes out.*]

DUNYASHA Do you know, Yermolay Alexeyevitch, I must confess, Yepikhodov has made me a proposal.

LOPAKHIN Ah!

DUNYASHA I'm sure I don't know. . . . He's a harmless fellow, but sometimes when he begins talking, there's no making anything of it. It's all very fine and expressive, only there's no understanding it. I've a sort of liking for him too. He loves me to distraction. He's an unfortunate man; every day there's something. They tease him about it—two and twenty misfortunes they call him.

LOPAKHIN [*listening*] There! I do believe they're coming.

DUNYASHA They are coming! What's the matter with me? . . . I'm cold all over.

LOPAKHIN They really are coming. Let's go and meet them. Will she know me? It's five years since I saw her.

DUNYASHA [*in a flutter*] I shall drop this very minute. . . . Ah, I shall drop.

[*There is a sound of two carriages driving up to the house. Lopakhin and Dunyasha go out quickly. The stage is left empty. A noise is heard in the adjoining rooms. Firs, who has driven to meet Madame Ranyevsky, crosses the stage hurriedly leaning on a stick. He is wearing old-fashioned livery and a high hat. He says something to himself, but not a word can be distinguished. The noise behind the scenes goes on increasing. A voice: "Come, let's go in here." Enter Lyubov Andreyevna, Anya, and Charlotta Ivanovna with a pet dog on a chain, all in travelling dresses. Varya in an out-door coat with a kerchief over her head, Gayev, Sem-*]

yonov-Pishtchik, Lopakhin, Dunyasha with bag and parasol, Servants with other articles. All walk across the room.]

ANYA Let's come in here. Do you remember what room this is, mamma?

LYUBOV [joyfully, through her tears] The nursery!

VARYA How cold it is, my hands are numb. [To Lyubov Andreyevna] Your rooms, the white room and the lavender one, are just the same as ever, mamma.

LYUBOV My nursery, dear delightful room. . . . I used to sleep here when I was little. . . . [Cries.] And here I am, like a little child. . . . [Kisses her brother and Varya, and then her brother again.] Varya's just the same as ever, like a nun. And I knew Dunyasha. [Kisses Dunyasha.]

GAYEV The train was two hours late. What do you think of that? Is that the way to do things?

CHARLOTTA [to Pishtchik] My dog eats nuts, too.

PISHTCHIK [wonderingly] Fancy that!

[They all go out except Anya and Dunyasha.]

DUNYASHA We've been expecting you so long. [Takes Anya's hat and coat.]

ANYA I haven't slept for four nights on the journey. I feel dreadfully cold.

DUNYASHA You set out in Lent, there was snow and frost, and now? My darling! [Laughs and kisses her.] I have missed you, my precious, my joy. I must tell you . . . I can't put it off a minute. . . .

ANYA [wearily] What now?

DUNYASHA Yepikhodov, the clerk, made me a proposal just after Easter.

ANYA It's always the same thing with you . . . [Straightening her hair] I've lost all my hairpins. . . . [She is staggering from exhaustion.]

DUNYASHA I don't know what to think, really. He does love me, he does love me so!

ANYA [looking towards her door, tenderly] My own room, my windows just as though I had never gone away. I'm home! To-morrow morning I shall get up and run into the garden. . . . Oh, if I could get to sleep! I haven't slept all the journey, I was so anxious and worried.

DUNYASHA Pyotr Sergeyevitch came the day before yesterday.

ANYA [joyfully] Petya!

DUNYASHA He's asleep in the bath house, he has settled in there. I'm afraid of being in their way, says he. [Glancing at her watch] I was to have waked him, but Varvara Mihailovna told me not to. Don't you wake him, says she.

[Enter Varya with a bunch of keys at her waist.]

VARYA Dunyasha, coffee and make haste. . . . Mamma's asking for coffee.

DUNYASHA This very minute. [Goes out.]

VARYA Well, thank God, you've come. You're home again [petting her]. My little darling has come back! My precious beauty has come back again!

ANYA I have had a time of it!

VARYA I can fancy.

ANYA We set off in Holy Week—it was so cold then, and all the way Charlotta would talk and show off her tricks. What did you want to burden me with Charlotta for?

VARYA You couldn't have travelled all alone, darling. At seventeen!

ANYA We got to Paris at last, it was cold there —snow. I speak French shockingly. Mamma lives on the fifth floor. I went up to her and there were a lot of French people, ladies, an old priest with a book. The place smelt of tobacco and so comfortless. I felt sorry, oh! so sorry for mamma all at once, I put my arms round her neck, and hugged her and wouldn't let her go. Mamma was as kind as she could be, and she cried. . . .

VARYA [through her tears] Don't speak of it, don't speak of it!

ANYA She had sold her villa at Mentone, she had nothing left, nothing. I hadn't a farthing left either, we only just had enough to get here. And mamma doesn't understand! When we had dinner at the stations, she always ordered the most expensive things and gave the waiters a whole rouble. Charlotta's just the same. Yasha too must have the same as we do; it's simply awful. You know Yasha is mamma's valet now, we brought him here with us.

VARYA Yes, I've seen the young rascal.

ANYA Well, tell me—have you paid the arrears on the mortgage?

VARYA How could we get the money?

ANYA Oh, dear! Oh, dear!

VARYA In August the place will be sold.

ANYA My goodness!

LOPAKHIN [*peeps in at the door and moos like a cow*] Moo! [*Disappears.*]

VARYA [*weeping*] There, that's what I could do to him. [*Shakes her fist.*]

ANYA [*embracing Varya, softly*] Varya, has he made you an offer? [*Varya shakes her head.*] Why, but he loves you. Why is it you don't come to an understanding? What are you waiting for?

VARYA I believe that there never will be anything between us. He has a lot to do, he has no time for me . . . and takes no notice of me. Bless the man, it makes me miserable to see him. . . . Everyone's talking of our being married, everyone's congratulating me, and all the while there's really nothing in it; it's all like a dream. [*In another tone*] You have a new brooch like a bee.

ANYA [*mournfully*] Mamma bought it. [*Goes into her own room and in a light-hearted childish tone*] And you know, in Paris I went up in a balloon!

VARYA My darling's home again! My pretty is home again!

[*Dunyasha returns with the coffee-pot and is making the coffee.*]

VARYA [*standing at the door*] All day long, darling, as I go about looking after the house, I keep dreaming all the time. If only we could marry you to a rich man, then I should feel more at rest. Then I would go off by myself on a pilgrimage to Kiev, to Moscow . . . and so I would spend my life going from one holy place to another. . . . I would go on and on. . . . What bliss!

ANYA The birds are singing in the garden. What time is it?

VARYA It must be nearly three. It's time you were asleep, darling [*going into Anya's room*]. What bliss!

[*Yasha enters with a rug and a travelling bag.*]

YASHA [*crosses the stage, mincingly*] May one come in here, pray?

DUNYASHA I shouldn't have known you, Yasha. How you have changed abroad.

YASHA H'm! . . . And who are you?

DUNYASHA When you went away, I was that high [*showing distance from floor*]. Dunyasha, Fyodor's daughter . . . you don't remember me!

YASHA H'm! . . . You're a peach! [*Looks round and embraces her: she shrieks and drops a saucer. Yasha goes out hastily.*]

VARYA [*in the doorway, in a tone of vexation*] What now?

DUNYASHA [*through her tears*] I have broken a saucer.

VARYA Well, that brings good luck.

ANYA [*coming out of her room*] We ought to prepare mamma: Petya is here.

VARYA I told them not to wake him.

ANYA [*dreamily*] It's six years since father died. Then only a month later little brother Grisha was drowned in the river, such a pretty boy he was, only seven. It was more than mamma could bear, so she went away, went away without looking back [*shuddering*]. . . . How well I understand her, if only she knew! [*A pause*] And Petya Trofimov was Grisha's tutor, he may remind her.

[*Enter Firs: he is wearing a pea-jacket and a white waistcoat.*]

FIRS [*goes up to the coffee-pot, anxiously*] The mistress will be served here. [*Puts on white gloves.*] Is the coffee ready? [*Sternly to Dunyasha*] Girl! Where's the cream?

DUNYASHA Ah, mercy on us! [*Goes out quickly.*]

FIRS [*fussing round the coffee-pot*] Ech! you good-for-nothing! [*Muttering to himself*] Come back from Paris. And the old master used to go to Paris too . . . horses all the way. [*Laughs.*]

VARYA What is it, Firs?

FIRS What is your pleasure? [*Gleefully*] My lady has come home! I have lived to see her again! Now I can die. [*Weeps with joy.*]

[*Enter Lyubov Andreyevna, Gayev and Semyonov-Pishtchik; the latter is in a short-waisted full coat of fine cloth, and full trousers. Gayev, as he comes in, makes a gesture with his arms and his whole body, as though he were playing billiards.*]

LYUBOV How does it go? Let me remember. Cannon off the red!

GAYEV That's it—in off the white! Why, once,

sister, we used to sleep together in this very room, and now I'm fifty-one, strange as it seems.

LOPAKHIN Yes, time flies.

GAYEV What do you say?

LOPAKHIN Time, I say, flies.

GAYEV What a smell of patchouli!

ANYA I'm going to bed. Good-night, mamma. [*Kisses her mother.*]

LYUBOV My precious darling. [*Kisses her hands.*] Are you glad to be home? I can't believe it.

ANYA Good-night, uncle.

GAYEV [*kissing her face and hands*] God bless you! How like you are to your mother! [*To his sister*] At her age you were just the same, Lyuba.

[*Anya shakes hands with Lopakhin and Pishtchik, then goes out, shutting the door after her.*]

LYUBOV She's quite worn out.

PISHTCHIK Aye, it's a long journey, to be sure.

VARYA [*to Lopakhin and Pishtchik*] Well, gentlemen? It's three o'clock and time to say good-bye.

LYUBOV [*laughs*] You're just the same as ever, Varya. [*Draws her to her and kisses her.*] I'll just drink my coffee and then we will all go and rest. [*Firs puts a cushion under her feet.*] Thanks, friend. I am so fond of coffee, I drink it day and night. Thanks, dear old man. [*Kisses Firs.*]

VARYA I'll just see whether all the things have been brought in. [*Goes out.*]

LYUBOV Can it really be me sitting here? [*Laughs.*] I want to dance about and clap my hands. [*Covers her face with her hands.*] And I could drop asleep in a moment! God knows I love my country, I love it tenderly; I couldn't look out of the window in the train, I kept crying so. [*Through her tears*] But I must drink my coffee, though. Thank you, Firs, thanks, dear old man. I'm so glad to find you still alive.

FIRS The day before yesterday.

GAYEV He's rather deaf.

LOPAKHIN I have to set off for Kharkov directly, at five o'clock. . . . It is annoying! I wanted to have a look at you, and a little talk. . . . You are just as splendid as ever.

PISHTCHIK [*breathing heavily*] Handsomer, indeed . . . dressed in Parisian style . . . completely bowled me over.

LOPAKHIN Your brother, Leonid Andreyevitch here, is always saying that I'm a low-born knave, that I'm a money-grubber, but I don't care one straw for that. Let him talk. Only I do want you to believe in me as you used to. I do want your wonderful tender eyes to look at me as they used to in the old days. Merciful God! My father was a serf of your father and of your grandfather, but you—you—did so much for me once, that I've forgotten all that; I love you as though you were my kin . . . more than my kin.

LYUBOV I can't sit still, I simply can't . . . [*Jumps up and walks about in violent agitation.*] This happiness is too much for me. . . . You may laugh at me, I know I'm silly. . . . My own bookcase [*kissing the bookcase*]. My little table.

GAYEV Nurse died while you were away.

LYUBOV [*sits down and drinks coffee*] Yes, the Kingdom of Heaven be hers! You wrote me of her death.

GAYEV And Anastasy is dead. Squinting Petruchka has left me and is in service now with the police captain in the town. [*Takes a box of caramels out of his pocket and sucks one.*]

PISHTCHIK My daughter, Dashenka, wishes to be remembered to you.

LOPAKHIN I want to tell you something very pleasant and cheering. [*Glancing at his watch*] I'm going directly. . . . There's no time to say much. . . . Well, I can say it in a couple of words. I needn't tell you your cherry orchard is to be sold to pay your debts; the twenty-second of August is the date fixed for the sale; but don't you worry, dearest lady, you may sleep in peace, there is a way of saving it. . . . This is what I propose. I beg your attention! Your estate is not twenty miles from the town, railway runs close by it, and if the cherry orchard and the land along the river bank were cut up into building plots and then let on lease for summer villas, you would make an income of at least 25,000 roubles a year out of it.

GAYEV That's all rot, if you'll excuse me.

LYUBOV I don't quite understand you, Yermolay Alexeyevitch.

The Cherry Orchard

LOPAKHIN   You will get a rent of at least 25 roubles a year for a three-acre plot from summer visitors, and if you say the word now, I'll bet you what you like there won't be one square foot of ground vacant by the autumn, all the plots will be taken up. I congratulate you; in fact, you are saved. It's a perfect situation with that deep river. Only, of course, it must be cleared—all the old buildings, for example, must be removed, this house too, which is really good for nothing, and the old cherry orchard must be cut down.

LYUBOV   Cut down? My dear fellow, forgive me, but you don't know what you are talking about. If there is one thing interesting—remarkable indeed—in the whole province, it's just our cherry orchard.

LOPAKHIN   The only thing remarkable about the orchard is that it's a very large one. There's a crop of cherries every alternate year, and then there's nothing to be done with them, no one buys them.

GAYEV   This orchard is mentioned in the "Encyclopædia."

LOPAKHIN   [glancing at his watch]   If we don't decide on something and don't take some steps, on the twenty-second of August the cherry orchard and the whole estate too will be sold by auction. Make up your minds! There is no other way of saving it, I'll take my oath on that. No, no!

FIRS   In old days, forty or fifty years ago, they used to dry the cherries, soak them, pickle them, make jam too, and they used—

GAYEV   Be quiet, Firs.

FIRS   And they used to send the preserved cherries to Moscow and to Kharkov by the wagon-load. That brought the money in! And the preserved cherries in those days were soft and juicy, sweet and fragrant. . . . They knew the way to do them then. . . .

LYUBOV   And where is the recipe now?

FIRS   It's forgotten. Nobody remembers it.

PISHTCHIK   [to Lyubov Andreyevna]   What's it like in Paris? Did you eat frogs there?

LYUBOV   Oh, I ate crocodiles.

PISHTCHIK   Fancy that now!

LOPAKHIN   There used to be only the gentlefolks and the peasants in the country, but now there are these summer visitors. All the towns, even the small ones, are surrounded nowadays by these summer villas. And one may say for sure, that in another twenty years there'll be many more of these people and that they'll be everywhere. At present the summer visitor only drinks tea in his verandah, but maybe he'll take to working his bit of land too, and then your cherry orchard would become happy, rich and prosperous. . . .

GAYEV   [indignant]   What rot!

[Enter Varya and Yasha.]

VARYA   There are two telegrams for you, mamma. [Taking out keys and opening an old-fashioned bookcase with a loud crack.] Here they are.

LYUBOV   From Paris. [Tears the telegrams, without reading them.] I have done with Paris.

GAYEV   Do you know, Lyuba, how old that bookcase is? Last week I pulled out the bottom drawer and there I found the date branded on it. The bookcase was made just a hundred years ago. What do you say to that? We might have celebrated its jubilee. Though it's an inanimate object, still it is a bookcase.

PISHTCHIK   [amazed]   A hundred years! Fancy that now.

GAYEV   Yes . . . it is a thing. . . . [Feeling the bookcase] Dear, honoured bookcase! Hail to thee who for more than a hundred years hast served the pure ideals of good and justice; thy silent call to fruitful labour has never flagged in those hundred years, maintaining [in tears] in the generations of man, courage and faith in a brighter future and fostering in us ideals of good and social consciousness.

[A pause]

LOPAKHIN   Yes. . . .

LYUBOV   You are just the same as ever, Leonid.

GAYEV   [a little embarrassed]   Cannon off the right into the pocket!

LOPAKHIN   [looking at his watch]   Well, it's time I was off.

YASHA   [handing Lyubov Andreyevna medicine]   Perhaps you will take your pills now.

PISHTCHIK   You shouldn't take medicines, my dear madam . . . they do no harm and no good. Give them here, honoured lady. . . . [Takes the pill-box, pours the pills into the hollow of his hand, blows on them, puts them in

ANTON CHEKHOV

his mouth and drinks off some kvass.] There!

LYUBOV [*in alarm*] Why, you must be out of your mind!

PISHTCHIK I have taken all the pills.

LOPAKHIN What a glutton!

[*All laugh.*]

FIRS His honour stayed with us in Easter week, ate a gallon and a half of cucumbers . . . [*mutters*].

LYUBOV What is he saying?

VARYA He has taken to muttering like that for the last three years. We are used to it.

YASHA His declining years!

[*Charlotta Ivanovna, a very thin, lanky figure in a white dress with a lorgnette in her belt, walks across the stage.*]

LOPAKHIN I beg your pardon, Charlotta Ivanovna, I have not had time to greet you. [*Tries to kiss her hand.*]

CHARLOTTA [*pulling away her hand*] If I let you kiss my hand, you'll be wanting to kiss my elbow, and then my shoulder.

LOPAKHIN I've no luck to-day! [*All laugh.*] Charlotta Ivanovna, show us some tricks!

LYUBOV Charlotta, do show us some tricks!

CHARLOTTA I don't want to. I'm sleepy. [*Goes out.*]

LOPAKHIN In three weeks' time we shall meet again. [*Kisses Lyubov Andreyevna's hand.*] Good-bye till then—I must go. [*To Gayev*] Good-bye. [*Kissing Pishtchik*] Good-bye. [*Gives his hand to Varya, then to Firs and Yasha.*] I don't want to go. [*To Lyubov Andreyevna*] If you think over my plan for the villas and make up your mind, then let me know; I will lend you 50,000 roubles. Think of it seriously.

VARYA [*angrily*] Well, do go, for goodness sake.

LOPAKHIN I'm going, I'm going. [*Goes out.*]

GAYEV Low-born knave! I beg pardon, though . . . Varya is going to marry him, he's Varya's fiancé.

VARYA Don't talk nonsense, uncle.

LYUBOV Well, Varya, I shall be delighted. He's a good man.

PISHTCHIK He is, one must acknowledge, a most worthy man. And my Dashenka . . . says too that . . . she says . . . various things. . . . [*Snores, but at once wakes up.*] But all the same, honoured lady, could you oblige me . . . with a loan of 240 roubles . . . to pay the interest on my mortgage tomorrow?

VARYA [*dismayed*] No, no.

LYUBOV I really haven't any money.

PISHTCHIK It will turn up. [*Laughs.*] I never lose hope. I thought everything was over, I was a ruined man, and lo and behold—the railway passed through my land and . . . they paid me for it. And something else will turn up again, if not to-day, then to-morrow . . . Dashenka'll win two hundred thousand . . . she's got a lottery ticket.

LYUBOV Well, we've finished our coffee, we can go to bed.

FIRS [*brushes Gayev, reprovingly*] You have got on the wrong trousers again! What am I to do with you?

VARYA [*softly*] Anya's asleep. [*Softly opens the window.*] Now the sun's risen, it's not a bit cold. Look, mamma, what exquisite trees! My goodness! And the air! The starlings are singing!

GAYEV [*opens another window*] The orchard is all white. You've not forgotten it, Lyuba? That long avenue that runs straight, straight as an arrow, how it shines on a moonlight night. You remember? You've not forgotten?

LYUBOV [*looking out of the window into the garden*] Oh, my childhood, my innocence! It was in this nursery I used to sleep, from here I looked out into the orchard, happiness waked with me every morning and in those days the orchard was just the same, nothing has changed. [*Laughs with delight.*] All, all white! Oh, my orchard! After the dark gloomy autumn, and the cold winter; you are young again, and full of happiness, the heavenly angels have never left you. . . . If I could cast off the burden that weighs on my heart, if I could forget the past!

GAYEV H'm! and the orchard will be sold to pay our debts; it seems strange. . . .

LYUBOV See, our mother walking . . . all in white, down the avenue! [*Laughs with delight.*] It is she!

GAYEV Where?

VARYA Oh, don't, mamma!

LYUBOV There is no one. It was my fancy. On the right there, by the path to the arbour, there is a white tree bending like a woman. . . .

[*Enter Trofimov wearing a shabby student's uniform and spectacles.*]

LYUBOV What a ravishing orchard! White masses of blossom, blue sky . . .

TROFIMOV Lyubov Andreyevna! [*She looks round at him.*] I will just pay my respects to you and then leave you at once. [*Kisses her hand warmly.*] I was told to wait until morning, but I hadn't the patience to wait any longer. . . . [*Lyubov Andreyevna looks at him in perplexity.*]

VARYA [*through her tears*] This is Petya Trofimov.

TROFIMOV Petya Trofimov, who was your Grisha's tutor. . . . Can I have changed so much? [*Lyubov Andreyevna embraces him and weeps quietly.*]

GAYEV [*in confusion*] There, there, Lyuba.

VARYA [*crying*] I told you, Petya, to wait till to-morrow.

LYUBOV My Grisha . . . my boy . . . Grisha . . . my son!

VARYA We can't help it, mamma, it is God's will.

TROFIMOV [*softly through his tears*] There . . . there.

LYUBOV [*weeping quietly*] My boy was lost . . . drowned. Why? Oh, why, dear Petya? [*More quietly*] Anya is asleep in there, and I'm talking loudly . . . making this noise. . . . But, Petya? Why have you grown so ugly? Why do you look so old?

TROFIMOV A peasant-woman in the train called me a mangy-looking gentleman.

LYUBOV You were quite a boy then, a pretty little student, and now your hair's thin—and spectacles. Are you really a student still? [*Goes towards the door.*]

TROFIMOV I seem likely to be a perpetual student.

LYUBOV [*kisses her brother, then Varya*] Well, go to bed. . . . You are older too, Leonid.

PISHTCHIK [*follows her*] I suppose it's time we were asleep. . . . Ugh! my gout. I'm staying the night! Lyubov Andreyevna, my dear soul, if you could . . . to-morrow morning . . . 240 roubles.

GAYEV That's always his story.

PISHTCHIK Two hundred forty roubles . . . to pay the interest on my mortgage.

LYUBOV My dear man, I have no money.

PISHTCHIK I'll pay it back, my dear . . . a trifling sum.

LYUBOV Oh, well, Leonid will give it you. . . . You give him the money, Leonid.

GAYEV Me give it him! Let him wait till he gets it!

LYUBOV It can't be helped, give it him. He needs it. He'll pay it back.

[*Lyubov Andreyevna, Trofimov, Pishtchik, and Firs go out. Gayev, Varya, and Yasha remain.*]

GAYEV Sister hasn't got out of the habit of flinging away her money. [*To Yasha*] Get away, my good fellow, you smell of the hen-house.

YASHA [*with a grin*] And you, Leonid Andreyevitch, are just the same as ever.

GAYEV What's that? [*To Varya*] What did he say?

VARYA [*to Yasha*] Your mother has come from the village; she has been sitting in the servants' room since yesterday, waiting to see you.

YASHA Oh, bother her!

VARYA For shame!

YASHA What's the hurry? She might just as well have come to-morrow. [*Goes out.*]

VARYA Mamma's just the same as ever, she hasn't changed a bit. If she had her own way, she'd give away everything.

GAYEV Yes. [*A pause*] If a great many remedies are suggested for some disease, it means that the disease is incurable. I keep thinking and racking my brains; I have many schemes, a great many, and that really means none. If we could only come in for a legacy from somebody, or marry our Anya to a very rich man, or we might go to Yaroslavl and try our luck with our old aunt, the Countess. She's very, very rich, you know.

VARYA [*weeps*] If God would help us.

GAYEV Don't blubber. Aunt's very rich, but she doesn't like us. First, sister married a lawyer instead of a nobleman. . . .

[*Anya appears in the doorway.*]

GAYEV And then her conduct, one can't call it virtuous. She is good, and kind, and nice, and I love her, but, however one allows for extenuating circumstances, there's no denying that she's an immoral woman. One feels it in her slightest gesture.

VARYA [*in a whisper*]   Anya's in the doorway.

GAYEV   What do you say? [*A pause*] It's queer, there seems to be something wrong with my right eye. I don't see as well as I did. And on Thursday when I was in the district Court . . . [*Enter Anya.*]

VARYA   Why aren't you asleep, Anya?

ANYA   I can't get to sleep.

GAYEV   My pet. [*Kisses Anya's face and hands.*] My child . . . [*weeping*] you are not my neice, you are my angel, you are everything to me. Believe me, believe . . .

ANYA   I believe you, uncle. Everyone loves you and respects you . . . but, uncle dear, you must be silent . . . simply be silent. What were you saying just now about my mother, about your own sister? What made you say that?

GAYEV   Yes, yes. . . . [*Puts his hand over his face.*] Really, that was awful! My God, save me! And to-day I made a speech to the book-case . . . so stupid! And only when I had finished, I saw how stupid it was.

VARYA   It's true, uncle, you ought to keep quiet. Don't talk, that's all.

ANYA   If you could keep from talking, it would make things easier for you, too.

GAYEV   I won't speak. [*Kisses Anya's and Varya's hands.*] I'll be silent. Only this is about business. On Thursday I was in the district Court; well, there was a large party of us there and we began talking of one thing and another, and this and that, and do you know, I believe that it will be possible to raise a loan on an I.O.U. to pay the arrears on the mortgage.

VARYA   If the Lord would help us!

GAYEV   I'm going on Tuesday; I'll talk of it again. [*To Varya*] Don't blubber. [*To Anya*] Your mamma will talk to Lopakhin; of course, he won't refuse her. And as soon as you're rested you shall go to Yaroslavl to the Countess, your great-aunt. So we shall all set to work in three directions at once, and the business is done. We shall pay off arrears, I'm convinced of it. [*Puts a caramel in his mouth.*] I swear on my honour, I swear by anything you like, the estate shan't be sold. [*Excitedly*] By my own happiness, I swear it! Here's my hand on it, call me the basest, vilest of men, if I let it come to an auction! Upon my soul I swear it!

ANYA [*her equanimity has returned; she is quite happy*]   How good you are, uncle, and how clever! [*Embraces her uncle.*] I'm at peace now! Quite at peace! I'm happy!

[*Enter Firs.*]

FIRS [*reproachfully*]   Leonid Andreyevitch, have you no fear of God? When are you going to bed?

GAYEV   Directly, directly. You can go, Firs. I'll . . . yes, I will undress myself. Come, children, bye-bye. We'll go into details to-morrow, but now go to bed. [*Kisses Anya and Varya.*] I'm a man of the eighties. They run down that period, but still I can say I have had to suffer not a little for my convictions in my life. It's not for nothing that the peasant loves me. One must know the peasant! One must know how . . .

ANYA   At it again, uncle!

VARYA   Uncle dear, you'd better be quiet!

FIRS [*angrily*]   Leonid Andreyevitch!

GAYEV   I'm coming. I'm coming. Go to bed. Potted the shot—there's a shot for you. A beauty! [*Goes out, Firs hobbling after him.*]

ANYA   My mind's at rest now. I don't want to go to Yaroslavl, I don't like my great-aunt, but still my mind's at rest. Thanks to uncle. [*Sits down.*]

VARYA   We must go to bed. I'm going. Something unpleasant happened while you were away. In the old servants' quarters there are only the old servants, as you know—Yefim-yushka, Polya, and Yevstigney—and Karp too. They began letting stray people in to spend the night—I said nothing. But all at once I heard they had been spreading a report that I gave them nothing but pease pudding to eat. Out of stinginess, you know . . . and it was all Yev-stigney's doing. . . . Very well, I said to my-self . . . if that's how it is, I thought, wait a bit. I sent for Yevstigney . . . [*yawns*]. He comes . . . "How's this, Yevstigney," I said, "you could be such a fool as to . . . ?" [*Looking at Anya*] Anitchka! [*A pause*] She's asleep.

[Puts her arm round Anya.] Come to bed . . . come along! [Leads her.] My darling has fallen asleep! Come. . . .
[They go. Far away beyond the orchard a shepherd plays on a pipe. Trofimov crosses the stage and, seeing Varya and Anya, stands still.]

VARYA 'Sh! asleep, asleep. Come, my own.

ANYA [softly, half asleep] I'm so tired. Still those bells. Uncle . . . dear . . . mamma and uncle. . . .

VARYA Come, my own, come along.
[They go into Anya's room.]

TROFIMOV [tenderly] My sunshine! My spring.

Act Two

The open country. An old shrine, long abandoned and fallen out of the perpendicular; near it a well, large stones that have apparently once been tombstones, and an old garden seat. The road to Gayev's house is seen. On one side rise dark poplars; and there the cherry orchard begins. In the distance a row of telegraph poles and far, far away on the horizon there is faintly outlined a great town, only visible in very fine clear weather. It is near sunset. Charlotta, Yasha, and Dunyasha are sitting on the seat. Yepikhodov is standing near, playing something mournful on a guitar. All sit plunged in thought. Charlotta wears an old forage cap; she has taken a gun from her shoulder and is tightening the buckle on the strap.

CHARLOTTA [musingly] I haven't a real passport of my own, and I don't know how old I am, and I always feel that I'm a young thing. When I was a little girl, my father and mother used to travel about to fairs and give performances —very good ones. And I used to dance salto-mortale and all sorts of things. And when papa and mamma died, a German lady took me and had me educated. And so I grew up and became a governess. But where I came from, and who I am, I don't know. . . . Who my parents were, very likely they weren't married . . . I don't know. [Takes a cucumber out of her pocket and eats.] I know nothing at all. [A pause] One wants to talk and has no one to talk to . . . I have nobody.

YEPIKHODOV [plays on the guitar and sings].

What care I for the noisy world!
What care I for friends or foes!

How agreeable it is to play on the mandoline!

DUNYASHA That's a guitar, not a mandoline. [Looks in a hand-mirror and powders herself.]

YEPIKHODOV To a man mad with love, it's a mandoline. [Sings]

Were her heart but aglow with love's mutual flame.

[Yasha joins in.]

CHARLOTTA How shockingly these people sing! Foo! Like jackals!

DUNYASHA [to Yasha] What happiness, though, to visit foreign lands.

YASHA Ah, yes! I rather agree with you there. [Yawns, then lights a cigar.]

YEPIKHODOV That's comprehensible. In foreign lands everything has long since reached full complexion.

YASHA That's so, of course.

YEPIKHODOV I'm a cultivated man, I read remarkable books of all sorts, but I can never make out the tendency I am myself precisely inclined for, whether to live or to shoot myself, speaking precisely, but nevertheless I always carry a revolver. Here it is [showing revolver]. . . .

CHARLOTTA I've had enough, and now I'm going. [Puts on the gun.] Yepikhodov, you're a very clever fellow, and a very terrible one too—all the women must be wild about you. Br-r-r! [Goes.] These clever fellows are all so stupid; there's not a creature for me to speak to. . . . Always alone, alone, nobody belonging to me . . . and who I am, and why I'm on earth, I don't know [walking away slowly].

YEPIKHODOV Speaking precisely, not touching upon other subjects, I'm bound to admit about myself that destiny behaves mercilessly to me, as a storm to a little boat. If, let us suppose, I am mistaken, then why did I wake up this morning, to quote an example, and look round, and there on my chest was a spider of fearful magnitude . . . [*shows with both hands*] like this. And then I take up a jug of kvass, to quench my thirst, and in it there is something in the highest degree unseemly of the nature of a cockroach. [*A pause*] Have you read Buckle? [*A pause*] I am desirous of troubling you, Dunyasha, with a couple of words.

DUNYASA Well, speak.

YEPIKHODOV I should be desirous to speak with you alone. [*Sighs.*]

DUNYASHA [*embarrassed*] Well—only bring me my mantle first. It's by the cupboard. It's rather damp here.

YEPIKHODOV Certainly. I will fetch it. Now I know what I must do with my revolver. [*Takes guitar and goes off playing on it.*]

YASHA Two and twenty misfortunes! Between ourselves, he's a fool. [*Yawns.*]

DUNYASHA God grant he doesn't shoot himself! [*A pause*] I am so nervous, I'm always in a flutter. I was a little girl when I was taken into our lady's house, and now I have quite grown out of peasant ways, and my hands are white, as white as a lady's. I'm such a delicate, sensitive creature, I'm afraid of everything. I'm so frightened. And if you deceive me, Yasha, I don't know what will become of my nerves.

YASHA [*kisses her*] You're a peach! Of course a girl must never forget herself; what I dislike more than anything is a girl being flighty in her behaviour.

DUNYASHA I'm passionately in love with you, Yasha; you are a man of culture—you can give your opinion about anything.
[*A pause*]

YASHA [*yawns*] Yes, that's so. My opinion is this: if a girl loves anyone, that means that she has no principles. [*A pause*] It's pleasant smoking a cigar in the open air. [*Listens.*] Someone's coming this way . . . it's the gentlefolk. [*Dunyasha embraces him impulsively.*] Go home, as though you had been to the river to bathe; go by that path, or else they'll meet you and sup-

pose I have made an appointment with you here. That I can't endure.

DUNYASHA [*coughing softly*] The cigar has made my head ache. . . . [*Goes off.*]
[*Yasha remains sitting near the shrine. Enter Lyubov Andreyevna, Gayev, and Lopakhin.*]

LOPAKHIN You must make up your mind once for all—there's no time to lose. It's quite a simple question, you know. Will you consent to letting the land for building or not? One word in answer: Yes or no? Only one word!

LYUBOV Who is smoking such horrible cigars here? [*Sits down.*]

GAYEV Now the railway line has been brought near, it's made things very convenient. [*Sits down.*] Here we have been over and lunched in town. Cannon off the white! I should like to go home and have a game.

LYUBOV You have plenty of time.

LOPAKHIN Only one word! [*Beseechingly*] Give me an answer!

GAYEV [*yawning*] What do you say?

LYUBOV [*looks in her purse*] I had quite a lot of money here yesterday, and there's scarcely any left to-day. My poor Varya feeds us all on milk soup for the sake of economy; the old folks in the kitchen get nothing but pease pudding, while I waste my money in a senseless way. [*Drops purse, scattering gold pieces. Annoyed*] There, they have all fallen out!

YASHA Allow me, I'll soon pick them up. [*Collects the coins.*]

LYUBOV Pray do, Yasha. And what did I go off to the town to lunch for? Your restaurant's a wretched place with its music and the table-cloth smelling of soap. . . . Why drink so much, Leonid? And eat so much? And talk so much? To-day you talked a great deal again in the restaurant, and all so inappropriately. About the era of the 'seventies, about the decadents. And to whom? Talking to waiters about decadents!

LOPAKHIN Yes.

GAYEV [*waving his hand*] I'm incorrigible; that's evident. [*Irritably to Yasha*] Why is it you keep fidgeting about in front of us!

YASHA [*laughs*] I can't help laughing when I hear your voice.

GAYEV [*to his sister*] Either I or he . . .

LYUBOV Get along! Go away, Yasha.

YASHA [*gives Lyubov Andreyevna her purse*] Directly . . . [*hardly able to suppress his laughter*] this minute. . . . [*Goes off.*]

LOPAKHIN Deriganov, the millionaire, means to buy your estate. They say he is coming to the sale himself.

LYUBOV Where did you hear that?

LOPAKHIN That's what they say in town.

GAYEV Our aunt in Yaroslavl has promised to send help; but when, and how much she will send, we don't know.

LOPAKHIN How much will she send? A hundred thousand? Two hundred?

LYUBOV Oh, well! . . . Ten or fifteen thousand, and we must be thankful to get that.

LOPAKHIN Forgive me, but such reckless people as you are—such queer, unbusiness-like people —I never met in my life. One tells you in plain Russian your estate is going to be sold, and you seem not to understand it.

LYUBOV What are we to do? Tell us what to do.

LOPAKHIN I do tell you every day. Every day I say the same thing. You absolutely must let the cherry orchard and the land on building leases; and do it at once, as quick as may be— the auction's close upon us! Do understand! Once make up your mind to build villas, and you can raise as much money as you like, and then you are saved.

LYUBOV Villas and summer visitors—forgive me saying so—it's so vulgar.

GAYEV There I perfectly agree with you.

LOPAKHIN I shall sob, or scream, or fall into a fit. I can't stand it! You drive me mad! [*To Gayev*] You're an old woman!

GAYEV What do you say?

LOPAKHIN An old woman! [*Gets up to go.*]

LYUBOV [*in dismay*] No, don't go! Do stay, my dear friend! Perhaps we shall think of something.

LOPAKHIN What is there to think of?

LYUBOV Don't go, I entreat you! With you here it's more cheerful, anyway. [*A pause*] I keep expecting something, as though the house were going to fall about our ears.

GAYEV [*in profound dejection*] Potted the white! It fails—a kiss.

LYUBOV We have been great sinners. . . .

LOPAKHIN You have no sins to repent of.

GAYEV [*puts a caramel in his mouth*] They say I've eaten up my property in caramels. [*Laughs.*]

LYUBOV Oh, my sins! I've always thrown my money away recklessly like a lunatic. I married a man who made nothing but debts. My husband died of champagne—he drank dreadfully. To my misery I loved another man, and immediately—it was my first punishment—the blow fell upon me, here, in the river . . . my boy was drowned and I went abroad—went away for ever, never to return, not to see that river again . . . I shut my eyes, and fled, distracted, and *he* after me . . . pitilessly, brutally. I bought a villa at Mentone, for *he* fell ill there, and for three years I had no rest day or night. His illness wore me out, my soul was dried up. And last year, when my villa was sold to pay my debts, I went to Paris and there he robbed me of everything and abandoned me for another woman; and I tried to poison myself. . . . So stupid, so shameful! . . . And suddenly I felt a yearning for Russia, for my country, for my little girl. . . . [*Dries her tears.*] Lord, Lord, be merciful! Forgive my sins! Do not chastise me more. [*Takes a telegram out of her pocket.*] I got this to-day from Paris. He implores forgiveness, entreats me to return. [*Tears up the telegram.*] I fancy there is music somewhere. [*Listens.*]

GAYEV That's our famous Jewish orchestra. You remember, four violins, a flute and a double bass.

LYUBOV That still in existence? We ought to send for them one evening, and give a dance.

LOPAKHIN [*listens*] I can't hear. . . . [*Hums softly.*]

For money the Germans will turn a Russian into a Frenchman.

[*Laughs.*] I did see such a piece at the theatre yesterday! It was funny!

LYUBOV And most likely there was nothing funny in it. You shouldn't look at plays, you should look at yourselves a little oftener. How grey your lives are! How much nonsense you talk.

ANTON CHEKHOV

LOPAKHIN That's true. One may say honestly, we live a fool's life. [*A pause*] My father was a peasant, an idiot; he knew nothing and taught me nothing, only beat me when he was drunk, and always with his stick. In reality I am just such another blockhead and idiot. I've learnt nothing properly. I write a wretched hand. I write so that I feel ashamed before folks, like a pig.

LYUBOV You ought to get married, my dear fellow.

LOPAKHIN Yes . . . that's true.

LYUBOV You should marry our Varya, she's a good girl.

LOPAKHIN Yes.

LYUBOV She's a good-natured girl, she's busy all day long, and what's more, she loves you. And you have liked her for ever so long.

LOPAKHIN Well? I'm not against it. . . . She's a good girl.

[*A pause*]

GAYEV I've been offered a place in the bank: 6,000 roubles a year. Did you know?

LYUBOV You would never do for that! You must stay as you are.

[*Enter Firs with overcoat.*]

FIRS Put it on, sir, it's damp.

GAYEV [*putting it on*] You bother me, old fellow.

FIRS You can't go on like this. You went away in the morning without leaving word. [*Looks him over.*]

LYUBOV You look older, Firs!

FIRS What is your pleasure?

LOPAKHIN You look older, she said.

FIRS I've had a long life. They were arranging my wedding before your papa was born. . . . [*Laughs.*] I was the head footman before the emancipation came. I wouldn't consent to be set free then; I stayed on with the old master. . . . [*A pause*] I remember what rejoicings they made and didn't know themselves what they were rejoicing over.

LOPAKHIN Those were fine old times. There was flogging anyway.

FIRS [*not hearing*] To be sure! The peasants knew their place, and the masters knew theirs; but now they're all at sixes and sevens, there's no making it out.

GAYEV Hold your tongue, Firs. I must go to town to-morrow. I have been promised an introduction to a general, who might let us have a loan.

LOPAKHIN You won't bring that off. And you won't pay your arrears, you may rest assured of that.

LYUBOV That's all his nonsense. There is no such general.

[*Enter Trofimov, Anya, and Varya.*]

GAYEV Here come our girls.

ANYA There's mamma on the seat.

LYUBOV [*tenderly*] Come here, come along. My darlings! [*Embraces Anya and Varya.*] If you only knew how I love you both. Sit beside me, there, like that.

[*All sit down.*]

LOPAKHIN Our perpetual student is always with the young ladies.

TROFIMOV That's not your business.

LOPAKHIN He'll soon be fifty, and he's still a student.

TROFIMOV Drop your idiotic jokes.

LOPAKHIN Why are you so cross, you queer fish?

TROFIMOV Oh, don't persist!

LOPAKHIN [*laughs*] Allow me to ask you what's your idea of me?

TROFIMOV I'll tell you my idea of you, Yermolay Alexeyevitch: you are a rich man, you'll soon be a millionaire. Well, just as in the economy of nature a wild beast is of use, who devours everything that comes in his way, so you too have your use.

[*All laugh.*]

VARYA Better tell us something about the planets, Petya.

LYUBOV No, let us go on with the conversation we had yesterday.

TROFIMOV What was it about?

GAYEV About pride.

TROFIMOV We had a long conversation yesterday, but we came to no conclusion. In pride, in your sense of it, there is something mystical. Perhaps you are right from your point of view; but if one looks at it simply, without subtlety, what sort of pride can there be, what sense is there in it, if man in his physiological formation is very imperfect, if in the immense majority of cases he is coarse, dull-witted, profoundly unhappy? One must give up glorification of self. One should work, and nothing else.

GAYEV One must die in any case.

TROFIMOV Who knows? And what does it mean—dying? Perhaps man has a hundred senses, and only the five we know are lost at death, while the other ninety-five remain alive.

LYUBOV How clever you are, Petya!

LOPAKHIN [*ironically*] Fearfully clever!

TROFIMOV Humanity progresses, perfecting its powers. Everything that is beyond its ken now will one day become familiar and comprehensible; only we must work, we must with all our powers aid the seeker after truth. Here among us in Russia the workers are few in number as yet. The vast majority of the intellectual people I know seek nothing, do nothing, are not fit as yet for work of any kind. They call themselves intellectual, but they treat their servants as inferiors, behave to the peasants as though they were animals, learn little, read nothing seriously, do practically nothing, only talk about science and know very little about art. They are all serious people, they all have severe faces, they all talk of weighty matters and air their theories, and yet the vast majority of us—ninety-nine per cent—live like savages, at the least thing fly to blows and abuse, eat piggishly, sleep in filth and stuffiness, bugs everywhere, stench and damp and moral impurity. And it's clear all our fine talk is only to divert our attention and other people's. Show me where to find the crèches there's so much talk about, and the reading-rooms? They only exist in novels: in real life there are none of them. There is nothing but filth and vulgarity and Asiatic apathy. I fear and dislike very serious faces. I'm afraid of serious conversations. We should do better to be silent.

LOPAKHIN You know, I get up at five o'clock in the morning, and I work from morning to night; and I've money, my own and other people's, always passing through my hands, and I see what people are made of all round me. One has only to begin to do anything to see how few honest, decent people there are. Sometimes when I lie awake at night, I think: "Oh! Lord, thou hast given us immense forests, boundless plains, the widest horizons, and living here we ourselves ought really to be giants."

LYUBOV You ask for giants! They are no good except in story-books; in real life they frighten us.

[*Yepikhodov advances in the background, playing on the guitar.*]

LYUBOV [*dreamily*] There goes Yepikhodov.

ANYA [*dreamily*] There goes Yepikhodov.

GAYEV The sun has set, my friends.

TROFIMOV Yes.

GAYEV [*not loudly, but, as it were, declaiming*] O nature, divine nature, thou are bright with external lustre, beautiful and indifferent! Thou, whom we call mother, thou dost unite within thee life and death! Thou dost give life and dost destroy!

VARYA [*in a tone of supplication*] Uncle!

ANYA Uncle, you are at it again!

TROFIMOV You'd much better be cannoning off the red!

GAYEV I'll hold my tongue, I will.

[*All sit plunged in thought. Perfect stillness. The only thing audible is the muttering of Firs. Suddenly there is a sound in the distance, as it were from the sky—the sound of a breaking harp-string, mournfully dying away.*]

LYUBOV What is that?

LOPAKHIN I don't know. Somewhere far away a bucket fallen and broken in the pits. But somewhere very far away.

GAYEV It might be a bird of some sort—such as a heron.

TROFIMOV Or an owl.

LYUBOV [*shudders*] I don't know why, but it's horrid.

[*A pause*]

FIRS It was the same before the calamity—the owl hooted and the samovar hissed all the time.

GAYEV Before what calamity?

FIRS Before the emancipation.

[*A pause*]

LYUBOV Come, my friends, let us be going; evening is falling. [*To Anya*] There are tears in your eyes. What is it, darling? [*Embraces her.*]

ANYA Nothing, mamma; it's nothing.

TROFIMOV There is somebody coming.

[*The wayfarer appears in a shabby white forage cap and an overcoat; he is slightly drunk.*]

WAYFARER Allow me to inquire, can I get to the

station this way?

GAYEV Yes. Go along that road.

WAYFARER [*coughing*] I thank you most feelingly. The weather is superb. [*Declaims*] My brother, my suffering brother! . . . Come out to the Volga! Whose groan do you hear? . . . [*To Varya*] Mademoiselle, vouchsafe a hungry Russian 30 kopeks.

[*Varya utters a shriek of alarm.*]

LOPAKHIN [*angrily*] There's a right and a wrong way of doing everything!

LYUBOV [*hurridly*] Here, take this. [*Looks in her purse.*] I've no silver. No matter—here's gold for you.

WAYFARER I thank you most feelingly! [*Goes off.*]

[*Laughter*]

VARYA [*frightened*] I'm going home—I'm going. . . . Oh, mamma, the servants have nothing to eat, and you gave him gold!

LYUBOV There's no doing anything with me. I'm so silly! When we get home, I'll give you all I possess. Yermolay Alexeyevitch, you will lend me some more . . . !

LOPAKHIN I will.

LYUBOV Come, friends, it's time to be going. And Varya, we have made a match of it for you. I congratulate you.

VARYA [*through her tears*] Mamma, that's not a joking matter.

LOPAKHIN "Ophelia, get thee to a nunnery!"

GAYEV My hands are trembling; it's a long while since I had a game of billiards.

LOPAKHIN "Ophelia! Nymph, in thy orisons be all my sins remember'd."

LYUBOV Come, it will soon be supper-time.

VARYA How he frightened me! My heart's simply throbbing.

LOPAKHIN Let me remind you, ladies and gentlemen: on the twenty-second of August the cherry orchard will be sold. Think about that! Think about it!

[*All go off, except Trofimov and Anya.*]

ANYA [*laughing*] I'm grateful to the wayfarer! He frightened Varya and we are left alone.

TROFIMOV Varya's afraid we shall fall in love with each other, and for days together she won't leave us. With her narrow brain she can't grasp that we are above love. To elimi-

nate the petty and transitory which hinders us from being free and happy—that is the aim and meaning of our life. Forward! We go forward irresistibly towards the bright star that shines yonder in the distance. Forward! Do not lag behind, friends.

ANYA [*claps her hands*] How well you speak! [*A pause*] It is divine here to-day.

TROFIMOV Yes, it's glorious weather.

ANYA Somehow, Petya, you've made me so that I don't love the cherry orchard as I used to. I used to love it so dearly. I used to think that there was no spot on earth like our garden.

TROFIMOV All Russia is our garden. The earth is great and beautiful—there are many beautiful places in it. [*A pause*] Think only, Anya, your grandfather, and great-grandfather, and all your ancestors were slave-owners—the owners of living souls—and from every cherry in the orchard, from every leaf, from every trunk there are human creatures looking at you. Cannot you hear their voices? Oh, it is awful! Your orchard is a fearful thing, and when in the evening or at night one walks about the orchard, the old bark on the trees glimmers dimly in the dusk, and the old cherry trees seem to be dreaming of centuries gone by and tortured by fearful visions. Yes! We are at least two hundred years behind, we have really gained nothing yet, we have no definite attitude to the past, we do nothing but theorise or complain of depression or drink vodka. It is clear that to begin to live in the present we must first expiate our past, we must break with it; and we can expiate it only by suffering, by extraordinary unceasing labour. Understand that, Anya.

ANYA The house we live in has long ceased to be our own, and I shall leave it, I give you my word.

TROFIMOV If you have the house keys, fling them into the well and go away. Be free as the wind.

ANYA [*in ecstasy*] How beautifully you said that!

TROFIMOV Believe me, Anya, believe me! I am not thirty yet, I am young, I am still a student, but I have gone through so much already! As soon as winter comes I am hungry, sick, careworn, poor as a beggar, and what ups and downs of fortune have I not known! And my soul was always, every minute, day and night, full of inexplicable forebodings. I have a foreboding of happiness, Anya. I see glimpses of it already.

ANYA [*pensively*]   The moon is rising.

[*Yepikhodov is heard playing still the same mournful song on the guitar. The moon rises. Somewhere near the poplars Varya is looking for Anya and calling "Anya! where are you?"*]

TROFIMOV   Yes, the moon is rising. [*A pause.*] Here is happiness—here it comes! It is coming nearer and nearer; already I can hear its foot-steps. And if we never see it—if we may never know it—what does it matter? Others will see it after us.

VARYA'S VOICE   Anya! Where are you?

TROFIMOV   That Varya again! [*Angrily*] It's revolting!

ANYA   Well, let's go down to the river. It's lovely there.

TROFIMOV   Yes, let's go.

[*They go.*]

VARYA'S VOICE   Anya! Anya!

Act Three

A drawing-room divided by an arch from a larger drawing-room. A chandelier burning. The Jewish orchestra, the same that was mentioned in the second act, is heard playing in the ante-room. It is evening. In the larger drawing-room they are dancing the grand chain. The voice of Semyonov-Pishtchik: "Promenade à une paire!" Then enter the drawing-room in couples first Pishtchik and Charlotta Ivanovna, then Trofimov and Lyubov Andreyevna, thirdly Anya with the Post-office Clerk, fourthly Varya with the Station Master, and other guests. Varya is quietly weeping and wiping away her tears as she dances. In the last couple is Dunyasha. They move across the drawing-room. Pishtchik shouts: "Grand rond, balancez!" and "Les Cavaliers à genou et remerciez vos dames."

Firs in a swallow-tail coat brings in seltzer water on a tray. Pishtchik and Trofimov enter the drawing-room.

PISHTCHIK   I am a full-blooded man; I have already had two strokes. Dancing's hard work for me, but as they say, if you're in the pack, you must bark with the rest. I'm as strong, I may say, as a horse. My parent, who would have his joke—may the Kingdom of Heaven be his!—used to say about our origin that the ancient stock of the Semyonov-Pishtchiks was derived from the very horse that Caligula made a member of the senate. [*Sits down.*] But I've no money, that's where the mischief is. A hungry dog believes in nothing but meat. . . . [*Snores, but at once wakes up.*] That's like me . . . I can think of nothing but money.

TROFIMOV   There really is something horsy about your appearance.

PISHTCHIK   Well . . . a horse is a fine beast . . . a horse can be sold.

[*There is the sound of billiards being played in an adjoining room. Varya appears in the arch leading to the larger drawing-room.*]

TROFIMOV [*teasing*]   Madame Lopakhin! Madame Lopakhin!

VARYA [*angrily*]   Mangy-looking gentleman!

TROFIMOV   Yes, I am a mangy-looking gentleman, and I'm proud of it!

VARYA [*pondering bitterly*]   Here we have hired musicians and nothing to pay them! [*Goes out.*]

TROFIMOV [*to Pishtchik*]   If the energy you have wasted during your lifetime in trying to find the money to pay your interest had gone to something else, you might in the end have turned the world upside down.

PISHTCHIK   Nietzsche, the philosopher, a very great and celebrated man . . . of enormous intellect . . . says in his works that one can make forged bank-notes.

TROFIMOV   Why, have you read Nietzsche?

PISHTCHIK   What next . . . Dashenka told me. . . . And now I am in such a position, I might just as well forge bank-notes. The day after tomorrow I must pay 310 roubles—130 I have procured [*feeling in his pockets, in alarm*]. The money's gone! I have lost my money! [*Through his tears*] Where's the money? [*Gleefully*] Why, here it is behind the lining. . . . It has made me hot all over.

ANTON CHEKHOV

[*Enter Lyubov Andreyevna and Charlotta Ivan-ovna.*]

LYUBOV [*hums the Lezginka*] Why is Leonid so long? What can he be doing in town? [*To Dunyasha*] Offer the musicians some tea.

TROFIMOV The sale hasn't taken place, most likely.

LYUBOV It's the wrong time to have the orchestra, and the wrong time to give a dance. Well, never mind. [*Sits down and hums softly.*]

CHARLOTTA [*gives Pishtchik a pack of cards*] Here's a pack of cards. Think of any card you like.

PISHTCHIK I've thought of one.

CHARLOTTA Shuffle the pack now. That's right. Give it here, my dear Mr. Pishtchik. *Ein, zwei, drei*—now look, it's in your breast pocket.

PISHTCHIK [*taking a card out of his breast pocket*] The eight of spades! Perfectly right! [*Wonderingly*] Fancy that now!

CHARLOTTA [*holding pack of cards in her hands, to Trofimov*] Tell me quickly which is the top card.

TROFIMOV Well, the queen of spades.

CHARLOTTA It is! [*To Pishtchik*] Well, which card is uppermost?

PISHTCHIK The ace of hearts.

CHARLOTTA It is! [*Claps her hands; pack of cards disappears.*] Ah! what lovely weather it is to-day!

[*A mysterious feminine voice which seems to be coming out of the floor answers her:* "Oh, yes, it's magnificent weather, madam."]

CHARLOTTA You are my perfect ideal.

VOICE And I greatly admire you too, madam.

STATION MASTER [*applauding*] The lady ventriloquist—bravo!

PISHTCHIK [*wonderingly*] Fancy that now! Most enchanting Charlotta Ivanovna. I'm simply in love with you.

CHARLOTTA In love? [*Shrugging shoulders*] What do you know of love, *guter Mensch, aber schlechter Musikant.*

TROFIMOV [*pats Pishtchik on the shoulder*] You dear old horse. . . .

CHARLOTTA Attention, please! Another trick! [*Takes a travelling rug from a chair.*] Here's a very good rug; I want to sell it [*shaking it out*]. Doesn't anyone want to buy it?

PISHTCHIK [*wonderingly*] Fancy that!

CHARLOTTA *Ein, zwei, drei!*

[*Quickly, Charlotta picks up rug she has dropped; behind the rug stands Anya; she makes a curtsey, runs to her mother, embraces her and runs back into the larger drawing-room amidst general enthusiasm.*]

LYUBOV [*applauds*] Bravo! Bravo!

CHARLOTTA Now again! *Ein, zwei, drei!* [*Lifts up the rug; behind the rug stands Varya, bowing.*]

PISHTCHIK [*wonderingly*] Fancy that now!

CHARLOTTA That's the end. [*Throws the rug at Pishtchik, makes a curtsey, runs into the larger drawing-room.*]

PISHTCHIK [*hurries after her*] Mischievous creature! Fancy! [*Goes out.*]

LYUBOV And still Leonid doesn't come. I can't understand what he's doing in the town so long! Why, everything must be over by now. The estate is sold, or the sale has not taken place. Why keep so long in suspense?

VARYA [*trying to console her*] Uncle's bought it. I feel sure of that.

TROFIMOV [*ironically*] Oh, yes!

VARYA Great-aunt sent him an authorisation to buy it in her name, and transfer the debt. She's doing it for Anya's sake, and I'm sure God will be merciful. Uncle will buy it.

LYUBOV My aunt in Yaroslavl sent fifteen thousand to buy the estate in her name, she doesn't trust us—but that's not enough even to pay the arrears. [*Hides her face in her hands.*] My fate is being sealed to-day, my fate . . .

TROFIMOV [*teasing Varya*] Madame Lopakhin.

VARYA [*angrily*] Perpetual student! Twice already you've been sent down from the University.

LYUBOV Why are you angry, Varya? He's teasing you about Lopakhin. Well, what of that? Marry Lopakhin if you like, he's a good man, and interesting; if you don't want to, don't! Nobody compels you, darling.

VARYA I must tell you plainly, mamma, I look at the matter seriously; he's a good man, I like him.

LYUBOV Well, marry him. I can't see what you're waiting for.

VARYA Mamma. I can't make him an offer myself. For the last two years, everyone's been talking to me about him. Everyone talks; but he says nothing or else makes a joke. I see what it means. He's growing rich, he's absorbed in business, he has no thoughts for me. If I had money, were it ever so little, if I had only a hundred roubles, I'd throw everything up and go far away. I would go into a nunnery.

TROFIMOV What bliss!

VARYA [*to Trofimov*] A student ought to have sense! [*In a soft tone with tears*] How ugly you've grown, Petya! How old you look! [*To Lyubov Andreyevna, no longer crying*] But I can't do without work, mamma; I must have something to do every minute.

[*Enter Yasha.*]

YASHA [*hardly restraining his laughter*] Yepikhodov has broken a billiard cue! [*Goes out.*]

VARYA What is Yepikhodov doing here? Who gave him leave to play billiards? I can't make these people out. [*Goes out.*]

LYUBOV Don't tease her, Petya. You see she has grief enough without that.

TROFIMOV She is so very officious, meddling in what's not her business. All the summer she's given Anya and me no peace. She's afraid of a love affair between us. What's it to do with her? Besides, I have given no grounds for it. Such triviality is not in my line. We are above love!

LYUBOV And I suppose I am beneath love. [*Very uneasily*] Why is it Leonid's not here? If only I could know whether the estate is sold or not! It seems such an incredible calamity that I really don't know what to think. I am distracted . . . I shall scream in a minute . . . I shall do something stupid. Save me, Petya, tell me something, talk to me!

TROFIMOV What does it matter whether the estate is sold to-day or not? That's all done with long ago. There's no turning back, the path is overgrown. Don't worry yourself, dear Lyubov Andreyevna. You mustn't deceive yourself; for once in your life you must face the truth!

LYUBOV What truth? You see where the truth lies, but I seem to have lost my sight, I see nothing. You settle every great problem so boldly, but tell me, my dear boy, isn't it because you're young—because you haven't yet understood one of your problems through suffering? You look forward boldly, and isn't it that you don't see and don't expect anything dreadful because life is still hidden from your young eyes? You're bolder, more honest, deeper than we are, but think, be just a little magnanimous, have pity on me. I was born here, you know, my father and mother lived here, my grandfather lived here, I love this house. I can't conceive of life without the cherry orchard, and if it really must be sold, then sell me with the orchard. [*Embraces Trofimov, kisses him on the forehead.*] My boy was drowned here. [*Weeps.*] Pity me, my dear kind fellow.

TROFIMOV You know I feel for you with all my heart.

LYUBOV But that should have been said differently, so differently. [*Takes out her handkerchief, telegram falls on the floor.*] My heart is so heavy to-day. It's so noisy here, my soul is quivering at every sound, I'm shuddering all over, but I can't go away; I'm afraid to be quiet and alone. Don't be hard on me, Petya . . . I love you as though you were one of ourselves. I would gladly let you marry Anya—I swear I would—only, my dear boy, you must take your degree, you do nothing—you're simply tossed by fate from place to place. That's so strange. It is, isn't it? And you must do something with your beard to make it grow somehow. [*Laughs.*] You look so funny!

TROFIMOV [*picks up the telegram*] I've no wish to be a beauty.

LYUBOV That's a telegram from Paris. I get one every day. One yesterday and one to-day. That savage creature is ill again, he's in trouble again. He begs forgiveness, beseeches me to go, and really I ought to go to Paris to see him. You look shocked, Petya. What am I to do, my dear boy, what am I to do? He is ill, he is alone and unhappy, and who'll look after him, who'll keep him from doing the wrong thing, who'll give him his medicine at the right time? And why hide it or be silent? I love him, that's clear. I love him! I love him! He's a millstone about my neck, I'm going to the bottom with him, but I love that stone and can't live without it. [*Presses Trofimov's hand.*] Don't think ill of me, Petya, don't tell me anything, don't tell me . . .

TROFIMOV [*through his tears*] For God's sake

ANTON CHEKHOV

forgive my frankness: why, he robbed you!

LYUBOV No! No! No! You mustn't speak like that. [*Covers her ears.*]

TROFIMOV He is a wretch! You're the only person that doesn't know it! He's a worthless creature! A despicable wretch!

LYUBOV [*getting angry, but speaking with restraint*] You're twenty-six or twenty-seven years old, but you're still a schoolboy.

TROFIMOV Possibly.

LYUBOV You should be a man at your age! You should understand what love means! And you ought to be in love yourself. You ought to fall in love! [*Angrily*] Yes, yes, and it's not purity in you, you're simply a prude, a comic fool, a freak.

TROFIMOV [*in horror*] The things she's saying!

LYUBOV "I am above love!" You're not above love, but simply as our Firs here says, "You are a good-for-nothing." At your age not to have a mistress!

TROFIMOV [*in horror*] This is awful! The things she is saying! [*Goes rapidly into the larger drawing-room clutching his head.*] This is awful! I can't stand it! I'm going. [*Goes off, but at once returns.*] All is over between us! [*Goes off into the ante-room.*]

LYUBOV [*shouts after him*] Petya! Wait a minute! You funny creature! I was joking! Petya!

[*There is a sound of somebody running quickly downstairs and suddenly falling with a crash. Anya and Varya scream, but there is a sound of laughter at once.*]

LYUBOV What has happened?

[*Anya runs in.*]

ANYA [*laughing*] Petya's fallen downstairs! [*Runs out.*]

LYUBOV What a queer fellow that Petya is!

[*The Station Master stands in the middle of the larger room and reads "The Magdalene," by Alexey Tolstoy. They listen to him, but before he has recited many lines, strains of a waltz are heard from the ante-room and the reading is broken off. All dance. Trofimov, Anya, Varya, and Lyubov Andreyevna come in from the ante-room.*]

LYUBOV Come, Petya—come, pure heart! I beg your pardon. Let's have a dance! [*Dances with Petya. Anya and Varya dance. Firs comes in,*

puts his stick down near the side door. Yasha also comes into the drawing-room and looks on at the dancing.]

YASHA What is it, old man?

FIRS I don't feel well. In old days we used to have generals, barons and admirals dancing at our balls, and now we send for the post-office clerk and the station master and even they're not overanxious to come. I am getting feeble. The old master, the grandfather, used to give sealing-wax for all complaints. I have been taking sealing-wax for twenty years or more. Perhaps that's what's kept me alive.

YASHA You bore me, old man! [*Yawns.*] It's time you were done with.

FIRS Ach, you're a good-for-nothing! [*Mutters.*] [*Trofimov and Lyubov Andreyevna dance in larger room and then on to the stage.*]

LYUBOV *Merci.* I'll sit down a little. [*Sits down.*] I'm tired.

[*Enter Anya.*]

ANYA [*excitedly*] There's a man in the kitchen has been saying that the cherry orchard's been sold to-day.

LYUBOV Sold to whom?

ANYA He didn't say to whom. He's gone away. [*She dances with Trofimov, and they go off into the larger room.*]

YASHA There was an old man gossiping there, a stranger.

FIRS Leonid Andreyevitch isn't here yet, he hasn't come back. He has his light overcoat on, *demi-saison,* he'll catch cold for sure. Ach! Foolish young things!

LYUBOV I feel as though I should die. Go, Yasha, find out to whom it has been sold.

YASHA But he went away long ago, the old chap. [*Laughs.*]

LYUBOV [*with slight vexation*] What are you laughing at? What are you pleased at?

YASHA Yepikhodov is so funny. He's a silly fellow, two and twenty misfortunes.

LYUBOV Firs, if the estate is sold, where will you go?

FIRS Where you bid me, there I'll go.

LYUBOV Why do you look like that? Are you ill? You ought to be in bed.

FIRS Yes. [*Ironically*] Me go to bed and who's to wait here? Who's to see to things without me? I'm the only one in all the house.

YASHA [to Lyubov Andreyevna] Lyubov Andreyevna, permit me to make a request of you; if you go back to Paris again, be so kind as to take me with you. It's positively impossible for me to stay here. [Looking about him; in an undertone] There's no need to say it, you see for yourself—an uncivilised country, the people have no morals, and then the dullness! The food in the kitchen's abominable, and then Firs runs after one muttering all sorts of unsuitable words. Take me with you, please do!

[Enter Pishtchik.]

PISHTCHIK Allow me to ask you for a waltz, my dear lady. [Lyubov Andreyevna goes with him.] Enchanting lady, I really must borrow of you just 180 roubles . . . [dancing] only 180 roubles.

[They pass into the larger room.]

YASHA [hums softly]

Knowest thou my soul's emotion.

[In the larger drawing-room, a figure in a grey top hat and in check trousers is gesticulating and jumping about. Shouts of "Bravo, Charlotta Ivanovna."]

DUNYASHA [has stopped to powder herself] My young lady tells me to dance. There are plenty of gentlemen, and too few ladies, but dancing makes me giddy and makes my heart beat. Firs, the post-office clerk said something to me just now that quite took my breath away.

[Music becomes more subdued.]

FIRS What did he say to you?

DUNYASHA He said I was like a flower.

YASHA [yawns] What ignorance! [Goes out.]

DUNYASHA Like a flower. I am a girl of such delicate feelings, I am awfully fond of soft speeches.

FIRS Your head's being turned.

[Enter Yepikhodov.]

YEPIKHODOV You have no desire to see me, Dunyasha. I might be an insect. [Sighs.] Ah! life!

DUNYASHA What is it you want?

YEPIKHODOV Undoubtedly you may be right. [Sighs.] But of course, if one looks at it from that point of view, if I may so express myself, you have, excuse my plain speaking, reduced me to a complete state of mind. I know my

destiny. Every day some misfortune befalls me and I have long ago grown accustomed to it, so that I look upon my fate with a smile. You gave me your word, and though I—

DUNYASHA Let us have a talk later, I entreat you, but now leave me in peace, for I am lost in reverie. [Plays with her fan.]

YEPIKHODOV I have a misfortune every day, and if I may venture to express myself, I merely smile at it, I even laugh.

[Varya enters from the larger drawing-room.]

VARYA You still have not gone, Yepikhodov. What a disrespectful creature you are, really! [To Dunyasha] Go along, Dunyasha! [To Yepikhodov] First you play billiards and break the cue, then you go wandering about the drawing-room like a visitor!

YEPIKHODOV You really cannot, if I may so express myself, call me to account like this.

VARYA I'm not calling you to account, I'm speaking to you. You do nothing but wander from place to place and don't do your work. We keep you as a counting-house clerk, but what use you are I can't say.

YEPIKHODOV [offended] Whether I work or whether I walk, whether I eat or whether I play billiards, is a matter to be judged by persons of understanding and my elders.

VARYA You dare to tell me that! [Firing up] You dare! You mean to say I've no understanding. Begone from here! This minute!

YEPIKHODOV [intimidated] I beg you to express yourself with delicacy.

VARYA [beside herself with anger] This moment! Get out! Away! [He goes towards the door, she following him.] Two and twenty misfortunes! Take yourself off! Don't let me set eyes on you! [Yepikhodov has gone out; behind the door his voice is heard, "I shall lodge a complaint against you."] You're coming back? [Snatches up the stick Firs has put down near the door.] Come! Come! Come! I'll show you! What! You're coming? Then take that! [She swings the stick, at the very moment that Lopakhin comes in.]

LOPAKHIN Very much obliged to you!

VARYA [angrily and ironically] I beg your pardon!

LOPAKHIN Not at all! I humbly thank you for

your kind reception!

VARYA No need of thanks for it. [*Moves away, then looks round and asks softly*] I haven't hurt you?

LOPAKHIN Oh, no! Not at all! There's an immense bump coming up, though!

VOICES FROM LARGER ROOM Lopakhin has come! Yermolay Alexeyevitch!

PISHTCHIK What do I see and hear? [*Kisses Lopakhin.*] There's a whiff of cognac about you, my dear soul, and we're making merry here too!

[*Enter Lyubov Andreyevna.*]

LYUBOV Is it you, Yermolay Alexeyevitch? Why have you been so long? Where's Leonid?

LOPAKHIN Leonid Andreyevitch arrived with me. He is coming.

LYUBOV [*in agitation*] Well! Well! Was there a sale? Speak!

LOPAKHIN [*embarrassed, afraid of betraying his joy*] The sale was over at four o'clock. We missed our train—had to wait till half-past nine. [*Sighing heavily*] Ugh! I feel a little giddy.

[*Enter Gayev. In his right hand he has purchases, with his left hand he is wiping away his tears.*]

LYUBOV Well, Leonid? What news? [*Impatiently, with tears*] Make haste, for God's sake!

GAYEV [*makes her no answer, simply waves his hand; to Firs, weeping*] Here, take them; there's anchovies, Kertch herrings. I have eaten nothing all day. What I have been through! [*Door into the billiard room is open. There is heard a knocking of balls and the voice of Yasha saying, "Eighty-seven." Gayev's expression changes, he leaves off weeping.*] I am fearfully tired. Firs, come and help me change my things. [*Goes to his own room across the larger drawing-room.*]

PISHTCHIK How about the sale? Tell us, do!

LYUBOV Is the cherry orchard sold?

LOPAKHIN It is sold.

LYUBOV Who has bought it?

LOPAKHIN I have bought it. [*A pause. Lyubov is crushed; she would fall down if she were not standing near a chair and table. Varya takes keys from her waist-band, flings them on the floor in middle of drawing-room and goes out.*] I have bought it! Wait a bit, ladies and gentle-men, pray. My head's a bit muddled, I can't speak. [*Laughs.*] We came to the auction. Deriganov was there already. Leonid Andreyevitch only had 15,000 and Deriganov bid 30,000, besides the arrears, straight off. I saw how the land lay. I bid against him. I bid 40,000, he bid 45,000, I said 55, and so he went on, adding 5 thousands and I adding 10. Well . . . so it ended. I bid 90, and it was knocked down to me. Now the cherry orchard's mine! Mine! [*Chuckles.*] My God, the cherry orchard's mine! Tell me that I'm drunk, that I'm out of my mind, that it's all a dream. [*Stamps with his feet.*] Don't laugh at me! If my father and my grandfather could rise from their graves and see all that has happened! How their Yermolay, ignorant, beaten Yermolay, who used to run about barefoot in winter, how that very Yermolay has bought the finest estate in the world! I have bought the estate where my father and grandfather were slaves, where they weren't even admitted into the kitchen. I am asleep, I am dreaming! It is all fancy, it is the work of your imagination plunged in the darkness of ignorance. [*Picks up keys, smiling fondly.*] She threw away the keys; she means to show she's not the housewife now. [*Jingles the keys.*] Well, no matter. [*The orchestra is heard tuning up.*] Hey, musicians! Play! I want to hear you. Come, all of you, and look how Yermolay Lopakhin will take the axe to the cherry orchard, how the trees will fall to the ground! We will build houses on it and our grandsons and great-grandsons will see a new life springing up there. Music! Play up!

[*Music begins to play. Lyubov Andreyevna has sunk into a chair and is weeping bitterly.*]

LOPAKHIN [*reproachfully*] Why, why didn't you listen to me? My poor friend! Dear lady, there's no turning back now. [*With tears*] Oh, if all this could be over, oh, if our miserable disjointed life could somehow soon be changed!

PISHTCHIK [*takes him by the arm, in an undertone*] She's weeping, let us go and leave her alone. Come. [*Takes him by the arm and leads him into the larger drawing-room.*]

LOPAKHIN What's that? Musicians, play up! All must be as I wish it. [*With irony*] Here comes the new master, the owner of the cherry orchard! [*Accidentally tips over a little table, almost upsetting the candelabra.*] I can pay for everything!

[*Goes out with Pishtchik. No one remains on the stage or in the larger drawing-room except Lyubov, who sits huddled up, weeping bitterly. The music plays softly. Anya and Trofimov come in quickly. Anya goes up to her mother and falls on her knees before her. Trofimov stands at the entrance to the larger drawing-room.*]

ANYA Mamma! Mamma, you're crying, dear, kind, good mamma! My precious! I love you! I bless you! The cherry orchard is sold, it is gone, that's true, that's true! But don't weep, mamma! Life is still before you, you have still your good, pure heart! Let us go, let us go, darling, away from here! We will make a new garden, more splendid than this one; you will see it, you will understand. And joy, quiet, deep joy, will sink into your soul like the sun at evening! And you will smile, mamma! Come, darling, let us go!

Act Four

Same as in first act. There are neither curtains on the windows nor pictures on the walls: only a little furniture remains piled up in a corner as if for sale. There is a sense of desolation; near the outer door and in the background of the scene are packed trunks, travelling bags, etc. On the left the door is open, and from here the voices of Varya and Anya are audible. Lopakhin is standing waiting. Yasha is holding a tray with glasses full of champagne. In front of the stage Yepikhodov is tying up a box. In the background behind the scene a hum of talk from the peasants who have come to say good-bye. The voice of Gayev: "Thanks, brothers, thanks!"

YASHA The peasants have come to say good-bye. In my opinion, Yermolay Alexeyevich, the peasants are good-natured, but they don't know much about things.

[*The hum of talk dies away. Enter across front of stage Lyubov Andreyevna and Gayev. She is not weeping, but is pale; her face is quivering—she cannot speak.*]

GAYEV You gave them your purse, Lyuba. That won't do—that won't do!

LYUBOV I couldn't help it! I couldn't help it! [*Both go out.*]

LOPAKHIN [*in the doorway, calls after them*] You will take a glass at parting? Please do. I didn't think to bring any from the town, and at the station I could only get one bottle. Please take a glass. [*A pause*] What? You don't care for any? [*Comes away from the door.*] If I'd known, I wouldn't have bought it. Well, and I'm not going to drink it. [*Yasha carefully sets the tray down on a chair.*] You have a glass, Yasha, anyway.

YASHA Good luck to the travellers, and luck to those that stay behind! [*Drinks.*] This champagne isn't the real thing, I can assure you.

LOPAKHIN It cost 8 roubles the bottle. [*A pause*] It's devilish cold here.

YASHA They haven't heated the stove to-day—it's all the same since we're going. [*Laughs.*]

LOPAKHIN What are you laughing for?

YASHA For pleasure.

LOPAKHIN Though it's October, it's as still and sunny as though it were summer. It's just right for building! [*Looks at his watch; says in doorway*] Take note, ladies and gentlemen, the train goes in forty-seven minutes; so you ought to start for the station in twenty minutes. You must hurry up!

[*Trofimov comes in from out of doors wearing a great-coat.*]

TROFIMOV I think it must be time to start; the horses are ready. The devil only knows what's become of my galoshes; they're lost. [*In the doorway*] Anya! My galoshes aren't here. I can't find them.

LOPAKHIN And I'm getting off to Kharkov. I am going in the same train with you. I'm spending all the winter at Kharkov. I've been wasting all my time gossiping with you and fretting with no work to do. I can't get on without work. I don't know what to do with my hands, they flap about so queerly, as if they didn't belong to me.

TROFIMOV Well, we're just going away, and you will take up your profitable labours again.

LOPAKHIN Do take a glass.

TROFIMOV No, thanks.

LOPAKHIN Then you're going to Moscow now?

TROFIMOV Yes. I shall see them as far as the town, and to-morrow I shall go on to Moscow.

LOPAKHIN Yes, I daresay, the professors aren't giving any lectures, they're waiting for your arrival.

TROFIMOV That's not your business.

LOPAKHIN How many years have you been at the University?

TROFIMOV Do think of something newer than that—that's stale and flat. [*Hunts for galoshes.*] You know we shall most likely never see each other again, so let me give you one piece of advice at parting: don't wave your arms about —get out of the habit. And another thing, building villas, reckoning up that the summer visitors will in time become independent farmers—reckoning like that, that's not the thing to do either. After all, I am fond of you: you have fine delicate fingers like an artist, you've a fine delicate soul.

LOPAKHIN [*embraces him*] Good-bye, my dear fellow. Thanks for everything. Let me give you money for the journey, if you need it.

TROFIMOV What for? I don't need it.

LOPAKHIN Why, you haven't got a halfpenny.

TROFIMOV Yes, I have, thank you. I got some money for a translation. Here it is in my pocket, [*anxiously*] but where can my galoshes be!

VARYA [*from the next room*] Take the nasty things! [*Flings a pair of galoshes onto the stage.*]

TROFIMOV Why are you so cross, Varya? h'm! . . . but those aren't my galoshes.

LOPAKHIN I sowed three thousand acres with poppies in the spring, and now I have cleared forty thousand profit. And when my poppies were in flower, wasn't it a picture! So here, as I say, I made forty thousand, and I'm offering you a loan because I can afford to. Why turn up your nose? I am a peasant—I speak bluntly.

TROFIMOV Your father was a peasant, mine was a chemist—and that proves absolutely nothing whatever. [*Lopakhin takes out his pocket-book.*] Stop that—stop that. If you were to offer me two hundred thousand I wouldn't take it. I am an independent man, and everything that all of you, rich and poor alike, prize so highly and hold so dear hasn't the slightest power over me—it's like so much fluff fluttering in the air. I can get on without you. I can pass by you. I am strong and proud. Humanity is advancing towards the highest truth, the highest happiness, which is possible on earth, and I am in the front ranks.

LOPAKHIN Will you get there?

TROFIMOV I shall get there. [*A pause*] I shall get there, or I shall show others the way to get there.

[*In the distance is heard the stroke of an axe on a tree.*]

LOPAKHIN Good-bye, my dear fellow; it's time to be off. We turn up our noses at one another, but life is passing all the while. When I am working hard without resting, then my mind is more at ease, and it seems to me as though I too know what I exist for; but how many people there are in Russia, my dear boy, who exist, one doesn't know what for. Well, it doesn't matter. That's not what keeps things spinning. They tell me Leonid Andreyevitch has taken a situation. He is going to be a clerk at the bank —6,000 roubles a year. Only, of course, he won't stick to it—he's too lazy.

ANYA [*in the doorway*] Mamma begs you not to let them chop down the orchard until she's gone.

TROFIMOV Yes, really, you might have the tact . . . [*walks out across the front of the stage*].

LOPAKHIN I'll see to it! I'll see to it! Stupid fellows! [*Goes out after him.*]

ANYA Has Firs been taken to the hospital?

YASHA I told them this morning. No doubt they have taken him.

ANYA [*to Yepikhodov, who passes across the drawing-room*] Semyon Pantaleyevitch, inquire, please, if Firs has been taken to the hospital.

YASHA [*in a tone of offence*] I told Yegor this morning—why ask a dozen times?

YEPIKHODOV Firs is advanced in years. It's my conclusive opinion no treatment would do him good; it's time he was gathered to his fathers. And I can only envy him. [*Puts a trunk down on a cardboard hat-box and crushes it.*] There, now, of course—I knew it would be so.

YASHA [*jeeringly*] Two and twenty misfortunes!

VARYA [*through the door*] Has Firs been taken to the hospital?

ANYA Yes.

VARYA Why wasn't the note for the doctor taken too?

ANYA Oh, then, we must send it after them. [*Goes out.*]

VARYA [*from the adjoining room*] Where's Yasha? Tell him his mother's come to say good-bye to him.

YASHA [*waves his hand*] They put me out of all patience! [*Dunyasha has all this time been busy about the luggage. Now, when Yasha is left alone, she goes up to him.*]

DUNYASHA You might just give me one look, Yasha. You're going away. You're leaving me. [*Weeps and throws herself on his neck.*]

YASHA What are you crying for? [*Drinks the champagne.*] In six days I shall be in Paris again. To-morrow we shall get into the express train and roll away in a flash. I can scarcely believe it! *Vive la France!* It doesn't suit me here—it's not the life for me; there's no doing anything. I have seen enough of the ignorance here. I have had enough of it. [*Drinks champagne.*] What are you crying for? Behave yourself properly, and then you won't cry.

DUNYASHA [*powders her face, looking in a pocket-mirror*] Do send me a letter from Paris. You know how I loved you, Yasha—how I loved you! I am a tender creature, Yasha.

YASHA Here they are coming!
[*Busies himself about the trunks, humming softly. Enter Lyubov Andreyevna, Gayev, Anya, and Charlotta Ivanovna.*]

GAYEV We ought to be off. There's not much time now. [*Looking at Yasha*] What a smell of herrings!

LYUBOV In ten minutes we must get into the carriage. [*Casts a look about the room.*] Fare-well, dear house, dear old home of our fathers! Winter will pass and spring will come, and then you will be no more; they will tear you down! How much those walls have seen! [*Kisses her daughter passionately.*] My treasure, how bright you look! Your eyes are sparkling like diamonds! Are you glad? Very glad?

ANYA Very glad! A new life is beginning, mamma.

GAYEV Yes, really, everything is all right now. Before the cherry orchard was sold, we were all worried and wretched, but afterwards, when once the question was settled conclusively, irrevocably, we all felt calm and even cheerful. I am a bank clerk now—I am a financier—cannon off the red. And you, Lyuba, after all, you are looking better; there's no question of that.

LYUBOV Yes. My nerves are better, that's true. [*Her hat and coat are handed to her.*] I'm sleeping well. Carry out my things, Yasha. It's time. [*To Anya*] My darling, we shall soon see each other again. I am going to Paris. I can live there on the money your Yaroslavl auntie sent us to buy the estate with—hurrah for auntie!—but that money won't last long.

ANYA You'll come back soon, mamma, won't you? I'll be working up for my examination in the high school, and when I have passed that, I shall set to work and be a help to you. We will read all sorts of things together, mamma, won't we? [*Kisses her mother's hands.*] We will read in the autumn evenings. [*Dreamily*] We'll read lots of books, and a new wonderful world will open out before us. Mamma, come soon.

LYUBOV I shall come, my precious treasure. [*Embraces her. Enter Lopakhin. Charlotta softly hums a song.*]

GAYEV Charlotta's happy; she's singing!

CHARLOTTA [*picks up a bundle like a swaddled baby*] Bye, bye, my baby. [*A baby is heard crying: "Ooah! ooah!"*] Hush, hush, my pretty boy! ["*Ooah! ooah!*"] Poor little thing! [*Throws the bundle back.*] You must please find me a situation. I can't go on like this.

LOPAKHIN We'll find you one, Charlotta Ivanovna. Don't you worry yourself.

GAYEV Everyone's leaving us. Varya's going away. We have become of no use all at once.

CHARLOTTA There's nowhere for me to be in the town. I must go away. [*Hums*]

What care I . . .

[*Enter Pishtchik.*]

LOPAKHIN The freak of nature!

PISHTCHIK [*gasping*] Oh! . . . Lct me get my breath. . . . I'm worn out . . . my most honoured . . . give me some water.

GAYEV Want some money, I suppose? Your humble servant! I'll go out of the way of temptation. [*Goes out.*]

PISHTCHIK It's a long while since I have been to see you . . . dearest lady. [*To Lopakhin*] You are here . . . glad to see you . . . a man of immense intellect . . . take . . . here [*giving money to Lopakhin*] 400 roubles. That leaves me owing 840.

LOPAKHIN [*shrugging his shoulders in amazement*] It's like a dream. Where did you get it?

PISHTCHIK Wait a bit . . . I'm hot . . . a most extraordinary occurrence! Some Englishmen came along and found in my land some sort of white clay. [*To Lyubov Andreyevna*] And 400 for you . . . most lovely . . . wonderful [*giving money*]. . . . The rest later. [*Sips water.*] A young man in the train was telling me just now that a great philosopher advises jumping off a house-top. "Jump!" says he; "the whole gist of the problem lies in that." [*Wonderingly*] Fancy that, now! Water, please!

LOPAKHIN What Englishmen?

PISHTCHIK I have made over to them the rights to dig the clay for twenty-four years . . . and now, excuse me . . . I can't stay . . . I must be trotting on. I'm going to Znoikovo . . . to Kardamanovo. . . . I'm in debt all round. [*Sips.*] . . . To your very good health! . . . I'll come in on Thursday.

LYUBOV We are just off to the town, and tomorrow I start for abroad.

PISHTCHIK What! [*In agitation*] Why to the town? Oh, I see the furniture . . . the boxes. No matter . . . [*through his tears*] no matter . . . men of enormous intellect . . . these Englishmen . . . never mind . . . be happy. God will succour you . . . no matter . . . everything in this world must have an end. [*Kisses Lyubov Andreyevna's hand.*] If the rumour reaches you that my end has come, think of this . . . old horse, and say: "There once was such a man in the world . . . Semyonov-Pishtchik . . . the Kingdom of Heaven be his!" . . . Most extraordinary weather. . . . Yes. [*Goes out in violent agitation, but at once returns and says in the doorway*] Dashenka wishes to be remembered to you. [*Goes out.*]

LYUBOV Now we can start. I leave with two cares in my heart. The first is leaving Firs ill. [*Looking at her watch*] We have still five minutes.

ANYA Mamma, Firs has been taken to the hospital. Yasha sent him off this morning.

LYUBOV My other anxiety is Varya. She is used to getting up early and working; and now, without work, she's like a fish out of water. She is thin and pale, and she's crying, poor dear! [*A pause*] You are well aware, Yermolay Alexeyevitch, I dreamed of marrying her to you, and everything seemed to show that you would get married. [*Whispers to Anya and motions to Charlotta and both go out.*] She loves you—she suits you. And I don't know— I don't know why it is you seem, as it were, to avoid each other. I can't understand it!

LOPAKHIN I don't understand it myself, I confess. It's queer somehow, altogether. If there's still time, I'm ready now at once. Let's settle it straight off, and go ahead; but without you, I feel I shan't make her an offer.

LYUBOV That's excellent. Why, a single moment's all that's necessary. I'll call her at once.

LOPAKHIN And there's champagne all ready too. [*Looking into the glasses*] Empty! Someone's emptied them already. [*Yasha coughs.*] I call that greedy.

LYUBOV [*eagerly*] Capital! We will go out. Yasha, *allez!* I'll call her in. [*At the door*] Varya, leave all that; come here. Come along! [*Goes out with Yasha.*]

LOPAKHIN [*looking at his watch*] Yes. [*A pause. Behind the door, smothered laughter and whispering, and, at last, enter Varya.*]

VARYA [*looking a long while over the things*] It is strange, I can't find it anywhere.

LOPAKHIN What are you looking for?

VARYA I packed it myself, and I can't remember. [*A pause*]

The Cherry Orchard

591

LOPAKHIN Where are you going now, Varvara Mihailovna?

VARYA I? To the Ragulins. I have arranged to go to them to look after the house—as a housekeeper.

LOPAKHIN That's in Yashnovo? It'll be seventy miles away. [*A pause*] So this is the end of life in this house!

VARYA [*looking among the things*] Where is it? Perhaps I put it in the trunk. Yes, life in this house is over—there will be no more of it.

LOPAKHIN And I'm just off to Kharkov—by this next train. I've a lot of business there. I'm leaving Yepikhodov here, and I've taken him on.

VARYA Really!

LOPAKHIN This time last year we had snow already, if you remember; but now it's so fine and sunny. Though it's cold, to be sure—three degrees of frost.

VARYA I haven't looked. [*A pause*] And besides, our thermometer's broken.

[*A pause. Voice at the door from the yard:* "Yermolay Alexeyevitch!"]

LOPAKHIN [*as though he had long been expecting this summons*] This minute!

[*Lopakhin goes out quickly. Varya sitting on the floor and laying her head on a bag full of clothes, sobs quietly. The door opens. Lyubov Andreyevna comes in cautiously.*]

LYUBOV Well? [*A pause*] We must be going.

VARYA [*has wiped her eyes and is no longer crying*] Yes, mamma, it's time to start. I shall have time to get to the Ragulins to-day, if only you're not late for the train.

LYUBOV [*in the doorway*] Anya, put your things on.

[*Enter Anya, then Gayev and Charlotta Ivanovna. Gayev has on a warm coat with a hood. Servants and cabmen come in. Yepikhodov bustles about the luggage.*]

LYUBOV Now we can start on our travels.

ANYA [*joyfully*] On our travels!

GAYEV My friends—my dear, my precious friends! Leaving this house for ever, can I be silent? Can I refrain from giving utterance at leave-taking to those emotions which now flood all my being?

ANYA [*supplicatingly*] Uncle!

VARYA Uncle, you mustn't!

GAYEV [*dejectedly*] Cannon and into the pocket . . . I'll be quiet. . . . .

[*Enter Trofimov and afterwards Lopakhin.*]

TROFIMOV Well, ladies and gentlemen, we must start.

LOPAKHIN Yepikhodov, my coat!

LYUBOV I'll stay just one minute. It seems as though I have never seen before what the walls, what the ceilings in this house were like, and now I look at them with greediness, with such tender love.

GAYEV I remember when I was six years old sitting in that window on Trinity Day watching my father going to church.

LYUBOV Have all the things been taken?

LOPAKHIN I think all. [*Putting on overcoat, to Yepikhodov*] You, Yepikhodov, mind you see everything is right.

YEPIKHODOV [*in a husky voice*] Don't you trouble, Yermolay Alexeyevitch.

LOPAKHIN Why, what's wrong with your voice?

YEPIKHODOV I've just had a drink of water, and I choked over something.

YASHA [*contemptuously*] The ignorance!

LYUBOV We are going—and not a soul will be left here.

LOPAKHIN Not till the spring.

VARYA [*pulls a parasol out of a bundle, as though about to hit someone with it; Lopakhin makes a gesture as though alarmed*] What is it? I didn't mean anything.

TROFIMOV Ladies and gentlemen, let us get into the carriage. It's time. The train will be in directly.

VARYA Petya, here they are, your galoshes, by that box. [*With tears*] And what dirty old things they are!

TROFIMOV [*putting on his galoshes*] Let us go, friends!

GAYEV [*greatly agitated, afraid of weeping*] The train—the station! Double baulk, ah!

LYUBOV Let us go!

LOPAKHIN Are we all here? [*Locks the side-door on left.*] The things are all here. We must lock up. Let us go!

ANYA Good-bye, home! Good-bye to the old life!

TROFIMOV Welcome to the new life!

[*Trofimov goes out with Anya. Varya looks*

round the room and goes out slowly. Yasha and Charlotta Ivanovna, with her dog, go out.]

LOPAKHIN Till the spring, then! Come, friends, till we meet!

[Goes out. Lyubov Andreyevna and Gayev remain alone. As though they had been waiting for this, they throw themselves on each other's necks, and break into subdued smothered sobbing, afraid of being overheard.]

GAYEV [in despair] Sister, my sister!

LYUBOV Oh, my orchard!—My sweet, beautiful orchard! My life, my youth, my happiness, good-bye! Good-bye!

VOICE OF ANYA [calling gaily] Mamma!

VOICE OF TROFIMOV [gaily, excitedly] Aa—oo!

LYUBOV One last look at the walls, at the windows. My dear mother loved to walk about this room.

GAYEV Sister, sister!

VOICE OF ANYA Mamma!

VOICE OF TROFIMOV Aa—oo!

LYUBOV We are coming.

[They go out. The stage is empty. There is the sound of the doors being locked up, then of the carriages driving away. There is silence. In the stillness there is the dull stroke of an axe in a tree, clanging with a mournful lonely sound. Footsteps are heard. Firs appears in the doorway on the right. He is dressed as always —in a pea-jacket and white waistcoat with slippers on his feet. He is ill.]

FIRS [goes up to the doors, and tries the handles] Locked! They have gone. . . . [Sits down on sofa.] They have forgotten me. . . . Never mind . . . I'll sit here a bit. . . . I'll be bound Leonid Andreyevitch hasn't put his fur coat on and has gone off in his thin overcoat. [Sighs anxiously.] I didn't see after him. . . . These young people . . . [mutters something that can't be distinguished]. Life has slipped by as though I hadn't lived. [Lies down.] I'll lie down a bit. . . . There's no strength in you, nothing left you—all gone! Ech! I'm good for nothing. [Lies motionless.]

A sound is heard that seems to come from the sky, like a breaking harp-string, dying away mournfully. All is still again, and there is heard nothing but the strokes of the axe far away in the orchard.

REVIEWERS AND AUDIENCES, like the producers of Chekhov's plays, have long assumed that his dramas are comedies that turn tragic at the last moment. The foolishness of that assumption is demonstrated by the generalization that Lynton Hudson makes about Chekhov's "state of mind" and the very important particularization that David Magarshack makes about The Cherry Orchard.

What is the secret of Chekhov's spell? It is surely not that he provides us with the maudlin pleasure of self-commiseration in recognizing the reflection of our own futility in his naive, pathetic children of a vanished epoch! The secret lies, I think, in the method of his play writing. He achieved, as he deliberately attempted, something new. When he began writing plays he announced his conviction that "the drama must either degenerate completely, or assume a completely new form." He rejected the realism that brought life into the debating hall or the dissecting room. He rejected drama, the drama of the *beginning-middle-end* tradition. "Life does not happen like that," we find him saying to Stanislavsky in his dressing-room after he has left the auditorium in the middle of an Ibsen play. His are the most undramatic of all plays, yet they are full of the stuff of drama. He discarded the event-plot of chosen, accentuated situations, because things did not happen that way in real life. His object was, in his own words, "to see life, not only through its rising peaks and sinking abysses, but also through the surrounding everyday life." He accomplished it, as William Gerhardi puts it, "not by dispensing with plot, but by using a totally different kind of plot, the tissues of which, as in life, lie below the surface of events and unobtrusively shape our destiny." [Lynton Hudson, *Life and the Theatre,* Roy Publishers, New York, 1954, p. 19.]

It is inevitable that Chekhov's plays should seem a little sad. The *Chekhovskoe nastroyenie,* the Chekhov state of mind, is suffused with a gentle melancholy. One is inclined to wonder that he thought of them as comedies. Even the richest comic moments . . . somehow fail of their full comic effect because of Chekhov's sympathetic pity for absurdity and foolishness. And, because he could prescribe no remedy for the Slav malady of inertia to which the society he depicted was inured, he was accused of pessimism. He was always exceedingly annoyed when people regarded him as a pessimist. Certain it is that his plays will never be properly presented if the idea of their essential gloom prevails. I think it is worth going to a little trouble to refute this accusation of pessimism. Chekhov himself was a merry fellow. His characters never whine. "It seemed to me," he wrote, "that all Russian novelists and playwrights had felt the need of drawing gloomy characters." He wrote *Ivanov,* one of his earlier plays, "to sum up all that had been written up to now about grumbling and sulky people and to put an end to those writings." "Rejoice," he says somewhere, "that you are not a tramhorse, not a Koch bacillus, not a pig, not an ass, not a bear led by a gypsy, not a bug . . . that you do not have to drive a sewage cart nor to be married to three women simultaneously. Isn't life wonderful? If your wife has been unfaithful, rejoice that she has betrayed merely yourself and not your country." Chekhov had a great belief in healthy self-respect and lofty human pride. We find him reproving his younger brother for a false humility thus: "There is one thing I do not like. Why do you call yourself 'your insignificant, inconspicuous kid brother'? You admit your insignificance? Not to everybody, brother. Do you know where to admit your insignificance? Before God, perhaps, before wisdom, beauty, Nature, but not before people. When among people, you must recognize your own worth." [*Ibid.,* pp. 27–28.]

To Anton Chekhov life was meaningless; it is just Life. His plays are like torn strips of underfocused cine-camera photographs. There are no clear-cut outlines, no apparent direction. There are no highlights on any of these people. We are not invited to pass moral judgment on them; we are not even asked to sympathize for their author's attitude is deliberately objective.

At the time they were created the Western mind, then so positive, was merely irritated or exasperated by their futility, because they were not *living* in the Western material sense; it did not then perceive that they were really living in their dreams. Chekhov was the first modern dramatist—and this is the essence of his modernity—to question the reality of life, of external life as contrasted with the greater reality of the inner dream-life of illusions. Of course, Romantics ever since Homer have known the part illusion plays in human life. Dreams have given man something to live up to, a dynamic urge to rise above himself. But the dreams that Chekhov's people dream, the illusions of our times, are not dynamos, but drugs. And Chekhov seems to be the first to ask the modern question: which is waking and which sleeping—the opium trance of our illusions or the active bustle of everyday affairs? For this is a question that perpetually recurs in modern thought. It haunts the modern writer. It was first raised implicitly by Anton Chekhov, then stated boldly in the plays of Luigi Pirandello. It was constantly at the back of the mind of Marcel Proust, prompting him to drag his shrimping-net industriously over the bottom of the clouded pools of the subconscious. It still underlies such recent works as Alfred Camus's Existentialist novel *L'Étranger,* which depicts a hero who never in the philosophical sense begins to be alive, and Eugene O'Neill's latest play, *The Iceman Cometh,* with its ghastly waxworks show of down-and-outs, "keeping up the appearances of life with a few harmless pipe dreams about their yesterdays and to-morrows." [*Ibid.,* pp. 32–33.]

The Cherry Orchard has been so consistently misunderstood and misrepresented by producer and critic alike that it is only by a complete dissociation from the current misconceptions about the play that it is possible to appreciate Chekhov's repeated assertions that he had written not a tragedy but "a comedy, and in places even a farce."[1] Structurally, this last play of Chekhov's is the most perfect example of an indirect-action play, for in it all the elements are given equal scope for the development of the action. . . . Long before Chekhov sat down to write his last play, he had made it clear that it was going to be a comedy. He told his wife, Olga Knipper, on March 7th, 1901, that is to say, barely six months after the completion of *The Three Sisters,* that his next play would be "an amusing one, at least in conception." In April of the same year he again wrote to her that he was overcome by a strong desire "to write a four-act vaudeville or comedy for the Moscow Art Theatre." [David Magarshack, *Chekhov, the Dramatist,* Hill and Wang, Inc., New York, 1962, p. 264.]

The misinterpretation of *The Cherry Orchard* as a tragedy (Stanislavsky, in the first flush of excitement after reading Chekhov's last play, rushed off a letter to Chekhov in which he vowed that it was a tragedy and not, as Chekhov insisted, a comedy) is mainly due to a misunderstanding of the nature of a comic character. A "comic" character is generally supposed to keep an audience in fits of laughter, but that is not always so. No one would deny that Falstaff is essentially a comic character, but his fall from favour is one of the most moving incidents in *Henry IV*. Don Quixote, too, is essentially a comic character, but what has made him immortal is his creator's ability to arouse the compassion and the sympathy of the reader for him.

[1] "I'm afraid my play has turned out to be not a drama but a comedy, and in places even a farce, and I fear Nemirovich-Danchenko will never forgive me for that." (Letter to Maria Lilina, Stanislavsky's wife and one of the leading actresses of the Moscow Art Theatre, Sept. 15, 1903.)

The same is true of the chief characters of *The Cherry Orchard:* the sympathy and compassion they arouse in the spectator should not be allowed to blind him to the fact that they are essentially comic characters. It should be the producer's aim to bring out their comic traits and not, as is all too often done, to sentimentalise them. All the characters in the play, in fact, with perhaps the single exception of the seventeen-year-old Anya, possess this unmistakably ludicrous streak in their natures which makes them into comic characters.

The main theme of the play is generally taken to be the passing of the old order, symbolised by the sale of the cherry orchard. But that theme was stale by the time Chekhov wrote his play. Alexander Ostrovsky had practically exhausted it, and so had many other Russian novelists and playwrights before Chekhov, who himself had already used it in *Platonov*. What is new about this theme is the comic twist Chekhov gave it. Stanislavsky, who was himself a member of the old order, could not help regarding the passing of the Gayev estate into the hands of a successful business man who had once been a peasant on it as a tragedy. But Chekhov belonged to "the lower orders" himself and he could therefore take a completely detached view of it. Not being personally involved, he saw the comedy of it all and gave it an artistic form of a play full of comic characters. Nothing indeed was further from Chekhov's thoughts than that his characters should spread a feeling of gloom among his audience. In reply to a telegram from Nemirovich-Danchenko who complained that there were too many "weeping characters" in the play, Chekhov wrote: "Where are they? There is only one such character—Varya, but that is because she is a crybaby by nature and her tears ought not to arouse any feelings of gloom in the audience. I often put down 'through tears' in my stage directions, but that shows only the mood of the characters and not tears."

The symbolism of the cherry orchard, then, has nothing to do with its sale. All it expresses is one of the recurrent themes in Chekhov's plays: the destruction of beauty by those who are utterly blind to it. "All Russia is our garden," Trofimov says to Anya at the end of Act II, and he adds: "The earth is great and beautiful and there are many wonderful places in it." And his words are meant not only as a consolation to Anya, but as a warning against the Lopakhins of this world, a warning that can be understood everywhere, since the menace of the speculative builder has been felt not only in Russia. The cherry orchard indeed is a purely aesthetic symbol which its owners with the traditions of an old culture behind them fully understand; to Firs it merely means the cartloads of dried cherries sent off to town in the good old days, and to Lopakhin it is only an excellent site for "development." [*Ibid.*, pp. 273–275.]

In their attempts to wring the last drop of pathos out of the final scene of *The Cherry Orchard,* many producers tend to sentimentalise even Firs by leading their audiences to believe that he has been left to die by his lackadaisical masters. But there is nothing in the play to indicate that Chekhov's stage direction: "lies motionless" means "dies." If Chekhov had meant Firs to die, he would have said so. But in fact nothing could have been further from Chekhov's thoughts than to end his play with the death of an abandoned old servant. That would have introduced a completely alien note in a play which Chekhov never meant to be anything but a comedy.

The dying, melancholy sound of a broken string of musical instrument (the Russian word does not specify the particular nature of the instrument, it might have been a balalaika), which first occurs in Act II and with which the play ends, is all Chekhov needed to convey his own attitude to the "dreary" lives of his characters. It was a sound Chekhov remembered from his own boyhood days when he used to spend his summer months at a little hamlet in the Don basin. It was there that he first heard the mysterious sound, which seemed to be coming from the sky, but which was caused by the fall of a bucket in some distant coal-mine. With the years this sound acquired a nostalgic ring, and it is this sad, nostalgic feeling Chekhov wanted to convey by it. It is a sort of requiem for the "unhappy and disjointed" lives of his characters.

So many unnecessary tears have been shed in this play both on the stage and in the auditorium that it would seem almost hopeless to re-establish it as a comedy. It is much easier to misrepresent it as a tragedy than to present it for what it really is, namely "a comedy, and in places almost a farce." [*Ibid.*, pp. 285–286.]

To recognize the comic texture of The Cherry Orchard *is not to discount its sociological significance. W. H. Bruford has made the most searching sociological study of Chekhov in English.*

In his last and finest play, *The Cherry Orchard,* Chekhov returns to the theme of the landowning class and its problems, but he presents their failure now not so much as a matter of personal or national character as of changing conditions of life. The play symbolises, poetically, yet without ever losing touch with reality, the transition from a purely agrarian to a more and more industrial Russia. It brings home to us the perplexity of the older generation of the aristocracy as the ground slips from under their feet, their attachment to the home and the way of life of their youth, with the sentiments of carefree ease and beauty associated with them

in their minds, and their inability to master either their economic or their personal problems by resolutely facing facts. The central characters are the mondaine Lyubov Andreyevna, the owner, with her brother Gayev, of an estate with a fine old cherry orchard, and Lopakhin, the merchant son of the village shopkeeper. We have come across him already as a representative of the peasant who has risen out of his class, in the new age of money, through his energy and business ability. Though he stands for another world, he is not hostile to Lyubov. On the contrary, he remembers with gratitude her kindness to him as a boy. But the aristocrats, almost in spite of

ANTON CHEKHOV

themselves, tend to look down on him, and his proposal for saving their estate, by letting the ground where the cherry orchard stands for building sites, fills them with horror. It is simply unthinkable, yet they see no other way out of their predicament. They watch their doom approaching with paralysed will, still vaguely hoping that somehow they will escape, and bringing their ruin nearer all the time by the reckless extravagance to which they are accustomed.

Gayev, the brother, and his friend Simeonov-Pishtchik, are merely background figures, not drawn in the round, but they suggest two types of decadent squire, the one seeking refuge from reality in fine words and sentiments, or solacing himself with billiards and lollypops, and the other, cruder, living on his friends, until minerals are found on his land by English prospectors. The Chekhov who wrote to Suvorin in 1891: "Alas, I shall never be a Tolstoyan. In women I love beauty above all things; and in the history of mankind, culture, expressed in carpets, carriages with springs, and keenness of wit"—was drawn emotionally, one feels, to his aristocrats, as Goethe had been to his poet Tasso. But just as Goethe's wisdom had seen something right too in the prosaic Antonio, because even poets must have some regard for the society around them, so Chekhov would have the Russians realise that Lopakhin is a good fellow, and that what he represents is something to which Russia has to reconcile herself. For post-revolutionary critics he is even too kind to this bourgeois. He

tries to marry him off with Varya, Lyubov's adopted daughter, but there is always a hitch, perhaps because their classes are not quite ripe for fusion. And he holds out hope for the future in his picture of Lyubov's young daughter, Anya, and the former tutor, Trofimov. Trofimov, the "eternal student," the raisonneur of the piece, is given lines which express Chekhov's own thought as we know it from his letters, that men have little till now to be proud of; they should cease to be so pleased with themselves and simply work, as at present few do in Russia. Anya, under his influence, is ready to part from her dear cherry orchard. There will be still better places in the world that is yet to be. "All Russia is our garden," Trofimov tells her, and the garden they are leaving is spoilt for them by the odour of serfdom which still clings to it. But this young man himself, who has not succeeded at thirty in taking a degree, is not a very promising leader towards the better world. As a representative of revolutionary youth he is not really convincing, and that not merely because of the caution imposed on any author by the censorship, say post-revolutionary critics.[1] It may be, as they assume, because Chekhov was here drawing a type he did not know sufficiently well. Or it may be that he saw a good deal of the Ivanov even in Trofimov, and could not help treating him with a certain irony. [W. H. Bruford, *Chekhov and His Russia*, Oxford University Press, New York, 1947, pp. 83–85.]

When all other conclusions or speculations about Chekhov have been made, the impression that remains is of his characters. Those in The Cherry Orchard *are perhaps the most durable of all and they have been written about with a fitting attention and discernment by several critics.*

He shows his people in their detachment from affairs. Their daily occupations, activities, and professional duties, where they have any, are not overlooked, but they are important only as the broad foundation of monotonous or purposeless or hopeless disillusioned lives. The immediate contrast is Ibsen's world, its people immersed in

their businesses, their undertakings, their newspapers, their mayors and councils, their clergymen; the public arena, the social cross-currents providing a great stir of character and plot. Chekhov, in selecting his scene, virtually elimi-

[1] See S. Balukhaty, in *Klassiki russkoi dramy*, Leningrad and Moscow, 1940.

nates the buzz of practical affairs, and presenting his persons without the rigidities of the "well-made" play, he allows us to observe them within the inner chamber of their character. He descends upon them in their leisure moments and discovers them not as servants of a job or a duty or a purpose, propelled by practical reason or animal egoism, but as men and women who, however paralysed their wills may be, are conscious of their souls and seem to wait on some great transfiguration. Setting them free in this way from all conventional appearances of work and economic struggle, Chekhov shows an essence of spiritual character. Whatever their intellectual degree or moral rank, whether they are odd, or bored, or aspiring, or fluttered, or empty, or intensely suffering, these people are laid bare in their spiritual condition. It is upon this end that the artistic process of selection is bent. If a form is the emergence of an idea in terms of sensibility, Chekhov gets his form by isolating in the lives of his men and women the moments in which they are spiritually awake, when they hear a profound inner voice that detaches them from a lifeless material world and plunges them into a vital sensitiveness; when they suddenly become alive to questions, mysteries, meanings and the lack of them; when they become, in feeling, revolutionary. They hear echoes of worlds transcending their own, where love is requited, where there is less suffering, where men are happy; and they then have their characteristic impulse to do something to make the dream real, an impulse which in an odd sort of way is part of the dream itself. With such a purpose in his selection Chekhov is really testing his people for the nature of their souls. When they fail the test outright he satirizes them; those who are sensitive at all he portrays at the least with tenderness and at the most with tragic pathos. [Ronald Peacock, *The Poet in the Theatre*, Hill and Wang, Inc., New York, 1960, pp. 96–97.]

As has often been pointed out, Chekhov makes the largest concession to realism by discarding the concept of the hero or heroine. Each character is to a degree a centre within itself and has its own story, just as in life each man is his own hero, an axis round which other people are merely players. But on a Chekhovian stage we look at a whole group, and all the actors act all the time, so that one "hero" cancels out another. An event, or even a general mood, will affect all the characters, but each in his own way, making one happy, another sad maybe. Adding up their sum we conclude within ourselves precisely what that event feels like, or what it is to experience that mood. We are made uncommonly aware in a new way of what it feels like to be alive. By refusing to put the usual theatrical emphasis on any one character, Chekhov's great achievement is to put the important stress on *relationships between* characters rather than on the characters themselves. Accordingly, events as such fade into the background of the play, and we are left only with their effect on relationships. For us to apprehend the links between characters, a method of shifting impressions must be prosecuted vigorously. The last interview between Lopakhin and Varya in *The Cherry Orchard* will demonstrate this facet of Chekhov's art.

In this scene we are not asked to show more sympathy for, or interest in, either Lopakhin or Varya. We know that the sale of the cherry orchard will take Varya to Yashnevo, seventy miles from her home, and that it will leave Lopakhin behind with more work to do, but we are not primarily interested in the individual futures of either of them. We are interested rather in what they feel towards each other. [J. L. Styan, *The Elements of Drama,* Cambridge University Press, New York, 1960, pp. 72–74.]

In *The Seagull* and *The Cherry Orchard* considerable emotional agility is necessary: there is a quick intermittent movement of farce and pathos. Or at least that is the usual view. My own question is whether Chekhovian farce and pathos are emotionally distinguishable, whether both in fact do not proceed from the same limited expression. The local point for analysis, in all the plays, is the practice of self-dramatisation by characters. . . . The key play is, of course, *The Cherry Orchard*, where Chekhov's particular method is most richly employed.

Under the shadow of a Russia which is passing away (the movement is expressed in the figure of the cherry orchard—a characteristic lyrical symbol) a group of characters is revealed. They are all, in a sense, *nedotepa,* which is a keyword in the play.[1] The elements of method which we have already noted are fully employed. There is a good deal of what I would call "rednose" characterisation: Gayev, with his continual billiards phrases. . . .

Then there is Trofimov, self-dramatised as the "perpetual student." Yepikhodov, whose nickname slogan is "twenty-two misfortunes," talks in sentimental officialese. . . .

He is never separated from his guitar, on which he accompanies his love-songs. Gayev, it is true, is less limited than Yepikhodov; he is the occasion for some very acceptable comedy, and is a relief in the very sense that in him is satirised the tendency to speechmaking about which one remains uneasy throughout the play. For it is blindness to assume that—however it may be placed by the author—there is no didacticism in *The Cherry Orchard.* Trofimov's speech in the second act, on a theme which constantly recurs in Chekhov's plays and which seems, from his letters and conversations, to have been also a personal belief—

> At present only a few men work in Russia. The vast majority of the educated people that I know seek after nothing, do nothing, and are as yet incapable of work.

—this indictment is set by design against the declaration of Lopakhin, the son of a serf, a figure of the new Russia, the man who will take over the cherry orchard and chop it down to build villas:

> I work from morning till night. . . . When I work for hours without getting tired I get easy in my mind and I seem to know why I exist. But God alone knows what most of the people in Russia were born for. . . . Well, who cares?

As Chekhov constructs this microcosm for us —the stupid, sentimental, generous Madame Ranevsky, the juggling, isolated Charlotte, the ineffectual Pishtchik—we assent. Our first glance confirms the impotence and the subsequent decay. The expository method is masterly of its kind. But there grows, implacably, a profound uneasiness, an uncertainty about the emotional quality of what is at the very heart of the work. It is the process, though infinitely more complicated, of one's evaluation of Galsworthy: a mastering suspicion of the emotional integrity from which the satire proceeds, a growing conviction that the author remains attached, by strings which in performance extend to and operate on us, attached to something lovable, something childlike, something vague; attached, in the human sense, to a residue of unexamined experience which for one reason or another cannot be faced, and to which, accordingly, renouncing his control, the author must submit. But to take the play beyond naturalism, to make it something more than an entertaining, but limited, collection of human sketches, this unexamined experience would have to be faced and understood. [Raymond Williams, *Drama from Ibsen to Eliot,* Oxford University Press, New York, 1953, pp. 133–135.]

[1] *Nedotepa* offers particularly difficult translation difficulties. It is a word invented in this play by Chekhov, and now established in the language. It is derived from *ne*—not, and *dotyapat*—to finish chopping. Applied to people its general significance is clear. English versions have variously offered: "joblot"; "those who never get there"; "botchment." An English idiom "half-chopped" would be literal, and "half-baked" probably the best translation. But it seems certain that the word is bound up in this context with the *chopping* down of the cherry orchard, for an effect one can apprehend.

GEORG KAISER

1878–1945

*Georg Kaiser was fascinated with the ways of business. But his
fascination was much more than merely theatrical. He came from
a family of businessmen. He was himself, at least to begin with,
a businessman in Germany and in Argentina. His condemnation
of the destructive forces of industrial civilization was not, then, the
facile distrust of an outsider for a world he did not know. Kaiser
wrote about business and industry with understanding and, at
least in the case of several self-sacrificing and altogether idealistic
capitalists who were determined to improve the lot of their workers
by revolutionary changes in the conduct of their plants, with great
respect. He did tend to think in round and spacious terms, about
businessmen, about workers, about society generally. The
generalizations about economic class and social type on which
Expressionism was founded were natural to Kaiser. When he
turned to the drama as a profession, after the production of*
The Jewish Widow *in 1911, he identified himself as a member of
a class of artists who were privileged as a result of their creative
gifts to break the law. And thus he defended himself when he was
arrested in 1920 for selling the furniture of a rented home. The
court did not see things his way, however; he spent four months
in prison. It all added to his equipment as a playwright of masses
and classes, constantly subjecting the moral structures of society,
especially the synthetic ones, to the closest scrutiny. He was a
prolific playwright. He was an inventive one. He dealt in as many
ways as possible with the emergence of a new society and new*

classes of men, almost all of them victims, as he saw them, of an uncontrollable technology or an annihilating greed. Among Kaiser's many dramas of high technical quality, the most striking perhaps, because of their introduction of new techniques of staging, are the trilogy The Coral *(1918)*, Gas I *(1918)*, and Gas II *(1920)*, and From Morn to Midnight *(1916)*. Before he died in Switzerland, in exile from Nazi Germany, Kaiser also wrote some novels and collaborated with the composer Kurt Weill in several dramas and a song cycle.

From Morn to Midnight

TRANSLATED BY ASHLEY DUKES

CASHIER

STOUT GENTLEMAN

CLERK

MESSENGER BOY

LADY

BANK MANAGER

MUFFLED GENTLEMAN

SERVING MAID

PORTER

THE LADY'S SON

THE CASHIER'S MOTHER

HIS DAUGHTERS

HIS WIFE

FIRST GENTLEMAN

SECOND GENTLEMAN

THIRD GENTLEMAN

FOURTH GENTLEMAN

FIFTH GENTLEMAN

SALVATION LASS

WAITER

FIRST MASK

SECOND MASK

THIRD MASK

FOURTH MASK

FIRST GUEST

SECOND GUEST

THIRD GUEST

OFFICER OF SALVATION ARMY

FIRST SOLDIER OF SALVATION ARMY

FIRST PENITENT

SECOND SOLDIER OF SALVATION ARMY

SECOND PENITENT

THIRD SOLDIER OF SALVATION ARMY

THIRD PENITENT

FOURTH SOLDIER OF SALVATION ARMY

POLICEMAN

CROWD AT VELODROME AND SALVATION ARMY HALL

The action takes place in a small town and a city in Germany at the present time.

SCENE ONE

Interior of a provincial bank. On the right, pigeon-holes and a door inscribed "Manager" Another door in the middle: "Strong Room." Entrance from the lower left. In front of the Cashier's cage on the left-hand side is a cane sofa, and in front of it a small table with a waterbottle and glass.

The Cashier at the counter and the Clerk at a desk, both writing. On the cane sofa sits a Stout

Gentleman, wheezing. *In front of the counter stands a Messenger Boy, staring at the door, through which some one has just gone out.*

Cashier raps on the counter. Messenger Boy turns, hands in a check. Cashier examines it, writes, takes a handful of silver from a drawer, counts it, pushes a small pile across the counter. Messenger Boy sweeps the money into a linen bag.

STOUT GENTLEMAN [*rising*] Now the fat fellows take their turn.

[*He pulls out a bag. Enter Lady, expensive furs; rustle of silk. Stout Gentleman stops short.*]

LADY [*smiles involuntarily in his direction*] At last!

[*Stout Gentleman makes a wry face. Cashier taps the counter impatiently. Lady looks at Stout Gentleman.*]

STOUT GENTLEMAN [*giving place to her*] The fat fellows can wait.

[*Lady bows distantly, comes to counter. Cashier taps as before.*]

LADY [*opens her handbag, takes out a letter and hands it to Cashier*] A letter of credit. Three thousand, please. [*Cashier takes the envelope, turns it over, hands it back.*] I beg your pardon. [*She pulls out the folded letter and offers it again. Cashier turns it over, hands it back.*]

LADY [*unfolds the letter, hands it to him*] Three thousand, please.

[*Cashier glances at it, puts it in front of the Clerk. Clerk takes the letter, rises, goes out by the door inscribed* "Manager."]

STOUT GENTLEMAN [*retiring to sofa*] I can wait. The fat fellows can always wait.

[*Cashier begins counting silver.*]

LADY In notes, if you don't mind.

[*Cashier ignores her.*]

MANAGER [*youthful, plump, comes in with the letter in his hand*] Who is—

[*He stops short on seeing the Lady. Clerk resumes work at his desk.*]

STOUT GENTLEMAN Ahem! Good morning.

MANAGER [*glancing at him*] How goes it?

STOUT GENTLEMAN [*tapping his belly*] Oh, rounding out—rounding out!

MANAGER [*laughs shortly; turning to Lady*] I

understand you want to draw on us?

LADY Three thousand marks.

MANAGER I would pay you three [*glancing at letter*]—three thousand with pleasure, but—

LADY Is anything wrong with the letter?

MANAGER [*suave, important*] It's in the proper form. [*Reading the headlines*] "Not exceeding twelve thousand"—quite correct. [*Spelling out the address*] B-A-N-C-O—

LADY My bank in Florence assured me—

MANAGER Your bank in Florence is quite all right.

LADY Then I don't see why—

MANAGER I suppose you applied for this letter?

LADY Of course.

MANAGER Twelve thousand—payable at such cities—

LADY As I should touch on my trip.

MANAGER And you must have given your bank in Florence duplicate signatures.

LADY Certainly. To be sent to the banks mentioned in the list to identify me.

MANAGER [*consults letter*] Ah! [*Looks up.*] We have received no letter of advice.

[*Stout Gentleman coughs; winks at the Manager.*]

LADY That means I must wait until . . .

MANAGER Well, we must have something to go upon!

[*Muffled Gentleman, in fur cap and shawl, comes in and takes his place at the counter. He darts angry glances at the Lady.*]

LADY I was quite unprepared for this . . .

MANAGER [*with a clumsy laugh*] As you see, Madame, we are even less prepared; in fact—not at all.

LADY I need the money so badly . . .

[*Stout Gentleman laughs aloud.*]

MANAGER Who doesn't? [*Stout Gentleman neighs with delight. Looking round for an audience*] Myself, for instance—[*To the impatient Muffled Customer*] You have more time than I—don't you see I'm busy with this Lady? Now, Madame, what do you expect me to do—pay you money on your—ah—

[*Stout Gentleman titters.*]

LADY [*quickly*] I'm staying at the Elephant.

[*Stout Gentleman wheezes with laughter.*]

MANAGER   I am very glad to know your address. I always lunch there.

LADY   Can't the proprietor vouch for me?

MANAGER   Has he already had the pleasure? [Stout Gentleman rocks with delight.]

LADY   Well, I have my luggage with me . . .

MANAGER   Am I to examine it?

LADY   A most embarrassing position. I can't . . .

MANAGER   Then we're in the same boat. You can't—I can't—that's the situation. [He returns the letter.]

LADY   What do you advise me to do?

MANAGER   This is a snug little town of ours—it has surroundings— The Elephant is a well-known house . . . you'll make pleasant acquaintances of one sort or another . . . and time will pass—days—nights—well you know?

LADY   I don't in the least mind passing a few days here.

MANAGER   Your fellow-guests will be delighted to contribute something for your entertainment.

LADY   But I must have three thousand today!

MANAGER   [to Stout Gentleman] Will anybody here underwrite a lady from abroad for three thousand marks?

LADY   I couldn't think of accepting that. I shall be in my room at the hotel. When the letter of advice arrives, will you please notify me at once by telephone?

MANAGER   Personally, Madame, if you wish.

LADY   In whatever way is quickest. [She folds up the letter, replaces it in the envelope, and puts both into her handbag.] I shall call again in any case this afternoon.

MANAGER   At your service. [Lady bows coldly, goes out. Muffled Gentleman moves up to counter, on which he leans, crackling his cheque impatiently. Manager ignoring him, looks merrily at the Stout Gentleman. Stout Gentleman sniffs the air. Laughs.] All the fragrance of Italy, eh? Straight from the perfume bottle. [Stout Gentleman fans himself with his hand] Warm, eh?

STOUT GENTLEMAN   [pours out water] Three thousand is not bad. [Drinks.] I guess three hundred wouldn't sound bad to her either.

MANAGER   Perhaps you would like to make a lower offer at the Elephant?—in her room?

STOUT GENTLEMAN   No use for fat fellows.

MANAGER   Our bellies protect our morals. [Muffled Gentleman raps impatiently on the counter. Indifferently] Well?

[He takes the cheque, smooths it out, and hands it to the Cashier. Messenger Boy stares after the departing Lady, then at the last speakers, finally stumbles over the Stout Gentleman on the sofa.]

STOUT GENTLEMAN   [robbing him of his wallet] There, my boy, that's what comes of making eyes at pretty ladies. Now you've lost your money. [Messenger Boy looks shyly at him.] How are you going to explain to your boss? [Messenger Boy laughs.] Remember this for the rest of your life! [Returning the wallet] Your eyes run away and you bolt after them. You wouldn't be the first.

[Messenger Boy goes out. Cashier has counted out some small silver.]

MANAGER   And they trust money to a young fool like that.

STOUT GENTLEMAN   Stupid!

MANAGER   People should be more careful. That boy will abscond the first chance he gets—a born embezzler. [To Muffled Gentleman] Is anything wrong? [Muffled Gentleman examines every coin.] That's a 25-pfennig piece. Forty-five pfennigs altogether; that's all that's coming to you.

[Muffled Gentleman pockets his money with great ceremony; buttons his coat over the pocket.]

STOUT GENTLEMAN   [ironically] You ought to deposit your capital in the vault. [Rising] Now it's time for the fat fellows to unload.

[Muffled Gentleman turns away from counter and goes out.]

MANAGER   [to Stout Gentleman, breezily] What are you bringing us this morning?

STOUT GENTLEMAN   [sets his attaché case on the counter and takes out a pocket-book] With all the confidence that your elegant clientele inspires. [He offers his hand.]

MANAGER   [taking it] In any case we are immune to a pretty face when it comes to business.

STOUT GENTLEMAN   [counting out his money] How old was she, at a guess?

MANAGER I haven't seen her without rouge—yet.

STOUT GENTLEMAN What's she doing here?

MANAGER We'll hear that tonight at the Elephant.

STOUT GENTLEMAN But who's she after?

MANAGER All of us, perhaps, before she gets through.

STOUT GENTLEMAN What can she do with three thousand in this town?

MANAGER Evidently she needs them.

STOUT GENTLEMAN I wish her luck.

MANAGER With what!

STOUT GENTLEMAN Getting her three thousand if she can.

MANAGER From me?

STOUT GENTLEMAN It doesn't matter from whom!
[*They laugh.*]

MANAGER I'm curious to see when that letter of advice from Florence will arrive.

STOUT GENTLEMAN If it arrives!

MANAGER Ah! If it arrives!

STOUT GENTLEMAN We might make a collection for her benefit.

MANAGER I dare say that's what she has in mind.

STOUT GENTLEMAN You don't need to tell me.

MANAGER Did you draw a winning number in the last lottery?
[*They laugh.*]

STOUT GENTLEMAN [*to Cashier*] Take this. What's the difference if our money draws interest here or outside. Here—open an account for the Realty Construction Company.

MANAGER [*sharply, to Clerk*] Account: Realty Construction Company.

STOUT GENTLEMAN There's more to come.

MANAGER The more the merrier. We can use it just now.

STOUT GENTLEMAN Sixty thousand marks, fifty thousand in paper, ten thousand in gold.
[*Cashier begins counting.*]

MANAGER [*after a pause*] And how are you, otherwise?

STOUT GENTLEMAN [*to Cashier, who pauses to examine a note*] Yes, that one's patched.

MANAGER We'll accept it, of course. We shall soon be rid of it. I'll reserve it for our fair client from Florence. She wore patches too.

STOUT GENTLEMAN But behind these you find—one thousand marks.

MANAGER Face value.

STOUT GENTLEMAN [*laughing immoderately*] Face value—that's good!

MANAGER The face value! Here's your receipt. [*Choking with laughter*] Sixty—thousand—

STOUT GENTLEMAN [*takes it, reads*] Sixty—thou—

MANAGER Face.

STOUT GENTLEMAN Value.
[*They shake hands.*]

MANAGER [*in tears*] I'll see you tonight.

STOUT GENTLEMAN [*nods*] The face—the face—value!

[*He buttons his overcoat, and goes out laughing. Manager wipes the tears from his pince-nez; Cashier fastens the notes together in bundles.*]

MANAGER This lady from Florence—who claims to come from Florence—has a vision like that ever visited you in your cage before? Furs—perfume! The fragrance lingers—you breathe adventure. Superbly staged. Italy . . . enchantment — fairy-tale — Riviera — Mentone — Pordighera — Nice — Monte Carlo — where oranges blossom, fraud blooms too. Swindlers —down there every square foot of earth breeds them. They organize crusades. The gang disperses to the four winds—preferably small towns—off the beaten track. Then—apparitions — billowing silks — furs — women — modern sirens. Refrains from the sunny south—*o bella Napoli!* One glance and you're stripped to your undershirt—to the bare skin—to the naked, naked skin. [*He drums with a pencil on the Cashier's hand.*] Depend upon it, this bank in Florence knows as much about the lady as the man in the moon. The whole affair is a swindle, carefully arranged. And the web was woven not in Florence, but in Monte Carlo. That's the place to keep in mind. Take my word for it, you've just seen one of the gadflies that thrive in the swamp of the Casino. We shall never see her again. The first attempt missed fire; she'll scarcely risk a second! I joke about it but I have a keen eye—when you're a banker —I really should have tipped off the police! Well, it doesn't concern me—besides, banks must be discreet. Keep your eye on the out-of-town papers—the police news. When you find something there about an adventuress, safe under lock and key—then we'll talk about it again. You'll see I was right—then we'll hear more of our Florentine lady than we'll ever see of her and her furs again.

[*Exit. Cashier seals up rolls of bank notes.*]

PORTER [*enters with letters, hands them to Clerk*] One registered letter. I want the receipt.

[*Clerk stamps receipt form, hands it to Porter. Porter rearranges glass and waterbottle on the table, and goes out. Clerk takes the letters into Manager's room, and returns.*]

LADY [*reenters; comes quickly to the counter*] I beg your pardon.

[*Cashier stretches out his hand, without looking at her. Raps.*]

LADY [*louder*] If you please! [*Cashier raps on the counter.*] I don't want to trouble the Manager a second time. [*Cashier raps on the counter.*] Please tell me—would it be possible for me to leave you the letter of credit for the whole sum, and to receive an advance of three thousand in part payment? [*Cashier raps impatiently.*] I should be willing to deposit my diamonds as security, if required. Any jeweler in the town will appraise them for you. [*She takes off a glove and pulls at her bracelet. Serving Maid comes in quickly, plumps down on sofa, and begins rummaging in her market-basket. Lady, startled by the commotion, looks round. As she leans on the counter her hand sinks into the Cashier's. Cashier bends over the hand which lies in his own. His spectacles glitter, his glance travels slowly upward from her wrist. Serving Maid, with a sigh of relief, discovers the check she is looking for. Lady nods kindly in her direction. Serving Maid replaces vegetables, etc., in her basket. Lady, turning again to the counter, meets the eyes of the Cashier. Cashier smiles at her. Lady, drawing back her hand*] Of course I shall not ask the bank to do anything irregular. [*She puts the bracelet on her wrist; the clasp refuses to catch. Stretching out her arm to the Cashier*] Would you be so kind? I'm clumsy with the left hand. [*Cashier stares at her as if mesmerized. His spectacles, bright points of light, seem almost to be swallowed up

in the cavity of his wide-open eyes. To Serving Maid*] You can help me, mademoiselle. [*Serving Maid does so.*] Now the safety catch. [*With a little cry*] You're pinching my flesh. Ah, that's better. Thank you so much.

[*She bows to the Cashier and goes out. Serving Maid coming to the counter, planks down her check. Cashier takes it in trembling hands, the slip of paper flutters and crackles; he fumbles under the counter, then counts out money.*]

SERVING MAID [*looking at the pile of coins*] That isn't all mine.

[*Cashier writes. Clerk becomes observant.*]

SERVING MAID [*to Clerk*] But it's too much! [*Clerk looks at Cashier. Cashier rakes in part of the money.*] Still too much!

[*Cashier ignores her and continues writing. Serving Maid shaking her head, puts the money in her basket and goes out.*]

CASHIER [*hoarsely*] Get me a glass of water! [*Clerk hurries from behind the counter; comes to table.*] That's been standing. Fresh water—cold water—from the faucet. [*Clerk hurries out with glass. Cashier goes quickly to electric bell, and rings. Porter enters from the hall.*] Get me fresh water.

PORTER I'm not allowed to go so far from the door.

CASHIER [*hoarsely*] For me. Not that slime. I want water from the faucet. [*Porter seizes waterbottle and hurries out. Cashier quickly crams his pockets with bank notes. Then he takes his coat from a peg, throws it over his arm, and puts on his hat. He lifts a flap in the counter, passes through, and goes out.*]

MANAGER [*absorbed in reading a letter, enters from his room*] Here's the letter of advice from Florence, after all!

[*Clerk enters with a glass of water. Porter enters with a full waterbottle.*]

MANAGER [*looking up*] What the devil . . . ?

SCENE TWO

Writing-room of a hotel. Glass door in background. On right, desk with telephone. On the left, sofa and armchair with table and newspapers.

LADY [*writes; Son, in hat and coat, enters, carrying under his arm a large flat object wrapped in green baize; with surprise*] Have you brought it with you?

SON Hush! The wine dealer is downstairs. The old fool is afraid I'll run away with it.

LADY But I thought this morning he was glad to get rid of it.

SON Now he's suspicious.

LADY You must have given yourself away.

SON I did let him see I was pleased.

LADY [*smiling*] That would open a blind man's eyes.

SON Let it. But don't be afraid, Mother, the price is the same as it was this morning.

LADY Is the man waiting for his money?

SON Let him wait.

LADY But, my dear boy, I must tell you—

SON [*kissing her*] Hush, Mother. This is a great moment. You mustn't look until I say so. [*He takes off his hat and cloak, puts the picture on a chair and lifts the green baize covering.*]

LADY Ready?

SON [*in a low tone*] Mother! [*Lady turns in her chair. Comes to her, puts his arm round her neck.*] Well?

LADY That was never meant to hang in a restaurant.

SON It was turned to the wall. The old fellow had pasted his own photograph on the back of it.

LADY Was that included in the price?

SON [*laughs*] Tell me, what do you think of it?

LADY I find it—very naïve.

SON Marvelous, isn't it? Extraordinary considering it's a Cranach.

LADY Do you really prize it as a picture?

SON Of course! But just look at the peculiar conception—unique for Cranach. And a new treatment of this subject in the entire history of art. Where can you find anything like it—in the Pitti—the Uffizi—the Vatican? Even the Louvre has nothing to compare with it. Here we have without doubt the first and only erotic conception of Adam and Eve. The apple is still in the grass—the serpent leers from behind the indescribable green foliage—and that means that the drama is played in Paradise itself and not in the banishment. That's the original sin—

the real fall! Cranach painted dozens of Adams and Eves—standing stiffly—always separated—with the apple bough between them. In those pictures Cranach says simply: "They knew each other." But in this picture for the first time, he cries exultantly, "They loved each other." Here a German proves himself a master of an eroticism intensely southern in its feeling. [*In front of the picture*] And yet what restraint in this ecstasy! This line of the man's arm as it slants across the woman's hip. The horizontal line of her thighs and the opposing line of his never weary the eyes. These flesh tones make their love a living thing—doesn't it affect you that way?

LADY I find it as naïve as your picture.

SON What does that mean?

LADY Please hide it in your room.

SON I won't get its full effect until we get home. This Cranach in Florence. Of course, I'll have to postpone finishing my book. I must digest this first. A man must live with a thing like this before he dares write about it. Just now I am overwhelmed. Think of finding this picture here —on the first stage of our trip!

LADY But you were almost certain that it must be in this neighborhood.

SON I am dazed nevertheless. Isn't it amazing! I am lucky.

LADY This is simply the result of your own careful research.

SON But not without your generosity? Your help?

LADY It makes me as happy as it does you.

SON Your patience is endless. I tear you from your beautiful quiet life in Fiesole. You are an Italian, but I drag you through Germany in mid-winter. You live in sleeping cars or third-rate hotels; rub elbows with Tom, Dick, Harry!

LADY [*smiling—patting his cheek*] Yes, I have had my fill of that.

SON But now I promise you to hurry. I'm madly impatient to get this treasure safely home. Let's take the three o'clock train. Will you give me the three thousand marks?

LADY I haven't them.

SON But the owner is here, in the hotel.

LADY The bank couldn't pay me. The letter of advice has somehow been delayed.

SON I've promised him the money.

LADY Then you must return the picture until the letter arrives.

SON Can't we hurry it in any way?

LADY [*smiles*] I've written a telegram; I'll have it sent now. You see, we traveled so quickly that—[*Waiter knocks at the door; Phone rings*]. Yes?

WAITER Someone from the bank.

LADY Send him up. [*To Son*] They must be sending the money.

SON Call me as soon as you've got it. I'd rather keep an eye on the old man.

LADY I'll send for you.

SON Then I'll wait downstairs.

[*Pauses in front of picture. Lady closes her portfolio. Cashier is seen behind the glass door, enters. Lady points to a chair, and starts to seat herself. Cashier stands.*]

LADY I hope the bank [*Cashier sees the picture, and starts violently.*]—my visit to the bank was closely connected with this picture.

CASHIER [*staring*] You!

LADY Do you find any point of resemblance?

CASHIER [*smiling*] In the wrist!

LADY Are you interested?

CASHIER I should like to discover more.

LADY Do such subjects interest you?

CASHIER [*looking straight at her*] Yes—I understand them.

LADY Are there any more to be found here? You would do me a great favor—that's more important than the money.

CASHIER I have the money.

LADY I fear at this rate my letter of credit will soon be exhausted.

CASHIER [*produces a roll of bank notes*] This will be enough.

LADY I can only draw twelve thousand in all.

CASHIER Sixty thousand!

LADY But—how did you—?

CASHIER That's my business.

LADY How am I to—?

CASHIER We shall bolt.

LADY Bolt? Where?

CASHIER Abroad. Anywhere. Pack your trunk, if you've got one. You can start from the station; I'll walk to the next stop and board the train. We'll spend the first night in—a time-table! [*He finds it.*]

LADY Have you brought more than three thousand from the bank?

CASHIER [*preoccupied with the timetable*] I have sixty thousand in my pocket—fifty thousand in notes and ten thousand in gold.

LADY And my part of that is—

CASHIER [*opens a roll of notes, and counts them with professional skill, then lays a bundle of them on the table*] Your part. Take this. Put it away. We may be seen. The door has a glass panel. That's five hundred.

LADY Five hundred?

CASHIER More to come. All in good time. When we're in a safe place. Here we must be careful . . . hurry up—take it. No time for love-making. The wheel spins. An arm outstretched will be caught in the spokes. [*He springs to his feet.*]

LADY But I need three thousand.

CASHIER If the police find them on you, you'll find yourself in jail!

LADY What have the police to do with it?

CASHIER You were in the bank. Your presence filled the air. They'll suspect you; the link between us is clear as daylight.

LADY I went to—your bank.

CASHIER As cool as a cucumber—

LADY I demanded—

CASHIER You tried to.

LADY I tried—

CASHIER You did. With your forged letter.

LADY [*taking a paper from her handbag*] Isn't my letter genuine?

CASHIER As false as your diamonds.

LADY I offered them as a security. Why should my precious stones be paste?

CASHIER Ladies of your kind only dazzle.

LADY What do you think I am? I'm dark, it's true; a Southerner, a Tuscan.

CASHIER From Monte Carlo.

LADY [*smiles*] No, from Florence!

CASHIER [*his glance lighting upon the Son's hat and cloak*] Ha! Have I come too late?

LADY Too late?

CASHIER Where is he? I'll bargain with him. He'll be willing. I have the means. How much shall I offer? How high do you put the indemnity? How much shall I cram into his pockets?

I'll bid up to fifteen thousand. Is he asleep? Still rolling in bed? Where's your room? Twenty thousand—five thousand extra for instant withdrawal! [*He picks up hat and cloak.*]

LADY [*in astonishment*] The gentleman is sitting in the lounge.

CASHIER Downstairs? Too risky! Too many people down there. Call him up; I'll settle with him here. Ring for him; let the Waiter hustle. Twenty thousand, cash down! [*He begins counting the money.*]

LADY Can my son speak for me?

CASHIER [*bounding back*] Your—son ! ! !

LADY I'm traveling with him. He's collecting material for a book on the history of art. That's what brought us from Florence to Germany.

CASHIER [*staring at her*] Son?

LADY Is that so appalling?

CASHIER But—but—this picture—

LADY A lucky find of his. My son is buying for three thousand marks; this was the amount needed so urgently. The owner is a wine dealer whom you will probably know by name . . .

CASHIER Furs . . . silk . . . rustle—glitter. The air was heavy with perfume!

LADY This is mid-winter. As far as I know, my way of dressing is not exceptional.

CASHIER The forged letter—

LADY I was about to wire to my bank.

CASHIER Your bare wrist—on which you wanted me to put the bracelet—

LADY We're all clumsy with the left hand.

CASHIER [*dully, to himself*] And I—have stolen the money—

LADY [*diverted*] Will that satisfy you and your police? My son is not utterly unknown in the art world.

CASHIER Now—at this very moment—they've discovered everything! I asked for water to get the clerk out of the way—and again for water to get the porter away from the door. The notes are gone; I'm an embezzler. I mustn't be seen in the streets; I can't go to the railway station; the police are warned, sixty thousand! I must slip away across the fields—through the snow—before the whole town is on my track!

LADY [*shocked*] Be quiet!

CASHIER I took all the money. Your presence filled the bank. Your scent hung on the air.

You glistened and rustled—you put your naked hand in mine—your breath came warm across the counter—warm—

LADY [*silencing him*] Please—I am a lady.

CASHIER But now you must—

LADY [*controlling herself*] Tell me, are you married? Yes? [*Violent gesture from Cashier.*] Ah, that makes a difference. Unless I am to consider the whole thing a joke, you gave way to a foolish impulse. Listen. You can make good the loss. You can go back to your bank and plead a passing illness—a lapse of memory. I suppose you still have the full amount.

CASHIER I've embezzled the money—

LADY [*abruptly*] Then I can take no further interest in the matter.

CASHIER I've robbed the bank.

LADY You grow tedious, my dear sir.

CASHIER And now you must—

LADY The one thing I must do, is to—

CASHIER After this you must—

LADY Preposterous.

CASHIER I've robbed for you. I've delivered myself into your hands, destroyed my livelihood. I've burned my bridges behind me. I'm a thief and a criminal. [*Burying his face in his hands*] Now you must! . . . After all that you must!

LADY [*turns*] I shall call my son. Perhaps he—

CASHIER [*with a change of tone, springs nimbly to his feet; grabbing her arm*] Aha! Call him, would you? Rouse the hotel, give the alarm? A fine plan! Clumsy. I'm not so easily caught as that. Not in that trap. I have my wits about me, ladies and gentlemen. Yours are asleep. I'm always five miles ahead of you. Don't move. Stay where you are until I . . . [*putting the money in his pocket*] until I . . . [*pressing his hat over his eyes*] until I . . . [*wrapping his coat closely about him*] until I . . .
[*Softly he opens the glass door and slips out. Lady rises, stands motionless.*]

SON [*entering*] The man from the bank has just gone out. You're looking worried, Mother. Is the money—?

LADY I found this interview trying. You know, my dear boy, how money matters get on my nerves.

SON Is there still trouble about the payment?

LADY Perhaps I ought to tell you—

SON   Must I give back the picture?

LADY   I'm not thinking of that—

SON   But that's the chief question!

LADY   I think I ought to notify the police.

SON   Police?

LADY   Send this telegram to my bank. In future I must have proper documents that will satisfy everyone.

SON   Isn't your letter of credit enough?

LADY   Not quite. Go to the telegraph office for me. I don't want to send the porter.

SON   And when shall we have the three thousand marks? [*Telephone bell rings.*]

LADY   [*recoils*]   They're ringing me up already. [*At the instrument*] Oh! Has arrived? And I'm to call for it myself? Gladly. [*Change of tone.*] I'm not in the least annoyed. Yes, of course. [*Change of tone.*] Florence is a long way off. And then the Italian post office—I beg your pardon? Oh, via Berlin—a roundabout way. That explains it. Not in the least. Thank you. In ten minutes. Good-by. [*To Son*] All settled, my dear boy. Never mind the telegram. [*She tears up the form.*] You shall have the picture. Your wine dealer can come along. He'll get his money at the bank. Pack up your treasure. We go straight from the bank to the station. [*Telephoning while the Son wraps up the picture*] The bill, please. Rooms 14 and 16. Yes, immediately. Please.

SCENE THREE

Aslant a field deep in snow. Through a tangle of low-hanging branches, blue shadows are cast by the midday sun.

CASHIER   [*comes in backward, furtively*]   What a marvelous contraption a man is. The mechanism runs in his joints—silently. Suddenly faculties are stimulated, action results. My hands, for instance, when did they ever shovel snow? And now they dig through snowdrifts without the slightest trouble. My footprints are all blotted out. I have achieved a complete incognito. [*Pause*] Frost and damp breed chills. Before you know it you've got a fever and that weakens the will—a man loses control over his actions if he's in bed sick. He's easily

tracked. [*Throws cuffs to ground.*] Lie there! You'll be missed in the wash! Lamentations fill the kitchen! A pair of cuffs is missing! A catastrophe in the tubs! Chaos! [*Pause*] Strange! How keen my wits are! Here I work like mad to efface my tracks and then betray myself by two bits of dirty linen. It is always a trifle, an oversight—carelessness that betrays the criminal. [*Pause*] I wonder what's going to happen. I am keyed up to the highest pitch! I have every reason to expect momentous discoveries. The last few hours prove it. This morning a trusted employee—fortunes passing through my hands. The Construction Company makes a huge deposit. At noon an out-and-out scoundrel. Up to all the tricks. The details of flight carefully worked out. Turn the trick and run. Marvelous accomplishment—and only half the day gone. I am prepared for anything. I know I can play the game. I am on the march! There is no turning back. I march—so out with your trumps without any fuss. I have put sixty thousand on a single card—it must be trumps. I play too high to lose. No nonsense—cards on the table—do you understand? Now you'll have to, my beautiful lady. Your cue—my silken lady, give it to me, my resplendent lady—or the scene will fall flat. [*Pause*] Idiot—and you think you can act! Perform your natural duties—breed children and don't bother the prompter. Ah, I beg your pardon—you have a son—you are completely absolved. I withdraw my aspersions. Good-by, give my compliments to the manager of the bank. His very glances cover you with slime, but don't let that worry you. He's been robbed of sixty thousand. His roof rattles and leaks—never mind, never mind—the Construction Company will mend it for him. I release you from all obligations—you are dismissed—you can go! Stop! Permit me to thank you! What's that you say? Nothing to thank you for? Yes! There is. Not worth mentioning? You are joking. You are my sole creditor. How so? I owe you my life! Good God—I exaggerate? You have electrified me—set me free. One step toward you and I enter a land of miracles. And with this load in my breast pocket I pay cash for all favors. And now fade away. You are outbid. Your means are too limited. Remember you have a son. Nothing will be knocked down to you. I'm paying cash down. [*Pause*] I have ready money. Come on— what's for sale? [*Pause*] Snow? Sunlight— stillness—. Blue snow at such a price. Outrageous, profiteering. I decline the offer. Your proposition is not *bona fide*. [*Pause*] But I must pay. I must spend, I've got the cash. Where are the goods that are worth the whole sum? Sixty thousand and the buyer to boot—flesh and bones—body and soul. Deal with me! Sell to me—I have the money, you have the goods —let us trade. [*The wind is blowing, the sun is overcast, distant thunder is heard.*] The earth is in labor—spring gales at last! That's better! I knew my cry could not be in vain. My demand was urgent. Chaos is insulted and will not be put to shame by my colossal deed of this morning. I knew it. In a case like mine never let up. Go at them hard—pull down their cloaks and you'll see something. [*The tree has changed to the form of a skeleton, the wind and thunder die down.*] Have you been sitting behind me all this time eavesdropping? Are you an agent of the police? Not in the ordinary narrow sense—but [*pausing*] comprising all. Police of Fate? Are you the all-embracing answer to my emphatic question? Does your rather well ventilated appearance suggest the final truth—emptiness? That's somewhat scanty —very threadbare—in fact nothing! I reject the information as being too full of gaps. Your services are not required. You can shut your rag and bone shop. I am not taken in as easily as that. [*Pause*] This procedure would be exceedingly simple—it's true—you would spare me further entanglements. But I prefer complications. So farewell—if that is possible, to you in your condition! I still have things to do. When one is traveling one can't enter every house on the road—not even at the friendliest invitations. I still have many obligations to fulfill before evening. You can't possibly be the first—perhaps the last—but even then only as a last resort. I won't want to do it. But, as I said, as a last resort—that's debatable. Ring me up at midnight—ask Central for my number. It will change from hour to hour. And excuse the coldness of my tone. We should be on friendlier terms, I know. We are closely bound. I really believe I carry you about with me now.

So, you see, we have come to a sort of understanding. That is a beginning which gives one confidence and backbone to face the future, whatever it is. I appreciate that fully. My most profound respects. [*After a peal of thunder and a last gust of wind the skeleton reverts to the tree. The sun comes out again.*] There—I knew it wouldn't last.

SCENE FOUR

Parlor in Cashier's house. In the window-boxes, blown geraniums. Table and chairs. Piano right. Mother (hard of hearing) sits near the window. First Daughter is embroidering at the table. Second Daughter is practicing the overture to Tannhäuser. *Wife comes and goes on the left. The clock ticks interminably.*

MOTHER What's that you're playing?

FIRST DAUGHTER The "Overture" to *Tannhäuser*.

MOTHER "O Tannenbaum" is another pretty piece.

WIFE [*entering*] It's time I began to fry the chops.

FIRST DAUGHTER Oh, not yet, Mama.

WIFE No, it's not time yet to fry the chops.

MOTHER What are you embroidering now?

FIRST DAUGHTER Father's slippers.

WIFE [*coming to Mother*] Today we have chops for dinner.

MOTHER Are you frying them now?

WIFE Plenty of time. It's not twelve o'clock yet.

FIRST DAUGHTER Not nearly twelve, Mama.

WIFE No, not nearly twelve.

MOTHER When he comes, it will be twelve.

WIFE He hasn't come yet.

FIRST DAUGHTER When Father comes, it will be twelve o'clock.

WIFE Yes. [*Exit.*]

SECOND DAUGHTER [*stops playing, listens*] Is that Father?

FIRST DAUGHTER [*listens*] Father?

WIFE [*enters*] Is that my husband?

MOTHER Is that my son?

SECOND DAUGHTER Father!

FIRST DAUGHTER Father!

WIFE Husband!

MOTHER Son!

[*Cashier enters right, hangs up hat and cloak. Pause.*]

WIFE Where do you come from?

CASHIER From the cemetery.

MOTHER Has somebody died suddenly?

CASHIER [*patting her on the back*] You can have a sudden death, but not a sudden burial.

WIFE Where have you come from?

CASHIER From the grave. I burrowed through the clods with my forehead. See, here's a lump of ice. It was a great effort to get through—an extraordinary effort. I've dirtied my hands a little. You need a good grip to pull yourself up. You're buried deep. Life keeps on dumping dirt on you. Mountains of it—dust—ashes—the place is a rubbish heap. The dead lie at the usual depth—three yards. The living keep on sinking deeper and deeper.

WIFE You're frozen from head to foot.

CASHIER Thawed. Shaken by storms, like the spring. The wind whistled and roared; I tell you it stripped off my flesh until my bones were bare—a skeleton—bleached in a minute. A boneyard! At last the sun welded me together again. And here I am. Thus I've been renewed from the soles of my feet up.

MOTHER Have you been out in the open?

CASHIER In hideous dungeons, Mother. In bottomless pits beneath monstrous towers; deafened by clanking chains, blinded by darkness!

WIFE The bank must be closed. You've been celebrating with the Manager. Has there been a happy event in his family?

CASHIER He has his eye on a new mistress. Italian beauty—silks and furs—where oranges bloom. Wrists like polished ivory. Black tresses—olive complexion. Diamonds. Real . . . all real. Tus . . . Tus . . . the rest sounds like Canaan. Fetch me an atlas. Tus-Canaan. Is that right? Is there an island of that name? A mountain? A swamp? Geography can tell us everything. But he'll burn his fingers. She'll turn him down—brush him off like a bit of dirt. There he lies . . . sprawling on the carpet . . . legs in the air . . . our snug little Manager!

WIFE The bank is not closed?

CASHIER Never, Wife. Prisons are never closed.

The procession is endless. An eternal pilgrimage. Like sheep rushing into the slaughterhouse. A seething mass. No escape—none—unless you jump over their backs.

MOTHER Your coat's torn in the back.

CASHIER And look at my hat! Fit for a tramp.

SECOND DAUGHTER The lining's torn.

CASHIER Look in my pockets. Left . . . right!

[*First Daughter and Second Daughter pull out cuffs.*]

CASHIER Inventory.

DAUGHTERS Your cuffs.

CASHIER But not the buttons. Hat—coat—torn—what can you expect—jumping over backs. They kick—they scratch—hurdles and fences—silence in the pen—order in the fold—equal rights for all. But one jump—don't hesitate—and you are out of the pen. One mighty deed and here I am! Behind me nothing and before me—What?

[*Sits. Pause. Wife stares at him.*]

MOTHER [*half whispering*] He's sick.

CASHIER [*to one of the Daughters*] Get my jacket. [*To the other*] My slippers. [*To the first*] My cap. [*To the other*] My pipe. [*All are brought.*]

MOTHER You oughtn't to smoke, when you've already been—

WIFE [*motioning her to be silent*] Shall I give you a light?

CASHIER [*in jacket, slippers, and embroidered skull-cap, with pipe in hand, seats himself comfortably at the table*] Light up!

WIFE [*anxiously*] Does it draw?

CASHIER [*looking into pipe*] I shall have to send it for a thorough cleaning. There must be some bits of stale tobacco in the stem. Sometimes way in . . . there are obstructions. It means I have to draw harder than is strictly necessary.

WIFE Do you want me to take it now?

CASHIER No, stay here. [*Blowing great smoke-clouds*] It will do. [*To Second Daughter*] Play something.

[*Second Daughter, at a sign from her mother, sits at piano and plays.*]

CASHIER What piece is that?

SECOND DAUGHTER The "Overture" to *Tannhäuser.*

CASHIER [*nods approval; to First Daughter*]

Sewing? Mending? Darning?

FIRST DAUGHTER Embroidering your slippers.

CASHIER Very practical. And you, Grandma?

MOTHER [*feeling the universal dread*] I was just having forty winks.

CASHIER In peace and quiet.

MOTHER Yes, my life is quiet now.

CASHIER [*to Wife*] And you, Wife?

WIFE I was going to fry the chops.

CASHIER [*nodding*] Mmm—kitchen.

WIFE I'll fry yours now.

CASHIER [*nodding as before*] Kitchen!
[*Exit Wife.*]

CASHIER [*to Daughters*] Open the doors.
[*Daughters exit right and left, returning immediately.*]

WIFE [*enters; pause*] Are you too warm in here?
[*She returns to her task.*]

CASHIER [*looking around him*] Grandmother at the window. Daughters—at the table embroidering . . . playing Wagner. Wife busy in the kitchen. Four walls . . . family life. Cozy . . . all of us together. Mother—son . . . child under one roof. The magic of familiar things. It spins a web. Room with a table. Piano. Kitchen . . . daily bread. Coffee in the morning . . . chops at noon. Bedroom . . . beds . . . in . . . out. More magic. In the end flat on your back . . . white and stiff. Table pushed against the wall . . . in the center a pine coffin . . . screw lid . . . silver mountings . . . but detachable . . . a bit of crepe on the lamp . . . piano unopened for a year.
[*Second Daughter stops playing, and runs sobbing into the kitchen.*]

WIFE [*enters*] She is practicing the new piece.

MOTHER Why doesn't she try something simpler?
[*Cashier knocks out his pipe, begins putting on his hat and overcoat.*]

WIFE Are you going to the bank? Are you going out on business?

CASHIER Bank—business? No.

WIFE Then where are you going?

CASHIER That's the question, Wife. I've climbed down from windswept trees to find an answer. I came here first. Warm and cozy, this nest; I won't deny its good points, but it doesn't stand the final test. No! The answer is clear. This is not the end of my journey, just a signpost; the road leads further on. [*He is now fully dressed.*]

WIFE [*distraught*] Husband, how wild you look!

CASHIER Like a tramp, as I told you. Never mind. Better a ragged wayfarer than an empty road!

WIFE But, it's dinner-time.

MOTHER [*half rising*] And you're going out, just before a meal?

CASHIER I smell the pork chops. Full stomach, drowsy wits.
[*Mother beats the air suddenly with her arms, and falls senseless.*]

FIRST DAUGHTER Grandma.

SECOND DAUGHTER Grandma! Mother.
[*Both fall on their knees, beside her. Wife stands motionless.*]

CASHIER [*going to Mother's chair*] For once in his life a man goes out before his meal—and that kills her. [*He brushes the Daughters aside and regards the body.*] Grief? Mourning? Overflowing tears? Can they make me forget? Are these bonds so closely woven that when they break there's nothing left to me in life but grief?—Mother—son! [*He pulls the roll of banknotes out of his pocket and weighs it in his hand, then shakes his head and puts the money away*]. Grief does not paralyze . . . the eyes are dry and the mind goes on. There's no time to lose, if my day is to be well spent. [*He lays his well-worn purse on the table.*] Use it. There's money honestly earned. That may be worth remembering. Use it.
[*He goes out on the left. Wife stands motionless. Daughters bend over the dead Mother.*]

MANAGER [*coming from the right*] Is your husband at home? Has your husband been there? I have to bring you the painful news that he has absconded. We missed him some hours ago; since then we have been through his books. The sum involved is sixty thousand marks, deposited by the Realty Construction Company. So far, I've refrained from making the matter public, in the hope that he would come to his senses and return. This is my last attempt. You see I've made a personal call. Has your husband been here? [*He looks around him, and observes jacket,* *pipe, etc.*] It looks as though . . . [*His glance lights upon the group at the window; he nods.*] I see! In that case . . . [*He shrugs his shoulders, puts on his hat.*] I can only express my personal sympathy; be assured of that. The rest must take its course. [*Exit.*]

DAUGHTERS [*coming to Wife*] Mother—

WIFE [*savagely*] Don't screech into my ears! Who are you? What do you want? Brats— monkeys. What have you to do with me? [*Breaking down*] My husband has left me. [*Daughters stand shyly, holding hands.*]

SCENE FIVE

The steward's box of a velodrome during a cycle race meeting. Jewish gentlemen, stewards, come and go. They are all alike; little animated figures in dinner jackets, with silk hats tilted back and binoculars slung in leather cases. Whistling, catcalls and a restless hum from the crowded tiers of spectators unseen, off right. Music. All the action takes place on the platform.

FIRST GENTLEMAN [*entering*] Is everything ready?

SECOND GENTLEMAN See for yourself.

FIRST GENTLEMAN [*looking through glasses*] The palms—

SECOND GENTLEMAN What's the matter with the palms?

FIRST GENTLEMAN I thought as much.

SECOND GENTLEMAN But what's wrong with them?

FIRST GENTLEMAN Who arranged them like that?

THIRD GENTLEMAN Crazy.

SECOND GENTLEMAN Upon my soul, you're right!

FIRST GENTLEMAN Was nobody responsible for arranging them?

THIRD GENTLEMAN Ridiculous. Simply ridiculous.

FIRST GENTLEMAN Whoever it was, he's as blind as a bat!

THIRD GENTLEMAN Or fast asleep.

SECOND GENTLEMAN Asleep. But this is only the fourth night of the races.

FIRST GENTLEMAN The palm-tubs must be pushed on one side.

SECOND GENTLEMAN Will you see to it?

FIRST GENTLEMAN Right against the wall. There must be a clear view of the whole track. [*Exit.*]

THIRD GENTLEMAN And of the royal box.

SECOND GENTLEMAN I'll go with you. [*Exit. Fourth Gentleman enters, fires a pistol-shot and withdraws. Fifth Gentleman enters with a red-lacquered megaphone.*]

THIRD GENTLEMAN How much is the prize?

FIFTH GENTLEMAN Eighty marks. Fifty to the winner, thirty to the second.

FIRST GENTLEMAN [*reentering*] Three times round, no more. We're tiring them out.

FOURTH GENTLEMAN [through megaphone] A prize is offered of eighty marks. The winner to receive fifty marks, the second thirty marks. [*Applause. Second and Third Gentlemen return, one carrying a flag.*]

FIRST GENTLEMAN We can start them now.

SECOND GENTLEMAN Not yet, Number 7 is shifting.

FIRST GENTLEMAN Off! [*Second Gentleman lowers his flag. The race begins. Rising and falling volume of applause, with silent intervals.*]

THIRD GENTLEMAN The little fellows must win once in a while.

FOURTH GENTLEMAN It's a good thing the favorites are holding back.

FIFTH GENTLEMAN They'll have to work hard enough before the night's over.

THIRD GENTLEMAN The riders are terribly excited.

FOURTH GENTLEMAN And no wonder.

FIFTH GENTLEMAN Depend upon it, the championship will be settled tonight.

THIRD GENTLEMAN The Americans are still fresh.

FIFTH GENTLEMAN Our lads will make them hustle.

FOURTH GENTLEMAN Let's hope His Royal Highness will be pleased with the victory.

FIRST GENTLEMAN [*looking through glasses*] The box is still empty. [*Outburst of applause*]

THIRD GENTLEMAN The result!

FOURTH GENTLEMAN Prizes in cash—fifty marks for Number 11, thirty marks for Number 4. [*Second Gentleman enters with Cashier. The latter is in evening clothes, with silk hat, patent shoes, gloves, cloak, his beard trimmed, his hair carefully brushed.*]

CASHIER Tell me what is this all about?

SECOND GENTLEMAN I'll introduce you to the stewards.

CASHIER My name doesn't matter.

SECOND GENTLEMAN But you ought to meet the management.

CASHIER I prefer to remain incognito.

SECOND GENTLEMAN But you seem interested in these races.

CASHIER I haven't the slightest idea what it's all about. What are they doing down there? I can see a round track with a bright moving line, like a snake. Now one comes in, another falls out. Why is that?

SECOND GENTLEMAN They ride in pairs. While one partner is pedalling—

CASHIER The other blockhead sleeps?

SECOND GENTLEMAN He's being massaged.

CASHIER And you call that a relay race?

SECOND GENTLEMAN Certainly.

CASHIER You might as well call it a relay rest.

FIRST GENTLEMAN [*approaching*] Ahem! The enclosure is reserved for the management.

SECOND GENTLEMAN This gentleman offers a prize of one thousand marks.

FIRST GENTLEMAN [*change of tone*] Allow me to introduce myself.

CASHIER On no account.

SECOND GENTLEMAN The gentleman wishes to preserve his incognito.

CASHIER Impenetrably.

SECOND GENTLEMAN I was just explaining the sport to him.

CASHIER Yes, don't you find it funny?

FIRST GENTLEMAN How do you mean?

CASHIER Why, this relay rest.

FOURTH GENTLEMAN A prize of one thousand marks! For how many laps?

CASHIER As many as you please.

FOURTH GENTLEMAN How much shall we allot to the winner?

CASHIER That's your affair.

FOURTH GENTLEMAN Eight hundred and two hundred. [*Through megaphone*] An anonymous gentleman offers the following prizes for an open race of ten laps: eight hundred marks to the winner; two hundred marks to the second; one thousand marks in all.

[*Loud applause*]

SECOND GENTLEMAN But tell me, if you're not really interested in this sort of thing, why do you offer such a big prize?

CASHIER Because it works like magic.

SECOND GENTLEMAN On the pace of the riders, you mean?

CASHIER Rubbish.

THIRD GENTLEMAN [*entering*] Are you the gentleman who is offering one thousand marks?

CASHIER In gold.

SECOND GENTLEMAN That would take too long to count . . .

CASHIER Watch me. [*He pulls out the money, moistens his finger and counts rapidly.*] That makes less to carry.

SECOND GENTLEMAN I see you're an expert.

CASHIER A mere detail, sir. [*Handing him the money*] Accept payment.

SECOND GENTLEMAN Received with thanks.

FIFTH GENTLEMAN [*approaching*] Where is the gentleman? Allow me to introduce—

CASHIER Certainly not!

THIRD GENTLEMAN [*with flag*] I shall give the start.

[*General movement from the stand*]

FIFTH GENTLEMAN Now we shall see a tussle for the championship.

THIRD GENTLEMAN [*joining group*] All the cracks are in the race.

FOURTH GENTLEMAN Off!

[*Outburst of applause*]

CASHIER [*taking First and Second Gentlemen by the collar and turning them around*] Now I'll answer your question for you. Look up!

SECOND GENTLEMAN But you must keep your eye on the track, and watch how the race goes.

CASHIER Childish, this sport. One rider must win because the other loses. Look up, I say! It's there, among the crowd, that the magic works. Look at them—three tiers—one above the other —packed like sardines—excitement rages. Down there in the boxes the better classes are still controlling themselves. They're only looking on but, oh, what looks—wide-eyed—staring. One row higher, their bodies sway and vibrate. You hear exclamations. Way up—no restraint! Fanatic—yells—bellowing nakedness—a gallery of passion. Just look at that group! Five times entwined; five heads dancing on one shoulder, five pairs of arms beating time across one howling breast! At the head of this monster is a single man. He's being crushed . . . mangled . . . thrust over the railing. His hat, crumpled, falls through the murky atmosphere . . . flutters into the middle balcony, lights upon a lady's bosom. There it rests daintily . . . so daintily! She'll never notice the hat; she'll go to bed with it; year in, year in, year out, she'll carry this hat upon her breast!

[*The applause swells.*]

FIRST GENTLEMAN The Dutchman is putting on speed.

CASHIER The second balcony joins in. An alliance has been made; the hat has done the trick. The lady crushes it against the railing. Pretty lady, your bosom will show the marks of this! There's no help for it. It's foolish to struggle. You are pushed to the wall and you've got to give yourself, just as you are, without a murmur.

SECOND GENTLEMAN Do you know the lady?

CASHIER Look! Someone is being pushed out over the railing. He swings free, he loses his hold, he drops—he sails down into the boxes. What has become of him? Vanished! Swallowed, stifled, absorbed! A raindrop in a maelstrom!

FIRST GENTLEMAN The fellow from Hamburg is making up ground.

CASHIER The boxes are frantic. The falling man has set up contact. Restraint can go to the devil! Dinner jackets quiver. Shirt fronts begin to split. Studs fly in all directions. Lips are parted, jaws are rattling. Above and below—all distinctions are lost. One universal yell from every tier. Pandemonium. Climax.

SECOND GENTLEMAN [*turning*] He wins! He wins! The German wins! What do you say to that?

CASHIER Stuff and nonsense.

SECOND GENTLEMAN A marvelous spurt!

CASHIER Marvelous trash!

FIRST GENTLEMAN [*about to leave*] We'll just make certain—

CASHIER [*holding him back*] Have you any doubts about it?

SECOND GENTLEMAN The German was leading, but—

CASHIER Never mind that, if you please. [*Pointing to the audience*] Up there you have the staggering fact. Watch the supreme effort, the lazy dizzy height of accomplishment. From boxes to gallery one seething flux, dissolving the individual, re-creating passion! Differences melt away, veils are torn away; passion rules! The trumpets blare and the walls come tumbling down. No restraint, no modesty, no motherhood, no childhood—nothing but passion! There's the real thing. That's worth the search. That justifies the price!

THIRD GENTLEMAN [*entering*] The ambulance column is working splendidly.

CASHIER Is the man hurt who fell?

THIRD GENTLEMAN Crushed flat.

CASHIER When life is at fever heat some must die.

FOURTH GENTLEMAN [*with megaphone*] Result; eight hundred marks won by Number 2; two hundred marks won by Number 1.

[*Loud applause*]

FIFTH GENTLEMAN The men are tired out.

SECOND GENTLEMAN You could see the pace dropping.

THIRD GENTLEMAN They need a rest.

CASHIER I've another prize to offer.

FIRST GENTLEMAN Presently, sir.

CASHIER No interruptions, no delays.

SECOND GENTLEMAN We must give them a chance to breathe.

CASHIER Bah! Don't talk to me of those fools! Look at the public, bursting with excitement. This power mustn't be wasted. We'll feed the flames; you shall see them leap into the sky. I offer fifty thousand marks.

SECOND GENTLEMAN Do you mean it?

THIRD GENTLEMAN How much did you say?

CASHIER Fifty thousand. Everything.

THIRD GENTLEMAN It's an unheard of sum—

CASHIER The effect will be unheard of. Warn your ambulance men on every floor.

FIRST GENTLEMAN We accept your offer. The contest shall begin when the box is occupied.

SECOND GENTLEMAN Capital idea!

THIRD GENTLEMAN Excellent!

FOURTH GENTLEMAN This is a profitable visitor.

FIFTH GENTLEMAN [*digging him in the rib*] A paying guest.

CASHIER [*to First Gentleman*] What do you mean—when the box is occupied?

FIRST GENTLEMAN We'll talk over the conditions in the committee room. I suggest thirty thousand to the winner; fifteen thousand to the second; five thousand to the third.

SECOND GENTLEMAN Exactly.

THIRD GENTLEMAN [*gloomily*] Downright waste, I call it.

FIFTH GENTLEMAN The sport's ruined for good and all.

FIRST GENTLEMAN [*turning*] As soon as the box is occupied.

[*All go out, leaving Cashier alone. Enter Salvation Lass.*]

SALVATION LASS The War Cry! Ten pfennigs, sir.

CASHIER Presently, presently.

SALVATION LASS The War Cry, sir.

CASHIER What trash are you trying to sell?

SALVATION LASS The War Cry, sir.

CASHIER You're too late. The battle's in full swing.

SALVATION LASS [*shaking tin box*] Ten pfennigs, sir.

CASHIER So you expect to start a war for 10 pfennigs?

SALVATION LASS Ten pfennigs, sir.

CASHIER I'm paying an indemnity of fifty thousand marks.

SALVATION LASS Ten pfennigs.

CASHIER Yours is a wretched scuffle. I only subscribe to pitched battles.

SALVATION LASS Ten pfennigs.

CASHIER I carry only gold.

SALVATION LASS Ten pfennigs.

CASHIER Gold—

SALVATION LASS Ten—

CASHIER [*seizing megaphone, bellows at her through it*] Gold! Gold! Gold!

[*Salvation Lass goes out. Many Gentlemen enter.*]

FOURTH GENTLEMAN Would you care to announce your offer yourself?

CASHIER No, I'm a spectator. You stun them with the fifty thousand [*handing him the megaphone*].

FOURTH GENTLEMAN [*through the megaphone*] A new prize is offered by the same anonymous gentleman. [*Cries of "Bravo!"*] The total sum is fifty thousand marks. Five thousand marks to the third, fifteen thousand to the second.

The winner to receive thirty thousand marks. [*Ecstasy*]

CASHIER [*stands apart, nodding his head*] There we have it, the pinnacle. The summit. The climbing hope fulfilled. The roar of a spring gale. The breaking wave of a human tide. All bonds are burst. Up with the veils—down with the shams! Humanity—free humanity, high and low, untroubled by class, unfettered by manners. Unclean, but free. That's a reward for my impudence. [*Pulling out a bundle of notes*] I can pay with a good heart!

[*Sudden silence. The Gentlemen have taken off their silk hats and stand with bowed heads.*]

FOURTH GENTLEMAN [*coming to Cashier*] If you'll hand me the money, we can have the race for your prize immediately.

CASHIER What's the meaning of this?

FOURTH GENTLEMAN Of what, my dear sir?

CASHIER Oh this sudden, unnatural silence.

FOURTH GENTLEMAN Unnatural? Not at all. His Royal Highness has just entered his box.

CASHIER Highness . . . the royal box . . . the house full.

FOURTH GENTLEMAN Your generous patronage comes at the most opportune moment.

CASHIER Thank you! I don't intend to waste my money.

FOURTH GENTLEMAN What do you mean?

CASHIER I find the sum too large . . . as a subscription to the society of back-benders!

FOURTH GENTLEMAN But pray explain . . .

CASHIER This fire that was raging a moment ago has been put out by the boot of His Highness. You take me for crazy, if you think I will throw one single penny under the snouts of these groveling dogs, these crooked lackeys! A kick where the bend is greatest, that's the prize they'll get from me.

FOURTH GENTLEMAN But the prize has been announced. His Royal Highness is in his box. The audience is showing a proper respect. What do you mean?

CASHIER If you don't understand my words, let deeds speak for me.

[*With violent blow he crushes the other's silk hat down upon his shoulders. Exit. Fourth Gentleman rushes after him, but is restrained by the others.*]

GEORG KAISER

SCENE SIX

Private supper room in a cabaret. Subdued dance music. A Waiter opens the door. The Cashier enters; evening clothes, coat, silk muffler, gold-headed bamboo cane.

WAITER Will this room suit you, sir?

CASHIER It'll do.

[*Waiter takes coat, etc. Cashier turns his back and looks into a mirror.*]

WAITER How many places shall I lay, sir?

CASHIER Twenty-four. I'm expecting my grandma, my mother, my wife, and several aunts. The supper is to celebrate my daughter's confirmation. [*The Waiter stares at him. To the other's reflection in the mirror*] Ass! Two! What are these private rooms for?

WAITER What brand would you prefer?

CASHIER Leave that to me, my oily friend. I shall know which flower to pluck in the ballroom . . . round or slender, a bud or a full-blown rose. I shall not require your invaluable services. No doubt they are invaluable . . . or have you a fixed tariff for that too?

WAITER What brand of champagne, if you please?

CASHIER Ahem! Grand Marnier.

WAITER That's the liqueur, sir.

CASHIER Then I leave it to you.

WAITER Two bottles of Pommery—extra dry. [*Producing menu card*] And for supper?

CASHIER Pinnacles!

WAITER *Oeufs pochés Bergère? Poulet grillé? Steak de veau truffé? Parfait de foie gras en croûte? Salade coeur de laitue?*

CASHIER Pinnacles, pinnacles from soup to dessert.

WAITER Pardon?

CASHIER [*tapping him on the nose*] A pinnacle is the point of perfection . . . the summit of a work of art. So it must be with your pots and pans. The last word in delicacy. The menu of menus. Fit to garnish great events. It's your affair, my friend. I'm not the cook.

WAITER [*sets a large menu-card on the table*] It will be served in twenty minutes.

[*He rearranges glasses, etc. Heads with silken masks peep through the doorway.*]

CASHIER [*sees them in the mirror; shaking a warning finger at them*] Wait, my moths! Presently I shall have you in the lamplight! [*The Masks vanish, giggling. Waiter hangs a notice—"Reserved"—on the outside of the door, then withdraws and closes it behind him.*]

CASHIER [*pushes back his silk hat, takes out a gold cigarette case, strikes a match, sings*]

Tor . . . ea . . . dor, Tor . . . ea . . . dor . . .

Queer, how this stuff comes to your lips. A man's mind must be cram full of it . . . cram full. Everything. "Toreador"—*Carmen*—Caruso. I read all this somewhere . . . it stuck in my head. There it lies, piled up like a snowdrift. At this very moment I could give a history of the Bagdad railway. And how the Crown Prince of Roumania married the Czar's second daughter, Tatjana. Well, well, let them marry. The people need princes. [*Sings*]

Tat . . . tat . . . ja . . . na, Tat . . . ja . . . na . . .

[*Twirling his cane, exit. Waiter enters with bottles on ice. Uncorks, pours out wine. Exit.*]

CASHIER [*reenters, driving before him a female Mask in a harlequin's red-and-yellow-quartered costume*] Fly, moth! Fly, Moth!

FIRST MASK [*running round the table*] Fizz! [*She drinks both of the filled glasses.*] Fizz!

CASHIER [*pouring out more wine*] Liquid powder. Load your painted body.

FIRST MASK [*drinking*] Fizz!

CASHIER Battery mounted, action front.

FIRST MASK Fizz!

CASHIER [*putting aside the bottles*] Loaded. [*Coming to her*] Ready to fire. [*The First Mask leans drunkenly towards him. Shaking her limp arm*] Look brighter, moth. [*First Mask does not respond.*] You're dizzy, my bright butterfly. You've been licking the prickly yellow honey. Open your wings, enfold me, cover me up. I'm an outlaw; give me a hiding-place; open your wings.

FIRST MASK [*with a hiccough*] Fizz!

CASHIER No, my bird of paradise. You have your full load.

FIRST MASK Fizz! [*Sinks onto sofa.*]

CASHIER Not another drop, or you'll be tipsy. Then what would you be worth?

From Morn to Midnight

FIRST MASK Fizz!

CASHIER How much are you worth? What have you to offer? [*Bends over her.*]

FIRST MASK Fizz!

CASHIER I gave you that, but what can you give me? [*First Mask falls asleep.*] Ha! You'd sleep here, would you? Little imp! But I've no time for the joke; I find it too tedious. [*He rises, fills a glass of wine and throws it in her face.*] Good morning to you! The cocks are crowing!

FIRST MASK [*leaping to her feet*] Swine!

CASHIER A quaint name. Unfortunately I'm traveling incognito, and can't respond to the introduction. And so, my mask of the well-known snoutish family . . . get off my sofa!

FIRST MASK I'll make you pay for this!

CASHIER I've paid already. It was cheap at the price.

[*Exit First Mask. Cashier drinks champagne; exit, singing. Waiter enters with caviar; collects empty glasses; exit. Cashier enters with two black Masks.*]

SECOND MASK [*slamming the door*] Reserved!

THIRD MASK [*at the table*] Caviar!

SECOND MASK [*running to her*] Caviar?

CASHIER Black as your masks. Black as yourselves. Eat it up; gobble it, cram it down your throats. [*Seating himself between them*] Speak caviar. Sing wine. I've no use for your brains. [*He pours out champagne and fills their plates.*] Not one word shall you utter. Not a syllable, not an exclamation. You shall be dumb as the fish that strewed this black spawn upon the Black Sea. You can giggle, you can bleat, but don't talk to me. You've nothing to say. You've nothing to shed but your finery. . . . Be careful! I've settled one already! [*Masks looks at one another, sniggering. Taking Second Mask by the arm*] What color are your eyes? Green . . . yellow? [*Turning to Third Mask*] And yours? Blue . . . red? A play of glances through the eyeholes. That promises well. Come, I'll offer a beauty prize! [*Masks laugh. To Second Mask*] You're the pretty one. You struggle hard, but wait! In a moment I'll tear down your curtain and look at the show. [*Second Mask breaks away from him. To Third Mask*] You have something to hide. Modesty's your lure. You

dropped in here by chance. You were looking for adventure. Well, here's your adventurer. Off with your mask. [*Third Mask slips away from him.*] This is the goal? I sit here trembling. You've stirred my blood. Now let me pay. [*He pulls out a bundle of notes and divides it between them.*] Pretty mask, this for your beauty. Pretty mask, this for your beauty. [*Holding his hand before his eyes*] One—two—three! [*Masks lift their dominoes. Looking at them, he laughs hoarsely.*] Cover them—cover them up! [*He runs round the table.*] Monsters—horrors! Out with you this minute—this very second—or I'll . . . [*he lifts his cane*].

SECOND MASK But you told us—

THIRD MASK You wanted us—

CASHIER I wanted to get at you! [*The Masks run out. Shaking himself, he drinks champagne.*] Sluts!

[*Exit, humming. Waiter enters with fresh bottles, and exit.*]

CASHIER [*kicking the door open, entering with Fourth Mask, a Pierrette in a domino cloak reaching to her shoes; he leaves her standing in the middle of the room, and throws himself in chair*] Dance! [*The Fourth Mask stands still.*] Dance! Spin your bag of bones. Dance, dance! Brains are nothing. Beauty doesn't count. Dancing's the thing—twisting, whirling! Dance, dance, dance! [*Fourth Mask comes halting to the mirror. Waving her away*] No interruption, no delay. Dance! [*Fourth Mask stands motionless.*] Why don't you leap in the air? Have you never heard of Dervishes? Dancing-men. Men while they dance, corpses when they cease. Death and dancing—signposts on the road of life. And between them— [*The Salvation Lass enters.*] Oh, Halleluja!

SALVATION LASS The War Cry!

CASHIER I know. Ten pfennigs. [*Salvation Lass holds out her box.*] When do you expect me to jump into your box?

SALVATION LASS The War Cry!

CASHIER I suppose you do expect it?

SALVATION LASS Ten pfennigs.

CASHIER When will it be?

SALVATION LASS Ten pfennigs.

CASHIER So you mean to hang on to my coat-tails, do you? [*Salvation Lass shakes her box.*] I'll shake you off! [*Salvation Lass shakes box. To Mask*] Dance!

SALVATION LASS Oh!

[*Exit. Fourth Mask comes to table.*]

CASHIER Why were you sitting in a corner of the ballroom, instead of dancing in the middle of the floor? That made me look at you. All the others went whirling by, and you were motionless. Why do you wear a long cloak, when they are dressed like slender boys?

FOURTH MASK I don't dance.

CASHIER You don't dance like the others.

FOURTH MASK I can't dance.

CASHIER Not to music, perhaps; not keeping time. You're right! that's too slow. But you can do other dances. You hide something under your cloak—your own particular spring, not to be cramped by step and measure! You have a quicker movement—a nimbler leap. [*Pushing everything off the table*] Here's your stage. Jump onto it. A boundless riot in this narrow circle. Jump now. One bound from the carpet. One effortless leap—on the springs that are rooted in your joints. Jump. Put spurs to your heels. Arch your knees. Let your dress float free over the dancing limbs!

FOURTH MASK [*sits on the edge of the table*] I can't dance.

CASHIER You arouse my curiosity. Do you know what price I can pay? [*Showing her a roll of bank notes*] All that!

FOURTH MASK [*takes his hand and passes it down her leg*] You see—I can't.

CASHIER [*leaping to his feet*] A wooden leg! [*He seizes a champagne cooler and upsets it over her.*] I'll water it for you! We'll make the buds sprout!

FOURTH MASK I'll teach you a lesson.

CASHIER I'm out to learn!

FOURTH MASK Just wait!

[*Exit. Cashier puts a bank note on the table, takes cloak and stick. Exit. Guests in evening dress enter.*]

FIRST GUEST Where is the fellow?

SECOND GUEST Let's have a closer look at him.

FIRST GUEST A blackguard who entices away our girls—

SECOND GUEST Stuffs them with caviar—

THIRD GUEST Drenches them in champagne—

SECOND GUEST And then insults them!

FIRST GUEST We'll find out his price—

SECOND GUEST Where is he?

THIRD GUEST Given us the slip!

FIRST GUEST He smelt trouble!

SECOND GUEST The place was too hot for him.

THIRD GUEST [*finding the bank note*] A thousand!

SECOND GUEST Good God!

FIRST GUEST He must stink of money.

SECOND GUEST That's to pay the bill.

THIRD GUEST He's bolted. We'll do a vanishing trick too. [*He pockets the money.*]

FIRST GUEST That's the indemnity for our girls.

SECOND GUEST Now let's give them the slip.

THIRD GUEST They're all drunk.

FIRST GUEST They'll only dirty our shirt-fronts for us.

SECOND GUEST Let's go to the district for a week.

THIRD GUEST Bravo! While the money lasts! Look out, here comes the waiter!

[*Waiter, entering with full tray, halts dismayed.*]

FIRST GUEST Are you looking for anyone?

SECOND GUEST You might find him under the table.

[*Laughter*]

WAITER [*in an outburst*] The champagne—the supper—the private room—nothing paid for. Five bottles of Pommery, two portions of caviar, two special suppers—I have to stand for everything. I've a wife and children. I've been four months out of a place, on account of a weak chest. You won't see me ruined, gentlemen?

THIRD GUEST What has your chest to do with us? We all have wives and children.

SECOND GUEST Did we do you? What are you talking about?

FIRST GUEST What sort of a place is this? Where are we? It's a common den of swindlers. And you lure people into a place like this? We're respectable people who pay for their drinks. Eh! What! Eh!

THIRD GUEST [*after changing the door key to the outer side*] Look under the table, there. Now we've paid you, too!

[*He gives the Waiter, who turns round, a push which sends him sprawling. Waiter staggers, falls. Gentlemen exeunt.*]

WAITER [*rises, runs to the door, finds it locked; beating his fists on the panels*] Let me out! Let me out! You needn't pay me! I'm going—into the river!

SCENE SEVEN

Salvation Army hall, seen in depth. The background is formed by a black curtain. In front of this stands the low platform on which is the penitent form.

In the body of the hall, the benches are crowded. A great hanging lamp, with a tangle of wires for electric lighting, is above the audience. In the foreground on the left, is the entrance. Music: "Jesus Lover of My Soul," played on an organ and sung by the audience. From a corner, applause and laughter centering in one man. Salvation Lass goes to this corner and sits near the disturber. She takes his hand in hers and whispers to him.

VOICE [*from the other side*] Move up closer. Be careful, Bill! Ha, ha! Move there!
[*Salvation Lass goes to the speaker, a young workman.*]

WORKMAN What are you after?

SALVATION LASS [*looks at him, shaking her head gravely*] Merriment.

OFFICER [*woman of thirty, coming to the front of the platform*] I've a question to ask you all. [*Some cry, "Hush" or whistle for silence. Others shout: "Speech!" "None of your jaw!" "Music!" Voices are heard: "Begin!" "Stop!"*]

OFFICER Tell me . . . why are you sitting crowded there?

VOICE Why not?

OFFICER You're packed like herrings in a barrel. You're fighting for places . . . shoving one another off the forms. Yet one bench stands empty.

VOICE Nothing doing!

OFFICER Why do you sit squeezing and crowding there? Can't you see it's a nasty habit? Who knows his next-door neighbor? You rub shoulders with him, you press your knees against his, and for all you know he may be rotting. You look into his face—and perhaps his mind is full of murderous thoughts. I know there are sick men and criminals in this hall. So I give you warning! Mind your next-door neighbor! Beware of him! Those benches groan under sick men and criminals!

WOMAN'S VOICE Next to me?

SECOND VOICE Or me?

OFFICER I give you this word of advice; steer clear of your neighbor! In this asphalt city, disease and crime are everywhere. Which of you is without a scab? Your skin may be smooth and white, but your looks give you away. You have no eyes to see, but your eyes are wide open to betray you. You haven't escaped the great plague; the germs are too powerful. You've been sitting too long near bad neighbors. Come up here, come away from those benches if you would not be as your neighbors are in this city of asphalt. This is the last warning. Repent. Repent. Come up here, come to the penitent form. Come to the penitent form, come to the penitent form.
[*Music, "Jesus Lover of My Soul." Salvation Lass leads in Cashier, in evening dress, who arouses some notice. Salvation Lass finds Cashier a place among the crowd, stands next to him and explains the procedure. Cashier looks around him amused. Music ceases, ironical applause.*]

OFFICER [*coming forward again*] One of our comrades will tell you how he found his way to the penitent bench.
[*First Soldier of Salvation Army, a young man, steps onto the platform.*]

VOICE So that's the mug!
[*Some laughter*]

FIRST SOLDIER I want to tell you of my sin. I led a life without giving a thought to my soul. I cared only for my body. I built up my body like a strong wall; the soul was quite hidden behind it. I sought for glory with my body, and made broader the shadow in which my soul withered away. My sin was sport. I practiced it without a moment's pause; vain of the quickness of my feet on the pedals; and the ring of the applause among the spectators. I

GEORG KAISER

sent out many a challenge; I won many a prize. My name was printed on every billboard; my picture was in all the papers. I was in the running for the world championship. . . . At last my soul spoke to me. Its patience was ended. I met with an accident. The injury was not fatal. My soul wanted to leave me time for repentance. My soul left me strength enough to rise from those benches where you sit, and to climb up here to the penitent form. There my soul could speak to me in peace. What it told me I can't tell you now. It's all too wonderful, and my words are too weak to describe it. You must come yourselves, and hear the voice speak within you!

[*He steps in. A man laughs obscenely.*]

[*Several cry* "Hush!"]

SALVATION LASS [*to Cashier, in a low voice*]   Do you hear him?

CASHIER   Let me alone.

[*Music plays and ceases.*]

OFFICER [*coming forward*].   You've heard our comrade's testimony. Can you win anything nobler than your own soul? And it's quite easy, for the soul is there within you. You've only to give it peace . . . once, just once. The soul wants to sit with you for one quiet hour. Its favorite seat is on this bench. There must be one among you who sinned like our comrade here. Our comrade will help him. The way has been opened up. So come. Come to the penitent bench. Come to the penitent bench. Come to the penitent bench.

[*Silence. The First Penitent, a young man of powerful build, with one arm in a sling, rises in a corner of the hall and makes his way through the crowd, smiling nervously. He mounts the platform. A man laughs obscenely. Another voice is heard, asking indignantly, "Where is that dirty lout?" The man rises abashed and makes his way toward the door. Others cry, "That's the fellow!" Salvation Lass hurries to him and leads him back to his place. A voice says facetiously, "Oh, let me go, Angelina!" Still others are heard crying "Bravo!"*]

FIRST PENITENT [*on the platform*].   In this city of asphalt there's a hall. Inside the hall is a cycle-track. This was my sin. I was a rider too. I was a rider in the relay races this week. On the second night I met with a collision. I was thrown; my arm was broken. The races are hurrying on, but I am at rest. All my life I have been riding without a thought. Now, I want to think of everything. [*Loudly*] I want to think of my sins at the penitent bench.

[*Led by a Soldier, he sinks onto the bench; Soldier remains at his side.*]

OFFICER   A soul has been won!

[*Music plays and ceases.*]

SALVATION LASS [*to Cashier*]   Do you see him?

CASHIER   My affair. My affair.

SALVATION LASS   What are you muttering?

CASHIER   The relay races.

SALVATION LASS   Are you ready?

CASHIER   Hold your tongue.

OFFICER [*stepping forward*]   Another comrade will testify.

[*A man hisses.*]

OTHERS   Be quiet there!

SECOND SOLDIER [*girl mounts the platform*]   Whose sin is my sin? I'll tell you of my sin without shame. I had a wretched home, if you could call it a home. The man, a drunkard, was not my father. The woman—who was my mother—went with smart gentlemen. She gave me all the money I wanted; her bully gave me all the blows—I didn't want. [*Laughter.*] No one thought of me; least of all did I think of myself. So I became a lost woman. I was blind in those days. I couldn't see that the miserable life at home was only meant to make me think of my soul and dedicate myself to its salvation. One night I learned the truth. I had a gentleman with me, and he asked me to darken the room. I turned out the gas, though I wasn't used to such ways. Presently I understood why he had asked for me; for I realized that I had with me only the trunk of a man whose legs had been cut off. He didn't want me to know that he had wooden legs, and that he had taken them off in the dark. Then horror took hold of me, and wouldn't let me go. I began to hate my body; it was only my soul that I could love. And now this soul of mine is my delight. It's so perfect, so beautiful; it's the bonniest thing I know. I know too much of it to tell you here. If you ask your souls, they'll tell you all—all! [*She steps down. Silence.*]

From Morn to Midnight

OFFICER [*coming forward*] You've heard our sister testify. Her soul offered itself, and she did not refuse. Now she tells you her story with joyful lips. Isn't a soul offering itself now, at this moment, to one of you? Let it come closer. Let it speak; here on this bench it will be undisturbed. Come to the penitent bench. Come to the penitent bench.

[*Movement in the hall. Some turn round.*]

SECOND PENITENT [*elderly prostitute, begins to speak as she comes forward*] What do you think of me, ladies and gentlemen? I was just tired to death of streetwalking, and dropped in by chance for a rest. I'm not shy—oh, dear no! I don't know this hall; it's my first time here. Just dropped in by chance, as you might say. [*Speaking from the platform*] But you make a great mistake, ladies and gentlemen, if you think I should wait to be asked a second time! Not this child, thank you—oh, dear no! Take a good look at me, from tip to toe; it's your last chance; enjoy the treat while you can! It's quite all right; never mind me; I'm not a bit shy; look me up and down. Thank you, my soul's not for disposal. I've never sold that. You could offer me as much as you pleased, but my soul was always my own. I'm obliged to you for your compliments, ladies and gentlemen. You won't run up against me in the streets again. I've got no time to spare for you. My soul leaves me no peace.

[*A Soldier leads her to the penitent form.*]

OFFICER A soul has been won!

[*Music. Jubilation of the Soldiers. Music ceases.*]

SALVATION LASS [*to Cashier*] Do you hear all?

CASHIER That's my affair. My affair.

SALVATION LASS What are you muttering about?

CASHIER The wooden leg. The wooden leg.

SALVATION LASS Are you ready?

CASHIER Not yet. Not yet.

[*A man stands upright in the middle of the hall, saying, "Tell me my sin. I want to hear my sin!"*]

OFFICER [*coming forward*] Our comrade here will tell you.

[*Voices excitedly call out "Sit down!" "Keep quiet; give him a chance."*]

THIRD SOLDIER [*elderly man*] Let me tell you my story. It's an everyday story.

VOICE Then why tell it?

THIRD SOLDIER That's how it came to be my sin. I had a snug home, a contented family, a comfortable job. Everything was just—everyday. In the evening, when I sat smoking my pipe at the table, under the lamp, with my wife and children round about me, I felt satisfied enough. I never felt the need of a change. Yet the change came, I forgot what started it; perhaps I never knew. The soul knocks quietly at your door. It knows the right hour and uses it.

SECOND PENITENT Halleluja.

THIRD SOLDIER However that might be, I couldn't pass the warning by. I stood out at first in a sluggish sort of way, but the soul was stronger. More and more I felt its power. All my born days I'd been set upon comfort; now I knew that nothing could satisfy me fully but the soul.

SOLDIERS Halleluja.

THIRD SOLDIER I don't look for comfort any longer at the table under the lamp, with a pipe in my mouth; I find it here alone at the penitent bench. That's my everyday story.

[*He stands back. Music plays and is interrupted by Third Penitent.*]

THIRD PENITENT [*elbowing his way up*] My sin! My sin! [*From the platform*] I'm the father of a family!

VOICE Congratulations!

THIRD PENITENT I have two daughters. I have a wife. My mother is still with us. We live in four rooms. It's quite snug and cozy in our house. One of my daughters plays the piano, the other does embroideries. My wife cooks. My old mother waters the geraniums in the window-boxes. It's cozy in our house. Coziness itself. It's fine in our house. It's grand . . . first-rate . . . it's a model—a pattern of a home. [*With a change of voice*] Our house is loathsome . . . horrible . . . horrible . . . mean . . . paltry through and through. It stinks of paltriness in every room; with the piano-playing, the cooking, the embroidery, the watering-pots. [*Breaking out*] I have a soul! I have a soul! I have a soul! [*He stumbles to the penitent bench.*]

SOLDIERS Halleluja.

OFFICER A soul has been won!

SALVATION LASS [to Cashier] Do you see him?

CASHIER My daughters. My wife. My mother.

SALVATION LASS What do you keep mumbling?

CASHIER My affair. My affair.

SALVATION LASS Are you ready?

CASHIER Not yet. Not yet.

[Jubilant music. Loud uproar in the hall.]

[A man stands upright, stretching out his hands, saying, "What's my sin? What's my sin? I want to know my sin. Tell me my sin."]

OFFICER [coming forward] Our comrade will tell you.

[Deep silence]

FOURTH SOLDIER [middle-aged, comes forward] My soul had a hard struggle to win the victory. It had to take me by the throat and shake me like a rat. It was rougher still with me. It sent me to jail. I'd stolen the money that was entrusted to me; I'd absconded with a big sum. They caught me; I was tried and sentenced. In my prison cell I found the rest my soul had been looking for. At the last it could speak to me in peace. At last I could hear its voice. Those days in the lonely cell became the happiest of my life. When my time was finished I could not part from my soul.

SOLDIERS Halleluja.

FOURTH SOLDIER I looked for a quiet place where we two could meet. I found it here on the penitent form; I find it here still each evening that I feel the need of a happy hour! [Stands aside.]

OFFICER [coming forward] Our comrade has told you of his happy hours at the penitent form. Who is there among you who wants to escape from this sin? Here he will find peace! Come to the penitent bench!

[A man stands up shouting and gesticulating, "Nobody's sin! That's nobody's sin! I want to hear mine! My sin! My sin!" Many join in: "My sin! My sin! My sin!"]

CASHIER My sin!

SALVATION LASS [above the uproar] What are you shouting?

CASHIER The bank. The money.

SALVATION LASS [shaking him] Are you ready?

CASHIER Yes, now I'm ready!

SALVATION LASS [taking his arm] I'll lead you up there. I'll stand by you—always at your side. [Turning to the crowd, ecstatically] A soul is going to speak. I looked for this soul. I found this soul! [The tumult ebbs into a quiet hum.]

CASHIER [on the platform, Salvation Lass by his side] I've been on the road since this morning. I was driven out on this search. There was no chance of turning back. The earth gave way behind me, all bridges were broken. I had to march forward on a road that led me here. I won't weary you with the halting-places that wearied me. None of them were worth my break with the old life; none of them repaid me. I marched on with a searching eye, a sure touch, a clear head. I passed them all by, stage after stage; they dwindled and vanished in the distance. It wasn't this, it wasn't that, or the next—or the fourth or the fifth! What is the goal, what is the prize, that's worth the whole stake? This hall, humming with crowded benches, ringing with melody! This hall! Here, from bench to bench, the spirit thunders fulfillment! Here glow the twin crucibles; confession and repentance! Molten and free from dross, the soul stands like a glittering tower, strong and bright. You cry fulfillment for these benches. [Pause] I'll tell you my story.

SALVATION LASS Speak, I'm with you. I'll stand by you.

CASHIER I've been all day on the road. I confess; I'm a bank cashier. I embezzled the money that was entrusted me. A good round sum: sixty thousand marks! I fled with it into your city of asphalt. By this time, they're on my track; perhaps they've offered a big reward. I'm not in hiding any more. I confess! You can buy nothing worth having, even with all the money of all the banks in the world. You get less than you pay, every time. The more you spend, the less the goods are worth. The money corrupts them: the money veils the truth. Money's the meanest of the paltry swindles in this world! [Pulling rolls of bank notes out of his breast pocket] This hall is a burning oven; it glows with your contempt for all mean things. I throw the money to you; it shall be torn and stamped under foot. So much less deceit in the world! So much trash consumed. I'll go through your benches and give myself up to the first policeman; after confession comes atonement. So the cup is filled!

[*With gloved hands he scatters bank notes broadcast into the hall. The money flutters down; all hands are stretched upward; a scrimmage ensues. The crowd is tangled into a fighting skein. The Soldiers leap from the platform; benches are overturned, blows of fisticuffs resound above the shouting. At last, the cramped mass rolls to the door and out into the street. The Salvation Lass, who has taken no part in the struggle, stands alone on the steps.*]

CASHIER [*smiling at her*] You are standing by me. You are with me still! [*Picking up an abandoned drum and a stick*] On we go. [*Roll of drum*] The crowd is left behind. [*Roll of drum*] The yelping pack outrun. Vast emptiness. Elbow room! Room! Room! Room! [*Drum*] A maid remains . . . upright, steadfast! Maiden and man. The old garden is reopened. The sky is clear. A voice cries from the silent tree tops. It is well. [*Drum*] Maiden and man . . . eternal constancy. Maiden and man . . . fullness in the void. Maiden and man . . . the beginning and the end. Maiden and man . . . the seed and the flower. Maiden and man . . . sense and aim and goal!

[*Rapid drumtaps, then a long roll. Salvation Lass draws back to the door, and slips out. Cashier beats a tattoo.*]

SALVATION LASS [*throws the door open; to Policeman*] There he is! I've shown him to you! I've earned the reward.

CASHIER [*letting fall the drumstick in the middle of a beat*] Here above you, I stand. Two are too many. Space holds but one. Space is loneliness. Loneliness is space. Coldness is sunshine. Sunshine is coldness. Fever heat burns you. Fever heat freezes you. Fields are deserted. Ice

overgrows them. Who can escape? Where is the door?

POLICEMAN Is this the only entrance? [*Salvation Lass nods. Cashier feels in his pocket.*]

POLICEMAN He's got a hand in his pocket. Switch off that light. We're a target for him!

[*Salvation Lass obeys. All the lights of the hanging lamp are put out. Lights from the left illuminate the tangle of wires, forming a skeleton in outline.*]

CASHIER [*feeling with his left hand in his breast pocket, grasps with his right a trumpet, and blows a fanfare toward the lamp*] Ah!—Discovered. Scorned in the snow this morning—welcomed now in the tangled wires. I salute you. [*Trumpet*] The road is behind me. Panting, I climb the steep curves that lead upward. My forces are spent. I've spared myself nothing. I've made the path hard, where it might have been easy. This morning in the snow when we met, you and I, you should have been more pressing in your invitation. One spark of enlightenment would have helped me and spared me all trouble. It doesn't take much of a brain to see that— Why did I hesitate? Why take the road? Whither am I bound? From first to last you sit there, naked bone. From morn to midnight, I rage in a circle . . . and now your beckoning finger points the way . . . whither? [*He shoots the answer into his breast.*]

POLICEMAN Switch on the light.

[*Salvation Lass does so. The Cashier has fallen back, with arms outstretched, tumbling headlong down the steps. His husky gasp is like an "Ecce," his heavy sigh is like a "Homo." One second later all the lamps explode with a loud report.*]

POLICEMAN There must be a short circuit in the main.

[*Darkness.*]

THE THEATER in the twentieth century has been much concerned with dramas of interiority. The movement that made this concern its special aim was Expressionism. Its first spokesman was Georg Kaiser.

Somehow, the Expressionists believed, the finite individual must discover his relation to this uncharted world of infinite reality, and then there would be a New Man and a New Era. They had varying conceptions of this New Dawn in which the individual would accept his cosmic responsibility. These ranged from a vague doctrine of personal suffering for the salvation of mankind and of self-sacrifice as an atonement for the past to the transformation of the world by a political revolution in which the masses should be converted from their materialism and society be recreated in the idea of love, brotherhood, and humanity. Their plays were alternatively "Ich-Dramas" ("I-plays"), dealing with the liberation of the individual soul, or pacifist, revolutionary, often communistic intuitions of a rebirth of the world. To the Expressionists the theatre is necessarily either a tribune for the propagation of spiritual ideas or a temple for the sharing of a mystical experience. As with the Hebrew prophets, their eyes were full of dreams and bright visions. It is all highly emotional, ecstatic—the last a favourite word of the Expressionists.

The creative task of the Expressionist dramatist was therefore not to construct a play in the accepted sense of the word, but to communicate to an audience these ecstatic and intuitive visions for which he generally abandoned the traditional nomenclature of the drama, giving them explanatory sub-titles, such as *Vision, Dramatic, Fantasy, Ecstatic.* As from the trance-like nature of their conception they were, as our dreams are, interfused with unreal or super-real elements, they could not obviously be presented in the conventional realistic form. A new form had to be invented. "Expressionism," said Georg Kaiser, "is not interested in depicting life, but ideas must be given external form. We have left the sphere of contemplation, and have entered the higher sphere of playing with ideas." But on the stage, ideas, abstractions, must be personified. So we get symbolic figures: Nightmare, Five Gentlemen in Black, the Veiled Figure of a Woman, symbolising human fear, the forces of capitalism, the suffering caused by war. The characters of the play had to be de-individualized; they became the Mother, the Woman, the Nameless One, or were dissolved in choral groups of Workers, Soldiers, Prisoners. A vision has no progressive plot, no conflict, no essential drama. It can only be presented in a series of often unrelated tableaux, with no unity except the unity of idea. . . .

The average playgoer, accustomed to find his interest in the action of recognizable individual characters, verisimilitude, and psychological motivation of the action, is inclined to dismiss impatiently as extravagant, highbrow nonsense these puzzling and often incomprehensible fantasies: plays written half in verse and half in prose, with lyrical soliloquies and sometimes almost wordless pantomime; plays with scenes laid in cemeteries and prison-yards and factories, in Hell or at the Last Judgment; with their symbolic choruses of bankers, prostitutes, and soldiers, and all the paraphernalia of apparitions, visionary voices, and veiled and headless figures. They seem as absurdly pretentious as the paintings of those contemporary artists who pasted tram-tickets and trouser-buttons on their bewildering, preposterous canvases. But Expressionism held the stage in Germany for fourteen years, and all the major dramatists of other countries have been in some degree affected by it.

But Expressionism is not for the average playgoer. We cannot begin to appreciate or understand it until we have revised our conception of what constitutes a play. Expressionist plays are not *Schauspiele* (spectacles) but *Denkspiele* (plays of ideas). Georg Kaiser defined their object thus: "to lead the audience on, by means of a grudging concession to the delight of the eye, to a joyous revelling in thought" (*aus karger Schaulust in glueckvolle Denklust einziehen*). Even here we must alter our conception of the play of ideas connected in our minds with the plays of Ibsen or Bernard Shaw. There is no logic in this drama. We are not asked to contemplate the outer world of perception, but an inner, psychical world, the world of our dreams and our desires, a world just as important, just as much a part of reality as what is immediate and actual. We are asked to think and feel about things that exist only in the mind. Our attitude must not be cerebral, but a "raptness of spirit" (*Beseeltheit*), says Paul Kornfeld: "Let us leave it to the working day to have character; let us be nothing but soul."

This drama is of necessity experimental and incomplete. It records experiences in the exploration of that greatest of mysteries, the human mind, discoveries which throw some light on our true inner nature. Being experimental, it requires new forms. The difficulty of the artist who transcends reality has always been to express his irrational ideas by means of recognizable conventions. The Expressionists found necessary a complete break with the tradition of realistic presentation. [Lynton Hudson, *Life and The Theatre*, Roy Publishers, New York, 1954, pp. 64–68.]

The special mode of Expressionism was generalization, of setting, of society, of character. Thus Kaiser's people are—and must be— types or symbols more than individuals.

In general the expressionist dramatists seized upon and developed further the kind of dramatic technique in which diverse experiments had already been made by Hauptmann, Wedekind, and Strindberg. Short scenes took the place of longer acts; dialogue was made abrupt and given a staccato effect; symbolic (almost morality-type) forms were substituted for "real" characters; realistic scenery was abandoned, and in its place the use of light was freely substituted; frequently choral, or mass, effects were preferred to the employment of single figures, or else single figures were elevated into positions where they became representative of forces larger than themselves.

Fundamentally, what these men sought to do was to escape from the detailed exploration of the psyche and from the rounded, indirect methods implied in the entirety of neo-romantic endeavour, and to substitute therefor the typical representation of humanity along with a sharp, economic, straight-line effect. In method the expressionists are closely associated with the school of cubism, which, born at Paris in 1908, endeavoured to get beneath the curves of reality to express basic flat planes.

The development of the new style is intimately bound up with a realization of the mechanistic nature of our civilization. For the neo-romanticist there is always the desire to escape from the machine—escape into a world inhabited by Pelléas and Mélisande, escape into the realm of vague emotional symbols, escape into the misty reaches of the human soul. In effect, the mechanistic is here deliberately avoided and, if possible, forgotten. The true expressionist takes a different line. Whether he shares [the Italian futurist] Marinetti's enthusiasm for the machine or whether he stands aghast at the way in which the machine is gradually imposing itself on the living organism, he accepts its existence and endeavours to deal boldly with the problems it raises. The expressionist often is a tortured, sometimes a desperate soul, but he does not wish to abnegate the world he lives in.

Although Kaiser makes free use of effects which would have been styled melodramatic had they appeared in plays of earlier vintage, there does exist in him a kind of tormented daimonic force. . . . In *From Morn to Midnight* he takes as central figure a petty bank-clerk, but in true expressionistic manner makes this character a

GEORG KAISER

symbol of a large class rather than an individual. Stealing some of his employers' money, the clerk is shown, in violently anti-realistic scenes, passing through a series of adventures in which his dreams of a fine and exciting life gradually crumble or are rudely shattered. All the persons he meets are symbols or type-representations of human groups: to condemn the author for failing to draw interesting individual characters here is absurd, since his central aim is to avoid that method of dramatic composition and to achieve, by other means, a larger concept than could otherwise be attained. We may legitimately condemn the object: we have no right to seek in such a work something which the playwright specifically sought to exclude. [Allardyce Nicoll, *World Drama,* Harcourt, Brace, and Company, Inc., New York, n.d., pp. 795–797.]

Kaiser's expressionist dramas have something in common with the medieval Morality play: they are essentially dramas of sin and regeneration—though the regeneration may only be contemplated and may actually dissolve into disillusionment.

The initial impetus of the dramatic action originates in sexual desire; but almost at once the issues grow wider, and the sexual becomes only one aspect incidental to others. For the stress is now laid on the social background of the drama: the tension arises out of the friction between the individual and the whole of his environment, which Kaiser seeks to compress into seven loosely-connected scenes, whose only unity is the presence in each of the central figure, and the fact that each attempts to present in its barest essentials a particular but representative aspect of modern life.

From Morn to Midnight is Kaiser's first *Stations-drama,* depicting the stations of the martyrdom of modern man—a dramatic technique whose popularity with the Expressionist writers was due largely to Strindberg's use of it in *Till Damaskus* (*The Road to Damascus,* 1898). Here a highly-developed drama looks back to its medieval origins in the mystery and passion-play, where the figure of Christ unifies the various scenes of his suffering.

That Kaiser intends here to represent the fate of modern man, and not of one specific man, is clear from a glance at the dramatis personae: we find, for instance, Cashier; Mother; Lady; Gentlemen in Evening Dress; Salvation Lass and a host of other nameless figures, who bear only the label of their social function. This accepted expressionist device of typification is intended to strip from the drama all that is merely contingent, and to achieve a maximum concentration of significance. Thus the bank-clerk stands for any bank-clerk; indeed, for any man who is condemned by social conditions and his passive acceptance of them to the monotonous drudgery of competitive bread-winning. . . .

But Kaiser chooses a bank-clerk as his protagonist for a very good reason: his purpose, in part at least, is to demonstrate the social effect of money as an irritant to cupidity—and who could be more appropriate to this purpose than one whose livelihood depends upon the organization of the modern financial system? [B. J. Kenworthy, *Georg Kaiser,* Basil Blackwell & Mott, Ltd., Oxford, 1957, pp. 24–25.]

The clerk reaches the last stage of his progress in a Salvation Army hall, to which he is led by a girl who has made several appearances in the second part of the play, selling copies of the *War Cry.* From the assembled men and women a number of penitents come forward to confess their sins; and each sin forms a part of the clerk's own guilt, which is distributed among them—a practice often used by Expressionist dramatists to give concrete form to the complex inner life of their characters. But here, in the early years of Expressionism, this device is modified. An audience seeing *From Morn to Midnight* is aware of the circumstances of the clerk's guilt, and is therefore able to evaluate it objectively. This the clerk himself cannot do, for he is so consumed by a newly-released flood of passion, by an overwhelming sense of deprivation, that his judgment is essentially subjective; his demands upon society and the manner of his attempts to realize them, stamp him as an egoist. Kaiser, then, uses dramatic division as a means of showing the clerk to himself; his own guilt is borne in upon him; and, caught up in the emotional appeal of this display of public penitence, he at last finds what he was seeking: regeneration through *"Bekenntnis und Busse"* [confession and atonement].

He confesses his sins, even though he knows that a reward has been offered for his capture, and goes on to voice the conviction which the stations of his journey had brought him. He has conquered in himself the materialism of money, of which he had first been a slave and then a dupe. . . . Scattering the remainder of the stolen money in the hall, he prepares to deliver himself up to justice and retribution. His fellow-penitents, however, are unregenerate; they scramble for the money, while the girl who had conducted him here betrays him to the police, in order to earn the reward. The individual may be regenerated, but not the mass.

Over this final disillusionment of the clerk, the skeleton thrones again, now formed in the tangled wires of the chandelier; the mad circle in which he has rushed from morn till midnight closes. He shoots himself, sinking against the draperies of the hall. . . .

The New Man of Kaiser's dramas of regeneration has appeared. But his regeneration has been shortlived, for he had expected more than society would concede. . . . So sharp is the contradiction between the reality of experience and the ideal vision that it can be resolved only by the destruction of one or the other. It is the materially weaker that is destroyed with the clerk's suicide. Nothing but the symbol of his search for a better life survives at the end.

Not only the form, but also the inspiration of *From Morn to Midnight* is expressionistic. The vision before the writer remains ideal, and consequently impossible of realization in the material world; as far as any action of the clerk is concerned, the play is negative: some of the ills of society are diagnosed, but no specific is prescribed for their cure. The fruitful deed must be sought elsewhere. . . .

There was for many years a half-resolved conflict in Kaiser himself—between the observing, analysing critic and the visionary creative writer, between the classicist and the romantic, the admirer of Plato on the one hand and of Buechner, Kleist and Nietzsche on the other. . . .

Besides this acute awareness of a duality in life, he was filled with a sense of its insecurity: a trifling incident may bring momentous consequences, or a coincidence may determine a fate. These are the sources of Kaiser's thought and feeling—and an inner necessity compelled him to give them expression and form; and the natural vehicle for their immediate and concise formulation is the drama. Kaiser himself maintained that this medium permitted the presentation of abstract ideas in the most concrete and readily comprehensible way. [*Ibid.*, pp. 28–30.]

JEAN GIRAUDOUX

1882–1944

*When Jean Giraudoux describes the negotiations between Greeks
and Trojans to forestall a war in* Tiger at the Gates (*1935*), *he
writes as an expert. He was by profession a diplomat as well as a
playwright, novelist, essayist, and film writer. He served the French
government up until the year of his death. In his last government
post, he acted as minister of propaganda during World War II,
a suitably ironic role for a lifelong pacifist. But ironies would
never have fazed Giraudoux. His career as a dramatist was
compounded of conditions contrary to fact. His first play,* Siegfried
(*1928*), *based on a novel of his own, presents a Frenchman turned
into a German as a result of a war accident. In his second,*
Amphitryon 38 (*1929*), *Jupiter, the arch-philanderer, is persuaded
by a wily logic any diplomat would be bound to admire to forego
seduction in favor of friendship. In the most successful of his plays
to reach the American stage,* The Madwoman of Chaillot (*1943*),
*a young woman who is a dishwasher by profession discovers when
she falls in love that she adores not only life but death. In the
same play, folly is the exclusive province of those the world regards
as sane. By the same token, it is only the demonstrably eccentric,
if not insane, who offer wisdom to a sorely beset Paris and bring
something like peace to a city about to be destroyed by its financial
exploiters by consigning the villains to dissolution in the sewers
of the French metropolis. The sewers serve Giraudoux well as
surrogates for hell, even as in* The Trojan War Will Not Take
Place—*the original title of* Tiger at the Gates—*the Palace of Troy*

*and its environs serve as stand-in for Geneva, Locarno, and all
the other places in which the diplomats sat and talked and signed
pacts outlawing war between the end of World War I and the
beginning of World War II. With irony, with elegance, with every
sort of theatrical ease, Giraudoux invites the world to contemplate
its own fate, in terms mythological, universal, and quite
unmistakably true.*

Tiger at the Gates

A PLAY IN TWO ACTS

TRANSLATED BY CHRISTOPHER FRY

Characters

ANDROMACHE

CASSANDRA

LAUNDRESS

HECTOR

PARIS

FIRST OLD MAN

SECOND OLD MAN

PRIAM

DEMOKOS

HECUBA

MATHEMATICIAN

LADY IN WAITING

POLYXENE

HELEN

MESSENGER

TROILUS

ABNEOS

BUSIRIS

AJAX

ULYSSES

A TOPMAN

OLPIDES

SENATOR

SAILOR

PEACE

IRIS

The action takes place in and around the Palace of Troy just before the outbreak of the Trojan War.

Act One

Ramparts of the palace.

ANDROMACHE There's not going to be a Trojan War, Cassandra!

CASSANDRA I shall take that bet, Andromache.

ANDROMACHE The Greeks are quite right to protest. We are going to receive their ambassador very civilly. We shall wrap up his little Helen and give her back to him.

CASSANDRA We shall receive him atrociously.

We shall refuse to give Helen back. And there *will* be a Trojan War.

ANDROMACHE   Yes, if Hector were not here. But he is here, Cassandra, he is home again. You can hear the trumpets. At this moment he is marching into the city, victorious. And Hector will certainly have something to say. When he left, three months ago, he promised me this war would be the last.

CASSANDRA   It is the last. The next is still ahead of him.

ANDROMACHE   Doesn't it ever tire you to see and prophesy only disasters?

CASSANDRA   I see nothing. I prophesy nothing. All I ever do is to take account of two great stupidities: the stupidity of men, and the wild stupidity of the elements.

ANDROMACHE   Why should there be a war? Paris and Helen don't care for each other any longer.

CASSANDRA   Do you think it will matter? If Paris and Helen don't care for each other any longer? Has destiny ever been interested in whether things were still true or not?

ANDROMACHE   I don't know what destiny is.

CASSANDRA   I'll tell you. It is simply the relentless logic of each day we live.

ANDROMACHE   I don't understand abstractions.

CASSANDRA   Never mind. We can try a metaphor. Imagine a tiger. You can understand that? It's a nice, easy metaphor. A sleeping tiger.

ANDROMACHE   Let it sleep.

CASSANDRA   There's nothing I should like better. But certain cocksure statements have been prodding him out of his sleep. For some considerable time Troy has been full of them.

ANDROMACHE   Full of what?

CASSANDRA   Of cocksure statements, a confident belief that the world, and the supervision of the world, is the province of mankind in general, and Trojan men and women in particular.

ANDROMACHE   I don't follow you.

CASSANDRA   Hector at this very moment is marching into Troy?

ANDROMACHE   Yes. Hector at this very moment has come home to his wife.

CASSANDRA   And Hector's wife is going to have a child?

ANDROMACHE   Yes; I am going to have a child.

CASSANDRA   Don't you call these statements a little over-confident?

ANDROMACHE   Don't frighten me, Cassandra.

[*A young laundress goes past with an armful of linen.*]

LAUNDRESS   What a beautiful day, Miss!

CASSANDRA   Does it seem so indeed!

LAUNDRESS   It's the most beautiful Spring day Troy has seen this year. [*Exits.*]

CASSANDRA   Even the laundrymaid is confident!

ANDROMACHE   And so she should be, Cassandra. How can you talk of a war on day like this? Happiness is falling on us out of the sky.

CASSANDRA   Like a blanket of snow.

ANDROMACHE   And beauty, as well. Look at the sunshine. It is finding more mother-of-pearl on the rooftops of Troy than was ever dragged up from the bed of the sea. And do you hear the sound coming up from the fisherman's houses, and the movement of the trees, like the murmuring of sea shells? If ever there were a chance to see men finding a way to live in peace, it is today. To live in peace, in humility. And to be immortal.

CASSANDRA   Yes, I am sure those cripples who have been carried out to lie in their doorways feel how immortal they are.

ANDROMACHE   And to be good. Do you see that horseman, in the advance-guard, leaning from his saddle to stroke a cat on the battlements? Perhaps this is also going to be the first day of true fellowship between men and animals.

CASSANDRA   You talk too much. Destiny, the tiger, is getting restive, Andromache!

ANDROMACHE   Restive, maybe, in young girls looking for husbands; but not otherwise.

CASSANDRA   You are wrong. Hector has come home in triumph to the wife he adores. The tiger begins to rouse, and opens one eye. The incurable lie out on their benches in the sun and feel immortal. The tiger stretches himself. Today is the chance for peace to enthrone herself over all the world. The tiger licks his lips. And Andromache is going to have a son! And the horsemen have started leaning from their saddles to stroke tom-cats on the battlements! The tiger starts to prowl.

ANDROMACHE   Be quiet!

CASSANDRA He climbs noiselessly up the palace steps. He pushes open the doors with his snout. And here he is, here he is!

[Hector's voice: "Andromache!"]

ANDROMACHE You are lying! It is Hector!

CASSANDRA Whoever said it was not?

[Hector enters.]

ANDROMACHE Hector!

HECTOR Andromache! *[They embrace.]* And good morning to you, too, Cassandra. Ask Paris to come to me, if you will. As soon as he can. *[Cassandra lingers.]* Have you something to tell me?

ANDROMACHE Don't listen to her! Some catastrophe or other!

HECTOR Tell me.

CASSANDRA Your wife is going to have a child.

[Cassandra exits.] Hector takes Andromache in his arms, leads her to a stone bench, and sits beside her. There is a short pause.]

HECTOR Will it be a son or a daughter?

ANDROMACHE Which did you want to create when you called it into life?

HECTOR A thousand boys. A thousand girls.

ANDROMACHE Why? Because it would give you a thousand women to hold in your arms? You are going to be disappointed. It will be a son, one single son.

HECTOR That may very well be. Usually more boys than girls are born at the end of a war.

ANDROMACHE And before a war? Which, before a war?

HECTOR Forget wars, Andromache, even this war. It's over. It lost you a father and a brother, but it gave you back a husband.

ANDROMACHE It has been too kind. It may think better of it presently.

HECTOR Don't worry. We won't give it the chance. Directly I leave you I shall go into the courtyard, and formally close the Gates of War. They will never open again.

ANDROMACHE Close them, then. But they will open again.

HECTOR You can even tell me the day, perhaps?

ANDROMACHE I can even tell you the day: the day when the cornfields are heavy and golden, when the vines are stooping, ready for harvest, and every house is sheltering a contented couple.

HECTOR And peace, no doubt, at its very height?

ANDROMACHE Yes. And my son is strong and glowing with life.

HECTOR *[embracing her]* Perhaps your son will be a coward. That's one possible safeguard.

ANDROMACHE He won't be a coward. But perhaps I shall have cut off the index finger of his right hand.

HECTOR If every mother cut off her son's right-hand index finger, the armies of the world would fight without index fingers. And if they put out their eyes, the armies would be blind, but there would still be armies: blind armies groping to find the fatal place in the enemy's groin, or to get at his throat.

ANDROMACHE I would rather kill him.

HECTOR There's a truly maternal solution to war!

ANDROMACHE Don't laugh. I can still kill him before he is born.

HECTOR What? Do you mean never to see your son?

ANDROMACHE It is your son that interests me. Hector, it's because he is yours, because he is you, that I'm so afraid. You don't know how like you he is. Even in this no-man's-land where he is waiting, he has all those qualities you brought to this life we live together. He has your tenderness, your silences. If you love war, he will love it. Do you love war?

HECTOR Why ask such a question?

ANDROMACHE Admit, sometimes you love it.

HECTOR If a man can love what takes away hope, and happiness, and all those nearest to his heart.

ANDROMACHE And you know it can be so. Men do love it.

HECTOR If they let themselves be fooled by that little burst of divinity the gods give them at the moment of attack.

ANDROMACHE Ah, there, you see! At the moment of attack you feel like a god.

HECTOR More often not as much as a man. But sometimes, on certain mornings, you get up from the ground feeling lighter, astonished, altered. Your whole body, and the armour on your back, have a different weight, they seem to be

Tiger at the Gates

made of a different metal. You are invulnerable. A tenderness comes over you, submerging you, a kind of tenderness of battle: you are tender because you are pitiless; what, in fact, the tenderness of the gods must be. You advance towards the enemy slowly, crush a beetle crossing your path. You brush off the mosquito without hurting it. You never at any time had more respect for the life you meet on your way.

ANDROMACHE And then the enemy comes?

HECTOR Then the enemy comes, you can see him there, behind the swollen veins and the whites of his eyes, the helpless, willing little man of business, the well-meaning husband and son-in-law who likes to grow his own vegetables. You feel a sort of love for him. Then you kill him. Such is war.

ANDROMACHE All of them: you kill them all?

HECTOR This time we killed them all. Quite deliberately. They belonged to an incorrigibly warlike race, the reason why wars go on and multiply in Asia. Only one of them escaped.

ANDROMACHE In a thousand years time, there the warlike race will be again, descended from that one man. His escape made all that slaughter futile after all. My son is going to love war, just as you do.

HECTOR I think, now that I've lost my love for it, I hate it.

ANDROMACHE How do you come to hate what you once worshipped?

HECTOR You know what it's like when you find out a friend is a liar? Whatever he says, after that, sounds false, however true it may be. And strangely enough, war used to promise me many kinds of virtue: goodness, generosity, and a contempt for anything base and mean. I felt I owed it all my strength and zest for life, even my private happiness, you, Andromache. And until this last campaign there was no enemy I haven't loved. It's hard to explain how all the sounds of war combined to make me think it was something noble. The galloping of horse in the night, the clatter of bowls and dishes where the cooks were moving in and out of the firelight, the brush of silk and metal against your tent as the night patrol went past, and the cry of the falcon wheeling high above the sleeping army and their unsleeping captain: it all seemed then so right, marvellously right.

ANDROMACHE But not this time: this time war had no music for you?

HECTOR Why was that? Because I am older? Or was it just the kind of weariness with your job which, for instance, a carpenter will be suddenly seized by, with a table half finished, as I was seized one morning, standing over an adversary of my own age, about to put an end to him? Up to that time, a man I was going to kill had always seemed my direct opposite. This time I was kneeling on a mirror, the death I was going to give was a kind of suicide. But after that nothing remained of the perfect trumpet note of war. The spear as it slid against my shield rang suddenly false; so did the shock of the killed against the ground. The cries of the dying sounded false. I had even come to that.

ANDROMACHE But it all still sounded right for the rest of them.

HECTOR The rest of them heard it as I did. The army I brought back hates war.

ANDROMACHE An army with poor hearing.

HECTOR No. When we first came in sight of Troy, an hour ago, you can't imagine how everything in that moment sounded true for them. There wasn't a regiment which didn't halt, racked to the heart by this sense of returning music.

ANDROMACHE You haven't understood, this is where things are falser than anywhere. War is here, in Troy, Hector. That is what welcomed you at the gates.

HECTOR What do you mean?

ANDROMACHE You haven't heard that Paris has carried off Helen?

HECTOR They told me so. What else?

ANDROMACHE Did you know that the Greeks are demanding her back? And their ambassador arrives today? And if we don't give her up, it means war.

HECTOR Why shouldn't we give her up? I shall give her back to them myself.

ANDROMACHE Paris will never agree to it.

HECTOR Paris will agree, and very soon. Cassandra is bringing him to me.

ANDROMACHE But Paris can't agree. His honor, as you call it, won't let him. Nor his love either, he may tell you.

HECTOR Well, we shall see. Run and ask Priam if he will let me speak to him at once. And set your heart at rest. All the Trojans who have been fighting, or who can fight, are against a war.

ANDROMACHE There are still the others, remember.

[*As Andromache goes out, Cassandra enters with Paris.*]

CASSANDRA Here is Paris.

HECTOR Congratulations, Paris. I hear you have been very well occupied while we were away.

PARIS Not badly. Thank you.

HECTOR What is this story they tell me about Helen?

PARIS Helen is a very charming person. Isn't she, Cassandra?

CASSANDRA Fairly charming.

PARIS Why these reservations today? It was only yesterday you said you thought she was extremely pretty.

CASSANDRA She is extremely pretty, and fairly charming.

PARIS Hasn't she the ways of a young, gentle gazelle?

CASSANDRA No.

PARIS But you were the one who first said she was like a gazelle.

CASSANDRA I made a mistake. Since then I have seen a gazelle again.

HECTOR To hell with gazelles! Doesn't she look any more like a woman than that?

PARIS She isn't the type of woman we know here, obviously.

CASSANDRA What is the type of woman we know here?

PARIS Your type, my dear sister. The fearfully unremote sort of woman.

CASSANDRA When your Greek makes love she is a long way off, I suppose?

PARIS You know perfectly well what I'm trying to say. I have had enough of Asiatic women. They hold you in their arms as though they were glued there, their kisses are like battering-rams, their words chew right into you. The more they undress the more elaborate they seem, until when they're naked they are more overdressed than ever. And they paint their faces to look as though they mean to imprint themselves on you. And they do imprint themselves on you. In short, you are definitely *with* them. But Helen is far away from me, even held in my arms.

HECTOR Very interesting! But, one wonders, is it really worth a war, to allow Paris to make love at a distance?

CASSANDRA With distance. He loves women to be distant but right under his nose.

PARIS To have Helen with you not with you is worth anything in the world.

HECTOR How did you fetch her away? Willingly, or did you compel her?

PARIS Listen, Hector! You know women as well as I do. They are only willing when you compel them, but after that they're as enthusiastic as you are.

HECTOR On horseback? I suppose. In the usual style of seducers? Leaving a heap of manure under the windows.

PARIS Is this a court of enquiry?

HECTOR Yes, it is. Try for once to answer precisely and accurately. Have you insulted her husband's house, or the Greek earth?

PARIS The Greek water, a little. She was bathing.

HECTOR You haven't disfigured the walls of the palace with offensive drawings, as you usually do? You didn't shout to the echoes any word which they would at once repeat to the betrayed husband?

PARIS No. Menelaus was naked on the river bank, busy removing a crab from his big toe. He watched my boat sail past as if the wind were carrying his clothes away.

HECTOR Looking furious?

PARIS The face of a king being nipped by a crab isn't likely to look beatific.

HECTOR No onlookers?

PARIS My crew.

HECTOR Perfect!

PARIS Why perfect? What are you getting at?

HECTOR I say perfect, because you have done nothing irrevocable. In other words: she was undressed, so neither her clothes nor her belongings have been insulted. Nothing except her body, which is negligible. I've enough acquaintance with the Greeks to know they will concoct a divine adventure out of it, to their own glory, the story of this little Greek queen who goes down into the sea, and quietly comes up again a few months later, with a look on her face of perfect innocence.

CASSANDRA We can be quite sure of the look on her face.

PARIS You think that I'm going to take Helen back to Menelaus?

HECTOR We don't ask so much of you, or of her. The Greek ambassador will take care of it. He will put her back in the sea himself, like a gardener planting waterlilies, at a particular chosen spot. You will give her into his hands this evening.

PARIS I don't know whether you are allowing yourself to notice how monstrous you are being, to suppose that a man who has the prospect of a night with Helen will agree to giving it up.

CASSANDRA You still have an afternoon with Helen. Surely that's more Greek?

HECTOR Don't be obstinate. We know you of old. This isn't the first separation you've accepted.

PARIS My dear Hector, that's true enough. Up to now I have always accepted separations fairly cheerfully. Parting from a woman, however well you love her, induces a most pleasant state of mind, which I know how to value as well as anybody. You come out of her arms and take your first lonely walk through the town, and, the first little dressmaker you meet, you notice with a shock of surprise how fresh and unconcerned she looks, after that last sight you have had of the dear face you parted from, her nose red with weeping. Because you have come away from such broken, despairing farewells, when you hear the laundry-girls and the fruit-sellers laughing their heads off, more than make up for whatever you've lost in the parting. By losing one person your life has become entirely repeopled. All the women in the world have been created for you afresh. Yes, you're quite right: when a love-affair is broken off it reaches its highest point of exaltation. Which is why I shall never be parted from Helen, because with Helen I feel as though I had broken with every other woman in the world, and that gives me the sensation of being free a thousand times over instead of once.

HECTOR Because she doesn't love you. Everything you say proves it.

PARIS If you like. But, if I had to choose one out of all the possible ways of passion, I would choose the way Helen doesn't love me.

HECTOR I'm extremely sorry. But you will give her up.

PARIS You are not the master here.

HECTOR I am your elder brother, and the future master.

PARIS Then order me about in the future. For the present, I obey my father.

HECTOR That's all I want! You're willing that we should put this to Priam and accept his judgment?

PARIS Perfectly willing.

HECTOR On your solemn word? We both swear to accept that?

CASSANDRA Mind what you're doing, Hector! Priam is mad for Helen. He would rather give up his daughters.

HECTOR What nonsense is this?

PARIS For once she is telling the truth about the present instead of the future.

CASSANDRA And all our brothers, and all our uncles, and all our great-great uncles! Helen has a guard-of-honor which includes every old man in the city. Look there. It is time for her walk. Do you see, there's a fringe of white beards draped all along the battlements?

HECTOR A beautiful sight. The beards are white, and the faces red.

CASSANDRA Yes; it's the blood pressure. They should be waiting at the Scamander Gate, to welcome the victorious troops. But no; they are all at the Sceean Gate, waiting for Helen.

HECTOR Look at them, all leaning forward as one man, like storks when they see a rat going by.

CASSANDRA The rat is Helen.

PARIS Is it?

CASSANDRA There she is: on the second terrace, standing to adjust her sandal, and giving careful thought to the crossing of her legs.

HECTOR Incredible. All the old men of Troy are there looking down at her.

CASSANDRA   Not all. There are certain clever-heads looking up at her.

[Cries offstage: "Long live Beauty!"]

HECTOR   What are they shouting?

PARIS   They're shouting "Long live Beauty!"

CASSANDRA   I quite agree with them, if they mean that they themselves should die as quickly as possible.

[Cries offstage: "Long live Venus!"]

HECTOR   And what now?

CASSANDRA   "Long live Venus." They are shouting only words without R's in them because of their lack of teeth. At least they imagine they're shouting, though, as you can hear, all they are doing is simply increasing a mumble to its highest power.

HECTOR   What has Venus to do with it?

CASSANDRA   They imagine it was Venus who brought Helen and Paris together.

HECTOR   Very likely; whenever she's at a loss for something to do, she throws as many people as possible into a different pair of arms. It's becoming a nervous habit with her. I'm surprised at Paris being taken in by it.

PARIS   Stop playing the older brother.

[Two old men enter.]

FIRST OLD MAN   Down there we see her better.

SECOND OLD MAN   We had a very good view.

FIRST OLD MAN   But she can hear us better from up here. Come on. One, two, three!

BOTH   Long live Helen!

SECOND OLD MAN   It's a little tiring, at our age, to have to climb up and down these impossible steps all the time, according to whether we want to look at her or to cheer her.

FIRST OLD MAN   Would you like us to alternate? One day we will cheer her? Another day we will look at her?

SECOND OLD MAN   You are mad! One day without looking at Helen, indeed! Goodness me, think what we've seen of her today! One, two, three!

BOTH   Long live Helen!

FIRST OLD MAN   And now down we go again!

[They run off.]

CASSANDRA   You see what they're like, Hector. I don't know how their poor lungs are going to stand it.

HECTOR   But our father can't be like this.

PARIS   Hector, before we have this out in front of my father, I suppose you wouldn't like to take just one look at Helen.

HECTOR   I don't care a fig about Helen. Ah: greetings to you, Father!

[Priam enters with Hecuba, Andromache, the poet Demokos, another old man, and a mathematician. Hecuba leads by the hand little Polyxene.]

PRIAM   What was it you said?

HECTOR   I said that we should make haste to shut the Gates of War, Father, see them bolted and padlocked, so that not even a gnat can get between them.

PRIAM   I thought what you said was somewhat shorter.

DEMOKOS   He said he didn't care a fig about Helen.

PRIAM   Look over here. [Hector obeys.] Do you see her?

HECUBA   Indeed he sees her. Who, I ask myself, doesn't see her, or hasn't seen her? She takes the road which goes the whole way round the city.

DEMOKOS   It is Beauty's perfect circle.

PRIAM   Do you see her?

HECTOR   Yes, I see her. What of it?

DEMOKOS   Priam is asking you what you see.

HECTOR   I see a young woman adjusting her sandal.

PARIS   I carried her off naked; she left her clothes in Greece. Those are your sandals, Cassandra. They're a bit big for her.

CASSANDRA   Anything's too big for these little women.

HECTOR   I see two charming buttocks.

HECUBA   He sees what all of you see.

PRIAM   I'm sorry for you.

HECTOR   Why?

PRIAM   I had no idea that the young men of Troy had come to this.

HECTOR   What have they come to?

PRIAM   To being impervious to beauty.

DEMOKOS   And, consequently, ignorant of love. And, consequently, unrealistic. To us who are poets reality is love or nothing.

HECTOR   But the old men, you think, can appreciate love and beauty?

HECUBA But of course. If you make love, or if you are beautiful, you don't need to understand these things.

HECTOR You come across beauty, Father, at every street corner. I'm not alluding to Helen, though at the moment she condescends to walk our streets.

PRIAM You are being unfair, Hector. Surely there have been occasions in your life when a woman has seemed to be more than merely herself, as though a radiance of thoughts and feelings glowed from her flesh, giving a special brilliance to it.

DEMOKOS As a ruby represents blood.

HECTOR Not to those who have seen blood. I have just come back from a close acquaintance with it.

DEMOKOS A symbol, you understand. Soldier though you are, you have surely heard of symbolism! Surely you have come across women who as soon as you saw them seemed to you to to personify intelligence, harmony, gentleness, whatever it might be?

HECTOR It has happened.

DEMOKOS And what did you do?

HECTOR I went closer, and that was the end of it. And what does this we see here personify?

DEMOKOS We have told you before: Beauty.

HECUBA Then send her quickly back to the Greeks if you want her to personify that for long. She's a blonde. They don't last forever.

HECTOR Listen, Father: we are just back from a war, and we have come home exhausted. We have made quite certain of peace on our continent for ever. From now on we mean to live in happiness, and we mean our wives to be able to love us without anxiety, and to bear our children.

DEMOKOS Wise principles, but war has never prevented wives from having children.

HECTOR Explain to me why we have come back to find the city transformed, all because of Helen? Explain to me what you think she has given us, worth a quarrel with the Greeks?

MATHEMATICIAN Anybody will tell you! I can tell you myself!

HECUBA Listen to the mathematician!

MATHEMATICIAN Yes, listen to the mathematician!

And don't think that mathematicians have no concern with women! We're the land-surveyors of your personal landscape. I can't tell you how we mathematicians suffer to see any slight disproportion of the flesh, on the chin or the thigh, any infringement of your geometrical desirability. Well now, until this day mathematicians have never been satisfied with the countryside surrounding Troy. The line linking the plain with the hills seemed to us too slack: the line from the hills to the mountains too taut. Now, since Helen came, the country has taken on meaning and vigor. And, what is particularly evident to true mathematicians, space and volume have now found in Helen a common denominator. We can abolish all the instruments we have invented to reduce the universe to a manageable equation. There are no more feet and inches, ounces, pounds, milligrams or leagues. There is only the weight of Helen's footfall, the length of Helen's arm, the range of Helen's look or voice; and the movement of the air as she goes past is the measure of the winds.

HECUBA The old fool is crying.

PRIAM My dear son, you have only to look at this crowd, and you will understand what Helen is. She is a kind of absolution. To each one of these old men, whom you can see now hanging like a frieze of grotesque heads round the city walls: to the old swindler, the old thief, the old pandar, to all the old failures, she has shown they always had a secret longing to rediscover the beauty they had lost. Helen is like a pardon to them: a new beginning for them, their whole future.

HECTOR These old men's ancient futures are no concern of mine.

DEMOKOS Hector, as a poet I approach things by the way of poetry. Imagine if beauty, never, at any time, touched our language. Imagine there being no such word as "delight."

HECTOR We should get on well enough without it. I get on without it already. "Delight" is a word I use only when I'm absolutely driven to it.

DEMOKOS Well, then the word "desirable": you could get on without that as well, I suppose?

HECTOR If it could be bought only at the cost

of war, yes, I could get on without the word "desirable."

DEMOKOS One of the most beautiful words there are was found only at the cost of war: the word "courage."

HECTOR It has been well paid for.

HECUBA And the word "cowardice" was inevitably found at the same time.

PRIAM My son, why do you so deliberately not understand us?

HECTOR I understand you very well. With the help of a quibble, by pretending to persuade us to fight for beauty, you want to get us to fight for a woman.

PRIAM Would you never go to war for any woman?

HECTOR Certainly not!

HECUBA And he would be unchivalrously right.

CASSANDRA If there were only one woman, then perhaps he would go to war for her. But we have exceeded that number, quite extravagantly.

DEMOKOS Wouldn't you go to war to rescue Andromache?

HECTOR Andromache and I have already made our secret plans for finding our way back to each other again.

DEMOKOS Even if there's no hope of it on earth?

HECTOR Even then.

HECUBA You have done well to unmask them, Hector. They want you to make war for the sake of a woman; it's the kind of lovemaking men believe in who are past making love in any other way.

DEMOKOS And doesn't that make you all the more valuable?

HECUBA Ah yes! No doubt!

DEMOKOS Excuse me, but I can't agree with you. The sex which gave me my mother will always have my respect, even its least worthy representatives.

HECUBA We know that. You have, as we know, shown your respect for instance to—

[*The servants who have stood by to hear the argument burst out laughing.*]

DEMOKOS It's painful to say so, but there's no one knows less what a woman is than a woman.

YOUNG SERVANT [*passing*] Oh dear, dear!

HECUBA We know perfectly well. I will tell you myself what a woman is.

PRIAM I have only to think of one of you, my dears, to know what a woman is.

DEMOKOS In the first place, she is the source of our energy. You know that, Hector. The soldiers who haven't a portrait of a woman in their kit aren't worth anything.

CASSANDRA The source of your pride, yes, I agree.

HECUBA Of your vices.

ANDROMACHE She is a poor bundle of uncertainty, a poor mass of fears, who detests whatever is difficult, and adores whatever is vulgar and easy.

HECTOR Dear Andromache!

HECUBA It's really very simple. I have been a woman for fifty years, and I've never yet been able to discover precisely what it is I am.

PRIAM My dear daughters, I can't conceive of any greater unselfishness than the way you now fight for peace, when peace will give you idle, feeble, chicken-hearted husbands, and war would turn them into men.

DEMOKOS Into heroes.

HECUBA Yes, we know the jargon. In wartime a man is called a hero. It doesn't make him any braver, and he runs for his life. But at least it's a hero who is running away.

ANDROMACHE Father, I must beg you to listen. If you have such a fondness for women, listen to what they have to say to you, for I can promise I speak for all the women in the world. Let us keep our husbands as they are. The Gods took care to see they were surrounded with enough obstacles and dangers to keep them brave and vigorous. Quite enough if they had nothing to cope with except floods and storms! Or only wild animals! It's better for a man to pit his strength and cunning against wolves, lions, hyenas, than against his fellow men. The smaller game, foxes and hares and pheasants, which a woman can scarcely distinguish from the heather they hide in, prove a man's quickness of eye far better than this target you propose: the enemy's heart hiding in flesh and metal. Why should you want me to owe Hector to the deaths of other men?

PRIAM I don't want it, my dear child. But why do you think you are here now, all looking so beautiful, and valiantly demanding peace? Why: because your husbands and your fathers, and their fathers, and theirs, were fighting men. If they had been too lazy and self-indulgent to spring to arms, if they hadn't known how this dull and stupid business we call life suddenly leaps into flame and justifies itself through the scorn men have for it, you would find *you* were the cowards now, and *you* would be clamoring for war. A man has only one way of being immortal on this earth: he has to forget he is mortal.

ANDROMACHE Why, exactly so, Father: you're only too right. The brave men die in war. It takes great luck or judgment not to be killed. Once at least the head has to bow and the knee has to bend to danger. The soldiers who march back under the triumphal arches are death's deserters. How can a country increase in strength and honor by sending them both to their graves?

PRIAM Daughter, the first sign of cowardice in a people is their first moment of decay.

ANDROMACHE But which is the worse cowardice? To appear cowardly to others, and make sure of peace? Or to be cowardly in your own eyes, and let loose a war?

DEMOKOS Cowardice is not to prefer death on every hand rather than the death of one's native land.

HECUBA I was expecting poetry at this point. It never lets us down.

ANDROMACHE Everyone always dies for his country. If you have lived in it, well and wisely and actively, you die for it too.

HECTOR And you can listen to all this without saying a word, Paris? Can you still not decide to give up an adventure to save us from years of unhappiness and massacre?

PARIS What do you want me to say? My case is an international problem.

HECTOR Paris, are you really in love with Helen?

CASSANDRA They've become now a kind of symbol of love's devotion. They don't still have to care for each other.

PARIS I worship Helen.

CASSANDRA [*at the rampart, crossing*] She is coming now.

HECTOR If I persuade her to set sail, will you agree?

PARIS Yes, I'll agree.

HECTOR Father, if Helen is willing to go back to Greece, will you hold her here by force?

PRIAM Why discuss the impossible?

HECTOR Do you call it impossible? If women are a tenth of what you say they are, Helen will go of her own free will.

PARIS Father, now *I'm* going to ask you to let him do what he wants. You have seen what it's like. As soon as the question of Helen cropped up, this whole tribe royal turned itself into a family conclave of all the poor girl's sisters-in-law, mother and father-in-law, brother-in-law, worthy of the best middle-class tradition. I doubt if there's anything more humiliating than to be cast for the part of the seducer son in a large family. I've had quite enough of their insinuations. I accept Hector's challenge.

DEMOKOS Helen's not only yours, Paris. She belongs to the city. She belongs to our country.

MATHEMATICIAN She belongs to the landscape.

HECUBA You be quiet, Mathematician.

CASSANDRA Here's Helen; here she is.

HECTOR Father, I must ask you to let me handle this. Listen; they are calling us to go to the ceremony, to close the Gates of War. Leave this to me. I'll join you soon.

PRIAM Do you really agree to this, Paris?

PARIS I am eager for it.

PRIAM Very well, then; let it be so. Come along, the rest of you; we will see that the Gates of War are made ready.

CASSANDRA Those poor gates. They need more oil to shut them than to open them.

[*Paris exits and the rest withdraw. Demokos stays.*]

HECTOR What are you waiting for?

DEMOKOS The visitation of my genius.

HECTOR Say that again?

DEMOKOS Every time Helen walks my way I am thrown into a transport of inspiration. I shake all over, break into sweat, and improvise. Good heavens, here it is! [*He declaims*]

642   JEAN GIRAUDOUX

Beautiful Helen, Helen of Sparta,
  Singular as the evening star,
The gods forbid that we should part a
  Pair as fair as you and Paris are.

HECTOR Those rhymes give me a headache.

DEMOKOS It's an invention of mine. I can obtain effects even more surprising. Listen: [*Declaims*]

Face the great Hector with no qualm,
  Troy's glory though he be, and the world's terror:
He is the storm, and you the after-calm,
  Yours is the right, and his the boist'rous error.

HECTOR Get out!

DEMOKOS What are you glaring at? You look as though you have as little liking for poetry as you have for war.

HECTOR They make a pretty couple! Now vanish.

[*Demokos exits, Cassandra enters.*]

CASSANDRA Helen!

[*Cassandra exits, Helen and Paris enter.*]

PARIS Here he is, Helen darling; this is Hector. He has a proposition to make to you, a perfectly simple proposition. He wants to hand you over to the Greeks, and prove to you that you don't love me. Tell me you do love me, before I leave you with him. Tell me in your own words.

HELEN I adore you, my sweet.

PARIS Tell me how beautiful the wave was which swept you away from Greece.

HELEN Magnificent! A magnificent wave! Where did you see a wave? The sea was so calm.

PARIS Tell me you hate Menelaus.

HELEN Menelaus? I hate him.

PARIS You haven't finished yet. I shall never again return to Greece. Say that.

HELEN You will never again return to Greece.

PARIS No, no, this is about you, my darling.

HELEN Oh, of course! How silly I am! I shall never again return to Greece.

PARIS I didn't make her say it.—Now it's up to you. [*He exits.*]

HECTOR Is Greece a beautiful country?

HELEN Paris found it ravishing.

HECTOR I meant is Greece itself beautiful, apart from Helen?

HELEN How very charming of you.

HECTOR I was simply wondering what it is really like.

HELEN Well, there are quite a great many kings, and a great many goats, dotted about on marble.

HECTOR If the kings are in gold, and the goats angora, that would look pretty well when the sun was rising.

HELEN I don't get up very early.

HECTOR And a great many gods as well, I believe? Paris tells me the sky is crawling with them; he tells me you can see the legs of goddesses hanging down from the clouds.

HELEN Paris always goes about with his nose in the air. He may have seen them.

HECTOR But you haven't?

HELEN I am not gifted that way. I will look out for them when I go back there again.

HECTOR You were telling Paris you would never be going back there.

HELEN He asked me to tell him so. I adore doing what Paris wants me to do.

HECTOR I see. Is that also true of what you said about Menelaus? Do you not, after all, hate him?

HELEN Why should I hate him?

HECTOR For the one reason which might certainly make for hate. You have seen too much of him.

HELEN Menelaus? Oh, no! I have never seen Menelaus.

HECTOR You have never seen your husband?

HELEN There are some things, and certain people, that stand out in bright colors for me. They are the ones I can see. I believe in them. I have never been able to see Menelaus.

HECTOR Though I suppose he must have come very close to you sometimes.

HELEN I have been able to touch him. But I can't honestly tell you I saw him.

HECTOR They say he never left your side.

HELEN Apparently. I must have walked across him a great many times without knowing it.

HECTOR Whereas you have seen Paris.

HELEN Vividly; in the clearest outline against the sky and the sun.

HECTOR Does he still stand out as vividly as he did? Look down there: leaning against the rampart.

HELEN Are you sure that's Paris, down there?

HECTOR He is waiting for you.

HELEN Good gracious! He's not nearly as clear as usual.

HECTOR And yet the wall is freshly white-washed. Look again: that is Paris. The one in profile.

HELEN It's odd how people waiting for you stand out far less clearly than people you are waiting for.

HECTOR Are you sure that Paris loves you?

HELEN I don't like knowing about other people's feelings. There is nothing more embarrassing. Just as when you play cards and you see your opponent's hand. You are sure to lose.

HECTOR What about yourself? Do you love him?

HELEN I don't much like knowing my own feelings either.

HECTOR When you make love with Paris, when he sleeps in your arms, when you are circled round with Paris, overwhelmed with Paris, haven't you any thoughts about it?

HELEN My part is over. I leave any thinking to the universe. It does it much better than I do.

HECTOR Have there been many others, before Paris?

HELEN Some.

HECTOR And there will be others after him, wouldn't you say, as long as they stand out in clear relief against the sky, or the wall, or the white sheets on the bed? It is just as I thought it was. You don't love Paris particularly, Helen; you love men.

HELEN I don't dislike them. They're as pleasant as soap and a sponge and warm water; you feel cleansed and refreshed by them.

HECTOR Cassandra! Cassandra!

CASSANDRA [*entering*] What do you want?

HECTOR Cassandra, Helen is going back this evening with the Greek ambassador.

HELEN I? What makes you think so?

HECTOR Weren't you telling me that you didn't love Paris particularly?

HELEN That was your interpretation. Still, if you like.

HECTOR I quote my authority. You have the same liking for men as you have for a cake of soap.

HELEN Yes; or pumice stone, perhaps is better. What about it?

HECTOR Well, then, you're not going to hesitate in your choice between going back to Greece, which you don't mind, and a catastrophe as terrible as war?

HELEN You don't understand me at all, Hector. Of course I'm not hesitating. It would be very easy to say "I will do this or that, so that this can happen, or that can happen." But you mustn't think, because you have convinced me, you've convinced the future, too. Merely by making children behave as you want them to, you don't alter the course of destiny.

HECTOR I don't follow your Greek shades and subtleties.

HELEN It isn't a question of shades and subtleties. It's a question of monsters and pyramids.

HECTOR Do you choose to leave here, yes or no?

HELEN Don't bully me. I choose what happens in the way I choose men, or anything else. I choose whatever is not indefinite and vague. I choose what I see.

HECTOR I know, you said that: what you see in the brightest colors. And you don't see yourself returning to Menelaus in a few days' time?

HELEN No. It's very difficult.

HECTOR We could no doubt persuade your husband to dress with great brilliance for your return.

HELEN All the purple dye from all the murex shells in the sea wouldn't make him visible to me.

HECTOR Here you have a rival, Cassandra. Helen can read the future, too.

HELEN No, I can't read the future. But when I imagine the future some of the pictures I see are colored, and some are dull and drab. And up to now it has always been the colored scenes which have happened in the end.

HECTOR We are going to give you back to the Greeks at high noon, on the blinding sand, between the violet sea and the ochre-colored wall. We shall all be dressed in golden armor with red skirts; and my sisters, dressed in green and standing between my white stallion and Priam's black mare, will return you to the Greek ambassador, over whose silver helmet I can imagine tall purple plumes. You see that, I think?

HELEN No, none of it. It is all quite sombre.

HECTOR You are mocking me, aren't you?

HELEN Why should I mock you? Very well, then. Let us go, if you like! Let us go and get ready to return me to the Greeks. We shall see what happens.

HECTOR Do you realize how you insult humanity, or is it unconscious?

HELEN I don't know what you mean.

HECTOR You realize that your colored picture-book is holding the world up to ridicule? While we are all battling and making sacrifices to bring about a time we can call our own, there are you, looking at your pictures which nothing in all eternity can alter. What's wrong? What picture has made you stop and stare at it with those blind eyes? I don't doubt it's the one where you are standing here on the ramparts, watching the battle going on below. Is it the battle you see?

HELEN Yes.

HECTOR And the city is in ruins or burning, isn't that so?

HELEN Yes. It's a vivid red.

HECTOR And what about Paris? You are seeing his body dragged behind a chariot?

HELEN Oh, do you think that is Paris? I see what looks like a flash of sunlight rolling in the dust. A diamond sparkling on his hand. Yes, it is! Often I don't recognize faces, but I always recognize the jewelry. It's his ring, I'm quite certain.

HECTOR Do I dare to ask you about Andromache, and myself, the scene of Andromache and Hector? You are looking at us. Don't deny it. How do you see us? Happy, grown old, bathed in light?

HELEN I am not trying to see it.

HECTOR The scene of Andromache weeping over the body of Hector, does that shine clearer?

HELEN You seem to know. But sometimes I see

things shining, brilliantly shining, and they never happen. No one is infallible.

HECTOR You needn't go on. I understand. There is a son between the weeping mother and the father stretched on the ground?

HELEN Yes. He is playing with his father's tangled hair. He is a sweet boy.

HECTOR And these scenes are there in your eyes, down in the depths of them. Could I see them there?

HELEN I don't know. Look.

HECTOR Nothing. Nothing except the ashes of all those fires. How innocent it is, this crystal where the future is waiting. But there should be tears bathing it, and where are they? Would you cry, Helen, if you were going to be killed?

HELEN I don't know. But I should scream. And I feel I shall scream if you go on at me like this, Hector. I am going to scream.

HECTOR You will leave for Greece this evening, Helen, otherwise I shall kill you.

HELEN But I want to leave! I'm prepared to leave. All that I'm trying to tell is that I simply can't manage to distinguish the ship that is going to carry me there. Nothing is shining in the least—

HECTOR You will go back on a grey sea under a grey sun. But we must have peace.

HELEN I cannot see peace!

MESSENGER [*entering*] Hector, Priam is asking for you. The priests are opposed to our shutting the Gates of War. They say the gods will consider it an insult.

HECTOR It is curious how the gods can never speak for themselves in these difficult matters.

MESSENGER They have spoken for themselves. A thunderbolt has fallen on the temple, several men have been killed, the entrails of the victims have been consulted, and they are unanimously against Helen's return to Greece.

HECTOR I would give a good deal to be able to consult the entrails of the priests— I'll follow you. [*The messenger exits.*] Well, now, Helen, do we agree about this?

HELEN Yes.

HECTOR From now on you will say what I tell you to say? You will do what I tell you to do?

HELEN Yes.

HECTOR When we come in front of Ulysses you won't contradict me, you will bear out everything I say?

HELEN Yes.

HECTOR Do you hear this, Cassandra? Listen to this solid wall of negation which says Yes! They have all given in to me. Paris has given in to me, Priam has given in to me, Helen has given in to me. And yet I can't help feeling that in each of these apparent victories I have been defeated. You set out, thinking you are going to have to wrestle with giants; you brace yourself to conquer them, and you find yourself wrestling with something inflexible reflected in a woman's eye. You have said yes beautifully, Helen, and you're brimfull of a stubborn determination to defy me!

HELEN That's possible. But how can I help it? It isn't my own determination.

HECTOR By what peculiar vagary did the world choose to place its mirror in this obtuse head?

HELEN It's most regrettable, obviously. But can you see any way of defeating the obstinacy of a mirror?

HECTOR Yes. I've been considering that for the past several minutes.

[*Messenger offstage:* "Hector."]

HELEN If you break the mirror, will what is reflected in it cease to exist?

HECTOR That is the whole question. [*Exits.*]

HELEN Cassandra, you can see what I can see. You could have helped him to understand me.

CASSANDRA He understands you only too clearly. And, besides, I see nothing; I never have seen anything colored or not. But I can feel the weight of every person who comes toward me. I know what is in store for them by the sensation of suffering which flows into my veins.

HELEN In fact, you feel what I can see.

CASSANDRA What I feel in Hector is a suffering too deep to be suffered. He may yet break the reflection in your mirror, Helen. He may have the hands great enough to strangle the tiger as it springs.

HELEN Do you suppose so?

CASSANDRA There is always something more than one supposes.

Act Two

A palace enclosure later. At each corner a view of the sea. In the middle a monument, the Gates of War. They are sliding gates, wide open.

HELEN [*calling*] You hoo, you hoo. Hey! You down there! Yes, it's you I'm calling. Come here.

TROILUS [*off*] No.

HELEN What is your name?

TROILUS Troilus.

HELEN Come here.

TROILUS No.

HELEN Come here, Troilus! [*Troilus draws near.*] That's the way. You obey when you're called by your name: you are still very like a puppy. It's rather beguiling. Do you know you have made me call out to a man for the first time in my life. You will pay for that. What's the matter? Are you trembling?

TROILUS No, I'm not.

HELEN You tremble, Troilus.

TROILUS Yes, I do.

HELEN Why are you always just behind me? If I walk with my back to the sun and suddenly stop, the head of your shadow stubs itself against my heel. Tell me what you want.

TROILUS I don't want anything.

HELEN Tell me what you want, Troilus!

TROILUS Everything! I want everything!

HELEN You want everything. The moon?

TROILUS Everything! Everything and more!

HELEN You're beginning to talk like a real man already; you want to kiss me!

TROILUS No!

HELEN You want to kiss me, isn't that it, Troilus?

TROILUS I would kill myself directly afterwards!

HELEN Come nearer. How old are you?

TROILUS Sixteen. Alas!

HELEN Bravo for that alas. Have you kissed girls of your own age?

TROILUS I hate them.

HELEN Yes. But have you kissed them?

TROILUS Well, yes, you're bound to kiss them, you kiss them all. I would give my life not to have kissed any of them.

HELEN You seem prepared to get rid of quite a number of lives. Why haven't you said to me frankly: Helen, I want to kiss you! I don't see anything wrong in your kissing me. Kiss me.

TROILUS Never.

HELEN And then, when the day came to an end, you would have come quietly to where I was sitting on the battlements watching the sun go down over the islands, and you would have turned my head towards you with your hands —from golden it would have become dark, only shadow now, you would hardly have been able to see me—and you would have kissed me, and I should have been very happy. Why this is Troilus, I should have said to myself: young Troilus is kissing me! Kiss me.

TROILUS Never.

HELEN I see. You think, once you have kissed me, you would hate me?

TROILUS Oh! Older men have all the luck, knowing how to say what they want to!

HELEN You say it well enough.

PARIS [*entering*] Take care, Helen; Troilus is a dangerous fellow.

HELEN On the contrary. He wants to kiss me.

PARIS Troilus, you know that if you kiss Helen I shall kill you?

HELEN Dying means nothing to him; no matter how often.

PARIS What's the matter with him? Is he crouching to spring? Is he going to take a leap at you? He's too nice a boy. Kiss Helen, Troilus. I'll let you.

HELEN If you can make up his mind to it you're cleverer than I am.

[*Troilus who was about to hurl himself on Helen immediately draws back.*]

PARIS Listen, Troilus! A committee of our revered elders coming to shut the Gates of War. Kiss Helen in front of them; it will make you famous. You want to be famous, don't you, later on in life?

TROILUS No. I want nobody to have heard of me.

PARIS You don't want to be famous? You don't want to be rich and powerful?

TROILUS No. Poor. Ugly.

PARIS Let me finish! So that you can have all the women you want.

TROILUS I don't want any, none at all, none.

PARIS Here come the senators! Now you can choose: either you kiss Helen in front of them, or I shall kiss her in front of you. Would you rather I did it? All right! Look!—Why, this was a new version of kiss you gave me, Helen. What was it?

HELEN The kiss I had ready for Troilus.

PARIS You don't know what you're missing, my boy! Are you leaving us? Goodbye, then.

HELEN We shall kiss one another, Troilus. I'll answer for that. [*Troilus goes.*] Troilus!

PARIS [*slightly unnerved*] You called rather too loudly, Helen.

DEMOKOS [*entering*] Helen, one moment! Look me full in the face. I've got here in my hand a magnificent bird which I'm going to set free. Are you looking? Here it is. Smooth back your hair, and smile a beautiful smile.

PARIS I don't see how the bird will fly any better if Helen smooths her hair and gives a beautiful smile.

HELEN It can't do me any harm, anyway.

DEMOKOS Don't move. One! Two! Three! There! It's all over, you can go now.

HELEN Where was the bird?

DEMOKOS It's a bird who knows how to make himself invisible.

HELEN Ask him next time to tell you how he does it. [*Exits.*]

PARIS What is this nonsense?

DEMOKOS I am writing a song on the subject of Helen's face. I needed to look at it closely, to engrave it, smiling, on my memory.

[*Hecuba, the little Polyxene, Abneos, the Mathematician, and some old men enter.*]

HECUBA Well, are you going to shut these Gates for us?

DEMOKOS Certainly not. We might well have to open them again this very evening.

HECUBA It is Hector's wish. And Hector will persuade Priam.

DEMOKOS That is as we shall see. And what's more I have a surprise in store for Hector.

POLYXENE Where do the Gates lead to, Mama?

ABNEOS To war, my child. When they are open it means there is war.

DEMOKOS My friends—

HECUBA War or not, it's an absurd symbolism, your Gate-way, and those two great doors always left open look very unsightly. All the dogs stop there.

MATHEMATICIAN This is no domestic matter. It concerns war and the gods.

HECUBA Which is just as I said: the gods never remember to shut their doors.

POLYXENE I remember to shut them very well, don't I, Mama?

PARIS And you even include your fingers in them, don't you, my pretty one?

DEMOKOS May I ask for a moment of silence, Paris? Abneos, and you, Mathematician, and you, my friends: I asked you to meet here earlier than the time fixed for the ceremony so that we could hold our first council. And it promises well that this first council of war should be, not a council of generals, but a council of intellectuals. For it isn't enough in wartime to have our soldiers drilled, well-armed, and spectacular. It is absolutely necessary to bring their enthusiasm up to fever pitch. The physical intoxication which their officers will get from them by a generous allowance of cheap wine will still be ineffective, against the Greeks, unless it is reinforced by the spiritual and moral intoxication which the poets can pour into them. If we are too old to fight we can at least make sure that the fighting is savage. I see you have something to say on the subject, Abneos.

ABNEOS Yes. We must make a war-song.

DEMOKOS Very proper. A war requires a war-song.

PARIS We have done without one up to now.

HECUBA War itself sings quite loud enough.

ABNEOS We have done without one because up to now we were fighting only barbarians. It was nothing more than a hunt, and the hunting horn was all we needed. But now with the Greeks we're entering a different region of war altogether.

DEMOKOS Exactly so, Abneos. The Greeks don't fight with everybody.

PARIS We already have a national anthem.

ABNEOS Yes. But it's a song of peace.

PARIS If you sing a song of peace with enough gestures and grimaces it becomes a war-song. What are the words we have already?

ABNEOS You know them perfectly well. There's no spirit in them:

We cut and bind the harvest,
We tread the vineyard's blood.

DEMOKOS At the very most it's a war-song against farm produce. You won't frighten the Spartans by threatening a wheatfield.

HECUBA It includes the word "blood," there's always that.

ABNEOS Why discuss it, when Demokos can invent an entirely new one in a couple of hours?

DEMOKOS A couple of hours is rather short.

HECUBA Don't be afraid; it's more than you need for it. And after the song will come the hymn, and after the hymn the cantata. As soon as war is declared it will be impossible to hold poets back. Rhyme is still the most effective drum.

DEMOKOS And the most useful, Hecuba: you don't know how wisely you speak. I know war. As long as war isn't with us, and the Gates are shut, each of us is free to insult it and execrate it as we will. But once war comes, its pride and autocracy is huge. You can gain its good will only by flattery and adoration. So the mission of those who understand how to speak and write is to compliment and praise war ceaselessly and indiscriminately, otherwise we shut ourselves out from his favor.

PARIS Have you got an idea for your song already?

DEMOKOS A marvelous idea, which no one will understand better than you. I have had the notion to compare War's face with Helen's. It will be enchanted by the comparison.

POLYXENE What does War look like, Mama?

HECUBA Like your Aunt Helen.

POLYXENE She is very pretty.

DEMOKOS Then the discussion is closed. You can expect the war song. Why are you looking worried, Mathematician?

MATHEMATICIAN Because there are other things far more urgent than this war song, far more urgent!

DEMOKOS You think we should discuss the question of models, false information, atrocity stories, and so on?

MATHEMATICIAN I think we should discuss the insulting epithets. Before they hurl their spears the Greek fighting-men hurl insults. You third cousin of a toad, they yell! You son of a sow — They insult their enemies like that! And they have a good reason for it. They know that the body is more vulnerable when self-respect has fled. We Trojans suffer from a grave shortage of insults.

DEMOKOS That Mathematician is quite right. We are the only race in the world which doesn't insult its enemies before it kills them.

PARIS You don't think it's enough that the civilians insult the enemy civilians?

MATHEMATICIAN The armies have to show the same hatred the civilians do. You know what dissemblers armies can be in this way. Leave them to themselves and they spend their time admiring each other. Their front lines very soon become the only ranks of real brotherhood in the world. So naturally, when the theatre of war is so full of mutual consideration, hatred is driven back on to the schools, the salons, the tradespeople. If our soldiers aren't at least equal to the Greeks in the fury of their epithets, they will lose all taste for insults and calumny, and as a natural consequence all taste for war.

DEMOKOS Suggestion adopted! We will organize a cursing parade this evening.

PARIS I should have thought they're big enough to find their own curses.

DEMOKOS What a mistake! Could you, adroit as you are, find your own effective curses?

PARIS I believe so.

DEMOKOS You fool yourself. Come and stand face to face with Abneos and begin.

PARIS Why Abneos?

DEMOKOS Because he lends himself to this sort of thing.

ABNEOS Come on, then, speak up, you piece of pie-crust!

PARIS No. Abneos doesn't inspire me. I'll start with you, if you don't mind.

DEMOKOS With me? Certainly. You can let fly at ten paces. There we are. Begin.

HECUBA Take a good look at him. You will be inspired.

PARIS You old parasite! You filthy-footed iambic pentameter!

DEMOKOS Just one second. To avoid any mistake you had better say who it is you're addressing.

PARIS You're quite right! Demokos! Bloodshot bullock's eye. You fungus-ridden plum-tree!

DEMOKOS Grammatically reasonable, but very naïve. What is there in a fungus-ridden plum-tree to make me rise up foaming at the lips?

HECUBA He also called you a bloodshot bullock's eye.

DEMOKOS Bloodshot bullock's eye is better. But you see how you flounder, Paris? Search for something that can strike home to me. What are my faults, in your opinion?

PARIS You are cowardly: your breath smells, and you have no talent.

DEMOKOS You're asking for trouble!

PARIS I was trying to please you.

POLYXENE Why are we scolding Uncle Demokos, Mama?

HECUBA Because he is a cuckoo, dearest!

DEMOKOS What did you say, Hecuba?

HECUBA I was saying that you're a cuckoo, Demokos. If cuckoos had the absurdity, the affectation, the ugliness and the stench of vultures, you would be a cuckoo.

DEMOKOS Wait a bit, Paris! Your mother is better at this than you are. Model yourselves on her. One hour's exercise each day for each soldier, and Hecuba has given us the superiority in insults which we badly need. As for the war-song, I'm not sure it wouldn't be wiser to entrust that to her as well.

HECUBA If you like. But if so, I shouldn't say that war looks like Helen.

DEMOKOS What would you say it looks like, in your opinion?

HECUBA I will tell you when the Gates have been shut.

[*Enter Priam, Hector, Andromache, the messenger, and presently Helen. During the closing of the Gates, Andromache takes little Polyxene aside and whispers a secret or an errand to her.*]

HECTOR As they nearly are.

DEMOKOS One moment, Hector!

HECTOR Aren't we ready to begin the ceremony?

HECUBA Surely? The hinges are swimming in oil.

HECTOR Well, then.

PRIAM What our friends want you to understand, Hector, is that war is ready, too. Consider carefully. They're not mistaken. If you shut these Gates, in a minute we may have to open them again.

HECUBA Even one minute of peace is worth taking.

HECTOR Father, you should know what peace means to men who have been fighting for months. It's like solid ground to someone who was drowning or sinking in the quicksands. Do let us get our feet on to a few inches of peace, touch it, if only with the tips of our toes.

PRIAM Hector: consider: inflicting the word peace on to the city today is as ruthless as though you gave it poison. You will take her off her guard, and undermine her iron determination. The soldiers will rush to buy the bread of peace, to drink the wine of peace, to hold in their arms the woman of peace, and in an hour you will put them back to face a war.

HECTOR The war will never take place!

[*There is the sound of clamor near the Gates.*]

DEMOKOS No? Listen!

HECTOR Shut the Gates. This is where we shall meet the Greeks. Conversation will be bitter enough as it is. We must receive them in peace.

PRIAM My son, are we even sure we should let the Greeks disembark?

HECTOR Disembark they shall. This meeting with Ulysses is our last chance of peace.

DEMOKOS Disembark they shall not. Our honor is at stake. We shall be the laughing-stock of the whole world.

HECTOR And you're taking it upon yourself to recommend to the Senate an action which would certainly mean war?

DEMOKOS Upon myself? No, not at all. Will you come forward now, Busiris. [*Busiris enters.*] This is where your mission begins.

HECTOR Who is this stranger?

DEMOKOS He is the greatest living expert on the rights of nations. It's a lucky chance he should be passing through Troy today. You can't say that he's a biased witness. He is neutral. Our

Senate is willing to abide by his decision.

HECTOR And what is your opinion?

BUSIRIS My opinion, Princes, is that the Greeks, in relation to Troy, are guilty of three breaches of international law. If you give them permission to disembark you will have sacrificed your position as the aggrieved party, and so lost the universal sympathy which would certainly have been yours in the conflict to follow.

HECTOR Explain yourself.

BUSIRIS Firstly, they have hoisted their flag hatchway and not masthead. A ship of war, my dear Princes and colleagues, hoists its flag hatchway only when replying to a salute from a boat carrying cattle. Clearly, then, so to salute a city and a city's population is an insult. As it happens, we have a precedent. Last year the Greeks hoisted their flag hatchway when they were entering the port of Orphea. The reply was incisive. Orphea declared war.

HECTOR And what happened?

BUSIRIS Orphea was beaten. Orphea no longer exists, nor the Orpheans either.

HECUBA Perfect.

BUSIRIS But the annihilation of a people doesn't alter in the least their superior moral position.

HECTOR Go on.

BUSIRIS Secondly, on entering your territorial waters the Greeks adopted the formation known as frontal. At the last congress there was some talk of including this formation in the paragraph of measures called defensive-aggressive. I was very happy to be able to get it restored under its proper heading of aggressive-defensive: so without doubt it is now a disguised form of naval blockade: that is to say, it constitutes a fault of the first degree! We have a precedent for this, as well. Five years ago the Greek navy adopted the frontal formation when they anchored outside Magnesia. Magnesia at once declared war.

HECTOR Did they win it?

BUSIRIS There's not one stone of Magnesia still standing on another. But my redraft of the paragraph is still standing.

HECUBA I congratulate you. We were beginning to be anxious.

HECTOR Go on.

BUSIRIS The third fault is not so serious. One of the Greek Triremes has crept close in to shore without permission. Its captain, Ajax, the most unruly and impossible man among the Greeks, is climbing up towards the city, shouting scandal and provocation, and swearing he would like to kill Paris. But this is a very minor matter, from the international point of view; because it isn't, in any way, a formal breach of the law.

DEMOKOS You have your information. The situation can only be resolved in one of two ways. To swallow an outrage, or return it. Choose.

HECTOR Send word to have Ajax headed off in this direction. [*Messenger exits.*]

PARIS And I'll be waiting here for him.

HECTOR You will be good enough to stay in the palace until I call you. As for you, Busiris, you must understand that Troy has no intention of being insulted by the Greeks.

BUSIRIS I am not surprised. Troy's incorruptible pride is a legend all the world over.

HECTOR You are going to provide me, here and now, with an argument which will allow our Senate to say that there has been no fault whatever on the part of our visitors, and with our pride untouched we welcome them here as our guests.

[*Messenger reenters.*]

DEMOKOS What nonsense is this?

BUSIRIS It isn't in keeping with the facts, Hector.

HECTOR My dear Busiris, all of us here know there's no better way of exercising the imagination than the study of law. No poet ever interpreted nature as freely as a lawyer interprets truth.

BUSIRIS The Senate asked me for an opinion: I gave it.

HECTOR And I ask you for an interpretation. An even subtler point of law.

BUSIRIS It goes against my conscience.

HECTOR Your conscience has seen Orphea destroyed, Magnesia destroyed; is it now contemplating, just as lightheartedly, the destruction of Troy?

HECUBA Yes. He comes from Syracuse.

HECTOR I do beg of you, Busiris. The lives of two countries depend on this. Help us.

BUSIRIS Truth is the only help I can give you.

HECTOR Precisely. Discover a truth which saves us. If you can't, there is one thing I can tell you, quite simply: we shall hold you here for as long as the war goes on.

BUSIRIS What are you saying?

DEMOKOS You're abusing your position, Hector!

HECUBA During war we imprison the rights of man. There seems no reason why we shouldn't imprison a lawyer.

HECTOR I mean what I say, Busiris. I've never failed yet to keep my promises, or my threats. And now either you will be taken off to prison for a year or two, or else you leave here, this evening, heaped with gold. With this in mind, you can dispassionately examine the evidence once again.

BUSIRIS Actually they are certain mitigating arguments.

HECTOR I was sure there were.

BUSIRIS In the case of the first fault, for instance, when the cattle-boat salute is given in certain seas where the shores are fertile, it could be interpreted as a salute from the sailors to the farmers.

HECTOR That would be, in fact, the logical interpretation. The salute of the sea to the earth.

BUSIRIS Not to mention that the cargo of cattle might easily be a cargo of bulls. In that case the homage would verge on flattery.

HECTOR There you are. You've understood what I meant. We've arrived at our point of view.

BUSIRIS And as to the frontal formation, that could as easily mean a promise as a provocation. Women wanting children give themselves not from the side but face to face.

HECTOR Decisive argument.

BUSIRIS Then, again, the Greek ships have huge carved nymphs for figureheads. A woman who comes towards you naked and open-armed is not a threat but an offer. An offer to talk, at any rate.

HECTOR So there we have our honor safe and sound, Demokos. The next step is to make this consultation with Busiris public. Meanwhile, Minos, tell the port authorities to let Ulysses disembark without any loss of time.

Tiger at the Gates

[*Busiris exits, messenger exits.*]

DEMOKOS It's no use even trying to discuss honor with these fighting men. They make the most of the fact that you can't treat them as cowards.

MATHEMATICIAN At any rate, Hector, deliver the Oration for the Dead. That will make you think again.

HECTOR There's not going to be an Oration for the Dead.

PRIAM But it's a part of the ceremony. The victorious general must always speak in honor of the dead when the Gates are closed.

HECTOR An Oration for the Dead of a war is a hypocritical speech in defense of the living, a plea for acquittal. I am not so sure of my innocence.

[*Messenger reenters.*]

DEMOKOS The High Command is not responsible.

HECTOR Ach, no one is: not even the gods. Besides, I have given my Oration for the Dead already. I gave it to them in their last minute of life, when they were lying on the battle-field, on a little slope of olive trees, while they could still attend me with what was left of their sight and hearing. I can tell you what I said to them. There was one, disembowelled, already turning up the whites of his eyes, and I said to him: "It's not so bad, you know; it's not so bad. You will do all right, old man." And one with his skull split in two; I said "You look pretty comical with that broken nose." And my little equerry, with his left arm hanging useless and his last blood flowing out of him; and I said "It's a good thing for you it's the left arm you've splintered." I am happy I gave them one final swig of life; it was all they asked for; they died drinking it. And there's nothing else to be said. Shut the Gates.

POLYXENE Did the little equerry die, as well?

HECTOR Yes, puss-cat. He died. He stretched out his right arm. Someone I couldn't see took him by his perfect hand. And then he died.

DEMOKOS Our general seems to confuse remarks made to the dying with the Oration for the Dead.

PRIAM Why must you be so stubborn, Hector?

HECTOR Very well: you shall have the Oration.

[*He takes a position below the gates.*] —You who cannot hear us, who cannot see us, listen to these words, look at those who come to honor you. We have won the war. I know that's of no moment to you. You are the victors, too. But we are victorious, and still live. That's where the difference is between us and why I'm ashamed. I don't know whether, among the crowd of the dead, any privilege is given to men who died victorious. But the living, whether victorious or not, have privilege enough. We have our eyes. We see the sun. We do what all men do under the sun. We eat. We drink. By the moon, we sleep with our wives. And with yours, now you have gone.

DEMOKOS You insult the dead!

HECTOR Do you think so?

DEMOKOS Either the dead or the living.

HECTOR There is a distinction.

PRIAM Come to the peroration, Hector. The Greeks are coming ashore.

HECTOR I will come to it now—Breathe in this incense, touch these offerings, you who can neither smell nor touch. And understand, since I speak to you sincerely, I haven't an equal tenderness and respect for all of you. Though all of you are the dead, with you as with us who survive there are men of courage, and men of fear, and you can't make me confuse, for the sake of a ceremony, the dead I admire with those I can't admire. But what I have to say to you today is that war seems to me the most sordid, hypocritical way of making all men equal: and I accept death neither as a punishment or expiation for the coward, nor as a reward to the living. So, whatever you may be, absent, forgotten, purposeless, unresting, without existence, one thing is certain when we close these Gates: we must ask you to forgive us, we, the deserters who survive you, who feel we have stolen two great privileges, I hope the sound of their names will never reach you: the warmth of the living body, and the sky.

[*The Gates slowly close.*]

POLYXENE The gates are shutting, Mama!

HECUBA Yes, darling.

POLYXENE The dead men are pushing them shut.

HECUBA They help, a little.

HECTOR Is it done? Are they shut?

GUARD Tight as a clam.

HECTOR We're at peace, Father, we're at peace.

HECUBA We're at peace!

POLYXENE It feels much better, doesn't it, Mama?

HECTOR Indeed it does.

POLYXENE I feel much better, anyway.

[*The sound of the Greeks' music is heard.*]

MESSENGER The Greeks have landed, Priam! [*Exits.*]

DEMOKOS What music! What frightful music! It's the most anti-Trojan music there could possibly be! Let's go and give them a welcome to match it.

HECTOR Receive them royally, bring them here safely. You are responsible.

MATHEMATICIAN At any rate we ought to counter with some Trojan music. Hector, if we can't be indignant any other way, you can authorize a battle of music.

[*Crowd, offstage:* "The Greeks! The Greeks!"]

DEMOKOS Strike up our Trojan anthem!

MESSENGER [*reentering*] Ulysses is on the landing-stage, Priam. Where are we to take him?

PRIAM Conduct him here. Send word to us in the palace when he comes. Keep with us, Paris. We don't want you too much in evidence just yet.

HECTOR Let's go and prepare what we shall say to the Greeks, Father.

DEMOKOS Prepare it somewhat better than your speech for the dead; you're likely to meet more contradiction.

[*Priam and his sons and lords exit.*]

If you are going with them, Hecuba, tell us before you go, what it is you think war looks like.

HECUBA You insist on knowing?

DEMOKOS If you've seen what it looks like, tell us.

HECUBA Like the bottom of a—baboon. When the baboon is up in a tree, with its hind end facing us, there is the face of war exactly: scarlet, scaley, glazed, framed in a clotted, filthy wig.

DEMOKOS So he has two faces: this you describe, and Helen's.

[*Demokos exits, Hecuba exits.*]

ANDROMACHE Here is Helen now. Polyxene, you remember what you have to say to her?

POLYXENE Yes.

ANDROMACHE Go to her, then.

HELEN [*entering*] Do you want to talk to me, darling?

POLYXENE Yes, Aunt Helen.

HELEN It must be important, you're so very tense.

POLYXENE Yes, Aunt Helen.

HELEN Do tell me, then; you make me feel terrible when you stand there like a little stick.

POLYXENE Aunt Helen, if you love anyone, please go away.

HELEN Why should I go away, darling?

POLYXENE Because of the war.

HELEN Do you know about war already, then?

POLYXENE I don't exactly know about it. I think it means we have to die.

HELEN And do you know what dying is?

POLYXENE I don't exactly. I think it means we don't feel anything any more.

HELEN What exactly was it that Andromache told you to ask me?

POLYXENE If you love us at all, please go away.

HELEN That doesn't seem to me very logical. If you loved someone you wouldn't leave them.

POLYXENE Oh, no! Never!

HELEN Which would you rather do: go right away from Hecuba, or never feel anything any more? Which?

POLYXENE Oh, never feel anything! I would rather stay, and never feel anything any more.

HELEN You see how badly you put things to me. If I'm to leave you, I mustn't love you. Would you rather I didn't love you?

HECUBA [*offstage*] Polyxene!

POLYXENE Oh, no! I want you to love me.

HELEN In other words, you didn't know what you were saying, did you?

POLYXENE No.

HECUBA [*offstage*] Polyxene! [*entering*] Are you deaf, Polyxene? Why did you shut your eyes when you saw me? Are you playing at being a statue? Come with me.

HELEN She is teaching herself not to feel anything. But she has no gift for it.

HECUBA Can you hear me, Polyxene? And see me?

POLYXENE Yes, I can hear you. I can see you, too.

HECUBA Why are you crying? Don't you like to see and hear me?

POLYXENE If I do, you will go away.

HECUBA I think it would be better, Helen, if you left Polyxene alone. She is too sensitive to touch the insensitive, even through your beautiful dress and your beautiful face.

HELEN I quite agree with you. I advise Andromache to carry her own messages in the future. Kiss me, Polyxene. I shall go away this evening, since that is what you would like.

POLYXENE No!

HELEN Bravo! You are quite loosened up again!

HECUBA Are you coming with us, Andromache?

ANDROMACHE No: I shall wait here.

[*Hecuba and Polyxene exit.*]

HELEN You want an explanation?

ANDROMACHE I believe it's necessary.

HELEN You've heard the way they're shouting and arguing down below. Isn't that enough? Do you and I have to have explanations, too? And what explanations, since I'm leaving here anyway?

ANDROMACHE Whether you go or stay isn't any longer the problem.

HELEN Tell Hector that. You will make his day easier.

ANDROMACHE Yes, Hector is obsessed by the thought of getting you away. All men are the same. They take no notice of the stag in the thicket because they're already chasing the hare. Perhaps men can hunt like that. But not the gods.

HELEN If you have discovered what the gods are after, in this affair, I congratulate you.

ANDROMACHE I don't know that the gods are after anything. But there is something the universe is after. Ever since this morning, it seems to me, everything has begged and cried out for it, men, animals, even the leaves on the trees and my own child, not yet born.

HELEN Cried out for what?

ANDROMACHE That you should love Paris.

HELEN If they know so certainly that I don't love Paris, they are better informed than I am.

ANDROMACHE But you don't love him! You could love him, perhaps. But, at present, you are both living in a misunderstanding.

HELEN I live with him happily, amicably, in complete agreement. We understand each other so well, I don't really see how this can be called a misunderstanding.

ANDROMACHE Agreement is never reached in love. The life of a wife and husband who love each other is never at rest. Whether the marriage is true or false, the marriage portion is the same: elemental discord. There is no tranquility for lovers.

HELEN And if I went pale whenever I saw Paris: and my eyes filled with tears, and the palms of my hands were moist, you think Menelaus would be delighted, and the Greeks pleased and quite satisfied?

ANDROMACHE It wouldn't much matter then what the Greeks thought.

HELEN And the war would never happen?

ANDROMACHE Perhaps, indeed, it would never happen. Perhaps if you loved him, love would call to the rescue one of its own equals: generosity or intelligence. No one, not even destiny itself, attacks devotion lightheartedly. And even if the war did happen, why, I think even then—

HELEN Then it wouldn't be the same war, I suppose.

ANDROMACHE Oh, no, Helen! You know what this struggle is going to be. Fate would never take so many precautions for an ordinary quarrel. It means to build the future on this war, the future of our countries and our peoples, and our ways of thinking. It won't be so bad if our thoughts and our future are built on the story of a man and a woman who truly love each other. But fate hasn't noticed yet that you are lovers only officially. To think that we're going to suffer and die only for a pair of theoretical lovers: and the splendor and calamity of the age to come will be founded on a trivial adventure between two people who don't love each other—that's what is so horrible.

HELEN If everybody thinks that we love each other, it comes to the same thing.

ANDROMACHE They don't think so. But no one will admit that he doesn't. Everyone, when there's war in the air, learns to live in a new element: falsehood. Everybody lies. Our old men don't worship beauty: they worship ugliness, they worship themselves. And this indignation the Greeks are showing us is a lie. Their boats, in the bay, with their patriotic anthems and their streamers flying, are falsehood of the sea. And Hector's life and my son's life, too, are going to be played out in hypocrisy and pretense.

HELEN So?

ANDROMACHE I beg of you, Helen. Love Paris! Or tell me that I'm mistaken! Tell me that you would kill yourself if Paris were to die! Tell me that you would even let yourself be disfigured if it would keep him alive. Then the war will only be a scourge, not an injustice.

HELEN You are being very difficult. I don't think my way of loving is as bad as all that. Certainly I don't get upset and morbid when Paris leaves me to play bowls or go fishing for eels. But I do feel commanded by him, magnetically attracted. Magnetism is a kind of love, as much as devotion. And it's an old and fruitful passion in its own way, as desperate devotion and passionate weeping are in theirs. I'm as content in this love as a star in a constellation. I shine there; it's the way I breathe, and the way I take life in my arms. What will it all become if I fill it with jealousy, with emotion, and anxiety. The world is nervous enough already: look at yourself!

ANDROMACHE Fill it with pity, Helen. That's the only help the world needs.

HELEN There we are; I knew it would come; the word has been said.

ANDROMACHE What word?

HELEN The word "pity." You must talk to someone else. I'm afraid I'm not very good at pity.

ANDROMACHE Because you don't know unhappiness.

HELEN Maybe. It could also be that I think of unhappy people as my equals, I accept them, and I don't think of my health and my position and beauty as any better than their misery. It's a sense of brotherhood I have.

ANDROMACHE You're blaspheming, Helen.

HELEN I am sure people pity others to the same extent that they would pity themselves. Unhappiness and ugliness are mirrors they can't bear to look into. I haven't any pity for myself. You will see, if war breaks out. I'll put up with hunger and pain better than you will. And insults. Do you think I don't hear what the Trojan women say when I'm going past them? They treat me like a slut. They say that the morning light shows me up for what they think me. It may be true, or it may not be. It doesn't matter to me, one way or the other.

ANDROMACHE Stop, Helen!

HELEN And of course I can see, in what your husband called the colored picture-book in my head, pictures of Helen grown old, flabby, toothless, sitting hunched up in the kitchen, sucking sweets. I can see the white enamel I've plastered over my wrinkles, and the bright colors the sweets are, very clearly. But it leaves me completely indifferent.

ANDROMACHE I am lost.

HELEN Why? If you're content with one perfect couple to make the war acceptable, there is always you and Hector, Andromache.

AJAX [*entering*] Where is he? Where's he hiding himself? A coward! A typical Trojan!

HECTOR [*entering*] Who are you looking for?

AJAX I'm looking for Paris.

HECTOR I am his brother.

AJAX Beautiful family! I am Ajax! What's your name?

HECTOR My name's Hector.

AJAX It ought to be pimp!

HECTOR I see that Greece has sent over her diplomats. What do you want?

AJAX War.

HECTOR Not a hope. Why do you want it?

AJAX Your brother carried off Helen.

HECTOR I am told she was willing.

AJAX A Greek woman can do what she likes: She doesn't have to ask permission from you. He carried her off. It's a reason for war.

HECTOR We can offer our apologies.

AJAX What's a Trojan apology? We're not leaving here without your declaration of war.

HECTOR Declare it yourselves.

AJAX All right, we will. As from this evening.

HECTOR That's a lie. You won't declare war. There isn't an island in the Archipelago that will back you if we aren't in any way responsible. And we don't intend to be.

AJAX Will you declare it yourself, personally, if I call you a coward?

Tiger at the Gates

HECTOR That is a name I accept.

AJAX I've never known such unmilitary reaction! Suppose I tell you what the whole of Greece thinks of Troy, that Troy is a cess-pit of vice and stupidity?

HECTOR Troy is obstinate. You won't get your war.

AJAX Suppose I spit on her?

HECTOR Spit.

AJAX Suppose I strike you, you, one of her princes?

HECTOR Try it.

AJAX Suppose I hit you in the face, you disgusting example of Troy's conceit and her spurious honor?

HECTOR Strike.

AJAX [*striking him*] There. If this lady's your wife she must be proud of you.

HECTOR I know her. She is proud.

DEMOKOS [*entering*] What's all the noise about? What does this drunkard want, Hector?

HECTOR He has got what he wants.

DEMOKOS What is going on, Andromache?

ANDROMACHE Nothing.

AJAX Two times nothing. A Greek hits Hector, and Hector puts up with it.

DEMOKOS Is this true, Hector?

HECTOR Completely false, isn't it, Helen?

HELEN The Greeks are great liars. Greek men, I mean.

AJAX Is it natural for him to have one cheek redder than the other?

HECTOR Yes. I am healthier on that side.

DEMOKOS Tell the truth, Hector. Has he dared to raise his hand against you?

HECTOR That is my concern.

DEMOKOS It's the concern of war. You are the figurehead of Troy.

HECTOR Exactly. No one is going to slap a figurehead.

DEMOKOS Who are you, you brute? I am Demokos, second son of Achichaos!

AJAX The second son of Achichaos? How do you do? Tell me: is it as serious to slap a second son of Achichaos as to strike Hector?

DEMOKOS Quite as serious, you drunk. I am the head of the senate. If you want war, war to the death, you have only to try.

AJAX All right. I'll try. [*He slaps Demokos.*]

DEMOKOS Trojans! Soldiers! To the rescue!

HECTOR Be quiet, Demokos!

DEMOKOS To arms! Troy's been insulted! Vengeance!

HECTOR Be quiet, I tell you.

DEMOKOS I *will* shout! I'll rouse the city!

HECTOR Be quiet! If you won't, I shall hit you, too!

DEMOKOS Priam! Anchises! Come and see the shame of Troy burning on Hector's face!

HECTOR Oh, very well then.

[*Hector strikes Demokos. Ajax laughs. During the scene Priam and his Lords group themselves ready to receive Ulysses.*]

PRIAM What are you shouting for, Demokos?

DEMOKOS I have been struck.

AJAX Go and complain to Achichaos!

PRIAM Who struck you?

DEMOKOS Hector! Ajax! Ajax! Hector!

PARIS What is he talking about? He's mad!

HECTOR Nobody struck him, did they, Helen?

HELEN I was watching most carefully, and I didn't notice anything.

AJAX Both his cheeks are the same color.

PARIS Poets often get upset for no reason. It's what they call their inspiration. We shall get a new national anthem out of it.

DEMOKOS You will pay for this, Hector. [*Exits.*] [*Voices off: "Ulysses! Here is Ulysses!"*]

AJAX [*going amicably to Hector*] Well done. Noble adversary. Plenty of pluck. A beautiful hit. Your slap must be stronger than mine is.

HECTOR I doubt it.

AJAX My deepest respect! My dear Hector, forgive me. I withdraw my threats, I take back my slap. We have enemies in common, in the sons of Achichaos. I won't fight with anybody who shares with me an enmity for the sons of Achichaos. Not another mention of war. I don't know what Ulysses has got in mind, but count on me to arrange the whole thing. [*He goes towards Ulysses offstage and comes back with him.*]

ANDROMACHE I love you, Hector.

HECTOR [*showing his cheek*] Yes; but don't kiss me just yet.

ANDROMACHE You have won this round, as well. Be confident.

HECTOR I win every round. But still with each

victory the prize escapes me.

[*Offstage crowd:* "Ulysses!" *Enter Ulysses, followed by Ajax, sailors, and others.*]

ULYSSES Priam and Hector?

PRIAM Yes. And behind us, Troy, and the suburbs of Troy, and the land of Troy, and the Hellespont.

ULYSSES I am Ulysses. There are many people here for a diplomatic conversation.

PRIAM And here is Helen.

ULYSSES Good morning, my queen.

HELEN I've grown younger here, Ulysses. I've become a princess again.

PRIAM We are ready to listen to you.

AJAX Ulysses, you speak to Priam. I will speak to Hector.

ULYSSES Priam, we have come to take Helen home again.

AJAX You do understand, don't you, Hector? We can't have things happening like this.

ULYSSES Greece and Menelaus cry out for vengeance.

AJAX If deceived husbands can't cry out for vengeance, what can they do?

ULYSSES Deliver Helen over to us within an hour. Otherwise it means war.

HECTOR But if we give Helen back to you give us your assurance, there will be peace.

AJAX Utter tranquility.

HECTOR If she goes on board within an hour, the matter is closed.

AJAX And all is forgotten.

HECTOR I think there's no doubt we can come to an understanding, can we not, Helen?

HELEN Yes, no doubt.

ULYSSES You don't mean to say that Helen is being given back to us?

HECTOR Exactly. She is ready.

AJAX What about her baggage? She is sure to have more to take back than when she came.

HECTOR We return her to you, bag and baggage, and you guarantee peace. No reprisals, no vengeance!

AJAX A woman is lost, a woman is found, and we're back where we were. Perfect! Isn't it, Ulysses?

ULYSSES Just wait a moment. I guarantee nothing. Before we say there are going to be no reprisals we have to be sure there has been no

cause for reprisals. We have to make sure that Menelaus will find Helen exactly as she was when she was taken from him.

HECTOR How is he going to discover any difference?

ULYSSES A husband is very perceptive when a worldwide scandal has put him on his guard. Paris will have had to have respected Helen. And if that isn't so—

TOPMAN Oh, no! It isn't so!

OLPIDES Not exactly!

HECTOR And if it is so?

ULYSSES Where is this leading us, Hector?

HECTOR Paris has not touched Helen. They have both taken me into their confidence.

ULYSSES What is this absurd story?

HECTOR The true story, isn't it, Helen?

HELEN Why does it seem to you so extraordinary?

OLPIDES It's terrible! It puts us Trojans to shame!

HECTOR Why do you have to smile, Ulysses? Do you see the slightest indication in Helen that she has failed in her duty?

ULYSSES I'm not looking for one. Water leaves more mark on a duck's back than dishonor does on a woman.

PARIS You're speaking to a queen.

ULYSSES Present queens excepted, naturally. So, Paris, you have carried off this queen, carried her off naked; and I imagine that you didn't go into the water wearing all your armor; and yet you weren't seized by any taste or desire for her?

PARIS A naked queen is dressed in her dignity.

HELEN She has only to remember to keep it on.

ULYSSES How long did the voyage last? I took three days with my ships, which are faster than yours.

TOPMAN What are these intolerable insults to the Trojan navy?

OLPIDES Your winds are faster! Not your ships!

ULYSSES Let us say three days, if you like. Where was the queen during those three days?

PARIS Lying down on the deck.

ULYSSES And Paris was where? In the crow's nest?

HELEN Lying beside me.

ULYSSES Was he reading as he lay beside you?

Or fishing for goldfish?

HELEN Sometimes he fanned me.

ULYSSES Without ever touching you?

HELEN One day, the second day, I think it was, he kissed my hand.

ULYSSES Your hand! I see. An outbreak of the animal in him.

HELEN I thought it was more dignified to take no notice.

ULYSSES The rolling of the ship didn't throw you towards each other? I don't think it's an insult to the Trojan navy to suggest that its ships roll?

OLPIDES They roll much less than the Greek ships pitch!

AJAX Pitch? Our Greek ships? If they seem to be pitching it's because of their high prows and their scooped-out sterns!

TOPMAN Oh, yes! The arrogant face and the flat behind, that's Greek all right.

ULYSSES And what about the three nights you were sailing? The stars appeared and vanished again three times over the pair of you. Do you remember nothing of those three nights?

HELEN I don't know. Oh, yes! I remember the number of stars in the Great Bear: seven, and in the constellation of Orion: twenty-three.

ULYSSES While you were asleep, perhaps, he might have taken you—

HELEN A mosquito can wake me.

HECTOR They will both swear to you, if you like, by our goddess Aphrodite.

ULYSSES We can do without that. I know what Aphrodite is. Go on with your story, Paris. It's an interesting contribution to the study of human behavior. What good reason could you have possibly had for respecting Helen when you had her at your mercy?

PARIS I—I loved her.

HELEN If you don't know what love is, Ulysses, I shouldn't venture on the subject.

ULYSSES You must admit, Helen, you would never have followed him if you had known the Trojans were impotent.

OLPIDES Shame! Muzzle him! Bring your women here, and you'll soon see!

TOPMAN And your grandmother!

ULYSSES I expressed myself badly. I meant that Paris, the handsome Paris, is impotent.

TOPMAN Why don't you say something, Paris? Are you going to make us the laughing-stock of the world?

PARIS Hector, you can see, this is a most unpleasant situation for me!

HECTOR You have to put up with it only a few minutes longer. Goodbye, Helen. And I hope your virtue will become as proverbial as your frailty might have done.

HELEN That doesn't worry me. The centuries always give us the recognition we deserve.

ULYSSES Paris the impotent, that's a very good surname! If you care to, Helen, you can kiss him for once.

PARIS Hector!

TOPMAN Are you going to tolerate this farce, Commander?

HECTOR Be quiet! I am in charge here!

TOPMAN And a rotten job you make of it! We've stood quite enough. We'll tell you, we, Paris's own seamen, we'll tell you what he did with your queen!

VOICES Bravo! Tell him!

TOPMAN He's sacrificing himself on his brother's orders. I was an officer on board his ship. I saw everything.

HECTOR You were quite wrong.

TOPMAN Do you think a Trojan sailor doesn't knows what he sees? I can tell the sex of a seagull thirty yards off. Come over here, Olpides. Olpides was up in the crow's nest. He saw everything from on top. I was standing on the stairs in the hatchway. My head was exactly on a level with them, like a cat on the end of a bed. Shall I tell him, Trojans?

VOICES Tell him! Go on and tell him!

HECTOR [*drawing his sword*] Silence!

PRIAM Hector! Let him talk.

TOPMAN And they hadn't been on board more than two minutes, wasn't that true, Olpides?

OLPIDES Only time enough for the queen to dry herself, being just come up out of the water, and to comb the parting into her hair again. I could see her parting, from her forehead over to the nape of her neck, from where I was.

TOPMAN And he sent us all down into the hold, except the two of us who he couldn't see.

OLPIDES And without a pilot, the ship drifted due north. There was no wind, and yet the sails were bellied out full.

TOPMAN And when I looked out from where I was hiding, what I should have seen was the outline of one body, but what I did see was in the shape of two, like a wheaten loaf and rye bread, both baking and rising in the oven together.

OLPIDES But from up where I was, I more often saw one body than two, but sometimes it was white, and sometimes it was golden brown.

TOPMAN So much for impotence! And as for respectful, inexpressive love, and unspoken affection, you tell him, Olpides, what you heard from your ledge up there! Women's voices carry upwards, men's voices stay on the ground. I shall tell you what Paris said.

OLPIDES She called him her ladybird, her little ewe-lamb.

TOPMAN And he called her his lion, his panther. They reversed the sexes. Because they were being so affectionate. It's not unusual.

OLPIDES And then she said: "You are my darling oak tree. I put my arms round you as if you were an oak tree." When you're at sea you think about trees, I suppose.

TOPMAN And he called her his birch tree: "My trembling silver birch tree!" I remember the word birch tree very well. It's a Russian tree.

OLPIDES And I had to stay up in the crow's nest all night. You don't half get thirsty up there, and hungry, and everything else. And when at last they got up from the deck to go to bed they swayed on their feet.

TOPMAN And that's how your wife Penelope would have got on with Trojan impotence.

VOICES Bravo! Bravo!

A WOMAN'S VOICE All praise to Paris.

A JOVIAL MAN Render to Paris what belongs to Paris!

HECTOR This is a pack of lies, isn't it, Helen?

ULYSSES Helen is listening enraptured.

HELEN I forgot they were talking about me. They sound so wonderfully convincing.

ULYSSES Do you dare to say they are lying, Paris?

PARIS In some of the particulars, yes, I think they are.

TOPMAN We're not lying, either in the general or the particular. Are we, Olpides? Do you deny the expressions of love you used? Do you deny the word panther?

PARIS Not especially the word panther.

TOPMAN Well, birch tree, then? I see. It's the phrase "trembling silver birch tree" that embarrasses you. Well, like it or not, you used it. I swear you used it, and anyway what is there to blush about in the word "birch tree"? I have seen these silver birch trees trembling against the snow in wintertime, by the shores of the Caspian, with their rings of black bark apparently separated by rings of space, so that you wondered what was carrying the branches. And I've seen them at the height of summer, beside the canal at Astrakhan, with their white rings like fresh mushrooms. And the leaves talked and made signs to me. To see them quivering, gold above and silver underneath, it makes your heart melt! I could have wept like a woman, isn't that true, Olpides? That's how I feel about the birch tree.

CROWD Bravo! Bravo!

ANOTHER SAILOR And it wasn't only the topman and Olpides who saw them, Priam. The crew came wriggling up through the hatches and peering under the handrails. The whole ship was one great spy-glass.

THIRD SAILOR Spying out love.

ULYSSES There you have it, Hector!

HECTOR Be quiet, the lot of you.

TOPMAN Well, keep this quiet, if you can!

[*Iris appears in the sky.*]

PEOPLE Iris! Iris!

PARIS Has Aphrodite sent you?

IRIS Yes, Aphrodite sent me, and told me that I should say to you that love is the world's chief law. Whatever strengthens love becomes in itself sacred, even falsehood, avarice, or luxury. She takes all lovers under her protection, from the king to the goat-herd. And she forbids both of you, Hector and Ulysses, to separate Paris from Helen. Or else there will be war.

PARIS AND THE OLD MEN Thank you, Iris.

HECTOR Is there any message from Pallas Athene?

IRIS Yes; Pallas Athene told me that I should say to you that reason is the chief law of the world. All who are lovers, she wishes me to say, are out of their minds. She would like you to tell her quite frankly what is more ridiculous than the mating of cooks with hens or flies. And she orders both of you, Hector and Ulysses, to separate Helen from this Paris of the curly hair. Or else there will be war.

HECTOR AND THE WOMEN Thank you, Iris!

PRIAM Oh, my son, it isn't Aphrodite nor Pallas Athene who rules the world. What is it Zeus commands us to do in this time of uncertainty?

IRIS Zeus, the master of the Gods, told me that I should say to you that those who see in the world nothing but love are as foolish as those who cannot see it at all. It is wise, Zeus, master of the Gods informs you, it is wise sometimes to make love, and at other times not to make love. The decision he gives to Hector and Ulysses is to separate Helen and Paris without separating them. He orders all the rest of you to go away and leave the negotiators to face each other. And let them so arrange matters that there will be no war. Or else—he swears to you: he swears there will be war.

[*Exit Iris.*]

HECTOR At your service, Ulysses!

ULYSSES At your service.

[*All withdraw. A great rainbow is seen in the sky.*]

HELEN How very like Iris to leave her scarf behind.

HECTOR Now we come to the real tussle, Ulysses.

ULYSSES Yes: out of which either war or peace is going to come.

HECTOR Will war come of it?

ULYSSES We shall know in five minutes' time.

HECTOR If it's to be a battle of words, my chances are small.

ULYSSES I believe it will be more of a battle of weight. It's as though we were one on each side of a pair of scales. How we weigh in the balance will be what counts in the end.

HECTOR How we weigh in the balance? And what is my weight, Ulysses? My weight is a young man, a young woman, an unborn child. Joy of life, belief in life, a response to whatever's natural and good.

ULYSSES And my weight is the mature man, the wife thirty-five years old, the son whose height I measure each month with notches against the doorpost of the palace. My weight is the pleasures of living, and a mistrust of life.

HECTOR Hunting, courage, loyalty, love.

ULYSSES Circumspection in the presence of the gods, of men, and everything else.

HECTOR I weigh a whole race of humble peasants, hard-working craftsmen, thousands of ploughs and looms, forges and anvils—Why is it, when I put all these on the scale in front of you, all at once they seem to me to weigh so light?

ULYSSES I am the weight of this incorruptible, unpitying air of these coasts and islands.

HECTOR Why go on? The scales have tipped.

ULYSSES To my side? Yes, I think so.

HECTOR And you want war?

ULYSSES I don't want it. But I'm less sure whether war may not want us.

HECTOR Our peoples have brought us together to prevent it. Our meeting itself shows that there is still some hope.

ULYSSES You are young, Hector! It's usual on the eve of every war, for the two leaders of the peoples concerned to meet privately at some innocent village, on a terrace in a garden overlooking a lake. And they decide together that war is the world's worst scourge, and as they watch the rippling reflections in the water, with magnolia petals dropping onto their shoulders, they are both of them peaceloving, modest and friendly. They study one another. They look into each others eyes. And, warmed by the sun and mellowed by the claret, they can't find anything in the other man's face to justify hatred, nothing, indeed, which doesn't inspire human affection, nothing incompatible in their languages any more, or in their particular way of scratching the nose or drinking wine. They really are exuding peace, and the world's desire for peace. And when their meeting is over, they shake hands in a most sincere brotherly fashion, and turn to smile and wave as they drive away. And the next day war breaks out. And so it is with us both at this moment. Our peoples, who have drawn aside, saying nothing while we have this interview, are not expecting us to win a victory over the inevitable. They have merely given us full powers, isolated here together, to stand above the catastrophe and taste the essential brotherhood of enemies. Taste it. It's a rare dish. Savor it. But that is all. One of the privileges of the great is to witness catastrophes from a terrace.

HECTOR Do you think this is a conversation between enemies we are having?

ULYSSES I should say a duet before the full orchestra. Because we have been created sensible and courteous, we can talk to each other, an hour or so before the war, in the way we shall talk to each other long after it's over, like old antagonists. We are merely having our reconciliation before the struggle instead of after it. But, as the universe well knows, we are going to fight each other.

HECTOR The universe might be mistaken. One way to recognize error is the fact that it's universal.

ULYSSES Let's hope so. But when destiny has brought up two nations, as for years it has brought up yours and mine, to a future of similar invention and authority, and given to each a different scale of values, the universe knows that destiny wasn't preparing alternative ways for civilization to flower. It was contriving the dance of death, letting loose the brutality and human folly which is all that the gods are really contented by. It's a mean way to contrive things, I agree. We are heads of state, you and I, we can say this between ourselves. It is destiny's way of contriving things, inevitably.

HECTOR And this time it has chosen to match Greece with Troy?

ULYSSES This morning I was still in doubt. As soon as I stepped on to your landing stage I was certain of it.

HECTOR You mean you felt yourself on enemy soil?

ULYSSES Why will you always harp on the word enemy? Born enemies don't fight. You will find the real antagonists in nations fate has groomed and made ready for the same war.

HECTOR And you think we have been made ready for the Greek war?

ULYSSES To an astonishing extent. Just as nature, when she foresees a struggle between two kinds of insects, equips them with weaknesses and weapons which correspond, so we, living well apart, unknown to ourselves, not even suspecting it, have both been gradually raised up to the level where war begins. Doom has transfigured everything here with the color of storm: the future has never impressed me before with such startling clarity. There is nothing to be done. You're already living in the light of the Greek war.

HECTOR And do the rest of the Greeks think this?

ULYSSES What they think is no more reassuring. The rest of the Greeks think Troy is wealthy, her warehouses bulging, her soil prolific. They think that they, on the other hand, are living cramped on a rock. And your golden temples and golden wheat-fields flashed from your promontories a signal our ships will never forget. It isn't very wise to have such golden gods and vegetables.

HECTOR This is more like the truth, at last. Greece has chosen Troy for her prey. Then why a declaration of war? It would have been simpler to have taken Troy by surprise when I was away with the army. You would have had her without striking a blow.

ULYSSES There's a kind of permission for war which can be given only by the world's mood and atmosphere, the feel of its pulse. It would have been madness to undertake a war without that permission. We didn't have it.

HECTOR But you have it now.

ULYSSES I think we do.

HECTOR But why against us? Troy is famous for her arts, her justice, her humanity.

ULYSSES A nation doesn't put itself at odds with its destiny by its crimes, but by its faults. Its army may be strong, its treasury well-filled, its poets at the height of inspiration. But one day, why it is no one knows, because of some simple event, such as the citizens wantonly cutting down the trees, or the children getting out of hand, or their prince wickedly making off with a woman, the nation is suddenly lost. Nations, like men, die by imperceptible disorders.

There's no doubt you carried off Helen badly.

HECTOR What fairness of proportion can you see between the rape of one woman, and the possible destruction of a whole people, yours or mine, in war?

ULYSSES We are speaking of Helen. You and Paris have made a great mistake about Helen. I've known her for fifteen years, and watched her carefully. There's no doubt it: she is one of the rare creatures destiny puts on the earth for its own personal use. They're apparently quite unimportant. But if you lay hands on them, watch out! It's very hard to know how to recognize one of these hostages of fate among all the other people and places. You haven't recognized it. Paris could have let himself go with perfect safety in a Spartan bed, or a Theban bed, with generous returns twenty times over; but he chose the shallowest brain, the hardest heart, the narrowest understanding of sex. And so you are lost.

HECTOR We are giving Helen back to you.

ULYSSES The insult to destiny can't be taken back.

HECTOR What are we discussing, then? I'm beginning to see what is really behind your words. Admit it. You want our wealth! You had Helen carried off to give you an honorable pretext for war! I blush for Greece. She will be responsible and ashamed for the rest of time.

ULYSSES Responsible and ashamed? Do you think so? The two words hardly agree. Even if we believed we were responsible for the war, all our generation would have to do would be to deny it, and lie, to appease the conscience of future generations. And we shall lie. We'll make that sacrifice.

HECTOR Ah, well, the die is cast, Ulysses. On with the war! The more I hate it, the more I find growing in me an irresistible need to kill. If you won't help me, it were better you should leave here.

ULYSSES Understand me, Hector; you have my help. Don't ask me to interpret fate. All I have tried to do is to read the world's hand, in the great lines of desert caravans, the wake of ships, and the track of migrant birds and wandering peoples. Give me your hand. There are lines there, too. We won't search to see if their lesson tells the same story. We'll suppose that these three little lines at the base of Hector's hand contradict the waves, the wings, and the furrows. I am inquisitive by nature, and not easily frightened. I'm quite willing to join issue with fate. I accept your offer of Helen. I will take her back to Menelaus. I've more than enough eloquence to convince a husband of his wife's virtue. I will even persuade Helen to believe it herself. And I'll leave at once, to avoid any chance of disturbance. Once back on my ship perhaps we can take the risk of running war on to the rocks.

HECTOR Is this part of Ulysses' cunning, or his greatness?

ULYSSES In this particular instance, I'm using my cunning against destiny, not against you. It's my first attempt, so I deserve some credit for it. I am sincere, Hector. If I wanted war, I should have asked for a ransom more precious to you than Helen. I am going now. But I can't shake off the feeling that the road from here to my ship is a long way.

HECTOR My guard will escort you.

ULYSSES As long as the road of a visiting king, when he knows there has been a threat against his life. Where are the assassins hiding? We're lucky if it's not in the heavens themselves. And the distance from here to the fountains is a long way. A long way, taking this first step. Where is it going to carry me among all these perils? Am I going to slip and kill myself? It's all new stonework here; at any moment a stone may be dislodged. But courage. Let us go. [*He takes a first step.*]

HECTOR Thank you, Ulysses.

ULYSSES The first step is safely over. How many more?

HECTOR Four hundred and sixty.

ULYSSES Now the second! You know what made me decide to go, Hector?

HECTOR Yes. Your noble nature.

ULYSSES Not precisely. Andromache's eyelashes dance as Penelope's do.

[*Ulysses exits, Andromache and Cassandra enter.*]

ANDROMACHE Hector!

HECTOR Were you there all the time, Andromache?

ANDROMACHE Let me take your arm. I've no more strength.

HECTOR Did you hear what we said?

ANDROMACHE Yes. I am broken.

HECTOR You see, we needn't despair.

ANDROMACHE We needn't despair for ourselves, perhaps. But for the world, yes. That man is terrible. All the unhappiness of the world is in me.

HECTOR A moment or two more, and Ulysses will be on board. You see how fast he is traveling. You can follow his progress from here. There he is, on a level with the fountains. What are you doing?

ANDROMACHE I haven't the strength any longer to hear any more. I am covering up my ears. I won't take my hands away until we know what our fate is to be.

HECTOR Find Helen, Cassandra!

AJAX [entering more drunk than ever, sees Andromache, her back toward him] Where is she?

CASSANDRA Ulysses is waiting for you down at the harbor, Ajax. Helen will be brought to you there.

AJAX Helen! To hell with Helen! This is the one I want to get my arms around.

CASSANDRA Go away, Ajax. That is Hector's wife.

AJAX Hector's wife! Bravo! I've always liked my friends' wives, my best friends' wives!

CASSANDRA Ulysses is already half way there. Hurry.

AJAX Don't worry, my dear. She's got her hands over her ears. I can say what I like, she can't hear me. If I touched her, now, if I kissed her, certainly! But words she can't hear, what's the matter with that?

CASSANDRA Everything is the matter with that. Go away, Ajax!

AJAX [while Cassandra tries to force him away from Andromache and Hector, slowly raising his javelin] Do you think so? Then I might as well touch her. Might as well kiss her. But chastely. Always chastely, with your best friends' wives! What's the most chaste part of your wife, Hector, her neck? Her ear? I'll tell you what I've always found the chastest thing about a woman—Let me alone, now; let me alone! She can't even hear when I kiss her— [Pushes Cassandra away. Hector moves toward him.] You're so cursed strong! All right, I'm going, I said I was going. Goodbye.

[He exits. Hector lowers his javelin slightly. At this moment Demokos bursts in.]

DEMOKOS What's this cowardice? You're giving Helen back? Trojans, to arms! They've betrayed us. Fall in! And your war-song is ready! Listen to your song of war!

HECTOR [striking him] Have that for your song of war!

DEMOKOS [falling] He has killed me!

HECTOR The war isn't going to happen, Andromache! [He tries to take Andromache's hands from her ears. She resists, her eyes fixed on Demokos. The curtain, which had begun to fall, is lifted little by little.]

ABNEOS [entering] They have killed Demokos! Who killed Demokos?

DEMOKOS Who killed me? Ajax! Ajax! Kill him!

ABNEOS Kill Ajax!

HECTOR He's lying. I am the man who struck him.

DEMOKOS No. It was Ajax.

ABNEOS Ajax has killed Demokos. Catch him! Punish him!

HECTOR I struck you, Demokos, admit it! Admit it, or I'll put an end to you!

DEMOKOS No, my dear Hector, my good dear Hector. It was Ajax! Kill Ajax!

CASSANDRA He is dying, just as he lived, croaking like a frog.

ABNEOS There. They have taken Ajax.

[Shouts and cries off.]

There. They have killed him!

HECTOR [drawing Andromache's hands away from her ears] The war will happen.

CASSANDRA It is still further off—the frustrating of the tiger!

[The Gates of War slowly open, to show Helen kissing Troilus.]

The Trojan poet is dead. And now the Grecian poet will have his word.

GIRAUDOUX'S THEATER *is one of antithesis, allusion, illusion. Ironic indirection spins the plot and fixes the theme. Rhetoric much of the time seems to be all. But, as his sympathetic critics have been quick to point out, all his devices have a purpose. He has strong convictions. Through the agile ironies, the expert allusions, the deft illusions, an idealist emerges.*

From the broader aspects of structure or composition to the stylistic detail, the rhetoric manual remains a handy reference in analyzing the mechanics of Giraudoux's art. A critical edition of his works could carry the sort of notes that we find in school editions of the classics, where examples of figurative language or devices of rhetoric are carefully pointed out. Illustrations would not be found wanting for many of the most forbidding terms invented by the Greeks. We shall forgo, however, the pedantic pleasure of classifying Giraudoux's figures thoroughly. It will serve our purpose well enough to demonstrate further his general tendencies, the type of figure in which his thought finds its characteristic expression. Parallels, paradoxes, and antitheses have already been studied as structural elements defining not only the broad patterns themselves, but also the patterns of their internal composition. In the mechanics of Giraudoux's writing, the principle of polarity is a fundamental factor. A second fundamental factor is unquestionably the image. "Je suis certes le poète qui ressemble le plus à un peintre," ["I am certainly the poet who most resembles a painter"] Giraudoux declares. No writer has indulged himself more unrestrainedly in the delights of imagery or exploited more thoroughly its manifold possibilities. . . .

As a censor, irony functions indubitably as an anti-lyric element, but it is so closely bound up with lyricism, so often dependent upon the lyrical urge to set itself in operation, that it is with some poets an integral part of their creation. Giraudoux, himself, sees nothing antithetical in the two terms irony and poetry: "Cette ironie," he says in his preface to Evelyn Waugh's book, "dont l'autre nom est la poésie." ["That irony, of which the other name is poetry."] This remark implies that, for him at least, the whim-

sical and fanciful play of irony belongs as much to poetry as does lyricism. In this notion he has, of course, many antecedents, extending back to the Romantic philosopher-poets of Germany, whom, as a young man, Giraudoux studied assiduously. Irony was for them, too, the means of maintaining control over their artistic creations, the necessary adjunct of inspiration, the mark of a free and agile spirit. . . .

Systematically, by a variety of means, Giraudoux keeps his work free from all illusion of reality. In his plays, there are the perpetual incongruities of character, situation, and discourse. . . . Ancient Troy is pictured in terms of the contemporary French bourgeoisie, with Cassandra appearing under the traits of a slightly idiotic maiden aunt, and Paris the younger brother who has got into a scrape. The episode of the rape of Helen is turned into farce with Menelaus being unable to pursue his wife's abductor because a crab has hold of his toe! In the same spirit of parody, the tragic heroes and heroines permit themselves flip and impertinent remarks which break the spell and bring the lofty down with a crash. . . .

Giraudoux depends greatly upon allusion as a comic device. Much in *La Guerre de Troie* would be lost on those of the audience who did not know their Homer, and a familiarity with La Motte Fouqué's *Märchen* adds to one's enjoyment of *Ondine*. . . . Sometimes, it is true, we mistake for allusions remarks that are purely fortuitous. *La Guerre de Troie* has numerous passages that one would take as humorous references to Homer, but which prove not to be. In Helen's vision of Hector's death there is mention of a ring. It sounds very much like an illusion, but we recall nothing of the sort in Homer. When an allusion is understood, however, its mixture of aptness and incongruity is bound to entertain, and if it has been a difficult one, the pleasure of self-congratulation makes us relish it all the more. [Laurent Le Sage, *Jean Giraudoux: His Life and Works,* Pennsylvania State University Press, University Park, Pa., 1959, pp. 176–177, 186–189.]

Giraudoux is an idealist, but he does not believe in miracles. He has confidence in man and prefers to leave him to search for his own solutions through debate and an appeal to the intellect. He does not believe that we live in the best of possible worlds, but he does not exclude the possibility that we could live in the best of possible worlds. His universe magnifies beauty, because he knows that it is an alternative to ugliness; the one would not exist without the other. Perhaps he remembers the verdict of Socrates—"Evils, Theodorus, can never pass away, for there must always remain something which is antagonistic to good." The antithesis of words, and the play on these words in the dialogue, is to be found throughout Giraudoux's plays. In *La Guerre de Troie n'aura pas lieu* the play is on the words 'guerre/paix'; in *Amphitryon 38* the play is on the words 'jour/nuit'; it is on 'vie/mort' in *Intermezzo* and 'vice/vertu' in *Sodome et Gomorrhe*. In *La Folle de Chaillot*, Irma, the Parisian dishwasher, has a soliloquy in which she invokes the following examples: "I detest the ugly, I adore the beautiful"; "I detest the wicked, I adore kindness"; "I detest the evening, I adore the morning"; "I detest the devil, I adore God"; "I adore freedom, I detest slavery"; "I don't much like women, I adore men"; "I adore life, I detest death."

In his strange land of reality and make-believe, Giraudoux brings together both human beings and those who are not subject to human laws. Frequently the humans lack those human virtues of love, forgiveness, understanding which the non-human characters may display, but in the end these are only human failings which can be redressed. Many questions are asked which are as perplexing as the songs of the Sirens, but no definite answers are attempted. Young girls can retain their youth and beauty for eternity, or turn into the mad old hags of Chaillot, and we may live in a world where the mad old hags are the sane inhabitants. The only certainty is death and everlasting life, which, indeed, is the riddle of the universe.

Many modern writers have been moved, like Giraudoux, to ask what is the place of man in life, and although most have given more excessive interpretations than Giraudoux, none has been a greater humanist. Life is neither a tragedy nor a comedy. Laughter can follow tears and laughter can lead to tears. All the threads are interwoven in the modern theatre, as a character observes in *Siegfried*. This, then, is the point of departure for Giraudoux's study of life, where there are no borders between laughter and tears, no frontiers between dreams and reality, and where always we can see our vision of the ideal in terms of the real world. . . .

There are those who accuse Giraudoux of being a literary dilettante in the theatre, presumably either those who do not hold so highly the purpose of the drama, or the existentialists, who see their paradise threatened by the influence of Giraudoux's universe, and who have therefore taken the critique of Giraudoux by their lord and master Sartre to heart. But all important writers have had their critics—Pirandello was responsible for riots in the streets of Rome and duels in Milan—and Giraudoux has had fewer than most. His reputation to-day in France stands exceedingly high, his plays have entered into the repertoires of the new provincial dramatic centres, and the possibility of Jouvet's prophecy that "if the language of Racine is still spoken in France in 200 years, the plays of Giraudoux will still be performed" should not lightly be dismissed. For Giraudoux believes in good theatre, the theatre of the great dramatists. And Giraudoux's success has been as remarkable as his plays were unorthodox and his ideas unlimited. He can have no imitators. Yet he does point a direction in which young writers can follow, he has led them to a point of departure from where they can advance. Just as Pirandello experimented gradually away from the naturalist camp, Giraudoux has succeeded in turning the semi-circle in theatrical fashions and has freed the theatre from the stifling atmosphere of naturalism. With his impressionistic interpretation of life Giraudoux has shown how the world we live in can respond to the poetic sweep of imagination. His way is always towards a less sophisticated universe, and his creation of this little world which is more than a world, inhabited by characters which are more than human, is the testament of faith which Giraudoux has bequeathed to a world in doubt. [Frederick Lumley, *Trends in 20th Century Drama*, Essential Books, New York, 1960, pp. 42–43, 58–59.]

The great risk of Giraudoux's method is that his essential seriousness will be lost in paradox and irony, that the considerable force of his convictions will not be felt at all.

That Giraudoux is a serious playwright, as well as a fantastical one, has been known for a long time to those familiar with his works in the original. That he has been accused of being an escapist is true, and it is also true that he has had his moments of escapism. As Claude-Edmonde Magny has pointed out, however, in her excellent *Précieux Giraudoux*, preciosity is a perilous enterprise. It risks blinding its audience with a surface brilliance which may hide what is going on beneath, and Giraudoux's frequent seriousness has at times been missed, despite his own statements about the function of his theatre. For these statements, like his plays, have been poetically conceived and put, and in the 'thirties and 'forties it was often hard to believe in a poet's seriousness, particularly if the poet was charming and witty and obviously in love, if not with life, at least with certain aspects of it. I would merely submit the following, which appeared in a volume entitled *Visitations* in 1947 but which dates from 1942. . . .

Epochs are in good order only if, in those radiant confessionals which are its theatres and arenas, the crowd comes, and in so far as possible in its most dazzling confessional dress, in order to augment their solemnity, to listen to its own avowals of cowardice and sacrifice, of hate and of adoration. And if it cries also, "Bring on the Prophet!" For there is no theatre without divination. Not that factitious divination which gives names and dates, but the real, which reveals to men these surprising truths: that the living must live, that the living must die, that autumn follows after summer, spring after winter, that there are the four elements, and happiness, and billions of catastrophes, that life is a reality, that it is a dream, that man lives by peace, that man lives by blood, in brief, what they will never know. . . .

[Bert M-P. Leefmans, "Giraudoux's Other Muse," *Kenyon Review*, Vol. 16, 1954, pp. 611–612.]

There is an instructive use of paradox in Tiger at the Gates. *Through paradox, something like a tragic view is presented. The question that remains, largely as a result of Giraudoux's method in this play, is whether men must wage war, and one possible answer, at least implicit here, according to Wallace Fowlie, is that he need not.*

'The Trojan War will not take place.' Through this clarion sentence, placed in the mouth of Andromache at the very opening of the play, the author gives notice that his intention is to present war as a paradox. Paradox it has always appeared to men of good-will, and paradox it

must continue to appear until a way is found to eliminate its causes. For a professional diplomat, well placed to observe the tortuous and futile negotiations which followed the war of 1914–18, the prospects of discovering these causes before a new cataclysm should befall humanity could scarcely seem favourable. To Andromache's cry of mingled joy and hope, Cassandra opposes a pessimism based on a sober view of facts as they strike her. The prophetess of doom explains that it is not by choice that she foretells disaster. 'I see nothing, Andromache, I foresee nothing. I merely take account of twin stupidities, the stupidity of men and the stupidity of the elements.' Although *The Trojan War,* presented for the first time on 21st November 1935, is not called a tragedy by the author, it is in fact a tragedy of a kind far more easily grasped than *Judith,* and as such it was understood by critics and public alike. If it is not, as many maintain, Giraudoux's greatest play, it is certainly the one in which he first rises to the heights as a moralist and as a thinker, without losing any of the skill of the practised dramatist. . . .

As in the case of *Amphitryon,* the starting point of *The Trojan War* is provided by Giraudoux's classical studies; but here the resemblance ends. Whereas in the writing of *Amphitryon* he makes use of a plot already in existence, for the second play only the characters and the basic situation are borrowed. The whole mechanism of suspense and dramatic development has been built up by Giraudoux himself, working onwards from the point at which war between Troy and Greece is as yet undecided to the moment at which it becomes inevitable. To maintain dramatic tension up to the very end about a hypothetical possibility which the audience knows from the start to be unrealizable, must be regarded as a *tour-de-force,* illustrating in advance the view of tragedy expounded by the Chorus at the opening of Jean Anouilh's *Antigone.* The tragic nature of tragedy lies not in the neglected chance of avoiding disaster, but in the inevitability with which disaster advances. 'Only God is really without pity,' says Giraudoux already in *Amica America,* published in 1919, when memories of war were still fresh in his mind.

There is much to be said for the point of view that by working forwards to a dénouement known in advance, Giraudoux adopted a kind of self-discipline highly profitable to dramatic concentration. Everything had necessarily to lead in one direction only: the war was going to come about. His originality reveals itself to the full in the imaginative power with which he conceives his characters; his technical skill in the ease with which the play advances from scene to scene until the climax is reached only in the very last lines. [Donald Inskip, *Jean Giraudoux: the Making of a Dramatist,* Oxford University Press, New York, 1958, pp. 80–81.]

When the opening of *La Guerre de Troie n'aura pas lieu (Tiger at the Gates)* was announced for November 1935, the mystifying title was looked upon by the Parisians as a trait of the *"normalien"* (Giraudoux had studied at the École Normale Supérieure) because everyone knew that the Trojan War had taken place. His art and his conception of tragedy are fully exemplified in this play, which is a combination of wit and seriousness, of the spectacular and the threat of war. . . .

Hector answers and defeats one after the other all the human reasons for declaring war. But he is on the losing side because war, in Giraudoux's conception, is a fatality not controllable by man. The profoundest reason for war comes from man's love of war, albeit a shameful and hidden love. What is war? It is risk, adventure, a liking for danger. It is that force able to separate man from the comfortable forms of happiness into which he sinks so easily. By contrast he takes delight in the convulsion of war which he sees on the battlefield or which he reads about in his daily newspaper. In Giraudoux's world, woman does not feel the same need for brutality. She has learned to offset the monotony of comfortable living by simple means. Andromache and Hecuba are horrified by the virile instincts that war arouses.

But even if man himself overcame his warlike instincts, Giraudoux would answer that destiny itself demands war. The dramaturgy of *La Guerre de Troie* shows how destiny, which wants the war, uses Hector himself as a pawn to bring it about. Giraudoux's conclusion is bleak and despairing. War is hateful, but it is eternal because it comes from the nature of man. And even if men reach some temporary agreement, destiny, for whom it is a favorite distraction, will release it.

Behind the legend of the Trojan War, Giraudoux seemed to be referring, in 1935, to the coming of the Second World War. This was the obvious interpretation ˉof a line in Act II [page 661], "Everyone knows it—we are going to fight." (*L'univers le sait, nous allons nous battre. . . .*) Despite such theories on war, Giraudoux's fundamental philosophy is not pessimism. It is not the vision of man placed in a world unsuited to him, in which his existence will appear absurd. Giraudoux's view is far less intrinsically tragic. If there is a lack of harmony between man and the world, the fault is man's. When man tries to bring about some kind of reconciliation between himself and the world, tragedy ensues, or what is called tragedy. We must learn to see the world from the viewpoint of universal harmony and not from the viewpoint of individual man. [Wallace Fowlie, *Dionysus in Paris: a Guide to Contemporary French Theater,* Meridian Books, Inc., New York, 1960, pp. 64–65.]

GLOSSARY

a brief list of some of the most frequently used terms in the theatre.

ACTING AREA   That part of the stage in which a performance takes place.

ACTING SPACE   That part of the stage, enclosed by the scenery, in which actors can perform.

ACTION   The main sequence of events in a play. See *Unities.*

AGON   In Greek drama, a verbal struggle or debate between two characters.

ALIENATION   See *epic theater.*

ANTAGONIST   The character or force opposed to the hero or protagonist.

ANTITHEATER   The deliberate eschewing of conventional theatrical devices, such as climax and dénouement, by such playwrights as Ionesco, Beckett, and Albee, usually for satirical purposes.

APRON   The part of the stage in front of the curtain.

ARENA STAGE   A central stage, without a proscenium, surrounded by seats on three sides or entirely surrounded by them. Also called *theater-in-the-round.*

ARETE   Among the Greeks, one's particular excellence or greatness.

ASIDE   A dramatic convention in which the actor's words are not heard by other actors on the stage with him; thus the audience is informed of a character's real thoughts or hidden intentions. Eugene O'Neill's *Strange Interlude* (1928) makes exhaustive use of this device.

ATMOSPHERE   The general mood of a play or the special effects of the play's setting. Frequently, the effect produced by scenery and lighting.

AT RISE (OF CURTAIN)   Beginning of play or of act.

AUTO   Religious play of the Spanish theater of the Middle Ages. A descendant of the Morality Play. Often accompanied by music.

BACKING   Scenery used behind openings to conceal off-stage areas from the audience's view.

BACKSTAGE   The parts of the theater behind the scenery, including storage areas, dressing rooms, etc.

BATTEN   Piece of lumber used to stiffen the canvas or board surfaces of scenery.

BLOCKING   Organization of the action of a play, often in the form of diagrams.

BORDER   Small drop or curtain used to mask overhead lights or the tops of scenery. A sequence of borders may act as a ceiling. Also called *drape.*

BORDER LIGHTS   Lamps mounted over a stage to produce overhead lighting.

BOX SET   Three walls and the ceiling of a room created by flats cleated together, with the proper openings for windows and doors, rather than by perspective painting on a single flat.

BROADWAY   Generic name for the commercially successful New York theater. Actually, most of the theaters on Broadway show films; those which house dramas are, with few exceptions, located east and west of Broadway.

BURLESQUE   In drama, a theatrical piece which parodies the sort of play with which it deals or which it pretends to resemble. Prominent examples in English drama are Buckingham's *The Rehearsal* (1671), Gay's *Beggar's Opera* (1728), and Fielding's *Tom Thumb the Great* (1730).

BUSINESS   A bit of action, a gesture, or grimace used to illuminate a character or a set of lines.

CATHARSIS   Literally, cleansing or purging. Aris-

669

totle's *Poetics* asserts briefly and enigmatically that tragedy, through pity and fear, effects a proper purgation of these emotions. The meaning of this statement has been the subject of much controversy.

CENTER Center of the acting space. Indicated by the letter C.

CHORUS In Greek drama, the group of actors who danced and sang choral odes in unison. Their dramatic function varied from direct participation in the action to supplying commentary on it. In Elizabethan drama the term was applied to a single actor who addressed the audience in a prologue introductory to the play as a whole or to some part of it.

CLASSICISM See *neoclassicism*.

CLIMAX The turning point of a play, the peak of emotional tension.

CLOSET DRAMA Supposedly a play written to be read rather than performed. In practice, usually a play which promises, or has proved, to be unsuccessful in performance.

COMEDY A play designed to amuse and to come to a happy ending. Like tragedy, the term covers a great variety of dramatic forms; see, for example, the three entries below.

COMEDY OF HUMOURS A kind of comedy built upon dominant traits in most of the characters; one trait, such as jealousy, greed, or braggadocio, is usually the only one in a character's make-up, and is employed to make him appear ridiculous. The form is based upon the humour psychology of the Middle Ages and the Renaissance.

COMEDY OF MANNERS Comedy which concerns the actions and attitudes of people with reference to a particular social code.

COMMEDIA DELL'ARTE Literally, "Comedy of the Guild," a form of comedy popular in Italy from the mid-sixteenth to the early eighteenth century. It was acted by professionals who were organized in small companies. The members were cast to type and went on stage with only a sketchy scenario prepared; they improvised the dialogue. The skeleton plots usually derived from Plautus and Terence. The comic style, as well as many of the character types, influenced such playwrights as Shakespeare, Jonson, and Molière.

CONFLICT An essential ingredient of most plots, in which a play's single protagonist or collective hero is opposed by a person or persons, a force or forces.

CONFIDANTE A secondary character in a play whose main function is to provide a main character with a friend to whom he can entrust confidences. The usual purpose, of course, is dramatic exposition.

CONTAMINATION A term which originally referred to the practice of mixing two plots from Greek drama to produce a single play, as in Plautus. It was extended to include the use of multiple plots in one play, as in Shakespeare's *Merchant of Venice*.

CONVENTION Any practice or rule which operates by common consent of the audience, even though it may be unrealistic or arbitrary. Asides and prologues are conventions of which modern audiences are acutely conscious, while the box set and three-act structure are generally accepted without notice.

COUP DE THÉÂTRE "Stroke of the theater." A sudden, startling turn of the plot used with great effect of surprise. It occurs most often in melodrama.

CROSS An actor's movement to change his location on stage.

CUE Last few words or business by one actor used as signal for another actor's entrance or speech or business.

CURTAIN RAISER One-act play, usually a farce, used particularly in the nineteenth century as an *apéritif* before the main course, a five-act drama.

CYCLORAMA Large drop, usually of canvas, hung at rear of stage to represent the sky. Any number of different kinds of light can be thrown upon it, to indicate times of day or night, changes of mood, etc.

DECORUM The quality of being proper or fitting. Originally, as in Aristotle, its importance resulted from the principle that order and proportion were essential to beauty. Later, especially in the neoclassic period, the concept of decorum came to be identified with fixed standards of what was fitting to a form or proper for polite society. The strained diction of Heroic Drama is an example of the former; an instance of the latter was the substitution, in the French adaptation of *Othello,* of a misleading note for Desdemona's handkerchief, an article which would have offended the sensibilities of the audience.

DÉNOUEMENT The final disentangling of the intricacies of plot. Also the point in the plot at which the unraveling occurs.

DEUS EX MACHINA "God from the machine." In the Greek theater a crane was usually employed to lower gods to the stage, simulating their descent from the heavens. Euripides's free use of the device was parodied by Aristophanes. The introduction of a god offered an easy, artificial means of resolving plot complications. Consequently, the phrase now usually refers to a dénouement achieved by a surprising turn of events and not growing naturally out of plot and character.

DIKĒ The Greek concept of justice, particularly seen as a working out of the proper order of things in the universe.

DOWNSTAGE The area of the stage nearest the audience. Indicated by the letter D.

DRAMA The imitation by one or more actors of one or more events. From the Greek *dran,* meaning to do, to act, to make.

DRAMATIC EXPOSITION The presentation to the audience of relevant background information which it must have in order to understand the action which follows. Historically this presentation makes varying approaches to and departures from realism. The prologues of some Greek and Roman plays are completely unrealistic; the bald exchange of information between characters in Elizabethan drama is somewhat less so. Most modern playwrights try to hide the exposition in natural, casual dialogue, but the opening telephone conversation or exchange between servants will not always bear up under close sceptical analysis.

DRAMATIC IRONY An irony growing out of a situation; the audience is aware of information of which one or more characters on the stage are ignorant.

DRAMATURGY The art of writing or producing plays.

DRAME Originally a French term for serious plays which included some comic touches, un-like French classical tragedy. It now sometimes refers to serious plays which do not conclude tragically.

DRAPE See *border.*

DROP Large sheet of cloth, usually canvas, dyed or painted as background scenery and suspended from a pipe or wooden batten.

DUMB SHOW A form of *pantomime* frequently used as part of another play as, for example, in *Hamlet.*

EPIC THEATER The drama of Bertolt Brecht and those who follow him, in which the audience is, as much as possible, held off from vicarious experience of the events on stage by a deliberate *alienation,* or estrangement, of the emotions. Brecht's effort was to convert the mind rather than to touch the emotions of his spectators, by truncated scenes, anticlimaxes, fragments of music, the use of placards and like devices.

EPISODIC PLOT A plot in which the incidents are linked not by probabilities of character in a unified action, but only by loose chronological treatment of a central figure.

EXODOS In Greek drama, the final scene in a tragedy; it follows the last choral ode.

EXPRESSIONISM A movement in drama which seeks to present subjective experience and psychological states rather than an objective view of affairs. Expressionistic drama makes extensive use of symbolism, in effects of staging as well as in plot and dialogue. Its chief source is Strindberg, its most important later playwrights, Kaiser, Toller, Čapek, and O'Neill.

FARCE A kind of comedy characterized by highly improbable situations, horseplay, and broad humor.

FLASHBACK An interruption of the normal chronological order of events through the introduction, out of sequence, of an incident which occurred at some time in the past.

FLAT A large piece of upright scenery consisting of a wooden frame covered with cloth or board, usually canvas.

FLIES Space over the stage into which scenery and lighting units are raised (or *flown*) to be stored. Scenery is raised by a system of weights and pulleys or loose ropes from a balcony high on the stage wall called the *fly gallery.*

FLOODLIGHTS Single lamps used to diffuse light over large portions of the stage.

FOIL A character who sets off or enhances another, as Laertes does Hamlet.

FOLIO A large printed volume (approximately 13½ × 8¾ inches), so called because a printer's sheet was folded once through the middle for binding, affording four printed pages. A long work or an author's collected works were usually printed in folio.

FOOTLIGHTS Sets of lights mounted on or recessed in the stage floor just in front of the curtains.

FOURTH WALL By convention, the open space that the proscenium frames is accepted as the fourth wall of a room. With the acceptance of this convention, an actor may behave as if the wall is there, turn his back to the audience, and all but lean upon the invisible partition.

GELATIN See *spotlights*.

GOOD THEATER A phrase ostensibly praising a stage production, or some device in it, which has achieved popular success; it is quite often used in defense of a piece which shows no merit beyond sheer theatrical effectiveness.

GRIDIRON An open framework over the stage from which scenery is suspended.

GROUND-ROW Low pieces of scenery, cut out and painted to represent hills, rocks, and shrubs.

HAMARTIA Aristotle's "tragic flaw." It is the fault of character or error of judgment which, ideally, brings misfortune to the tragic hero.

HEROIC PLAY A type popular in England between 1664 and 1678. It was characterized by dialogue written in rhymed iambic pentameter couplets (hence "heroic couplets"), the theme of love and honor, and a style marked by much posturing and bombast. Dryden was its chief practitioner.

HISTORY PLAY A type of play, especially popular in Elizabethan England, which has as its immediate purpose the dramatization of a series of historical events. History Plays which employ episodic plot structure and achieve only this limited end are sometimes called *chronicle plays,* as distinguished from History Plays with more complex structure, greater depth of characterization, and more profound didactic pur-

poses. Most of Shakespeare's History Plays belong to the latter group.

HOUSE That part of the theater in which the audience sits.

HYBRIS The Greek term (sometimes also Anglicized as *hubris*) for overweening pride; its presence in an individual led him to forget or to ignore his proper relationship to the gods, and consequently to transgress against their explicit command or the moral law.

IMITATION Representation; frequent appearance of the term in criticism is largely a result of Aristotle's definition of tragedy as the imitation of an action that is serious, complete, and of a certain magnitude.

INNER PROSCENIUM A false proscenium used to narrow the proscenium opening.

INTERLUDE A kind of play which developed out of the Morality. Its name seems to derive from its presentation, between other entertainments, at a banquet. It increasingly dealt with political and social themes, rather than maintaining the distinctly moral character of the Morality Play, and was often satirical.

LIGHT-CUE SHEET A list of the signals by which the electrician can see the moments at which each of a number of lighting effects will be required.

LIGHT PLOT Detailed lighting plans for a play.

LITURGICAL DRAMA Any of a number of dramatic forms which developed from the Mass, as, for example, the *trope.*

LIVING NEWSPAPER An episodic stage presentation, usually employed to dramatize news events or to instruct. Developed by the Federal Theater Project of the WPA, it owes some of its technical innovations and motivating force to the German Expressionist theater.

MASK To conceal any area from the audience's view.

MASQUE A Renaissance entertainment, usually of an allegorical nature, performed at court by the nobility. Ben Jonson's *antimasque,* performed by professionals, was a kind of burlesque version of the masque, in which the clown's role was usurped by the nobleman.

MELODRAMA A form of drama which pretends to treat serious conflicts, but actually deals in sensationalism in order to provide the audience with thrills. Motivation is usually oversimplified or obscure, characterization shallow, and dramatic logic ignored. Spectacular elements—music used to excite emotion, weird or lurid stage effects—and an elaborate acting style often accompany the profusion of unlikely incidents.

MESSENGER A character in a play who is used to bring news of events represented as having occurred offstage.

METAPHOR A figure of speech in which one thing is called another. Now often analyzed, as by I. A. Richards, into *tenor* (the central idea or emotion) and *vehicle* (the image attached to the idea or emotion).

MIRACLE PLAY Medieval drama based on Scripture or a saint's life, more frequently the latter.

MISE-EN-SCÈNE A French term, now in general use, for stage setting (scenery and properties).

MONOLOGUE Generally, a speech spoken by one person, relatively long, and forming either a whole or a self-contained part. It is distinguished from the soliloquy by being addressed to an audience, either present or understood. A type of monologue which enjoys a fitful popularity is that which presents one side of a telephone conversation.

MORALITY PLAY Late medieval drama designed to instruct. Generally an allegory of the conflict between good and evil with humor provided by the characterization of the devil and by figures of vice.

MYSTERY PLAY A Miracle Play which concentrates on a Biblical story, produced in cycles by the medieval guilds as part of their "mysteries." Each episode was assigned to a different guild. Among the most famous of the surviving cycles are the long York sequence and the Towneley (or Wakefield) cycle, which contains *The Second Shepherd's Play*.

NATURALISM In the theater, a late nineteenth-century movement directed against the artificialities of the romantic drama and the *well-made play*. Zola's version insisted upon the presentation of one small *slice of life*, in precise detail. The naturalism of the early Strindberg, as, for example, in *Miss Julie*, is much broader. As a movement naturalism is generally deterministic in attitude, presenting its

characters as inflexibly conditioned by society or psychological or physiological elements or some combination thereof.

NEOCLASSICISM Generally, a literary movement in Europe from the sixteenth through the eighteenth century. The term has different applications in different countries and different times: sometimes *classicism* and *pseudoclassicism* are used in connection with it. As a literary ideal, it refers generally to an adherence to certain aesthetic principles, alleged to be derived from the study of Greek and Latin literature. Foremost among these principles are an insistence on tradition, including the imitation of models, rather than on uninhibited originality; the exertion by the artist of conscious and constant discipline and restraint; an emphasis on the representative and universal rather than on the limited and particular. In its more narrow application, neoclassicism suggests rigid adherence to the "rules" supposedly drawn from Aristotle and Horace, including the Unities, decorum, etc.

NEW COMEDY A kind of comedy popular in Greece in the fourth and third centuries B.C.; its chief exponent was Menander (d. 292 B.C.), none of whose plays is extant in complete form. New Comedy stressed character types and smoothly constructed (although rather conventionalized) plots. It furnished Plautus and Terence with characters and incidents for use in Roman comedy.

OFFSTAGE That part of the stage which the audience cannot see.

OLD COMEDY Greek comedy of the fifth and fourth centuries B.C. which made use of a single basic incident in the action to satirize individuals and attitudes in politics, literature, etc. Its master was Aristophanes (c. 448–385 B.C.).

PANTOMIME While this term has historically possessed a number of widely varying meanings, it is now usually used to denote a theatrical performance in which one or more actors, using no dialogue, employ movement, gesture, and facial expression to convey meaning.

PARODOS The "entering ode" in Greek tragedy, the first ode which the chorus sings in the play.

PASTORAL DRAMA A form of drama which origi-

Glossary

nated in Renaissance Italy; Tasso's *Aminta* (1573) and Guarini's *Il Pastor Fido* (c. 1590) were the most successful there. The form employs rural settings and stylized shepherds in presenting a rustic life which is idyllic and artificial. In England Fletcher and Jonson attempted pastoral plays, and Shakespeare used the form critically in *As You Like It*.

PERIPETEIA A reversal or turning about. Aristotle considers it one of the regular elements of plot: a change of the situation into its opposite. He furnishes as example the character who tries to cheer Oedipus by revealing his parentage, thereby changing the whole situation.

PLACES Positions of the actors at the beginning of an act or scene.

PLOT One of the most difficult of literary terms to define. Perhaps the simplest and most useful definition of a dramatic plot is the plan of action of a play. Secondary actions provide *subplots* (see below), as distinguished from the *main plot*. Two equally important and interrelated actions produce what is called a *double plot*.

PROBLEM PLAY A serious play which has as its primary purpose the investigation, and usually the suggested solution, of a particular social or political problem. While at one extreme such plays shrink to mere propaganda, at the other they extend to treat generalized human problems not limited to a specific time and place. Some of Ibsen's Problem Plays, for example, are of the latter sort.

PROLOGUE In ancient Greek drama an introductory speech, usually expository in nature. Euripides relied upon it heavily, and the device was adopted by Plautus. The Elizabethans sometimes used a prologue and called it a chorus. During the Restoration and eighteenth century in England the prologue was usually a poem spoken by one of the actors but distinct from the play; it commented on the nature of the play, and even on topical issues apart from it.

PROPERTIES All that is added to the scenery on stage—furniture, pictures, window draperies, books, vases, etc.

PROSCENIUM The architectural opening through which a play is seen and by which the stage is divided from the audience.

PROSCENIUM ARCH The arch that frames the proscenium opening.

PROTAGONIST Originally, in Greek drama, the first actor; now applied to the central figure in a play.

QUARTO A volume prepared by folding the printer's sheet twice, the result being four divisions on each side or twice those of a folio. In Renaissance England individual plays were published in quarto.

REALISM The result of the close observation of appearances. The emphasis in the theater of realism is on language, gesture, situation, and scene as they might be found in the world. Ibsen led the revolt of the realists against the distortions of the early nineteenth-century theater. As a movement, realism is more moderate than naturalism; its progenitors and followers never surrendered to an all-encompassing biological, psychological, or sociological determinism.

RECOGNITION SCENE Also called the *discovery*. A scene in which a character (usually the protagonist) first recognizes some crucial fact about his own identity or that of another character. Aristotle, who considered it a standard element of the plot, thought it most effective when it coincides with the reversal, as in *Oedipus Rex*.

REVENGE PLAY A type of tragedy which turns upon the initial necessity for vengeance by the central character; a delay, occasioned by obstacles which arise; and finally the accomplishment of the revenge. Developing in the English Renaissance from the influence of Seneca, the form was seemingly initiated by Kyd's *The Spanish Tragedy* and found its most complex development in Shakespeare's *Hamlet*.

SCRIM A light fabric which can be painted to serve as a backdrop. Because of its transparency, it allows an additional stage set behind it to appear when the rear area of the stage is lighted. Thus, for instance, the scrim can represent the wall of a room, through which the street outside can be seen when lights are used behind the scrim.

SENECAN DRAMA The type of play associated with the Roman dramatist, prose writer, and politician, Lucius Annaeus Seneca (c. 4 B.C.–A.D. 65). He was probably the author of nine tragedies based on Greek plays, particularly those of Euripides. Seneca's plays seem to have been written for declamation by one actor rather than for acting out by several. Violent in plot, Stoic in attitude, alternately sententious and epigrammatic in style, the plays of Seneca strongly influenced English Renaissance dramatists.

SENTIMENTAL COMEDY A type of comedy popular in France and England in the eighteenth century. It attempted to engage the sentimental sympathies of the audience, and had little or nothing to do with arousing laughter. Goldsmith and Sheridan wrote their "Laughing Comedies" as correctives to Sentimental Comedy.

SET or **SETTING** Scenery for any given act or scene.

SHIFT To replace the sets and properties of one scene with those of another.

SIGHT LINES The audience's lines of vision to all parts of the acting space.

SOLILOQUY A speech in which a character talks to himself, or to no one in particular. It is distinguished from the *aside* by its greater length and complexity, usually presenting not only some intention of the speaker but also his motivation and, at times, his psychology.

SOPHROSYNE Moderation or self control, one of the most important ethical norms of ancient Greece.

SPECTACLE A display, sometimes incorporated into drama, which appeals largely or wholly to the senses (for instance, through lavish settings, opulent costumes, etc.).

SPOTLIGHTS Powerful lamps equipped with focusing devices. A sheet of colored *gelatin* framed in front of a spotlight is used to produce colored light on stage.

STAGE DIRECTIONS Notes added to the text of a play, explaining details of movement, gesture, setting, and properties. They vary in length from the mere fragments in Elizabethan plays to the elaborate pieces of exposition of Shaw.

STAGE LEFT and **STAGE RIGHT** Areas to the actor's left and right when he faces the audience. Indicated by the letters L and R.

STAGE WHISPER A loud whisper by an actor, designed to be heard by the audience.

STASIMON In Greek tragedy, any choral ode after the first one, or parodos. *Oedipus Rex* has four stasima.

STICHOMYTHIA Dialogue in which characters speak in alternate single lines of verse. Often used for disputation or scenes of high emotional tension, the device was a favorite one of Euripides and of his imitator Seneca, from whom it passed to Elizabethan drama. There it was broken down further, so that each character may have only one-half or one-third a line at times. Kyd's *Spanish Tragedy* and Shakespeare's *Richard III* furnish numerous examples.

STRIKE To take down scenery from the stage.

SUBPLOT A plot which is developed in addition to the main plot in a play. The methods and degrees of linkage between main plot and subplot vary greatly from play to play. Most often the mechanical link is furnished by one or more characters who function in both plots. In Elizabethan drama there is probably always a thematic relationship between subplot and main plot, with the two plots compared or contrasted. While critics with a psychological bias sometimes make much of the idea that the function of a subplot is to furnish "comic relief," relieving the strong tension which the main plot has produced in the audience, it is obviously impossible to think of many subplots —that of Gloucester in *King Lear*, for instance —in terms of "comic relief."

SWITCHBOARD The board on which appear all the switches which control stage lighting.

TEMPO The rate of speed at which a scene or a whole drama plays or at which an actor speaks.

TENOR See *metaphor*.

THEATER-IN-THE-ROUND. See *arena stage*.

THEATRICALITY The quality of artificiality or sheer sensationalism in stage presentations. Striking effects are introduced for their own sake rather than with regard to meaningful function in an organic whole.

TIRADE In French drama, a long, rhetorical speech in which the speaker somewhat formally analyzes or describes his emotions.

TRAGEDY Like *comedy*, a term of such breadth and varying usage as almost to defy definition. In almost every theatrical era, it has been the dramatic form in which both the largest potentialities and the most upsetting failures of human beings have been examined. In almost every significant tragic drama, there is some form of self-reversal or self-betrayal, ending with death. The conventions of classical drama as described by Aristotle are generally the basis for all examinations of tragedy; the terms of Aristotle's discussion are described above and below under *catharsis, decorum, hamartia, hybris, imitation, peripeteia, recognition scene,* and *Unities.*

TRAGEDY OF BLOOD A name sometimes applied to the Elizabethan Revenge Play, which derived from Seneca.

TROPE A brief dialogue used to illustrate or explicate a portion of the Mass. The Easter trope of the Abbey of St. Gall is generally accepted as the beginning of *liturgical drama.* The trope, known as *Quem quaeritis?* (Whom do you seek?), parallels the Gospel narrative of the confrontation of the angel by the three Marys at the tomb on Easter morning. Somehow it was separated from its position at the beginning of the Easter Mass and given its own dignity as a drama to be enacted at matins on Easter morning.

UNITIES The three Unities were formal limitations on tragedy (and extended to drama generally) introduced into neoclassic criticism and practice by Castelvetro's commentary on Aristotle's *Poetics.* Unity of Action prescribes a single plot; Unity of Time limits the time represented to twenty-four hours (some critics allowed thirty-six, but the ideal was a succession of incidents which occupied no longer a period than that required to present them on the stage); Unity of Place forbids changing the scene throughout the play, or, at its most lenient, forbids representing more than a single city. It should be noted that the Unities were not the invention of Aristotle, who was describing, not prescribing, and who spoke only of "one action and that a whole" and the tendency of the drama with which he was directly concerned to endeavor, "as far as possible, to confine itself to a single revolution of the sun, or but slightly to exceed this limit."

UP or UPSTAGE That part of the stage which is farthest removed from the audience.

VEHICLE See *metaphor.*

WELL-MADE PLAY Now a derogatory term for a play that is carefully motivated, smoothly plotted, and neatly resolved with all loose ends gathered and everything explained, but which has nothing to recommend it besides this neatness and plausibility, and is consequently found to be essentially artificial and shallow. The French playwright Eugène Scribe (1791–1861) was its most influential champion and, with more than 400 plays to his credit, perhaps its most prolific.

WINGS Offstage areas right and left of the acting space; used for actors' entrances and exits.

BIBLIOGRAPHY

SOPHOCLES

Sophocles: The Seven Plays in English Verse, translated by Lewis Campbell, Oxford, 1906. (World's Classics)

The Dramas of Sophocles, translated by Sir George Young, London, 1906. (Everyman's Library)

Adams, S. M.: *Sophocles the Playwright, The Phoenix,* supplementary vol. 3, Toronto, 1927.

Greene, William C.: *Moira: Fate, Good, and Evil in Greek Thought,* Cambridge, Mass., 1944.

Kirkwood, G. M.: *A Study of Sophoclean Drama,* Cornell Studies in Classical Philology, vol. 31, Ithaca, N. Y., 1958.

Knox, Bernard M.: *Oedipus at Thebes,* New Haven, 1957.

Moore, J. A.: *Sophocles and Arete,* Cambridge, Mass., 1938.

Opstelten, J. C.: *Sophocles and Greek Pessimism,* Amsterdam, 1952.

Webster, T. B. L.: *An Introduction to Sophocles.* Oxford, 1936.

EURIPIDES

The Plays of Euripides, translated by E. P. Coleridge, 2 vols., London, 1891. (Bohn's Classical Library)

The Plays of Euripides, translated by Gilbert Murray, London, 1914 (includes six plays), 1931 (with two additional plays). [Also see *Five Plays of Euripides,* translated by Gilbert Murray, New York, 1934.]

Appleton, R. B.: *Euripides the Idealist,* London, 1927.

Decharme, Paul: *Euripides and the Spirit of the Dramas,* translated by James Loeb, New York, 1906.

Greenwood, L. H.: *Aspects of Euripidean Tragedy,* Cambridge, 1953.

Grube, G. M. A.: *The Drama of Euripides,* London, 1941.

Lucas, F. L.: *Euripides and His Influence,* Boston, 1923.

Norwood, Gilbert: *Euripides and Shaw,* Boston, 1921.

Verrall, A. W.: *Essays on Four Plays of Euripides,* Cambridge, 1905.

————: *Euripides the Rationalist,* Cambridge, 1895.

PLAUTUS

The Works of Plautus, edited and translated by Paul Nixon, 5 vols., London, 1916–38. (Loeb Classical Library)

The Complete Roman Drama, edited by G. E. Duckworth, 2 vols., New York, 1942.

Three Plays of Plautus, translated by F. A. Wright and H. Lionel Rogers, London, 1925.

Beare, W.: *The Roman Stage,* London, 1950.

Bieber, Margarete: *The History of the Greek and Roman Theater,* Princeton, 1939.

Conrad, C. C.: *The Technique of Continuous Action in Roman Comedy,* Chicago, 1398.

Duckworth, G. F.: *The Nature of Roman Comedy,* Princeton, 1952.

Dunkin, P. L.: *Post-Aristophanic Comedy,* Urbana, Ill., 1946.

Fields, D. E.: *The Technique of Exposition in Roman Comedy,* Menasha, Wis., 1915.

Norwood, Gilbert: *Plautus and Terence,* London, 1932.

Perry, Henry Ten Eyck: *Masters of Dramatic Comedy and Their Social Themes,* Cambridge, Mass., 1939.

Wright, F. A.: *Three Roman Poets,* New York, 1938.

SIR DAVID LYNDSAY

Ane Satyre of the Thrie Estaits, edited by F. Hall. Part IV, *Works of Sir David Lindsay,* Early English Text Society, Original Series, No. 37, Edinburgh, 1869.

Ane Satyre of the Thrie Estaitis, edited, with an Introduction and Notes, by Douglas Hamer, vols. 2 and 4 of *The Works of Sir David Lindsay,* Scottish Text Society, Third Series, Nos. 2 and 8, Edinburgh, 1931, 1936.

Chief Pre-Shakespearean Dramas, edited by Joseph Quincy Adams, Boston, 1924.

English Miracle Plays, Moralities, and Interludes, edited by A. W. Pollard, 5th ed., rev., Oxford, 1909.

Everyman and Other Interludes, edited by Ernest Rhys, London, 1909. (Everyman's Library)

Gayley, C. M.: *Plays of Our Forefathers,* New York, 1907.

Mill, Anna J.: *Mediaeval Plays in Scotland,* Edinburgh, 1927.

Nicoll, Allardyce: *Masks, Mimes and Miracles,* New York, 1932.

Schelling, Felix E.: *English Drama,* New York, 1914.

Smith, Janet M.: *The French Background of Middle Scots Literature,* Edinburgh, 1934.

Ward, A. W.: *A History of English Dramatic Literature to the Death of Queen Anne,* 3 vols., 2d ed., London, 1899.

BEN JONSON

Ben Jonson, edited by Brinsley Nicholson, with an Introduction by C. H. Herford, 3 vols., London, 1893–1894. (Dramabooks)

Ben Jonson, edited by C. H. Herford and Percy Simpson, 10 vols., Oxford, 1925–1950.

Complete Plays of Ben Jonson, with an Introduction by Felix E. Schelling, 2 vols., London, 1910. (Everyman's Library)

Five Plays, Oxford, 1953. (World's Classics)

Bamborough, J. B.: *Ben Jonson,* London, 1959. (Writers and Their Works, No. 112)

Bentley, G. E.: *Shakespeare and Jonson: Their Reputations in the Seventeenth Century Compared,* 2 vols., Chicago, 1945.

Noyes, R. G.: *Ben Jonson on the English Stage (1660–1776),* Cambridge, Mass., 1935.

Palmer, John: *Ben Jonson,* London, 1934.

Partridge, A. C.: *Studies in the Syntax of Jonson's Plays,* Cambridge, 1953.

Pennanen, E. V.: *Chapters on the Language of Ben Jonson's Dramatic Works,* Turku, Finland, 1951.

Sackton, A. H.: *Rhetoric as a Dramatic Language in Jonson,* New York, 1948.

JOHN WEBSTER

Webster and Tourneur, edited by John Addington Symonds, 2d ed., London, 1903. (Dramabooks)

Plays by Webster and Ford, with an Introduction by G. B. Harrison, London, 1933. (Everyman's Library)

Bluestone, Max, and Norman Rabkin, (eds.): *Shakespeare's Contemporaries,* Englewood Cliffs, N.J., 1961.

Bowers, Fredson T.: *Elizabethan Revenge Tragedy,* Princeton, 1940.

Bradbrook, Muriel C.: *Themes and Conventions of Elizabethan Tragedy,* Cambridge, 1935.

Dent, R. W.: *John Webster's Borrowing,* Berkeley, Cal., 1960.

Ornstein, Robert: *The Moral Vision of Jacobean Tragedy,* Madison, Wis., 1960.

Schelling, Felix E.: *Elizabethan Drama, 1558–1642,* 2 vols., Boston, 1908.

Schelling, Felix E.: *Elizabethan Playwrights,* New York, 1925.

Spencer, Theodore: *Death and Elizabethan Tragedy,* Cambridge, Mass., 1936.

Wells, Henry W.: *Elizabethan and Jacobean Playwrights,* New York, 1939.

MOLIÈRE
(JEAN BAPTISTE POQUELIN)

Eight Plays by Molière, translated by Morris Bishop, New York, 1957. (Modern Library)

Molière: Plays, translated by John Wood, 2 vols., London, 1960. (Penguin Books) [Vol. 1, *Five Plays,* 1958; vol. 2, *The Misanthrope and Other Plays,* 1959.]

Chatfield-Taylor, H. C.: *Molière: A Biography,* New York, 1906.

Marzials, Frank T.: *Molière,* London, 1906.

Matthews, Brander.: *Molière: His Life and His Works,* New York, 1910.

Palmer, John: *Molière,* New York, 1930.

Tilley, Arthur: *Molière,* Cambridge, 1921.

Trollope, Henry M.: *The Life of Molière,* London, 1905.

Wilcox, John: *The Relation of Molière to Restoration Comedy,* New York, 1938.

JEAN RACINE

Racine: Five Plays, translated by Kenneth Muir, New York, 1960. (Dramabooks)

Phaedra and Figaro: Racine's Phèdre translated by Robert Lowell and Beaumarchais's Figaro's Marriage translated by Jacques Barzun, New York, 1961.

Baring, Maurice: *Have You Anything to Declare?,* New York, 1937.

Barrault, J.-L.: *Reflections on the Theatre,* London, 1949.

Brereton, Geoffrey: *Jean Racine,* London, 1951.

Lockert, Lacy: *Studies in French-Classical Tragedy,* Nashville, Tenn., 1958.

Poulet, Georges: *Studies in Human Time,* Baltimore, 1956.

Raphael, D. D.: *The Paradox of Tragedy,* Bloomington, Ind., 1960.

Taine, H. A.: *The Ideal in Art,* New York, 1868.

Turnell, Martin: *The Classical Moment,* London, 1947.

Vinaver, Eugene: *Racine and Poetic Tragedy,* New York, 1959.

WILLIAM CONGREVE

Complete Plays of Congreve, edited by Alexander C. Ewald, London, 1887. (Dramabooks)

Comedies by William Congreve, edited by Bonamy Dobrée, London, 1925. (World's Classics)

Dobrée, Bonamy: *Restoration Comedy,* Oxford, 1924.

Fujimura, Thomas H.: *The Restoration Comedy of Wit,* Princeton, 1952.

Krutch, Joseph Wood: *Comedy and Conscience after the Restoration,* New York, 1924.

Loftis, John: *Comedy and Society from Congreve to Fielding,* Stanford, 1959.

Lynch, Kathleen: *The Social Mode of Restoration Comedy,* University of Michigan Publications in Language and Literature, vol. 3, New York, 1926.

Nettleton, George: *English Drama of the Restoration and Eighteenth Century,* New York, 1914.

Nicoll, Allardyce: *A History of Restoration Comedy, 1660–1700,* Cambridge, 1923.

Perry, Henry Ten Eyck: *The Comic Spirit in Restoration Comedy,* New Haven, 1925.

Spingarn, Joel E. (ed.): *Critical Essays of the Seventeenth Century,* 3 vols., Oxford, 1908.

HENRIK IBSEN

Ibsen: An Enemy of the People, The Wild Duck, Rosmersholm, translated by J. W. McFarlane, London, 1960.

Six Plays by Henrik Ibsen, translated by Eve Le Gallienne, New York, 1960. (Modern Library)

Bradbrook, M. C.: *Ibsen the Norwegian,* London, 1948.

Downs, B. W.: *Ibsen: The Intellectual Background,* London, 1946.

Koht, Halvdan: *The Life of Ibsen,* New York, 1931.

McFarlane, J. W.: *Ibsen and the Tempo of Norwegian Literature,* New York, 1960.

Northam, John: *Ibsen's Dramatic Method,* London, 1952.

Shaw, G. B.: *The Quintessence of Ibsenism* (1913), New York, 1957. (Dramabooks)

Tennant, P. F.: *Ibsen's Dramatic Technique,* Cambridge, 1948.

Weigand, H. J.: *The Modern Ibsen,* New York, 1925.

AUGUST STRINDBERG

Strindberg: Seven Plays, translated by Arvid Paulson, New York, 1960. (Bantam Books)

Five Plays of Strindberg, translated by Elizabeth Sprigge, New York, 1960. (Anchor Books)

Letters of Strindberg to Harriet Bosse, edited and translated by Arvid Paulson, New York, 1959.

Bentley, Eric: *In Search of Theater,* New York, 1954. (Vintage Books)

Bulman, Joan: *Strindberg and Shakespeare,* London, 1933.

Dahlström, C. E. W. L.: *Strindberg's Dramatic Expressionism,* Ann Arbor, Mich., 1930.

Mortensen, B. M. E., and B. W. Downs: *Strindberg,* New York, 1949.

Shaw, G. B.: *The Quintessence of Ibsenism* (1913), New York, 1957. (Dramabooks)

Sprigge, Elizabeth: *The Strange Life of August Strindberg,* New York, 1949.

BERNARD SHAW

Shaw, G. B.: *Complete Plays and Prefaces,* 6 vols., New York, 1962.

Shaw, G. B.: *Plays and Players: Essays on the Theatre,* London, 1952. (World's Classics)

Shaw on Theatre, edited by E. J. West, New York, 1958. (Dramabooks)

Beerbohm, Max: *A Selection from Around Theatres,* New York, 1960. (Anchor Books)

Bentley, Eric: *Bernard Shaw,* New York, 1957.

————: *The Playwright As Thinker,* New York, 1949.

Chesterton, G. K.: *George Bernard Shaw,* London, 1909.

Downer, Alan S.: *The British Drama,* New York, 1950.

Ervine, St. John: *Bernard Shaw,* New York, 1956.

Henderson, Archibald: *Bernard Shaw, Playboy and Prophet,* New York, 1932.

Huneker, James: *Iconoclasts,* New York, 1905.

Irvine, William: *The Universe of G. B. S.,* New York, 1949.

Kronenberger, Louis (ed.): *George Bernard Shaw: A Critical Survey,* New York, 1953.

Peacock, Ronald: *The Poet in the Theatre,* New York, 1960. (Dramabooks)

ANTON CHEKHOV

Chekhov: Plays, translated by Elizaveta Fen, Baltimore, 1959. (Penguin Books)

The Life and Letters of Anton Tchekhov, edited and translated by S. S. Koteliansky and Philip Tomlinson, New York, 1925.

The Personal Papers of Anton Chekhov, New York, 1948.

Bruford, W. H.: *Chekhov and His Russia,* New York, 1947.

Hingley, Ronald: *Chekhov,* London, 1950.

Hudson, Lynton: *Life and the Theatre,* New York, 1954.

Magarshack, David: *Chekhov the Dramatist,* New York, 1962. (Dramabooks)

Peacock, Ronald: *The Poet in the Theatre,* New York, 1960. (Dramabooks)

Stanislavsky, Constantin: *My Life in Art,* New York, 1924.

Styan, J. L.: *The Elements of Drama,* New York, 1960.

Williams, Raymond: *Drama from Ibsen to Eliot,* New York, 1953.

GEORG KAISER

Kaiser, Georg: *The Coral, Gas I,* and *Gas II,* translated by Winifred Katzin and Hermann Scheffauer, in S. M. Tucker and A. S. Downer (eds.), *Twenty-five Modern Plays,* New York, 1953.

Hunton, Lynton: *Life and the Theatre,* New York, 1954.

Nicoll, Allardyce: *World Drama,* New York, n.d.

Kenworthy, B. J.: *Georg Kaiser,* Oxford, 1957.

Samuel, R., and R. H. Thomas: *Expressionism in German Life, Letters and the Theatre,* Cambridge, 1939.

JEAN GIRAUDOUX

Jean Giraudoux: Four Plays, adapted by Maurice Valency, New York, 1958. (Dramabooks)

Giraudoux, Jean: *Electra,* translated by Winifred

Smith, and *Judith,* translated by John K. Savacool, in Eric Bentley (ed.), *The Modern Theatre,* vols. 1 and 3, New York, 1955. (Anchor Books)

Giraudoux, Jean: *Sodom and Gomorrah* and *Song of Songs,* translated by Herma Briffault, in Barry Ulanov (ed.), *Makers of the Modern Theater,* New York, 1961.

Fowlie, Wallace: *Dionysus in Paris,* New York, 1960.

Grossvogel, D. I.: *The Self-Conscious Stage in Modern French Drama,* New York, 1958.

Inskip, Donald: *Jean Giraudoux,* New York, 1958.

Leefmans, B. M-P.: "Giraudoux's Other Muse," *Kenyon Review,* vol. 16, 1954.

Le Sage, Laurent: *Jean Giraudoux,* University Park, Pa., 1959.

Lumley, Frederick: *Trends in 20th Century Drama,* New York, 1960.

CHRONOLOGY

CHRONOLOGY

B.C.

525–456 Aeschylus, tragic poet, said to have written 90 plays. Titles of 79 plays are known; seven are extant: the *Suppliants* (c.490), the *Persians* (472), *Seven Against Thebes* (469), *Prometheus Bound* (c.460), the *Oresteia* (made up of the *Agamemnon*, the *Choephori* or *Libation-bearers*, and the *Eumenides*; 458). Winner of first prize at festival of Dionysus, where tragedies were performed, 13 times.

496–406 Sophocles, winner of 18 victories for his tragedies (first over Aeschylus in 468). Said to have written over 100 plays, of which seven and part of a satyr-play are extant: *Ajax* (c.450), *Antigone* (c.442), *Trachiniae*, *Oedipus Rex* (c.425), *Electra*, *Philoctetes* (409), *Oedipus Coloneus* (posthumous), and the *Ichneutae* (the satyr-play).

484–406 Euripides, more skeptical than the earlier tragic poets, more self-assertive, gains five victories. Said to have written 92 plays of which 17 survive. Best known, perhaps, are *Alcestis* (438), *Medea* (431), *Hippolytus* (428), *Andromache*, *Electra*, *Trojan Women* (415), *Iphigenia in Tauris* (414), the *Bacchae* and *Iphigenia in Aulis* (both posthumous).

447–380 Aristophanes, poet of Old Comedy (c.435–405), which emphasizes criticism of well-known figures and combined high burlesque and moving lyrics. Author of about 40 comedies, of which 11 survive. Best known: *Clouds* (423), *Wasps* (422), *Birds* (414), *Lysistrata* (411), *Thesmophoriazousae* (410), *Ecclesiazousae* (392).

476 First Olympian ode of Pindar.

460 Birth of Hippocrates, physician who makes medicine a practical art.

438 Parthenon completed.

432 Death of Phidias, sculptor of giant statues of Athene (at Athens) and Zeus (at Olympia).

525 Cambyses makes Egypt a Persian province.

522–486 Darius the Great, king of Persia.

499–479 Period of Persian Wars: Battle of Marathon (490), Battles of Thermopylae and Salamis (480).

461 Pericles emerges as a figure of importance in Athens.

431–404 Peloponnesian War.

B.C.

425 Death of the historian Herodotus.

400 Death of the historian Thucydides.

404–371 Sparta supreme in Greece.

399 Socrates put to death.

385 Academy founded by Plato, most prolific and influential of Greek philosophers.

359 Accession of Philip II of Macedon.

351 Demosthenes delivers first Philippic.

343–292 Menander, foremost writer of New Comedy, which is highly plotted, features romantic love, and stays close to contemporary life. Author of some 100 plays, of which the substance of 5 remain, along with fragments of others.

347 Aristotle at Macedonian court as tutor to Alexander.

336 Assassination of Philip II; accession of Alexander the Great.

323 Death of Alexander.

300 Euclid: *Elements.*

285 Arts and sciences flourish at Museum of Alexandria. Translation of Hebrew Scriptures into Greek begins at Alexandria.

285 Ptolemy Philadelphus, king of Egypt.

264–241 First Punic War.

246 Building of Great Wall of China begun.

240 Roman drama begins to mature with production of adaptations of a Greek tragedy and a Greek comedy by Livius Andronicus. Naevius (270–199) and Ennius (239–169) not only write on Greek models but choose subjects from Roman history for their tragedies.

254–184 Plautus, though he uses Greek models, gives Roman comedy a flavor of its own. Author of about 130 plays of which 20 survive. Among the best known: *Amphitryo, Menaechmi, Miles Gloriosus* (*The Braggart Warrior*), and *Rudens.*

224 Archimedes's discoveries in mechanics made known.

218–202 Second Punic War.

B.C.

195–159 Terence, second of surviving masters of Roman comedy, models 4 of his 6 plays on those of Menander. Best known are the *Eunuch* (161), *Phormio* (161), and *Adelphoe* (160).

149–146 Third Punic War. Carthage and Corinth destroyed by the Romans.

133 Tiberius Gracchus tribune.

60 First Triumvirate (Pompey, Caesar, and Crassus).

44 Assassination of Caesar.

31 War between Octavian and Antony; Octavian triumphs in Battle of Actium.

19 Death of Virgil.

8 Death of Horace.

5 Birth of Jesus.

A.D.

4–65 Seneca, philosopher, author of 9 tragedies taken from the Greek, including a *Medea,* a *Phaedra,* an *Agamemnon,* and an *Oedipus.*

14 Death of Augustus.

17 Death of Livy, the historian, and Ovid, the poet.

35 The Crucifixion.

54–68 Nero, Roman Emperor.

70 Earliest of gospels, St. Mark's, written.

79 Eruption of Vesuvius: Pompeii and Herculaneum buried.

130 Pantheon built at Rome.

138 Death of Juvenal, the poet.

132–135 Destruction of Jewish community in Palestine.

A.D.

200 Tertullian warns Christians in his *De Spectaculis* against the dangers of heathen shows, races, and the theater.

270 Death of Plotinus, the philosopher.

200 Canon of New Testament fixed.

251 Death of Origen, theologian and scriptural exegete.

285–305 Absolutism of Emperor Diocletian; persecution of Christians.

324 Constantine wins control of entire Roman Empire.

387 Conversion of Augustine.

400 Little remains of Roman drama except crude outlines preserved by the mimes, mixing dance, music, and touches of both tragedy and farce in their performances.

410 Visigoths under Alaric sack Rome.

476 Deposition of last Roman Emperor of the West, Romulus Augustulus.

523 Boethius: *Consolation of Philosophy.*

590–604 Pope Gregory the Great.

622 Mohammed's Hegira to Medina.

700 *Beowulf* epic.

731 Bede: *Ecclesiastical History of England.*

732 Battle of Tours: Charles Martel defeats Arabs.

800 Charlemagne crowned Emperor by Pope Leo III.

804 Death of Alcuin, scholar-educator.

871–899 Alfred the Great, king of Wessex.

A.D.

930 Conjectural date of *Quem quaeritis* (Whom do you seek?) trope, beginning of liturgical drama in Easter Mass. Additions to the four-line playlet in succeeding centuries produce full-sized Passion and Nativity Plays and celebrations of other events in the Church year.

980 Roswitha, Benedictine abbess of Gandersheim in Saxony, writes six prose plays based on Terence but using Christian subjects for her mixtures of morality and farce.

962 Otto I crowned Roman Emperor.

1000 *Chanson de Roland.*

1036 Death of Avicenna, Arab philosopher.

1066 Battle of Hastings: Normans conquer England.

1096–1099 First Crusade.

1134–1150 Western façade of Chartres Cathedral built.

1173 Chretien de Troyes: *Yvain.*

c.1180 Anglo-Norman *Adam,* religious drama complete with stage directions. Outdoor performances of such plays are given in booths or pageant wagons, clustered together in town market places. Sequences or cycles of dramas develop, to be given over a period of days or a week or more. The great collections become known as Mystery Cycles.

1198–1216 Pope Innocent III.

1215 Magna Carta.

A.D.

c.1250 Rutebeuf (c.1230–c.1285) in *The Miracle of Theophilus,* Jean Bodel in *The Play of St. Nicholas,* and Adam de la Halle (c.1240–c.1286) in *The Play of Robin and Marion* broaden characterization and setting in the drama and provide it with playwriting personalities.

1226–1270 Louis IX (St. Louis), king of France.

1274 Death of St. Thomas Aquinas.

1311 Corpus Christi festival established, a feast specially dedicated to the performances of mysteries by the trade guilds.

1321 Death of Dante.

1336 Death of Giotto.

1338–1453 Hundred Years' War.

1341 Petrarch crowned poet on the Capitol in Rome.

1348 Black Death (plague) in Europe.

1385 Chaucer: *Troilus and Cryseide.*

1402 Founding of Confrérie de la Passion at Paris, most famous of amateur groups organized to perform the mysteries (*mystères* in French; *sacre rappresentazioni* in Italian; *Passionsspiele* in German). Most famous of the English cycles are those of York, Wakefield, Coventry, and Chester, performed by the guilds in pageant wagons.

1410 Paul, Hans, and Hermann of Limburg: *The Book of Hours of the Duke de Berry.*

1416 Donatello: *St. George.*

1440 Gutenberg invents art of printing by movable type.

1415 Thomas a Kempis: *The Imitation of Christ.*

1453 Conquest of Constantinople by the Turks.

1492 Columbus discovers America.

1495 *Everyman,* most famous of Morality Plays, written in Dutch. As its name suggests, the Morality is designed to instruct; its characters are usually abstractions of vice and virtue.

1496 Leonardo da Vinci: *Last Supper.*

A.D.

1500 Erasmus: *Adagia.*

1501–1504 Michelangelo: *Statue of David.*

1509 Lodovico Ariosto: *The Supposes.*

1506 Bramante begins to build St. Peter's, Rome.

1509–1547 Henry VIII reigns.

1516 Thomas More: *Utopia;* Ariosto: *Orlando Furioso;* Raphael: *Sistine Madonna.*

1516 Charles V, king of Spain (1519—Holy Roman Emperor).

1517 Luther affixes 95 theses to door of Wittenberg Palace church.

1520 Machiavelli: *La Mandragola,* Italian satire; John Heywood: *The Four P's,* interlude given at court.

1527 Castiglione: *The Book of the Courtier.*

1534 Rabelais: *Gargantua.* Michelangelo begins work on Sistine Chapel.

1534 Act of Supremacy: Severance from Rome of Church of England.

1540 Sir David Lyndsay: *The Satire of the Three Estates.*

1541–1564 John Calvin in Geneva.

1543 Copernicus publishes his system of heliocentric astronomy.

1545 Council of Trent opens.

1549 The group of poets who call themselves La Pleiade publish their *Défense et Illustration de la Langue Française,* in which French classicism finds its best support. Several members of the group write plays following the principles set forth in this book.

1550 Nicholas Udall: *Ralph Roister Doister,* first known English comedy.

1553–1558 Mary Tudor, queen of England.

A.D.

1561 Scaliger: *Poetics,* establishing important precedents for literary criticism.

1558–1603 Elizabeth I, queen of England.

1561–1567 Mary Stuart reigns in Scotland.

1562 Sackville and Norton: *Gorboduc,* first English tragedy in blank verse.

1562–1598 Civil Wars in France.

1570 Palladio: *Treatise on Architecture.*

1573 Tasso: *Aminta.*

1575 William Stevenson: *Gammer Gurton's Needle,* drama notable for its native English materials.

1577 Raphael Holinshed: *Chronicles.*

1579 North's translation of Plutarch's *Lives.*

1580 Last Mystery Play performed at Coventry.

1581 Tasso: *Jerusalem Delivered;* Sidney: *Defense of Poesie.*

1585 Thomas Kyd: *The Spanish Tragedy;* Guarini: *The Faithful Shepherd,* the tragicomedy which ranks with Tasso's *Aminta* in establishing the Pastoral Drama.

1587 Mary Stuart beheaded.

1588 The Spanish Armada formed.

1589 Christopher Marlowe: *Doctor Faustus.*

1589 Henry of Navarre claims French crown.

1590 Edmund Spenser: *The Faerie Queene,* I–III.

1592 Remains of Pompeii discovered.

1593 Shakespeare: *Richard III, Comedy of Errors, Venus and Adonis.*

A.D.

1595 Shakespeare: *Romeo and Juliet.*

1596 Shakespeare: *King John, The Merchant of Venice.*

1597 Shakespeare: *Richard II.*

1600 Thomas Dekker: *The Shoemaker's Holiday;* Shakespeare: *Henry V, As You Like It, Much Ado about Nothing.*

1601 Shakespeare: *Troilus and Cressida, Twelfth Night.*

1602 Shakespeare: *Hamlet.*

1604 John Marston: *The Malcontent;* Shakespeare: *Othello.*

1605 Shakespeare: *King Lear, Macbeth.*

1606 Ben Jonson: *Volpone.*

1608 Shakespeare: *Coriolanus, Antony and Cleopatra.*

1610 Jonson: *The Alchemist.*

1611 Shakespeare: *The Tempest.*

1613 Beaumont and Fletcher: *The Knight of the Burning Pestle.*

1614 John Webster: *The Duchess of Malfi.*

1615 Publication of Cervantes's plays, eight comedies, and eight *entremeses* (comic interludes).

1623 First Folio edition of Shakespeare's plays.

1625 Philip Massinger: *A New Way to Pay Old Debts.*

1595 Montaigne: *Essays* published in definitive edition.

1602–1604 Galileo discovers laws of gravitation and oscillation.

1605 Cervantes: *Don Quixote;* Bacon: *Advancement of Learning.*

1609 Kepler: *The New Astronomy.*

1612 Rubens: *Descent from the Cross.*

1600 Patent to East India Company.

1600 Founding of English East India Company.

1607 Founding of Jamestown in Virginia.

1608 Founding of Quebec.

1618–1648 Thirty Years' War.

A.D.

1627 *Daphne,* first German opera, written by Martin Opitz, composed by Heinrich Schütz.

1628 William Harvey discovers double circulation of blood.

1633 John Ford: *'Tis Pity She's a Whore.*

1633 John Donne: *Poems;* George Herbert: *The Temple.*

1635 Death of Lope de Vega, most prolific of all playwrights, said to have written over 2,000 plays. Known titles are 725, of which 470 survive.

1636 Pierre Corneille: *Le Cid.*

1637 Descartes: *Discourse on Method.*

1640 Corneille: *Horace.*

1642 Corneille: *Polyeucte.*

1642–1648 Civil War in England.

1649–1660 Commonwealth in England.

1651 Hobbes: *Leviathan.*

1660 Death of Velasquez.

1660 Restoration of Monarchy in England (Charles II).

1662 Foundation of Royal Society in England. Death of Pascal.

1664 George Etherege: *The Comical Revenge,* or *Love in a Tub;* Molière: *Tartuffe.*

1666 Molière: *The Misanthrope.*

1667 Jean Racine: *Andromache.*

1667 Milton: *Paradise Lost.*

1668 Dryden: *Essay of Dramatick Poesy.*

1669 Death of Rembrandt.

1671 Molière: *The Would-be Gentleman.*

1673 Calderón de la Barca: *Life Is a Dream,* best known, perhaps, of 200 plays (of which 100 survive).

A.D.

1674 William Wycherley: *The Country Wife.*

1675 John Dryden: *Aurengzebe.*

1677 Racine: *Phaedra.*

1678 Dryden: *All for Love.*

1680 Comédie Française established.

1680 Henry Purcell: *Dido and Aeneas.*

1682 Thomas Otway: *Venice Preserved.*

1688 "Glorious Revolution": Accession of William and Mary.

1690 John Locke: *Essay Concerning Human Understanding.*

1695 William Congreve: *Love for Love.*

1696 Sir John Vanbrugh: *The Relapse.*

1700 Congreve: *The Way of the World.*

1701–1714 War of the Spanish Succession.

1707 George Farquhar: *The Beaux' Stratagem.*

1711 Alexander Pope: *Essay on Criticism;* Addison and Steele: *The Spectator.*

1713 Joseph Addison: *Cato.*

1713 Peace of Utrecht.

1714 Leibnitz: *Monadology.*

1719 Defoe: *Robinson Crusoe.*

1725 Vico: *The New Science.*

1726 Swift: *Gulliver's Travels.*

1728 John Gay: *Beggar's Opera.*

1729 Bach: *St. Matthew Passion.*

1730 George Lillo: *The London Merchant;* Marivaux: *The Game of Love and Chance.*

1732 Voltaire: *Zaïre.*

1733 Bach: *B Minor Mass.*

A.D.

<table>
<tr><td></td><td>1739 Hume: Treatise of Human Understanding.</td><td></td></tr>
<tr><td></td><td>1741 Handel: Messiah.</td><td>1740–1786 Frederick the Great of Prussia.</td></tr>
<tr><td>1743 Voltaire: Mérope.</td><td></td><td></td></tr>
<tr><td></td><td>1744 Hogarth: Marriage à la Mode.</td><td></td></tr>
<tr><td></td><td>1749 Fielding: Tom Jones.</td><td></td></tr>
<tr><td>1753 Carlo Goldoni: The Mistress of the Inn.</td><td>1755 Samuel Johnson: Dictionary of the English Language.</td><td>1756–1763 Seven Years' War (French and Indian War).</td></tr>
<tr><td>1761 Carlo Gozzi: The Love of the Three Oranges.</td><td>1762 Rousseau: Social Contract.</td><td>1762–1796 Catherine the Great of Russia.</td></tr>
<tr><td>1767 Gotthold Ephraim Lessing: Minna of Barnhelm.</td><td>1767 Sterne: Tristram Shandy.</td><td></td></tr>
<tr><td>1769 Lessing: Hamburg Dramaturgy.</td><td>1769 Patent for James Watt's steam engine.</td><td></td></tr>
<tr><td>1773 Oliver Goldsmith: She Stoops to Conquer; Goethe: Goetz von Berlichingen.</td><td></td><td></td></tr>
<tr><td>1775 Beaumarchais: The Barber of Seville.</td><td></td><td>1775–1783 War of American Independence.</td></tr>
<tr><td>1777 R. B. Sheridan: The School for Scandal.</td><td></td><td></td></tr>
<tr><td>1779 Lessing: Nathan the Wise.</td><td></td><td></td></tr>
<tr><td>1781 Schiller: The Robbers.</td><td>1781 Kant: Critique of Pure Reason.</td><td></td></tr>
<tr><td>1784 Beaumarchais: The Marriage of Figaro.</td><td></td><td></td></tr>
<tr><td></td><td>1785 Mozart: Marriage of Figaro.</td><td></td></tr>
<tr><td></td><td>1786 Robert Burns: Poems.</td><td></td></tr>
<tr><td>1787 Schiller: Don Carlos.</td><td>1787 Mozart: Don Giovanni.</td><td></td></tr>
<tr><td>1789 Goethe: Tasso.</td><td></td><td>1789 Estates-General opens at Versailles.</td></tr>
<tr><td></td><td>1790 Burke: Reflections on the French Revolution.</td><td></td></tr>
<tr><td></td><td>1791 Boswell: Life of Johnson.</td><td></td></tr>
</table>

A.D.

		1794 Execution of Robespierre.
	1798 Wordsworth and Coleridge: *Lyrical Ballads.*	
1799 Schiller: *Wallenstein.*		1799 Napoleon's *coup d'état.*
1800 Schiller: *Mary Stuart.*		
		1801–1825 Alexander I of Russia.
		1804–1814 Napoleonic Empire.
1808 Goethe: *Faust, Part I;* Kleist: *The Broken Jug.*		
		1812 Napoleon's Russian campaign.
		1814–1815 Congress of Vienna.
		1815 The Hundred Days. Battle of Waterloo.
1819 Shelley: *The Cenci.*	1819 Byron: *Don Juan;* Keats: *Eve of St. Agnes;* Scott: *Ivanhoe.*	
	1822 Beethoven: *Missa Solemnis.*	
	1824 Beethoven: *Ninth Symphony.*	
1825 Pushkin: *Boris Godunov.*		
1830 Victor Hugo: *Hernani.*	1830 Tennyson: *Poems Chiefly Lyrical.*	1830 *July Revolution in France.*
1831 Griboyedov: *Wit Works Woe.*	1831 Constable: *Waterloo Bridge.*	
1832 Goethe: *Faust, Part II.*		1832 Great Reform Act in England.
1835 Georg Büchner: *Danton's Death.*	1835 Gogol: *Dead Souls.*	
1836 Nikolai Gogol: *The Inspector General;* Büchner: *Woyzeck.*	1836 Dickens: *Pickwick Papers.*	
		1837–1901 Victoria, queen of England.
1844 Friedrich Hebbel: *Mary Magdalen.*		

A.D.

1845 Poe: *Tales of Mystery.*

1846 Repeal of Corn Laws in Great Britain.

1848 *Communist Manifesto.* Revolutions in France, Germany, Austria, Italy, Hungary.

1849 Eugene Scribe: *Adrienne Lecouvreur.*

1850 Dickens: *David Copperfield;* Wagner: *Lohengrin.*

1851 Ruskin: *Stones of Venice.*

1852 Alexandre Dumas, fils: *Camille.*

1852 Stowe: *Uncle Tom's Cabin.*

1854 Thoreau: *Walden.*

1854–1856 Crimean War.

1855 Whitman: *Leaves of Grass.*

1857 Flaubert: *Mme. Bovary;* Baudelaire: *Les Fleurs du mal.*

1859 Darwin: *Origin of Species;* Mill: *On Liberty.*

1860 Alexander Ostrovsky: *The Storm*; Eugene Labiche: *The Journey of M. Perrichon.*

1861 Kingdom of Italy. Abolition of serfdom in Russia.

1862 Hugo: *Les Misérables;* Turgeniev: *Fathers and Sons.*

1861–1865 Civil War in the United States.

1864 Newman: *Apologia pro Vita Sua.*

1865 Tolstoy: *War and Peace.*

1866 Ibsen: *Brand.*

1867 Ibsen: *Peer Gynt.*

1869–1870 Vatican Council.

1870–1871 Franco-Prussian War.

1871 First Impressionist exhibition at Paris. Verdi: *Aida.*

1870–1940 Third French Republic.

A.D.

1870 Italian unification completed; Rome the capital.

1871–1918 Second German Empire.

1875 Mark Twain: *Adventures of Tom Sawyer.*

1876 Invention of telephone by Bell.

1877 Brahms: *First Symphony.*

1879 Ibsen: *A Doll's House.*

1880 Dostoevsky: *Brothers Karamazov.*

1881 Ibsen: *Ghosts.*

1881 James: *Portrait of a Lady.*

1882 Mallarmé: *L'Après-midi d'un faune.*

1884 Ibsen: *The Wild Duck.*

1885 Pater: *Marius the Epicurean;* de Maupassant: *Bel Ami;* Zola: *Germinal.*

1886 Ibsen: *Rosmersholm.*

1886 Nietzsche: *Beyond Good and Evil.*

1887 Théâtre Libre opened in Paris. August Strindberg: *The Father;* Chekhov: *Ivanov.*

1888 Strindberg: *Miss Julie.*

1888–1918 William II of Germany.

1889 James: *Principles of Psychology.*

1891 Ibsen: *Hedda Gabler;* Franz Wedekind: *Spring's Awakening.*

1892 Gerhart Hauptmann: *The Weavers.*

1892 Hardy: *Tess of the D'Urbervilles.*

1893 Victorien Sardou: *Mme. Sans-Gêne;* Hauptmann: *Hannele;* Bernard Shaw: *Mrs. Warren's Profession.*

1893 Verdi: *Falstaff;* Tchaikovsky: *Pathétique Symphony.*

1894 Kipling: *Jungle Book.*

1895 Oscar Wilde: *The Importance of Being Earnest.*

1895 Invention of wireless telegraphy by Marconi.

A.D.

1896 Hauptmann: *The Sunken Bell;* Anton Chekhov: *The Seagull;* Ibsen: *John Gabriel Borkman.*

1897 Rostand: *Cyrano de Bergerac.*

1898 Strindberg: *To Damascus, I* and *II;* Shaw: *Caesar and Cleopatra.*

1899 Chekhov: *Uncle Vanya.*

1901 Strindberg: *Dance of Death;* Chekhov: *Three Sisters.*

1902 Strindberg: *A Dream Play;* Maxim Gorki: *Lower Depths;* James M. Barrie: *The Admirable Crichton;* W. B. Yeats: *Cathleen ni Houlihan.*

1903 Shaw: *Man and Superman;* Hugo von Hofmannsthal: *Electra;* Arthur Schnitzler: *Hands Around;* Wedekind: *Pandora's Box.*

1904 Chekhov: *The Cherry Orchard;* Yeats: *On Baile's Strand.*

1905 Shaw: *Major Barbara;* J. M. Synge: *The Well of the Saints.*

1907 Synge: *The Playboy of the Western World.*

1908 Shaw: *Getting Married.*

1909 Maurice Maeterlinck: *The Blue Bird.*

1912 Shaw: *Pygmalion.*

1896 Puccini: *La Bohème.*

1901 Croce: *Aesthetics.*

1902 Débussy: *Pelléas et Melisande.*

1903 First successful airplane flight by Wright brothers.

1905 Einstein's special theory of relativity. The Fauvists—Vlaminck, Derain, Matisse.

1907 Bergson: *Creative Evolution;* Picasso: *Young Ladies of Avignon.*

1909 Manifesto of Futurism.

1910 Mahler: *Ninth Symphony.*

1911 Braque: *Man with a Guitar.*

1912 Ravel: *Daphnis and Chloë;* Schönberg: *Pierrot Lunaire.*

1899–1902 Boer War.

1904–1905 Russo-Japanese War.

1905 Revolution in Russia.

A.D.

	1913 Lawrence: *Sons and Lovers;* Stravinsky: *Rite of Spring;* Freud: *Totem and Taboo;* Proust: First volumes of *Remembrance of Things Past.*	
	1914 De Chirico: *Nostalgia of the Infinite.*	**1914–1918** World War I.
1916 Georg Kaiser: *From Morn to Midnight.*	**1916** Dadaism. *Intolerance* (directed by Griffith).	
1917 Luigi Pirandello: *It Is So! (If You Think So).*	**1917** Alexander Blok: *The Twelve.*	**1917** Russian Revolution.
1918–1920 Kaiser: *Gas I and II.*	**1918–1921** Spengler: *The Decline of the West.*	
1919 Shaw: *Heartbreak House;* Ernst Toller: *Masses and Man.*	**1919** Bauhaus established.	**1919–1920** Peace treaties of Versailles, St. Germain, Neuilly, Trianon, Sèvres.
1920 Eugene O'Neill: *Beyond the Horizon, The Emperor Jones;* Shaw: *Back to Methuselah.*	**1920** Berg: *Wozzeck;* Pound: *Hugh Selwyn Mauberley.*	
1921 Pirandello: *Henry IV, Six Characters in Search of an Author;* Karel Căpek: *R.U.R., The Insect Comedy.*	**1921** Picasso: *Three Musicians.*	
	1922 Joyce: *Ulysses;* Berg: *Wozzeck;* Lewis: *Babbitt;* Klee: *The Twittering Machine.* Radio broadcasting on national scale in U.S. Eliot: *The Wasteland.*	**1922** Fascist march on Rome.
1923 Elmer Rice: *The Adding Machine.*	**1923** Rilke: *Duino Elegies.*	
1924 Shaw: *Saint Joan;* Sean O'Casey: *Juno and the Paycock;* Anderson–Stallings: *What Price Glory?*	**1924** Kafka: *The Trial;* Mann: *Magic Mountain;* Jung: *Psychological Types. The Navigator* (starring Buster Keaton). Forster: *A Passage to India.*	**1924** Death of Lenin.
	1925 Fitzgerald: *The Great Gatsby. Potemkin* (directed by Eisenstein). *The Gold Rush* (starring Charlie Chaplin).	
1926 O'Neill: *The Great God Brown;* O'Casey: *The Plough and the Stars.*	**1926** Kafka: *The Castle;* Gide: *The Counterfeiters;* Hemingway: *The Sun Also Rises.*	**1926** General strike in Great Britain.

A.D.

1927 Toller: *Hoppla! Such Is Life!*

1928 Bertolt Brecht: *Threepenny Opera;* O'Neill: *Strange Interlude;* Jean Giraudoux: *Siegfried.*

1929 Giraudoux: *Amphitryon 38;* Rice: *Street Scene;* Paul Claudel: *Satin Slipper.*

1930 Philip Barry: *Hotel Universe;* Pirandello: *Tonight We Improvise.*

1931 O'Neill: *Mourning Becomes Electra;* Gabriel Marcel: *The Funeral Pyre.*

1932 Ugo Betti: *Landslide at the North Station.*

1933 O'Casey: *Within the Gates;* Garcia Lorca: *Blood Wedding.*

1934 Jean Cocteau: *The Infernal Machine;* Lorca: *Yerma.*

1935 Robert Sherwood: *The Petrified Forest;* Giraudoux: *Tiger at the Gates;* T. S. Eliot: *Murder in the Cathedral.*

1936 Marcel: *Ariadne;* Lorca: *The House of Bernarda Alba.*

1937 Giraudoux: *Electra.*

1938 Albert Camus: *Caligula;* Giraudoux: *Song of Songs;* Yeats: *Purgatory;* Rodgers–Hart: *Boys from Syracuse.*

1927 Benda: *The Treason of the Intellectuals.* Stravinsky: *Oedipus Rex.* First solo transatlantic flight by Lindbergh.

1928 *The Way of All Flesh* (starring Emil Jannings). Huxley: *Point Counter Point.*

1929 Wolfe: *Look Homeward, Angel.* Graf Zeppelin flies around the world. Faulkner: *The Sound and the Fury.*

1930 Waugh: *Vile Bodies.*

1931 First ascent into the stratosphere by Auguste Piccard.

1932 Invention of television. Mauriac: *Vipers' Tangle.*

1933 Malraux: *Man's Fate.*

1934 Hindemith: *Mathias the Painter;* Stein–Thomson: *Four Saints in Three Acts;* Bernanos: *Diary of a Country Priest.*

1936 *Modern Times* (starring Charlie Chaplin). Silone: *Bread and Wine.*

1937 Picasso: *Guernica.*

1938 Dos Passos: *U.S.A.*

1929 Great Depression begins. Lateran Treaties between the Pope and Mussolini.

1933 Hitler seizes power in Germany.

1935 Conquest of Abyssinia by Italy.

1936–1939 Spanish Civil War.

1938 Munich Pact.

A.D.

1939 Barry: *The Philadelphia Story;* Eliot: *Family Reunion.*

1940 O'Casey: *Purple Dust;* O'Neill: *Long Day's Journey into Night.*

1941 Brecht: *Mother Courage.*

1942 Henry de Montherlant: *Port-Royal;* Jean Anouilh: *Antigone;* Jean-Paul Sartre: *The Flies.*

1943 Giraudoux: *Sodom and Gomorrah, The Madwoman of Chaillot.*

1944 Betti: *Corruption in the Palace of Justice;* Sartre: *No Exit;* Tennessee Williams: *Glass Menagerie.*

1945 Camus: *Cross Purpose;* Montherlant: *The Master of Santiago.*

1947 Williams: *A Streetcar Named Desire.*

1948 Eugene Ionesco: *The Bald Soprano;* Brecht: *Good Woman of Setzuan, Caucasian Chalk Circle.*

1949 Arthur Miller: *Death of a Salesman;* Christopher Fry: *The Lady's Not for Burning;* Eliot: *Cocktail Party.*

1950 Anouilh: *The Rehearsal.*

1951 Betti: *The Queen and the Rebels;* Ionesco: *The Chairs;* Anouilh: *The Waltz of the Toreadors;* Sartre: *The Devil and the Good Lord.*

1953 Williams: *Camino Real;* Miller: *The Crucible;* Eliot: *The Confidential Clerk.*

1939 Joyce: *Finnegans Wake.*

1940 Greene: *The Power and the Glory. The Baker's Wife* (Raimu).

1941 Koestler: *Darkness at Noon.*

1943 Mondrian: *Broadway Boogie Woogie;* Eliot: *Four Quartets.*

1946 Thomas: *Deaths and Entrances.*

1947 Camus: *The Plague;* Auden: *Age of Anxiety.*

1948 Pollock: *Number 1.*

1949 Orwell: *1984.*

1951 Matisse: Chapel at Vence, France.

1952 De Kooning: *Woman, I.*

1954 Dubuffet: *Eyes Closed.*

1939 German–Russian Pact.

1939–1945 World War II.

1945 Deaths of Roosevelt, Mussolini, Hitler.

1946 First meeting of United Nations General Assembly.

1947 Marshall Plan.

1949 North Atlantic Treaty. People's Republic of China proclaimed; Mao Tse-tung rules.

1950–1953 Korean War.

1953 Death of Stalin.

1954 U.S. Supreme Court declares racial segregation in schools unconstitutional. Nasser rules in Egypt. Southeast Asia Treaty.

A.D.

1955 Samuel Beckett: *Waiting for Godot;* Williams: *Cat on a Hot Tin Roof;* Miller: *A View from the Bridge.*

1956 Lerner–Loewe: *My Fair Lady;* John Osborne: *Look Back in Anger.*

1957 Williams: *Orpheus Descending, Suddenly Last Summer.*

1958 Archibald MacLeish: *J.B.*

1959 Ionesco: *Rhinoceros;* Anouilh: *Becket;* Peter Shaffer: *Five Finger Exercise.*

1960 Shelagh Delaney: *A Taste of Honey;* Edward Albee: *Zoo Story;* Sartre: *The Siege of Altona.*

1961 Robert Bolt: *A Man for All Seasons;* Williams: *The Night of the Iguana.*

1956 Muir: *One Foot in Eden.*

1958 Pasternak: *Doctor Zhivago;* Lampedusa: *The Leopard;* Stravinsky: *Threni.*

1960 Durrell's *Clea* completes *"The Alexandria Quartet."*

1961 Hughes: *The Fox in the Attic.*

1955 Baghdad Pact.

1956 Suez Canal Crisis.

1958 De Gaulle rules in France. End of Fourth Republic.

1959 Cyprus achieves independence.

1960 Congo crisis.

1961 War for independence in Algeria.